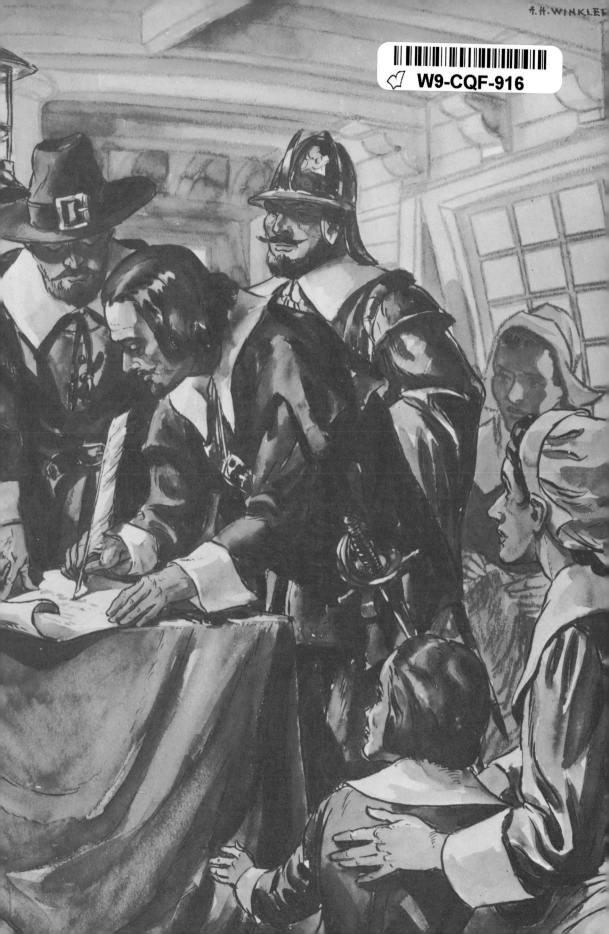

SIGNING OF THE MAYFLOWER COMPACT
Famous First Step in American Self-Government

AMERICAN SCHOOL children have for generations been rightfully taught that the hardy souls who came to this country on the *Mayflower* were pioneers of freedom. It is true that the Mayflower Compact, signed by the Pilgrim Fathers on Nov. 11, 1620, in Provincetown harbor, is not a notably democratic document. It is true also that the Pilgrims not only did not extend religious liberty to everyone, but in 1635 expelled Roger Williams from their colony for advocating it. Nevertheless, through the sacrifices they made to secure it for themselves, they gave impetus to an attitude which ultimately resulted in the universalization of religious freedom in the United States.

Their influence with regard to government in general was similar. The Compact which they drew up and signed emphasized allegiance to the then reigning king of England and said nothing directly about the rights of individuals. However, it was the dramatic first step in the long and eventful history of American self-government.

The story of the Pilgrims is familiar. A group of Puritans with mildly Calvinistic principles in 1606 organized a congregation in the English village of Scrooby, declaring themselves independent of the Church of England. Later they went to Holland mainly to get away from contact with that church and its members. But they did not approve of the relatively radical religious groups permitted to be active in Holland. In addition they were afraid that they, and particularly their children, would, under the pressure of Dutch influence, lose their English way of living.

About half of them decided, therefore, to migrate to the New World. Plans were made for some of them to cross the Atlantic in a small vessel called the *Speedwell* and for others to do that in the *Mayflower*. The *Speedwell*, however, did not prove seaworthy. So as many of her passengers as possible were crowded on the *Mayflower*, which then set sail from Plymouth, England, on Sept. 6, 1620, with 102 persons aboard. After a stormy voyage it reached Provincetown bay in Massachusetts on Nov. 11. From there they cruised along the coast until December 21. On that day the Pilgrims landed near a large boulder which has become famous as Plymouth Rock. They gave the name Plymouth also to the colony which they established close to it.

In well-known poems, Whittier, Lowell, Holmes, and Longfellow, among others, have glorified the *Mayflower* and the Pilgrims as shining symbols of American tradition. See ALDEN, JOHN; BREWSTER, WILLIAM; CARVER, JOHN; MASSACHUSETTS, History; MAYFLOWER; MAYFLOWER COMPACT; PILGRIMS; PLYMOUTH COLONY; PURITANISM; ROBINSON, JOHN; STANDISH, MYLES; WILLIAMS, ROGER.

THE
American Peoples
ENCYCLOPEDIA

WALTER DILL SCOTT, B.A., Ph.D., LL.D.
President Emeritus, Northwestern University
Chairman of the Editorial Board

FRANKLIN J. MEINE, Ph.B., M.A.
Editor-in-Chief

Chicago
The SPENCER PRESS, Inc.

INDIAN, AMERICAN. See INDIANS, AMERICAN.

INDIAN ARCHITECTURE. The history of architecture in India is inextricably connected with the history of its religion. Since the worship of God in the form of nature was one of the main tenets of ancient Brahminism, the national religion until the third century B.C., the erection of temples was forbidden as being unholy. It was not until the reign of of Asoka, who established Buddhism as the state religion, that the history of Indian architecture begins. The earliest monuments yet discovered are a series of columns erected by Asoka to commemorate the doctrines of Buddha. The sacred buildings of Buddhism may be considered in two classes—the *topes*, or *stupas*, and the *chaityas*, or temples. The *topes* are moundlike erections, rising from a low circular wall and containing in the center or at the top a small chamber for the preservation of the relics of some saint. Of the temples, or *chaityas*, only rock-cut examples now exist. These, having only the façade on the face of the rock, show mainly an interior architecture, interesting as being in many points a copy of a wooden building. In plan they consist of a three-aisled, columned hall, having a semicircular apse at the end farthest from the entrance, in which stood the shrine, and a semicircular ribbed roof, closely resembling woodwork. These interiors are lighted by one large opening at the entrance, admitting a single volume of light, which falls direct on the shrine at the farther end, leaving the side aisles and columns in comparative obscurity. Beside the topes and chaityas, there are also *viharas*, or monasteries, placed near the temples as residences for the priests and consisting of courtyards surrounded by cells. Sometimes there is a sanctuary for the shrine.

The Jain Style. The early Buddhist style was followed by that of the Jains (A.D. 100–1300), which extended over the whole of India from the Himalayas to Cape Comorin. While this style seems to have taken many of its features from some older non-Buddhist style, it lacks the vigor and boldness of the Buddhist, but far surpasses it in delicacy of detail.

The normal type of temple consists of a square cell, the *vimana*, lighted from the door only, containing a cross-legged figure of one of the 24 saints or Tirthankaras of the Jain religion, and surmounted by a pyramidal, spirelike roof, the *sikra*. To this is attached a portico or pillared hall of varying extent, cruciform in plan. The center of the portico is roofed by a dome

Dilwarra temple, in Jain style, on Mount Abu

carried on eight columns, with bracket capitals and sloping struts, which form the most characteristic and beautiful features of the style. In the temple of Vimala Sah, on Mount Abu (Rajputana), this portico consists of 48 pillars, and both portico and cell are placed in a courtyard surrounded by a double colonnade, which forms a portico to a range of cells, each occupied by a cross-legged image. Externally the temple is perfectly plain, and gives no indication of the magnificence within. Sculptured ornament of great richness and delicacy.

Partly contemporaneous with the Jain is the Hindu or Brahmanical style. It may be divided into three branches: (1) the northern Hindu, A.D. 600 to the present time; (2) the Chalukyan, or central Indian, A.D. 1000–1300; (3) the Dravidian, or southern Indian, A.D. 1350–1750. All three styles have the small shrine and portico, and the excessive richness of carving and sculpture, of the Jain style.

The Brahmanical Style. The great temple at Orissa (A.D. 617–637) is a fine example of the northern style. In the Chalukyan style the vimana is star-shaped in plan and is surmounted by a roof, formed either by a straight-sided cone with richly ornamented steps and vaselike finial or with a curved outline. The windows are filled in with elaborately pierced marble slabs, and the whole temple is placed on a terrace three or four feet in height. The principal monuments are in the province of Mysore. As in the Jain examples, the normal type of Dravidian temple has a square vimana with a many-storied pyramidal roof. The porch, a square building having a door on each side and a pyramidal roof lower than that over the cell, is placed similarly against the door of the cell. The Hindus seem to have disliked the use of columns in these cells, and never use them except in the largest examples. Cell and porch, forming the temple proper, are enclosed in a rectangular court entered under *gopuras*, or gate pyramids, of great size and magnificence. Within these courts are grouped lakes and ranks for ritual purposes, and the *choultries*, or halls of a thousand columns, where the dancing girls attached to the temple danced and sang, and where various ceremonies were performed. They are of extreme richness, often no more than two columns being alike in the one hall.

Indo-Saracenic Architecture. A fourth style of Indian architecture is the Indo-Saracenic, which may be divided into two parts, the Pathan and the Mogul. It begins with the 11th century and ends with the 15th. The early Pathan style, whether in stone, as at Ahmedabad, near the west coast, or in brick, as at Gaur, in Bengal, far eastward, consists, with one notable exception, of the Hindu architecture already described, but adapted for a simple worship and modified with a certain breadth of conception to which the Hindus never attained. The exception is this, that sculpture of the human form is excluded, as being idolatrous. The later Pathan style was based on northern models. Plainness and grandeur are its characteristics. The dome, the arch, the minaret are nobly developed.

The Mogul style began with Akbar the Great in the 14th century. At first it appeared in a somewhat Hinduized form, but it soon became purified from a Moslem point of view and assumed the severe simplicity and grandeur of the later Pathan style. At first the materials were red sandstone and marble intermixed. But by degrees marble was used more and more, till the culminating example of this style, the Taj Mahal at Agra, was encased entirely with this material, inlaid with precious and parti-colored stones. The Pearl mosque (marble) at Agra and the palace fortresses at Agra and Delhi, and the Jama mosques at Delhi and Lahore (Punjab) are the most renowned later examples of the style. See also MOSLEM ARCHITECTURE.

None of the Indian styles has influenced European architecture unless we except the buildings erected

The Pearl mosque, in Mogul style, at Agra

divided into three periods. The Buddhist period, best represented by the murals in the Ajanta caves, covers the first to the seventh century A.D. The work is flat, but extremely rhythmic with emphasis on contour. There is a thousand year gap between the frescoes of the Buddhist period and those now extant of the Rajput and Mongol periods. Mohammedan and Persian influences had meanwhile molded Indian style, and while the Rajput paintings (those produced in the Rajput domain after 1550) show a continuation of the Indian tradition, they are smaller and show many scenes from secular life. They are, however, lyrical and religious compared to the work of the Mongol school and more indigenous to India, for the Mongols brought Persian artists with them when they settled in India. Thus Mongol art is that of secular miniatures combined with Hindu elements. Court life under the Mongol rulers is emphasized as subject matter.

Minor Arts. Due to the caste system in which the craftsman passed his trade to his descendants generation after generation, the minor arts of India have a high quality of workmanship. Since jewelry was an important element in Indian dress, goldsmithing and damascening were highly developed arts. The weaving of cotton and CASHMERE was also artistically perfected. Yet in all the arts of India conventions of technique stringently influence the design. It is the inner soul of the subject that is represented rather than the outward form: symbolism is emphasized. M. R.

BIBLIOG.–Albert Grünwedel, *Buddhist Art in India* (1901); A. K. Coomaraswamy, *The Indian Craftsman* (1909), *The Arts and Crafts of India* (1914), *Rajput Painting* (1916); L. Binyon, *The Court Painters of the Grand Moguls* (1921); P. Brown, *Indian Painting Under the Mughals* (1924); A. K. Coomaraswamy, *History of Indian and Indonesian Art* (1927); P. Brown, *Indian Painting* (1929); V. A. Smith, *A History of Fine Art in India and Ceylon* (1930); Anand Mulk Raj, *The Hindu View of Art* (1933); L. Warner, *Buddhist Wall Paintings* (1938).

INDIAN ART, AMERICAN. See INDIANS, AMERICAN, *Indian Art*.

INDIAN CAPTIVITIES. Prisoners were taken by most Indian tribes, and although a surprising number were not ill-treated, men captured in battle were often tortured. Colonel William Crawford was burned at the stake in 1792, but possibly no other officer was so treated. Indians were apt to be merciless with those who could not keep up in the retreat from a raid. On arrival at a village the captives were divided among families, often being assigned as slaves in families where male members had been killed. Adoption into the tribe often followed. Many children raised among the Indians later had no desire to return to their families. Women sometimes were forced to become wives of Indians, but often accepted the relationship voluntarily. It has been stated that no cases of rape are known east of the Mississippi River; many aggravated cases of rape are charged against the Plains tribes and the Apaches.

"The Narrative of the Captivity and Restoration of Mrs. Mary Rowlandson," who was taken in KING PHILIP'S WAR, was published in 1682, the first of a long line of "captivity" literature. Increase and Cotton Mather collected and printed many early narratives. Other notable accounts were written by John Gyles, 1736, Robert Eastburn, 1758, and Elizabeth Hanson, 1780. HANNAH DUSTIN, captured in 1697, with the aid of her nurse and a boy killed 10 Indians and brought back their scalps.

During the French wars, many captives were redeemed from the Indians and distributed among families in Canada, where they were so well treated many refused to return home. During the Revolution and War of 1812 the British ransomed many captives from the Indians and sometimes arranged for their exchange. Captivity for ransom became a lucrative traffic in the Southwest from 1835–1875, bringing sums as high as $500.

Some former captives became notable scouts. Simon Kenton's "Mazeppa ride" in 1778 is a frontier classic.

---

by Emmanuel of Portugal (1495–1521) at Tromar and Batalha in Portugal, shortly after the Portuguese settlement in India. These show detail of a type utterly unlike that of any other European building, but having many points of resemblance to the rich work of the Jain style. S. W. X.

BIBLIOG.–E. B. Havell, *Indian Architecture: Its Psychology, Structure, and History* (1913); *Handbook of Indian Art* (1920); J. F. Blacker, *ABC of Indian Art* (1922); A. Nawrath, *India and China* (1939).

INDIAN ART begins simultaneously with the rise of Indian architecture in the third century B.C. Like architecture it, too, is closely related to the religion of the country. Temple decoration constitutes the greatest outlet for Indian art, and sculpture far exceeds painting in the ornamentation of religious buildings. In many structures there is little wall space that is not fully carved in reliefs so luxuriant that they resemble the lavish natural growth of the tropical jungles of India. The stories represented in profuse carvings, like those on the Sanchi Gates, are taken from the life of Buddha. However, none of the earlier reliefs depict Buddha in human form, but substitute his symbol, the stupa, or represent him reincarnated as an animal. The personification of Buddha as a human being did not begin until several hundred years after his death.

Sculpture in the Round. Indian sculpture in the round is characteristically a single male figure, usually a deity of the Indian religion. Because of the divinity inherent in all figures, there is no attempt at carving individuality or personality; the abstract symbol of spirituality is emphasized. Trends, such as the monumentality and formalism of the Gupta period, compared with the grace and lightness of the next style, have arisen and departed in Indian sculpture without influencing its transcendental quality.

Mural Painting. At one time there was a great fresco tradition in Indian art, but it has long since been forgotten. Great gaps occur in the history of Indian mural painting of past ages, yet it can be

MUSEUM OF FINE ARTS, BOSTON

Stone statue of Siva, 10–11th century

FREER GALLERY OF ART, WASHINGTON

Indian painting of the Rajput period

BOSTON MUS. OF FINE ARTS

Champleve enamel pendant

MUSEUM OF FINE ARTS, BOSTON

Rajput painting, 17th century, depicts scene from "Ramayana"

PICTURES

Detail of frieze from one of Sanchi gates

PICTURES

Detail of rock-cut relief at Mamallapuram

Captain William Wells, killed at Fort Dearborn (1812), had been a captive of Little Turtle. Frank Gruard, scout under Crook in 1876, was said to have been a Hawaiian once captive among the Sioux.

Frances Slocum, captured in Wyoming, Pennsylvania, in 1778, lived happily among the Miamis in Indiana until 1847. Cynthia Ann Parker, taken in Texas in 1836, became the mother of the notable Comanche chief Quanah Parker.   DON RUSSELL

LYNWOOD M. CHACE

Indian pipes

BIBLIOG.–Isabel M. Calder, *Colonial Captivities, Marches and Journeys* (1935); Carl Coke Rister, *Border Captives* (1940), *Tragedies of the Wilderness, or True and Authentic Narratives of Captives* (1841).

INDIAN FIG. See BANYAN TREE.

INDIAN FIRE, also known as Bengal lights, colored fires (red, white, green, blue or yellow) used as signals and in pyrotechnics. Potassium chlorate, antimony sulfide, and sulfur are the chief ingredients.

INDIAN HEMP. See DOGBANE.

INDIAN OCEAN, one of the oceans of the globe, stretches from Africa E to Indonesia and Australia, and from Asia S to the Antarctic regions; area about 27,500,000 sq. mi. In the north it is divided by the peninsula of India into two basins: the Arabian Sea on the west and the Bay of Bengal on the east. Outside these two relatively shallow arms, the uniform average depth is from 2,200 to 2,300 fathoms, except for three small depressions which sink below the 3,000 fathom line. These are the Wharton and Maclear deeps to the northwest of Australia, and the Jeffreys deep to the south of Australia. The greatest depth thus far ascertained is 3,232 fathoms. North of 13° S lat. the surface water has a mean annual temperature of 80°; but from that line it gradually decreases as the Antarctic regions are approached. Below 2,000 fathoms the temperature remains fairly constant at 35° F.

Along the line of 13° S lat. a strong current of warm water flows west toward Madagascar, and there dividing, gives rise to the swift Agulhas current, which sweeps southward along the coast of South Africa. This is compensated by an easterly flowing equatorial current, which remains constant throughout the year, and by a cold current which runs northward along the western coast of Australia. Also, there is a deep-sea flow of cold water from the Antarctic. During the summer months, the southwestern monsoon blows steadily toward the continent of Africa. Although in great part a fairly tranquil region, this ocean is sometimes visited, expecially at the changes of the monsoons, by violent hurricanes.

The Indian Ocean is fed by several large rivers, notably the Indus, Ganges, Brahmaputra, Irrawaddy, Salween, and Tigris-Euphrates on the north, and by the Zambezi and Limpopo on the west. The principal islands which stud its waters are Madagascar, Mauritius, Réunion, Rodriquez, Socotra, Ceylon, and the archipelagoes of the Andamans, Nicobars, Mergui, Maldives, and Laccadives. Deep-sea investigations do not favor the existence of the fabled continent of Lemuria, reputed to have been the cradle of the human race.   S. W. X.

INDIAN PAINT BRUSH, common wild flower of the western region of the United States and state flower of Wyoming. The leaves of *Castilleja coccinea* are olive or grass green, alternate on the stem, and the flowers are yellow, reddish, or purple, closely crowded at the tip.

INDIAN PIPE, a low-growing parasitic plant native to Asia and the United States which attaches itself to roots or to decomposing vegetable matter. It is waxy white in color but turns black on drying. It has a solitary nodding flower. An infusion of the root was once thought to be beneficial in the treatment of cancer, hence it is sometimes known as Cancer Root. It is called Corpse Plant, *Monotropa uniflora*.

INDIAN PLANTAIN, a genus of tall perennial herbs of the eastern and middle United States. The Great Indian Plantain, *Cacalia reniformis*, occurs in damp woodlands from New Jersey and Illinois southward. It bears thin leaves, green on either side, and large corymbs of white flowers. The Pale Indian Plantain, *C. atriplicifolia*, is a smaller plant, also bearing perfect white flowers in corymbs.

INDIAN POKE, or **WHITE HELLEBORE,** a hardy perennial with large broad leaves and yellowish green flowers, growing in swamps and marshy ground from Canada to North Carolina. Its powdered roots form the basis of various insect powders. It is sometimes cultivated as a border plant.

INDIAN RIVER, a long narrow lagoon, paralleling and near the E coast of Florida, about one to five miles wide and 100 miles long. It is a part of the GULF INTRACOASTAL WATERWAY and is connected with the Atlantic Ocean at several points. Many popular winter resorts have been built along its course and the Indian River country is famous for its citrus fruits. The river was once called Ais, the Indian word meaning "deer."

INDIAN SCHOOLS. See INDIANS, AMERICAN, *Education.*

INDIAN SHOT. See CANNA.

INDIAN RESERVATIONS. See INDIANS, AMERICAN, *Social and Economic Progress.*

INDIAN SUMMER, a spell of mild and generally hazy weather occurring in October or November after the first days of freezing temperature. The term originated in the U.S. in the 18th century. Indian Summer may last only a few days, or over a more extended period. In some years it does not come at all. The haziness in the quiet, warm air is supposedly due to smoke from the fall burnings over large tracts.

INDIAN TAILORBIRD, a small sparrow-like bird of India and adjacent countries, about five inches long, yellowish green in color on the upper parts and white beneath. In the summer the male acquires much lengthened middle tail feathers. The bird is remarkable chiefly for its skill in constructing its nest, which consists of fine grass, hair, or down placed in a receptacle made by fastening the edges of a leaf together with plant fibers.

INDIAN TERRITORY, a term at first loosely applied to unorganized U.S. territory; later specifically to all of Oklahoma except the panhandle. It was never organized. Treaties with the CHOCTAWS (1820), CREEKS (1825), CHEROKEES (1828), SEMINOLES (1832), and CHICKASAWS (1837), opened this area to these "Five Civilized Tribes." A formal policy of moving other Eastern tribes there was adopted in 1830. "Indian Territory" was first used officially in 1848 to indicate all of the Louisiana Purchase south of the Platte River, and after the establishment of Nebraska and Kansas Territories in 1854 the term Indian Territory was applied to present-day Oklahoma except the panhandle. A treaty with the Osage in 1825 set aside a strip 50 miles wide between Indian Territory and their reservation; it became known as the neutral land. The neutral land was added to Indian Territory, establishing its northern boundary north of the southern boundary of Missouri. In 1833 the Quapaws were given a reservation at the northeast corner of Indian Territory without reference to the Five Tribes. Later a number of Eastern tribes were admitted to this area. In 1825 a treaty was made between the tribes moved to Oklahoma and those originally there, principally the Comanches and Wichitas, giving the Western tribes hunting rights in the western half of the Territory. During the Civil War the Territory was largely under Confederate control and after the war new arrangements were made with the Five Tribes whereby they agreed to admit other tribes and ceded land. From 1879 to 1889 there was considerable organized illegal entry into the western half of the Territory by "boomers." In 1889 a small "Oklahoma District" was opened to settlement. In 1890 the western half, including the Public Lands strip, was designated Oklahoma Territory, leaving the eastern half as Indian Territory. Oklahoma areas were opened to settlement from time to time, and less official settlement continued in Indian Territory. In 1907 the two territories were re-united and admitted as the state of Oklahoma. See OKLAHOMA, *History*.   DON RUSSELL

BIBLIOG.–Roy Gittinger, *The Formation of the State of Oklahoma* (1939); Grant Foreman, *Indians and Pioneers* (1930), *Advancing the Frontier* (1933), *The Five Civilized Tribes* (1934), *A History of Oklahoma* (1942), *The Last Trek of the Indians* (1946).

INDIAN TOBACCO, a poisonous plant belonging to the family *Lobeliaceae*. Indian tobacco is found extensively in pastures, dry open fields, and wooded areas. It has branched stems, bractlike leaves, and tubular flowers. The leaves, stems, and fruits contain two narcotic alkaloids, *lobeline* and *lobelidine*, small amounts of which are used in medicine to relieve the distress of laryngitis. Overdoses of these alkaloids cause nausea, convulsions, and death in man, and livestock are poisoned by feeding upon the foliage. Indian tobacco is the species *Lobelia inflata*.

INDIAN TURNIP. See JACK-IN-THE-PULPIT.

INDIAN WARS occurred intermittently in American history from the years of early settlement until the closing of the frontier about 1890. Much of the conflict involved depredations (committed by both sides) and bloody guerrilla warfare, leading usually to punitive wars conducted by the whites against their savage opponents. Some of the wars were well-organized attacks made by the Indians to exterminate the settlers who were taking their homeland; examples were King Philip's War and Pontiac's War. At other times, as during the Colonial wars, the American Revolution, and the War of 1812, the Indians fought as allies of one of the contending governments. The causes of these wars were usually numerous and often confused, but essentially there was one fundamental cause: the dispossession of savage tribes by the inexorable power of civilized peoples. It was inevitable that a few hundred thousand redmen, making little use of their territory beyond exploiting it as a hunting ground, should give way before agricultural homeseekers, but the displacement involved deep injustice to the first Americans. The history of these wars is a record of broken treaties; agreements to be effective "as long as the grass shall grow" were flagrantly violated by individualistic settlers who coveted the lands solemnly promised to the Indians. The latter resisted the inevitable with savage cruelty, inflicting a long series of massacres upon the white men. The self-reliant but half-lawless pioneers retaliated in kind, inflicting perhaps as many atrocities as they suffered.

Colonial Indian Wars. In early Virginia the Indians were hostile and friendly by turns; in 1622, 347 persons perished in the Great Massacre; again in 1644 about 500 were killed in a second uprising. Another prominent Indian uprising in Virginia occurred in 1675–76 and played a part in BACON'S REBELLION. The Plymouth colony enjoyed friendly relations with the Indians through its treaty of peace with Massasoit, chief of the Wampanoags, but after his death came King Philip's War (1675–76), which for a time threatened the existence of the colony. The Massachusetts Bay colony early came into conflict with the Pequots, until this tribe was destroyed in the Pequot War of 1637. The settlers of Connecticut were also involved in this Pequot War. Rhode Island, under the leadership of ROGER WILLIAMS, who advocated fair treatment for the aborigines, lived at peace with the Indians until the Narragansetts joined in King Philip's War. In New York the original Dutch settlers had considerable trouble with the Indians; oppressive policies led to two Indian uprisings (1637–45 and 1659–64), the latter often called the Esopus War. On the Delaware the colony of New Sweden enjoyed uneventful relations with the Indians. William Penn established terms of friendship with the red men, and as a consequence Pennsylvania lived at peace until the French and Indian War. New Jersey and Delaware had little difficulty with the Indians. Maryland during a period of internal discord (1642–47) suffered minor Indian attacks. South of Virginia from 1711 to 1714 the settlements in North Carolina suffered severely from attacks by the Tuscaroras, while the Yamasee War (1714–15) caused the death of about 400 persons in South Carolina. Georgia had no troubles with the Indians until after the Revolution.

The northern colonies suffered severely from Indian attacks during the long series of imperial conflicts which broke out between England and France in 1689. In KING WILLIAM'S WAR (1689–97) the Indian allies of the French attacked English frontier settlements from Maine to New York, the most notable event being the destruction of Schenectady. In QUEEN ANNE'S WAR (1702–13) the towns of Wells, Saco, Deerfield, Reading, Sudbury, and Haverhill were the victims of French and Indian attacks. Such attacks were renewed in KING GEORGE'S WAR (1744–48) and in the FRENCH AND INDIAN WAR (1754–63). After the final defeat of the French, occurred the Pontiac War (1763–64), a determined uprising of the western Indians to keep the British from taking control of their new territory. A decade later the Indians of the Ohio region, incensed at the encroachments of frontiersmen, committed a series of attacks, which led to Dunmore's War (1774) in retaliation.

Revolutionary Period. Widespread Indian warfare took place during the American Revolution. Induced by British agents, motivated also by pioneer encroachments on their hunting grounds, many tribes began to terrorize the frontier. The Iroquois (except the Oneidas and the Tuscaroras) under the leadership of Joseph Brant participated in many border campaigns, including Burgoyne's expedition, being responsible for massacres at Cherry Valley and Wyoming Valley, but were finally defeated by an American expedition in 1779. Cherokee uprisings, directed at American pioneers on the Virginia-North Carolina frontier, took place in 1776 and 1780, but were quickly crushed. Most of the tribes north of the Ohio River were active allies of the British; they directed most of their hostility toward the incoming settlers in Kentucky. Daniel Boone and George Rogers Clark took prominent roles in these rear-guard campaigns of the Revolution. In Georgia the Creeks gave last-minute assistance to the losing British cause.

Midwestern and Southern Indian Wars. With the British retaining the western forts after the Revolution, contrary to the territorial provisions of the treaty of 1783, most of the tribes of the Northwest Territory continued hostile to the United States. When the new nation attempted to establish control over its western lands in 1790 warfare broke out, resulting in defeats for expeditions led by Harmar (1790) and St. Clair (1791); the Indians were finally defeated in 1794 by General Wayne at the Battle of Fallen Timbers, and soon thereafter the British abandoned the western forts. As American settlers began to pour into the Midwest another Indian uprising occurred, led by the able Shawnee chief Tecumseh, who organized a great Indian confederation against the whites; the Indians were defeated at the Battle of Tippecanoe (1811) by William Henry

ST. CLAIR Expedition 1791
Surprised and surrounded,
St.Clair in desperation ordered
a charge through the circle.
His subsequent retreat
turned to a wild flight and
overwhelming defeat—

'794
'ined
'1793
'bers,
'ians.

© NORTHERN TRUST CO., CHICAGO

Indian Wars scene from map, "The Old Northwest Territory"

Harrison. During the War of 1812 the Indians again fought as allies of the British; Tecumseh's leadership proved invaluable until he was killed at the Battle of the Thames (1813). A tragic incident of the Indian warfare in Illinois was the Fort Dearborn Massacre. Abandoned by their British allies in the treaty of peace of late 1814, the Indians were forced to make terms with the Americans. Thereafter the only important Indian campaign in the Midwest was the Black Hawk War (1832). In the South the Creeks with British encouragement took the warpath in 1813; they were defeated by Andrew Jackson at the battles of Talladega (1813) and Horseshoe Bend (1814). Later as they were facing removal west of the Mississippi the Creeks made raids on settlements in Georgia and Alabama (1836–37) but they were soon forced to abandon their homeland. Much more serious and destructive were the Seminole Wars (1816–18, 1835–42) in Florida.

Western Indian Wars. In Oregon the murder of the missionary MARCUS WHITMAN by the Cayuse Indians led to the Cayuse War, which dragged on from 1847 until 1850. After the American annexation of Texas and New Mexico the United States had to send a series of expeditions against the Navahos, Cheyennes, Lipans, and Kickapoos (1849–63). During the same time minor Indian wars were fought in California and Utah. More serious were the Yakima Indian Wars in Oregon (1855–58). The most determined of all the Western tribes in resisting the encroachments of the whites were the Sioux. The numerous Sioux tribes were involved in the following uprisings and campaigns: uprising near Fort Laramie in 1854, leading to a punitive expedition by General Harney the next year; a bloody uprising near Mankato, Minn. (1862); uprising in Wyoming in 1865, followed by the indecisive Powder River campaign; the Red Cloud War (1866–68); uprising of the Sioux and other tribes after the opening of the Black Hills in 1874, ending in the defeat of the Indians in 1877, following the annihilation of Custer's force at Little Big Horn (1876); a final uprising in 1889 under religious frenzy, put down by defeat at the Battle of Wounded Knee (1890). The Cheyennes were associated with the Sioux in most of these campaigns; it is said that they suffered greater battle casualties than any other tribe in proportion to numbers in numerous engagements from 1866 to 1878. The Arapahoes also participated in many of these battles. A series of campaigns were fought against the Kiowas, Comanches, and other tribes from 1863 to 1881 in Kansas, Colorado, New Mexico, Texas, and Indian Territory. In the Southwest the Apaches were especially troublesome; in 1860 they went on the warpath, and for ten years they dominated what is now Arizona; in a determined campaign (1872–74) General Crook defeated them, but even after that time they often escaped from their reser-

vations and continued their raids; final defeat came in 1886 with the surrender of Geronimo to General Miles. The Utes were also troublesome. There were campaigns against them in Colorado and Utah (1878, 1879–80). Other Indian wars of prominence were the following: the Modoc War (1872–73) in southern Oregon and northern California; the Nez Percé War (1877) in Utah; and the Bannock War (1878) against the Bannocks, Piutes, and Shoshones in Idaho, Washington, and Wyoming. A minor expedition was led (1898) against the Chippewas in Minnesota. For details concerning Indian wars see the following entries:

Indian Wars	Battles and Massacres
BLACK HAWK WAR	DEARBORN, FORT
CHEROKEE WARS	DUMMER, FORT
DUMMER'S WAR	FALLEN TIMBERS, BATTLE OF
DUNMORE'S WAR	LITTLE BIG HORN BATTLE
ESOPUS WAR	MOUNTAIN MEADOWS MASSACRE
KING PHILIP'S WAR	POINT PLEASANT, BATTLE OF
OUACHITA INDIAN CAMPAIGN	SAND CREEK MASSACRE
PEQUOT WAR	SLIM BUTTES, BATTLE OF
RED CLOUD WAR	SPIRIT LAKE MASSACRE
RED RIVER INDIAN WAR	TALLADEGA, BATTLE OF
SEMINOLE WARS	TIPPECANOE, BATTLE OF
YAKIMA INDIANS	WOUNDED KNEE, BATTLE OF
YAMASEE WAR	WYOMING MASSACRE

Indian Tribes	Indian Leaders
FOX INDIANS	BLACK HAWK
IROQUOIS INDIANS	BRANT, JOSEPH
KICKAPOO INDIANS	CRAZY HORSE
KIOWA INDIANS	GERONIMO
MODOC INDIANS	GIRTY, SIMON
MOHAWK INDIANS	JOSEPH, CHIEF
NARRAGANSETT INDIANS	OSCEOLA
NATCHEZ INDIANS	PONTIAC
NAVAHO INDIANS	RED CLOUD
NEZ PERCE INDIANS	SITTING BULL
ONEIDA INDIANS	TECUMSEH
ONONDAGA INDIANS	
OTTAWA INDIANS	Indian Fighters
PAIUTE INDIANS	BOONE, DANIEL
POTAWATOMIE INDIANS	CLARK, GEORGE ROGERS
SAUK INDIANS	CROOK, GEORGE
SENECA INDIANS	CUSTER, GEORGE
SHAWNEE INDIANS	CARSON, CHRISTOPHER
SHOSHONE INDIANS	FORSYTH, GEORGE A.
SIOUX INDIANS	GIBBON, JOHN
TUSCARORA INDIANS	HARMAR, JOSIAH
UTE INDIANS	HARRISON, WILLIAM HENRY
WAMPANOAG INDIANS	JACKSON, ANDREW
WINNEBAGO INDIANS	KENTON, SIMON
	MILES, NELSON A.
	SHERIDAN, PHILIP
	ST. CLAIR, ARTHUR
	STANDISH, MYLES
	WAYNE, ANTHONY

See also UNITED STATES HISTORY; REVOLUTION, AMERICAN; WAR OF 1812; also the sections on history for the various states.　　　　　　　F. M.

BIBLIOG.—G. Foreman, *Advancing the Frontier, 1830–1860* (1933), *Indians and Pioneers* (1930, ed. 1936); C. J. Brill, *Conquest of the Southern Plains* (1938); G. F. Brimlow, *Bannock Indian War of 1878* (1938); J. M. Oskison, *Tecumseh and His Times* (1938); F. Haines, *Red Eagles of the Northwest* (1939); G. T. Hunt, *Wars of the Iroquois* (1940); T. Cruse, *Apache Days and After* (1941); F. D. Downey, *Indian Fighting Army* (1941); C. C. Rister, *Border Command, General Phil Sheridan in the West* (1944); G. Crook, *General George Crook* (1946); L. H. Gipson, *Great War for the Empire* (1946); M. F. Schmitt and D. Brown, *Fighting Indians of the West* (1948); W. S. Campbell, *Warpath and Council Fire* (1948); J. G. Bourke, *On the Border with Crook* (1950).

INDIANA

The Hoosier State

INLAND STEEL COMPANY

This thriving state evolved from the old Northwest Territory is one of the leading producers of limestone, of coal, and of steel and iron

INDIANA, known as the "Hoosier State," N central United States; bounded on the N by Lake Michigan and Michigan; on the E by Ohio; on the S by the Ohio River and Kentucky; on the W by Illinois; and on the SW by the Wabash River; area, 36,291 sq. mi., including 309 sq. mi. of inland water; pop. (1950) 3,934,224. The state is 276 miles long and 177 miles wide. Indianians are popularly called "Hoosiers." There are several versions of the origin of the name: it may be a contraction of the pioneer's hail to visitors, "Who's yere"; or it may have developed from the name given to Indiana canal laborers hired by Samuel Hoosier to work on the Ohio Falls Canal at Louisville. The state motto is "The Crossroads of America," and the flower is the zinnia. The song is "On the Banks of the Wabash Far Away."

Topography. Indiana is in the valley of the Mississippi River and in the basin of the Great Lakes. It is partly in the great central prairie and for the most part has an undulating surface, sloping southwestward. The highest point in the state is in Randolph County in the eastern tier of counties where the estimated altitude is about 1,200 feet; the southwestern corner of the state is about 300 feet above sea level. The region near Lake Michigan is a sandy tract, bordered on the south by low marshes, among which are a number of lakes. The largest of these is English Lake, formed by the broadened bed of the Kankakee River. There are also a number of lakes in the northeast corner. The southwest corner is broken and covered with timber.

Drainage is chiefly through the WABASH River and its main tributaries: the WHITE, Tippecanoe, Mississinewa, Salamonie, Wild Cat, and others. The northern part of the state drains into Lake Michigan through the Calumet and ST. JOSEPH rivers, or into the Mississippi through the KANKAKEE River. The southeastern part drains into the Ohio River.

Climate. Indiana has a humid continental climate characterized by long, warm summers and cold winters. The growing season is 170 days long in the northern part of the state, and 190 days in the south. The average annual temperature since 1886 was 52.7° F.; extremes of 116° (1936) and −33° (1887) have been recorded. An average of 147 days a year are cloud-free. Precipitation, which is evenly distributed throughout the year, increases from north to south: in the north, 35.85 inches is the average; in the center, 39.10; and in the south, 42.83; the state average is 39.26 inches. Unmelted snowfall amounts to 22.5 inches annually and is heaviest in the north.

Drought is known in the southeastern hill section. The prevailing wind is from the west in winter and from the southwest in summer. Gales, tornadoes, and other damaging winds are rare.

Plants and Animals. Plants and wild life are conserved in the state parks and in the 781,000 acres of national forests located in southern Indiana, including Lafayette, Lost River, Patoka, and Pleasant Run forests. Although variations in soil and terrain between the dune country around Lake Michigan and the prairie and woodland in the south of the state are slight, Indiana has a great variety of plants and animals. White pine, jack pine, arctic lichen moss, and some varieties of cactus thrive in the sand hills. In the southern woodlands the trunks of beech and sycamore gleam white, and the leaves afford magnificent coloring in autumn. A particular favorite is the tulip, or yellow poplar, voted the state tree. Poplars, hickories, and several varieties of oaks are among the more than 120 kinds of trees which are native to the state. Although much of the swampland around the northern lakes has been drained, some of the swamp plants survive, notably the peppermint which is harvested commercially. Native Indiana shrubs are the elderberry, bittersweet, trumpet creeper, dogwood, and sumac. Goldenrod, asters, sunflowers, fringed gentian, and Queen Anne's lace are familiar roadside flowers.

The red fox is the only carnivorous animal which is still found in Indiana. Among the small animals are the rabbit, muskrat, raccoon, woodchuck, mink, and opossum. In the dunes are many waterfowl: marsh birds, herons, bitterns, geese, and ducks; while in the central and southern part are such familiar meadow and orchard birds as the warbler, oriole, robin, lark, woodpecker, swallow, thrush, flicker, bluebird, wren, and bluejay. The cardinal is the state bird. Among the fish found in Indiana's lakes and streams are catfish, pike, bass, pickerel, and sunfish.

PRINCIPAL CITIES	POPULATION	
	Census 1940	Census 1950
Indianapolis (Capital)	386,972	427,173
Gary	111,719	133,911
Fort Wayne	118,410	133,607
Evansville	97,062	128,636
South Bend	101,268	115,911
Hammond	70,184	87,594
Terre Haute	62,693	64,214
Muncie	49,720	58,479
East Chicago	54,637	54,263
Anderson	41,572	46,820

PURDUE UNIVERSITY

Memorial Union building at Purdue University

PEOPLE

Population. According to the Federal census for 1950 the population of Indiana was 3,934,224, an increase of 506,428, or 14.8 per cent, over 1940 (compared with an increase of 5.8 per cent during 1930–40).

Education. Administration of education is vested in a state superintendent of public instruction. Education is free for all persons in the state between 6 and 21 years of age, compulsory for all between 7 and 16. The state provides for the instruction of teachers in the State Normal School, the western division being at Terre Haute and the eastern at Muncie. The institutions of higher learning supported by the state are Indiana University at Bloomington, Purdue University, and a school of technology at Lafayette. Other institutions of higher learning include DePauw University, at Greencastle; NOTRE DAME UNIVERSITY, near South Bend; Earlham College, at Richmond; Hanover College, at Hanover; Franklin College, at Franklin; Goshen College, at Goshen; Rose Polytechnic Institute, at Terre Haute; Wabash College, at Crawfordsville; Indiana Central College, at Indianapolis; Oakland City College, at Oakland City; Manchester College, at North Manchester; Butler University, at Indianapolis; Valparaiso University, at Valparaiso; Marion College, at Marion; and Evansville College, at Evansville.

Public Welfare. In 1936, a Department of Public Welfare was created to administer all of the state welfare services and control state institutions. Mental cases are handled by the Central State Hospital at Indianapolis, the state hospitals at Evansville, Logansport, Madison, and Richmond; the Fort Wayne State School, Muscatatuck State School at Butlersville, and

Howard and Morrissey Halls at Notre Dame

UNIVERSITY OF NOTRE DAME

the Village for Epileptics at New Castle. Penal and correctional institutions include the state prisons at Michigan City and Greencastle, the Reformatory at Pendleton, the Boys' School at Plainfield, the Women's Prison at Indianapolis, and the Girls' School near Indianapolis. Other state institutions include the Soldiers' Home at Lafayette, the Soldiers', Sailors' and Children's Home at Knightstown, and the School for the Blind and the School for the Deaf at Indianapolis.

ECONOMIC LIFE

Minerals and Mining. Indiana has considerable wealth in its mines and quarries. It has ranked first among the states in the value of the limestone industry and high in coal production. Coal mining is the state's leading mineral industry. Important by-products are gas, coke, and producer gas. Indiana has ranked among the four top states in the output of coke. The coal-producing area, comprising about 7,000 square miles in the southwestern part of the state, is part of the Eastern Interior Coal Field, which extends also into Illinois and Kentucky.

More than two-thirds of the limestone used for building in the United States comes from Indiana, the Bedford-Bloomington district in Lawrence and Monroe counties being the largest producer of this mineral. The presence of fine clay deposits and the immense supply of limestone account for the state's high rank in the manufacture of Portland cement. Indiana has held third or fourth place among the states in the production of pig iron. In the 1880's immense wells of natural gas were tapped, but the supply was squandered in the period 1890–1910. At about the same time and in the same area petroleum was found and exploited; after an oil boom of a few years, production declined but in recent years new wells, in the southwestern part of the state, have increased production. In 1948 Indiana ranked 18th among the states in mineral production, with its total output valued at $166,803,000.

MINERAL PRODUCTION OF INDIANA

MINERAL	UNIT (Thousands)	1946	1947	1948
Clay	Short Tons	983	1,181	1,210
Coal	Short Tons	21,696	25,449	22,500
Iron, Pig	Short Tons	4,823	6,385	6,496
Natural Gas	M. Cu. Ft.	1,094	877	553
Petroleum	Barrels	6,726	6,095	6,710
Sand and Gravel	Short Tons	8,752	9,231	9,439
Stone	Short Tons	5,767	5,589	6,574

Agriculture and Stock Raising. The soil of Indiana is generally fertile and exceptionally so in the valleys of the Wabash and White rivers. The surface soil of the northern and central parts of the state is made up of deposits of glacial drift, with alluvial silt in the river bottoms. The most common type of farm in the state is the fairly small general farm; excessive crop specialization has generally been avoided. Nearly a fourth of the entire state acreage is planted in corn, which is by far the state's most important crop.

PRINCIPAL CROPS OF INDIANA

CROP	UNIT (Thousands)	1939-1948 Average	1949	1950
Apples	Bushels	4,640	3,900	4,845
Corn	Bushels	207,605	249,548	213,790
Hay	Tons	2,580	2,253	2,622
Oats	Bushels	45,047	55,825	52,577
Popcorn	Pounds	25,103	29,520	35,530
Potatoes	Bushels	4,640	3,900	4,845
Rye	Bushels	1,292	756	826
Soybeans	Bushels	22,958	34,608	35,002
Wheat	Bushels	28,258	39,150	31,798

INTERNATIONAL HARVESTER CO.

Indiana corn, the state's most important crop

INDIANA DEPT. OF COMMERCE

Guernsey cows, part of Indiana's dairy industry

STANDARD OIL CO. (IND.)

Whiting oil refinery, one of world's greatest

UNITED AIR LINES

Aerial view of the vast steel mills at Gary

Operations in an Indiana limestone quarry

INDIANA DEPT. OF COMMERCE

U.S. BUREAU OF MINES

Strip mining operations by a coal company

Truck gardens and fruit orchards are important in the agricultural economy of the state. Purdue University has been of prime importance in the development of the state's agriculture. The Indiana Farm Bureau, a unit of the American Farm Bureau Federation, has been the leading co-operative agency for Indiana farmers. Besides its educational work and attention to farm legislation, it has conducted co-operative sales and marketing activities, and participated in the rural electrification program.

Livestock constitutes a large part of the state's farm wealth, including cattle, horses, swine, mules, and sheep. Though conducted most intensively around the larger cities and in the northwestern area for the Chicago market, dairying is well distributed around the state. The poultry industry is important; several fur farms breed silver fox, skunk, and raccoon; and the breeding of rabbits, guinea pigs, pigeons, frogs, and goldfish has sometimes been profitable.

Forestry. Indiana has declined in importance as a lumber producing state, and tree planting has been resorted to. A century ago forests covered about seven-eighths of the state. Destruction of the forests, after protracted waste, has been followed in turn by floods, drought, and soil erosion. Nevertheless, the supply of timber is still an important resource. The trees include oak, ash, walnut, poplar, hickory, maple, elm, Norway spruce, pine, and hemlock. A state department of conservation, established in 1919, has been concerned, notably, with conserving and propagating wild life and guarding against drought, flood, and soil erosion. The department has charge of the state forests, state parks, game preserves, and historical memorials. It also maintains nurseries for reforestation purposes and sponsors a forest-fire prevention campaign.

Fisheries. The fisheries of northern Indiana are carried on in Lake Michigan and those of southern Indiana in the Ohio, Wabash, White, and other rivers. The state department of conservation maintains five major fish hatcheries; the first distributed include black bass, bluegills, yellow perch, crappie, rock bass, sunfish, catfish, carp, and pike perch.

Manufactures. Indiana showed a wonderful in-

Pioneer village in Spring Mill State Park

INDIANA DEPT. OF COMMERCE

INDIANA DEPT. OF COMMERCE

A shifting white sand hill in Dunes State Park

crease in manufactures up to the second decade of the 20th century. An abundant supply of timber, important agricultural products, and a large output of petroleum and natural gas were factors in this growth. The falling off of supplies of these natural resources in recent years has hurt the industries depending on them, but manufacturing has nevertheless continued to grow, lumber being shipped in from outside the state to supplement the local supply; while the increasing amount of coal mined has compensated largely for the smaller supply of natural gas and stimulated other lines of manufacturing. The 1947 Census of Manufactures showed that there were 5,408 industrial establishments in Indiana; the total value added by manufacture was $2,977,508,000.

Iron and steel, steel works, and rolling mills constitute the most important industry. The Calumet region, including Gary, East Chicago, Hammond, and Whiting, is the center of this industry in the state, and also of petroleum refining, another of the more valuable enterprises. Highly important, too, is the manufacture of motor-vehicle bodies and parts, and of motor vehicles; Indiana was one of the leading states in the development of the automobile industry. Other important industries or products include: electrical machinery, apparatus, and supplies; slaughtering and meat packing; refrigerators and ice-making apparatus; furniture (including store and office fixtures); glass; flour and other grain mill-products; blast-furnace products; drugs and medicines; canned and dried fruits and vegetables; and canned and bottled juices, preserves, and jellies; coke oven products; printing and publishing; wearing apparel; machine shop products; the making and repair of railroad cars; and distilled liquors.

Transportation. The location of the state has been conducive to the development of railway facilities; nearly all the great trunk lines connecting the East with the West pass through it, and, with Chicago to the northwest and Louisville and Cincinnati to the south and southeast, many important lines cross from north to south. There are more than 7,000 miles of steam railway within the state. Indiana was one of the leading states in the construction of electric railways, with extensive interurban systems. Motorbus lines have been expanding and more than 2,000 truck lines use the nearly 60,000 miles of surfaced roads which reach into every community. Three major air lines serve Indiana. Indianapolis is served by the TWA, American, and Eastern air lines; South Bend is on the American Airlines, and Fort Wayne is served by the TWA, while more than 50 airports and landing fields are in operation. Four important lake ports, Gary, Buffington, East Chicago, and Michigan City, move 16,000,000 tons of freight annually to supply the concentrated Calumet industrial region. On the Ohio River, Evansville is the chief port for barge lines running both north and south. Indiana manufacturers also use the ports of Louisville, Ky., and Cincinnati, Ohio. Along the southwest corner of the state, the Wabash River carries some water traffic.

L. B. READ

George Rogers Clark Memorial in Vincennes

Tourist Attractions. Indiana displays to advantage its scenic attractions, protecting them in 12 state parks which offer excellent accommodations for visitors. In the hill country is Brown County State Park, a rugged woodland which is beautiful in any season; Clifty Falls Park, overlooking a sweeping arc of the Ohio River; McCormicks Creek Park, containing woodlands and a carved limestone canyon; Spring Mill Park, enclosing a re-created pioneer village; and Turkey Run Park, an area of virgin forest rich in botanical and geological items of interest. Within Lincoln State Park is the Nancy Hanks Lincoln Memorial, the grave of Abraham Lincoln's mother.

Thirteen state forests, several game farms and preserves, and a large area of national forests protect the beauty and the wild game native to the state, and at the same time make these attractions available for public enjoyment. The dune country along Lake Michigan offers a picturesque region of shifting white sand hills bordering miles of white beaches. In the Northern section of the state myriads of little lakes, set in rich prairies, lure fishermen. French Lick Springs in central Indiana has been a famous health and recreation resort for more than 100 years. Wyandotte Cave, one of the largest caves on the North American continent, is near White Cloud, Crawford County.

Indiana has marked many historic spots and the birthplaces of famous Hoosiers. Among these are Vincennes, the first settlement and the first capital of Indiana Territory; Corydon, the site of the first capital of the state, and Fort Wayne, once a historic trading post and fort. Northeast of Lafayette, site of Purdue University, is Tippecanoe Battlefield (1811). Remains of the Harmonites' communistic experiment (1815) may be seen at New Harmony. The stately Lanier mansion (1842), now a state memorial, is at Madison, and the home of Lew Wallace, Hoosier writer, is preserved at Crawfordsville. In Indianapolis may be seen the World War Memorial Plaza and the homes of James Whitcomb Riley and Benjamin Harrison. Fort Benjamin Harrison is near by.   F. C. W.

Government. The present constitution of Indiana was ratified in 1851. It may be amended by propositions submitted in either house of the state legislature, approved at two consecutive sessions by a majority of each house, and later ratified by a majority vote of the electorate. The usual suffrage requirements are in effect.

The legislature is composed of the senate, limited to 50 members, and the house of representatives, limited to 100 members. Senators are chosen for four years, and representatives for two years. Regular sessions are held every two years, and are limited to 61 days.

The chief executive officers are the governor and lieutenant governor, chosen by popular vote for four-year terms but ineligible to succeed themselves, the secretary of state, attorney general, treasurer, auditor, and superintendent of public instruction, all elected for two-year terms without any restriction as to re-election. The governor has a veto over all legislation,

but his disapproval may be overridden by a majority vote of both houses of the General Assembly. Bills sent to the governor for signature become law automatically if not returned in three days.

The state judicial system is composed of a supreme court of five justices elected from the state at large for six years, an appellate court of six judges elected for four years, a system of circuit courts with judges elected for six years, and justices of the peace.

Indiana is represented in the national Congress by two senators and 11 representatives. Indianapolis is the state capital.

HISTORY

Early History. The first white persons to enter the present limits of Indiana were French explorers and traders. In the winter of 1679–80 La Salle crossed the portage from St. Joseph to the Kankakee River. In 1702 the French built a fort at Vincennes, and soon after made the first permanent settlement. Previous to the occupation of the territory by the English in 1763, the population was very small and consisted almost entirely of Indians and French. Through the expedition of the Virginians under GEORGE ROGERS CLARK, in 1778–79, the region west of Ohio and north of the Ohio River, known as the "Illinois country," was conquered for Virginia.

This region, ceded in 1783 to the United States, four years later became part of the Northwest Territory under the Ordinance of 1787. Settlement was hindered by Indian hostilities, leading to the expeditions of Harmar, St. Clair, and "Mad ANTHONY" WAYNE (1790 to 1794). In 1800 the Indiana Territory was organized, including the present Indiana, Illinois, and Michigan.

Statehood. Agitation for slavery by many early settlers from across the Ohio began previous to admission into the Union in 1816. But the first constitutional convention carried out the spirit of the Ordinance of 1787 by prohibiting slavery. An era of wild speculation in lands culminated in 1837 in general bankruptcy and a state debt of $14,000,000. The construction of the National Road and the beginning of railway building in 1847 renewed good

Wooded canyon in Turkey Run State Park

INDIANA DEPT. OF CONSERVATION

Battle of Tippecanoe in 1811 was a blow to the Indian opposition to the westward surge of settlers

CHICAGO HISTORICAL SOCIETY

McKinley Inn, built near Brazil on old Cumberland Road in 1832, was prominent in the stagecoach era

CLAY COUNTY HISTORICAL SOCIETY

INDIANA
High Lights of History

INDIANA HISTORICAL BUREAU

George Clark, leader of the Northwest expedition, captured fort at Vincennes from the British in 1779

INDIANA STATE LIBRARY

Communal Colony founded at New Harmony in 1825 by Robert Owen was experiment in a new social order

First Studebaker Shop, left, opened in 1852 at South Bend, played big role in development of West

STUDEBAKER CORP.

Marschall Residence, built at Vincennes about 1800, served as the first Indiana territorial capitol

STATE OF INDIANA

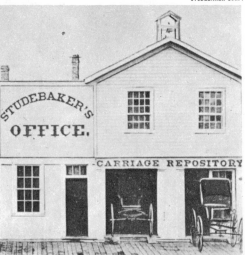

times; and between 1850 and 1860 was built the Wabash and Erie Canal from Evansville to Toledo, Ohio. During the Civil War, Indiana furnished a full quota of men, and was an important source of food supplies. The development of extensive coal deposits from about 1870 and the discovery of an abundant supply of natural gas in 1885 greatly stimulated the industries of the state. In 1905 a new municipal code went into effect. During World War I, 130,670 Indiana citizens served in the armed forces.

Under Gov. Paul V. McNutt (1933–37) the state governmental structure was drastically reorganized. The southern part of the state suffered heavily in the Ohio River flood in 1937. During World War II about 385,000 Indiana men and women served in the armed forces; in 1949 the legislature authorized a $105,000,000 veterans' bonus. In May, 1949, tornadoes caused heavy damage in the state.   F. M.

BIBLIOG.–L. Esarey, *A History of Indiana* (2 vols. 1924); Robert and Helen Lynd, *Middletown: A Study in Contemporary American Culture* (1929); E. Lilly, *Prehistoric Antiquities of Indiana* (1937); W. E. Wilson, *The Wabash* (1940); Indiana Writers Project, *Calumet Region Historical Guide* (1939), *Indiana: A Guide to the Hoosier State* (1941); H. Bowman, *Hoosier* (1941); P. S. Sikes, *Indiana State and Local Government* (ed. 1946); J. B. Martin, *Indiana: An Interpretation* (1947); K. M. Stampp, *Indiana Politics During the Civil War* (1949); *The Indiana Year Book*, published annually.

INDIANA, borough, SW central Pennsylvania, county seat of Indiana County, on the Baltimore and Ohio and the Pennsylvania railroads, and U.S. highways 119 and 422; about 46 miles NE of Pittsburgh. Indiana, the trade center of a bituminous coal-mining area, was settled in 1805. Before the Civil War it was an important station in the underground railroad. Indiana State Teachers College is located here. Tires, hosiery, leather goods, and concrete blocks are the chief manufactures. Pop. (1950) 11,743.

INDIANA CENTRAL COLLEGE. See COLLEGES.

INDIANA STATE TEACHERS COLLEGE. See COLLEGES.

INDIANA UNIVERSITY. Located in Bloomington and Indianapolis, Indiana, Indiana University can trace its history back to an act of the Indiana Territorial Legislature in 1806. This act created the Vincennes University in the borough of Vincennes. The institution did not survive, and in 1820 the General Assembly of the state established a new school, then called the State Seminary, from which the present university grew. Opened in 1824, the seminary became a college in 1827 and, on February 15, 1838, was given a new charter as Indiana University. A fourth charter, granted to the university in 1852, provides the basis for its present government, under which the institution is supported by public funds.

Instruction at first was limited to the classics, although the curriculum was gradually extended to other fields. Graduate degrees were first granted in 1881, and a graduate school was organized in 1904. Courses in law began in 1842, lapsed from 1877–89, and were resumed with the establishment of the School of Law. Teacher training began in 1852 and, after considerable reorganization, culminated in the School of Education in 1923. The School of Business, established in 1938, was an outgrowth of the commercial course begun in 1902. Similarly the School of Music (1921) goes back to instruction begun in 1893. The university has been affiliated with medical schools in Indianapolis since the 1870's. The School of Medicine was established there in 1903. In 1914 a Training School for Nurses was added at the Long Hospital; and in 1925 the Indiana University School of Dentistry was established. A School of Health, Physical Education, and Recreation was organized in Bloomington in 1946.

In 1942 the Junior Division of the university was established to deal with the problems of freshman students. The University Extension Division, first organized in 1912, offers lectures and college work to citizens of seven Indiana communities and thus extends the scope of the university to cover the entire state. Indiana University has been coeducational since 1867. It is a member of the Association of American Universities.   ROBERT MARSH

INDIANAPOLIS, city, Indiana, state capital and county seat of Marion County, on the W bank of the White River, 184 miles SE of Chicago and 240 miles NE of St. Louis. It is served by the Baltimore and Ohio, the Erie, the Illinois Central, the Chicago, Indianapolis, and Louisville, the New York Central, the Pennsylvania, the Nickel Plate, and the Indianapolis Union railroads; U.S. highways 31, 36, 40, and 52; the American, the Chicago and Southern, the Eastern, and the Transcontinental and Western air lines; and by more than 100 established truck lines operating out of the city. Pop. (1950) 427,173.

Indianapolis, the largest city in Indiana, is not only the state capital of the commonwealth, but its physical, economic, and cultural capital as well. Situated in almost the exact center of Indiana and within 60 miles of the center of the population of the United States, it has come to be known as the "Crossroads of America." Indianapolis is a great livestock and grain market and the center of a large trade area. Embracing 54.13 square miles in the heart of a fertile, undulating agricultural area, it is the largest city in the United States not on navigable water.

Features of Interest. The city, built on level ground, follows the L'Enfant street pattern of Washington, D.C. In the exact center of the original tract of four sections, surrounded by a circular park, is the Soldiers' and Sailors' Monument of Indianapolis. The 284-foot monument has an observation platform which gives a beautiful view of the city and many miles of surrounding country. From this central circle four avenues radiate to the four corners of the city. The other streets run at right angles to one another. North of the circle is the Indiana World War Memorial Plaza, which covers five blocks and contains, among other buildings, the national headquarters of the AMERICAN LEGION.

Indianapolis has parks and playgrounds which occupy more than 3,000 acres of public land. The

Start of Memorial Day auto race at Indianapolis Speedway

F. M. KIRKPATRICK

Indianapolis

largest of these is Riverside Park with 930 acres. The State Fairgrounds, located here, are the site of the State Fair held annually in the first week of September since 1852. The Indianapolis Motor Speedway is the scene of the world famous 500-mile Memorial Day automobile race. This annual race attracts more than 150,000 people from all over the United States and many foreign countries. In addition, the two-and-one-half mile asphalt oval, built in 1909, is a proving ground and outdoor laboratory where many of the improvements in automobile engines and tires have been developed. Northeast of the city is Fort Benjamin Harrison, established in 1903, a U.S. Army Post covering 2,702 acres.

Indianapolis is the seat of many institutions of higher learning. These include the Indiana Central College, Butler University, Marian College, and several law schools. The Indiana University Medical Center occupies 93 acres and consists of three hospitals, a nurses' school and home, a medical and a dental school, and a convalescent park. The John Herron Art Institute houses one of the finest permanent collections of art works in the Middle West. An art school, which has won national recognition, is conducted in connection with the museum. The Children's Museum has a collection of 30,000 objects and is managed in part by children through a junior board of directors. The State Library of Indiana, located here, contains 33,000 books on the state and an outstanding collection of books in Braille for circulation. The city has been the home of many of the country's most illustrious citizens. The homes of James Whitcomb Riley, the "Hoosier Poet," and Benjamin Harrison, the 23rd president of the United States, have been preserved as shrines. Other famous citizens include Henry Ward Beecher, Booth Tarkington, Albert J. Beveridge, statesman and author of *The Life of John Marshall*, and "Kin" Hubbard, noted humorist. Indianapolis is the center of religious activity, being the seat of an Episcopal bishop, a Methodist bishop, and a Roman Catholic bishop.

Industry. Indianapolis enjoys the advantages of a wide diversification of industrial products. In 1947 there were 944 industrial plants in the area, some of them the largest of their kind in the world; these normally produce around 1,200 different commodities. These include aviation motors, parts, and bearings, motor trucks, electrical parts and equipment, metallurgical specialties, radios, phonograph records and players, rubber products, meat packing products, flour and feeds, paint, automotive parts and accessories, pharmaceuticals, heating equipment, precision instruments, brass, saws, tools, hosiery, clothing, steel, petroleum products, containers, fertilizers, wood products, and power transmission chains.

History. The earliest settlers near what is now Indianapolis were George Pogue and John McCormick and their families, who came here in February, 1820. By the following summer a dozen or more cabins had sprung up along the young river settlement which was known as Fall Creek. After Indiana's entrance into the Union, Congress granted to the new state four sections of public land for its capital city. On June 7, 1820, the commissioners decided on the Fall Creek site because it was located as near as possible to the center of the state. Attracted by the prospect of settling in the future seat of the state government, many settlers soon arrived. The town was laid out, a mile square, in 1821 and named Indianapolis, "Indiana" plus the Greek "polis" meaning city. The first legislative meeting was held here in 1825, and in 1836 the first state capitol was erected. The first steam train came to the town in 1847 and that same year Indianapolis was incorporated as a city. The introduction of train service and the discovery of natural gas gave impetus to industry, and the future of the city was decided. The growth of Indianapolis in population, industry, and importance has been steady.   A. M. K.

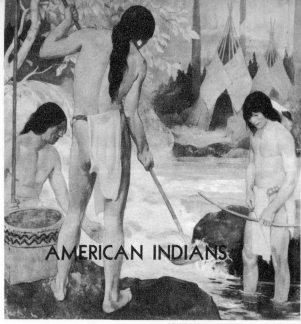

Once the lords of America, they fought a losing battle to save their lands from the white man and his "manifest destiny"

INDIANS, AMERICAN, the aborigines of the New World, so called from the original misconception of Columbus, who supposed that the land discovered by him was India and its inhabitants the Indians of the Eastern Hemisphere. The name Indian is therefore a misnomer, but its usage is so wide that the proposed substitute, AMERIND, is not often seen.

The oldest traces of man in this hemisphere are found at Folsom, N.M., Fort Collins, Colo., and Ventana Cave in Arizona. These sites make it clear that men were there at least 18,000 years ago. Almost all anthropologists agree that the origin of the Indian was Asia and that the bulk of the population came across Bering Strait. The migration probably started around the end of the GLACIAL EPOCH and continued for thousands of years; the ESKIMOS are thought to be the latest arrivals. There is little basis for belief that the Indians brought with them anything more than a simple STONE AGE culture.

The American Indians belong to the Mongoloid stock; they usually have straight black hair, a broad face, shovel-shaped incisors, and complexions that range from reddish to brown colors. The nose is often prominent and they rarely have much facial or body hair. Only the Eskimo differs greatly in appearance from the "Red Indian." The rest of the American aborigines are essentially one people, although there are wide variations in living habits, physical types and languages.

Native Civilization. In Peru, Colombia, Central America, Yucatán, and Mexico there were tribes 500 years ago who had attained a relatively high degree of native civilization. In New Mexico and Arizona, the rather numerous PUEBLOS or native Indian towns are the relics of what may have been in part a northern extension of the Mexican civilization. These influences began to be exerted first on the early population known as Basket Makers by the introduction of corn and pottery. By continued contact and local development came the period of massive CLIFF DWELLINGS and finally the pueblos. In the Mississippi Valley somewhat similar southern influence led to the development of higher cultures. Some of these people built mounds for burial purposes, some as substructures for ceremonial buildings. These remains have given rise to the name Mound Builder and often have been ascribed to a mysterious vanished people.

Archaeology has shown that the Mound Builders were simply North American Indians who built mounds. They did not form any single tribe, nation or even a unified culture. The Mexicans and Peruvians excelled in architecture. Neither of them had iron; both had native copper and gold, and the Peruvians seem to have had some cutting tools of bronze. The Mexicans had no domestic animals but the dog; the Peruvians had also the llama and alpaca. Both grew cotton as well as maize; both could spin and weave.

CLASSIFICATION

North America. Rejecting the Aleuts and Eskimos from the category of "Indian" peoples, the principal stocks or recognized families of North America are as follows: (1) The Athabascans (Tinné), including many tribes of Alaska and north Canada, as well as the Apaches, Navahos, and others in the United States. (2) The Algonquins, a great and clearly marked people which once covered a large part of the Atlantic slope from Labrador to Virginia, and reached westward to the Rocky Mountains. Here belong the Abnaki, the Delawares, the Crees, the Chippewas, and many now historic tribes. Most authorities assign the Cheyennes, the Arapahoes, and even the Blackfeet to this stock. (3) The Iroquois, a once powerful and warlike people, formerly dwelling for the most part in the St. Lawrence Valley and what is now New York state. This was one of the most clearly defined families of North America. It includes the Cherokees, Mohawks, Senecas, and numerous others. (4) The important Sioux family, including the great Dakota group, and the Omahas, Osages, Winnebagoes, Crows, Catawbas, and others. (5) The Muskhogeans, including the Alibamus, Apalachis, Choctaws, Creeks, Chickasaws, and Seminoles. In point of intelligence and adaptiveness to civilization, these tribes take a high rank. (6) The Caddoan family, including the Pawnees, Arickarees, Wichitas, Caddos, and others. All were plainsmen, and many of them have excelled as horsemen and warriors. (7) The tribes of the northern Pacific coast, among which are the Tlingit of Alaska, and many tribes of western Canada and the United States. (8) The Yuman family, in the valley of the Colorado River and California, including the Maricopa and other tribes. (9) The Shoshones, with whom are classed the Utes, the warlike Comanches, and the half-civilized Hopi, and many of the degraded Diggers. They live mostly among or near the Rocky Mountains. (10) The Pueblo Indians of New Mexico and Arizona, a composite division, including the Zuñi and the Keresan family. (11) The Mexican tribes, of which the number is very great and the family unity questionable. Here are placed the celebrated Aztecs, the half-mythical Toltecs, the interesting and semicivilized Nicaraguans, and many others. (12) The Maya stock of Yucatán and Central America. (13) A number of independent Central American and Isthmian stocks.

Peruvian Indian of South America

South America. A comprehensive classification of the South American tribes is much more difficult. In the mountainous district of the northwest belong the Chocos, Chibchas, Paniquitas, and Paezes, the tribes of Cauca and Antioquia, and the Coconuca, Barbacoa, and Mocoa stocks. The linguistic stocks of the Peruvian region include the Quichuas, Aymaras, Puquinas, Yuncas, Atacamenos, and Changos. The Amazonian Indians are grouped in a great number of bands or tribes, and have, as a rule, a very low position. Most of these tribes would appear to have few linguistic or other characters in common. They include the Tupi-Guarani stock, the Tapuyas, the Arawaks, the Caribs and Orinoco Indians of many tribes, and the Indians of the Upper Amazonian basin and the Bolivian highlands. In the Pampean region are the linguistic stocks of the Gran Chaco, the Charruas, the nomadic Pampean tribes, the Araucanians and the tribes of the Fuegian family.

S. W. X.

LANGUAGES

Multiplicity and Diversity. In native America there are more aboriginal languages than linguists engaged in their study. Indeed, there are probably more language families in both North and South America than there are professional linguists studying them. Compare this with Europe, where there are two big language families represented (Finno-Ugric for Finnish and Hungarian, and Indo-European for all the rest: for English, German, and Scandinavian languages, for the Celtic languages like Irish, for the Latin languages like French, Spanish, Italian and Rumanian, for the Slavic languages like Russian, Czech, Serbo-Croatian, Bulgarian, and for others). In Europe, also, there is one language spoken in the mountains between Spain and France which is related neither to Finno-Ugric nor to Indo-European. This language is called Basque, and it is unique in Europe in being unrelated to other languages. If Basque were an American Indian language, either in North or South America, it would not be unique. There are little Basquelike languages scattered from the Atlantic to the Pacific, as the Yuki in California, the Kutenai in the Rocky Mountains, and Beothuk in Newfoundland. Besides these little, isolated, unrelated Indian languages, there are also great, far-flung language families, like Algonquian. Before we turn to the great language families of native America, we should note that no linguistic relationship has ever been demonstrated between a language in America and one outside of America. Basque itself has been compared to Algonquian, as have the earlier Germanic languages; more seriously, some scholars have fancied a relationship between Eskimo and the Ural-Altaic extension of the Finno-Ugric family, or even more tenuous, between the Athabascan family, to which Navaho belongs, and the Tibeto-Sinitic family to which the Chinese languages belong.

Cognates and Loan Words. More impressive than theories of genetic relationship between languages of the Old and New Worlds are a few cases in which the same object in the two areas was called by the same name at the first contact period. Thus, the Maori of New Zealand and the Aztec of Mexico used kuma (kumari, kumatl, respectively) for *sweet potato*. Borrowings of this order were sometimes found between unrelated languages in native America (as words for tobacco); perhaps more place names have been borrowed by English from American Indian languages than names for material objects. Of river names, the Mississippi is from Algonquian, where it means *big river;* the Ohio, meaning *beautiful river*, is supposed to be from an Iroquois language, but this is hard to attest; and the numerous names beginning in Mini- are from Siouan and mean *water*. Thus Minneapolis is half Siouan (*water*) and half Greek (*city*).

The Linguistic Problem. The immediate conclusion is not only apparent but highly significant. In contrast to what we are accustomed to for European languages: (1) there is virtually no international vocabulary in native America; (2) there is much greater diversity of languages and language families in America than in Europe. We might say, despite (2), (1) obtains. But the significant implication is rather: because of (1), that is, isolation of speech communities in native America, it follows, (2), that whatever the ancient source, whether common or not, of the American Indian languages, they have become (or are found) so differentiated as we study them today, that we cannot prove relationships beyond what is demonstrable by the comparative method alone: since we lack written records of earlier stages of any given language, we rely upon reconstruction alone; this gives us less knowledge of historical growth than if we had written records of earlier forms. Attention is accordingly often diverted from historical statements about native America to statements of classification of structural types and phonetic areas, and to questions of underlying psychological and physiological causes, as Boas once phrased it.

Indian Language Families. Let us begin with a list of language families which have actually been studied by the comparative method in native America.

1. The Eskimo family extends across Arctic America from Greenland to Alaska (one language) and in Alaska (a second Eskimo language), with two related Aleut languages spoken in the Aleutian Islands.

2. Of Algonquian languages south of the Eskimo, we note Cree and Ojibwa, with the latter found also in the Great Lakes area together with such languages as Menomini, Fox, Shawnee, Pattawatomie, and formerly the Delaware, which was carried to the east coast to join the Penobscot, Micmac and other eastern languages before being removed by the whites to Oklahoma. In Oklahoma the present day Delawares meet Algonquian speakers removed from the Plains, as Cheyenne and Arapaho, while all the Blackfeet remain today in the northern Plains.

3. Of Athabascan languages south of the Eskimo in the Mackenzie River drainage, we might note more than a half-dozen names like Dogrib, Yellowknife, Kutchin and Sarsi; but we would have to turn to another area in northwest California and southern Oregon to account for the Hupa, Mattole and other anguages, and to the southwest for still additional Athabascan languages, as Navaho and Apache.

4. The Uto-Aztecan languages extend from the international line between Canada and the states in the west, down to Panama Canal in middle America.

5. Some Penutian languages or language families, as Yokuts, Maidu, Miwok and Wintun of California, have recently been shown to be related by the comparative method; others are scattered to the north beyond Vancouver Island.

6. Siouan languages have a wide distribution parallel to Algonquian, but more Siouan languages are found in the Plains, fewer in the Woodlands. Iroquois languages are surrounded by Algonquian or by Algonquian and Siouan languages in the eastern Woodlands.

7. In Mexico and Central America, besides Uto-Aztecan languages, we have such language families as the Mayan, Tarascan, Mixtecan, Zapotecan, Tototanacan and others on which little comparative work has been done.

8. Languages of the Chibchan family are spoken in the West Indies, Central America, and South America. Other than this, no language family shows demonstrable affinities in both South and North America.

9. In South America we have such language families postulated as Arawakan, Aymaran, Cariban, Chonean, Kechuan, Matako, Panoan, Pehuelchen, Timotean, Tukanan, Tupi-Guarani, Witotan, Xibaran, the Ge family and many others. They are neither properly described nor properly compared; but enough information has been published to enable us to say that the linguistic picture (as also the cultural picture) in South America is roughly parallel to that in North America. For example, in one language of California (Maidu) a very rare type of sound is produced: implosive stops (air sucked into a vacuum in the mouth to make a reverse b, and reverse d, as it were); again, in South America, implosive stops are produced in one of the Ge languages.

We can gain some idea of the total diversity of all languages of the New World by multiplying the diversity found in the United States and Canada by 3;

that is to say, by assuming that when the languages have all been described we will find as much diversity in Mexico and Central and South America as we found north of the Rio Grande.   C. F. VOEGELIN

BIBLIOG.–F. Johnson, *Linguistic Map of Mexico and Central America* (1942); C. F. and E. W. Voegelin, *Map of North American Indian Languages* (1944).

SOCIAL CONDITIONS

Villages and House Types. In many sections of the United States area the Indians had permanent settlements or villages in which they resided for the greater part of the year, excepting during the periodical hunts or other functions in which the whole community joined. In the East this generally meant the summer and fall hunts between crop seasons, and the sugarmaking time in early spring, the exodus and return being according to regular program and along regular lines. In the same way the Pawnee and Mandan divided the time between their crops and winter games at home and the recurring buffalo hunt on the open plains. The sedentary Pueblo tribes seldom stirred far from their own villages. The popular impression that the Indian was an aimless wanderer is entirely false. His coming and going were of regular sequence, except where the inhospitable nature of the country had all seasons alike, in necessity, or until the acquisition of the horse by the plains tribes gave unlimited opportunity for roving. The great tribal migrations were of slow accomplishment. Compared to the white man, however, the Indian was at all times an outdoor man.

The prevailing house type east of the Mississippi was the wigwam, a framework of saplings, covered with bark or mats, with a door at either end and one or more fireholes in the roof; in general shape resembling a wagon top set upon the ground. It was usually communal, in some cases accommodating as many as 20 families and of corresponding length. In the Gulf States we find square or circular houses of upright logs, chinked with clay and sometimes whitened with lime wash with conical roofs also covered with a foot or more of clay. In Florida the house consisted chiefly of a thatched roof raised upon poles. Every principal settlement had one large central structure for dances, councils, and other public purposes, and some towns, especially among the Iroquois, were compactly built and stockaded for defense. In general, however, the houses of a settlement were scattered at wide intervals without much regard to arrangement.

Along the Missouri, among the semisedentary Mandan, Arikara, Pawnee, etc., the permanent dwelling was the earth lodge, a large circular or octagonal log structure, with roof rising to a rounded point in the center and covered with a foot or more of hard packed clay. From 15 to 20 persons, comprising closely related families, usually occupied the same lodge.

The nonagricultural and purely hunting tribes of

Plains Indians on a buffalo hunt

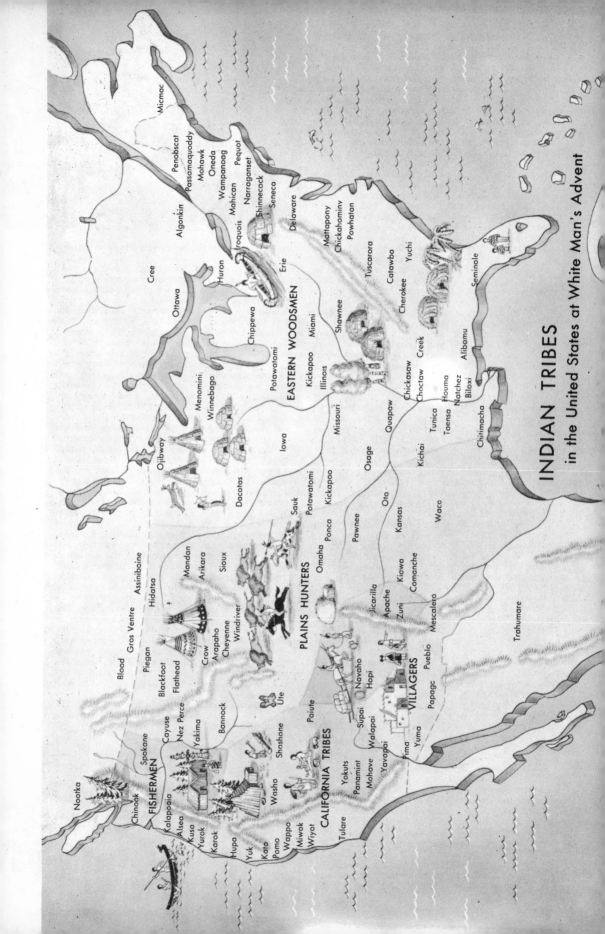

INDIAN TRIBES
in the United States at White Man's Advent

the plains, as well as those just mentioned, when away from their permanent villages, occupied the tepee—a name adopted from the Sioux language—a high conical tent composed of some 20 dressed buffalo skins sewn together in proper form and brought over a framework of about the same number of poles. The open top allowed the smoke to escape and two movable flaps regulated the draft. At ceremonial gatherings the tepees were set up in a great circle, those belonging to the principal families being painted and otherwise decorated with totemic designs.

In the Columbia region the typical structure was the rectangular board house, with elaborate painted and carved designs, and was sometimes semisubterranean. It was generally communal, and some for public purposes were as much as 500 feet in length. Board houses, subterranean dwellings, and earth-covered beehive structures were found in California.

The Navaho hogan of New Mexico and Arizona was a round earth-covered log structure, open at the top and with a covered passageway for entrance. The Piute, Apache, and lower Colorado tribes built only a light brushwood or tule structure, commonly known as a *wickiup*. The rectangular many-roomed and many-storied stone or adobe houses of the Pueblo tribes are too well known to more than mention here, as also the related "cliff dwellings" of the same region.

Social Organization and Religion. Each larger group usually acting together as a single independent body and speaking the same language was commonly known as a tribe, but the word is merely a convenient designation, as we know too little of the Indian organization to give it fixed meaning. In some cases the tribe comprised but a single village or band; in other cases, as with the Sioux or Navaho, it numbered thousands of souls, in many bands with varying dialects, scattered over a large territory. In either case the organization was so loosely democratic that there was rarely any compelling single authority to weld the body into united action. It was a bond rather of friendship than authority and seemed frequently to have its origin in community of religious ritual. Tribes were sometimes grouped into confederacies, as the Iroquois and the Creeks.

Kinship systems were much more intricate than among Europeans. There were numerous military, ritual, medicine, and work societies, among both men and women, each with its special function, dress ceremonial, and initiation forms. The priesthood as a rule represented the highest intelligence of the tribe and exercised more influence than the governing chiefs. Among the great religious ceremonials may be noted the Green Corn Dance thanksgiving festival of the eastern (agricultural) tribes; the Sun Dance of the Plains; the Snake Dance of the Hopi; and the Salmon Dance of the Columbia region. Of general but minor importance were the so-called war dance and scalp dance, the dance itself in each case being only the spectacular part of an elaborate ritual. The universal religion, however varying in detail of myth or ceremony, was an animistic polytheism in which animals, plants and the phenomena of nature were deified, or, perhaps more properly speaking, regarded as the embodiment of deities. The Sun, the Rain, the Buffalo, the Snake, the Eagle, the Corn, and the Peyote Cactus were among the highest divinities. There was no supreme "great spirit," no heaven or hell, only a shadowy counterpart of the present life. Besides the gods there was a host of fairies, water spirits, and monsters, not counting witches, while every important tribe had its culture hero, its sacred genesis tradition and mythology, and frequently its tribal medicine or sacred bundle, the contents of which were exposed only on great ceremonial occasions. Human sacrifice as a religious rite was rare, but existed among the Pawnee and certain southern tribes. The marriage ceremony in most tribes was a simple affair, consisting only of the giving of a present by the young man to the girl's parents, after the matter had been debated

Interior of the earth lodge of a Mandan chief

by the older people of both families and the girl's consent obtained. Polygamy was recognized, but not frequent. Divorce was a simple process, and in some tribes the children followed the mother.

Subsistence. The main dependence of all the tribes east of the Plains as well as of the Pueblos and those of the lower Colorado was agriculture, while hunting, fishing, and the gathering of wild fruits, nuts and seeds, were only auxiliary. The Plains Indians as a body lived by the buffalo hunt; those of Nevada and California depended largely upon the piñon and acorn; while in Oregon and throughout the Columbia region the camas root and salmon held the principal place. About the Upper Lakes wild rice was an important crop, and maple sugar—an aboriginal discovery—was manufactured in the Ohio Valley and the north Atlantic region. Corn was everywhere the great agricultural staple, supplemented by beans, pumpkins, and tobacco. The sheep industry of the Navaho is a legacy from early Spanish missionaries and the horse also is of Spanish introduction. The dog was the only regularly domesticated animal in early times, except for a few birds sometimes caged for the feathers.

Dress. The dress was scanty, excepting on ceremonial occasions, and consisted, for the man, of loin cloth, leggings, and moccasins with a shirt and blanket for cold weather. The woman wore a skirt belted at the waist, with leggings and moccasins, the two sometimes made as one piece. The material was usually soft, dressed deerskin, or among the Pueblos, a cotton fabric of native weaving. The blanket was more often of buffalo skin; dressed with the hair on the inside, or in the Southwest, of rabbit skin, in woven strips. The decoration of fringe, paint and porcupine quills, or the peculiar style of wearing the hair, marked the tribal distinctions. In everyday life, the warrior wore usually only the loin cloth and moccasins, while young children went naked. The face and sometimes the upper body was painted according to individual design. In the East the head was generally shaven with

Indian chieftains clad in tribal dress

the exception of a ridge along the crest and a single scalp lock. On the Plains the hair was worn full length, but usually gathered into a large plait hanging down in front on each shoulder with the smaller scalp lock behind. West of the mountains it was usually cut above the eyes in front and about at the shoulder behind, or, as with the Navaho, was bunched up behind in club fashion.

Home Life. The home life was diversified by feasting, dancing, games and storytelling. Every important household celebration was accompanied by a feast, from the setting up of the new tepee to the piercing of the ears of a newborn child. In the same way, almost every religious function from the annual thanksgiving festival to the ordinary doctor's performance over a sick patient had an accompaniment of song and dance, the instruments being the drum, rattle, whistle, and sometimes the flute or flageolet. There were songs for every occasion of ritual, war, love, and medicine, lullaby songs, serenade songs, and songs to call up the game and fish.

Customs. Cannibalism, while rare, is reported to have been found in several regions; it reached its greatest development on the coast of Texas and western Louisiana. Ceremonial adoption by the family or by the tribe in council existed in many sections. The mother-in-law tabu, which forbade a man to have any communication with or even to look at his wife's mother, and vice versa, was common to most of the Plains tribes, the Navaho, and Apache. Name tabus were almost universal.

The dead were disposed of in different ways, the most widespread being probably by interment in the ground. Urn burial was frequent along the eastern Gulf coast, and a custom of mummy preservation existed along the south Atlantic coast from Virginia to Florida. With some Plains tribes, as the Cheyenne, the corpse was fastened upon a scaffold in the tree tops, to be eaten as carrion. The Piute and many tribes of California and the lower Colorado practiced cremation. The personal property of the deceased was usually sacrificed at the grave or upon the funeral pyre; the relatives showed their grief by lacerating their bodies with knives and by cutting off the hair, and for weeks thereafter the death wail was heard night and day.

Weapons and War. The warrior's weapons were the bow, the club of wood or stone with attached handle, the knife of reed or flint, the stone-headed lance, and the round shield of buffalo hide in the open country; body armor of wicker work or tough hide in certain eastern districts and about Puget Sound, with the blowgun of cane for hunting small game in the Gulf region. Boys were initiated into the war societies at about the age of 14. The original war trophy was the head, and the custom of scalping, so far from being general, was confined to a limited eastern territory until the introduction of firearms and the establishment of scalp premiums by the rival colonial governments. Even in recent times it was practically unknown west of the Rockies.   S. W. X.

INDIAN ART

The most striking thing about the Indian arts and crafts is that they possess the indefinable magic associated with the Indian people. The work has a character which is universally distinguished for its integrated sensitivity and its instinct for form and rhythm, unless the creative urges have been tampered with by commercial influences.

Art forms followed life needs. In the Southwest, where the Indian's close communion with nature has been less disturbed by the white man's infringements, the arts have remained more traditional. Decoration is often symbolic, particularly in religious objects, but many patterns are inspired purely by love of design.

Weaving. Baskets, one of the earliest art forms, are now made mostly by the Apaches. These are often larger than a clothes hamper, with endless styles of geometric patterns in decoration. The Pomo and other tribes in California make excellent tiny baskets.

Weaving was an early skill in the Southwest. Remarkable fragmentary examples are found in the ruins of the oldest culture groups. Wild cotton was used. Wool was not used for weaving until the arrival of the Spaniards. Today, the Navaho women and Hopi men are the main weavers. The Hopis make the ceremonial costume cloth for all the New Mexico tribes. Much of this has rich borders in geometric design, laid in or embroidered. The Navaho blanket has now come to be made for white man's rugs, tightly woven, using the homespun wool of the local sheep. The best designs today are in the saddle blankets, still made for tribal use.

Pottery. POTTERY did not develop until the migrants became sedentary. It reached its peak in the Southwest in the 11th to 14th centuries. At this time the Mimbres Valley tribes were producing distinguished designs both in geometric and stylized human and animal forms, using a dark gray line against a light, almost white, background. Hopi potters used rich yellow and deep red clay colors in bolder motifs. A glazing technique was developed earlier, particularly on the Pajaritan Plateau. Each area and era had styles and colors peculiar to it, which aid archaeologists in dating sites and tracing intercourse.

Jewelry. Jewelry has always been important to the Indians, who are famous for their adornment. Since the coming of the white man, the Navaho and Zuñi tribes have developed fine silverwork. The Navaho style is massive, showing off the metal itself. Zuñi work has more intricate detail, with a recent trend to use inlay. Turquoise settings are often used by both tribes. The squash blossom necklace of the Navaho is made of petaled silver bells at intervals on strings of round silver beads. The Navaho concha belt has large round or oval silver disks strung on a thin leather strip. The bracelets of this tribe are very wide or very thick. Bow guards decorated with a large oblong silver top are used as bracelets. Bridles are gorgeously trimmed with bands of silver. While most of the Navaho silver is hammered from strips of silver, some of it is made by a special sand-cast process, with great success.

Beadwork. Beadwork has been more characteristic of Plains and Eastern tribes, using white man's glass beads (famous for trade in the past). These are best used in massive, all-over designs for yokes on women's deerskin dresses, or for moccasins. Santo Domingo Pueblos made turquoise bead necklaces, shaping the stone into a tiny cylinder. The Navahos make similar beads from coral, and in early days from shells and minerals.

Painting and Drawing. The ability of the Indians to paint and draw is seen in prehistoric kiva decorations, paintings on the façades of the mission churches and in the interiors, as well as in the exquisite pottery figures and the skin paintings. Also the remarkable religious symbols done in colored sands have a fine

An elaborate sand painting by Navaho Indians

quality of integrated design. When ethnologist and school teachers in recent times provided crayons or paints, an amazing expression took place, combining primitive and modern instincts. Ceremonial and animal subjects prevail. The style is two-dimensional, with occasional developments toward the third dimension. Generally there is no background, but the figures are placed to suggest space; colors are strong; figures are clear; detail is exquisite. There is a fine sense of design and rhythm. The impression of life and movement is often uncanny. The government school and the state museum, both in Santa Fe, were the first agencies to encourage this rare talent. Water color is the medium most successfully used. There are delightful touches of humor, especially in the less studied work of the younger children. HESTER JONES

INDIAN DANCES

The dances of the Southwest are carried on, in general, according to earliest tradition. Elsewhere, the original forms and meanings have largely disintegrated. The ceremonies symbolize the Indian's sense of man's oneness with nature. The tribes follow an annual calendar, performing dances pertaining to the seasons and to the life-giving forces of the universe. They are powerful so that we feel their significance even before we begin to understand it. They produce a spell which removes us from our familiar world. The Indians become more than themselves in these dances; they are transfigured into a living expression of the will to unite with cosmic forces for human good. Sky, earth, sun, rain; sowing, growing, breathing, begetting; the harvest, the hunt; the harmonizing of spiritual elements, the healing—all are synthesized in a mystic interweaving of color, sound, movement, drama, music, rhythm, design, and form.

The Pueblo Corn Dance is an enacting of the forces of the sky by the men, and of the earth by the women, the two clans of the pueblo dancing alternately all day, in the sequences of changing forms. A large men's chorus chants the accompaniment in time with the throbbing beat of the large tom-tom. The Koshari, painted ashen, with dead corn husks in their hair, transformed into ancestral spirits, carry on pantomime, leaping and occasionally calling with an unearthly cry, while they move in contrasting freedom among the formal lines of dancers. Their arms are lifted, then lowered in shimmering motion, suggestive of falling rain. They are dancers superb.

The Animal Dances of the Pueblos are symbolic of the hunt and of the co-operation of animal life with humans. Head masks suggest the animals, and the rhythms and movements are in keeping with the mood of the pantomime.

The Shalako Dance at Zuñi is an annual masked dance of the winter solstice, mainly for blessing the new houses. The culminating ceremony is held in these houses from midnight till dawn. Mudheads and the Council of the Gods (masked figures) take part with the six giant Shalako gods. The masks of carved wood cover the whole head and are beautifully painted to represent supernatural beings.

The Snake Dance is an annual event in the Hopi villages. The dancers pick up snakes and dance with them in their teeth. The snake is symbolic of power emerging from the lower regions to the upper.

The Navaho dances are held in the winter at night. Thousands in colorful blankets gather around huge fires. Preliminary ceremonies include making sand paintings in the medicine hogan, where rites are held over sick people for whose healing the dance is given. The meaning of the symbolism of the ceremony is to bring the patient back into harmony with nature. The sand paintings must be destroyed before sunset, as the gods are not to be represented in permanent form. At night, a *Yebetchei* or fire dance is held.

Other especially meaningful dances are the *Niman Katchina* dance of the Hopi, symbolic of the time the gods departed to return in spirit while their effigies dance; and the *Ha-Ko* of the Pawnees, symbolic of intertribal good will.

The Apache and Plains Indians perform spectacular dances, such as the Apache Devil Dance (so-called), the Kiowa Scalp Dance, and the Sun Dance which teaches stoicism and courage. See SUN DANCE.
                                        HESTER JONES

GOVERNMENT POLICY

In North America, at least, the forcible expatriation and deportation of tribes is a thing of the past. Since the Indians are now increasing in number, it is apparent that the race is not destined to die out, and it may be that a gradual assimilation of the red and white races will take place in the United States. The ordinary operations of government work have not always borne the best fruit among the Indians. The plan adopted years ago, in the United States, of paying annuities to the deported tribes, no doubt took its rise in the desire to deal equitably with them; but the result, in many cases, has been the pauperization and consequent moral degradation of the beneficiary tribes.

In 1887 the Dawes General Allotment Act inaugurated the policy of making the Indian an individual landholder, with citizen rights and duties, and throwing open the reservations to white settlement. The ration system practically terminated in 1901, and the autonomous Indian governments in the Indian Territory were formally dissolved, after long negotiation, in 1906 under the amendment to the General Allotment Act known as the Burke law. Under the prevailing allotment agreements, each Indian man, woman, and child was made the individual owner of 80 acres of agricultural or 160 acres of grazing land, inalienable and free of taxes for a term of 25 years, with restricted citizenship privileges and a per capita share in all tribal funds. Allotments have usually been selected from reservation lands, though the Indians may take advantage of the Homestead law (1863) to settle on any unoccupied public land.

Early Policy. The original theory of the government, inherited from the colonies, was that the tribes were independent nations, with treaty-making powers. Treaties to the number of 370 were negotiated in accordance with this theory from 1778 to 1871. In some cases, as with the five principal southern tribes of Cherokees, Choctaws, Chickasaws, Creeks, and Seminoles, the Indians acted in agreement with the theory so far as to form autonomous governments under the title of "nations." It was expected that certain tribes would be organized into states and be granted representation in Congress. Between 1815 and 1840 the great majority of the treaties were concluded. Practically all of them stipulated that the Indians should yield to white settlement certain portions of territory which, either by long occupation or former compact, had been recognized as belonging to the tribes. In return, the government furnished tools and supplies, and created interest-bearing funds to be held for the future use and benefit of the tribes. In this respect, therefore, the government, from the beginning, denied their actual independence. Their political status was exceedingly hard to define, and that difficulty has stood in the way of the race's progress.

While the tribes held the terms of the old treaties to be binding the government looked upon them merely as expedients to pacify temporarily a people angered by the encroachments of white settlers. Washington argued that since they were practically "subject" peoples no real treaty could be negotiated. Since they were nominally independent nations, they could have no share in the conduct of the government. As a consequence, the Indians have been without representation at Washington, and without political influence in the states that grew up around their reservations. A logical result of the government's uncertain theory of Indian autonomy, its vacillating treaty

BUR. AMER. ETHNOLOGY

Blackfeet Indian chief

PAUL'S PHOTOS

Blackfeet tepees in the foothills of Montana

Seminole squaw

MIAMI NEWS BUREAU

Seminole thatched-roof hut in the Florida Everglades

CHICAGO NATURAL HISTORY MUSEUM

Pueblo Indian girl

CHICAGO NATURAL HISTORY MUSEUM

Adobe homes of Hopi Indians at pueblo in Walpi, Arizona

B. C. GOVT. TRAVEL BU.

Koksilah squaw

CANADIAN NATIONAL RAILWAYS

British Columbian Indians smoke salmon for winter use

BU. OF AMERICAN ETHNOLOGY
Pawnee Indian chief

policy, and its complete denial of political rights, was the suspicion and hatred that culminated in the Western Indian wars of the late sixties and the seventies. General Sheridan's classic remark that "the only good Indian is a dead Indian" seems to have been passively accepted by many persons in the western states as an excuse for exploiting the "Red Man." When, in 1871, Congress abandoned the term "treaty" and adopted "agreement" instead, it declared tentatively for the guardian and ward theory that has since been generally accepted. The government's right of eminent domain was insisted upon. Once the impression was lodged in Washington that the government regarded the Indians as minor children and orphans, the question arose as to how the strict authority flowing from such a relationship had best be exercised. Settlers complained that these government orphans ranged too far in their hunting expeditions and had too vague a conception of property rights. Therefore it became the duty of the guardian to limit the wanderings of its wards. But if the Indians were to remain self-supporting, most of them must hunt, and hunting meant wide ranging. A new series of agreements were made with tribal chiefs and councils pledging the government to support the Indians and covenanting that the Indians should remain on certain restricted and defined reservations. For a quarter of a century, therefore, most of the Indians were barred from contact with the white populations and were pauperized by gratuities of food and clothing. Their only means of communication with the government was through agents appointed by the president.

Schools were established, however, wherever practicable. As these grew in size and scope, their superintendents were sometimes heavily bonded, and placed in charge of the reservations on which they were situated, supplanting the political agents, and giving the Indians concerned a higher conception of the importance of the educational work in progress among them. With the gradual introduction of the merit system of appointment into the school and clerical services, the quality of the superintendents improved. During Theodore Roosevelt's administration practically all the agencies were brought under bonded superintendents from the classified civil service. The other employees—teachers, physicians, etc.—serve under the superintendent.   S. W. X.

Indian Removal. From the earliest colonial times the white settlers sought to remove Indians from their immediate neighborhood in order to gain possession of the land and to prevent conflict. Treaties were usually negotiated with Indian tribes providing for land cession, after which the displaced savages were left to find new homes wherever they could. Such negotiations were often marked by gross frauds, whisky being the means to facilitate many a deal. After the Revolution both states and Federal government made Indian treaties. Early in the 19th century

discussion began on a plan to move all Indians west of the Mississippi. President Jefferson, who had serious doubts about the constitutionality of the LOUISIANA PURCHASE, regarded this plan as partial justification for the cession; hence the 1804 act which organized the new territory authorized the president to exchange Indian lands east of the river for land to the west. Under this authority some tribes were removed, but the general removal awaited a specific act passed in 1830.

This Indian Removal Act provided for the removal of all Indians east of the Mississippi to an area designated as "Permanent Indian Country." This included land west of Arkansas and Missouri and a line running through western Iowa, central Minnesota, and northwestern Wisconsin. The War Department was to conclude treaties with eastern Indians providing for the exchange of land and with western Indians to secure the land needed for their new neighbors. This act had widespread support, although a few Americans, notably the Quakers, opposed it as unjust. Prevailing opinion regarded the western territory as desert land, and therefore uninhabitable. President JACKSON put this act into execution with vigor and enthusiasm; a westerner himself, he had little concern for moral principles in dealing with Indians. Hence pressure and sharp practices were used to get Indian agreement to the necessary treaties. The weak northern tribes offered little opposition; most of them had already been dispossessed of their ancestral homes, and for this reason they felt little attachment to their lands. The short BLACK HAWK WAR of 1832, involving a faction of the Sauks and Foxes under Chief Black Hawk, was the only serious opposition. Other northern tribes removed were the Chippewas, Winnebagoes, Pottawatomies, Iowas, Kickapoos, Delawares, Shawnees, Ottawas, Kaskaskias, Peorias, and the Miamis.

The southern Indians, however, were moved only after considerable resistance. These Indians, the Creeks, Cherokees, Choctaws, Chickasaws, and Seminoles, often called the Five Civilized Tribes, had adopted some of the features of civilization; the Creeks and Cherokees especially had permanent homes and farms and had established representative government. Their removal required threats and even force. The SEMINOLE WARS (1835–42) cost some 1,500 lives and about $10,000,000, but finally all except a remnant of this Florida tribe was transported to the West. Even after treaties were signed the actual movement of the Indians was difficult, the army having the task of escorting the 60,000 Indians to their new homes. The march became an Indian epic of tragedy; much of the suffering was caused by grafting contractors who were unscrupulous about the quality of supplies which they furnished.

By 1837 the removal was practically complete. As a result of some 94 treaties, several million acres of Indian land east of the Mississippi were vacated. The Indians were settled in the "Permanent Indian Country," where according to law and treaty they were not to be molested "as long as grass shall grow and water run." But almost immediately the American westward movement pushed

BUR. AMER. ETHNOLOGY
Crow Indian chief

into this territory. In the 1850's they were moved from Kansas and Nebraska into the new INDIAN TERRITORY, now Oklahoma. In 1868 the idea of a permanent Indian country was dropped and the system of reservations was adopted. FRANK L. ESTERQUEST

Wheeler-Howard Act. In 1924 all Indians were made citizens of the United States, but this did little to improve their status. For years friends of the Indian and Indian leaders themselves agitated for reforms. In the late 1920's a thorough factual study of the whole system was made by a committee under the Institute of Government Research headed by Dr. Lewis Meriam. Publication of the Meriam report in 1928 was followed by a lengthy investigation by a committee of the U.S. Senate whose voluminous hearings and exposures heralded the changes to come. President Hoover appointed to the Indian Office commissioners of a wholly new type, pledged to a reform program—Messrs. Charles J. Rhoads and J. Henry Scattergood. Under their administration the groundwork was laid for a new policy, embodied in the Indian Reorganization (Wheeler-Howard) Act of 1934. Under the provisions of the Act a $10,000,000 revolving fund was established to make loans to Indian tribes. It provided for the purchase of millions of acres of land to permit Indians to attain a standard of living equal to that of the non-Indian rural population of the country. Further allotment was prohibited, while restricted lands were to stay restricted, and the period of trust was extended indefinitely. An appropriation of $2,000,000 a year for land purchase was fixed, these purchases to be made rather for the tribe than for the individual, with title to remain in the government. The tribes accepting the Act could exercise veto power over the spending of their own tribal funds, hitherto at the discretion of the Indian Office. Tribes were given authority to incorporate for business purposes, to buy up heirship land, and to arrange for voluntary exchanges and consolidations of land among members. A scholarship loan fund of $250,000 a year was set up. The employment of qualified Indians was permitted in the Indian Service irrespective of any civil service status.

In 1946 an Indian Claims Commission was established. By 1951, claims totaling $1,750,000,000 had been filed against the government; the commission had awarded $3,490,000 on the claims.

Suffrage. Although all Indians were made citizens in 1924, as recently as 1940 seven states barred them from voting, either by discriminatory state laws or by interpretations of state law resulting in discrimination. Lack of enforcement of these restrictions by five of these states, however, permitted their Indian citizens to vote. The last legal barriers between Indians and their franchise rights were removed in 1948 when favorable court decisions in Arizona and New Mexico, the other two states, granted full voting privileges to Indians. In 1950 Rhode Island officially granted the vote to the Narragansett Indians, and Idaho granted full citizenship to its Indian residents.

Administration. The commissioner of Indian Affairs has, under the direction of the secretary of the interior, management of all Indian affairs and of all matters arising out of Indian relations. This includes the economic development and relief of the Indian, both tribally and as an individual; the organization of Indian tribes, including credit organizations; Indian education in boarding schools, day schools, and community centers operated by the government, and in public schools and other nongovernmental institutions; health, medical, and sanitation activities; the land program, involving land acquisitions and adjustment, tribal enrollment, land sales, and contracts; forestry, involving forest management, fire protection, grazing; the furtherance of an agricultural extension program; irrigation, both construction, maintenance and operation; the construction and upkeep of buildings at field units; the con-

struction and maintenance of roads and bridges on Indian lands; Indian emergency conservation work and other emergency activities; also health, education, and other activities in behalf of the natives of Alaska.   B. F. C.

SOCIAL AND ECONOMIC PROGRESS

Under provisions of the Indian Reorganization (Wheeler-Howard) Act of 1934 tribal government was accepted by 195 tribes, bands, communities and groups, including 14 groups that had previously been organized in the manner contemplated. Elections in 181 tribes accepted the plan, which was rejected by 77 tribes, including the Navaho. Tribal government takes many forms. Many are chartered as business corporations. Some adapted earlier tribal organizations. Some provided for a modern council and invested some power in chiefs. In nearly all cases new constitutions and charters were adopted.

Along with recognition of tribal functions went encouragement of a return to original native culture and art. Traditional Indian beliefs were brought under the constitutional guaranties of freedom of religion. All of this was a reversal of most previous official and welfare policies. In many cases traditional arts and handicrafts had been forgotten within the tribes and it was found necessary to teach them anew from recorded white sources. But the economic values were stressed; in addition to the continuing demand for Indian products by collectors and souvenir hunters, many articles were in demand within the producing group itself and others had a wide general acceptance. Navaho rugs and silver jewelry, for example, although not derived from any pre-Columbian native culture, had developed in a peculiarly Indian pattern and had become a considerable factor in trade. These and other policies, advocated by John Collier as commissioner, Office of Indian Affairs (1933–1945), were criticized by many sincere friends of the Indian who saw in them a step backward. They ridiculed attempts to teach basket weaving to Indians of tribes which had never practiced that art, and the encouragement given Indians who had made some success in normal pursuits of white communities to adopt Sioux headdresses and beadwork for purposes of showmanship. More seriously, they opposed the return to tribal government where it had been abandoned as retarding the assimilation of the Indian into normal American life, and as encouraging continued segregation and wardship.

Reservations. In early years lands reserved for Indian use were on an impermanent basis, with the result that the reservations east of the Mississippi River are today few and small. The policy of concentrating all Indians in an INDIAN TERRITORY was long favored. The reservation system became a definite policy in 1853. The Dawes General Allotment Act of 1887 was an attempt to provide for its extinction. Unfortunately it was based on the theory that the Indian was a vanishing race, whereas increasing populations made the division of reservations into lands held in severalty impracticable. Indian-owned lands are known variously as reservations, communities, colonies, rancherias, pueblos, and the like, so that an exact accounting is difficult.

Some of the larger reservations are: Menominee in Wisconsin; Greater Leech Lake, White Earth and Red Lake in Minnesota; Fort Berthold and Fort Totten in North Dakota; Standing Rock (mostly in South Dakota), Cheyenne River, Crow Creek, Sisseton, Pine Ridge and Rosebud in South Dakota; Winnebago and Omaha in Nebraska; Osage in Oklahoma; Blackfeet, Fort Belknap, Fort Peck, Flathead, and Crow in Montana; Wind River in Wyoming; Uintah and Ouray in Utah; Jicarilla, Mescalero, Canoncito in New Mexico; Navaho, Hopi, San Carlos, Papago, Kaibab, Havasupai and Hualapai in Arizona; Fort Hall, Coeur d'Alene, and Nez Perce in Idaho; Colville, Spokane, and Yakima

CHICAGO NAT. HIST. MUS.

Navaho silversmith at work in front of his home

in Washington; Warm Springs, Klamath, and Umatilla in Oregon; Western Shoshone, Pyramid Lake, and Walker River in Nevada.

Largest is the Navaho Reservation, exceeding 16,000,000 acres, mostly in Arizona, but extending into New Mexico and Utah, which has been found inadequate to support a population which has increased from 8,000 at the time of the treaty of 1868 to 65,000, and additional lands have been purchased.

A great change in the basic organization of the Bureau of Indian Affairs went into effect in 1950. The present organization provides three areas of operation: Washington, headquarters office; area offices; and field offices. The field service consists of 54 agencies, several nonreservation boarding schools, and some detached sanitoriums. There has been a tendency to consolidate agencies, with one agency in many cases administering the affairs of several reservations.

Lands. The Office of Indian Affairs has jurisdiction over some 57,000,000 acres, nearly all of which is held in trust for Indian tribes and individuals. More than 13,000,000 acres, however, are located in regions having 10 inches or less of annual rainfall. Actually, the Indians have only 3,000,000 acres classified as farm-crop land, and of this amount, approximately one-half must be irrigated; in 1950, 845,000 acres were under irrigation. Approximately 45,000,000 acres are range lands used for grazing, about 34,000,-000 being used by the Indians themselves.

The land available is judged insufficient in quantity and quality to support its population. A program of land acquisition has been in effect since passage of the Indian Reorganization act (1934). Lands open to public settlement but unclaimed have been restored to tribal ownership; for example, 236,790 acres on the Uintah and Ouray Reservation in 1946 and 157,000 acres on the Red Lake Reservation in 1945. Tribal funds have been used to purchase lands, $177,000 for 63,000 acres on 12 reservations in 1945; $203,000 for 49,000 acres on 13 reservations in 1946; and $304,000 in 1947. Congress appropriated $350,-000 for the purchase of lands for needy Indians and returning veterans in 1947—the first appropriation following World War II. Under the tribal government plan individual allotments and heirship inter-

ests have been returned, in many cases, to tribal control where an improved use of the land is considered probable.

Conservation policies have been adopted to reduce soil depletion; in 1950, irrigation projects affecting 845,000 acres were in operation. Improvement in the quality of livestock has been marked; numbers have increased from 167,000 beef cattle and 16,400 dairy cattle in 1933 to 363,350 beef cattle and 47,-580 dairy cattle in 1948, producing an income of $30,973,800. Other agricultural income increased from $9,124,000 in 1940 to $25,377,500 in 1948.

Sources of Wealth. Livestock raising is the principal industry of Indians. Of other sources of income the most spectacular has been oil. In the 10-year period ending 1945, total petroleum production on Indian lands was 251,000,000 barrels; in 1949, total output of Indian wells exceeded 23,000,000 barrels. The most productive fields are those on the Osage Reservation and the restricted lands of the Five Civilized Tribes in Oklahoma. Other fields have been developed on the Wind River Reservation in Wyoming and the Blackfeet Reservation in Montana. In 1950, leases were taken on three reservations on which there had been no previous development; these leases were on Fort Peck land, Montana; Jicarilla tribal land, New Mexico; and the Uintah and Ouray reservations, Utah.

During World War II lead and zinc concentrates totaling 415,000 tons valued at $38,000,000 were mined on Quapaw lands. The total income from mining during 1948 amounted to about $12,000,000.

About 2 per cent of the estimated total volume of standing timber in the United States is on Indian land and is estimated at 35 billion feet. Cuts have averaged a half billion feet a year. Sawmills on the Menominee, Red Lake, Navaho and Fort Apache Reservations have been important Indian industries. Fish and game continue to be important sources of income and 60,000 furs and skins valued at $1,250,000 were taken in 1945. Arts and crafts bring income of $350,000 to $500,000 annually.

Population. Probably few of the Indians of today are of pure Indian blood and although sometimes estimated as high as 60 per cent, it is, of course, impossible to determine how many there are. Some persons have claims to Indian allotments or other rights who have no Indian blood, as, for example, descendants of white captives or of Negro slaves. The Census Bureau counts as Indians those who are considered Indians in the communities in which they live, which might exclude some Indians having valid tribal rights. The Office of Indian Affairs counts Indians under its jurisdiction, which excludes many who have passed into the white community. The census of 1910, which made a thorough breakdown of Indian tribes (excluding Alaska) counted 265,683; in 1930 the number was 332,397. Office of Indian Affairs figures for 1947 totaled 398,050. The round number 400,000 is commonly used.

Estimates for the pre-Columbian period have ranged from 350,000 to 3,000,000. Clark Wissler estimated Indian population in the United States in 1780 at 750,000. There is much opinion that the Indian population has remained relatively constant.

Health. In pre-Columbian times Indians were certainly not subject to many of the diseases that later afflicted them, although there is some question whether they were as healthy as has been generally assumed. From 1781 to 1840 smallpox ravaged many tribes, some of which were greatly reduced, as, for example, the Mandans. Measles took a heavy toll. Reservation life increased the incidence of colds, diphtheria, pneumonia, trachoma and tuberculosis. In recent years tuberculosis has been the leading cause of death and much effort has been devoted to its prevention and eradication. Trachoma, an eye infection formerly a major problem, has been reduced to an incidence of 7.2 per cent. The Indian

INDIAN: CEREMONIES

In the Eagle Dance, Tesque Indians paint their bodies, and wear symbolic beaks and feathers of the bird

Devil Dance, the weird and savage ceremony of the Apache Indians, is performed each year on July 4th at the Mescalero Apache Indian Reservation in southern New Mexico

The Hoop Dance of the Pueblo Indians is an exhibition of great skill. It is performed upon many important occasions

A Laguna Drummer and Dancers take part in the yearly powwow of more than 31 tribes, held at Gallup, N.M.

NEW MEXICO STATE TOURIST BUREAU; SANTA FE RAILROAD

The Navaho Sun and Wand Dance is performed yearly as a thanksgiving. Both men and women participate. The wands carried in the ceremony are symbolic of the harvest

INDIAN: ARTS & CRAFTS

Drums, made of hollowed-out logs and animal skins, are closely associated with Indian culture. They are used in ceremonies and communications

A Navaho Weaver in Monument Valley practices her tribe's best known art. Each rug has a deliberate flaw, since a perfect rug signifies bad luck

Wool for Navaho Blankets is carded and spun by primitive methods which were outmoded in white communities before the Revolutionary War

Belt Weaving again exhibits Indian skill in using geometric design. This weaver wears a squash-blossom necklace, the Indian symbol of fertility

Pottery Making is an outstanding Indian craft. It has survived since earliest times as an important trade. This is one of San Ildefonso's best ceramists

FRED CLARK; JOSEF MUENCH; SANTA FE RAILROAD; PATRICIA BAILEY

This Apache Family represents a typical picture of present-day home life. The cradle board containing the baby is an ancient custom still used

A Navaho Woman brushes the hair of a young girl with a yucca brush. The Navahos are essentially a nomadic group, and seldom have permanent villages

Home Life in the Everglades of Florida is peaceful. These Seminole Indians are cooking their dinner over an open fire. Their costumes are colorful

Beehive Bakeries, a common sight on the reservations of the Southwest, are one of the cultural contributions of the Spanish explorers

JOSEF MUENCH; SANTA FE RAILROAD; F.N. & P.S.; FRED CLARK

A Corn Grinder bends to her ancient task in the costume bequeathed to the Navahos by the Basques in their first contacts with the Indians

INDIAN: TRIBES

Apaches, a tribe of the Athabascan family, are related to the totem-pole builders of Alaska. Once warlike, they are now adopting modern civilization

Navahos, a southwestern tribe, are believed to have migrated from Canada at about A.D. 1000. They are noted for their rugs and silver work

Many Tribes are represented at the yearly powwow of the Pendleton, Ore. roundup. Pictured are Walla Wallas, Umatillas, Cayuses, and Nez Perces

Hopi Indians are a comparatively small Arizona tribe known as Village Dwellers. This Indian girl is wearing the traditional unmarried woman's costume

This Yakima Chief is a descendant of a tribe which numbered 3,000. Living in the woodlands of Washington, they were the state's first fishermen

SOUTHERN PACIFIC; MILTON SNOW; UNION PACIFIC; GORDON PALMQUIST

Service in 1950 maintained 71 hospitals. In that year a new hospital was completed at Mount Edgecumbe, Alaska, and work was begun on new hospitals at Anchorage, Alaska, and Galen, Montana.

Education. Dartmouth College was founded as an "Indian Charity School" and for many years mission schools dominated Indian education, receiving Federal aid until 1896. Captain R. H. Pratt established the Carlisle Indian School at Carlisle, Pennsylvania, in 1879 and gave a new impetus to Indian education. Carlisle was closed in 1918, but it inspired the establishment of such nonreservation boarding schools and Indian Service schools as Haskell Institute, Lawrence, Kansas; Chilocco Indian Agricultural School, Chilocco, Oklahoma; Sequoyah Training School at Tahlequah, Oklahoma; Flandreau School, Flandreau, South Dakota; Sherman Institute, Riverside, California; and Chemawa School, Chemawa, Oregon.

The Indian Service also maintains reservation boarding schools, special consolidated schools and day schools. Total enrollment in all Indian schools reached a new high of 26,716 in 1950. The inadequacy of this education program is shown by the fact that the Navahos alone have petitioned for schools for 20,000 children in accordance with treaty provisions. In 1950 there were 33 Federal Indian high schools, all accredited by the states in which they operated; since World War II, the number of Indian students attending high school has quadrupled. In 1949, between 2,000 and 3,000 Indian veterans were studying under the G.I. Bill of Rights.

Indians in the War. During World War II, 30,000 Indians were enrolled in the armed forces, to whom more than 200 decorations were awarded, including two congressional medals of honor. During the war 40,000 to 45,000 Indians annually left reservations to engage in war work. One especial service performed by Indians in both World Wars I and II was their use in communications work where Indian languages such as the Navaho were used as codes. In World War II the Marine Corps established a special school to train Navaho code talkers.

Assimilation into American Life. When John Rolfe married POCAHONTAS in 1614 some objection was expressed in London to allowing Rolfe a commoner to marry a "princess" and several "First Families of Virginia" are proud to trace their ancestry to her. On the other hand some states still segregate Indians in schools and elsewhere. An act of Congress in 1924 conferred citizenship on all Indians, but Indians in New Mexico and Arizona are excluded from voting if they are wards of the Federal government and not taxed. Indians on reservations, however, are not subject to state law.

However in 1947 the Indian Commissioner presented a program for the gradual withdrawal of Federal control from certain Indian tribes with the idea of eventually ending all wardship. The excellent record made by Indians in World War II emphasized the practicability of assimilation into American life generally, which many had demonstrated over the years by achievement. Such names as General Ely Parker, Vice President Curtis and Will Rogers are examples.

No count has ever been taken of the thousands of Indians assimilated over the years and lost to record as Indians. It is probable that full assimilation is only a question of time.   Don RUSSELL

CANADIAN POLICY

In Canada the Indian problem was less critical than in the United States. The French character and methods of dealing suited the ideas of the aborigines, and the two races amalgamated to a surprising extent under French rule. The British and colonial authorities of Canada, however, have always endeavored to deal fairly and generously with the Indians, and have made the local French traditions fully their own.

CANADIAN NATIONAL RAILWAYS
British Columbian Indians

Canada never had a real Indian war. Under the Hudson's Bay Company's rule in the Northwest no Indian ever had cause to complain of injustice, and as a consequence the Indians committed few crimes.

But it must be remembered that the Indian population of Canada was never nearly so dense as farther south, nor so hard pressed by the influx of white settlers as it has been in the United States from the first. Nothing but the absolute prohibition of immigration could have prevented Indian wars in the United States. The influx of settlers has been incessant; and as a consequence, Indian wars were formerly almost continually waged.

The number of Indians in Canada was 127,941 in 1901; 110,596 in 1921; and 118,316 in 1941. The affairs of the Indians of Canada are administered by the Indian Affairs Branch, Department of Citizenship and Immigration. In 1949, 386 Indian schools were in operation, including 72 residential schools with an enrollment of 9,368 and 309 day schools with an enrollment of 12,615.

See INDIAN CAPTIVITIES; INDIAN TERRITORY; INDIAN WARS. See also the entries for the separate tribes and for individual Indian leaders; also UNITED STATES, *People*; CENTRAL AMERICA, *People*; NORTH AMERICA, *People*; and SOUTH AMERICA, *People*.

BIBLIOG.–F. W. Seymour, *The Story of the Red Men* (1929); F. C. MacGregor, *Twentieth Century Indians* (1941); Oliver La Farge, *As Long as the Grass Shall Grow* (1940), *The Changing Indian* (1942); L. B. Priest, *Uncle Sam's Stepchildren* (1942); C. T. Loram and T. F. McIlwraith, *The North American Indian Today* (1943); B. A. DeVoto, *Across the Wide Missouri* (1947); C. Wissler, *North American Indians of the Plains* (ed. 1948); R. M. Edwards, *American Indians of Yesterday* (1948); F. H. Douglas and R. D'Harnoncourt, *Indian Art of the United States* (ed. 1949); M. W. Smith, ed., *Indians of the Urban Northwest* (1949); C. E. Hamilton, ed., *Cry of the Thunder Bird* (1950).

INDICAN is a GLUCOSIDE which occurs in the indigo plant, from which it can be extracted. It has the formula $C_{14}H_{17}O_6N$. On HYDROLYSIS in the presence of enzymes or acids, indican is converted into the sugar glucose (DEXTROSE) and a compound called indoxyl. The latter is oxidized by air into INDIGO. At one time indigo was made commercially from this natural source, but synthetic indigo has replaced it.

Indican is also a name used for potassium indoxyl sulfate, a compound which occurs normally in the urine. Excessive amounts of indican in the urine have been observed in diseases of the small intestine, such as intestinal obstruction, in intestinal indigestion, and in stomach ailments, such as gastritis, caused by a deficiency of hydrochloric acid in the gastric juice. See INDOLE.

INDICATOR, in chemistry, is a substance which, by means of a change in color, is used to identify some particular kind of substance. The commonest application of indicators is in the detection of acids and bases. Litmus, methyl orange, and phenolphthalein are commonly used as indicators; they change color when the solution is neutral, slightly acid, and slightly basic respectively. Any litmus turns blue in the presence of bases, and red in the presence of acids. Methyl orange is orange in basic solutions, and red in acidic solutions. Phenolphthalein is red in basic solutions, and colorless in acidic.

INDICTMENT, in criminal law, a formal, written accusation of a crime made by a public prosecutor and submitted to a grand jury in order that it may determine from competent evidence whether there is a *prima facie* case against the accused (sufficient evidence to raise the presumption of guilt). Upon such a finding the grand jury presents a *true bill* (of indictment) to the proper court, so that the accused may be tried.

The indictment differs from a *presentment* which originates with the grand jury and is founded on its own knowledge and observations; and from an *information* which is an accusation presented directly to the court by a proper public official without the intervening process of a grand jury hearing.

The office and purpose of an indictment are to notify the accused of the offense with which he is charged and the elements thereof, so that he may properly prepare his defense, and to initiate his trial. Among the essential requisites of a valid indictment generally are that it be presented to a court having jurisdiction of the offense with a specific allegation of such jurisdiction and that it be drawn with sufficient certainty as to identify the crime of which the defendant is accused.

The indictment may contain several *counts* charging different offenses arising out of the same set of facts and it has been held proper to join distinct offenses in separate counts. The indictment may also join two or more individuals. While formerly at common law the court was not permitted to amend indictments (that right being reserved to the grand jury and any amendment required its concurrence), the law has been changed by statutes in both United States and England to permit amendments which do not work an injustice and which seem reasonable to the court, such as correction of mistakes of time or place. The accused cannot be convicted of a higher degree of offense than charged in the indictment, but can be convicted of a lesser one. A single good count in the indictment is sufficient to sustain a verdict of guilty, it not being required to prove at the trial all of the allegations contained in the indictment.

In the United States the forms and requirements of indictments differ among the various states, there being a trend to simplify them and to reduce the technical strictness which existed in the common law. The Federal constitution, as well as many of the state constitutions, provide a guaranty to an accused person of a trial "on a presentment or indictment by a grand jury." Where the constitution or the statutes do not require an indictment, other methods of accusation are frequently employed, particularly that of INFORMATION. See CRIMINAL LAW; JURY.   S. G.

INDIES. See INDONESIA, UNITED STATES OF; WEST INDIES; INDIA.

INDIGESTION is a term used loosely to describe various disturbances of the upper digestive tract, including nausea and vomiting, heartburn, regurgitation and belching, and pain and distention of the stomach. The causes of these symptoms may or may not be located within the digestive system. See DYSPEPSIA; DIGESTION; STOMACH; INTESTINE; LIVER; GALLBLADDER; APPENDICITIS; CONSTIPATION; COLITIS; DIARRHEA; FOOD POISONING; ULCERS; CANCER; NAUSEA AND VOMITING; ALLERGY; HUNGER AND APPETITE; ANTACIDS; CATHARTICS.

Gastric Neuroses. Frequently the symptoms that patients call indigestion are the result of "nervous indigestion." Doctors call these disturbances *functional gastric neuroses* to distinguish them from disorders caused by organic disease. This is not to say that the discomfort is imaginary. The disturbances of function are real enough, but calling them functional neuroses means that they are produced by nerve impulses conveyed via the AUTONOMIC NERVOUS SYSTEM as a result of some emotional or psychological conflict. In such cases the affected organ may at first be organically sound, but if the disturbing influence continues, lesions and deformities may eventually develop. See PSYCHOSOMATIC MEDICINE.

When the disturbance is related to an increase in the activities stimulated by the vagus nerve (parasympathetic division of the autonomic nervous system) the neurosis is said to be *hypersthenic*. This means that there will be increased secretion of the digestive glands, increased acidity of the gastric secretion, increased flow of mucus, and a continuous and excessive flow of gastric juice. Similarly there will be increased muscular activity of the digestive organs, including spasm of the stomach and of the sphincters guarding its entrance and exit. Symptoms of these increased secretory and motor activities may include abnormally intensified hunger, distress in the upper middle portion of the abdomen, and failure to feel satisfied after a meal. Symptoms may vary from day to day, tending to be intensified by fatigue or emotional tension.

When the disturbance is related to a decrease in the activities stimulated by the vagus nerve the neurosis is said to be *hyposthenic*. Distress in neuroses of this type is usually less acute than in the hypersthenic. Patients may complain of lack of appetite and a feeling of drag in the upper middle portion of the abdomen. It is not unusual for the same patient to be troubled by this neurosis at some times, by a hypersthenic state at others.

A third type of neurosis is *reverse peristalsis*, which is frequently found associated with the other two. In this condition waves of muscular contraction tend to force the contents of the digestive tract backward rather than forward. This gives rise to additional discomforts, including belching, regurgitation, heartburn ("burning" sensation in back of the sternum), and nausea.

Treatment of the gastric neuroses must be based on careful diagnosis. Self-medication is inadvisable. Thorough examination is required to locate any possible organic lesion. Equally important in most cases is discovery of the source of the anxiety, frustration, or other conflict at the root of the personality problem. Drugs can be prescribed to relieve immediate distress, but PSYCHOTHERAPY is usually the only measure for permanent relief.   M. B. C.

BIBLIOG.–C. Binger, *The Doctor's Job* (1945); H. T. Hyman, *Integrated Practice of Medicine* (1946).

INDIGIRKA RIVER, U.S.S.R., the Russian Soviet Federated Socialist Republic, in the Yakut Autonomous Soviet Socialist Republic, between the Yana and the Kolyma rivers. It rises in the Stanovoi Range, flows west, north, and northeast for nearly 1,200 miles, and empties into the Arctic Ocean.

INDIGO, a blue coloring matter occurring in various species of *Indigofera* and other plants. It originated in India and is one of the oldest known dyes. It was generally prepared by the fermentation of a glucoside (INDICAN), existing in a number of plants, of which *Indigofera tinctoria*, grown largely in India, and *Indigofera anil*, a product of the West Indies, are most important. *Isatis tinctoria*, or the woad plant, is also a source of indican.

Indigofera tinctoria is a shrub from four to six feet high, with silvery branches, small, yellowish-red flowers borne in racemes, and long, nearly straight pods. *Indigofera anil* is similar but has smaller flowers and shorter curved pods. The plants are easily cultivated, requiring a rich well-watered soil. The seeds are sown in rows about two feet apart and the flowers appear about three months from the time of seeding. The plants are cut when beginning to flower, and as this can be done at frequent intervals, four or five crops a year can be obtained. The plants are extremely hardy and if neglected will propagate themselves as weeds.

To prepare the dye the leaves and stems of the plants are macerated, and soaked in water. Fermentation soon commences, producing a solution of "indigo white," which is run off and agitated with air. During this oxidation the liquid becomes green, then blue, as the indigo white is changed to indigo blue. The latter is allowed to settle out and is washed and dried. The yield of the crude indigo is about 0.3 per cent of the weight of the plant.

Natural indigo has now been almost completely replaced by synthetic indigo, first prepared by A. Bayer in 1870. In one of the commercial processes in use, aniline ($C_6H_5NH_2$) is treated with chloroacetic acid ($ClCH_2COOH$) to form phenyl glycine (C_6H_5-$NHCH_2COOH$), which is next converted into indigo white, then, by oxidation into indigo. The formula for indigo is $C_6H_4NH(CO)C=C(CO)NHC_6H_4$.

Pure indigo blue can be obtained from the crude products by SUBLIMATION under reduced pressure. It forms a purplish blue powder which is insoluble in water. It is reduced by many agents, sodium hydrosulfite for example, to soluble indigo white. Fabrics to be dyed are immersed in the solution, then exposed to the air which reconverts indigo white into insoluble indigo blue. This process is called *vat dyeing*. See DYES AND DYEING.

Indigo may be converted by sulfuric acid into indigodisulfonic acid, the sodium salt of which is called *soluble indigo*. Soluble indigo is a permissible blue food dye.

INDIGO BUNTING, a small FINCH, less than six inches long. The indigo bunting, *Passerina cyanea*, is found in the groves and thickets of eastern United States but winters in Central America. The striking male bird is a deep indigo blue, the color being due to light refraction rather than pigmentation. Females and young males are grayish-brown. Indigo buntings have a cheerful, characteristic song.

INDIGO, FALSE, a name given to several perennial herbs of the genus *Baptisia*, of the eastern and middle United States. They bear trifoliolate or, rarely, simple leaves, which turn black on drying, and racemes of yellow, white, or blue bell-shaped flowers. An inferior grade of indigo is obtained from some species. *B. tinctoria*, wild indigo, or the horsefly weed, has loose terminal racemes of yellow flowers. It blooms from July to September. *B. australis*, blue false indigo, is a tall handsome plant, bearing bright blue flowers in midsummer.

The name false or bastard indigo is also applied to *Amorpha fruticosa*, a tall shrub growing along streams from southern Pennsylvania to Wisconsin and the Rocky mountains, southward to Florida and Texas. It has dense racemes of violet or purple flowers with long conspicuous orange anthers.

INDIGO SNAKE. See GOPHER SNAKE.

INDIO, city, S California, Riverside County; on the Southern Pacific Railroad and U.S. highways 60, 70, and 99; about 69 miles SE of Redlands in a fruit and vegetable-growing region. The city was founded in 1876 as a distribution point for railroad freight; it was named for the large number of Indians who comprised the settlement when it was a railroad construction camp. Indio is a trading center and a packing and shipping point for grapefruit, dates, and truck crops grown on near-by irrigated lands. Pop. (1950) 5,300.

INDIUM, a distinctly metallic element, somewhat like tin in appearance but softer than lead, formerly very rare but now available commercially. It is malleable and ductile, has a density of 7.3, a melting point of 156°C., and boiling point of 2100°C. It is present in very small quantities, usually only a few hundredths of a per cent, in most zinc blende ores. The principal commercial sources from which indium is derived are various residues or by-products of zinc metallurgy.

The symbol for indium is In. Its atomic weight is 114.76 and its atomic number 49. Indium belongs to the same periodic group as aluminum, and it precipitates with iron and aluminum as the hydroxide, $In(OH)_3$. Sodium sulfite or bisulfite is often used to

precipitate indium from a solution without precipitating much of the iron. Zinc amalgam in a slightly acid solution will also leave iron in the solution and transfer the indium into the amalgam. Indium, like cadmium, can be precipitated from solutions in the form of a metallic sponge by zinc. Metallic indium dissolves easily in most acids.

Indium resembles aluminum by having a principal valence of three, by having an easily sublimed trichloride (obtained by heating the metal in chlorine gas), by forming ALUMS, and by its inertness in dry air or in water. Heated in the air it is oxidized to the pale yellow oxide, In_2O_3.

Indium differs from aluminum in being unattacked by sodium hydroxide; by forming with hydrogen sulfide, in alkaline or very weak acid solutions, a stable pale-yellow sulfide, In_2S_3; by the fact that it can be electroplated from alkaline or weakly acid solutions; and by the formation of compounds of lower valence, such as $InCl$.

Its salts impart a blue violet color to a gas flame and show two lines in the spectroscope in that part of the SPECTRUM; this is the most delicate test.

The metal is easily obtained from its salts by electrolysis, by heating the oxide in hydrogen, or by replacement from dilute acid solutions with metallic zinc.

Uses. The most important use for indium is in lead bearings (0.1 to 0.4 per cent) to reduce corrosion by acids that may be present or may be formed in the lubricating oils. The finished lead bearings, after receiving the very light electrolytic deposit of indium, are heated at 140°–150° C. and later at 170°–180° C., to cause diffusion of the indium into the lead layer.

Silver containing 25 per cent of indium is usually free from tarnishing. The inclusion of 18 per cent of indium in Woods' metal will reduce the melting point to 46° C., a temperature low enough for making castings or impressions of animal tissues. Indium has been suggested for use in dental alloys and in high temperature thermometers because of its high vaporizing and boiling point and its low melting point. In alloys, it usually hardens, strengthens, and increases the resistance to tarnishing and corrosion.

Indium is very toxic, similar to lead, and care is necessary for those using it or its salts. F. C. MATHERS

BIBLIOG.–M. T. Ludwick, *Indium, its Occurrence, Metallurgical and Chemical Characteristics* (1950).

INDIVIDUAL, a term used in the history of thought with two shades of meaning. In one, it signifies an indivisible unit or atomic thing; in the other, that which is unique—a real existence with a distinctive nature of its own. "Individuality," in which the element of uniqueness is emphasized, is used as a rule in a good, or at least a neutral, sense.

INDIVIDUAL DIFFERENCES. The ways in which one individual differs from another have long been of interest to people. Evidence for this interest lies in age-old records of races and contests of various types. Efforts at demonstrating differences and superiority are seen in these manifestations.

The psychological interest in individual differences received its greatest impetus from GALTON. Working in the last half of the 19th century, he collected evidence for differences in individuals with regard to their sensory acuity, perceptual modes, etc. A contemporary, WUNDT, working in Germany, became interested in individual differences in attention, memory, and other measurable psychological traits. Following this lead, much of the work of laboratory psychologists was directed toward the determination of differences in various psychological processes.

Starting about 1890 CATTELL and his students experimented with MENTAL TESTS. These tests were merely a modification of laboratory methods of demonstrating individual differences. In these early attempts the principal traits measured were strength of grip, rote memory, reaction time, weight discrimination, etc. Higher mental processes did not become susceptible of measurement until the work of EBBINGHAUS, BINET, Henri, and Simon. The failure of Cattell and his workers to get differentiation of higher mental processes was due to poor sampling of subjects and tests, and to inadequate statistical treatment of the data. Later work remedied these defects and led to further research. Measurement of individual differences has progressed by leaps and bounds since the work of Binet and those who followed. Not only was intelligence measured, but testing spread into the fields of educational achievement, emotions, personality, vocational preferences, industrial selection, clinical evaluation, etc.

Although Galton's early work indicated the presence of differences in individuals in type of memory (e.g., one was "visual" in his recall; another "verbal"; another "olfactory," etc.), subsequent research demonstrated no such exclusive types, but rather mixed types in which there were variable degrees of predominance of one or another of these sensory impressions. Thus, while one person recalls his breakfast primarily as a visual image, he also may have some olfactory, gustatory, and verbal recollections. Another may recall primarily in terms of verbal memory with elements of other factors operating with variable degrees of effectiveness. The importance of these findings with regard to memory were demonstrated when it was found that other human traits and abilities were present in much the same way. As research data accumulated it was seen that a continuum was the rule, rather than a dichotomy. It became evident also that the usual form for the distribution of human attributes was the bell-shaped, or normal, curve. Not only do anthropometric data, such as height, weight, strength of grip, vital capacity, etc., conform to the normal curve, but psychological traits, such as memory span, intelligence, emotional stability, attention, learning, etc., also tend to be distributed in this way. Earlier efforts at grouping people into neat compartmentalized types have met with little success, since any one individual is a unit which is composed of a kaleidoscopic collection of traits in an infinite variety of possible combinations. See CONSTITUTIONAL TYPES.

The import of this concept becomes apparent when one attempts to classify individuals in terms of aptness for military, academic, or industrial pursuits. The factor of quantitative possession of a given attribute or of several of them is less important, than is the proper proportion of the pertinent qualities. Concretely, some students with less native ability than others may achieve more because of a stronger drive (motivation) and of more stable personality integration. To be sure, ability is important, but the unique utilization of that ability to its fullest potential is more important, and this depends on other factors which are not always apparent.

In the clinical situation this problem is encountered with regularity. A very common illustration is one in which two persons with the same IQ are vastly different in physique, temperament, personality makeup, vocational interests, etc. To evaluate these two solely in terms of intelligence is of little or no real importance. It should be pointed out that even with identical IQ's they may vary widely in the respective degrees of various components of the intelligence tests, since the IQ is merely the summation of a number of scores on a variety of tasks. See INTELLIGENCE.

Culturally, the problem of individual differences is characterized by two diametrically opposite drives. On the one hand, each individual wishes to conform and to be a member of the group. Deviant behavior generally is frowned upon. On the other hand, each individual wishes to be distinguished from the others and to possess some individuality. As ADLER has put it, for each one there is his own "style of life" which is his effort to maintain his individuality. In the last analysis, the solution lies in achieving a balance between conformity and individuality which will be satisfying to the individual and to society. See INDIVIDUAL PSYCHOLOGY.   WILLIAM SLOAN

BIBLIOG.–R. S. Ellis, *The Psychology of Individual Differences* (1928); O. Klineberg, *Race Differences* (1935); A. Anastasi, *The Psychology of Individual Differences* (1937).

INDIVIDUAL PSYCHOLOGY is a systematic interpretation of human nature based upon the work of ALFRED ADLER.

The Life-Style. The central thesis of individual psychology is that the human personality is a unity which reflects the individual's concept of his relationship to the world. This concept, which Adler called the life-style, carries with it a purposeful yet unconscious striving toward some goal. It is built during the first few years while the child is trying to define for himself his role in life. It is usually maintained throughout life with no major change other than a decreasing awareness of it.

The Striving for Significance. Each individual develops an "inferiority-feeling" early in his life. This feeling has its origin in the child's bodily defects and his evaluation of his relative weakness in comparison with the strength of older members of the family. Out of this feeling of inferiority, the child develops compensations with which he attempts to make up for his weakness. (See COMPENSATION.) While the compensations may change in character, the need for compensation of some kind generally persists throughout life due to the permanence of the inferiority-feeling. These attempts to escape from a status of inferiority constitute the "striving for significance." See INFERIORITY COMPLEX.

Social Interest. The traditional upbringing of the child emphasizes the development of compensatory activities whose purpose is to establish the status of the individual in the adult community. This encourages a striving for significance which, in its extreme forms, manifests itself either by an aggressively competitive attitude with emphasis upon success and prestige, or by an intense discouragement and withdrawal from social tasks. Most life-styles are based upon the individual's concept of his weakness and the need for independent competitive activity to gain status.

Adler found that such attitudes toward life, while they may result in outward evidence of success, rarely bring emotional balance and good social relationships to the individual. These latter factors, essential for happiness and adequate functioning, proceed from the development of "social interest." Individual psychology defines social interest as a feeling of belonging to the community. It involves an awareness of one's obligation to participate with others for the welfare of the community in which the individual shares. This concept of social interest as an essential element in the development of the healthy personality is perhaps the most important contribution of individual psychology to the fields of medicine, and the other social sciences. See PSYCHOANALYSIS; FREUD, SIGMUND.   ARTHUR ZWEIBEL, M.D.

BIBLIOG.–A. Adler, *Understanding Human Nature* (1927), *The Practise and Theory of Individual Psychology* (1927), *Social Interest: A Challenge to Mankind* (1938); N. E. Shoobs and G. Goldberg, *Corrective Treatment for Unadjusted Children* (1942).

INDIVIDUALISM is the development of opportunities for individuals to plan and manage their lives in accordance with their own tastes and ideals. Individualism is not a doctrine or set of institutions, though it has found partial expression in various doctrines, attitudes, and institutions. It is a characteristic or a direction of movement common to many institutions and fields of action; and it is one of the basic forces or drives of modern civilization.

Some opportunity for the development of individuality has appeared in other cultures and at other periods, and some degree of individualism may be characteristic of the advanced stages of any culture; but comprehensive and effective attainment of conditions favorable to individual judgment and responsibility has been a notable peculiarity of Western Europe. Only in recent centuries in Western Europe has individualism become a central ideal and a basic principle of social organization.

Manifestations of Individualism. During the entire modern period individualism has seemed to many men the essential foundation for any really civilized society, but has been regarded by other men as a threat to social order and stability and as a potential destroyer of all the institutions upon which civilization rests. Men's fear of individualism has stemmed in part from their attachment to traditional institutions and to the apparent stability and security provided by long established custom and respected authority. A more reasoned uneasiness has resulted from the fact that individualism has been a part of, and undoubtedly one of the dynamic causal factors in, a series of political, social and industrial revolutions. These revolutions have produced societies of tremendous size and intricate organization, within which the failure of one small part of the machinery may threaten the welfare of a nation or even of the world, and within which changes innocently initiated by individuals may have cumulative, unforeseen effects which turn out to be disastrous. Alarmed by the complexity of modern social machinery, the speed at which it runs, and its apparent vulnerability to accident, ignorance or sabotage, many men have felt an imperative need for measures of social discipline and control difficult to reconcile with individualism. The 20th century is a critical period for individualism; and no one knows with certainty whether it is in its old age, soon to die, or is now growing from a brash adolescence into a vigorous maturity.

Certainly the worst enemies of individualism are mistaken when they caricature it as a system in which each individual goes his own way regardless of other people, tries to be as different as possible, and refuses to adapt himself to social action. Individualists believe that men who understand what they are doing and follow their own judgments will make agreements among themselves and will enter into forms of co-operation which are at once more stable and more flexible than types of association resting on custom or obedience to authority. There can be no doubt that individualism has actually produced systems of economic and political co-operation of a size, intricacy, vigor and effectiveness never previously attained. Individualism is not anarchism; but whether individualistic organization can solve contemporary problems remains to be seen.

An individualistic society may be contrasted in general with a society in which customary patterns of thought and action are so stable that little possibility for individual variation exists. It may be contrasted more specifically with the feudal order, in which an established set of relations assigned to each individual a social role complete with rights and duties, or with totalitarian, paternalistic or planned societies, whether democratic or autocratic, in which emphasis on social or governmental action narrows the range within which the individual may follow his own choices.

Sources of Individualism. Some light may be thrown on the positive meaning of individualism by consideration of three of its main sources. One of the pervasive sources was certainly the growth of modern science. DESCARTES, who may be taken as representative of 17th-century scientists, expressed a profound distrust of prevailing beliefs and established authorities. The authorities disagreed and the beliefs conflicted with each other and with experience. He resolved, consequently, to set aside all traditional beliefs, to doubt everything he had been taught, and to accept as true only beliefs whose proof he himself could clearly see. Like Descartes, many of his contemporaries felt that truth could be attained only if the individual freed himself from tradition and authority in order to follow discoverable evidence by the light of his own reason.

During the 17th and 18th centuries this scientific ideal exerted a widespread influence in politics, morals, and religion. Seeking a cure for civil strife, religious dissension and a series of wars, many intellectual leaders concluded that a basis for peace and harmony could be found in individual reason. If the individual could be freed from superstition, tradition, and tyrannical authority, he could follow the light of his own reason to fundamental principles upon which all reasonable men could agree. The ideal of a reasonable religion, a reasonable morality, and a reasonable political order was for a century or more a great intellectual force; and the foundation of this ideal was the belief that the best way of attaining political order and social harmony is to develop in each individual the capacity to follow his own judgment.

Another notable source of modern individualism was the violent conflict among various religious sects following the Reformation. An outcome of this conflict was the doctrine, at first accepted merely as a means of obtaining peace but later regarded as essential to religion, that each individual should have the right, as indeed he has the duty, to follow his own conscience in regard to religious beliefs and forms of worship. Because of the close relation between religion and morals, individualism in religion opened the way for the individual to follow his conscience or judgment in other matters; and this effect was increased by the principle, accepted as part of the formulation of the relation between church and state, that the state should confine its action to matters essential to the welfare of society.

A third source of individualism was the extensive contact between different societies, from the time of the Crusades to the present, resulting from war, trade, exploration, colonization, and travel. An individual who has known only the ways of his own society is likely to follow them as a matter of course; but an individual who has moved from one culture to another may have occasion to select from the old and the new in accordance with his own judgment. Instead of taking it for granted that he is to live where his father lived and as his father lived, an individual may decide that another kind of life or even life in another country is better suited to his needs or ideals. In America the frontier for many generations offered an alternative to individuals who found life in their communities not to their liking. The extensive changes resulting from inventions have had a similar effect. These and other occasions for decision, initiative, and responsibility over several centuries have developed both capacities and tastes for individualism and have resulted in the formation of individualistic institutions.

Phases of Individualism. The individualism which has pervaded the structure of modern society has been reflected in various ideals, doctrines, and institutions. Though these different phases of individualism have not been harmonized in a comprehensive social theory which might furnish clear guidance for future action, they have nevertheless been fused, at least in England and America, into a coherent and recognizable pattern of social organization.

In economic life individualism has been expressed in the system of laissez faire or free enterprise. In politics its product has been governments of limited power, operating mainly through general laws intended to formulate fair rules within which each individual may act in accordance with his own judgment. The main impact of individualism on law has been to promote the development of contract, permitting individuals to make mutually satisfactory arrangements among themselves, and of the system of private property, whereby the individual may acquire resources to be used in accordance with his own judgment. Similar changes, increasing the individual's opportunity to shape his life and to assume responsibility for the result of his decisions, have occurred in education, in the family, and indeed in all phases of social life.

Future of Individualism. Though the past of individualism can be seen with some clarity and constitutes one of the major advances in civilization, its present is troubled and its future uncertain. Despite its successes, individualistic social organization may be unable to deal with the problems of a world torn apart by two world wars and threatened by atomic bombs. As individualism spreads to the East, it is attacked in the West both by men who are in principle opposed to it because they think individual intelligence too wavering and uncertain to serve as a basis for society and by men who favor it in principle but fear that present problems are too grave to be met by individual reason. Individualism is not identical, however, with the institutions in which it has found partial expression; and if individualists are able to develop their institutions to meet new problems, individualism may be the organizing principle and the dynamic force in the construction of a world civilization. See FREEDOM; LIBERTY; LIBERALISM; EQUALITY; DEMOCRACY; CAPITALISM; LAISSEZ FAIRE; FREE ENTERPRISE; FEUDAL SOCIETY; LAW.   CHARNER PERRY

BIBLIOG.–F. Warner, *Individualism* (1911); H. Hoover, *American Individualism* (1922); J. M. Keynes, *The End of Laissez Faire* (1926); J. Dewey, *Individualism, Old and New* (1930); F. A. von Hayek, *Individualism: True and False* (1946); J. Schwartzman, *Rebels of Individualism* (1949).

INDOCHINA, or Farther India, the southeastern peninsula of Asia. See INDOCHINA, FRENCH; ANNAM; TONKIN; SIAM; CAMBODIA; COCHIN CHINA; LAOS; VIET NAM.

INDOCHINA, FRENCH, a federation within the French Federal Union; located in the E part of the great SE Asian peninsula; bordered on the N by China; on the W by Burma, Siam, and the Gulf of Siam; and on the S and E by the China Sea; area 286,000 sq. mi.; pop. (U.N. 1949 est.) 27,460,000.

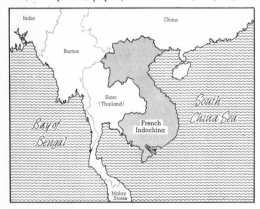

Location map of French Indochina

Under the former political status as a dependency of France, French Indochina included the colony of COCHIN CHINA, the protectorates of TONKIN, ANNAM, CAMBODIA, and LAOS, and KWANGCHOW-WAN Territory (leased from China, 1898–1945); within the Federation it consists of the three associated states of Viet Nam, Cambodia, and Laos.

Topography and Climate. Most of French Indochina lies between the Tropic of Cancer and the 10th south parallel. The area lies wholly within the tropic zone and is hot and humid; the southwestern monsoon brings the long rainy season. The area is generally mountainous, a chain extending from China through Tonkin and the length of Annam, rising in the south to 7,890 feet; in central Annam to 8,524 feet; and in Tonkin, near the Chinese border, to 10,310 feet. Near the Gulf of Siam the Monts des

Cardamomes, rising to 5,722 feet, extend southward to the Cochin China border through western Cambodia. A number of short, unimportant rivers flow from the eastern slopes the short distance to the China Sea, and longer rivers flow westward from the western slopes to add to the Mekong, entering the China Sea through a number of mouths in southern Cochin China. One other important river, the Red, rises in China, enters central northwestern Tonkin, and flows southeastward past Hanoi, and into the China Sea at Haiphong. Both the Red and the Mekong are navigable in Indochina. Great Lake, or Tonle Sap, covers a large area in Cambodia.

People. French Indochina's population included an estimated 43,000 French and 600,000 other foreigners in 1949. Natives of Indochina are the Annamese (four-fifths of the whole), the Khmers (Cambodians), the Chams, the Siamese, the Laotians, and various indigenous tribes.

National education is administered by local authorities. There are schools for French children, and also private denominational and Chinese schools. There are numerous professional schools, and the University of Hanoi (est. 1917). The chief religion is Buddhism.

PRINCIPAL CITIES	POPULATION	
	1940 Est.	1949 Est.
SAIGON-CHOLON	256,000	1,179,000
PNOMPENH	103,000	260,000
HANOI	135,000	160,000
HAIPHONG	122,000	90,000
HUE	28,000	25,000

Economic Life. There are three well established economic areas. The Saigon region—including Cochin China, Cambodia, and southern Laos and Annam—affords extensive fisheries off its coasts and in Great Lake However, the region is largely agricultural, one of the world's greatest rice-producing areas. Around the Tonkin port of Haiphong are great anthracite coal mines; and in northern Annam and Tonkin zinc, tin, and wolfram are mined. Central Annam, between Porte d'Annam and Cape Varella, has Tourane as its chief port for the shipment of cinnamon, sugar, tea, corn, and manico raised in the area. In the northern mountains are valuable tropical hardwoods, bamboo, lacs, herbs, and essential oils. Fish is a major item of diet, but fishing is second to agriculture in importance. The chief exports are rice (about 1,700,000 tons per year), rubber (70,000 tons), coal (2,000,000 tons), fish, pepper, cinnamon, cattle, hides, corn, zinc, tin, wolfram, and cement. Among the principal imports are cotton and silk for Indochina's weaving industries, metal goods, chemicals, pharmaceuticals, oil, motor cars, and fertilizers.

The country has some 27,000 miles of roads, of which about 5,000 are paved, and is serviced by some 2,100 miles of railway. There are about 50,000 miles of telephone and telegraph lines, and radio-telephone service with Europe has been established. There is international air service from Hanoi and Saigon.

Government. Under the political status existing before World War II the whole dependency was under a French governor general, who had general supervision over all the separate divisions. Under the present status, the governor general has been replaced by a high commissioner representing the French Union. Assisting him are eight counselors, nominated by him, and the commander in chief as counselor for military affairs; this group forms the government council. A commissioner of the republic represents the high commissioner in each state. In 1949 Viet Nam received sovereignty in internal affairs.

History. French influence in Indochina can be traced to the missionary efforts begun in the 17th century in Siam, from which missionaries entered Tonkin and Annam. But it was not until 1861–62 that the French mastered the principal part of Cochin China and established a protectorate over Cambodia. In 1882 the French assumed a more aggressive colonial

Harbor of coastal village in French Indochina

Royal palace in city of Pnompenh, Cambodia

Lunch in Saigon barracks

Boy in Saigon region

City street in Saigon

Native orchestra plays before ancient temple of Angkor Wat

Wall of giant stone statues surrounds temple in Cambodia

policy, which was heightened following the weakening of the Chinese in the Sino-Japanese War of 1894–95, and pressed their penetration so that they gained territory east of the Mekong—Tonkin, Laos, and Annam. The capital was first established at Saigon, but was moved to Hanoi in 1902. Following the French defeat early in World War II, the Japanese demanded control over imports and exports, and the use of naval facilities for their fleet. In 1941 the French were forced to cede a strip of Laotian territory on the bank of the Mekong and a portion of northern Cambodia to Siam; and before the year had ended, Japanese and Siamese troops had occupied commercial and strategic areas. In March, 1945, the Japanese disarmed the French army and seized complete control of Indochina, and in August, 1945, proclaimed the independence of French Indochina. Japanese control was not relinquished until after their defeat by the Allies in September, 1945. During the Japanese occupation much damage was done to the communications and industrial installations of French Indochina by the exploitation policy of the Japanese and the bombing attacks of the Allies. An attempt by the Indochinese nationalists to exploit the defenseless position of the French and try to gain independence was put down by British occupation forces and by captured Japanese troops under orders of French officials. Nevertheless, on March 7, 1946, the French announced an agreement recognizing the Viet Nam republic as a free state within the Indochinese federation and the French Union. The Cambodian kingdom willingly accepted the re-establishment of French protection. The French also established the former colony of Cochin China as a free state within the French Union. However, fighting broke out in 1947 between the French and the Communists in Viet Nam. The Communist government of the Viet Minh party began to lose some ground but continued to be entrenched in some parts of the country. In December, 1949, the power of the French was transferred to the Viet Nam authorities and the latter became a part of the French Union. But the Communist forces continued to fight the French. In 1950 the Soviet Union and its satellites recognized the Communist regime in Viet Nam.   C. S.; G. B. DE H.

INDO-EUROPEAN LANGUAGES. The Indo-European language family contains about 140 languages stretching from Iceland to India. Its existence was discovered in the early part of the 19th century, independently by a German scholar, FRANZ BOPP, and a Danish scholar, RASMUS RASK. The Indo-European family forms the following branches: Tokharian, Indo-Iranian, Armenian, GREEK, Albanian, Italic, Celtic, Germanic, Baltic, Slavic, and possibly Hittite. The inclusion of Hittite in the Indo-European family is controversial; some scholars claim that Hittite is a sister language of Indo-European, and that the Indo-European languages and Hittite together form a large group, the Indo-Hittite family.

All languages of the Indo-European family have been demonstrated to have developed from a common ancestral language. This common parent language, called Proto-Indoeuropean, has been reconstructed on the basis of existing languages and data from dead languages. Of the various branches of the Indo-European family, some are occasionally brought into closer relationship. Thus, one often finds mention of an Italo-Celtic branch, composed of the Italic and Celtic languages, or of a Balto-Slavic branch, composed of the Baltic and Slavic languages. Of late, both of these groupings have been proved to be the result of parallel development, rather than common ancestry. The Italic and Celtic languages thus probably do not go back to a common Italo-Celtic parent language, but rather the development of the separate Italic and Celtic parent languages seems to have been similar in many respects. The importance of the Indo-European family lies not only in the fact that the most powerful and influential nations of the world speak Indo-European languages, but also in the great opportunity it has given scholars to create and verify linguistic theories and methods.

Celtic Branch. Languages of the Celtic branch of the Indo-European family were once spoken in most of western and central Europe; today they are restricted to some areas in and around the British Isles. Some scholars divide the Celtic branch into two groups, Continental Celtic and Island Celtic. The former group includes the language of Gaul before its Latinization, Gallic. The latter group includes all the Celtic languages spoken today: Irish, Scotch, Gaelic, Welsh, and Breton. Some scholars suggest a common origin for the Celtic and Italic branches of the Indo-European family, but this theory has of late been abandoned.

Germanic Branch. The Germanic branch of the Indo-European family includes the English language, most important of the languages of the West Germanic group. Other West Germanic languages are German, Frisian, and Dutch. The North Germanic group includes the Scandinavian languages: Swedish, Danish, Norwegian, and Icelandic. The East Germanic group is now extinct. Its only known member is Gothic, studied on the basis of a Bible translation from the fourth century. The parent language of the Germanic branch, Proto-Germanic, has been reconstructed on the basis of data from Gothic and earlier stages of present-day Germanic languages, such as Old English, Old High German, and Old Norse.

Italic Branch. The Italic branch is one of the most important in the Indo-European family, since it contains Latin, from which the Romance languages are derived. It is divided into two groups, Latin and Osco-Umbrian. Osco-Umbrian contains the Oscan and Umbrian languages, both known from inscriptions and spoken in parts of central Italy in prehistoric and early historic times.

Romance Languages. Romance languages are present-day stages of Latin, one of the languages of the Italic branch of the Indo-European family. Latin, as spoken by the common people of the Roman Empire in the first centuries of the Christian Era (Vulgar Latin), has undergone many changes in the various areas into which it had penetrated, and has given rise to a number of languages. Differences between the Romance languages, however, are not only due to different developments in the various areas, but also to the fact that these areas were Latinized at different times and consequently populated by people speaking different brands of Latin. The most important Romance languages are (from East to West) Rumanian, Ladinian, Italian, French, Provençal, Catalan, Spanish, and Portuguese.

Slavic Branch. The Slavic branch contains one of the most important modern languages—Russian. Russian, formerly called Great Russian, is a member of the East Slavic group of the Slavic branch, the other members being Ukrania, formerly called Little Russian, and White Russian or Byelorussian. Other groups of the Slavic branch are West Slaviac, containing Polish, Czech, Slovak, and Serbian or Lusatian (the language of about 100,000 Slavs in Lusatia, Germany), and South Slavic, containing Bulgarian, Serbocroatian, and Slovene. The parent language of the Slavic branch, Proto-Slavic, has been reconstructed on the basis of data from earlier stages of the Slavic languages, and from Old Church Slavonic, formerly called Old Bulgarian. The latter is the language used in the Slav Bible translation of the ninth century and was spoken by all Slavs at that time and up to the 11th century, when the various Slavic dialects developed into independent languages, mainly because of the geographic separation of the Slavs during the Magyar invasion.

    THOMAS A. SEBEOK

INDO-IRANIAN LANGUAGES form a branch of the Indo-European language family. The branch is divided into two subbranches, Indic and Iranian.

Indole

The Indic subbranch comprises Old Indic, from which developed Sanskrit and Prakrit, the ancient literary and popular languages of India, and their many modern offspring, such as Hindustani and Bengali. The Iranian subbranch contains Old Persian (Avestan), which through several stages has developed into present-day Modern Persian, and Ossete, a language spoken by one of the mountain tribes of the Caucasus.   THOMAS A. SEBEOK

INDOLE, or benzopyrrole, is an aromatic, low-melting, organic AMINE having the formula $C_6H_4NH-(CH)_2$. It is present in coal tar and in the oil of jasmine flowers and orange blossoms. In concentrated form indole has a fecal odor but in dilute solutions its odor is pleasant. It has been used as a base in perfumery.

Indole is formed, together with skatole, in the large intestine by the action of putrefactive bacteria on the AMINO ACID tryptophane which occurs in many proteins in the diet. Most of the indole is excreted in the feces, but some may be absorbed from the intestinal tract and converted in the liver to potassium indoxyl sulfate (INDICAN), which is excreted in the urine.

INDONESIA

From the Netherlands East Indies after World War II arose the Autonomous United States of Indonesia

INDONESIA, REPUBLIC OF, or **Malay Archipelago,** formerly known as the **Netherlands East Indies,** now a partner in the Netherlands-Indonesian Union, consisting of the great island territories off the coast of SE Asia, extending in two roughly parallel chains from 95° to 141° E long. (a linear distance of about 3,200 mi.) and lying between 5° N and 11° S lat., made up of the political units of the Indonesian Republic (Java, Sumatra, and Madura), East Indonesia (the islands lying E of Java and Borneo and W of New Guinea), East and West Borneo, Netherlands New Guinea, and the autonomous territories of the mineral-rich Riouw-Lingga Archipelago, Bangka Island, and Billiton Island; area about 735,260 sq. mi.; pop. (U.N. 1949 est.) 79,260,000, including about 290,000 Europeans. The upper chain includes the Greater Sunda Islands (chiefly Sumatra, Java, Dutch Borneo, and Celebes), the Moluccas (including the Kei and Aru islands), and Netherlands New Guinea; the lower chain includes the Lesser Sundas (those small islands lying between, and including, Bali and Netherlands Timor) and the Tanimbar Islands. The capital is Batavia, on Java.

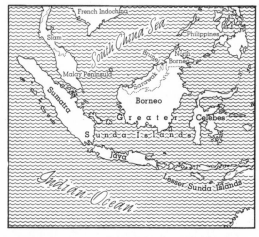

Location map of United States of Indonesia

NETHERLANDS INFORMATION BUR.

Indonesian Restaurant on the island of Java is located at the approach to a picturesque foot bridge

Physical Features. The prevailing geographical features are irregular coast lines, mountains (some with active volcanoes, especially on Java), swamps, and thick jungles; the chief marks of tropical climate (high temperatures and humidity) diminish with altitude rather than with latitude, and the rainfall is heavy throughout. Leeches, ants, scorpions, and hundreds of small insects abound. Borneo and Sumatra have some of the large jungle mammals (such as the tiger, elephant, and orangutan), and marsupials are found on the eastern islands. The crocodile is practically ubiquitous and always dangerous. The primary domestic and draft animal is the carabao.

People. The indigenous population, called Indonesians, are Malays, a branch of the Mongoloid race. They are generally short and brown-skinned, but there are many physical, cultural, and temperamental divergences. Some Negrito and Papuan elements are found. Most of the Indonesians are friendly, polite, and endowed with remarkable grace and poise, resulting in a generally slow but not awkward demeanor. In addition to the European and Indonesian population there are about 1,200,000 Chinese and 115,000 Arabs and Hindus; the Chinese, Arabs, and Hindus have a legal identity separate from the Europeans and Indonesians. The hub of the population is Java (with Madura one of the most densely populated areas of the world: 1,000 persons to the sq. mi.). Efforts are being made to ease the population pressures of Java and Madura by encouraging emigration to outer islands.

Allegiance to Mohammedanism is professed by more than 90 per cent of the Indonesians, Christianity by about 2,500,000, and Buddhism by 1,000,000, while in Bali and in some other isolated parts Brahmanism is still practiced. All are strongly adulterated with paganism (ancestor and spirit worship), as well as magic, which is practiced throughout the archipelago.

Until well into the 20th century literacy among the Indonesians remained at a low level, but the government has considerably broadened the scope of existing educational facilities. The system is liberal but not free, tuition being required in many of the lower schools. There are private and public schools for Europeans, Indonesians, Chinese; and others, and, in 1940, 21,370 schools had a total enrollment in excess of 2,373,000. There is a university at BATAVIA with four faculties (law, medicine, civil service, and arts), an engineering college at BANDUNG, and other specialist schools and colleges in other centers. Of the some 250 languages and dialects spoken, including Dutch, French, and English, Malayan is the *lingua franca.*

Economic Life. Endowed with abundant natural resources and self-sufficient as to food (rice, the food staple is grown), Indonesia has provided the Netherlands and other countries with a considerable number

OSTRANDER—EWING GALLOWAY

School Girl in Borneo uses her huge hat as a parasol to protect herself from rays of burning sun

of items essential to modern industry and civilization. Indonesian industry, crippled by World War II and the subsequent civil war, was again approaching prewar figures in 1949. Exports of rubber, the leading export product, amounted to 636,000 tons in 1940, and to 405,696 tons in 1949. Sugar, the second export product, is cultivated chiefly in Java, as is coffee. Other agricultural products are tea, cinchona, tobacco, cacao, and palm oil. Spices, copra, and gutta percha are also produced in quantity. Cattle raising and lumbering are important occupations. The textile and shipbuilding industries are increasing in importance, as are numerous light industrial products such as soap, margarine, cigarettes, beer, leather goods, and chemicals. Oil and tin are the most important mineral products, although output is far below prewar figures of 8,000,000 tons of oil and 44,000 tons of tin. Coal, gold, silver, manganese, bauxite, and phosphate are found in commercial quantities.

Foreign trade, an important item in the economy of Indonesia, is carried on with the United States (which took about 15 per cent of the exports in 1949), the United Kingdom, the Netherlands, and with other countries. Imports, largely textiles and machinery, come mostly from the United States, the Netherlands, and Japan.

Before World War II, Indonesia had 3,355 miles of railway, 33,000 miles of hard-surfaced roads, and 16,920 miles of telephone line. All were severely damaged during the war, but are being restored slowly to prewar figures. There is regular airplane service between the chief cities, and international routes make stops at Jakarta and other places. There are radio broadcasting and commercial stations.

Government. By the Netherlands constitution of 1922 the islands of the archipelago became an integral part of the Kingdom of the Netherlands; constitutionally, it was made an overseas territory of the home state. In practice, however, the islands continued to be governed as a Dutch dependency. The government was headed by a governor general, who was appointed by the Crown.

After World War II the Indonesian nationalists, who had set up a *de facto* republic, known as the Indonesian Republic, demanded complete independence, or at least dominion status with complete autonomy. The Netherlands government during 1946–47 recognized the Indonesian Republic, and set up

the Netherlands puppet states of East Indonesia, East Borneo, West Borneo, and the autonomous territories of the Riouw-Lingga Archipelago, Billiton Island, and Bangka Island. In 1948 a provisional government was set up in Jakarta. As the result of a round table conference at The Hague in 1949, Dutch rule in the East Indies came to an end, and the Netherlands-Indonesian Union was created; the Republic of the United States of Indonesia was established as a sovereign state within the framework of the union.

The Republic of the United States of Indonesia was replaced on Aug. 15, 1950, by the Republic of Indonesia. The 15 other states created by the Dutch were merged with the new Republic, and the country was divided into ten provinces: West Java, Central Java, East Java (including Madura), North Sumatra, Middle Sumatra, South Sumatra, Kalimantan (Indonesian Borneo), Sulawesi (Celebes), Sunda Kechil (Lesser Sundas), and Maluku (Moluccas).

In July, 1950, a provisional constitution was adopted by a joint conference of the parliaments of the Republic of the United States of Indonesia and the Republic of Indonesia. The provisional constitution was to be in effect until a constituent assembly framed a constitution for the new Republic. The transitional government was based upon a unicameral provisional parliament, the People's Representative Council, with a membership of 235. Executive power was vested in the prime minister and his cabinet, who were responsible to the Council. The president had the power to dissolve parliament and call new elections. All legislation had to be approved by him as well as by the cabinet, and he could initiate legislation. The vice president was elected by the People's Representative Council with the approval of the president.

History. Indonesia's place in the prehistoric chronology of the human race was ascertained by the discovery of the Java Man (*Pithecanthropus erectus;* see RACE). In the first centuries after Christ, the Hindus invaded the islands and created a number of kingdoms. By the 7th century Sumatra had become the political center of the region but by the 14th century Java established hegemony extending from the Malay Peninsula to the Moluccas. It fell at the end of the 15th century, due in part to the increasing spread of Mohammedanism throughout the archipelago, and the subsequent period was dominated by Islam and the various occidental powers which began to exploit the opulent Indies. The first of these latter was Portugal, which established a trading post at Malacca (on the Malay Peninsula) in 1511 and built installations at other strategic points. Christianity made its way into Indonesia with the coming of St. FRANCIS XAVIER in 1546, and the Dutch entered the scene in 1596, their ships touching at the Moluccas. The Dutch East India Company, founded in 1602, developed and protected Dutch interests in the Indies (against Spanish, Portuguese, and English) until its dissolution in 1799, after which the Netherlands' own continental difficulties prevented her from proceeding with expansion and trade in Indonesia. During the period from 1811 to 1816 the territory was ruled by the British. In 1818 the Dutch relinquished claims on the Malay Peninsula in return for a reciprocal action by the British in respect to Sumatra. A stable and effective Dutch administration was not achieved throughout Indonesia, however, until 1910, after which industry was developed and trade and commerce brought the riches of the area to Europe and the Americas.

The Dutch East Indies ceased to be Dutch colonies in 1922. The natives, particularly of Java, demanded equality with the Dutch and autonomy. Controversies over these questions went on for years, and revolutionary movements in Java twice (1927 and 1933) placed the Dutch in precarious positions.

The Japanese had long coveted the Dutch and British possessions in the archipelago, and many

NETHERLANDS INFO. BUR.

Native of Borneo

OSTRANDER—EWING GALLOWAY

Wedding party traveling by boat on a river in Borneo

NETHERLANDS INFO. BUR.

Javanese woman

NETHERLANDS INFORMATION BUREAU

Nuts are offered for sale in market place in West Java

MASON WARNER

Balinese dancer

NETHERLANDS INFORMATION BUREAU

Balinese dancers perform to music of a native orchestra

NIEUWENHUIS

Sumatran bride

CHICAGO NATURAL HISTORY MUSEUM

Saddle roofs mark the Menangkabau houses in Sumatra

Harbor at Batavia, on island of Java, offers modern docking facilities for ocean-going vessels

years before World War II Japanese agents infiltrated the region under various kinds of camouflage. The Japanese invasion started in northwestern Borneo on Dec. 17, 1941. During 1942 most of Indonesia fell to Japanese aggression, and its immense wealth was exploited by Japan. On May 2, 1945, the Allies began the reconquest of Borneo, and slowly the other islands came back into Allied control. But when the Japanese surrendered on Sept. 2, 1945, they still held large areas of the archipelago and a relatively long time was needed to capture and disarm them.

Although the capitulation of the Japanese was followed by the restoration of Dutch authority, a revolutionary nationalist movement seized power in Java, Madura, and Sumatra. On Aug. 17, 1945, the nationalists proclaimed the Indonesian Republic, claiming jurisdiction over Java, Sumatra, and Madura. British forces sent to occupy Java after the Japanese surrender refused to intervene in local affairs, but were attacked by some of the Javanese nationalists. Desultory warfare resulted while the Japanese were being repatriated. Later an agreement between Great Britain and the Netherlands was reached, providing for the withdrawal of British troops from Java and their replacement by Dutch forces.

On Nov. 7, 1945, the Dutch government issued a declaration of principles according to which Indonesia should become a partner in a kingdom so con-

structed that the self-respect of all people participating in it would be guaranteed. Meetings between Dutch and Indonesian representatives in February, 1946, resulted in a statement of policy calling for increased representation by Indonesians. In July, 1946, the Netherlands government regained administrative control of all Indonesia except Sumatra, Java, and the Riouw Archipelago. Dutch forces were steadily increased over the following months amid constant guerrilla warfare. On Mar. 25, 1947, Dutch and Indonesian officials signed the Basic Agreement of Linggadjati at Batavia, recognizing the *de facto* authority of the republic for Java, Madura, and Sumatra. Late in July, 1947, warfare broke out again between the reinforced Dutch and the Republican forces. The Indonesian Republic appealed to the United Nations to intervene; the Security Council appointed a commission under whose auspices negotiations were renewed. The Renville Agreement, signed on Jan. 17, 1948, secured a truce.

On Dec. 18, the Dutch again resorted to "police action" against the Republic on the ground that the Republican government did not suppress Communist rebels, could not keep order in its regions, and was unwilling or unable to carry out the agreements of Linggadjati and Renville. Dutch forces occupied the capital of the Republic and made its leaders political prisoners. As a result of a Mar. 23, 1949, United Nations resolution, negotiations were resumed between the Dutch and the Indonesians with respect to the proclamation of a cease-fire order, the return of the Republican government to its capital, and the time and conditions for holding a round table conference at The Hague. As a consequence of this conference, held at The Hague from Aug. 23 to Nov. 2, 1949, complete and unconditional sovereignty was transferred to the Republic of the United States of Indonesia; it was further agreed that the Netherlands and the Republic would co-operate with each other on a basis of equality and complete independence. The basis of this relationship was laid down in a Statute of the Union which provided a loose partnership under the Dutch crown and established a court of arbitration to settle future disputes.

On July 20, 1950, the cabinets of the United States of Indonesia and the Indonesian Republic, the largest state in the federation, agreed to set up a unified Indonesian nation under a strong central government. The new state applied for membership in the United Nations and announced that it would not take sides in the "cold war." See WORLD WAR II, UNITED NATIONS, and the articles on the principal islands.   G. A.; C. S.; F. M.; B. F.-C.; G. B. DE H.

BIBLIOG.–E. S. de Klerck, *History of The Netherlands East Indies* (2 vols. 1938); A Hyma, *Dutch in The Far East* (1942); B. H. M. Vlekke, *Nusantara* (1943); H. Daniel, *Islands of The East Indies* (1944); D. G. Fairchild, *Garden Islands of The Great East* (1944); F. C. Cole, *Peoples of Malaysia* (1945); J. Kunst, *Peoples of The Indian Archipelago* (1946); B. A. Ubani and others, *Indonesian Struggle for Independence* (1946); J. H. Boeke, *Structure of Netherlands Indian Economy* (1942), *Oriental Economics* (1947); J. S. Furnivall, *Colonial Policy and Practice; A Comparative Study of Burma and Netherlands East Indies* (1948); J. F. Collins, *The United Nations and Indonesia* (1950).

INDOOR BASEBALL. Basically the same as outdoor baseball, this game is played in gymnasiums. Seven to ten players, depending upon the size of the hall, make up each team. Two shortstops may be used. It is said to have originated in Chicago in 1887, George W. Hancock and fellow members of the Farragut Boat Club being its sponsors. The ball must be not less than 16¾ nor more than 17¼ inches in circumference, and not less than eight nor more than 8¾ ounces in weight. The bat must be 2¾ feet long and 1¾ inches in diameter at its largest part. Superseded by the outdoor game of softball, indoor baseball is a vanishing sport. See SOFTBALL.

INDORE, a former feudatory state, India, merged with other states in 1948 to form the Madhyabharat Union; area 9,934 sq. mi.; pop. (1941) 1,513,966.

Japanese-Held Oil Field in Borneo was target of many bombings by the A.A.F. in World War II

The state's area is broken up into parcels which are interspersed with portions of other states. The Vindhya Range crosses, east to west, the northern part of the main section of Indore, and the southern part belongs to the Narbada Valley. Indore is served by the state-owned Holkar State Railway, and by two British-owned lines. The state lies within the famine district of India, and has introduced a large measure of irrigation and other means of preventing famine. The chief imports are textiles, machinery, sugar, salt, spices, rice, coal, and petroleum; the exports: cotton, cloth, tobacco, and cereals. The state has a growing industrial economy, principally in weaving.

The bulk of the people are Hindus, and there are savage Bhils in the mountains. Indore has a school system which includes three colleges, 10 high schools, 81 medical institutions, and a deaf and dumb school at the capital city, Indore. Schooling for girls is free throughout the system; for boys, through the primary grades.

Government and History. Indore has individual representation on the Constituent Assembly of India. In 1948 it was merged with Madhya Bharat. The native ruler of Indore is Yeshwant Rao Holkar Bahadur, who was granted ruling powers in May, 1930. The founder of the state was Malhar Rao Holkar, a peasant officer in the service of the Mahratti, who by 1761 had been granted and gained territories that extended from the Deccan to the Ganges. His successors were defeated in war with the British in 1804, and were deprived of large sections of territory. In 1818 the state entered into treaty relations with the British. In the 1857 mutiny the ruler remained loyal to the British, although his army did not.   G. B. DE H.

INDORE, city, India, capital of the former state of INDORE, is situated on the bank of the Saraswati River near its junction with the Khan, some 1,730 feet above the sea, 87 miles N of Khandwa. It is a rail and highway junction, and a thriving trading center, and has cotton mills, a hospital, a college, the maharaja's palace and gardens, as well as the cenotaphs of the ruling house. East of the city lies the area where are the government offices of the Central India Agency. Here also is Daly college, a school for the education of princes and nobles. Pop. (1941) 203,695.

INDORSEMENT, the signature, or words and signature, usually written on the back of commercial paper or legal documents (by the *indorser*) generally for the primary purpose of transferring title thereto (to the *indorsee*). The indorsement may also be made on the face of the instrument or on another paper (*allonge*) attached to the original, when convenience or necessity prompts it. It is in the transfer of NE-GOTIABLE INSTRUMENTS that indorsements are most common.

The legal effects of indorsements of negotiable instruments are varied, the most important (besides the transfer of title with delivery of the instrument), being the liability of the indorser in the nature of a guarantor or surety (see GUARANTY; SURETYSHIP). Where there are several indorsers, the general rule is that each is liable to those subsequent. However, it is difficult to make general statements of the legal effects of indorsements, because they differ with jurisdictions and the nature of the instruments, as well as with the several types of indorsements.

Among the most common types and their distinctive legal effects are: (1) *blank* indorsement—the indorser merely writes his name, the general effect being to make the instrument payable thereafter to the *bearer* (whoever possesses it) and subsequently title may pass merely by delivery and without further indorsements; (2) *conditional* indorsement—a stipulation of some condition which renders the instrument payable upon the happening of some contingency; (3) *qualified* indorsement—a stipulation by the indorser which alters the ordinary legal effect of his indorse-

ment, whether it be to enlarge or limit his liability (the most common limitation being "without recourse") which may relieve him of liability for non-payment, but not of such things as implied warranties that the previous signatures are genuine, that he has title to the instrument, and that the instrument is valid between the original parties); (4) *restrictive* indorsement—a stipulation which limits the negotiability of the instrument to a particular person or for a particular purpose, such as "For Deposit" or "Pay to John Doe for my use"; (5) *special* indorsement or indorsement *in full*—one in which the indorser stipulates the name of the indorsee, such as "Pay to John Doe" or "Pay to John Doe, or order." (The usual effect is to require a further indorsement in order to pass title, a device often employed to prevent commercial paper, such as checks, from being "cashed" or "negotiated" by improper persons.)

The indorsement of a non-negotiable instrument generally does not have the effect of guaranteeing payment, but merely that of warranting that the instrument is genuine and that it is what it purports to be. See ASSIGNMENT; NEGOTIABLE INSTRUMENT.
                                                                    S. G.

INDRA, in Indian mythology, the god of heaven, of thunder, lightning, storm, and rain. In Vedic hymns he is described as the relentless foe of drought and darkness, and nearly a fourth of the hymns in the *Rig-Veda* are dedicated to him. His chief weapon is the thunderbolt, and as a mighty warrior he gives battle to the dragon enemies of his people. Under Brahmin influences, Indra became the SIVA of Hinduism, whose beneficent work is to destroy only that he may grant new life.

INDRE, department, central France, bounded by the departments of Loir-et-Cher on the N, Cher on the E, Creuse and Haute-Vienne on the S, and Vienne and Indre-et-Loire on the W; area 2,664 sq. mi.; pop. (1946) 252,075. The chief rivers are the Cher in the north, and the Indre and the Creuse, which drain toward the Loire. The characteristic divisions are the Champagne in the north, the Brenne in the West, between the Indre and the Creuse, and the marshy, wooded Boischaut in the south. The department is chiefly agricultural, growing grain and fruit and producing red and white wines. Sheep, cattle, and pigs are raised. Iron ore is worked, and lithographic stones are obtained. The chief industries are woolen and linen weaving, paper and pottery manufacturing, and leather tanning. The principal town is Châteauroux.

INDRE-ET-LOIRE, department, central France, is bounded on the N by the department of Sarthe, E by Loir-et-Cher and Indre, S by Vienne, and W by Maine-et-Loire; area 2,377 sq. mi.; pop. (1946) 349,685. It is drained toward the west by the Loire River and its tributaries. North of the Loire lies La Gâtine, a plateau region diversified by woods and plains. To the south of the river and between the Cher and the Indre, stretches the plateau of Champeigne. The climate is mild and vegetable gardens, orchards, and vineyards are numerous. Cereals and hemp also are grown, and sheep are raised. The department is famous for its wines. Industries include distilleries, flour mills, printing, and manufactures of iron and steel goods, rope and paper. Tours is the capital.

INDRE RIVER, in central France, rises in the department of Creuse, flows NW and joins the Loire 17 miles SE of Tours. It has a total length of about 150 miles. See LOIRE RIVER.

INDUCED CURRENT. See ELECTRICITY: ELECTROKINETICS; ELECTROMAGNET.

INDUCTANCE. Somewhat over a century ago Michael Faraday (1791–1867) discovered that when the magnetic flux passing through a closed circuit changed, an induced *electromotive force* was established which persisted during the change only. The value of the emf depends on the time rate of change of the flux at which the change is taking place. Thus analytically expressed

$$E = \frac{-d\phi}{dt}$$

the minus sign indicating that the emf is in such a direction as to oppose by the current it sets up in the circuit the change in the flux. This latter statement is the contribution of H. F. E. Lenz (1804–64) who indicated that the induced electromotive force was such as to oppose the course producing it. This statement must not be construed too literally. For example, the change in the flux may be set up by closing a switch in a simple circuit. It does not follow that the induced emf will proceed to open the switch.

If the flux is expressed in terms of oersteds or gauss and the time in seconds, then the emf will be expressed in abvolts. Since the volt is equivalent to 10^8 abvolts, then

$$E \text{ (volts)} = \frac{d\phi}{10^8 dt} \left(\frac{\text{oersteds}}{\text{seconds}} \right)$$

Mutual Inductance. If the change in the flux through a given circuit is brought about by a changing flux in a second neighboring circuit, then there will be induced an emf E_1 in the first circuit, such that

$$E_1 = \frac{M d\phi_2}{10^8 dt}$$

where $d\phi_2/dt$ is the time rate of change of the flux in the second circuit. M is a factor of proportionality known as the coefficient of mutual inductance. Since the change in the flux depends upon the rate of change of the current in the second circuit then

$$E_1 = \frac{M d\phi_2}{10^8 dt} = \frac{M di_2}{10^8 dt}$$

when the emf is expressed in volts and the rate of change of the current in amperes per second, then the coefficient of mutual inductance is expressed in henrys. Thus, when the current in the secondary, varying at the time rate of one ampere per second, induces an emf of one volt in the primary circuit, its mutual inductance is said to be one henry. The unit is named after JOSEPH HENRY (1797–1878) who discovered the phenomenon of self-induction.

Self-Induction. When the current imposed in a circuit is a varying one, it produces a varying magnetic flux through that circuit. Obviously, this varying flux through the circuit is the necessary condition for the production of an emf of self-induction which attempts to counteract the changing flux due to the impressed current. The phenomenon is known as self-induction and was discovered by Joseph Henry. When the current in the circuit varies at the rate of one ampere per second and produces a counter emf of one volt, the coefficient of self-induction is one henry.   B. J. SPENCE

BIBLIOG.–F. A. Laws, *Electrical Measurements* (1938); N. H. Frank, *Introduction to Electricity and Optics* (1940); F. W. Sears, *Principles of Physics* (1944).

INDUCTION, the process of inference by which we pass from particular data to general principles or propositions, thus contrasted with *deduction*, in which we are said to apply general principles to particular cases. Induction is further distinguished as *perfect* or *imperfect*, according as the enumeration of the particular instance on which is based the general conclusion is or is not exhaustive. Such a view of induction, is, however, inadequate, and the logic of modern science seeks to exhibit induction as a process of discovery and proof in which the character of the process, if properly carried out, is a guarantee of the truth of the results. The third book of Mill's *Logic* is an elaborate analysis of induction from this point of view.

The theory of induction perhaps most widely accepted defines it as the "inverse process of deduction."

The process of induction in physical science may be represented as passing through the corresponding stages of framing a hypothesis assumed to be true, deducing conclusions from it, and then, by comparison of these conclusions with the data from which we started, verifying (or disproving) the truth of the hypothesis. See DEDUCTION; LOGIC.

Mathematical Induction is a method of proving propositions about the "natural numbers," 1, 2, 3, ... For example, consider the proposition: The sum of the first n even numbers is $n(n+1)$ or, in symbols, $2+4+6+ \ldots +2n = n(n+1)$. If $n=1$, this becomes $2 = 1(1+1)$; if $n=2$, it becomes $2+4 = 2(2+1) = 2 \times 3 = 6$; if $n=3$, it becomes $2+4+6 = 3(3+1) = 12$, etc. Thus the proposition is true when n has the values 1, 2, or 3. To prove it true for *all* natural numbers, *assume* it is true for $n=K$, i.e., for $2+4+6+ \ldots +2K = K(K+1)$. The next even number after $2K$ is $2(K+1)$. Add this to both numbers, obtaining $2+4+6+ \ldots +2K+2(K+1) = K(K+1)+2(K+1)$. The number on the right may be written

$$(K+1)[(K+1)+1],$$

which is the same *form* as the original $K(K+1)$, with K replaced by $(K+1)$. Thus, if the proposition is true for n equal to some integer K it is also true for n equal to the next greater integer $(K+1)$.

Stated more formally, the method of mathematical induction depends on the following postulate: If S represents any set of natural numbers such that (a) the number 1 is in S, and (b) if any natural number K is in S, its successor $(K+1)$ must also be in S, then *all* natural numbers are in S. In the example it is shown that the numbers 1, 2, and 3 are in the set S of values of n for which the proposition is true; and also, that if K is in S, then $(K+1)$ must also be in S. Since the proposition is true for $K=1$, it must be true for all values of K; that is, for any number of terms. Many important theorems are proved by this method.   M. L. HARTUNG

INDUCTION COIL, an electrical device which makes use of small electromotive forces or, as some writers prefer, voltages either direct or alternating (usually direct), to produce high electromotive forces or voltages, either semidirect or alternating. Strictly speaking, any device which performs the function indicated above may be classified, as an induction coil, but generally the name is restricted to a particular device designed many years ago for the production of high electromotive forces and it is this device to which this article will confine its particular attention. Up until the advent of the high voltage mercury arc rectifier and the high voltage electron tube rectifier used in conjunction with the high potential transformer, the induction coil was in use. During the latter half of the last century small units whose potentials were not too high were used for electrical therapy and much later larger units were used for the operations of x-ray tubes.

The induction coil makes use of a discovery of MICHAEL FARADAY (1791–1867). Faraday first proved that if the number of lines of magnetic force or flux threading a coil of wire changes, there is produced at the terminals of the coil an electromotive force or potential difference whose value depends upon the rate change of the number of lines of force or flux. See INDUCTANCE.

INDUCTION FURNACE, an electrical furnace used extensively in the production of high-grade steels in making steel alloys and for the manufacture of high-speed cutting tools. The generation of heat in an induction furnace results from the resistance offered by the metal being heated to the current induced in it by an electromagnetic field set up by a coil which surrounds it. A modern high frequency induction furnace consists of a cylindrical or cup-shaped, non-conducting crucible surrounded by a water-cooled coil. The coil is supplied with alternating current of several thousand cycles frequency. The alternating current in the coil sets up a field of force which gives

REVERE COPPER AND BRASS INC.

Induction furnace for special and tool steels

rise to induced eddy currents in the charge of metal placed in the crucible. The resistance of the metal to the induced currents results in the generation of sufficient heat to melt the metal. In induction furnaces more effective sealing against contamination of the charge results in producing steels and alloys which are highly desirable from the metallurgical point of view.

Aside from its use in the production of high-grade steel, the basic principle embodied in the induction furnace lies behind a vast and constantly growing group of recent scientific and industrial developments. While at first glance many of these developments might seem to bear no relationship to each other, an important common denominator binds them together—the application of heat in a basically different way. It is in this field that the vacuum tube, the keystone of electronics, is finding one of its significant uses. Through the use of an electron tube and the appropriate circuits, currents of electricity are now being produced which alternate so rapidly that they can produce heat not only in what are normally considered electrical conductors but literally in any material. The heating results not from the eddy currents induced, as is the case in the melting of metals, but from the molecular vibration caused by the field.

Already the fast-moving plastics industry is using this principle to soften its multisyllabic pellets to workable consistencies; doctors are applying it in fever therapy; and meat, fish, and vegetables are being electronically dehydrated successfully. Other present-day uses of high frequency heating include the killing of insects or larvae in grain and cereals, baking bread, drying lumber, textiles, and paper, and drying glue in laminated aircraft propellors. A recently developed coin-operated vending machine delivers a high-frequency cooked hot dog—with mustard. D. M. MacMaster.

INDUCTION HEATING. See Heating, High Frequency.

INDUCTION MOTOR. See Generator and Motor; Electricity: Electrokinetics.

INDULGENCE, a doctrine of the Roman Catholic Church, the application of which signifies the remission of the temporal punishment attached to sin after the guilt has been forgiven. The basis for this theory rests on the teaching that every sin is a violation of God's law, through which the violator incurs guilt, eternal punishment, and temporal punishment. Catholicism maintains that the guilt and the eternal punishment is removed by Confession, but that the temporal punishment remains to be paid.

In the early stages of Christianity the church imposed upon sinners certain public penances in varying degrees of arduousness according to the seriousness of the crime. These penances were considered as atonement for the temporal punishment. By the 12th century these penances had been relaxed and the use of indulgences had taken their place.

According to Catholic doctrine the church has inherited a *Treasury of Merits*—a limitless storehouse of the superfluous meritorious acts of Jesus Christ and the saints. This "treasury" the church has charge over and may apply its "merits" to sinners through the practice of indulgences. These indulgences may be acquired by Catholics through the performance of certain acts and prayers designated by their church. Precisely how much temporal punishment is obliterated by indulgences, in point of time, is not known. A "forty days indulgence" is said to atone for the same amount of temporal punishment as 40 days of public penance accomplished in the early centuries. A *plenary* indulgence is considered to delete all of the temporal punishment; a *partial* indulgence takes away only part. If a person dies free from the guilt of sin, so goes the Catholic belief, but who has not paid the full debt of temporal punishment due for his sins, he is consigned to Purgatory until the debt is cleared.

Many glaring abuses were practiced in the distribution of indulgences, particularly the "sale" of them for money offerings, until the Catholic Reformation of the Council of Trent. (See Trent, Council of.) Eminent churchmen of the years preceding the Council strongly condemned these practices, as shown in such quotations as the following from Berthold of Regensburg (c. 1270): "Fie, penny-preacher" .... thou dost promise so much remission of sins for a mere halfpenny or penny, that thousands now trust thereto, and fondly dream to have atoned for all their sins with the halfpenny or penny, and thus go to hell." History records numerous early disagreements among theologians regarding the application of indulgences and their theory. There was also a popular misunderstanding that indulgences are a permission to sin. The various abuses and the teachings of indulgences were the subjects of Luther's first attacks. See Reformation; Wycliffe, John.

INDULGENCE, DECLARATION OF, proclaimed by James II of England, in 1687, promised to suspend all laws which tended to force the consciences of his subjects. His aim was to relieve the Roman Catholics; hence the declaration was very unpopular, and the refusal of the Seven Bishops to command their clergy to read it from their pulpits was the culminating point of public dissatisfaction. Two similar indulgences in English history were those issued by Charles II in 1662 and 1672, both of which were equally unpleasing to church people and to dissenters alike in England and Scotland.

INDUS RIVER, Sanskrit **Sindhu,** Pakistan, rises among the glaciers of the Kailas Mountains (19,796 ft.) in Tibet, near the sources of the Brahmaputra and Sutlej, in 32° N lat. and 81° E long. Its general

A junk on the broad waters of the Indus River

GOVT. OF INDIA INFORMATION SERV.

course is at first toward the northwest through Tibet and Kashmir, where it turns abruptly southward between Gilgit and Hunza, and follows that direction right down to the sea. In the mountains the current is very rapid; it passes through deep, wild gorges (one near Skardu, in northwestern Kashmir, having a depth of more than 10,000 ft.), and is liable to tremendous floods. The Indus enters the Punjab 812 miles from its source. Near Attock, 48 miles lower down, the Indus receives the Kabul River from Afghanistan, and then becomes navigable. Here it is only 2,000 feet above sea level. About 450 miles below Attock it receives, on the left, the accumulated waters of the Punjab through the single channel of the Panjnad. Each of the "five water courses" as well as the Kabul, is navigable for inland craft to the mountains. The delta of the river covers an area of about 3,000 square miles, and extends for some 125 miles along the Arabian Sea. The main channel is constantly shifting. The delta is bare and not fertile. In both Punjab and Sind the bed of the river is littered with islands and sand banks. The value of the river for irrigation purposes is enormous, and the Indian government has carried out a series of works which have given rise to remarkable agricultural development in Sind. The total length of the river is estimated at 1,800 miles, and the area of its drainage basin at 372,000 square miles. The Indus abounds in fish of excellent quality and is infested by crocodiles.   C. S.

INDUSTRIAL ACCIDENTS. See Accidents, *Occupational*; Occupational Diseases and Industrial Hygiene; National Safety Council; Accidents, Accident Prevention.

INDUSTRIAL ARBITRATION. See Arbitration, Industrial.

INDUSTRIAL CHEMISTRY. See Chemical Industry; Chemical Engineering.

INDUSTRIAL COLLEGE OF THE ARMED FORCES. The National Defense Act of June 4, 1920, placed the responsibility for industrial mobilization planning on the assistant secretary of war, including the procurement of all military supplies by the War Department, as well as the mobilization of material and of industrial organizations. On Oct. 11, 1923, the Assistant Secretary of War, Dwight W. Davis, recommended to Secretary John W. Weeks that a special course of instruction be instituted in order to train officers for the necessary industrial mobilization planning duties. Accordingly, the Army Industrial College was established on Feb. 25, 1924. On April 11, 1946, the college was redesignated as The Industrial College of the Armed Forces, and was placed under the Joint Chiefs of Staff. It is situated in Washington, D.C., in the grounds of the old Army War College, adjacent to the National War College, with which its course is closely integrated. The first course under the new name began in September, 1946. The stated mission of the college was to train officers of the armed forces for duties involving all the aspects of procurement planning, procurement, mobilization of the national economy and economic warfare; evaluate the economic war potential of foreign nations; conduct studies and research in the above fields; and foster close relationship between the armed forces and civilian engineering, scientific, educational and industrial groups in the study of the social, political and economic impact of war. See National War College.

                          J. B. Heffernan

INDUSTRIAL CRISES. See Business Cycle.

INDUSTRIAL DISEASES. See Occupational Diseases and Industrial Hygiene.

INDUSTRIAL EDUCATION. See Manual Training and Industrial Education.

INDUSTRIAL HAZARDS. See Occupational Diseases and Industrial Hygiene; Accidents, Accident Prevention.

INDUSTRIAL HYGIENE. See Occupational Diseases and Industrial Hygiene.

INDUSTRIAL INSURANCE. See Insurance, Life Insurance.

INDUSTRIAL LEGISLATION. See Factory Acts; Child Labor; Employers' Liability; Labor Legislation; Labor, Hours of; Women, Rights of, Industrial; Workmen's Compensation; Social Security; Labor Management Relations Act.

INDUSTRIAL ORGANIZATION

Modern management employs systematic and scientific methods to increase production and reduce costs

INDUSTRIAL ORGANIZATION AND MANAGEMENT. Through the years of the last two centuries industry grew out of the simplicity of the *domestic system* of household work, and the *factory system*, to that of the complex structure of modern industry. The basic causal factor in this radical change was the Industrial Revolution. During the period from 1765 to 1785, the methods and conditions of manufacturing in England underwent a change that altered the face of western civilization. The consequences of this revolution were vast and immediate. Primarily, however, the great inventions of that era changed the character of man in relation to his work from that of having the tool act as an auxiliary to the worker to that of the worker becoming an auxiliary to the machine. No longer was man the controlling factor in his work. No longer did he own the means of his production. The consequences of this separation from the tools of industry was that the laborer became degraded from his previous role of craftsman and his market value was reduced to that of an unskilled laborer. His prosperity was no longer for the larger part subject to his ability and willingness to work. It depended upon the ability of business to furnish him with the opportunity to labor.

Industry, at first, did not understand the new roles labor and machinery were playing. The worker was still regarded as the controlling factor in production. It was believed that the harder a man worked and the more hours he put into his work, the more total and and per unit output would be produced. This had been true in the past when the working man owned his tools and determined his rate of work. However, with the advent of machinery into the picture, labor could no longer be considered the sole determiner of the rate and quality of work. The two—man and machine—counterbalanced each other and became interdependent. This factor in industry was not realized until the close of the 19th century, and then only because of the struggles that resulted from the inability of the individual worker to maintain long-run productivity and economic security for himself within a framework of outmoded legal, social and industrial institutions.

Industrial organization may be defined as those systems of modern management that have been developed in the 20th century to facilitate the work of man and machinery. The effect that the scientific method had upon other phases of human endeavor at last caught up with industry. In the latter part of the 19th century the old methods of doing business were first realized to have become inefficient. With the advent of an increasing complexity, and a growing scale of manufacturing operations, it became necessary to discard outmoded systems. During this period of time Specialization of men and machines increased with the passing of each year. Standardization, or the limitation in type, size, and characteristics of products, developed. In addition, or perhaps as a consequence of all this, industry grew. No longer was the "shop" the predominant feature on the industrial landscape. Large scale business and mass enterprise took its place.

The most predominant characteristic of American

business since the latter part of the 19th century has been the growth in number and size of industrial establishments. Some plants merely grew through accretion. Others developed by consolidation as organizations combined with similar industrial establishments under one head. Still other companies grew by integration, or extension of the control of manufacturing processes back towards the sources of their raw material. At the same time these developments were taking place, some organizations engaged in combinations of similar and related industries. The economic advantages accruing from large scale enterprise aided the expansion of national production.

It was noted that certain tangible economies could be realized by new structural organizations within business. The era of individual ownership and partnership gave way largely to the corporate structure. This form of organization was also espoused as a means whereby the liability of ownership was limited to that of the value of the stock held. The advantages of such a system were also understood by state and municipal governments when they went into the fields that were not adequately covered by private industry. Furthermore there were some individuals who still wanted the permanence inherent in individual or partnership ownership, but wished to include some of the advantages accruing to corporations. Thus joint-stock associations and closed corporations were developed. In order to control industry further and eliminate the hazards of competition in certain fields, trusts and holding companies were instituted. These organizations were associations of corporations interested in controlling a field of business. Of late, co-operatives have been formed to better obtain and sell goods for its individual members. During the 30's, the government itself began to enter business, and built such projects as the Hoover and Columbia dams. During the great Depression, it participated in many public works programs.

Thus the circumstances of competition and free enterprise in a large and rapidly expanding country have tended to result in large and closely integrated industrial organizations, which have in some respects restricted that very competition and individual enterprise. In such instances the government has attempted to correct what were claimed to be abuses in corporate practices. The CLAYTON ANTITRUST ACT of 1914 prohibited corporations from creating monopolies by individual dealings, and outlawed trusts. The SECURITIES EXCHANGE COMMISSION was set up to correct the abuses in the issuance of corporate stock. The NATIONAL LABOR RELATIONS Act and the FAIR LABOR STANDARDS ACT were passed in the late 30's to insure organized labor bargaining rights and the security of a minimum wage. During World Wars I and II whole series of Acts were promulgated to control and regulate the industrial life of our country. These were only a few instances when the government entered into the field of business, for purposes of regulation.

Scientific Management. It has been realized only recently that the work of FREDERICK W. TAYLOR completely altered the perspective of modern business. Before Taylor began his work, it had been the practice in industry to get the most out of men and machines in an extremely haphazard way. Our present practices of study, planning and control were only distant dreams in the minds of forward thinking engineers. How to achieve these goals were not then realized. Taylor, at the turn of the century, told business that it must understand its media, otherwise it could not develop. He stated that before management could enter into a field of endeavor, it would first have to measure all the forces and factors involved in a given business situation. Then certain laws and patterns of action would need to be derived from this experimental research. Working in conjunction with the establishment of these laws, definite standards would have to be evolved. These standards should be the

sole criteria for the operation of the business. Before attempting any work, a planned layout of the necessary procedures should be developed. A definite distinction should always be made between the planning and operating functions of a business. Among Taylor's specific recommendations were the payment of high wages, concentration upon measures to reduce per unit cost of production and a progressive improvement and standardization of working conditions.

At present considerations in inaugurating new factory organizations cover the following research of the existing field for the proposed product: analysis of competition, price levels, costs, profits, research of consumer and distributor attitudes, technical and competitive tests of proposed articles; study of trade-mark or patent situations; study of raw material status and prospects; study of plant location from the angles of raw materials, labor, distribution cost; budgetary plan for five years of operation; study of capital needs, capital structure best suited; analysis of manufacturing process, machinery; study of unit costs on volume production ratios; study of proposed prices, discounts, margins, analysis of sales and advertising cost, merchandising methods, packaging; layout of functional organization; study of available personnel; blueprint or schedule of five-year plan and procedure; detail of policies and principles.

Specific factory organization, in the sense of production solely, starts with the research of the product, chemically or mechanically or both. Then it goes on from there to purchase and storage of raw materials, the routing of the processes of manufacture on a continuous line basis, mechanization of processes, power plant, consultation with designer's of special machinery, designing or remodeling of factory buildings to fit location of skilled labor, negotiation with unions, arrangements for supervision and inspection, special counsel on power or scientific management on motion study, tuning up, setting of standards of work, and maintenance of morale.

The Structure of modern industry has become so vast and complex that it has proved impossible for any one man to control adequately anything but a specific field of endeavor. Therefore, it has proved necessary to break down and classify the various types of managerial functions, and then attract men to these positions who fulfill the necessary requisites. Thus, in present-day establishments, the officers of the concern generally fall into one of the three categories of administrative, staff, and operative executives.

The *administrative officer* is one who usually deals with the abstract planning processes. He is a man who must possess a wide range of abilities and intelligence. It is he who decides what products are to be produced, whether expansion is necessary, and who is, in general, the planner of the organization. The *staff executive* is a man who organizes the various functions of investigation, interpretation, and co-ordination of data within the company. The *operative executive* is responsible for control over the operations in the various plants.

The *staff executive* is generally the secretary of the organization, but can also be the comptroller. The office manager works directly under this person, and supervises the necessary office work; he expedites and co-ordinates all clerical activities. The comptroller is responsible for controlling costs, budgeting, auditing, accounting, and the pay roll. Directly under him there is a chief accountant who keeps records of the financial status of the company. Working along with this official are the cost department, which compiles expenditures used for labor and material, and the auditor, who makes sure the accounts are correct. In many organizations the credits and collections department works under the supervision of the comptroller, but in most cases it is a separate depart-

Industrial Organization

ment. The sales manager, who also works with the staff executive, insures the company of adequate, or as the case may be, inadequate distribution of its product.

The title that is usually applied to the executive responsible for the operation of a business establishment is *general manager*. Some organizations term him a "works manager" or "general superintendent." It is this person who, in the initial stages of a business, is responsible for the location and layout of buildings. After the plant is ready to operate he then assumes authority over the various functions of production. He makes sure that the physical equipment is kept in order, that production processes adhere to a standard, and that the working force of supervisors and skilled and unskilled men is adequate. He guides the work loads in relation to sales estimates, approves the necessary purchases and changes in design, and helps formulate standard procedures for work. Naturally, the manager is merely the over-all controlling element in these varied activities. The actual work involved is done by delegated subordinates.

To help the executive control his plant, and to help his subordinates know what the executive desires, certain charts and records are kept. These charts and records are made by men whose positions are further down on the hierarchial ladder of the organization, but under the direct supervision of the manager. The charts that are compiled generally include the past progress of the plant, and the future estimates of plant activity. They may also show relationships between productive ability of various departments or between periods of time. A good example of these reports is the Gantt chart, which purports to give a visual record of projected operations. Of late, the study of the workingman in relation to varied factors has come to the fore. These charts include studies of absenteeism, labor turnover, productitivy, earnings while working rated operations, and latenesses. The charts are always at the disposal of the plant manager. Records are kept of production, orders and machinery breakdowns. Shipping reports and returns are compiled into easily-read documents for managerial study. Financial reports are made stating the income of the organization and expenses. A cost report is compiled which includes statements of the material, labor, and other expense items.

Industrial Engineering can be defined as that phase of management involved in the more technical details of business. It includes the various fields of production, inventory, and quality control, the standardization of procedures and operations, and the wage rate setting functions of the time study specialist. The industrial engineer has been the tool by which management has changed the face of business practices from one of haphazard, chance responses to challenges, to one of analytical and empirical study. The necessity of making the best product with the cheapest method has become the ranking problem in modern business. The competition of other concerns, and the discriminatory buying habits of the public have made it imperative for industry to change its methods and practices.

A specific example of the type of problem which requires the attention of an industrial engineer is that of material handling. How can the plant manager supply the productive men with adequate material while maintaining a minimum working force for the job? How can he situate his machines so that he will have a lessened material handling cost? How can he decrease the handling of material after it is produced? These are real problems in everyday industry, and every manager has to face them. What does he generally do? He calls his industrial engineer to his office and presents him with the problem. The industrial engineer welcomes the manager's suggestion that something has to be done about the great cost in material handling, and then begins to study his problem.

Industrial Engineering developed this special machinery to handle 130 cylinder heads at one time

Material handling has reached very unusual lengths of development, due to need for elimination of human labor and as a result of industrial engineering practice. Special electric trucks and cranes, plant trolley systems, the use of chutes and gravity feed, and the teaming up of processes, machinery, building arrangements, railway unloading machinery, moving belts, elevating apparatus, pumps, tractor hauled cars, pipe pressure systems, and all manner of ingenious devices are being made use of in manufacture to eliminate handling. In many instances the entire process becomes automatic from the first movement of raw material to the packing of the finished product. In a large plant general systematization of routine and mechanization of supply for workers is of utmost importance, because a fractional difference repeated thousands of times makes a worth-while total per day. A skilled workman should be using his skill a large part of the time, not merely his muscles for material handling which an unskilled worker or a conveyor could do for him.

Production Control. All projects in a plant must be accomplished with a maximum economy and a minimum effort. It is the duty of the production control department to work toward that goal. The job of controlling production falls under the head of the *production control manager*. He is the person who heads the department that plans, schedules, and expedites the work loads in the plant. His department must make sure that the customer receives his allotted supply of the product on the date promised. To accomplish this end, the production manager must make sure that there is a rapid turnover of the work in process, that the working capital is kept low, that a minimum amount of overtime is used to finish the job, that overhead expense is kept reasonably low, and that the least possible amount of time is spent in moving the material. In other words, it is the function of production control to maintain an even flow of material throughout the plant at all times, and to prevent stoppages in this even distribution of work.

It can be said that a production control manager performs a function of the staff. This may be true, but only in the initial stages of control. After all, no control could possibly be instituted without planning. To insure this over-all planning the production department must keep records of time consumed in the production of previous similar orders, of operations necessary for the completion of the project, of potential bottlenecks in the production process, and of the production abilities of men and machines. These records form the basis of any future planning that the production manager may undertake.

From planning, schedules can then be devised. This function of control is a major phase in the process. Without it there could be no effective operation. The function of scheduling is to determine the rate of speed that is necessary for the accomplishment of each successive operation. The most widely used means of visually determining the time lag that is essential for each phase of work is the Gantt chart. This is generally made in the form of a control board. It shows, in horizontal line form, the proposed and actual work performed.

When the preparation for a production order has been completed, the next step is to start it moving. Dispatching serves the function of assuring that work is started at a proper time and that the work follows the schedule set in the planning office. A dispatcher assigns work orders to successive operators in every department and instructs each department head about the desired machines that are to be used and the work that is to be accomplished in the order. He also assigns cost figures to the order for future use by the accounting department. His main objective is to gain good co-ordination in the operative functions of the plant.

Once an order is given to a department, the function of control in a shop becomes the duty of the foreman. Until recent years it was the practice to use men for this position who had proved themselves able and willing workers. It was believed that knowledge of the machine was adequate qualification for leadership. Of late, however, this belief has largely been discarded. It is now the common practice to appoint men to the position of foreman who, though having a good work background, are known to be capable administrators. In the past, these supervisors controlled the work of a group of men. At present, this system of "bossing" is no longer used, and more definite control is established through functional foremanship. The foreman is now considered to be a supervisor of operations and not of men.

No organization could stay in business for any length of time without adequate quality control. The task of this inspection is to certify that the finished article fulfills specifications. Good systems of inspection make for quick turnover of defective materials, places responsibility, checks losses, keeps clerical work at minimum, and prevents customer ill will. Alert, adequate inspection systems are an integral part of modern production technique.

Time and Motion Study first came to the fore when Taylor began his work in the Midvale Steel Company in 1881. He discovered that by breaking down a job into its elements he could study the time necessary for the completion of each phase in the work. By so doing, he was capable of determining what could be considered a fair day's pay. The stop watch was the means through which he got his information. The statistical evaluation of this information gave him his needed data.

Through the years that followed Taylor's work, time and motion study developed to such an extent that, at present, few efficiently run businesses do without it. Decreased production costs, increased production, fair wages, operation standardization, production control, all depend upon the work of the time study engineer. Specifically, time and motion study involves the investigation of movements in relation to their environment and time element. From the empirical studies that are made, standards and rates of pay are set, and incentive scales of pay increments are derived. This latter item should not be confused with any "speed up" system. The time and motion engineer is not interested in worker exploitation. He merely desires to give an incentive to work with the added injection of reward into the condition of work. Of course there is a general increase in the work performed after time study methods are put into practice, but this increase normally comes from sources other than a "speed up." The time study engineer is basically interested in stepping up production in the most efficient way possible. The result of his efforts usually culminate in improved working conditions and techniques, and the definition of an equitable and productive day's labor. This engineer makes a study of all elements involved in the work situation—the machine, the man, and his movements. He understands the scientific method and aptly applies it.

Stock Control is a specific function for conservation and care of raw materials, parts and supplies, and is usually under the administration of a rigid system. Such systems include (1) main office central control, (2) territorial or branch or subsidiary control, (3) local or individual plant control. The stock control

JOHN A. PATTON- MANAGEMENT ENGINEERS, INC.

Industrial organization through job analysis reduced the eight movements required in the operation at the left to a bare minimum through the use of the holder and suspended screw driver pictured at the right

technique includes inspection of materials coming in, care and accurate classification (usually in vertical wire bins), complete records in detail and periodic inventory. Its functions are as follows:

1. Furnish material and supplies when and where needed.

2. Inspect and check goods received and report promptly all receipts with description of condition, etc.

3. Record all goods received and dispatched in such way that the amount on hand may be estimated at a glance (records kept in this way serve as a perpetual inventory).

4. Maintain vigilance over stock and issue none save on proper authority.

5. Establish a maximum and minimum stock mark and hold stock within those limits.

6. Place requisitions for reorder with the purchasing executive far enough ahead to insure judicious purchasing and receipt of goods before stock on hand is exhausted.

7. Maintain standards established by standardization plans by seeing that the correct name and description of all material for reorder are furnished fully to the purchasing executive.

Modern science of inventory control, in the effort to keep inventories at lowest practical point, calls for alert management and watchfulness.

Purchasing is a major industrial science and a specialized profession, emerging from a haphazard exercise of the purchasing function of the past. Today the scientific view prevails, and purchase by guesswork, favor, or "pull," or high pressure salesmanship is disappearing. Instead, purchasing agents have their own codes and professional ethics, national and local associations and co-operative committees, and operate laboratories where not only are purchases tested, but new specifications worked out for goods to be purchased. In some instances firms unable to purchase goods of the qualifications desired have put their own experts into the factories of supply companies, or even organized or financed factories to make the goods as per specification. A purchasing agent must not only buy what is offered, but sometimes also stimulate the seller to make goods.

Purchasing must distinguish between sellers as to their standing, experience and likelihood of continued service and ability to deliver. There is a difference between a reliable and a dependable source of supply; the reliable one being one competent to produce the right quantity and quality; the dependable one being the firm not only equipped for quantity and quality, but in addition able and willing to make any sacrifices to deliver without fail. The purchasing department must be in close touch with knowledge of all important sources and study all changes going on. It must buy basic commodities which are subject to world or general market fluctuations and volume of supply (such as wool, cotton, silk, vegetable oils, etc.); it must study crop and other conditions which affect prices, and be "market wise." While speculation in raw materials as a policy for factory executives is now generally condemned, the speculative element is ever present in such commodities. Long-range prognostication is often necessary. General price tendencies on a short or long term basis need to be studied, since price levels have definite long term swings, up or down.

A purchasing department needs for its guidance in making efficient purchases the following information:

1. Full specifications as to quantity, quality, and intended use of materials, requisitioned.

2. Advance information as to curtailment or expansion of production.

3. Changes in specifications, even though these changes do not have a direct bearing upon the materials purchased.

4. Date of receipt and condition in which goods are received.

5. Maximum and minimum limits of storage spaces.

6. Amount received, requisitioned and on hand in storeroom.

7. Rate of production.

8. Rate of sales.

9. Cost of production and selling.

10. Selling price and gross or net profit.

11. Overhead expense of entire organization.

12. Financial standing and resources.

13. Specific duties and responsibilities of each department, and the relation of these departments to purchasing.

Large purchases often use the "blanket" order, covering any desired length of time and any quantity, at an agreed-upon price or the market price, or a sliding quantity scale.

Knowledge of the laws of contract are also vital to purchasing science; rights and liabilities of contracting parties; when and how contracts may be canceled or the seller forced to live up to it, etc.

Industrial purchasing falls into classifications, such as (1) contract buying, (2) buying direct, (3) buying from jobbers, (4) buying through brokers, (5) buying from salesmen, (6) buying by mail through samples, (7) buying on open market, (8) buying through exchanges, (9) buying through competitive bids.

"Standardization" is a purchasing term used to designate the installation of equipment all of one type or make, to facilitate and simplify repair, supply, and operation. It also usually involves concession on the part of the seller. Standardization is a term also more widely used, such as standardization of catalog sizes, or other forms, policies, plans. Standard order system, invoices, purchasing orders are used.

Personnel Organization and Labor Relations. The human element is receiving more and more importance in the industrial setup of our country. No longer are men merely hired, worked, and fired. Men and women are now employed and properly fitted into a job they can do. Industrial tests are being given in increasing numbers of organizations to determine the qualifications of applicants for positions within a firm. Health maintenance and medical service is now a part of every plant's organization. Safety measures and devices are used to decrease accidents. Better relations are carefully being built between management and unions. No longer are complaints handled in an offhand manner. The industrial relations department of all larger industries and the union representatives get together and discuss the grievances of the workers. Management is engaging in vast education and training programs to better fit its men and women for their jobs. It continually engages in research in personnel matters to further develop better relations with the workers. It supports schools of industrial and personnel relations to study these matters and to offer solutions to the many problems. See INDUSTRY AND COMMERCE, GOVERNMENT REGULATION OF; FINANCE, BUSINESS; CORPORATION; INDUSTRIAL REVOLUTION; CAPITALISM; MONOPOLY; BUSINESS; INDUSTRIAL RELATIONS; PERSONNEL MANAGEMENT; COLLECTIVE BARGAINING; SPECIALIZATION; ENTREPRENEUR; PRODUCTION, COST OF; MASS PRODUCTION; JOB ANALYSIS; WAGE.   E. HOFFMAN

BIBLIOG.—F. W. Taylor, *Shop Management*, Transactions of the American Society of Mechanical Engineers (1903); D. S. Kimball, *Principles of Industrial Organization* (1939); W. Clark, *The Gantt Chart, a Working Tool of Management* (1942); E. H. Schell, *The Technique of Executive Control* (1942); W. Rautenstrauch, *Principles of Modern Industrial Organization* (1943); L. L. Bethel et al, *Industrial Organization and Management* (1945); E. H. Hempel, *Top-Management Planning* (1945); D. S. Shybekay, *Industrial Management: Standardization and Simplification* (1945); E. Buckingham, *Production Engineering* (ed. 1946).

INDUSTRIAL PSYCHOLOGY has been defined as "that branch of applied psychology which investigates problems and situations found in the various industries." This definition will here be narrowed to those classes of problems which arise out of the relations of the employed worker to his employer and his work, namely: improving the worker's efficiency by training; influence on worker efficiency of motivation and attitudes; increasing efficiency by improved working conditions; increasing efficiency by improved work methods; analysis and evaluation of the job; evaluation of the worker. Other related problems, such as choice of a vocation, selection and placement of employees, and distribution of product, are dealt with elsewhere. See ADVERTISING; BUSINESS PSYCHOLOGY; APTITUDE TESTING; PERSONNEL MANAGEMENT; VOCATIONAL GUIDANCE.

Industrial psychology developed from several origins: (1) Early laboratory experiments on work, fatigue, motor learning, work and learning curves, etc.; (2) the study of INDIVIDUAL DIFFERENCES and the development and use of aptitude and achievement tests; (3) the "scientific management" movement, initiated late in the 19th century by FREDERICK W. TAYLOR, an industrial engineer, who first actively applied scientific methods to the analysis and improvement of human efficiency; and also the extension of Taylor's methods by F. B. Gilbreth and other disciples of his; (4) the early experimental efforts of the Harvard psychologist, MUNSTERBERG, to select workers in terms of their special aptitudes, and to discover and provide work conditions conducive to the greatest and most satisfactory output; his *Psychology and Industrial Efficiency* (1913) was the first systematic treatise on the subject, and had considerable influence. World War I brought rapid extension of psychological research to the study of practical military problems and later to industrial problems. In England, industrial psychology has been extensively practiced since 1921 when the National Institute of Industrial Psychology was established to supplement the work of the older National Fatigue Research Board. German psychologists and industrialists have also been very active, as well as some in Russia.

Although little more than a generation old, industrial psychology has developed a considerable body of literature and corresponding practice which falls roughly into two types: (1) Practical utilization of psychological knowledge and insight in the various industrial arts; (2) Psychotechnology, i.e., experimental and statistical research on industrial problems. Adequate training and skill in both these aspects is necessary for effective achievement.

Training. Conditions in modern specialized industry require that much of the training for particular occupations shall be done after, rather than before, an employee has been hired. It is accomplished by several means, including instruction on the job by an experienced co-worker, foreman, or special instructor, use of instruction cards or manuals, preliminary training in vestibule or company schools, or some apprenticeship plan. Economy and efficiency in learning motor skills are increased by the use of methods and devices found by psychological experiment or educational experience to be more effective, such as use of motion pictures to show sequences of movements, keeping the learner informed of his progress, emphasis on accuracy before speed, judicious praise, practice on sequences rather than on separate elements (except in correcting specific errors), and other conditions known to affect efficiency of learning. Foreman training has also come to be recognized as a vitally important duty, and increased use is made of such methods as scheduled conferences, discussions, lectures, and demonstrations, to supplement or replace the earlier informal and sporadic attempts.

Motivation and Attitudes. The old view, that workers are interested only in high pay and keeping their jobs, has given way to recognition that conditions influencing worker-attitudes are complex, varied, poorly understood by the worker himself, and by no means confined to shop and working hours. Financial incentives, such as wage and piece rates, group-quota, task-, bonus-, and profit-sharing systems, as well as stock-purchase, savings, and pension plans, have been extensively tried; but their relative success has been found so dependent on varying social and local conditions that few generalizations are possible. Incentives not directly financial have been found very potent in numerous investigations, among them opportunity for advancement (especially among younger workers), steady work (for older), opportunity to use one's ideas, opportunity to learn a trade, good supervision, fair treatment, consideration of grievances, good working conditions, congenial surroundings and companions, etc. Attitudes of employees toward their work, company, foreman, and working conditions have been investigated by various means, such as supervisors' reports, encouragement of voluntary criticisms and suggestions, and spontaneous or periodic interviews and questionnaires. A recent practice has been the provision of counselors with whom the employee is free to discuss his vocational and personal problems at any time. The use of so-called nondirective counseling has met with considerable success in revealing the nature and extent of workers' feelings of frustration and in stimulating individuals to discover and apply their solutions for themselves. Out of such conferences may come evidence of some work condition needing to be corrected, a trouble-making foreman who should be removed, a company policy which needs to be altered or clarified. A frequent problem is that of the recognition, diagnosis, and treatment or reassignment of chronically maladjusted workers who somehow escaped being screened out in the employment process, and who should not be discharged if any other remedy is possible. No aspect of industrial psychology is receiving more serious consideration today than the problem of improving industrial relations.

Conditions of Work. Conditions affecting efficiency may be physiological or environmental. Causes of decreased efficiency include FATIGUE (especially "unnecessary" fatigue), use of drugs (chiefly narcotics), accident proneness, poor ventilation, poor illumination, distractions, monotony, and occupational hazards. See ACCIDENTS.

The drugs chiefly studied in this connection have been alcohol, tobacco, and caffein. Neither of the two latter has been shown to have markedly deleterious effects on output when used moderately. Alcohol, however, has been proved a depressant on motor and mental performance, not a stimulant as often supposed; and experimental evidence offers no justification for its habitual use where work efficiency is used as criterion. With all these drugs, effects are so complicated by habituation, tolerance, and by emotional, personal, and social factors, that unequivocal conclusions are possible only when carefully selected control groups and control experiments are used. Accident proneness varies with several physiological and psychological conditions, including experience, emotional stability, physical condition, sensory defects, fatigue, habitual recklessness, alcohol habits, and attitude toward work; but little if any with mental level. It is known that a large majority of industrial and driving accidents happen to a small minority of workers and drivers. See ALCOHOLISM.

Accidents vary also with atmospheric conditions, illumination, rate of production, occupational hazards, etc., which call for investigation and correction, as well as the adoption and enforcement of safety programs and adequate accident compensation laws and insurance. Regarding defective ventilation, experiments have shown that rarely is excess of carbon dioxide or oxygen deficiency responsible for the bad effects on output, but primarily atmospheric temperature and moisture which hinder bodily evaporation and radiation and thus lower efficiency and increase mental inertia. The beneficial effects of electric fans are therefore not illusory but real, in accelerating radiation and evaporation. In general, circulating air at a temperature of 68° and a 50 per cent humidity approximates the optimal condition for

Ventilated Workbench increases efficiency of workman by exhausting grinding dust below work

work. The optimal illumination has been found to be that amount sufficient to reveal clearly all details, and uniformly distributed over the contrasts which produce eyestrain and fatigue. Noises which are intermittent have been found more distracting than continuous noises; those which carry meaning (e.g., conversation), more distracting than meaningless noises. One can readily become adapted to noisy surroundings so that his output is not decreased, but often at the expense of extra muscular effort. On the other hand, many firms have found properly chosen music beneficial to rate and uniformity of output, and decreased tension and fatigue. Monotonous work which may decrease the output of some people (and hence is often confused with fatigue), may have no such effect on others, particularly those who temperamentally prefer repetitive activity, or those whose mental equipment finds the routine operations more challenging, and hence more satisfying, than persons with different mental equipment would.

Job Appraisal. Job descriptions and analyses are made for various purposes; time and motion studies for speeding or economizing operations, descriptions of job-responsibilities for employment routine, improving working conditions, establishing training programs, making promotional schedules and charts, and setting wage standards. The methods used vary to fit the purposes. The importance of providing machinery for individual advancement has been suggested; and attention is given in many companies to tracing out the possible lines of promotion and transfer between positions, both in order to facilitate advancement of promising talent, and to discover suitable human material for promotion as vacancies occur. Much progress has also been made in devising uniform procedures for classifying and rating jobs in terms of their complexity, responsibility, requisite-qualifications, etc., in order to set equitable wage and salary standards on an impersonal basis; although this is often subject to modification by the wage-scale demands of organized labor. See JOB EVALUATION.

Worker Evaluation. What a worker should be paid depends not only upon the demands of his position but also on his relative efficiency in that kind of work. Consequently, not only for purposes of wage-setting, but for other purposes such as promotion, transfer, evaluating of the original selection techniques, or discovery of present or latent problems, periodical efficiency-rating of employees is a routine feature in many organizations. Where comparable and objective production records are not available, rating-scales are likely to be used. These are devices by which the appraisals of an employee by supervisors, department heads, or other responsible ad-

ministrators can be expressed in numerical form. Yet no matter how elaborate or refined they be, such ratings are still records of personal opinions, and subject to all the errors characteristic of such opinions, including hasty and unconsidered judgments, perfunctory or careless ratings, variations in observation of different traits, inaccurate discrimination between traits, bias or partiality, "halo effect" (i.e., too high or too low over-all ratings due to some one conspicuously high or low trait), lenient, severe, or changing standards, insufficient knowledge of ratee, and failure to record real differences between ratees. Methods suggested for discovering and correcting these tendencies include the description of habits to be judged instead of bare trait-names, rating all employees on one trait at a time, checking frequency distributions in each set of ratings, cross-checking for internal inconsistencies, and training raters. The chief types of rating scale are: Simple ranking in order of efficiency, simple point-scale grading, man-to-man comparison scales, trait check lists, graphic rating scales (probably the most used type), and frequency scales in which the various gradations are defined in terms of prescribed fractions of a representative work-population such as highest, middle, or lowest one-third, or divisions of a normal probability distribution such as low 5 per cent, next 20 per cent, middle 50 per cent, next 20 per cent, and highest 5 per cent. In spite of their subjectivity and proneness to error, the scarcity of more objective methods of evaluation and the ready availability of ratings has led to their wide adoption and use.

FORREST A. KINGSBURY

BIBLIOG.–H. Munsterberg, *Psychology and Industrial Efficiency* (1913); F. B. and L. M. Gilbreth, *Applied Motion Study* (1919); M. S. Viteles, *Industrial Psychology* (1932); J. G. Jenkins, *Psychology in Business and Industry* (1942); J. Tiffin, *Industrial Psychology* (1942); M. A. Bills, *The Psychology of Efficiency; A Discussion of the Hygiene of Mental Work* (1943).

INDUSTRIAL RELATIONS is broadly defined as a study to acquire theoretical knowledge and understanding which leads to the development of administrative and operating techniques in the labor field.

The necessity for the study of industrial relations has come about as a result of the passing of small-scale industry where it was possible to maintain a close personal relationship between employer and employee. The evolution of the large corporation with its thousands of scattered owners has tended to create a lack of understanding between employer and employee.

One of the marked characteristics of an industrial society is the impersonality of group to group relationships. The problems arising from this aspect of industrialism have received tardy attention and study in the fields of the social sciences. Executives have been schooled to understand the economics of the business, to be adept in analyzing the cost situation to increase sales, or to invent better equipment, yet the greatest portion of the executive's time and effort is consumed in dealing with people, in handling problems of morale and co-operation, in manipulating human relations. Analysis has shown that good employee relations do not depend on written contracts and company recreation facilities, but on what is said and done between people.

Today the whole structure of industry and society is impaired by labor-management problems. The present need for the objective study of industrial relations springs from the past neglect of the human factor in industry. Hence, there has begun such study of industrial relations from the viewpoint of "human relations in industry," and many universities have initiated research programs and courses of study. The frameworks of study may vary from ordinary theory and research emphasizing the ethical rather than the economic aspects of work relations, to workers' educational programs, to administrative techniques

for union leaders, to a many-faceted program including all of these. Many industries and states have
considered this subject of sufficient importance to
set aside funds for foundations and schools for the
study of industrial relations.

At Yale University, training of management and
trade union leaders is conducted in joint classes under
the theory that the two groups, put in the context
of an educational setting, can better understand the
nature of differing labor-management concepts in
the field of industrial relations.

At Harvard University Graduate School of Business
Administration, the "case method" is used in which
actual industrial situations and problems are studied.
Unlike Yale, the program for trade union men is
distinct and separate from that for management.
The University of Chicago's Industrial Relations
Center gives services to management and labor as
two separate units. It has carried out experimental
projects in 1945 seeking new approaches for labor
administration.

State funds have been set aside for courses in many
universities to build up a systematic knowledge of
industrial relations and also to train students under
special formal academic programs. These are to be
distinguished from the trade union and management
fellowship programs. Sectarian schools and some state
universities with their extension programs are centering attention on the rank and file worker to increase
his effectiveness as a member of labor. As yet, no
professional school of industrial relations exists in the
independent sense of a law or business administration school.

Recent Studies have attempted to show why relations between management and labor are unhappy
and what improvements can be made. The basic
issue in problems of industrial relations is that both
management and labor are striving for individual
survival. Both are fighting to preserve familiar goals,
opportunities, integrity and independence. Both dislike anything that threatens their own survival needs.
Conclusions of many studies attempt to show objectively why each should recognize the need for
each other and help strengthen the other; why each
should know why the other does and thinks as he
does. Many experts in this field have concluded if
industrial relations cannot be agreed upon and allow
mutual survival, public regimentation will become
necessary. See LABOR UNION; PERSONNEL MANAGE-
MENT; COLLECTIVE BARGAINING.

BIBLIOG.–E. D. Mayo, *The Social Problems of An Industrial
Civilization* (1945); B. B. Gardner, *Human Relations in Industry*
(1945); E. W. Bakke, *Mutual Survival* (1946).

INDUSTRIAL RESEARCH. See RESEARCH.

INDUSTRIAL REVOLUTION

Changes in Britain's economic system were
accelerated in the late 18th century with
the introduction of steam and machinery

INDUSTRIAL REVOLUTION, a name applied
to the era of economic and social development in
Great Britain introduced by the mechanical inventions of HARGREAVES and ARKWRIGHT, and covering
approximately the years 1760 to 1830. Its principal
features were the substitution of the factory system
for the domestic system of industry, and the social
and economic readjustments involved therein.

Prior to 1760 British industry was conducted
chiefly in the home by domestic workers, who often
combined with their handicraft the cultivation of
small tracts of ground. The mechanical arts had advanced but little, and the machines in use for spinning, weaving, and other manufacturing processes
were of the simplest type. In 1733 the fly shuttle, the
first of a long series of labor-saving inventions, was
patented by KAY. In 1764 Hargreaves invented the

spinning jenny; Arkwright followed with his spinning
machine in 1769, CROMPTON with the spinning mule
in 1779, and CARTWRIGHT with the power loom in
1785. In the meantime new methods of smelting gave
a great impetus to the iron industry, and the invention of the steam engine rendered obsolete old methods
of hand production in all industries.

The inevitable outcome of these great changes
was the disappearance of domestic manufacture, the
concentration of labor in factories, and the development of large-scale industry, with the consequent
differentiation of the agricultural and industrial
classes, the growth of great industrial centers, the
division of labor, the substitution of the unskilled
laborer for the skilled workman, production for profit
rather than for use or exchange, and the rise of a
capitalist class. Accompanying this transformation
in methods of industry and closely related to it were
important agrarian changes, including the application of capital to agriculture, the consolidation of
farms, and the introduction of more intensive tillage.
Transportation facilities were also improved, and
British foreign trade expanded markedly.

The term "Industrial Revolution" is usually applied to the movement in Great Britain inasmuch as
the first and most drastic manufacturing and social
changes occurred there. A simultaneous change and
movement could not occur in other countries for
various political and economic reasons. Although
similar developments followed at later dates in France,
Germany, the United States, etc., the change was
from agriculture and commerce to manufacturing
rather than from widespread domestic manufacture
to a factory system. This difference together with the
relative slowness of industrial development in these
countries prevented the sudden economic and social
changes which occurred in Great Britain. However,
similar growth, if not revolution, occurred and may
be traced in all modern industrial countries, particularly Russia and Japan as well as those mentioned.

France. In the years preceding 1789, France succeeded in keeping pace with the English in developing the new industrial techniques. After this time, she
lagged steadily. The French Revolution followed by
the Napoleonic wars depleted the country through loss
of colonies, checking of commerce and wasting of resources. Further, restrictive commercial policies designed to protect home industries followed the war
period with the result that high duties prevented the
adequate importation of machinery. In the earlier
part of the era, the great inventions had been designed for the utilization of water power, but the discoveries of Colt, Wilkinson, Darby, and others in
England suddenly replaced water with coal as a
source of industrial power. The coal deposits of
France were of poor quality and widely scattered,
so that real industrial development was delayed until about 1830.

Although factories sprang up and industrial centers appeared, the social consequences of the industrial
revolution were not as extensive in France as in England. A fair amount of domestic manufacture was retained, the centers of industry formed more slowly
and were fewer in number. As a result of the French
Revolution in 1789, which gave the peasant permanent ownership of his land, there remained in
France a peasant class majority, while in England
enclosures and industrialization had led the yeomen
to move into the cities.

Germany. Until 1871, the area of modern Germany was divided among small independent states.
Industry lacked the free access to raw materials and
the concentration of capital necessary for large-scale
development. In 1848, the German states were
dominated by agricultural and feudal concepts, but
by 1860 there were numerous factories, towns were
expanding into cities, and a network of railroads took
outline. This development gave rise to economic
groups, with important political consequences.

Industrial Revolution marked the change from production in the home by domestic workers, as typified by woman at left spinning wool for Harris tweed, to the widespread use of power driven machines, right

The new industrialists and powerful merchant groups were interested in identical currency, a unified postal system, the abolition of all tariff barriers, and free access to raw materials in backward areas, along with the other powerful European countries. Agitation on the part of these new economic groups was helpful to Bismarck and other German political leaders in uniting the many autonomous German states into the German Empire of 1871.

The Franco-Prussian War, which ended in 1871, also gave impetus to the developing German industrial revolution. During the war, industry was stimulated to greater production efforts, and the fight against a common enemy broke down remaining political barriers among the German states. With the war's end, the vanquished French were compelled to pay an indemnity of five billion francs to the victorious Germans. This vast sum provided German industry with a large capital reserve for industrial expansion.

United States. Although manufacturing had become important by 1812, the most rapid industrial development occurred after 1865 when Northern industry received its stimulus from the Civil War. The Bessemer steel process invented in England in 1856 was not used in the United States until 1864, but expansion was so rapid that by 1875 the country was producing 375,000 tons of steel. Railroad mileage increased from 30,000 miles in 1860 to 60,000 in 1870. New industries arose and grew rapidly. For example, only 3,700 automobiles and trucks were produced in 1899, as against 4,360,000 passenger automobiles and 820,000 commercial vehicles in 1929. Steel production rose to 32 million tons by 1913, and railroad mileage to 406,000 miles by 1920. Industrialization reduced agriculture to secondary economic importance, so that the majority of the population live now in towns and cities.

Russia. A trend toward industrialization existed in Russia before the advent of the first Five Year Plan in 1928. In 1897, about 2,000,000 workers were employed by industry and there was some production of steel and iron. It was necessary to import machinery and technical experts, however, and the important railway from Moscow to St. Petersburg remained single track until World War I.

Under the Soviets the first Five Year Plan called for systematic industrialization, relocating factories, training engineers and mechanics and mechanizing agriculture. It may be said that while an industrial revolution had been slowly developing in the late

19th century, its rapid progress did not begin until the advent of the first Five Year Plan.

Japan. With the commencement of the Meiji Era (Enlightenment) in 1868, Japan opened her ports to world trade and launched upon a period of industrial progress similar to that which had been taking place in Europe. Large-scale expansion occurred after Japan's victory in the Sino-Japanese war in 1895. The war indemnity of £35,000,000 paid by China initiated a period of development in Japan as the French indemnity had done in Germany after the Franco-German War. In 1893, there were an estimated 1200 factories. By 1909, the number had grown to more than 32,000. Cotton yarn production rose from 13,000,000 pounds in 1888 to 425,000,000 in 1909. A further increase in industrialization occurred as a result of Japanese participation in World War I, in which she gained control of new Asiatic markets, and established factories in Manchuria. Despite modernization of her industries, Japan retained much domestic manufacture. In World War II, many essential aircraft and motorcar parts were made in workers' homes.

New Industrial Revolution. The industrial revolution was a period in which new sources of power and energy were discovered and put to use by industry. The term is generally applied to the last half of the 18th century and the early part of the 19th century. The later 19th century and 20th century

Components of a synthetic fiber are tested

developments are referred to as part of the *new* industrial revolution.

In the 18th century, water was the chief source of industrial power. Later, water and coal were combined in the steam engine, and industry moved into what is sometimes called the Age of Steam. In 1841, MICHAEL FARADAY announced a series of discoveries which turned the last half of the century into an era of electrical power. Although much of our electrical power is derived from coal, and steam power is still important in industry, electricity provides the means for transmitting power a distance from its source. This has made possible our modern cities, with well-lighted homes, offices, and factories widely scattered but supplied with power economically from a central generator. In addition to electric dynamos and motors, the late 19th and early 20th centuries saw the development of the gas engine, the Diesel engine, and jet-propulsion, bringing about a revolution in transportation so extensive that today no two parts of the globe are more than 60 hours apart.

The most characteristic development of the 20th century has been the application of science to industry, first advanced in Germany and quickly adopted by other nations. Chemistry was applied to industry, with the development of cellulose; plastics; textiles, such as rayon and nylon; fertilizers; and synthetics of every description. In recent years, physics has vied with chemistry in the industrial research laboratories, leading to such valuable discoveries as the vacuum tube, and the electronic industry surrounding it. Nuclear physics gives promise of enabling us to draw power directly from the atom, making the smallest particles of matter potential sources of unlimited energy. See MERCANTILISM; LAISSEZ FAIRE; INDUSTRIAL ORGANIZATION AND MANAGEMENT; GUILD; CAPITALISM; INVENTION AND DISCOVERY; MASS PRODUCTION; BANKS AND BANKING; IMPERIALISM; LABOR MOVEMENT. WILLIAM R. SPARKS

BIBLIOG.–B. K. Sarkar, *The Industrial Development of Japan* (1916); J. L. Hammond, *The Rise of Modern Industry* (1926); N. S. B. Gras, *Industrial Evolution* (1930); A. Nevins, *The Emergence of Modern America* (1935); S. Fabricant, *The Output of Manufacturing Industries, 1899–1930* (1940).

INDUSTRIAL SAFETY. See ACCIDENTS, *Accident Prevention;* OCCUPATIONAL DISEASES AND INDUSTRIAL HYGIENE.

INDUSTRIAL SCHOOLS. See MANUAL TRAINING AND INDUSTRIAL EDUCATION.

INDUSTRIAL WORKERS OF THE WORLD, popularly known as the I.W.W., a revolutionary labor organization including men of many trades and crafts, having as its objective the overthrow of the wage system and the rebuilding of society on a socialistic basis. Advocating direct action in the form of strikes and sabotage instead of collective bargaining and political action, it was really the American manifestation of syndicalism, a labor movement which had considerable support in France and other Latin countries shortly after 1900. The American organization was established in 1905 by EUGENE V. DEBS, W. D. Haywood, Daniel De Leon; the principal constituent body was the Western Federation of Miners, a powerful labor union of that day. The aim of the I.W.W. was to unite in one body all skilled and unskilled workers as a revolutionary instrument for the overthrow of capitalism. In 1908 the organization split on the issue of political action; most of the socialists withdrew, leaving control in the hands of the anarchists and syndicalists. The I.W.W. developed most of its strength in the Northwest, especially among workers in the lumber camps; it spread also to Canada and to Australia. Its maximum strength in the United States was about 100,000 in 1912. The I.W.W. was responsible for some 150 strikes, which were used less for collective bargaining demands than as a revolutionary weapon. Among the most prominent of the I.W.W. strikes were the textile workers' strike at Lawrence, Mass. (1912); the strike

in the rubber industry at Akron, Ohio (1913); the Minnesota mine workers' strike (1916); the lumber workers' strike in the Northwest (1917); and the general strike in Seattle (1919). During World War I the I.W.W. took a militant stand against the war, and as a result many of its members were prosecuted under the antisyndicalist laws of various states. The organization was subjected to persecution and ridicule—a popular term of contempt being "I Won't Work." After 1920 it declined as it lost many members to the Communist party and to other left-wing groups. In recent years the I.W.W. has played an insignificant role in the labor movement. See SYNDICALISM; ANARCHISM; LABOR UNION; SABOTAGE; REVOLUTION. F. M.

BIBLIOG.–P. F. Brissenden, *History of the I.W.W.* (1920); J. S. Gambs, *Decline of the I.W.W.* (1932).

INDUSTRY. See INDUSTRIAL ORGANIZATION AND MANAGEMENT; INDUSTRIAL REVOLUTION; CAPITALISM; MASS PRODUCTION; PRODUCTION, COST OF; FREE ENTERPRISE; MONOPOLY; BUSINESS; INDUSTRY AND COMMERCE, GOVERNMENT REGULATION OF; FINANCE, BUSINESS; INDUSTRIAL RELATIONS; CORPORATION; SPECIALIZATION; ENTREPRENEUR.

INDUSTRY AND COMMERCE
Government Regulation

Government regulation has been extended in great variety over economic life

INDUSTRY AND COMMERCE, GOVERNMENT REGULATION OF. Regulation of business by government and by other agencies of control is not a new idea or concept. The exercise of governmental restrictions on business is virtually as old as business itself. The policies, methods, and objectives of control may change, but the control of individual and group behavior is an inherent characteristic of every organized society. Among the early primitive tribes, control was exerted by moral force; the economic practices of its members were further controlled by the customs of "taboo." With the extension of social groups and the growth of a caste system including the military, the aristocracy, and slaves, rule by custom was partially supplanted by the use of actual force.

HISTORICAL BACKGROUND OF GOVERNMENTAL CONTROL

During the Middle Ages various forms of control developed. Custom, the arbitrary power of the feudal lords, the power of the Church, the guilds, all assumed significant roles as regulators of economic activities. With the growth of towns and the rise of strong national monarchs, an organized system of control of business was ushered in. There have been three important periods in the development of governmental control. The first was from the 11th to the 15th century; the second from the 15th to the 18th century, the third from the latter part of the 18th century to the present day.

The First Period, which is often designated as the late Middle Ages, was marked by the growth of towns and the development of trade. These centuries were characterized by the desire of those in control of government and commerce to maintain the *status quo.* Custom was an important regulatory device. Illustrative of the controlling force of custom were the laws limiting the price of bread and ale, setting limits on the size of loaves of bread as well as on the wages of labor, and the restraint upon the freedom of workers to move to jobs at will. The Church engaged actively in the regulation of economic practices. The charging of interest on money loaned was held to be sinful, but with the continued growth of trade and commerce exceptions to the usury law permitted the lender some compensation. Another form of economic regulation by the Church was the development and application of the doctrine of the "just price" for goods sold. The merchant and craft GUILDS regulated economic practices of members in minute detail, while the towns, which were almost synonymous with guilds, applied the rules of the guilds to outsiders. The guilds operated under codes which sought to protect members against competition. In addition to market controls, rules were established and enforced as to the rights and duties of apprentices, the hours of work, the quality of workmanship, introduction of inventions, prices, wages, use of undesirable selling methods and materials, and advertising.

The 13th and 14th centuries witnessed the growth of fair and staple towns and markets. The king exercised close supervision over the selection of the town to be designated as a fair or staple

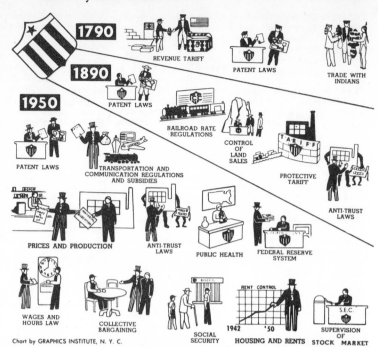

Chart by GRAPHICS INSTITUTE, N. Y. C.

How government's regulatory functions have increased, 1790-1950

town. It was in these towns that a body of rules, based upon custom, business practices, and trade usages, developed into the LAW MERCHANT. This body of rules regulated contracts, notes, bills of exchange, weights and measures, sales, trade practices, prices, and the liability of persons engaged in private, public, and quasi-public ventures.

In the Second Period the former pattern of control was continued but with a change in purpose and methods. The control which had previously been exercised by towns and guilds passed gradually into the jurisdiction of the strong national states. Through the policy which came to be called MERCANTILISM kings and their ministers sought to unify and strengthen the state in competition with other states by means of public control over economic activities. Government aid was granted in the form of SUBSIDIES to manufacturing and shipping interests; tariffs on imports were used to protect home industries. Patent monopolies were issued to encourage the introduction of new processes and products. Goods had to pass governmental inspection, unethical practices were prosecuted, wages were controlled, combinations of employers and manufacturers as well as workers were held to be criminal conspiracies, and the right of collective bargaining was not recognized. There were restrictions on free trade and regulations imposed in the interest of fiscal policy. The aim was to make the state self-sufficient.

The Third or Modern Period has been characterized by an insistent demand for the removal of governmental restraints on business as a reaction to the control exercised under mercantilism. Emphasis has been placed on individual freedom and "natural laws" in human relationships, on the inherent and inalienable rights of man such as freedom of speech, of the press, and of association, the right to life, liberty, and the pursuit of happiness, the right of property, and the right of equality before the law. The predominant philosophy of the period has been individualism and the prevailing doctrine has been "laissez faire." In practice, however, the doctrine did not lead to a completely "hands-off" policy by government. With the advent of the INDUSTRIAL REVOLUTION and the factory system there developed

many external forces, such as the growth of large enterprises, the use of technological changes and mass production, the development of modern transportation and marketing devices, which brought about unforeseen problems necessitating constant intervention by government in business activities.

In the United States government aid to industry by means of TARIFF protection has been accepted ever since 1789. Early in the 19th century banks, shipping companies, and railroads were made subject to public regulation. After the Civil War the Granger movement, a strong political action campaign in the farm states, gave impetus to public demand for the regulation and control of rates and practices of businesses affected with a public interest or those in which certain forms of monopoly might be deemed desirable. In 1887 Federal regulation of railroads was begun. Since 1900 the government has instituted further regulation in order to preserve the free competitive system and to raise the plane of competition. See GRANGE, THE.

METHODS AND MACHINERY OF CONTROL

The patterns and programs of governmental control are many, varied, and interrelated. The motives are numerous and diverse: certain programs are instituted because of broad social objectives, others for the protection of particular business groups against competition; some policies are based upon a desire to preserve the small business unit, while others are designed to protect the consumer. The official statement of purpose may aim at the reduction of risks which inhere in our economic order, the elimination of unfair and undesirable business practices and conduct, the control of price, output, quality of product or service, or the designation of the areas of allowable competition between various individuals, groups, or institutions. Because of such diverse—and sometimes conflicting—motives the controls may appear conflicting and inconsistent.

Methods of Control. A wide choice of machinery is available to the government for the regulation of business. Control may be exercised through legislation, judicial decisions, administrative orders, or codes, by means of taxation, tariffs, or subsidies, and through regulatory commissions or government ownership. Statutes may be general or specific, allowing for a wide or narrow area of discretion in the administrative agencies established for enforcement. These agencies provide an important method of control, serving as continuous, expert bodies to give practical application to the general principles established by law. (See ADMINISTRATIVE LAW; ADMINISTRATIVE RULE MAKING.) Taxation, although primarily designed for revenue, is often employed as a technique of regulation; business activities which are regarded with disfavor may be subjected to discriminatory taxation, while those which are favored may be helped through exemptions. Public aid is also granted through TARIFFS, SUBSIDIES, and special privileges. Other types of control are exercised through the issuance of franchises, charters, licenses, and certificates of convenience and necessity. Codes, either self-imposed under public pressure or subject to government supervision and participation, constitute another method of regulation. Finally, if public regulation proves unsatisfactory the government may use the threat of GOVERNMENT OWNERSHIP as a threat against business.

Objects of Control. Both the states and the Federal government have laid down the conditions for entry into many services and businesses. Some state laws impose conditions in the form of procedural requirements for the formation of the business organization, such as are found in business corporation acts (enacted by all states) and the uniform partnership acts (in force in 25 states). The Uniform Limited Partnership Act has been passed by 28 states (1947). The power of the states to grant charters to private corporations and franchises to public utilities or public service corporations has enabled the states to subject such companies to regulation of rates, prices, services rendered, returns on investment, and discontinuances of service. Occupations and activities which require state licenses or permits may be regulated in the same manner. In cities ZONING laws impose limitations on the freedom of choice in the location of business enterprises. The so-called BLUE-SKY LAWS, which have been enacted by all states, are designed to protect the investing public from worthless stocks and bonds.

The government has regulated the prices, rates, wages, and services of businesses affected with a public interest and those which are considered public utilities. Both the states and the national government have actively engaged in the regulation of transportation agencies, public utilities, financial organizations, organized exchanges, extractive industries, labor, and labor unions. Such regulatory laws have been held constitutional under the POLICE POWER of the states and the interstate commerce clause of the Federal Constitution. In recent years the role of the Federal government has increased while the jurisdiction of the state has been more and more limited. This trend has resulted in part from the increase in the size of business units and in part from the fear that state regulation—varying in strictness from one state to another—would lead to competitive inequalities.

REGULATION IN SPECIFIC FIELDS

Transportation. The general types of activities of transportation facilities which have been subjected to control and regulation with varying degrees of emphasis are: (1) entry into service, (2) abandonment of service, (3) adequacy of service, (4) discrimination in service, (5) safety of service, (6) financial practices and security issues, (7) rates and rate structures, (8) rate discrimination, (9) combinations, (10) pooling agreements, (11) interlocking directorates, (12) holding companies, (13) consolidations and reorganizations, (14) accounting methods and reports, (15) industrial relations. (See COMMON CARRIER; FREIGHT RATES.) Prior to 1887 railroad regulation was in the hands of the states, but in that year the Federal

government stepped into the field with the passage of the Interstate Commerce Act. Since the enactment of this law Congress has passed many acts providing direct and indirect aid as well as control and regulation of the railroads. The Interstate Commerce Commission has authority to enforce legislative provisions by making rules and regulations against unjust and unreasonable charges, discrimination between persons, places, or kinds of traffic, and to require the publication of rates and fares and the posting of public notice of all rate increases. Not until 1920 with the passage of the Transportation Act of that year was the Commission given authority to regulate service; by the provisions of this act the agency was granted authority over new construction and extension of roads, abandonment of service, and standards as to adequacy of service. Various legislative enactments provide the Commission with authority to regulate the financial practices of railroad management, the issuance of securities, reorganizations, accounting practices, and to supervise loans to carriers. Railroads are also subject to the regulatory provisions of the SHERMAN ANTITRUST ACT and the CLAYTON ANTITRUST ACT, but exemptions are provided in the transportation acts of 1920, 1933, and 1940. Mediation and arbitration machinery for the settlement of labor disputes and legislative recognition of the right of workers to join labor organizations and to bargain collectively are the subjects of the Railway Labor Acts of 1926 and 1934. Provisions for unemployment insurance and retirement pensions are found in the Railroad Unemployment Insurance Act of 1938 (amended 1940) and the Railroad Retirement Act of 1937. For details see INTERSTATE COMMERCE COMMISSION; RAILROAD, Railroads and the Government; INTERSTATE COMMERCE.

Motor carriers have been subjected to a maze of state regulatory enactments lacking uniformity and effectiveness. State regulation has been difficult to enforce because of the numerous types of legislation and agencies, inadequate funds, and the narrow interpretation of the laws as to the powers of the commissions. The Motor Carrier Act of 1935 placed the regulation of interstate motor carriers under the jurisdiction of the Interstate Commerce Commission; under its provisions a regulatory system similar to that of railroads has been set up for motor carriers. See BUS TRANSPORTATION.

Water and pipe line carriers have been made subject to the regulation of the Interstate Commerce Commission by the Natural Gas Act of 1938 and the Transportation Act of 1940. Prior to these laws the regulation of these carriers was piecemeal and divided. Petroleum pipe lines are under the jurisdiction of the FEDERAL POWER COMMISSION. Every state has enacted some type of control over pipe line operations of oil and gas carriers. See PETROLEUM.

Air transportation has been subjected to both state and Federal regulation. (See AIR TRANSPORTATION.) Government aid and control has assisted and nurtured agencies of water transportation. The states and municipalities have sought to improve harbors and waterways and water facilities, sometimes with Federal grants-in-aid. The Merchant Marine Act of 1936 created a Maritime Commission which exercises the powers and functions formerly vested in the Shipping Board created in 1916. Further regulation and control are to be found in the policy and administration of the Transportation Act of 1940 by the Interstate Commerce Commission and the Inland Waterways Commission. See MERCHANT MARINE; SHIPPING.

In agriculture the program of government control has emphasized the use of direct and indirect financial aids and subsidies, the regulation of foreign agricultural product, and the imposition of tariff duties. The positive program of government aid has involved the problem of disposal of surplus agricultural products and the stabilization of price. For details see AGRICULTURE; AGRICULTURAL ADJUSTMENT AGENCY.

For Coal and Oil governmental programs of control have been motivated by three principal objectives: the conservation of resources, the control of production, and the stabilization of prices. (See COAL AND COAL MINING.) The pattern for the control of oil has been quite similar to that in coal. See PETROLEUM.

Security Issues and Organized Exchanges. The stated aim of regulatory legislation dealing with corporate security issues is the protection of the capital market and the investor. The states have enacted blue-sky laws which vary as to type and method of control; some of the laws are of the "fraud-type," while others require licensing and registration. Although the Federal government attempted to control the issuance of securities in 1909, the first effective control was instituted with the enactment of the Securities Act of 1933 and the Securities Exchange Act of 1934. Under the provisions of these acts, as amended, and the Public Utility Holding Company Act of 1935 the SECURITIES AND EXCHANGE COMMISSION is vested with broad discretionary and administrative powers. The regulatory powers of the commission over interstate holding company systems controlling gas and electric utilities and over trading on commodity exchanges are contained in the Public Utility Holding Company Act of 1935 and the Grain Futures Act of 1922. See BOND; STOCK; STOCK EXCHANGE; SECURITIES AND EXCHANGE COMMISSION; PUBLIC UTILITY REGULATION.

The first attempt at regulation of trading on commodity exchanges was the Future Trading Act of 1921; the next year Congress enacted the Grain Futures Act to regulate trading of certain commodities on the exchanges. Later amendments, especially those provided in the Commodity Exchange Acts of 1936 and 1938, set up administrative machinery in the Department of Agriculture to regulate contract markets and commodity exchanges. See EXCHANGE, COMMODITY.

Employer-Employee Relations. Both business and labor have been subjected to regulation since the Middle Ages. In the United States during much of the 19th century the regulation of business as an employer was deemed a local matter and was left to the jurisdiction of the states under their POLICE POWER. There was little or no regulation of hours, wages, working conditions, child labor, and collective bargaining practices prior to 1900.

Regulatory labor legislation of the states and the Federal government involve limitations on the supply of labor, restrictions on the labor market, equalization of the bargaining position of labor, and distribution and allocation of income and economic risks. State and Federal control of the supply of labor and the labor market include compulsory education laws, regulation of child labor, restrictions on the use of convict labor, antialien laws, immigration laws, the establishment of public employment agencies and the control of private employment agencies, hours laws for women and men on government contracts, in transportation, and in hazardous occupations. Few states have attempted to limit the hours of employment of men except for employment on state work, government contracts, work financed by the government, or in industries and occupations deemed hazardous, as in mining, smelting, work under compressed air, etc. See LABOR, HOURS OF; CHILD LABOR; WOMEN, RIGHTS OF, Industrial; LABOR LEGISLATION; FAIR LABOR STANDARDS ACT; LABOR MANAGEMENT RELATIONS ACT; WAGES; WORKMEN'S COMPENSATION; COLLECTIVE BARGAINING; APPRENTICE; MINIMUM WAGE; UNEMPLOYMENT; STRIKE.

Competition and Monopoly. Public regulation of business involves a complicated mass of regulations and methods of control, some of which encourage monopoly, restrain competition, or attempt to maintain effective competition. Regulatory legislation in specific fields may restrict as well as encourage competition. The antitrust policy of the Federal government is an attempt to preserve competition as a guarantee of protection to the public as a whole. The SHERMAN ANTITRUST ACT (1890) was enacted because of the inadequacy of the common law and state regulation; it provides remedies and penalties for injuries resulting from contracts, combinations, and conspiracies in restraint of trade. The CLAYTON ANTITRUST ACT (1914) attempted to clarify and make specific certain provisions of the earlier law with regard to price discriminations and exemptions of labor and agricultural associations. Many laws enacted as antitrust laws contain special exemptions from the Sherman and Clayton acts. The following governmental agencies have important roles in the attempt to establish and enforce fair standards of competition: FEDERAL TRADE COMMISSION, FEDERAL POWER COMMISSION, INTERSTATE COMMERCE COMMISSION, Food and Drug Administration, SECURITIES AND EXCHANGE COMMISSION, and the secretary of agriculture among many others. For further details see CARTEL; COMBINATIONS AND MERGERS; MONOPOLY; TRUSTS AND TRUST REGULATION; MARKETING.

Other Governmental Functions. The programs of public regulation and patterns of control in specific fields are further implemented by government aid to business and government ownership of properties and business. The Federal government is actively engaged in the establishment of standards of value, weight and measure and quality of agricultural products, foods, drugs, and cosmetics (see FOOD AND DRUG REGULATION). Special services have been provided to shipping, mining, foreign trade, and other businesses in the form of statistical information on foreign commerce, manufacturing and distribution, labor, consumer needs, etc. Tariff provisions, bankruptcy laws, and bankruptcy privileges have furnished indirect financial aids to business; loans made by the RECONSTRUCTION FINANCE CORPORATION and subsidies provide direct financial aid. See TARIFF; SUBSIDY; BANKRUPTCY.

Government Ownership has been found to be a desirable form of regulation in certain ventures, especially those which constitute natural monopolies, and in some cases where the public welfare has been jeopardized by the litigation and delays encountered in the government's attempts to enforce less stringent types of control. Thus government has entered the fields of transportation, electric power, finance, shipping, banking, and others.

The task of making a free enterprise system operate effectively and efficiently enlarges the scope of the problem of control. The need for determining the proper spheres of activity for business and government in the face of conflicting interests has resulted in an expansion of public regulation. The absence of unanimity as to the proper spheres of activity and the weight to be accorded the various interests in our economic and political order tends toward an increasing amount of more minute regulation of business with less laxity in enforcement by state and Federal agencies of control. See FREE ENTERPRISE; BUSINESS; COMMUNICATION; TRANSPORTATION; CONSERVATION MOVEMENT.   GERTRUDE S. METTEL

BIBLIOG.—John Stuart Mill, *Principles of Political Economy,* Book V, Chapter XI (1848); J. M. Clark, *Social Control of Business* (1939); U.S. Congress, Temporary National Economic Committee, *Investigation of the Concentration of Economic Power* (1940); U.S. Department of Labor, Division of Labor Standards, *Handbook of Labor Legislation* (1941), *Principal Features of Workmen's Compensation Laws* (1943); H. D. Koontz, *Government and Business* (1942); U.S. Department of Labor, Bureau of Labor Statistics, *Trend in Child Labor, 1939–1942* (1943); Stuart Chase, *Democracy Under Pressure* (1944); U.S. Federal Security Agency, *State Unemployment Compensation Laws of 1945* (1945); U.S. Bureau of the Budget, *United States Government Manual* (1947); U.S. National Labor Relations Board, *Tenth Annual Report of the NLRB* (1946), *A Guide to the NLRA, Practices and Procedures* (1946).

INDUSTRY, FORT, a military outpost on the present-day site of Toledo, Ohio, built in 1794 by order of Gen. ANTHONY WAYNE after his victory at the Battle of FALLEN TIMBERS as a safeguard against the British garrison at Fort MIAMI. Here on July 4, 1805, was signed an important treaty with the Indians by which the leading tribes of Ohio, Michigan, and Indiana gave up a great tract of 2,726,812 acres for settlement.

INDUSTRY, GOVERNMENT IN. See MUNICIPAL OWNERSHIP; TENNESSEE VALLEY AUTHORITY; RAILROAD.

INDY, VINCENT D'. See D'INDY, VINCENT.

INE, d. 726, king of Wessex, was chosen king in 688. He subjugated Kent, Essex, and Middlesex; and by his victory over the British king, Geraint (710), conquered West Somerset. About 693 he published the earliest extant code of West Saxon laws, whereby the great Celtic population of his kingdom was emancipated. Having abdicated (726), he made a pilgrimage to Rome, and died there.

INEBOLU, ancient Ainobol, or Ionopolis, seaport, N Turkey, Kastamonu Vilayet, on the Black Sea; 72 miles W of Sinop. It is the port of the inland city of Kastamonu and has a fair roadstead. Exports are copper, wool, mohair, and woolen fabrics and blankets. Pop. (1940) 6,315.

INEQUALITY, in mathematics, a statement that one quantity is greater or less than another. In symbols: $a>b$ means that a is greater than b; $c<d$, that c is less than d; $x>0$, that x is a positive number because it is greater than zero; $w<0$, that w is a negative number; and $a\geqq b$, that a is greater than or equal to b. If the same number is added to or subtracted from both members (sides) of an inequality, or if both members are multiplied or divided by a *positive* number other than zero, the statement of inequality remains true and the *sense* (or direction) of the inequality is not changed. If both members of an inequality are multiplied or divided by a *negative* number, however, the sense of the inequality is changed. For example:

(1) $3+8>5+2$; $3+8+4>5+2+4$
(2) $12>3$; $12/3>3/3$; $4>1$
(3) $5>-2$; $4\times5>4(-2)$; $20>-8$
(4) $5>-2;(-4)5<(-4)(-2)$; $-20<+8$

These are examples of *absolute inequalities*, which are always true. When letter symbols are used, the inequality may be either absolute or *conditional;* in the latter case, as in conditional EQUATIONS, the statement is true only for some values of the symbols, but not for all, and may be thought of as posing the question, "For what value of the symbol is the statement true?" For example, if it is given that

$$12x-2>10x+2, \text{ then}$$
$$12x>10x+4$$
$$2x>4$$
$$x>2$$

The successive operations above were: the addition of 2 to both sides; subtraction of $10x$ from both sides; and finally, division of both sides by 2. The result shows that the original equality holds provided x has any value greater than 2. Note that for $x=2$ the two members are equal.   A. T. M.

INERT GASES, a group of six gaseous chemical elements which form no stable compounds. These gases, in the order of increasing density, are: HELIUM (He), NEON (Ne), ARGON (A), KRYPTON (Kr), XENON (Xe), and RADON (Rn). The inert gases were discovered and isolated by Sir WILLIAM RAMSAY and co-workers near the end of the 19th century, with the help of the SPECTROSCOPE. These elements are placed in group O of the periodic table because their atoms contain outer shells completely filled with electrons. The inert gases neither exchange nor share electrons with other elements, hence form no stable compounds. See PERIODIC ARRANGEMENT OF THE ELEMENTS.

INERTIA, a universal property of a body which resists change in velocity or direction of motion. It is a fundamental experimental fact which was known

to Galileo and later formulated by Sir ISAAC NEWTON as the First Law of Motion, that "every body perseveres in its state of rest or of uniform motion in a straight line except in so far as it is compelled by force to alter that state."

From personal experiences in attempting to set bodies in motion comes the basic knowledge of motion and its causes. Muscular effort is the cause, in these cases, and experience teaches that the greater the muscular effort expended, other things being equal, the greater is the motion which results. A given amount of effort, however, produces greatly differing results depending upon the characteristics of the body being moved. A small ("light") object is affected more profoundly than a large ("heavy") one, with the same amount of muscular effort. It therefore is a fundamental experimental fact that response to a given cause of motion is determined by some property of the object. This property is called inertia. The greater the inertia of a body, the greater is its tendency to resist a change in velocity or direction of movement. Our understanding of inertia, or mass, as it is frequently called, is based on these considerations.

Only when a body is accelerated does its inertia become observable. While the word inertia infers inaction, it is actually an opposition to any change in motion. Any acceleration of a body, or change in direction of motion requires the application of force proportional to the mass of the body and the amount of acceleration. Acting through the center of mass, the reaction of the body to the force is a measure of the inertia of the body.

When it is rotational motion which is to be given to a body, the distribution of the matter of the body with respect to the axis of rotation is of importance and leads to the recognition of a quantity known as the "moment of inertia." It may be established experimentally that for a given axis of rotation the rotational inertia is constant. The moment of inertia about a given axis is equal to the sum of the products of the elements of mass that comprise the object by the square of the distance of each element of mass from the given axis of rotation. See KINETIC ENERGY.

INFALLIBILITY, the immunity from error in all that pertains to faith and morals, which is claimed by the Roman Catholic Church. This claim involves the positive and constant assistance of the Spirit of God to protect against the possibility of error at all times. From the positive view, by virtue of this claim, the church must permanently teach the essential truths of God without fear of error. From the negative standpoint, the church assumes divine protection from ever receiving or teaching erroneous doctrines. Although the question of infallibility arose in discussions among theologians and was implicitly presumed to be present in the church by most of the Christian world, it was not defined as a tenet of the church until 1870. In that year the VATICAN COUNCIL decreed "that when the Roman Pontiff speaks *ex cathedra*—that is, when he, using his office as pastor and doctor of all Christians, in virtue of his apostolic office defines a doctrine of faith and morals to be held by the whole church—he, by the divine assistance promised him in the Blessed Peter, possesses that infallibility with which the Divine Redeemer was pleased to invest his church in the definition of doctrine on faith or morals, and that therefore such definitions of the Roman Pontiff are irreformable in their own nature and not because of the consent of the church."

On matters to which the prerogative of infallibility extends, Catholics consider that it embraces only those subjects which are necessary for the maintenance of divine truth in the church. It is not believed to pertain to questions of science, history, and so forth. Nor is it considered a part of infallibility when the pope issues private or personal opinions concerning such matters as politics and international affairs. See PAPACY.

INFANT CARE

Essential for the normal development of a child is the understanding and care given it in the very early years

INFANCY AND INFANT CARE. Infancy is usually regarded as the first 12 to 15 months of human existence, the period before the baby begins to walk and talk. However, some authorities consider the duration of infancy to include the first two or two and a half years, or, until the baby has his first set of teeth.

Growth and Development. There is an orderly and regular sequence of growth, maturation, and development through which each individual will pass from birth to adulthood. Each child will follow his own individual rate of progress and will attain the size, shape and functional capacities which are inherent in him. His development will be limited by his inheritance, but it will be conditioned by the forces in his environment.

Recent studies in child development have shown that the rate of growth differs widely among children who are regarded as normal. It is now believed that young children should not be forced or urged to develop various skills and abilities before they are structurally and functionally mature enough for such abilities. Demands made on a child before he is ready to accept them usually lead to frustrations which endanger normal adjustments. If he is given an opportunity to perform fully and freely at each stage of his development and if denials are made when he is ready to accept them, the child will be less likely to suffer from warped feelings and personal maladjustments.

The newborn baby is from 18 to 22 inches long and weighs between 5 and 10 pounds, or, an average of about seven and a half pounds. His head is large in relation to his trunk, his body is small, and his legs are drawn up in the position in which they were folded in prenatal life. His jaw is not fully developed at birth, but it develops more rapidly than the rest of the face during the first year of life, so the baby has a well developed chin by the time he is one year old.

During the first week of life a baby loses about 10 per cent of his birth weight (about 10 ounces), but he generally regains this loss by the end of the second week. The healthy normal child generally doubles his birth weight in five months, triples it at one year, and quadruples it at two years of age. The average weekly gain during their first six months is about four to eight ounces; during the second six months it is about two to four ounces. The child grows about one inch a month in length during the first half year, and a half inch a month during the second half year. At six months the average height is about 26 inches and at one year about 29½ inches.

At birth the baby has more bones than he will have at maturity. As he grows, new bones develop and others are fused together. The soft spot, or anterior fontanelle, in the child's head should be closed by the time he is 18 months old. During childhood the growth of the head, which is disproportionately large at birth, slows up and the other parts of the body grow increasingly faster: the arms most rapidly, the trunk next, and the legs and feet next. See GROWTH.

All of the teeth of the first set and many of those of the second set are already formed in the baby's jaw when he is born. However, the teeth do not begin to erupt until the baby is six or seven months old. Although some variation from these figures may be expected, the approximate time of eruption of the temporary or milk teeth is as follows:

2 lower central incisors	6–9 months
4 upper incisors	8–12 months
2 lower lateral incisors . . .	12–15 months
4 anterior molars	12–15 months
4 canines (eye teeth) . . .	18–24 months
4 back molars	24–30 months

Seeing. The special cells which are used for seeing are not fully developed in the baby's eyes at birth. These cells develop gradually. By the time the baby is a month old he can see large objects, and by the time he is four months old he is able to distinguish shapes and colors quite well. The baby can follow a moving light with his eyes by the first or second month, and soon after this he shows that he recognizes familiar objects.

Hearing. Many authorities believe that hearing is well developed at birth. However, most babies are totally or partially deaf during the first few days, until the amniotic fluid which may have filled the middle ear has drained off. A young baby is easily startled by noises, and he evidences disturbance at loud sounds. He is able to distinguish sounds at an early age; he stops crying when he hears his mother's voice. As the baby grows older he imitates the sounds he hears. In this manner the baby thus begins to learn how to talk.

Fontanelle, or soft spot, on head of baby

A healthy baby at the age of three months

PHOTOS FROM "BABY CARE", BY E. G. LAWLER, M. D., WILCOX AND FOLLETT. 1947

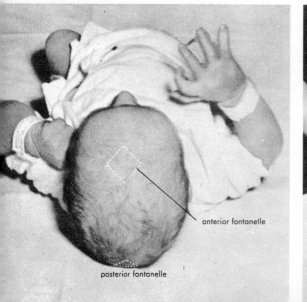

anterior fontanelle

posterior fontanelle

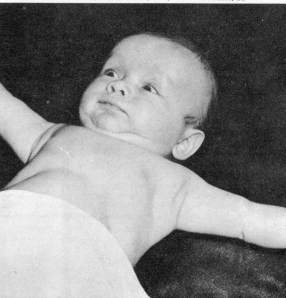

INFANT CARE

The health and happiness of the individual depends to a considerable degree upon the care he receives in the first year of his life. During that period are laid the foundations for habits and adjustments necessary for him in later years. A happy baby has the best chance of becoming a well-adjusted adult

PHOTOS. "BABY CARE," E. G. LAWLER, M. D. WILCOX AND FOLLETT CO., 1947

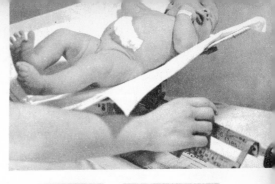

Weighing Baby on a beam scale, with a blanket on the scale to prevent chilling

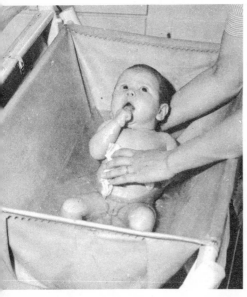

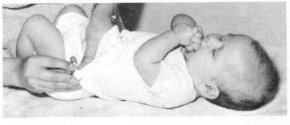

The Baby's Bath, left. Dressing the baby, above. Slipover shirt is gathered and put on first over the head; the diaper is brought up snugly between the baby's legs and then pinned

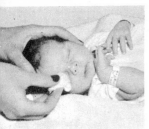
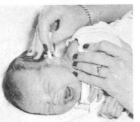
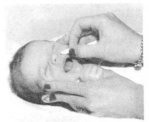
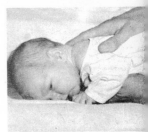

Baby Care. Left to right: Eyes are wiped from the nose outward; external ear and the nose are cleaned with a soft cotton swab moistened in oil or sterile water; correct method of turning baby on his abdomen

Baby Feeding. Cod liver oil given daily supplies needed amount of vitamins A and D, left; for a normal baby, bottle feeding, center, is a satisfactory substitute for breast feeding; "bubbling" the baby, right

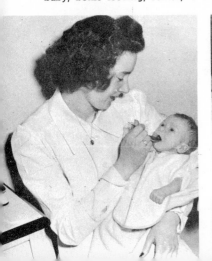
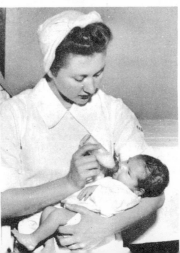

Tasting. The sense of taste is present in early infancy. Most babies seem to prefer sweet-tasting substances, but some may prefer sour tastes.

Smelling. It is believed that the sense of smell is well developed at birth. By the time the baby is seven or eight months old he knows how to sniff and smell and seems to enjoy various odors.

Feeling. A young baby has a delicate sense of touch, especially in the tongue and lips, but his sensitiveness to pain is thought to be very slight, especially in early infancy. He reacts early to heat and cold and may refuse food if it varies a few degrees in temperature.

Nutrition. Breast milk is the ideal food for the baby, since the composition of breast milk is better suited to meet the baby's needs, is more easily digested than the milk of other mammals, and is safe from contamination. Studies have shown that breast-fed babies have less indigestion, less rickets, fewer respiratory infections and a lower mortality than bottle-fed babies. Furthermore, breast feeding provides a close physical contact of the child with its mother and furnishes an important means for fulfilling the infant's need for affectional security, which is a basis for wholesome emotional adjustment.

Most mothers who really want to, can nurse their babies if they are careful to eat the proper food and live healthy and well adjusted lives during the months in which they are nursing their babies. Since milk secretion is stimulated by the sucking of a hungry baby, more frequent nursing periods, as often as every two or three hours during the first few days, serve to increase the quantity of breast milk which the mother has for her child. A baby who cannot be breast-fed is usually given a mixture of boiled cow's milk. The milk may be fresh, evaporated, or dried, and some form of sugar and water is usually added as prescribed by the pediatrician to make the milk more readily digestible and adapted to the baby's needs. Since milk does not supply all food factors that the baby needs supplementary foods are added. (See NUTRITION.) The following extracts from the Children's Bureau Publication No. 8, *Infant Care*, presents the foods in addition to milk that are recommended for babies at different ages.

At two weeks: One teaspoonful orange juice; one teaspoonful cod liver oil.

At one month: One ounce orange juice; two and one-half teaspoonfuls cod liver oil.

At two months: Three ounces orange juice; two and one-half teaspoonfuls cod liver oil.

At four months: Three ounces orange juice; two and one-half teaspoonfuls cod liver oil; cereal; egg yolk.

At five to six months: Three ounces orange juice; two and one-half teaspoonfuls cod liver oil; cereal; egg yolk; vegetables.

At seven months: Three ounces orange juice; two and one-half teaspoonfuls cod liver oil; cereal; egg yolk; vegetables; scraped meat.

At eight to twelve months: Three ounces orange juice; two and one-half teaspoonfuls cod liver oil; cereal; whole egg; vegetables; fruit; scraped meat; dry toast, as soon as the baby has some teeth.

Recent investigations have shown that young babies tolerate strained meat at a very early age. See NUTRITION.

Habits. The health, happiness and normal adjustments of the older child and of the adult are influenced by the habits formed in early childhood. To promote good habits, the adult must see that the baby gets satisfaction out of actions which are desirable and that he does not get satisfaction from actions which are undesirable.

Training in elimination habits should begin when the child is psychologically ready and has established a rhythm of evacuation. For bowel control this is usually at eight or ten months or later. Bladder control is more difficult and is therefore begun later, usually after bowel control is well established. (See ENURESIS.) Most babies will develop daytime bladder control by the time they are two years old or earlier, and night-time control about six months later.

An ever increasing number of pediatricians are advising mothers to feed their newborn babies on a self-demand schedule: that is, to feed them as long and as much as they demand whether they are breast- or bottle-fed. It is believed that the early gratification of the infant's desires serves to promote psychological well-being by building up pleasant conditioning toward food and the process of eating. Studies have shown that the self-demand schedule is very successful and popular with mothers who have used it. By the fifth or sixth week most babies establish themselves on rather regular schedules which are similar to those which are artificially imposed on many babies. Furthermore, these babies seem to adjust themselves to this regular schedule with a minimum of frustration, and they reduce the total number of daily feedings they require more rapidly than do babies who are fed on a strict schedule with a prescribed number of feedings from the start.

Motor and Mental Development. The baby learns first to control the muscles of the head and the neck, then the muscles of the arms and chest, and finally the muscles of the feet and legs. When he is about a month old he can hold up his chin when lying on his abdomen. Soon after this he is able to lift his head and chest by putting his weight on his hands, and by the time he is four months old he can roll from side to back. At the age of six months his muscular control has developed so much that he can turn over from his back onto his stomach. Some children stand as early as seven months; others do not attempt it until as late as 10 or 11 months. The average age of walking is 13 or 14 months, although many children walk before then, and many others do not walk until 15 or 16 months. A baby should never be urged to walk. He will do so without coaxing as soon as he is ready.

Language Development. At about six weeks of age a baby begins to make random sounds which are single syllables. A little later he begins to double these single syllables and produces such "babble" sounds as lul-lul and buh-buh. He is praised if some of these combinations sound like real words, and is urged to repeat them. Many babies have a vocabulary of two or three words when they are a year old. Some girls, and a few boys, use from 10 to 100 words at around 18 months of age. However, some children, usually boys, do not have as many as five words in their vocabularies until they are two years or two and one-half years old.

Social and Emotional Development. During his first year, through his successes and failures, and through the encouragement and disapproval of those around him, the baby gradually develops definite abilities and lays the foundation for certain personality traits. He is very conscious of people's actions and attitudes, and he learns by imitation of those around him. The baby's love is centered in himself at first, but soon it extends to those things and persons that give him physical satisfaction. By about nine months he has extended his affection from himself to his mother and to others who care for him.

The baby shows anger if his wishes are not granted or if he is thwarted in any way. By six months his desire for companionship, or desire for a toy that he cannot reach, may cause anger. But gradually he learns to control his anger by making satisfactory adjustments and by developing a feeling of security in his family group.

Immunization. The baby should be inoculated against diphtheria and smallpox, and when the doctor recommends it, against whooping cough, tetanus (lockjaw), and typhoid fever. (See COMMUNICABLE DISEASES.) The following plan for immunization of the infant is recommended by the Children's Bureau of the U.S. Dept. of Labor: (1) Have the baby vaccinated against smallpox at three months of age; (2) Have him vaccinated against whooping cough at seven months (three injections); (3) Have the infant immunized against diptheria at nine months (three injections). Tetanus immunization may be given at the same time. (4) Have a Schick test made from six months to a year after the diptheria immunization is given. See CHILD; CHILD GUIDANCE; CHILD PSYCHOLOGY; CHILD TRAINING; GIFTED CHILDREN; FEEBLE-MINDED, TRAINING OF; MATERNITY.   ANNE M. LEE

BIBLIOG.–R. M. Smith, *Baby's First Two Years* (1937); C. A. and M. M. Aldrich, *Babies Are Human Beings* (1938); L. W. Sauer, *From Infancy Through Childhood* (1942); L. R. Schultz and M. S. Smart, *Understanding Your Baby* (1942); U. S. Dept. of Labor, Children's Bureau Publication No. 8, *Infant Care* (1942); E. B. Hurlock, *Modern Ways with Children* (1943); M. A. Ribble, *Rights of Infants* (1943); H. N. Bundesen, *Baby Manual* (1944); A. L. Gesell, *Infancy and Human Growth* (1928), *The First Five Years of Life* (1940), *Infant and Child in the Culture of Today* (1943), *How a Baby Grows* (1945); C. A. Smith, *Physiology of the Newborn Infant* (1945); W. P. H. Sheldon, *Diseases of Infancy and Childhood* (5th ed. 1946); B. M. Spock, *Common Sense Book of Baby and Child Care* (1946); J. Gibbens, *Care of Child from One to Five* (1947); F. T. King, *Feeding and Care of Baby* (1947); B. Reyher, *Babies Keep Coming* (1947); B. Sullivan, *Babies Don't Bounce* (1947); L. De Lissa, *Life in the Nursery School and in Early Babyhood* (ed. 1948); J. C. Montgomery and M. J. Suydam, *America's Baby Book* (1951).

INFANT, the common law term for one who, from lack of age, has not full legal capacity. The synonomous term, *minor*, is in more popular usage in the United States. At common law the age of legal capacity for both sexes is 21 years. An infant comes of age the day before the 21st anniversary of his birth. Some of the states of the United States have reduced the age to 18 in the case of females.

The rules governing the legal relations of normal persons are modified in some important respects to meet the conditions of infancy. An infant can neither sue nor be sued in his proper person, but only through his guardian or person appointed to protect his interests by the court. He cannot bind himself irrevocably by contract except for necessaries, and he may avoid or confirm a deed, gift, payment, or transfer of property made by him during infancy within a reasonable time after he comes of age. Infants may acquire property by descent, devise, gift, or purchase, and, unless under guardianship, may hold and manage same.

Generally, an infant under seven is deemed incapable of crime; between 7 and 14 there is a presumption that he is so incapable, but this may be overcome by such evidence as may convince the jury that a criminal intent was really present. However, an infant is usually held responsible for his torts. See AGE, *In Law*; GUARDIAN; CHILD LABOR; MARRIAGE.

INFANT CARE AND DEVELOPMENT. See CHILD WELFARE; INFANCY AND INFANT CARE; MATERNITY.

INFANT MORTALITY. See VITAL STATISTICS.

INFANTE, the title given in Spain and Portugal to the princes of the royal family, the corresponding title of infanta being given to the princesses.

INFANTICIDE, or the killing of newborn infants, in the law of modern civilized communities, is not regarded in a different light from other cases of homicide. The practice was, however, regularly sanctioned in the states of the ancient world, such as Sparta and early Rome, in order to prevent the rearing of unhealthy citizens. The same idea was prevalent among the Norsemen, Gauls, and other primitive tribes. The Poles continued to destroy deformed children until the 13th century. Infanticide is still practiced by certain barbarous races, though the progress of civilization is gradually rendering the custom extinct.

INFANTILE PARALYSIS. See POLIO OR POLIOMYELITIS.

INFANTILE PARALYSIS, NATIONAL FOUNDATION FOR. With funds raised by the annual "March of Dimes" campaign, the National Foundation for Infantile Paralysis conducts a fight against this disease by making research grants to hospitals, universities, and laboratories and by conducting an educational program throughout the country. Founded by President Franklin D. Roosevelt in 1938 the foundation now has chapters in every county in the nation as well as in Alaska, Hawaii, and Puerto Rico. Half of the sum contributed each year is employed in the area from which it was donated. The rest is used by the foundation to obtain the best medical minds for its research program, to disseminate their findings and to aid during infantile paralysis epidemics. See POLIO OR POLIOMYELITIS.

INFANTRY, foot soldiers collectively; that part of an army trained to march and maneuver on foot, usually forming the mass of an army and equipped with the standard and most prevalent arm.

History. The history of armies begins with the separation of picked fighting men, or champions, from the mass of soldiers armed with sword and spear, bow and arrow. As described in the Old Testament and the Iliad, these champions often decided the issue; they were especially equipped with armor and arms of greater weight that lesser men could not bear. But the first development of a separate arm was in the appearance of horsemen and chariots. The invention of stirrups made cavalry shock action possible. The residue of infantry first regained leadership with the first tactical development, the PHALANX, a hedgehog formation of spears of varying length wielded by a carefully drilled and trained mass. Epaminondas developed an oblique attack that was copied by Philip and Alexander. But as the phalanx became formalized and inflexible it was replaced by the Roman legion, a highly flexible formation derived from the already-developed light infantry. Hannibal brought against it cavalry and elephants, but Rome, under Scipio, was quick to adopt these modifications. Neglect of auxiliary arms and flexible formations brought the downfall of infantry at Adrianople, and the triumph of the armed knight, who formed the decisive arm for 1,000 years. But even in the Middle Ages the bulk of armies, in most cases, were foot soldiers. Swiss and Spanish archers, Genoese crossbowmen, and English archers demonstrated on many fields that the knightly cavalry was not invincible. Yet pikemen lacked mobility and archers the power fully to protect themselves. Infantry overcame these defects with the invention of FIREARMS, at first used in combination with pikes, a combination made unnecessary by the invention of the bayonet.

Under Gustavus Adolphus the period of modern infantry begins with the Swedish king's use of fire power. From the 17th to the 20th century armies were divided, in varying proportions, in the three dominant branches of infantry, cavalry, and artillery. Cromwell, Conde, and Turenne put emphasis on cavalry; Marlborough and Frederick the Great returned it to infantry, the Prussian king by a return to the ancient oblique order, a mass attack in echelon that depended as much on shock as it did on fire power. Meanwhile in America, under the influence of Indian fighting, there had been developing a system of light infantry. The smooth-bore musket's volley firing had dominated Europe's battlefields. Although the rifle had been invented, it remained for the American frontiersman to demonstrate its practicality by using a patched ball instead of hammering an oversized ball home against the grooves of the rifling.

Morgan's riflemen of the Revolution proved that accurate rifle firing could be depended upon on the battlefield. Napoleon increased mobility by employing the division. He employed masses of cavalry and artillery, but after his day increasing fire power caused a decline of cavalry which was less and less employed in shock action, although retained for reconnaissance and for raids on the vulnerable and extending supply lines. This was its role in the American Civil War, but it became of decreasing importance until its almost complete disappearance during World War II.

The reverse was true of artillery, which has increased proportionately through the same period. In the 18th century the standard was two guns to 1,000 men, increased to five in some of Napoleon's battles, although two remained the standard of his total organization. By 1870 the proportion had only been increased to three guns to 1,000 men, but at the opening of World War I it had increased to six, and by 1917 to 20, with some attacks using a gun to every five or six yards, or 300 to the mile of front. This tendency increased in World War II. American and British artillery were used in huge concentrations in the closing months of the war.

At the same time, other branches of service became an increasingly large proportion of armies. In the United States Army, in World War II, infantry totaled only 20 per cent, although suffering 70 per cent of the casualties. Only 90 divisions were formed, although very nearly as many divisions of much larger size had been organized in the much smaller army of World War I.

Despite the vast increase in other arms, the infantry itself has become a diversified force armed with a wide variety of weapons. The early period of pike and firelock soon saw the addition of the grenade, and for a time, in the late 18th and early 19th century a separation was made of heavy infantry armed with the musket and light infantry armed with the rifle. For a succeeding century the rifle and bayonet formed the only infantry arm. When the Gatling gun, and later the machine gun, were invented, they were at first attached to the artillery. Shortly before World War I a machine gun company appeared in each infantry regiment, and during the war three machine gun battalions were brigaded with the four infantry regiments in a division. The grenade and the rifle grenade returned, and there was some use of the light machine gun or automatic rifle, but the trench mortar remained with the artillery. Infantry regiments had a one-pounder gun section. After the war each infantry battalion consisted of three rifle companies and one machine gun company.

In World War II this became a heavy weapons company, armed with light and heavy machine guns, mortars, and 37 mm guns. Although the automatic rifle had replaced the bolt-action Springfield, each rifle squad also had a Browning or other automatic rifle, and other members of the squad were grenade specialists. Officers and noncommissioned officers replaced the revolver or automatic pistol with an automatic carbine. The infantry was armed with antiaircraft and antitank guns of various calibers, including the "bazooka" rocket gun. The 75 mm gun, which had been the principal artillery weapon of World War I, became an infantry weapon.

All of this meant an increasingly intensive and variegated training of infantry, recognized in the United States Army by the creation of the expert infantryman's badge for proficiency in infantry specialities. The infantryman of course was also an engineer; he was taught to dig in and take cover at every opportunity. But his duty was to take ground as well as to hold it.

While the increased fire power developed by the infantry division, using weapons of various type and caliber, vastly increased the ammunition supply problem, some of the difficulties long forecast with the increase in automatic weapons did not develop. General George S. Patton complained that he had difficulty in getting his men to fire enough ammunition to get results; apparently they had been oversold on the necessity for conserving ammunition. He named the Garand rifle and the 2½-ton truck as the most valuable infantry weapons, paying his tribute

U.S. ARMY SIGNAL CORPS

U.S. Infantrymen, headed for the front lines on one of the Palau Islands, pause on a tropical road

to the supply problem, so important in warfare.

Most of the formations and tactics before the war—the advance in columns, the deployment in thin skirmish lines, the holding of one-third of each force in support or reserve—proved of value in combat. The smaller infantry division was sometimes broken down into regimental combat teams, where a smaller infantry-artillery team seemed advisable.

Infantry of the Present and Future. While the lessons of World War II would seem valid for future infantry training, only experience can show what will be the effect of atomic warfare on the future of armies. One critic has visualized that "Ordinary infantry will only be useful as the static garrison of bases on the overseas lines of communication—and such bases may have a diminished value in the coming era—besides being more vulnerable." Training at present continues along the lines indicated by experience in World War II, largely in such formations as the division and the regimental combat team. A large part of the infantry remaining in the armies of the victorious powers at present is employed in garrisoning seized territories. See ARMY; ARMY OF THE UNITED STATES; FIELD ARMY; ARMY CORPS; DIVISION; BRIGADE; REGIMENT; COMBAT TEAM; BATTALION; COMPANY.   DON RUSSELL

BIBLIOG.–B. H. Liddell Hart, *Science of Infantry Tactics* (1923), *The Future of Infantry* (1936), *The Revolution in Warfare* (1946); O. L. Spaulding, Hoffman Nickerson, and J. W. Wright, *Warfare* (1924); Paul W. Thompson, *Modern Battle* (1941).

INFECTION. See COMMUNICABLE DISEASES; IMMUNITY AND RESISTANCE TO DISEASE; INFLAMMATION; DISINFECTANTS; FIRST AID; CHEMOTHERAPY; ANTISEPTICS.

INFERIORITY COMPLEX. The inferiority COMPLEX, as a psychological concept, was developed by ALFRED ADLER. It is a pattern of behavior based upon the universal feeling of inferiority, in which the individual characteristically withdraws from the solution of his problems. The original inferiority-feeling may be traced in the personalities of all individuals, including those who have compensated successfully and those whose social interest is highly developed. (See COMPENSATION.) The "inferiority complex," however, is found typically in those individuals who present a characteristic pattern of failure in such life tasks as friendship, marriage, and work. The inferiority complex involves an inferiority-feeling unsuccessfully handled by the individual, and attended by an expectation of failure together with appropriate rationalizations for failure. See INDIVIDUAL PSYCHOLOGY; RATIONALIZATION.

ARTHUR ZWEIBEL, M.D.

INFINITE. In philosophy, infinite is that which is without limitation, and, like absolute and unconditioned, is used especially of the Infinite, of God. It is now usual to distinguish, after the manner of Hegel, between a lower or false notion of infinity, as mere immensity or indefinite extension, and a higher or genuine notion of infinity, as that which transcends finite limitations. The character of the finite as such is that it is limited from without, and to get the true notion of infinity it is not enough merely to set back this external limit indefinitely far. On the contrary, it is only when such limitation from without is altogether transcended that we get the true notion of infinity—viz., as that self-sufficient existence in which all determination is internal, and in which, therefore, determination is no longer in any degree a restriction, but simply the expression of the nature of this existence itself. See ABSOLUTE.

INFINITE AND INFINITESIMAL. In mathematics a variable x is said to "become infinite" or to "approach infinity" if its numerical value ultimately becomes and remains greater than any preassigned number N, no matter how large N may be. In symbols, this is written $x \to \infty$. A variable is sometimes said to become "infinitely small" if it approaches zero as a limit. Such a variable is called an *infinitesimal*. Thus, as x becomes infinite, its reciprocal $1/x$ approaches zero; in symbols, as $x \to \infty$, $1/x \to 0$. In the CALCULUS, infinitesimals play a fundamental role in the study of derivatives and integrals.

In geometry, it is usually assumed that *a line is infinite in extent*. Although a segment or "piece" of a line may be extended indefinitely in either direction, it will not include this entire "line." Similarly, *a plane is assumed to be infinite*. It is customary to assign meanings to such statements so that other statements can be made which appear to have no exceptions. Consider, for example, the statement "two straight lines in the same plane have one (and only one) point in common *except when they are parallel*." The italicized part can be omitted if it is agreed that on every line there is a single "point at infinity," and that two lines which have a common "point at infinity" are parallel.   M. L. HARTUNG

INFIRMARY. See HOSPITAL.

INFLAMMATION. When the tissues of the body are injured by a blow or by germs a reaction develops which is called inflammation. Pain, heat, redness, and swelling develop around the injured area. This is caused by a rush of blood to the injured spot, the blood circulation is slowed, so that the blood near the injury is not circulating rapidly, and there is an escape of fluid and some of the blood cells out of the small blood vessels into the surrounding tissues. This is what makes the swelling. Inflammation is one of nature's methods of defending the body against injury. (See IMMUNITY AND RESISTANCE TO DISEASE.) For example, if the cause of the inflammation is an infection, this rushing of blood and slowing of circulation help to prevent the spread of the germs to the rest of the body. Inflammation helps to keep the injury confined to the one spot and thus to speed recovery.   EDWIN P. JORDAN, M.D.

INFLATION AND DEFLATION. Inflation is an increase in the quantity of purchasing power sufficiently large in relation to commodities available and the concurrent level of production to bring about, within a relatively short time, a marked rise in prices. Deflation, the opposite of this process is a reduction in purchasing power relative to current commodities

available and current level of production, accompanied by falling prices.

Economic Basis for Inflation and Deflation. Economic theorists are not in total agreement as to the precise economic phenomena which merit being known as inflation or deflation. Most commonly it is associated with increases and decreases in the amount of MONEY in circulation. Proponents of this theory support the quantity theory of money and assert that price changes deviate in accordance with changes in the quantity of currency in circulation; in some cases they also take into account as a contributing factor changes in the velocity of circulation of money. Others add changes in credit outstanding, especially bank credit extended on the basis of unliquid assets, to changes in currency supply and velocity as a prime factor. On the other hand Keynes, Cassel, and some present-day authorities view inflation and deflation solely from the point of view of price change. Keynes in particular points out the relationship between prices and profits as an inflationary factor, that is an increase in prices which is not absorbed by increased cost of production, but increases profit per unit leads to inflationary business expansion. Likewise unchanging prices and decreasing costs of production would also increase profits and bring into force inflationary tendencies.

In many aspects of business and industry it is almost impossible to disentangle the various factors which cause price shifts and to designate those which appear inflationary and those which tend to maintain an economic equilibrium. However it may be said that any expansion in the quantity of money, increase in the velocity of circulation of money, or expansion in credit which has the effect of increasing prices rapidly may start an inflationary trend inasmuch as the increased prices may be reflected in increased profits and these in turn stimulate an expansion in business activity which may necessitate further expansion of credit, etc. The opposite is true of deflation. More or less minor tendencies of this type occur in connection with the upward and downward swings of the BUSINESS CYCLE.

The Role of Government Financing. Throughout history notable inflations have been caused by the measures taken by governments to increase their own purchasing power. A serious emergency, such as war or economic disaster, makes it necessary for centralized governments to obtain increased funds. Such funds may be obtained by borrowing, by taxing, or by increasing the amount of money available through debasing the metallic currency itself, through the issuing of paper money, or by a deliberate expansion of bank credit.

The raising of funds through taxes has frequently been avoided throughout history because it is an unpopular political measure. However taxation is not usually an inflationary factor, and the general level of prices is not raised by increased income taxes inasmuch as they merely effect a transfer of purchasing power from the individual to the government. Particular prices may change, those of commodities necessary to the government program rising in relation to those of consumer items.

Likewise government borrowing from private individuals through the issuance and sale of bonds does not necessarily cause inflation if the funds come primarily from the actual savings and current income of the lenders. However if individuals use savings or bank credit to maintain their regular purchasing power, there may be an increase in money and credit in relation to goods available which results in increased prices in general.

When inflation is brought about by the issue of government paper money or through the expansion of bank credit, the increased purchasing power (measured in money units) raises prices; rising prices necessitate larger expenditures—by the government as well as by individuals—thus calling for a further increase in the rate of creation of paper money or bank credit. This kind of inflation tends to be cumulative and is extremely difficult to stop. These circumstances occurred in France during World War I when the government found it necessary to borrow from the Bank of France; the government borrowing plus the impetus to expansion of commercial loans given by the initial price rise supported further price rises which in turn caused more borrowing. This spiral continued up to 1926.

Deflation by government action is intended to correct the evils of inflation and restore the stability of currency. This may be done by redeeming the paper at par, by complete repudiation, or by such compromise measures as retiring a part of the paper and restoring the rest to relationship with a metallic standard. Devaluation of the currency in the past has been the principle generally followed as opposed to raising funds for redemption by heavy taxation.

Effects of Inflation and Deflation. Usually the results of inflation appear beneficial for a period. The differential between selling prices and production costs stimulates production; the time lag between wage increases and price increases benefits those who can add to their profits through these conditions. Banks extend large amounts of short-term credit regardless of the rise in interest rates. For these reasons those whose incomes are rising often are in favor of measures which will increase the inflation. Those who suffer during this period are those whose real incomes decrease; wage and salary earners whose money incomes do not keep pace with the price rise and creditors who are repaid in money the real value of which has decreased since they extended the credit.

Periods of rapid deflation are also accompanied by widespread adjustment and dislocation. When inflation reaches the stage where it is realized that the value of money is falling, there is a general scramble for protection against a further fall. Credit becomes difficult to obtain and businesses find it necessary to liquidate. Production shrinks and unemployment results. Prices and total volume of credit may decrease to a point considerably below that necessary to the functioning of the economy. Those with fixed incomes gain through the increased value of their money, but debtors find it difficult to repay their borrowings and business profits become negligible.

The over-all social-economic results of such a surge and decline are often serious and widespread. A large percentage of the property of a nation may change ownership with individuals becoming dispossessed and financial and credit institutions acquiring title. Geographic shifts in population sometimes take place; business and political leaders are discredited; certain industries are retarded in their normal long-term development; and perfectly legitimate aspects of business are avoided as dangerous.

History. Inflation and deflation may be traced throughout the course of history. In 217 B.C., after the defeat of Hannibal, Fabius Maximus increased the volume of currency by reducing the size of the bronze *as*, and by the introduction of the first gold coins. In Nero's reign, the draining away of gold into foreign trade led to a debasement of the coinage. Price fluctuations followed Diocletian's reorganization of the currency so that A.D. 301 he issued a list of maximum prices. Inflation of currency was a frequently practiced policy of medieval princes. It was usually carried out through debasement of coins or through the issuance of newly minted coins with smaller metal content. The number of such monetary devaluations which were undertaken to make up deficits due to costly wars or excessive private spending by the ruler, goes well into the hundreds.

In the 17th century speculation in the stocks of the India Companies ushered in a period of inflation in the Netherlands; and in the 18th century there occurred the MISSISSIPPI BUBBLE inflation, the English inflation connected with the South Sea Company speculations, and the issue of the French ASSIGNATS (1790).

After World War I Germany experienced a disastrous inflation. During the war the government had borrowed heavily from the Reichsbank (just as the government of France had borrowed from the Bank of France), and the Reichsbank had been allowed to suspend specie payments and substitute noncash cover for its bills. After the war reconstruction expenses and reparations necessitated further borrowing from the Reichsbank and the ensuing rise in prices created a near-panic situation with people spending rapidly in an attempt to obtain goods rather than retain money which they feared would lose further value. During this period prices tended to lag behind foreign exchange rates which contributed to the country's need to borrow progressively larger amounts. Russia experienced a similar situation at this time, but in England, partially as a result of the return to the gold standard, inflation was obviated.

In the United States during the pre-Revolutionary period the colonies issued paper money known as colonial bills of credit to defray expenses. In the Revolutionary War, the Continental Congress as well as the individual colonies issued paper money, the former being driven to this action by its lack of power to levy taxes. The appetite for easy money from the printing press grew and the outcome was disastrous with the paper worth practically nothing; as a result we still have the expression "not worth a Continental." During the Civil War GREENBACKS were issued by the Northern states in the total amount of $450,000,000; this money began to depreciate shortly after February 1862, the date of first issue.

During the 1920's the United States experienced an inflation as a result of the expansion of bank credit buttressed by widespread installment selling. The deflation which followed this over-expansion resulted in the depression of the 1930's. To restore the economy the government followed a program of credit inflation through the medium of easy credit advances by governmental agencies such as the RECONSTRUCTION FINANCE CORPORATION. From 1933 to 1937 the price level rose steadily, but dropped again late in 1937 almost to the 1934 level. By the end of 1941, owing to the influence of the European war the price level reached the mid-1937 level and began to rise beyond it. With the entrance of the United States into World War II serious efforts were made to prevent war inflation by price control measures and rationing. During 1943 and 1944 the general price level rose only about 30 or 40 points above what it had been at the outbreak of the war; agricultural commodities as a group, however, doubled in price between 1941 and 1944. See COST OF LIVING INDEX.

Inflation After World War II. During the six years from August, 1939, to August, 1945—approximately the duration of the war—the wholesale price index for all commodities rose from 75.0 to 105.7 (based on an index of 100 in 1926), an increase for the war years of 40.9 per cent. For the period, Aug. 1, 1945 to June 29, 1946, while price controls were still functioning, it increased to 112.9, or 6.8 per cent over August, 1945. By June, 1947, it had reached 147.6. Since 1947, the index established the following pattern: January, 1948, 165.6 per cent of 1926; March, 1949, 158.4; and January, 1950, 151.6. Prices in most commodities rose following the outbreak of the Korean conflict in mid-1950, and by February, 1951, the index stood at 183.4.

The effect of the Korean war on U.S. prices, combined with the extensive defense mobilization planned, made certain by late 1950 that price controls were inevitable as a curb on runaway inflation. The administration announced that "our primary defense against inflation will be credit control, higher taxes, and reduced non-military expenditures," along with some form of price stabilization. Congress quickly approved the Defense Production Act of 1950 giving the President power to impose anti-inflationary controls, including authority to fix price controls and ration consumer goods, if necessary. An Economic Stabilization Agency was created and a Director of Price Stabilization appointed. On Jan. 26, 1951, price ceilings were imposed on most commodities at their highest points during the period Dec. 19, 1950–Jan. 25, 1951.

Rising prices, however, were not the only inflationary pressure exerted after the outbreak of the Korean war. Pressure developed from the money side of the trade relation, as well. Although there was a great increase in production of goods (normally a deflationary condition), the diversion of production to war purposes beyond the reach of the spending citizen actually left fewer goods for public consumption. At the same time there was an acceleration in the continual increase in money and credit which had served to treble the money supply between 1940 and 1951. This was caused by the government's policy of supporting its bonds at par (i.e., buying them whenever they threatened to drop in open market value, and in the process throwing more money into circulation). This policy, in turn, was the effect of the government's position as a debtor: it must support its bonds in order to be able to sell them easily to finance its war production. In 1951 a plan was effected which attacked the money side of inflation by: (a) raising interest rates on government bonds so they would attract investors, and require less government support; (b) tightening loan restrictions on banks and private agencies, thus reducing the available money supply.

Recent Effects of Inflation. Inflation in the United States has tended to afflict white-collar "fixed-wage" workers, most of whom lack the power to strike, and few of whom have been placed under "cost-of-living" wage-scale provisions. On the other hand, it has favored the self-employed—businessmen and farmers—and has been no worse than neutral in its effect on organized labor.

Others afflicted have been owners of fixed-return securities, such as savings-bank deposits, bonds, mortgages, and life insurance policies, who have suffered heavy losses through decline in the purchasing power of these assets.

Inflation has struck hard at pensioners, because between 1940–49 when the cost of living increased 70 per cent, the average Federal old-age and survivors' pension increased only 15 per cent, affecting over 2,000,000 recipients.

Also, while the average of all items in the cost-of-living index rose 52 per cent between 1940–50, the item of rents rose only 19 per cent, creating an effect of discrimination against landlords. See GOLD STANDARD; CYCLE; TAXATION; BOND; PRICE; PRICE CONTROL; RENT REGULATION; SUPPLY AND DEMAND; PAPER MONEY; COINAGE; EXCHANGE, FOREIGN; BANKS AND BANKING.   I. H.

BIBLIOG.–J. M. Keynes, *Monetary Reform* (1924); T. Frank, *An Economic History of Rome* (1927); R. G. Hawtrey, *Trade and Credit* (1928); J. M. Keynes, *A Treatise on Money* (1930); F. D. Graham, *Exchange, Prices and Production in Hyperinflation: Germany 1920–1923* (1930); E. Sparling, *Primer of Inflation* (1933); B. Woodward and M. A. Rose, *Inflation* (1933); E. V. Kemmerer, *A.B.C. of Inflation* (1942); W. J. Fellner, *Treatise on War Inflation* (1942); Tax Institute, *Curbing Inflation Through Taxation* (1944); S. E. Harris, *Inflation and the American Economy* (1945); T. D. Waage, *Inflation: Cause and Cures* (1949).

INFLECTION, in grammar, either indicates the relation of the inflected word to others in the same sentence (e.g., by case endings), or denotes some aspect of the conception which the word expresses (e.g., by tense forms). It is an important feature in the Semitic and Indo-European languages, but outside of these groups does not appear to be common. Prefixes and suffixes that are inflectional in a strict sense have no independent existence or significance. Presumably, however, the earliest of them were at first actual independent words, whose transformation lies beyond the reach of historical inquiry. The Indo-European parent language possessed a most elaborate system of inflections. The daughter languages have greatly modified and to a large extent ceased to use the inflections transmitted to them.

The history of the English language itself exemplifies this process of change. Early English was much more highly inflected than modern English. The complete loss of the old adjective inflections (for gender, number, and case), and the disappearance of the special case forms of the nominative, accusative, and dative of nouns, may be cited as illustrations of the changes which have taken place. See GRAMMAR.

INFLORESCENCE, a cluster of flowers. Inflorescences are classified in either of two major groups: (1) *indeterminate or racemose,* or (2) *determinate or cymose.* In indeterminate inflorescences the tip of the cluster continues to grow, forming new flowers in indefinite succession, the youngest at the growing apex. In determinate inflorescences the tip of the cluster ceases its growth very early. The terminal growing tissue is used up in the formation of a terminal flower, and other flowers develop farther down on the axis of the inflorescence. The youngest flowers are those farthest from the apex of the cluster. Examples of plants with cymose inflorescences are crab apple, phlox, and forget-me-not.

A flower that is not borne in a cluster is termed solitary, exemplified by the rose and magnolia.

INFLUENZA, often called "The Flu" or "The Grippe," is an acute virus disease characterized by severe weakness, aching, cough, and sometimes chills. It usually appears rather suddenly, often following a cold. The disease is usually over in four or five days, but it leaves the patient in a weakened condition and may be followed by a relapse or complications such as pneumonia, arthritis, or inflammations of the nose and throat.

Epidemics. Influenza has been characterized by peculiar epidemic behavior. Most of the COMMUNICABLE DISEASES are reasonably predictable, but influenza is not. Although records of communicable diseases were not systematically kept before 1890, there is evidence that epidemics of influenza occurred long before this time. The all-time peak of U. S. influenza deaths, 1,500 per 100,000 people, occurred in the 1918–1919 epidemic. Lesser peaks occurred in 1922, 1923, and 1926, when the deaths were 500 per 100,000. In the 1929 epidemic there were 600 deaths per 100,000 population. In the winter of 1950–51 a spotty epidemic occurred in Europe and the United States, caused by a variant of the type A virus. It was mild in character, probably because the complications were controlled by the newer drugs. Earlier epidemics which were probably due to influenza occurred in 1847, 1857, 1874, and 1890.

Cause. Not until 1933 was influenza identified as a virus disease. Previously, many different organisms had been blamed by various investigators, but as the true picture unfolded, it was recognized that these were simply secondary invaders, many of them more or less constant inhabitants of the average person's respiratory mucous membranes. Perhaps the most widely blamed of the germs in that classification was the one known as Pfeiffer's bacillus.

In epidemics in 1936 and 1940 it was found that more than one influenza virus existed; the 1933 virus was called "A" and the new one "B." Now it is known that in addition to viruses A and B, variants of these may be responsible.

Vaccine. Mice have been protected against influenza A by giving mild doses of the virus, and ferrets can be protected sufficiently to reduce the severity of subsequent influenza attacks. This is not equivalent to full protection, but in view of the havoc wrought by influenza in previous epidemics it would be distinctly worth while if we had a vaccine which would provide even partial protection. Chief difficulty in

Same scene made on panchromatic film without filter, left, and on infrared film, right

this connection is the fact that unless the specific virus causing a given epidemic is known, there is little to be gained by vaccination. No composite vaccine that is effective against all the various strains has been developed. Widespread use of this form of protection is not advised by health authorities.

Treatment and Control. Mortality from influenza itself, uncomplicated, has always been low. Only when complications appear has the death rate mounted. These complications have included pneumonia, lung or chest abscess, overwhelming acute generalized sepsis, and heart failure. Influenza appears to have a more serious course in pregnancy. Lesser complications not involving death have already been mentioned. Medical science now has better weapons for the control of influenza than have been available at any previous time. Influenza, a virus disease, is not susceptible to treatment with sulfa drugs or antibiotics, but most of its complications have been due to organisms other than the virus; for these, notably the streptococcus, the staphylococcus, and the pneumococcus, the new drugs have been of very great value. By combining the use of preventive vaccinations as a means of reducing the severity of influenza with the prompt treatment of its complications with sulfa drugs or antibiotics, it is possible that future influenza epidemics will be robbed of much of their worst features.

It must not be supposed that the influenza problem has now been solved. We do not yet understand why a virus which must undoubtedly pass from person to person many times in the course of a winter should remain mild and of little consequence for long periods of time, ranging up to 30 years, and then suddenly become explosively deadly, attacking all and sundry with almost unbelievable virulence. We do not know how to predict an epidemic of influenza with the relative certainty vouchsafed us in the case of diphtheria, measles, scarlet fever, or whooping cough. Our influenza vaccines are as yet experimental and imperfectly developed. Fighting complications with chemical medication is not the method we would choose if we could have a more effective means of control. Nevertheless, there should be no such helplessness and terror in the next epidemic of influenza as occurred during the last. The death toll should be lower even if the prevalence of sickness is not greatly reduced. There is even reason to hope that if influenza vaccines can be made readily available, and if people can be educated to accept them, some curtailment of the prevalence of this disease may be achieved.   W. W. BAUER, M.D.

INFORMATION is a process by which crimes are prosecuted not on INDICTMENT found or presentment made by a grand jury, but on complaint of a public office. More strictly the term denotes the complaint itself. Private persons are often allowed to bring accusations in the name of the attorney general or other officer, and are then technically known as *relators*. No capital or other infamous crime can be tried by information in the Federal courts, but many states have made this process competent for all or nearly all offenses.

INFRARED SPECTRUM. In order to make clear what is meant by the infrared spectrum, one must go back to the very early experiments of NEWTON (1672). He passed sunlight through a triangular glass prism and found that it was broken up in a gamut of colors which he named the spectrum. The white light is dispersed and refracted, the blue more than the red. He concluded that white light was a composite of the various colors which he observed in the spectrum. He did not correctly identify the nature of the colors.

Building upon the earlier work of Huygens, Young, Fresnel, Faraday, and others, CLERK MAXWELL (1862) developed his celebrated electromagnetic theory of light, which indicates that the colors in the spectrum discovered by Newton were electromagnetic waves; those corresponding to the blue were shorter than those corresponding to the red. In space these waves traveled with a speed of 186,000 miles per second.

About 1800 Sir William Herschel (1738–1822) discovered that a thermometer placed in the region beyond the red end of the solar spectrum indicated a rise in temperature, and that it was higher at one point than at others. Herschel investigated the reflection and refraction of this invisible or infrared radiation and found that it behaved similarly to the visible radiation.

The observations of Herschel were left undeveloped largely because of the lack of adequate techniques for accurate study. About 1830, as the result of the development of the thermopile and the use of rock salts, prisms, and lenses, Leopoldo Nobili and Macedonio Melloni undertook a series of researches dealing with the infrared spectrum. It is well to note that at that time photography had not been adapted to the recording of the infrared spectrum. The advance in the art of detection of infrared radiation has been wholly dependent on the development of techniques and instruments.

The work which gave impetus to the study of infrared radiation was that of S. P. LANGLEY (1834–1906) of the Smithsonian Institution in Washington, D.C. Langley set himself the task of studying the solar spectrum in the infrared range. In 1881 he perfected the bolometer as a detector. The bolometer is essentially a balanced Wheatstone's Bridge; two arms of which are made of narrow strips of very thin platinum foil. When one of these strips is exposed to radiation, its temperature rises, increases the resistance of the foil, and throws the bridge out of balance, as indicated by a very sensitive galvanometer. Using a rock salt prime which is permeable to the radiation, Langley studied the solar spectrum between 0.76μ and 5.3μ. The micron (designated by the letter μ) is 1/1000 of a millimeter. He not only got the general distribution of the radiation in the spectrum but discovered some 700 new absorption, or Fraunhofer, lines. Langley's work in this field was epoch-making in that it stimulated a feverish activity in infrared manifestations. In the literature between 1890 and 1910 appear the names of Rubens, Paschen, Nichols, Wood, and others. By 1924 the gap between the shortest radio wave and the longest infrared wave had been bridged. Nichols and Tear at that time extended the study of infrared radiation to wave lengths corresponding to 420μ. This long radiation came from a mercury arc and was isolated by means of absorbents and the wave lengths measured by the Fabry and Perot interferometer. They also constructed minute Hertzian oscillators which emitted a short radio wave of length only 220μ. The identity of infrared or heat radiation and the electromagnetic or short radio waves was thus established.

The study of infrared radiation has been responsible for the initiation of quantum mechanics into modern physics. Between 1890 and 1900 the German physicists were studying the relationship between temperature and radiation from a black body. Using data from such experiments, Planck in 1905 arrived at the conclusion that radiation consists of discrete quanta. See QUANTUM THEORY.

Prior to and during the second World War, developments were going on which made the infrared spectroscope a most useful tool in the study of molecular structure. The complicated structures of organic compounds can in some measure be resolved by a study of the absorption by the compounds of different infrared wave lengths. Industrial research laboratories interested in this type of work are now equipped with infrared spectroscopes. The detectors, usually vacuum thermocouples, are incorporated in electronic circuits with amplifiers so that the spectra can be recorded. Certain types of semiconductors incorporated in the form of a bolometer with associated electronic circuits bid fair to surpass the thermocouple. Inasmuch as both the thermocouple and the bolometer require temperature changes on the absorption of radiant energy, they respond to the longest infrared radiation as well as the shortest, and they are the only receivers, including the radiometer, that have such a response.

It has long been known that a system of communication may be had by properly modulating the radiation from an arc light and using a suitable receiver. Due to demands for secrecy in communication, a system that cannot be jammed was developed by the nations at war. The systems modulated a source of infrared radiation. All of radiation is comprised in a narrow band of wave lengths. Such systems have the advantage of not becoming jammed largely because of the secrecy of the beam direction and receiver. This is not wholly true of radar. Radar has the advantage of much greater range.

It would appear at present that the use and study of infrared radiation, aside from military purposes,

Sniperscope on carbine uses infrared sighting

has come into its own where molecular structure is concerned, particularly in the more complicated structures. See LIGHT.   B. J. SPENCE

INFRARED APPLICATIONS

Infrared radiation is utilized in a variety of different ways. One of the principle applications is in the field of photography, where it extends the usefulness of the camera far beyond the limits of human vision. Infrared radiation and visible light often are transmitted and reflected quite differently by common objects. The chlorophyll in green plants absorbs a large percentage of visible light but reflects the invisible infrared radiation. Atmospheric haze permits free transmission of infrared, while prohibiting transmission of visible light. Ordinary photographic plates and films are not sensitive to infrared. Sensitivity is conferred through the treatment of the emulsion with special dyes. When this is done, infrared photography is useful in revealing information not visible through the use of ordinary light. It is successfully used in criminology, photomicrography, botany, paleontology, and other scientific fields. In infrared photographs the sky appears nearly black, clouds and snow are white, grass and leaves appear very light, as though covered with snow, and distant details are revealed with remarkable clarity and sharpness.

In the textile industry the detection of irregularities in the dyeing and weaving of cloth is successfully accomplished through infrared photography. Other uses include the study of the interiors of furnaces while they are in operation and the detection of carbonaceous material in oils used in the lubrication of internal combustion engines.

Infrared Heating. An entirely different use of infrared radiation is to be found in the industrial application of infrared heating. Examples of the baking, drying, and heating uses to which infrared radiation equipment is being put include the rapid drying of motor and transformer windings, the removal of moisture from granulated cellulose acetate before it is placed in an injection molding press, the expansion of automobile engine pistons to permit insertion of closely fitting piston pins, the dehumidification of paper, the fusing of paint to glass bottles, the drying of paint and lacquer finishes on automobile bodies and other products, etc.

Among the advantages of infrared heating for a variety of purposes is the fact that no medium of transmission is required, as is the case in applying heat by conduction or convection. Infrared heating is radiant in nature; the heat is transferred from the source to the object to be heated with a minimum of loss. The common source of such infrared radiation is an especially engineered incandescent lamp, which produces a minimum of visible light and a maximum of radiation in the useful part of the infrared spectrum. Other advantages of infrared heating include low initial cost, the elimination of elaborate insulated ovens, speed of operation, immediate response, the elimination of long waiting periods for furnaces to come up to working temperatures, and the use of lightweight, inexpensive portable installations.

Detection. An unusual development during World War II in the field of infrared radiation resulted in

Infrared heating dries car-body paint

two devices, the "sniperscope" and the "snooper-scope." The sniperscope is a viewing device using infrared radiation and is mounted on a carbine. It permits the soldier to see his target in the dark. Similar devices had been developed by Germany and Great Britain. It was effectively used by American troops to stop night infiltration tactics of the enemy. The device was given credit for causing 30 per cent of the Japanese casualties on Okinawa. The snooper-scope is used for night observation and signaling. It utilizes the same unit as does the sniperscope. Infrared radiation is beamed through a black-faced light source that is attached to a telescope. A third device, the metascope, is a pocket-size unit used to observe and detect infrared radiation.

Communication. Infrared beams used in ship-to-ship and ship-to-shore communication over moderate distances during the war are now on a commercial basis. Words spoken into a microphone cause a cae-sium-vapor lamp alternately to brighten and dim thousands of times a second following the tonal char-acteristics of the speaker's voice. A reflector beams the rays toward a sensitive receiver in which a photo-electric cell picks up the rays. Amplification repro-duces them into spoken words.

There can be no eavesdropping or jamming of the infrared. The included angle of the beam is about 30 degrees and its present range is ten miles. The advantages of the infrared beamcast in bad radio weather and where wire connections are down are obvious.   D. M. MacMaster

INFRINGEMENT. See Copyright; Patent; Trade-Mark.

INFUSORIA, a class of small, one-celled animals that belongs to the phylum Protozoa. All members of the class move about by means of cilia (hairlike extensions of the body wall) and for this reason the class is sometimes called Ciliata. Most are free-living (a few are colonial) in fresh water or in the sea. Some, however, are parasitic, e.g., *Balantidium coli*, parasitic in the intestine of the chimpanzee, pig, and man.

These animals are largest of all the protozoa. Most have two nuclei (see Cell), a large *macronucleus* and a smaller *micronucleus*. Reproduction is by means of binary fission and Conjugation. In conjugation the macronucleus is thought to function as the vegetative element that maintains metabolism (respiration and other chemical processes) and the micronucleus that initiates reproduction. *Paramecium caudatum* and *Stentor coerulus* are two common representatives of the group.

INFUSORIAL EARTH. See Diatomaceous Earth.

INGE, WILLIAM RALPH, 1860–   , English clergyman and theologian, was born in Crayke, Yorkshire. After receiving his education at Eton and at King's College, Cambridge, he returned to Eton as assistant master from 1884 to 1888. The following year he went to Hertford College, Oxford, where he was fellow and tutor for the next 15 years. He was appointed vicar of All Saints, London (1905–7), was repeatedly select preacher at Oxford and Cam-bridge, and became professor of divinity at Oxford (1907–11). Chosen dean of St. Paul's Cathedral in 1911, Inge was given the name of "the gloomy dean," because of the recurrent pessimism in his teachings and writings. He was a prolific author, and his numerous works display a great originality of thought. A few of his books are: *Society in Rome under the Caesars* (1886); *Truth and Falsehood in Religion* (1906); *Personal Realism and Mysticism* (1907); *The Church in the World* (1927); *Christian Ethics and Modern Problems* (1930); *God and the Astronomer* (1931–33); *Talks in a Free Coun-try* (1943); *Diary of a Dean* (1949).   R. M. Leonard

INGELOW, JEAN, 1820–97, English poet, was born in Boston, Lincolnshire. Her first notable work was *Poems* (1863), a book of lyrics and ballads about life on the Lincolnshire seacoast which was long popular both in England and America. Among her most familiar poems were "The High Tide on the Coast of Lincolnshire," "Supper at the Mill," and "Divided." The best of her later verse appeared in *A Story of Doom and Other Poems* (1867) and *Poems, Third Series* (1885). She was also the author of many books for children, including *Tales of Orris* (1860), *Mopsa the Fairy* (1869), and *The Little Wonder-Horn* (1872).

INGEMANN, BERNHARD SEVERIN, 1789–1862, Danish poet and novelist, was born in Thorkild-strup and received his education at the University of Copenhagen. His best works were a series of historical novels in the manner of Scott—*Valdemar Seier* (1826), *Erik Menved's Childhood* (1828), *King Erik* (1833), and *Prince Otto of Denmark* (1835). His poems, which like his novels were based on incidents of Danish national history and tradition, include *Waldemar the Great and his Men* (1824), *Queen Margaret* (1836), and *Holger Danske* (1837).

INGERSOLL, CHARLES JARED, 1782–1862, American public official and writer, was born in Philadelphia, Pa. He was a member of Congress in 1813–15, and again in 1841–49; U.S. district attorney for Pennsylvania (1815–29); a member of the con-stitutional convention of Pennsylvania (1837); and secretary of the U.S. legation in Berlin (1837–38). He was the author of *Edwy and Elgiva* (1801), a tragedy; *Inchiquin the Jesuit's Letters* (1809), a spirited defense of the government, manners, and customs of the Ameri-cans; *Historical Sketch of the Second War between the United States and Great Britain* (4 vols. 1845–52); *Recollections* (1861).

INGERSOLL, ROBERT GREEN, 1833–99, Amer-ican lawyer, lecturer, and writer, was born in Dresden, N.Y., the son of a Congregational minister of very broad views. He practiced law in Illinois; served on the Federal side during the Civil War, with the rank of colonel; and in 1867–69 was attorney general of Illinois. He became a Republican campaign orator, and in a famous speech proposed James G. Blaine for the presidential nomination at the National Con-vention of 1876. Later he entered the lecture field, and was widely known for his strong opposition to Christianity, as manifested in a forceful series of agnostic lectures. He wrote: *The Bible; The Gods, and Other Lectures* (1876); *Some Mistakes of Moses* (1879); *Lectures Complete* (1883); *Great Speeches* (1887); *Founda-tions of Faith*. His *Works* were published in 12 vols. in 1900.

INGERSOLL, ROYAL EASON, 1883–   , U.S. naval officer, was born in Washington, D.C. A graduate of the U.S. Naval Academy, he was a com-mander in World War I and was decorated for his services as communications officer for the Peace Commission during the Paris Conference (1918–19). Assistant to the Chief of Naval Operations (1940–42), he became commander in chief of the Atlantic Fleet (1942–43) and was raised to the rank of admiral. He commanded the Western Sea Frontier (1944–45), and retired in 1946, the year he testified at the Pearl Harbor inquiry.

INGERSOLL, town, Canada, in the province of Ontario, Oxford County, on the Thames River and the Canadian National and the Canadian Pacific railways; 19 miles NE of London. The region was settled by Thomas Ingersoll of Massachusetts in 1793, and the town was named in his honor in 1821. It is an agricultural center and has manufactures of agricultural implements, flour, wood products, cheese, and condensed milk. Pop. (1949 est.) 6,428.

INGLEWOOD, city, S California, in Los Angeles County, on the Santa Fe Railroad and U.S. High-way 101; 10 miles SW of Los Angeles. Inglewood was settled in 1873 by Daniel Freeman. It is the home of the famous Hollywood Turf Club, and there are large aviation plants near by. The first chinchilla farm in the United States was founded in Inglewood and is still in existence. The chief manufactures are electrical equipment, sporting goods, millinery, and textiles. Pop. (1950) 46,185.

INGOLDSBY, Sir RICHARD, d. 1685, British soldier, was born in Buckinghamshire. He commanded a regiment on the Parliamentary side in the Civil Wars, and was a member of the court that condemned Charles I to death. On Richard Cromwell's resignation he entered into negotiation with the agents of Charles II. Although distrusted, he was sent in 1660 by Charles to suppress the rising organized by John Lambert, whom he captured at Daventry. For this service he received a full pardon.

INGOLDSBY LEGENDS. See BARHAM, R. H.

INGOLSTADT, town and fortress, Germany, in the upper part of the state of Bavaria, situated on a plain on both sides of the Danube, 52 miles by rail N of Munich. Features of interest include the cathedral (1439) containing the tombs of Tilly and Duke Stephen, a 15th century castle, and the first Jesuit college founded in Germany (1555). Ingolstadt was formerly the seat of a famous university founded by Louis the Rich in 1472, later transferred to Landshut (1800), and then to Munich (1826). Manufactures include locomotives, machinery, bells, bake ovens, brushes, furniture and wood wares, frame houses, beer, and dairy products. Trade is carried on in wool, grain, and hops. Ingolstadt was first mentioned as a royal villa in the eighth century, and incorporated as a town in 1310, becoming part of Upper Bavaria. Its fortress, constructed in 1539, was vainly attacked by Gustavus Adolphus (1632), razed by the French general, Moreau, in 1800; and reconstructed from 1828 to 1848. Pop. (1946) 36,530.

INGRAHAM, DUNCAN NATHANIEL, 1802–91, American naval officer, was born in Charleston, S.C. He served as midshipman during the War of 1812; accompanied Commander David Porter's expedition against the West Indian pirates in 1824; and became lieutenant in 1825 and commander in 1841. He is best known for his connection with the Koszta affair. His course in this matter was approved by the U.S. government, and brought him much popularity at home. During the Civil War he was chief of the Bureau of Ordnance, Construction, and Repair of the Confederate Navy, with the rank of commodore.

INGRAM, JONAS HOWARD, 1886– , American naval officer, was born in Jeffersonville, Ind., was graduated from the U.S. Naval Academy (1907), and was promoted through the grades to admiral (1944). He was awarded the Medal of Honor as turret officer of the *Arkansas* (1914) and the Navy Cross as aide to the commander of Division 9, Atlantic Fleet (1918). After directing athletics at the Academy (1926–30), he commanded the South Atlantic Force, Atlantic Fleet (1942) and the Atlantic Fleet (1944). He retired in 1947, and became commissioner for the professional All-America Football Conference until it was disbanded in 1949.

DON RUSSELL

INGRES, JEAN AUGUSTE DOMINIQUE, 1780–1867, French historical painter, the leader of the classical school, as opposed to the romanticists under DELACROIX, was born in Montauban. He became a pupil of David in 1796, and five years later gained the Prix de Rome. He did not go to Rome, however, until 1806. After 14 years spent in that city, he was four years in Florence, and there painted "The Vow of Louis XIII," which on its exhibition at the Paris Academy in 1824, broke down the indifference of the public to his work. To this period belong also his best portraits and his "Oedipus and the Sphinx," "Venus Anadyomene," "Romulus and Acron," "Virgil Reading the Aeneid," "Raphael and Fornarina," "Roger and Angelique."

Returning to Paris in 1826, Ingres was appointed professor of fine arts at the Academy, and became the recognized head of a great school. But the acrimonious criticisms inspired by his "Apotheosis of Homer" (1827) and "Martyrdom of St. Symphorian" (1834)

made him gladly embrace the opportunity of returning to Rome, where he succeeded Horace Vernet as director of the French Academy in 1834. There he painted "Stratonice" and the "Portrait of Cherubini." The exhibition of these and other pictures in Paris at length turned the tide of popular admiration in his favor, and he again returned to that city in 1841. At the exhibition of 1855 he was awarded the grand medal of honor for his collection of pictures, and was nominated a grand officer of the Legion of Honor. See CLASSIC REVIVAL.

INHAMBANE, seaport, E Africa, Mozambique, the chief town of Inhambane District, situated at 23° 50′ S lat. and 35° 25′ E long., on Inhambane Bay. It has a good harbor, and exports copal, rubber, ivory, wax, and nuts. The town was founded in the middle of the 16th century and was taken by natives early in the 19th century, after which its trade declined. The town has been of increasing importance since late in the 19th century. Pop. (1946 est.) 12,000, including about 10,000 natives.

INHERITANCE, BIOLOGICAL. See HEREDITY.

INHERITANCE, IN LAW. A person who dies leaving no will is said to die *intestate*. In the absence of a will, a property owner's lands and personal property pass by law to certain designated next-of-kin, who are denominated *heirs*. Such persons are said to acquire title by *inheritance* or *descent*. In some states real estate and personal property are inherited by different classes of persons. In such states it is preferable to designate as *heirs* those who take the real estate and to describe as *distributees* those who receive the personal property. In practice, however, this distinction in terminology is largely ignored and both classes are referred to as heirs.

The right to inherit property is generally regarded as not being a natural or inherent right, but as a creature of the law, and in all states it is minutely regulated by statute. The descent of real property is generally governed by the laws of the states in which the property is located. The right to inherit personal property is governed by the law of the state in which the deceased had his legal residence at the time of his death. As a general rule, all vested rights and interests owned by deceased at the time of his death are subject to inheritance. Statutes generally confer rights of inheritance only on blood relatives, adopted children, adoptive parents, and a surviving husband or wife, but laws relating to inheritance differ widely from state to state. It is the rule in some states that on the failure of direct descendants (children, grandchildren, etc.) an estate inherited from one ancestor shall go to the intestate's next-of-kin who are of the blood of the ancestor from whom the estate was inherited.

At some point in the inheritance law of each state, after enumerating the closest kindred of the deceased and the order in which and what share they take, the law concludes with a provision giving the property in default of all previously named kindred, to the nearest of kin in equal degrees. In computing such degree of kinship it is usual to reckon by the method of ascending the intestate to a common ancestor and descending from him to a claimant, reckoning one degree for each generation, both in the ascending and descending lines. Thus, uncles, aunts, nephews, nieces, and great grandparents of the deceased are related to him in the third degree. The fourth degree includes first cousins, great-uncles and great-aunts, and great, great grandparents. A person related to the deceased in the fourth degree will take all the property to the exclusion of persons related in the fifth and higher degrees, and so on. Parents and children are, of course, related to the deceased in the first degree, but the law usually provides that the children take in preference to parents.

Inheritance by representation (*per stirpes*) occurs when the children or other descendants of a child, brother or sister who died before the intestate did, take the same share of the estate that their ancestor would have taken if living. While under the early common law a widow had no rights of inheritance in the estate of her deceased husband, under the statutes in most states rights of inheritance are now conferred upon her. The extent of her share depends upon the terms of the statute applicable to the facts in the particular case. The prospective interest of an expectant heir is a mere possibility and gives him no interest in property which he may subsequently inherit. See INHERITANCE TAX; CONSANGUINITY; KIN, NEXT OF; HEIR; DESCENT AND DISTRIBUTION.

ROBERT KRATOVIL

INHERITANCE TAX, a tax or charge imposed upon the devolution of the property of a deceased person to his heirs or legatees. This is a very old form of taxation. While a tax on the transfer of property on death was used by the Egyptians and Greeks in classic times, the first true inheritance tax was that imposed in the Roman Empire to raise money for the support of the army. The legal philosophy underlying the tax is that there is no natural right on the part of an heir or legatee to succession to the property of a deceased person; and that since the privilege is conceded and protected by the state, the latter has a constitutional right to declare the terms upon which the estate shall devolve.

Social Theory. From a social point of view, there are conflicting theories, such as that inheritance taxation ought not to be so high as to discourage the individual from saving and of setting aside something for the support of those naturally dependent upon him, that is to say, his wife and children; and on the other hand, that it is neither ethically fair nor socially expedient for individuals to be provided with an income derived from the earnings of others. The inheritance tax has often been regarded as a means for breaking down family fortunes and leveling social inequalities. As such it was one of the principal reform planks of the St. Simonian socialists whose guiding principle was equality of opportunity; but other socialist schools, particularly the Marxians, have regarded inheritance taxation as of small consequence. Most statutes make a distinction between direct, or lineal, and collateral heirs. Where the property goes to direct heirs, a certain amount is generally exempt, so that no hardship may result to those who have been dependent upon the deceased for support; and upon the surplus over this amount the rate is usually less than if the property devolved upon collateral heirs. Inheritance taxes are now in force in practically all the countries of Europe, in Great Britain and her colonies, and in the United States.

Federal Law. In the United States, estate or inheritance taxation was made a part of the General Revenue Act, effective Sept. 8, 1916, and has since remained a permanent source of Federal revenue. While there had been revisions in the rate since 1916, the principle of the law up to 1948 remained as follows: the tax was imposed upon the net estate —i.e., the gross estate less deductions for the expenses of administration, debts, and losses—of every decedent whether a resident or a nonresident of the United States. Gifts made "in contemplation of death" were taxed as part of the inheritance, and any gift made within two years of death was presumed to have been intended as in anticipation of death. In addition to the deductions already mentioned, there was an exemption of $60,000 in all cases except for estates of nonresidents. The rates were progressive from 5 per cent to 30 per cent on the first $140,000 over the exemption, from 30 per cent to 39 per cent on the next $1,000,000, from 42 per cent to 53 per cent on the next $2,000,000, and so on up at increasing rates of tax to 77 per cent on the amount an estate exceeded $12,390,000. As a World War II measure, an additional flat tax rate of 10 per cent was levied.

A fundamental change in the tax was made in 1948 when the community-property principle was applied. This stated, in effect, that one half of an estate already belonged to the surviving wife or husband, and was therefore not subject to tax. After this was deducted from the net estate, the next $60,000 was exempt under former provisions of the law (already referred to). The tax rates, then, beginning at 3 per cent and running as high as 77 per cent were applied to the remaining net estate.

State Inheritance Taxation. Inheritance taxes are imposed in all states. In most of the states all receipts from inheritance taxes are paid directly to the state treasury.

The rates and exemptions provided by various state laws differ widely both with respect to the amount of the estate or inheritance and the grade of relationship between the decedent and the beneficiary. In general, property passing to parents, husband, wife, or direct descendants is subject to partial exemption, the amounts varying from $1,000 to $100,000. The amount most commonly exempted is $10,000.

Smaller exemptions are frequently allowed in the case of inheritances of brothers and sisters, aunts and uncles, and their descendants. Both exemptions and rates of taxation in the case of these classes are commonly graded with reference to the closeness of blood relationship. In most instances the tax rate increases with the value of the estate, but nowhere does the highest rate equal that in the schedules of the Federal government.

In most of the states property left by an individual for charitable, educational, religious, historical, or municipal purposes is totally exempt from taxation. In Utah, property left to organizations in this class is exempt from tax up to $10,000, which is an ordinary amount. In general, the state inheritance taxes are more lenient than the Federal estate tax.

The most acute problem of inheritance taxation has been that of multiple taxation of the same property by different states in consequence of varying rules of situs. Situs of real estate is ordinarily assignable to the state in which the property is located, but in the case of personal property, varying rules of situs including domicile of the decedent, domicile of the corporation, location of the securities and of the property represented by the securities, make it possible for the same property to be taxed by different states.

A tangible step in the direction of relieving the consequences of multiple taxation was the Federal Estate Tax Act of 1926, authorizing deduction from Federal taxes of all state inheritance taxes paid, up to 80 per cent, of the Federal tax payable. See TAXATION.   B. NOSKIN

BIBLIOG.–R. E. Paul, *Federal Estate and Gift Taxation*, (1942); R. H. Montgomery and J. O. Wynn, *Federal Taxes on Estates, Trusts and Gifts* (3 vols. 1944–46); E. N. Polisher, *Estate Planning and Estate Tax Saving* (ed. 1948); W. J. Bowe, *Tax Planning for Estates* (1949); Prentice-Hall, Inc., *How The Tax Law Affects Your Will and Estate Plans* (1949); W. C. Warren, and S. S. Surrey, *Federal Estate and Gift Taxation* (1950); K. McFarlane, *Death Duties* (ed. 1950).

INHIBITION. The term inhibition as used in psychology refers to the unconscious blocking of incompatible impulses and painful memories which are highly emotional. These inhibited impulses and memories although banished from consciousness continue to be active in the unconscious, and find expression indirectly in slips of the tongue, dreams, hypnotic states, and other devious ways.

INIA, (*Inia geoffrensis*), a toothed fresh-water cetacean, not unlike a dolphin. It is found in some of the upper tributaries of the Amazon, and in the lakes near the Cordilleras. It measures about 8 feet in length, has a long cylindrical snout with stiff hairs and a very slight dorsal fin.

INISFAIL, ancient poetic name for Ireland, alluding to the LIA FAIL. Inis is the Gaelic word for island.

INITIATIVE, REFERENDUM, AND RECALL. Among the political reforms advocated during the Progressive movement in the United States, 1900–1914, were the initiative, the referendum, and the recall. The purpose was to bring political control closer to the people and to make government more responsive to the popular will. Although all three methods of controlling legislation and public officials go back to the Greek city states, and have been practiced in Switzerland for 500 years, they are essentially a 20th century development in the United States, at least as far as ordinary lawmaking is concerned.

Initiative. The initiative is a political device by which the people can enact directly new laws or repeal old laws. As usually practiced it requires several steps. A citizen or a group of citizens draws up a proposed law. A specified number of legally qualified voters must then sign a petition requesting a vote on the law proposed. The number is usually expressed as a per cent of the registered voters, varying from 3 to 25 per cent. After the petition has the required number of signatures, it is filed with an official, who in some states must immediately arrange for a popular vote on the question. In other states the legislature is required at this point to vote on the proposed law and it is not submitted to popular balloting unless the legislature defeats the bill. In the states requiring legislative action a second petition with a larger number of signers is required in some instances to bring the legislative-defeated bill before the people. In any case, if the bill goes before the people and secures a majority vote it becomes a law without further legislative action and the governor is not permitted to veto it.

The Greek city states used a system of initiative and both the Swiss cantons and the Swiss federal government permits its use. The German republican constitution of 1919 provided for this method of law enactment. Since 1777, certain American states have made use of the initiative to inaugurate constitutional changes. It was also used at times in specific fields of lawmaking. But the first use of the initiative for general lawmaking was provided for in South Dakota in 1898. Eight states adopted this device in the next 10 years and 11 others followed by 1918. Since that date there have been no additions to the 20 states permitting its use. Even where permitted, the initiative is not excessively used. The average seems to be about one popularly initiated law appearing on the ballot every two years. Of those proposed about one-third are adopted. The initiative is also used in many cities, often in states where there is no provision for its state-wide use.

Referendum. The referendum is a democratic check on legislative action. More common than the initiative it is frequently adopted independently and is almost always provided for when the initiative is adopted. There are two types: the optional and the obligatory. The American states have always felt that they had the right to submit questions to popular balloting and have made use of this optional referendum from time to time. But the obligatory referendum was adopted during the period of initiative popularity and was usually a companion to it. Varying somewhat in procedure, the people are given the right to petition that a law passed by the legislature be submitted to popular vote. If a sufficient number of qualified voters sign the petition the question must be submitted at the next election, or at a special election. The popular vote determines whether the legislative act shall be valid or void. In some cases the law is suspended between the time the petition is filed and the vote is cast, but even in such instances certain types of laws are made not subject to suspension.

Those non-American governments which make use of initiative also have adopted the referendum. As far as American constitutional history is concerned, ratification of constitutions and of constitutional amendments is essentially a referendum operation and has been used since the Revolutionary period. State legislatures in the 19th century used the optional referendum to permit counties to choose their county seats, to permit districts to determine liquor laws, and for other special purposes. The mandatory referendum was likewise required in some states during the nineteenth century on specific subjects, such as the sale of state-owned lands. But the popularly controlled, mandatory, general referendum came into operation in South Dakota in 1898. All the states adopting the initiative, and in addition Maryland and New Mexico, have provided for the general referendum. It has also been adopted for use in several hundred local governments, many of these in states which do not authorize its use in state legislation. A study of referendum elections shows that the legislative acts referred to the people have been revoked about 65 per cent of the time.

Recall. Usually associated with the initiative and the referendum is the recall by which elected, and less frequently appointed, officials may be removed from office by popular vote before the expiration of their term. First adopted by Los Angeles in 1903, it is a legal device in several hundred American cities. Only 12 states, beginning with Oregon in 1908, have authorized its use. No state has adopted it since 1926. Four of the twelve do not make judges subject to recall. In a few states the recall has been enlarged to provide for the submission of judicial decisions to popular referendum.

The procedure for recalling public officials is similar to that of the initiative and the referendum. A petition must be signed by a specific per cent of the qualified voters. This varies from 10 per cent to 35 per cent in the 12 states. When such a petition has been signed an election must be held, usually within 40 days. In this election the voters have the opportunity of voting the official out of office. If they so vote by either a majority of the votes cast in that election or by a total equal to the number which elected him, another election is held to determine his successor. In some cases these two elections are combined, and the voters actually cast their ballots for the incumbent or for some other candidate for the office. In order to insure a public officer the opportunity to prove his fitness the law usually provides that no recall election may take place for six months after inauguration. Also only one recall attempt may be made during a term.

Only twice—in North Dakota in 1921 and in Oregon in 1922—have state officials been recalled. Most of the local officials who have been recalled are Californians. Actually the confusion usually found in elections befogs recall actions, and the difficulty of making an honest appraisal of the complex functioning of a public office has largely defeated the practical operation of the recall.

Results of Direct Legislation. During the 1900–1914 reform movement there was much hope that the initiative, referendum, and recall would correct much of the abuse and political corruption found in state government. It was argued that the legislature would be checked by the people and that these devices were a means for greater democratic government. Today these hopes have been somewhat dimmed by the observation of popular legislation in practice. Use of these devices have tended to lessen legislative responsibility, and special groups have a favorable opportunity of securing a vote on legislation affecting their special interests. Furthermore, at a time when the short ballot is being urged to reduce the complexity of elections, the initiative and referendum is a movement in the opposite direction. In summary, most political scientists would agree that the initiative, referendum, and recall are not panaceas but are political devices that may or may not serve the public, as the public determines.

FRANK L. ESTERQUEST

BIBLIOG.–C. A. Beard and B. E. Schulty, *Documents on the State-Wide Initiative, Referendum and Recall* (1912); E. P. Oberholtzer, *Referendum in America* (1912); W. B. Munro, *The Initiative, Referendum and Recall* (1912); J. S. L. Strachey, *The Referendum* (1924); B. V. Hubbard, *Making America Safe for Democracy* (1926); J. M. Turner and E. E. White, *Initiative and Referendum* (1924); V. O. Key and W. W. Crouch, *Initiative and Referendum in California* (1939); J. K. Pollock, *Initiative and Referendum in Michigan* (1940).

INJECTION. The invention of the hollow needle syringe in 1853 by Alexander Wood and Charles Gabriel Pravaz was a great advance for pharmacotherapy, making possible the use of many drugs and biologicals that are ineffective or irritating when taken by mouth. With this instrument fluids can be introduced into various tissues and cavities of the body. Injection in this way into the skin is called *intracutaneous*, or *intradermal;* allergens and vaccines are administered in this way. Injection beneath the skin is called *subcutaneous*, or *hypodermic;* water-soluble nonirritant drugs and biologicals, such as local anesthetics and insulin, are given in this way. Injection into muscle is called *intramuscular;* this method is employed when more rapid effects of water-soluble drugs are desired, and is used for irritant water-soluble drugs, for suspensions, for oil-soluble drugs, and for biologicals. Injection directly into a vein is called *intravenous;* blood and plasma are given in this way, as are some water-soluble drugs when a rapid action is desired. *Intra-arterial* injection of blood or plasma is often practiced in cases of profound shock, or when the heart has stopped beating. *Parenteral* administration of a drug means administration by some route other than the digestive tract, and includes all methods of injection.

INJUNCTION, a writ or order of a court of equity either forbidding an act or ordering that an act be done.

Jurisdiction. For many years, the granting of an injunction was the special prerogative of the chancery courts of England and the courts of equity jurisdiction in the United States. During the last century this power has been granted by statute to many common law courts in England and the United States.

Classes of Relief. There are three general classes of injunctions; temporary restraining orders, temporary injunctions and permanent injunctions. A *temporary restraining order (ad interim)* may issue upon the filing of a bill, without notice to the opposing party or giving him opportunity to be heard, on the ground that irreparable damage would result before a hearing could be had. Its sole object is to preserve the status quo until the merits can be heard. A *temporary injunction (pendente lite)* may issue after notice to the opposing party and some opportunity to be heard. The hearing is full enough to enable the judge to determine the probabilities and the court's discretion is very broad and seldom interfered with. In the case of both the temporary restraining order and the temporary injunction, the court may require that security be given by the person seeking relief to cover possible damage if the injunctive relief was not warranted. A *permanent injunction*, sometimes called a *final* or *perpetual* injunction, may issue after notice to the opposing party and a full opportunity to be heard. It is a final decision of the merits of the case and it will not be granted when the plaintiff's rights are in doubt or there are disputed questions of fact or law.

Enforcement. An injunction is usually directed at a specific person or at specific persons, but it may also be directed at all persons; and to be subject to its terms it need only appear that one has had actual knowledge of it. In the event of the violation of an injunction the court may punish the person violating the order of the court by holding him to be in contempt of court. An injunction may restrain actions outside the jurisdiction of the court if the person enjoined was within the jurisdiction of the court. An injunction will not usually be modified or dissolved except by the court which issued it. It is a protection

for the future and not a punishment for past transactions. It must protect a present right and cannot be used to allay fears and apprehensions, and it must be based on a reasonable probability that acts will occur. However, threats are not a condition precedent to relief.

INJUNCTIONS IN LABOR DISPUTES

History. First known use of the injunction in a labor dispute was made by a British court in 1868. Since that time, however, it has rarely been used outside the United States and has become a distinctly American institution. Although labor injunctions were issued by courts in several states during the 1880's, such a writ was first issued by a Federal court in 1891 and did not come into frequent use until after its employment in the famous Pullman strike of 1894, when an injunction was issued by a Federal court on the initiative of the Justice Department. From that time until the 1930's the labor injunction was used with increasing frequency, and the power of the courts was invoked in most of the important strikes.

Although used occasionally by labor against the employer, the labor injunction has in general been a weapon of management against labor and the labor union. In 1908 the Supreme Court in the Danbury Hatters Case established that trade unions were within the scope of the Sherman Antitrust Act, thus supporting a position which had previously been taken by lower Federal courts and sanctioning the use of the injunction in cases of labor violation of the Sherman law. Through the Hitchman Case of 1917, the so-called "yellow dog" or individual antiunion contracts, in which the employee agreed not to join a union, were declared by the Supreme Court to be entitled to injunctive protection. Blanket injunctions came into increasing use as the only type of restraining order effective in labor disputes. These writs were directed not only at specific individuals but also at "all persons generally," as in the Northern Pacific Case of 1893, or at "all persons combining and conspiring with them (the defendants), and all other persons whomsoever," as in the Debs Case of 1895.

Legal Basis for Use of the Injunction. In theory the injunction is issued in labor disputes only in extraordinary cases where there is no remedy at law for some threatened damage to property rights or interests, as may occur, for example, through unlawful boycotting or violent picketing. In such instances the employer may file a complaint with the district court requesting an order restraining the actions in question. If protection was needed immediately a temporary restraining order has often been issued without a hearing, remaining in effect until a hearing could be held to determine whether a temporary injunction should be issued. In many instances the temporary restraining order was bypassed and a hearing on a temporary injunction held immediately. Such a hearing involves neither jury nor witnesses, the decision being reached by the judge alone on the basis of affidavits. The temporary injunction, in turn, is intended only to control the parties until a full hearing is held. In most labor cases, however, settlement is made before the full hearing stage is reached and the permanent injunction rarely used. Violation of the injunctive order constitutes contempt of court.

Labor's Arguments Against the Injunction. Labor has constantly opposed the injunction as a handicap to the organized labor movement and as a strike-breaking agency. Actually the injunction has been more effective in hindering union efforts to organize workers under nonunion contracts than in defeating STRIKES and BOYCOTTS. One of the arguments most frequently used by labor against the injunction is that it has deprived the accused of constitutional rights of jury trial by trying as contempt cases, heard by the judge alone, criminal cases which require trial by jury. Labor has also argued that the injunction has restrained lawful as well as unlawful actions.

Labor has also objected that the injunction has placed too much emphasis on the right to do business and that in the majority of cases injunctions were issued not to protect tangible property but rather to prevent business from being interfered with. The main difficulty has probably been in the law and in the procedure of using the injunction rather than in the injunction as an instrument in itself. But its use created hostility toward the courts and the injunction was consistently one of labor's chief legislative issues from the 1890's to the 1930's.

Controlling Legislation. Increasing agitation by labor led to the passage in 1914 of the Clayton Act, designed to control the granting of temporary restraining orders, improve the practice in issuing injuctions, and limit contempt penalties. Organized labor expected the Clayton Act to liberalize Federal law as to what it might do, but court interpretation soon proved that only the parts of the Act relating to jury trial in contempt proceedings and to promptitude of hearings were really of value.

The Norris-LaGuardia Act, passed in 1932, was designed to change the substantive law as enforced by equity proceedings in Federal courts, to regulate the granting of restraining orders, and to provide for trial by jury in contempt cases. A broad definition was given to the term "labor dispute" and this, combined with the strict procedural requirements, made it impossible for many labor injunctions to be issued by Federal courts. The "yellow-dog" contract was made unenforceable, payment of strike benefits, picketing, and peaceable assembly were protected, and the blanket injunction could be issued only "against the person or persons, association, or organization making the threat or committing the unlawful act or actually authorizing or ratifying the same." Procedure in issuing restraining orders and injunctions was made stricter and the right of trial by jury greatly extended. Restraining orders were to be effective for only five days, and injunctions could be granted only after a hearing with witnesses and upon the determination of strict factual requirements. The Norris-LaGuardia Act was followed by the passage of many state anti-injunction acts directly modeled upon its provisions, and some of the states went even further in curbing the use of the labor injunction.

Relevant Provisions of the Taft-Hartley Act. The provisions of the Norris-LaGuardia Act were modified, however, under the Federal Labor Management Relations Act (Taft-Hartley Act) of 1947, in which provision was made for the issuance of temporary restraining orders or injunctions in the event of unfair labor practices or work stoppages.

See Equity; Labor Union; Labor Movement; Sherman Antitrust Act; Clayton Antitrust Act; Pullman Strike.   C. F.

Bibliog.–Felix Frankfurter and Nathan Greene, *The Labor Injunction* (1930); Edwin Witte, *The Government in Labor Disputes* (1932); Cleon Swayzee, *Contempt of Court in Labor Injunction Cases* (1935); Harry A. Millis and Royal E. Montgomery, *Organized Labor* (1945).

INJURY. See First Aid; Fracture; Dislocation; Bleeding; Burn; Blast Injuries; Head Injury; Wound; Shock.

INJURY, LEGAL. A legal injury is a wrong affecting the right of a person in respect to his person, his property or his reputation, or a breach or violation of rights or duties affecting the whole community. The former are called civil injuries and may be the basis for the recovery of compensation. The latter are called public injuries and may be crimes, misdemeanors, nuisances, etc. Civil and public injuries may overlap and there may be recovery for civil injury and prosecution for public injury arising from the same act. See Contract; Tort; Master and Servant; Crime; Misdemeanor; Nuisance.

INK, a fluid or pasty substance which leaves a wholly or partially indelible impression when applied to a suitable surface. The identity of the inventor of writing ink is unknown. The first writings were characters either cut in stone tablets or marked in damp clay with a stylus and later baked in kilns, as the Assyrians and Babylonians formed their cuneiform blocks. As nations and trade expanded the need arose for writing materials more portable and convenient than brick or stone. Papyrus sheets, first made about 2500 b.c. or before, were probably the first substitutes. The nature of the early inks used on papyrus is uncertain; probably the pigment was soot or iron oxide suspended in a varnish in which a drying oil was the principal ingredient (see Oils). In any case it is certain that the pigments used have retained their colors over a span of almost 5,000 years. An old ink recipe dating from the beginning of the Christian Era called for one part of bluestone (copper sulfate), one part of hoof glue and 16 parts of soot, to be ground with water by the purchaser as needed. It was also prescribed for cases of burns and baldness. The development of the modern iron tannate inks came with the invention of printing about a.d. 1400 and from that time to the present they have largely displaced the carbon inks for pen use.

Writing Ink. The writing ink industry is old but relatively small and highly competitive. While the exact composition of a commercial writing ink is usually the manufacturer's trade secret, the majority of the black inks are water solutions of ferrous sulfate and tannin (nut gall extract) with a small amount of blue dye to provide initial color intensity. The chemical change which such ink undergoes is more complex than the simple oxidation of colorless ferrous tannate to an insoluble, black, ferric tannate; nevertheless oxidation plays an important part. A solution of oxalic acid which reverses this reaction by reducing the ferric iron to the ferrous state is an effective ink stain remover.

The manufacture of writing ink involves first, careful purification of the water either by distillation or by Ion Exchange in order to forestall secondary color reactions produced by dissolved salts. Other important matters to be considered are the suppression of insoluble sludges, attained by the addition of a mineral acid, and the problem of pen corrosion that the presence of the acid promotes. The pH Values of commercial blue-black inks lie in the range of 1.0 to 3.0 (fairly high acidity). The various ingredients are mixed in tanks ranging in size up to 5,000 gallons. Besides the iron tannate which makes up about 3 per cent of the solution, glycerine may be added to regulate the drying rate and a little phenol to serve as a preservative. The ink is aged for a few days, then filtered; bottling and packaging procedures, which are entirely mechanized, follow the pattern used in other manufacturing processes.

Soluble Inks including most of the colored varieties are mainly solutions of dyes with small additions of gums to give them colloidal stability (see Colloid). Thus, the reds are made with eosin, carmine, or magenta; the blues with Prussian blue and a little oxalic acid, and so on. The common formulary books contain numerous recipes for a wide variety of such writing fluids. Stains made by inks of this type may be removed by the use of a bleaching agent such as sodium hypochlorite.

Indelible Inks are made up according to various chemical principles. Some are colloidal suspensions of insoluble dyes such as indigo or aniline derivatives stabilized by the addition of gums; others are solutions of metallic salts that undergo reduction to the metal in contact with the fabric. Thus, silver nitrate leaves a black stain on reduction to metallic silver by the cloth. A pen mark of gold chloride solution shows a gold streak on contact with paper previously treated with a solution of oxalic acid which serves as the Reducing Agent. Similarly, a platinic chloride mark on paper treated with sodium carbonate develops into an intense purple-red when moistened with stannous chloride solution. The so-called *India, China,* and *Japan* inks are extremely permanent by virtue of the chemical inertness of the carbon black with which they are pigmented. These inks are used extensively by architects, engineers, and others to make permanent drawings. *Typewriter, mimeograph*, and *stamp-pad inks* are made by mixing organic dyes or carbon with glycerin to the desired consistency.

The action of *sympathetic* or *invisible inks* is based on the principle of producing a color reaction on a mark made with a colorless reagent. Thus, starch paste marks assume the familiar starch-blue on contact with iodine vapor, and sodium carbonate writing turns pink with the application of an indicator such as phenolphthalein.

Printing Ink. The properties of a printing ink are governed by the type of printing and the press employed. In general the basic requirements are: (1) uniform consistency with absence of undispersed pigment; (2) a viscosity (rate of flow) suited to the speed of the press and the rate at which it is to be applied to the roller; (3) optimum drying characteristics to prevent smudging or "setting off" on the one hand or the sticking of the paper to the forms on the other; and (4) ease of removal of the ink from the type. Makers of printing ink work from definite formulas based on long experience, which in their fine points are largely secret. The raw materials include boiled linseed oil, with or without driers, rosin and rosin oil, petroleum oils and waxes, soaps, and carbon black. These are mixed and ground in stone mills to complete uniformity. *Lithographic inks* contain a higher percentage of pigments than common printing inks. These pigments are dispersed in high-viscosity varnishes to prevent "bleeding" or spreading.

Intaglio inks, which include those used in steel and copper engraving and in photogravure, dry mainly by evaporation, and so are made up with a large proportion of a volatile solvent such as toluene or xylene with no drying oil of the linseed class. They must have sufficient cohesion to lift readily from the depression of the plate in their transfer to the paper and to dry without lateral spread.

Books and magazines using glossy paper need an ink that dries rapidly on the surface without blurring or spreading. "Driers" such as salts of lead or manganese are incorporated into the linseed oil to accelerate the drying process. A similar ink must be used to prevent the blurring of illustrations. Newspapers use a more absorbent paper, drying occurs more readily, and less drier is used. H. L. OLIN

BIBLIOG.–C. A. Mitchell, *Inks; Their Composition and Manufacture* (1937); C. F. Waters, *Inks*, U.S. Dept. of Commerce Circular C-426 (1940); C. Ellis, *Printing Inks* (1940); G. D. Hiscox, *Henley's Twentieth Century Book of Formulas* (1944); R. S. Casey, *Writing Ink*, Chemical Industries (1946).

INKBERRY, or **WINTERBERRY,** an evergreen shrub of the Holly family, growing from two to four feet high, found along the east coast of North America in sandy soil. It bears shining, lanceolate leaves, clusters of sterile flowers and solitary fertile ones followed by small black berries, from which the name is derived.

INKERMAN, village, U.S.S.R., the Russian Soviet Federated Socialist Republic, in Crimea Region, four miles E of Sevastopol. The Battle of Inkerman in which the Russians were defeated by the British and French armies was fought here on Nov. 5, 1854 (see CRIMEAN WAR). The "rock of Inkerman" near the village is honeycombed with troglodytic dwellings and passages.

INKSTER, village, SE Michigan; on the New York Central Railroad and U.S. Highway 112, about 13 miles W of Detroit. Inkster is a residential village incorporated in 1926 and inhabited largely by industrial workers in the Detroit metropolitan area. Pop. (1950) 16,728.

INKY CAP. See MUSHROOM.

INLAND MARINE. See INSURANCE, *Combination Policies.*

INLAND SEA, Japanese **Setonaikai,** extends NE from the NE shore of Kyushu, between Shikoku and the main Japanese island of Honshu, some 310 miles to Osaka. It has an average width of 20 miles, and is studded with unusually beautiful islands. On the shores of the Inland Sea are the important industrial and commercial towns of Osaka, Kobe, Himeji, Okayama, Moji, Yawata, and also Kure, where the Japanese had one of their three primary naval bases to the end of World War II. The salt-recovery, fishing, shipping, and granite industries are important. Connecting the Inland Sea with the Pacific and the Sea of Japan are three straits that the Japanese had heavily fortified: Kii Channel enters the eastern end of the sea between Honshu and Shikoku, and is about 20 miles wide; Bungo Channel, about 20 miles wide, lies between Kyushu and Shikoku; and two-mile-wide Shimonoseki Strait connects with the Sea of Japan between Kyushu and Honshu. Although the Inland Sea is rarely over 100 feet in depth, it accommodates large ocean vessels and was regarded by Japan, in World War II, as an invulnerable refuge for her fleet, before American planes attacked and sank many Japanese ships there in early 1945. P. W.

INLAND WATERWAYS. See WATERWAYS, INLAND.

INLAYING is a method of ornamenting an object by inserting a panel of foreign material into its surface.

Inlaid Directoire walnut commode of about 1810

The first example of inlay work is thought to be an Egyptian stool, dating from 2000 B.C., which is adorned with ebony and ivory inlays. In the *Odyssey* of Homer, mention is made of inlay work, which indicates its ancient origin. Chinese and Indian craftsmen have long been masters of the art. Inlay is a general term referring to many varieties of decorative work, among them MOSAIC, which is the piecing together of small bits of glass, marble or stone to make a pattern on the surface of an object; *pietra dura*, a variety of mosaic utilizing precious stones; *damascening*, which is the inlaying of iron or steel with gold wire; *niello*, a process of inlaying silver and gold with other metals; and *intarsia*, which is a general term referring to all wood inlaying. The art of inlaying, and particularly a branch of intarsia known as marquetry, was brought to its fullest development in 17th-century France. Jean Mace of Blois was the founder of a family which was to practice this delicate art for 150 years. Particularly adapted to cabinet work, the process used by the Boulles (descendants of Jean Mace) was as follows; a pattern was drawn on paper of the design to be used; a piece of the decorative wood was cut to the design; the surface of the object to be ornamented was chiseled out by wood-carving tools to the desired shape; and, lastly, the inlay piece was driven in with tools designed for this purpose. The pieces to be used in intarsia work varied from ⅛ to ¼ inches thick. Parquetry, another form of intarsia, is inlay work on a wood floor. The materials used for inlay work vary. Ivory and ebony were favorite materials in early times; gems, rare woods, and other materials have since been used. See also CLOISONNÉ.   HELEN STEWART

INMAN, HENRY, 1801–46, American painter, was born in Utica, N.Y. After securing an appointment in the U.S. Military Academy, he paid a visit to the studio of John Wesley Jarvis, and thereupon determined to become an artist. In 1822 he opened a studio of his own, and gained a reputation as a portrait painter. He was one of the founders and the first vice-president of the National Academy of Design. While in England (1844) he completed portraits of Wordsworth, Macaulay, and others. His portrait of William Penn hangs in Independence Hall, Philadelphia. His genre and historical pictures include "The Boyhood of Washington," "Trout Fishing," "Bride of Lammermoor"; his landscapes "Birnam Wood," "Rydal Falls," "England," "An October Afternoon."

INN, the English name for a place where a traveler is furnished with both food and lodging. A restaurant, lodging house, tavern, or boarding house is not an inn. With few exceptions, an innkeeper is required to accept all unobjectionable guests seeking accommodations, who can pay for their entertainment, if he has facilities to do so. For this reason, he has historically always been entitled to a lien upon the baggage and personal effects of his guests for their entertainment. Historically, an innkeeper has also been liable for loss of a guest's property by theft on the premises. However, in the United States, innkeepers' liens and innkeepers' liability are now largely governed by state statutes. See LIEN, *The Possessory Lien;* HOTEL.

INN RIVER, Germany, rises in the Alps, in the Swiss canton of Grisons, flows NE through the Engadine and onward through the Tyrol and Bavaria to its junction with the Danube at Passau. Its length is about 320 miles.

INNER MONGOLIA. See MONGOLIA.

INNESS, GEORGE, 1825–94, American painter, was born in Newburgh, N.Y. His formal schooling ended when, at 16, he went to New York City as an engraver's apprentice. Finding his medium in painting, he soon set up a studio, studying under Régis Gignoux. His earliest work was influenced by the Hudson River Group, an example of this period being "Afternoon," which was exhibited in 1846. Two years in Rome, studying the masters of Renaissance painting, were followed by a year in France. Here he first saw the work of the Barbizon school, whose style influenced him profoundly. Returning to America, he set up a studio in New York City. After his marriage to Elizabeth Hart (1850), he moved to Medfield, Mass. During the years 1859–64 he painted New England landscape, developing his technique and putting into practice his theories of color and light. In 1870 he again sailed for Europe, painting in Italy and France for six years. At this time he became interested in religious philosophy. Always a student of metaphysics, his study of Swedenborg deepened his mystic strain. Alive to the thought of his day, he was an advocate of the Single Tax and interested in the symbolist movement in American poetry. On his return from Europe, he settled in Montclair, N.J. In the late 1870's his work, which before this time was known only to a small group of artists and art lovers, grew more popular, and soon he became the best known landscape artist in America. Though his subject matter remained the New England countryside throughout his life, his technique evolved from a photographic rendering of nature in his earlier years to the harmony of light, air, and color which marked his mature work. Distinctly original in his manner, he took from Corot, Daubigny, and other European

ART INSTITUTE OF CHICAGO
"After a Summer Shower," by George Inness

masters, their artistic ideas rather than their techniques. Always, however, his subject was what he termed the "civilized landscape," as opposed to the dramatic. A member of the National Academy and the Society of American Artists, his paintings "Millpond" and "Rainbow in the Storm" hang in the Chicago Art Institute; "Autumn Oaks" in the Metropolitan Museum in New York; "Gray Lowering Day," "Niagara," and many others in private collections and various museums throughout the country. See AMERICAN PAINTING for illustration.   HELEN STEWART

INNESS, GEORGE, 1854–1926, American painter, was born in Paris, France. Having studied art under his father, GEORGE INNESS, in Rome, and subsequently under Bonnat in Paris, he devoted himself to animal and landscape painting. From 1895 to 1899 he exhibited annually at the Paris salon, and in 1899 was elected to the American National Academy. His works include: "The First Snow at Cragsmoor" and "Shepherd and Sheep" (Metropolitan Museum of Art); "The Ford"; "Monarch of the Herd"; "After the Combat"; "A Mild Day"; "The Coming Storm"; "Morning on the River"; "The Only Hope."

INNKEEPER. See INN.

INNOCENT. See POPE.

INNOCENT I, SAINT, d. 417, pope, was born in Albano, Italy. During his pontificate from 402 to 417, the last martyrdom of a Christian in the Roman amphitheater took place, when the monk, Telemachus, trying to separate the combatants in the arena, angered the mob and was stoned to death. His heroic action ended that barbarism and helped to add greater respect for Innocent's reign. Innocent, zealous for the progress of the church, opposed the Montanists, with the help of Emperor Honorius, quelled the Arian schism at Antioch, and condemned the heretical doctrine of Pelagius.

INNOCENT II, d. 1143, pope, was born in Rome. The choice of the Frangipani faction, he was hastily elected as soon as Pope Honorius II died in 1130 and ruled until his death. The opposing faction, the Pierleone family, seized upon the opportunity created by the technicality that not all of the cardinals had been consulted for the election, called together the slighted cardinals, and chose another man to wear the tiara who took the name of Anacletus II. Again the question arose as to who was the valid pope. The powerfully influential monk, St. Bernard of Clairvaux, gave his support to Innocent, and caused France, England, Castille, Aragon, and Germany to follow. A truce was effected with the Pierleone, but not until 1138 was Innocent completely recognized by everyone. In that year he convoked the Tenth Ecumenical Council, attended by almost a thousand church dignitaries; but nothing of great importance was decided. A quarrel began, concerning whose right it was to choose and invest bishops, between the pope and Louis VII, and resulted in Innocent's placing all the regions of France, which would be visited by the king, under interdict.   R. M. LEONARD

INNOCENT III, c. 1160–1216, pope, was born in Anagni, Italy. He was only 36, the son of a Roman noble, when he was elected in 1198. He was also the nephew of Pope Clement III, had received his education in Paris, Rome, and Bologna, and had already written a book, *On the Contempt of the World.* Capable, clever, and energetic, he soon was the actual ruler of Italy. His lofty ideals made the power of the church and the dignity of the papacy felt throughout Europe. In the disagreement concerning who had proper claim to rule Germany, Otto of Brunswick or Duke Philip of Swabia, the Pope supported Otto and crowned him emperor of the Holy Roman Empire. When Otto adopted antipapal policies, Innocent immediately excommunicated him. When Philip Augustus of France and Alphonse IV of Leon refused to follow the marriage laws of the church, he placed their kingdoms under the penalty of interdict, until they conformed. England was also put under the ban and King JOHN was excommunicated for plotting against the appointment of a cardinal. In the selection of rulers for Norway, Hungary, and Poland, Innocent was chosen as the arbitrator. The Moors of Spain were defeated by a crusade which the pope inaugurated through uniting the kings of Navarre, Castille, and Aragon. However, a fourth CRUSADE to the Holy Land was unsuccessful, and Constantinople was captured contrary to the pope's wishes. He tried to quiet the Albigenses by sending missionaries to them; but when they persisted in heresy he organized a crusade against them. In 1215 the Fourth Ecumenical Council of the Lateran was convoked by Innocent. Attended by almost 1,400 prelates, the Council pronounced the famous obligation for church members of annual confession and communion, and defined the doctrine of TRANSUBSTANTIATION in the Eucharist. Although his government in church affairs had far-reaching effects, even these were overshadowed by his great political achievements. See OTTO I.   R. M. LEONARD

INNOCENT IV, d. 1254, pope, was born in Genoa, Italy. Trouble brewed between the pope and Emperor Frederick II almost immediately after Innocent's election in 1243. He was forced to flee Rome and escaped to Genoa. At Lyons a General Council was convened by Innocent, which excommunicated Frederick and inaugurated the Sixth CRUSADE to the Holy Land. The campaign lasted six years, but suffered defeat. In the meantime, Innocent carried on his battle against Frederick, which ended when the emperor died in 1250, after making his peace with the church. Innocent's courageous pontificate did much to build the strength of the church against the anarchy that threatened it. See FREDERICK II.

INNOCENT XI, 1611–89, pope, was born in Como, Italy. From the very beginning of his pontificate in 1676 until its close, the pope and LOUIS XIV of France were in violent disagreement. The pope refused to be intimidated by the king. When Louis assembled the French clergy to define church rights in France, the result was the "Declaration of the French Clergy," which stated that ecclesiastical power had no jurisdiction over kings and princes in things temporal, and that any decision of the pope needed the approval of the church before it became final. Innocent quickly retaliated by condemning the group and its definitions, and denied canonical investure to ecclesiastics who followed those views, resulting in 36 bishoprics in France becoming vacant since they were devoid of ecclesiastical jurisdiction. The French king reacted by having his soldiers seize the territory of Avignon from the papacy. Louis's persecution of the Protestants in France grew, and Innocent sought help from the English king, James II, on their behalf. The pope remained adamant, however, in matters of faith. The Jesuits in France, who were fighting the teachings of the Jansenists, were leaning to the new school of flexible theology called "Casuistry," which tried to teach moral principles through practical cases. A series of writings from these moral theologians was condemned by the pope, which the Jansenists loudly hailed as a moral victory, and this action brought suspicion for some time upon the pope as being Jansenistic. Pursuing his policy of reform, Innocent reduced taxes, condemned immodesty in dress, censured laxity in moral theology, and disapproved the imprudent measures adopted by James II in restoring Catholicism to England.
          R. M. LEONARD

INNOCENT XII, 1615–1700, pope, was born in Spinazzolo, Italy. Before his election he had been governor of Perugia, nuncio to Poland and Vienna, bishop of Faenza, archbishop of Naples, and a cardinal. Immediately after his election in 1691 he issued the bull *Romanum decet Pontificem,* directed against the church abuse of nepotism and simony. The bull placed great limitations on all future popes in the appointments of relatives to any offices under papal patronage. Insuring it permanency, Innocent instituted an obligatory declaration of it under oath for all future popes. From Louis XIV of France he won a repeal of the "Declaration of the French Clergy," which was supplanted by an edict in accord with canon law. By advising Charles I of Spain to establish the French prince, Philip of Anjou, as his heir to the Spanish territories, Innocent inadvertently brought on the terrible War of the Spanish Succession after his death. His own pontificate, however, closed in glory with the institution of the year 1700 as the Holy Year of Jubilee which brought huge crowds to the papal states on pilgrimage to receive the aging pope's blessing.   R. M. LEONARD

INNS OF COURT are the noncorporate law societies of England and are located in London. The four principal *Inns* are Inner Temple, Middle Temple, Lincoln's Inn, and Grey's Inn. The term sometimes also includes the two *Serjeant's Inns* and the nine *Inns of Chancery,* which are connected with the four principal Inns. The origin of the Inns of Court is lost in antiquity and their present importance is much less than their former greatness. After the clergy was forbidden by law to appear as advocate in the secular courts and to lecture on law outside the monasteries, the Inns grew up as a part of the GUILD system in which the candidate for admission to the bar became a member of the household of some duly qualified master and satisfied his master as to his qualifications for admission. In the later MIDDLE AGES, the Inns of Court became the great schools of law of England. The legal instruction furnished by the universities has generally been theoretical and academic. (See FEUDAL SOCIETY.) The Inns are self-governing and distinct from each other. Each one is governed by a board of "benchers" or "parliament" composed of senior counsel or king's counsel appointed to office by the then existing board. Lectures are delivered by experienced members of the Inn who also conduct the examinations. Attendance at lectures is assured by requiring that the candidate eat a prescribed minimum number of meals at the Inn. The four principal Inns of Court have the exclusive privilege of admitting persons to practice at the bar and may accept or reject candidates in their discretion, for no member of the public has an absolute right to be called to the bar. Each Inn has the power to disbar one of its members for misconduct and there is no appeal from its decision. The Inns own extensive buildings which have been constructed over a period of several centuries and follow no definite architectural design or plan, but include some features of interest and beauty. A valuable source of revenue is the rental of "chambers" to members of the bar, thereby centralizing the location of the offices of barristers in the several Inns of Court.   E. N.

INNSBRUCK, town, Austria, capital of the province of Tyrol, in the Inn Valley at the foot of the Alps, on the railway and highway leading to the

A little country church in the Innsbruck region

Brenner Pass, 19 miles S. The town is situated at a height of 1,800 feet, nearly surrounded by mountains, and is much visited by tourists. The old town's narrow streets, tall houses with dormer windows, and the old inns are unchanged, while the new town has modern buildings and wide streets. Chief of these is the broad Maria-Theresen Strasse, with a triumphal arch at its southern end commemorating the marriage of Leopold II, Maria Theresa's son, to Maria Ludovica of Spain. The street continues as Friedrich Strasse through the old town. Among its notable buildings are the Royal Palace (1766–70); the Hofkirche, a Franciscan church (16th century) containing a colossal monument to the memory of the Emperor Maximilian I, and the tomb of Andreas Hofer, Tyrolese patriot; the Ferdinandeum, a museum of Tyrolese art; and the university (founded 1672). Leopold's Fountain (1893) and the statue of Hofer, on the height of Berg Isel outside the town, are of interest. Innsbruck's manufactures include woolen cloth, glass, and machinery. Pop. (1948 est.) 97,221.

INOCULATION. See VACCINES AND SERUMS; IMMUNITY AND RESISTANCE TO DISEASE; COMMUNICABLE DISEASES.

INÖNÜ, ISMET, 1884–　　　, Turkish statesman and soldier, born in Smyrna. He received his training in military schools, and became a captain of the general staff in 1906. During World War I he served on the Syrian front, and during the Allied occupation of Constantinople he became chief of staff. In 1922 as commander in chief of the Turkish army on the western front, he signed the Armistice with the Allies. He was prime minister for 12 years under President Kemal Atatürk and upon the death of the "Strong Man of Turkey" in 1938, Inönü became president of Turkey. He remained in this post until 1950 when he was defeated by Celâl Bayar in the first free election in the history of the country. Inönü supported the Allies in World War II.

INOSITOL, one of the several compounds comprising VITAMIN B.

INOWROCLAW, German **Hohensalva,** town, Poland, the province of Pomorze, 25 miles by rail SW of Torum (Thorn). It has a 13th-century romanesque church, salt-water baths, and salt works. The town's manufactures include machinery, iron products, chemicals, and flour. There is trade in grain and livestock. Inowroclaw is first mentioned in 1185, was chartered as a town in 1267, and fell to Prussia in 1772. It became Polish in 1919 under the provisions of the Treaty of Versailles. During World War II Inowroclaw was occupied by the Germans. Pop. (1946) 35,808.

INQUEST, an inquiry into the facts of a case, usually by a jury appointed for that purpose. The finding of the jury is occasionally called an inquest. The term sometimes refers to the jury itself. A *coroner's inquest* inquires into the manner of death of one who has been slain or dies suddenly, dies under unusual circumstances, or dies in prison. An inquest may be used in a judicial proceeding to ascertain the amount of damages when the suit is uncontested. In practice in the New York courts, there is a procedure known as an inquest where the defendant, in a civil action, has not filed an affidavit of merit or verified his answer. An *inquest of office* both in England and in the United States is an inquiry into the possible forfeiture or escheat of lands to the crown or to the state. See CORONER; ESCHEAT.

INQUISITION, a general term for a type of administrative tribunal of the Roman Catholic Church. Also referred to as the Holy Office, its purpose was to investigate the practice of faith and morals of Christians. Apparently first organized early in the 13th century, this organ looked upon HERESY as anarchy—a threat to the welfare of state and church alike. Drawn chiefly from the Dominican Order, the "inquisitors" were appointed by the pope. These men were sent into districts where heretics were considered most notorious. A month of grace was given to violators in which time they must rectify their beliefs and practices. Those persisting in heresy were then summoned before the inquisitors, given trial, and sentenced. At first the heresy-hunters were lenient. Then abuses began to creep in.. Tortures were adopted, the property of heretics was confiscated and usurped by the inquisitors for their own or church use, and burning at the stake was incorporated as penalty for the obstinate. Since heretics were considered to be undermining the government itself, those sentenced were delivered to the civil authority for proper punishment. Condemnations of severe practices came repeatedly from the papacy, but abuses continued.

The most notorious point of the inquisition was reached in Spain. Organized there by the king and queen, appointments of inquisitors and direction of their courts was under the civil government. Even though the Holy See interfered persistently, the only prerogative it was permitted was that of appointment over the Inquisitor Generalship. The Spanish Inquisition was mainly directed against the converts from Islamism and Judaism. The name most frequently associated with the inquisition in Spain is that of TORQUEMADA.

The Holy Office, or the Congregation of the Holy Roman and Universal Inquisition, exists in the administrations of the papacy today. Its functions, however, are far more limited, and it is entirely devoid of earlier abuses connected with the Inquisition. Its main duty is to defend the purity of faith and morals. Besides the cases directly applying to these matters brought before it, this office also has charge of the Catholic INDEX, which investigates and condemns books considered injurious to, or erroneous in, Catholic faith and morals.

INSANITY, now regarded as strictly a legal term, formerly applied to all serious mental disorders or psychoses. (See PSYCHOSIS.) It covers two concepts: the traditional so-called "right and wrong test" and the more liberal concept involved in the so-called "irresistible impulse" test. The first test assumes that a person without an appreciation of the rightness or wrongness of an act cannot have a criminal mind or formulate a criminal intent. The second test assumes that, if a person, because of mental illness, is deprived of the power of choice or of volition, he does not possess the mental attitude and freedom of action essential to criminal responsibility. Note that the standard is not limited to a determination of the existence of "insanity," which is popularly used to denote the existence of a psychosis, but also covers every type of mental illness, including neurosis, when such illness results in involuntary behavior. (See PSYCHONEUROSIS.) The ultimate mental and criminal accountability of an accused person must be made by a court composed of laymen whose attention must be centered upon the difficult, factual problem of answering the two following all-important questions.

The first question is: Was the accused person at the time of the alleged offense "so far free from mental defect, disease or derangement, as to be able to distinguish right from wrong concerning the particular act involved?" The "right and wrong" test is the sole criterion of criminal responsibility in 29 states. These are: Arizona, California, Florida, Georgia, Idaho, Iowa, Kansas, Maine, Maryland, Minnesota, Mississippi, Missouri, Nebraska, Nevada, New Jersey, New York, North Carolina, North Dakota, Oklahoma, Oregon, Pennsylvania, South Carolina, South Dakota, Tennessee, Texas, Utah, Washington, West Virginia, and Wisconsin. In 17 other states, it is one of the rules followed.

The second question is: Was the accused at the time of the alleged offense "so far free from mental defect, disease, or derangement as to be able concerning the particular act charged to adhere to the right?" This is recognized in seventeen states as the "irresistible impulse" test. These states are: Alabama, Arkansas, Colorado, Connecticut, Delaware, Illinois, Indiana, Kentucky, Louisiana, Massachusetts, Michigan, Montana, New Mexico, Ohio, Vermont, Virginia, and Wyoming.

If either of the answers is in the negative, the accused should be found not guilty by reason of mental defect, disease, or derangement.

Some states accept the "mistake of fact" test. According to this rule, an accused person suffering from insane delusions must be judged by the supposed facts presented by the delusion.   A. A. SHARP

CIVIL RESPONSIBILITY

In England the early common law subjected an insane person to civil responsibility for both his contractual and tortious acts. In America, the law has manifested greater solicitude for the insane in the field of contract, albeit not in tort.

Contracts. A basic requirement for the creation of a contract is the participation of persons having legal capacity to contract. American courts have consistently ruled that one incapable of understanding the effect and force of a contract does not possess such capacity and hence is not responsible on the contract. In some jurisdictions, the fact that a litigant has been adjudged insane is accepted as conclusively demonstrating his contractual disability. In others, the adjudication is regarded as establishing a rebuttable presumption of incapacity. In all, the inability of a litigant to understand his contractual undertaking because of insanity may be proved as a defense.

Although the rule that an insane person does not have the capacity to contract should logically lead to the conclusion that his efforts to enter into a contract are utterly unavailing, preponderant judicial authority regards his contract as merely voidable, and gives him (or one acting for him) the option of avoiding or enforcing the contract.

The insane individual is not relieved from complete responsibility for the consequence of his contractual excursions. While he will not be liable on the contract, as such, he may be held accountable on a "contract implied in law" to the extent of benefits actually received. Thus, if an insane person contracts to, and does, receive necessary services or benefits, he will be called upon to pay for them—not because of his efforts to contract for them, but because the law imposes upon him an obligation to pay. The measure of recovery is not the contract price but the reasonable value of the benefits conferred or services rendered.

Torts. The tort responsibility of an insane person is not affected by his criminal or contractual irresponsibility. Common law jurisdictions, in contrast to civil law states, are prone to hold insane persons responsible for all torts, except those which require a wrongful intent. If the tort consists of both act and intent, the mental infirmities of an insane person are said to preclude his exercising the necessary intent. Consequently, an insane person may be held responsible for assault and battery, which require no specific intent, but he would not be responsible for libel and slander, which do require proof of intent. When a tort judgment is entered against an insane person, a more clement rule of damages will be applied: the successful plaintiff will be limited to compensatory damages; exemplary damages will be denied.

Procedure. Persons are presumed to be sane. When a litigant files suit he is under no obligation to establish the sanity of the defendant. However, if in the course of the proceedings it appears that the defendant is insane, the court will protect his interests by appropriate action, such as the appointment of a guardian *ad litem* or attorney to represent him. A. B. TETON

BIBLIOG.—F. A. Moss, *Your Mind in Action* (1929); P. M. Lichtenstein, *A Doctor Studies Crime* (1934); A. Deutsch, *The Mentally Ill in America* (1937); E. Mortenson, *You Be the Judge* (1940).

INSECTS ❖ Rivals of Man

Three fourths to five sixths of all known kinds of animal life are insects

INSECT, an animal belonging to the class Insecta, or Hexapoda, of the phylum Arthropoda, the largest class of organisms known. So many species of insects have been described in so many different publications over the past 180 years that no accurate figure is available; three recent estimates place the number of known species at 1,500,000, 640,000, and 750,000. It is certain, however, that insects compose from three-fourths to five-sixths of all known kinds of animals. No one can say how many kinds of insects exist today, unknown to science, but they are being described at the rate of about 5,000 to 6,000 species a year.

Insects are notable not only for diversity of species but for the size of their populations. Depending upon the kinds of soils, it is estimated that there are from 1,000,000 to 50,000,000 insects per acre of land. As many as 24,000 aphids, or plant lice, have been taken from a single tomato plant. Insects are numerous in the leaf mold of the forest floor; for example, from 500 to 5,000 minute individuals per kilogram of mold or topsoil can be collected. With the advent of spring, insects begin feeding upon almost all kinds of vegetation, upon the roots, stems, foliage, flowers, and fruits. They attack stored grains, and devour packaged food products, such as flour and breakfast cereals. Hides, woolen goods, and many wooden articles are also subject to attack. Many parasitic species attack other organisms, including man and his domesticated animals. Hosts of insects feed upon other insects. In general, as a consequence of their diverse feeding habits, their occupation of so many kinds of habitats, and their great abundance, the economic importance of insects is large.

The injurious aspects of insect life are so obvious, and their control, or attempted control, costs so much, that one is apt to think of insects as wholly undesirable. It is true that they compete with man for his food, and that they transmit a number of dangerous diseases (see section on *Insects in Relation to Disease*). For example, in the United States in 1938, plant losses resulting from insect attack, plus the cost of control measures, amounted to $1,601,527,000.

These two major aspects of the harmful relation of insects to human welfare generally are much better known than the equally important beneficial relations. Of the beneficial insect activities two deserve broad appreciation. First, the great majority of our fruit trees, berry bushes, and garden vegetables are pollinated by insects; this is an essential operation, without which man's food supply eventually would be seriously impaired. The second beneficial relation of insects to man is their role in soil formation. Plant life is dependent upon sunlight and mineralized salts in the soil. These salts are made available by bacteria, from decomposing plant and animal bodies. The numerous earthworms, mites, and insects that live in the litter and soil of prairies and forests chew up, transfer, digest, and aerate dead plant and animal products, and consequently play an important intermediate part in this vital process.

The intelligent approach, then, is to foster the beneficial insects and to eradicate or control the injurious insects. There are countless numbers of beneficial insects, relatively few injurious insects. Of the nearly 1,000,000 species of insects known, about 10,000 species are definitely dangerous. Only about 2,000 species of these are considered highly injurious, and in the United States not more than 600 species are major pests or disease carriers. Research, scientific control measures, and conservation are necessary in our understanding of insect problems.

External Structure. The insect body wall is known as the *exoskeleton*. It protects the animal from excessive dryness, moisture, physical shock, rapid fluctuations in temperature, and certain kinds of disease organisms and parasites, as well as injury from certain predators. It also acts as a framework and supporting mechanism for the soft, internal structures. The exoskeleton is formed by three layers: the *basement membrane*, a very thin, delicate, internal lining that lies against the hypodermis; the *hypodermis*, a layer of rather large cells with prominent nuclei; and the *cuticula*, the external portion of the body wall, which is secreted by the hypodermis. The cuticula is a lifeless layer, consisting of from 20 to 50 per cent chitin, a nitrogen polysaccharide. Due to the deposition of pigments, known as melanins, and other substances, the chitin undergoes a hardening process (sclerotization) to form a tough, dense impermeable layer. The cuticula bears many structures: solid or hollow spines; pits, known as foveae; the external orifices of many glands; receptors or sense organs for sight, sound, taste, and touch; and hairs or setae formed from enlarged hypodermal cells, known as trichogens. The setae of an insect are called, collectively, *pubescence;* most insects are pubescent. The cuticula also forms internal extensions into the body cavity. These internal cuticular ingrowths are known collectively as the *endoskeleton*, and individually as apodemes. The endoskeleton of the head is called the tentorium. Apodemes increase the attachment surface for muscles.

The chitinous body wall is divided into a number of *segments*. From embryological and paleontological evidence, the number of segments is generally thought to be 20 or 21; the segments are, however, subject to fusion, modification, and specialization through evolution and embryological development. In most insects the body is divisible into three major portions, head, thorax, and abdomen. The *head* consists of about six segments, largely fused into the head capsule; the *thorax* is composed of three segments, prothorax, mesothorax, and metathorax; the *abdomen* consists of 10 or 11 segments, but may have only as few as two visible segments. Joining the head and thorax is a membranous region known as the cervicum. The body segments and their associated appendages receive mobility by having the connecting surfaces of the body wall relatively thin and less sclerotized. Such connecting, or articular, membranes are known as conjunctivae. The hardened cuticula of the segments is composed of several separate areas, called sclerites, separated from one another by cuticular grooves, or sutures.

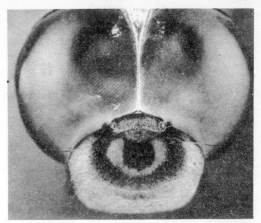

Two huge compound eyes of a dragonfly

Eyes. Compound eyes are present in the adults of most species, one on each side of the head, and are composed of many separate units known as *ommatidia*. Each ommatidium has an external, hexagonal facet, or cornea, formed from the cuticula. Beneath the cornea are two hypodermal cells, which in certain species may be greatly reduced. Next to the corneal hypodermis are, as a rule, four elongate crystalline cone cells, or a body known as the crystalline cone; at the base of the cone, or cone cells, are several visual cells, forming a retinula and an elongated rhabdom. From the basal ends of the visual cells, delicate retinal nerve fibers pass through the basement membrane to form, collectively, the optic tract. Surrounding the cone cells and visual cells are iris pigment cells.

The theory that insects have *mosaic vision* was proposed by J. Müller in 1826. Mosaic vision is considered to be well adjusted for the perception of moving objects. In this type of vision only the light that falls on the crystalline cone reaches the visual cells, and other light rays are absorbed by the iris pigment. Since each ommatidium receives light from a very limited field of vision, the numerous rhabdoms contribute a mosaic of the object seen on the combined retinal cells. This produces a single, erect image. The distinctness of the object seen increases with the number of ommatidia. Many cave-dwelling, parasitic, or deep-soil inhabiting species have no compound eyes or have the facets reduced to one facet or a few facets. At the other extreme are the dragonflies, with as many as 28,000 facets in each eye.

Simple eyes, or *ocelli*, occur in many immature stages in the insect life cycle, as well as in adults, and in some species are entirely absent. It is thought that an ocellus enables the insect to distinguish between darkness and light, and possibly to form a very faint, single image from its single cornea.

Head Appendages. Included as appendages of the head are the *antennae* and mouth parts. The single pair of jointed antennae located on the insect's head is a diagnostic feature. These organs vary among the orders, families, genera, species, and even between the sexes. They differ in length, width, shape, ornamentation, color, and in the structure and number of segments. Antennae are organs of smell and touch. Certain organs of smell, the sensoria, are developed on the antennal segments of many insects; these sense organs are especially well developed on the antennae of aphids. See ANTENNA.

The mouth is surrounded by the *mouth parts*, which are subject to great variation. Two rather distinct types, different in appearance and physiology but derived from homologous parts, are recognized: the *mandibulate* or chewing type, and the *haustellate* or sucking type. In the chewing type a pair of jaws,

INSECT

The Classification of Insects

The many kinds of insects are separated into approximately 33 orders. Their classification is based chiefly on structure of mouth parts, type of metamorphosis, presence of wings, and wing structure. Only a few of the better known orders are illustrated

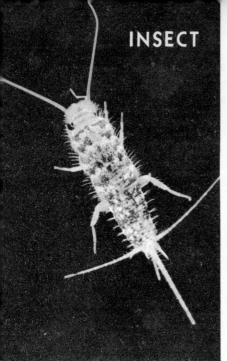

P. S. TICE

L. W. BROWNELL

U.S.D.A.

CONN. AGR. EXPT. STA.

Order Thysanura, represented here by the firebrat, is considered one of the more primitive insect orders

Order Orthoptera includes destructive grasshoppers

Order Isoptera. Termites, the only members of this order, are social insects. A wingless worker and winged adult are shown

L. W. BROWNELL

U.S.D.A.

Order Odonata consists of the dragonflies and damsel flies. The finely veined wings seen on the dragonfly are characteristic of these insects

Order Hemiptera includes squash bugs

Order Homoptera, often classified as a suborder of the Hemiptera, or true bugs, contains the cicada

Order Coleoptera, the beetles. The Mexican bean beetle, a crop pest, is a typical coleopteran

AMERICAN MUSEUM OF NATURAL HISTORY

LYNWOOD M. CHACE

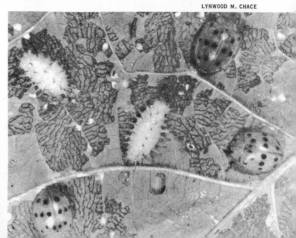

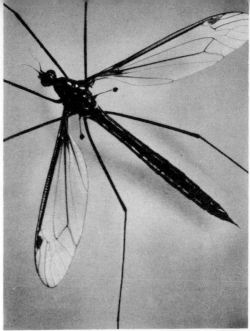

Order Lepidoptera consists of the familiar butterflies, moths, and skippers. Like other Lepidoptera,
the polyphemus moth above has scaly wings and body

Order Diptera. Members of this order, the flies,
have only one pair of wings, the second pair being
reduced to balancers. The crane fly is shown

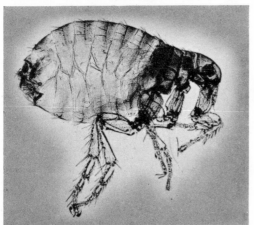

Order Siphonaptera includes the small, wingless
insects known as fleas. The dog flea, shown above,
may infest man as well as dogs and cats

Order Hymenoptera. Such diverse forms as the
bumblebee, left, and ant, above, are classified as
hymenopterous. Many of the insects of this order are
social. The bumblebee with the pollen basket on its
hind leg is useful in fertilizing certain flowers

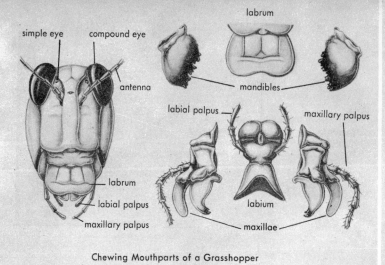

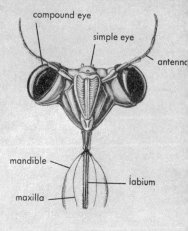

Chewing Mouthparts of a Grasshopper

Piercing and Sucking Mouthparts of a Cicada

Insect mouth parts

the mandibles, is a conspicuous feature. Located above them is a head sclerite, known as the labrum or upper lip. Back of the mandibles is a pair of maxillae, each of which gives off a segmented maxillary palpus. The lower lip or labium, with its pair of segmented labial palpi, may be found just behind the maxillae. On the floor of the oral cavity is a tongue-like organ, the hypopharynx. The mandibles, maxillae, and labial palpi operate in a horizontal plane, and chew up or otherwise manipulate food, finally passing it into the mouth. The mandibulate type of mouth parts is considered the most primitive. It is well developed in grasshoppers and beetles.

In the haustellate type of mouth parts the labrum tends to be short and inconspicuous, the mandibles and maxillae are long slender piercing stylets, and the labium is usually greatly enlarged to form a long, protective sheath about the other mouth parts. Together these specialized organs form a more or less tubular beak, through which plant sap or blood can be sucked. In the case of bloodsucking insects (bedbugs, mosquitoes, stable flies, fleas) the secretion of the salivary glands may act as an anticoagulant, as an anesthetic, or as both, since the host's blood must be prevented from coagulating in the slender beak, and there is less danger of interruption from the host if the pain of the bite is lessened. Haustellate mouth parts are found in true bugs, butterflies, moths, and flies.

In some insects, such as ANTS, the mandibles are developed for chewing, and the other mouth parts are adapted for licking and sucking. This condition is often spoken of as a *composite* type of mouth parts.

Other insects, such as the large, showy saturniid moths (Cecropia moths and their allies) and the adult May flies, have rudimentary mouth parts in the adult stage and take no food. Most immature insects have mandibulate mouth parts, or a modification of these. Examples are the immature termites, caddis flies, caterpillars of butterflies and moths, grubs of beetles, and the young of certain bees and wasps. Immature bugs have sucking mouth parts, like their parents; many immature flies have mouth hooks attached to an internal pharyngeal skeleton.

Thoracic Appendages. The thorax bears the wings and legs. *Wings* arise as baglike, membranous outgrowths of the notum (the dorsal part of each thoracic segment) and are strengthened by sclerotized wing veins. Most adult insects are winged. Where two pairs of wings occur, the first pair (mesothoracic) is developed from the mesothorax and the second pair (metathoracic) from the metathorax. No modern insects have a pair of prothoracic wings but certain fossil insects had expansions from the prothorax, which indicated that insects may have had three pairs of wings in some part of their ancestry.

Typical four-winged insects are BUTTERFLIES and BEES. In these the anterior wings are usually larger than the posterior pair, and the two wings on each side are more or less fastened together by a variety of hooks, or holding devices, so that they beat in unison. BEETLES also usually have two pairs of wings, but the anterior pair is sclerotized to form a pair of hardened wing covers, the *elytra*. In grasshoppers the anterior wings are leathery and form wing covers called *tegmina*. Flies have only one pair of wings, the posterior

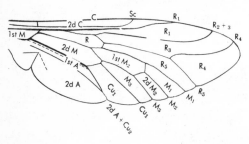

Wing of a Horsefly

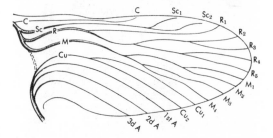

Hypothetical Wing Venation

J. H. COMSTOCK, "AN INTRODUCTION TO ENTOMOLOGY"

The primitive, hypothetical wing venation merely serves as a pattern for the study of wing venation, since the wings of most modern insects, such as the horsefly, are modified through fusion or loss of veins. Longitudinal veins include the costa, C; subcosta, Sc; radius, R; media, M; cubitus, Cu; anals, A. Each wing cell takes its name from the longitudinal vein above or anterior to it

pair being represented by small capitate structures known as *halteres*. In the Strepsiptera, the females are without wings; males have the anterior pair of wings reduced to a pair of pseudohalteres, and the posterior wings are large and fan-shaped with reduced venation. In one suborder (Heteroptera), the true bugs (Hemiptera), the basal half of each anterior wing is leathery, forming a basal *hemelytron*, or *corium*, and an apical membrane; the posterior pair of wings is wholly membranous. Another suborder of bugs (Homoptera), which includes the aphids or plant lice, has some members with both pairs of wings membranous, others totally lacking wings, and the males of the scale insects (*Coccidae*) with the anterior pair of wings present and the posterior pair replaced by a pair of spines. See FLY.

The silverfish of the order Thysanura, and the springtails of the order Collembola are *apterous*, i.e., have no wings. These two orders are very primitive and are thought to have lacked wings through the course of evolution. True lice (Anoplura), bird lice (Mallophaga), and fleas (Siphonaptera) are also wingless, but are believed to have lost their wings as a consequence of the evolution of their parasitic habits. Almost all winged orders of insects have exceptions to the typical winged condition. For example, among the beetles (Coleoptera) the elytra usually cover the abdomen, but certain families, such as the *Staphylinidae* and the *Pselaphidae*, have very short elytra. This condition is spoken of as *brachypterous*.

Generally speaking, adult insects and most larval stages have three pairs of *legs*, a pair on each segment of the thorax. Some larvae, however, are without legs (*apodous*). Included among these are the larvae of some weevils, flies, moths, and certain parasitic wasps. Insect legs are usually highly adapted for certain kinds of activity. There are legs fitted for running (cursorial), as in tiger beetles; digging (fossorial), as in the mole crickets; swimming (natatorial), as in the water beetles; and for holding prey (raptorial), as in the mantids. In some species the legs of the male are adapted for holding the female during the act of mating. In others the legs are used for rasping or producing sounds (*stridulation*).

Abdominal Appendages. Embryologically, each abdominal segment except the last bears a pair of appendages. Certain larvae have *prolegs* on the abdomen, as for example, the larvae of sawflies and the caterpillar larvae of butterflies and moths. Adult insects are usually without abdominal appendages except on the eighth and eleventh segments of females and the ninth segment of males. These appendages are concerned with copulation, egg laying (oviposition), or allied reproductive functions and are termed collectively *genitalia*, or gonapophyses. An exception is seen in certain Thysanura, or silverfish, where some genera have minute, paired abdominal appendages on several anterior sternites.

Photogenic Organs. The light-producing organs of the FIREFLIES are also abdominal. These organs lie above the fourth to the sixth sternites, near the hypodermis. Such organs produce relatively cold luminescence and are called photogenic organs. Their physiology is obscure. Two complex organic compounds are produced, *luciferin* and *luciferase*. Luciferase, a catalyst and strong oxidizing agent, acts upon luciferin in the presence of oxygen. Oxygen is supplied by a rich network of respiratory tubes. The light is produced by rapid oxidation and is very efficient since little energy is lost through heat production. The efficiency is calculated to be between 92 and 100 per cent.

Circulation. The internal body cavity (hemocoel) of insects is largely filled by the internal organs. These are bathed in the circulating *hemolymph*, which consists of a greenish or a straw-colored plasma and corpuscles. The corpuscles are of numerous kinds, including several types of white corpuscles (leucocytes) that are capable of engulfing foreign bodies, such as

bacteria. Such cells have a protective, or phagocytic, role. The "blood," or hemolymph, is circulated by the heart, a tubular, pulsating organ located in the median dorsal part of the abdominal cavity. This organ is open anteriorly but closed posteriorly and lies on a thin dorsal diaphragm, just beneath the body wall. Along each side of the heart is a series of small valves (osteoles) that open and close periodically. Blood sucked through the osteoles into the heart (which may be divided into a number of chambers) is forced forward by rhythmic pulsations through the open anterior end. It is sent into the head and the appendages, and over the various organs, generally moving posteriorly along the lower side of the body cavity, and completes the circulatory movement by once again being drawn upward into the heart.

The blood of insects has many functions. It distributes food, absorbed from the digestive system, to all parts of the body; it transports dissolved waste products from all parts of the body to the excretory organs; it carries endocrine secretions; it clots over wounds in the body wall. In a few aquatic insects, such as the larvae of certain chironomid flies, the blood is red as a consequence of the respiratory pigment, hemoglobin. Unlike the hemoglobin of vertebrates, which is carried in special red blood cells, insect hemoglobin is dissolved in the plasma. Another difference between vertebrates and insects is that vertebrates have a closed circulatory system, whereas insects have an open system, i.e., lacking a system of veins, arteries, and capillaries.

Digestion and Excretion. The digestive system of insects is divisible into three chief portions, *stomodaeum*, *mesenteron*, and *proctodaeum*. Both stomodaeum and proctodaeum are ingrowths of the external body wall from the anterior and posterior ends respectively. Hence, in the embryonic period these two ectodermal portions grow inward and meet the middle portion, the mesenteron. Eventually the blind ends of the stomodaeum and proctodaeum fuse with the ends of the mesenteron and break through to form a continuous gut. It will be noted that the structure of the stomodaeum and proctodaeum is that of the body wall, that is, each has an internal basement membrane bathed by the hemolymph, a layer of modified hypodermal cells, and a chitinous lining of the gut, known as the *intima*. Since the intima of the stomodaeum and proctodaeum is relatively impermeable, most absorption of food takes place in the mesenteron. Food is ingested at the mouth, after being masticated by the mandibles and maxillae of mandibulate insects or sucked up by the labial tube of haustellate insects. It is sent into the short pharynx, into which the saliva secreted by the paired salivary glands usually enters by means of the salivary ducts. From the pharynx the food goes to the esophagus, crop, and in some insects from the crop directly into the mesenteron, in other insects from the crop to the proventriculus or gizzard. The gizzard may have the intima greatly thickened and dissected into complicated ridges and teeth and its walls greatly thickened with muscles, so that the food can be ground up and strained. This is the condition in many crickets.

Digestion by enzymes takes place both in the stomodaeum and mesenteron. These enzymes are of several kinds: lipolytic, that break down fats; proteolytic, that break down proteins; amylolytic, that break down carbohydrates; and xylases, that break down cellulose. Since many insects feed upon wood, and plant cells have cellulose walls, xylases are usually associated with wood-devouring species. An interesting exception, however, is found in certain families of termites (Isoptera) that have a gut fauna of minute flagellate protozoans, which break down the wood ingested by the TERMITES. This mutual co-operation between two organisms is known as *symbiosis*. Cleveland demonstrated experimentally (1925) that termites can ingest cellulose but die unless the flagellate gut protozoans are present to digest it for them.

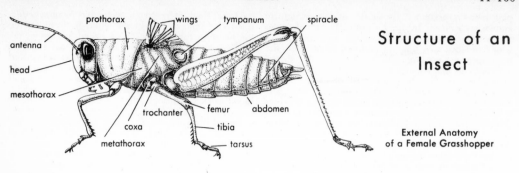

External Anatomy
of a Female Grasshopper

Structure of an Insect

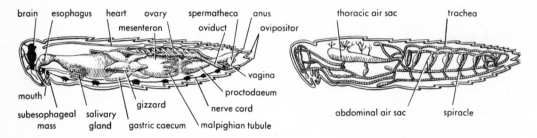

Internal Anatomy of a Female Grasshopper   Respiratory System of a Grasshopper

The unabsorbed contents of the mesenteron pass backward into the proctodaeum. This portion of the gut is usually divided into ileum, colon, rectum, and anus. The ileum also receives the waste products from the principal excretory organs. Waste from these organs and unabsorbed food products from the mesenteron are pushed backward by waves of muscular energy and voided from the anus as feces. The anus of insects lies near the dorsal, or upper, side of the posterior end of the body.

The chief excretory organs are the *Malpighian tubules*, which vary in size, shape, and number. The cavity of each tubule is continuous with that of the ileum and the closed end of the tubule lies in the hemocoel. Wigglesworth (1939) has demonstrated the action of the Malpighian tubules. The distal portion of the tubule absorbs waste products from the hemolymph; in the proximal portion, the waste is dehydrated, the water extracted and resecreted into the hemolymph; finally the concentrated wastes that remain in the tubule enter the ileum.

Respiration. The respiratory system of insects is quite different from that of vertebrate animals. Air is inspired and expired from a series of paired, minute pores, the *spiracles*. There are typically 10 pairs of spiracles, a mesothoracic pair, a metathoracic pair, and eight abdominal pairs located on the lateral walls of the segments. Each spiracle is the orifice of a tube called the *trachea*. Since tracheae are ingrowths of the body wall, they have the usual basement membrane, layer of hypodermal cells, and chitinous cuticula. The respiratory cuticula, however, is in the form of a tightly coiled spiral known as the tracheal intima, or *tenidium*, and serves to keep the trachea open. When the immature insect sheds its cuticle during molting, the tenidia are shed also, as are the intimal linings of the stomodaeum and the proctodaeum. The tracheae ramify, branch, and join one another throughout the hemocoel, the finer subdivisions of each trachea being continuous with still finer tubes, the *tracheoles*. Each tracheole forms from within a tracheal hypodermal cell, has no chitinous intima, and therefore is not shed with each molt. Tracheoles carry the air to all parts of the body, oxygen diffusing from their thin walls into active organs, and carbon dioxide diffusing into the tracheoles from the organs.

Respiratory movements, chiefly rhythmic move-

ments of the abdomen, force used air from the system and suck fresh air into it. In many insects there is a special spiracular apparatus that rhythmically closes and opens each tracheal trunk, near its spiracle. The great majority of insects have functional spiracles. Some, however, have no spiracles; among these are the aquatic immature stages of MAY FLIES (Ephemerida), Stone Flies (Plecoptera), DRAGONFLIES and DAMSEL FLIES (Odonata), and others. In these forms the spiracles are replaced by gills, and respiration takes place between the surrounding water and the thin gill wall. The chironomid fly larvae, with blood gills supplied with hemoglobin, are of this type.

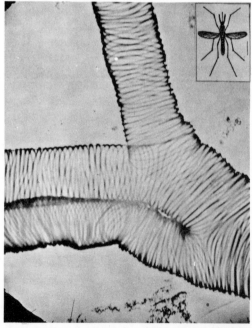

R.C.A. LABORATORIES

Respiratory Trachea of mosquito larva is kept open by the spiral tenidium, arranged in a tight coil

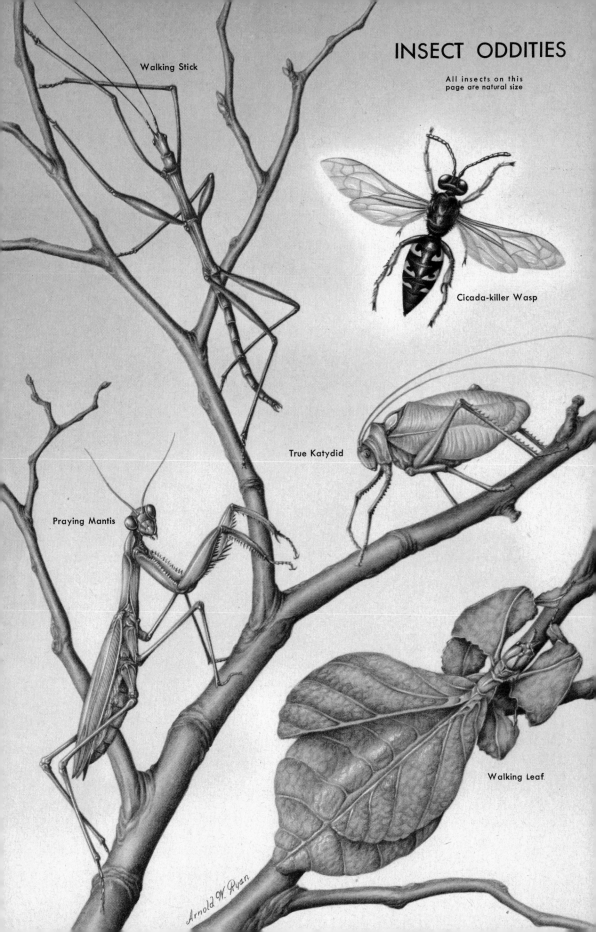

INSECT ODDITIES

All insects on this page are natural size

Walking Stick

Cicada-killer Wasp

True Katydid

Praying Mantis

Walking Leaf

Arnold W. Ryan

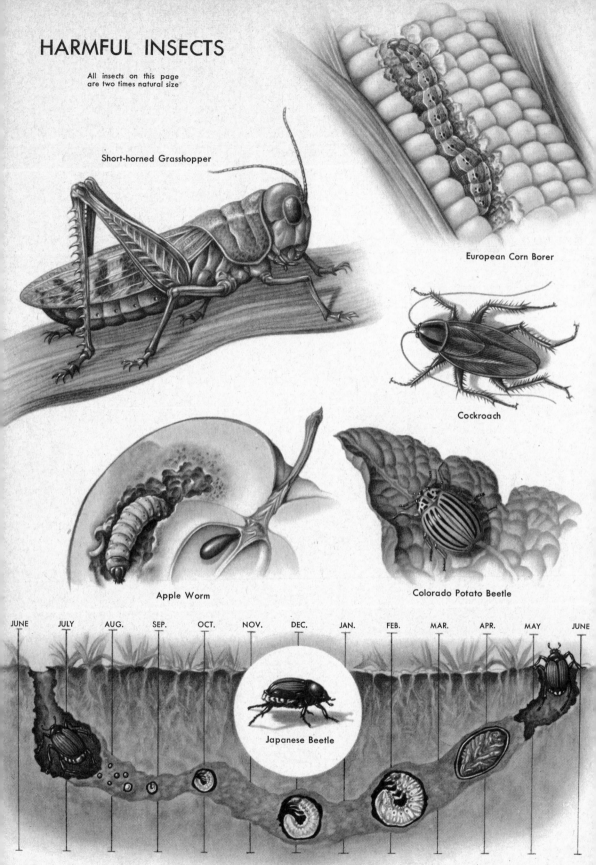

HARMFUL INSECTS

All insects on this page
are two times natural size

Short-horned Grasshopper

European Corn Borer

Cockroach

Apple Worm

Colorado Potato Beetle

JUNE   JULY   AUG.   SEP.   OCT.   NOV.   DEC.   JAN.   FEB.   MAR.   APR.   MAY   JUNE

Japanese Beetle

The Japanese beetle attacks almost all plants and trees. It destroys throughout its life cycle from the time it lays its eggs in early summer through the larval or grub winter stage to the early spring pupa, the newly-hatched beetle finally emerging to begin the destructive cycle over again

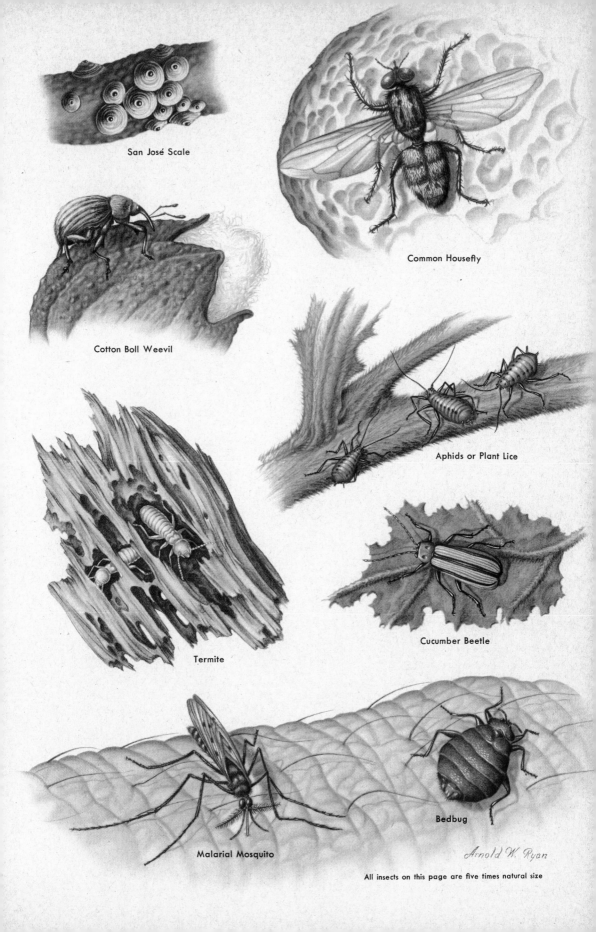

San José Scale

Common Housefly

Cotton Boll Weevil

Aphids or Plant Lice

Termite

Cucumber Beetle

Malarial Mosquito

Bedbug

Arnold W. Ryan

All insects on this page are five times natural size

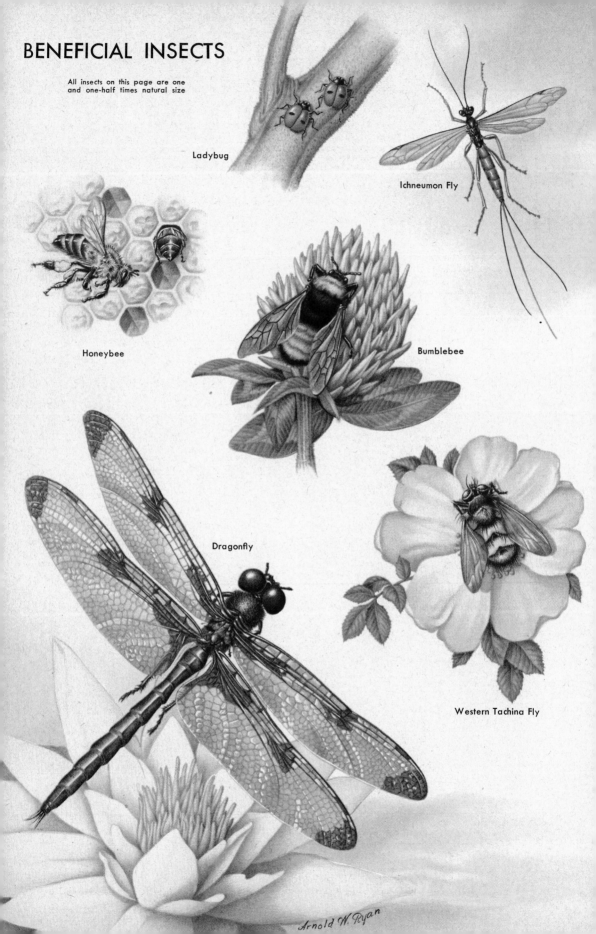

BENEFICIAL INSECTS

All insects on this page are one
and one-half times natural size

Ladybug

Ichneumon Fly

Honeybee

Bumblebee

Dragonfly

Western Tachina Fly

Arnold W. Ryan

Nervous System. As in vertebrates, there are two systems of co-ordination, the nervous system and the endocrine system. The insect nervous system is very complex. The *brain* consists of a relatively large supraesophageal mass, composed of the protocerebrum, deutocerebrum, and tritocerebrum. The protocerebrum has two hemispheres, which give rise to the optic lobes; it sends nerves to the ocelli and contains the important association centers of the nervous system. The deutocerebrum is also divisible into right and left hemispheres, each of which sends a nerve to the dorsal part of the body and a large antennal nerve to the respective antennae. The tritocerebrum sends a large nerve to each side of the labrum and continues downward on either side of the esophagus, as a pair of *crura cerebri*, to the subesophageal mass. In addition to the crura, there is a subesophageal commissure which passes beneath the esophagus and unites the two tritocerebral lobes.

The *subesophageal mass*, composed embryologically of four ganglia or neuromeres, sends paired nerves to the mandibles, hypopharynx, maxillae, salivary ducts, labium, and cervicum. It is continuous posteriorly with the *ventral nerve cord* on the ventral body wall and is covered by a thin ventral diaphragm. Along the cord are several ganglia, one in each thoracic segment and often five in the abdomen; these innervate muscles, digestive tract, and genital tract. In general, there is a reduction or consolidation of cord ganglia within the life history, from larva to adult, and within the phylogeny, from primitive to specialized species.

The supraesophageal and subesophageal masses, together with the ventral nerve cord, make up the *central nervous system;* the motor and sensory nerves from the central nervous system constitute the peripheral nervous system. In addition, insects may have two, rather separated *autonomic nervous systems.* The first of these is associated with the stomodaeum and has several pairs of ganglia and associated nerves that innervate the crop, salivary ducts, heart, and a pair of endocrine glands, known as the corpora allata. This system is connected with the brain by one or two pairs of nerves. The second autonomic system consists of a slender ventral nerve that lies just beneath the ventral nerve cord and gives off a pair of tracheal nerves to the vicinity of each pair of spiracles.

Muscular System. Insects have many more muscles than vertebrates, between 2,000 and 3,000 muscles having been found in certain species. Insect muscles are always striated and innervated. They receive food and give off wastes through the hemolymph and take in oxygen and give off carbon dioxide through the tracheoles. In addition, they are responsible in whole or in part for respiratory movements, circulation of the hemolymph, flight and locomotion, mastication, and copulation. During flight, for example, the large thoracic muscles alternately elevate and depress the top of the thorax and indirectly release from pressure and press upon certain sclerites of the wing bases so that the wings lower and raise in flight. Other flight muscles also act directly upon the wing sclerites. Flying insects have rapid wing vibration, their wings beating from 9 to 300 times a second, depending upon the species. Insects are relatively strong. In general, however, the larger the insect, the relatively weaker it becomes (Hiestand, 1928). A beetle (*Platynus*) weighing .017 gram has been shown to have a strength/weight ratio of about 45, with friction not present.

Reproduction. The reproductive systems of male and female insects are essentially homologous and occupy much of the abdominal hemocoel. The male produces spermatozoa in the paired testes, each of which consists of testicular tubes. Sperms are conveyed down paired vasa deferentia to a common sperm reservoir, or into an ejaculatory duct. They are injected into the female by the male copulatory organ, the *aedeagus*. The ova are produced in paired ovaries, each of which consists of ovarian tubes. As the ova mature they pass down paired oviducts and receive an eggshell in which is a minute pore, the micropyle. At copulation the sperm of the male are deposited by means of the aedeagus in the female's bursa copulatrix, or further inward, into the female's spermatheca. Here the sperm may be kept alive for a number of years. As the ova pass from the oviducts into the common vagina, which is continuous with the bursa, they are fertilized by sperm. Each spermatozoan, released from the spermatheca, enters through the micropyle of the eggshell. The fertilized eggs are then laid (oviposited) to start a new life cycle.

Most insects develop from fertilized eggs, the zygotes. Some, however, hatch from unfertilized eggs, that is, eggs oviposited by parthenogenetic females. In certain species the females are ovoviviparous, the young being born alive from eggs that hatch within the genital tract. Both types of females may be found in the complex aphid cycle.

Endocrine System. There are in insects at least four hormones which are of prime importance in growth and metamorphosis. The *brain factor* is secreted by nerve cells in the brain and functions to activate secretion of the *growth and differentiation hormone* (GDH) by the prothoracic glands. GDH factor initiates molting and controls metamorphosis. The *juvenile hormone*, secreted by the corpora allata glands which flank the esophagus, is antagonistic to GDH and prevents untimely metamorphosis. A fourth hormone, the *metabolic hormone*, also from the corpora allata, regulates egg production.

Metamorphosis. During the development of insects from egg to adult, many complicated changes occur. This general process is known as metamorphosis and is one of the most characteristic features of insect life.

There are five different types of metamorphosis shown by various groups of insects: (1) *Ametabola* is a type in which there is no change in structure but only increase in size; it is found in primitive insects such as silverfish (Thysanura). (2) *Paurometabola* is metamorphosis in which the young upon hatching resemble the adult somewhat and the resemblance is increased with each molt; it is found in grasshoppers (Orthoptera), bugs (Hemiptera), and termites (Isoptera). (3) *Hemimetabola* is incomplete metamorphosis in which aquatic gilled larvae (naiads) molt to become adults; it is exemplified in May flies (Ephemerida), stone flies (Plecoptera), and dragonflies (Odonata). (4) *Holometabola* is complete metamorphosis in which the successive stages are egg, wormlike larva, pupa, and adult; it is shown by butterflies and moths (Lepidoptera), flies (Diptera), fleas (Siphonaptera), beetles (Coleoptera), and bees and ants (Hymenoptera). (5) *Hypermetabola* is complicated metamorphosis with several different types of larvae; certain parasitic flies, blister beetles, and the peculiar, parasitic Strepsiptera are the main examples.

Recently the relationship between hormones and metamorphosis has been extensively investigated in the fruit fly and the silkworm (the larva of the Cecropia moth). It was shown that early in the development of the egg, hormones from the future thoracic region cause some cells to be pre-determined as larva-forming cells, and others as pupa and adult-forming cells. The larva-forming cells grow rapidly but those set aside to become pupa and adult form tiny "imaginal disks" and remain scattered throughout the larval body. When the larva reaches full size the brain factor stimulates the prothoracic gland to release the *growth and differentiation hormone* (GDH) which in turn activates the imaginal disks to start growing to form the pupa. The old larval cells die and are absorbed by the developing pupa. The pupa remains quiescent throughout the winter since the brain stops secreting its hormone. In the spring the brain releases it hormone and activates again the secretion of GDH, which causes metamorphosis from pupa to adult. It is in this way that the secretory activity of the brain synchronizes the life history of the animal with the seasons.

Fossil Insects. Geologically speaking, insects are moderately ancient. Apparently they appeared in the Carboniferous period, many millions of years ago. The first group to leave recognizable fossil traces were orthopteroid insects, the *Blattaria* or forerunners of the modern cockroaches. Over 200 species of roaches are described from Carboniferous deposits of North America and Europe. From the Carboniferous to the present, various insect groups have evolved, reached a zenith, and declined; others have steadily evolved and just now may be reaching their evolutionary peak. *Blattaria*, the primitive cockroaches, comprised about 34 per cent of the known Permian insects, but now number less than half of 1 per cent of the insect population. Beetles, on the other hand, have increased in species with the passage of time, 1 per cent in the Permian, 37 per cent through the Mesozoic and Tertiary periods, and about 41 per cent of the known insects at the present time.

Distribution. Within the class Insecta there are about 33 orders which are chiefly classified on the basis of the kind of mouth parts, type of metamorphosis, presence or absence of wings and wing structure. Insects are widely distributed but disproportionately so in the three major habitats: terrestrial, fresh water, and marine. They are one of the dominant groups of animals in the terrestrial habitat, from 93 to 95 per cent of all insect species living on land. Here they are found in almost every known situation, from below sea level almost to the tops of tall mountains, and from about 800 miles south of the North Pole to at least 1,200 miles north of the South Pole. They appear to increase with the amount of vegetation, moisture, and mean air temperature. Consequently it is in the tropics that insects are especially notable. From 5 to 7 per cent of the species inhabit fresh water, but these have dispersed into all available marshes, ponds, lakes, streams, and springs. Immature stages of May flies, damsel flies, dragonflies, and stone flies, are good examples of orders in which the adults are terrestrial and the nymphs or larvae are aquatic. Hot Springs and chemically charged waters often have a natural insect fauna. The marine habitat is almost uninhabited by insects. There are, however, two notable exceptions, the water striders of the genus *Halobates* and the chironomid flies (*Pontomyia*).

Terrestrial insects include a number of social and subsocial species. The subsocial groups exhibit a certain amount of co-operation between members, and include representatives among the beetles (Coleoptera), wasps and bees (Hymenoptera), earwigs (Dermaptera), and tube-spinning or web-spinning embiids (Embioptera). The social insects have complex societies and have developed a certain amount of control over their natural environment. The chief difference between these insect societies and those of man is that the former have their behavior patterns regulated in great part by instinctive mechanisms, whereas human societies are regulated in great part through plastic behavior, or intelligence. The social insects are termites (Isoptera), wasps, bees, and ants (Hymenoptera).

Size Ranges Among Insects. Although insects as a group are small in size as compared with vertebrates, they have a spectacular size range. The smallest species, certain parasitic wasps and certain families of beetles, are much smaller than the largest single-celled animals, the Protozoa. On the other hand, the largest insects are much larger than the smallest vertebrates. The size range of insects is from about 0.21 mm. in a mymarid wasp, *Alaptus magnanimus*, to 275 mm., which is the wing expanse of a Brazilian moth, *Erebus agrippina*. Many fossil insects were much larger, the extinct dragonfly (*Meganeura*), for example, having had a wing expanse of 600 mm., or two feet.

ORLANDO PARK

INSECTS IN RELATION TO DISEASE

Insects play an extremely important part in relation to diseases of man and animals. In their capacity as disease transmitters they are rivaled only by MITES and TICKS. These arthropods belong to the class Arachnida and although not true insects, are popularly called insects. The term "insect," therefore, as used here, in its popular, broad sense, includes mites and ticks as well as the members of the class Insecta.

Comparatively few insects are themselves important as causers of disease; it is in their capacity as *vectors* (carriers and transmitters of germs) or as intermediate hosts for other parasites that insects play their most important role in relation to disease. The principal insects that themselves cause disease are: various kinds of mites that live on or in the skin, causing *scabies* (itch) in human beings and mange or scab in animals; lice and fleas that live as external parasites, causing not only local effects but often allergic reactions as well; and larvae of many kinds of flies (bots, screwworms, etc.) that invade various parts of the body or infest wounds or natural cavities, causing a condition known as *myiasis*. Tick paralysis is another disease caused directly by an arthropod. Many insects and ticks inject poisonous substances with their bites or stings that produce painful or dangerous symptoms.

Some of the most important diseases of man and animals depend exclusively, or almost so, upon insects for their transmission and therefore do not exist except where the insect transmitters are present. Included in this category are diseases caused by filterable viruses, bacteria, protozoa, and worms. Some of the most important among virus diseases are yellow fever, dengue, and sand fly fever; among rickettsial or bacterial diseases, various forms of typhus, spotted fever, Q fever, Oroya fever, relapsing fever, plague, and tularemia; among protozoan diseases, malaria, various trypanosome diseases of man and animals, forms of leishmaniasis (kala azar, espundia, oriental sore), and piroplasmosis in animals (Texas fever and red water fever in dogs); and among helminthic (worm) diseases, filariasis, and many other kinds of nematode, spinyheaded worm, fluke, and tapeworm infections. In addition to these diseases, transmitted exclusively by insects, there are many others in which transmission by insects plays a more or less important though not exclusive part. Such are various forms of encephalomyelitis (sometimes called sleeping sickness), and possibly poliomyelitis (infantile paralysis); yaws; trachoma and different forms of conjunctivitis; anaplasmosis; fowl pox; anthrax; and such intestinal infections as dysentery and typhoid.

The first evidence of the role of insects in disease transmission was the discovery of the development of filarial worms in mosquitoes, made by Sir Patrick Manson in 1879. The first demonstration of the importance of insects as vectors of protozoan parasites was made by two Americans, Smith and Kilbourne, in 1893. Transmission of malaria by mosquitoes was independently worked out by Ross and Grassi, from 1898 to 1900, and the transmission of yellow fever by mosquitoes was proved by an American Army commission in Havana in 1900.

Insect Vectors. Insects transmit disease by a number of methods, some mechanical, some biological. The simplest method is *indirect mechanical transmission*, in which the insects function merely as passive carriers of bacteria, viruses, protozoan cysts, or worm eggs, picking them up from the bodies or excretions of man or animals and depositing them on food which is later ingested. The importance of any particular insect in this type of transmission depends upon the efficiency with which it carries the germs and the extent to which its habits bring it in contact with the source of the germs and later with food. The housefly is outstanding in this respect; not only do germs readily adhere to its body and feet, but they also survive well in its alimentary canal. To feed and lay its eggs it frequents excreta, then readily enters houses to partake of human food. It may pollute the food by depositing germs carried on its feet, in its droppings, or in regurgitations. The most important diseases transmitted in this manner are dysentery, typhoid, infantile diarrhea, and intestinal protozoan infections. It is possible that poliomyelitis also may be transmitted in this manner.

Slightly more specialized is *direct mechanical transmission*, in which the insects pick up the germs from the body of a diseased individual and then directly inoculate them into skin sores, wounds, or the blood stream of other individuals. Biting flies, such as mosquitoes, stable flies, and horseflies, transmit blood diseases in this manner, e.g., anthrax, fowl pox, and encephalomyelitis. Flies that feed on sores or open wounds, such as eye flies and many relatives of the Housefly, transmit skin or eye diseases, including yaws, trachoma, and oriental sore. Usually the disease organisms do not live in these vectors for more than a few minutes to a few days at most.

When an insect plays some further part in the life of the parasite or germ than merely as a means of transportation, and multiplication or some phase of development in the life cycle of the organism is entailed, the process is called *biological transmission*. In the simplest cases there is mere propagation of the infective organisms, without any special phase of the life cycle being involved. This is probably the case with all virus, rickettsial, bacterial, and spirochete infections; examples are yellow fever, dengue, encephalitis, typhus, spotted fever, plague, tularemia, yaws, and probably relapsing fever. In the case of plague a special mechanism is involved. The plague bacilli multiply so prodigiously in fleas that they block the alimentary canal of the insect; when the "blocked" fleas vainly try to suck blood, the bacilli are regurgitated into the bite. With regard to protozoan parasites, there is not only multiplication of the disease-causing organism within the insect vector, but also a special phase in the life cycle of the protozoa that prolongs the time required for an insect to become infective after feeding on an infected man or animal. Examples are malaria, trypanosome and leishmania infections, and various forms of piroplasmosis (Texas fever) in animals.

In helminthic infections for which insects serve as vectors, no multiplication of the parasites occurs, but in most cases the worms undergo a necessary part of their life cycle in insects that serve as intermediate hosts (organisms infected by larvae which as adults are parasites of other organisms). Many tapeworms and spinyheaded worms develop larval stages in insects; and many flukes, although they use snails as their primary intermediate hosts, later penetrate and encyst in insects, using them as a means of access to the final hosts. Among nematode worms there are two groups that utilize insects as necessary intermediate hosts, but in very different ways. In one, the filarial worms, the embryos of the worms are sucked from the blood or skin by blood-sucking insects and, after undergoing development within the body of the insect, enter another host through the skin while the insect is biting. In the other, the spiruroids, insects such as dung beetles, white grubs, and roaches, become infected by eating the eggs of the worms passed in the feces of the final host. Transfer to the final host is made when the infected insect is eaten. A special case is that of the gapeworm of poultry, which develops to the infective stage while still within the egg. The infective egg of the worm leaves the body of the infected fowl and may gain access to a host through contaminated food or water; but if the eggs are eaten by insects or by other invertebrates, such as earthworms or slugs, the larvae hatch and become encapsulated. Thus the invertebrates serve as "transport" hosts.

A very remarkable instance in which an insect serves as a vector for another insect is demonstrated by certain Mosquitoes that are captured by the tropical American Botfly, *Dermatobia hominis*. The botfly glues its eggs to the abdomen of a captured mosquito and then frees the captive. When the mosquito bites animals, especially cattle or human beings, the warmth of the body causes the fly's eggs to hatch. The little maggots then bore into the opening made by the mosquito's bite and undergo development in the skin, producing painful boils.

Of all insect disease carriers, mosquitoes are pre-eminent, being vectors of malaria, yellow fever, dengue, filariasis, and encephalomyelitis. Ticks are next in importance and transmit spotted fever, Q fever, relapsing fever, tularemia, various forms of piroplasmosis, anaplasmosis, and some virus diseases. Fleas are important as carriers of plague and endemic typhus; lice, of relapsing fever and epidemic typhus; chiggers, of scrub typhus; triatomid bugs, of Chagas' disease; Tsetse Flies, of African trypanosomiasis; sand flies, of leishmaniasis, sand fly fever, and Oroya fever; black flies, of onchocerciasis; horse and deer flies (tabanids), of anthrax, tularemia, etc.; and houseflies, of dysentery, typhoid, and other intestinal infections. See Parasites and Parasitism; Louse; Reed, Walter.   Asa C. Chandler

Bibliog.–W. M. Wheeler, *The Social Insects* (1928); R. A. Wardle, *Problems of Applied Entomology* (1929); F. M. Carpenter, *Review of Our Present Knowledge of the Geological History of Insects* (1930); J. W. Folsom and R. A. Wardle, *Entomology with Special Reference to Its Ecological Aspects* (1934); F. E. Lutz, *Field Book of Insects* (ed. 1935); H. L. Sweetman, *Biological Control of Insects* (1936); W. B. Herms, *Medical Entomology* (1939); C. L. Metcalfe and W. P. Flint, *Destructive and Useful Insects* (1939); V. P. Wigglesworth, *Principles of Insect Physiology* (1939); J. H. Comstock, *An Introduction to Entomology* (1940); J. Smart, *Insects of Medical Importance* (1943); C. T. Brues, *Insect Dietary* (1946); E. A. Steinhaus, *Insect Microbiology* (1946); W. Harvey and H. Hill, *Insect Pests* (1947); A. D. Imms, *General Textbook of Entomology* (ed. 1949); F. A. Urquhart and E. B. S. Logier, *Introducing the Insect* (1949).

INSECTICIDE, a chemical used to kill insects and related pests. As used here, the term includes various non-insect forms, as spiders, scorpions, mites, and ticks. It is distinguished from other special pesticides, such as Fungicides, herbicides (see Weed), and rodenticides (see Rat Poisons).

Some insects transmit disease, and others destroy or damage valuable plants. Over 6,000 kinds of insects in the United States attack plants that produce food and textile fibers, causing an annual loss of about 10 per cent. The apple tree alone, it has been estimated, is afflicted with 18 different insect pests, including the codling moth, canker worm, and aphids. Among insects that transmit disease germs to man are mosquitoes (malaria and yellow fever), lice (typhus), and ticks (rocky mountain fever). Flies, fleas, bedbugs, and roaches are also common pests.

The outstanding development of 1940–50 was the synthesis and introduction of new organic insecticides. In many fields these replaced or supplemented the older agents, but the latter continued useful.

Agricultural Insecticides. Three types of agents are generally recognized when dealing with plant pests: (1) *stomach poisons*, for foliage-eating insects, (2) *contact poisons*, for insects that do not eat foliage, and (3) *fumigants*, used indoors, or for tunneling pests (see Fumigation).

DDT acts both as a stomach and contact poison, but its chief action is by contact (see DDT). Of the older chemicals, the chief stomach poisons are compounds of arsenic and fluorine. *Lead arsenate* has had wide use on fruit trees, especially protecting apples against the codling moth. For many years *calcium arsenate* was a standard protection against the cotton boll weevil. The usual method of application is dusting, either by ground machines or low-flying airplane. Paris Green is effective against the potato bug. The principal fluorine insecticide is CRYOLITE, which has been useful on a small scale against the boll weevil and Mexican bean beetle.

Contact insecticides are most effective against soft bodied insects. In the form of fine dusts and oils, they seal the breathing pores, or cause paralysis and death when absorbed through the pores. *Sulfur* dust or *lime-sulfur* sprays have been widely used for many years, and have created one of the principal markets for sulfur in this country. *Nicotine sulfate*, made from waste tobacco, is usually sold as a 40 per cent solution, then diluted with water or soap solution as desired. Ground PYRETHRUM flowers and *rotenone* (from derris root), both contact poisons, have been widely used in horticulture.

The best known synthetic contact insecticide is DDT, which first won popular attention as a de-louser in World War II. It has increasingly taken the place of the older compounds. Another important discovery is the gamma isomer of benzene hexachloride, in its purified form known as LINDANE. A report by the U.S. Dept. of Agriculture states that a mixture of 5 per cent DDT and 3 per cent lindane promises to provide the best all-round protection against cotton insects. Lindane is also used against cattle flies and ticks. Other chlorinated organics that have won favor are CHLORDANE, methoxychlor, and toxaphene.

All organic insecticides are more or less poisonous to man and domestic animals. Some, however, have been fatal when absorbed through the skin or inhaled, and must be applied with extreme precaution. These include TEPP (tetraethyl pyrophosphate), HETP (hexaethyl tetraphosphate) and *parathion*. They are used to control aphids, mites, and thrips, and are several times as toxic as nicotine.

Insecticides in Disease Control. Contact insecticides are generally used against germ carriers. Films of kerosene over mosquito-breeding ponds have considerable effect against mosquito larvae, but DDT and the newer synthetics have proven more effective. For large-scale outdoor applications it has been found practicable to spray solutions or suspensions of DDT in kerosene from low-flying airplanes. See DISINFECTANTS. Indoors, a common dispensing method is by an aerosol bomb released from the "bug bomb" type container. The bomb contains a DDT solution together with some inert gas, such as freon, sometimes liquefied under pressure. The gas vaporizes when released, distributing the solution as a very fine mist. Low pressure aerosol containers have now become popular for household use.

Household Insecticides. The common "fly spray" was formerly composed of pyrethrum flowers in kerosene, and "insect powder" contained ground pyrethrum. At present, extracts containing the active pyrethrins are used to supplement other household insecticides, because they immobilize the insect almost immediately. DDT sometimes takes hours or days to kill, but may be sprayed or painted on woodwork for its residual effect. Other synthetics now taking the place of pyrethrum for household use include *phenothiazine*, *gammexane* (or lindane), *chlordane*, and *lethane*.

Among the organics, several thousand compounds of wide chemical composition are insecticidal. Of the inorganics, *sodium fluoride* is used against cockroaches and against lice on chickens and livestock, while *sodium fluosilicate* solution is used to mothproof clothing.

Organic stomach poisons which mothproof garments for long periods have begun to replace the familiar naphthalene mothballs and dichlorobenzene. One such compound, a dye, is a salt of dinitro-alpha-naphthol.

Repellents, while not insecticides, frequently discourage insect activity in a locality. Pine oil distillates, dimethyl phthalate, and "6-12" (ethyl hexandiol) are effective mosquito repellents. Wood *preservatives* are also important for insect control. Hot creosote oil has long been successful for protective treatment of railroad ties. See SHIPWORM. Sodium arsenite and other *ground poisons* are used to kill TERMITES in the soil.

The U.S. Dept. of Agriculture and the state agricultural experiment stations provide information on the selection and proper use of insecticides. It is possible to select specific insecticides for specific insects. A few insecticides are effective against many different insects, but no single agent will kill every variety.   R. L.

BIBLIOG.–D. E. H. Frear, *Chemistry of Insecticides, Fungicides, and Herbicides* (ed. 1948); E. Riegel, *Industrial Chemistry* (ed. 1949); H. H. Shepard, *The Chemistry and Action of Insecticides* (1951); U. S. Department of Agriculture, *Agricultural Statistics* (annual).

INSECTIVORA, an order of small, primitive mammals with representatives in all parts of the world except Australia and the southern two-thirds of South America. They range in size from tiny shrews, some species of which are not heavier than a ten cent piece, to those about the size of a small cat. Practically all have five toes on each foot, a long pointed snout extending considerably beyond the jaw, and a wedge-shaped skull. The simple brain has smooth cerebral hemispheres. The teeth are sharp, with well defined cusps, and the canines, while always present, are small and shaped like the adjoining incisors. The fur of MOLES and SHREWS is soft and silky, while that of tenrecs and hedgehogs is coarse, with prominent spines covering the body of the latter. All possess minute eyes, often hidden by the fur. In moles and shrews the eyes probably serve only to distinguish light from darkness. The insectivores are of particular interest to the biologist, for although they are very generalized mammals, they are primitive and were forerunners of the primates,

Insecticide is sprayed on orchard by machine

INTERNATIONAL HARVESTER CO.

Lime-sulfur spray is applied to potato plants

CATERPILLAR TRACTOR CO.

the order to which man belongs. Some of the tree shrews of Borneo exhibit characters of both the lemurs and the insectivores. Many insectivores have changed little during the past 60,000,000 years.

Among the most common insectivores are moles and shrews. Moles are subterranean in habit, being well adapted for an underground existence. The large paddle feet and the tremendous development of the fore limbs are modifications for digging. The tiny mouselike shrews, most abundant in moist forests, are found throughout the temperate regions of the world. Some species of shrews have a life span of little more than a year. The Old World hedgehog has a wide distribution from western Europe to China. Some insectivores are adapted for an aquatic existence (see DESMAN), while others are partly arboreal. All feed primarily upon insects and other small invertebrates, such as crayfish, spiders, and mollusks. The group is of minor economic importance. Pelts of moles are of commercial value; and the destruction of injurious insects probably offsets the damage the animals do to lawns and golf greens.

W. J. HAMILTON, JR.

INSECTIVOROUS PLANTS. See CARNIVOROUS PLANTS.

INSECURITY. The feeling of insecurity is grounded in fear. It can be seen in an infant when his blanket is suddenly pulled from under him or when he is dropped ever so small a distance from a higher to a lower level. The infant shrinks, wails, and exhibits a variety of diffuse random movements. In later life we learn to tense up inwardly (shrink invisibly), repress our cries, and control our random movements. But the state of fear is still there. It is there when we feel emotionally insecure, and may continue as long as the conditions responsible for it continue.

When a child's basic desires are satisfied, the foundation is laid for his emotional security. If the love of a favored person is endangered, or if he fears that some event may break up his home or some relationship upon which he is dependent, he experiences insecurity. Home, school, and other social relationships which produce a feeling of insecurity are frequently found in the case of children with conduct problems and delinquency. Undesirable behavior is in every case the child's attempt to bolster up his threatened ego. It is a desperate attempt to achieve security when all other means have failed.　　　　FRED MCKINNEY

INSIGNIA, MILITARY, the various devices used to indicate rank and branch of service or specialty of members of armed forces. In the United States Army, Air Force, and Marine Corps, officers wear rank insignia on their shoulders and collars. Corps insignia is worn on coat lapels. In the United States Navy, officers wear rank and branch insignia on their shoulders, coat sleeves, or collars, depending on the uniform worn. Naval enlisted men wear their insignia on one arm. For illustration of U.S. insignia see pages 11-171-2.

INSOMNIA is ordinarily defined as inability to sleep, but it would be better to define it in terms of degree. There are many degrees of insomnia, ranging from complete inability to fall asleep down through very light sleep, being easily awakened, waking in the middle of the night and being unable to fall asleep again, and so on.

Causes. Various external conditions may occasionally help cause insomnia, e.g., noise, light, physical discomfort, cold, heat, insufficient oxygen, etc. These external causes are ordinarily given far more weight than they deserve by the insomniac. He is apt to think that he is being kept awake by noise or an uncomfortable bed whereas it is much more likely that these are merely unimportant excuses. The physically healthy, relaxed, and emotionally secure person can go to sleep when the time comes under almost any external conditions.

It is now widely agreed that any degree of insomnia is most likely to be a joint product of physiological and psychological causes, i.e., psychosomatic. This has been learned partly through clinical observation and partly through everyday experience. It is well known that people may have disturbed sleep because of worry, grief, tension, anxiety, anger, or excitement as well as through glandular, nervous, or cardiovascular disorders, or through pain, itching, or coughing. Clinical observation and various experiments show that those people who are in an emotional state most of the time, that is, neurotic or maladjusted people, tend strongly in many instances to develop a mild or a severe degree of insomnia. In such people this condition tends to be chronic, i.e., to persist over a long period of time, as contrasted with the cases of insomnia in relatively normal people who are going through a temporary period of stress. The weight of the evidence would indicate that most cases of insomnia are explicable ultimately as inability to relax the muscles, and that such inability may come either from organic, or physiological or psychological causes—more usually from combinations of these causes.

Treatment. Mild cases which are not chronic are usually treated by measures which attempt to achieve muscular relaxation, e.g., hot baths, soothing music, correct temperature in the bed, reading, hot drinks, etc. Where such measures do not work, the problem is one for a physician or psychotherapist. Immediate success can be obtained with various sedative drugs, but there is no known drug which can be used over a long period of time without danger. They ought never to be used except when prescribed by a physician. Where insomnia is severe and chronic, and a physical examination is negative, psychotherapy is indicated. This may range from immediate measures like hypnosis and various other forms of suggestion through a profound analysis and reorganization of the personality. Jacobson has made many experiments that show a relationship between mental and muscular activity and has worked out a technique of teaching patients to relax their muscles much more completely than can be done by the ordinary person. By this means he claims to be able to cure (occasionally) not only insomnia, but also stomach disorders, high blood pressure, and other sicknesses due primarily or in part to muscular tension.

One interesting form of insomnia is seen in certain people who are afraid to go to sleep because of the expectation of horrible nightmares. This is sometimes found, for instance, in those afflicted with the traumatic neuroses of war. These sufferers tend to dream regularly of their original traumatizing situation, for example, falling out of an airplane, being buried by a shellburst, being torpedoed. There are also other individuals who are subject to this type insomnia because of dread of nightmares in milder degree. For such individuals no superficial therapy will do. Only discovering the cause of insecurity or neurosis will remove the nightmare. A. H. MASLOW

INSPECTOR GENERAL'S DEPARTMENT, in the U.S. Army. The mission of this department is to inquire into and report upon all matters that affect the efficiency and economy of the Army, and to make such inspections, investigations, or reports as may be prescribed by law or directed by superior authority. It assists the Army by supplying information when appropriate, by recognizing and reporting meritorious conduct and performance of duty, and by suggesting ways and means to improve conditions.

The department consists of an inspector general with the rank of major general, who reports directly to the chief of staff, and a number of field officers detailed from the various arms and services. It has no permanent officers.

A similar system of inspection exists in all modern armies, but generally organized so as to have a separate inspector general for each arm of the service. For historical sketch, see ARMY OF THE UNITED STATES.

INSIGNIA OF RANK—U.S. ARMED FORCES

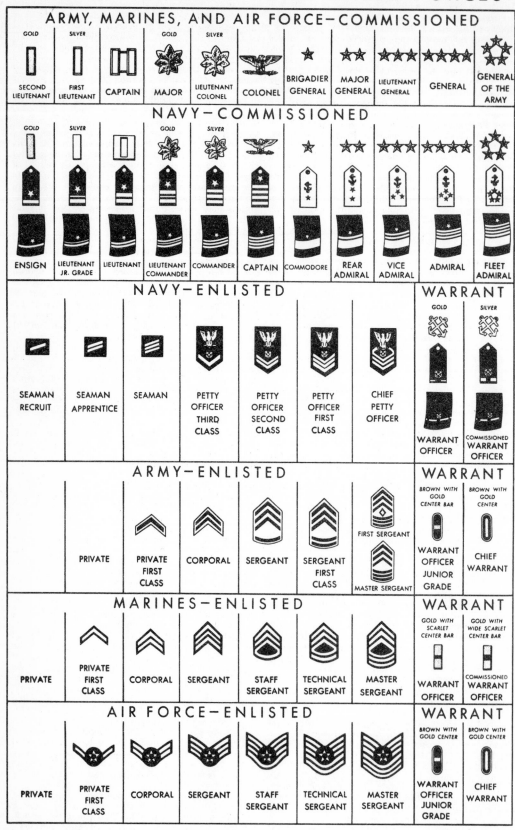

INSPECTOSCOPE. See X-ray.

INSTALLMENT SELLING is the selling of goods to be paid for in uniform installments at regular intervals after delivery of the goods. Possession of the goods passes immediately to the purchaser, but most installment sales are conditional, allowing the seller to retain some control over the goods, either by holding the title until the final payment has been made or by giving the title to the purchaser immediately in exchange for a chattel mortgage. Default in payment customarily means the repossession of the goods by the seller and the forfeiture of those installments already paid.

Because of the element of possible repossession, installment selling has been confined almost entirely to goods with a resale value, or more specifically to durable consumer goods. Among the products which have been most commonly sold on this plan are automobiles, houses, furniture, radios and phonographs, pianos, washing machines, farm machinery, stoves, and refrigerators.

Although the technique of installment selling has been known for centuries and was used to some extent during the 1900's in the sale of furniture, sewing machines, and books, it was not until the coming of the automobile that selling on the installment plan became an important factor in the national economy. Introduced into the automobile business around 1915 as a sales promotion measure, it proved extremely successful and spread rapidly into other fields of industry, especially during the business depression of 1920–21. Expansion continued throughout the 1920's, both as to types of products sold and number of consumers reached, until at the end of 1929 the installment sale debt outstanding reached $2,515,000,000 for the entire nation.

The depression in the early 1930's saw a sharp decline in the volume of installment selling, with only $999,000,000 installment sale debt outstanding at the end of 1932. From that time on, however, with the exception of the year 1938, installment sales steadily increased until 1941 when the installment sale debt outstanding reached an all-time high of $3,744,000,000.

During World War II the Federal government, in an effort to prevent inflation and limit production for consumer use, placed heavy restrictions on installment selling and consumer credit, causing the installment sale debt outstanding at the end of 1943 to drop to less than one-fourth of the 1941 figure. These restrictions, issued as "Regulation W" by the Federal Reserve Board of Governors, specified the minimum amount of down payment which must be made (in most instances $1/3$ of the cash price), established the maximum maturity period, and required that installments be equal in amount, payable at equal intervals, and not less than $5 a month or $1.25 a week.

In 1947, these government consumer credit controls were discontinued. In 1950, however, following the outbreak of the Korean war, the Federal Reserve Bank reinstituted "Regulation W," as amended. Under the new controls, payment periods were reduced to 15 months for automobiles and household electrical appliances and furniture. Down payments were raised to 25 per cent for appliances and 15 per cent for furniture. These controls applied to all purchases amounting to more than $50.

The history of installment selling in the United States reflects the correspondingly rapid growth of the consumer-credit business. Many of the earliest cash-credit agencies were established for the express purposes of financing the purchase of automobiles, and as installment selling spread to other industries the small loan agencies extended their services to cover these fields as well as many others in the retail trade field.

See Credit; Retail Trade; Finance, Personal; Department Store.   C. F.

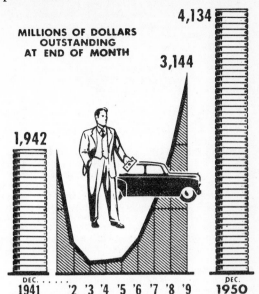

MILLIONS OF DOLLARS OUTSTANDING AT END OF MONTH

4,134

3,144

1,942

DEC. . . . . .
1941   '2 '3 '4 '5 '6 '7 '8 '9   DEC. **1950** EST.

SOURCE: FEDERAL RESERVE BOARD

Automobile Installment Credit in the United States in millions of dollars, 1941-50

INSTERBURG, or **Chernyakovsky,** town, U.S. S.R., the Russian Soviet Federated Socialist Republic, in Kaliningrad Area (former Königsberg in East Prussia), above the confluence of the Inster and Angerapp rivers, 55 miles by rail E of Königsberg, and 16 miles W of Gumbinnen. Manufactures include candies, sausages, flour, textiles, feathers, brushes, furniture, and machinery. There is trade in horses, timber, and grain. Insterburg was founded by the Teutonic Order in 1337; it was chartered as a town in 1583. In World War I the town was occupied by Russian forces from Aug. 24 to Sept. 11, 1914. In World War II it fell to Soviet forces on Jan. 22, 1945, and in August was incorporated into the Soviet Union. Pop. (1950 est.) 50,000.

INSTINCT, the ancient dogma that "animals are controlled by instinct and man by reason" was challenged by William James in 1890. James asserted that man has more, not fewer, instincts than animals, but that they are transitory and quickly pass over into habits, with practice and modification by experience. McDougall, arguing that instincts are not merely chain reflexes but innate psychic dispositions, published in 1908 the theory, widely held for some years, that human behavior is the modified expression of one or more basic instincts: flight, repulsive, pugnacious, parental, gregarious, acquisitive, etc. About 1914 the doctrine of the instinctive bases of human behavior began to be severely criticized on several grounds. Proof that many supposedly innate fears and other reactions can be learned through social conditioning, and realization that most published lists of human instincts are a priori and unsupported by experimental evidence, led to widespread skepticism in regard to the theory; although the instincts demonstrated in lower species, especially invertebrates, continue to be generally assumed. There is, however, a marked disposition to demand controlled experimental evidence of their innate origin, even in animals, and to exclude the possibility of their having been learned early, as has been shown to be true among mammals. The word "instinct" is and always has been used ambiguously. It is employed even today to designate such different things as (1) reflexes, (2) the general drive to be active, and (3) types of human behavior which are universal or widespread, even though presumably learned under similar conditions. Other current tendencies are, to use the adjective "instinctive" in preference to the noun, often as roughly equivalent to impulsive, spontaneous, or automatic; and to substitute for the older descriptive lists of instincts, lists of "wants" or "motives" with no necessary implication of their innate origin. In short, the role of human instincts in the psychology of 1900 is now largely replaced by that of widespread cultural habits. See WATSON, JOHN B.

FORREST A. KINGSBURY

BIBLIOG.–L. L. Bernard, *Instinct: A Study in Social Psychology* (1924); C. L. Hull, *Principles of Behavior, an Introduction to Behavior Theory* (1943); J. A. Bierens de Haan, *Animal Psychology* (1950).

INSTITUTE FOR ADVANCED STUDY. In 1930 a donation of $5,000,000 by Louis Bamberger and Mrs. Felix Fuld enabled Abraham Flexner, a distinguished American educator, to found the Institute for Advanced Study. The Institute is for young scholars and research workers who have obtained the doctorate and who show such promise that additional training in informal association with the leaders of their fields seems highly desirable. Admission to the institute is based entirely on ability without any consideration as to race, sex, political or religious affiliations. Housed at first in Fine Hall of Princeton University, Princeton, New Jersey, the institute moved in 1940 to its own building near the university campus. From 1933 until his retirement in 1945, Albert Einstein was one of the distinguished professors on the staff of the institute. See FLEXNER, ABRAHAM; EINSTEIN, ALBERT.

INSTITUTE OF ARTS AND LETTERS, NATIONAL, a society for the protection and advancement of literature, sculpture, painting, music, and architecture, organized in 1898 by members of the American Social Science Association nominated for the purpose.

Qualification for membership in the Institute, which is limited to 250, is "notable achievement in art, music, or literature." The insignia of the Institute consists of a purple ribbon bearing two bars of old gold. The American Academy of Arts and Letters was organized in 1904 by the National Institute. See ACADEMY OF ARTS AND LETTERS, AMERICAN.

INSTITUTE OF HUMAN RELATIONS, YALE, a research center in Yale University, where members of the faculty and advanced students study various aspects of human behavior. The principal objective of its research program is the development of a science of social behavior basic to the practical problems of human welfare. The facilities of the Institute provide for inter-disciplinary training for groups of sociologists, psychologists, psychiatrists, and anthropologists. Research funds are obtained mainly from a grant by the Rockefeller Foundation.

INSTITUTIONS, SOCIAL. See SOCIAL INSTITUTIONS.

INSTRUMENTATION, the use or method of using instruments. For many years the term concerned only musical instruments and the arranging of music for various instruments. However, the increased use of measuring and controlling instruments has led to specialization in this field, and the term instrumentation has had this additional meaning attached to it. So widespread has this work developed that a branch of engineering has grown around it and an association, the Instrument Society of America, represents the workers in this field. In addition to trade magazines published by various instrument companies, The Instrument Publishing Co. of Pittsburgh, Pa. publishes *Instruments*, a magazine of Measurement and Control; and the Institute of Physics in co-operation with the National Physical Laboratories publishes the *Journal of Scientific Instruments*.

INSULAR POSSESSIONS OF THE UNITED STATES. See UNITED STATES, *Territories and Outlying Possessions*.

INSULATION, the process of greatly reducing the passage of heat, cold, sound, vibration or condensation from one area or material to another. This is accomplished by the use of various nonconductors called "insulating materials."

Thermal Insulation restricts the passage of heat to or from a certain area. Thermal insulation may be used in air-conditioning systems, in refrigeration, on roofs, walls or partitions, as coverings for industrial piping, and in ovens, furnaces, etc.

Most of the material required for thermal insulation in residential buildings can be grouped into three general classes: (1) Fill type, which is shredded or granulated siliceous material that is used to fill the spaces within wall, floor and roof structure. (2) Flexible type, which comes in rolls or "batts," and is placed between joists, studs and rafters. It consists of loosely felted or fibrous materials, such as mineral wool, and is covered on one or both sides with asphalt paper. (3) Rigid or board form insulation which consists of panels, usually 4 feet wide, $\frac{1}{2}$ to 2 inches thick and from 6 to 12 feet in length. This type is placed over rafters and studs and may preclude the use of plaster.

Heat loss from an average six room house is reduced 25% by use of such insulating measures as weather stripping and "storm windows," 35% when weather stripping, "storm windows" *and* attic fill-type insulation is used, and 60% when complete "weatherproofing" or insulation is added.

Industrial Insulation materials are largely derived from five mineral products: ASBESTOS, magnesium carbonate, diatomaceous silica (celite), rock or mineral wool, and refractory clay. Vegetable cork is also used. These products furnish insulation in the form of sectional pipe covering; insulating sheets, blocks, bricks, and blankets; insulating papers, felts, and millboards; and insulating fillers, finishes, and cements. The latter are often used as a surface finish over block or sheet insulation to seal joints and provide a durable, smooth surface. There are several types of industrial insulating cements, each designed for certain purposes. MINERAL WOOL, vermiculite and asbestos fiber serve as bases for these cements. The steam fitting and plumbing trade uses such cements for insulating domestic boilers and low-pressure piping.

Efficient insulation is just as important to a refrigerating plant as is efficient heat removal. An uninsulated refrigerant line of $1\frac{1}{2}$ inch pipe 200 feet long, carrying brine at 15° F. through an area with a 90° F. temperature, wastes 450 tons of refrigeration in a year by conduction to surrounding space.

The materials generally used for refrigeration insulating purposes are cork in granulated and board form. This is the most efficient form of refrigeration insulation. The function of cork insulation in this case is to keep *out* heat. This cork insulation usually comes in slabs of one, two or three inch thicknesses, in varying widths and lengths. It is prepared by cementing cork granules together by baking or by use of a cement.

Sawdust and wood shavings are also used for insulation in refrigeration, as well as animal wool (hair felt) mineral and rock wool, waterproof paper, metal foil sheets, redwood bark, and kapok.

Hair felt is used in blanket form, one to two inches thick. Mineral wool is obtained from the slag of blast furnaces; crushed rock is mixed with coke and placed in furnaces at a temperature of 3000° F. As the molten slag runs from the furnace, it is blown by high-pressure steam into a fleecelike, brittle mass. Rock wool is made in the same manner as mineral wool, but granite and limestone are added to the slag. From 92% to 96% of the bulk of this "wool" consists of tiny air spaces. It is made into slabs one to two inches thick.

Sound Insulation is used where the "absorption" of sound waves is desired whether originating inside or outside of a building, room, or vehicle. This type of insulation is being increasingly utilized in such places as offices, gymnasiums, broadcasting studios, theaters, skating rinks, bowling alleys, schoolrooms, hospitals, and auditoriums.

In a classroom or auditorium with plaster walls and ceiling, a large part of the sound waves striking such a wall surface is reflected back into the room or hall. Like a rubber ball, these reflected sound waves (known as reverberations) continue bouncing back and forth from walls and ceiling until they are spent.

The cellular character of cork admirably suits it as a sound insulating material. To prevent "reflection of sound," sound waves must be trapped and held the *first* time they strike the walls and ceiling, and the myriad openings in the granulated particles making up the surface of cork help to break up and absorb sound waves. Manufactured in board form, cork is applied to ceilings, walls, and as a floor base. It is usually 1½ inches thick, of various widths and lengths, and is installed by cementing or nailing to an under wall of wood, metal or plaster.

Acoustical corkboard is similar to thermal insulation corkboard, and it is a highly effective heat or cold barrier. Therefore it performs a two-fold insulation function. This is very important when sound insulation is used in air-conditioned buildings.

The interiors of many modern passenger airliners are soundproofed with fiber-glass or blown fiber-glass insulation. Other sound insulating materials include finely perforated steel plates mounted on balsam wood. A light, sound-absorbent, plastic artificial stone can be molded into various designs.

Vibration Insulation is used to prevent machinery in motion or connecting parts of various devices in operation from transmitting undesired or destructive vibration to attached parts or immediate surroundings. Cork, rubber or felt, depending upon the type of usage, are generally preferred for this type of insulation. "Isolation corkboard," one form of industrial vibration control, is densely-packed cork "boards" and comes in a standard 12 by 36 foot size with a 1- to 6-inch thickness. When installed under the base of industrial machinery, such as belt driven wheels, or presses, motors, etc., it absorbs or isolates most of the shock, vibration, and noise which would otherwise be transmitted to the floor and thus to other equipment.

Specially treated heat- and oil-resistant rubber is used as a vibration insulator in the motor mountings of modern automobiles. Formerly the motor was rigidly bolted to the frame at three points and transmitted excessive vibration to the car body. In those cars not having frame and body as one unit, the body is insulated from the frame at a number of points by vibration "dampeners" (blocks or pads of rubber). See ACOUSTICS.   R. L.

INSULATION OF WIRES AND CABLES. See ELECTRIC CABLES.

INSULATOR, ELECTRIC, a device used to confine electric currents to desired paths, and provide mechanical support for electric wires or apparatus Insulators are commonly seen connecting power transmission lines, telephone and telegraph wires, and trolley wires to the supporting structure. Insulators fitted with a pin, usually steel, for fastening and support are known as "pin-type." The pin is threaded to engage the porcelain or glass body of the insulator from the hollow under side. The insulator may be several inches high and is made with one or more "skirts." A grooved top holds the current-carrying wire which is secured with a tie-wire. For power lines carrying 70,000 volts or more, suspension-type insulators are used. These are made up of disks 10 inches in diameter which are strung by means of cap and pin attachments. The power line is hung at the bottom of the string at a distance of perhaps 15 feet from the supporting cross arm. The line-post type of insulator, also used for high voltages, is characterized by a hollow corrugated

shape with a metal pin cemented to the bottom and the usual grooves for line and tie-wires at the top.

Under high-voltage conditions, the outer shape of the insulator is an important consideration. Leakage current over the surface of the insulator may be appreciable if the surface is moist or dusty. This factor accounts for the "skirted" shape which shields the under side from moisture and gives a long and more difficult leakage path. Insulators are tested for mechanical strength and for flaws in material. Wet and dry "flashover" tests are made by applying voltage until a visible electric arc crosses the surface. The insulator is then examined for surface damage. Resistance to electrical puncture is tested in an insulating oil bath where an increasing voltage is applied until the insulator fails.

In addition to suitable insulators, transmission lines are also provided with lightning arresters as one means of protection against the damaging effects of lightning. The arrester functions as an insulator under normal operating conditions. When a sudden surge of excess voltage appears on the line, the arrester conducts the discharge to the earth and then blocks the follow-current. The outer case of the lightning arrester is made of insulating material. The interior consists of a spark-gap in series with the arrester elements which allow current to pass readily only if the voltage is high. Thyrite, a semiconductor of electricity, is commonly used in arrester elements. The function of the spark-gap is to isolate the arrester from the power line unless a voltage appears which is sufficient to leap the gap. Lightning arresters are connected with one end attached to the power line and the other end fastened to a ground wire, and are most efficiently located as close as possible to the equipment which requires protection, particularly power machinery. See POWER TRANSMISSION; LIGHTNING.   AARON L. ZOLOT

INSULIN ❖ Life-Saving Hormone Secreted by the Pancreas

Before the discovery of insulin, the onset of diabetes usually meant an early death

INSULIN is a hormone produced by certain cells in the islets of Langerhans of the pancreas. This hormone plays an important part in the metabolism and utilization of sugar in the body. Insulin has been isolated from the pancreas, even prepared in crystalline form, and is now used universally in the treatment of diabetes mellitus. See DIABETES; ENDOCRINE GLANDS.

Electric insulators on a high tension line
WESTINGHOUSE

Its Discovery. An English physician, T. Cawley, was probably the first to suggest the relationship between diabetes and the pancreas because he noted the presence of a stone in the pancreas of a patient who died of diabetes (1788). Almost a century later the French Claude Bernard (1877) and the German Langendorff (1879) performed operations on the pancreas of birds and observed that they rapidly lost weight and died within two weeks. Langendorff even reported the presence of sugar in the urine of hawks following extensive injuries to the pancreas. In 1889 the famous German physicians, von Mering and Minkowski, removed the entire pancreas in dogs and proved that severe, and eventually fatal, diabetes followed this operation. Suggesting the involvement of the pancreas in human diabetes, this great discovery was followed by many reports that changes in the pancreas, particularly in its islets, accompany this disease.

In 1892 Minkowski showed that transplantation of the pancreas underneath the skin prevents the onset of diabetes in completely depancreatized animals. Interpreting this observation to mean that the pancreas elaborates a vital substance, many scientists attempted to isolate substances from this gland that would keep depancreatized dogs alive, or alleviate the symptoms of human sugar diabetes—the high blood sugar, and the presence of sugar in the urine. In 1893 the Italian Capparelli made a brew of the pancreas and injected it into diabetic dogs, and his colleague Battistini used it for the treatment of two diabetic patients. Although they reported good results they dropped their work, possibly as a result of the scathing criticism of the medical authorities of the time.

Zuelzer, Dohrn, and Marxer (1908) improved the method of the extraction of an active substance from the pancreas and injected their extract into diabetic patients. These patients showed a marked reduction of sugar and acetone in the urine, gained weight, and felt better. Unfortunately, however, fever and chills followed each injection, and this work also had to be abandoned. Slowly it dawned upon scientists that, since not the entire pancreas is involved in the antidiabetic action, better results might be obtained if the islet tissues alone were used for the experiment. In several species of fish such tissues form a separate organ, and Rennie and Fraser (1907) prepared an extract of these organs. This was effective in the treatment of diabetes but still too toxic for routine use. American investigators also obtained potent but still somewhat poisonous extracts (Murlin, Scott).

To Banting, Best, and Macleod, University of Toronto investigators, belongs credit for the successful preparation of a pancreatic extract effective in lowering blood and urine sugar in diabetic animals and man. Shortly after the first World War (1921–22) Banting suggested to Professor Macleod that since ligating the pancreatic duct leads to degenerative changes in the pancreas and leaves only the islet tissue intact, it would be better to look for the active antidiabetic principle in glands previously prepared in this way. This suggestion was promptly acted upon; and from degenerated dog pancreas macerated with salt solution the first active extract was obtained. Later it was found that alcohol is a better extractor than salt solution, and that for a complicated alcohol extraction the entire untreated pancreas can be utilized because alcohol doesn't dissolve the substances responsible for the toxic effects noted in earlier extracts. Banting and his colleagues named their extract insulin, a name that was suggested for the active principle of the pancreas by De Meyer (1909) and by Schafer (1916).

Abel, Geiling, and their associates of Johns Hopkins University purified commercial insulin preparations and finally obtained insulin in a pure crystalline form. Crystalline insulin is a typical protein and contains a number of amino acids and sulfur. Since both commercial and crystalline insulin are quickly absorbed, necessitating oft-repeated administration, attempts were made to prepare insulins with a prolonged action (Hagedorn, 1936). Such modified insulins are *protamine, globin,* and *histone* insulins. These are prepared by combining fish protamine or globin and histone of the blood pigment, hemoglobin, with insulin. When these various insulins are injected the combination is broken down slowly, and the rate of liberation of insulin is even and slow.

How Insulin Acts. In diabetic patients with hyperglycemia (high blood sugar), glycosuria (sugar in the urine), and acidosis (acetone and similar bodies in the blood and urine), insulin decreases the blood sugar to a normal level and causes disappearances of acidosis and the voiding of sugar. These actions of insulin are complex and not yet fully understood. Lowering of the blood sugar is a result of deposition of the blood sugar in the liver and muscles. Once this deposition is effected, less sugar leaks out from the liver into the blood. In diabetics the liver loses a great deal of its carbohydrates, and insulin helps to regain them. Insulin also produces a lowering of the phosphates and potassium in the blood. See METABOLISM; PANCREAS; DIABETES.

Methods of Administration. In the routine treatment of diabetes insulin is always given by hypodermic injection. No preparation of insulin (nor any other drug) is useful in the treatment of diabetes when taken by mouth. Insulin is administered into the loose tissue beneath the skin, usually one half hour to one hour before meals. With "regular" insulin the maximum action takes place in about 2½ hours, so that this form of insulin must usually be given three times per day. With the newer insulin preparations, including protamine zinc insulin, globin, histone, and NPH50 insulin, the greatest effects are seen from 6 to 24 hours after injection, so that one daily injection usually suffices. Intravenous injection is possible only with regular insulin, which is often administered in this way for its rapid effect in aiding patients with diabetic coma or acute alcohol poisoning.

Diabetic Coma is due to a sudden increase in the severity of diabetic symptoms. Administration of large amounts of insulin is imperative. Fluids and alkalies must also be given to correct the acidosis, and carbohydrates to restore the depleted glycogen deposits in the liver.

Insulin Appetizer. It has been known for some time that the injection of insulin activates the movements of the stomach and the intestines, and shortens the sojourn of food in the stomach. It also produces an intense craving for food. This is why small doses of insulin are sometimes prescribed to increase appetite and body weight. Food, particularly sugar, temporarily relieves the sensation of hunger caused by insulin.

Preparations. Insulin is an aqueous solution of an active principle from the pancreas, the potency of which is expressed in units. One *insulin unit* is equivalent to 0.125 milligrams of the international standard preparation of dry insulin hydrochloride. In the biological assay of insulin 3 units barely suffice to produce such a low blood sugar in rabbits as to cause convulsions. Insulin should never be given in terms of cubic centimeters (cc.) or minims, but always in units. The average insulin preparation is so standardized that 1 cc. contains either 20, 40, 80, or 100 insulin units. *Protamine zinc insulin* is insulin modified by the addition of protamine and a zinc salt. Usually each cc. contains 40 units of insulin, 0.4 milligrams of protamine, and 0.1 milligram of zinc. *Globin insulin with zinc* contains either 40 or 80 units of insulin in each cc. Protamine zinc insulin is commonly combined with regular insulin; speedy onset of action is thus retained while the maximum effect is prolonged. Globin and histone insulin are longer acting than regular insulin but shorter acting than protamine zinc insulin.

The latest and perhaps the most promising insulin preparation is a modified crystalline protamine zinc insulin called NPH50. The N is for neutral, the P for protamine, the H for Hagedorn, and the 50 for the amount of protamine (0.50 mgm.) that has been used with every 100 units of insulin. NPH50 insulin contains less protamine and less zinc than protamine zinc insulin. It is longer acting than regular insulin but shorter acting than the conventional protamine zinc insulin. It has been especially useful in the treatment of severe diabetes, including the juvenile form.   THEODORE KOPPANYI; C. F. MORGAN

INSULIN SHOCK. See DIABETES; PSYCHO-THERAPY.

INSULL, SAMUEL, 1859–1938, American public utility executive, was born in London, England, and educated in public schools in Reading and Oxford. He came to the United States in 1881 and became private secretary to Thomas Alva Edison, whose vast business affairs he managed for many years in the various Edison companies and organizations. When these were consolidated (1892) with the Thomson-Houston Company as the General Electric Company, he became a vice president, resigning the same year to assume the presidency of the Chicago Edison Company and the Commonwealth Electric Company until 1907, when a consolidation of other public utilities effected by Insull made him the ruler of a vast business "empire" which collapsed in 1932. Charges of unethical conduct were leveled against him; he fled to Greece, and then to Turkey, from where he was extradited (March, 1934). With many associates Insull was tried by Federal court, and acquitted.

INSURANCE

With insurance, an individual shares his risk with a group and thus is protected against unexpected loss

INSURANCE. The subject of insurance is treated as a complete entity in this article. For purposes of clarity the analysis is divided as follows: *History* (Ancient Forms, Middle Ages, Modern Development); *Casualty Insurance* (Development, Accident and Health, Automobile, Burglary, Credit, Crop, Fidelity and Surety Bonds, Liability, Title, Workmen's Compensation, Other Types, Rates); *Fire Insurance* (Types of Companies, Rates, The Policy); *Life Insurance* (Functions, History, Calculation of Premiums, Mortality Tables, Policy Forms, Surrender Value, Disability Benefits, Industrial Insurance, Mutual Benefit Associations, Savings Bank Life Insurance, Service Life Insurance); *Marine Insurance* (Development, Policy Form, Average); *War Risk Insurance; Combination Policies* (Recent Trends, Inland Marine, Floater Policies); *Group Insurance* (Development, Modern Types; Requirements and Procedure, Multi-Employer, Life Coverage); *Fraternal Insurance; Government Supervision* (Jurisdiction, State Laws, Federal Supervision); *Social and State Insurance*).

Definition. Insurance is an economic device used for protection against financial loss from perils or hazards inherent to living. It is designed to substitute certainty for uncertainty through the sharing of one person's risk by a large number of persons. This is accomplished by a contract of insurance, the policy, in which, for a moderate premium, one party, the insurer, agrees to pay a sum of money to another, the insured, upon the occurrence of a certain casualty or event.

The benefits of such risk sharing are: (1) risk is transferred from an individual to a group; (2) loss contingency reserves are made unnecessary, making money available for investment; (3) facilitation of credit transactions, permitting the free flow of credit;

(4) premiums collected become funds for investment; (5) providing of security for individuals.

HISTORY

Ancient Forms. Insurance is not a recent development; actually, the first record of a transaction resembling it is found in the Code of Hammurabi, 2250 B.C. A section reads "If a man has a debt upon him and a thunderstorm ravaged his field or carried away his produce, or the corn has not grown through lack of water, in that year he shall not return corn to his creditor; he shall alter his tablet and shall not give interest for that year."

Ancient Chinese merchants using the Yangtze River, distributed parts of an entire cargo to all of their ships, rather than risk it in a single vessel, so that if one were lost, the cargo loss to each shipper was insignificant. Chaldean merchants employed a similar method but, in addition, each merchant and *his family* guaranteed safe delivery of the merchandise which, if lost, was repaid by the entire family working for the shipper.

It is believed the Phoenicians developed bottomry, a form of marine insurance, by which an individual made a loan on a ship and the cargo. If the voyage were completed, the shipowner repaid the loan at a high interest rate, but if the ship were lost, he paid nothing.

By 1000 B.C. such protection was regularly used and laws were enacted to regulate it. One portion of the Rhodian Sea Laws sets forth a principle—*general average*—which is still used in modern marine insurance. If part of a cargo is jettisoned (thrown overboard for the safety of the ship) each of the merchants having cargo on board share proportionately for the losses in direct ratio to the value of their merchandise.

Middle Ages. After the fall of the Roman Empire in the 5th century, European commerce was greatly decreased until the 12th century Crusades, and by that time bottomry changed. Instead of a loan arrangement, a stipulated premium was paid by the shipowner to the individual insurer.

During the next 400 years Florence, Genoa and Venice led in maritime commerce. However, in northern Europe, a group of cities bordering the North and Baltic seas organized a mutual protection group known as the HANSEATIC LEAGUE. As commerce increased cities grew and accentuated fire hazards, but nothing was done during the Middle Ages to protect property with insurance until Guilds were formed in the textile cities of Flanders and Holland. They levied assessments on their members for paying benefits such as burial expenses and reimbursement for fire losses.

Modern Development. Once, insurance was written only by individuals, known as *underwriters* because they signed their names *under* the contract. The term is commonly used today to describe the person who examines a risk. (He is usually an employee of a company.) He passes, recommends improvements in, or rejects the policy application and in doing this is said to be underwriting. Five factors always considered are: (1) moral hazard; (2) physical hazard; (3) financial condition; (4) ability to perform duties; (5) risk location. Emphasis is placed on some factors more than on others, depending upon the coverage desired, i.e., life, burglary, fire.

Insurance as it is known today probably began with the formation of LLOYD'S of London and in America with the organization in 1752 of a company known as *The Philadelphia Contributionship for the Insurance of Homes from Loss by Fire.*

In addition to Lloyd's there are now several kinds of insurers—capital stock companies, pure assessment mutual associations, advance premium mutual associations, fraternal orders, reciprocals, state funds, and self-insurers.

Stock companies organize for profit and insure for a fixed premium. Policies are sold by agents. The *pure* assessment mutuals assess members proportionately after a loss. The advance premium mutuals collect a premium stipulated in advance and the policyholder may receive a portion of the profits or be assessed if a deficit results. Policies usually are sold by paid employees.

Fraternal orders operate similarly to mutuals except that they only insure members of their group. A reciprocal's business is conducted by an attorney in fact appointed by the "subscribers." Each of them is insured by and is an insurer of other members, each of whom pays an advance premium against which his pro rata share of the annual losses is charged. Should it exceed his "deposit," he is required to make up the deficit. See FRATERNAL SOCIETIES.

State funds are conducted by or for some governmental agency. They operate similarly to advance premium mutuals. This is chiefly used in the WORKMEN'S COMPENSATION line. Self insurance is often undertaken by large corporations which set aside a fund for their losses. Many buy insurance from regular insurers above this to protect against catastrophes.

Four general types of risk bearers operate in the United States—life, casualty, fire, and marine. Until recently, one chartered to write in one phase was generally not permitted to write any of the others as a risk bearer may do in other countries. (For recent developments changing this pattern, see Government Supervision, Multiple Line Underwriting.) For further historical data see discussion below of the development of various types of insurance.

CASUALTY INSURANCE

Development. Casualty insurance is the name given to a wide variety of insurance forms which cover innumerable hazards arising out of the complexities of modern life. There are as many as 60 different forms of casualty insurance, one-half of which have originated since 1900. In general, it may be said that casualty insurance is the child of the industrial and mechanized age and its forms protect against the hazards created by motor vehicles, mechanized conveyances, factory processes and the ever-increasing exposure of property owners to suits under the law of NEGLIGENCE.

Accident and Health Insurance is not a single form of insurance, although commonly associated and frequently written in conjunction with one another. Accident insurance has been described as "income interruption" insurance, as it is designed to pay an individual for loss of time, earnings, and expenses caused by accidental bodily injuries. Accident insurance is frequently sold separately, but health insurance is also issued if an equal amount of accident insurance is taken out. The coverages are often combined in a joint accident and health, or "disability," policy.

The principal types of the coverage are (1) commercial, which is sold chiefly to risks in the less hazardous occupations and on which the premiums are payable annually, semiannually or quarterly; (2) industrial, which is sold, as the name implies, to the industrial type of worker and on which the premiums are payable in weekly or monthly installments; (3) noncancellable, similar to the commercial form except that it cannot be canceled by the company and the insured has the right of renewal each year, usually until the insured reaches a certain age (generally 65 years) or else until the company has paid a certain aggregate indemnity, and (4) group policies, often written in connection with group life insurance. (See Group Insurance, below.)

Accident and health insurance was once confused by the multiplicity of policies being offered, all vying with one another in an effort to attract favor by the provision of special benefits. There has since been a tendency to simplify and liberalize the terms of policies, and this has led to the use of forms more clearly understandable. To protect the public interests and those of the insurance business, state requirements govern the approval, form, contents, format, and provisions of accident and health insurance contracts.

The basic purpose of most accident and health policies is to provide income protection. In addition, policy supplements and separate policies are available which provide indemnity to help pay hospital, medical, and surgical expenses. This expense form of accident and health coverage has become so popular that some companies specialize in it alone.

The typical basic accident insurance coverage in the commercial type of policy includes principal sum for loss of life and weekly or monthly indemnity for loss of time. Also usually included are indemnities for certain dismemberment losses and loss of sight, termed specific losses. The weekly or monthly indemnity is payable if the injury causes loss of time, occasioned either by total disability or partial disability. Similar benefits for loss of time caused by sickness under treatment of a physician are provided by health insurance.

The loss-of-time indemnity payments in many policies do not take effect from the first day of disability, but, for a lower premium, are effective after 3, 7, 14, 30, or more days. This applies more frequently to sickness coverage alone, and the days are usually counted from the first date of medical treatment. Also, most policies require that the policy be in effect for a certain number of days before coverage begins. Some policies include expense of treatment coverage for accidents. Most accident or health policies provide hospital benefits, either 50 or 100 per cent of the amount of weekly or monthly indemnity or a named amount daily for hospital board and room plus miscellaneous hospital expenses up to a specified maximum either in total amount or in total days in hospital.

There are secondary coverages included in many policies. Coverage for aviation accidents (if the insured is a fare-paying passenger in a commercial airline on its regularly scheduled route) is usually included. Most policies provide that a small sum will be paid if injuries received do not disable but are treated by a physician.

Many policies provide double indemnity, whereby double the principal sum or loss-of-time indemnity, or both, is paid if the injury resulted from travel in a public passenger conveyance or in elevators, was sustained while in a burning building, or was the result of an explosion of a steam boiler, lightning, hurricane, or tornado. Aviation accidents are usually excluded from the double benefits.

Every accident and health policy contains clarifying definitions and sets forth exclusions that affect the coverage. A typical contract will exclude disabilities resulting from war or any act of war and while the insured is in military service. Also excluded are disabilities resulting from suicide or any attempt threat, or self-inflicted injuries. Territorial limitations are sometimes defined, outside of which the insurance does not apply. Accident coverage includes neither losses caused by disease or bodily or mental infirmity (except pyogenic infections from an accidental cut or wound) nor hernia. Also, accident as well as sickness insurance does not apply except while the insured is under care of a physician. Sickness coverage generally does not include childbirth, except in family hospital-expense policies up to a limited amount.

The application for accident and health insurance identifies the insured and describes his occupation, required to determine the hazard, premium rating, and amount of weekly or monthly indemnity, which is limited to a person's earnings. Most companies limit the amount to from 75 per cent to 80 per cent of the income. Two main factors determine the premium —the occupational hazard and the age of the insured.

Special Policies: The most common form is the newspaper policy, which was developed by the London press. Limited benefits are available for certain injuries or death. In the United States the typical policy of this kind is sold for as little as one dollar as annual premium.

Another is the automobile accident policy. Its cost ranges from as little as $3.00 per year and upward.' Coverage is provided against injuries sustained from accidents while riding as a passenger in a passenger motor vehicle. This form is also somewhat limited.

Ticket policies, railway or aviation, are descendants of the Travelers Insurance Company and the Railway Passenger Assurance Company original single trip insurance for protection against accidental death or injury.

Some large companies have special risks departments that specialize in insuring unusual situations, e.g., covering a summer camp for loss of income as a result of epidemic or disease. Another type is installment purchase insurance available to those wishing to make sure installments on time purchases are met when due should the insured become unable to earn his regular income because of injury or illness.

An accident insurance development of recent years is the providing of aviation coverage—other than ticket policies previously mentioned. Protection for the flying man or woman ranges from a single trip contract to one written on an annual basis.

It is now possible for a tourist, businessman, or diplomat traveling world-wide to buy a special trip policy covering him anywhere in the world for periods ranging from 3 days to 6 months. Protection may be for aviation accidents only or include all ground accidents while on the journey. Even broader so-called "tailored" coverage may be had to meet special needs.

Insurance of pilots, crews, aviation students, etc., and indemnity purchased by an employer to cover employees' deaths as a result of using air transport for business trips, are also written today.

A form of sickness insurance that has become popular, principally because of the type of protection against catastrophe which it provides at a low premium, is the *poliomyelitis expense policy* for individuals and families. The typical policy provides for payment up to an aggregate of $5,000 for expense of treatment, appliances, and transportation, because of poliomyelitis (infantile paralysis) for each person insured, usually during a 3-year period. The annual premium ranges from $3 for one person to about $10 for a family group. An extension of this coverage is the specified disease or "dread disease" policy, which usually covers poliomyelitis and certain other serious diseases, such as leukemia, encephalitis (sleeping sickness), spinal and cerebral meningitis, tetanus, rabies, smallpox, diphtheria, and scarlet fever.

Policies to pay doctors' bills, in the form of *medical treatment policies*, may be purchased on an individual or a family basis to insure against emergency medical expenses. W. B. BORGEL

Automobile Insurance has become the largest single casualty line. It is a direct result of the invention and mass production of the automobile. In general there are two distinct types of coverage: (1) *liability* for death or injury to a person and the destruction or damage of property; (2) *damage* to the insured's vehicle by collision, fire, windstorm, etc., or theft of vehicle.

The first insurance on an automobile was written for "public liability" in 1898 by endorsement on a Teams Policy, and the first auto damage policy was written in 1902. Forms were not standardized until state legislatures became interested in auto insurance, some enacting compulsory auto insurance laws. Now standard contracts have been adopted by the National Bureau of Casualty Underwriters (which is a stock company bureau) and the American Mutual Alliance.

These policies provide two coverages with a third optional indemnity. The first is known as *bodily injury* liability and indemnifies the insured for liability imposed by law for the death of or injury to a person or persons caused by accident resulting from the ownership, maintenance, or use of his or another's vehicle which he had permission to use. This has two limits (selected by the insured), the lower for injury to one person in one accident, and the upper for two or more persons injured in one accident.

The second coverage, *property damage* liability, indemnifies the insured for liability imposed by law for damage or destruction, including the loss of use of property, caused by accident resulting from the ownership, maintenance, or use of his auto or another which he has permission to drive.

The third coverage is *medical payments*, which provides for payment of medical and hospital expenses, regardless of the insured's legal liability if he, his family, or his guests, while in, entering, or leaving, the vehicle are injured as a result of an accident. Physical damage to autos generally cannot be covered by a company writing liability insurance, unless it is licensed to write both lines. (See *Multiple Underwriting*.) Collision insurance may be written by either a fire or casualty company. A company not licensed to write fire and casualty insurance can, with an affiliated company, write what is known as a combination policy.

Physical damage coverage includes: comprehensive, an "all-risk" insurance against falling objects— hail, earthquake, submersion in water, etc; collision with another him; fire; lightning; transportation hazards; theft (including larceny, robbery, and pilferage); towing and labor costs. The insured may buy some or all of the enumerated coverage. Collision coverage and property damage coverage are not synonymous. Collision means damage to the insured's vehicle, and property damage indemnifies for damage to any type of property belonging to others.

Aviation Insurance, similar to automobile, provides two general coverages: damage to the plane and legal liability for injury to persons or property.

Because of the dissimilarity of the two types of insurance involved, damage and legal liability, each is underwritten differently. Physical damage, known as hull coverage, includes provision for inspection of planes, fields, and hangars to maintain low cost insurance and to contribute to safer operation. Unlike automobiles, hulls are considerably more expensive and depreciation and obsolescence are more rapid.

Liability underwriting requires consideration of the physical condition, experience, and training of pilots' and crews, plus the condition of the grounds.

Aviation is a more hazardous risk than other phases of liability insurance, because the aircraft owner is held completely liable for injury to or death of persons; damage to or destruction of property. This is a result of various court decisions and the adoption of the Uniform State Law of Aeronautics, by 20 states.

Burglary Insurance is commonly described as burglary, robbery, and theft insurance. Basically, all forms of coverage insure the property owner against loss or damage by actual or attempted burglary, robbery, or theft caused by someone other than the insured. Since there are no universal legal definitions of these words, the insurer states in the policy what is meant by the terms.

While coverage of this nature has been written for many years, the demand for it has increased considerably because of the mounting value of movable personal property (jewels, clothing, furnishings, silver, securities, money, etc.). The existence of a variety of risks resulted in a multitude of policy forms to meet the needs of each.

Credit Insurance indemnifies manufacturers, jobbers, wholesalers, dealers, etc. against "above normal" loss caused by the insolvency of customers. The loss ratio is determined by comparing the number of "nonpayers" to the applicant's total credit extensions during a period of normal business years.

The insurance recoverable on any debtor of the insured must be in excess of the normal loss but cannot exceed the amount of insurance stipulated for that debtor, providing the debtor has a capital and credit rating in a credit or mercantile agency selected by the insured.

Prior to 1898, when the National Bankruptcy Act was passed, the policies excluded bankruptcy as a cause of loss. They were gradually liberalized and, today, insolvency is understood to include at least 12 different meanings, among them being: absconding, death, or insanity of the debtor; receivership; the sale or transfer in bulk of all the debtor's stock in trade. The benefits of credit insurance to the businessman include: (1) maintenance of a good bank standing; (2) availability of an efficient collection and salvage service; (3) guidance for credit extension.

Crop Insurance. This form of insurance protects farmers from the loss of yield for specified agricultural products. It does not include hail insurance, which is an important form of commercial insurance. Crop insurance has made little progress. Attempts to develop all-risk insurance for agricultural crops have generally proved unsuccessful.

A limited form of crop insurance is provided under title V of the Agricultural Adjustment Act of 1938, cited as the Federal Crop Insurance Act. In practice this system has not been successful; since it is voluntary, relatively few farmers have made use of the insurance, and these are generally those with the greatest risks.

Fidelity and Surety Bonds are written by casualty insurance companies although the coverage is not insurance in the strict sense of the word. Suretyship is an ancient practice and Biblical and other references show its use as early as 1000 B.C. For centuries, the furnishing of surety for the fidelity of persons in positions of trust was in the hands of individuals. The Guaranty Society of London, established in 1849, was the first company to write fidelity bonds in Great Britain; and the Guarantee Company of North America, a Canadian corporation, was the first to offer this form of insurance in the United States. The object of fidelity insurance is to guarantee the integrity, good faith, and honesty of an employee against misuse or misappropriation of money or property in his keeping. In the United States it is always purchased by the obligee, in whose favor the bond runs, who may insure the fidelity of each principal, or party primarily liable, separately, or may purchase a "schedule" bond covering all the principals. The insuring company is known as the obligor or surety. Fidelity bonds may be, and usually are, secured by employers to cover possible losses through dishonesty of an employee or groups of employees. It is also possible to secure a fidelity bond for a given position.

Of *surety bonds* there might be listed several hundred individual types applying to various positions and situations where the guarantee of the performance of an agreement is required. These include public official bonds, executed for state, county and municipal officials guaranteeing the faithful performance of their duty; judicial bonds, for persons in charge of estates in court and of other court actions; bail bonds; bonds guaranteeing the performance of contracts; bid bonds; construction bonds; bonds guaranteeing bank deposits; license and permit bonds; importation bonds; forgery bonds; appeal bonds, and a host of others. See SURETYSHIP.

Liability Insurance. The company, in return for a consideration, assumes the liability for injury to others which legally attaches to the person or persons insured; agreeing to settle with the injured person, to defend possible law suits, and to pay judgments up to the policy limits. An important application of liability insurance is in connection with employers' liability and workmen's compensation. (See discussion of Workmen's Compensation Insurance below).

The modern development of liability insurance has centered around automobile liability coverage. (See discussion of Automobile Insurance above).

Public liability insurance is purchased by owners of buildings, factories, stores, private homes, and apartments, to protect them against injuries suffered by the general public in and about their premises for which they may be liable.

Liability insurance is also available to individuals and families, both city dwellers and farmers, in what is called a *personal liability* policy. It is separately available or written in conjunction with other forms of protection, in combination contracts.

Title Insurance secures and safeguards ownership of real estate. The title policy guarantees the owner clear title (free of claims) for all time to come against all loss caused by an undisclosed defect in the title which existed at the time the policy was issued. Only one premium is paid—when the contract is issued. Premiums vary, depending upon the type of coverage. In large cities it is usually one half of one per cent of the purchase price. The insurance terminates with cessation of the insured's ownership of the property, but it can be assigned to the new owner with no guarantee covering the period subsequent to the date of transfer.

Owning real property involves the question of good title. During the years prior to the existence of title guaranty companies, a landowner hired a lawyer to search the records and prepare an *Opinion of Title*. Should a "cloud" (a fault affecting the ownership) subsequently appear, and the lawyer had not been negligent or dishonest, the owner could not hold him liable for loss. To remedy this uncertainty of undisputed ownership, professional title guarantors came into existence, the first being the Real Estate Title Insurance Company, organized in Philadelphia in 1876. Present day companies still specialize in one line and usually operate in a limited territory because of the expense of building an "abstract plant." This is an index on every tract of land in the vicinity. By use of this index and maps the status of each tract is kept up to date. See TITLE GUARANTY COMPANY.

Workmen's Compensation Insurance indemnifies an employer for liability (imposed by statute) to an employee who is injured or contracts a disease while engaged in his occupation. See WORKMEN'S COMPENSATION.

Other Types. Among other forms of casualty insurance are live stock, glass, elevator, contractors' and manufacturers' liability, and a multitude of other risks which may arise involving loss or injury to person or property or liability therefor. It is virtually safe to say that insurance coverage may be obtained for almost every variety of possible known risk.

Rates. Generally speaking, casualty insurance rates, exclusive of accident and health rates, are under the close surveillance of state government authorities. It is not the general practice in the United States for the states to fix the rates, but in most states the companies are required to file their rates for the information and approval of the state insurance department.

The general dictum in casualty insurance rate making is that the rates must be adequate, reasonable, and entirely nondiscriminatory. It is not for the benefit of the companies alone that the rates must be adequate.   ROBERT F. STEINKE

FIRE INSURANCE

Forms of protection against fire losses existed even among the commercial peoples of antiquity, especially the Romans. In its present form, fire insurance developed as an adjunct to the insurance of marine risks. As early as 1635 efforts were made in England to establish it upon a separate footing, but none of these seems to have borne fruit until after the great fire of London in 1666.

Early in the history of fire insurance in England two distinct ideas developed as to the manner in which it should be conducted—that of the stock company, and that of the mutual. Groups of private speculators, the forerunners of our modern stock companies, were the first to write insurance in large volume; and when, about 1684, the mutual idea was launched, those already in the field invoked the aid of the government against the newcomers. In 1687 a *modus vivendi* was established, and it was agreed that both stock companies and mutuals might lawfully engage in the business of fire insurance, each enjoying exclusive privileges, exempt from competition with the other, during alternate periods of three months. In 1706 Charles Povey introduced the insurance of personal property, and by 1720 fire insurance was established in most of Great Britain's large cities.

The first fire insurance company of importance to be organized in the United States was the Philadelphia Contributionship, a mutual organization founded in 1752. The Mutual Assurance Company of Philadelphia was established in 1784; the Insurance Company of North America, the Baltimore Equitable Society, and the Insurance Company of the State of Pennsylvania in 1794; the Mutual Assurance Company of the City of Norwich (Conn.) in 1795; the Provident-Washington Insurance Company of Providence in 1799; the Eagle Fire Insurance Company of New York in 1806; the Hartford Insurance Company of Hartford in 1810; and the Aetna Insurance Company of Hartford in 1819. By 1820 there were 17 stock companies in New York, 6 in Pennsylvania, 2 in Connecticut, and one each in Rhode Island, New Jersey, and Massachusetts. From an early period many English and Continental fire insurance companies have also been represented in the United States under laws designed to protect American policyholders; and these have transacted a considerable portion of the total insurance.

Types of Companies. Fire insurance companies are of two main types: Stock companies and mutuals. Many *stock companies* require the local agent to report all his transactions, both underwriting and financial, to the head office; while an equal amount of business is done by stock companies which have extensive geographical departments. Most of these latter are located in Chicago, Boston, Philadelphia, New York and San Francisco; while some companies further subdivide the country into New England, Middle States, Southern States, Middle West, Northwest, and Pacific Coast. *Mutual companies* are further classified as town or local, state, and factory mutuals. These furnish insurance upon the payment of a small cash premium, and depend upon assessments to make up possible losses.

A third type of fire insurance organization is the so-called *Lloyds.* These are voluntary associations in which each of the members is held liable for the payment of losses up to a specified amount; and most of these associations issue policies upon the property of members only. Reciprocal and inter-insurance exchanges are variations of the mutual and Lloyds ideas. The limit of risk accepted by one company varies, but insurance over and above the company's limit is placed in the other companies by means of reinsurance treaties (see discussion of Reinsurance above). Fire insurance companies also carry catastrophe coverage with other companies.

The two fundamental necessities in connection with any successful scheme of fire insurance are (1) that it shall be absolutely *dependable*, and (2) that its *rates* shall be reasonable. Fire insurance is a hazardous, unpredictable business and the pendulum of profits swings back and forth. The National Association of Insurance Commissioners set a standard for what might be considered a "fair profit" for fire insurance underwriting. It was the consensus of this body of state supervisors that a profit of 5 per cent was equitable, but they further recommended an additional profit of 3 per cent as a conflagration reserve making an over-all underwriting profit of 8 per cent. This "fair" profit the companies have never been able to achieve.

Rates. Fire insurance rates are determined largely by schedules prepared on the basis of the hazards involved. Minimum rates are given to the best risks; specific charges are added for all deficiencies from the required standards; and reductions from such rates are made when the deficiencies charged for are eliminated. The rating of mercantile property is especially difficult, and a number of attempts have been made to evolve a universal schedule for rating risks of that character. The first of these, the *Universal Mercantile Schedule*, or some modification of it, is now used in many of the large cities of the United States. The *Dean* or *Analytic Schedule* is another important method. Fire insurance rates have generally been higher in the United States and Canada than in western Europe because the fire waste in those two countries has been much greater. Among the immediate causes of this excessive loss, and the consequent excess in rates, are the incendiary fires—deliberately caused for the sake of insurance.

Much of the improvement in the American fire waste situation must be attributed to the National Board of Fire Underwriters, an organization supported by most of the capital stock fire insurance companies (American and foreign) operating in the United States. The board maintains an expert staff of investigators who are trained to detect incendiarism and who are well versed in the histories and habits of professional arsonists. They have tracked such criminals all over the country and have aided in their arrest and conviction by the state and Federal authorities. The legal department of the board also prepared and fostered a model arson law which is now in force in many of the states. Another function of the board which has had an incalculable effect in reducing the fire loss is its establishment of the *Underwriters' Laboratories*, an admirably equipped institution which tests and approves all electrical devices, household equipment and the like. The standards set up by this organization have greatly minimized the number of home fires which commonly occurred as a result of faulty or inadequately insulated equipment.

The Policy of fire insurance in the United States is a standardized contract, the current one being the so-called *1943 New York Standard Form.* This is used, in many cases verbatim, or at least as a model, in forty-five states, the District of Columbia, and two territories. New Hampshire, Minnesota, and Massachusetts use what is referred to as the *New England Form.*

The present standard policy has, on the face, the name of the company, a listing of the amount of insurance, rates, and premiums for the *basic* coverage as well as for any additional coverage for risks insured by separate endorsements attached to the policy.

Next is shown the terms of insurance, premium, dates, and amount of coverage, followed by a space provided for the signature of the issuing agent on behalf of the company. On the reverse of this page are the conditions, exceptions and statements of duties of both parties to the contract.

The property covered is not usually described in the *policy* itself, but is shown in a form that is pasted to the contract, thus allowing for greater flexibility in listing the property, be it a building or contents. The forms also modify the conditions of the policy and, in practice, most fire insurance contracts are a combination of the standard policy and a descriptive form.

The policy insures for the actual cash value to the limit of the insured's interest for all direct loss or damage by fire, lightning, and removal from premises endangered by perils insured in the policy. In the event of willful concealment or misrepresentation the policy is void.

Bullion or manuscripts, ordinarily not included, can be covered by endorsement, but negotiable and similar instruments are not and cannot be covered.

Fire from certain hazards such as enemy attack by armed forces, civil war, etc., but not riot and civil commotion, is excluded. The policy also excludes: loss caused by laws or ordinances requiring construction or repair beyond the actual fire damage; interruption of business or manufacturing process.

Other provisions require the insured to notify the company in the event of a fire, protect the property from further damage, prepare an inventory, and within 60 days after the fire, present a sworn proof of loss. Should there be disagreement about settlement, each party can select an appraiser; these, in turn, appoint an umpire for the purpose of settling the differences.

The amount of insurance is reduced by any partial loss and the contract terminates upon the payment of a total loss.

Many "forms" attached to fire insurance policies (depending upon the risk) carry what is known as a "co-insurance" or "average" clause. This clause is a warranty on the part of the insured that the amount of the insurance in force shall be equal to a given percentage of the actual value. In case of *total* destruction, the "average" clause has no effect, the amount collectible being limited by the amount of the insurance.

In cases of *partial* loss the amount that is collectible is determined by the ratio which the insurance in force bears to the percentage of value specified in the average clause. For example, if the average clause specifies 80 per cent of insurance to value, and if the actual insurance that is in force when fire occurs is only 70 per cent of the value, the owner becomes a co-insurer for the deficiency, and collects only seven-eighths of the total amount of any partial loss.

If, however, the insurance that is in force equals 80 per cent of the value, the average clause would have no effect. The insertion of a co-insurance clause is optional with the insured, but if he should wish such a clause with his policy, his rate is reduced according to the amount of insurance that he carries related to the value of the property that he is insuring.

A large variety of miscellaneous coverages can be added at the price of an additional premium. Both private and commercial risks can purchase what is known as *extended coverage*. This type of coverage includes indemnity for loss or damage caused by: windstorm, hail, explosion, riot, aircraft, vehicle, or smoke to the insured property.

Other protections available include: (1) *business interruption*, providing for payment of stipulated sums for as long a period as the insured is unable to resume operations because of complete or partial shutdown due to fire or to other insured perils; (2) *extra expense*, if an insured must continue to operate in spite of damage his plant may have suffered. This insurance pays the expenses above his normal operating costs.

Water damage, sprinkler leakage, riot and civil commotion, explosion, vandalism and malicious mischief, and fire legal liability are other types of protection also available from contemporary fire insurers, and frequently sold with fire coverage policies.

BIBLIOG.–A. W. B. Welford and W. W. Otter-Barry, *Law Relating to Fire Insurance* (1932); B. C. Remington and H. G. Hurren, *Dictionary of Fire Insurance* (1936); S. S. Huebner, *Property Insurance* (1938); J. H. Magee, *Property Insurance* (1941).

LIFE INSURANCE

Functions. Life insurance may be defined as a guarantee, on the part of the insurer, of a certain payment to the person insured, or his beneficiary in case of death or other specified event, in consideration of a present cash payment or series of payments called the *premium*. During the 20th century the practice of insuring lives has developed into one of the foremost institutions of the civilized world. Its uses are such and its policies so varied that it is purchased by all classes of people from those of low-level income to the most prosperous. Originally designed to relieve the financial worries of widows and orphans brought about by the death of the breadwinner, it continues to perform that function but also pays a large portion of its beneficences to living policyholders, thus protecting against the hazards of living too long as well as dying too soon.

History. As in the case of fire insurance, the business of insuring lives originated as an offshoot of marine insurance. Vessel owners and over-sea merchants and speculators desired protection against the pecuniary loss which would follow upon the death or capture of their trusted captains and supercargoes, with whom the success of trading voyages was usually bound up; and the underwriters who insured the property interests involved in such ventures began to insure, also, the safe return of the responsible men in charge of them.

The first company in Great Britain to devote itself exclusively to life insurance and to transact business on scientific principles, was the Equitable, founded in 1762. Both the sum insured and the premium were fixed at the time of making the insurance contract; the rate of premium was regulated by the age at entry; and the scale adopted was derived from the Northampton Table of Mortality. As this overstated the mortality throughout the greater part of life, by far the majority of premiums were too high; and after paying all claims and expenses, and making the necessary reserves for future claims, a surplus was gradually accumulated. This was divided among the members from time to time, thus originating the modern system of dividend payment.

In the United States, life insurance had its beginning with the Presbyterian Ministers' Fund of Philadelphia, founded in 1759, and still in active business. The Insurance Company of North America, established in 1794, issued a few life policies and then discontinued writing life insurance in 1804; while the first actual life insurance company was the Pennsylvania Company for Insurance on Lives and Annuities, chartered in 1809. Later ones were the Massachusetts Hospital Life Insurance Company (1818), the New York Life Insurance and Trust Company (1830), and the Girard Life and Trust Company of Philadelphia (1836).

Insurance as it is conducted today, however, began with the incorporation of the Mutual Life Insurance Company of New York in 1842, beginning operations in 1843. In the next ten years 25 other companies began operations, among them the New England Mutual Insurance Company, Boston (1843, though chartered in 1835); Mutual Benefit Life Insurance Company, Newark, N.J. (1845); New York Life Insurance Company (1845); State Mutual Life Assurance Company, Worcester, Mass. (1845); Connecticut Mutual Life Insurance Company, Hartford, Conn. (1846); Penn Mutual Life Insurance Company, Philadelphia (1847); Aetna Life Insurance Company, Hartford (1850); Manhattan Life Insurance Company, New York (1850); and Phoenix Mutual Life Insurance Company, Hartford (1851). By 1860 there were 47 life insurance companies in the United States; 60,000 persons were insured for the amount of $180,000,000, paying annual premiums of $7,000,000.

State supervision of insurance companies began early in the 19th century. The first general insurance act was passed by the state of New York in 1849, and its insurance department was established in 1859; Massachusetts established its insurance department in 1855; and the other states gradually fell into line. Each state now has an insurance division, which in almost all cases is a distinct department, though in a few states it is a subdivision of the banking or treasury department. Almost all states have their own insurance codes. (See Government Supervision discussed below.)

Calculation of Premiums. Life insurance, when properly conducted, is not a speculative or hazardous enterprise, but an exact science, controlled and regulated by actuarial computations. The two fundamental requirements are (1) a reliable mortality table and (2) an assumed rate of interest to be used in computing the earning power of a company's reserves. From these two factors the net cost of the insurance, or pure premium, is mathematically figured.

(1) The individual, when he takes out a policy, cannot know, in the nature of things, whether he will have to pay one or fifty annual premiums before his policy finally matures upon his death. But to the insurance company, dealing with hundreds of thousands of individual policyholders, the *Table of Mortality* furnishes a means of making definite estimates in advance; and the outcome is at all times as absolutely sure as the inexorable law of averages can make it. No matter whether the policyholder dies the day after taking out his policy, or lives until a ripe old age—no matter what individual freaks of fortune may occur— the ultimate result to the company must be about the same.

(2) The other dominant factor in determining the cost of life insurance is the *assumed rate of interest*. The rates now used by the companies in estimating the income which their reserves will earn are down to $2\frac{1}{2}$ per cent in most cases, due to the low yield of investments to which life insurance companies are restricted.

In the calculation of premiums, the *net premium* is the figure arrived at before any allowance has been made for expenses and contingencies, and represents only enough to pay the cost of insurance and furnish the requisite *reserve*, which has been called the sheet anchor of life insurance, is a sinking fund maintained to the credit of each policy until it matures; and it is swelled each year by contributions from the premium. On any given policy the amount that the company has at risk—that is to say, the amount which in case of death will have to be made up by contributions from other policies—diminishes each year.

The net or pure premium takes no account of the expenses of conducting the business; so that, in fixing the amount of the premium actually charged, an additional item, called the *loading*, must be included. The amount of loading now permitted under the insurance laws of New York and other states usually exceeds the expenses of properly conducting the business; the interest actually received is nearly always more than the net interest assumed in the calculations; and the actual mortality is, in practice, generally less than is given in the tables now in use in the United States. From these three sources comes the *surplus*. This surplus is the source of contingency reserves, set aside to meet unusual developments, for example, in mortality (such reserves may not exceed 10 per cent of the policy reserve), and is the source of dividends to policyholders and stockholders.

Mortality Tables. Until recently the table in general use was the *American Experience Table* prepared and adopted in New York in 1868. For several years considerable criticism was directed at the *American Experience Table* and other tables used by insurance companies. It was suggested that actual longevity be compared with current tables.

Criticism became so intense that the National Association of Insurance Commissioners, in 1937, decided to investigate the situation. It appointed a committee headed by Alfred N. Guertin, actuary, then with the New Jersey department of Banking and Insurance. The committee sought to find: the levels of population mortality, the levels of insurance mortality, and to survey the research already completed on tables, premiums, etc.

As a result of this work it proposed: (1) new legislation providing that life policies have a provision for equitable nonforfeiture benefits calculated on a basis of appropriate mortality tables representing current experience; (2) adoption of a new table; (3) divorcing mortality and interest rates used for calculating nonforfeiture benefits from that used in calculating premium reserves.

The committee's proposal was redrafted after the commissioners met with company representatives. The result was a model bill approved at the Commissioners' convention in New York, 1942. It was popularly referred to as the *Guertin Laws* but its formal name is: the *Standard Nonforfeiture and Valuation Law*.

Its purpose is to modernize the actuarial bases on which a life company operates and remove cause for criticism of state supervision. It also modernizes antiquated standards established in some statutes. The law includes the *Commissioners 1941 Standard Ordinary Mortality Table*. In compiling this the committee made use of mortality data collected by the Actuarial Society of America since 1925. This included the experience of 15 or 16 of the largest life companies in the country. Also, considerable data was contributed by life companies and the result was a merger of old and new statistical data.

The model bill has been enacted into law in most states.

Policy Forms. With the increasing public interest in life insurance, the companies set about devising attractive policy forms, calculated to appeal to every taste. The practice of declaring dividends to policyholders out of the profits was inaugurated; and these dividends, now declared annually, may be received in cash or used either to reduce the premium, to purchase paid-up insurance, or to accumulate at the current interest rate, thus swelling considerably the sum payable at maturity.

The many varieties of policies now issued may be reduced to four general types:

(1) *whole life policies*, in which premiums are paid during the whole life of the insured, the insurance being payable at death only;

(2) *limited-payment life policies*, in which premiums are paid during a limited period, the insurance being paid at death;

(3) *endowment policies*, in which premiums are paid during a limited period, the insurance being payable at death if it should occur during this term or payable to the insured at the end of the term, if he is living;

(4) *term policies*, which provide for the payment of the insurance at death if it occurs at any time within a specified term, at the end of which the policy expires.

Term policies are pure protection contracts and therefore have no value upon or after expiration of the coverage.

Special Forms include the following two types: (1) *retirement income policies*, which provide a life income to the insured at a certain retirement age, or the cash value or face amount of the policy (whichever of these is the greater) in cash or under an income option to the beneficiary in the event of the insured's death before retirement; and (2) *family income policies*, which provide a high income to the family (usually $10 monthly per thousand of the face amount of the policy) payable for a specified period of years in the event of the insured's death, and then the face amount of the policy in cash or in installments payable for life or a certain number of specified years.

See ANNUITY.

There is no standard life insurance policy required

by any state, but most states prescribe certain standard provisions which must be incorporated in all policies. Following the Armstrong investigation in 1905 the New York Legislature passed a standard policy law. Companies found it too restrictive and at a meeting in Chicago, one year after the investigation, officials from various states appointed the Committee of Fifteen to draw up a more acceptable legislative code. The more important recommendations of this committee were subsequently written into the statutes of the majority of the states.

In 1909, New York repealed its standard policy law, substituting a law requiring the use of standard provisions and the approval of the insurance commissioner of all policy forms. The standard provisions require (1) a 30-day grace period for the payment of premiums; (2) a clause making the policy incontestable after two years; (3) that the policy constitutes the entire contract between the parties; (4) that in case of misstatement of age, the amount payable shall be for the correct age; (5) that the policy in a participating company shall participate in the company's surplus annually; (6) that the options must be specified to which the policyholder is entitled in the event of default of premium payment after three full annual premiums have been paid; (7) that all the loan values of the policy shall be stated; (8) that a table be printed in the policy showing loan values and options available in default of premium payments each year during at least the first 20 years of the policy; (9) that where the policy is payable as an annuity or in installments a table shall show the amount of such annuity or installment payments; (10) that reinstatement shall be covered. Such provisions safeguard policyholders adequately, and their uniform adoption precludes any necessity for a standard policy.

Surrender Value. When the policyholder desires to give up his policy, the company is required by law to return to him a part of the premiums he has already paid. This return, which is called the *surrender value*, varies from one-third to one-half of the premiums paid in ordinary cases; but it may be as much as or even more than, the whole of the premiums, if the policy has been in force for many years and the insured is of advanced age. Some companies provide that in case of lapse of policy through discontinuance of the premiums, the surrender value, if not withdrawn by the insured, shall automatically purchase insurance equal to the face value of the policy— such insurance to be in force for a certain number of years, depending upon the amount of the surrender value

and the age of the insured. Most of the companies will grant loans on the security of their policies to an extent equal to their surrender value. The nonforfeiture law passed by Massachusetts in 1861 required the insurance companies to recognize the equities of retiring policyholders in the company's funds. It was followed by similar laws in other states, and initiated the practice of allowing surrender values.

Disability Benefits. In the early part of the 20th century, disability benefits were introduced as a feature of the life insurance contract. Their first manifestation took the form of a clause waiving payment of premium in the event of total or permanent disability. This *waiver of premium* clause remains today as a feature of most life insurance policies. Other disability benefits were added, however; and during the expansive years of 1925 to 1929 disability benefits were used freely as a competitive weapon and many companies adopted liberal forms which provided for annuity payments in the event of total or permanent

STANDARD ORDINARY MORTALITY TABLE

AGE	NUMBER LIVING	NUMBER DYING	RATE OF MORTALITY	AGE	NUMBER LIVING	NUMBER DYING	RATE OF MORTALITY
1	1,000,000	5,770	.00577	50	810,900	9,990	.01232
2	994,230	4,116	.00414	51	800,910	10,628	.01327
3	990,114	3,347	.00338	52	790,282	11,301	.01430
4	986,767	2,950	.00299	53	778,981	12,020	.01543
				54	766,961	12,770	.01665
5	983,817	2,715	.00276				
6	981,102	2,561	.00261	55	754,191	13,560	.01798
7	978,541	2,417	.00247	56	740,631	14,390	.01943
8	976,124	2,255	.00231	57	726,241	15,251	.02100
9	973,869	2,065	.00212	58	710,990	16,147	.02271
				59	694,843	17,072	.02457
10	971,804	1,914	.00197				
11	969,890	1,852	.00191	60	677,771	18,022	.02659
12	968,038	1,859	.00192	61	659,749	18,988	.02878
13	966,179	1,913	.00198	62	640,761	19,979	.03118
14	964,266	1,996	.00207	63	620,782	20,958	.03376
				64	599,824	21,942	.03658
15	962,270	2,069	.00215				
16	960,201	2,103	.00219	65	577,882	22,907	.03964
17	958,098	2,156	.00225	66	554,975	23,842	.04296
18	955,942	2,199	.00230	67	531,133	24,730	.04656
19	953,743	2,260	.00237	68	506,403	25,553	.05046
				69	480,850	26,302	.05470
20	951,483	2,312	.00243				
21	949,171	2,382	.00251	70	454,548	26,955	.05930
22	946,789	2,452	.00259	71	427,593	27,481	.06427
23	944,337	2,531	.00268	72	400,112	27,872	.06966
24	941,806	2,609	.00277	73	372,240	28,104	.07550
				74	344,136	28,154	.08181
25	939,197	2,705	.00288				
26	936,492	2,800	.00299	75	315,982	28,009	.08864
27	933,692	2,904	.00311	76	287,973	27,651	.09602
28	930,788	3,025	.00325	77	260,322	27,071	.10399
29	927,763	3,154	.00340	78	233,251	26,262	.11259
				79	206,989	25,224	.12186
30	924,609	3,292	.00356				
31	921,317	3,437	.00373	80	181,765	23,966	.13185
32	917,880	3,598	.00392	81	157,799	22,502	.14260
33	914,282	3,767	.00412	82	135,297	20,857	.15416
34	910,515	3,961	.00435	83	114,440	19,062	.16657
				84	95,378	17,157	.17988
35	906,554	4,161	.00459				
36	902,393	4,386	.00486	85	78,221	15,185	.19413
37	898,007	4,625	.00515	86	63,036	13,198	.20937
38	893,382	4,878	.00546	87	49,838	11,245	.22563
39	888,504	5,162	.00581	88	38,593	9,378	.24300
				89	29,215	7,638	.26144
40	883,342	5,459	.00618				
41	877,883	5,785	.00659	90	21,577	6,063	.28099
42	872,098	6,131	.00703	91	15,514	4,681	.30173
43	865,967	6,503	.00751	92	10,833	3,506	.32364
44	859,464	6,910	.00804	93	7,327	2,540	.34666
				94	4,787	1,776	.37100
45	852,554	7,340	.00861				
46	845,214	7,801	.00923	95	3,011	1,193	.39621
47	837,413	8,299	.00991	96	1,818	813	.44719
48	829,114	8,822	.01064	97	1,005	551	.54826
49	820,292	9,392	.01145	98	454	329	.72467
				99	125	125	1.00000

disability, with such disability to be presumed permanent if it lasted more than three months. In most instances the rates were inadequate, and with the advent of the depression a serious situation in respect to disability benefits was unveiled. From 1932 on, there was a general trend toward reduction of disability benefits, and an increase in the rates charged for them. Some companies abandoned the monthly disability benefit altogether. *Double indemnity* for accidental death is commonly included for a modest charge in most life insurance policies. The clause provides for twice the payment of the face amount of the policy where death is due to accidental injury.

H. P. GRAVENGAARD

Industrial Insurance (or weekly and monthly premium insurance) is an outgrowth of the burial clubs, guilds, and friendly societies that originated in England. The term "industrial" stems from the fact that it was originally written on industrial workers. In modern times it has developed from a strictly burial fund into an all-purpose emergency fund for the average family in the event of death, and also as a savings fund to meet emergencies. The early societies which furnished "burial" insurance were frequently unsound actuarially because of the lack of adequate mortality tables, and the dissatisfaction with this system cleared the way for commercial companies to enter the field on a sounder basis. Early companies specializing in industrial insurance were the Industrial and General Insurance Company of England (1949) and the Prudential Assurance Company of London (which entered this field in 1854).

In America the first company to write industrial insurance was the Prudential Insurance Company of America (no connection with the British company), which began business in 1875 as the Prudential Friendly Society. In 1879 the Metropolitan Life and the John Hancock Mutual Life insurance companies entered the field. These companies, although now large writers of ordinary insurance, today lead all others in the volume of industrial insurance in force.

Industrial insurance is written largely on a weekly or monthly premium basis and is customarily referred to in these terms. The premiums are collected by company representatives calling at the insured's home, and this home service may be considered one of its distinguishing characteristics. It was customary for many years to sell the policies for a stated weekly premium such as five, ten, or fifteen cents, rather than on the basis of the face amount of the policy. Whole life policies were the original basic forms for industrial insurance, but eventually limited payment and endowment forms came to be written. Industrial life insurance companies reserve the right to require a medical examination, but in general practice they waive this right. Weekly or monthly premium insurance is written both on adults and children, and they were at one time the only insurance available on the lives of juveniles in the lower age brackets.

Mutual Benefit Associations. For many years Employees' Benefit Associations have been in existence, but it is only within the last few decades that employers have become an integral part of these organizations. In the early days these associations were organized and managed by the employees. In recent years the tendency has been toward a co-operative organization between the employer and the workmen, both contributing to the fund, with the financial benefits, however, going to the sick employee. Today the main types of Mutual Benefit Associations are those managed and financed by employees alone, and those operated jointly with the employer.

Savings Bank Life Insurance, originated by Louis D. Brandeis for the state of Massachusetts in 1907, authorizes savings banks to sell life insurance to citizens of the state. Soliciting agents are not permitted to be employed. Each bank is limited to $1,000 on a single life although there is nothing to prohibit a citizen's purchasing the maximum coverage from several or all of the banks authorized to sell insurance. Criticism of the Massachusetts system is made that the insurance, designed for the benefit of the poorer citizens, is not applied for by them in substantial numbers or amount, but on the contrary is popular with wealthier individuals who secure the limit in several of the banks because of the low rate. In 1938 the state of New York enacted a savings bank insurance law and, taking cognizance of the criticism directed at the Massachusetts law, provided that no individual might insure in more than three banks, thus making maximum coverage available, $3,000.

Service Life Insurance. Life insurance was provided servicemen during each world war. The National Service Life Insurance Act of 1940 established a new system of life insurance for those persons who were in the active service in the land or naval forces, including the Coast Guard, of the United States on Oct. 8, 1940, or who entered those services after that date. Included were those selected for training and service under the Selective Training and Service Act of 1940.

The plan is known as *The National Service Life Insurance* and, like its predecessor, is supported by an independent trust fund comprised of the premium payments and the earnings therefrom.

Coverage is available to any qualified person in any multiple of $500, but not for less than $1,000 or more than $10,000 and if the applicant is serving under active duties for a period of not less than 31 days. Coverage is available to both sexes.

No person can carry more than an aggregate of $10,000 "NSLI" and United States Government Life insurance. Premium payments, which had been low, were eliminated in 1951, making NSLI free to all armed forces personnel on active duty. This provision was retroactive to June 27, 1950.

In 1949, dividends were paid (at the rate of 55¢ per $1,000 of insurance for each month the insurance had been held between 1940 and 1948). This plan for dividend payments resulted from the unexpectedly low volume of payments to next-of-kin of holders of the insurance, which took only a portion of the accumulated income from premium payments. In 1951, a second dividend payment began, based on the period the insurance was held after 1948. In 1951 a law was passed authorizing World I and II veterans to continue their 5-year term policies indefinitely.

MARINE INSURANCE

Marine insurance indemnifies for loss of ships, goods, or profits of voyage by perils of navigation.

Development. It is by far the oldest insurance in the world, fire and life risks all being, until recently, too liable to vast and unpredictable destruction. The first and, till modern times, the only form was the *bottomry bond* (see BOTTOMRY), where a loan in security of ship and cargo was repayable only if the ship returned safely, its loss canceling the bond. The interest on the loan thus included insurance, and was very high and outside any usury laws—a common rate being 15 per cent. It was a favorite investment of Roman patricians and medieval Shylocks, but its high gambling risk is evinced by ages of literature as well as history. Modern marine insurance dates from the 13th century in Flanders and Portugal, and probably among the Lombard merchants in Italy, who carried it to England early in the 16th century. The oldest extant document upon it is a Barcelona (Spain) ordinance of 1435.

A large portion of the marine insurance of the world is taken out in Great Britain. The business is done by stock or mutual companies (alone or with other forms of insurance); by associations of individual underwriters, the oldest and chief of which is Lloyd's; or by the large shipping companies keeping a book account as insurance on their own vessels, and charging the losses against a set per cent of earnings. Until recent years Lloyd's almost monopolized British marine insurance; but the regular companies have now obtained a great proportion'—largely written, it is true, in their capacity as members of Lloyd's. See LLOYD'S.

In the United States, much of the marine insurance was formerly placed in foreign markets. Although the American marine market has regained control of the local business, the larger share of marine insurance is written by American branches of foreign companies, mostly British. There is only one American company whose business is predominantly marine insurance. Since World War I, however, a number of American fire companies have been attracted to the marine field. At the close of World War I the United States government had in its possession a large mercantile fleet which it set out to transfer to private ownership. Adequate insurance facilities were needed for such ships, and at the instance of the government the marine companies operating in America gathered together in the American Marine Insurance Syndicates to provide it. The syndicates largely control the underwriting of ocean hulls by the American insurance offices and share with the London underwriters the hull insurance on most of the vessels registered under the United States flag. (See discussion of War Risk Insurance below.)

Policy Form. There is no standardized marine policy, but all of those in use are essentially alike and derive from the common Lloyd's form of marine insurance policy. This has been in use for over a century and a half, and its retention is most advantageous to both insurers and insured, because every clause has had judicial interpretation many times over, so that each side can make a contract with a comparatively exact knowledge of risks and rights. This policy contains blanks for the name or names of the insured; the property insured, and its value; the name of the ship and master; the commencement and termination of the risk; the voyage; and the ports at which the vessel may touch and stay. It specifies the perils of the sea: "men-of-war, fire, enemies, pirates, rovers, thieves, jettisons, letters of marque, surprisals, takings at sea, arrestments; restraints and detainments of all kings, princes, and people of what nation, condition, or quality soever; barratry—i.e., unlawful conduct involving loss or damage—of the master or mariners; and all other perils, losses, and misfortunes that have or shall come to the detriment or damage of the said goods, merchandise, and ship, or any part thereof."

The usual term is for the voyage, between specified ports, the ship being warranted seaworthy at starting. Sometimes it is for a year or other period, without warranty.

While the fire company may always replace the lost property, the marine company never does. Another difference, peculiar to marine among all forms or property insurance, is that the anticipated profits of a voyage may be insured. Fire insurance companies only approach this in *use and occupancy insurance* which insures net normal earnings during the period a business is interrupted by fire or other catastrophe.

The marine policy does not cover all injuries to vessel or cargo on the voyage, but only abnormal ones. Nor does it provide for those where the normal procedure is pushed to abnormal extent. It covers all navigation perils proper, as wind and wave, grounding, leaks, fire, collisions, etc.; also risks of war, piracy, theft, and barratry. It does not cover the using up of coal, or cracking masts by overpress of sail, or warping boilers by over-pushing fires, to escape enemies; these belong merely to "wear and tear." Centuries of lawsuits over this sometimes tenuous distinction have made a volume of minute legal definitions.

By custom and law, "total loss" of ship, cargo, or freight means something beyond the common understanding of the words. When the loss is more than half the value of vessel or cargo; when the vessel is captured or embargoed; when damage to cargo obliges it to be sold at an unintended place at a loss; or when the voyage cannot be completed, so that the freight cannot be earned, it is a legal "total loss." This also confers a right which exactly inverts the fire-insurance practice: that of claiming the full insurance and abandoning the property to the insurers, who are thus subrogated to all claims against it. In fire insurance the company itself, on assuming a total loss, takes the property for salvage.

Average. Perhaps the most distinctive single feature of marine insurance is a custom not related to insurance at all, but taken over from general maritime law—a custom almost as old as navigation itself, copied by Romans from ancient Rhodian law, and indeed intrinsic in basal justice. This is "average" of losses deliberately inflicted on part of the venture to save the whole; that is, distributing the loss among all who are to share the profits—including, of course, the sacrificed owner. The term "average" was long ago curiously expanded to mean any loss *not* averaged. Such apportionment is called *general average;* a loss borne solely by the owner is *particular average.*

These discriminations, fought unendingly by the interests at stake, have again loaded the law with multifold decisions, differing much in different countries. A given loss is *general* or *particular* according to circumstances, the broad line being that general is voluntary, and particular is involuntary—part of the understood risks of the voyage, or in marine insurance the things which the policy is primarily written to cover.

The policy itself usually limits the company's liability in varying degree on particular averages. Some it does not cover at all; others, only for losses over a certain (commonly five) per cent, or in special contingencies; and to fix that percentage, all partial losses at different times during the voyage are added together.

Inland Marine. Although this form of coverage is comparatively new, there is some evidence of primitive forms of land transportation risks recorded in the trading loans of the Babylonians and Hindus.

Actually, it grew from *Ocean Marine*—coverage on a shipment from the time it was on board until off the ship. Necessity for broader insurance caused merchants to demand it, until there was developed the "warehouse to warehouse" form and, ultimately, the "all-transit" risk by the time of World War I.

Since the government operated the railroads during that period and there were considerable shipping losses with inevitable claim delays, shippers went to insurers for protection and received the transit policies. Marine underwriters handled this coverage because they were familiar with transportation risks and subsequently created many forms of "Inland" marine contracts to cover specific situations. The volume of business annually transacted in the United States has grown tremendously and is considered a major phase of the industry today.

WAR RISK INSURANCE

The additional risks to shipping due to the conditions created by World War I led to the creation by the U.S. Congress (Sept. 2, 1914) of a Federal Bureau of War Risk Insurance, to insure American vessels, freight, and cargo, when it proved impossible to secure adequate marine insurance on reasonable terms from private companies; a fund of $5,000,000 being provided for the purpose. By act of June 12, 1917, the Bureau was empowered to extend insurance to officers and seamen of American merchant ships, and by Act of July 11, 1918, (1) to vessels of foreign friendly flags (including their freight and passenger moneys, and personal effects of masters, officers and crews) when such vessels were chartered or operated by the U.S. Shipping Board, or by a citizen of the United States, and (2) to cargoes shipped in such vessels of foreign friendly flags, whether or not they were so chartered.

Before World War II Britain announced the formation of a War Risk Pool to cover shipments to and from Great Britain and keep shipowners from avoiding the British Isles. American marine underwriters minimized individual risk by forming the American Cargo War Risk Re-insurance Exchange in 1939.

The Merchant Marine Act of 1920 provided for a fund to be used by the U.S. Shipping Board to offer insurance considered necessary on the interests of ships sold by the board subject to mortgage. The Merchant Marine Act of 1936, Title II, gave the Maritime Commission which succeeded the U.S. Shipping Board all of its powers and the use of this fund.

The act was amended in 1940 and the fund was known then as the Marine and War Risk Insurance Fund and this act authorized the commission to provide direct war risk insurance and reinsurance on U.S. shippers. Coverage, then, did not apply to contraband cargo. In 1942 this restriction was eliminated.

Some war risks were written by private carriers, but most of it was handled by the fund of the War Shipping Administration. Rates fluctuated with conditions, but government action stabilized them somewhat. The fund did not compete with private carriers.

For war damage insurance, other than marine, on Dec. 13, 1941, the Reconstruction Finance Corporation established the War Damage Corporation with capital of $100,000,000 to insure against war damage, and in a subsequent act (March 27, 1942) its functions were defined.

This corporation insured individuals "against direct physical loss or damage to the property described in the attached application which may result from enemy attack including any action taken by the military, naval or air forces of the United States in resisting enemy attack." (Protection applied only to war risks and did not include perils such as damage by enemy civilian agents, since the latter is covered by standard contracts protecting against the perils involved, i.e., fire, explosion, vandalism, etc.)

This insurance was written through the facilities of existing fire insurance companies who were appointed to serve as fiduciary agents of the corporation. Premiums collected were placed on deposit with the nearest Federal Reserve Bank to the account of the WDC. Later, coverage was extended to money and securities with casualty companies and their agents similarly participating.

Six million policies were issued for about $140,-000,000,000 in insurance in 1942. Up to December, 1943, claims were made for $72,899 and the corporation received about $218,000,000 in premiums after paying all expenses. Renewal premiums were charged in 1943, but cover was renewed in 1944 for no charge. Policies renewed and in force at the time were continued for no additional charge as of Feb. 28, 1945, for one year after their expiration date. Operations of this program were finally discontinued in 1946.

Floater Policies. Among the types of policies now written are the so-called *floaters* covering property anywhere in the world against practically any cause. This form is an outgrowth of the transportation form called the "open" policy. There are at least 20 different types of which the following are representative: personal property, fur, jewelry, fine arts, musical instrument, radium, patterns, jeweler's block, physicians' and surgeons' instrument, camera, silverware, neon signs, registered mail, morticians, and wedding presents.

In addition inland marine underwriters can insure bridges, tunnels, and other instrumentalities of transportation.

Thus it will be seen that insurance is coming closer to the multiple-line idea, although considerations of safety still make it advisable that fire and casualty

companies maintain their separate existences, thus making more certain the proper allocation of reserves for each class of risk. Thus far the western states seem to be more liberal than the eastern states in permitting combination policies.

GROUP INSURANCE

Group insurance is a plan of insurance similar to that issued individuals but offered to all members of a certain group. Every member is eligible for the same plan—there is no discrimination, and involved applications or physical examinations are not required.

Today, group insurance is easily sold because regular payroll deductions made by the employer reduces the cost of the plan. It is available to industrial and commercial firms, stores, associations, teachers' groups, medical societies, auto clubs, schools, credit unions, and public employees. Coverage can be sold by either life insurance companies or casualty companies, as well as regular accident and health companies.

Development. While individual accident and health insurance is not new, the "Group" plan dates back only to 1890. In that year the Travelers Insurance Company issued the first group contract to the Board of Fire Commissioners covering the fire fighting force. The coverage as it is known today evolved when Montgomery Ward & Co., in 1910, sought a plan for their employees. It was created and written by the London Guarantee and Accident Company.

Modern Types. Present day group accident and health insurance falls into three types: (1) group accident and health, (2) group hospitalization, (3) group accidental death and dismemberment. The first provides, usually, weekly indemnity for loss of time caused by nonoccupational injury or sickness. Some companies occasionally are willing to include occupation accidents. The policy may have a 13-, 26- or a 52-weekly maximum benefit with waiting periods ranging from 3 days to one month. The second provides a daily allowance for hospital confinement and reimbursement for certain fees such as room and board, operating room, x-rays, anesthesia, etc. Surgery can also be included. Some plans permit the coverage of an employee's family. This phase was given considerable impetus by the origin of mutual plans such as the well-known Blue Cross Plan for Hospital Care.

The third plan insures against loss of life, limb, or sight. None of the three follows the same policy forms exactly for all groups. Modifications are made to suit each risk.

Requirements and Procedure. The typical group plan can be had by almost any group, providing there are 50 or more members in it. This can include an entire personnel or a particular class. In many states the minimum is as low as 25; and in others a miniature form, or 10, is permitted. Seventy-five per cent of the group must accept the plan or it will not be written, because the company estimates this as the minimum necessary to make the plan profitable.

Ordinarily a probationary period is stipulated for employees. They must be with the employer a certain length of time and also must accept the plan before a specified date to avoid a physical examination. Otherwise some might delay participating until illness is imminent and thus work the plan to the insurer's disadvantage.

Usually the amount of insurance per employee is based upon the averaged group income and the type of plan desired. Certain industries are rated higher, and if a larger amount of females or non-Caucasians are employed the cost is higher.

A *master policy* is issued to the employer who ordinarily pays part of the cost. He administers the plan and distributes the certificates of insurance to the participants. Such plans are generally considered as one year term insurance and the rates are based, partially, on the experience of the group. It is customary for a group specialist to visit the plant at least once each year to determine how the plan is functioning. Individuals are seldom canceled by the insurer unless a disastrous loss ratio develops, and then only with the consent of the employer.

Multi-Employer. A recent development in group plans was that brought about by World War II—the *Multi-Employer* group. It started with local unions whose members were all employed by the same concern and then gradually transferred to other firms engaged in the same business.

The insurer's group requirements presented a problem, but it was solved in New York by a law passed in 1943 making trustees of funds established and maintained by the contributions of the employer members of a trade association for the sole benefit of its employees eligible for group cover.

Under the plan, a union can negotiate with all of the employers of the association. The plan is mutually selected by both. Groups such as the garment, hosiery, jewelry, leather, and textile workers are successfully using the system.

Franchise and Blanket Insurance. Franchise accident and health insurance is sold when group requirements cannot be met, usually because of the smallness of the group. Popular forms of blanket accident insurance are those issued for volunteer fire departments and school or college students. Some companies also issue policies to insure high school athletic teams and others, usually providing medical expense coverage for accidents arising out of specified types of athletic games or training for athletic events.

Statutory Disability Insurance. Since 1943, several states have enacted laws to provide statutory disability insurance whereby workers are insured mainly for loss of time due to accidents or sickness occurring away from their occupations. These laws are in principle an extension of workmen's compensation insurance. They provide basically for the payment of a small weekly indemnity either by the state or through private insurance companies for a period of thirteen or twenty-six weeks, after a waiting period of seven days has elapsed.

Life Coverage. Group life insurance was advanced originally in 1911 by the Equitable Life Assurance Society of America and has, since then, had a rapid growth.

Technically, it is one-year renewable term insurance. Its popularity has been based on the low wholesale rates charged and the fact that it can include all employees without regard to their health or family history. For an average premium rate, which is determined from all ages represented, the life of each member of the group is insured for an announced amount, often increasing with length of service or increase in salary. The total premium was formerly paid by the employer, and the insurance certificate given to each employee as a gratuity to increase and improve industrial goodwill. Since about 1922, however, the more usual practice is for the employer and employee to bear jointly the cost of the insurance. It has been shown that such a cooperative plan, providing low-cost insurance for every active employee, improves the morale in an organization.

In addition to health, accident, hospitalization, and life coverage by group plan there are additional features offered, such as thrift plans and annuities, which represent a recent development in the field and offer a possible solution of the industrial pension problem.

FRATERNAL INSURANCE

Fraternal Insurance is an agreement whereby a fraternal beneficiary society pays to its members or to their beneficiaries, as prescribed in its constitution and laws, death or other benefits in return for stated annual or monthly premiums. Fraternal insurance differs from old-line insurance chiefly in being an obligation to pay under stipulated conditions, rather than a contract for indemnity against loss. Owing to the mutual character of fraternal organizations and their lack of soliciting agents, their rates are comparatively low.

Originally, the financial methods of fraternal societies in the United States and Canada closely resembled those of the English friendly societies. Uniform assessments were made according to need, and the amount and occasion of benefit were not explicitly defined. The failure of many early societies demonstrated the need of more adequate provision for the inevitable rise in death rate due to the increased age of members. The level premium system was thereupon introduced, grading the premiums of each member according to his age at entrance. This plan, though an improvement, was in turn found defective. In recent years the natural premium system, based upon attained age, and making the payment of each cover the year's risk, has been adopted by many societies. Variations of this are the step-rate plan peculiar to fraternal insurance, whereby the rates are increased at five-year intervals; and several modifications involving higher rates in youth to counteract insufficient later rates. The reserve is limited to one year, and is supplied by making premiums payable in advance.

The most influential agent in procuring these reforms has been the National Fraternal Congress, which in 1913 became The National Fraternal Congress of America when it merged with the Associated Fraternities of America. It was organized in 1886 primarily for the purpose of establishing uniform minimum rates throughout the United States. These were urgently needed, for the temptation to gain membership by low assessments had led many societies to organize on a basis which invited ultimate failure. Voluntary agreement on the part of the various orders proving impossible, and existing legislation being inadequate, a bill was drafted in 1910 for introduction into the state legislatures. This bill provided in part for sufficient rates based on sound mortality tables, and stipulated that societies found insolvent by their annual reports should be readjusted according to certain regulations. Laws have been passed in a majority of states containing the chief articles of the bill, and embodying the provision that future rates shall be calculated from mortality tables at least equal to those of the National Fraternal Congress.

See FRATERNAL SOCIETIES.

GOVERNMENT SUPERVISION

Insurance as a quasi-public activity is under governmental supervision for the protection of the policyholders and the citizens of the state. In the United States, states and territories have passed laws regulating the forms, rates, manner of acquisition, and company qualifications. All of the laws and the departments controlling insurance are not similar, but they tend to accomplish the same results.

The first state to assert supervisory authority over insurance was Massachusetts which passed a law in 1827. Later, in 1852, it enacted a law regulating insurance and requiring the appointment of a commission to perform limited duties. In 1855 an independent board was created to carry the burden of controlling insurance activities. Elizur Wright, of Massachusetts, is considered the father of insurance supervision. He studied the need for financial security of companies and, in 1858, the state legislature required the posting of adequate reserves for all life insurance companies to protect its contracts with the public.

Jurisdiction. The United States government's broad jurisdiction over foreign relations makes it capable of excluding, expelling, or admitting an alien firm without regard to state regulation. The Federal government, however, recognizes the jurisdiction of various states over alien insurance companies. All states have passed regulations stating what may or may not be done and provide for the appointment of a commissioner or superintendent of insurance.

State Laws provide for deposits of securities, cash, or corporate surety bonds from newly licensed companies. There are two varieties: *compulsory*, required before permission to operate is granted; and *optional*, a voluntary plan usually used by life companies. Agents are generally required to post bonds. In dealing with rate problems, the commissioner has the authority to make rulings in response to hearings or complaints. Hearings are common although not required by law. While the insurance supervisor has tremendous power he seldom is accused of using it unfairly. In most states the governors have no way of removing him from his appointed office.

As a consequence of the McCarran Act (discussed under *Federal Supervision*) all states, by the end of 1948, had some type of rate regulatory law in force. Briefly, these laws were intended to promote public welfare by regulating rates so they would not be excessive, inadequate or unfairly discriminatory and to authorize and regulate co-operative action among insurers in rate-making and other matters.

Insurance officials out of common interest organized the National Association of Insurance Commissioners in 1871. It encourages the promotion of higher professional standards and the solution of common problems. The biggest one today is the development of a uniform law controlling insurance adaptable in all states to conform with significant Federal legislation and court decisions. The Association has prepared a uniform insurance code and forms for financial statements. It makes recommendations to states to follow uniform practices.

Multiple Line Underwriting. Until recently, U.S. insurance companies were not permitted to write several different kinds of insurance, since they would be licensed to write only Fire or only Casualty, etc. Some companies organized in eastern states had such broad powers in their charter, but they seldom availed themselves of the privilege since practically all states prohibited such freedom in underwriting.

However, following recommendations by the National Association of Insurance Commissioners in 1944, most states authorized both Fire and Casualty insurers to write all forms of Automobile and Aircraft insurance, the Personal Property Floater, and some forms of Inland Marine coverages. In 1951, 31 states and the District of Columbia permitted complete multiple-line underwriting—Fire and Casualty—while other state laws varied from no provision to limited authority.

Federal Supervision. Insurance first attracted Federal interest in *Paul* v. *Virginia*, a case heard by the U. S. Supreme Court, which decided in 1869 that issuing a policy of insurance was not commerce. Insurance remained purely a state problem until 1942 when the Southeastern Underwriters Association (composed of nearly 200 stock companies and 27 officers and executive members of the group) was charged by the U.S. Department of Justice with violating Federal antitrust laws. In the decision of 1944 the Supreme Court held that the *Paul* v. *Virginia* case did not establish that the Federal government had no authority or that the laws applying to interstate commerce did not apply to insurance. It also asserted that there was no intent in the antitrust laws to exclude insurance. This decision created a furor in the insurance world and caused concern as to whether the business would be subject to the Federal Trade Commission regulations. However, the McCarran-Ferguson Act, passed in 1945, provided that, until Jan. 1, 1948: (1) insurance is subject to state laws regulating and taxing it; (2) no Federal law shall supersede a state law except that after that date the Sherman, Clayton, and Federal Trade Commission acts shall apply to insurance to the extent that the business is not regulated by the state; (3) the Sherman,

Clayton, Federal Trade Commission, and Robinson-Patman acts shall not apply to insurance until after Jan. 1, 1948 (see TRUSTS and TRUST REGULATION). This enabled the states and the industry jointly to fashion "model laws" so that the Federal control of insurance as interstate commerce would apply with no ill effect to the degree that the states do not regulate it. Two subsequent U.S. Supreme Court decisions rendered in June, 1946—*Robertson* v. *California*, and *Prudential* v. *Benjamin*—indicated that no Federal law will invalidate or impair a state law regulating the business. ROBERT F. STEINKE

SOCIAL AND STATE INSURANCE

The details of the various branches of social and state insurance are covered under their individual headings. See CHARITY; CHILD WELFARE; HEALTH INSURANCE, STATE; PENSIONS; POOR LAW; POVERTY AND POOR RELIEF; SOCIAL SECURITY; UNEMPLOYMENT; UNEMPLOYMENT COMPENSATION; WORKMEN'S COMPENSATION. T. G.

INSURGENCY. See INSURRECTION.

INSURRECTION, an uprising against political authority less extensive than a rebellion or a REVOLUTION. Although the terms are never precise and are often used interchangeably some distinctions in meaning may be noted. A revolution usually involves a well-planned and organized uprising to bring about a radical modification of the existing political order; the classic examples are the French Revolution and the Russian Revolution. The word "rebellion" is most often used to refer to the attempt of a part of a state to break away from the rest; thus the American Revolution was properly a rebellion, as was also the attempt of the Confederate States to break away from the Union in 1861. An insurrection involves the use of force against the established government for more limited objectives; often it is the means used by a minority group when it has failed to gain its ends by constitutional means. The WHISKY INSURRECTION of 1794 was actually an insurrection, being an uprising against the payment of taxes on liquors. The word "insurrection" is also applied to the initial stages of movements which later develop into either revolutions or rebellions.

Insurgency in international law is an ill-defined condition of public disorder between mob violence and civil war. The recognition of insurgency does not carry the rights and obligations of a state of BELLIGERENCY. Usually in a full-scale civil war other states, whose interests are affected by the conflict, recognize the existence of belligerency, thus granting to the rebel group the rights of warfare and imposing on it the corresponding obligations. The status of insurgency grants only limited belligerent rights, but if the movement gains strength it may be replaced by full belligerency. In 1895 when the revolt against Spain broke out in Cuba President Cleveland recognized the state of insurgency, and similar action has frequently been taken in regard to uprisings in various Latin American states. Such action is merely the recognition of a widespread condition of public disorder; its principal effect is to bring about changes in legal rights and obligations. FRANK L. ESTERQUEST

INTAGLIO, the term applied either to a method of engraving, or to a gem engraved in that particular style. *Etching* is one of the chief methods. In it the lines drawn by the artist upon the prepared surface are bitten by acid into the plate and form hollows in its face. In photogravure and allied mechanical processes, an intaglio is produced by photographic and scientific means in a metal plate, from which impressions are printed.

In a stricter sense, an intaglio is a gem, usually of onyx or some other variety of chalcedony, in which a design has been hollowed out, so that, when the gem is pressed upon any soft material, such as wax, it gives an impression in relief of the nature of a CAMEO. Intaglio gems are of very ancient origin, and fine examples are highly esteemed as works of art. In Egypt and early Greece and Etruria they were either of scarab or seal form; while in Babylonia and Assyria they took the form of cylinders round which the subject was engraved. See GEMS AND PRECIOUS STONES.

INTAGLIO PRINTING. A method of producing a print from a plate on which the image is engraved or etched below the surface. Examples of this method are found in ENGRAVING and PHOTOGRAVURE.

INTEGRAL AND INTEGRATION. See CALCULUS; NUMERICAL INTEGRATION.

INTEGRATION (mental) refers to the process of organizing mental elements into more complex units. Experiences are not merely piled up in the mind; they are synthesized and systematically arranged. Thus images are integrated into ideas, ideas again are integrated into concepts, these again into principles, etc. Each of these levels may be simple or extremely complex.   J. L. HIRNING

INTEGUMENT. See SKIN.

INTELLIGENCE has been defined as "a general capacity of an individual consciously to adjust his thinking to new requirements." The capacity is general for it does not bear upon the specific nature of the task or problem upon which it works, and it is essentially adaptive since it is considered to be in operation when a human being or animal successfully meets a novel environmental situation. Recently human intelligence has been described as "mental alertness," a phrase that emphasizes rapidity of adaptation. No final definition of intelligence, however, can be laid down. A widespread use of the term has come about because of an extensive and successful employment of "intelligence tests." It is found that persons who do well in one mental test are apt also to do well in a great variety of different tests, so that intelligence has among psychologists the practical meaning of a general capacity for success in widely diverse mental tests. A working definition of intelligence is therefore general ability in the performance of such tasks (e.g., MENTAL TESTS) as demand rapid adjustment to novel requirements. In any practical situation, however, such as school or occupation, an individual's efficiency depends not only on his general intelligence but also on his special training, instruction, experience, and practice, on his possession of some special aptitude such as manual co-ordination or musical talent, and on certain qualities of temperament and personal-social adjustment. Some of these can be appraised by means of tests of special aptitudes or personality traits, although not so reliably as can intelligence and actual achievement.

Measurement of Intelligence. Intelligence is measured by intelligence tests, the actual measure being an arbitrary score in a particular test. Such "raw" or point scores, usually the number of problems correctly solved in a given time, are often supplemented by derived or equivalent scores based on comparing the individual's score with scores (norms) made by a large and representative sampling of the test-population. The most common kinds of equivalent score are (1) dispersion scores, such as standard score or percentile score, and (2) mental age scores. (1) The standard score tells where the individual stands among others with whom he is compared, in terms of "standard deviation units"; thus, if his standard score is +1.00 he scores one standard deviation ("sigma") unit above the average or median of the group, which is to say that he equals or surpasses approximately 84% of the comparable group; so we can state the same fact by saying his percentile score is 84. (2) A more generally used measure is the "mental age."

Development of Intelligence constitutes the major mental change in childhood, whereas in adulthood intelligence is practically constant or decreases slightly, while mental development continues with respect to special abilities and the accumulations of knowledge. (See GROWTH.) In late maturity and more markedly in old age mental ability declines in those acitivities which do not depend upon accumulated knowledge or skills, but some of this decrease is due to the increase with age of sensory and motor deficiency and some of it is due to diminished motivation and decreased desire to excel. It is not known how much intelligence as such diminishes in senescence.

Stupid and feeble-minded persons have mental ages less than normal. (See MENTAL DEFICIENCY.) A common classification in terms of IQ is as follows: normal, 90–110; dull, 80–90; borderline defective, 70–80; moron, 50–70; imbecile, 20–50; idiot, 0–20. Perhaps 5% of the population of the United States has an IQ less than 70. Only a very few of the least competent of these—about one in two thousand in the United States—receive institutional care.

Genius has often been defined as high intelligence, an IQ, say, of 140 and over. The biographical records of great men have been studied in an attempt to determine posthumously their IQ's. FRANCIS GALTON had an IQ very near 200. LEIBNITZ, GOETHE, JOHN STUART MILL and a few others seem to have had IQ's above 180. CHARLES DARWIN's IQ was computed as 135, but that is nevertheless very high. Many of these great men were child prodigies, reading several languages at eight and attaining in adolescence distinctions that belong to adulthood.

Intelligence Tests. No single mental test is ever an adequate test of intelligence for the reason that intelligence must be regarded as general ability, whereas any particular test involves always some kind of special ability. Intelligence tests consist, therefore, of "batteries" of various tests, each depending in part on intelligence and in part on some specific ability. The variations in these special aptitudes cancel each other out, and general ability is thus indicated by the sum of the scores in all the tests. Recently, owing to factor analyses of test data, there has been a growing tendency to recognize the existence of several "group factors" or "primary abilities," intermediate in generality between specific abilities and general intelligence. Among these psychologists have specified verbal comprehension, number facility, perceptual speed, space visualization, word fluency, memory, inductive thinking, and, with less certainty, others. Some of these abilities are known to be further analyzable. Since different intelligence tests tap different combinations of these primary abilities, it follows that "test intelligence" is a complex entity, a somewhat variable combination of general abilities which are important in processes of adjustment. This explains discrepancies among the scores of an individual on different intelligence tests, and the failure to find as high correlations between different tests as would be expected if all intelligence tests measured exactly the same thing.

The earliest series of intelligence tests was the Binet-Simon scale which has undergone various revisions. The most recent English form (1937) is known as the revised Stanford-Binet test. It consists of two equivalent forms, each of which contains 129 test-items that are scaled in difficulty from what is normal for two years of age up to the maximum for the superior adult. Above this level, there are three successive levels of superior adult intelligence. The passing of every item in the scale would yield, according to certain calculations, a mental age of 22 years and 10 months, and an adult attaining this score would have an IQ of 152.

Some early test-makers assumed, and many people still believe, that intelligence-test scores measure some exclusively hereditary capacity and are not affected by differences in environment and training. This has been demonstrated to be untrue. Indeed, some have gone so far as to deny that mental ages reflect hereditary endowment. The generally accepted view among psychologists is that an individual's mental level is fixed to some extent by hereditary determinants, and that, while this family strain influences the kind of home environment to which the growing child will be exposed, any marked deviation from a normal environment tends, nevertheless, to raise or lower his expected score. Intelligence, as the tests test it, depends on both nature and nurture.

Intelligence tests do not function independently of cultural acquisition. No successful inter-racial or international test of intelligence has ever been devised. On the average the test scores of children are favored by the high social and economic status of their fathers, a relationship which, while not precluding the inheritance of intelligence, is probably dependent upon the fact that the tests are so "bookish" and "linguistic" in character that an intellectual environment fits the child to do well in them. Tests that closely resemble the accepted intelligence tests are administered to college students in America under the title "scholastic aptitude tests," a term which avoids the connotation of intelligence as something that is inherited and not acquired. As a matter of fact performance in the Stanford-Binet test is improved by practice and experience with it tends to raise the IQ on the scholastic aptitude tests about two points.

Concepts of Intelligence. Intelligence, as general ability, is most readily thought of as a "common factor" entering in different degrees into a large number, or even all, human abilities. Some psychologists regard this common factor as a general fund of "mental energy" that can be employed in any activity. There is some evidence that intelligence, at least as it is measured in animals, is directly related to the total amount of tissue in the cerebral cortex, and that destruction of some of the cortex, irrespective of what part it is, reduces capacity in learning and in test-performance proportionately. This fact may mean that the intelligent person or animal is the individual who has available within his nervous system many different means for solving a single problem. His quick success in adjusting to a novel situation comes about because he has so many solutions at hand that he soon pitches upon an adequate one, whereas the individual with less cortex is handicapped by the loss of some of the various normal means of meeting the situation. See INDIVIDUAL DIFFERENCES.

Intelligence in Animals. In animals, intelligence is usually considered to be the ability to profit by experience, and it is measured by the capacity of the animal for learning. Most tests consist in measuring the animal's capacity to learn a path to food through a maze, or to learn to operate some combination of mechanical devices which will release him from a "puzzle-box." Higher levels of intelligence can be tested by the "multiple-choice method" in which the animal is required to learn some rule by which, from a series of boxes, he can select at once the box which contains his food. The correct box may always be the middle box when the total number of boxes varies, or it may always be the second box from the left, or it may be the box at the opposite end from the end that was previously right. See COMPARATIVE PSYCHOLOGY.

The animal scale of intelligence may be considered as overlapping the human, for the mature chimpanzee is approximately as intelligent as the average child of three years. As we go down in the evolutionary scale we find less and less intelligence. Even the very simplest animals, however, can learn in the sense that their behavior may be modified by past experience; and they must thus be considered to have intelligence. The conception of intelligence as a capacity for giving attention would mean that it was always to be found wherever there was consciousness or animal life.

EDWIN G. BORING

BIBLIOG.–L. M. Terman and M. A. Merrill, *Measuring Intelligence* (1937); L. L. Thurstone, *Primary Mental Abilities* (1938); E. B. Greene, *Measurements of Human Behavior* (1941); G. K. Bennett and D. Wechsler, *The Measurement of Adult Intelligence* (1944); W. C. Halstead, *Brain and Intelligence* (1947); S. Lall, *Mental Measurement* (1948); J. Piaget, *Psychology of Intelligence* (1950).

INTELLIGENCE, GOVERNMENTAL, is, in its broadest sense, the vast body of information on which governments base all their plans, policies, and actions, both domestic and foreign. In its narrower and more common sense, it refers to the information a nation gathers concerning other nations on which it bases its plans, policies, and actions in war and peace.

In this latter meaning, governmental intelligence may be classified as either *strategic*, or long-range, in nature; or as *tactical*, or short-range. It may also be classified as to type: MILITARY INTELLIGENCE; political, technical, and industrial and commercial intelligence; and counter intelligence.

Intelligence is collected by governments in a number of ways. Clandestine intelligence is usually gathered through ESPIONAGE or cryptanalysis (see CRYPTOGRAPHY). But much intelligence is collected in more prosaic ways, such as by reading of open publications and by collating and analyzing data made public in various ways.

Intelligence collection is basically a function of the military forces and of the diplomatic services of a nation, as well as of special intelligence bureaus which may be set up. In the United States, intelligence is gathered by the state and defense departments as well as the Central Intelligence Agency. These agencies gather, collate, analyze, and distribute to the proper authorities all possible intelligence information.   R. W. M.

BIBLIOG.–S. T. Felstead, *Intelligence* (1941); W. R. Hall and A. J. Peaslee, *Three Wars with Germany* (1944); E. M. Zacharias, *Secret Missions* (1946); S. Kent, *Strategic Intelligence for American World Policy* (1949).

INTELLIGENCE, MILITARY. See MILITARY INTELLIGENCE.

INTELLIGENCE QUOTIENT. See I. Q.

INTELLIGENCE TEST. See MENTAL TESTS.

INTENT, in law, the purpose for which an act is done. In civil law responsibility for a wrong attaches without inquiry into the intent. In criminal law, at least in the countries where the English common law is basic, the *mens rea* or *criminal intent* is a necessary element. However, the criminal intent in violation of a statute may be the intent to do a forbidden act even when the ultimate objective is the public good.

Historically the mens rea or criminal intent has had an interesting development, starting with the earliest recorded *theocratic* law where the question of evil purpose was the important factor. On the other hand those early societies and governments where compensation or restitution was the basis for the action in crimes against the person, the intent was immaterial. However, the ancient Greek law, the Roman law, and the English law have as a basic element the inquiry into intent to determine whether a crime was committed. In the German and the French laws negligence and consequences are the determinative factors in determining the crime committed, rather than the question of intent.

Common Intent concerns the natural sense given to words. When words have a natural meaning or sense and also an artificial sense to be made out by argument and influence, the natural sense should prevail, as a rule of construction.

Criminal Intent, the intent to commit a crime, is a state of mind accompanying a forbidden act which is an element material to making the act a crime or determining the nature of the crime committed, as, for instance, in distinguishing manslaughter from murder. The principle underlying the responsibility for one's acts is that one is able to understand the effect of an act and intends the natural consequences of his acts.

In civil cases, where a written instrument is involved, the intent must be determined from the instrument regardless of what went on in the minds of the parties or in their discussions regarding it. This rule of construction is of course subject to other factors vitiating the express terms as where the parties were not all competent, or there was coercion or fraud. However, in the case of a will a construction must be based on the purpose of the testator and the intent determined in the light of human feelings and affections.

Legislative Intent arises as a concept in circumstances where a legislature has enacted inconsistent statutes or a statute in conflict with the state or Federal constitution resulting in ambiguity; the courts in interpreting the statute will look beyond their words to the legislative purpose.

INTER-AMERICAN HIGHWAY. See Pan American Highway; Alaska Highway.

INTERCOASTAL WATERWAY, a system of canals connecting protected bays, inlets, and rivers on the Atlantic Coast. It is designed to extend from Boston, Mass., to Miami, Fla., and to connect with the Gulf Intracoastal Waterway in Florida. See Waterways, Inland.

INTERDICT, an ecclesiastical penalty placed upon the faithful by the Roman Catholic Church. This form of censure was notably used in the Middle Ages. An interdict may be imposed on a whole nation, a certain locality, or individuals of the church. Unlike Excommunication, the faithful under interdict remain in communion with the church. While an interdict is in effect, however, no public church services may be held. Only certain sacraments, particularly baptism and sacraments for the dying, may be administered; but the dead may not receive Christian burial. An example of a recent interdict, rarely used in the present day, took place in 1933–34. Cardinal Faulhaber, archbishop of Munich, placed a parish under interdict because of a disagreement between the German government and the church.

INTERDICT, in law. See Injunction.

INTEREST. The often used definition of interest as "payment for the use of money" is a rather limited one, and a more comprehensive definition is essential to a real understanding of the problem. Interest is the money income (after a depreciation allowance has been subtracted) paid to those who, as creators, owner, or lenders of capital, sacrifice the present use of that capital or its liquidity (its ability to be turned into "cash" quickly and without loss) in favor of future benefits. It is therefore the monetary adjustment or compensation made in all purchase-sale or loan agreements wherein one or both of the contracting parties must choose between the present or future benefits of economic resources or between liquidity or nonliquidity. Capital may for this discussion be defined as all resources, including loan funds, held for use over an appreciable period of time. Interest is commonly of two varieties, simple and compound. *Simple* interest is interest computed at a fixed rate on the original capital involved. *Compound* interest, on the other hand, is computed not only on the original capital but also on the interest which has previously accumulated.

However, interest has been associated in the minds of many with only institutionalized Capitalism and the productive processes carried on in it. As a matter of fact a type of interest appears in any situation wherein an individual or society sacrifices present enjoyments or satisfactions in favor of satisfactions in the future. A consumer will not pay $2,000.00 in the present for an automobile unless he expects its future services to be worth, as a cumulative aggregate, somewhat more than this amount—the overplus is interest. If he did not expect this extra value from the services of the automobile, his rational choice would be to invest the money at the best possible rate of interest. Thus we might say that certain of the long-run advantages inuring to Robinson Crusoe as a result of his laborious and abstemious creation of capital equipment, and which resulted in no im-

mediately compensating enjoyments, were in a very real sense interest.

Interest manifests itself in connection with successful forward planning, wherever a *rational* adjustment is made between the needs and desires of the present and those of the future, no matter what the basic institutional structure of the economy may be.

History. The role of interest in the economic structure as we know it today is primarily a modern development. In ancient and medieval times, when economic life involved little use of roundabout production and marketing methods and was for the most part static or slow-moving, the role of the interest rate as a time-binder and as one of the bases for evaluating capital was largely unknown. The Greeks, with whom the word for interest etymologically related to the word for offspring, were disturbed over the fact that "money did not breed." Under Roman law and finally under canon law interest was regarded as legitimate only when it could be interpreted as payment for damages resulting from deferred repayment of loans. Medieval churchmen opposed the payment of interest on the largely consumer loans of that period and from them our word Usury, the medieval name for interest, acquired its present meaning of interest at exorbitant or illegal rates.

With the commercial and industrial revolutions, however, the productive contributions of man-made capital became increasingly evident. Interest and the "profit" theory were incorporated into an economic philosophy which included the Ricardian theory of rent and the subsistence theory of wages. The English writers Senior and Jevons and more especially the Austrian Böhm-Bawerk pioneered during the 19th century in emphasizing the time factor in interest, a theory which was further developed by the Americans Fisher and Fetter. To these theories modern economic philosophy has added the concepts of the "liquidity preference" emphasized by Keynes and of interest as reflecting rate and nature of change in the economic balance, as interpreted by Schumpeter. See Fisher, Irving.

Rate of Interest. When yearly interest in money may be expressed as a per cent of the principal sum of a loan or of the money value of a piece of capital it is known as a rate of interest. As the interest rate serves to equate the present and future by allowing variously-timed benefits and services, as well as the basic desire for some degree of liquidity, to be incorporated into a general movement toward price equilibrium, the study of interest today is mainly concerned with an examination of the factors which determine the rate of interest.

Basic to the solution of this problem are two simple economic laws. The first law is: Free market transactions reflect subjective human preferences. This means that, assuming some degree of equality in bargaining power, anyone who renders a service or submits to an inconvenience does so for a compensation, and anyone who secures a special advantage must ordinarily pay for it. The second law is: Any two truly alternative devices for achieving the same economic end can, in a free market, be secured on approximately the same terms. Sacrifices which are essentially the same are approximately equally compensated. Market imperfections may result, of course, in these principles, operating, as do all economic laws, only as tendencies, and operating above all laws is the uncontrovertible factor of dynamism, or constant change. Changes in the rate and nature of this dynamism are especially important in creating fluctuating expectations of return on new investment.

Theories of Interest. Modern economists have sought to explain the rate of interest in three ways. These three interpretations are suggested by the phrases time preference, liquidity preference, and capital productivity or investment opportunity. The first of these explanations is based on the human tendency to place more importance on present wants or needs than on future ones. For example, the subjective significance of the purchasing power of a hundred dollars now available is greater than the significance of the same amount of money available one year hence, other factors remaining the same. The time preference of individuals varies, of course, with differing circumstances.

The phrase liquidity preference refers to the preference for holding some economic resources in liquid rather than nonliquid form, for the holder of liquid resources is relatively immune to the danger and risks of physical deterioration of capital and of monetary losses due to unwise speculative investments or of deflation. Liquidity preference may be a reflection of business outlook and is, like time preference, constantly changing.

Third, is the influence of capital productivity or investment opportunity. While in a static economy the rate of return on new investment will roughly equal the rate of interest, in a dynamic situation of technological change or of abruptly shifting consumer tastes, new capital may be built or old capital drawn from now present uses with the expectation, at least for the time being, of somewhat higher returns.

Loan Fund Market Factors and Interest. The most easily observable manifestation of interest is as "the money paid for the use of money" in the money market. Individuals and firms enter this market with varying degrees of time and liquidity preference, in situations of slow or rapid economic change, in order to borrow or lend as the case may be. Those with low time preference may set up savings accounts and trust funds, put money into life insurance and annuities, or, as stockholders or owners, acquiesce in the amassing of undistributed business surpluses. These are the chief sources of the supply of loan funds. Whether or not a large or small part of these funds enter as supply into the money market depends on liquidity preference, i.e., the desirability of large cash balances. The prospect of high return on new investment may cause the withdrawal of these funds from the loan market into the direct purchase of new, or the reactivation of old productive capital equipment. Demand for such funds comes from those having high time preferences, to a less degree from those having high liquidity preferences, and from those who wish to borrow for investment.

At some rate of interest the supply will equal the demand and the loan fund market be cleared. Imperfections in this market, as well as its highly discriminatory nature, result, however, in a wide spread of interest rates around a mode or central point. Governments, for example, may usually borrow at lower rates than private individuals or corporations, while loan sharks may push the rate to enormous heights. The modal rates of interest, however, have for a long time hovered around the 4, 5, or 6 per cent levels.

Commercial banks have customarily provided a highly specialized substitute for some types of loan funds in the form of bank credit. The costs of such lending are not the sacrifice of present use of resources or of liquidity but rather the expenses involved in the banking business. Because of the high fixed overhead costs involved in banking much of this credit may be obtained at very low rates, although regular bank discount rates are usually slightly above the modal money rates in the wider market.

Changes in time or in liquidity preference or in the speed of economic change and resulting return expectations on new investments may, by influencing the demand or supply of loan funds, push the rate of interest up or down. Money which is held out of the loan market because of high time preference will ordinarily be spent in the purchase of usable goods and will thus indirectly promote production. Money held because of high liquidity preference, however, will ordinarily not be spent at all and may serve to paralyze the industrial economy.

Capital Facilities Market and Interest. Interacting with the loan fund, or money, market is the capital facilities market. The buyer or holder of capital sacrifices the use of part of his resources and liquidity in favor of a future income. A general rise in time or liquidity preference will, therefore, cause a selling movement in the capital facilities market, as the seller will gain the right to use presently enjoyable resources or liquidity. Conversely a fall in time or liquidity preference will result in a period of buying and the enhancement of capital values.

Interactions of the Two Markets. If the interest rate in the money market is higher than in the capital facilities market, owners will sell to lend. If the money market rate is lower people will borrow to buy. The rates, then, will tend toward equality. If the expected rate of return on new investment is above both these rates there will be borrowing in the money market and selling in the capital facilities market for the purpose of new investment. Thus rates throughout tend to be equalized. If the expected rate of return on new investment is less than the other rates there will be little new investment until expectations improve. If the rates are held up by high time preference, consumer spending will counteract low investment, eventually improving the prospects of investment return. If the factor keeping the rates up is high liquidity preference, the economy may get into a state of paralysis. A situation of rapid change will, by stimulating new investment, exert an upward push on the rates of interest by increasing the demand for loans and stimulating the sale of pre-existent capital.

Thus the active factors determining the rate of interest in any market are time preference, liquidity preference, and investment opportunity, influencing every transaction involving choice between present and future and between liquidity and specialization. The recipient of interest receives it as a compensation for his sacrifice of present resources or liquidity. The

INTEREST LAWS OF THE VARIOUS STATES*

STATES AND TERRITORIES	LEGAL RATE	RATE ALLOWED BY CONTRACT	STATES AND TERRITORIES	LEGAL RATE	RATE ALLOWED BY CONTRACT
	%	%		%	%
Alabama..	6	8	New Hampshire.....	6	Any rate
Alaska....	6	10	New Jersey	6	6
Arkansas..	6	6 to 10	New Mexico.......	6	10 or 12
Arizona...	6	8	New York.	6	6
California.	7	10	North Carolina..	6	6
Colorado..	6	Any rate	North Dakota...	4	7
Connecticut	6	12	Ohio......	6	8
Delaware..	6	Any rate	Oklahoma.	6	10
Dist. of Columbia	6	8	Oregon.....	6	10
Florida....	6	10	Pennsylvania....	6	6
Georgia...	7	8	Puerto Rico	6	8 or 9
Hawaii....	6	12	Rhode Island....	6	Any rate
Idaho.....	6	8	South Carolina..	6	7
Illinois...	5	7	South Dakota...	6	8
Indiana...	6	8	Tennessee..	6	6
Iowa......	5	7	Texas.....	6	10
Kansas....	6	10	Utah......	6	10
Kentucky..	6	6	Vermont...	6	6
Louisiana..	5	8	Virginia...	6	6
Maine.....	6	Any rate	Washington	6	12
Maryland.	6	6	West Virginia..	6	6
Massachusetts......	6	Any rate	Wisconsin.	5	10
Michigan..	5	7	Wyoming..	7	10
Minnesota.	6	8			
Mississippi.	6	8			
Missouri...	6	8			
Montana..	6	10			
Nebraska..	6	9			
Nevada...	7	12			

* For legal rates of small loan company credit see FINANCE, PERSONAL.

payer of interest renders it because he gains access to present resources or liquidity or is able to cash in on a profitable investment opportunity.

The chief theoretical controversy is concerned with the relationship between prospective return on new investment and the rate of interest. This relationship is of particular significance because of the relationship between the amount of such investment and the BUSINESS CYCLE. Those who maintain that a high rate of interest deters all but the prospectively most gainful new investments have arithmetic and logic on their side. The critics of this position claim that the facts indicate the contrary—heavy investment seems to accompany high interest rates. This argument is analogous to an attempted disproof of the basic law of purchase, the inverse relationship between demand and price (see SUPPLY AND DEMAND), by saying that prices of goods and the demand for them may, under certain circumstances, both rise at the same time. When demand is expanding this is true. When expectations are optimistic, borrowing for investment will pull the rate of interest up. But given expectancies of a certain degree of optimism the response of investors will be affected by the rate of interest.

Legal Regulation of Interest. Rates of interest have been subjected to strict legal regulation. The states in the United States have widely varying maximum interest rates, applicable ordinarily, however, only when no other rate is actually specified in contracts. (See Table.) All states with the exception of Colorado, Maine, Massachusetts, and New Hampshire have qualified restrictions on contract rates. These are called usury laws. Thirty-eight states regulate small loans in the interest of protecting borrowers against exploitation. Federal banking powers are exercised in such a way as to affect commercial bank lending. Securities exchange regulations partially control borrowing by bond sales. Those numerous manifestations of interest outside the loan fund market are generally outside all regulative influences. See CAPITAL; USURY; INVESTMENT; VALUE; SAVINGS; BOND; BANKS AND BANKING; LOAN; LIMITATIONS, STATUTES OF.   GEORGE J. CADY

BIBLIOG.–Bohm-Bawerk, *Capital and Interest* (1890); F. A. Fetter, *Economic Principles* (1915); I. Fisher, *The Theory of Interest* (1930); J. M. Keynes, *The General Theory of Employment Interest and Money* (1936); K. E. Boulding, *Economic Analysis* (1941); H. C. Wallich, "Changing Significance of the Interest Rate," *The American Economic Review*, Vol. XXXVI.

INTEREST TESTS. See VOCATIONAL INTEREST TESTS.

INTERFERENCE AND INTERFEROMETER. The term interference may be applied to a number of physical phenomena; but as considered here, it will be regarded as a wave phenomenon, dealt with chiefly in connection with LIGHT. The phenomenon was discovered about 1809 by THOMAS YOUNG (1773–1829), a British physician, in connection with his study of light. The effects that Young discussed are represented in Fig. 1a, b, and c. Fig 1a depicts two wave trains moving with the same speed in opposite directions with their crests and troughs superimposed. The resultant wave is one of double amplitude, and is the result of helpful interference. Fig. 1b shows two trains of equal amplitude moving with the same speed in opposite directions, crests superimposed on troughs; the result is destructive interference. The wave motion is completely destroyed. Fig. 1c indicates two waves of equal amplitude traveling in opposite directions and out of phase, such that the resultant wave is one of the same amplitude as the original wave.

In the case of sound, it is possible to combine two sounds in such a manner as to produce silence. With light it is possible to combine two beams and produce darkness. This is precisely what Young did. The two sources of interfering light were obtained

by making two pinholes or very fine slits in a card and then viewing a distance source through both holes or slits close to the eye. In the case of slits a series of bright and dark waves was observed. If one views the source through one slit, no such pattern is observed. The dark bands are the regions in which crest meets trough in the wave forms with complete destructive interference.

To carry the exposition further, the reader is urged to consult a good text on Physics, of the college level, or any good text on Optics. A number of examples and uses of interference phenomena will be mentioned.

One of the curious anomalies in the interpretation of physical phenomena is the fact that while Newton observed interference phenomena and actually produced interference ring colors by placing the convex surface of a plano-convex lens against a flat piece of glass, he nevertheless refused to accept the wave interpretation of the phenomenon. He chose to explain the phenomenon by the assumption of easy or difficult transmission of the light corpuscles constituting the light. Because of his persistence in the belief in the corpuscular theory, the acceptance of Young's wave theory was seriously retarded.

One of the most frequently observed phenomena of light interference is the production of color in very thin oil films over a water surface. The colors in soap films or bubbles are produced in the same manner. When white light falls on such a thin film, part of it is reflected from the top surface and part from the lower surface. Since that traveling from the lower surface transverses a longer path than that from the top surface, it is possible to bring about a condition whereby crest meets trough for a particular wave length. This color or wave length will be absent from the reflected light and it will no longer be white, but a composite of the waves, with the destructively interfering ones absent.

The colors produced by seashells, the abalone pearl, the "pearl button," are produced as a reflection and interference from the multiple very thin layers of material laid down in the shell growth.

The use of interference phenomena in industrial testing has become a fine art in which high degrees of precision of measurement and production are required. In the optical industry, for example, a degree of flatness is required to the extent of 1/50 of a wave

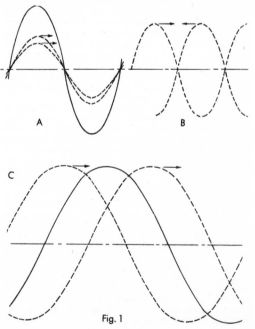

Fig. 1

length of yellow light. The wave length of yellow light is approximately 5/10000 centimeters. By placing the surface, whose flatness is desired, against a flat master plate and observing the shape or contour of the interference fringes, the degree of flatness can be determined.

The Interferometer. The earliest form of interferometer was developed by ALBERT MICHELSON in conjunction with Professor Morley in an attempt to determine whether or not there was a relative motion between the ether, the medium through which it was assumed that the electromagnetic light waves were transmitted, and the earth. Fig. 2 indicates schematically the design of the instrument and its operation.

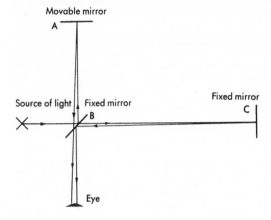

Movable mirror

A source of yellow light, or any monochromatic source, sends radiation to the half-silvered mirror B. (A half-silvered surface is one on which the silver film is so thin that about equal parts of the incident light are reflected and transmitted.) The transmitted beam is incident on mirror C and reflected portion of the incident beam passes onto mirror A, where it is reflected back to mirror B, where a portion of it is transmitted to the eye.

The eye receives the two beams, and a set of interference fringes are observed, the shape of which depends upon relative positions of mirrors A and C and their flatness. The mirror A is mounted on a nut which may travel backward or forward by means of a very precise screw. Assume that the paths traveled by the two beams on arrival at the eye are exactly the same length. A set of fringes will be observed when the mirrors are properly adjusted. If the mirror B is moved backward or forward a distance equal to a half wave length of the light used, the whole set of fringes will be displaced by a distance equal to the distance between the fringes.

In 1892 Professor Michelson, then of Clark University, was invited to Paris to measure the standard meter in terms of a wave length of light. The red cadmium wave length was chosen, and it was found that there were 1553163.5 waves to the standard meter. Hence the wave length of the red cadmium wave was 6.4384700×10^{-5} cm, a precision of one part in 2 million, and unexcelled by any other measurement in the realm of science.

In 1908 the Frenchmen Messrs. Benoit, Fabry and Perot, repeated the measurements with an interferometer designed by Messrs. Fabry and Perot. Their measurements of the wave length of the red cadmium line was 6.4384696×10^{-5} cm. The value differs from the Michelson value by one part in 16,000,000.

The interferometer in conjunction with a spectroscope is today the precision method for measuring wave length. It is thus the means of establishing length values grounded on invariable natural facts. However, instead of cadmium, the U.S. Bureau of Standards has adopted mercury-198, an isotope formed by

transmutation from gold. Its spectral line is sharper than that of cadmium because of the smaller Doppler effect, and sharper than that of ordinary mercury, since mercury-198 is isotopically pure.

B. J. SPENCE

INTERIOR DECORATION
Making Each Room Harmonious
Interior decoration strives for a combination of beauty and utility

INTERIOR DECORATION may be interpreted as the art which aims to harmonize in the interior of a building, the requirements of utility and of beauty. This interior stands in such close relation to its exterior, that the design of the one cannot well be regarded as separate and distinct from that of the other. In the greatest epochs of artistic production, architecture was the controlling spirit that determined style. The subordinate arts which included all decoration were but parts of a concerted scheme, of which architecture was the all-embracing genius of the age. All the arts grew and developed together with equal significance, but they took their proper places in helping to build up the glory of a structure as a whole. The intimate relation between architecture and all the arts was very important and it is only within comparatively recent years that this spirit of homogeneity has passed away. Interior decoration today has become a glib term used loosely to include any form of house furnishing and decoration.

The history of interior architecture does not begin with the great baronial halls of the Middle Ages. High standards of comfort and the ability to execute luxurious appurtenances for the home are known to have existed in the early days of Egypt, Greece and Rome, and to have been well established in the second, third and fourth centuries. But because these interiors are so remote from our own and because information concerning them can mostly be gleaned only from fragments and from pictorial scenes and sources, this article will concern itself only with significant styles which come within our present-day understanding. See FURNITURE.

Gothic. The greatest of the Romantic styles, developing from the Romanesque, came into being during the latter part of the 12th century in northern France, and continued to develop in western Europe during the 13th, 14th and 15th centuries. It was the expression of Christian religious fervor. The soaring perpendicular lines and the pointed arches, characteristic of this style, reached upward with aspiring effect, suggestive of, and inspired by, the lofty peaks and towering heights in nature. Circles, trefoils, quatre foils, triangles, intermingling with the elongated shapes of religious figures, all played a dramatic part in decoration as well as in architecture. These motifs were used again and again, resulting in exquisite traceries, or in a more robust form of carvings upon woodwork and furniture. Designs for brocades, damasks and embroideries were based upon these underlying Gothic forms, accounting for the intimate relation between Gothic architecture and the lesser arts. The finest flowering of Gothic art occurred in the 15th century, from which date remarkable tapestries, furniture and paintings. Color was introduced on frescos and fabrics and applied to sculpture. Stained glass was one of the most remarkable developments of the Gothic period and glass of equal quality and beauty has not been made since that time. It was used to modify the light filtering through open window spaces and to enhance the beauty of interior wood and stone by its vibrating, explicit color.

In the early Middle Ages in the north, when conditions of living were shaped by constant warfare and castles were used more as fortresses than dwellings, decoration and furniture were naturally only of that type which could be quickly packed and carried away. The bare walls of the medieval castles and dwellings were hung with tapestries, and woven cloths were stretched across open-timbered roofs. Long after these conditions of life in Europe changed, houses still retained many of those feudal features. But not so in Italy. At the end of the Middle Ages, though still untouched by the spell of the Renaissance, Italy had produced architecture which already revealed her native genius, and which was well on the way toward a riper development. The preceding century was one of peace which fostered the accumulation of wealth, luxury and comforts, allowing the prosperous Italian to express his inherent artistic taste in his house, furnishings, and surroundings.

The period rejoiced in the use of color as shown in gold on ceilings and the use of frank reds, blues and greens, or black and white on ceilings and walls. The great fireplace consisted of a hearth, topped by a deeply projecting, sloping hood which sometimes was decorated with carved escutcheons or other symbolic ornament. Though only a few pieces of furniture are extant that can actually be assigned to the 14th century, there is sufficient evidence to show that they were large, heavy and strongly built, rich in carving and often enlivened with color.

The salient qualities of this era's style were strength and breadth of line, largeness of scale, plain surfaces, scarcity of unnecessary architectural detail—all characteristic of this medieval, nonclassic, pre-Renaissance period whose inherent simplicity and naturalness was hardly anticipatory of the rich, classic, exuberant style that was to follow.

The Renaissance, signifying a rebirth of the classic, was a return to the inherent Italian love for Latin and Lombard forms. Beginning in Italy in the early part of the 15th century, the Renaissance was a revolt against the Gothic, so transcendently fulfilled in the North, never entirely accepted or assimilated in the South. The soaring, perpendicular, pointed arches of the Gothic now gave way to the horizontal solidarity of rounded arches. The main features of the style were the classic orders—the Doric, Ionic and Corinthian, but these classic columns and decorative forms, though distinctly Roman in origin, became vivid forces in the hands of these worshipers of the past, who, while imitating, really transformed them anew. Never in ancient times did classic forms yield themselves to such new and mobile treatment.

Decoration now took first place, claiming ascendency over structural achievement. Color was obtained through fresco painting and mosaics, which were lavishly applied to interiors. The superb friezes and panels are the best the world has known. The fine and decorative arts were brought to their highest perfection to enhance and emphasize the beauty of the architectural lines and masses. Great artists were great craftsmen as well, and no object was too mean or insignificant for their consideration. A splendid co-operation of painting with sculpture and carving gave to early Renaissance interiors a radiant, jewel-like quality which presented a brilliant background for the free and worldly splendor of those days. The Renaissance in Italy antedated its spread through France, Germany, Spain, the Netherlands and England by 100 years. During the late Renaissance, a revolt in Italy against prevailing art traditions and against prevailing rule and order resulted in what is known as the BAROQUE. This effort to produce something new and "different" developed a style complex and profuse and often lacking in restraint.

The Elizabethan style in England (1558–1603) following the Tudor, which developed from the late Gothic during the reigns of Henry VII and Henry VIII, was complex in character, because many Gothic features were retained, combined with Renaissance details. Though classic predominated, they were modified and Anglicized under the rule of Elizabeth. Henry VIII, dispensing with fortifications during his

peaceful reign and suppressing the erection of monasteries, directed all building activities toward domestic architecture. He imported Italian artists and builders to design and erect palaces for himself and the nobility, but these foreign architects were not able to fuse successfully their own classic Renaissance style with the romantic type of English Gothic. Elizabeth, however, succeeded in creating a characteristic English style by engaging only English designers and craftsmen, who brought back from travels in France and Italy ideas for erecting great English Renaissance manor houses whose design was adapted to English country life. These great houses were the ancestors of our English and American country houses of today. They were well lighted, ample and informal and in them interior architecture found its beginning in England.

Those early English builders combined a fine feeling for balance with a real knowledge of native materials. The open timberwork, the plastering of walls, the wainscoting and paneling of wood, all were treated with sympathetic understanding. They knew and loved all the peculiarities of oak, rough plaster and stone. The fireplace was built for service as well as for decorative effect. It was framed elaborately and its overmantel of wood or stone was ornately carved in strapwork pattern or embellished with coats of arms. It became the nucleus of the other decoration and furnishings of the room. Ceilings were treated in an elaborate manner with intricate designs in plaster. When walls were of plaster and not paneled in oak, they were hung with elaborate tapestries. Velvets, damasks, and brocades were imported from France and Italy and embossed leather from Spain.

Jacobean (1603–1649) was a transitional style, the name derived from James I, the successor of Elizabeth, but covering the period that occupied the reign of Charles I. Classic conceptions were more fertilely planted, a more definite Renaissance influence prevailed and foreign styles and tastes were voluntarily adopted. Plaster and woodwork became classically conventional and severe in comparison with Elizabethan freedom and flowering, but a better understanding of the correct classical proportions gave Jacobean rooms a look of greater homogeneity and planned arrangement. Rich fabrics and lavish draperies and upholsteries offset the restraint of ornament and their color cheered the potential coldness of white plaster ceilings and dark wood-paneled walls.

Though all decoration under Francis I of France was a mixture of the two styles, Italian Renaissance and French Gothic, it began to take on a truly national French flavor which in the reigns of Henry II and Henry IV became French decoration, transfused with classic. It further developed into the splendor of the style known as Louis XIV.

Louis XIV. The magnificence of the style of Louis XIV adequately expressed the spirit that animated the age of "Le Grand Monarque" (1643–1715) who, as patron and enthusiast, raised France to an undisputed leadership in all the arts. The style influenced and was imitated by all the other countries of western Europe. Though basically classic in design, strong touches of the Baroque gave to it a character entirely different from 16th century Renaissance. Magnificence and a studied dignity, though often overloaded with ornament, achieved a fitting background for so great a monarch. Interiors and furnishings were grand and impressive, made rich and luxurious with gold, with beautiful velvets and silks and elaborate damasks, following classic models. Interiors were arranged architecturally and the orders were used in correct classical proportions. Large plate glass mirrors, the height of extravagant luxury at that time, were often used between pilasters for entire walls in palace rooms. Walls were covered with fabrics or decorated in painted leather or wood. Furniture, tapestry and rugs were superb. Architecture, which had been growing more and more monumental since the coming of

PHILADELPHIA MUSEUM OF ART

French Gothic room of the 15th century

ART INSTITUTE OF CHICAGO

French Renaissance bedroom of late 16th century

ART INSTITUTE OF CHICAGO

Elizabethan great hall of an English home

CITY ART MUSEUM, ST. LOUIS

Jacobean room of early 17th century

PHILADELPHIA MUSEUM OF ART

Louis XVI parlor

CITY ART MUSEUM, ST. LOUIS

Queen Anne hall of early 18th century

11-221

11-222

the Renaissance, now reached its climax. An age of conquest, this period also became a pliable age of adaptation and absorption. The real productive art years of Louis XIV began in 1667 when the Manufacture Royale was established to aid all the allied arts that helped to promote the greatest magnificence in building and decoration. The Gobelin, and later the Beauvais, factories were part of this enterprise and from the establishment of the former dates the grandeur of a true French national art.

Charles LeBrun, chief court painter, became the director of the Gobelin factory. He surrounded himself with the greatest artists and craftsmen of his day and with him are associated such names as Mansart, Boulle, Monnoyer, Coypel brothers, the ebonists, Cucci, Poitou, Jean and Daniel Marot, Jean Berain. Many others of equal distinction gave themselves wholeheartedly to the production of one of the most finished styles known in history, a style, however, essentially created for royalty, a glowing tribute to a monarch whose great palace of Versailles typifies all that this period implies. See GOBELIN, GILLES AND JEHAN.

Louis XV. The classic Renaissance principles observed by Louis XIV in decoration now yielded to the sophisticated, ostentatious period of Louis XV. There was an eager reaching out for the new which expressed the exaggeration, frivolity and extravagance of social life. Decorators turned to nature, but an artificial nature, for inspiration and gay landscapes, flowers, garlands, rocks (rocailles) and shells (coquilles) were utilized as decorative motifs and from the reiterated use of the two latter forms, the style came to be known as Rococo. The use of straight lines in all forms of decoration was avoided, and the symmetry that dignified the preceding period, disappeared. Riotous and fantastic curves with a sensuous appeal were used at every possible opportunity. Large wall paintings and massive bas-reliefs in the great rooms of palaces were displaced by gay paintings in lighter vein, and by the glitter of mirrors which were more appropriate embellishments for smaller dwellings and apartments. Furniture was also made smaller in scale, more coquettish, more affected in style, and color schemes became daintier and lighter. Watteau, Boucher, Fragonard, and Lancret emphasized this lighter spirit in their remarkable decorations and paintings.

Louis XVI style was a reversion to the early classic—a return to forms and interiors whose prototypes had been unearthed at Pompeii and Herculaneum. Curved lines and exaggerations were abandoned, both in construction and in decoration, in favor of an exquisite simplicity, in which proportion, symmetry and refinement reached a perfect consummation. Exaggerations and extravagance in decoration had run their limit. Fashion dictated a desire for intimate salons and boudoirs, so a smaller, daintier scale in architecture, decoration and furniture was demanded. Legs of furniture were delicately fluted and tapered, oblong panels and oval frames became popular.

Love of the pastoral was added to classic chasteness in the form of fruit, flowers, ribbons, shepherd's crooks and festoons which appeared as decorative motifs. Sentimental and allegorical allusions were shown by the use of the bow and quiver, the urn and burning torch. Classic vases and urns were graceful and delicate in line. Many of these forms appeared in the contemporary English work of Adam, thus revealing a close relationship between the two. Muslins, hand-blocked prints and silks were used in profusion for upholstery and hangings. Ceilings were beautifully painted and the walls were either painted or paneled in silk. It was a style that reflected a desire for less ostentatious living, with no wish to awe by grandeur but to bring exquisite grace and beauty into more intimate houses and apartments. It was a period perfect of its kind—and the makers of furniture,

decorative painters and designers of fabrics, brought their different arts to such a high state of perfection that they stood on a perfect equality with those artists who devoted themselves to the fine arts.

The grandeur of the court of Louis XIV greatly influenced the taste of Charles II, as an exile in France, and on his return to England he surrounded himself with luxurious appurtenances more pretentious than were ever before used in England. Magnificent hangings, furniture of solid silver, and the most costly imported embroideries were a few of his extravagances.

James II (1685–1688) and William and Mary (1689–1702), his successors, were deeply influenced by Dutch taste. Flat surface decoration, paint and lacquer, veneer and marquetry replaced the old liking for carving. Bright color was introduced in upholstery made of needlepoint, damasks, or gilded Cordovan leather. Walls were treated with panels three to five feet wide, which were covered with tapestry, leather or silk.

Queen Anne. The reign of Queen Anne (1702–1714) was a comfort-loving age and at that time began what is known as the period of modern comfort. Furniture shorn of carving emphasized forms that were comfortable and relaxing. The smooth splat back and shell detail, cabriole leg and soft flowing curves are characteristic. It was the age of walnut, not only for furniture but also for interior woodwork, superseding oak. The simplicity of interiors called for lower-keyed tones and brightly colored fabrics were replaced by quiet-toned velvets. Comfortable upholstered armchairs now appeared for the first time. The developing trade of the joiner made possible fittings for interiors which showed high standards of taste and a nice sense of appropriateness that were reflected in even the most modest homes.

The desire for comfort pervaded all classes and furniture now became plentiful. The simple, strong types, so satisfying to both eye and body, are as appealing today as they were then. Coffee and tea were introduced at this time, and with them came the necessity for designing coffee and tea pots, and the making of small tables for serving these beverages. The best known names of this period are Sir CHRISTOPHER WREN, the great architect who rebuilt a large part of London after the great fire of 1666, and his master-carver GRINLING GIBBONS whose woodcarvings gave to many interiors of his day a distinction which has never been equaled.

The Georgian is fundamentally an architectural style both in form and decoration. The 18th century was a critical age when architecture keenly interested, and was understood by, those of culture; when the classics were deeply reverenced and when men enjoyed living in formal homes surrounded by examples of classic art and decorative forms. If this architecture and its interiors founded on Roman and Italian authority and derived from various French motives, was cold and austere, it was also aristocratic and elegant and perfectly suited a correct and intelligent people and their formal way of living. The pure classicism of the early Georgian later grew rather heavy and too profuse in the use of columns and pilasters, but there was a return to an exquisite refinement under the influence of the Adam Brothers who dominated the whole art of the last third of the century.

During the reigns of George I (1714–1727) and George II (1727–1760) elaborate woodwork for wall panels, window and door trims, and large heavy mantelpieces, and plastered walls were much in vogue. They were painted white, cream or some very light tint which was a distinct departure from wood in the natural, used in the 17th century. Indeed no one feature is more expressive of the change from the late Stuart days than this pervading whiteness. Walls, ceilings, mantels—all were very light, generally white in tone, a quality revealing a love of architectural form which was more significant at this time than any concern with color or material. If it presented an austere background, it was relieved by the satiny glow of mahogany furniture upholstered in silks, velvets and gay chintzes; by oriental rugs, carpets, curtains and hangings in various delightful fabrics.

Wallpapers came into common use during the middle of the century (1756). Of Chinese origin, these gay landscapes, flowers and figures proved daring and amusing, and the craze for everything Chinese, from pottery to furniture, grew. Chinese motifs were also copied by French and English manufacturers of wallpaper which, when the process of printing in long rolls was discovered, became the popular wall covering at the end of the century. Mahogany which was then the accepted wood for furniture lent itself admirably to carving, and CHIPPENDALE, the famous cabinetworker of the time, took full advantage of it in making his designs.

ROBERT AND JAMES ADAM, architects, decorators, and designers, with their pre-eminent influence during the second half of the Georgian period, put an end to Chinese and Rococo tendencies, and revived the English classic which was contemporary with the French classic of Louis XVI. Under the Adam Brothers, interiors were brought to a rare unity of design, for they were architects who not only designed the decoration for walls, ceilings and mantelpieces in their rooms, but furniture, carpets, silver, linen and all accessories as well. Though SHERATON and HEPPLEWHITE were two great names associated with the furniture making of the day, they were responsive to classic ideas and were glad to carry out many Adam designs.

As in the style of Louis XVI, the Adam Brothers reflected the spirit of Pompeii and Herculaneum which was revealed particularly in their designs for ceilings, walls and mantelpieces. Perhaps the most striking feature in these rooms was their ornament in which light graceful moldings, rich yet restrained, were arranged with the greatest skill and finesse. The designs for ceilings, friezes and panels were greatly diversified. Much of their success was due to a secret process of casting plaster ornament in molds, brought back by Adam from Italy, a process found to be much cheaper and more easily applied than carving or hand-modeled plasterwork. Workmen imported from Italy were adept craftsmen and produced this type of work with great delicacy and finish. Painting was also employed to embellish ceilings, panels, and furniture, but such remarkable results could never have been attained without the co-operation of such great artists as Zucchi, Cipriani, Pergolesi, Angelica Kauffmann and others of less repute, who were engaged to decorate furniture as well as small spaces—ovals, panels, decorative forms that were applied as pure architectural decorations. Though the large neutral surfaces of these walls did not differ fundamentally from those of the earlier Georgian period, they were broken by panels, niches, bas-reliefs and various other ornamental accents. The too-white wall expanse was toned down with color— pale green, cream or gray. The walls of smaller, more informal rooms were covered with quiet patterned silks. Urns and vases of Etruscan origin were favorite' Adam motifs. Besides mahogany, satinwood and beechwood were utilized for furniture, and painting and inlay were used as decoration. Very little carving appeared.

Directoire and Empire. At the close of the period of Louis XVI followed what is generally called the Directoire (1795–1804). Both France and England developed contemporaneously, inspired by common enthusiasm for new and different classic ideals. David was the great master who dominated France after Louis XVI, and all England, except perhaps Chippendale, was affected by the change. It was a time of transition in which the refined classicism of Pompeii was transformed into a grosser, more masculine

type called EMPIRE STYLE. Roman influence now became dominant, but Napoleon, wishing to attain greater pomp and dignity in his surroundings, turned to Egypt for certain decorative forms and motifs. The style now became overwhelmingly massive, heavy and ostentatious. The wreath and laurel branch, the torch, winged figures and most of all, the crown and bee of Napoleon became conspicuous emblems. Mahogany, rosewood and ebony were employed for woodwork and furniture, and little or no carving was used. Ornamentation took the form of classic appliqués, color became harsh and pronounced.

American Decoration. In the 17th and 18th centuries, American taste was but a reflection of that prevailing in Europe, and though decoration and furnishings possessed distinct, individual characteristics in the United States, no real national style was developed. French and English furniture was either imported, copied or adapted, crudely at first but later by expert cabinetmakers in native woods—oak, ash, elm, walnut, cherry, pine, maple and cedar. These native woods often help to identify American from English woodwork and furniture. English interiors from the time of Queen Anne to Late Georgian were copied and followed as closely as possible. The term "Colonial furniture" is elastically used to signify furniture in the colonies during the 17th, 18th and 19th centuries, but this term applied to 19th century furniture is really incorrect. Early 19th century furniture is more exactly termed Federal or American Empire—later pieces are American Victorian. American Empire evolved from a type which developed in France and spread to England and then to America, but which in America was shorn of European embellishments, retaining, however, the heavy mahogany frame, classic columns or carved scrolls.

Wallpaper was used in the United States contemporaneously with its use in England. Cotton, linen, chintzes, silks, velvets, brocades and Eastern prints were utilized for hangings and upholsteries. Interiors associated with the Empire were rather heavy and pompous in style. With the close of the Georgian Era, the great creative period of the decorative arts ended. From that time, there have been but sporadic revivals of various past styles.

The Victorian period beginning in 1837, introduced machine-made products and brought craftsmanship to a low ebb. Taste and discrimination were submerged by an overpowering output of mechanically produced furnishings. It was the dark age of the decorative arts. Interiors were heavy and gloomy, colors were oppressive and inharmonious, spaces were crowded with ugly furniture, bric-a-brac and hangings.

As a reaction from such an age, William Morris and his associates battled for a new awakening to the meaning of art. Their work was far-reaching and splendid in its aim to re-establish craftsmen's ideals in England, reviving the Gothic which they expressed in a modern spirit. The pre-Raphaelites were also seekers of finer art ideals, who banded themselves together to try to bring back the early fervor for beauty. Walter Crane, Ruskin and others labored for the redemption of decadent art, yet no well-founded style developed. Sporadic attempts to create something new and different ensued and Art Nouveau in France, England and Austria and a similar movement in Germany developed. A style appeared in America called the Mission which was simple in line without any ornament to break the straight, bleak structure of furniture, which was heavy and massive in form. It was a commercial style, turned out easily and in great quantities by furniture factories. Interiors retained their Victorian aspects.

Again in the late 19th century there arose a brief and feeble revolt against straight lines in favor of curves, which resulted in decorative motifs, gleaned from nature, which were not bad for smaller accessories, but which did not lend themselves well to the

Georgian room of late 18th century

American Empire bedroom, 1820-50

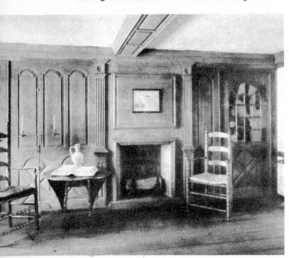

American Colonial room, 1725-50

American Victorian double parlor, about 1850

American penthouse apartment of the 1930's

American modern functional design

broader schemes needed for interior decoration. The style of Art Nouveau has been experimented with, modified and reformed, appearing in many guises and under various names—New Art, Secession, Arts and Crafts, etc., some of them genuine attempts to re-establish old precedents in the association of Art with Labor; others advocating individualism, still others only aiming to eliminate the past and to produce something new and startling. Eventually the desire to produce a really new style became the dominant trend of all this experimentation and various "modernistic" forms were introduced. Although these were supposed to be based on the principles of functionalism and pure design, functionalism was not always well understood at first. Many bizarre styles, ramifications of the "modernistic," were concocted—Cubistic, Futuristic, Modernique, etc.—many of unsound design and in atrocious taste. However, all these fads indicated a groping for a new style that would be suitable for modern living and methods of machine manufacture.

Modern Functionalism. At the present time there is an ever-growing interest in all the arts, particularly in interior decoration. Naturally, a modern interior is at its best in a modern building because it is often impossible to create a completely modern interior in an old building without making costly architectural changes. Nevertheless, adaptations of varying degree can be made and a skillful decorator can often create a very harmonious interior with a mixture of modern and traditional styles. A good indication of the immense interest in interior decoration today is the increasing number of professional interior decorators. These people are skilled in the practical application of decorating principles and can often give invaluable aid and advice to the individual with a problem.

Modern interiors stress functionalism because usefulness is the prime requisite of the present era and a house that does not meet the demands for light, heat, storage, and space would be of little value in an age of speed and scientific progress. The need now for economy is space and maintenance has created many rooms suited to more than one function. Built-in furniture and movable unit furniture are used for their space-saving characteristics and their quality of unity with the architecture. Very strict functionalists will permit nothing that is not absolutely necessary, whether in the design of an individual piece or in the furnishings of a complete house. As important as functionalism is, usually interest and beauty are also needed and sometimes the theory that "pure utility creates its own beauty" is not enough. A room can "function" perfectly without a fine painting or growing plants, but their presence often makes the whole room much more enjoyable to the occupant than it would be without them. The best modern planning makes such accessories as pictures and flowers an integral part of the design of the room as a whole. Modern interiors strive for a unified and harmonious composition of the whole—the whole house as well as one room. Uncluttered space and broad, sweeping lines are their dominant characteristics and overly-elaborate detail has given way to the contrast of large, plain masses of color and texture. This is an era of transition and all forms are not definitely established, so almost any contemporary design that follows the tenets of simplicity, functionalism, and sound design can be classified as modern. Modern is sometimes called "The International Style" because of the similarity of design, construction and materials used all over the world.

In the new interiors, various hitherto unused woods are being utilized for furniture and woodwork, which are so cut that the grain is revealed in all its beauty, and the finish is admirable. Furniture is also being fashioned from metal. Form is still in a transitional state. Wood, glass, metal, cork, paper, silks and velvets are utilized for wall coverings. Interiors are frequently so designed that they show "pattern" and the forms that express this pattern are a combination of straight lines and compass curves. The problem of illuminating interiors correctly for aesthetic effects as well as adequately for working and reading, the design and texture of fabrics, glass, and pottery all are significantly expressive of modern tendencies. So many new methods and materials are constantly entering the market that the present problem of interior decorating is a very dynamic one and there can be no excuse for drabness or monotony.   CATHERINE SHAW PHILLIPS

BIBLIOG.–C. R. Clifford, *Period Furnishings: An Encyclopedia of Historic Decorations and Furnishings* (1927); B. Ionides, *Colour in Everyday Rooms* (1934); H. Koues, *On Decorating the House* (1936); H. D. Eberlein, A. McClure, and E. S. Holloway, *The Practical Book of Interior Decoration* (1937); S. Whiton, *Elements of Interior Decoration* (1937); G. Miller, *Decoratively Speaking* (1939); V. Seeley, *Harmony in Interiors* (1940); J. Ford and K. Morrow, *Design of Modern Interiors* (1942); M. D. Gillies, *All About Modern Decorating* (1942); H. Koues, *How to Be Your Own Decorator* (1945); F. B. Terhune, *Decorating for You* (1944); E. Lewis, *Decorating the Home* (1945); D. Patmore, *Colour Schemes and Modern Furnishing* (1945); W. Murray, *Interior Decoration for Today and Tomorrow* (1946).

INTERIOR, U.S. DEPARTMENT OF THE, one of the departments of the Federal executive establishment, organized in 1849 under the name of the Home Department. It is charged with the direction and administration of national internal affairs concerning the domestic welfare and the conservation of natural resources. Its head, the secretary, is a cabinet member, appointed by the president, and a number of the chiefs of its establishments are similarly appointed, but serve under the supervision of the secretary of the department. The personnel and functions of the department are spread throughout the United States, the territories, and possessions.

The Bureau of Land Management, established in 1946, supervises the survey, management, and disposition of the public lands and the resources therein. The Bureau of Reclamation is charged with the construction and operation of a large number of projects in 17 western states, including the Missouri Basin Project. The Bonneville and the Southwestern Power Administrations market federally controlled power. The National Park Service and the Fish and Wildlife Service care for the National Park System and carry out the wild-life conservation programs, and the Office of Land Utilization co-ordinates and integrates the departmental land programs. The Geological Survey surveys, maps, and classifies all American territory. The Solid Fuels Administration, the Oil and Gas Division, and the Division of Power are other departmental agencies working in the field of conservation and effective utilization of natural mineral resources. The Bureau of Mines explores mineral deposits, conducts investigations into new production and use processes, prepares statistics on mining, and promotes safety in the mineral industries. It is the world's only commercial producer of helium.

The department's affairs extend to the Indians of the United States and Alaska. The Office of Indian Affairs provides education, medical services, social services, police assistance, agricultural and industrial guidance for the Indians; administers Indian monies; and provides Indians with needed credit. The Division of Territories and Island Possessions is the principal agency for the development of Federal territorial policy in Alaska, Hawaii, Puerto Rico, and the Virgin Islands. It forms the liaison between these territories and the various branches of the Federal government in Washington, advises them on needed legislation, and supervises enterprises such as the Puerto Rico Reconstruction Administration (1935), the Virgin Islands Company and the Alaska Railroad.
                    ALFRED DE GRAZIA

INTERJECTION, in grammar, the part of speech that expresses excitement, feeling, or emotion, as *Oh!* or *Alas!* Expressions in the vocative case—as *O Lord!* and *Dear me!*—and imperatives—as *Wait!* and *Go on!*—are also classed as interjections.

Interlaken children in Swiss national dress

INTERLAKEN, resort, Switzerland, in Bern Canton, on the Aar River, 17 miles SE of the town of Thun and 26 miles SE of Bern. It is situated at an altitude of 1,864 feet in the heart of the Bernese Oberland between Lakes Thun on the west and Brienz on the east. Unterseen is across the river. The principal avenue of Interlaken, the Hoheweg, is lined with huge hotels and shops. The town has a 12th century castle. Thousands of tourists annually visit Interlaken for its bracing air and the wonderful view of the JUNGFRAU (13,668 ft.) to the south, the Schreckhorn (13,386 ft.), and the Bernese Alps. Pop. (1930) 3,703.

INTERLOCHEN, village, NW Michigan, in Grand Traverse County; on the Chesapeake and Ohio Railroad and U.S. Highway 31, about 12 miles SW of Traverse City. Two miles southwest of the village, lying between Lake Wahbekaness and Lake Wahbekanetta, is the National High School Orchestra and Band Camp, a nonprofit summer school of music for high school students and alumni. Bordering the lakes on the south is Interlochen State Park. Pop. (1950 est.) 120.

INTERMARRIAGE. See MARRIAGE; MISCEGENATION.

INTERMEDIATE STATE. See PURGATORY.

INTERMENT. See BURIAL.

INTERMEZZO, Italian musical term for an interlude, a piece of incidental music played for a ballet or between the acts of an opera. In Italy in the 16th century, as in the English mystery and morality plays, the intermezzo was frequently a madrigal or a chant. Later, the several pieces of *entr'acte* music were sometimes connected so as to form a secondary action, and these small operas, afterward played separately, formed the beginning of *opera bouffe.* The Intermezzo from Mascagni's *Cavalleria Rusticana* is a celebrated present-day example.

INTERNAL COMBUSTION ENGINE

Converting the heat of natural fuel into work within the cylinder of the engine

INTERNAL COMBUSTION ENGINE, an engine in which air and fuel are burned in a combustion space in direct contact with a working cylinder carrying a piston. The fuel charge is drawn or forced into the cylinder and fired. The resulting combustion increases the pressure within the cylinder and drives the piston away from the cylinder heads. As the piston starts its return to its head position, the confined gases expand through the exhaust ports to a lower pressure. The residue of gases remaining in the cylinder after expansion is then forced out by the

returning pistons or is blown out. The common automotive-type gasoline engines as well as diesels (oil burners) convert the heat of fuel into mechanical energy within the cylinders. In the GAS TURBINE, combustion occurs in a separate chamber, and combustion products are then conducted to the turbine.

Compression Ratio. Types of engines differ in their compression ratio, the ratio between volumes above the piston at the bottom and top of its stroke. The compression ratio for most gasoline engines is approximately 7:1; for diesel engines the ratio is far above this value, approximately 16:1. In an internal combustion engine, either gasoline or diesel, the higher the compression ratio, the greater the efficiency obtained.

The compression ratio of automobile engines has been increased year by year, and each increase resulted in more efficient engines with greater power output, less fuel consumption, higher speed, and greater acceleration. When the charge in the cylinder of a diesel is compressed to as much as 16 times, it is heated to approximately 1000° F. If the compression ratio of a gasoline engine were increased to 16:1, the resulting high temperature would start the mixture of gasoline and air burning in the cylinder long before it should. Ignition would start while the piston was on its upstroke and cause a violent knock, or it might even force the piston back down the cylinder, causing engine reversal. The best commercial antiknock gasoline would not eliminate this. For that reason, to prevent premature burning in gasoline engines the compression ratio must be held to limits such as 6–7:1. In the diesel engine only the air is compressed, and the fuel is injected at the top of the stroke; consequently, the compression ratio can be much higher.

Fuels. Gasoline, because of its volatile nature, is readily converted into vapor at ordinary temperatures when under atmospheric or slightly below atmospheric pressure. In addition, gasoline has other inherent characteristics that tend to make it an excellent internal combustion engine fuel. Among these are quick starting, low rate of corrosion and gum forming, and high antiknock qualities. It is admirably adaptable, therefore, as a fuel for engines used in motorcars, airplanes, and small boats. Because of the relatively high price of gasoline, there is now a strong tendency toward the use of heavier fuel oils in engines of the diesel or similar types. These heavier fuels do not vaporize at ordinary temperatures, so some means must be used to effect their vaporization in internal combustion engines. See FUEL.

ENGINE CYCLES

Gasoline and oil engines are either of the two-stroke cycle or the four-stroke cycle type, a cycle being the series of events that occur in the cylinder and that are repeated continuously in the same order while the engine is working. There are, however, many variations of each cycle, incorporating features that were not included in the original cycles. There are also engines operating on cycles that embody parts of both the Otto and diesel cycles. In the two-stroke cycle engine (frequently called the two-cycle type) two strokes of the piston or one revolution of the crankshaft is required to complete a cycle. In the four-stroke cycle engine (sometimes known as the four-cycle type) four strokes of the piston or two revolutions of the crankshaft are required. See OTTO, NIKOLAUS A.

The Two-stroke Cycle Engine, in which exhaust and charging are carried out by means of ports, may be explained by Fig. 1, a section of the elementary engine with crankcase compression. The piston A is near the bottom of the cylinder and has just started its upward stroke, which compresses the explosive charge of air and gasoline vapor in the space B to a pressure somewhat less than that which will ignite the charge. In its movement upward, the piston

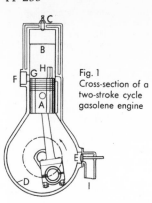

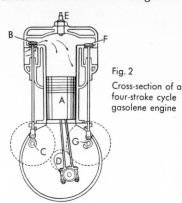

Fig. 1

Cross-section of a two-stroke cycle gasolene engine

Fig. 2

Cross-section of a four-stroke cycle gasolene engine

creates a partial vacuum in the crankcase D. As a result, the atmospheric pressure opens the valve E and allows the air and gasoline vapor mixture to flow into the crankcase from the carburetor (not shown) through the port I. The upward stroke of the piston, then, is a combined suction and compression stroke. When the piston reaches the upper end of the stroke, a spark from the plug C ignites the mixture of air and gasoline vapor. The rapid combustion of the mixture greatly increases the pressure and temperature of the products of combustion. The pressure developed forces the piston downward on its working stroke.

Near the end of its stroke, the piston uncovers the exhaust port G and the products of combustion

escape through it. In the meantime, the descent of the piston on its working stroke compresses the air and gasoline vapor mixture in the crankcase and forces the valve E to its seat. At the end of its stroke, after the exhaust port is opened, the piston uncovers the port F, which opens the transfer passage from the crankcase to the cylinder. The higher pressure in the crankcase then forces air and gasoline vapor through the port F past the baffle H into the cylinder. The baffle is used to force the incoming charge of explosive mixture to the upper end of the cylinder to prevent it from discharging through the exhaust port. This deflection also tends to utilize the incoming mixture to drive out the products of combustion, an action known as "scavenging." The piston now starts its upward stroke and the cycle of operation just described is repeated.

The Four-Stroke Cycle Engine gives one power or working stroke in every four strokes of the piston or in two revolutions of the engine crankshaft. Fig. 2 shows a diagrammatic section of a four-stroke cycle engine, wherein the piston A is nearing the bottom of its suction stroke and a charge of the explosive mixture from the carburetor (not shown) is being drawn through the inlet valve B into the piston cylinder. This valve has been opened by the action of the cam on the camshaft C, which is gear-driven from the crankshaft D at half the speed of the crankshaft; thus the valve is opened once in every two revolutions of the crankshaft.

When the piston has reached the end of its suction stroke, the valve B is closed and on the next upward stroke of the piston, the compression stroke, the explosive mixture is compressed. Just as this stroke is completed, the mixture is ignited from a spark produced by the spark plug E, and the expansion of the gases caused by the heat of explosion forces the piston downward on its power or working stroke. When the piston nears the bottom of the working stroke, the exhaust valve F is opened by the cam on the camshaft G, which, like camshaft C, is gear-driven from the crankshaft at half the crankshaft speed. The burnt gases then escape through the exhaust valve. During the next upward stroke, the exhaust stroke, the exhaust valve F is held open so that all of the burnt gases remaining are driven from the cylinder. When the piston reaches the end of this stroke the exhaust valve is closed and the cycle is repeated.

CARBURETION

Carburetors are devices for discharging into the air stream the desired quantity of gasoline. They atomize the gasoline and produce a homogeneous air-fuel mixture. The most important and difficult function is the automatic production and delivery of this desired air-fuel ration to the engine under varying operating conditions; in stationary engines this ratio is the one which gives the maximum economy. In transportation engines, where speed must be changed within wide ranges, the air-fuel ratios must also change, depending upon whether maximum economy or maximum power is desired.

A simple carburetor is one having a fuel chamber, a single air entrance, and a single jet. Fig. 3 shows a simple *updraft carburetor*. Suction created by the movement of the piston causes air and fuel to flow through the carburetor into the engine. Each alternate downward stroke of the piston draws a fresh charge of mixed fuel and air into its own particular cylinder, where it is compressed and exploded. As engine speed

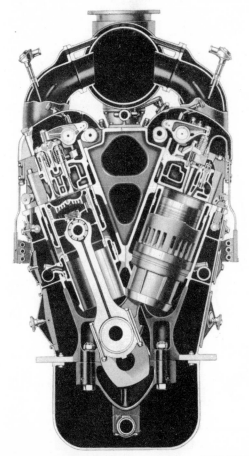

GENERAL MOTORS

Section of a two-cycle, V-type diesel engine

increases, however, the flow of fuel in response to this suction increases faster than the flow of air. Therefore the mixture becomes too rich and there is no longer the perfectly balanced mixture which the engine

Fig. 3

Schematic diagram of a
simple carburetor

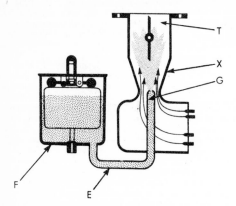

F, Float Chamber; E, fuel outlet; G, nozzle; X, venturi; T, throttle valve (fully open)

needs. Increased speed requires larger quantities of fuel rather than richer mixtures. Different methods are used to overcome the tendency of the mixture supplied by the single carburetor to become rich. One method of overcoming the variation of flow through the simple jet is by introducing another jet into the carburetor. This is arranged so that it allows the mixture to become leaner under increasing suction (directly opposite to the action of the simple jet). Combining the two jets results in obtaining, at all speeds, a mixture with essentially the correct portions of air and fuel, actually controlled by varying the sizes of holes in the jets.

Figure 4 shows a cross sectional view of a carburetor. All fuel for part-throttle operation is supplied through the main jet orifice. Its influence is greatest at the higher speeds. When the manifold depression drops, the power-jet system comes into operation to supply the additional fuel for maximum power. The main jet fuel passes through the main discharge jet (1) and into the air stream to the secondary Venturi (2). The main jet (3) is located in the fuel bowl. The compensating system consists of the main discharge jet (1) and a well vent (4). The flow of fuel from the main jet (3) and power jet (5) is controlled by the size of the well vent (4) and the size of the main discharge jet (1).

The *power-jet system* consists of the power jet (5) which regulates the volume of fuel and the power-jet piston (6) which, actuated by the manifold vacuum, causes the power-jet valve (7) to open. A series of channels (D) connects the power-jet vacuum piston with the carburetor barrel below the throttle plate. At part-throttle operation, the manifold vacuum is sufficient to overcome the tension of the power-jet piston spring, and the piston is held up in its cylinder. Under certain conditions, such as those during sustained high speed, or when the throttle

is opened suddenly, the manifold vacuum drops. This permits the vacuum piston to descend in its cylinder and causes the power-jet valve (7) to open and permit fuel to flow through the power jet (5). This fuel adds to the main jet supply and furnishes the proper mixture for full power development.

The *idling system* consists of the idling jet (9) which measures the fuel and the idling-adjusting needle (8) which regulates the air. The idling jet is calibrated in the side; it receives fuel from the main jet (3) and then the fuel goes through the small calibration in the idling jet (9), where it is mixed with air going through the center of the jet. This system functions only at idling and at low speeds, when the throttle plate is almost closed and there is very strong suction past the edge of the plate. The mixture from the idling jet is discharged through the priming plug (10).

The accelerating system of this carburetor consists of an accelerating-pump piston, a series of channels, check valves, and an accelerating jet. The pump piston is actuated by throttle movement, and the accelerating jet and pump spring control the rate of fuel discharge. As the throttle is opened, it causes a downward stroke of the accelerating-pump piston in its cylinder and supplies pressure on the fuel. This closes a check valve, and moves the fuel through a ball-check valve. The pressure of the fuel closes the air-vent check valve, and the fuel is discharged into the air stream through the accelerating jet. When the fuel has been discharged, there is no more pressure against the ball-check valve or the air-vent check valve. The ball-check valve then drops on its seat and the upper check valve opens, admitting ventilation from the bowl and eliminating direct suction on the fuel through the accelerating jet. No further fuel discharge comes from the accelerating jet until the throttle is closed and the accelerating procedure is repeated.

Supercharging. The supercharger is a device such as a blower, compressor, or pump, used to increase the weight of the air charge for an internal combustion engine over that which would normally be drawn in through the pumping action of the piston. It is used to compensate for the lower density of air in the operation of aircraft engines at high altitudes, or for the deficiency of air charge in high-speed automotive

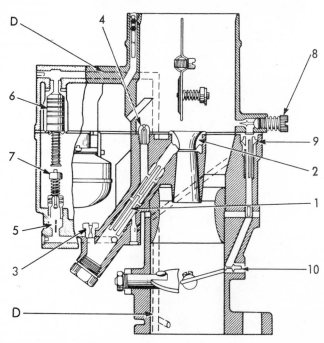

Fig. 4. Cross-sectional view of a downdraft carburetor

Internal Combustion Engine

operation. The turbo-supercharger has been used successfully in both military and commercial aircraft. In this device, the exhaust gases of the engine are utilized to run a gas turbine, which in turn runs an air compressor supplying the carburetor. Such compound engines, in which the turbine salvages waste energy, have seen best use at high speeds or altitudes, and have yet to be perfected for automobiles.

LOWER AND MEDIUM PRESSURE ENGINES

Automobile and Aircraft Engines are the most common and the most highly developed types of gasoline engines. Those used almost exclusively for both automobile and airplane are of the multicylinder type and operate on the Otto four-stroke cycle. Automobile engines are usually of the in-line or V types, the first with a single row of cylinders, and the latter with two rows arranged in a V shape. Automobile engines can also be classified as the L-head type or the valve-in-head type, depending on the location of the inlet and exhaust valves. The valves of the L-type engine are located in the side of the cylinder and are poppet valves that are lifted directly by the cam on the camshaft. The valves of the valve-in-head engine are located directly in the cylinder head and are operated by a small lever, known as a tappet, which is placed in motion by the cam. Airplane engines may be divided into three main classes: radial, in-line, and V types. Rotary engines, used in World War I, are now obsolete. They resemble radial engines, but the cylinders and crankcase rotate around the crankshaft. Radial engines have the cylinders arranged at equal angular intervals around a circle and the number of cylinders may vary, those of more than nine cylinders being arranged in two or more rows. Radial motors are always air-cooled, the circular arrangement exposing the cylinders equally to the air current. A system of fins around each cylinder also helps disperse heat. In-line and V type engines are usually cooled by water or glycol. Both air- and liquid-cooled engines were used extensively in World War II. In-line and V type drives are similar to those of motorcars, while the radial engine imparts its power to a specially-designed, very short, rotary crankshaft.

Compound engines employ a combination of cylinder and gas-turbine elements. The turbines, fed by exhaust gases from the cylinders, are themselves geared to the crankshaft. It is claimed that the Wright Turbo-cyclone, a compounded model built for the U.S. Navy, utilizes about 20 per cent of the energy normally wasted. The engine is so compact that it fits the cowling lines of comparable cylinder engines.

Marine Engines. Both gasoline and diesel engines are used for boats and ships. Gasoline engines similar to automobile engines are used in small boats, but for most of the larger ships diesel engines are used. Marine engines are either two-stroke cycle or four-stroke cycle vertical engines. Single-acting, two-stroke cycle marine engines are built up to 7,000 hp, and double-acting, two-stroke cycle engines up to 25,000 hp; four-stroke cycle engines have been built up to 3,000 hp.

Marine engines are similar in all respects to the types of engines described, but a few modifications are made to adapt them to marine service. Reverse gears for change of direction of the propeller are used in sizes up to 150 hp, but the larger engines are directly reversible. They are usually built for moderate speed operation in order to obtain better propeller efficiencies and, in two-stroke cycle engines, to make scavenging easier. Both the lubricating and cooling systems of marine engines must be designed to function properly regardless of the listing and pitching of the ship. Since sea water is used for cooling the marine engine, the cooling system must be corrosion-resisting.

The Oil Engine differs from the gasoline engine in that it uses a fuel which cannot be vaporized by a carburetor or mixing valve. Instead the oil is sprayed

Radial engines of a modern airliner

into the cylinder near the end of the compression stroke, and only the air is compressed. There are three classes of oil engines: the surface ignition or semi-diesel, the spark ignition, and the compression ignition or diesel.

The *spark ignition oil engine* has been on the American market for industrial machinery since 1931. Later developments and refinements have extended its field of application to bus and truck operations as well as heavy duty, moderate, and slow speed industrial work. It is a low compression engine which operates on the Otto four-stroke cycle. On the downward or intake stroke of the piston, air alone is admitted to the cylinder. At the bottom dead-center point, the intake valve closes and the compression stroke of the piston compresses the air in the cylinder to a pressure of about 125 lbs. per sq. inch. Just before the end of the stroke the fuel oil is injected into the combustion chamber by the fuel injection pump. Because of the form of the combustion chamber, the air is compressed in a definite turbulence pattern. The whirling air picks up the finely atomized fuel from the injector, mixes with it, and sweeps it past the spark plug. At the proper moment the spark ignites the highly combustible mixture and the piston is driven downward on its working stroke. At the end of that stroke, the exhaust valve opens and the piston returns, forcing out the exhaust gases.

This low-compression type of engine can be hand cranked and is started on gasoline supplied to the manifold by a conventional primer pump. When the engine is started, it operates on fuel oil, the ignition of the fuel oil being accomplished because the residual heat of the initial combustion is sufficient to vaporize a part of the spray before it reaches the spark plug.

DIESEL ENGINES

The chief differences in the Otto cycle and the diesel cycle are (1) fuel is injected before compression in the Otto cycle and after compression in the diesel cycle; (2) lower compression pressures are used in the Otto cycle than in the diesel cycle; (3) Otto cycle engines require an outside source of ignition while none is required in the diesel cycle; and (4) the Otto cycle engine employs approximately constant-volume combustion, while the diesel cycle engine, on the other hand approaches constant pressure combustion of the fuel.

The Diesel Four-Stroke Cycle consists of four strokes. Fig. 5, A to D, shows the valve action and the conditions existing in the cylinder of a four-cycle diesel when the piston is at different points in the engine cycle. The pressure in the cylinder at any point in the piston stroke is indicated by F, while E shows that part of the crank circle swept by the crank during any of the several events in the engine cycle. A shows suction, or admission stroke of piston. Valve at J is open at point *a* just before the piston has reached the upper dead center. This valve remains open from point *a* to point *b*, during which time the piston moves downward, drawing in the cylinder's charge of air, reverses, and starts to move upward.

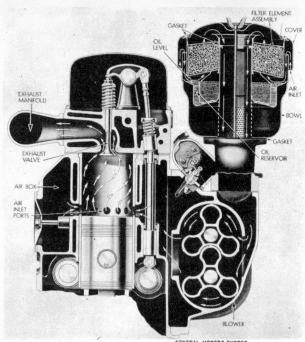

GENERAL MOTORS PHOTOS

Air Intake through a diesel engine blower, as shown in photodiagram

This admission stroke is shown in Fig. 5, E and F. In the latter the indicator diagram shows this line as being slightly below atmospheric pressure line XY. In B the admission valve J has closed and the pure air charge is compressed by the piston up to the point a. This is top dead center. This process is indicated by the compression line bc on the indicator diagram in F. The clearance volume is very small and the maximum or final compression pressure rises to a comparatively high pressure. The work done on the air charge in compression causes the temperature to rise to a point above the ignition temperatures of the oil fuel. At point c in C, the injection valve K opens and a charge of fuel is forced into the cylinder by means of the high-pressure air in an air-injection engine and by means of the pressure pump in the solid-injection engine. The fuel-injection valve, or spray valve, is designed to cause the rate of flow through the valve to be regulated so that the entire oil charge is not injected simultaneously, but takes place while the engine crank turns through a considerable angle. In C the injection of the fuel starts when the crank is at c and ends when the crank is at d. In F the line cd represents the fuel admission and combustion, and the desired condition is obtained when the line cd is practically horizontal, showing that the rate of heat addition is such that there is no increase in cylinder pressure.

The injection and combustion of fuel ceasing at the point d, the piston continues to the end of its stroke under the influence of the expanding gases. Before the completion of the stroke the exhaust valve L opens and the crank is at e. This allows gases to rush out through the exhaust passage. The exhaust valve continues to remain open until the piston again advances to the top of the cylinder, expelling all of the exhaust gases. This part of the cycle is shown in E and D as continuing from e to f. In F this forms the exhaust ef. Before the exhaust valve L closes, the admission valve opens at a, allowing a fresh air charge to be induced into the cylinder during the stroke shown in A.

Two-Stroke Cycle Diesel Engine. Fig. 6 represents the working diagram of a two-stroke cycle diesel engine. In F the air charge is compressed from b to c. The fuel is injected when the piston nears the top dead center, and the piston, forced downward on the working stroke, makes the lines cd and de in C; at e, in D, the piston uncovers the ports in the side of the cylinder, through which the exhaust gases pass. As the piston moves downward to the point a, scavenging valves in the cylinder head open, and a charge of pure air from the scavenging pump blows into the cylinder, clearing it of all exhaust gases. At b, or slightly before this point, the scavenging valve closes, and as the piston moves upward it seals the exhaust ports which are located at point b. Continued upward motion compresses the air charge until upper dead center is reached, whereupon the cycle is repeated.

Fuel Injection Systems. In general there are two distinct types of fuel injection systems for diesel engines; air injection and solid injection. Two solid

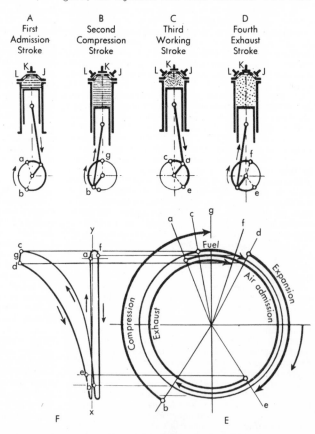

Fig. 5. Diagram of four cycle Diesel engine operation

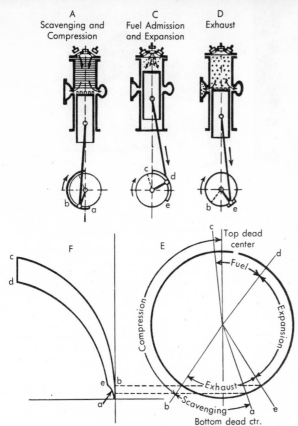

Fig. 6. Diagram of two cycle Diesel engine operation

injection systems of fuel injection are used by diesel engine builders, namely, the "common rail" system and the pump injection system. Either an open or closed type fuel nozzle is used with these systems. The open type nozzle is not provided with means for stopping the flow of fuel, while the closed type is provided with a spring-loaded valve at or near its orifice. The system of solid injection which embodies a common rail supplies fuel to all cylinders continuously. Its pressure is maintained by cam- or eccentric-driven fuel pumps with cranks staggered to maintain a supply and pressure of fuel that is almost constant. The valve in the closed type nozzle used in the individual cylinder in this system is mechanically operated and timed from the engine camshaft. Quantity fuel control is accomplished by the lift of the valve, the timing, the area of the nozzle holes, and the pressure on the common rail.

The pump injection system generally employs an individual fuel pump for each cylinder. The open type nozzle in the pump injection system is generally furnished with a check valve to prevent cylinder combustion gas from entering the valve. A helix in this type of nozzle rotates the fuel spirally, and thus it issues from the nozzle orifice into a precombustion or turbulence chamber in a cone-shaped spray. When the pump pressure drops, the check valve reseats. Some pump injection systems use a single pump to supply fuel to all of the cylinders. The allocation of the fuel is accomplished by the use of a distributor, which connects each cylinder valve to the pump in sequence.

Governing Devices. To obtain maximum thermal efficiency at all loads and to maintain constant speed of any type of oil or gasoline engine, some type of speed governor is required. On automobile, marine, aircraft, and some of the high-speed diesels, hand governing is usually used. On most of the other types of engines, automatic governors are furnished either as an integral part or as an accessory to the engine. In general there are three types of governors: hit-and-miss governors, quality governors, and quantity governors. The hit-and-miss type controls the admission of fuel to the cylinder and gives a complete charge or no charge at all. Quantity governors control the amount of fuel mixture admitted to the cylinder, and quality governors control the proportions of the fuel-air mixture. The hit-and-miss type governors are used generally on small gasoline engines where close regulation of speed is not essential. Automobiles, boats, etc. employ engines that are manual quantity type governing. Diesel engines incorporate quality type governors.

In the hit-and-miss type governor a cam on the camshaft gives a reciprocating motion to the pick blade, which has a sharp end shaped to engage with a nick in a block that is fastened to the stem of the valve through which the mixture is drawn into the cylinder. The pick blade is hinged near the end, and is attached by means of a vertical rod to the sliding collar of a flyball governor. So long as the engine maintains a certain speed the pick blade is held in the closed position, and in each revolution of the cam, the inlet valve is forced open, admitting an explosive charge. If the speed increases beyond the desired normal speed, the flyballs move outward, raise the collar, and so lift the rod connected to the pick blade, which draws the blade up and prevents it from engaging with the block on the valve stem. As a result no charge is taken into the cylinder and explosions are missed until the speed drops to such a point that the governor again lowers the pick blade. Hit-and-miss governing, however, cannot be used on engines that must run at uniform speed.

A common method of *quantity governing* is to put a throttle valve in the pipe leading from the carburetor to the inlet valve and to connect this throttle valve to the governor. Thus, with variations of load and consequently of the speed, the governor will automatically adjust the quantity of explosive charge admitted, which, of course, will determine the force exerted during the working stroke and, therefore, the speed of the engine.

Since 1926 one of the greatest advances in diesel engine design has been the development of the solid injection engines. Air injection has been almost entirely eliminated, though it was popular years ago.

Low-Speed Diesels. Two-cycle diesel engines with trunk piston design and mechanical fuel injection are available in three cylinder sizes and with several different numbers of cylinders. In size they range from 750 hp to 5,800 hp, operating on the port scavenging system, which has several advantages. There are relatively few moving parts, and system is adapted to fuels of widely varying characteristics.

Scavenging air for the power cylinders is provided by a double-acting pump located on the bedplate at the end opposite the flywheel. This pump is driven from the crankshaft and delivers low-pressure air into the scavenging manifold, which extends the full length of the engine and connects with the power cylinders. In the larger sizes a separate motor-driven scavenging blower can be supplied if desired, and can be connected directly to the scavenging manifold. Inside the scavenging manifold are placed the automatic scavenging valves that control the passage of

Internal Combustion Engine

NORDBERG MFG. CO.   NORTHWESTERN UNIVERSITY

Internal Combustion Engines are made in such varying sizes as the huge stationary Diesel of a power plant, left, and tiny air-cooled gasoline motor, right, used to power airplane and automobile models

air from the manifold to the power cylinders. These valves consist essentially of a multiplicity of disks set in cages. In the system of scavenging the air flows from the manifold, through the scavenging valves and ports into the cylinder. With the air deflected upward, the cylinder is filled with clean, cool, uncontaminated air, the exhaust gases having been forced out through the exhaust ports.

These engines are available with either cross-head or trunk-piston construction, and with mechanical or air injection. While each cylinder has its own fuel pump, these pumps are combined into a single unit mounted on the frame directly above the camshaft and driven from it.

A pressure lubrication system provides complete positive lubrication to all working parts. The oil, after passing through the main bearings, is carried into the crankshaft and up the hollow connecting rods to the top of the pistons, thereby keeping the pistons cool. After circulating through the pistons, the oil spills into the base, is passed through a strainer and a cooler, and then is again circulated through the system.

Another heavy-duty, stationary diesel engine of the vertical two-cycle-with-port-scavenging, single-acting, trunk-piston, mechanical injection type operates at 240 rpm, develops 330 brake hp per cylinder, and is furnished with from 4 to 12 cylinders. The engine is completely enclosed by means of large, oil-tight crankcase doors which, when removed, expose all vital parts for inspection. All moving parts are pressure-lubricated and working cylinders are automatically lubricated by force feed lubricators. The pistons are of the three-piece, oil-cooled, trunk type. The piston head is machined from a steel forging and is grooved for six snap rings. The fuel injection valves are located in a central port in the cylinder head. The starting valves are of the nonreturn poppet type and are mounted on the cylinder head in separate cages; valves are arranged to time properly the admission of starting air to the cylinders and are so designed that they will close immediately when the pressure in the cylinder exceeds the starting air pressure. The method is simple and effective.

Scavenging of the working cylinder after combustion of fuel is effected through two rows of ports in the cylinder wall on the back side of the engine. The ports of the upper row are controlled by automatic valves and do not open until the pressure within the cylinder has fallen to nearly atmospheric levels during the expulsion of the gases through the exhaust ports on the front side of the engine. Thus the scavenging air assists in expelling the burned gases and fills the cylinder with fresh air at a slight overpressure. As a result, at the beginning of actual compression the cylinder contains a greater weight of air than it would contain at atmospheric pressure.

High-Speed Diesels. Recent years have shown the greatest advance in diesel engine design, particularly in the trend toward the higher engine speeds in the automotive, transportation, and industrial fields, where engine weight and space must be kept to a minimum. In the smaller size engines, speeds have been raised to as high as 2,600 rpm for truck and tractor service, to 1,800 rpm for industrial service, and to 1,000 rpm for locomotive service. Nearly all of the modern engines under 150-hp capacity are of the four-cycle type, while the high-capacity, high-speed engines may embody either the two-cycle or four-cycle construction. One type is available in several sizes either as a tractor engine or a power unit. The largest is an eight-cylinder engine with 5¾-inch bore and 8-inch stroke, developing 160 maximum brake hp at the governed speed of 850 rpm. The smallest is a 4-cylinder engine with a 3½-inch bore and a 5-inch stroke, developing 32 maximum brake hp at 1,525 rpm. Several intermediate sizes are available, arranged with various numbers of cylinders and different full load speeds. All of these engines are of the four-stroke cycle construction with valves located in the cylinder head. Each cylinder has its own injection pump, calibrated and set at the factory.

There is another line of two-cycle, vertical diesels for automotive, general industrial, and marine service. They are available in 3-, 4-, and 6-cylinder designs. The largest engines rate 125 hp maximum at 1,200 rpm, the 4-cylinder engine rates 84 hp maximum at 1,200 rpm, and the 3-cylinder size rates 63 hp maximum at 1,200 rpm. These engines operate on the full diesel principle with a compression ratio of 16:1.

LUBRICATING AND COOLING

Lubricating systems are divided into two parts: one provides the lubricant to the surfaces to be lubricated, and the other provides a means for maintaining the quality of the lubricant. In some engines it may not be necessary to furnish a means for maintaining the quality of the lubricant. If a means is necessary for this purpose, the device used should remove the impurities from the lubricant as rapidly as contamination takes place. The quality of the lubricant is maintained in various engines by a number of different devices. Present-day engines may use singly or in combination the following devices: filters, coolers, acetylene tanks, reclaimers of various designs, separators, and centrifugal purifiers. Splash lubrication is employed on many engines, particularly those in automobiles. The crankcase is completely enclosed, forming an oil-tight chamber. A quantity of oil is poured into the tank. At each revolution of the tank, the end of the connecting rod dips into the oil and splashes it over the bearings as well as over the running surface of the piston. This method naturally is not satisfactory on two-stroke cycle engines because too much of the oil would be carried through the transfer port into the cylinder with the fuel charges.

About one third of the heat generated through the combustion of the fuel in an internal combustion engine is useful in delivering work to the crankshaft. Another third is carried away by the exhaust gases, and the rest must be removed by the *cooling system* to prevent excessive temperatures in the engine parts. Such temperatures might cause reduction of the strength of the materials in the engine so that harmful strains would occur, or expansion and distortion of parts, which would make the engine inoperative, or cause breakdown of the lubricating oil film.

In general, engines may be classified as *air-cooled* or *water-cooled*. Smaller engines can be cooled successfully by the use of the air-cooling method. The outside of the cylinder is formed with a series of ribs or fins to increase the heat-radiating surface. Air currents over the cylinder carry off enough heat to keep the working parts at a sufficiently low temperature to assure satisfactory operation. The cooling air may be circulated by means of a fan or by the motion of the engine itself. Because air cooling is not successful for larger engines, water cooling is used. Between inner and outer walls of the cylinder casting, a space known as the outer jacket is formed, through which water is circulated to carry off excess heat.

In ship propulsion there has been lively competition between steam and internal combustion engines since World War I. In that time the improvement in metals to withstand higher temperatures and stresses has led to improved efficiencies in both types. The Scandinavian countries which led off with the diesel for shipping, still seem to favor that type.

The strong position and growth of the internal combustion engine are cited. In 1919 the approximate shipbuilding figures indicated that steam reciprocating was 70 per cent; steam turbines, 28 per cent; diesels, two per cent. In 1938 the steam reciprocating was approximately 39 per cent; steam turbines, 14 per cent; diesels, 56 per cent. In 1947 the steam reciprocating engine had fallen to approximately 14 per cent; the steam turbine had risen to about 32 per cent; and the diesels were 54 per cent; and this in the face of increased burner efficiency under boilers and bunkering advantages in fuel oil.

BIBLIOG.–L. C. Lichty, *Internal Combustion Engines* (1939); A. W. Judge, *Testing of High-Speed Internal Combustion Engines* (ed. 1943); G. C. Boyer, *Diesel and Gas Engine Power Plants* (1943); H. A. Everett, *Internal Combustion Engine Lubrication Research at Pennsylvania State College* (1944); B. H. Jennings and E. F. Obert, *Internal Combustion Engines, Analysis and Practice* (1944); V. L. Maleev, *Internal Combustion Engines, Theory and Design* (ed. 1945); A. T. J. Kersey, ed. *Internal-Combustion Engineering* (1949).

INTERNAL IMPROVEMENTS. The question of whether state and Federal funds should be used to help finance the construction of roads, canals, and railroads, and to what extent, was a source of political controversy in the United States, especially in the early decades of the 19th century. The matter became an issue after the settlement of the region beyond the Appalachian Mountains; the lack of means of communication with the eastern states was the principal reason for the separatism in the Old Southwest during the 1780's. As the western states grew in numbers and political influence the issue gained support. The sketchy roads of the interior were unsuited to the swiftly growing traffic in merchandise and farm products; the rivers, although well adapted as inland waterways, led away from the eastern markets. Settlers on the frontiers and farm interests throughout the country stood to benefit from better transportation; these groups were supported by certain business interests and by land speculators. Private capital had developed the early roads and some of the short eastern canals, but it was not adequate for the construction of hundreds of miles of roads and canals into the thinly-settled West. Hence the demand was made for government-financed improvements.

In 1817 New York State began the construction of the ERIE CANAL, and soon other states started similar projects of their own. The Federal government pushed the CUMBERLAND ROAD (or NATIONAL ROAD) west from the Potomac River, reaching the Ohio in 1818, and continuing on into Illinois; this was the first of the great new roads which opened up the continent. No strong constitutional objection was raised to the financing of the Cumberland Road by the Federal government since the project was clearly interstate in character. But when the Bonus Bill of 1816 sought to grant Federal funds to internal improvement schemes in the separate states President Madison vetoed the bill as contrary to the Constitution; also under Monroe a narrow view was taken of the role of the Federal government in the matter. During the late 1820's, however, the so-called AMERICAN SYSTEM advocated by Henry Clay gained the ascendancy, resulting in the appropriation of immense sums for internal improvements. A decade later the clamor for new improvements reached a fever pitch, but culminated in the panic of 1837. This disaster put great numbers of government-launched companies into bankruptcy, with the result that when construction got under way again in the 1840's there was more reliance on private funds. By 1850 the demand for canals had given way to the demand for railroads, in the construction of which the initiative was in the hands of private companies, aided by Federal land grants in many cases. Also, numerous counties, townships, and cities subscribed stock for the construction of railroads (often an outright or partial subsidy); such action was often motivated by the fear that the region concerned might otherwise be bypassed by the railroad. Although there was much graft and abuse in these different forms of aid, the result was a magnificent network of railways.

The coming of the automobile age likewise caused a great demand on the Federal government, this time for improvements in the form of hard-surfaced roads. The result was again a system of improved transportation, binding together the whole country and altering the life of its people. See WATERWAYS, INLAND; RAILROAD.   R. W. QUINN.

INTERNAL REVENUE, the taxes collected under the Bureau of Internal Revenue of the United States Department of the Treasury. In Great Britain, the corresponding taxes, including in general all levies except customs, are called *inland revenue*. In 1789, when the Federal government was organized under President Washington, tariff duties were levied as the sole source of revenue. Two years later, however, it was found necessary to levy excise taxes on distilled spirits. These taxes were soon repealed because of their unpopularity. Excise taxes have been constantly levied since 1862, at which time the Bureau of Internal Revenue was established. At the present time the principal sources of internal revenue are excise taxes, personal and corporate income taxes, estate and gift taxes, railroad employment compensation taxes, and social security taxes. These taxes now provide most of the revenue for the Federal government. In 1794 customs yielded $4,801,000, while internal revenue brought in only $274,000. In 1950 internal taxes were estimated at $38,947,000,000 and customs were only $428,891,788. See EXCISE; INCOME TAX; INHERITANCE TAX; NATIONAL INCOME; TAXATION; WHISKY INSURRECTION.

INTERNATIONAL, THE, the term applied to a number of world-wide groupings of socialist and communist political organizations. The stimulus for such union came from the closing words of the Communits Manifesto (1848) of Marx and Engels: "Workers of the world, unite." In 1864 at a mass meeting held in London there was organized the International Workingmen's Association, usually called the International, but in retrospect spoken of as the First International. The organization soon spread to the continent, but the British labor unions were the mainstay of it. Congresses were held at Geneva (1866), Lausanne (1867), Brussels (1868), Basle (1869), The Hague (1872), Geneva (1874), and Philadelphia (1876). After 1870, however, the British unions lost interest in the International because of the radicalism of the continental organizations and for this reason they soon dissociated themselves from it. Also, a factional quarrel broke out between the followers of Marx and those who looked to Bakunin; the latter, expelled at the Hague congress, formed their own International, which ended in 1879. The parent organization passed out of existence after the Philadelphia congress in 1876.

The Second International was established at Paris in 1889 as an association of socialist parties. Frequent congresses were held at which the two most prominent problems debated were the question of Socialist participation in "bourgeois" ministries and the socialist attitude toward the coming war. When World War I broke out, the Socialists in various countries, with some exceptions, supported their respective nations. After the war the Second International was reconstituted at Hamburg in 1923, as the "Labor and Socialist International," following the break with the more radical elements, which had joined the Communist Third International. The Second International's most important constituent parties were the Labor party of Great Britain and the Social Democratic party of Germany. It continued its existence until 1939.

The Third International came into existence after the Russian Revolution as a union of communist parties throughout the world. Headquarters of the organization (often called Comintern) were in Moscow; the Communist who dominated the Soviet government also controlled the Third International. The Comintern was a world revolutionary organization which aimed to overthrow capitalism in all nations. It followed a flexible policy and adjusted its tactics as the exigencies of the moment required. The Third International was officially abolished in May, 1943, during World War II when the Soviet government felt it desirable to co-operate with the other United Nations.

The Cominform (Communist Information Bureau) came into being in Belgrade, Yugoslavia, in October, 1947. This new organization aimed to present a united front against the United States and its allies as well as against social democratic leaders in France, Great Britain, Austria, and other nations. The Cominform was in effect a new Communist International, aiming to realize communism on a world-wide scale, although it was claimed not to be so. In addition, it was the main instrument of Soviet Russia in the attempt to tighten its control over the satellite states. In June, 1948, the Cominform began its attack on the Yugoslav government and at the end of 1949 it met in Hungary and denounced Tito's government on the ground that it conducted a provocative campaign against Soviet Russia. Yugoslavia was ousted from the Cominform.

See Communism; Socialism; Labor Movement; Marx, Karl; Bakunin, Michael. F.M.; G. B. de H.

Bibliog.–R. M. Roy, *Communist International* (1943); William Henry Chamberlain, *Blueprint for World Conquest as Outlined by the Communist International* (1946); Martin Ebon, *World Communism Today* (1948); Committee on Foreign Affairs, House of Representatives, *The Strategy and Tactics of World Communism* (1948).

INTERNATIONAL ARBITRATION. See Arbitration, International.

INTERNATIONAL ASSOCIATIONS. For organizations beginning with International, see under significant title, as Chamber of Commerce, *The International Chamber of Commerce.*

INTERNATIONAL BANK FOR RECONSTRUCTION AND DEVELOPMENT. See Bretton Woods; Banks and Banking; International Finance; United Nations.

INTERNATIONAL BANKING. See Banks and Banking; International Finance.

INTERNATIONAL CIVIL AVIATION ORGANIZATION. See United Nations; Air, Law of the; Freedom of the Air.

INTERNATIONAL COURT OF JUSTICE. See United Nations; Courts, International.

INTERNATIONAL DATE LINE. See Time, Measurement of.

INTERNATIONAL FALLS, city and port of entry, N Minnesota, county seat of Koochiching County; at the falls of the Rainy River near Rainy Lake; on the Northern Pacific and the Minnesota, Dakota, and Western railroads and U.S. highways 53 and 71, about 135 miles NW of Duluth. A bridge connects the city with Fort Frances, Ontario. Although the first settler, Alexander Baker, arrived in 1881, the village was not incorporated until 1901. In 1904, a paper company secured American and Canadian riparian rights and contracted for the development of water power and industrial plants. During succeeding years, the falls have supplied power for sawmills and paper mills, a fiberboard plant, and other extensive wood industries. International Falls is the headquarters of several branches of the U.S. International Border Patrol. Pop. (1950) 6,269.

INTERNATIONAL FINANCE is essentially the same as internal finance in any particular country. It consists in making available monetary resources and credit by those who are disposed to invest to those who require additional funds in order to carry out productive economic ventures.

Purpose and Scope. International finance may be private or public and may involve short- or long-term transactions. It may consist of lending and borrowing operations, or of operations in which the provider of funds acquires the ownership of the enterprise he is financing. The urge behind international financial operations is usually, as in domestic operations, the anticipation of and quest for financial returns: interest payments in the case of lending operations, profits or dividends in the case of ownership investments.

When international financial transactions take place not between persons or businesses, but between governments or countries, there arise additional considerations. When one government gives a loan to another, it is animated by motives other than the realization of an income, the motives are, on the contrary, either political or economic in a very broad sense of the word. Typically international finance involves a movement of capital from countries which are highly developed economically, and which have an excess of Savings over current requirements toward less developed countries which cannot provide themselves with an adequate volume of available financial resources to give impetus to their economic vitality. We speak in that connection of creditor and debtor countries, by which we mean countries which are net exporters and those which are net importers of Capital. International financial transactions are not limited, however, to only a flow of funds from developed to under-developed countries. Financial transactions take place between countries which are on an equal level of economic development—either high or low. There were, for example, before World War II, large American investments in Britain and large British investments in the United States.

The scope of international finance is much greater than the *net* flow of funds between countries. Unless restrained by government restrictions, private capital moves across boundary lines whenever its owners or administrators find an attractive field of Investment for the funds that they control. The effect of these investments is to allow the accumulated savings to find the most productive outlets, thus contributing to the welfare of both the investing owners of capital and society in general.

As has been already intimated, international finance may have objectives other than those in connection with the normal ways of business. Countries which have been afflicted by war or by natural cataclysms may require foreign funds in order to improve their positions rapidly even though they may not be able to provide tempting opportunities for the private businessman. Intergovernmental loans then become necessary, and governments granting them do so in the conviction that the restoration of the economic health of the afflicted areas will have a favorable effect on their own future foreign trade and their economic security. Certain intergovernmental loans serve the purpose of buttressing the monetary reserves of a country having undergone great economic strain. These "stabilization loans" are granted either by one central bank to another or by one government to another; combined with appropriate domestic measures in the country receiving them, they help to restore and maintain international monetary stability which in turn is indispensable for the stability of international economic relations. Finally intergovernmental loans may be granted for the purpose of helping a friendly nation in difficulties, thus making stronger the links of political friendship between the two countries. Political loans are on the borderline between international finance and international power-political relationships.

Methods. As has been suggested, international finance can, just as internal finance, operate by the method of lending or that of ownership investment. Intergovernmental transactions are generally of the former kind; in the field of private investment both methods are frequently encountered. Finance, through lending, gives to the creditor a reasonable assurance of the returns he will get year after year from his investment, and involves at the end of the period the repayment of the loan. The returns it offers can never be as high, of course, as those that an investor may obtain by accepting the risks inherent in an ownership investment. The latter gives the investor a right to the profits realized or to a pro-rata share in these profits (dividends).

Ownership investment can take the form of purchases of stock in a foreign company or can consist of so-called "direct business investments" made abroad. The second method of international finance consists in establishing a business enterprise abroad with the creditor's money or in setting up a branch factory in another country. The investor accepts the normal business risks, and the amount of risk he is going to accept depends on his anticipations of the profits he can achieve if the business goes well.

In the 19th century and up to World War I, one form of international finance consisted of so-called "venture capital," daring and large scale private investments in countries rich in resources, but underdeveloped economically. The rewards were very great in case of success and losses equally considerable in case of failure. In those days venture capital often enjoyed special privileges in the country to which it went and these were an added incentive for undertaking the venture. The two World Wars and the interwar period of unsettled economic conditions have dealt a heavy blow to the venturesomeness of capital. Other factors worked in the same direction, as will be set out below. As of 1947 venture capital, namely, the opening up of vast unused natural resources, has become largely a function of public bodies. The International Bank for Reconstruction and Development established in 1944 (see below) has as its function the bridging of the gap between purely private and purely public capital investments. It will be noted that ownership investments do not generally raise the question of repayment. A lender has a legal claim to repayment; an ownership investor does not. The latter can of course sell his shares or his enterprise and transfer the proceeds to another country for the financing of new projects. But the transfer problem

involved in ownership investments is much smaller in scope than that incident in international loans.

Special Problems. Whereas, fundamentally, international finance represents an extension into the foreign field of financial transactions that take place at home, there are nevertheless certain special problems which arise internationally but not domestically. All of these problems are due to the existence in the world of multiple political sovereignties, each state having the power to control to a larger or lesser extent the conditions under which economic activity takes place in its territory. The existence of many separate sovereignties and the existence of NATIONALISM make the position of a foreign investor different from that of a capitalist investing at home. Reference has already been made to the particularly favorable treatment given to foreign venture capital in certain parts of the world before World War I. More recently the contrary has been frequently true, foreign capital having become the object of discriminatory treatment on the part of nationalistic governments.

The spread of state socialism throughout certain parts of the world has also created special problems for the foreign investor. If his capital has been placed in an industry which becomes the object of a nationalization program, he runs the risk of being expropriated along with the nationals of the socialistic country who have made investments in the same branch of industry. The methods of the nationalization program may be such that the foreign capitalist receives a fair compensation and is able to take his funds out of the country again to use them to better advantage elsewhere. But it may also happen that the compensation is not fair and that the foreign investor is prohibited through exchange control regulations from repatriating his funds. In view of nationalistic discriminations and of the growth of state socialism it becomes necessary to reach intergovernmental agreements which would determine the legal status of foreign capital in the country to which it has come to work. Proposals have been made recently by the International Chamber of Commerce and other bodies for the working out of an international code of fair practice in the field of foreign investment. The acceptance of such a code would greatly facilitate overcoming the above-mentioned special difficulties inherent in foreign investments.

The transfer problem is another special feature of international finance. Because the world consists of many separate states it also has several separate currencies. An international payment generally involves a transfer from one currency into another and this, at times, may create more or less serious difficulties for balances of payments of particular countries. A *net* payment from one country to another can be accomplished in a definitive way only through the achievement of an export surplus by the country which is making a net payment and of an import surplus by the country which is receiving the net payment. The commercial transactions involved need not take place exclusively between the two countries in question; the network of multilateral international trade makes it unnecessary to have the commercial settlement take place between pairs of countries; placed against the broader background of the world economy, the problem of achieving the required export and import surplusage is greatly facilitated. Nevertheless if the net payment to be made is very considerable and if the need to make it arises suddenly rather than gradually, the making of the payment might encounter serious difficulties. These difficulties will be the greater the more restrictions that are placed on the path of the free flow of goods and services between countries. Economic nationalism aggravates the transfer problem which would be considerably eased in a free-trade world.

It is important to keep in mind that net international payments are usually very much smaller than gross payments. A country which has to pay off at a given date a large foreign loan may at the same time receive a new loan which may be equal in size, smaller, or even larger than the loan to be repaid, with the result that the country will have either no net payment to make or only a small net payment, or it may even have a receipt on current account in place of a payment. There are also compensatory short-term credit operations which can extend the period in which foreign trade must make the adjustment to the financial requirements in order to avoid a default of payments. Under stable international conditions a country can always attract short term capital from abroad by raising sufficiently its short term interest rate. Prior to World War I the mechanism of international payments was greatly assisted by movements of short-term funds in response to differential changes in interest rates; this was an important feature of the successful operation of the international gold standard.

International Bank for Reconstruction and Development. Even before World War II came to an end it became apparent that the problem of postwar reconstruction would require substantial international financing and that private capital could not be expected to undertake that responsibility alone. It was also realized that under anticipated postwar conditions one could not expect a sufficient revival of venture capital to enable underdeveloped areas of the world to take rapid strides toward a higher level of economic activity, a goal toward which many governments have become committed. It was also realized that it was undesirable to make the financing of reconstruction and development entirely dependent upon intergovernmental loans. There was a feeling that it was necessary to find a way by which capital could be provided for these purposes on less onerous terms than those which could attract private funds and with less likelihood of political considerations in the granting of loans than is typical of purely intergovernmental finance.

The International Bank for Reconstruction and Development, which was adopted at the BRETTON WOODS Conference (1944), is conceived as a cooperative intergovernmental scheme for providing to members loans for reconstruction and development purposes on terms more favorable than those of the private market and for purposes which can stand up to a strict economic scrutiny. The bank can make loans with its own funds or with money raised in its own name in the private capital market, or it can give its guarantee to loans issued with its consent by member countries in the private capital market. A country which could obtain funds on reasonable terms in the private market would not be expected to apply to the International Bank. The bank's loans would be given for specific projects, each of which would be carefully examined by an appropriate committee of experts. It may be possible for the bank in this way to establish much-needed standards for sound international investments. The bank is authorized furthermore to extend loans for stabilization purposes. Its capital has been set at $10,000,000,000 on the assumption of a full participation by all nations. The financial strength of the International Bank is considerably less than would be necessary to allow it to engage in very considerable investment transactions; in the early postwar period foreign investment remained very largely in the realm of direct intergovernmental relations. The International Bank and its twin institution, the International Monetary Fund (the aim of which is to assist in the maintenance of stable international monetary relations) have a forerunner in the shape of the BANK FOR INTERNATIONAL SETTLEMENTS which was established by The Hague Conference of 1930 with its headquarters in Basle, Switzerland. That institution, the purpose of which was and remains monetary rather than financial, has accumulated a vast fund of experience in both these fields and remains a very active meeting ground for

the heads of central banks of a great many countries of the world.

Post-World War II Trends. In a world which has endured two great wars and one great depression in one generation, the tasks of reconstruction are enormous and therefore the opportunities and responsibilities of international finance are very considerable. They are further increased by the needs and desires of underdeveloped countries for a substantial speeding-up of their rate of economic progress. These are the reasons for creating an environment favorable to the expansion of foreign investments throughout the world. During the chaotic period following World War II and before private investment (mainly American, since the United States was the principal source of exportable funds) had ventured to resume its former position, the Marshall Plan served as a stop-gap measure in opening again the international arteries of trade.

European Payments Union. Acting on a proposal first put forward by ECA Administrator Paul C. Hoffman, the 17 European Marshall Plan countries established a Payments Union in 1950. The union was, in effect, a new European central bank, a clearing house for debts and credits in Europe's international trade, which would greatly simplify transactions between separate countries. The operation of the Union served to make the currencies of all Western European countries interconvertible. The plan was unanimously accepted by the 17 nations and the United States July 7, 1950, at a conference in Paris, and it commenced functioning shortly thereafter. The United States turned over more than $200 million in Marshall Plan funds to be used as the union's initial working capital.

See TRADE, United States Foreign; TRADE, International; CREDIT; IMPERIALISM; CAPITAL; EXCHANGE, FOREIGN; BALANCE OF TRADE; TARIFF; RECIPROCITY; GOLD STANDARD; PUBLIC DEBT; REPARATIONS; CONCESSION; DRAGO DOCTRINE.

M. A. HEILPERIN

BIBLIOG.–J. T. Madden and M. Nadler, *International Money Markets* (1935); R. C. McGrave, *Foreign Bondholders and American State Debts* (1935); E. Staley, *War and the Private Investor* (1935); P. Einzig, *Fight for Financial Supremacy* (1935); G. F. Luthringer and others, *Money, Credit and Finance* (1937); J. Viner, *Studies in the Theory of International Trade* (1937); J. T. Madden and others, *America's Experience as a Creditor Nation* (1937); Royal Institute of International Affairs, *Problem of International Investment* (1937); J. P. Young, *International Trade and Finance* (1938); C. Lewis, *America's Stake in International Investments* (1938); G. S. Teng, *International Finance* (1939); S. E. Harris, ed., *Postwar Economic Problems* (1943); J. R. Bellerby, *Economic Reconstruction* (1943); P. A. Volpe, *International Financial and Banking Crisis, 1931–33* (1945); E. Staley, *World Economic Development* (1945); League of Nations, Economic and Financial Organization, *Conditions of Private Foreign Investment* (1946); G. B. de Huszar, ed., *Persistent International Issues* (1947); M. A. Heilperin, *Trade of Nations* (1947).

INTERNATIONAL HARVESTER COMPANY, the leading manufacturer of farm implements, organized in 1902 as a consolidation of five companies, the most important of which were the McCormick Harvesting Machine Company and the Deering Harvester Company. The first president of the consolidated company was Cyrus H. McCormick, the son of the inventor of the reaper. International Harvester began a great program of expansion, and within two decades it was offering a full line of farm implements. World War I gave a great impetus to farm mechanization, especially tractor-power equipment. A suit brought by the Federal government against the company in 1914 under the Sherman Antitrust Act ended in nonprosecution. However, in 1918 the company divested itself of three manufacturing lines, the two others being retained and merged into the McCormick-Deering line. In World War II, the company at governmental request continued production of farm machinery while devoting remaining facilities to war production. International Harvester maintains branches, transfer warehouses, and truck sales and service stations in over 200 U.S. communities. It also has an investment in subsidiaries overseas of nearly $100,000,000. Members of the McCormick family are active in company management. See AGRICULTURE, Historical Survey; FARM MACHINERY.   JAMES COLVIN

INTERNATIONAL LABOR ORGANIZATION, an autonomous institution established in fulfillment of the pledge made in Article 23 of the Covenant of the LEAGUE OF NATIONS, in which league members promised to "endeavor to secure and maintain fair and humane conditions of labor for men, women, and children, both in their own countries and in all countries to which their commercial and industrial relations extend." The constitution of the I.L.O. was incorporated in the treaties of Versailles, St. Germain, Neuilly, Trianon, and Sèvres.

The machinery of the organization consists of: the International Labor Conference, a world parliament for the consideration of labor and social questions; the International Labor Office, the secretariat of the organization which serves as a world center for information research and advice and prepares reports for the conference; and the Governing Body, which serves as an executive council of the organization and comprises 32 members, 16 representing governments, 8 labor and 8 employers. The conference held its first annual session in Washington in 1919. Each member nation is represented at sessions by four delegates, two of them representing the government, one labor, and one employers. A principal function of the conference is the formulation of standards of employment conditions. Conference decisions, requiring a two-thirds majority, are embodied in conventions and, less formally, in recommendations. The governments of the member states are obliged to submit these conventions and recommendations to their national legislatures. After 1948 in the United States these were referred to state legislatures as having proper authority rather than to the Federal government. When a convention is ratified by a government, it becomes in effect an international labor treaty, and annual reports must be made to the convention as to what measures have been taken to make the convention effective. In the 20 years before World War II the conference held 25 sessions and adopted 67 conventions and 66 recommendations. The conventions received nearly 900 ratifications by governments. The subjects dealt with in the conventions and recommendations included: hours of work, vacations with pay, regulation of working conditions of women, protection of child workers, prevention of and compensation for industrial accidents, social insurance, colonial labor, and living and working conditions of seamen.

In 1940 the headquarters were moved from Geneva, Switzerland, to Montreal, Canada, and the annual sessions interrupted by the war were not resumed until 1944. In 1948 the passage of a convention guaranteeing the right of workers and employers to establish and join organizations of their own choice was considered the most significant action taken in the history of the Conference. Ratification is not the sole test of the importance of conventions, for they serve as standards of social legislation in other countries as well.

Soviet Russia, which is not a member of the I.L.O., led in setting up the rival World Federation of Trade Unions, with which the C.I.O. was once affiliated. See CONGRESS OF INDUSTRIAL ORGANIZATIONS; LABOR MOVEMENT; UNITED NATIONS.   IRVING FRYER

BIBLIOG.–J. T. Shotwell, ed., *The Origins of the International Labor Organization* (2 vols., 1934). The International Labor Office publishes a *Year Book of Labour Statistics*, the *International Labour Review* (monthly), a *Legislative Series* (quarterly) giving texts and translations of important labor and social legislation in all countries, the *Industrial Safety Survey* (quarterly), and numerous studies and reports on particular subjects. Most of these are published in two or three languages (English, French, and Spanish).

INTERNATIONAL LAW

Rules to guide relations between nations have helped toward world peace

INTERNATIONAL LAW, formerly called the Law of Nations, consists of the principles and rules which may, under the principles of that law itself, be regarded as binding upon the otherwise independent states of the world in their relations with one another. Any rule which has received the general assent of the states of the world is valid law and therefore binding. Such assent may be given either explicitly or implicitly, that is, by formal agreement (treaty or convention) or through long-continued practice. Sometimes rules which are followed by the great majority of the international community are regarded as universally binding even in the absence of explicit acceptance by one or more minor states. It is also possible for international law to be enacted by majority vote (international legislation or statutes) as by organs of the United Nations or special international conferences, but such practice is a rather recent development. There is a growing tendency for international law to be formulated by or in multipartite (having many signatories) treaties or conventions dealing with such common problems as communications, weights and measures, and health. Such international agreements are often loosely called international legislation.

Persons in International Law. Just as national law (usually called municipal law) deals primarily with individuals so does international law deal with states. Traditionally sovereign states are referred to as the persons of international law. In theory each independent state is subject to no outside political authority and therefore it cannot be bound except by its own consent. International law usually touches individuals only indirectly. Individuals whose rights are affected by international law must therefore seek recourse through municipal law or through the diplomatic action of their own state.

Although it is still accurate in the main to describe international law as made by states and for states important changes are taking place. Even during the 19th century international law began to deal directly with individuals in certain situations, as in the outlawry of PIRACY and in the regulations pertaining to CONTRABAND OF WAR. With increasing frequency in recent decades the states of the world have been concluding conventions which define the rights and obligations of individuals and other substate entities directly. For example, international conventions dealing with river navigation must inevitably deal with persons as individuals no less than with states as political entities. Also, the independent states are admitting, slowly, irregularly, and reluctantly, numerous substate entities, such as dependencies, governmental agencies, and even private groups, to share in the process of making international law through the multipartite conventions and international statute just mentioned, although this practice is limited in scope and perhaps also in value.

History of International Law. This legal system is a development of modern times, but its roots go back to ancient times, especially to the rules and principles which governed the intercourse of the Greeks, Romans, and other peoples of the Mediterranean world. Early writers on international law relied heavily on the Roman *jus gentium*, which was a body of law developed to govern relations between Roman citizens and foreigners; though drawn from the practice of different countries, this system was often regarded as the law which natural reason had established among all nations. Modern international law appeared after the Renaissance had revived the study of ROMAN LAW. It developed because of the need for a legal system to regularize the relations between the new national states of western Europe.

HUGO GROTIUS (1583–1645) is generally called the father of international law. His famous work, *De jure belli ac pacis* (*On the Law of War and Peace*), was a systematic treatise dealing with the bases and principles of both positive and natural law. Many of the rules and principles enunciated by Grotius were recognized in the negotiations leading up to the Peace of Westphalia (1648) at the end of the Thirty Years War. Then followed a century and a half of rather slow growth; the development accelerated early in the 19th century, becoming very rapid during the decades before 1900. War, even when world-wide in scope, has not destroyed international law, although the changed conditions of international life have profoundly affected it.

Sources of International Law. The materials which must be consulted to discover the rules of international law are widely scattered. The most important sources are the following:

(1) Treaties, conventions, and other agreements between states. While all such agreements bind only the signatory parties, they are very important either as affording evidence of practice or as declaratory of what the law is to be.

(2) Practice and custom. The records of international practice must always be consulted to find out how states actually behave in their relations to each other and to discover how agreements are interpreted and applied.

(3) International legislation. In recent decades a certain amount of international statute law had been enacted by duly constituted agencies, conferences, and commissions of international organizations (such as the Universal Postal Union) and the League of Nations.

(4) Decisions of international tribunals. Included in this category are the special tribunals of arbitration (numerous in the decades before and after 1900), the World Court under the League of Nations and the United Nations.

(5) The opinions of experts. Partly because of the relative lack of international legislative and judicial bodies in the international sphere, the conclusions of textbook writers have been influential in the development of international law, but since such opinions are entirely private and are also subject to personal bias and national prejudice they must be carefully checked against usage.

(6) Diplomatic papers. All governments issue manuals and send instructions to their diplomatic agents to explain and interpret the principles of international law.

(7) Decisions on questions of international law by national courts. All domestic courts recognize the legal validity of international law and apply it in appropriate circumstances. The International Court of Justice may itself give consideration to the decisions of municipal courts. (Article 38 of the Statute.)

Codification of International Law. In view of the scattered character of the materials to be consulted for discovery of the rules of international law and the danger of differences of perception and interpretation in that process, a movement for the codification of international law has recently attained large proportions. Such action, involving a systematic statement of the law from the sources, has been taken in many legal fields. In general, continental European jurists have favored such action, while Anglo-Americans have opposed it, but today this opposition has greatly declined.

Important instances of official codification were made by the Declaration of Paris (1856), the HAGUE CONFERENCES (1899 and 1907), and the Declaration of London (1908–9). (See PARIS, DECLARATION OF; LONDON, DECLARATION OF.) (While the Declaration of London was not ratified it was regarded as a statement of the law of sea warfare for the period before World War I.) A more ambitious effort at codification

made under the League of Nations came to grief in 1930. Rather pretentious efforts under Pan-American auspices have produced elaborate statements on numerous topics, few of which have been finally adopted. An effort is under way (1946) to have the United Nations resume and continue the program begun by the league, with appropriate modifications based on that experience.

Private scholars have contributed to the cause of codification. The most interesting examples were produced by JOHANN BLUNTSCHLI the German Swiss, DAVID DUDLEY FIELD the American, and Pascal Fiore the Italian. Of course the statements of private scholars have no binding authority whatever, but they have been frequently quoted by national and international courts because they constitute secondary records of practice and state policy.

Content of International Law. This legal system has been traditionally divided into the law of peace, the law of war, and the law of neutrality, with further subdivisions under each heading. Some publicists now believe that this old division of the field should be replaced by one or more new classifications—such as common law or legislation, substantive law or procedural law. Also, the great expansion of international law in the last 25 years into fields of economic relations, public health, communications, social questions, and still other matters, should be adequately recognized.

The law of peace deals with the rights and duties of nations at peace. The law of war is concerned with the relations of nations at war. (See WAR, LAW OF.) The law of neutrality deals with the rights and duties of neutral states toward other nations which are at war. (See NEUTRALITY.) The law of peace involves the normal relationships between nations and it defines the nature of states and their principal rights and duties toward each other. In wartime a belligerent nation is under the law of war toward its enemy but under the law of peace toward other states. Likewise a neutral nation lives under the law of neutrality toward the belligerents but under the law of peace toward other neutrals.

The Law of Peace. International law is based on the foundation of state sovereignty. From this basic proposition are derived certain principles which are widely accepted. Every state recognized as a member of the family of nations has the following rights:

(1) The right to independence. Every state has the right of independence, and according to the traditional view it is justified in going to war to preserve this right and the principal rights derived therefrom. It has the right to be free from interference in matters which international law leaves to its exclusive control.

(2) The right to its own integrity as a state. Every state may control its own nationals (citizens or subjects), subject to certain limitations when they are found in other states; it may exercise complete control over its own territory and may maintain its sovereignty over such land as it possessed when it is recognized as a member of the family of nations. It may acquire new territory by any one of several methods recognized by international law. It may exclude aliens from its territory or admit them on its own terms; it may determine the rules under which foreigners may be admitted to citizenship. It may establish any kind of government it desires and may make whatever political changes it may wish.

(3) The right of equality. Every state may claim equality of rights with every other state without regard to the size of its territory, its population, or its industrial and military power. It may enter into diplomatic relations with every other nation and conclude treaties and other agreements with them. It can be bound only by its own free will. Rights and duties are always correlative. In other words, every state has the duty of recognizing the rights of all other states.

International law contains many detailed rules which are derived from the above-mentioned principles. Some of these rules are uncertain and even conflicting. For the detailed rules and for varying interpretations reference must always be had to standard, recent textbooks on international law, and also to such primary documents as were suggested above.

Law and International Relations. Law, or legal rules, must not be regarded as the only important aspect of international relations. Many important phases of this great field are not regulated by international law. Because nations are very jealous of their national sovereignty many matters have been left exclusively under national control even though they do concern the rest of the world. Such a matter is immigration; each country may entirely exclude immigrants or admit them on its own terms. Nations do, however, often make treaties which regulate these so-called domestic problems, which then cease to be purely domestic to this extent.

The phases of international relations outside international law are of basic importance since they are economic, social, and political in character. They give rise to the rules and principles of international law. They give rise also to institutions for conducting and controlling the business or activities of common interest to the states. These institutions are referred to by the phrase "international organization," which was almost unknown 25 years ago, but is now in common use. The United Nations is only one, although the largest and most important, among several hundred such institutions. Now international law deals with various aspects of international relations other than international organizations, and it also serves to define the structure of the latter. In turn international institutions display certain aspects, particularly on the margin where they are growing and changing, which are not embodied in legal rules. The law can be and actually is both master and agent for organized international institutions.

Authority and Enforcement of International Law. The twin problems of the authority of international law and its enforcement call for special attention. It is often denied that international law has any authority over the sovereign state, or can have such authority, or actually enjoys much respect or obedience, on the part of the latter. It is also alleged that no machinery or procedure exists for enforcing international law comparable with the policeman and the sheriff in the individual state and it is then denied that international law is effective or is entitled to be regarded as true law at all.

The reply to the first point seems to be fairly clear. The principle of sovereignty does not deny to the state the right to accept limitations upon its discretion voluntarily, nor does it impair the binding force—in principle or logic—of such limitations once they are accepted; it only denies that such limitations may be imposed without the state's consent. As for the practical aspects of the situation history seems to show clearly that this practice of self-limitation is recognized by the states and that in fact they live up to their obligations under international law about as well as individuals and corporations live up to the law in the national state, at least in time of peace. It is certainly not the states or governments—very rare dictatorships aside—which deny the binding force of international law or in practice defy or violate it extensively.

Several points must be emphasized respecting the enforcement of international law. It is often asserted that there are no facilities for enforcement of international law; it is added that this defect deprives international law of true legal character. The last point, based on the theories of the English jurist John Austin, seems to involve confusion between law and government and an exaggeration of the power of the latter. International law may derive binding force from other sources than physical enforcement and in

any case this latter function (the action of the policeman or sheriff) is a phase of governmental action, not of law itself. Finally, administration of law by force is by no means infallible or completely superior to the other factors compelling respect for law. Individual states have always done what they could by diplomatic protest, retaliation, or war to enforce the law against one another, a type of enforcement (self-help) entirely familiar in all early legal systems. In recent years a great number of experiments have been made, some of them very successful, in the direction of community international enforcement.

International Law and National Law. The relations between international law and national law are both interesting and important. For nearly two centuries it has been held in all Anglo-American countries that international law is part of the law of the land; in other states this point is not so clear. In the American constitution treaties and "the law of nations" are given special recognition and the courts apply their rules whenever cases involving them arise. There is, however, some hesitation in recognizing international law as superior to national law, although the United States Supreme Court has admitted on several occasions that this country may not relieve itself of obligations under international law on the ground of conflicting provisions in congressional statutes or even the constitution.

As has been implied, international law is applied by both national and international courts. Indeed it may be, and continually is, applied by both international and national administrative officials of all ranks, including the traffic policeman on the corner (in granting certain immunities to a motorcar carrying a diplomatic license, for example). In this field the trend is in the direction of creating distinct international agencies for administration of the law rather than to remit this function to national agencies, although the latter method of administration has real advantages of economy, convenience, and even effectiveness if properly supervised. For this reason national administration of international law will probably never entirely disappear.

Effects of Two World Wars. Sometimes it is implied or asserted that international law has been ruined or rendered impotent by the events of the past 30 years, particularly the two world wars. At other times it is argued that international law is too rudimentary a system, and is based on too reactionary a conception of the universe, to compete today with advanced international institutions such as the United Nations and its Security Council or with more ambitious schemes of world government which are now actually in being or are being seriously and vigorously proposed.

As for the effects of war on international law there are a number of points to be strongly emphasized. (Incidentally, this question is not entirely new but has arisen following various wars in the past.) The first point is that in such cases it is only the law of war or, at most, the law of war and neutrality which is called in question, while the law of peace, which is the more important, extensive, and normal aspect of the law, is left untouched. Secondly, it is universally admitted that violations of law do not destroy the legal rules (not even the common law which is based on practice), until and unless they become so general as to constitute an admitted revision of the law, which is very seldom the case. Thirdly, it is necessary to wait for the final reckoning in such matters, for violations of the law during war can only be punished in the main at the end of hostilities; then if the parties guilty of violations have been defeated they can be made to pay for their crimes, although this condition in the case raises far-reaching problems which cannot be explored here. Finally, it is historically a fact that in modern times there has always occurred a reaction at the end of war, growing in strength from Napoleonic times down to the present, in favor of extending and strengthening international law and its application. This trend is in some measure an admission that the effect of war has not been beneficial, but in the main it has nothing to do with the effect of the war and relates to the law of pacific settlement of disputes and to other aspects of the law of normal INTERNATIONAL RELATIONS.

Can International Law Survive? The real source of danger for the continuation of the existing rules of international law (as of all law) lies in the possibility —nay the certainty—that the circumstances or conditions on which present law is based will change and thus render those rules unsuitable or even meaningless. This has been the case in recent times especially of the law of war, but it has been felt also in the law of peace. For example, in a day when states and governments are entering the fields of industry, trade, and finance extensively, the old rules granting wide immunity to state-owned property seem to demand reconsideration. In the face of such changes efforts to maintain the law unaltered would only be unsuccessful in the long run; indeed if such attempts should be successful they would be harmful.

The existence of international institutions of advanced type does not, on the other hand, render international law superfluous by any means. Law is needed to create, define, and regulate these institutions and to express their acts of authority and their other operations. What is more to the point, no development of such institutions can cover or treat adequately all the range and detail of interstate relations. Every international constitution, such as the Covenant of the League of Nations and the Charter of the United Nations, assumes the continued existence of international law and relies largely upon it for support and assistance. If the establishment of international institutions were the only challenge to international law its continuation would not be seriously threatened, although its scope would certainly be modified somewhat.

Another challenge to international law arises out of the current movement to establish a unitary world state which would entail a degree of centralization far beyond what any system of international federal union would provide. Such a unitary world state, even though it might originally be set up by state units, would derive its authority directly from the people themselves, and it would act directly upon individuals all over the world without passing through the states or calling upon them for their assistance. Under such a world state international law would disappear in favor of world government, based on a world constitution with world law.

It is believed, however, that such a world unitary government is unattainable. Also, in view of what may more easily be accomplished through federal union, it might be undesirable. Most advocates of world organization favor some kind of federal union based on the model which has proved so successful in the United States. Under such a system international law could probably continue, although with considerable modifications. See WAR; WAR, LAW OF; NEUTRALITY; PARIS, DECLARATION OF; LONDON, DECLARATION OF; HAGUE CONFERENCES; FREEDOM OF THE SEAS; MARITIME LAW; DIPLOMACY; DIPLOMATIC SERVICE; LEAGUE OF NATIONS; UNITED NATIONS; ARBITRATION, INTERNATIONAL; COURTS, INTERNATIONAL.   PITMAN B. POTTER

BIBLIOG.–H. W. Briggs, *The Law of Nations* (1938); G. Hackworth, *Digest of International Law* (1940); C. A. Riches, *Majority Rule in International Organization* (1940); S. Glueck, *The Nuremberg Trial and Aggressive War* (1946); Philip C. Jessup, *A Modern Law of Nations* (1948); L. F. L. Oppenheim, *International Law* (1948); C. G. Fenwick, *International Law* (1948); E. S. Colbert, *Retaliation in International Law* (1948); J. L. Brierly, *Law of Nations* (ed. 1949); M. O. Hudson, *International Legislation* (1950); L. B. Sohn, ed., *Cases and Other Materials on World Law* (1950); E. D. Dickinson, *Cases and Materials on International Law* (1948), *Law and Peace* (1951); G. Schwarzenberg, *Manual of International Law* (1951).

INTERNATIONAL LEGISLATION. See INTERNATIONAL LAW.

INTERNATIONAL MEDIATION AND ARBITRATION. See ARBITRATION, INTERNATIONAL.

INTERNATIONAL MONETARY CONFERENCES. See MONETARY CONFERENCES, INTERNATIONAL.

INTERNATIONAL MONETARY FUND. See UNITED NATIONS; BANKS AND BANKING; INTERNATIONAL FINANCE; BRETTON WOODS.

INTERNATIONAL ORGANIZATION may exist on two levels: private and public There are hundreds of private international organizations which express the unofficial world community, e.g., ROTARY INTERNATIONAL, and the International CHAMBER OF COMMERCE. Public international organizations are concerned with the regulation of the interests of various nations. The aim of international organization is to promote the co-operation of various nations in the realm of common interests and to avoid friction and violence.

The subject of international organizations is wide. In recent decades a number of such organizations have come into existence dealing with legal, economic, medical, political, artistic, scientific, and other matters.

The rudiments of public international organizations can be found in the practice of DIPLOMACY, treaty negotiations, and international conferences. Diplomacy is concerned with the political relations between nations. Treaty negotiations signify the legalization of agreements reached through the practice of diplomacy. International conferences are wider in scope and involve the attendance of delegates from many nations.

There are three major forms of public international organizations. Imperial unity is a form of international organization. In the ancient world the most lasting attempt of this kind was the Roman Empire, which preserved peace throughout the civilized world and established an order which came to be known as the *Pax Romana*. Imperial universality does not allow for the existence of independent nations living side by side on the basis of equality. It is based on the superiority of one nation.

The appearance of modern nations,' after the breakdown of the medieval world, made it impossible to achieve a universal organization under the imperial system. A new concept of international organization came into being: the association of nations on the basis of equal and voluntary co-operation. In view of the existence of many nations only such an association could serve the interest of all. But the realization of a community interest between nations grew slowly and only in the 20th century did it lead to the establishment of a permanent association of sovereign states. The League of Nations represented such a form of international organization. The United Nations is an international organization which is likewise based on the principle of the association of sovereign states.

The third major form of international organization is a close federation between states. The United States of America and the Swiss Confederation are examples of such federations. Especially in recent decades, there have been a number of persons advocating the idea of the extension of the federal principle and the creation of a world federation. This type of international organization would be a world state based on a cosmopolitan society where the sovereignty of nations would be abandoned. See: INTERNATIONAL RELATIONS; INTERNATIONALISM; LEAGUE OF NATIONS; UNITED NATIONS; IMPERIALISM.   G. B. DE H.

BIBLIOG.–C. Eagleton, *International Government* (1932); C. D. Burns, *Modern Theories and Forms of International Organization* (1939); C. A. Riches, *Majority Rule in International Organization* (1940); P. B. Potter, *An Introduction to the Study of International Organization* (1947).

INTERNATIONAL PEACE GARDEN consists of an area of 2,200 acres of great natural beauty located in the Turtle Mountains on the boundary line between the United States and Canada, 12 miles N of Dunseith, N.D., and 15 miles S of Boissevain, Manitoba, and dedicated to the perpetuation of peace between the two nations. The chief feature of the park is a cairn of stones gathered from both countries and built exactly on the international line. A plaque on the cairn reads "To God in his glory, we two nations dedicate this garden and pledge ourselves that as long as men shall live we will not take up arms against one another." An area of 888 acres in North Dakota and 1,451 acres in Manitoba is administered by a board of directors chosen jointly from the citizens of the United States and Canada. The garden contains an ornamental driveway through the park, accommodations for visitors, and a formal garden where re-dedication ceremonies are held each year. The idea for an international peace garden was first suggested in 1929 by Henry J. Moore of Islington, Ont. The site of the Turtle Mountains was selected because of its scenic beauty and its central location on the boundary line in the heart of the North American continent.   F. C. W.

MANITOBA TRAVEL BUREAU

International Peace Garden. A view on the Canadian side, above. Plaque bearing pledge of peace between Canada and United States appears at left

INTERNATIONAL POSTAL UNION. See UNIVERSAL POSTAL UNION.

INTERNATIONAL REFUGEE ORGANIZATION. See UNITED NATIONS; DISPLACED PERSONS; REFUGEES.

INTERNATIONAL RELATIONS. The study of international relations is basically concerned with interstate relations. It is the newest and least developed of the social sciences, having been evolved only in the last 50 years.

History. Both international law and study of international relations were developed because of practical needs. International law dates back to Victoria and Suarez of the Spanish school of the 16th century, to Gentilis of the same century, and to Grotius of the early 17th century. The rules of modern warfare date back to the Middle Ages, but it was the emergence of sovereign national states in the 16th century which necessitated the development of international law.

The study of international relations was the fruit of increasing contacts between nations in the 18th and 19th centuries and of World War I. In the 19th century contacts between nations became extensive and frequent. Imperialism, trade, and colonization were its most obvious aspects, but contacts extended to many other realms as well. It was only after international contact had become a well-established fact that fields of study arose reflecting on it. The international implications of various fields of human endeavor, such as economics, science, and literature, were beginning to be realized.

The greatest impetus to the development of the field of international relations was provided by World War I. The war created a demand for information, leading to the greater employment of foreign correspondents and to the acceleration of systematic study of international relations. Before the war there were very few chairs for its study, but today practically all universities offer courses on international relations. After the war it was realized by many that international public law, being limited to rules of law between sovereign states, was not sufficient for an understanding of the relations between nations. This realization has been brought about partly by the League of Nations, which officially recognized the existence of international economic and social problems.

International Relations—International Law. The study of international relations is traditionally related to law. Public international law is concerned with nations as juristic entities. Thus, it is the study of formal phenomena, while on the other hand the study of international relations is concerned with the interaction between peoples who form social groups called "nation-states."

International law has contributed to the development of the study of international relations. This is especially true of those who have viewed international law functionally—that is to say, sociologically. The Chilean jurist Alejandro Álvarez has long insisted that the most important aspect of international politics is psychological. Probably the earliest statement of the sociological foundation of international law was made by Max Huber in 1910. More recent contributions along these lines have been made by two Swiss jurists, Dietrich Schindler and Paul Guggenheim, and by Ranyard West.

Development of the Study of International Relations. As in the case of political science, there has been a tendency in recent decades to give the study of international relations a broader scope, and to relate it to other social sciences. But this trend has not gone so far in international relations as in political science. The study of international relations has been dominated by international law. On the whole the study of international relations has been entrusted to international lawyers, who have often limited it to the formalistic character of international law. Besides law, the study of international relations is mainly composed of diplomatic history, geography, and current affairs. Like the earlier political science, it is mostly juristic and historical. Its approach is institutional; it tends to treat exclusively the structure of international organizations or their history. Its method is mainly descriptive. International relations conceived along these lines are static and limited.

As in political science the formal study of the state has been replaced to some extent by its study as related to other social phenomena, so in recent years some students of international relations came to be concerned not with formal interstate (legal relations between sovereign states) but with internation relations which may occur on the economic, psychological, and social level. Growing knowledge of international economic relations, of cultural and racial contacts, of the social psychology of peoples, has facilitated the basing of international relations on a broader foundation. If one compares the present status of the field with that which existed before World War I, the trend becomes apparent.

Within the last decade there has been a growing realization that the subject matter of international relations is wide, including all factors which play a part in the relations between peoples. The inclusive nature of the study of international relations was recognized by many members of the International Studies Conference, held in Prague in 1938. This conference attempted to examine critically the fundamentals of the field of international relations. Several members maintained that it is essentially a synthesis of many fields of study. Experts attending this conference decided to ask themselves the question of what these fields consisted. Alfred Zimmern maintained that international relations is sociology in the widest sense. Edouard Lambert, however, went so far as to maintain that the study of international relations is practically identical with all of the social sciences.

Scope of the Study of International Relations. It would be a mistake to assume that international relations is the sum total of the various social sciences. The realistic school of political science is based on various social sciences but is not identical with them; likewise, international relations depends on the various social sciences but does not include the total range of their data. International relations is not the synthesis of all the social sciences, but is based on a synthesis of certain data provided by these sciences. Only certain material is relevant to international relations. From anthropology, data on race relations and on culture contacts are very relevant, the study of kinship system is less germane, and archaeology is of little pertinence. From sociology, knowledge of population pressure is more relevant than material on family structures or on juvenile delinquency. From economics, information on trade is more pertinent than statistics or marketing research. From psychology, generalizations concerning collective behavior are more applicable than physiological or statistical psychology. From political science, the results of studies of propaganda and comparative government are more useful than medieval political theory or data on municipal administration. From geography, data on raw materials and land utilization are more relevant than cartography. From law, international law is obviously more appropriate than torts. From history, knowledge about the Roman Empire or modern imperialism is more pertinent than the history of the ancient Near East.

International relations, thus, is a frame of reference which includes aspects of the social sciences and other fields. While each social science does not necessarily study international problems, each has material which is relevant to such problems. Viewed from such a point of view, international relations is not static and limited in scope. It deals with dynamic forces and includes social, economic, and psychological as well as legal, geographical, and historical data.

Specifically international relations is divided into the following aspects:

A. Legal Aspect: International Law. (See INTERNATIONAL LAW; CONFLICT OF LAWS; DIPLOMACY; HAGUE CONFERENCES; ALLIANCE; ARBITRATION, INTERNATIONAL; TREATY.)

B. Historical Aspect: Diplomatic, Economic and Social History. (See HISTORY and the history of various nations.)

C. Structural Aspect: International Organization. (See LEAGUE OF NATIONS; UNITED NATIONS; INTERNATIONAL LABOR ORGANIZATION; INTERNATIONAL ORGANIZATION; BRETTON WOODS.)

D. Functional Aspect: International relations on economic, diplomatic, psychological and ideological levels. (See WORLD WAR I; WORLD WAR II; PROPAGANDA; PEACE; TRADE AND COMMERCE, International, United States Foreign; INTERNATIONAL FINANCE; INTERNATIONALISM; ISOLATIONISM; EXCHANGE, FOREIGN.)

E. Spatial Aspect: Physical, economic, and cultural geography. (See POPULATION; GEOPOLITICS; GEOG-

RAPHY and the geography sections of the articles on the various nations.)   G. B. DE H.

BIBLIOG.–P. T. Moon, *Syllabus on International Relations* (1925); L. L. and Jessie Bernard, *Sociology and the Study of International Relations* (1934); G. B. de Huszar (ed.) *New Perspectives on Peace* (1944); T. V. Kalijarvi, *Modern World Politics* (1945); R. Strausz-Hupé and S. T. Possony, *International Relations* (1950).

INTERNATIONAL SETTLEMENTS, BANK FOR. See BANK FOR INTERNATIONAL SETTLEMENTS.

INTERNATIONAL SOCIALIST CONGRESS. See INTERNATIONAL, THE.

INTERNATIONAL TRADE. See TRADE, INTERNATIONAL.

INTERNATIONAL Y.M.C.A. COLLEGE. See COLLEGES.

INTERNATIONALE, THE, a Communist song, which served as the national anthem of the Soviet Union until 1943. The song is French in origin; it was written in that language by Eugène Pottier in 1871, the music being supplied later by Adolphe Degeyter. The Internationale is frequently sung wherever Communists gather.   R. W. QUINN

INTERNATIONALISM, as opposed to nationalism, favors close co-operation between nations. It stresses those elements which are common to all men and all nations rather than those elements which differentiate one nation from another. Internationalism aims to transcend national sovereignty but accepts the principle of nationalism in a modified form.

The medieval church maintained the aspirations of world unity. With the rise of national states in the 15th century, co-operation of states declined in importance. But many scholars, statesmen and writers championed internationalism. William Penn in the 17th century proposed a plan for peace based on the principle of internationalism. In the 18th century a number of historical writers contributed to the cause of internationalism by showing the unity in mankind's history. In the same century, the German philosopher IMMANUEL KANT, in his *Zum ewigen Frieden* formulated a theory of internationalism which would lead to peace. Internationalism found concrete expression in the Holy Alliance which was an informal union of states that wanted to preserve peace by maintaining the *status quo*.

An important manifestation of internationalism was the Hague Peace Conferences. The first of these had its origin in the desire of Nicholas II of Russia to initiate measures for the creation of peace. On May 20, 1899, delegates from 26 states met at The Hague. President Theodore Roosevelt took the initiative for the second Peace Conference which met at The Hague in the summer of 1907.

At the end of World War I, internationalism found concrete expression in the creation of the League of Nations. This agency was the first permanent association of nations for the maintenance of peace and for international collaboration in political, economic, social, cultural and medical fields. Up until the establishment of the League of Nations, permanent international organizations were only concerned with postal and quarantine services. Two allied agencies of the League further strengthened internationalism. The International Labor Organization fostered international co-operation in the field of labor and social problems. The Permanent Court of International Justice, which was founded in September, 1921 at The Hague, provided for the peaceful settlement of international legal disputes. The League of Nations and its allied agencies were based on the principle of internationalism, according to which the principles of nationalism and sovereignty were not abandoned but modified.

The League of Nations had an enormous influence on the development of internationalism. A number of international conferences were held after its establishment and many international agencies and declarations were inaugurated. But the forces of international collaboration were not strong enough to prevent the disintegration of the international community and the subsequent outbreak of World War II.

World War II has fostered the spirit of internationalism and led to the creation of a number of international agencies, most of which are affiliated with the United Nations. See NATIONALISM; INTERNATIONAL ORGANIZATION; INTERNATIONAL RELATIONS; ISOLATIONISM; LEAGUE OF NATIONS; UNITED NATIONS; HAGUE CONFERENCES.   G. B. DE H.

BIBLIOG.–P. C. Jessup, *International Security* (1935); C. Meyer, *Peace or Anarchy* (1947); L. Bryson, L. Finkelstein, and R. MacIver (eds.), *Learning and World Peace* (1948).

INTERNMENT, the detention of persons or property as permitted by the laws of war or as required by the obligations of neutrality. By international law neutrals must seize and intern belligerent ships, troops, and airplanes which either seek asylum in the neutral state or violate its neutrality or jurisdiction. Thus in World War II German and Allied planes which made forced landings in neutral Sweden were taken over by the Swedish government and the crews placed in custody. International law grants the interning state considerable leeway as to the degree of restriction to be imposed on such personnel. Since 1914 most countries at war have interned resident enemy aliens. Previously the nationals of an enemy state were given a limited time after the declaration of war to return to their countries, but with the development of total war internment has been the general practice. The notable exception has been the United States, which has interned only those enemy aliens considered dangerous; in World War II, however, Japanese and persons of Japanese descent on the west coast were removed from their homes and placed in relocation centers. See INTERNATIONAL LAW; WAR, LAW OF; NEUTRALITY; ALIEN.

                        FRANK L. ESTERQUEST

INTEROCEPTORS are receptor-organs located in the linings of the alimentary canal and in other deep tissues. These organs are involved in the adjustment of the organism to special conditions inside the organism. Feelings of hunger, thirst, nausea, and the desires to micturate and to defecate are mediated by the interoceptors.   T. F. KARWOSKI

BIBLIOG.–T. F. Troland, *Psychophysiology* (Vol. I, 1930).

INTERPLEADER, in law, is the proceeding by which a person having a debt or goods seeks, upon being sued, to have a third party claiming the same property to be made a party to the proceeding. The person having the debt or goods thereby admits that the debt or property is not his but expresses doubt as to which of the claimants is entitled to it. This proceeding settles the rights of the two claimants to the debt or property.

INTERPOLATION, in mathematics, is the process of finding one or more numbers between two known numbers such that the entire set satisfies, at least approximately, some mathematical relationship. In the following table, for example, what values of b correspond to $a=4$ and to $a=5.4$? Corresponding to a difference

a	1	3	5	7	9
b	5	45	125	245	405

D_1	40	80	120	160
D_2		40	40	40

of $5-3=2$ in the value of a is a difference of $125-45$ $=80$ in the value of b. *If the relationship between a and b is linear* (see LINEAR RELATION), then a difference of $4-3=1$ in a should produce a difference of $80/2=40$ in b. Then, if $a=3+1=4$, $b=45+40=85$. Similarly when a changes from 5 to 7, b changes from 125 to 245, a difference D_1 of 120. The value of b corresponding to $a=5.4$ may be estimated by computing the proportionality factor $p=(5.4-5.0)/(7-5)=$ $0.4/2=0.2$; then $pD_1=0.2\times120=24$, and finally,

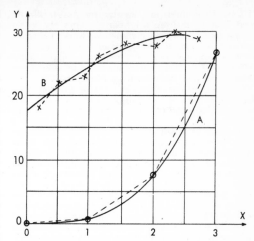

Linear Interpolation between plotted points is made along the broken lines, but better interpolation routes in these two cases are the continuous lines A and B. A is the actual graph of the function used, and B is a graphical "smoothing" of scattered data

$b=125+24=149$. If the tabular differences D_1 are small, this method is sufficiently accurate for most purposes. In the example above, the relationship between a and b is not linear, the tabular differences are not small, and the error is appreciable. Hence the second differences D_2 may be used; in this case $D_2=40$. For $a=5.4$, compute
$$p(p-1)D_2/2=0.2(0.2-1.0)40/2=$$
$$0.2(-0.8)20=-3.2,$$
then $b=149.0-3.2=146.8$. For $a=4$,
$$p=(5-4)/(5-3)=\tfrac{1}{2}=0.5;\text{ hence}$$
$$p(p-1)D_2/2=0.5(0.5-1.0)40/2=-0.25\times20=-5,$$
and finally, $b=85-5=80$.

In the example given, the relationship between a and b happens to be given by the formula $b=5a^2$, and it may be verified that the interpolation process, by using the second differences, produces the proper values for b when $a=4$ and $a=5.4$. Often a carefully drawn graph of the relationship between the tabulated number pairs makes it easy to interpolate with sufficient accuracy for practical problems. General methods exist for treating much more complex problems of interpolation, using the theory of finite differences (see DIFFERENCES, FINITE) and other more advanced theories.   M. L. HARTUNG

BIBLIOG.–J. B. Scarborough, *Numerical Mathematical Analysis* (1930); P. Mitra, *Calculus of Finite Differences* (1943); E. T. Whittaker and G. Robinson, *Calculus of Observations* (4th ed. 1947).

INTERSTATE BARRIERS. See INTERSTATE COMMERCE.

INTERSTATE COMMERCE. The Federal Constitution vests in Congress the power "to regulate commerce with foreign nations and among the several states." The commerce clause of the Constitution was conceived as a means of composing the commercial rivalry among the states following the American Revolution. Beginning in 1784 protective tariffs were enacted by New England and most of the middle states, and additional tribute was exacted from the coastal trade, notably by New York, through the imposition of clearance fees. Retaliatory measures invited attacks and reprisals. The founders of the nation, by vesting in Congress the power to regulate interstate commerce, aimed to overcome this intolerable situation that threatened to deter the economic development of the nation.

Referring to that eight-year period under the Articles of Confederation, Charles Beard thus described the impediments to interstate commerce:

"Under local influences legislatures put tariffs on goods coming in from neighboring states just as on foreign imports, waged commercial wars of retaliation on one another, raised and lowered rates as factional disputes oscillated, reaching such a point in New York that duties were levied on firewood from Connecticut and cabbages from New Jersey."

The achievement of the Federal Constitution lifted this nation from the unhappy Balkanization which has so handicapped the full commercial development of Europe.

Progress of Regulation. Though the Constitution vested in Congress the right to regulate interstate commerce, it was not until the 1870's that a demand for such regulation arose. State regulation preceded Federal regulation (see INTRASTATE COMMERCE), the turning point to the latter being a decision of the Supreme Court in the Wabash Case (*Wabash Railway* v. *Illinois*, 1886) which held that while the state of Illinois might regulate intrastate traffic, it could not regulate rates on traffic from points within the state to points outside. This decision was one of the influences that caused Congress, in 1887, to enact the Federal Act to Regulate Commerce, establishing the Interstate Commerce Commission. It was not until 1906 (Hepburn Act) and 1910, however, that Congress passed laws giving the I.C.C. definite power to make rates.

Federal authority to modify interstate rates was established by Supreme Court decisions in the Minnesota Rate Cases (1913), the Shreveport Rate Case (1914), and the Wisconsin Passenger Fares Case (1922).

In the case of *Simpson* v. *Shepard*, decided in 1913, the Supreme Court decided the inevitable question as to whether the states, by regulating commerce within their borders, could limit the power of the Federal government over interstate commerce. The court ruled that the power of Congress to regulate interstate commerce is "supreme and plenary," but that the states may be permitted to regulate intrastate rates, even though interstate commerce may be affected, until such time as Congress may see fit definitely to exercise its plenary powers.

In its Shreveport decision a year later, the court ruled that "wherever the interstate and intrastate transactions of carriers are so related that the government of one involves the control of the other, it is Congress and not the state, that is entitled to prescribe the final and dominant rule . . . ."

In 1918, in the Illinois Passenger Fares Case, the court made it clear that when the I.C.C. issues an order that in fact results in the setting aside of state-made charges, its order may not be vague and indefinite.

Congress, in the Transportation Act of 1920, authorized the I.C.C., after investigation disclosing unjust discrimination against interstate or foreign commerce, to prescribe directly the railroad rates, classification, regulation, or practice that shall thereafter apply in intrastate commerce. It further authorized the Commission to conduct such an investigation even though a specific complaint had not been filed. Congress ordered the I.C.C. to notify the interested states of all proceedings involving intrastate rates, and authorized it to confer with the proper state authorities, to hold joint hearings with state regulatory agencies, and to avail itself of the co-operation of such agencies.

When the I.C.C. in its general rate increase decision of 1920 ordered horizontal freight-rate advances on intrastate as well as on interstate traffic, many states protested and some refused to advance their intrastate rates. The I.C.C. then investigated the rates and rate structures in these states, and in 28 related cases decided that its power to regulate intrastate charges is not limited to specific discriminations that affect injuriously persons or localities in interstate commerce. It decided that it had power to regu-

late intrastate rates as a whole when general discrimination against interstate commerce as a whole is apparent. When two states appealed to the Supreme Court, that body upheld the contention of the I.C.C., in 1922.

The principles established in the foregoing railroad cases also apply in general to highway transportation. In *Buck* v. *Kuykendall*, decided in 1925, the Supreme Court ruled that the states could not regulate the interstate business of motor carriers.

In 1925 Congress passed the Hoch-Smith Resolution, which represented an attempt by Congress to afford special relief for a particular industry, agriculture. In its joint declaration, Congress declared that the "true policy" to be pursued by the I.C.C. in fixing freight rates requires consideration of the conditions which at any time prevail in the various industries, to the end that commodities may move freely. As to agriculture, the I.C.C. was ordered to effect without delay such changes in rate structure as would promote the free movement of agricultural products affected by the postwar depression, at the lowest lawful rates compatible with the maintenance of an adequate transportation system.

The last important bit of transportation legislation was the act of 1940, a product of the long business depression and the intensely competitive situation in transportation. The act aimed to restrain competition to some extent, and to bolster up the transport industry, particularly the railroads. The act declared it to be the national transportation policy of Congress "to provide for fair and impartial regulation of all modes of transportation subject to the provisions of this Act, so administered as to recognize and preserve the inherent advantages of each . . . . to the end of developing, co-ordinating, and preserving a national transportation system by water, highway, and rail, as well as other means, adequate to meet the needs of the commerce of the United States, of the Postal Service, and of the national defense."

The act brought the regulation of highway carriers and inland and intercoastal water carriers under the I.C.C. and led to the elimination of land-grant rail rates on Federal government traffic.

The relative powers of the Federal and state governments over railroad rates may be summarized somewhat as follows: The Federal government has the exclusive power (1) to regulate interstate commerce, (2) to require the states to raise particular intrastate rates when they discriminate against interstate commerce to a material extent, (3) to control intrastate rate levels as a whole so that intrastate traffic will bear its due share of the total revenue, and (4) to require the states to raise a particular intrastate rate when such rate does not produce its fair share of revenue necessary to maintain an adequate national railroad system. Subject to these limitations, the states retain the power to determine intrastate rates.

Court Review. This conflict between the Federal and state regulatory authorities has had its counterpart in the controversy over judicial review of rate-making laws and commission decisions by the Federal and state courts. The general principle established by the Supreme Court is that, in reviewing railroad rates, the courts must confine themselves to considering whether rate laws or commission orders are lawful and constitutional. State courts are confined to review of state-made intrastate rates, while the Federal courts review rates that are determined by either the Federal or state rate authorities.

Regulation of Water Transportation. The first Federal regulation of water transportation in general, as distinct from transportation rendered jointly by railroads, was partly established by the Shipping Act, 1916, which required common carriers by water operating in interstate commerce to file with the U.S. Shipping Board and keep open for public inspection maximum local and joint rates. Such rates were to be reasonable and might be fixed by the board if found unreasonable. Water lines tended to control rates, apportion traffic, pool earnings, and compete with outside lines by means of agreements or "conferences" and the act recognized these devices as useful tools of stabilization. When approved and filed with the board, conference agreements were exempted from the antitrust laws.

The Intercoastal Shipping Act of 1933, as amended in 1938, required common carriers engaged in the intercoastal, coastwise, and Great Lakes services to publish and observe the actual rates of charge; to give 30 days' notice of changes in rates; and authorized the Shipping Board to suspend proposed changes in rates for a period of four months. The Maritime Commission was empowered, after 1938, to prescribe maximum and minimum rates for common carriers on the high seas, and maximum rates for such carriers on the Great Lakes.

Through the Transportation Act of 1940, Federal regulation by the I.C.C. was extended to all interstate transportation on the inland waters and the oceans, and the regulatory functions of the Maritime Commission was transferred to the I.C.C. The Maritime Commission, while retaining regulation over ocean steamship rates, became a promotional body, owning several steamship lines, and administering the subsidization of the merchant marine.

Highway and Air Transportation. The Motor Carrier Act of 1935 created a special motor-carrier division of the I.C.C., with general jurisdiction over motor carriers engaged in transporting persons or property in interstate or foreign commerce, with numerous exceptions.

Prior to 1938 Federal regulation of air transport was divided among the Post Office Department, the Secretary of Commerce, and I.C.C. The Civil Aeronautics Act of 1938, and the Executive Order of 1940, brought about comprehensive regulation of air transportation, creating a Civil Aeronautics Board to regulate rates, prescribe safety standards and rules, and investigate accidents; and a Civil Aeronautics Authority, to exercise administrative functions, such as the development and operation of airways, aircraft inspection, licensing of pilots, enforcement of safety rules, and supervision of the pilot-training program.

By the close of the World War II, transport regulation was reasonably thoroughgoing in scope and in substance. All forms of intercity transportation were subject to commission supervision with respect to rates, service, accounts, intercorporate relations, and other matters. Excepting air carriers, the predominant authority was centralized in the hands of the I.C.C. This far-reaching control is the product of a gradual evolution over many years. New laws have been passed from time to time in response to clearly defined needs as set forth by representatives of carriers, shippers, and the I.C.C.

Goods Banned in Interstate Commerce. While transportation agencies holding themselves out as common carriers must accept and transport at published rates all commodities offered for transportation, there are various commodities which, under certain conditions cannot legally move in interstate commerce. Such commodities are narcotics, diseased plants and animals, lottery tickets, the products of child labor or prison labor, obscene literature, explosives unless packed according to specifications, and other goods of a character dangerous to the public. In practice, the common carriers handle anything that is offered to them, since the enforcement of these provisions is not in the carriers' hands, and they must accept cargo offered them.

Responsibility for seeing that banned commodities are not handled by the common carriers rests with whatever Federal department is concerned. The Department of Agriculture, through its bureaus, administers Federal acts regarding animal quarantine, diseased animal transportation, and the humane handling of livestock while in the course of interstate transportation. The department's bureau of entomology and plant quarantine is responsible for enforcing the Federal plant quarantines and regulatory orders to prevent the introduction into or spread within the United States of injurious insect pests and plant diseases. Various state governments maintain similar quarantine departments.

The Post Office Department, through its chief inspector, administers the laws governing the mailing of explosives, poisons, firearms, intoxicants, and obscene matter, which are prohibited transmission in the mails. The Department of Justice is empowered to prevent the sale to the public of goods or articles made in the Federal prison system.

The Treasury Department has the responsibility for preventing the smuggling of contraband merchandise and the release of smuggled articles and administering the laws controlling the traffic in marijuana and other narcotics, and in firearms. The Food and Drug Administration is empowered to remove from the channels of trade all those products which fail to comply with the terms of the acts against misbranded or adulterated foods, drugs, and cosmetics.

Other Federal departments have varying degrees of control over interstate commerce. The Department of Labor, for example, has, in addition to enforcing the ban on the transport of products of child labor through its wage and hour division, the power to see that employees engaged in interstate commerce or in producing goods for interstate commerce, are compensated in conformity with the wage and hour standards; to bring suit to enjoin employers who do not meet these standards; and to bring suit to enjoin the shipment in interstate commerce of goods produced in violation of the act.

Recent Developments. The so-called Reed-Bulwinkle Act, passed in 1948 (incorporated as Section 5a of the Interstate Commerce Act), exempts common carriers and freight forwarders subject to the Interstate Commerce Act from operation of the antitrust laws against them in certain procedures of joint consideration of rates and other matters. The first decision under the new section provided for a district organization among railroads in the western district, covering certain jurisdictional matters. The commission agreed that such an organization was necessary for the perpetuation of a competitive rate system and gave it its approval.

Public Regulation with private ownership and operation has appeared to work well in the United States, though at an undetermined cost involved in the duplication of transportation facilities. Other nations, such as Australia, Brazil, and Argentina have recognized the unsurpassed strength of the American transportation system and these countries have copied closely the commerce clause in the United States Constitution and have modeled regulation of their transport facilities after that achieved in the United States.

See INTRASTATE COMMERCE; ROADS AND HIGHWAYS; INDUSTRY AND COMMERCE, GOVERNMENT REGULATION OF; FREIGHT RATES; INTERSTATE COMMERCE COMMISSION.   N. C. HUDSON

BIBLIOG.–I. L. Sharfman, *The Interstate Commerce Commission* (1931); National Resources Planning Board, *Transportation and National Policy* (1942); T. C. Bigham, *Transportation Principles and Problems* (1946); M. Ramaswamy, *Commerce Clause in the Constitution of the United States* (1950); Annual Reports of the I.C.C.

INTERSTATE COMMERCE COMMISSION, an independent commission to regulate railroads and other aspects of interstate commerce, set up by the Federal government under the Interstate Commerce Act of 1887. It was a momentous departure from precedent in several respects. A great part of the American transport and communications system was brought under government control for the first time when the I.C.C. was given the power to supervise certain railroad practices. The form of the I.C.C. allowing considerable independence of the legislative and executive branches of the government to its bipartisan and impartial members, was a novelty in government, and the combination of judicial, legislative, and executive powers over certain areas in one commission diverged from the traditional insistence on the SEPARATION OF POWERS in government. The imposing example of the I.C.C. led to further trials of the independent regulatory commission idea in the form of the Federal Reserve Board, the FEDERAL TRADE COMMISSION, the FEDERAL POWER COMMISSION, the FEDERAL COMMUNICATIONS COMMISSION, and several others.

The I.C.C. was created in response to an intense public demand for governmental regulation of the railroads, among which monopolistic, discriminatory, and illicit practices against the public interest were commonly found. More than 20 states, though limited in their jurisdiction over interstate commerce, had established commissions to regulate the railroads. Between 1868 and 1886 more than 150 bills were introduced in Congress providing for some kind of control over the railroads by the Federal government. Finally the original Interstate Commerce Act of 1887 created the Commission, forbade certain objectionable railroad practices such as rate discriminations, pooling, rebating, and the charging of unreasonable rates. The I.C.C. could not fix rates but could issue an order against a malpractice for which a complaint was brought and then could rely on the courts for enforcement of its orders.

The Hepburn Act of 1906 strengthened the I.C.C., gave it the power to fix joint rates, and allowed it to issue orders with immediate effect. The Mann-Elkins Act of 1910 extended the rate power to all rates and created a Commerce Court to hear all appeals from the orders of the I.C.C. In 1911 the Locomotive Boiler Inspection Act increased the I.C.C.'s power over safety requirements. In 1913 the Commerce Court was abolished and its powers turned over to the regular Federal courts, and also in 1913 the Valuation Act imposed upon the I.C.C. the heavy burden of assessing the valuations of all railroads as a basis for rate-fixing. The Clayton Antitrust Act of 1914 charged the I.C.C. with enforcing its antimonopoly rules in the railroad industry.

The Federal Railroad Control Act of 1918 authorized the unified control of American railroads under a single director general appointed by the president, but the I.C.C. still performed its functions of reviewing the rates although the government was setting them. The railroads were returned to private management by presidential proclamation early in 1920; and in the same year the Transportation Act was passed, giving new powers to the I.C.C. It could initiate new rates and set joint and minimum rates, and it was asked to prepare broad plans for consolidating the entire national railroad structure. Mergers of competing railroads were permitted to a limited extent, and a "recapture clause," repealed in 1933, allowed the I.C.C. to help weaker railroads establish themselves economically by forcing the co-operation of more successful railroads. The Emergency Transportation Act of 1933 established the post of Co-ordinator of Transportation, provided further for the softening of competition, and empowered the division of railroads into southern, eastern and western sections under regional co-ordinating committees. In 1935, interstate motor traffic and in 1940 domestic water carriers were placed under the I.C.C. Since 1920 the Commission, appointed by the president for staggered terms of seven years at $10,000 per annum, has had 11 members. See INTERSTATE COMMERCE.   ALFRED DE GRAZIA

BIBLIOG.–I. L. Sharfman, *The Interstate Commerce Commission*, 4 Vols. (1931 et seq.); R. E. Cushman, *The Independent Regulatory Commissions* (1941).

INTERSTATE RELATIONS. See UNITED STATES, *Government*.

INTERSTELLAR MATTER. The scale of astronomical distances is so enormous that the existence of even a small amount of matter in the space between the stars may have important effects. Both gas and dust occur in the form of a general substratum of low density in which concentrations visible as dark nebulae exist. This material is concentrated toward the central plane of the Milky Way, little being observed at distances greater than 100 PARSECS from it. Clouds of dust and gas have also been observed in extragalactic nebulae, especially those of the spiral type (see GALAXY); but so far matter has not been detected in the space between the galaxies.

Interstellar Gas. In that part of our galaxy near the sun the dominant gas is atomic hydrogen. Its density in space is between 1 and 10 atoms per cubic centimeter (cc.) as compared with the 10^{19} molecules in each cc. of the earth's atmosphere. In 30 cubic parsecs of space the total mass of hydrogen is about equal to that of the sun; this is about the same as the average density of stars in space. Interstellar hydrogen may be of fundamental significance in theories of the origin of the universe and of the stars. It is probable that the heavier elements have been built up from hydrogen, with liberation of energy, by nuclear processes in the interiors of stars or in some primitive pre-stellar state. Thus interstellar hydrogen may be the débris left after the stars were formed; however, it has also been suggested that stars are now being formed as condensations in the denser parts of the gas clouds. Hydrogen produces no observable *absorption lines* in space; it is detected spectroscopically by its *emission lines*, produced in faintly glowing nebulae filling most of the Milky Way.

The spectra of stars that are seen through long distances (more than 100 parsecs) show sharp absorption lines produced by gases of the elements sodium, potassium, calcium, and titanium. These elements and many others exist in space as atoms. A few simple molecules are observed also, although their spectra are unusual, not showing complex *bands* (see BAND SPECTRUM); instead, a few sharp weak lines of the simple hydrocarbon (CH) and cyanogen (CN) are seen. Lines of ionized calcium atoms have proved to be reliable indicators of distance since their intensity increases in a regular fashion with increasing distance of the stars. It is also possible to measure Doppler shifts (see DOPPLER EFFECT) of interstellar lines and thus study the motions of the interstellar atoms. The gases are found to share in the general rotation of the Milky Way and also to show considerable stream motions in large clouds.

Starlight provides the energy for the ionization and excitation of interstellar atoms (see ION; ATOM); but, because of the great distances between stars, the quantity of this radiation available is small. A solid particle would be heated to a temperature of only 3° Kelvin (about −454° F.) if exposed to starlight in space. The temperature is so low that frozen gases, except hydrogen and helium, would remain solid and would not evaporate. The ultraviolet radiation of the stars, however, ionizes the interstellar gas and thereby releases electrons that move with speeds corresponding to a temperature of about 10,000° K. (17,500° F.).

Interstellar Solid Particles. Study of the interstellar solid particles likewise makes important contributions to our knowledge of the distances of stars. Small dust particles weaken the light of the stars, making them appear fainter and therefore more distant than they really are. Many stars are known whose brightness is diminished as much as five MAGNITUDES by absorbing material in space. Accompanying this absorption is a reddening of the starlight due to the greater absorption at the blue end of the spectrum. A similar but relatively greater reddening is observed at sunset when the sun shines through a

YERKES OBS., ASTROPHYSICAL JOURNAL, UNIV. OF CHICAGO PRESS

Dark interstellar matter in the Milky Way north of the star Theta Ophiuchi

long path in the earth's atmosphere; here the absorption (or scattering) is molecular in origin. The reddening in space seems to be proportional to the amount of absorption, and therefore the measurement of the color of a distant star (that appears more red than its spectral type indicates it should) provides an estimate of the absorption and the amount of dust.

Observation and theory show that small dust particles near the wave length of light in size, about 1/100,000 inch, are enormously efficient in scattering and absorbing light, and produce the type of reddening observed. Absorption along the galactic plane weakens the starlight, on the average, by one magnitude for each 1,000 parsecs of distance. A density no greater than one dust particle per cubic mile is sufficient to do this, and the total density of dust in space is probably less than that of hydrogen.

The dust often collects in enormous, relatively dense clouds—the dark nebulae, which blot out the more distant stars and appear as blank, star-free spaces in the Milky Way. Even in such clouds the space density of matter is far below that of the most perfect vacuum attainable on the earth. The chemical constitution of the interstellar dust is not yet known; it may be metallic in nature or it may be frozen gas, its particles built up by condensation of the gas. On the other hand, when particles collide in space they will be vaporized, so that an equilibrium must exist between the gas and the dust. See NEBULA; MILKY WAY.

JESSE L. GREENSTEIN

BIBLIOG.–L. Goldberg and L. H. Aller, *Atoms, Stars and Nebulae* (1943).

INTERVAL, in music, is the difference between two notes of unequal pitch. The smallest interval used in practical music is a semitone, and in tempered intonation all semitones are of equal interval. The modern chromatic scale consists of twelve consecutive notes of different pitch, which, beginning with the tonic or keynote, are each a semitone higher than the preceding note. All other scales are constructed from these 12 semitones. The number of semitones contained in the interval between two notes of different pitch determines the *size* of the interval, but the numerical name depends on the number of degrees of the scale included. Thus, though the interval C to E contains four semitones, it is termed a third, because it includes only three degrees of the scale—viz., C, D, E. Intervals calculated upward from the tonic to the other degrees of the major scale are *major* (seconds, thirds, sixths, and sevenths) and *perfect* (unisons, fourths, fifths, and eighths). These may be increased or augmented by raising the higher note or depressing the lower note, and may be lessened by reversing the process. Major intervals lessened a semitone become minor; minor and perfect intervals lessened a semitone become diminished; and major and perfect intervals increased a semitone become augmented; a second with its upper note an octave higher becomes a ninth, a third becomes a tenth, etc. All intervals are either *consonant* or *dissonant*. Unisons, fourths, fifths, and eighths are *perfect* and *consonant* when in their primary relationship to the tonic or keynote of the major scale; they become *imperfect* and *dissonant* when augmented or diminished. Major and minor seconds, major, minor, and diminished sevenths, are all dissonant; major and minor thirds and sixths are consonant, but when augmented or diminished become dissonant.

INTESTACY, the act of dying without having effectively disposed of one's property by will. When a person dies without leaving a will he is said to die *intestate*. His property is distributed according to the laws of descent or inheritance. In the event of intestacy, the law prescribes the persons who are entitled to be appointed *administrator* of the estate and thus to have charge of the payment of the decedent's debts and the distribution of his personal property. These are usually near relatives of the decedent in a certain order of priority. There may be partial intestacy of an estate where a will leaves certain property undisposed of. As to this portion, the rules of intestacy apply. See DESCENT AND DISTRIBUTION; INHERITANCE, IN LAW.   ROBERT KRATOVIL

INTESTINAL FLU. It is possible that occasionally the virus which causes true INFLUENZA may attack the intestinal tract and may cause symptoms. Intestinal upsets, however, are unusual in epidemics of influenza. More often what is called "intestinal flu" is probably a form of FOOD POISONING.

INTESTINE

In this long coiled tube occur the vital processes of digestion and absorption commonly attributed to the stomach

INTESTINE. The entire length of the ALIMENTARY CANAL beyond the stomach constitutes the intestine. In general plan the intestine is like a tubular continuation of the stomach, the same four layers that form its walls extending from esophagus to rectum (see STOMACH). The inner layer is the mucous membrane, whose cells secrete mucus and digestive juices; outside this is a layer of connective tissue supporting blood vessels, lymph vessels, and nerve fibers (*intrinsic nerve supply*); the third layer is muscular, composed of inner circular fibers and outer longitudinal fibers; the fourth and outer layer is the serous coat composed of visceral peritoneum (see ABDOMEN). The intestine is supplied with two sets of nerve fibers (*extrinsic nerve supply*)—all belonging to the AUTONOMIC NERVOUS SYSTEM; the vagus nerves (parasympathetic) carry augmentary impulses, the splanchnics (sympathetic) carry inhibitory impulses.

Length and Time. Because of differences in caliber, the intestine is regarded as divided into two portions: The *small intestine*, which is relatively narrow but in man is 20–30 feet long, extends from the pylorus (sphincter that guards the exit from the stomach) to the colic valve. The *large intestine*, which is relatively wide but in man is only about 5 feet long, extends from the colic valve to the anus (opening to the exterior). By the addition of insoluble pigments or colored glass beads to a meal, it is possible to determine the time required for the journey through the alimentary canal. In man it ordinarily takes 16–24 hours; in the hog, 40–50 hours; in the steer, 70–80 hours. In man it usually takes 4–5 hours for completion of the journey through the small intestine. As the last charge of food may not be ejected from the stomach till 5–6 hours after a meal is eaten, 9–11 hours are required for the stomach and small intestine to be completely cleared—for the person to be in what is called the *postabsorptive state* (see BASAL METABOLISM).

Small Intestine Most Important. Man can live without a stomach, and can survive removal of long sections of the intestine, but preservation of at least one-third of the small intestine is essential for life. In the stomach food is reduced to chyme (a thick liquid) and some of it is partially digested. But the stomach serves primarily as a storage chamber, and it is the small intestine where digestion is completed and through whose walls digested food is absorbed for distribution by the blood stream. In man and other carnivorous animals the large intestine is relatively unimportant, digestion and absorption being practically completed before the chyme reaches it. The principal function of the large intestine is the removal of water from the chyme, reducing it to semisolid feces. In herbivorous animals the large intestine is very long, the cecum often enormous, particularly in nonruminants, and digestion and absorption of nutrient materials continue on a large scale. In such animals bacterial action in the large intestine causes hydrolytic breakdown of cellulose, for which neither herbivores nor carnivores have any digestive enzyme.

Bacterial Flora. A variety of bacteria are found as natural inhabitants of the intestine. Species commonly found in the small intestine are fermentative, decomposing carbohydrates to form organic acids, carbon dioxide, etc., while those in the large intestine are putrefactive, decomposing proteins to form skatole, indole, hydrogen sulfide, etc. The significance of the bacterial flora in the intestines is not clear; in normal circumstances they appear to be harmless (see AUTOINTOXICATION; CONSTIPATION) and some investigators have even suggested that the bacteria may perform some essential physiological functions. That some of their actions are at least useful seems probable; in addition to those that digest cellulose, some intestinal bacteria have been discovered to be capable of producing vitamin K and at least two members of the vitamin B complex—biotin and pantothenic acid.

In man each of the two major divisions of the intestine is further subdivided, by names, on the basis of differences in function and microscopic structure. For lower vertebrates see FISH; FROG; TORTOISES AND TURTLES; BIRD; CARNIVORA; HERBIVORE.

SMALL INTESTINE

The three sections of the small intestine are fundamentally similar in structure and function, though muscular activity, secretory activity, and absorption all proceed at a gradually diminishing rate, with a maximum near the pylorus, a minimum near the junction with the large intestine. This gradient is apparent too in hydrogen ion concentration, the

INTESTINE

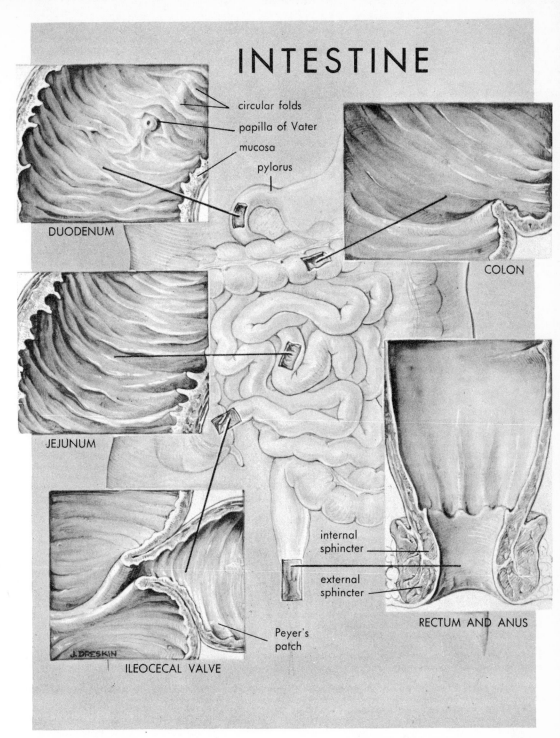

circular folds

papilla of Vater

mucosa

pylorus

DUODENUM

COLON

JEJUNUM

internal
sphincter

external
sphincter

RECTUM AND ANUS

J. DRESKIN

ILEOCECAL VALVE

Peyer's
patch

chyme gradually becoming less acid as it approaches the large intestine.

Duodenum, Jejunum, and Ileum. The first short section of the small intestine is the only part firmly fixed in place, and is shaped like an incomplete circle. Called the *duodenum* because it is about 12 fingerbreadths long, this section receives the bile from the liver and the digestive secretion from the pancreas. Of the remainder of the small intestine, the second section, the *jejunum* ("empty"), makes up about two-fifths, and the third portion, the *ileum* ("twisting"),

about three-fifths. The jejunum and ileum are freely movable in the abdominal cavity, but are attached to the posterior wall of the abdominal cavity by a double layer of peritoneum (serous lining of the abdomen) that encloses the blood and lymph vessels and the nerves supplying the intestine. The "root" of the mesentery along the backbone is only about 6 inches long (in man), yet in flaring out it supplies over 20 feet of jejunum and ileum.

Muscular Activity. On the basis of experiments similar to those used in studying the stomach, two types of motility in the small intestine have been observed: (1) Local contractions occur simultaneously in a number of evenly spaced points in a stretch of intestine. When observed by means of x-rays the band of the particular "loop" acquires the appearance of a beaded necklace, or a string of tiny sausages. A moment later the necklace "dissolves," and new constrictions develop where the beads were-thickest. By this process of alternate contraction and relaxation, which is called *rhythmic segmentation*, the intestinal chyme is thoroughly mixed with the digestive juices, and already digested materials are brought into closer contact with the absorbing villi. Rhythmic segmentation is probably independent of nervous regulation. In man Alvarez reported a rate of segmentation of 17–21 per minute in the duodenum, with a gradual decrease to 10–12 per minute in the ileum. (2) Propagated motility, or *peristalsis*, involves shorter or longer stretches of intestine and consists essentially of a traveling constriction that pushes the liquid contents in the direction in which the constriction moves. Waves traveling backward (toward the stomach) are said to be *antiperistaltic*. Normal motility is made up of peristaltic and antiperistaltic waves, the former naturally predominating, thus easing the chyme toward the large intestine. Peristalsis is dependent upon the intrinsic nervous network, or plexus, in the wall of the intestine, and is influenced by the extrinsic visceral innervation.

Secretion. The mucous membrane of the small intestine contains two types of GLANDS. Those in the duodenum, called *Brunner's glands*, are deep, compound, and not quite tubular. Those in the rest of the small intestine, called *Lieberkuehn's crypts*, are simple tubular depressions, not exceeding in depth the thickness of the mucosa. The volume of juices poured into the small intestine of man, on a normal diet, totals 6–10 pints per 24 hours: 1–2 pints of pancreatic juice, 1–2 pints of bile, and 4–6 pints of intestinal juice (*succus entericus*). These juices are all markedly alkaline, and the chyme, acid as it comes from the stomach, becomes progressively less acid while it proceeds along the small intestine. Even in the ileum, however, the chyme doesn't normally become actually alkaline during digestion, partly because of the fermentative activities of the bacteria present. But under certain circumstances, as during starvation or when the diet is deficient in carbohydrates and fats, the chyme in the ileum may become alkaline. This inhibits the activity of the fermentative bacteria, and promotes that of any putrefactive bacteria that may have migrated from the large intestine, which may lead to severe toxemia.

The secretory activity of the different sections of the small intestine has been studied on isolated loops made by cutting through the intestine in two places, several inches apart, and either bringing one end of the loop to the surface of the abdomen, while closing the other end (*Thiry fistula*), or bringing both open ends to the surface to facilitate emptying and rinsing (*Thiry-Vella fistula*). With the mesentery intact, the isolated loop preserves its blood, lymph, and nerve supply, and thus reflects fully the secretory activity of the particular region of the gut. Continuity of the severed intestine is re-established by joining the upper and lower openings (end-to-end anastomosis). On intact animals and human beings secretory activity of the intestine is investigated by intubation (see STOMACH).

By the several methods available, it has been shown that intestinal secretion is under a triple control. (1) Chyme received from the stomach evokes a flow of intestinal juice by stimulating the mucosa mechanically and chemically. (2) Impulses conveyed by the vagus nerves enhance the flow, while those from the splanchnics inhibit it. These effects are accomplished by regulating the caliber of the intestinal arterioles, vasodilatation leading to increased secretion, vasoconstriction to decreased secretion (see VASOMOTOR SYSTEM). (3) Hormones produced by the intestine are perhaps the most important of the factors influencing intestinal secretion. *Secretin*, a hormone that is liberated by the duodenal mucosa when stimulated by the presence of hydrochloric acid (received from the stomach), stimulates the flow of intestinal juice, pancreatic juice, and bile—all of which act simultaneously on the chyme in the small intestine. The small intestine produces another hormone, called *enterocrinin*, that stimulates the intestinal glands.

Digestion. All classes of hydrolyzable substances are acted upon and completely digested in the small intestine (see DIGESTION; ENZYME). Proteins, which may or may not have been partially broken down to peptones by the pepsin-hydrochloric acid digestion in the stomach, are decomposed into their ultimate "building stones," the amino acids. The intestinal juice contains a co-enzyme, *enterokinase*, that transforms trypsinogen of the pancreatic juice into *trypsin*. Trypsin acts on unbroken protein molecules, while *erepsin*, an enzyme of the intestinal juice, hydrolyzes peptones. Fats are decomposed by *steapsin* (pancreatic lipase) into fatty acids and glycerin. This is hastened by the emulsifying action of the bile, which leads to a mechanical subdivision of large fat globules into a much greater number of tiny droplets. Since the lipase is dissolved in the "watery" pancreatic juice, immiscible with fat, it can act only on the surface of the fat. Emulsification leads to a tremendous increase in the surface exposed to pancreatic lipase. Carbohydrates, in part digested to maltose by the ptyalin of the saliva during storage in the nondigesting region of the stomach, are hydrolyzed to simple sugars (hexoses). *Amylase* of the pancreatic juice converts starches to maltose. Though similar in its action to ptyalin, pancreatic amylase acts much more rapidly, and is capable of hydrolyzing raw as well as cooked starch. Disaccharide-splitting enzymes (*sucrase, maltase, lactase*), which are found in the intestinal juice and in the cells of the villi, complete the digestion to simple sugars.

Absorption. In the small intestine digestion and absorption go on simultaneously. The absorbing structures are called *villi*. These minute finger-like projections are so numerous (10–20 million) that they give the mucosa a velvety appearance when viewed with the naked eye. A villus resembles a simple tubular gland turned inside-out, having its blood and lymph supply on the inside, with its outer surface of cells exposed to and projecting into the lumen of the intestine. The capacity of the small intestine for absorption, which can occur only at cell surfaces, is increased considerably by the numerous internal folds, but even more by the villi, whose presence is estimated to increase the absorbing surface about 20 times.

When an animal's intestine is split, and the lining kept moist, movements of the villi can be seen through a low-power microscope. In a fasting animal's gut the villi are motionless, but hydrochloric acid, bile salts, various amino acids, and the B vitamins evoke activity. If an excised loop of intestine from a fasting dog is perfused with blood obtained from another dog at the height of digestion, its resting villi begin to move. A specific villi-stimulating hormone has been isolated and named *villikinine*. In addition, villi are influenced by the extrinsic innervation of the intestine. Unlike a muscle fiber, which gets thicker when it shortens, a contracting villus keeps its diameter unchanged. This means, considering the incompressibility of liquids, that the villus empties, or "milks," itself inwardly. The self-squeezing is followed by "relaxation," when the blood and lymph capillaries of the villus become filled again, and the shortening process is repeated.

All the water-soluble products of digestion find their way into the blood capillaries, then into the veins, and finally into the portal vein, which carries them to the liver. Here some are stored (usually as larger insoluble molecules), some are modified, and others are passed through unchanged (see LIVER).

Digested fat, absorbed as fatty acids and glycerin (with the aid of or in actual combination with bile salts), appears in the cells of the villi as neutral fat "dust." These fat globules, apparently transported by white blood cells, find their way into the lymph capillaries, then into lymphatics, and finally into the large veins in the neck (see LYMPH AND THE LYMPHATIC SYSTEM). At the height of absorption of a meal rich in fat, the lymph ("chyle") in the lymphatics of the mesentery is so charged with fat droplets that the lymph vessels appear creamy white and are therefore called lacteals ("milk carriers"). It is interesting to note that the fat from intestinal lymph enters directly into the circulation, whereas water-soluble molecules that are absorbed into the blood capillaries must first run the gauntlet of liver cells, and may not pass, unchanged, into the circulation for some time if at all. See METABOLISM; NUTRITION.

The mechanism of absorption is not well understood and cannot be explained solely in terms of the three physical forces that may cause passage of molecules through membranes—filtration, diffusion, and osmosis. That it is neither ordinary filtration nor diffusion is evident from the fact that the pressure in the intestine

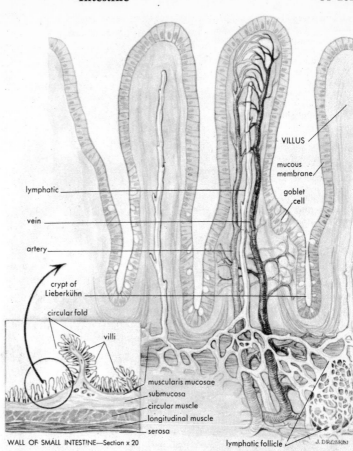

WALL OF SMALL INTESTINE—Section x 20

Diagram showing intestinal villi, where absorption takes place

is lower than that in the blood capillaries, and that substances with the same "diffusion velocities" are absorbed unequally. And if the usual laws of osmosis were operating, the concentration of a salt dissolved in the chyme should determine whether water would pass out of or into the intestinal lumen. Yet sodium chloride will be absorbed from the intestine regardless of its concentration in the chyme— whether it is in a solution isotonic with the blood (same osmotic pressure or freezing point as the blood plasma) or in a markedly hypotonic or hypertonic solution. Certain "foreign" salts, however, will draw water into the intestine, the cell walls of the villi behaving like nonliving semipermeable membranes. Thus when taken in hypertonic solution, magnesium sulfate (Epsom salt), both of whose ions are found in the blood in very low concentration, will draw so much water into the lumen of the intestine as to produce marked distention of the gut (see CATHARTICS). Pending further research we are left with the unsatisfactory explanation that "vital activity of the cells of the villi results in selective absorption."

Several variable factors are known to influence absorption. Calcium absorption is reduced if the chyme is alkaline, if vitamin D is absent, or if the diet contains large quantities of spinach and other foods containing oxalic acid or of oatmeal and other cereals containing phytic acid; calcium absorption is increased by diets rich in sugars and proteins. Absorption of iron is reduced by alkalinity of the chyme and by the presence of excess mucus, is increased by the presence of chlorophyll, bile pigments, calcium, and vitamin C. Absorption of carotene (precursor of vitamin A) and the fat-soluble vitamins D, E, and K

depends on the presence of bile salts. Continued research will undoubtedly reveal other factors important in regulating absorption.

LARGE INTESTINE

The small intestine opens at right angles into the large intestine. At the junction of the two there is a two-lipped valve (colic, or ileocecal), that acts as a sphincter and makes it easier for the chyme to leave than to return to the small intestine. In general, the muscular wall of the large intestine resembles that of the small intestine, except that the longitudinal fibers, instead of forming a continuous layer around the tube, are confined to three narrow bands (called taeniae) that "shirr" it into pouches called haustra. The mucous lining, too, is similar, but in the large intestine there is no villi, and the glands, microscopically like the crypts of Lieberkuehn, produce a secretion devoid of digestive enzymes. In its course toward the anus the large intestine makes certain characteristic turns, which appear to divide it into several parts, the majority of which are named in accordance with the positions relative to man's upright posture.

Cecum, Colon, and Rectum. The cecum in man is a short blind pouch (two to three inches long) below the junction of the small and large intestines, a vestigial portion of which is called the vermiform appendix (see APPENDICITIS). The colon forms such a large percentage of the large intestine that some writers use "colon" and "large intestine" as synonymous terms. The ascending colon bends sharply in the upper right region (hepatic flexure); the transverse colon proceeds across the upper abdomen and takes a down-turn in the upper left (*splenic flexure*); the *descending colon* makes a double S-shaped bend (*sigmoid flexure*) and enters the *rectum*, a straight portion that ends in the anal sphincters, two bands of circular muscle that guard the opening to the exterior. The upper of these, called the *internal sphincter*, is composed of smooth muscle controlled by the autonomic nervous system, while the lower, called the *external sphincter*, is composed of striated (voluntary) muscle controlled by the central nervous system.

Muscular Activity. With respect to motility there are three distinct functional divisions of the large intestine. The first part, made up of cecum, ascending colon, and the right half of the transverse colon, is the site of peristaltic and antiperistaltic shifting of the chyme, with absorption of water. The second part, comprising the rest of the colon as far as the lower sigmoid flexure, is

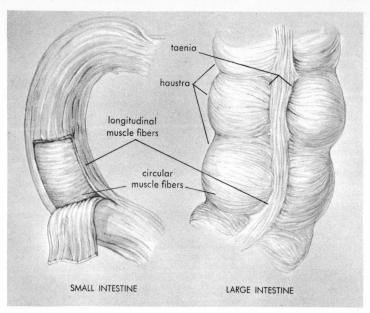

Muscular Layer of Intestine. All of these are fibers of the kind of muscle called smooth, or involuntary, muscle

usually empty when viewed by x-rays, but once in a while, as a rule immediately after a meal, there occurs along its entire extent a rushlike wave known as *mass peristalsis*, or the *gastrocolic reflex*. The remainder of the large intestine, the rectum, is concerned with defecation. In man, at least, the entrance of feces, propelled by mass peristalsis, into the rectum leads to a desire to empty the bowel. Defecation may be prevented by voluntary contraction of the external anal sphincter. But at times distention of the rectum evokes such powerful reflex contractions of the gut, from the middle of the transverse colon downward, that voluntary inhibition becomes impossible. *Straining*—voluntary contraction of the abdominal muscles, with the glottis closed—exerts a squeezing action on the abdominal viscera and is used to help empty the rectum (see LUNG). Thus defecation is usually a complex of reflex and voluntary activity and easily becomes habitual (see CONSTIPATION).

Absorption and Excretion in the Colon. Normally about 400 grams of fluid material is passed into the large intestine every 24 hours, during which time only about about 150 grams is evacuated. The difference, which is even greater than these figures suggest (because of the large amount of bacterial matter added during passage through the large intestine), is accounted for by absorption of water. The cecum and ascending colon are most active in this process, though some water may be removed at all levels. When introduced through the anus (see ENEMA) solutions of glucose, inorganic salts, and anesthetics may be absorbed, but rectal feeding of proteins and fats is of negligible value. Some substances, if carried in excess in the blood, notably calcium, magnesium, iron, phosphates, and the heavy metals, are excreted as salts through the mucosa into the lumen of the large intestine, from which they are evacuated in the feces.

Feces. Even during starvation feces not markedly different in composition from those produced on an ample diet continue to be formed. This is striking evidence of the fact that food residues constitute a surprisingly small proportion of the feces. On a normal diet the feces are made up of bacteria, intestinal secretions, white blood cells, cellular débris from the linings of the alimentary tract, excretory products from

the blood and bile, cellulose and other undigestible food residues, fecal fat, and traces of undigested food. The fecal fat is derived mainly from the action of intestinal bacteria, and continues to appear even on a fat-free diet. The characteristic odor of the feces is due mainly to various products (such as skatole and indole) formed during bacterial putrefaction. From two-thirds to four-fifths of the total weight of the feces is water. Bulk is varied mainly by increasing or decreasing "roughage" in the diet. Variable amounts of gases (methane, carbon dioxide, hydrogen, nitrogen, and hydrogen sulfide), derived mostly from bacterial action, are normally present in the large intestine and may be evacuated with the feces.

HYGIENE AND DISEASES OF THE INTESTINAL TRACT

Proper hygiene of the bowel involves establishment of regular habits of evacuation and deliberate consumption of a certain amount of fruits and vegetables to furnish "roughage" (indigestible matter). Self-treatment with drugs that irritate the intestine is dangerous and tends to become less and less efficacious (see CATHARTICS). Bran, often used to excess as roughage, may scratch the lining of the gut, and indigestible mineral oils or jellies, while they furnish bland bulk, are likely to carry away some of the fat-soluble vitamins. Occasional ENEMAS, when made up of salt and water, are probably harmless. Prevention, of course, is better than cure, and with the right habits and diet, there is usually no chance for constipation to develop. Of equal importance in prevention and treatment of disorders of the intestinal tract is MENTAL HYGIENE. It has been estimated that 50 per cent of all ailments of the digestive system are of emotional origin (see INDIGESTION; PSYCHOSOMATIC MEDICINE).

Constipation—the infrequent passage of hardened fecal matter—is the most common minor ailment of the digestive system of civilized man. The usual minimal rate of evacuation in normal individuals is once daily, though defecation two or three times per week is compatible with well-being (see CONSTIPATION). The notion of "autointoxication" by the absorption of toxic materials from retained feces has been largely exploded by Alvarez. He found that by stuffing cotton into the patient's rectum he could evoke lassitude, biliousness, and headache, the usual symptoms of constipation. It seems that it is not the absorption of poisons but rather the reflex effect of the failure to heed the call to defecate as soon as feces enter the rectum that is the cause of the malaise of constipation.

The initial portion of the duodenum (the duodenal cap) is often looked upon as functionally belonging to the stomach and is a more frequent site of *peptic ulcer* than the stomach itself (see STOMACH; ULCERS). Of the cancers of the alimentary tract, about 50 per cent occur in the stomach, 40 per cent in the colon, and less than 10 per cent in the small intestine (see CANCER). *Ileus* (intestinal obstruction) may be high or low, mechanical or inflammatory, dynamic (due to tonic contraction of the muscular coat) or paralytic. Stagnation of chyme promotes putrefactive bacterial activity in the small intestine, and absorption of the resultant toxic products may lead to pain, vomiting, a general state of prostration, and death in a few days. *Colitis* is a frequent cause of abdominal distress accompanied by rumbling or gurgling sounds and diarrhea (see COLITIS). *Hemorrhoids*, or piles, are vascular tumors of the rectum, produced by the enlargement and subsequent inflammation of local veins. They tend to ulcerate and bleed, and at times are very painful, especially during defecation (see HEMORRHOIDS; VARICOSE VEINS). Also see DIARRHEA; DYSENTERY; FOOD POISONING; HERNIA; HOOKWORM; TAPEWORM; TYPHOID.   NATHANIEL KLEITMAN

BIBLIOG.–W. C. Alvarez, *Nervous Indigestion* (1930); H. H. Dukes, *The Physiology of Domestic Animals* (1937); B. P. Babkin, *Secretory Mechanism of the Digestive Glands* (1944); C. H. Best and N. B. Taylor, *The Physiological Basis of Medical Practice* (ed. 1950).

INTOLERANCE, in sociology, is a social attitude characterized by the dislike of the beliefs, mode of life, or national or racial descent of members of groups other than one's own. It differs from prejudice in being less ingrained in the individual's emotional structure, and, is, therefore, more amenable to correction.

Problems caused by intolerance can be found at any level of interaction—person-to-person, within the family, within the community, the nation, or on the international level. Individuals often have little acceptance of others whose mode of life differs markedly from theirs. Similarly, within the family group in a rapidly changing culture such as the United States, children are often intolerant of what they consider to be the outmoded behavior standards of their parents and grandparents. American soldiers stationed outside of the United States during World War II often were intolerant of the alien cultures in which they found themselves. Such intolerances expressed themselves in disparaging remarks and nicknames about the native peoples.

Despite the persistence of intolerance at the present time, there is some evidence to show that medieval and ancient society was more militantly intolerant than modern society. During the early days of Christianity, Christians were viciously persecuted for their religious beliefs. During medieval times, the Church took a militant stand against heretics and waged active warfare against dissidents. In contrast to these earlier eras the world-wide interrelations of modern life have required a certain degree of tolerance. The unfamiliar or what may seem to be the undesirable must often be accepted in practice, even if not tolerated in theory, in order that varying social groups may live in harmony and commerce continue.

Education, one of the greatest weapons against intolerance, decreases suspicions and dislikes through teaching individuals about one another's ways of life. In the United States, various agencies such as the American Council on Race Relations, the National Education Association, the American CIVIL LIBERTIES UNION, the American Friends' Service Committee, the Catholic Inter-Racial Council, the NATIONAL COUNCIL OF THE CHURCHES OF CHRIST IN THE UNITED STATES, the NATIONAL CONFERENCE OF CHRISTIANS AND JEWS, the NATIONAL ASSOCIATION FOR THE ADVANCEMENT OF COLORED PEOPLE, and the National URBAN LEAGUE are endeavoring to combat intolerance by education and the dissemination of information. Whether education can succeed in eradicating intolerance has not as yet been adequately demonstrated. See PREJUDICE; FRIENDS, SOCIETY OF.

                                MAXINE CROW

INTOXICATION. See ALCOHOLISM; DIPSOMANIA; DRUNKENNESS; POISONS AND ANTIDOTES.

INTRACAINE. See COCAINE.

INTRACOASTAL WATERWAY. See GULF INTRACOASTAL WATERWAY; WATERWAYS, INLAND.

INTRASTATE COMMERCE, that commerce which originates and terminates within the boundaries of a single state. In the early days of this nation, almost all commerce was intrastate, as were the CANALS, TURNPIKES, and RAILROADS which bore the traffic. The individual states were the first to regulate commerce and transportation in the United States. As the nation developed, commerce became more extended, transportation agencies became interstate in character, and the Federal government gradually assumed the dominant role in regulating not only inter- but intrastate commerce.

State Regulation began with turnpike and canal companies and was extended to railroads, motor carriers, and air carriers as these later forms of transportation developed. The first form of state regulation of transportation was, as in England, by charter, the charters permitting the corporations owning the turnpikes and canals to fix rates, frequently with the proviso that charges should not exceed a stated maximum. Charter regulation failed, chiefly because of its inflexible character. States then attempted to act through constitutional or statute law, the first such law being passed in 1833, and dealing with applications for railroad charters, safety, taxation, stock subscriptions and transfers, annual reports, and a variety of other items.

Early general legislation marked an advance in the direction of standardized treatment of railroad companies, but accomplished little in the way of effective railroad control. Such regulation by general law failed because it tended to be rigid. Meeting infrequently, state legislatures were not able to modify their laws as conditions changed, and they lacked the administrative machinery and the personnel essential to effective control. Eventually the states set up commissions, which permitted flexible, continuous, and informed regulation.

The most important of the early efforts to establish a system of railroad regulation was made in the early seventies, as a result of the Granger movement among farmers in Illinois, Minnesota, Iowa, and Wisconsin, who organized to protest the drop in farm prices and the discriminatory practices of the railroads. See GRANGE, THE.

The first Illinois law, passed in 1869, declared that railroads should be limited to just, reasonable and uniform rates. An amendment in 1870 declared railroads to be public highways, forbade stock-watering and consolidations of competing lines, required annual reports, and directed the legislature to pass laws to correct abuses and to prevent unjust discrimination and extortion by railroad carriers in the state. Acting under this constitutional mandate, the Illinois legislature passed the law of 1873 which constituted the permanent basis for state regulation and remained unchanged for 40 years. This law declared that railroad rates should be reasonable, prohibited unjust discrimination which was defined in detail, provided for heavy fines against violators, and directed the state commission to prepare a schedule of maximum freight and passenger fares for each railroad. The Granger law in Illinois served as a model for other states.

Though the Granger laws were later repealed, due partly to opposition from the railroads, they are significant in that they made certain experiments and provoked certain statements of principle from the courts which proved of great importance in the development of state and Federal regulatory legislation.

The leading court case which tested the constitutionality of the Granger laws was that of *Munn* v. *Illinois*, 1876, in which the Supreme Court, in upholding the law, stated that transportation is "affected with a public interest," and the public has a right to control this business. This was followed by other Supreme Court decisions upholding the constitutionality of the Granger laws in other states. By the end of 1876 there had been enacted in the states a body of statute law attempting the regulation of railroad companies in various ways, and the constitutionality of this legislation has been upheld by the Federal courts. The Granger legislation of the seventies led directly to the Interstate Commerce Act of 1887. From that point on, the story of public regulation of transportation is the story of the gradual assumption by the Federal government of the power to regulate both interstate and intrastate commerce, and the gradual relinquishment by the states, often under protest, of such power.

By 1890 advisory or mandatory commissions, with some power as to railroads, existed in 34 states. By 1928 every state except Delaware had a commission with jurisdiction over railroads. The state statutes resemble in a general way the Federal acts (see INTERSTATE COMMERCE).

Federal Regulation. In the eighties it became clear that states could not regulate the entire field of transportation because interstate commerce was a Federal matter. Local authority is now almost entirely excluded from the field of railroad, air, and inland water regulation, and there is reason to believe that the course of control over motor carriers will ultimately be the same, as an increasing proportion of highway traffic is interstate in character. Behind the predominance of Federal authority in the regulation of commerce lies the simple fact of the growing importance of interstate as compared with local commerce. The absence of local tariff barriers in the United States, and the presence of cheap transport, has made specialization possible, which encourages the interstate movement of goods and passengers.

Interstate Trade Barriers. Of recent years a tendency has become apparent (temporarily halted during World War·II) on the part of various states to pursue local policies or prescriptions which restrict the flow of interstate commerce. Many shippers believe that certain state tax and quarantine regulations, for instance, which restrict the flow of interstate commerce, have the main purpose of protecting local industry. Some states have passed local quarantine laws which bar cattle raised in one area from entrance into another because of the alleged prevalence of diseases which do not actually exist.

In the case of state motor vehicle control, the burden of complaint has been directed against the variety as much as the content of local ordinances which fix permissible gross weights, and width and height of motor vehicles. Some states have allowed no full truck trailers. Others have limited the number of trailer units. State laws vary in the prescription of lights, windshield wipers, fire extinguishers, and other facilities; and sometimes a truck is required in one state to be fitted out in ways which are illegal in the adjoining states. Many trucking concerns have experienced unduly increased costs and unnecessarily impaired service, through reduction in pay loads and equipment capacity, increased mileage in "going around" states with low load limits, and in other ways.

As to state regulation of air-borne commerce, it has been noted that air transportation, unlike rail and highway transportation, was from the beginning interstate in character, and that only since 1945 did it begin to develop locally. The various state regula-

tory bodies, joined in the National Association of Railroad and Utilities Commissioners, have expressed a determination to regulate local air transportation, terming it a matter "of vital local interest."

Co-operation with Federal Authority. As the states have steadily retreated before the Federal assumption of the power to regulate commerce, co-operation between the Federal and state commissions has grown. An amendment of the Interstate Commerce Act in 1920 permitted the Interstate Commerce Commission to confer with authorities in any state when rates and fares imposed by the state were brought in question because of their relationship to interstate rates and fares. The I.C.C. was empowered to hold joint hearings in such instances and to avail itself of the co-operation, services, records, and facilities of the state regulatory bodies. The Motor Carrier Act of 1935 was even more explicit, requiring the I.C.C. to refer to joint boards, in instances where not more than three states are involved, certain types of cases. In the ten-year period 1930–39, there were 360 railroad cases alone in which there was co-operation between the I.C.C. and various state commissions. In important rate cases today, a co-operating committee of state commissioners sits with the I.C.C. Often, state commissioners or their spokesmen appear before the I.C.C. in rate cases.

When the Supreme Court, in 1922, upheld the I.C.C. in the Wisconsin Case (in which the I.C.C. ordered the Wisconsin commission to raise intrastate passenger fares), the National Association of Railroad and Utilities Commissioners wrote the chairman of the I.C.C. suggesting that if the state commissions were useless, they should be abolished. The Commission reply served to clarify the role of the state commissions in transportation regulation. The I.C.C. stated, in part: "Under existing Federal law there are important regulatory fields embracing one-half of the passenger traffic and one-fifth of the freight traffic of steam railroads, as well as the bulk of the telephone service, which are left untouched and uncared for unless the states continue to maintain their own regulatory bodies, empowered to cover these fields. It is perhaps unnecessary to add that most state commissions have very important rate and security regulation jurisdiction over utilities such as water, gas, telephone, electric and local transportation companies over which this Commission exercises no authority whatsoever. In our opinion the continued existence and proper maintenance of the state commissions is essential to adequate railroad regulation."

Since this exchange of letters, public opinion has generally accepted the conclusion that state railroad and public utility commissions should be retained. It is evident that the Federal government is unprepared to take over the work of the state commissions. The tendency has become more pronounced, however, for state authorities to emphasize local regulation of water, gas, telephone, electric, and local transportation companies, rather than the contentious function of state railroad control. Only in the field of motor vehicle regulation is the distribution of control between state and Federal commissions genuinely uncertain.

It is noteworthy that Federal regulation of motor carrier rates does not extend as far as in the case of railroads. With respect to intrastate motor rates, the Motor Carrier Act of 1935 declares "that nothing in this part shall empower the I.C.C. to prescribe, or in any manner regulate, the rate, fare, or charge for intrastate transportation or for any service connected therewith, for the purpose of removing discrimination against interstate commerce or for any other purpose whatever."

A similar clause in the Transportation Act of 1940 relates to water carriers. In other words, Congress has acknowledged the large amount of local movement by highway and water.

Most authorities believe that in the case of railroads, the paramount authority should be lodged with the Federal government. In motor transportation the case for centralized control is not so strong, owing to the fact that highway hauls are more largely local.

This is especially true of the larger states, where a considerable portion of all motor-borne commerce originates and terminates within the state's boundaries. The state of California would be a striking example of this.

As to intrastate air transportation, the N.A.R.U.C. has declared its "unalterable opposition" to Federal legislation which would destroy or interfere with the rights of the states to regulate the rates and service of air carriers operating in intrastate commerce. See INTERSTATE COMMERCE; COMMERCE AND INDUSTRY, GOVERNMENT REGULATION OF; RAILROAD; TRUCK; TRANSPORTATION; FREIGHT RATES.

N. C. HUDSON

BIBLIOG.–*Regulation of Transportation Agencies*, Report of Federal Coordinator of Transportation (1934); E. R. Johnson et al., *Transportation* (1940); S. Daggett, *Principles of Inland Transportation* (1941); T. C. Bigham, *Transportation Principles and Problems* (1946); W. J. Knorst, *Transportation and Traffic Management* (1947).

INTRAVENOUS TREATMENT. It is possible to inject many different kinds of substances into the veins. When these substances are used for treatment purposes it is called intravenous treatment (therapy). Intravenous treatment has an important place in medicine. It can be used to give substances which cannot be absorbed into the body in any other way. Some diseases can be treated best in this way. Various preparations containing arsenic, for example, are given intravenously for the treatment of syphilis. Some other chemicals which are poorly absorbed or irritating when injected into the muscles or under the skin are given intravenously for other conditions, particularly the tropical diseases. For people who have lost a great deal of blood, a lifesaving measure consists in giving blood from some other person into the veins; this form of intravenous therapy is called blood transfusion.

Nutritious substances and fluids are frequently given intravenously. For people who have lost a great deal of blood and where blood transfusion is not immediately possible, the fluid loss can be quickly made up by injecting into a vein water to which salts have been added in proper portions. Dextrose (sugar) solutions are a source of quick energy and can easily be given intravenously. Recently food proteins have been prepared which can be given directly into the blood stream through a vein. This has been helpful for people who have had extremely poor nutrition for long periods and are unable to eat or digest food in the usual manner. This can also be used for some who are unable to eat adequate quantities because of interfering operations or diseases. At least one case is on record where a patient without taking any food by mouth, was kept alive for eight weeks by intravenous injection of such a protein preparation, together with sugar and salt solutions to supply other types of energy and fluid.

EDWIN P. JORDAN, M.D.

INTROIT, the verse, psalm, or hymn which is sung as the priest goes up to the altar. It consists in the Roman Catholic Church of an antiphon, gloria, and part of a psalm or other passage of Scripture. Being sung as the priest enters within the precincts of the altar, it was named the *Introitus.* Introits are ascribed to Pope Gregory the Great (590–604) or even to Celestine (422–32). Introits were provided in the first English Prayer Book of King Edward VI (1549).

INTROSPECTIVE PSYCHOLOGY. See PSYCHOLOGY, Schools.

INTROVERSION-EXTRAVERSION. This pair of contrasting traits was named and described by CARL G. JUNG in 1920. Introverts, he said, direct their thoughts and attentions inward upon their own feelings; extraverts, outward toward people and events. Many tests, mostly questionnaires, have been widely used since then in diagnosing personal maladjustments and in vocational guidance and selection (e.g., extraverts for selling and public contact occupations). The earlier idea, that they represent distinct types, has yielded to the view that they are opposite extremes of one continuous variable along which people distribute approximately normally, the large majority being "ambiverts," i.e., (neither pronounced introverts nor extraverts but exhibiting both characteristics in varying proportion. It is also recognized that these are not "pure" but composites of several general traits. Guilford's analysis of introvert-extravert items produced evidence of several identifiable factors, including depression, meditative thinking, shyness or seclusiveness, carefree disposition, and alertness to surroundings. See PERSONALITY.

FORREST A. KINGSBURY

INTUITION, a term in philosophy and psychology for that knowledge which seems to be had without previous experience, reason, or learning. In philosophy, it has frequently been applied to a direct perception or awareness of principles not arrived at by conscious thinking. Thus, when the German philosopher IMMANUEL KANT spoke of space and time as "the pure forms of our intuition," he implied that our knowledge of space and time preceded any experience of them and gave meaning to such experience.

As intuition may be knowledge of right and wrong, it has been given a place in nearly all ethical systems. And, as it has been held to be an immediate experience of truth, unattainable by reason or sense observation, intuition has been considered important in religious knowledge. Considering intuition as an inner harmony with reality, the French philosopher HENRI BERGSON made it the source of all essential knowledge of the universe.

Intuition, in psychological usage, is the immediate grasping of the significant point in a mass of data. Although often confused with insight, it carries the further meaning of understanding which supposedly occurs without any preliminary knowledge or sense perception that can be identified. In addition, intuitive knowledge is sometimes assumed, without verification, to be innate or instinctive.

Psychological study suggests that intuition may simply be perception based on cues or stimuli which are marginal or obscure rather than in the center of attention. Hence, shrewd guesses or hunches about the personality, motives, thoughts, or possible behavior of another might make use of subtle hints in gesture or expression. Reactions to such clues may become so completely automatic from long use that they no longer depend upon conscious deduction.

Insight into esthetic values is sometimes ascribed to intuition, as are other judgments which involve sensitivity, feeling and emotion. This suggests a possible source of the common notion that women are more intuitive than men. See PSYCHOLOGY. H. V. M.

INVAR, an alloy of nickel and steel (36 per cent nickel) discovered by Dr. C. E. Guillaume. On account of the small percentage of variation in its volume from changes of temperature it is suitable for delicate instruments, such as those used in geodetical surveying. See STEEL.

INVASION. See OCCUPATION, MILITARY; INTERNATIONAL LAW; CONQUEST.

INVENTION, in patent law, is the contrivance or creation of something which did not exist previously, and was not known before. It differs from a discovery, for a discovery is finding out something which previously existed. For instance, steam and electricity were discovered; but the machines which put them to use, as the steam engine and electric motor, are inventions. To be patentable in the United States, an invention must be useful, advantageous, or give enjoyment. See PATENT.

INVENTION AND DISCOVERY

INVENTION AND DISCOVERY have lifted the status of man from that of a cave dweller, waging a constant struggle for his survival, to master of the earth and sky. Invention is defined as contriving that which had not existed before, such as the first wheel; discovery is finding out something hitherto unknown, such as atomic energy.

In many instances, from prehistoric times to the present day, there is often a close and sometimes overlapping relationship in particular cases of invention and discovery. Also, these two major factors in the development of the civilized world as we know it today can be projected into the abstract, thus embracing the entire history of mankind. Consideration here will necessarily be limited to a discussion of the physical fields of invention and discovery.

THE GENESIS OF A SCIENTIFIC DISCOVERY

Almost every article in use in the world today, as well as the 20th century by-product of any major discovery, has a history that goes back hundreds and even thousands of years. A dramatic example of this is atomic energy which may herald the dawn of the Atomic Age. The world became aware of the frightening potentialities of atomic energy with the dropping of the atom bomb on the Japanese city of Hiroshima, Aug. 6, 1945. The development of the atom bomb, however, goes back to ancient Greek times and to a man named DEMOCRITUS. Late in the 5th century B.C. he taught that all matter was made up of infinitely small particles which he called atoms. Epicurus, another Greek philosopher, taught this

UNIVERSITY OF CHICAGO
Cyclotron, invented in 1931, has developed into this enormous synchrocyclotron, completed in 1951

same theory a century later, but hundreds of years were to elapse before it was revived in 1803 by the English physicist, John Dalton. In 1911 another English physicist, Lord RUTHERFORD, discovered that the atom resembles a solar system in construction. In the center is a heavy mass of positively charged protons around which negatively charged electrons revolve like planets. Rutherford succeeded in splitting the atom and thus for the first time achieved the dream of the ancient alchemists in bringing about the transmutation of the elements.

Albert Einstein developed about 1905 a mass-energy theory, in accordance with which matter—which can be broken down into atoms—can be changed under certain conditions into energy, and energy can be changed into matter. Other discoveries and inventions which pushed man across the threshold into the Atomic Age were the discovery of the isotopes of elements (1919) by Francis W. Aston and other physicists, invention of the Geiger-Müller counter for ionization (1929), invention of the cyclotron by Ernest O. Lawrence (1931), and discovery of the neutron by James Chadwick and of the positron by Carl D. Anderson (1932). Under the direction of Enrico Fermi the first self-maintaining nuclear chain reaction pile was erected at the University of Chicago (1942). After the atom bomb proved to be a success, the project sought to harness atomic energy to produce power for industry in the Oak Ridge, Tenn., plant (1947).

The harnessing of the atom demonstrates a procedure that has been long evident in other fields. This development would have been impossible without other advances in chemistry, electricity, metallurgy and the funneling of vast knowledge accumulated in the past for one specific purpose. No complex modern invention is conceived in a vacuum.

EARLY DISCOVERIES AND INVENTIONS

Back in prehistoric times it is probable that most inventions and discoveries were stumbled upon by accident. For example, the discovery of fire—one of the basic discoveries of all time. Its earliest use probably dates to some prehistoric man who chanced across a tree that had been struck by lightning and was in flames. Possibly he warmed himself by the fire. It was also undoubtedly an accident that man made the tremendously important discovery that plants grow from seed. This marked the beginnings of agriculture. The first sharp-edged tool may have been the outgrowth of a glimmer of knowledge painfully acquired when some early man cut his foot on a sharp piece of flint.

Housing, Pottery, Transport. The earliest buildings used by man may have combined discovery and subsequent invention. The discovery of shelter provided by a fallen tree with thick leafage may have suggested the adding of other branches and the removal of inner limbs. This crude effort may have resulted in the first building. POTTERY, which has reached its zenith today in beautifully-wrought porcelain and a great variety of cooking utensils, goes back to dim prehistoric times. The development of pottery and even glazing is an indication of positive ingenuity in early man. This is also true in regard to the invention of the wheel and the first boat. The latter was in the form of a hollowed-out log or raft; it is also known that early man traveled on water in crude boats made of the skins of animals. Remote as it may seem, these humble craft started man on his way to circling the globe on palatial ocean liners.

Weights and Measures. Other important early discoveries closely allied with inventions include crude systems of measurement, weight scales, timing devices, and the calendar.

The first measuring device might well have been a sample arrowhead used by some cave dweller who wanted all of his arrowheads the same size. This probably was followed by a crude marked stick—the first ruler. Rulers as we know them today are much more refined, but the principle is the same. This applies to weight scales which are basically the same as the balance used by the merchants of Biblical times.

Most of the advances in measuring instruments have been developed during the last two centuries. These advances have made the greatest strides since the discovery of electricity which has resulted in voltmeters, ammeters, and similar devices. The discovery of the electron eventually resulted in the modern seemingly miraculous measuring and timing devices which can time billionth of a second intervals. Similarly, the electron microscope has made possible the enlargement of materials at least 100,000 times and with subsequent photographic enlargements to 200,000 times. This microscope makes it possible to see and study a speck only 10/1,000,000ths of an inch in diameter.

Exact measurements have provided man with a method for production—mass production—which has revolutionized the world in which he lives and works. The 18th-century American inventor, ELI WHITNEY (best known for his invention of the cotton gin) may have started the evolution of mass production with his invention of a gun with interchangeable parts. A few decades after this invention (about 1840) the Vernier caliper and micrometer were invented. These tools made possible the fine precision necessary for the making of interchangeable parts.

Back in the early days micrometers varied in their adjustments, thus limiting mass production to single shops. Seldom would parts made in one shop fit those produced in another. This stumbling block was removed in 1897 when C. E. Johansson made a set of steel blocks which varied less than 2/1,000,000 of an inch. These blocks were called "Jo" blocks and used to check gauges which make possible the assembly of complicated machines with parts made in a dozen plants.

As far back as 150 B.C. astronomers invented the astrolabe, forerunner of the mariner's sextant and the surveyor's theodolite. Despite the fact that the sextant and the theodolite are hundreds of years old, they long reigned supreme in their respective fields of navigation and surveying. Modern systems of navigation utilizing radio and radar are now extensively used, and the tri-metrogon aerial camera is used for mapping and surveying as well as reconnaissance. In the winter of 1946–47, Admiral Richard E. Byrd made use of the aerial camera in mapping vast areas in the Antarctic.

Clocks and Calendars. Man has concerned himself with the measurement and passage of time as far back as records of his existence are known. Early man divided his days with a semblance of hours by burning a piece of rope tied with equally spaced knots. This was a great and ingenious advancement over what was probably the first method discovered for telling time: observing a shadow cast by a tree or rock.

The ancient Chinese invented a water-clock which was cleverly devised. When a small dish in the clock filled with water, the dish sank, causing the figure of a boy to strike a gong. The Chinese also used burning ropes under crude shelters to protect them from the weather. The best known

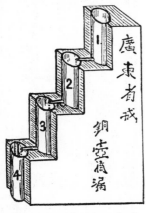

One type of water clock

nonmechanical timekeepers of all time are the hourglass and sundial.

It was not until the 16th century that Galileo discovered the pendulum. This made possible the precise timekeepers which set the pace until the advent of the modern electric quartz-crystal clocks.

On a larger scale, the measurement of CALENDAR time also dates back to the primitive. Days, weeks, months, seasons, and years were roughly gauged by the position of the sun, the stars, shape of the moon, fall of rain and snow, falling leaves and the ripening of grain and fruit.

The great difficulty throughout history in seeking to determine some standard for the measurement of months and years is the difference between 12 lunar months and a solar year. A lunar month contains 29½ days, thus making a lunar year only 354 days compared with the 364¼ days of the solar year. The Egyptians, Babylonians, Greeks, Chinese, and all ancient nations struggled with this problem, finding a variety of solutions or lack of solutions. Finally, Julius Caesar did something about those "excess" days. He decreed that the calendar year should have 365 days with the exception of every fourth year which should have 366. This was the origin of the Julian calendar. This calendar was used widely until 1582 when Pope Gregory XIII brought out the Gregorian or New Style calendar which is now in use in almost all Christian nations. See HOROLOGY.

Currency. The invention of MONEY as a convenient medium of exchange also goes back to the early days of civilized man as is evidenced by ancient coins found in tombs and among the excavations of archaeologists. The Romans set up a mint in the Temple of Juno Moneta and the word "money" is believed to be derived from the location of this ancient Roman mint.

TOOLS AND MATERIALS THROUGH THE AGES

While discoveries by mankind range far afield, with ramifications extending even into the realm of the social sciences, the great inventions by which man has improved his lot through the centuries are thought of largely as "mechanical." These inventions date back to the days of prehistoric man and proceeded at a slow pace until the dawn of the Machine Age when mechanical genius came into flower. The origin of some of man's most valuable basic mechanical inventions are unknown. These include the wheel, lever, wedge, saw, pulley, hammer, chisel, bellows, treadmill, waterwheel, pump, and scores of others.

Throughout history the available materials with which man has had to form his tools, houses, or means of conveyance have been an important factor in invention and discovery. Tracing man's use of these materials—wood, stone, bronze, iron, steel, light metals, plastics—provides a revealing record of the flowering of civilization.

The Stone Age. The first material used as such by primitive man was undoubtedly wood. His hut was made of wood in the form of branches or poles, and his first tool was a stick. Gradually, as the centuries rolled by and he became more ingenious, he began to make use of stones as implements. Sharp stones were used as weapons and for the skinning and cutting up of animals. Crude hammers, such as the tomahawk used by the American Indian, made their appearance, and stone utensils for preparing food. It is believed that at first man made little attempt to shape his tools from stone. He depended on finding rocks of the proper shape for a particular task. When the first man decided to fashion a piece of stone for his own purpose the development of homo sapiens took a long step forward. The first chisel or sharp hammer used for making an arrowhead was the direct ancestor of modern machinery tools—the precise and intricate tools which are the backbone of the manufacturing industry today. One has only to go to the great museums of the world to look upon the stone works of ancient man. Some of the tools,

Invention and Discovery

Gutenberg inspects a proof in his print shop

such as those used for grinding grain or the production of weapons, are amazingly ingenious. In some parts of the world early man constructed elaborate caskets, tombs, and religious symbols of stone.

The Bronze Age. Gold and copper were probably the first metals used by man, but he made no great progress in metal working until he discovered an alloy. This alloy, consisting principally of copper and tin, was bronze. Bronze was much easier to work with than stone, and so important was its discovery that an entire age in the history of mankind takes its name from this material—the Bronze Age. Bronze was used in Egypt as early as 2500 B.C., but Western Europe did not enter the Bronze Age until about 2000 B.C. when the use of this metal became widespread in the forming of swords, awls, hunting knives, eating utensils, gouges, hammers, arrowheads, and decorative pieces such as amulets and coronets. During the Bronze Age man made his first real strides in artistic as well as practical craftsmanship. Gold was used as an ornamental material during this period.

The Iron Age. Man made no sudden transitions in his quest for materials to aid his inventions and improve his way of living. The use of stone overlapped for centuries into the Bronze Age just as the use of bronze extended for many years into the Iron Age. The formation of iron from its ore required intense heat and for this reason it is believed that the discovery of iron was accidental. It was probably first found in the ashes from a fire of charcoal mixed with the ore. Later man duplicated such a fire with the earliest smelter, made in a rock cavity. These rock cavities were filled with iron ore and charcoal with an opening provided for the wind to create the draft required for intense heat.

The oldest piece of iron (on exhibit in the British Museum) is believed to be about 6,000 years old. It was found in Egypt. Archaeologists have discovered a gap of several thousand years between the age of this piece of the metal and the working of iron in Assyria, Chaldea, Greece, China, and India. Perhaps, as in the case of bronze, the discovery of iron was made and then lost many times before its wide usage. The Romans used bars made of iron as a medium of exchange, and Biblical references indicate that the ancient Hebrews were also acquainted with this metal. Iron was the favored metal for making tools and weapons in India and China by 500 B.C. Even steel had made its appearance in these countries, as well as Greece, at this time. Indian iron and steel were highly prized during the Middle Ages and Persia imported this steel to make into the famed Damascus blades of the Saracens. Some metallurgists believe that most of the metals and alloys were known in scattered parts of the world by 300 B.C. It was 50 B.C., however, before iron replaced bronze in the northern European nations.

The Machine Age. By the 10th century iron working was in full swing in England, in 1611 an Englishman took out a patent for smelting iron with coal, and during the latter part of the 18th century Henry discovered a way to purify iron by puddling. Until 1870 the principal metallic materials for construction work, tools, and weapons were cast and wrought iron. The Machine Age was really to get under way with the discovery in 1856 by Sir HENRY BESSEMER of a process for making steel. He devised the well-known Bessemer process for making steel from pig iron in a pneumatic converter. This great metallurgical discovery, coupled in time with the development of proper fuels, was a boon to inventors in harnessing machines as the servants of man.

However, man had already come a long way with inventions many years before the discovery of an economical method for producing great quantities of steel. Before 1500, a German printer, JOHANN GUTENBERG, had invented movable type (1440) which was to revolutionize the education of man. An Italian,

Galileo, had invented the telescope (1609) and a Frenchman, Denis Papin, had built a steamboat (1707). The steamboat, as every schoolboy knows, was perfected later by an American, ROBERT FULTON. JAMES WATT, the son of a Scotch shipbuilder, invented the "modern" steam engine in 1765. He worked for years perfecting this engine and by 1783 had built an engine containing nearly all the principles of the modern reciprocating engine. This engine provided a new and undreamed of source of power at small cost. About the same time (1764), another Englishman, JAMES HARGREAVES, had invented the spinning jenny to revolutionize the ancient art of making cloth. The coupling of Watt's steam engine with the spinning machine was the basis for England's great textile industry which continues to this day. Another boon to this industry was the power loom invented by Edmund Cartwright in 1785. Also allied to the textile industry, as well as agriculture, was the appearance in America of the cotton gin, the invention of Eli Whitney in 1793. In the year 1800 gas lighting was developed in Scotland by William Murdock, and an

NEW YORK MUSEUM OF SCIENCE AND INDUSTRY

Watt's Walking Beam Engine, using a separate condenser, was made to pump water from mines

Italian, Alexander Volta, made the first electric battery.

The first half of the 19th century saw the invention of the common match in England (John Walker, 1827); the reaping machine (CYRUS H. McCORMICK, United States, 1831); the locomotive engine (George Stephenson, England, 1814); the revolver (Samuel Colt, United States, 1835); the vulcanizing of rubber (Charles Goodyear, United States, 1840), and scores of other inventions of lesser importance.

COMMUNICATIONS

Also during the first half of the 19th century great strides were made in the field of communications which were to forge a close link between nations of the civilized world. Since man uttered the first spoken word, dispatched the first messenger, made the first "X" on a piece of bark or in the sand, or sent up the first smoke signal, he has been struggling to communicate with his fellows. The smoke signal or drum beat that spread the word of the approach of any enemy actually produced a similar effect to that of the radio °flash which reported that the Japanese had bombed Pearl Harbor. Primitive signals, however, were not concerned with the transmission of words but merely the confirmation or revocation of prearranged messages.

One of the earliest needs for communication facilities became evident when man began to sail the mysterious and uncharted seas. The sea-going Venetians devised a system of communication over short distances—either between one vessel and another or between a vessel and land—with flags. Later they developed lantern and sound signals.

Writing and Printing. The gradual development of speech and symbols for writing were the two greatest factors in communication up to the 15th century. That century saw the production of movable type which foreshadowed the newspaper, periodical and printed book. This invention greatly expedited mass communication, but until the harnessing of electricity all lines of communication were dependent on ordinary transportation facilities. Messages written on papyrus or printed on paper had to be carried by man, such as the runners of ancient Greece, by horse, coach, sailing boat, or other conveyance. Man had known paper for hundreds of years before the invention of movable type. Paper was invented in China in 105 A.D. and reached Europe from Damascus. It was not made in Europe, though, until the 12th century, when returning crusaders erected mills in Italy and other countries.

Electricity. The discovery of how to produce and control electricity and its subsequent development is almost synonymous with advances in communication. The actual discovery of electricity goes back hundreds of years to the Greeks. They are believed to be the first to discover that rubbing amber with a piece of cloth would give the amber a strange power to attract to it such objects as pieces of paper or feathers. Man observed the effects of electricity for thousands of years before he knew what it was or gave it a name. It was named by William Gilbert, an English scientist, who published a book on his experiments in 1600. He used the term "electric," derived from the Greek word "elektron" which means "amber." Dr. Gilbert experimented not only with amber, but with glass, resin, sulfur, and other materials. (In recent years knowledge of the electrons and their behavior was to bring about a reversion to the Greek term with the word "electronics.")

In 1663 a frictionizing machine was built by Otto von Guericke to create this strange energy, but a hundred years passed before man discovered that electricity could be carried through certain materials such as metal. During the 18th century, Volta made exhaustive studies of electric currents and Benjamin Franklin conducted his experiments with lightning (1752) to prove its identity with electricity.

MICHAEL FARADAY (1791–1867), British scientist, reached the profound conclusion in 1831 that magnetism can produce electricity. From this discovery came the electric dynamo. This was to pave the way for developments which were to reach into every walk of life, every branch of science and industry, and to unlock eventually one of the great secrets of the universe—the splitting of the atom and the release of atomic energy.

The dynamo is basically a simple machine. Coils of insulated wire are rotated between the poles of a magnet. and these moving coils pick up an electromotive force as they cut the lines of force in the magnetic field. The same result is obtained by moving a magnet around stationary coils.

The Telegraph. Soon after Faraday's discoveries were made known, SAMUEL F. B. MORSE invented the electric telegraph (1837) and the Morse Code of dots and dashes. From this time forward man was no longer dependent on boats or coaches or carrier pigeons (the latter dating back to the days of Genghis Khan) to carry his messages. Electricity was the new and speedy messenger in the field of communications.

Photography. About this time photography was developed in England (1835) by Fox Talbot, and across the channel in France what were to be known as daguerrotypes were being produced by Daguerre and an associate named Niepce. A few years later (1846) an American, Richard Hoe, invented the cylindrical printing press. This made the daily newspaper, books, and magazines available to the great mass of people at small cost.

The Typewriter, Telephone, and Linotype. The typewriter made its appearance in 1868 and in 1876

Typewriter invented by Charles Thurber

ALEXANDER GRAHAM BELL patented the telephone. This sensational invention was the first great forward stride in voice communications. Otto Mergenthaler, another American, invented the linotype in 1883— the greatest boon in printing since the advent of movable type.

Motion Pictures. The next important development was in the realm of visual messages in the form of moving pictures. The moving picture camera was patented by Thomas A. Edison in 1893. (A few years earlier in 1879 Edison had given the world the electric light with the invention of the incandescent bulb.) To this present day, motion pictures have continued in a state of evolution which has produced "talking" and technicolor pictures. The next development for this form of amusement and education is three-dimensional effects.

Radio, which did not become widely known until after World War I, also made its debut in the 19th century. It was known as the wireless telegraph. Sir Oliver Lodge of England demonstrated in 1894 that electromagnetic waves, first discovered by Hertz, could be used for signaling by guiding these waves for practical purposes. The 20th century was to see the refinement of radio. This refinement was not the work of any one inventor but was brought about by the pooling of knowledge and the gradual evolution of improvements. The Italian scientist, GUGLIELMO MARCONI, is known as the father of radio.

Other high lights of communication of the 20th century are television, facsimile, and the transmission of photographs by radio.

TRANSPORTATION

In the field of transportation nearly all of the important inventions have occurred in the last 150 years—a mere speck in the span of recorded history. The steamship was the first invention in the modern trend which was to cause the earth to "shrink" to a point where it can now be encircled by man in a few days. (Milton Reynolds, United States, flew around the world in 1947 for an unofficial record of three days, six hours and 55¼ minutes.)

The Steamboat. Just as Leonardo da Vinci had dreamed of flying many years before the Wright brothers, boat builders of the 16th, 17th, and 18th centuries had attempted to devise some method for powering a boat with steam. The French inventor, Papin, built such a boat with four paddle wheels in 1707. He launched this craft at Cassel, Germany. A mob of angry boatmen—symbolic of the resistance to any modern invention that threatens the jobs of any group—almost killed Papin and destroyed the steamboat, thus setting the progress of transportation back for an entire century. For just a hundred years later, in 1807, modern transportation got under way when Robert Fulton launched his famed steamboat, the *Clermont*, on the Hudson River. Twelve years later the first steamship, the *Savannah*, crossed the Atlantic Ocean from Savannah, Ga., to Liverpool, England.

The Automobile. With the development of the locomotive engine by GEORGE STEPHENSON in 1814 man thought that at last he had conquered the world as far as transportation was concerned. He had the steamship to cross the oceans and would now have the railroads to traverse the land. For personal transportation he not only had a horse and carriage, but the bicycle, invented by Kirkpatrick Macmillan (1839). In 1860 a Frenchman, Étienne Lenoir, invented the internal combustion gasoline engine. This was to eventually result in man's favorite mode of personal transportation—the automobile. The German engineers, Carl Bing (1884) and Gottlieb Daimler (1887), built the first successful gasoline automobiles. American automotive engineers in the

early years of the 20th century played a leading part in developing the automobile from a high-cost luxury item to a mass-produced comparatively low-cost means of transportation. HENRY FORD, Charles F. Kettering of General Motors, and other famous pioneers in the industry helped revolutionize this popular American means of transport.

Railroads, too, were to experience advancement with the advent of the Diesel-electric locomotive, the Pullman car and other improvements. The Diesel engine, invented by Rudolf Diesel (German, 1893) has been improved and adapted for use in trucks, busses, tractors, military tanks, ships and submarines.

The Airplane. In 1903 man began his mastery of the skies when ORVILLE and WILBUR WRIGHT flew the first airplane. It was not until World War I, however,

UNIVERSITY OF MICHIGAN

Contemporary Artist's Idea of the Great Steam Duck, an 1841 design for an airship that never flew

that the possibilities of the airplane for both civilian and military uses were fully appreciated. Following the war aviation made great strides and in a few years regular transport lines were established. World War II saw the flowering of international air travel and the development of the jet type aircraft which may carry man beyond the speed of sound.

INVENTION AND MODERN WARFARE

New Weapons. Throughout history every important invention has had as profound an effect upon the way man conducts his military tactics as it has had on his peacetime pursuits. Modern methods of transportation and communication have changed warfare from a long drawn out process of siege and infantry operation to that of the "blitzkrieg" of World War II. The recoil-operated machine gun (Sir Hiram Maxim, England, 1885), the air-cooled machine gun (Isaac N. Lewis, United States, 1911), the tank (1917), high-powered artillery, mass air raids with aerial bombs—the latter including "block busters," incendiaries and the atom bomb—have made warfare so deadly as to threaten the very existence of mankind. Despite camouflage, the "aerial eyes" of a modern army have made it literally impossible to launch a large surprise land or sea operation. Even submarines can be spotted by sonar (sound detection) when deep in the water and radar (reflected radio beams whose "echoes" reveal the distance and location of an object) when on the surface. World War II also saw the development of the miraculous proximity fuse which causes a bomb to explode as it nears a target. The "buzz bomb" V-1 and the deadly V-2 carried long-distance attacks via the stratosphere. These rocket bombs carry their own propellant and travel hundreds of miles to their targets.

Total Warfare. World Wars I and II were the first to take the lives of civilians on a broad scale—a factor that can be blamed directly on the resources

Robert Fulton's steamboat, the "Clermont"

of invention and discovery of warring mankind. Once wars were far removed from stay-at-home civilians in cities and industrial areas. Now key cities and manufacturing districts are prime targets and the lives of millions of civilians during time of war are in constant peril. Modern aerial warfare also holds a new threat to humanity in the form of germ warfare, the spreading of disease germs, such as typhus, over large congested areas.

War years give great impetus to inventors and scientists. Some of these developments, such as those in the medical field, are of lasting value to man. The history of the discoveries of medical science since the Middle Ages seems to offset man's inventive ability directed in wartime toward the destruction of his fellow man.

The Progress of Chemistry

Man has concerned himself with the structure of matter and the nature of chemical change since the ancient days of alchemy. Efforts to produce gold synthetically drove him on to many important early discoveries. Quests into the composition of matter were eventually to lead to the discovery of molecules, atoms, the electrical basis of matter, and eventually the splitting of the atom and release of atomic energy.

Every science has been dependent on chemical discoveries as a basis for progress. Chemists found that the universe is composed of nearly 100 known elements and compounds. The latter were found to be composed of two or more elements whose atoms are united by heat or electricity or other means.

Scientists have discovered through the centuries countless combinations of elements to produce fuels (from kerosene to high-test aviation gasoline), textiles, foods, drugs, dyes, and chemicals.

The first modern conception of the elements was presented by a noted French chemist ANTOINE LAURENT LAVOISIER (1743–94). His discoveries provided the foundation for modern chemistry and created a sharp dividing line between old and new practices. In 1772 he informed the Academy of Science that sulfur and phosphorus increased in weight when burned because "air" was absorbed in the process. Later (after the preparation of oxygen by Priestley in 1774) Lavoisier deduced that the air absorbed in his earlier experiments was oxygen. Oxygen was known as "dephlogisticated" air until he gave it the name of oxygen in a report explaining combustion which was published by the Academy in 1782. A year later, in conjunction with another noted French chemist, Laplace, he announced the discovery of the composition of water.

Many chemical discoveries have consisted largely of solving the secrets of the greatest chemist—Nature. Man has yet to solve the complete process of photosynthesis in plants—conversion of carbon dioxide from the air and nutrients of the soil into starches and cellulose.

Basic chemical discoveries have given inventors the new materials needed for progress: hard heat-resistant metals for engines from the internal combustion type of the 19th century to 20th century jet, fireproof plastics for building construction and thousands of other uses. The knowledge of the composition of steel brought that useful metal into reality. Steel alone

wrought infinite changes: modern machines of all types, skyscrapers, battleships, the powerful engines that lift tons of aircraft into the sky.

Prior to and during World War II chemists produced artificial rubber, high octane gasoline, liquids which would not freeze at 100° below zero, butter that would not melt in the tropics, fabrics to resist mildew or decay, the silicon lubricants and scores of other intriguing, important or amazing aids to mankind. Atabrine and other drugs with which medical science fights disease first came to light in the great chemical laboratories of the world.

Exploring the World and the Universe

Long before man had acquainted himself with the lands and seas of the earth, he had been scanning the heavens to solve their mysteries and relationship with the planet on which he lived. The earliest belief, which had persisted for centuries, was that the sun was stationary and the earth flat. It was feared that if one got too near the edge of the earth he would fall off into space. This belief existed long after the explorations of the Norsemen. A contemporary of COLUMBUS, COPERNICUS (1473–1543), Polish astronomer, astounded the world by refuting the accepted beliefs of astronomers. The reasoning of Copernicus was founded on the principle of the relativity of motion. He taught that the earth rotated on an axis directed toward the celestial pole and that the sun remained stationary. Fifty years after the death of Copernicus, the Italian astronomer GALILEO (who discovered the refracting telescope and the principle of the pendulum) supported the beliefs of Copernicus in regard to the solar system. Despite prejudice directed against his research, Galileo advanced the findings of Copernicus, strengthened them with discoveries of his own and paved the way for Sir ISAAC NEWTON's research. Newton was born the year of Galileo's death (1642). He discovered that the sun and planets behaved as "centers of force" and worked out his Laws of Gravitation. His findings have served as a searchlight to guide astronomers and other men of science in their quest for knowledge. Another great astronomer of the 17th century was Johann Kepler (Germany) whose discoveries helped to establish the foundations of a mechanical theory of the solar system.

In more recent years, ALBERT EINSTEIN, physicist, opened up new vistas to scientists with his special theory of relativity (1905) and his general theory of relativity (1915). Einstein's theory of energy and

Man's Interest in the myriad heavenly bodies is an ancient one. Herschel's 40-foot telescope was designed early in the 19th century

matter was later to be proved by the splittings of the atom which has given man a discovery that brings him to the dawn of a new age.   WAYNE WHITTAKER

BIBLIOG.–J. A. Maloney and others, *Great Inventors and their Inventions* (1938); G. Hartman, *Machines and the Men Who Made the World of Industry* (1939); R. Burlingame, *Engines of Democracy* (1940); A. Rogers, *From Man to Machine* (1941); M. Crawford, *Influence of Invention on Civilization* (1942); E. R. Montgomery, *The Story Behind Great Inventions* (1944); C. J. Hylander, *American Inventors* (ed. 1945); E. Larsen, *Inventors' Cavalcade* (ed. 1945); V. Stefansson, ed., *Great Adventures and Explorations* (1947).

PAINTING BY WILLIAM S. SCHWARZ

American Scientists in artist's portrayal are, left to right, Edison, Steinmetz, Bell, and Morse

LIST OF PRINCIPAL INVENTIONS

INVENTION	INVENTOR	DATE
Adding Machine	William Burroughs	1888
Air Brake, Railway	George Westinghouse	1868
Air Conditioning (Dew Point Control)	Willis H. Carrier	1911
Airplane	Orville and Wilbur Wright	1903
Air Pump	Otto von Guericke	1654
Airship, Navigable	Henri Giffard	1851
	Ferdinand von Zeppelin	1900
	Alberto Santos-Dumont	1901
Aluminum Reduction Process	Charles M. Hall	1886
	Paul L. T. Héroult	
Ammonia, Synthetic	Fritz Haber	c.1910
Anesthesia (Nitrous Oxide)	Sir Humphry Davy	1800
(Chloroform)	Samuel Guthrie	1831
Aniline Dyes	Sir William H. Perkin	1856
Arc Lamp, Electric	Charles F. Brush	1878
Atomic Bomb	Arthur H. Compton	1945
	Enrico Fermi	
	Ernest O. Lawrence	
	Lise Meitner	
	J. Robert Oppenheimer	
	Harold C. Urey	
Autogiro	Juan de la Cierva	1925
Automobile	Carl Benz	1884
	Gottlieb Daimler	1887
Balloon (Hot Air)	Joseph and Jacques Montgolfier	1783
Balloon (Hydrogen)	Jacques A. C. Charles	1783
Barometer	Evangelista Torricelli	1643
Barbed Wire	Joseph F. Glidden	1874
Bicycle	Kirkpatrick Macmillan	1839
	Pierre Lallement	1862
Blowpipe, Oxyhydrogen	Robert Hare	1801
Bunsen Burner	Robert W. Bunsen	1855
Canning	Nicolas Appert	1804
Car Coupler, Automatic	E. H. Janney	1873
Carborundum	Edward G. Acheson	1891
Cash Register	James J. Ritty	1879
Cathode-ray Tube	Sir William Crookes	1879
Cement, Portland	Joseph Aspdin	1824
Chronometer, Marine	John Harrison	1749
Coherer	Edouard Branly	1890
Comptometer	Dorr E. Felt	1884
Concrete, Reinforced	Joseph Monier	1867
Cotton Gin	Eli Whitney	1793
Cyclotron	Ernest O. Lawrence	1931
Diesel (Oil) Engine	Rudolf Diesel	1893
Dynamite	Alfred B. Nobel	1866
Dynamo	Michael Faraday	1831
Electric Light, Incandescent	Thomas A. Edison	1879
	Sir Joseph W. Swan	
Electric Light, Wire Tungsten Filament	William D. Coolidge	1911
Electric Light, Gas-filled Tungsten	Irving Langmuir	1913
Electroplating Process	Luigi Brugnatelli	1805
Elevator	Elisha G. Otis	1852
Embossed Printing for the Blind	Valentin Haüy	1784
	Louis Braille	1829
Engraving, Mezzotint	Ludwig von Siegen	c.1640
Fly Shuttle	John Kay	1733
Fountain Pen	Lewis E. Waterman	1884
Furnace, Regenerative	Sir William Siemens	1856
Garand (Gas-operated) Rifle	John C. Garand	1934
Gas, Illuminating	William Murdock	1800
Gas Engine	Etienne Lenoir	1860
	Nikolaus A. Otto	1876
Gatling (Machine) Gun	Richard J. Gatling	1861
Glider	Otto Lilienthal	1877
Guncotton	Christian Schonbein	1845
Gyroscope	Jean B. L. Foucault	1852
Gyroscopic Compass	Elmer A. Sperry	1905
Hydroairplane	Glenn H. Curtiss	1911
Ironclad Steam Battery (*Monitor*)	John Ericsson	1861
Jacquard (Pattern) Loom	Joseph M. Jacquard	1801
Jet Propulsion	Frank Whittle	1937
Kodak (Box Camera)	George Eastman	1888
Lewis (Air-Cooled Machine) Gun	Isaac N. Lewis	1911
Lightning Rod	Benjamin Franklin	1752
Linotype	Ottmar Mergenthaler	1883
Lithography	Alois Senefelder	1796
Lock, Cylinder	Linus Yale	1860
Locomotive, Railroad	Richard Trevithick	1804
	George Stephenson	1814
Loom, Power	Edmund Cartwright	1785
Match, Chemical Friction	John Walker	1827
Match, Safety	J. E. Lundstrom	1885
Maxim (Recoil-operated Machine) Gun	Sir Hiram Maxim	1885
Mercerized Cotton	John Mercer	1850
Mercury-vapor Arc Lamp	Peter Cooper Hewitt	1903
Microphone	David E. Hughes	1878
Milk, Condensed	Gail Borden	1853
Milk, Evaporated	John B. Meyenberg	1880
Milk, Irradiated	Harry Steenbock	1924
Miner's Safety Lamp	Sir Humphry Davy	1815
Mirror Foiling Process	Andrea and Domenico del Gallo	1507
	Baron Justus von Liebig	1836
Monotype	Tolbert Lanston	1887
Motion Pictures (Kinetoscope)	Thomas A. Edison	1893
(Phantascope)	Charles F. Jenkins	1894
Nail-making Machine	Nathan Read	1798
Neoprene	Julius A. Nieuwland	1930
(Synthetic Rubber)	Wallace H. Carothers	
Nernst Lamp	Walther Nernst	1897
Nitroglycerine	Ascanio Sobrero	c.1847
Nylon	Wallace H. Carothers	1937
Paper	Ts' ai Lun	A.D. 105
Paper-Making Machine, Web or Fourdrinier	Nicolas L. Robert	1798
	Bryan Donkin	1806
Phonograph	Thomas A. Edison	1877
Photo Transmission by Wireless	Arthur Korn	1904
Photography (Calotype)	Henry Fox Talbot	1835
(Daguerreotype)	Joseph N. Niepce	
	Louis Daguerre	1839
Piano	Bartolommeo Cristofori	1711
Pin-making Machine	Lemuel W. Wright	1824

Plastics		
(Celluloid)	John Wesley Hyatt	1869
(Bakelite)	Leo H. Baekeland	1909
Plow, Cast-iron	Charles Newbold	1797
Plow, Steel	John Deere	c.1846
Plow, Chilled-steel	James Oliver	1868
Pneumatic Rubber		
Tire	John Boyd Dunlop	1887
Porcelain, European	Johann Friedrich	
	Bottger	1709
Printing with	Pi-shing	c.1045
Movable Type	Johann Gutenberg	c.1440
Printing Press, Steam	Friedrich Konig	1811
Printing Press, Rotary	Richard M. Hoe	1846
Pulley, Compound	Archimedes	3d Century B.C.
Radio	Lee De Forest	1907
Radiolocator (Radar)	Sir Robert Watson-Watt	1935
Rayon	Count Hilaire de Chardonnet	1884
Reaper	Cyrus H. McCormick	1831
	Obed Hussey	1833
Refrigerator	Ferdinand P. E. Carré	1858
	Carl Linde	1874
Refrigerator Car	G. F. Swift	1875
Revolver	Samuel Colt	1835
Rubber Vulcanization	Charles Goodyear	1840
Screw, Water	Archimedes	3d Century B.C.
Sewing Machine	Thomas Saint	1790
	Barthélemy Thimonnier	1830
	Elias Howe	1846
Shield Tunneling	Sir Marc Brunel	1823
Shoe Sewing Machine	Lyman R. Blake	1858
Shrapnel Shell	Henry Shrapnel	c.1784
Silverware, Plated	Thomas Boulsover	1743
Sleeping Car	George M. Pullman	1864
Soda (Produced from Salt)	Nicolas Leblanc	c.1790
	Ernest Solvay	1861
Spectacles, Bifocal	Benjamin Franklin	c.1760
Spectroscope	Gustav R. Kirchhoff	1859
	Robert W. Bunsen	
Spinning Frame	Sir Richard Arkwright	1768
Spinning Jenny	James Hargreaves	1764
Spinning Mule	Samuel Crompton	1779
Steamboat	Denis Papin	1707
	John Fitch	c.1785
	Robert Fulton	1803
Steam Engine		
(Atmospheric)	Thomas Newcomen	1705
(Condensing)	James Watt	1765
Steam Hammer	James Nasmyth	1839
Steel Converter	William Kelly	c.1850
	Sir Henry Bessemer	1856
Stereotyping Process	William Ged	1725
Stethoscope	René Laennec	1819
Stocking Frame	William Lee	1589
Submarine	David Bushnell	1775
	John P. Holland	1881
Talking Pictures	Theodore W. Case	c.1922
	Lee De Forest	
Telautograph	Elisha Gray	1888
Telegraph	Samuel F. B. Morse	1837
	Sir Charles Wheatstone	
Telephone	Alexander Graham Bell	1876
Telescope		
(Refracting)	Galileo Galilei	1609
(Reflecting)	Sir Isaac Newton	1668
Television	John L. Baird	1926
Thermit	Hans Goldschmidt	c.1895
Thermometer	Gabriel D. Fahrenheit	1714
Thresher	Andrew Meikle	1784
Tool Steel, High-speed	Frederick W. Taylor	
	J. Maunsel White	c.1900
Transformer	William Stanley	1885
Turbine		
(Hydraulic)	Benoit Fourneyron	1827
(Steam)	Carl G. P. de Laval	1889
	Sir Charles A. Parsons	1884
Typewriter	Christopher L. Sholes	1868
	Carlos Glidden	
Voltaic Pile (Battery)	Alessandro Volta	1800
Welsbach (Gas)		
Mantle	Carl Auer von Welsbach	1885
Wireless	Guglielmo Marconi	1896
Telegraphy	Reginald A. Fessenden	1902
Zipper	W. L. Judson	1893

INVENTORY, a formal list of items of personal property, sometimes with the actual or estimated value of each item set over against it. An inventory may be an ordinary incident of commercial business, or it may be required by law as an incident of legal proceedings. It is thus required of executors and administrators on taking possession of a decedent's estate; of bankrupts and insolvents or their assignees or trustees; of receivers of corporations; of the guardians of infants; and of others acting in a fiduciary capacity. In all such cases the inventory is filed in court and becomes the basis of the accounting which the executor, assignee, or receiver must subsequently make before being discharged from liability. See EXECUTOR.

INVERARAY, royal burgh, county town, and port, Scotland, in Argyllshire, on the S shore of the bay where the Aray River enters Loch Fyne; 45 miles NW of Greenock and 51 miles NW of Glasgow. Near by is the 18th-century Inveraray Castle, seat of the dukes of Argyll. The town has a herring fishery. Pop. about 500.

INVERCARGILL, port, New Zealand, South Island, Otago Provincial District, seat of Southland County, on the S coast, 140 miles by rail WSW of Dunedin. The town is on an estuary named New River Harbor, which receives a number of famed trout streams. It is a deep and well-sheltered harbor, second in importance, however, to Bluff Harbor, to which there is connection by rail. Invercargill is a center of a prosperous dairying and farming district and has breweries, foundries, woolen mills, and sawmills. Pop. (1945) 23,470, including Maoris.

INVERELL, town, Australia, New South Wales, Gough County, situated on the W edge of a vast granite plateau, 341 miles by rail N of Sydney, on the Macintyre River. Inverell lies in the center of an agricultural district producing wheat, corn, sheep, dairy products, and cattle. Tin, silver, and diamonds are mined near by. The town became a municipality in 1872. Pop. (1947) 6,140.

INVERNESS, royal and large burgh and seaport, NW Scotland, country town of Inverness-shire, situated near the mouth of the Ness River, at the junction of the Beauly and Moray firths, and at the head of the Great Glen; 108 miles W of Aberdeen and 118 miles NW of Perth. It is called the "Capital of the Highlands," because of the beauty of its surrounding scenery and its position as an important northwest Scottish railway center and shipping port. The Caledonian Canal passes one mile west of the town, connecting it with inland and west coastal Scotland. Inverness is a large sheep and wool market. Its chief industries are shipbuilding, brewing, distilling, iron founding, and the manufacture of woolens and tweeds. There are also extensive tree nurseries, sawmills, and granite quarries. Features of interest include the St. Andrews Episcopal Cathedral; Castle Wynd, built in 1835 on the site of an ancient fortress supposed to have belonged to Macbeth and

PHILIP GENDREAU
Inverness Castle overlooks historic drawbridge

now a museum of Jacobean relics; Crowell's Fort (1652); the house where Mary, Queen of Scots, lived in 1562; and the Royal Academy. The curiously shaped Hill of Tomnahurich has been laid out as a cemetery.

Inverness was the ancient capital of the Picts, and, until 1228, of the Mormaers of Moray, who maintained their independence of the Scottish kings. The town was then clustered about the Hill of Tomnahurich. The battle of Culloden Maor (1746) was fought here. Pop. (1950 est.) 28,400.   K. E. H.

INVERNESS-SHIRE, maritime county, N central Scotland, largest of the Highland counties, bounded on the N by Beauly and Moray firths and Ross and Cromarty; E by Nairn, Moray, Banff, and Aberdeen; S by Perth, Argyll; W by the Atlantic and islands of the Inner and Outer HEBRIDES; area 4,383 sq. mi.; pop. (1950 est.) 88,500. The island section comprises in the two groups of the Hebrides (with the exception of Lewis) one-third of the shire's land area. The surface of the shire is generally mountainous, counting among its lofty summits Ben Nevis (4,406 ft.), Great Britain's highest peak; Ben Alder (3,757 ft.); the Cairngorm Mountains (4,084 ft.); and the Monadhliath Range (3,093 ft.). Inverness-shire has many of Scotland's most famous glens, including Urquehart, Nevis, Garry, Coe, Desdarry, Finnan, Cannich, Moriston, Roy, and Spean. Their wild and scenic beauty and extensive deer forests are preserved as national parks. The more important lakes of the county are Lochs Ness, Oich, and Lochy, which connect the course of the Caledonian Canal, a waterway dividing the shire almost exactly in half. The Great Glen, or Glen More, follows this canal southwest from Moray Firth to the sea loch, Linnhe. Other lakes are Mullardock, Beinn, Affric, Garry, Quoich, Arkaig, Moror, Monar, Shiel, and Frisa on Mull, lying northwest of the canal; and on the south and east side are Lochs Dunna, Laggan, Lush, Ruthven, Morlich, Ericht, Treig, Ossian, and Leven. Sea lochs indenting the coastline are the Beauly Basin on the northeast and Hourn, Nevis, Arisaig, Sunart, Line, Linnhe, Lorn, and Leven on the west coast. The principal rivers are the Beauly, Lochy, Farrar, Glass, Ericht, Ness, Nairn, Spey, Findhorn, Moriston, Spean, Nevis, and Leven. Because of the shire's rugged surface only about 5 per cent of the land is under cultivation; the chief crops are oats, barley, wheat, turnips, and potatoes. Great flocks of Cheviot sheep and a shaggy breed of horned cattle are raised in the highlands. Slate and granite are quarried and a valuable variety of smoky quartz, used for jewelry, is found in the Cairngorm Mountains. Herring fisheries head the list of industries, followed by brewing, distilling, wool and flax spinning, the manufacture of tweeds and chemicals, and sawmills. The chief towns of the mainland are Inverness, the county town, Fort William, Kinlochleven, and Spean Bridge; all three are ports.   K. E. H.

INVERT SUGAR. See SUGAR.

INVERTASE, INVERTIN, or **SUCRASE,** an unorganized ferment or enzyme, which inverts sugars of the higher orders to lower forms; as in the inverting of cane sugar ($C_{12}H_{22}O_{11}$) into dextrose (grape sugar, $C_6H_{12}O_6$) and fructose (fruit sugar, $C_6H_{12}O_6$). Invertase occurs in yeasts and other fungi, and in some of the animal digestive fluids. See FERMENTATION; DEXTROSE; FRUCTOSE.

INVERTEBRATES comprise all those animals not possessing a vertebral or spinal column (vertebrates) and hence include all animals except fishes, amphibians, reptiles, birds, and mammals. The invertebrates constitute a heterogeneous assemblage of animals that includes about 95 per cent of all known animal species. See ANIMAL LIFE.

The chief divisions of invertebrates are the Protozoa, unicellular species usually of microscopic dimensions, the Parazoa, multicellular animals called sponges, which have only a low degree of tissue differentiation and of organismic integration, and the Enterozoa, multicellular animals with differentiation of organs and organ systems (digestive, nervous, reproductive, etc.) having a high degree of organismic unity. The principal groups of the Enterozoa, the last and largest division, are the following: Coelenterates (jellyfishes, corals); Ctenophores (comb jellies); Platyhelminthes (unsegmented flatworms); Nemathelminthes (unsegmented roundworms, rotifers); Tentaculata (moss-animals, lampshells); Mollusca (snails, clams, octopus); Annelida (segmented worms); Arthropoda (crustaceans, insects, spiders); Echinodermata (starfishes, sea urchins, sea cucumbers); and some of the Chordata (balanoglossids, sea squirts).

FRANK A. BROWN

BIBLIOG.–L. A. Borradaile and F. A. Potts, *The Invertebrata* (1936); L. Hyman, *The Invertebrates. Protozoa through Ctenophora* (1940).

INVESTITURE, a juridical term of the feudal age, meaning an act on the part of a suzerain investing a vassal with land or office. In line with various traditions the suzerain presented the vassal with a clod, banner, branch or other suitable symbol after receiving the vassal's oath of fealty. The term is mainly used as investiture of clerics with their offices.

The question as to whether the worldly powers or the church were entitled to exercise this right of investiture led to one of the main conflicts of the Medieval Ages. The struggle between Papacy and Empire was fought over this right. In the beginning of the medieval ages the church had at least tolerated the king's right to confirmation of promotions within the ranks of the church. This tendency became even more pronounced under the reign of Charlemagne. In this respect as in so many others the great emperor tried to assert the supremacy of the imperial powers.

The question became more important under the reign of the Ottones (912–1002). The German emperors were faced with the growing power of their vassals who had succeeded in establishing the right of succession to their domains. A way to avoid the creation of rivaling dynasties offered itself by vesting fiefs in the hands of ecclesiastics. The emperor's hold seemed assured as long as the fief automatically returned into his hands for arbitrary disposition after the death of the vassal. No hereditary rights interfered with such welcome vacancies in the case of the celibate man of the church. Thus the emperors bestowed large grants of land upon archbishops, bishops and abbots. In its turn the church had become land owner in its own right by gifts of estates received from the faithful from early times. As long as the emperor retained the last word in the promotion of the clergy by exercising the right of investiture he retained supreme power over a very important sector of medieval life. The emperors misused this right greatly. Benefices were kept vacant for long periods in an attempt to increase the suzerain's income. Simony became fairly common and persons without any qualifications were promoted and installed in high church offices. See HOLY ROMAN EMPIRE.

The reform movement within the church which had its early center in the monastery of Cluny attacked these practices bitterly during the 10th century. It took a long time, however, until these reformist forces within the church were able to elect their candidate Hildebrand as Pope GREGORY VII (1073–1085). He forcefully tried to establish the principle that it was the pope's exclusive privilege to confirm promotions within the rank of the church. His famous decrees of 1075 and 1078 declared that investiture by laymen was a sacrilege punishable with excommunication of the ecclesiastic accepting and the layman bestowing it. Likewise the assent of the pope or archbishop became necessary for any investiture of laymen with ecclesiastical property. The ensuing fight between Gregory VII and the German Emperor HENRY IV over the validity of these decrees forms one of the most dramatic chapters of medieval history.

The struggle between Emperor and Papacy continued for two more centuries. But the question of investiture was brought to an end by the Concordat of Worms (1122). Its decisions were ratified for the church by the General Lateran Council of 1123. By the terms of this concordat the emperor recognized the church's privilege to free promotions and elections and finally renounced his right to investiture with ring and crozier (spiritual investiture). But he retained a right of confirmation by being confirmed in his right to confer the "regalia" through investiture by the touch of the scepter (temporal investiture). This right became a pure formality in Italy and Burgundy. However, for Germany the concordat specifically established the principle that the imperial investiture had to precede the Papal investiture and thus permitted the emperor to influence strongly the church's decisions on promotions within Germany. See FEUDAL SOCIETY; TENURE; KNIGHT AND KNIGHTHOOD; MANORIAL SYSTEM; PAPACY; FIEF.

FRANK POLLACZEK

INVESTMENT is the employment of capital in the expectation of INCOME and PROFIT. A broad interpretation of the term may include such things as the purchase of an education which will increase the future earning power of the individual or the purchase of durable consumer goods which will yield a psychological rather than a monetary return. In the great field of investment made up by the country's some 16,000 banks, insurance companies, investment companies, and building and loan associations, however, investment is measured solely in terms of money and the requirements are precise, demanding that the investment preserve the money invested, produce an income for the investor, and perform a social service.

Social Value. The importance of investment to society is that it increases the nation's capital and income-producing power. In any community where more is produced than is consumed there results a supply of surplus funds or savings. Through the investment process savings are placed in the hands of those elements of society which can best use them in the production of more capital and capital equipment. Thus individual investors, who provide a large part of the capital used by industry and government, corporations putting profits into expanded producing power, and the government, when it puts taxation funds into public works and other productive uses, all perform a service to the community.

The total of all investments made in any given year cannot be greater than the total amount of money saved by individuals and institutions during that year, for investment can only be made with that portion of the national income which exceeds the national expenditure on current consumption. In practice, however, total investment is less than total savings, since some saving, such as hoarding, takes place which cannot be considered investment. Hoarding meets only one of the three requirements of an investment: it preserves, but it neither produces nor accumulates. In times of depression fear may cause individuals to withhold their savings from the investment market, thus preventing any addition to productive equipment and adding to the general business slump, since in an industrialized capitalistic society a free flow of investment is essential to prosperity.

Investment and Risk. A certain degree of risk is present in all investment. In an absolute sense no investment is completely safe, although from a practical standpoint such securities as United States government obligations may be thoroughly relied upon. Investment is commonly associated with the idea of safety, however, and when the risk factor is high the investment is termed a speculation. One invests in a high grade bond for the secure and fixed rate of interest plus the promised return of the original amount of capital on a specified maturity date. If one seeks capital gain and more than the prevailing rate of return he speculates.

The technique of making a safe investment has become more complex with each passing year because of the vast amount of information which must be assembled and studied in order to determine the merit, legality, and qualifications of a given security in regard to stated investment objectives. In an advanced industrial society investments are in large degree carried on through the medias of the investment bank and the stock exchange. Here organized markets exist where through the intermediary of brokers, owners of stocks and bonds are brought into contact with the investor whenever it becomes desirable to effect a sale. This greatly facilitates the flow of investment, although it tends to remove the investor from any control over the use to which his money is put once it is invested.

Government Regulations. Although the average individual is free to invest as he pleases, institutional investors and others with fiduciary responsibilities are subject to rigid restrictions in the making of investments. The Investment Advisers Act of 1940 provides for the registration and regulation of investment com-

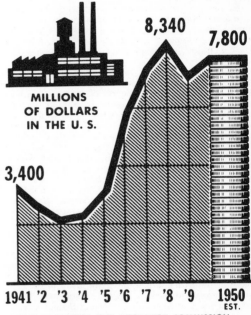

MILLIONS OF DOLLARS IN THE U. S.

8,340   7,800   3,400

1941 '2 '3 '4 '5 '6 '7 '8 '9   1950 EST.

SOURCE: SECURITIES AND EXCHANGE COMMISSION

Expenditures on new plant and equipment

panies and investment advisers, and in an effort to protect the public from tipsters and fraudulent stock promoters, forbids investment advisers and counselors to make use of the mails unless registered with the SECURITIES AND EXCHANGE COMMISSION. Extensive restrictions are placed on the operations of investment trusts, which solicit large sums of money from the public and reinvest the funds under the guidance of professional managers.

Criteria of Good Investment. From the individual investor's point of view, safety and the earning power of the assets back of his investment are of first consideration. For many years loans, in the form of well-secured corporation bonds and notes, formed the great bulk of investments. They were called the "top slice of value," and if they did not pay the specified interest the property pledged as security could be sold for the benefit of the investor. Certain stocks of well-established businesses were also considered investments. But for the most part stocks were considered largely as employment for venture capital since they did not yield as dependably as bonds.

In recent years certain factors growing out of the

depression, taxation, and governmental fiscal policies have greatly complicated the problem of determining sound investment policies. Interest rates have declined during the last half century to relatively low levels, so that the modest investor has turned to stocks for a larger portion of his investments in the hope of gaining greater income. Wealthy investors have been driven to very low-yield state and municipal bonds to avoid in some measure the Federal income tax. Investors in urban real estate have been deterred by the government regulation of rents, and farm land has been held at too high a price to attract conservative investors.

For the uninformed investor the first consideration in any investment is the avoidance of risks and the safety of principal. Such factors as age, present income, prospective earning capacity, and outside sources of income are important in determining any individual's investment program. Savings accounts, life insurance, and annuities, when handled by reliable firms, are excellent investments for the inexperienced investor or the individual who wants to be assured of a steady income.

In the field of securities government, state, and municipal bonds rank among the safest investments, their security resting upon the government power of taxation. Next come first mortgage bonds, followed by debentures, preferred stock, and common stock. Investment in stocks should follow a program of diversification, both as to types of products and geographic distribution, so as to insure the investor the maximum of safety. Records of previous earnings and the reputation of the company should be considered in choosing a bond or stock, as well as the marketability of the security itself. Real estate mortgages are one of the most important groups of private investments in the United States, although they are generally lacking in the marketability factor. A new business is an extremely dangerous risk as is land-purchase speculation. Buying securities on tips from persons whose reliability and experience is not fully known is only gambling. See INVESTMENT BANKING; SAVINGS; BUSINESS CYCLE; CAPITAL; INTEREST; STOCK; BOND; CREDIT.   C. F.

INVESTMENT BANKING is distinguished from commercial banking in that the former is primarily concerned with long term fixed capital loans, whereas the latter generally specializes in short term working capital loans. During the period of capital development in the 19th century these two forms of banking were often performed by a single institution. However, in the United States and Great Britain a tendency to specialize arose along with increasing capital expansion in these countries, until the two branches have become fairly well separated.

Functions. Since the passage of the Securities Act of 1933 it has been illegal in the United States for a commercial bank to undertake investment banking operations. In continental Europe banks still generally perform both investment and commercial banking functions. The chief business of the investment banker is the raising of relatively permanent funds to be used as fixed capital in business organizations, and to provide deficit financing for governments. The prospective borrower usually requires large sums which are only available in the widely distributed funds of numerous small savers. The most important function of the investment banker is the formation of this capital into an accessible fund. He is the middleman who operates between the lender and the borrower of savings, using securities as his stock in trade. Thus investment banking is primarily a merchandising business through which stocks and bonds are distributed and savings flow into permanent capital resources.

There are several classifications of investment bankers: first of all, the large houses which originate security issues; secondly, large retailers who distribute the securities; and finally, small retailers or dealers who sell the securities to the ultimate holder, the saver. Large houses often perform several of these operations, but in the usual case a syndicate consisting of all classes of investment bankers is formed to buy and dispose of a given issue.

Procedures. When a business organization is in need of capital for expansion, for the refunding of current debts, or for reorganization of its capital structure, it calls in an originating investment bank. This bank carefully analyzes the company, its probable earnings, and the collateral behind the proposed issue, and, if it finds everything acceptable, makes an offer to buy the issue at a certain price. If the issue is very large, other houses will be called in to assist in the purchase, thus sharing the risk and also providing the machinery for more rapid distribution to the investor.

Theoretically the issue is sold to the bank making the highest bid. Actually, however, the general practice is for a firm to deal continuously with a particular banking house so long as it receives satisfaction. The advantage in this is that continued close relationship between the borrower and his bank puts the latter in a much better position from which to advise the former and to judge properly any proposed security issue. The disadvantage lies in the fact that the borrower often receives a lower price for the issue than he would otherwise under a system of competitive bidding.

Because of the large scale of modern securities operations, it is seldom that one house is able to assume the responsibility for buying and selling an entire issue. Consequently syndicates are usually formed to share the risk and also to widen and hasten the final distribution. Generally the house of origin provides the management for the issue. The purchase group first takes over the securities. Then they are turned over to a second group called the banking group, which includes the purchase group and also other houses which have large retail facilities. Finally a selling group, composed of the above groups and also numerous small dealers scattered across the entire country, distribute the securities to the ultimate purchasers. Because of the banker's close operating margin, usually two or three points, and the fluctuations of the securities market, the risk in handling an issue increases with the length of time it remains unsold, necessitating this elaborate organization to obtain speed in selling, as well as to secure wide and permanent distribution. The final sale to the investor is accomplished by mail-order methods and by direct personal salesmanship, assisted by wise advertising.

Each operation of the syndicate earns a percentage of the "spread," the difference between the buying and selling prices, for the amount of the issue handled. If the issue remains partly unsold the selling group is usually free of all liability to buy the unsold securities, that liability falling back upon the preceding banking group, depending of course upon the actual terms of the formal syndicate agreement.

Occasionally the investment banker acts purely as an underwriter. This usually occurs when the issue is first offered only to stockholders rather than to the general public. The underwriting syndicate guarantees, at a given price, the purchase of all unsubscribed securities, and in return for this guarantee obtains a commission based on a flat rate for the entire issue.

Secondary Services of Investment Banks. While performing his primary function, the formation of capital, the investment banker also performs other protective and advisory services for both the borrowing corporation and the investor. These are (1) the maintenance of a market for the security, (2) advice to the borrower, (3) advice to the investor, and (4) protection of the investor while holding the security. The investor would have little interest in a stock or bond if he were unable to sell it if necessary. Consequently he looks to the investment banker to provide a market for the security. During its life a syndicate maintains a fixed bid for the security in order to uphold its market. After the syndicate is dissolved the security is allowed to seek its own price level, but the house of origin occasionally purchases it at request or in the open market in order to protect the investor.

The investment banker feels a responsibility toward the investor, since in the usual case the small investor relies almost entirely upon his banker's judgment when purchasing a security. Therefore he undertakes the moral responsibility of protecting the investor. As stated above he occasionally repurchases securities when absolutely necessary to protect his business reputation; but more often, he is instrumental in forming protective committees and in planning a reorganization of the corporation if the corporation fails to meet its obligations on the security issue.

Legal Regulation. Because of the importance of the investment banker in a capitalistic economy, he is subject to some degree of public control. Both state and Federal legislation attempt to protect the investor from fraud. In 1911, Kansas passed the first BLUE-SKY LAW, requiring that investment bankers be licensed, and that securities be fully qualified. Most other states followed with similar laws. In New York, legislation took the form of an antifraud act, authorizing the attorney general to obtain an injunction if fraudulent practices are suspected. The Securities Act of 1933 requires that the investor be fully informed of the issue and of the financial history and condition of the issuing corporation, thus relying on this information and the rule of *caveat emptor* to protect the prospective buyer. It also attempts to control the security by requiring its registration with the Securities Exchange Commission 20 days before it is offered for sale. If the registration statement is found fraudulent or misleading, the security is denied selling privileges. See BANKS AND BANKING; BOND; INVESTMENT; SAVINGS BANK.   I. H.

BIBLIOG.—H. Parkinson, *Scientific Investment* (1946); J. P. Allison, *Investors' Tax Planning* (1946); H. G. Carpenter, *This is Investment Management* (1946); J. R. Rood, *Family Security* (1946); R. C. Effinger, *ABC of Investing* (1947); L. V. Chandler, *Economics of Money and Banking* (1948); J. M. Peterson and D. R. Cawthorne, *Money and Banking* (ed. 1949); L. G. Whyte, *Principles of Finance and Investment* (1950).

INVESTMENT, FOREIGN. See INTERNATIONAL FINANCE.

INVISIBLE INK. See INK.

INVOLUCRE, a group or circle of bracts surrounding a single flower, a flower cluster, or a head of flowers. Involucres are particularly characteristic of such plants as daisies, chrysanthemums, and sunflowers.

INVOLUNTARY BEHAVIOR may be either random or purposive (but irrational), instinctive or habitual (acquired), unconscious or conscious (if irrational), normally adjustive or compensatory and rationalized. Its essential characteristic is that it is not the result of previous planning. Random behavior in infants is the raw material from which most matured behavior patterns are constructed by conditioning. Instinctive behavior is confined chiefly to visceral functioning. Habituation is an economical reduction of behavior to involuntary responses. Normal involuntary behavior is confined chiefly to instincts and socially approved habits and is distinguished from abnormal involuntary behavior chiefly by being socially accepted, although elements of irrationality may enter into it. Involuntary behavior may be definitely conscious when it is motivated by either socially approved or disapproved impulsions. Compensatory or rationalized involuntary behavior is essentially neurotic or psychotic and arises from the need to escape from maladjustment.   L. L. BERNARD

BIBLIOG.—K. Young, *Source Book for Social Psychology* (1927).

INVOLUTE. See CURVE.

INVOLUTION AND EVOLUTION, in mathematics, are the two *inverse operations* of raising numbers to *powers* and extracting the *roots* of numbers. For example, the third power of the cube root of 8 is the number 8; the two operations, extracting the cube root and then raising the root to the third power, exactly cancel each other. In general, the nth power of the nth root of any number k is k itself; in symbols, $(\sqrt[n]{k})n = k^{n/n} = k$ (see EXPONENT). If k is any positive integer, there is only one nth power of a number k, but there are always n different nth roots of k. See POWER AND ROOT.

INVOLUTIONAL MELANCHOLIA, a psychosis appearing at the time of the waning of the sexual function, in women generally between 40 and 55, in men between 50 and 65. Typical cases are depressed, fearful, agitated, self-accusatory, and may have delusions about their physical conditions. Many cases also show schizophrenic symptomatology.

J. KEPECS

INYOKERN, town, S California, in Kern County, on the Southern Pacific Railroad; about 75 miles ENE of Bakersfield. Inyokern is situated in the flat Indian Wells Valley west of Death Valley National Monument. A Naval Ordnance Testing Station is located here. Pop. (1950) 264.

IO, in greek legend the daughter of Inachus, first king of Argos. She was beloved by Zeus, whose wife, Hera, in jealousy, turned her into a heifer, and set the hundred-eyed Argus to watch her; but the latter was slain by Hermes at the command of Zeus. Hera then sent a gadfly to torment Io, which drove her from land to land, until she reached Egypt, where she regained her true shape, and bore a son, Epaphus. According to the tradition, the Bosporus (which means Oxford) got its name from her crossing it. Io appears to be identical with the moon goddess. The fullest account of her wanderings is given in Aeschylus' *Prometheus Vinctus*.

IOÁNNINA. See EPIRUS.

IOÁNNINA, also **Janina,** or **Yanina,** town and episcopal see, NW Greece, Epirus Division, capital of Ioánnina Department; 80 miles W of Lárisa, 44 miles N of Arta. It is a picturesque town not far from the Albanian frontier, built at the foot of Mount Mitzekeli (1,500 ft.), on Lake Ioánnina (ancient Pambotus). Most of its ancient Byzantine buildings and fortifications, including the fortress, are now in ruins. Manufactures include gold and silver ware, gold and silver embroideries, and silk goods and textiles. The town fell into the hands of the Turks in the 15th century, and from 1788 to 1818 was a stronghold of Ali Pasha. During the Balkan War of 1912–13 it was captured by the Greeks, and by the treaties of London and Bucharest, was ceded to Greece. In World War II the town and district were annexed, with Albania, by the Italians in 1941, but were liberated in 1944 by English troops. The mountainous region around Ioánnina was the scene of recurrent fighting between government troops and guerrilla forces in the political unrest within Greece following the war's end. Pop. (1950 est.) 20,000.

IODIC ACID is a white, crystalline, water-soluble solid obtained by the oxidation of IODINE with hot concentrated nitric acid. It has the formula HIO_3. Sodium iodate, the most important salt of iodic acid, occurs in Chilean *caliche*, mixed with sodium nitrate, and is used to prepare iodine. When iodic acid is heated, it changes into water and iodine pentoxide, I_2O_5. A mixture of the latter compound and sulfuric acid on pumice stone (called hoolamite) will absorb poisonous carbon monoxide gas, changing to a green color as it does so. This is a sensitive test for carbon monoxide.

IODINE is a nonmetallic element of the halogen group. It occurs sparingly in the form of iodides, chiefly of sodium, in sea water, from which it is assimilated by SEAWEEDS. Those growing below low-water mark (such as *Laminaria digitata* and *L. stenophylla*) contain the most—up to about 0.5 per cent. About 12 pounds of iodine can be extracted from a

Iodine goes through blowing-out process in this tower, emerging in a granular or crystallized form

ton of seaweed, which when dried and charred yields an ash containing sodium iodide. The latter is heated with manganese dioxide and sulfuric acid to produce iodine. Iodine is chiefly prepared, however, as a by-product in the purification of Chile saltpeter (sodium nitrate), or caliche, in which it occurs as sodium iodate, averaging 1 part of iodine to 1,000 parts of sodium nitrate. In the preparation from caliche, the mother liquors, from which the sodium nitrate has as far as possible been separated by crystallization, and which contain about 20 per cent of sodium iodate, are heated with sodium bisulfite. As a result, iodine is set free, and separates in the solid form. This is washed, pressed, dried, and purified by sublimation. More iodine can be prepared from caliche than there is a demand for; hence the price is maintained by limiting the output. Exports from Chile before World War II averaged 500–600 tons per year, one-half to two-thirds of which went to the United States. Iodine is now obtained in considerable quantities from the oil-well brines of Louisiana, California, and Japan.

Properties. Iodine is a lustrous, grayish-black crystalline solid of specific gravity 4.95. The symbol for iodine is I. It has an atomic weight of 126.92 and its atomic number is 53. Iodine was discovered by Courtois in 1811. It volatilizes at ordinary temperatures into a blue-violet gas with a very irritating

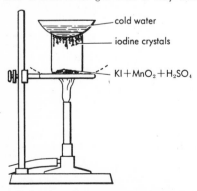

cold water

iodine crystals

$KI + MnO_2 + H_2SO_4$

Laboratory preparation of iodine

smell. At ordinary atmospheric pressure iodine sublimes without melting; but under slightly greater pressures it melts at 114° C., and boils at 184° C. It is not easily soluble in water, but dissolves readily in alcohol and freely in a solution of potassium iodide, forming a brown solution in each case. Iodine also dissolves freely in carbon disulfide, chloroform, ether, and glycerin, in which solvents the solution is purple. Iodine is less active chemically than the other halogens. Thus, though it readily unites with many metals, phosphorus, etc., it combines only in part with hydrogen when heated with it. Iodine has little or no action on hydrocarbons, and is a weak bleaching agent. It stains the skin a brownish-yellow, and is easily recognized by the intense blue color it gives with a cold cream of half-boiled starch.

Industrial Uses. Iodine is used in the preparation of its compounds, and in the manufacture of coal-tar dyes, drugs, and many other organic compounds. IODOFORM, CHI_3, is used as an antiseptic. Silver iodide, AgI, is used in PHOTOGRAPHY. Iodine is also employed to stimulate the growth of certain plants.

Iodine is absorbed by unsaturated fatty acids and glycerides. (See OIL.) The determination of the amount of iodine absorbed by 100 grams of an oil or fat (*iodine number*) is useful in ascertaining the per cent of unsaturated fatty acids or glycerides present. This value also aids in identifying oils and fats. Iodine is also used in volumetric chemical analysis. A standard solution of it is employed as an oxidizing agent in the quantitative determination of many reducing agents. These processes are called "iodimetry."   E. M. W.

MEDICAL USES

Iodine and iodine compounds are widely used in medicine. Iodine and the inorganic iodides are rapidly absorbed from the alimentary tract and are promptly excreted in the urine. Some of the organic iodides, however, are absorbed slowly and with difficulty, and hence their elimination may be delayed.

Antiseptic Action. Iodine in 1.5–3.0 per cent alcoholic solution (*tincture of iodine*) is an effective antiseptic, and is used to sterilize the site of an incision on the skin before a surgical operation. Iodine was at one time extensively used also to disinfect wounds. But its action is due to protein precipitation, which makes it so irritating that it may do more harm than good, tending to produce smarting, inflammation, blisters, and sometimes even corrosion. In fungus infections, such as chronic infestations by the ray fungus (actinomycosis) and other similar FUNGUS DISEASES such as blastomycosis and sporotrichosis, internal administration of tincture of iodine in milk, or of large doses of sodium or potassium iodide, is beneficial and often curative.

Chemotherapeutic Action. It is the belief of some of the most eminent authorities in the field that the iodine compounds are generally the most efficient and the safest therapeutic agents for the elimination of amebiasis (see DYSENTERY, *Amebic*). CHINIOFON, *diodoquin*, *vioform*, and *enterovioform* have a direct action on the ameba in the intestine, which depends on the iodine content of the drug. In over 90 per cent of cases with uncomplicated amebiasis recovery and permanent disappearance of the organism from the stools occurs after one course of treatment with these drugs. In countries where amebiasis is endemic these drugs may also be used as prophylactic agents. Their general toxicity is almost nil, partly because they are difficultly, if at all, absorbed from the intestinal tract.

Lytic Action of Iodine Compounds. It has been observed that low-grade, inflammatory lesions and exudates take up more iodine than normal tissues, and then are dissolved and finally absorbed. This lytic action on pathological tissues may be related to the well-known effect of sodium iodide in preventing a gelatin solution from setting. For their lytic action iodine compounds are prescribed in late syphilis, where they dissolve granulomatous, devitalized tissue, exposing the contained germs to effective antisyphilitic agents (arsenicals, bismuth, penicillin). Iodine compounds are, however, contraindicated in tuberculosis; they break down the tuberculosis lesions, but because no safe antitubercular agent has yet been discovered, the bacilli are freed to spread the infection.

Relation to the Thyroid. Iodine is indispensable for the normal functioning of the THYROID GLAND. The human thyroid contains about 15 milligrams of iodine, about 65 per cent of it combined in its hormone, thyroxine. Without adequate iodine intake the thyroid becomes abnormal and diseased, and most of the iodine ingested in the food goes to the thyroid for synthesis of the hormone. It can be demonstrated by means of administration of radioactive iodine that within 24 hours about one-half of the amount given is taken up by the thyroid. Iodine is thus unique among the elements in that it is vitally important and has special affinity for one particular organ in the body.

Iodine for Goiter. In areas where the soil is deficient in iodine, as in the Austrian Tyrol, in Switzerland, and in the Great Lakes region and the upper Mississippi Valley, large, but not overactive, thyroid glands are common. These are the so-called simple GOITERS. In these "goiter belts" steps have been taken to make iodine generally available by putting very small amounts of sodium iodide into the table salt (*iodized salt*) or by placing solutions containing iodine in public school classrooms so that iodine vapors may be inhaled by the children. The development of large thyroids can be prevented by the daily administration of as little as one milligram of iodine per day. Such small doses have little therapeutic effect once the goiter has become fully developed. In this event the administration of larger doses of iodine often reduces the size of the goiter.

Iodine may also be used in the treatment of toxic or exophthalmic goiter (Graves' disease). In this disease iodine medication produces a marked but temporary improvement, and the metabolic rate falls from an initial high level to normal. The action of iodine is probably the inhibition of thyroid hormone synthesis by the cells of the gland. It has no effect upon the iodine-concentrating action of the thyroid. The resulting decrease in thyroid hormone in the blood lowers the metabolic rate, reduces the heart rate, and lessens nervous irritability. Since this action is short-lasting, iodine is employed chiefly as a diagnostic agent and in preparing the patient for surgical removal of the thyroid. It improves the patient's chances as a surgical risk.

Iodine Compounds as Diagnostic Aids. Iodized oils, sodium iodide, and a large number of organic iodine compounds are satisfactory *contrast media*, i.e., radio-opaque substances. Their presence enables soft tissues to cast shadows on the x-ray plate. In this way it is possible to diagnose abnormalities of the bronchial tree, blood vessels, gallbladder, kidneys, genital and urinary passages, and other structures otherwise invisible. Iodized oils are used to visualize the respiratory organs and the uterus, while water-soluble iodine compounds, such as DIODRAST, *hippuran*, *neoiopax*, and *skiodan* are used for examination of the kidneys, the ureters, and the bladder. A concentrated diodrast solution may also be employed for the visualization of the heart and main blood vessels following intravenous injection. *Sodium phenoltetraiodophthalein* is used for the visualization of the gallbladder and also as a test for liver function.

Radioactive Iodine, from the fission of uranium (I-131) or from the bombardment or tellurium with deuterons (I-125 or I-132), is used as a tracer element in the study of the physiology of iodine and the thyroid hormone. It is also used in the treatment of some cases of toxic goiter and cancer of the thyroid. Since iodine is collected and then concentrated by thy-

roid tissue, the radioactive element is thus accurately placed in a position where it can destroy overactive or cancerous gland cells.

Iodine Poisoning. Iodine poisoning with suicidal or criminal intent is now exceedingly rare. Tincture of iodine taken by mouth acts as an irritant poison; pain beginning in the mouth follows its passage down the alimentary canal. Subsequently there is vomiting, purging, extreme thirst, dizziness, fainting attacks, and collapse. Iodine is excreted by way of the kidneys, and may cause a suppression of urine. Treatment should start at once, and should include use of a stomach pump or EMETICS, and administration of large quantities of starch water, which may be given in a decoction of ordinary laundry starch.

Chronic iodine poisoning, commonly referred to as *iodism*, is a result of daily administration of large doses of iodine compounds. Symptoms resemble those of a common cold and of skin affections such as acne, hives, and boils. These symptoms may or may not be accompanied by a slight fever. They disappear rather promptly when the medication is discontinued. Long-continued administration of iodides may lead to emaciation, restlessness, sleeplessness, mental depression, and even anemia.   THEODORE KOPPANYI

IODOFORM is a pale yellow, crystalline solid having a strong, characteristic odor. It is almost insoluble in water, but dissolves in alcohol, ether, and many other organic solvents. Chemically, iodoform is tri-iodomethane and has the formula CHI_3. It may be prepared by the electrolysis of alkaline solutions of iodides containing ethyl alcohol or acetone, or by the action of IODINE and sodium hydroxide on ethyl alcohol or acetone. The latter reaction is sometimes used to test solutions for the presence of ethyl alcohol ("iodoform test").

Iodoform may be used as a mild antiseptic and analgesic on open wounds, either in an ointment or as a dusting powder. Injections of an oil suspension have been used to treat tubercular joints. It is toxic when swallowed.

IODOGORGOIC ACID. See AMINO ACIDS.

IOLA, city, SE Kansas, county seat of Allen County; on the Neosho River, the Missouri Pacific, the Santa Fe, and the Missouri-Kansas-Texas railroads and U.S. highways 54, 59, and 169, near the Missouri border, about 40 miles W of Fort Scott, in an agricultural region. The city was founded in 1859 by Kansans who disapproved of the location of the county seat at Humboldt. Iola became the county seat in 1865, and was chartered as a city in 1870. The discovery of natural gas in the late 1890's caused great expansion until the 1920's when the diminishing supply of gas caused some industries to close. Iola is a farm-trading center; has a milk condensery, and manufactures creamery products, clothing, cement, and brick. Pop. (1950) 7,094.

IOLITE. See CORDIERITE.

ION. Ions are electrically charged particles of molecular or atomic size. They were named by Faraday from the Greek *ιον* meaning "going" because of the fact that they move to the positive (anode) and negative (cathode) poles in an electrolytic cell. Positively charged ions go to the cathode and are called cations; negatively charged ions go to the anode and are called anions.

Ions may originate from atoms of elements by the transfer of an electron or electrons (see ATOMIC THEORY). When metallic sodium and chlorine, each of which is electrically neutral, react with each other to form sodium chloride, the atom of sodium loses one electron and becomes positively charged thereby. This electron passes to the adjacent chlorine atom which becomes negatively charged. The two ions thus formed attract one another electrostatically and are held together in solid sodium chloride by this attractive force. This is characteristic of all salts.

Pure water has a high dielectric constant; that is, it is a good insulator. When a salt is dissolved in water, the water seems to have the power of weakening the attraction between the oppositely charged ions causing them to separate farther. Conversely, the removal of solvent by evaporation brings the ions closer together. This separation of ions is commonly called *ionization*. The ions in solution are free to move about through the liquid. See DISSOCIATION; SOLUTION.

Solutions containing ions can conduct the electric current and are called electrolytes. If an electric field is present, the ions will move toward the electrodes of opposite charge (see ELECTROLYSIS). Solvents other than water, having relatively high dielectric constants, e.g., liquid ammonia, accomplish a similar separation of ions. High temperatures also weaken the attractive forces between ions. This explains why many molten substances are able to conduct the electric current.

The charge of the ion corresponds to its valence. Thus ferric nitrate, $Fe(NO_3)_3$ has the ions Fe^{+++} and $3 NO_3^-$; cupric sulfate, $CuSO_4$, has Cu^{++} and SO_4^{--}; potassium chloride, KCl, has K^+ and Cl^-. In the case of the $Fe(NO_3)_3$, one atom of Fe has lost three electrons to the three NO_3 groups. Such groups as NO_3 or SO_4 cannot exist in the absence of the extra electrons. The properties of molecules are very different from those of the corresponding ions. Thus the chlorine molecule is a greenish gas and gives a greenish solution in water while the chloride ion is colorless.

Many substances are not ionized until they come in contact with the solvent. Such substances are held together by the sharing of electrons to form a connecting pair, as in the case of hydrogen chloride, $H:Cl$. When the HCl comes in contact with water, hydrogen splits off as H^+ to unite with a molecule of water, leaving its electron with the Cl to form the chloride (Cl^-) ion. The H^+ unites with water to form the hydronium ion, H_3O^+. This is the common behavior of ACIDS with water.

The "strength" of acids and their degree of conductivity depend upon how completely they react with water to form ions.

Many other compounds, such as sugar and glycerin, do not form ions even in water solution. Such solutions do not conduct the electric current and are known as nonelectrolytes.

It is also possible to cause elements to ionize by applying various forms of energy. Heat, ultraviolet light, x-rays, and the rays from radioactive substances may force the formation of small numbers of ions by causing electrons to be driven out of atoms or molecules. In a photoelectric cell sunlight falls on a thin surface of alkali metal such as potassium or cesium. This causes some of the metallic atoms to form ions, the electrons expelled by the light being sufficient to cause a flow of electricity. In radio tubes, the metallic filament is a source of electrons expelled during the ionization of the metal by the high voltage and by its heat.

Gaseous elements may become ionized by the same means. When a high tension current is sent through a partially evacuated tube ions are always formed (see VACUUM TUBE). If these ions and their electrons are allowed to recombine, energy in the form of light is emitted. The illumination of neon tubes is produced in this manner (see LAMP, ELECTRIC). Resolution of the light emitted into different wave lengths produces spectra, characteristic of the atoms, molecules, and ions of elements present in the tube. The atmosphere of the sun has been found, by spectrographic analysis, to consist essentially of the same elements found on the earth. See BRÖNSTED THEORY; SPECTRUM; ION EXCHANGE.   P. A. BOND

ION EXCHANGE, a reaction in chemistry in which undesirable ions are removed from solution usually by an interchange with other ions. (See ION.) The most important practical application of the principle of ion exchange is in water softening. Hard water contains calcium or magnesium ions which react with soap to form insoluble curds, thereby inhibiting the cleansing process.

In Water Softening, ZEOLITES, which are complex silicates of aluminum and the alkali metals, exchange their sodium or potassium ions for the calcium or magnesium ions in hard water forming insoluble calcium or magnesium compounds. A typical zeolite with the formula

$$Na_2O \cdot Al_2O_3 \cdot 2 SiO_2 \cdot 3H_2O,$$

which may be abbreviated to Na_2Z, in contact with a hard water containing calcium or magnesium salts reacts for example as follows:

$$Na_2Z + CaSO_4 \rightarrow Na_2SO_4 + CaZ.$$

The net result is a softening of the water. The zeolite reaction is reversible so that brief contact of the calcium saturated zeolite with a strong sodium chloride brine, followed with a back wash with pure water, results in the regeneration of the mineral to its original condition. It is then ready for another softening period.

$$CaZ + 2NaCl \rightarrow CaCl_2 + Na_2Z.$$

The only chemical agent used in reversing the action is common salt.

A new development of the ion exchange principle, known as two-step demineralizing, makes possible the complete removal of dissolved salts from raw supplies containing chlorides, sulfates, or sodium bicarbonate. In the first stage or step, a cation exchanger (H_2Z) made by the sulfonation of organic substances such as coal, paper waste, or synthetic RESINS removes the metallic ions:

$$CaCl_2 + H_2Z \rightarrow CaZ + 2HCl.$$

On reaching saturation the CaZ mass may be regenerated by treatment with sulfuric acid. In the second step, the acid remaining in the water after the first treatment is taken up by a "deacidizer," which may be an amino derivative of a synthetic resin (R_3N), thus:

$$HCl + R_3N \rightarrow R_3N \cdot HCl.$$

On reaching its full capacity this agent in turn may be regenerated by treatment with sodium carbonate. De-ionized water is as pure as distilled water, though economically it cannot always compete with distillation, especially in cases of waters of high mineral content, such as sea brines. See HARD WATER, *Methods of Softening.*

Synthetic Resins. The synthesis in 1935 of resins with ion-exchange power has led to many new applications. Chemically analagous to bakelite, these synthetics include polyhydric phenol formaldehyde condensates (cation exchangers) and polyamine formaldehyde condensates such as Amberlite IR-4B (anion exchangers). Resins have been used to remove sodium ions from the body in the relief of edema due to high blood pressure, while palatable forms, taken by mouth, neutralize stomach acidity in cases of gastric ulcer. Resins are employed in recovering precious metals from solutions. A resin developed in World War II exchanged silver ions for the metal ions in sea water. The resulting silver chloride was insoluble, and could be filtered out, producing good drinking water. Alkaloids, such as quinine, are being recovered from extracts of low grade cinchona bark by the same principle. Resins are also employed to remove impurities or undesirable properties from foods. An example is the production of "soft curd milk" for infants by replacing calcium ion with sodium. A recent sugar refining process uses ion-exchangers to reclaim molasses that was formerly inedible. Through ion exchange in connection with the process of CHROMATOGRAPHY, it is possible to perform difficult chemical separations. Notable are separations of amino acids and of rare earths. Chemists can now prepare rare earth samples 99.99 per cent pure.   H. L. OLIN

BIBLIOG.–G. D. Norcom and K. W. Brown, *Water Purification for Plant Operators* (1942); F. C. Nachod, *Ion Exchange: Theory and Application* (1949); H. Kunin and R. J. Myers, *Ion Exchange Resins* (1950).

IONA, or **Icolmkill**, island, W central Scotland, Argyllshire, Inner Hebrides, lying SW of Mull and S of Staffa; area four sq. mi.; pop. about 150. In 563, St. Columba, with twelve of his disciples, landed here from Ireland. He founded a monastery, which was burned in 802 by invading Danes, but rebuilt in 812. St. Oran's chapel is believed to have been built in the 11th century by St. Margaret, wife of Malcolm Canmore. St. Martin's cross (dating from the ninth century), one of the few remaining sculptured stone crosses, stands near the 12th century abbey of St. Mary, and there are ruins of a Benedictine monastery, founded in 1203. To the southwest of the abbey is the "kings' burial place," containing the tombs of 48 Scotch kings, four Irish kings, and eight Danish monarchs. These ecclesiastical remains were bequeathed by the eighth duke of Argyll to the Church of Scotland, and in 1905 the restored cathedral was reopened for public service. The inhabitants engage in marble quarrying; fishing; raising cattle, sheep, and horses; and farming. Crops include oats, potatoes, and barley. World War II interrupted a program to restore many of the ancient buildings of Iona; the project was resumed in 1947.

IONIA, that part of the W coast of Asia Minor which was colonized mainly by settlers from Athens and others dispossessed by the Dorian invaders—probably in the 11th and 10th centuries B.C. It adjoined the Aegean Sea, and was bounded on the east by Lydia. In historical times there were 12 important cities which claimed to be Ionian, and formed a confederacy—Miletus, Myus, Priene, Samos, Ephesus, Colophon, Lebedus, Teos, Erythrae, Chios, Clazomenae, and Phocae. Smyrna (of Aeolic origin) was afterward added to the league. Their common sanctuary was a temple of Poseidon on the promontory of Mycale, called the Panionium, where the national assembly was held. The Ionians were wealthy and luxurious; and the fine arts were cultivated amongst them at a much earlier date than among their kinsmen in the mother country. During the eighth, seventh, and sixth centuries B.C. Ionia was the most advanced and most prosperous part of Greece. Its colonists settled in large numbers especially on the Propontis and the Euxine; and it was in Ionia that philosophy, science, and history arose, and many famous poets were born.

The Ionians were conquered by Croesus about 560 B.C.; then by Harpagus, general of Cyrus, in 545. In 500–499 they revolted from the Persians, but were again subdued in 494. The defeat of Xerxes left them free to join Athens in a league, in which eventually they became her subjects. This league was formed in 477, and dissolved by the defeat of Athens in the Peloponnesian War in 404. Thereafter except for a renewal of the alliance with Athens from 378 to 357 B.C., the Ionian cities were autonomous, until they became merged in the kingdom of Alexander and his successors. Eventually they passed under Roman rule, by which time some of them were in a languishing condition. They formed part of the Empire of the East, and were for centuries under Turkish dominion.

IONIA, city, SW Lower Michigan, county seat of Ionia County, on the Grand Trunk and the Pere Marquette railroads, 33 miles E of Grand Rapids. Ionia is the trade center of a farm country pleasantly located in a region dotted with lakes and woods. The town was founded in 1833 by settlers from New York. The Ionia Fair Grounds are the scene of an annual exposition. Ionia is the seat of the Michigan Reformatory and the Michigan State Hospital. Furniture, pottery, flour, and beer are the principal manufactures. Pop. (1950) 6,412.

IONIAN ISLANDS, an irregular chain of seven large islands lying in the Ionian Sea close to the NW coast of Greece, and constituting a geographical division of Greece, and forming the departments (nomarchies) of Cephalonia, Corfu, and Zante; total area 1,115 sq. mi.; pop. (1940) 219,562. Extending north to south into the Sea of Candida the chain includes CORFU (Kérkyra), Paxos (with Antipaxos), Santa Maura (Levkàs, Leucas), Ithaca (Ithaké, Thiaki), CEPHALONIA (Kephallenía), Zante (Zácynthus), and Cerigo (Cythera, Kýthera), and the islets of Fanno, Merlera, Meganisi, Strophádes Servi, and Cerigotto (Antikýthera).

The surface of the islands is in general mountainous, with richly fertile plains and valleys. One half the area is under cultivation and yielded wheat, maize, pulse, cotton, and flax. There are olive and almond groves, peach, citron, pomegranate, and other semitropical and tropical fruit orchards, and vineyards bearing wine and currant grapes. These items with olives, olive oil, wines, salt, currants, honey, and soap are exported from the entire island group. Industries on the main islands are shipbuilding, fishing, farming, and the manufacture of carpets, goats-hair shawls and rugs, woolen and silk textiles, linen goods, and processing plants for olive oil and dried fruits and currants. The majority of the population of the islands is Greek, although there are many of part Italian, part Turkish and other mixtures. The climate and scenery of the islands are considered ideal by visitors, who tour the isles in great numbers via steamers from Athens and other Greek ports.

Paxos (area 10 sq. mi.; pop. 3,050), smallest of the seven largest islands, lies 10 miles southeast of Corfu off the southwest coast of Epirus. Its area is mostly grazing land for large flocks of long-haired goats. Gayo, situated on the east coast, is the chief city. The two tiny islets of Antipaxos lie two miles off the southeast end of Paxos.

Santa Maura (area 111 sq. mi.; pop. 11,000) is separated from Acarnania, with which it was at one time connected, by a mile-wide channel. A small

Picturesque section of Ithaca, an island in Ionian group which is famed as home of Odysseus

mountain chain runs from north to south through the center, terminating in Mount St. Elias (alt. 3,000 ft.) on Cape Ducato. About one-eighth of the land is under cultivation, and there is a large salt lagoon, from which salt is exported. The chief towns are Levkás (pop. 5,800), and Vliko, both situated on the east coast. At the south end of the island a great temple of Apollo crowns a 2,000-foot promontory. This spot is known as "Sappho's Leap," because of the poetess' suicide here in 557 B.C. The Corinthians founded the town of Amaxichi (near Levkàs) in the seventh century B.C. The island was then called Leucadia. The Caernanian League met here during the wars between Philip of Macedon and the Romans. See SAPPHO.

Ithaca (area 36 sq. mi.; pop. 8,115), lying two miles east of Cephalonia and just west of Acarnania, is famous as having been the home of Odysseus. It is mountainous; fishing and sheep and goat herding are the chief occupations. The very modern town of Vathy (pop. 3,120), is situated on the southern half of the island on a deep and beautiful bay.

Zante (area 277 sq. mi.; pop. 41,165), 10 miles south of Cephalonia and 16 miles west of the Peloponnese, is known as the "golden isle," because of the manufacture of gold and silver ornaments and religious articles, the chief industry. Gypsum is found here, and there are pitch wells. Pyrene, made from huckleberry stones, is also produced on the island for tanning. The chief town is Zante (pop. 11,500). The island was colonized by the Achaeans.

Cerigo (area 116 sq. mi.; pop. 7,900), 10 miles south of Cape Malea and 60 miles northwest of the island of Crete, is with Antikythera, the most southerly of the Ionian group. It is very hilly and parts of the island are heavily wooded. Cattle, sheep, and goats are grazed on the grassy slopes and exported to Greece. Colonized by the Phoenicians, Cerigo was once called Aegilia or Ogylos, and was celebrated for the worship of Venus (APHRODITE), who was said to have risen from the sea and come ashore on this island. There are interesting caves, some lined with red and purple feldspar. Farming, livestock raising, and fishing are occupations pursued by the people. Kythera, situated at the head of Kapsali Bay at the southern end, is the chief town. The towns of St. Nikolo and Potomo are on the southeast and northern ends of the island.

The lesser-known islands of the Ionian chain are Fanno (14 mi. NW of Corfu), Merlera (7 mi. N of Corfu), Meganisi (2 mi. E of Santa Maura) Strophádes, or Strivali (28 mi. S of Zante), a tiny quartette of islets, Servi (6 mi. N of Cerigo), and Cerigotto, or Antikythera, lying midway (12 mi.) between Cerigo and Crete. These are pastoral, and one or two have convents.

History. Levkàs, Ithaca, Cephalonia, and Zante, according to Homer, once belonged to the kingdom of Odysseus. The chain was originally colonized by the Corinthians and then the Ionians, who settled on the largest islands, especially on Corfu, in the seventh century B.C. The islands were Hellenic until invaded by the Romans. They became a part of the Byzantine Empire A.D. 1081; they were Venetian from 1386 to 1797, passing then into French hands. They came under Russian domination at the beginning of the 19th century. The French again took them in 1807 and held control until 1814, when the islands were taken under protection by the British, who held the islands until 1864, when they were returned to Greece. In 1941 at the beginning of World War II, the islands were invaded by Italian and then German troops, who did not surrender until 1944.

K. E. H.

IONIAN SEA, that part of the Mediterranean which lies between Italy and Greece, S of the Adriatic.

IONIC ORDER, one of the three classic architectural orders, features a scroll-shaped capital, the section crowning a column and acting as a decora-

tive link between the arch or lintel and the supporting column. Early forms of this capital have been found in Asia Minor, where the order originated in the Ionian colonies and had reached its height in development by the sixth century B.C. Later made of marble and stone, the Ionic column's prototype was

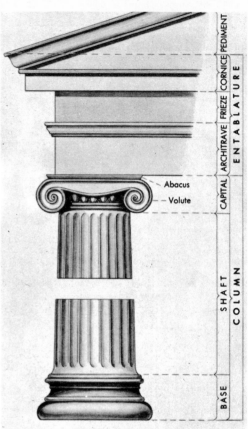

Ionic order

a wood shaft supporting a flared bracket carved in the copy of nature's scroll patterns, such as shells and animal horns. Not until the fifth century B.C. did the Ionic style appear in Greece itself, where its completed form is shown in the Erechtheum built in Athens around 420 B.C. Ionic columns in Greece were noted for graceful slenderness. Carved with numerous flutings, and supporting the decorative scroll capital, the Ionic column was especially suited for use at the corners of a portico. The Ionic Order was later adopted by the Romans, who did little in the advancement of its style, and actually used it with heavier detail and less attractive results. Numerous variations of the order have appeared in later period architectures. See ENTABLATURE.   JOAN C. CAMERA

IONOSPHERE, in physics, two and sometimes three regions (depending on conditions), in the earth's upper atmosphere which contain large numbers of electrically charged particles; these act as conductors in reflecting radio waves back to earth.

The lowest or E-region of ionized air is about 60 miles above the earth's surface; the other two regions, or F_1 and F_2, are located about 130 miles and 185 miles, respectively, above the earth's surface.

The upper atmosphere is also known as the Kennelly-Heaviside layer because Heaviside surmised its existence, which later was verified by Kennelly. See ATMOSPHERE; TERRESTRIAL MAGNETISM; WAVE.

IOS. See CYCLADES ISLANDS.

IOWA
The Hawkeye State

This fertile prairie state between the Mississippi and Missouri rivers, famed for its tall corn, is one of the greatest food producing areas in the world

IOWA, known as the "Hawkeye State," N central United States; between the Mississippi and the Missouri rivers; and bounded on the N by Minnesota, on the E by Wisconsin and Illinois, on the S by Missouri, and on the W by Nebraska and South Dakota; area 56,280 sq. mi., including 294 sq. mi. of inland water; pop. (1950) 3,261,073. It extends 310 miles from east to west and 210 miles from north to south. The name Iowa is an Indian word believed to mean "Beautiful land," and is also applied to the Indians who once lived in the area. The name was once spelled "Aiouez" and later "Ioway" and so it is spelled in many works relating to the Indians. A strictly etymological pronunciation would be "Iooway" or "Iyooway." This was the prevalent pronunciation during the pioneer period of the nation's history. The standard pronunciation, however, is "Iowuh." The state motto is "Our liberties we prize and our rights we will maintain." The state flower is the native wild rose. Des Moines is the capital.

Topography. The surface of Iowa is undulating prairie, sloping gently from the northwest corner toward the southeast. The highest point is at Primghar (1,800 ft.); the lowest points are the low-water marks at Keokuk (477 ft.) and Montrose (500 ft.). The average elevation is somewhat more than 1,000 feet above sea level. The surface is unusually smooth, even for a prairie country, the only rough places being the steep bluffs along the river, and the fantastic dolomite crags near Dubuque. Fully two-thirds of Iowa drains directly into the Mississippi River, which forms the whole of the eastern boundary, and the remainder into the Missouri, which forms most of the western boundary. The highland dividing the two drainage systems runs across the state irregularly north-northwest from a line west of the center of the southern boundary. The principal tributaries of the Mississippi are the DES MOINES, IOWA, Turkey, Wapsipinicon, CEDAR, Maquoketa, and Skunk rivers. Flowing into the Missouri are the BIG SIOUX, on the western border, the Rock, Floyd, LITTLE SIOUX, Boyer, West Nishnabotna, East Nishnabotna, and Nodaway rivers. Among the numerous small and beautiful lakes in the north-central part of the state are SPIRIT, Okoboji, Clear, Swan, and Storm lakes, several of which are popular health resorts.

Climate. Iowa is sunny with an average of 215 cloudfree days. The long summer has periods of prolonged heat and hot winds. It is said that the heat and not the drought damages crops. Temperatures vary greatly with the season and may vary by as much as 50° within a summer day. The average annual temperature over a period of 73 years was 48.1° F. An extreme high of 118° was recorded on July 20, 1934, and an extreme low of −47° was recorded Jan. 12, 1912. The average annual precipitation is 31.66 inches. The peak of the rainy season is the summer when the rain comes with the south wind; winter is somewhat drier; 30.2 inches of snowfall is the annual average. Hail frequently damages crops. Drought is experienced but seldom over the whole state. The prevailing wind is from the northwest. Twisters are common. Cold winds from the north bring winter cold waves.

Plants and Animals. Although half of Iowa's virgin timberlands have been cleared, the state still has 2,500,000 acres of natural woodlands bordering the streams and scattered on the knolls of pasturelands. Shelter groves have been planted around the farm buildings. The common varieties found are maple, oak, elm, hickory, basswood, birch, cottonwood, and willow. Pines, cedars, and deciduous trees line the river bluffs. Many of the native wild flowers that once turned the prairie into a garden of riotous color have disappeared along with the miles of waving prairie grass that once grew as high as the wheels of prairie schooners. Among the prairie flowers which still grow luxuriantly are the single pink rose, the state flower. Mulleins thrive in the pasturelands, and along the roadsides are sunflowers, goldenrod, asters, and blue phlox. In woods and hollows there is a succession of early wild flowers followed by the snow trillium, May apple, jack-in-the-pulpit, Solomon's-seal, and yellow or pink moccasin flower.

Iowa has had little wild game since the farmland has been developed. In some sections, there are herds of white-tailed deer, protected by law. Other common varieties of native animals are the red fox, coyote, raccoon, jack rabbit, and cottontail rabbit. The Mississippi and Missouri rivers are a natural passageway for migratory birds, and a nesting haven for many species of song birds that feed on the open farmland or the rush-grown sloughs and nest in the woodlands along the streams. Thousands of species visit Iowa at some time during the year. Most numerous are the meadow lark, red-winged blackbird, mourning dove, bluebird, robin, rose-breasted grosbeak, Baltimore oriole, thrush, whippoorwill, quail, and the eastern goldfinch or wild canary, which is the state bird. Ring-necked pheasants have become plentiful since their introduction into the state a few years ago, and open hunting seasons are permitted. Wild life is conserved in the state parks and Iowa has three national forests: Chariton, Chequest, and Keosauqua, comprising 218,000 acres in the southeastern section of the state.

PEOPLE

Population. According to the Federal census for 1950 the population of Iowa was 2,621,073, an increase of 82,805, or 3.3 per cent, over 1940 (compared with an increase of 2.7 per cent during 1930–1940). About 52 per cent of the population was urban, compared with 58 per cent in 1940. Of the foreign-born white population, Germans were the most numerous. Iowa, 20th in population among the states in 1940, dropped to 22nd rank in 1950.

PRINCIPAL CITIES	POPULATION Census 1940	Census 1950
DES MOINES (capital)	159,819	177,965
SIOUX CITY	82,364	83,991
DAVENPORT	66,039	74,549
CEDAR RAPIDS	62,120	72,296
WATERLOO	51,743	65,198
DUBUQUE	43,892	49,671
COUNCIL BLUFFS	41,439	45,429
OTTUMWA	31,570	33,631
BURLINGTON	25,832	30,613
CLINTON	26,270	30,379

Education. The chief executive of the public school system is the superintendent of public instruction, chosen every four years. There are also county superintendents. School attendance is compulsory for children between the ages of seven and sixteen years. Iowa has ranked first or second among the states in literacy.

Institutions for higher learning include the State University of Iowa at Iowa City; Iowa State College of Agriculture and Mechanic Arts, at Ames; Iowa State Teachers' College, at Cedar Falls; Buena Vista College, at Storm Lake; Central College, at Pella; Coe College, at Cedar Rapids; Cornell College, at Mount Vernon; Drake University, at Des Moines; University of Dubuque, at Dubuque; Kletzing College, at University Park; Grinnell College, at Grinnell; Iowa Wesleyan College, at Mount Pleasant; Luther College, at Decorah; Morningside College, at Sioux City; Parsons College, at Fairfield; Simpson College, at Indianola; St. Ambrose College, at Davenport; Upper Iowa University, at Fayette; Wartburg College, at Waverly; Western Union College, at Le Mars; William Penn College, at Oskaloosa.

Administration building of Drake University

The School for the Deaf, at Council Bluffs, and the School for the Blind, at Vinton, are under the state board of education. There are also numerous public and private junior colleges. In 1945 the legislature adopted state aid as part of its educational policy.

Public Welfare. Iowa has a number of boards and agencies which supervise the welfare activities of the state. The first to be established was the Board of Control of three members, originating in 1898 to manage the state's institutions. In 1907, the Board of Parole was instituted; in 1926, the Commission for the Blind was established to aid the adult blind, educationally and industrially in their homes. In 1937, the Department of Social Welfare was set up to administer state and Federal funds for old-age assistance, aid to the needy blind, child welfare, and to dependent children, and general relief. The charitable and penal institutions managed by the Board of Control include the institution for feeble-minded children, at Glenwood; a hospital for epileptics and a school for the feeble-minded, at Woodward; hospitals for the insane at Cherokee, Clarinda, Independence, and Mount Pleasant; a men's reformatory, at Anamosa; the state penitentiary, at Fort Madison; a training school for boys, at Eldora, and one for girls, at Mitchellville; a soldiers' orphans' home at Davenport; a juvenile home at Toledo; a women's reformatory at Rockwell City; the state sanatorium for tuberculous patients, at Oakdale.

ECONOMIC LIFE

Agriculture. Iowa ranks as one of the greatest food-producing areas of the world because of the exceptionally fertile soil and the plenteous rainfall during the months when crops are growing.

The surface soil of almost the entire state is glacial débris, or till, the covering being from 15 to 20 feet, with small areas reaching 200 feet. It is quite free from boulders, shows no typical moraines, and is everywhere fertile, particularly the drift of the great stretches of prairie and the alluvial soil of the river bottoms. The drift is black loam of sand, silt, and clay, which is easily worked and is of unsurpassed fertility. In the valleys of the Mississippi and Missouri rivers is a layer of fine yellowish sand and clay. The soil of other river bottoms is alluvial, formed from the erosion of the prairie drift.

According to the National Resources Board, Iowa has grade-one land in 25 per cent of its area. Ninety-five per cent of all the land is laid out in farms and more than two-thirds of this area is improved. The state has ranked second to Texas (which is five times as large) in the total value of farm crops. In 1950 Iowa ranked first in the production of corn, oats, and popcorn, and second in hay. In 1951, it led all states in the number of swine, and was second only to Texas in the number of cattle.

Farmers are aided by the State Department of Agriculture, the Agricultural Experiment Station, numerous co-operative associations, and favorable legislation by a state government well attuned to the needs and interests of the agricultural population.

PRINCIPAL CROPS OF IOWA

CROP	UNIT (Thousands)	1939–1948 Average	1949	1950
Apples	Bushels	1,333	1,715	1,020
Corn	Bushels	207,605	249,548	213,790
Hay	Tons	2,580	2,253	2,622
Oats	Bushels	45,047	55,825	52,577
Popcorn	Pounds	25,103	29,520	35,530
Potatoes	Bushels	4,640	3,900	4,845
Rye	Bushels	1,292	756	826
Soybeans	Bushels	22,958	34,608	35,002
Wheat	Bushels	28,258	39,150	31,798

Manufactures. With abundant coal, excellent railway transportation facilities, and large supplies of various kinds of raw agricultural products, the manu-

IOWA DEVELOPMENT COMM.

Aerial view of main section of Cedar Rapids

C. & N. W. RY.

Scene along the Mississippi River

IOWA DEVELOPMENT COMM.

Band shell in Grandview Park at Sioux City

IOWA DEVELOPMENT COMM.

Picturesque covered bridge in Madison County

IOWA STATE PRINTING BD.

Lake Laverne on grounds of Iowa State College

STATE HISTORICAL SOC. OF IOWA

Boats and barges on the Mississippi at Dubuque

Barnyard scene on a prosperous Iowa farm

factures of Iowa increased at a rapid rate during the 20th century. The value of manufactured products increased 140.3 per cent between 1910 and 1920. The 1947 Census of Manufactures showed there were 2,965 industrial establishments; the value added by manufacture was $671,100,000. By far the most important industries are those connected with the agriculture and livestock resources of the state. The industry ranking first has been slaughtering and meat packing. The second product in value has been butter. Great in value also are bread and other bakery products; flour, feed, and grain-mill products; corn products, including oil, syrup, and starch; and the canning and preserving of foods. Poultry killing and dressing is important.

Iowa holds high position in the manufacture of washing machines, wringers, driers, and ironing machines for household use. Other leading industries are printing and publishing, railroad shop construction and repairs; engines, turbines, and water wheels; foundry and machine-shop products, planing-mill products, cement, and furniture. There are, besides, such industries as the manufacture of wall plaster, wallboard, and floor composition, buttons, paving materials (other than brick or granite), stoves and ranges (other than electric) and warm-air furnaces, agricultural implements, clay products (other than pottery) and nonclay refractories.

Sioux City is the most important manufacturing center of the state, followed by Cedar Rapids and Des Moines and such other cities as Ottumwa, Waterloo, Davenport, Dubuque, Mason City, Clinton, and Muscatine.

MINERAL PRODUCTION OF IOWA

MINERAL	UNIT (Thousands)	1946	1947	1948
Cement	Barrels	6,145	6,155	6,835
Clay	Short Tons	696	896	893
Coal	Short Tons	1,788	1,684	1,750
Gypsum	Short Tons	560	656	729
Sand and Gravel	Short Tons	7,938	6,473	8,039
Stone	Short Tons	5,162	5,586	6,387

Port of Burlington on the Mississippi River

Mining. Coal mining is the leading mineral industry of Iowa. The coal area, comprising about 19,000 square miles, is part of the Western Interior Coal Field, and extends over the south-central and southwestern parts of the state. Other important minerals are clay, cement, and limestone. Lead and zinc were formerly mined in large quantities. In 1948 Iowa ranked 31st among the states in mineral production, with an output valued at $45,129,000.

Transportation. The principal means of transportation are the railways, though the Mississippi is of considerable importance to the cities on its banks. Railway construction began in 1854 and was carried on rapidly until 1900, when the mileage was about 9,400 (a total which has changed little since). The extensive mileage is in part due to the great number of trunk lines that pass through the state. Most of the lines run east and west, and seven are part of the great transcontinental railroad routes. There is at least one railroad in each of the 99 counties. The principal lines are the Rock Island, the Burlington, the Great Northern, the North Western, the Minneapolis and St. Louis, the Illinois Central, and the Milwaukee. Des Moines is the chief railroad center. Iowa once had an extensive system of electric interurbans which have gradually decreased in importance since truck and bus lines have offered competition. There are about 8,500 miles of state-maintained roads of which 6,000 miles are paved highways. U.S. 30, the Lincoln Highway, crosses the state between Clinton and Council Bluffs. The United Airlines, the Mid-Continent Airlines and Braniff Airways cross the state and serve Des Moines, Mason City, Burlington, Moline, and Sioux City.

Extensive river traffic has been revived since the construction of 11 large dams across the Mississippi between Illinois and Iowa. They extend from the eastern bend of the river at Allamakee County south to the gigantic Keokuk dam and were built by the Federal government to improve river navigation and provide power. Extensive locks for the passage of river craft have made it possible to operate steel barge lines which offer inexpensive freight transportation.

Tourist Attractions. Although Iowa has made little effort to attract tourists, it has developed many recreational areas which are widely used by its own people. There are 74 parks and preserves within its borders, having extensive facilities for picnicking and camping. The state has 65 public lakes and 800 miles of parkways bordering the lakes and streams. The high bluffs along the Mississippi in northeast Iowa afford fine scenic drives in contrast to the prairie land. Fishing is a good sport on the lakes, especially on Okoboji and Spirit lakes and Lake Keokuk which has been formed by waters impounded by the Mississippi dam. Historic sites, concerned with early state history, are well marked. A popular spot in Bradford, Chickasaw County, is the Little Brown Church in the Vale, which inspired the well-known hymn of that name. The Amana colony of seven villages in Iowa county has carried on its co-operative industry since 1855 (see AMANA SOCIETY). F. C. W.

Hybrid seed corn on a farm in Grundy County

GOVERNMENT

The present constitution dates from 1857; since that time 17 amendments have been adopted. The question of revising the constitution is submitted to the state electorate every 10 years. An amendment is initiated by a majority vote in two successive legislatures and ratified by a majority vote of the electors. The general assembly, consisting of a senate and a house of representatives, holds biennial sessions in every odd year. Representatives are elected for two-year terms and senators for four-year terms, one half of the latter being elected every two years. The house consists of not more than 108 and the senate of not over 50. Bills may originate in either house, and require a majority vote in each for passage. Members are paid $1,000 for two years and not over $10 a day additional for special sessions.

The elected administrative officers are the governor, lieutenant governor, secretary of state, attorney general, treasurer, auditor, secretary of agriculture, and superintendent of public instruction, the last two being statutory officials rather than constitutional. All have two-year terms, except the superintendent of public instruction, who serves for four years. The governor has the customary veto over legislation, subject to overriding action by two-thirds vote of each house. The governor may convene the general assembly for special sessions. State officials may be impeached by the house with the trial before the senate.

The supreme court is composed of a chief justice and eight associate justices, all elected for six-year terms. The state is divided into 21 districts, each of which has a district court with from two to six judges elected for four-year terms. Within each district sittings of the court must be held annually in each county. Below these courts are the municipal, superior, police, and mayors' courts.

For local government the state is divided into 99 counties, which are in turn subdivided into civil townships. At the head of each county is a board of supervisors which decides most of the policies of county administration; other county officials are the sheriff, coroner, clerk of court, auditor, treasurer, recorder, attorney, county superintendent of schools, and additional officials in some counties. The township is not an important governmental unit, the assessor being the only official of much consequence. State law provides for the mayor-council form of municipal government, but any city may vote for either the commission or the city manager form instead. Four cities—Muscatine, Camanche, Wapello, and Davenport—have special charters dating back to pioneer days, and therefore enjoy special privileges in local government.

HISTORY

The Coming of the White Man. The state takes its name from the Iowa Indians, who found a temporary home there at the beginning of the century. Spain was the first nation to claim the region of which Iowa is a part. England disputed the claim by virtue of the landing of the Cabots on the mainland of North America in 1497, but it remained for the French actually to explore and occupy the country, following the voyage of FATHER MARQUETTE and Louis Joliet down the Mississippi in June, 1673. They landed on Iowa soil, near the mouth of the Des Moines River, taking possession in the name of France. The first settlement was made in 1788 by French Canadians, under Julien Dubuque at the site of the city which bears his name. They were attracted by the lead mines in the vicinity and remained until 1810. In 1763, by secret treaty, the whole tract was ceded to Spain. It was receded to France in 1800 and was ceded to the United States, as part of the Louisiana purchase, in 1803.

When the state of Louisiana was created, and admitted to the Union, in 1812, the country northward,

State capitol of Iowa at Des Moines

including the present state of Iowa, was called Missouri. In 1821 the state of Missouri was created, leaving Iowa without government. In 1833 companies from Illinois and other states made permanent settlements near Burlington; Dubuque was founded; and in the course of the next few years many settlements were made along the Mississippi. In 1834 Iowa became a part of Michigan, and in 1836 a part of Wisconsin.

Statehood. Wisconsin having been set off as a separate state, Iowa was organized as a territory on June 12, 1838, with its capital at Burlington. It embraced the greater part of the present state of Minnesota and all of the Dakotas. The next year the government was removed to Iowa City. On Dec. 28, 1846, the state was admitted to the Union, with its present limits. In 1857 the constitution was revised, giving Negroes the right of suffrage and the obligation of military duty, and Des Moines became the capital. In the same year occurred a massacre by the Sioux at Spirit Lake, but the flow of immigration was not retarded. During the Civil War Iowa was loyal to the Union and furnished nearly 80,000 men to the Federal Army.

Railroad growth was rapid, and railroad legislation became an important issue. In 1872 an act was passed taxing railroad property; and as a result of the Grange agitation, a board of commissioners was established the following year to fix a minimum rate and to prevent discrimination. An amendment to the constitution prohibiting the sale of intoxicating liquors was adopted in 1882, and a more adequate law was passed in 1884; but in 1894 the courts declared the prohibition laws unconstitutional.

In 1907 a new municipal government for cities was put into operation in Des Moines, which has become known as the "Des Moines Plan" (see LOCAL GOVERNMENT). In 1911 the Iowa legislature ratified the Federal income tax amendment, and in 1919 the Federal prohibition amendment. During World War I, 113,000 Iowa men served in the armed forces.

In 1927 a measure was enacted establishing junior colleges in the public educational system; and the

Farm machinery manufacturing plant at Dubuque

Fort Madison was abandoned and burned in 1813

IOWA
High Lights of History

PIONEER ROOM MURAL, HOTEL KIRKWOOD, DES MOINES

Pere Marquette entered what is now Iowa in 1673

NEWBERRY LIBRARY
Historic river crossing site at Council Bluffs

Railway bridge at Davenport, completed in 1856

Old Shot Tower at Dubuque was erected in 1855

Old Capitol at Iowa City, erected in 1840 was the second capitol building of the state

"Little Brown Church" at Bradford was built in 1864

PAUL'S PHOTOS

IOWA STATE HISTORICAL SOCIETY

IOWA ST. HIST. SOC.

highway commission (five members) was given complete control over the primary road system. The farmers of Scott, Muscatine, and Cedar counties attempted in 1931 to resist the test for tuberculosis in cattle. Also in 1931, construction of a dam at Davenport was begun, as part of a project to canalize the upper Mississippi River by means of successive dams and locks; Dam No. 13, north of Clinton, was dedicated in 1939. In World War II, about 260,000 Iowa men and women served in the armed forces. In 1951, the spring floods of the Mississippi River, reaching the highest crest in years, caused extensive damage to Iowa river towns and cities.   F. M.

BIBLIOG.–B. F. Stambaugh, *The Constitution of Iowa* (1934); Federal Writers Project, *Iowa: A Guide to the Hawkeye State* (1938); C. Cole, *Iowa; Through the Years* (1940); P. D. Strong, *Hawkeyes: A Biography of the State of Iowa* (1940); W. J. Petersen, *Iowa: The Rivers of Her Valleys* (1941); A. E. Aitchison and M. Uttley, *Geography of Iowa* (1948); W. A. Lunden, *Basic Social Problems* (1950).

IOWA CITY, city, SE Iowa, county seat of Johnson County, on both sides of the Iowa River, on the Rock Island Railroad, U.S. highways 6 and 218, and the United Air Lines, about 120 miles E of Des Moines. Iowa City was founded as the capital of the Territory of Iowa in 1839. In 1857 the seat of the government was moved to Des Moines because of its more central position. Iowa City was incorporated in 1853 by the General Assembly. It is the seat of the University of Iowa, which houses its administrative offices in the old Capitol. The university medical center is one of the largest in the country and services the entire state. Advertising calendars, iron and sheet metal products, and gravel and other rock products are the chief manufactures. Pop. (1950) 27,212.

IOWA INDIANS, a Siouan tribe from the Winnebago stem, who early migrated from the Great Lake region to Missouri. The word "Iowa" has been variously explained as meaning "sleepy ones" or "dusty faces." At an early date they cultivated the soil and made and traded catlinite pipes, which, together with oxhides, constituted their original wealth and medium of trade. After the settlement of the country by the whites they carried on an active trade in furs. They removed in 1836 to a reservation in Kansas, and later to Oklahoma. Their numbers were estimated at 1,100 in 1760, but they have since declined. The tribal descendants now number under 300 but the group identity (especially in Oklahoma) has been largely lost.

IOWA RIVER, totally within the state of Iowa, rises in Hancock County and flows SE to join the Mississippi 22 miles below Muscatine. Its chief tributary is the Cedar which rises in southern Minnesota. Flood control dams have been authorized for both streams, at Coralville on the Iowa and at Rochester on the Cedar. Neither stream is commercially navigable.

IOWA STATE COLLEGE OF AGRICULTURE AND MECHANIC ARTS, an accredited, coeducational, land-grant, technical institution at Ames, Iowa, was founded in 1858 and opened in 1868. Curricular programs are provided in: agriculture, aeronautical engineering, architecture, veterinary medicine, home economics, forestry, engineering, landscape architecture, industrial and vocational education, technical journalism, graduate and secondary education. Degrees offered include the B.S., M.S., D.V.M., and Ph.D. Noncollegiate programs are provided in agriculture, and short courses are given in the winter. Extension courses are conducted at various points throughout the state, and research is carried on in the agricultural and industrial science research institutes. A visual education program is conducted throughout the state.

Iowa State College is controlled by the State Board of Education. Its campus covers about 3,000 acres, of which more than 250 are college grounds. There are also experimental farming plots and a forestry

plantation. Several national fraternities and sororities have chapters there. For statistics see COLLEGES.

IOWA STATE TEACHERS COLLEGE. See COLLEGES.

IOWA, UNIVERSITY OF. Established in February, 1847, by an act of the First General Assembly, the State University of Iowa represents one of the earliest acts of the commonwealth. When the state capitol moved to Des Moines in 1857, the old capitol building at Iowa City became a central part of the university. Instruction was begun in nine departments of the College of Liberal Arts. Law was added in 1868, medicine in 1870, dentistry in 1882, and pharmacy in 1885. The School of Nursing opened in 1898. The Graduate College was organized in 1900. The College of Engineering dates from 1905, the College of Education from 1913, and the College of Commerce from 1921. Through correspondence courses and a series of sponsored activities, the Extension Division has carried the work of the university to the state as a whole since 1913. The Iowa Child Welfare Research Station, established in 1917, is located at the university.

The Iowa State Board of Education, organized in 1909, is the central controlling body for the three state-operated, higher educational institutions. In addition to the State University of Iowa the board has authority over Iowa State Teachers' College at Cedar Falls, founded 1876, and the Iowa State College of Agriculture and Mechanical Arts at Ames, chartered in 1858. The college offers work in agriculture, engineering, home economics, veterinary medicine, and the sciences. The two colleges are accredited by the Association of American Universities of which the State University is a member.   ROBERT MARSH

IOWA WESLEYAN COLLEGE. See COLLEGES.

IPECAC, or **IPECACUANHA,** is the name applied to a drug and to the small shrub from which it is derived. The shrub, *Cephaelis ipecacuanha,* belongs to the dicotyledonous family *Rubiaceae* and is a native of forests of Brazil and Colombia. The drug is extracted from the rhizomes and roots of the plant and consists of a mixture of several alkaloids. It is employed in medicine as an irritant, expectorant, and EMETIC. Ipecac has been used in the treatment of amebic dysentery but now EMETINE (one of the alkaloids of ipecac) is usually prescribed instead.   H. J. FULLER

BIBLIOG.–E. N. Gathercoal and E. H. Wirth, *Pharmacognosy* (1936); A. F. Hill, *Economic Botany* (1937).

IPHIGENIA, in Greek legend, the daughter of AGAMEMNON and Clytaemnestra. When the Greek expedition was about to set sail against Troy from Aulis, the prophet Calchas advised Agamemnon to sacrifice Iphigenia to appease the goddess Artemis, which he did. Later accounts say that Artemis carried off Iphigenia to the Tauric Chersonese, to be her priestess. Pausanias tells us that, at Hermione, Artemis had a temple under the name of Iphigenia; and it is probable that, in her connection with Artemis, Iphigenia is but the goddess herself under another name. She is the protagonist in Euripedes' *Iphigenia in Aulis* and *Iphigenia in Tauris,* which were the basis of numerous adaptations, including tragedies by Racine and Goethe and two operas by Gluck.

IPIALES, town, Colombia, Nariño Department, at an altitude of about 10,000 feet, on the Simón Bolívar Highway, SE of Pasto near the Ecuador frontier. A branch of the Pan American Airways serves the city. A rock grotto below the Chapel of Las Vegas is an interesting point for sightseers. Pop. about 8,500.

IPIN, Suchow, or **Suifu,** commercial town, central China, SW Szechwan Province, on the Yangtze (at this point known as the Kinsha) at its junction with the Min River; 150 miles SW of Chungking. Ipin has salt and coal mines and a large trade with Yunnan in wax and cotton goods. Several American missionary societies have made the town their headquarters. Pop. about 125,000.

IPOMOEA, a genus of plants belonging to the Convolvulus family, *Convolvulaceae.* The plants are twining or creeping vines, with conspicuous, usually trumpet-shaped corollas. Each corolla is composed of five fused petals, and the calyx consists of five sepals, the stamens number five, and the ovary consists of two or three carpels and as many cells. The fruit is a capsule with four to six seeds. The corolla is commonly white, less frequently red, blue, or purple. *I. batatas* is the sweet potato; *I. bona-nox* is the moonflower, cultivated for its large, white, night-opening, sweet-scented flowers; and *I. purpurea* is the cultivated

J. H. MCFARLAND CO.-BODGER SEEDS

Morning glory vines, with flowers in inset

MORNING-GLORY. *I. quamoclit,* or CYPRESS VINE, cultivated in gardens, has deeply pinnately-parted leaves and scarlet, slender corollas, and *I. pes-caprae* is a common beach creeper in the American tropics. Some of the wild species in the United States are known as BINDWEEDS, because of their habit of twining about plants, posts, and other erect objects. Most bindweeds, however, are members of a closely related genus, *Convolvulus.*   H. J. FULLER

IPSAMBUL. See ABU SIMBIL.

IPSUS, small town in Greater Phrygia, in Asia Minor, where in 301 B.C., Seleucus and Lysimachus defeated Antigonus.

IPSWICH, originally known as **Limestone,** town, Australia, Queensland, on the Bremer River; 24 miles W of Brisbane by rail. It is situated in a coal-mining district and has manufactures of woolens, lumber, and ironwork. Pop. (1947) 26,218.

IPSWICH, municipal, county, and parliamentary borough, E England, Suffolk, on the Gipping River at its junction with the Orwell, at the head of the Orwell estuary; 69 miles NE of London. In the old sections of the town along the river the streets are narrow and irregular and still retain many picturesque old buildings decorated with carved oak. Of interest are Sparrowe's House (1567); Neptune Inn (1638); Archdeacon's Place (1471); Wolsey's Gateway (1528), a relic of Wolsey's College; and a grammar school founded in 1565 by Queen Elizabeth. Ipswich has an arboretum and a natural history museum. Interesting churches are those of St. Mary-at-Quay (15th century), St. Mary-at-the-Tower, St. Margaret, St. Mary Stoke, St. Nicholas, St. Peter, and St. Stephen. There are Roman and Saxon remains and ruins of a castle built by William the Conqueror. The manufacture of agricultural implements is important. Other industries include an engineering works, railway repair shops, a chemical plant, breweries, tanneries, and factories manufacturing electrical equipment, furniture, woolen goods, clothing, soap, paper, sailcloth, and sacking. There is a large cattle and foods market. During World War II the aircraft and war plants located here were badly damaged by German bombers. Pop. (1950 est.) 104,130. K. E. H.

IPSWICH, town, NE Massachusetts, in Essex County, on both sides of the Ipswich River and on Ipswich Bay; served by the Boston and Maine Railroad, 27 miles NE of Boston. Ipswich, known originally as Agawam (fish place), was founded in 1633 by John Winthrop and a group of 12 settlers. It was named for Ipswich, England. There are many well-preserved 17th-century homes in Ipswich. The Rebellion Tablet marks the spot where in 1687, nearly 100 years before the Revolution, the townsfolk of Ipswich gathered in anger to protest certain New England tax levies. The Choate bridge, which spans the river here, was built in 1764, the oldest arched bridge in America. In 1927, the machinery of the hosiery mills, which were the town's principal industry, was sold to Russia. Today Ipswich is a popular resort town with a few minor industries; digging and marketing clams support many of the residents. Pop. (1950) 6,895.

IQUIQUE, seaport town, Chile, capital of the province of Tarapacá, on the Pacific Coast, about 75 miles S of Arica with which it is connected by highway, rail, air, and steamer routes. The city, located on a high desert plateau, receives its water supply from the island oasis of Pica. Iquique is laid out with broad streets, the chief of which converge on a popular meeting place, the Plaza Prat. Opposite the excellent harbor is Serrano Island which is connected with the mainland by a causeway and a mole. A substantial foreign commerce, notably shipments of iodine and nitrates, passes through the port which ranks second in volume in the country. Iquique was founded in the 16th century soon after the Spanish Conquest. Earthquakes destroyed much of the port in 1868 and 1875. In 1879, Iquique was the scene of a battle between Chile and Peru and was ceded to Chile in 1883. Pop. (1944) 38,094.

IQUITOS, town, Peru, capital of the department of Loreto, on the upper Amazon River, about 210 miles W of Loreto. It is served by a branch of the Pan American Airways. Once a center of wild rubber production, the city has greatly declined in population, although it is still an important trade center for the tropical regions of Peru and the terminus for river steamers of the Amazon. The city's leading industries are lumbering, cotton ginning, soap making, distilling, and the making of straw hats. Pop. (1947 est.) 39,630.

IQUITOS INDIANS, a South American tribe who formerly occupied a wide domain about the rivers Tigre, Nanay, Napo, and other affluents of the upper Amazon. Many adopted Christianity in the 18th century, but wooden idols carved in the shape of birds and beasts are still secretly worshiped.

IRAK AJMI, former name of the central part of Iran, almost corresponding to the ancient Media; area about 138,000 sq. mi. It consists largely of elevated tablelands with fertile valleys, yielding cereals and fruits. In the east is the Great Salt Desert of Khurasan, the Dasht-i-Kavir.

IRAN, in early times, the name applied to the great Asiatic plateau which comprised the entire region from the Caucasus, the Caspian Sea, and Russian Turkestan on the N to the Tigris, the Persian Gulf, and the Arabian Sea on the W and S, and extended to the Indus on the E, likewise comprising the modern Afghanistan and the territory to the N of it as far as the Jaxartes River. The extremes of climate over this wide area were as great, and the diversity of features and characteristics as prominent, in ancient times as is the case today. Both in ancient and in modern times the land of Iran, although a somewhat ill-defined unit, has been of great importance, geographically and ethnologically, and in its influence on history and on the diffusion of the Indo-Germanic tongues. It obtained its name from its early inhabitants, who belonged to the Iranian branch of the so-called Aryan family. The name is now the official designation of Persia.

IRAN

EWING GALLOWAY

The Modern Persia

Farming, mining, and oil are the chief industries of this Mediterranean monarchy

IRAN, formerly **Persia**, a kingdom of Asia, occupying with Afghanistan and Baluchistan the Iranian Plateau extending W from the Indus River Valley to the Euphrates River Valley; bounded on the N by the Armenian and Azerbaijan Soviet Socialist Republics, the Caspian Sea, and the Turkmen Soviet Socialist Republic; on the E by Afghanistan and Indian Baluchistan; on the S by the Gulf of Oman and the Persian Gulf; and on the W by Iraq and Turkey; area about 628,000 sq. mi.; pop. (U.N. 1949 est.) 18,387,000. Portions of both the east and west boundaries have not been definitely fixed.

PHYSICAL FEATURES

Topography. More than a third of Iran is a desolate desert waste, with much of the remaining area arid. Iran's great plateau is generally barren, sandstone desert, or steepe, spotted with low hills or rugged rocks of peculiar shape and brilliant colors.

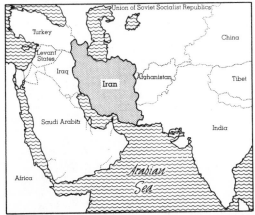

Location map of Iran

Iran

The great Dasht-i-Kavir waste lies south of the Elburz Mountains, and the Dasht-i-Lut occupies much of southeast Iran. These steppes and deserts are a part of the great steppe and desert zone which begins at Africa's Atlantic coast and extends across North Africa, Iraq, and Iran into central Asia. The only oasis in the two great deserts is Tabas, at their juncture in east central Iran; the saline nature of the soil prohibits settlement and almost all forms of vegetable and animal life. Other arid areas, however, have numerous oases watered by wells or natural springs, and surrounded by shrubs and pine trees. Among the great Iranian oases are Isfahan, Shiraz, Teheran, and Meshed.

Except for the lowlands in the southwest and the Caspian littoral, Iran is enclosed within mountain ranges, and geologically is within the great Alpine fold belt. From the Armenian highlands northwest of Lake Urmia a great mountain chain extends south, running through the Kurdistan region, and then, as the Zagros Chain, swings southeast along the Persian Gulf, making up most of the area of Luristan and Bakhtiari country. The Zagros Chain consists of several ranges separated by deep valleys, and is cut transversely from the east and the west by a few other valleys. Northeast of Kermanshah the mountains rise to 11,470 feet, east of Ahwaz to 10,509 feet, southeast of Shiraz to 10,500 feet, and north of Bandar Abbas to 10,706 feet. Inland and parallel to the Zagros another somewhat lower range, its greatest height reaching 11,000 feet west of Ardistan, starts west of the great salt lake (Darya-gi-Namak) and merges into the greater mountains in Iranian Baluchistan. In this range, the Kuh-i-Basman volcano rises to 11,447 feet. Another great chain also starts north of Lake Urmia, circles the Tabriz depression, and extends southeast to the Caspian Sea, on the way reaching 15,815 feet in Kuh-i-Savalan; thence it curves south of the Caspian Sea in the Elburz Mountains, from which rises Iran's highest point, Mount Demavend (18,550 ft.). Extending eastward with a northerly inclination south of the Atrek River, the Elburz diminish in height, and form the border between Khurasan and the Turkmen Soviet Socialist Republic. Less high mountains and hills extend south along the Afghanistan border to the mountains of Baluchistan, where they rise to 13,034 feet in Kuh-i-Taftan.

Iranian coat of arms

Iran has few rivers, the only navigable one being the KARUN, which rises in the Bakhtiari Mountains and flows past Ahwaz to empty into the Shatt-al-Arab at Khorramshahr. The ATREK flows into northeast Iran from Afghanistan, forming in its lower course the boundary between the Turkmen Soviet Socialist Republic and Iran, and empties into the Caspian north of Bandar Shah. The Sefid Rud descends from the Elburz Mountains and empties into the western Caspian southeast of Pahlevi. Other streams lose themselves in swamps in Iran's interior. Many of these rivers are dry for a large part of the year. Lake URMIA, so salty that it has no marine life, is in Azerbaijan in northwest Iran and Lake Helmand, in the Seistan Basin at the eastern border; both are more than 100 miles long.

Climate. Because of the range in elevation the climate of Iran varies considerably. On the heights the winter temperatures sometimes fall below zero, and in the lower altitudes of the plateau, summer temperatures often mount higher than 100° F. In the Persian Gulf coastal areas temperatures sometimes mount to 120° F. The heights, because there is little cloud formation to shield against the steady, direct rays of the sun, have hot day temperatures that descend rapidly with the coming of night. The summers are almost rainless; the heavier rainfall comes from November to March. Teheran has an average annual rainfall of only 9.3 inches, while Bushire on the Persian Gulf has only 11 inches. Much of the interior has no more than four or five inches of rainfall, and this rain is due to weak cyclonic storms that have an erratic distribution. The Caspian coastal plain, on the other hand, has too much rain, and parts of the area are unhealthful because of the prevalence of malaria. The north slopes of the Elburz, where there is heavy rainfall, are the only heavily forested region of Iran; the south slopes are almost barren.

Plants and Animals. The Zagros Mountains are rich in fruits, and the maritime areas of the Caspian readily produce rice, tobacco, tea, and fruits of all kinds. The north slopes of the Elburz support virgin forests of oak, beech, sycamore, and a luxuriant undergrowth. Date palms are plentiful on the littoral of the Persian Gulf. In areas other than the well-watered mountain slopes, trees, largely fruit, are cultivated. The forested slopes of the Elburz hide both large and small game. Among the wild animals are stags, foxes, lynx, leopards, and wild boars. Wild sheep, mountain goats (ibex), deer, wolves, and wildcats are found on the mountain slopes.

PEOPLE

The population is predominantly Mohammedan of the Shi'a sect. There are also smaller Kurdish, Armenian, Nestorian, and Jewish groups. The language is Persian which is of Indo-European stock. The physical type is basically Mediterranean (of the "Irano-Afghan" variant).

Recent estimates of Iran's population have varied widely, ranging from 10 to 18 million; of the population, about 3,000,000 are nomads. The officially estimated population in 1949 was 18,387,000.

PRINCIPAL CITIES	POPULATION 1942 Est.	1947 Est.
TEHERAN, the capital.........	699,110	850,000
MESHED.....................	176,000	250,000
TABRIZ.....................	214,000	214,000
ISFAHAN....................	205,500	205,000
ABADABN...................	40,000	150,000

Education. The old system of education in Iran was religious. Today, however, lay educational opportunity is generally available. The foreign schools supported by the American Presbyterian Mission, the Church Missionary Society, and the French Roman Catholic Mission have almost all been liquidated or absorbed into the Ministry of Education by order of the Iranian government. Iranian children are prohibited by law from attending other than government schools. A law providing for compulsory primary and general education, to be placed in force over a period of 10 years, was promulgated in 1943. Iran has more than 5,000 schools of all categories, topped by the University of Teheran, which has faculties in all branches of science and art, and which is largely staffed by instructors trained abroad under the Iranian plan for enlarging educational opportunities. A number of schools are still maintained by foreign agencies for the education of foreign children. See PERSIAN LANGUAGE AND LITERATURE; PERSIAN ARCHITECTURE.

ECONOMIC LIFE

Agriculture. Farming is the chief occupation of the Iranians, although the methods in use assure only minimum yields that, under better farming techniques, could be much increased. Because of the lack of rainfall in all but the Caspian region, dry farming can only be practiced at altitudes above 6,000 feet; at lower levels irrigation must be used. The Iranian irrigation system is very old and unique. There are few open irrigation streams. Instead, underground tunnels, called qanats, have been used for many centuries. The qanat is usually from 10 to 20 miles in length and about two to three feet in diameter. It is constructed with just sufficient slope to afford a slow water flow. At intervals shafts lead to the surface for the purpose of clearing debris from the qanat. At the water source lateral tunnels are dug to increase the water collection. The route of the qanat is lined with villages, with a well tapping the water at approximately every 20 yards. At the point where the qanat reaches ground surface irrigation ditches carry the water into cultivated fields. The system is excellent, but is expensive and needs frequent repair. The scanty river systems of Iran prohibit large irrigation projects, but many small ones are practicable, and the Iranian government has a number of small systems under construction, with more planned.

The farming population lives in villages, where a village headman supervises all farmers. Few farmers own their own land, and title to farming areas is held in great blocks by landlords or the religious sects, who seldom live in the area owned. The three-field system is largely in use: autumn-sown crops such as wheat, rye, and opium that are harvested in the summer; spring-sown crops such as corn, peas, and rice that are harvested in the autumn; and fallow fields.

The eastern part of Azerbaijan produces wheat, barley, almonds, and sugar beets. Gilan raises rice, jute, tobacco, tea, olives, and mulberry trees for the formerly large and, in recent years, increasing sericulture. The Fars area produces citrus fruits; Isfahan, leguminous plants; Khuzistan, dates; Khurasan, raisins, cotton, and gum tragacanth; Teheran, fruits; Semnan, pistachios; and Khamzeh, castor oil.

Much stock is also raised: sheep, asses, and goats in Khurasan, milch cattle and oxen in Azerbaijan and Mazanderan; mules in Isfahan, and horses in Kermanshah.

Mining. Numerous minerals are known to occur in Iran, but the sources have scarcely been touched, largely because of the transport difficulties. Coal is mined near Teheran, and there are turquoise mines at Nishapur west of Meshed in eastern Iran. The latent mineral resources of Iran include coal, iron, copper, lead, manga-

Road in Iran is leveled with roller drawn by water buffalo

ACME

Iranian farmer

ACME

Home of a rice farmer in the Caspian seacoast lowlands

EWING GALLOWAY

Zoroastrian woman

EWING GALLOWAY

Houses in a Zoroastrian town near religious center of Yezd

EWING GALLOWAY

Nomad-type woman

EWING GALLOWAY

Nomad's tent, made of black goat's hair woven into cloth

EWING GALLOWAY

Iranian schoolboy

EWING GALLOWAY

Street scene in a walled oasis town in the Iranian desert

EWING GALLOWAY

nese, marble, borax, nickel, cobalt, iron oxide, sulfur, sodium sulfate, other sodium salts, and rock salt.

Iran is the fourth largest oil-producing country of the world, and petroleum products make up about 60 per cent of Iran's exports. The oil fields have been developed mostly by foreign capital. The largest field, controlled by the Anglo-Iranian Oil Company, which in part is owned by the British government, lies about 150 miles north of the head of the Persian Gulf. The oil from this field is piped to Abadan, where the controlling company has one of the largest refineries in the world, complete with modern residential, business, and government buildings. Oil fields in northeastern Azerbaijan were at one time held by British, Dutch, and American interests, but these leases were canceled by Iran in 1944. It is believed that more than 20 per cent of the Iranian government's income is derived from oil royalties. Oil was struck in the Masjid-i-Sulaiman field in 1908 after some seven years of fruitless drilling, and the Anglo-Iranian Oil Company was formed the next year. The field is one of the world's richest. The production of a third Iranian oil field, the Naft-i-Shah field in Kermanshah, is used within Iran itself.

Fisheries. Iran's commercial fishermen ply the waters of both the Persian Gulf and the Caspian Sea, but although some 10,000 tons of fish products are shipped from the gulf area each year, the more important fisheries are in the Caspian and its rivers, from which the fishermen net salmon, pike-perch, carp, and sturgeon. Caspian sturgeon yield some of the world's highest quality caviar, and canning factories at Pahlevi and a Bandar Shah prepare the products for export. Most caviar goes through Russia, where the cans receive Russian labels because of the world's belief that Russian caviar is superior.

Manufactures. Although there has been a decided increase in manufacturing interest and effort, Iran is not a manufacturing nation. Manufactures are largely government monopolies and, since the country is mostly agricultural, most manufactures are processed vegetable and animal products. Mazanderan's present silk manufacture is the result of Reza Shah's interest in reviving the silk industries. Persian carpets are world-famed, and provide one of the country's largest exports. Carpets are produced largely at Tabriz, Kerman, Sultanabad, and Hamadan. Woolen and cotton cloths and yarns are manufactured at Isfahan. Teheran produces glass, small arms, ammunition, and chemicals. There is a match industry with factories at Tabriz, Zenjan, Teheran, and Isfahan. Tobacco and cigarettes are produced in the northern areas. Sugar refineries, processing principally beet sugar, are also found in the Caspian area. Other productions include wine, shawls, woolen felts, tea, and tanned hides.

Commerce. Iran's chief ports on the Persian Gulf are Abadan, important for its oil shipments; Khorramshahr, lend-lease port during World War II; Bushire; Bandar Abbas (Gombroon), one of the hottest places in the world, chiefly engaged in coastwise trade; and Gwatar, on the Arabian Sea at the border of Indian Baluchistan, a relatively unimportant shipping point. The chief ports on the Caspian shores, serving Iran's coastal trade and trade with Russia, are Astara, Pahlevi (Enzeli), Chalus, and Bandar Shah, the latter the terminus of the Trans-Iranian railway. The chief imports are manufactured goods, beverages and foodstuffs, raw materials, and precious metals. The chief exports are oil, carpets, wool, hides and skins, dried fruits, cotton, wool, gums, opium, silk, and sausage casings.

Communications. The Trans-Iranian railway, from Khorramshahr at the head of the Persian Gulf to Bandar Shah on the southeast coast of the Caspian Sea (870 mi.) was completed in 1938. A much earlier line, completed in the early part of the 20th century, runs northwest from Tabriz to connect with Russian lines in the Armenian Soviet Socialist Republic at Dzhulfa. A proposed line will connect Teheran with Tabriz. A branch of the Trans-Iranian line runs east of Teheran through Samnan as far as Damghan. It is planned to complete this line to Meshed in northeastern Iran. A short branch line in Azerbaijan connects Sharifkhaneh at the north of Lake Urmia with the Tabriz-Dzhulfa line.

The trade routes to the east have passed through Iran for many centuries. During the 20th century the government has made road construction and maintenance one of its principal concerns. There are some 5,000 miles of roads open to motor traffic throughout the year, among which is the road used and maintained by the United States and Russia during World War II for the transport of lend-lease supplies from Khorramshahr at the head of the Persian Gulf through Hamadan into Azerbaijan. Motor busses and trucks, mostly government-owned, travel these roads. However, there is still much of Iran which can only be reached through the use of such transport animals as horses, camels, mules, and asses.

The air base which the United States Persian Gulf Command constructed during World War II at Abadan was turned over to Iran after the war. Air services are carried on between Europe and Teheran by British, Dutch, French, and Scandinavian air lines. A Soviet air service from Moscow makes stops at Pahlevi, Teheran, and Bushire. An Iranian air line stops at Kermanshah on its flight to Baghdad, where connection is made with British and other European lines.   C. S.

GOVERNMENT AND HISTORY

Government. Iran is a constitutional monarchy. Executive power, under the shah, is vested in a cabinet headed by a prime minister, appointed by the shah and responsible to the legislature. The bicameral legislature is made up of an upper house, the senate, and a lower house, the Majlis (National Assembly). The people elect the members of the Majlis and half the members of the senate. The shah appoints the other half of the senate's members. The court system, modeled after that of France, is headed by a court of cassation or supreme court; below it are eight courts of appeal, and on the lowest level, justices of the peace, police magistrates, and other minor courts. Administratively, Iran is divided into 10 provinces (ostan). These are subdivided in turn into counties, districts, village groups, and finally villages. Officials appointed by and responsible to the central government head each province and district. There are no real political parties in the American sense in Iran.

History. The long history of the nation as old Persia came to an end with the revolution of 1925

EWING GALLOWAY
Pahlevi, caviar center, on the Caspian Sea

when Reza Shah Pahlavi took the throne. He assumed dictatorial powers and restored internal order, rejuvenated the army, reorganized the government, improved transportation, and ended the special rights exercised by Great Britain and other nations. In 1935 the name of the country was officially changed from Persia to Iran, and in 1937 Reza Shah granted U.S. oil companies concessions in eastern Iran. Next year the Trans-Iranian Railway, built in seven years, was opened. When war was declared in 1939, the government announced its neutrality.

In World War II the British needed control of the Middle East to insure the security of the Suez Canal and access to the Middle Eastern oil resources. Germany and Italy hoped to obtain control over Iran, Iraq, and Syria in order to acquire oil and to end eager British position with reference to the Suez and India. In April, 1941, the Iranian government drew closer to Germany, and Britain decided to take military measures. With Soviet aid, Britain occupied Iran in the late summer of 1942 and eliminated the German influence. Reza Shah was deposed and his son Mohammed Reza Shah put on the throne.

Iran declared war on Germany in September, 1943, and on Japan in 1945. At the Teheran Conference in 1943, the United States, the Soviet Union, and Great Britain guaranteed Iran's independence and territorial integrity. Iran became one of the original members of the United Nations in 1945. The date for the withdrawal of foreign troops was set as March 2, 1946. In November, 1945, a pro-Soviet government set itself up in the province of Azerbaijan in northwestern Iran. This government was backed by Soviet troops who remained in that region beyond the agreed evacuation date. In January, 1946, Iran appealed to the United Nations on the ground that Soviet officials were interfering in Iran's internal affairs. The Soviet forces were finally withdrawn on the promise that a joint Soviet-Iranian oil company would be formed pending approval by the Iranian parliament, which rejected the proposal. Elections were held in January, 1947, and the popularity of the central government candidates assured the reunion of Azerbaijan with Iran. To supervise the election the Iranian army moved into the province.

At the end of 1947 the Soviet government charged that Iran, in refusing to grant oil concessions to the U.S.S.R., had violated the agreement under which Soviet troops withdrew. Early next year the Iranian government rejected the Soviet charges and stated that the Soviet government had continued to plot against the independence of Iran. On February 4, 1949, an attempt was made on the life of the Shah by a member of the left-wing Tudeh underground party. In late 1949, the Shah visited the United States. On Oct. 10, 1949, the United States allotted funds to Iran under the Point 4 program. At the same time Iran and the U.S.S.R. reached a barter agreement. In March, 1951, a fanatic belonging to a sect proposing to nationalize Iran's oil industry assassinated Iran's premier. Parliament confirmed a strongly pro-Western premier in spite of a protest walkout by pro-Soviet leftist and extreme nationalist deputies. But he soon resigned to be succeeded by a nationalist premier, and parliament approved nationalization of Iran's oil industry in the face of a British protest against the confiscation of the Anglo-Iranian Oil Company. For earlier history see Persia.   G. B. de H.

Bibliog.–V. Sheean, *New Persia* (1927); W. S. Haas, *Iran* (1946); E. E. Groseclose, *Introduction to Iran* (1947); G. Lenezowski, *Russia and the West in Iran* (1950).

IRAPUATO, town, Mexico, province of Guanajuato; on the National Railway and a highway connecting with Guanajuato, near the geographic center of the country. Irapuato is a distributing point and an important agricultural and industrial center. Ancient churches and convents and fine modern buildings add to the city's charm. The manufacture of cigarettes is the chief industry. Pop. (1950) 78,017.

ORIENTAL INSTITUTE OF CHICAGO

Independent State Since 1932

Date palms, rice fields, and oil wells abound in this ancient land of Asia

IRAQ, or **Irak,** an independent kingdom of W Asia Minor, embracing all but the northernmost parts of Mesopotamia and the former Turkish vilayets of Baghdad, Basra, and Mosul, bounded on the N by the rugged Taurus Mountains of SE Turkey, on the NE by Iran, on the SE by the Persian Gulf, S by Kuwait, Uqubba (also called Neutral Territory), and Saudi Arabia, SW by Jordan, and W by Syria; area 116,000 sq. mi.; pop. (U.N. 1949 est.) 4,990,000.

The modern country of Iraq measures 600 miles from its northeast to southernmost tips, and 450 miles from east to west at its greatest width. Iraq has only about 26 miles of seacoast, which borders the southern edge of the peninsula extending along the estuary of the Shatt al Arab River into the Persian Gulf.

Coat of arms of Iraq

Physical Features

Topography. There are three great geographical divisions: the mountainous northeastern section, of southern Kurdistan; the arid desert-steppeland of the west and southwest; and the fertile plains and rolling hills between and along the three great rivers, the Euphrates, Tigris, and Diyala and their tributaries. The hot, dry steppeland, or desert fringe, lying west and southwest of the Euphrates is divided by that river into Upper and Lower Iraq, the section including part of Mesopotamia, a large portion of the Syrian Desert, Al Jazira, Al Wadyan, and Al Hajara. The surface of this desert land is composed of gravel, sand, and a light loam. It is a broad, treeless plain with frequent scarps rising from 50 to 100 feet in height. The area west of the Euphrates, called the Jazira ("Island"), is often referred to as the "Cradle of Humanity"; in spring it provides excellent pasturage for the livestock of the nomadic tribes of the country. Irrigation wells and canals permit a limited cultivation of about 15,000 square miles in this region, with additional fertile patches along streams and at oases. East of this grassland, along the Euphrates and Tigris, are some intensely cultivated fertile lands. The lower plain of this division, formed by the deltas of the rivers, extends south 400 miles in wide, terraced plains to the Persian Gulf, and is cultivable except in its lower reaches, where much of the area is low and marshy. Away from the rivers,

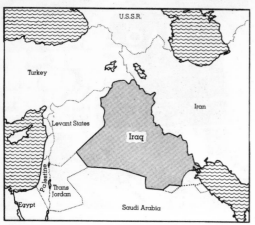

Location map of Iraq

irrigation ditches, or oases, all is arid and wasteland except in flood times. The character of the sections called Al Wadyan and Al Hajara is best described by the translation of their names "wadi or stream-fed," and "stony plain."

Iraq's third distinct natural division is the northern and eastern Kurdish Highlands, the foothills of the eastern end of the Anatolian Plateau, consisting of high limestone terraced ridges, which decrease in gently undulating slopes to the southwest plains. This is a semiwild region, lying along the borders of Turkey and Persia, though a great deal of it is the pastoral area of Sulaimaniya, where nomad tribes graze their cattle, sheep, and goats above the clouds, and cultivate small valley gardens in summer.

In northeastern Iraq, the land culminates in peaks reaching an altitude of from 10,000 to 12,000 feet; from the east central frontier into Iran extends the Pusht-i-kuh Range of the Zagros Mountains, whose highest peaks rise well over 8,000 feet. West of Mosul the Sinjar Hills (4,500 ft.) separate Iraq from Syria. There are a few wooded spots in the mountains where small forests of scrub oak, walnut, poplar, and pine grow. In the plains and desert, except by the rivers, or at oases, trees are almost entirely absent.

Iraq is drained by the three largest, longest, and most famous rivers of Asia Minor, the EUPHRATES, TIGRIS, and Diyala and their tributaries, the Khabur, Hauran, Great and Little Zabs, Aq, Shatt al Adhaim, and Sirwan. These are the lifeblood of this desert country. Most of them rise in snowclad mountains and flow across the arid land into the marshy delta to join as one in the Shatt al Arab, before emptying into the Persian Gulf. In southern Iraq both the Euphrates and Tigris have low gradients and great evaporation and are overloaded with silt. The Tigris is the swiftest and is navigable for steam craft for more than 450 miles as far as Baghdad. Levees hold the waters of the two great rivers above the level of the land in many areas. The Euphrates is not very useful for navigation except by native cargo boats called "dhows" and the curious bowl-shaped basket boats called "gufas," boats made of plaited reeds covered with pitch. In northern Iraq the rivers flow in normal valleys rather than on the plain. All of the rivers overflow in May and June, the rainy season. The floodwaters are created not from local rainfall, but from heavy storms in the mountain regions. There are numerous large lakes dotted over the country, chief among which are Habbaniya, Sunaisala, Bahr al Milh, Sanniya, Dalmaj, Sawaigiga, Auda, and Hor al Hammar (a small sea).

Climate. The summer temperatures of Iraq range from extreme heat in the desert to Alpine coolness in the mountains. The winters are mild and last from December to April. Only in the highlands are there

snowstorms. There is hardly any spring or autumn. The humidity is low except in the delta and around Basra. At the time of the rainy season there are usually cyclonic storms in the lowlands. The average rainfall throughout the year is 10 inches in Lower Iraq, 14.6 inches at Mosul, and 16.5 inches at Kirkuk. From June to October is the dry season. The highest temperature recorded in 50 years at Baghdad for July and August was 190° F., the coldest 48° F. The northern 200 miles of the country normally receives enough rainfall from October to May to raise winter crops, but the southern 400 miles would be an arid wasteland away from the rivers if irrigation were not practiced. The prevailing wind is from the northwest and is strongest from May to August when it is called the "Shimal." It brings storms that sometimes last three days. In winter the wind from the mountains is penetrating and cold, and the wind from the gulf is relatively cold and high in humidity with heavy morning fogs.

Plants and Animals. The plants of Iraq are largely like those of the Mediterranean areas in the irrigated districts; reeds grow in the marshy areas. Wild animals found are the cheetah, gazelle, antelope, wild pig, jackal, hyena, dwarf wolf, wild donkey, rabbit, and jerboa. Grouse and partridge are seen, and in the populated districts there are large owls, ravens, and vultures.

PEOPLE

Population. The population of Iraq is mainly Mohammedan (predominantly Arabs with some Kurds in the north), with smaller Christian, Jewish, and Yezidi communities. Arabic is the predominant language. The physical type is basically Mediterranean. About 90 per cent of the people live along the rivers or canals, especially in the south; two-thirds of the total population live in towns; the rest are nomad tribesmen.

PRINCIPAL CITIES	POPULATION	
	1938 Est.	1947 Census
BAGHDAD, the capital.........	400,000	552,047
MOSUL......................	260,000	340,541
BASRA......................	180,000	206,302
Kirkuk.....................	30,000	148,349

Other cities of note are HILLA, near the site of Babylon; Kurnah, Amara, and Kut-al-Imara, market centers. Karbala and Nejef are important pilgrimage centers, as is Baghdad. UR and Eridu, 14 miles south of Ur, are thought to be the world's oldest cities. Remains of the fourth millenium B.C., including a prehistoric temple, have been unearthed at Eridu. The vicinity also is claimed as the legendary site of the Garden of Eden. The most dense concentration of people is along the Shatt al Arab.

THE DIVISIONS OF IRAQ

	1947		1947
Amara.......	308,108	Hilla.........	261,903
Arbil........	240,273	Karbala......	276,670
Baghdad.....	805,293	Kirkuk.......	285,878
Basra........	352,039	Kut..........	224,792
Diwaniyah....	383,787	Mosul........	601,589
Diyala.......	273,336	Muntafiq.....	369,806
Dulain.......	193,294	Sulaimani....	222,732

The great majority of the people of Iraq are Moslems, divided into various sects such as the Shi'ites, and Sunnis. The Christians of Iraq live in Baghdad, Mosul, and many of the hill towns of upper Iraq.

Education. The children of Iraq from the ages of 6 to 12, are compelled to attend free primary schools. Instruction is in Arabic, Kurdish, and frequently in English. In 1945 there were 897 state elementary schools, of which 665 were for boys, and 176 were for girls. There are 76 additional private elementary schools. Of the 51 intermediate and secondary schools 33 were for boys, and 18 were for girls. There were five teachers colleges, two for women. Secondary

PHILIP GENDREAU
Kurdish Man

EWING GALLOWAY
Wheat is trampled and dragged in a primitive threshing yard

PHILIP GENDREAU
Arabian woman

EWING GALLOWAY
Homes clustered about a mosque in the city of Al Kadhimain

schools require fees but are so conducted as to permit poor boys of high scholastic standing the chance to continue specific training. In Baghdad, Mosul, and Kirkuk, are located three technical colleges for men and there are colleges in agriculture, medicine, engineering, pharmacy, law, military science, police work, home arts, nursing, and fine arts. Nearly all of the higher schools of learning of Iraq are now co-educational. Iraq has no university. The government receives large royalties on its exported petroleum, and this revenue is used for education, public health, and the improvement of the irrigation system.

Economic Life

In order of their importance, the industries of Iraq are: the production of oil, agriculture, manufactures, mines, fisheries, and shipping. There are only about 100 manufacturing concerns throughout Iraq; these produce bricks and tiles, cigarettes, woolen and cotton textiles, distilled liquors, knitted goods, vegetable oils, soap, glassware, tanneries, leather goods, and oriental rugs. In 1929 Iraq passed a law offering tax relief and many other concessions to stimulate the establishment of new industries.

Agriculture. Iraq annually has about 1,000,000 acres of land under cultivation. In the upper stretches of the country tillable areas lie largely in the valleys of the Tigris, Euphrates, and Great and Little Zab rivers. Enough rainfall is received from October to May to raise winter crops of wheat, barley, beans, rice, and maize in this area. Elsewhere, Iraq's agricultural development is largely dependent on the efficiency of its irrigation system. Most of the irrigated territory lies between the Euphrates, Tigris, and Diyala rivers. Considerable progress was made in improving the irrigation canal system during the British occupation between World Wars I and II.

Two harvests can be gathered in the year in the eastern and northern sections, one in April, the other in October. The permanent farmlands are usually located on the canals and rivers or at oases and lakes. Primitive methods are used by most of the farmers, although modern machinery is being acquired. The most important crop of Iraq, especially in the south, is the date crop. More than 200 varieties are produced to supply about 80 per cent of the world's date demands. The largest groves are located along 100 miles of the Shatt al Arab River, especially at the Great Basra Oasis, an area of 200 square miles. The fronds of the date palm are used to weave floor matting, rope, and other plaited articles; the palm timber serves for bridge and light construction work and the making of small polished wooden articles. The over-ripe fruit is utilized to make syrup, vinegar, and distilled spirits; the seeds are ground to make food for cattle and sheep.

Second in importance in food production is rice, which is grown largely in the lower reaches of the Tigris and Euphrates and to the east around Amara and Diwaniya. Wheat, barley, and beans are grown in Kirkuk and Mosul provinces; Indian corn and oats around Basra and Diyala; tobacco in Sulaimaniya; giant millet, sesame, vetch, lentils, licorice, and small millet are also grown in most of the irrigated districts. Cotton is gradually coming into favor throughout the country. About 14,000 acres of cotton are now annually cultivated. From 10,000 to 15,000 acres are planted in permanent orchards of apricots, pears, apples, oranges, lemons, and mulberries. There are fig and olive groves, and a variety of berry thickets. All kinds of melons are grown.

Livestock assets of the country are estimated at 8,000,000 sheep, 2,000,000 goats, 650,000 cattle. Camels and donkeys are other domestic animals raised. Thousands of the fine purebred Arabian horses, pride of the Moslem world, are raised yearly for domestic use, trading with near-by countries, and export all over the world.

Mineral Resources and Mining. Minerals found in Iraq, apart from oil, are not important and include salt and a little coal. Oil production, however, is great. Iraq has some of the richest oil fields of the world. The three great oil belts are the eastern belt, linked with that of Iran; the middle Tigris belt; and the Euphrates Valley (southwestern and southern Iraq) belt. These belts are centered in the provinces of Baghdad, Kirkuk, Mosul, and Basra. The two most important fields of the country are the Baba Gurgur wells north of Kirkuk, and those at Khanagin, southeast of Kirkuk near the Iranian border. The Baba Gurgur fields are operated by the Iraq Petroleum Company under British management on behalf of an international group. From these wells, via the refinery at Kirkuk, pipe lines run south and west across Syria to Tripoli and southwest across the desert of Iraq and Trans-Jordan and Palestine to Haifa. The Khanagin Oil Company, subsidiary of the Anglo-Iranian Oil Company, operates a large refinery 30 miles south of Kirkuk. In this belt also are Naft-i-Shah, and Naft Khaneh, twin oil cities on the Iranian border, from which pipe lines run to the Kermanshah (Iran), refinery.

Mosul's oil fields are near ancient Nineveh, and are operated by the Mosul Petroleum Company, associate of the Iraq Petroleum Company. This company holds the concession in all parts of the country west of the Tigris. The Basra Petroleum Company holds the concession for all the areas southwest of the Tigris and covering the southernmost liwas to the Gulf of Persia. The total normal production of oil per year in Iraq amounts to about 30,000,000 barrels.

Commerce. The total value of imports into Iraq in 1944 amounted to $58,480,321; exports (not including shipments of oil) amounted to $33,651,536. Imports (in order of amount) were cotton, woolen, silk, and rayon piece goods, coffee, tea, sugar, iron and steel goods, metal ores, machinery, vehicles, electrical machinery, equipment, and appliances, matches, tools, soap, chemicals and drugs, paper, and sacking. Exports are petroleum, dates (107,023 tons in 1944), Arabian horses, hides, lambskins, purebred sheep and goats, raw wool, angora goat's wool, gold and silver filigree and inlaid work, licorice roots, tobacco, barley, wheat, rice, maize, hemp, millet, sorghum, and date palm fiber for thatching and plaiting. Trade is carried on (in order of importance) with India, Syria, the United States, Great Britain, Iran, Trans-Jordan, Palestine, and one or two of the European countries. Baghdad is the principal commercial center; the port of Basra is the chief receiving and shipping center. Kirkuk and Mosul are commercially important as oil centers and because they are linked by railroads with the west coast ports on the Mediterranean.

Transportation. The Iraq State Railroad, operating over 966 miles of one-meter and standard gage main lines, is the country's only railway system. These lines run from Basra to Baghdad (354 mi.) and on to Kirkuk (200 mi.); from Baghdad to Quaraghan (92 mi.) and on to Khanagin (17 mi.); from Baghdad via Mosul to Tel Kotchek (328 mi.) where it connects with the Syrian-Turkish system. Steamer passenger and freight lines operate between Basra, the chief seaport, and Baghdad, via the Tigris. Tonnage shipping is handled by the Euphrates and Tigris Steam Navigation Company and three smaller companies beyond the steamer limits. Basra, 60 miles from the head of the Persian Gulf, is the only port for seagoing vessels and handles more than 50 per cent of Iraq's foreign trade. The port of Basra has 3,300 feet of docks and wharves with warehousing facilities. Iraq has nearly 4,000 miles of improved roads, 680 of which are fine macadamized highways that connect with highways of bordering countries and their chief cities and ports. There are 50,000 miles of secondary roads. Air routes link Baghdad with England, Egypt, Europe, India, Australia, via the Imperial Airways

Lines, and the British, Dutch, and Persian Overseas Airways. The Iranian State Airlines operates a biweekly flight between Teheran and Baghdad and Rutba and between these cities and Damascus. Seaplane bases are maintained at Basra and Habbaniya; on Lake Habbaniya and the Euphrates.

All forms of communication in Iraq are under government control, which maintains telephone, telegraph, and radio. Mail is carried by air, railway, truck transport, waterway, pack and mountain runners more than 17,078 miles.

GOVERNMENT AND HISTORY

Government. Iraq is a constitutional, hereditary monarchy. Its constitution came into being on March 21, 1925. The senate of 20 members is appointed by the king for eight-year terms and the lower house of 140 members is elected by manhood suffrage. The cabinet is responsible to the legislature. The judicial system consists of the Court of Cassation of Baghdad, four courts of appeal, 13 courts of first instance, and 42 peace courts. For administrative purposes the country is divided into 14 liwas, each headed by an official responsible to the central government. The Independence party is rightist and nationalist; the Liberal party is moderate nationalist and favors representative government; the Nationalist Democratic party is left of center; the People's party was banned in 1947 on the ground that it was subversive.

History. For the history of Iraq until the end of World War I see MESOPOTAMIA. During the war the country was liberated from Turkish rule and in November, 1920, a provisional Arab government was set up by the British Commissioner. In August, 1921, the Emir Feisal was elected and crowned king of Iraq. By the Treaty of Sèvres, Turkey renounced sovereignty over Iraq, and its administration was entrusted under mandate to Great Britain. In 1925 the nation became a constitutional monarchy. In 1932 Iraq entered the League of Nations as a sovereign, independent state; her former status as a British mandate was replaced by a 25-year treaty of alliance with Great Britain.

In 1936 a military revolt resulted in an army-dominated government which lasted less than a year. In April, 1939, the king was killed in an accident which was blamed by some on the British. The four-year-old child Feisal II became the king under the regency of Abdul Ilah. Riots against the Jews complicated the political crisis.

When World War I broke out, Iraq severed diplomatic relations with Germany but some elements continued to be pro-German. When these pro-Axis forces obtained control of the government of Iraq the British position was threatened. Britain launched military operations and by the end of May, 1941, British forces reached Baghdad. With the disappearance of German influence, the moderates assumed office and attempted to solve the economic dislocations which were caused by the military conflict. On January 16, 1943, Iraq declared war on the Axis powers. Iraq became an original member of the United Nations. With Soviet influence reaching into Iran on Iraq's eastern border, the government became concerned with the activities of radical groups. The political crisis, especially the opposition to Zionism, led to the resignation of the government on May 30, 1946. The new government brought some stability to Iraq. By October 26, 1947, the withdrawal of all British land forces was completed. On January 15, 1948, a new treaty of alliance and mutual assistance with Great Britain was signed, but the government which negotiated the treaty had to resign and the new government repudiated it on the ground that it did not realize the aspirations of Iraq.

Iraq, together with other members of the Arab League, fought in 1948 against the newly-formed state of Israel. In March and April, 1949, the forces of Iraq in Palestine were withdrawn. In the early part of 1949 the government took strong action to suppress Communist activities. In this year the government undertook a long range economic development program with particular emphasis on agricultural development. On Feb. 26, 1950, Iraq signed a treaty of friendship with Pakistan. On May 20, 1949, the exodus of Jews from Iraq started but relations between Iraq and the new state of Israel continued to be strained. On June 15, Iraq obtained a loan from the International Bank to help to finance a flood-control system for the Tigris River. In January, 1951, the Premier of Iraq urged the Arab nations, meeting in Cairo under the auspices of the Arab League, to renounce neutrality in the cold war, to line up firmly with the West, and to organize a joint Middle Eastern army. See FEISAL AL HUSSEIN.

K. E. H.; F. M.; G. B. DE H.

BIBLIOG.–S. H. Longrigg, *Four Centuries of Modern Iraq* (1925); M. F. Jamali, *New Iraq* (1934); H. Foster, *Making of Modern Iraq* (1935); E. Main, *Iraq from Mandate to Independence* (1936); P. W. Ireland, *Iraq, a Study in Political Development* (1938); H. Field and J. B. Glubb, *Yezidir, Sulubba, and other Tribes of Iraq and Adjacent Regions* (1943); S. Lloyd, *Iraq* (1943); M. Khadduri, *Government of Iraq* (1944); S. Lloyd, *Twin Rivers* (1947); F. H. Gamble, *Iraq: Economic and Commercial Conditions* (1950).

IRAQ ARABI, formerly a Turkish vilayet, now a district of SE Iraq. Its boundaries generally correspond with the ancient country of Babylonia, between the lower courses of the Tigris and Euphrates rivers. It contains the ruins of the ancient Babylon, Borsippa, Seleucia, and Ctesiphon, and the modern towns of Baghdad and Basra. It is mostly peopled by nomadic tribes. That part under cultivation produces dates, millet, grain, and cotton.

IRAWADI. See IRRAWADDY RIVER.

IRAZÚ, peak, Costa Rica, an active volcano, 11,319 feet in altitude. A modern concrete highway runs from the village of Cartago, at the foot of the mountain, to the summit. From the summit both the Atlantic and the Pacific oceans can be seen on a clear day.

IREDELL, JAMES, 1751–99, American jurist, was born in Lewes, England. He emigrated to North Carolina about 1768, was admitted to the bar in 1775, became prominent as a lawyer, and having embraced the cause of the colonists in the Revolutionary War, was made in turn a judge of the State Superior Court (1777) and attorney general of the state (1779). After the war he advocated the establishment of a strong central government, strove, as a member of the North Carolina convention, to secure the ratification by the state of the Federal Constitution, and in the early years of the national government was an ardent Federalist in politics. From 1790 until his death, he was an associate justice of the U.S. Supreme Court. The first to express the doctrine of judicial review in a United States court opinion, he was also largely responsible for the enactment of the 11th Amendment.

IRELAND, JOHN, 1838–1918, American Roman Catholic prelate. Born in Burnchurch, county Kilkenny, Ireland, he came to St. Paul, Minn., in early childhood. After receiving his education at seminaries in France, he returned to the United States and was ordained in 1861. As an enlisted chaplain, he served in the Civil War in 1862–63 with the 5th Minnesota Regiment, after which he became rector of the cathedral in St. Paul. Here he gained prominence by his rigid advocacy of total abstinence, opposing liquor traffic, and preaching against political corruption. In 1875 he was consecrated bishop of Maronea and coadjutor bishop of St. Paul, succeeding in 1884. His see was made archiepiscopal in 1888. He was influential in founding Catholic University in Washington.

IRELAND, JOHN, 1879–   , English composer, was born in Bowden. He wrote several sonatas, but his songs are considered his most important creations. Composed to poems by Hardy, Housman, Masefield, and Symons, they number over 70. Ireland's utilization of old scales and the Dorian and Lydian modes make his music of great interest to musicians, but his rather austere style prohibits much general popularity.   ANNE AND MARX OBERNDORFER

IRELAND, WILLIAM HENRY, 1777–1825, English literary forger, was born in London. In 1794 he was apprenticed to a London attorney, in whose office he had access to a collection of old deeds. From one of these he cut a piece of parchment, on which he wrote what purported to be a mortgage deed bearing the signature of Shakespeare. This he presented to his father (an enthusiast for everything Shakespearean), who accepted it as genuine, as did many more qualified critics. Subsequently, Ireland forged a large assortment of interesting relics, including a transcript of *King Lear*, and a new Shakespeare play, *Vortigern and Rowena*, which was purchased by Sheridan and produced at the Drury Lane theater. Later, the hostile attacks of Edmond Malone and other Shakespeare experts compelled Ireland to make a full confession.

BIBLIOG.–J. Mair, *The Fourth Forger* (1938).

IRELAND, an island in the Atlantic Ocean, one of the British Isles, separated from Great Britain by the North Channel, the Irish Sea, and St. George's Channel; area 31,839 sq. mi.; pop. about 4,062,000. The north, west, and south coasts of the island face the Atlantic Ocean. The island is about 300 miles long and has an average width of about 110 miles. The island is divided into two political units: Northern Ireland, in the northeast, and Ireland.

Topography. The island is like a bowl, rimmed by bold hills of high relief which dip inward to hills of low relief; the interior is a rolling plain. The coast line is irregular, having been inundated at the close of the Ice Age; since that time it has had a tendency to rise. The west coast is marked by many bays and headlands and a few small islands; among the most important are Donegal Bay in the northwest; Achil

The sheer side of a mountain in county Kerry

IRISH TOURIST ASSN.

Island and Clow Bay on the west-central coast; Galway Bay; the estuary of the River Shannon; Dingle Bay; the Kenmare River estuary; Bantry Bay; and other small bays formed by sandstone headlands on the southwest coast. The mountains range from 500 to 3,000 feet in altitude. In the north are the mountains of Donegal, in the west the mountains of Mayo, Connemara, and Kerry. The Kerrys rise to 3,414 feet at Carrauntoohil, the highest elevation on the island. On the east coast there are two ranges: the Wicklow Mountains, south of Dublin, and the Mourne Mountains, in Northern Ireland. The central plains of the island are composed of Carboniferous limestone; to the north there are pre-Cambrian crystalline schists and gneisses and in the northeast, a lava-capped plateau. In the southwest there are coal measures and Devonian and Old Red sandstone formations. Fault and faultline scarps in the northern hills are similar to those of Scotland.

Drainage. The central plain is an area of karst topography, it contains many sinks and surface lakes, and is the source of the streams which drain to the Atlantic. Lough Ree in the center of the plain is drained by the River Shannon. In its southwest course it receives the Suck River and widens to form Lough Derg before entering its long, wide estuary. The Shannon is 250 miles long, and is navigable for large steamers for about 120 miles; smaller craft can go upstream and cross the island by either the Grand or Royal canals which go to Dublin. There is a line of smaller lakes at the line of contact between the limestone and igneous rocks in the lee of the mountains of Mayo and Connemara. From north to south there are Lough Conn, Lough Carra, Lough Mask, and Lough Corrib, which drains into Galway Bay. The Erne River flows northeast from Lough Gowna through Upper Lough Erne and Lough Erne to enter Donegal Bay. The source and the mouth of the system are in Eire, but the lakes are in Northern Ireland. Also in Northern Ireland is Lough Neagh, the largest lake of the island; it covers nearly 100,000 acres and occupies a depression in the lava plateau. Lough Neagh is drained northward by the Bann River which enters the Atlantic just west of the GIANT's CAUSEWAY. Ulster Canal, navigable for small craft, connects Belfast to the River Shannon, it crosses the southern tips of Lough Neagh and Upper Lough Erne. Foyle River forms part of the west boundary between Eire and Northern Ireland. It enters a large semi-enclosed bay, called Lough Foyle, and has been canalized up to Londonderry. In the south Lee River enters Cork Harbor, which is navigable to the town of Cork; and the Suir River enters Waterford Harbor, which is navigable for large vessels up to Waterford and for smaller vessels for almost 50 miles above the town.

Climate. Ireland has a marine climate. The west coast is washed by the warm Rennell Current, part

A jaunting car on the shore of a Killarney lake

of the North Atlantic Drift. West winds carrying moisture are forced upwards by the coastal hill lands and precipitate between 60 and 80 inches of rain on the windward slopes. The hills cast a slight rain-shadow, and the average annual precipitation decreases to about 30 inches near Dublin. The island has a mean annual temperature of 50° F. with a small annual range. The average January temperatures are between 40° and 44°; the central plain is the coldest section. The average July temperatures are between 58° and 60°; the southeast coast and part of the central plain are the warmest sections. The maximum precipitation comes during the winter, but the light drizzly rain is well distributed in all seasons. Fogs are common, and there is almost constant cloud cover. Under these conditions the famous green grasses thrive. There is some forest cover of broadleaf and mixed broadleaf conifers which covers only 1.4 per cent of the land. The soils are podzols (like those of Great Britain and Canada) with much bog. Fishing is only a minor island industry because of the fogs and gales of the Atlantic and lack of native lumber for ships.

The Plants and Animals are similar to those of Great Britain, but the number of species is much less. The lizard is the only reptile found. The mole, shrew, wildcat, polecat, weasel, bear, beaver, and other mammals are unknown. Grass is abundant all over the country; sedges, rushes and ferns flourish; oak, beech, pine, and birch trees are found but to a limited extent. For the people, their work, and their government, see EIRE; NORTHERN IRELAND.

HISTORY

Early Ireland. The ancient inhabitants of Ireland, as of certain other parts of the British Isles, were the Picts. They were overcome by the CELTS at some time after 400 B.C. These tall blond invaders set up a number of small states, each with its king and assembly of freemen. At the time of the Christianization of Ireland by ST. PATRICK in the fifth century A.D., Ireland was organized into five kingdoms, Ulster, Meath, Munster, Connaught, and Leinster, all ruled over by the high king, at Tara in Meath. Christianity rapidly secured a foothold, and an era began during which Latin culture was cherished, peace was firmly established, and Irish missionaries carried Christianity to other portions of the British Isles and into parts of continental Europe. During the so-called Dark Ages Ireland was both a custodian and a focus of culture and classical knowledge. The Danes invaded Ireland in the 8th century, and occupied a portion of the country, but their power was broken by King Brian Boru in 1016.

English Occupation. English invasions beginning in the 12th century secured a foothold in Dublin and along the east coast, but the stubborn resistance of the Irish prevented English occupation of the whole island until the time of Elizabeth. From that time on the history of Ireland was one of repeated Irish rebellion against the English overlords, met by forcible efforts of the latter to subdue the island, by means of persecutions of Catholics, armed intervention with much bloodshed, and confiscation of lands, which were then awarded to English or Scottish settlers. Through missionary efforts and through the policy of granting lands to Scotch Presbyterians, the northeastern part of Ulster province became Protestant. The traditional hostility between Ulster and the rest of Ireland was thus increased by racial and religious differences which persist at present. During the 19th century four armed uprisings were vigorously repressed. At the beginning of the century the population was four and a half million, but by 1846 it had nearly doubled. In that and the following year the potato blight which swept over Europe and the British Isles ruined the potato crop so vital to the Irish people. A severe famine resulted, and large numbers emigrated to the United States and elsewhere.

Pilgrimage to Croaghpatrick in county Mayo

The famine intensified the craving for Irish autonomy which in the 1870's came to be known as the Home Rule Movement. The movement was led by CHARLES PARNELL, in return for whose support Gladstone introduced the first HOME RULE Bill in 1886, which failed in Parliament. A third such bill was passed in 1912, but the old antagonism between Ulster and the rest of Ireland prevented its being put into effect.

Independence. Meantime, since early in the 20th century the SINN FEIN movement had been gaining ground, advocating complete political and economic isolation for Ireland, and a return to its distinctly Celtic elements. Other revolutionary organizations, the Irish Volunteers and the Citizen Army, joined forces with the Sinn Fein in the Easter rebellion in Dublin of 1916, hoping to take advantage of German aid during British preoccupation with the World War. The rebellion was put down, but two years later the Sinn Feiners formed a national assembly called the Dáil Eireann, which proclaimed Ireland an independent republic. From that time until 1921 Irish revolutionaries and the forces of the British government maintained a guerrilla warfare, in which terrorism, arson, and murder were resorted to by both sides. This situation came to an end in December, 1921, when the Anglo-Irish treaty went into effect. The Irish Free State, consisting of 26 southern counties, was given a status similar to that of the Dominion of Canada; while 6 northeastern counties in Ulster were given a parliament subordinate to the British Parliament. For the government and history of Ireland after 1922 see EIRE; NORTHERN IRELAND.

BIBLIOG.–S. W. Bryant, *Celtic Ireland* (1889); W. E. H. Lecky, *History of Ireland in the Eighteenth Century* (1893); M. Davitt, *Fall of Feudalism in Ireland* (1904); C. G. Walpole, *Short History of the Kingdom of Ireland* (1908); G. H. Orpen, *Ireland under the Normans* (4 vols. 1911); G. Keating, *History of Ireland* (4 vols. 1902–14); J. G. S. MacNeill, *Constitutional and Parliamentary History of Ireland Till the Union* (1917); W. B. Wells and N. Marlowe, *History of the Irish Rebellion of 1916* (1917); *Irish Convention and Sinn Fein* (1918); J. Hogan, *Ireland in the European System* (1920); P. W. Joyce, *Social History of Ancient Ireland* (2 vols. 1913 ed. 1920); E. J. Riordan, *Modern Irish Trade and History* (1920); G. A. T. O'Brien, *Economic History of Ireland in the Eighteenth Century* (1918); *Economic History of Ireland from the Union to the Famine* (1921); R. Dunlop, *Ireland from the Earliest Times to the Present Day* (1922); B. Fitzpatrick, *Ireland and the Foundations of Europe* (1927); E. Hull, *History of Ireland and her People* (1931); S. Gwynn, *Charm of Ireland* (1934); R. A. S. Macalister, *Ancient Ireland* (1935); E. Curtis, *History of Medieval Ireland from 1014–1513* (1923, ed. 1938); C. M. Arensberg and S. T. Kimball, *Family and Community in Ireland* (1940); N. D. Palmer, *Irish Land League Crisis* (1940); S. O'Sheel, ed., *Seven Periods of Irish History* (1940); R. Clarke, *Short History of Ireland* (1941); N. Mansbergh, *Ireland in the Age of Reform and Revolution* (1941); S. MacManus. *Story of the Irish Race* (ed. 1944); T. F. O'Rahilly, *Early Irish History and Mythology* (1946); S. O'Faolain, *Irish* (1949); T. H. Mason, *Islands of Ireland* (ed. 1950); T. W. Freeman, *Ireland* (1950).

IRELAND, CHURCH OF, the independent Anglican church in Ireland, which considers itself the only true successor of the medieval Irish Church. At the time of the Reformation, Elizabeth (1533–

1603) and James I (1566–1625) extended the Anglican State Church over Ireland, taking possession of properties owned by the two rival and hostile Irish religious bodies, the Church of the Pale and the Celtic Church. Despite the fact that the Anglican Church received the support of the rulers in Dublin, the Celtic inhabitants of Ireland and most of the population of the Pale continued to be Catholic, the Celtic Church becoming even more Roman than it was prior to the Reformation.

Politics and Church Government. As provided by the Act of Union, which took effect Jan. 1, 1801, the Anglican Church became the legally established Church of Ireland. The Catholics, who represented more than three fourths of the population, resented greatly the establishment of a protestant church under English domination. Not only did the Anglican Church receive large state revenues, but Catholics also were forced to contribute toward the support of the Established Church through the collection of tithes. In 1833, the archbishoprics of the Established Church were reduced from 4 to 2, and the bishoprics from 18 to 10. By 1868, public opinion had become so strongly opposed to the Anglican Church in Ireland that Gladstone proposed that the Irish Anglican Church be disestablished. The House of Commons passed the bill, but it was rejected by the House of Lords. Another bill, likewise introduced by Gladstone in 1869, was finally passed by Parliament after much debate and intense national interest had been aroused. The act called for the complete disestablishment of the Irish Church, and the removal of all state endowments. In 1870, a general convention of Anglican Church representatives met in Dublin and drew up a constitution for the disestablished church. The government of the Church, which resembled that of the Protestant Episcopal Church in America, was vested in the General Synod, made up of a House of Bishops and a House composed of clergy and laity. The House of Bishops was given the authority to elect the Primate of Armagh.

Membership. The Church of Ireland was greatly influenced by CALVINISM, and has opposed High Church doctrines, though considering itself the only true Apostolic Irish Church. After disestablishment, the PRAYER BOOK was modified by the General Synod of the Irish church (1877) to accord with its theology and antiritualistic practices. The Anglicans in Ireland have numbered between 10 and 15 per cent of the population, with the Presbyterians and Methodists, the other two principal protestant denominations, and the Roman Catholics in the majority. The Church of Ireland is the most evangelical in its theology of all the churches belonging to the Anglican Communion. See ENGLAND, CHURCH OF; PROTESTANT EPISCOPAL CHURCH. W. G. D.

BIBLIOG.–W. Phillips, *History of the Church of Ireland, from Earliest Times to the Present Day* (1934).

IRELAND ISLAND. See BERMUDA.

IRELAND, NATIONAL UNIVERSITY OF, was established in Dublin in 1909 under the Irish Universities Act of 1908. It has nine faculties, embracing medicine, law, engineering, agriculture, philosophy, music, civil service, commerce, and the ancient Irish language. Three representatives of the university sit in Parliament. The university has three constituent colleges in Dublin, Cork, and Galway.

IRELAND, NORTHERN. See NORTHERN IRELAND.

IRENAEUS, SAINT, c. 120–202, Christian prelate, one of the fathers of the church and bishop of Lyons. An apostle of the Gauls, he sent many missionaries among them. He is best known for his repeated journeys to Rome to calm the storm of papal condemnation against MONTANISM and against those who persisted in celebrating EASTER on the 14th day of the paschal moon. Of his writings, two are extant: *Against the Heresies*, main source for the doctrines of gnosticism and of several heresies, and a complete explanation of Catholic doctrine; and *In Proof of the Apostolic Teaching*, a brief exposition of Catholic teachings for the layman.

IRENE, 752–803, Byzantine empress, was born in Athens and married Leo, later Leo IV, in 769. She was regent for their son, Constantine VI, following Leo's death in 780. Greatly devoted to the religious crisis, she was pleased with the decision of the Council of Nicaea (787) which ordered the worship of images. Forced to retire in 790, she was recalled by Constantine in 792 as co-ruler but plotted his downfall in 797 and became sole ruler until 802 when Nicephorus banished her. She is a saint of the Greek church.

IRETON, HENRY, 1610–51, English soldier, born in Attenton, near Nottingham; joined the Parliamentary forces, and fought at Newbury (1644), and at Naseby (1645). He won the favor of Cromwell, whose daughter, Bridget, he married (1646). A republican zealot, he advocated and signed the warrant for the king's execution. Becoming Cromwellian lord-deputy in Ireland, he ruled with relentless severity, until carried off by fever at Limerick. His remains, buried in Westminster Abbey, were disinterred at the Restoration, and hanged at Tyburn.

IRGIZ RIVER, U.S.S.R., in the Kazakh Soviet Socialist Republic, fully within Aktyubinsk Region. It rises in the southeastern slopes of the Urals and flows east for 300 miles into Lake Chelkar Tengiz.

IRGIZ RIVER, or *Great Irgiz*, U.S.S.R., in the Russian Soviet Federated Socialist Republic, a left tributary of the Volga. It rises in Kuibyshev Region and flows southwest for 600 miles through Saratov Region to enter the Volga below the city of Volsk.

IRIARTE, TOMÁS DE, 1750–91, Spanish poet, was born in Tenerife. His most serious efforts were his plays, *El señorito mimado* and *La señorita mal criada*, but these were obscured even in his own time by the fame of *Fábulas literarias* (1782), a book which was read and discussed throughout Europe. His critical attacks on contemporary writers provoked a host of bitter replies, which culminated in Juan Pablo Forner's *El asno erudito*, one of the most vicious libels in literary history.

IRIDESCENCE, the name given to the lustrous, delicately tinted sheen observed on certain surfaces, such as mother-of-pearl and the wings of certain insects. The phenomenon depends on the principle of interference.

IRIDIUM, a metallic element of the PLATINUM family, occurs in crude platinum in quantities varying from about one to eight per cent. The usual method of separation from the other platinum metals depends upon the insolubility of iridium in AQUA REGIA, unless it is alloyed with a high percentage of platinum. However, the separation is incomplete and commercial platinum usually contains 0.4 to 0.45 per cent of iridium.

Iridium was discovered by TENNANT in 1803. It is white, tin-colored in appearance, brittle at ordinary temperatures but malleable at a white heat, very hard (6.5 on Mohs' Scale), has a sp gr of 22.4 and a melting point of 2254° C. The symbol for iridium is Ir. It has an atomic weight 193.1, and its atomic number is 77.

Iridium is much more resistant to attack by most of the ordinary acids and chemicals than any of the other platinum metals, but fused sodium hydroxide or carbonate slightly attacks it as well as the other platinum metals. Pure iridium and also an alloy with platinum containing above 0.25 per cent of iridium is unattacked by aqua regia. Both iridic compounds, e.g., potassium iridic chloride, K_2IrCl_6, and iridous compounds, e.g., potassium iridous chloride, $K_3IrCl_6 \cdot 3H_2O$, are known. The salts are similar in most ways to the corresponding platinum compounds but are more highly colored. The many different brilliant colors shown by the various iridium compounds suggested its name.

Iridium is usually used in alloys with platinum (more than 30 per cent gives too great brittleness for most uses) to increase the hardness, tensile strength, and resistance to chemical attack. Pure iridium is too brittle for mechanical uses. High percentages of iridium in platinum crucibles is undesirable, because the formation of a volatile iridium oxide causes loss in weight during heating.

The high cost of iridium—four times that of platinum—limits its use to those special places where the improved properties are of sufficient importance. The alloy with platinum is used for surgical instruments, such as hypodermic needles, dental pins, jewelry, electrical contacts, standard weights and measures, corrosion-resistant chemical apparatus, spark plugs, detonation and electric fuses, resistors, electrodes, safety rupture discs for corrosive liquids or gases, spinnerets for fibers, tips for gold pens, etc.

Finely divided or spongy iridium has catalytic properties similar to the other platinum metals.

F. C. MATHERS

IRIGA, city, Philippine Islands, SE Luzon, Carmarines Sur Province, on the Bikol River, near the SW base of Mount Iriga, and 20 miles by rail SE of Naga, provincial capital. The surrounding fertile country produces rice, corn, sugar, pepper, cocoa, cotton, hemp, tobacco, and copra, and has forests of valuable hardwood. Pop. (1948) 42,049, made up of Bikols.

IRIS, in Greek mythology, was the daughter of Thaumas and Electra, and a sister of the Harpies. The *Iliad* represents her as the messenger of the gods. In earlier writers Iris appears as a virgin goddess, but later poets represent her as the wife of Zephyrus and mother of Eros. In Greek, the word Iris, as a common noun, means "rainbow."

IRIS, a popular garden plant belonging to the family *Iridaceae*. There are over 150 species distributed throughout the United States. Irises are perennials with simple or branching stems and sword-shaped leaves. Their showy flowers are divided into segments that are in turn united into a tube at the base. The three outer segments are reflexed and bearded on their upper surfaces, while the three inner segments or "standards" are arched and narrowed into claws. Three colored style branches, expanded and petal-like, ascend from the center of the corollas. Irises are propagated by seeds, bulbs, or rhizomes. Small roots and bulbs that divide naturally are separated from the parent plant to be stored or planted. Irises grow

J. H. MCFARLAND
White Queen Iris, above. Rhizomes of the iris at right

in any good garden soil and require little cultivation. They are attractive in gardens but are not useful as cut flowers since they are too delicate to transport.

IRIS, in optics. See IRITIS.

IRISH CHURCH. See IRELAND, CHURCH OF.

IRISH FREE STATE. See IRELAND; EIRE.

IRISH LITERATURE. See GAELIC LANGUAGE AND LITERATURE; ENGLISH LITERATURE.

IRISH MOSS. See CARRAGEEN.

IRISH SEA, a small but important sea lying between England and Ireland. It is connected with the Atlantic on the south by St. George's Channel, and on the north by St. Patrick's or North Channel. It is generally shallow, but in St. Patrick's Channel it has a depth of 850 feet.

IRISH TERRIER, a medium size dog of the terrier class, noted for its pluck, good temper and affectionate disposition. It is an ancient breed and is an excellent hunting dog. The Irish terrier is bright red, golden red, or red wheaten in color, with a hardy, wiry coat, rather short and perfectly straight.

Irish terrier

The head is long and narrow, eyes dark hazel, and nose black. The legs are straight and strong, the docked tail set high and the back straight but not short. This dog averages between 25 and 27 lbs. and stands 18 inches high. It is one of the gamest and most courageous of all dogs and shows extraordinary devotion to its master.

IRISH WOLFHOUND, one of the oldest breeds of dogs. Its general appearance is similar to that of the Scottish deerhound. In color it may range from light cream or fawn brindles through varying shades of grey to dark brindles. This dog is the tallest of all breeds, standing from 32 to 34 inches at the shoulder.

LEROY E. FESS

Irish wolfhound

The coat is rough, hard, and wiry, the head long, ears small, and muzzle moderately pointed. The back is long, and the legs are straight. These powerful dogs make fearless guards but are characterized by loyalty and sweetness of disposition, being wonderfully companionable and especially docile with children.

IRITIS. The circular membrane in the eye containing the coloring matter that determines eye color is called the *iris*. Any inflammation of this membrane may be called iritis. In *acute iritis* the inflammation comes on suddenly; in *chronic iritis* the inflammation is usually not so severe but lasts longer. The principal symptoms of iritis are pain in the eye, sensitivity to bright light, poor vision, and excessive watering of the eye. Iritis can be extremely painful; it usually feels as though the entire eyeball were involved. As a general rule the discomfort is worse at night and the whole eyeball is tender to even the slightest pressure. Although the symptoms of acute iritis are severe, recovery may come rapidly, sometimes in a few weeks. However, there is always a danger of complications and the possibility of developing chronic iritis.

The cause of iritis cannot always be discovered. When a cause can be found it needs to be treated as promptly as possible and often results in clearing up the inflamed iris. Iritis is sometimes associated with rheumatism, tuberculosis, diabetes, syphilis, or injury. In some cases it may be connected with what is called a focus of infection, such as an abscessed tooth or chronically inflamed tonsils. Highly skilled treatment is necessary for iritis in order to decrease the danger of permanently impaired vision or the development of chronic inflammation. Heat applied locally is important, as is the choice of drugs. The eye must be given rest from close work, often with the use of a black patch or protective glasses. Sometimes iritis can be successfully treated by injecting boiled milk or some other similar protein. This produces a reaction in the body, usually with fever, which seems to stimulate resistance and may produce a favorable effect on the iritis.   EDWIN P. JORDAN, M.D.

IRKUTSK, city, U.S.S.R., the Russian Soviet Federated Socialist Republic, capital of Irkutsk Region, situated on the Angara River, the Trans-Siberian Railway, and the highway leading to the head of navigation on the Lena River. Founded in 1661 by the Russian Cossacks, Irkutsk grew as a highway-and-river center of trade with Yakutia, Mongolia, the Far East, and the West. In the 18th century, Irkutsk merchants sent expeditions to Alaska and the Aleutian Islands to form the Russian-American Company which, in partnership with the czars, ruled Alaska and traded in the furs of Siberia and "Russian America." During this era the city was a place of exile for offenders against the czars. The Soviets developed Irkutsk as an air line and motor-road junction. The city, a growing industrial center, has manufactures of airplane engines, machine tools, machines for mining and gold-dredging, plywood, furniture, soap, railway cars, and footwear. There are also sawmills, flour mills, a mica factory, and one of the largest meat combines in southern Siberia. Irkutsk is the seat of the State University of Eastern Siberia, many colleges, and a biological-hydrological institute. Pop. (1951 est.) 250,000.

IRKUTSK REGION, U.S.S.R., an administrative area of the Russian Soviet Federated Socialist Republic; bounded on the N by the Yakut Autonomous Soviet Socialist Republic and the Evenki National District, on the W by Krasnoyarsk Territory, on the SW by Tuva Autonomous Region, on the S and SE by the Buryat-Mongol Autonomous Soviet Socialist Republic, and on the E by Lake Baikal and Chita Region; area 356,260 sq. mi.; pop. (1950 est.) 1,200,000. Within the Irkutsk Region lies the Ust-Ordyn Buryat Mongol National District. The Region is drained by the Angara and the Lena rivers. Its winters are long and severe; its summers, short and warm. Irkutsk Region is extremely rich in natural

Near Irkutsk, workers assemble main framework of new automobile plant located in Kaiskaya Valley

resources. The coal fields at Cheremkhovo, just southwest of Lake Baikal, are the largest in the Far East having estimated reserves of one hundred billion tons. The Region is one of the most important gold-producing areas of the U.S.S.R., and there are vast deposits of iron ore. Manganese, bauxite, and iron are also obtained from the western shores of Lake Baikal. Lime and some of the most important salt deposits of the entire Soviet Union are found to the north of the city of Irkutsk. Huge deposits of gypsum and mica provide other materials not available elsewhere in the Far East. These raw materials, together with the timber from the vast Siberian forests and agricultural products, provide for the many new chemical, iron and steel, aluminum, machine-tool, engineering, and synthetic rubber factories. In addition, situated as it is on the shore of Lake Baikal, the Region has limitless water-power potentials which are estimated at 20,000,000 kilowatts. The Angara hydroelectric stations supply power to the Region's factories, most of which are located in the cities of Irkutsk and Cheremkhovo. The southern part of the Region is agricultural, but cattle-raising is of greater importance. Its fur trade is also outstanding. Lake Baikal is a major source of fish with many canneries along its shores. The capital and industrial center of the Region is the city of Irkutsk.

A. M. K.

IRNERIUS, Italian jurist who flourished during the early part of the 12th century. He was born in Bologna, where about 1084 he founded a school of law, and at the instance of the Countess Matilda directed his attention to the laws of Justinian. He appears to have held some office under Henry V after 1116. According to ancient opinion, he was the first of the glossators, and was the author of an epitome of the *Novellae* of Justinian, called the *Authentica*.

IRON, RALPH. See SCHREINER, OLIVE.

IRON ❖ The Hard Metal

Prehistoric man used his iron ore for weapons and tools; its modern conversion into steel expanded all industry

IRON, one of the oldest, and most used of all metals, having been in use by man for some 3,000 years. The earliest source was probably meteorites, composed chiefly of iron, but alloyed with small percentages of nickel; later it was obtained by crude reduction methods from some iron mineral, usually the oxide. Iron of extremely high purity has been a commercial product only since about 1910, and even yet is used only in a comparatively small degree. Most of the ordinary commercial varieties of iron are alloys of the metal with various other elements in varying amounts, chief among these being carbon, manganese, silicon, sulfur and phosphorus; in some cases, other metals are also added to the combination, such as nickel, chromium, tungsten, and vanadium.

Iron

Properties. The symbol for iron is Fe. Iron has an atomic weight of 55.84 and its atomic number is 26. When pure, it has an almost silver-white color. It crystallizes in the isometric system, with two prominent allotropic forms, the so-called *Alpha* and *Gamma* irons; in the alpha variety the arrangements of the atoms in the crystal lattice is the body-centered cube, while the gamma variety is the face-centered cube. Beta iron for many years was considered as another allotropic form intermediate between the alpha and the gamma forms. Recent investigations with the x-ray spectrometer have demonstrated that both alpha and beta iron have a body-centered crystal arrangement, and are therefore only subdivisions of the same allotropic form, with the loss of magnetism in the beta form as the chief characteristic distinguishing it from the alpha form. The temperature points at which these transformations take place are 750° C. for alpha to beta, and 890° for beta to gamma. The pure metal melts at 1,535° C., and has a specific gravity of 7.86. It has a high degree of ductility and malleability, and a moderate tenacity. The magnetic quality of the metal is exceptional, and is one of its most outstanding characteristics.

Pure iron was first prepared by the reduction of iron oxide by hydrogen; later larger amounts were produced by electrodeposition from a pure solution of the sulfate or chloride; and finally, large tonnages of high purity metal have been obtained by a specially developed differential oxidation process, by which practically the entire content of impurities was oxidized away from a bath of liquid iron; this product is known as ingot iron. Iron is one of the few metals which will not directly amalgamate with mercury, although it may be forced into combination by the use of metallic sodium, or by the electrodeposition of one metal on the other. Iron is readily soluble in practically all of the common acids, forming "ferrous" or "ferric" compounds, corresponding to a valence of 2 or 3, respectively. The metal is not attacked by dry air or oxygen, but in the presence of moisture, oxidation proceeds readily with either, forming the common iron rust, a hydrated oxide of the metal. Oxidation or rusting is frequently prevented by covering the iron with a waterproof coating of paint or varnish, or by a coating of protective metal; besides the ordinary electroplating with a metal-like nickel or sherardized iron), tin (tin plate), tin and lead (terne plate), aluminum (calorized iron), and cadmium (Udylite process).

Classes of Iron. From an industrial standpoint, iron may be classed in the six following varieties: (1) Pure iron, approximating 99.9 per cent Fe, is made by electrodeposition, or by differential oxidation, as mentioned above. This product is used for special electrical uses where high magnetic properties are required or, in considerably greater amounts, where use is made of the exceptional resistance to oxidation and corrosion that the high purity imparts to the metal. (2) Pig iron, the crude product of the blast furnace reduction of iron ore with coke, usually carries 92–94 per cent Fe, 3–5 per cent carbon, and smaller amounts of silicon, manganese, sulfur and phosphorus, with frequently traces of several other metals. The large amounts of impurities rob the iron of all malleability and ductility, and materially reduce its strength in tension, but do not materially affect the strength in compression. The impurities also cause a reduction of 200–300° C. in the melting point of the iron. (3) Cast iron is pig iron that has been cast into some useful shape, usually after remelting in a cupola or a reverberatory furnace, although castings are sometimes made directly from the liquid pig iron as it comes from the blast furnace. Cast iron therefore does not differ materially in composition or properties from the pig iron from which it is made. (4) Wrought iron is the product of the puddling process and hence is frequently known as puddled iron. It is moderately pure, usually having not more than a few tenths of a per cent of total impurities, of which carbon is the chief one, but in addition also carries small particles of slag distributed throughout the body of the metal. Wrought iron is similar to pure iron in strength, malleability and ductility, and in addition is readily joined by plastic welding, while pure iron can be welded only by autogenous processes. (5) Simple STEEL is an alloy primarily of iron and carbon, the carbon content varying between 0.15 and 1.7 per cent depending on the physical properties desired; in addition to the carbon, all steels carry varying small percentages of the usual impurities in commercial iron. (6) Special or ALLOY steel contains, in addition to the carbon, some other metal, added for the purpose of imparting to the combination some extra degree of hardness, strength, or some other physical characteristic. The elements used for this purpose include manganese, nickel, chromium, silicon, tungsten, molybdenum, vanadium, and several others of lesser importance. More detailed information on the subject of steel may be found in the article under that heading.

Iron Ores. The ores from which commercial iron is produced are almost exclusively oxides, carrying lime, clay, or siliceous materials as impurities, or "gangue." The chief ores are MAGNETITE, magnetic iron oxide, Fe_3O_4, Fe = 72.5 per cent; red HEMATITE, iron sesquioxide (specular), Fe_2O_3, Fe = 70 per cent; brown hematite or brown ore, hydrated sesquioxide of iron, $Fe_2O_3 \cdot H_2O$, Fe = 52 to 66 per cent; small amounts of iron carbonate, $FeCO_3$, Fe = 48.2 per cent, are also used. During recent years the production of iron ore in the United States has usually amounted to 65 to 85 million tons, a maximum of 127 million tons was reached during the war in 1942 and 1943. Of the total amount, about 85–90 per cent is usually red hematite, 5–6 per cent brown hematite, and 6 per cent magnetite. In addition to these iron ores, other iron minerals are used for other purposes: pyrite, FeS_2, is burned to make sulfuric acid; Franklinite, a mixed oxide of zinc, manganese and iron, is used in the production of spiegeleisen, an alloy of manganese and iron, after the zinc has been removed and recovered; chromite, $FeO \cdot Cr_2O_3$, is used for its chromium content, and also as a refractory material in furnace construction.

The methods used in the production of these various ores depend on the character of the material in question; the soft red hematite and the brown ores are mined in open pits by steam shovels; the hard

Experimental Heats are under observation in an experimental cupola with combustion air conditioned

BATTELLE MEMORIAL INSTITUTE

hematites and other ores are mined by the usual underground methods, the details of the operation varying with the character of the ore, its manner of occurrence, and the locality. See MINING; LIMONITE; SIDERITE.

Electrolytic Iron. Iron of exceptionally high purity may be made by electrodeposition, and is being produced on a limited commercial scale in two different types of process. One type of process involves the electrolytic refining of an already comparatively pure iron in order still further to eliminate impurities; the other consists in the direct electrolytic precipitation of iron from a purified solution obtained by the action of an acid on an iron bearing raw material. This raw material may be either an iron ore or a crude metallic iron.

Ingot Iron. Ingot iron is the name that has been given to a product of high purity (99.85 to 99.95 per cent Fe) produced by a modification of the basic open-hearth steel process. See STEEL.

Pig Iron. The majority of iron ores go directly to the blast furnace just as mined; some ores, however, are given some preliminary treatment to put them in better shape for reduction. Brown ores are put through a washing operation in order to remove most of the clay and sand; some other ores, particularly magnetites, are given a preliminary concentration to improve the iron content; finely divided ores may be "sintered" or "nodulized" by heating to put them into better physical condition; heating or "calcining" may also be used to eliminate the carbon dioxide from a carbonate ore and convert the iron to the ferric form before reduction; the heating or nodulizing also serves to remove moisture and improve the richness of the ore, and also partially to oxidize the sulfur of the ore, and thus improve its quality.

The ore, either with or without preliminary treatment, is charged into the blast furnace, together with the requisite amount of fuel, usually coke but sometimes charcoal or anthracite, and sufficient limestone to combine with the siliceous gangue of the ore and form a fusible slag. In a few cases the ore itself contains a sufficient amount of limestone to render it partially or entirely self-fluxing. The blast furnace varies somewhat in size and shape, depending on the fuel that is used; in most cases, however, it consists of an irregular cylindrical shaft about 90 feet high, and from 16 to 22 feet in diameter in its various sections, usually 3 in number. The upper section, or "shaft" of the furnace is a truncated cone, into the top of which the charge (ore, fuel and flux) is periodically introduced from a skip hoist through a pair of hoppers closed by bells to prevent the escape of the furnace gases while charging. The preliminary heating, the calcining of the limestone to form lime, and most of the reduction of the iron ore to spongy, solid metallic iron, take place in the shaft; the resulting spongy iron, with its gangue and the lime from the decomposed limestone, then pass to the second section, an inverted truncated cone known as the "bosh"; here the remnants of unreduced ore are converted to iron, the gangue and the lime unite to form a fusible slag, and the iron melts. The liquid iron and slag then trickle down over the solid white-hot coke which fills the bosh and collect in the third section, a straight cylindrical section known as the "hearth" or "crucible." In some furnaces a short cylindrical section is interposed between the shaft and the bosh. Since the liquid iron is much heavier than the slag, it collects in the bottom, and the slag floats on top. After several hours' operation the hearth will be practically full of iron and slag, and ordinarily they are removed four times a day through tap holes provided in the side of the hearth. The necessary heat for carrying on the operation is produced by the combustion of the coke of the charge by means of several blasts of air introduced under a pressure of 15 to 20 pounds to the square inch through 12 to 16 openings known as "tuyeres," located just at the

130,000-pound steel ingot remained white-hot during 200-mile shipment because of vermiculite insulation

bottom of the bosh, and uniformly distributed around the circumference of the furnace. The hot carbon burns with the oxygen of the air blast to form carbon monoxide and a high temperature is generated. The pressure of the blast carries this hot mixture of carbon monoxide and nitrogen up through the openings of the charge, to which it imparts the necessary heat to carry on the fusion operations in the bosh and the heating operations in the shaft; also in the shaft the hot carbon monoxide serves as a reducing agent to abstract the oxygen from the iron oxides of the charge, converting them to spongy metallic iron, and in turn being converted to carbon dioxide.

Since it is impossible to balance the reactions in the furnace in such a way as to use up all of the carbon monoxide, the gases issuing from the top of the furnace carry 25 to 30 per cent of the unused carbon monoxide; this is equivalent to a low grade producer gas in heating value and is used to furnish heat around the plant, and for the generation of power in gas engines. The blast used in modern furnaces is always preheated to a temperature of about 550° C. before used in order to increase the working efficiency of the furnace and the temperature generated in combustion. This is accomplished by burning about one third of the gas produced by the furnace in supplementary devices called "stoves," in such a way that the heat generated may be absorbed into the air being fed into the furnace.

The iron as melted in the upper part of the bosh is quite high in purity, but as it passes through the higher temperature in the lower portion of the bosh, in contact with the slag and the hot coke, it takes up carbon from the coke and other impurities from the slag so that as finally removed from the furnace it contains considerable amounts of carbon, manganese, silicon, sulfur, and phosphorus. When the tap holes are opened and the accumulated slag and iron removed in separate ladles, the slag goes to the waste pile, while the iron is cast, sometimes in sand molds, but now more frequently in metal molds in an automatic casting machine, into ingots weighing about 100 lbs. each, known as "pigs," from which the product has come to be known as pig iron. In case the iron is to be used in the same plant for direct conversion into steel, the ladle of liquid pig iron, instead of going to the casting machine, will be poured into a heated storage vessel known as a "mixer," from which it is drawn as needed. The average production of the modern blast furnace is 500 to 600 long tons of pig iron per day. Depending on the amount of impurities and the condition of the carbon in the iron, the quality and appearance of the pig iron may vary considerably. The usual commercial grades of pig iron are:—No. 1, No. 2, No. 3, and No. 4 foundry; forge; mottled, and white—the different varieties being progressively finer in structure and harder.

Small amounts of pig iron are also produced in certain sections of the world in electric furnaces, where the entire heat requirements of the furnace are satisfied by electric energy and only such carbon need be supplied as is required to carry on the reduction. For economic reasons, this type operation can be carried on only in localities where electric power is cheap, fuel costs high, and high grade ore is available. This combination of conditions restricts the operation to only a few localities, such as Scandinavia, the mountainous section of northern Italy, and Brazil.

The world's production of pig iron (including ferro-alloys) in recent years has averaged about 100 million metric tons. Of this total the production of the United States has averaged a little over half.

Other important world producers are, in order of importance, the U.S.S.R., United Kingdom, France, Germany, and Belgium.

Cast Iron. Cast iron may be made by the direct casting of the pig iron as it comes from the blast furnace, but this method is little used except for the production of rough castings used around the blast furnace plant itself. Most cast iron is the result of the remelting in a cupola or reverberatory furnace of a pig iron of such composition as will give an iron of the desired physical properties; since it is difficult to obtain a pig iron of exactly the desired composition for the large variety of requirements to be fulfilled, the charge for remelting is usually made up of a mixture of two or more irons of different composition, in such proportions as to approximate the desired composition. The operation of the cupola is purely one of melting, and no material chemical change takes place in the charge other than a slight loss of the more readily oxidizable impurities of the iron, particularly silicon and manganese, by the oxygen of the air blast used to burn the fuel. The weakness of cast iron is due to carbon (graphite) in the form of flakes. The resultant iron fractures easily along the flakes. A recent development, called nodular iron, has a minute amount (less than 0.1 per cent) of cerium or magnesium, which causes the graphite to form into nodules, i.e., roughly spherical form. This iron is less expensive than malleable iron (annealed cast iron) or steel, but has many of their desirable properties. See FOUNDING; WROUGHT IRON.   R. L.

Iron Compounds. Iron forms two series of compounds, *ferrous* and *ferric*, in which the valence of iron is two and three, respectively. Ferrous compounds are usually formed by the action of acids on iron; ferric compounds may be prepared by the oxidation of the corresponding ferrous compounds. This oxidation occurs slowly at ordinary temperatures and ferrous compounds should therefore be protected from the air.

Ferric oxide, Fe_2O_3, occurs in nature as the ore HEMATITE or, in hydrated form, as the ore LIMONITE. In pure form, the finely ground red powder is sold commercially as *jeweler's rouge* for polishing and as *Venetian red*, a pigment used in painting barns, freight cars, etc., or as a pigment in rubber and pottery. A specially purified form, *rouge*, is used in COSMETICS.

Ferrous oxide, FeO, prepared by the partial reduction of ferric oxide, is a black powder easily oxidized at high temperatures into a ferrous-ferric oxide, Fe_3O_4, or *magnetic oxide of iron*. The latter compound occurs in nature as the ore MAGNETITE. It is also formed when iron burns and when iron is heated with steam. Iron scale, formed in forges and steel mills, is chiefly Fe_3O_4. A film of this material on gun barrels protects the metal against rusting. A mixture of magnetic or ferric oxide with powdered aluminum is known as THERMIT and is used in welding.

Iron PYRITE, FeS_2, is the most abundant sulfide found in nature. Oxidation of pyrite produces sulfur dioxide, used to make SULFURIC ACID.

FERROUS SULFATE, $FeSO_4$, is prepared by treating

Iron

iron with sulfuric acid. It is the most important of the ferrous salts.

Ferric chloride (FeCl₃ or Fe₂Cl₆), the most important ferric salt, is made by the direct combination of iron and chlorine. Commercial ferric chloride is a yellow hydrate which dissolves readily in water. It is used in medicine to stop bleeding and as a tincture to counteract anemia. It is also used as a mordant in dyeing (see DYES AND DYEING) and in purifying water and sewage. See WATER SUPPLY AND TREATMENT.

Iron cyanides are intermediate in the formation of complex compounds called FERROCYANIDES and FERRICYANIDES.   E. M. W.

BIBLIOG.–H. P. Tiemann, *Iron and Steel* (1933); D. G. Wilhelm, *Story of Iron and Steel* (1935); A. Allison, *Outline of Steel and Iron* (1937); Pan American Union, *Coal and Iron in Latin America* (1939); S. H. Holbrook, *Iron Brew* (1939); G. Brown and A. Orford, *Iron and Steel Industry* (1940); R. Hudson, *The Blast Furnace* (1942); E. Teichert, *Ferrous Metallurgy* (1944); American Iron and Steel Institute, *Annual Statistical Report*.

PHYSIOLOGICAL ROLE OF IRON

Iron Content of the Body. Iron is an essential element for the maintenance of life and health. The role of iron in the body is associated with production of hemoglobin (see BLOOD). It is an essential component of certain respiratory enzymes (see RESPIRATION) and other biologically active substances (chromatin of cell nuclei). The total iron content of the body is about 4.5 grams. Of this the circulating hemoglobin contains somewhat less than 65 per cent; iron available for hemoglobin formation, stored principally in the liver, bone marrow, and spleen, comprises about 30 per cent; and tissue iron, which is unavailable for hemoglobin formation, about 5 per cent. The fact that of the total iron in the body about 65 per cent is circulating in the blood, and that about half as much is available to supply more hemoglobin if necessary, agrees with the clinical experience that a patient may lose about half the circulating hemoglobin and replace it from the reserves without requiring iron administration.

Dietary Requirements. The iron requirement of an individual depends primarily on his age and sex. Babies are born with a reserve of iron normally adequate to supply their needs for the first few months. After this has been depleted anemia will develop if the child's diet contains no foods other than milk, which is deficient in iron. From the age of approximately four years to the period of adolescence the amount of iron that has to be supplied in the diet reaches a steady level. In adolescence the growth rate increases very rapidly, necessitating an increase in iron supply. In women, with the beginning of the menstruation the iron requirement is increased. Replacement of about 20 milligrams of iron lost with the blood of the menstrual flow is necessary for each monthly period. Pregnancy also makes an increased demand for iron intake. The recommended daily allowances of iron range from 6 mg. for children under one year of age to 15 mg. for adolescents of both sexes. The adult intake should be from 5 to 10 mg. per day to replenish the iron which may be lost. If no iron is lost this amount will certainly do no harm. Iron is present in small amounts in many foods. The iron content in milligrams per 100 grams of some foods is: *beef*, 3.5; *liver*, 6.7; *herring*, 1.0; *haddock*, 0.75; *egg*, 2.5; *cheese*, 1.5; *oatmeal*, 4.1; *bread*, 1.1; *split peas*, 5.4; *potato*, 0.6. Milk is practically iron free. See DIET; ENRICHED OR FORTIFIED FOOD; DEFICIENCY DISEASES; ANEMIA.

History of Iron in the Body. The course of iron transport, storage, and excretion can be followed most conveniently after ingestion of radioactive iron, which behaves in the body exactly like ordinary iron but can be readily detected at any point in its passage through the body. Hydrochloric acid of gastric juice aids in splitting iron from its organic combinations in food, liberating it in an inorganic form that is

WESTINGHOUSE

Three huge ladles pour an 82-ton base

soluble and more absorbable. It is therefore unreasonable to prescribe the more expensive complex iron preparations, because their effectiveness depends on their inorganic iron content. When hydrochloric acid is lacking in the gastric juice, iron absorption may be impaired.

Iron is absorbed chiefly in the upper part of the small intestine, enters the blood plasma, and soon reaches the bone marrow, where it is used in the formation of new red blood cells. Experiments in animals show that the amount of iron absorbed depends on the physiological state of the animal; an anemic dog will absorb approximately 36 times as much iron as a normal dog. It is not known how absorption is adjusted to physiological requirements. Even in states of severe anemia, however, only a relatively small fraction of iron is absorbed, most of it being eliminated in the feces. The iron in the stools represents the amount which has not been absorbed plus the fraction which may have been excreted into the intestine. The amount of iron excreted is by no means definitely fixed, but it has been established that normal males kept for long periods on diets containing very little iron excrete minimal amounts and appear to maintain a balance between iron intake and excretion.

Medical Uses of Iron. Some salts of iron are ASTRINGENTS and are useful in stopping superficial hemorrhages and in allaying irritation of mucous membranes, particularly those in the throat. They are chiefly employed, however, in the treatment of various types of anemia where the hemoglobin content of the blood cells is abnormally low, as in anemias of pregnancy, of adolescent girls, of malnutrition, and following severe blood loss. Because of their poor absorption from the intestine iron compounds should be administered in large amounts. There is no proof that injection of iron compounds yields superior results.

In the treatment of anemia iron may be used in its metallic form (reduced iron), as ferric salts, or as ferrous compounds (ferrous lactate, ferrous sulfate, iron and ammonium citrates). Ferrous salts are the drugs of choice because they are more easily absorbed and less irritating. Gram for gram of ingested iron, ferrous salts have been shown to cause a greater rise in hemoglobin percentage than ferric salts. This is due in part to the fact that ferric salts precipitate proteins, producing insoluble and unabsorbable iron compounds. Metallic (reduced) iron yields ferrous chloride in the stomach in the presence of hydrochloric acid. It should not be used when the acid is greatly diminished or lacking in the gastric juice. In this condition, exceptionally large doses of ferrous salts should be employed because in the absence of acid they precipitate and are poorly absorbed.

The toxic action of iron is relatively unimportant.

Most patients tolerate ferrous compounds very well. In some patients ferric salts, and occasionally even ferrous compounds, will cause abdominal cramps, nausea, vomiting, diarrhea, and a metallic taste in the mouth resembling that of ink. Solutions of most iron compounds should be taken through a straw because when in contact with the teeth they are apt to produce a black discoloration. Iron excretion in the intestine may also turn the feces black due to the formation of iron sulfide.   A. E. VIVINO

IRON AGE, the name given to that division of time which follows the BRONZE AGE in the Near East and Europe. There is no sharp break between the two, for some iron was used long before it became common. At first it was so highly prized that the victors in the Greek contests were rewarded with small pieces, and objects of gold were inlaid with iron designs. When later it was learned that the simpler ores could be reduced by means of charcoal fires and the bellows, it became more abundant, but it was a refractory metal, less useful than bronze. A new era began when a method of converting iron into steel was discovered. Just where this discovery took place is uncertain. Some scholars claim that it occurred in the Hallstatt area of Austria, because all stages of transition can be followed there. Others look to the Assyrians as the originators, while not a few claim that it was first known in Africa. The spread of the Iron Age into Central and Northern Europe was slow and is known under two period names—the HALLSTATT, 900 to 500 B.C., and LA TÈNE, 500 B.C. to the time of Christ.

Taken as a whole, the Iron Age is a time of change nearly equaling that of the Bronze Age. The search for metals, and the opening and extending of trade routes led to a great exchange of cultural materials and set the stage for rapid advance. At the same time the discovery of steel made possible the industrial revolution of our times.   FAY-COOPER COLE

IRON AND STEEL INSTITUTE, AMERICAN, was founded in 1908 for the purpose of promoting the interests of the iron and steel industry, collecting and publishing statistics and other information concerning the industry, providing a forum for the exchange of information and discussion of problems, and carrying out activities to promote the use of iron and steel.

Membership, which totaled 2,300 in 1950, is composed of residents of the United States, Canada, and Mexico directly engaged in the iron and steel industry. Annual meetings are held and a library containing 1,500 volumes on statistical, historical, and technical phases of the industry is maintained. Publications of the institute include: *Annual Statistical Report; Directory of Iron and Steel Works of the United States and Canada; Steel Facts,* issued several times a year; and the *Yearbook.* Institute headquarters are at 350 Fifth Avenue, New York City.

IRON CROSS, a German Decoration. See DECORATIONS AND MEDALS, MILITARY.

IRON CURTAIN, a term used by Winston Churchill in his March 5, 1946, speech at Fulton, Missouri, to refer to the establishment of police states in Eastern Europe. Churchill's actual phrase was the following: "the iron curtain which at present divides Europe in twain." Since 1946 the term has been used to refer to the Soviet Union's domination of Eastern Europe, which is economically and politically separated from Western Europe. See EUROPE; SATELLITE COUNTRIES.   G. B. DE H.

IRON GATE, a narrow, two-mile-long gorge where the Danube River has cut through steep cliffs of the Transylvanian Alps in SW Rumania. Although the gorge has been widened by blasting and a two-mile canal with a small railway paralleling the canal has been built, the Iron Gate is still an obstruction to navigation on the Danube. Donkey engines tow the barges through the canal to navigable waters above the difficult passage.

AMERICAN HOSPITAL SUPPLY CORP.

Iron lung

IRON LUNG. The iron lung is an intermittent negative pressure chamber designed to maintain artificial respiration over long periods in persons unable to breathe normally, especially in patients paralyzed by poliomyelitis. The principles involved in an iron lung are based on air pressure and the physiology of normal breathing. At sea level air pressure is about 15 pounds per square inch. This external force on the body is matched by an equal internal pressure. In normal breathing the chest cavity enlarges, creating a negative pressure. To equalize the pressure on the inside of the chest, air rushes into the lungs through the nose and mouth. The enlargement of the chest cavity is brought about partly by the contraction of the muscles between the ribs (intercostals), which raises the rib cage, and partly by the diaphragm, whose contraction depresses the floor of the chest. With the relaxation of the intercostals and the diaphragm the chest cavity returns to its original size and air is exhaled. See LUNG; RESUSCITATION.

The iron lung brings about respiration directly. The patient is placed in an airtight chamber, his head remaining outside. To prevent leakage of air through this opening a soft sponge rubber collar encircles the patient's neck. The iron lung, when in

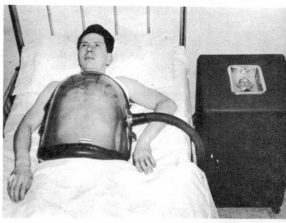

WARREN E. COLLINS, INC.

Portable iron lung

operation, automatically and regularly reduces the pressure within. This negative pressure causes the air cavities of the body to expand and the patient inhales. When the pressure within the chamber returns to normal the patient exhales. As in normal breathing, an iron lung patient rests during exhalation. The negative pressure cabinet induces breathing even though the muscles of the ribs and diaphragm are completely paralyzed, as they often are in poliomyelitis. Since activity of the chest muscles is not necessary for breathing in an iron lung, many "polio" victims have been saved. The artificial respiration permits these paralyzed muscles to rest. In a severe case of "polio" the patient may remain in the iron lung for months before he recovers enough muscle power to breathe alone. Until the patient is well enough to be removed from the respirator for short periods he must be attended through openings in the sides of the iron lung. These ports are surrounded by rubber cuffs which prevent air from escaping around the nurses' arms. Windows in the cabinet allow attendants to observe the patient.

There are several commercial models of iron lungs. The designs vary but their basic principles remain the same. Bellows, or a diaphragm made of rubber or leather, cause the decrease in pressure when they are extended. As the bellows fold up or as the leather diaphragm becomes flat, the pressure within the chamber returns to normal. A satisfactory respiratory range is 14–18 inhalations a minute. However, when necessary, this rate may be increased to as high as 36. A negative pressure varying between 14 and 20 is usually satisfactory. This pressure may be regulated and registers as negative pressure on the gauge. The amount of negative pressure determines the depth of respiration. These respirators may vary from the orthopedic tilting-rotating model to the emergency construction of an oil drum which uses a vacuum cleaner to create negative pressure. Although poliomyelitis patients are not the only users of the iron lung, they have created the greatest demand for prolonged artificial respiration. See DRINKER, PHILIP.
R. W. CUMLEY

IRON MASK, MAN IN THE, a political prisoner in the Bastille under the reign of Louis XIV, king of France. Being kept constantly masked, his identity remains a mystery to this day. He was carried in the prison records under the name of Marchioly and is known to have died in 1703 aged "about 45." Governor Saint-Mars had brought him to the Bastille from Pinerolo, Piedmont in 1698.

It is now generally assumed that the prisoner's real name was either Count Mattioli or Eustache Dauger. Count Mattioli was minister of Mantua and involved in an intrigue centering around the transfer of fortress of Casale to France. It is definitely established that he was arrested by Louis' agents. It is more likely, however, that the prisoner was Eustache Dauger. Little is known about him or the reasons for his imprisonment. Various theories have been advanced, but none has succeeded in establishing Eustache Dauger's exact identity.

The presence of this mysterious personality in the Bastille gave life to a number of legends and books. Speculations started during his lifetime. Voltaire described the mask as of iron—it was probably a mask of black velvet—and Alexandre Dumas, Sr., popularized him in his novel "Vicomte de Bragelonne" as a half brother of Louis XIV.   FRANK POLLACZEK

IRON MOUNTAIN, city, SW Upper Michigan, county seat of Dickinson County, on the North Western and the Milwaukee railroads and U.S. highways 2, 8, and 141; about 53 miles NW of Escanaba. Iron Mountain is a trade center and distributing point for the Menominee Range district. It was settled in 1879 and incorporated in 1887. The city was named for its location near a bluff heavily stratified with iron ore. Tourists are drawn to Iron Mountain for summer and winter sports. The city claims the world's highest artificial ski slide. Iron ore mining, lumber, automobile parts, clothing, picture frames, toys, and chemicals are the chief products. Pop. (1950) 9,679.

IRON MOUNTAIN, an eminence in Missouri, St. François County, once thought to be an almost solid mass of iron ore covering 500 acres and rising 200 feet above the valley. Beginning in 1836, a large volume of low grade ore was produced until mining operations became unprofitable after World War I.

IRON PYRITES. See PYRITE.

IRONDEQUOIT, town, NW New York, in Monroe County, bordering Irondequoit Bay. The town contains several villages in the Rochester metropolitan area. Pop. (1950) 34,417.

IRONSIDES, the nickname given to Oliver Cromwell's famous regiment, had been originally applied to Cromwell himself. The force consisted of 1,000 horse, recruited from the sturdy, God-fearing yeomen of the eastern counties. The regiment repeatedly distinguished itself in the English Civil War, notably at Winceby (Lincolnshire); at Marston Moor, where they scattered Prince Rupert's cavalry; and at Naseby, where they converted a rout into a decisive victory.

IRONSIDES, OLD. See CONSTITUTION, THE.

IRONTON, city, S Ohio, county seat of Lawrence County, on the Ohio River opposite Russell, Ky.; the Chesapeake and Ohio, the Detroit, Toledo, and Ironton, and the Norfolk and Western railroads; and U.S. Highway 52, about five miles N of Ashland, Ky. Ironton is a dairying, truck garden, and fruit-growing center. It was founded in 1848 by John Campbell, one of the first ironmasters in this region. Ironton was originally a strategic center of the iron industry. Gradually after the Civil War the ore deposits began to give out until the industry was completely exhausted. Today Ironton manufactures coke, cement, brick, athletic goods, road materials, engine parts, and machine tools. Pop. (1950) 16,333.

IRONWOOD, city, W Upper Michigan, in Gogebic County, on the Montreal River opposite Hurley, Wis., on the Michigan-Wisconsin border; served by the Chicago and North Western and the Soo Line railroads and U.S. highways 2 and 51. Ironwood is the trade and shipping center of Gogebic Range, an area rich in iron ore, timber, farm lands, and stock raising. It was settled in 1885 and probably named for John R. Wood whose interest in ore deposits caused him to be nicknamed "Iron" Wood. Ironwood has an extensive tourist trade. Mining and logging are the chief industries. Pop. (1950) 11,466.

IRONWOOD, a tree found in rich woods throughout the United States. Ironwoods are characterized by brown furrowed bark, simple leaves, and very hard, tough wood of little or no commercial value. The leaves are typically oblong ovate with cut edges and are downy beneath. Ironwoods, *Ostrya virginiana*, belong to the Birch family, *Betulaceae*.

IRONWORK has had a long history in the art products of most civilizations. The early Assyrian, Chaldean, and Egyptian cultures show traces of wrought ironwork in relics discovered by archaeologists. In India, iron was known as early as 1000 B.C. Smelting of iron by a primitive process made this metal available for use in the making of swords, whose fame spread throughout Europe in the Middle Ages. These weapons were made of tempered iron or steel, and decorated by carving and by damascening, a process of inserting gold and silver wire into grooves cut in the handle of the weapon to form a design. Swords were not the only products of the Indian ironworker; Buddhist begging bowls, wrought-iron finials, and elaborately decorated iron pillars, ranging from 10 feet to 23 feet in height, were all products of Indian ironwork. In China, iron first came into general use about 500 B.C. Soon this metal replaced all others as the material for tools and utensils of every kind. By the ninth century A.D..

sculptors, architects, and other artists were using iron extensively. A pagoda dating from the 13th century gives evidence of the Chinese ironworker's intricate art. This pagoda, built entirely of iron, is furnished with iron chairs and many decorative iron figures. Another example of Chinese ironwork is the iron picture, a reproduction in this metal of etchings and ink sketches which required a high degree of skill from the Chinese ironworker. At the present time, though the standard of craftsmanship is lower, ironwork continues to be a popular mode of decoration in China. In Japan, much of the ironwork was done on the swords and armor of the traditional army caste, the Samurai. Often the handle of a sword was decorated with combinations of metals and with intricate inlay work. When the period of

ART INSTITUTE OF CHICAGO
Beautifully wrought iron lock for a door

Samurai dominance passed, Japanese iron craftsmen turned their attention to the creation of small figures and decorative bowls.

In the Western world, wrought iron did not come into general use until the medieval period. In England, iron was particularly adapted to the needs of the time. Its first use was as a protection against attack; the massive doors of English castles were encrusted with iron, and iron grilles protected the narrow windows. When the need for protection diminished, wrought iron was used for decorative purposes. Intricately wrought hinges, delicate grilles, gates, and other architectural details in buildings of the 15th and 16th centuries are examples of early English wrought ironwork. In medieval France, wrought iron was used for much the same purposes as in England, but examples of French wrought ironwork show greater delicacy and more variety in pattern than their English counterparts. The ironwork on doors of the Cathedral of Notre Dame is a magnificent example of French work in this period. In Germany, iron was not as popular as in France or England, though several examples of the Gothic era show an understanding of the possibilities of this medium. The Gothic period in the rest of Europe saw an increase in the use of iron, but the Renaissance saw the greatest wrought ironwork.

Renaissance Ironwork. During the Renaissance, Spain developed the art of wrought iron and brought it to a degree of perfection that has never been surpassed. Spanish craftsmen in the 15th and 16th centuries concentrated on armor, but their greatest achievements are wrought-iron screens, called rejas, which enclose the chapel in Spanish cathedrals. Reaching a height of 30 feet, these screens, worked by

hand, are characterized by hammered arabesques, delicately patterned columns, and a profusion of ornamental figures. The Renaissance era in Italy saw an abundance of wrought ironwork, and in Florence, Niccoto Grosso became famous for his wrought-iron screens and lanterns. Though examples of wrought iron are found in abundance in Italy, work in this field did not attain the heights that other of the decorative arts achieved. In France progress in ironwork did not keep pace with other European countries, and it was not until the reign of Louis XIV that ironworkers began to explore the potentialities of this medium. The designs of craftsmen such as Daniel Marot, Jean Berain, and Jean Lepautre included panels in the form of scrolls, and such artisans treated iron as a plastic material, giving it a flexibility never previously achieved. Ironwork in England began its renaissance toward the end of the 17th century when a Frenchman, Jean Tijou, was commissioned by William III to construct screens and gates for the king's Hampton Court palace. Tijou's work is very ornate, and the plan of construction is often lost in a profusion of ornamental detail. Other English artisans of this time, including Robert Davies, Robert Bakewell, and others, followed Tijou's lead, though they adapted his ornate French style to more sober British designs. In Germany, iron during the Renaissance and early Baroque periods was used for many purposes, such as stove guards, church screens, fountain railings, doorknockers, in addition to locks for doors and chests. A German chest dating from the 17th century shows a typical use of iron, bands of which metal enclose the chest and the top is almost completely covered by a massive lock. Nuremberg, Munich and Innsbruck were centers of wrought ironwork in Germany.

From the 17th to the 19th century, ironwork was practiced by only a handful of artisans, and the great work of the Renaissance was not repeated. By the end of the 19th century, wrought iron was once again established as a popular ornamental art. At this time, the machine has made iron easier to handle, and though some of the hand-wrought details of earlier ironwork are missing, modern wrought iron has a beauty that rivals that of the Renaissance. An example of a modern iron figurine is Samuel Yellin's figure of St. Eloi, and stair railings, fire screens, and other wrought ironwork of this American craftsman are some of the finest examples of the art.

HELEN STEWART

BIBLIOG.—J. Aston, *Wrought Iron* (1939); A. Deas, *Early Iron Work of Charleston* (1941).

IROQUOIS INDIANS. The Iroquoian or Huron-Iroquois linguistic stock includes the HURONS, ERIES, Attawendaronks, Andastes and remotely the TUSCARORAS and CHEROKEES, as well as several smaller tribes in the eastern United States. Specifically Iroquois refers to the Iroquois League or Five Nations dwelling in New York from near Schenectady to the Genesee River. According to tradition Deganawida and HIAWATHA (only in part the subject of Longfellow's poem, derived largely from the Ojibway Manabozho) aided by Jikonasa and Totadaho, in the late 16th century united the MOHAWKS, ONEIDAS, ONONDAGAS, SENECAS and CAYUGAS into a league called "the great peace." A Great Council governed the league in which the Mohawks and Senecas formed the senior house and the Oneidas and Cayugas the lower house; the Onondagas furnished the presiding officer, and intervened in case of disagreement. Voting was by nations. The nations could—and did—make war separately on outsiders. Descent was maternal and women nominated the chiefs; they might also have a vote in council. The League was often known as "the Long House," a metaphor based on the long houses, rectangular and gabled, in which the Iroquois lived, often surrounded by stockades for defense. There were three principal clans existing in all the Five Nations; the principal clans named 49 sachems; chiefs of other clans could speak, but not vote in council. The Iroquois were largely agricultural. About 1710 the Tuscaroras, migrating from North Carolina, were admitted to the League, thereafter sometimes called the Six Nations, but the Tuscaroras had no rights in council.

When Samuel de Champlain aided the Hurons with his arquebus in a fight with the Iroquois in 1609 he alienated them from French influence. The Iroquois entered into friendly relations with the Dutch, obtained firearms, and virtually destroyed the Hurons, Wyandots, Eries and the Neutral Nation. With never more than 3,000 fighting men, they enslaved the Delawares, fought and defeated other Algonquin tribes of the North and East, raided against the Cherokees in the South and by 1684 had driven the Illinois westward to the river named for them. When the British took New York in 1664 the Mohawks made a treaty with them, the other tribes made an agreement with the French, which was broken by the de Denonville in 1687, after which the Mohawks destroyed La Chine and attacked Montreal. Frontenac had some success in making peace. In 1710 the British took a delegation of sachems, headed by King Hendrick (Thoyanoguen) to the court of Queen Anne. In 1738 WILLIAM JOHNSON came to settle and trade among the Mohawks. His influence was great among the Iroquois until his death in 1774. He led the Mohawks to victory at Lake George in 1755 and won the surrender of Niagara in 1759, but more important, he held the Iroquois firm in the British alliance in the final French war. Sir John Johnson, the son of Sir William, and Colonel Guy Johnson, the nephew, sought to attach the Iroquois to the British cause in the American Revolution. JOSEPH BRANT (Thayendanegea) went to England in 1775; he afterward led the Mohawks on St. Leger's expedition against Fort Schuyler in 1777, the battle of Oriskany, and with Captain Walter Butler at the Cherry Valley massacre. Burgoyne got little good of his Indian allies; the murder of Jane Macrea, a Loyalist, inflamed the border, as did the Wyoming massacre of 1778. In 1779 General JOHN SULLIVAN led an expedition against the Iroquois that burned forty villages and crippled their power. The Oneidas and Tuscaroras had generally remained peaceful; treaties were made with all tribes allowing them to retain reservations in New York, although many Mohawks under Brant and other hostiles went to the Bay of Quinté on the northern shore of Lake Ontario, and many still remain in the Grand River valley in Canada. Five thousand reside on six reservations in New York, and the Cornplanter reservation in Pennsylvania recalls a notable Seneca chief of the Revolutionary period. An Oneida group lives in Wisconsin. Senecas from Ohio, Cayugas from Canada, and other Iroquois from New York are in Oklahoma, a group of Senecas from Sandusky being among the first eastern Indians to agree to go to Indian Territory in 1831. See INDIANS, AMERICAN.   DON RUSSELL

BIBLIOG.—Cadwallader Colden, *History of the Five Indian Nations of Canada* (1755); Lewis H. Morgan, *The League of the Hodenosaunee or Iroquois* (1851); Arthur C. Parker, *Constitution of the Five Nations* (1916); Mabel Powers, *The Indian as Peacemaker* (1932); John Wolfe Lydekker, *The Faithful Mohawks* (1938); Jesse J. Cornplanter, *Legends of the Longhouse* (1938).

IRRADIATED FOOD. See ENRICHED OR FORTIFIED FOOD.

IRRADIATION SICKNESS. See RADIATION SICKNESS.

IRRATIONAL NUMBER; SURD. Many numbers needed in mathematics cannot be expressed exactly as *rational* numbers, that is, as the quotient (or ratio) of two integers. Such nonrational numbers are called *irrational*. For example, there is no rational number whose square is 3, but the irrational number $\sqrt{3}$ is defined so that $(\sqrt{3})^2 = 3$. The term *surd*, which means an indicated root of a rational number which cannot be extracted exactly, is now obsolescent; it is

replaced by *radical*, which includes both rational and irrational roots. In theoretical work, irrational numbers are represented by symbols like $\sqrt{5}$, $\sqrt[3]{2}$, $\sqrt[3]{10}$, etc., and the rules for operating with them are proved. For example, $\sqrt{2} \times \sqrt{5} = \sqrt{10}$ or, in general, the product of the square roots of two positive numbers is equal to the square root of the product of the numbers. In practical problems, rational *approximations* are used in place of irrational numbers. Thus 7/4, or $17/10 = 1.7$, or $173/100 = 1.73$ are rational numbers which approximate $\sqrt{3}$. The symbol $\sqrt{3}$ may be interpreted in two ways: (a) as an irrational number symbol; and (b) as an *operational* symbol meaning "find a rational number whose square is approximately 3." The general symbol is $\sqrt[n]{a}$, where a is a *positive number*, $a > 0$; but in special cases this symbol may also represent rationals, e.g., $\sqrt[3]{8} = 2$.

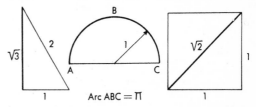

The Irrational Numbers $\sqrt{2}$, π, and $\sqrt{3}$ constructed geometrically

Surds are so-called *algebraic* numbers; other irrational numbers that are *nonalgebraic*, that is, which cannot be roots of a polynomial equation with integral (whole number) coefficients, are called *transcendental* numbers, of which π (see PI) and e are examples. See EQUATION; EXPONENT; COMPLEX NUMBER; POLYNOMIAL.   M. L. HARTUNG

IRRAWADDY RIVER, or **Irawadi,** the chief river of Burma, is formed by the confluence of the Mali and the Nmai, both of which rise at uncertain sources in Tibet. Its general course is from north to south for 1,500 miles; it discharges through nine principal mouths into the Bay of Bengal between the Gulf of Martaban on the east and Pagoda Point on the west, the mouths forming a wide, and fertile delta, chiefly planted to rice. Below the confluence of its two main arms, the river swirls and foams through a number of narrow defiles, some of which are not navigable during high water. It is navigable for small steamers for 140 miles north of Bhamo, or 1,170 miles from the sea. The chief tributary is the CHINDWIN RIVER, which joins the Irrawaddy below MANDALAY. The river is a main highway of commerce, and a railway follows its course from RANGOON to MYITKYINA.

IRREDENTISM, a corollary of nationalism which looks toward the redemption of foreign-held territory inhabited by people of its nationality. The term is derived from the phrase *Italia irredenta* (unredeemed Italy). The cession of Venetia to the kingdom of Italy after the war of 1866 left Italian minorities in various provinces of Austria. About 400,000 Italians lived in the southernmost part of Tyrol. The region itself had no particular economic value being a mountainous area but was considered of strategic value. Trento, its capital, was heavily fortified by the Austrians. A somewhat larger group of Italians were living in the Austrian provinces of Goricia, Trieste, Istria and Dalmatia. While Italian was spoken in most of the cities and coastal areas the hinterland with its rural sections was largely settled by Slavs. Slovenes lived in Gorizia while Croats and Serbs surrounded the small ports along the Dalmatian coast which retained their Italian character as an heritage of the Venetian expansion along the shores of the Adriatic. The Italian city of Trieste, surrounded by Slovene villages, was the main port of entry for the otherwise landlocked empire of the Hapsburgs.

Irrigation

Italy had claimed these territories, but Bismarck, Italy's ally in the war of 1866, did not support these claims. Italian nationalism, however, never renounced its intention to annex these territories to the kingdom in fulfillment of the political program for a united Italy. The expression irredentism was coined by an Italian patriot Matteo R. Umbriani in the year 1877 speaking of the "unliberated" territories of Trieste and Trento. A political organization called "Associazione in pro dell, Italia irredenta" was founded in the same year. Various other organizations worked in Austria to foster Italian language and culture among the Italian minorities. In line with its general policy the Austrian government did not interfere with these activities. On the whole the cause of irredentism was spread by peaceful propaganda among the Italian minorities, fostered to a varying degree by the governments of the Italian mother country. Its political goal was attained by the treaties after World War I, ceding Trieste and Trento with surrounding territories to Italy. However, some of these territories came to Yugoslavia after World War II with Trieste becoming a free city.　　　　　FRANK POLLACZEK

Strong irredentist sentiment has been found in many other countries of Europe. The treaties at the end of World War I satisfied some of these claims but in doing so they created others. German irredentism led to the absorption of Austria, the annexation of the Sudentenland from Czechoslovakia, and the armed attack on Poland in 1939. Since the end of World War II the various countries of Europe have been trying to settle this issue through the mass expulsion of foreign elements and the exchange of national minorities. See NATIONALISM; MINORITY.　　F. M.

IRRIGATION

Lands in areas with too little rainfall for agriculture are made productive by the science of irrigation

IRRIGATION, the artificial application of water to land, for the purpose of supplying the water essential to plant growth. While its object is agricultural, on account of the nature of the works required for the control of water, it includes a special branch of engineering, which involves a knowledge of the available water supply, its conservation and application to the land, the characteristics and needs of different soils, and the requirements of the particular crops to be produced.

Ancient Times. Irrigation, probably one of the oldest occupations of civilized man, antedates recorded history. Various countries in Asia, Africa, Europe, and America have remains of irrigation works of unknown antiquity, and the hieroglyphic records of the Pharaohs of the 12th dynasty give evidence of its practice in Egypt as early as 2500 B.C. In the NILE country, as in Mesopotamia, the land of the Euphrates, the rainfall is so slight as to be almost negligible and yet both were formerly renowned for their rich crops, great prosperity, and advanced civilization. These two great rivers annually flooded the lands bordering their lower reaches forming a natural system of irrigation, which was successfully assisted and controlled, particularly in Egypt, by artificial banks and other means of regulation. This irrigation system, which grew out of the natural peculiarities of the Nile, is known as the basin system and is in use today on a vaster and more elaborately developed scale in Egypt than anywhere else in the world. In Mesopotamia, where the flood season occurs six months later, it is probable that there was a system of perennial irrigation such as we now call "modern." Historical records of irrigation in India date back as far as 300 B.C., and it is estimated that that country has now over 55,800,000 acres under irrigation. In no other country is irrigation practiced

EWING GALLOWAY

Water for Irrigation of a rice field in India is raised by a cow pump, a popular water lift in Asia

on so large a scale and the activities of the British government in irrigation projects were very extensive.

Methods of Irrigation. Rainfall is the primary source of all water supply, but since rain does not always fall at the time when it is needed, means have been devised whereby water is conserved and conveyed, when necessary, to those places where it is required. Rivers are the principal channels of water supply but there is also an important underground supply tapped by springs and wells. In India irrigation by means of wells is of great importance, and in Egypt and in California artesian wells are extensively employed. This means of irrigation is well adapted to individual effort and seldom requires engineering enterprise.

By far the most important method of irrigation, and the one most widely used, is by means of open canals and laterals. The use of cement pipes in place of open canals in order to prevent losses due to percolation and evaporation is, however, constantly increasing.

There are in general two systems of applying the water to land to be irrigated: the flooding system and the furrow system. The flooding system in its turn may be subdivided into free flooding and flooding between borders. Free flooding, the oldest and crudest means of irrigation, is accomplished by providing sublaterals across the field on a fall of 1 to 3 feet per thousand. To apply the water, a temporary dam of wood or canvas is inserted in the ditch, causing it to overflow on the lower side or to discharge its water through openings in the lower bank. With his shovel the irrigator makes and mends these openings as he distributes the water to all parts of the ground; with skill an entire field may be quickly irrigated in this way. This system may be modified, especially in hilly countries, to the terrace system whereby a series of dikes is provided roughly parallel to the lateral, the ground above the dike being leveled so that it can be readily flooded. Each dike forms a sort of terrace, and the water is drawn from one level to the next through a pipe or tile, or it is carried down in a small sublateral. In flooding between borders parallel dikes are provided running nearly normal to the farm laterals, generally down the steepest slope of the field. These dikes or borders may be from 40 to 60 feet apart and from 5 to 8 inches high. To apply the water, the lateral is obstructed by a temporary dam at the second border at the top of the field, thus causing the lateral to overflow uniformly between the first and second borders. When a sufficient amount of water has been used to wet thoroughly the strip between the borders, the temporary dam is removed from the head of the second to the lateral at the head of the third border, causing an overflow between the second and third borders; this process is repeated until the entire field has been covered. This system requires careful preparation of the field. Border flooding is suitable to soils of rather wide variation in texture. Rather impervious subsoils overlain by compact loam permit long border strips, whereas open soils having porous gravelly subsoils necessitate narrow strips.

Furrow irrigation is especially suited to the watering of crops growing in rows. It consists in turning the water into furrows which run across the field in the direction of suitable slope. The furrows should be from 2 to 4 feet apart depending on the slope, the steeper slope requiring the lesser space In orchard irrigation, furrows may be spaced from 3 to 6 feet apart. Soils having unusually favorable capillary properties, or impervious subsoils, may permit orchard furrows 10 to 12 feet apart. Furrows from 8 to 12 inches deep facilitate control of water and penetration into the more impervious soil. They are well suited to orchards and to some furrow crops. Other furrow crops as sugar beets are best irrigated with furrows from 3 to 5 inches deep. One way of regulating the flow of water to bean plants is by spacing them in alternate 18- and 26-inch furrows. The farmer can send the water down the 18-inch furrow first while the plants are younger and require less water. Later he levels off the 18-inch furrow and diverts the flow to the 26-inch furrow. The water is allowed to run in each furrow until the lower end is reached, a distance of from 100 to 600 feet. Furrow irrigation is better adapted to undulating fields and steep slopes than is flooding, since it encourages deep rooting and is more economical of water. Corrugations or shallow furrows are applicable to crops such as grain and alfalfa. After the crops are planted and while the ground is still soft, a series of parallel grooves is made, several inches in depth and from 2 to 3 feet apart. These grooves have a gentle grade longitudinally to conduct the water in the required direction and prevent its running down the steepest slope.

A semifurrow system, sometimes called the ridge or bed system, is suitable for row crops where the ground is nearly level and the soil rather shallow. The land is plowed in straight furrows close enough together to form ridges. The large stream of water that can be run in the large furrows of the bed method flows quickly over the flat land, thus giving a more uniform penetration throughout the length of the rows.

Spray irrigation or irrigation by sprinkling is being used increasingly more on lands where the topography is irregular and flood irrigation is impractical and in humid sections to assure continuous and rapid growth of valuable crops despite the occasional occurrence of periods of drought. This system consists of applying water to the surface of the soil in the form of a fine spray somewhat as it comes in ordinary rain. Both the overhead pipe system and the circular spray system are used. The overhead pipe system consists of parallel lines of pipe about 50 feet apart, supported on rows of posts from 2 to 6 feet high, each line equipped with small nozzles spaced 3 to 4 feet apart. Each nozzle discharges a tiny stream of water perpendicularly to the pipe line, all streams emerging parallel The water falls upon the ground and plants in tiny drops or as a mist; the entire width of about 50 feet may be irrigated uniformly by turning the pipe. The water for irrigation is pumped through underground pipes, to which the end of each nozzle line is connected by an up ight pipe. A portable spray system, such as is used in some localities, consists of one or more nozzle lines that are carried from one part of the field to another. The circular-spray system distributes water from circular-spray nozzles fixed to the tops of upright pipes distributed uniformly through the field.

In a properly planned canal system the probable "duty of water," by which is meant the area which can be served by a unit quantity of water, must be decided upon. Much study has been made of the various factors affecting the duty of water, such as length of season, natural rainfall and evaporation, soil conditions, and crops raised. A large amount of valuable data on the subject is available. Water measurements are important in any irrigation system. These are of two main classes: first, the measurements of the stream, the main canal and the larger laterals which are of use in the operation of the system; and second, the measurement of water delivered to the irrigators.

Structures. The structures necessary to the working of an irrigation system, generally known as the "canal structure," consists of works for controlling the canal water, drainage crossings, and highway crossings. The control works include headworks, turnouts, spillways, drops and checks, and measuring devices.

The main object of the headwork, erected at the point where the water supply is diverted from the river, is to regulate the water supply admitted at the head of the canal system. A diversion weir or dam is generally necessary, with headgates at one or both ends of the weir, depending on whether one or two diversion canals are employed. The diversion weir serves to raise the water level in the river so that the desired flow may be secured through the headgates into the canal. Weirs are of two types: (1) closed weirs, as log weirs, pile weirs, crib weirs and framed weirs of wood, steel or concrete; and (2) open weirs, which consist of a series of piers of wood, iron or masonry set at regular intervals across the stream bed on a masonry or wooden floor. Lateral branches from the main canal and sublaterals from these, bringing the water to the individual farms, are also provided with regulatory structures known as "turnouts." These are usually located in an artificial bank of the canal, and near the bottom so that if the canal is running at part capacity a supply of water may still be drawn. For the sake of safety, large canal systems are provided also with a number of spillways to discharge surplus water, to prevent overtaxing the capacity of the canal, and to

Irrigation channels which supply water to field

Water-carrying conduit of an irrigation project

make it possible to empty the canal in case of a break. Spillways may be provided by so locating the canal that the water surface, at capacity, will be just even with the natural ground level on the downhill side, and omitting any bank for a considerable distance. When the water rises above the normal level, it flows gently over this natural spillway. Artificial spillways, known as wasteways, by which the canal may be quickly emptied in case of a break, are also employed. A check is a bulkhead, designed to hold the water above it at a higher level than it would otherwise stand, so that when a canal is carrying only part of its capacity, water may be taken into a turn-out which, for special reasons, has been located a distance above the bottom of the canal. A drop is a vertical or inclined structure in which a surplus grade can be concentrated and the canal transferred from a higher to a lower elevation without injury.

GROWTH OF IRRIGATION IN THE U. S.

	ACRES		ACRES
1890....	3,715,945	1929......	19,547,544
1899....	7,744,492	1939......	21,003,739
1909....	14,433,285	1948......	21,500,000
1919....	19,191,716		

If the country has considerable slope it may be necessary to provide hundreds of drops in the lateral system. These drops are sometimes constructed of wood and sometimes of concrete.

When a canal location intercepts a natural drainage line, some disposition must be made of the natural drainage water to prevent injury to the canal. This may be accomplished in various ways: the drainage, if not extensive, may be taken into the canal; the canal may be carried over the drainage channel in a flume or on an embankment with a culvert by which the drainage water may pass under the canal; or the canal may be carried under the ravine in an inverted siphon; or the drainage carried over the canal in a broad flume called a superpassage.

In addition to the canal structures just described the modern irrigation project commonly involves large engineering works, such as reservoirs; storage dams of masonry, loose rock, or earth; diversion works and large pumping plants. Sand, which is often a serious nuisance, is removed from the canal by means of sand traps, sand boxes and sluicing devices.

United States. As far back as the time of the Spanish conquests in America, extensive and well-built irrigation systems existed. Traces of such works have been found in southern Arizona, New Mexico, Colorado, and California. Modern irrigation began about the middle of the 18th century with the watering of the gardens in the hills and deserts of California by the adventurous missionaries from Mexico. One hundred years later the Mormons in Utah, separated by a thousand miles of desert from all cultivated land, found in irrigation their only escape from starvation. In a sense, therefore, BRIGHAM YOUNG may be called the pioneer of irrigation in the United States.

In August, 1894, Congress passed a law, known as the Carey Act, granting to each of the arid states 1,000,000

CROPS GROWN ON
FEDERAL RECLAMATIONS PROJECTS (1949)

CROP	PER CENT OF ACREAGE	PER CENT OF TOTAL VALUE
Vegetables and truck....	13.8	28.8
Cereals................	25.0	11.9
Alfalfa hay.............	22.5	12.2
Cotton and cotton seed...	15.5	16.4
Fruits and nuts.........	4.0	8.9
Sugar beets............	3.5	5.2
Seed..................	8.1	7.0
Pasture, hay, and forage..	41.4	5.2
Miscellaneous..........	3.7	1.8

acres of public land on the condition that it be irrigated. Many of the states have taken advantage of the grant, contracting with private parties to build works to supply water for the lands selected, the contracts specifying the price at which water rights shall be sold to water users. The states sell the land at 50 cents per acre, but will sell only to those who have contracted for water rights. The states of Wyoming and Idaho have selected their full allotment, and Congress has granted to Wyoming an additional area of 1,000,000 acres and to Idaho 2,000,-000 acres.

Prior to 1902, irrigation development in the United States had been the result of private enterprise. The larger canals had, as a rule, been built by corporations, some being constructed with money provided by the sale of bonds by irrigation districts, corporations in the nature of a municipal organization. At that time, about $200,000,000 had been invested and about 10,000,000 acres irrigated. In 1902 Congress passed the Reclamation Act which set aside the proceeds of the sales of public lands for the construction of irrigation works in the 17 arid states (see UNITED STATES, *Economic Life*).

The work done as a result of this Reclamation Act is under the direction of the Bureau of Reclamation, a bureau of the Department of the Interior. The Federal government had an investment of about two billion dollars in projects in the 17 western states, as of June 30, 1950. Practically the entire sum this investment was repayable to the United States Treasury under Federal Reclamation Laws by the

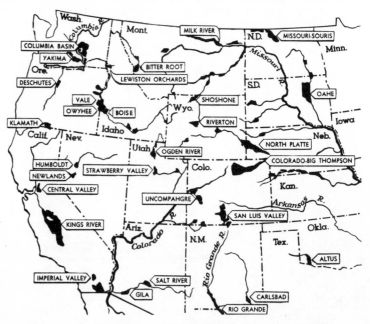

The great reclamation projects of the western United States

Water being delivered to irrigation ditch

NUMBER OF FARMS AND FARM POPULATION OF FEDERAL RECLAMATION PROJECTS—1947

STATE	PROJECT	IRRIGATED FARMS	
		NUMBER	POP.
	Regular Projects		
Arizona........	Salt River.......	5,500	19,250
	Gila (Yuma Mesa Division)......	108	311
Ariz.-Calif.......	Yuma...........	583	1,458
California.......	Orland..........	685	2,195
Colorado.......	Grand Valley....	452	1,539
	Uncompahgre....	1,746	5,247
Idaho..........	Boise...........	4,602	12,500
	Minidoka........	3,640	14,252
Montana.......	Bitter Root......	309	1,143
	Frenchtown......	37	112
	Huntley.........	277	1,492
	Milk River......	635	2,708
	Sun River.......	643	2,503
Mont.-N.D......	Lower Yellowstone	687	2,490
Neb.-Wyo......	North Platte.....	2,747	8,590
Nevada.........	Newlands........	889	3,064
New Mexico....	Carlsbad........	345	1,417
	Tucumcari.......	296	1,092
New Mexico-Texas........	Rio Grande......	8,440	43,975
Oklahoma......	W. C. Austin.....	349	787
Oregon.........	Deschutes (North Unit).........	514	1,428
	Umatilla (East and West Divisions).	553	1,757
	Vale...........	511	1,660
Ore.-Calif.......	Klamath........	1,219	3,669
Oregon-Idaho...	Owyhee.........	1,845	6,202
South Dakota...	Belle Fourche....	404	1,605
Utah..........	Strawberry Valley	1,963	....
Washington.....	Okanogan.......	401	1,357
	Yakima.........	6,233	25,348
Wyoming.......	Kendrick........	46	120
	Riverton........	525	1,510
	Shoshone........	1,140	2,403
	Subtotals......	48,324	173,184
	Supplemental Storage Projects		
California.......	All-American Canal: Imperial Valley........	4,779	27,000
Colorado.......	Fruitgrowers Dam	84	281
	Pine River.......	425	1,313
Idaho..........	Minidoka (Fremont-Madison I.D.)..........	1,718	5,627
Nevada.........	Humboldt.......	103	279
	Truckee River....	281	1,500
Oregon.........	Baker..........	39	142
	Burnt River......	118	800
	Deschutes (Central Oregon I.D.)...	755	2,320
	Stanfield.......	171	591
	Westland........	109	387
Utah..........	Hyrum.........	596	3,000
	Moon Lake......	683	2,480
	Ogden River.....	1,136	6,250
	Provo River (Deer Creek Div.)....	2,031	6,500
	Sanpete.........	225	390
	Subtotals......	13,253	58,860
	Water Conservation & Utilization Projects (Farms furnished partial or whole water supply under Warren Act or other special contracts)		
Idaho..........	Rathdrum Prairie (Post Falls Unit)	76	....
Montana.......	Buffalo Rapids...	202	638
	Intake..........	6	16
Nebraska.......	Mirage Flats.....	115	376
North Dakota...	Buford-Trenton...	70	307
Utah..........	Newton.........	123	572
	Scofield........	450	2,700
	Subtotals......	1,042	4,609
	TOTAL.....	62,619	236,653

water users and from electric power revenues. Approximately 5,000,000 acres of land were under irrigation from Bureau of Reclamation facilities in 1949. The gross value of food and forage crops on this land totaled approximately $516,000,000 for 1950. In addition, hydroelectric power plants on Bureau projects produced more than 18,000,000,000 kilowatt hours of electric energy.

The real arid region in the United States lies west of the 97th meridian between the Rocky Mountains and the Sierra Nevada and Cascade mountains, extending from Mexico to central Washington. In Arkansas, Louisiana, and eastern Texas, the normal precipitation is ample for all crops except rice.

Laws relating to the rights and use of water are enacted by several states. In general the laws of the arid states recognize the rights of persons needing water for irrigation to appropriate it from streams and other sources. Each state prescribes the manner in which the water may be appropriated.

Canada. Irrigation in Canada is confined chiefly to the semi-arid regions in Saskatchewan, Alberta, and the fruit growing districts of British Columbia. The property in and the right to use water are vested in the crown, and the government therefore issues licenses for the use of water. All construction work is under the irrigation districts act of the provinces, but before such construction can be started a license must be obtained for the use of the water from the Canadian government. After the construction work is completed the government inspects the systems annually. It is estimated that the total area irrigated in Canada is about 1,000,000 acres. The construction of large irrigation projects has been confined to the province of Alberta.

The chief available streams are the North and South Saskatchewan, Bow, Red Deer, Watertown, Belly, St. Mary, Milk, and Oldman rivers. Irrigation development is narrowly circumscribed by the

IRRIGATION PROJECTS BY TYPE OF ENTERPRISE (1940)

TYPE OF ENTERPRISE	ACREAGE	PER CENT
Individual and Partnership........	7,314,152	34.8
Co-operative....................	6,652,488	31.7
Irrigation District................	3,514,702	16.7
Commercial.....................	1,017,781	4.9
U.S. Office Indian Affairs........	515,765	2.4
U.S. Reclamation Service.........	1,824,004	8.7
Other—city, state, etc...........	164,847	.8
		100.0

small amount of available water and although it is being increased from year to year the fact remains that only a small fraction of the area for which water is needed can be irrigated. See also CANADA, *Economic Life*.

Other Countries. Mention has already been made of irrigation in India and Egypt. It is being increasingly practiced in New Zealand and Australia, and millions of acres are irrigated in China, where such work has been carried on from time immemorial. In Europe, France, Italy, and Spain are the chief countries in which irrigation is carried on. In northern and central France irrigation is not a necessity for raising crops but it is employed to increase the fertility of meadow land for hay. In southern France, where the summers are hot and dry, irrigation is useful, if not absolutely necessary, particularly for market gardening. In Italy irrigation is in an advanced stage of development. The plains of Piedmont and Lombardy are striking examples of what can be done by the artificial control of natural water supplies. Spain owes many of her irrigation laws and customs to the Moors. In Valencia the irrigation works are supposed to have been built about A.D 800. In the latter part of the 18th century much attention was given to the building of dams and the use of irrigation and as a result the value of land was greatly enhanced. In 1929 Argentina had an irrigated area estimated at over 3,000,000 acres, and Japan an estimated irrigated acreage of over 7,000,000. See RECLAMATION; DAM.
                                         MICHAEL W. STRAUS

BIBLIOG.–U.S. Dept. of Interior, Bureau of Reclamation, *Reclamation Handbook* (*Conservation Bulletin No. 32*) (1942); U.S. Dept. of Interior, Bureau of Reclamation, *Farmer's Irrigation Guide* (1939); Bureau of Reclamation, *Annual Reports;* Bureau of Reclamation monthly publication, *The Reclamation Era.*

IRTYSH RIVER, or **Irtish,** the principal tributary of the Siberian Ob River of the U.S.S.R. The Irtysh rises in China on the western slopes of the Mongolian Altai Mountains and flows northwest through the Kazakh Soviet Socialist Republic into the Russian Soviet Federated Socialist Republic. Here in Omsk Region the river flows past the city of Tobolsk to join the Ob after a course of about 2,520 miles, 2,000 of which are navigable. The chief tributaries of the Irtysh are the Ishim and the Tobol rivers.

IRÚN, town, Spain, in the province of Guipúzcoa, on the left bank of the Bidassoa River, eight miles E of San Sebastián. Situated on the French frontier, it is an important customs station of the Spanish Northern Railway, main Spanish overland route to the rest of Europe. Irún is also an industrial center, with paper mills, ironworks, tanneries, and potteries. During the Spanish Civil War (1936–39), it was the scene of bitter fighting; it fell to the forces of General Franco on Sept. 4, 1937. Pop. (1940) 7,790.

IRVING, EDWARD, 1792–1834, Scottish clergyman, and one of the originators of the Catholic Apostolic Church, was assistant to Dr. Chalmers at St. John's, Glasgow, until 1822, when he was called to Cross Street Chapel, London. Here his fiery eloquence attracted great crowds, the sensation being heightened by his book of discourses, *For the Oracles of God*, published in 1823, and he soon occupied the pulpit of a large and fashionable church in Regent Street. His popularity waned after he inclined toward mysticism and announced himself a prophet. Deposed from the ministry (1832) on the charge of heresy, he formed, with Henry Drummond, the banker, a community of Christians, who later became the Catholic Apostolic Church, and are frequently designated Irvingites.

IRVING, Sir HENRY, real name **John Henry Brodribb,** 1838–1905, English actor, was born in Somersetshire. He was given a private education in preparation for a business career, but early in life manifested his desire to identify himself with the theater. He made his debut at Sunderland in 1856, enacting the role of Gaston in *Richelieu,* and then went to Edinburgh, where he appeared with a stock company for a period of two years. He first excited the admiration of the critics in 1866 with his portrayal of Doricourt in *The Belle's Stratagem* at the St. James' Theater, London. As Digby Grant in *The Two Roses* (1870), he earned additional favor, but achieved his first considerable triumph after he began his tenure at the Lyceum in 1871. Thereafter for nearly 30 years Irving was intimately associated with this celebrated house, appearing there as Mathias in *The Bells.*

In 1878 Irving leased the Lyceum in association with ELLEN TERRY, who had first appeared with him in 1867 in *The Taming of the Shrew.* Among the plays produced by these two at the Lyceum, Shakespearean dramas predominated. They were performed on a scale of magnificence and with a meticulous attention to detail unknown before. Irving's interpretations, melodramatic and florid in tone and accompanied by exaggerated gestures, awoke controversy as to his stature as an artist, even in his own day. Nevertheless, his great vitality, amazing versatility, and earnestness of purpose were recognized by all. His dignified and sympathetic version of Shylock aroused both applause and condemnation.

In 1895 Irving was knighted by Queen Victoria. He first visited the United States in 1883, with Ellen Terry and his Lyceum company, opening in New York in his familiar and popular character of Mathias in *The Bells.* This was the first of several cordially received tours of the United States. Sir Henry died suddenly at Bradford, England, immediately after appearing with great success in the title role of Tennyson's *Becket,* and was buried in Westminster Abbey.

BIBLIOG.–C. Craig, *Henry Irving* (1938); H. A. Saintsbury and C. Palmer, eds., *We Saw Him Act* (1939).

IRVING, WASHINGTON, 1783–1859, American essayist, story writer, historian, and diplomat, descended from the Irvines of the Orkneys, was born in New York, a place with which he remained closely associated in spite of the fact that he spent approximately one-third of his life abroad. He thanked God later in life that he was "born on the banks of the Hudson," and he was indeed responsible through his writings for creating a kind of mythology of his beloved city. In his early days he wandered north into the Catskills; but, somewhat delicate in health, he early formed lasting tastes for literature and the theater. The latter formed the subject of his first youthful book, published when he was 19, a slight volume of dramatic criticism, *The Letters of Jonathan Oldstyle, Gent.* (1802).

His first journey abroad, a gift from his fond brothers in recognition of his talents in the literary and social life of the city occurred from 1804 to 1806, in an extended tour of France, Italy, Holland, and England. When he returned, in his luggage were manuscript notes and journals destined to aid him later in his writing, and in his memory the sophisticated scenes demanding his return. He now attempted to enter the law, but we see him more clearly in the social life of New York and Philadelphia and in the writing of *Salmagundi* (1807–8), a sheaf of charming essays in the Addison vein. In this he was aided by his old friend James K. Paulding, and by his talented brother, William Irving. The little volume was a success, and Irving was soon engaged on a more ambitious and more enduring piece of satire, the first American comic chronicle, Diedrich Knickerbocker's *A History of New York* (1809). Just as he was putting this rollicking book to press, grief overtook him in the sudden death of his betrothed, Matilda. This event, leaving him shattered and purposeless, profoundly affected his life and art. He never married.

During the next few years Irving studied German, was editor of *The Analectic Magazine,* and served as a staff officer in the War of 1812. Yet he was restless, and in 1815 he again sailed for Europe, this time as

Washington Irving, American essayist, story writer, and historian, pictured at the age of 26 against a background of his home, "Sunnyside," on the Hudson River, and an illustration, "The Lovers," from "Bracebridge Hall," published in 1822

it turned out, to remain for 17 years. This period abounded in personal adventure. He shared his brothers' distress in the collapse of the family hardware business in Liverpool; he rejoiced with all England at the downfall of Napoleon; and through a letter from Thomas Campbell he spent a few days at Abbotsford with Sir Walter Scott. This friendship moved him deeply, and either from the inspiration of the great novelist or from financial necessity or as a culmination (he was now in his thirties) of his literary ambitions, he began in 1819 to send to America in installments his masterpiece, Geoffrey Crayon's *Sketch Book*, which included "Rip Van Winkle" and "The Legend of Sleepy Hollow." "Crayon is very good," said Byron; and Irving, like Byron, became famous overnight. He was now on friendly terms with Cambell, Scott, Moore, and John Murray. Instead of the wandering American he was a successful author.

The other adventures of the 17 years included a romantic winter (1822–23) at the court of Frederick Augustus in Saxony; playwriting in Paris with Thomas Paine (1824), and, finally, the thrilling and productive three years in Spain (1826–29). For he now became a pioneer interpreter of this fascinating and mysterious country. When he left Spain in 1829 to serve until 1832 as American attaché in London, he was not only the author of *The Sketch Book* and of its mild sequel, *Bracebridge Hall* (1822), but of *Tales of a Traveller* (1824), a Gothic version of recollections of Germany, Italy, and New York, of *A History of the Life and Voyages of Christopher Columbus* (1828), of *The Conquest of Granada* (1829) and, published after his return to America, of *The Alhambra* (1832). These last three books marking the apogee of Irving's literary career, reveal his competence as a romantic historian and as a somewhat casual scholar. *The Alhambra*, in particular, is a memorial to his mastery of Spanish legend and his sensitivity to the romance of this semibarbaric country.

On his arrival home in 1832 Irving was feted at a public dinner. Toasts were drunk to "Geoffrey Crayon," our first man of letters, and to the characters in his stories. At the same time he was urged to transfer his talents from the celebration of European scenes to those of America. Amiable, even ductile in character, Irving yielded to the popular wish, and after an extended journey in the West wrote of Western subjects in a series of books almost ludicrous in their sophisticated treatment of the rough frontier: *A Tour on the Prairie* (part of a series called *The Crayon Miscellany*, 1835), *Astoria* (1836), and *The Adventures of Captain Bonneville* (1837). In them, however, are delightful glimpses of the life among the Osages and of the settlements of the Far West.

After his return from this pilgrimage, Irving, seemingly unaware of the change in fashions in the literature of his country (the powerful intellects of Concord and Cambridge had now appeared), continued to write his pleasant essays. He was, thought Longfellow, as he read these pensive, graceful studies, repetitious in theme and technique, writing himself out. This may have been true, but something of the magic of the born stylist still hovered over Irving's afterpieces, such as his *Oliver Goldsmith* (1849); *Ma-*

homet and His Successors (1849–1850); *Wolfert's Roost* (1855); or even over the tired biography of George Washington, whose final volume was completed in the year of his death.

Meanwhile Irving had made his third journey to Europe (1842–46), serving his country as minister to Spain so well, that like Lowell's, his memory is still cherished in the peninsula. Yet during this period he did no writing save the charming letters of an old man to his beloved nieces at home. For he now lived officially and happily at "Sunnyside," his picturesque little villa on the Hudson, the river which, through "Rip Van Winkle" and other sketches, will ever be associated with his name. Here, during the last two or three decades of his life, he had become, it was clear to his admiring contemporaries, instead of the genial idler of old New York, the literary arbiter of America, influencing younger writers, such as the devoted Hawthorne.

To the world he was much more than a writer; he was a famous American. His name had been suggested as a candidate for mayor of New York; he had been the friend of both Jackson and Van Buren; he was a public-spirited citizen. Yet, despite his sallies into public life, Irving was the literary man in essence; the browser and the antiquarian rather than the scholar; the romancer rather than the historian; the dreamer rather than the thinker. He was the first great American prose stylist and in this respect he still ranks high among the writers of all time.
STANLEY T. WILLIAMS

BIBLIOG.–P. M. Irving, *The Life and Letters of Washington Irving* (1935); S. T. Williams, *The Life of Washington Irving* (1935); Van Wyck Brooks, *The World of Washington Irving* (ed. 1950).

IRVINGITES. See IRVING, EDWARD.

IRVINGTON, town, NE New Jersey, in Essex County, on the Lehigh Valley Railroad, three miles W of Newark of which it is a residential suburb. Irvington was settled in 1692 as Camptown. In 1852 its name was changed to honor Washington Irving, then at the height of his fame. The industrial section of Irvington makes electric toy trains, hardware specialties, insulators, and tools. Pop. (1950) 59,201.

IRWIN, WALLACE, 1875– American author, brother of WILL IRWIN, was born in Oneida, N.Y., and educated in Denver and at Leland Stanford University. He began his career as a journalist, editing the *Overland Monthly* (1902) and writing feature stories for the *San Francisco Examiner*. From 1906 to 1907 he was on the staff of *Collier's Weekly*. He published a number of novels in a popular vein, as *Seed of the Sun* (1921), *Days of her Life* (1931), and *Young Wife* (1936), but is principally known for his humorous poems and sketches, including *The Love Sonnets of a Hoodlum* (1902), *Letters of a Japanese Schoolboy* (1909), and *Mr. Togo, Maid of All Work* (1913).

IRWIN, WILL, full name **William Henry,** 1873–1948, American writer, brother of WALLACE IRWIN, was born in Oneida, N.Y., and graduated from Leland Stanford University in 1899. From 1904 to 1906 he was a correspondent for the *New York Sun*, and became widely known for his graphic report of the San Francisco earthquake of 1906. In 1914 and 1915 he was war correspondent for several American and British publications and in 1916–18 for the *Saturday Evening Post*. His works include fiction: *The Picaroons* (with Gelett Burgess, 1903), *Confessions of a Con Man* (1909), *The Red Button* (1912); analyses of social and political trends: *Christ or Mars?* (1923), *How Red is America?* (1927), *Propaganda and the News* (1936); plays: *The Thirteenth Chair* (with Bayard Veiller, 1916), *Lute Song* (with Sidney Howard, 1930); and his autobiography, *Making of a Reporter* (1942).

ISAAC, in the Bible, second of the Hebrew patriarchs. In fulfillment of God's promise, he was born of ABRAHAM and Sarah in their old age. As a test of Abraham's faith and obedience, it was commanded by God that Isaac be offered as a sacrifice. When the offering was about to be carried out, a divine intervention saved Isaac's life. He married Rebekah, his cousin, who bore him twin sons, ESAU and JACOB. The history of his life and death are written in the Book of Genesis 17:17–19, 21; 22:2–18; 35:27–29.

ISAAC I COMNENUS, d. 1061, Byzantine emperor, the earliest of the house of Comnenus to occupy the throne at Constantinople. Chosen emperor by the army (1057), he reigned only two years, then abdicated, and entered a monastery, where he died. He was a ruler of high character and was a zealous reformer.

ISAAC II ANGELUS, d. 1204, Byzantine emperor, was raised to the throne of Constantinople by a revolution (1185), but was a dissolute and worthless prince. Compelled to resign by his brother Alexius (1195), he was restored by the Crusaders (1203), but was again thrown into prison on their departure, and died there.

ISAACS, Sir ISAAC ALFRED, 1855–1948, Australian jurist and governor general, was born in Melbourne, studied at Melbourne University, and was admitted to the practice of law in 1890. Rising rapidly in the colonial legislature, he entered the Dominion parliament (1901–6) and became attorney general of Australia (1905–6). Isaacs served as justice of the high court of Australia (1906–30) and chief justice of Australia (1930–31). He was governor general from 1931 to 1936, the first to be appointed following the recommendation of a Dominion ministry.

ISABELA, town, Philippine Islands, Negros Island, in Negros Occidental Province, situated near the W coast on the main highway 37 miles S of the provincial capital of Bacolod. It is a thriving trade center. Pop. (1948) 33,743, mostly Visayan.

ISABELA ISLAND, or **Albemarle,** the largest of the Galápagos, in the western part of the group. See GALÁPAGOS.

ISABELLA, 1292–1358, daughter of Philip the Fair of France, married Edward II of England at Boulogne in 1308. She and the king did not agree, and she often sided with his enemies. She was probably privy to his murder, and she and her paramour, Mortimer, ruled England for some time after the accession of her son, Edward III.

ISABELLA II, 1830–1904, queen of Spain, was born in Madrid, the daughter of Maria Christina and Ferdinand VII. She succeeded her father in 1833, and her mother was regent for her (1833–40) during the Carlist War, when DON CARLOS claimed the throne under the Salic Law. In 1840 the queen mother abandoned the regency to General Espartero, who in turn was ousted by General Narváez in 1843. Isabella, at the age of 13, was declared of age, and Narváez became her lieutenant governor (1843–51). Important events in Isabella's reign were her marriage to the Bourbon Don Francisco of Assisi (1846), which, with the simultaneous marriage of her sister to the Duke of Montpensier, caused a strain in Anglo-French diplomatic relations; a papal concordat (1851), making Roman Catholicism the only recognized faith in Spain; a war with Chile (1865–66); and constant internal revolutions and political battles, culminating in the successful revolution of Serrano and Prim in 1868, when Isabella, deposed, fled to France. She relinquished her claims in 1870 to her son ALFONSO XII.

ISABELLA OF CASTILE. See FERDINAND V.

ISAEUS, c. 420–338 B.C., Greek orator, was probably a native of Chalcis, but went to Athens at an early age. No particulars of his life are known, but he is said to have been a pupil of Isocrates and to have taught rhetoric to Demosthenes. All but one of his surviving speeches were made in behalf of clients involved in inheritance suits, and provide valuable information on Athenian laws of succession and domestic relations in general. Ten complete speeches are still extant, and the greater part of another was preserved by Dionysius of Halicarnassus in his treatise *On the Ancient Orators*.

ISAIAH, biblical prophet, is considered the greatest of the Old Testament prophesiers. Son of the prophet Amoz, Hebrew tradition assigns him a place in the line of royal blood of the kings of Judah. Isaiah's prophecies, recorded in the Book of the Prophet Isaiah, foretell of the coming of Immanuel, the longed-for Messiah. This may explain the origin of the prophet's name, since Isaiah in Hebrew language signifies "the salvation of the Lord." Isaiah complains of the sins of the nation and exhorts the people to repent of their ways; he predicts further evils that are to befall them because of sin; but foretells that Israel will be restored as a whole when the nation's enemies will be confounded. As with many other books of Old Testament writings, much controversy has taken place regarding various sections of the Book of Isaiah; there has been disagreement among scholars as to how much of the writing is actually that of the great prophet, and how much might have been incorporated by later writers. Regardless of conclusions reached, Isaiah has definitely been accorded the place of being one of the greatest of the Hebrew theologians, statesmen, and religious writers. A legend informs that, after living a holy life, the prophet died through martyrdom by being sawed in half at the command of his son-in-law, King Manasseh, whose hatred Isaiah incurred by reproving the king for his evil life.

R. M. LEONARD

ISAR RIVER. See DANUBE RIVER.

ISAROG, extinct volcano, Philippine Islands, SE Luzon, Camarines Sur Province. It reaches a height of 6,450 feet.

ISAURIA, an ancient district in Asia Minor, bounded on the S by Cilicia and Pisidia. It was inhabited by a barbarous people, who in Roman times were notorious as brigands and pirates. In 78 B.C., P. Servilius subdued them; but they soon broke loose again, and were a perpetual source of trouble. In the third century A.D., one of their chiefs, Trebellianus, assumed the title of emperor. He was conquered and executed, but his people were not permanently subjugated. At length an Isaurian, Zeno, became emperor (A.D. 474–491). In the next century, however, they were finally overpowered by the Emperor Anastasius. The Emperor Leo III (718–741) was also an Isaurian.

ISCHIA, Latin **Aenaria,** island, W central Italy, Campania Division, off the coast of Napoli (Naples) Province, in the bay of Naples; area 26 sq. mi.; pop. (1948) 30,418. It is six miles southwest of Naples, with which it has steamer connections. The highest point on the island is Mont Epomeo (alt. 2,608 ft.). There are extensive orchards, olive groves, and vineyards, and corn is grown. Ischia has shipbuilding and fisheries and manufactures pottery; straw plaiting for hats, baskets, and furniture; and tiles and bricks. The chief towns are Ischia, on the northeast coast; Casamicciola on the north; and Forio on the west. In 1883 the island was shaken by an earthquake resulting in great local destruction in Casamicciola and the loss of 1,900 lives. The island was occupied by the Germans in 1941, and freed from their control by Italian partisans and Allied troops in October, 1943.

Ischl

ISCHL, BAD, town, Austria, in the province of Upper Austria, in the Salzkammergut, at the confluence of the Ischl and Traun rivers, 39 miles SE of Salzburg. A fashionable spa, on a peninsula at an altitude of 1,530 feet and is almost surrounded by the two rivers. There are saline and other baths, and salt is produced at the Ischl mine near by. Bad Ischl has been a spa since 1822, and from 1856 to 1918 was the summer residence of the Austrian imperial family. Pop. (1946 est.) 14,721.

ISEO, LAGO D', ancient **Lacus Sebinus**, N Italy, in Lombardy Division, at the S foot of the Bergamasche Alps, in a valley lying midway between Lago di Garda, in Brescia Province, and Lago di Como, in Bergamo Province; area 24 sq. mi. Its length is 17 miles; greatest width, three miles; and depth, about 1,000 feet. The Oglio River enters the lake on the north at Lovere, leaving it on the south at Sarnico to join the Po. Lake Iseo has several islands including Siviano, with Monte Isola (1,965 ft.), which is crowned by a chapel; San Paola, with a Franciscan convent; Loreto, with a ruined chapel containing remains of frescoes. On the south side of the lake are the small towns of Iseo, 16 miles northwest of Brescia, and Sarnico, 15 miles west of Bergamo. At the head of the lake is Oglio Valley, with Adamello (alt. 11,660 ft.) to the northeast.

ISÈRE, department, SE France, bounded on the N by Ain, E by Savoie, S by Hautes-Alpes and Drôme, and W by Loire and Rhône; area 3,178 miles; pop. (1946) 574,019. The Isère, crossing the department from east to west, and the Rhône, on the northern boundary, are the chief rivers. South and east of the Isère the terrain is very mountainous, reaching heights of over 13,000 feet on the southeastern border, while the north and west consist of plateaus broken by valleys. Iron ore is mined, and marble and slates are quarried. Textiles, paper, iron, and steel are manufactured, and there are many hydroelectric plants along the Isère and its tributaries. The valleys are fertile, and cereals, vines, and mulberry trees are cultivated. The mountain pastures afford grazing for cattle. Grenoble is the chief city.

ISÈRE RIVER, ancient **Isara**, in SE France, rises on the Italian frontier, and winds W and SW 150 miles, through the departments of Savoie, Isère, and Drôme, to join the Rhône on its left bank a few miles N of Valence. Important hydroelectric plants have been installed on the Isère and its tributaries, the Drac, Arc, and Romanche. The total length of the river is 180 miles, of which 100 miles are navigable, though with difficulty.

ISERLOHN, town, Germany, in the Prussian province of Westphalia, on the Baar River, 36 miles by rail SE of Dortmund. Interesting features are the Upper Church and the old market place. It has an important iron and steel industry, a varied metal goods industry, and trade in timber, grain, and livestock. Iserlohn is beautifully situated, with a state park and a state forest in the vicinity. It was originally known as the site of a mint (11th century); it was chartered as a town in 1260. Pop. (1946) 30,800.

ISEULT. See TRISTAN.

ISEZAKI, city, Japan, Honshu, Gumma Prefecture, situated on a railway some 65 miles NW of Tokyo, and 10 miles SE of Maebashi, prefectural capital. During World War II Isezaki was more than half destroyed by American bombing attacks. Pop. (1946) 43,556.

ISFAHAN, W central Iran, the ancient **Aspadana** of Ptolemy, on the N bank of the Zaindeh River, 240 miles by road S of Teheran. The city is situated in the center of a fertile oasis having an altitude of over 5,000 feet, with bare, rugged mountains closing in on the north, south, and west. Temperatures range from a maximum of over 97° F. in July to a low of 24° F. in January. Isfahan is an important commercial center, with the bazaars having a large trade in tobacco, glassware, rice, carpets, and leather goods.

IRANIAN TRADE COMMISSION

Masjid-i-Shah, royal mosque at Isfahan

There are manufactures of calico and other printed cottons, felt, brocades, saddles, lacquered ware, pottery, tiles, leather goods, metalwares, and gold and silver filigree work ranging from small articles of jewelry to huge wall screens. Julfa, a suburb on the opposite bank of the Zaindeh, was established as a Christian Armenian community by Shah Abbas I early in the 17th century, when thousands of Armenian families were moved here from the city of the same name on the banks of the Araxes (Aras). Julfa is the seat of an Armenian bishop, and has a handsome cathedral and a number of fine churches, decorated with fine Iranian polychrome tile.

Three ancient bridges still in use cross the Zaindeh at Isfahan. The city has been called the treasury of Persian architecture. Many of its finer buildings are arranged about the Royal Square, or Maidan, a great rectangle more than 1,500 feet long and some 520 feet wide. These include the Masjid-i-Shah, royal mosque, dating from 1611, which is covered with an enameled tile of great beauty; the mosque of Sheik Lutfullah, with an interior of faience mosaics and painted tile; the Ale Qapu palace, a vast audience hall with a balcony that served as a royal box for the watching of various court games; the Chihil Situn, or Hall of Forty Pillars; the shrine of Safi and Din; and, on the east side of an avenue laid out by Shah Abbas I, the Masjid and the Madrassa Mader-i-Shah Sultan Husain, built in 1710 as a college for the training of dervishes and mullahs. The Masjid-i-Jami, or Cathedral Mosque, is historically and architecturally the most important building of Isfahan, some parts of it having been erected as early as the 10th century. These and several other buildings were surveyed by a royal commission in the early part of the 20th century and have since been magnificently restored.

As early as the seventh century B.C the Aryan Iranians, having gained their independence, established their seat of government at Gabae, on the site of modern Isfahan. The town was visited and probably sacked during the wars of Alexander and his successors. During the Sassanian period the name was corrupted to Jaï, the name by which it was known during the Arab invasion. Jaï subsequently was replaced by the name Medíneh. Medíneh was gradually superseded in importance by a suburb called Yahudíeh (Jews' town). Both cities have been described as independent, and each was protected by its own surrounding wall. Rukn-addaula, the Buyid king, united the two and near-by villages about the middle of the 10th century, and the city was called Isfahan. Isfahan continued to flourish until the time of Tamerlane (14th century), who is reputed to have built a tower of 70,000 human heads at the gate of the city as a warning to other cities not to resist his arms. Isfahan rose to its greatest power when the new Safavid dynasty moved its capital here from Kazvin. Shah Abbas I encouraged European merchants and embassies, and originated many of the buildings and gardens for which Isfahan was famed. Chardin, the great 17th century traveler, who spent much of his later life in Isfahan, estimated the population at 600,-000. Isfahan suffered as a result of the Afghan invasion of 1722, but continued as the capital until the end of the 18th century. The city has dwindled in size and power since, but has regained some of its former importance during the 20th century. Pop. (1947 est.) 205,000.   B. F. C.

ISHERWOOD, BENJAMIN FRANKLIN, 1822–1915, American mechanical engineer and naval architect, was born in New York City. As engineer in chief of the U.S. Navy (1861) and first chief of the Bureau of Steam Engineering (1862–70), he supervised design and construction of machinery for the rapidly expanding navy during the Civil War. His *Experimental Researches in Steam Engineering* (2 vols. 1863–65) became a standard engineering text.

ISHMAEL, in the Bible, son of ABRAHAM by Hagar, Egyptian maid to Sarah, Abraham's wife. Because of her own barrenness, Sarah suggested this means of obtaining a son. When Hagar bore Ishmael, her accomplishment prompted her to despise her mistress. Sarah retaliated by having the mother and son sent into the wilderness of Beer-sheba. Ishmael eventually settled in Paran and became a famous archer. He is considered by some to be the eponymous ancestor of the Ishmaelites. It is through him that the Mohammedans trace their descent to Abraham, claiming that he and his father constructed the Ka'aba at Mecca, where they point out his tomb. See Gen. 16:4–16; 17:18–26; 21:8–21; 25:9, 12–17; 28:9; I Chron. 1:29–30.

ISHPEMING, city, N Upper Michigan, in Marquette County, on the North Western, the Duluth, South Shore and Atlantic, and the Lake Superior and Ishpeming railroads and U.S. Highway 41; about 15 miles W of Marquette and Lake Superior. Ishpeming is an important iron mining center situated in the heart of the Marquette range. It was settled in 1854 and its name is from the Ojibway language meaning "high place" or "heaven." An annual ski tournament is held in Ishpeming. The principal industries include iron ore and gold mining, lumbering, and the manufacture of clothing and explosives. Pop. (1950) 8,962.

ISHTAR, or **ISTAR.** See ASTARTE.

ISIDORE, SAINT, c. 560–636, bishop of Seville, noted writer and scholar. His tremendous contributions to Western learning by preserving much of the classics in his works, gained him great popularity. A leading figure of Visigothic Spain, he attacked the doctrine of ARIUS, worked to establish educational institutions, and is credited by some with being originator of much of his day's legislation. His *Etymologiae* or *Origines* is an amazingly comprehensive digest of all the learning of the time; it is frequently referred to as the first encyclopedia. He also wrote numerous treatises on theology, natural history, language, and other subjects.

ISINGLASS, a variety of gelatin prepared by cutting the dried swimming-bladder of various fish into very fine shavings. It is employed in cookery, but chiefly, on account of its peculiar structure, for clarifying wine and beer.

ISIS, ancient Egyptian deity, wife of OSIRIS, and mother of Horus. She was originally the goddess of the earth, afterward of the moon. The Greeks identified her with both Demeter and Io. Her worship was introduced into Rome, toward the end of the republic, and became very popular; though, because of its licentious orgies, it was more than once checked by the government.

ISIS RIVER. See THAMES RIVER.

ISKENDERON. See ALEXANDRETTA.

ISLA, JOSÉ FRANCISCO DE, 1703–81, Spanish Jesuit writer, was born at Vidanes in León. He won international renown for his *Historia del famoso predicador Fray Gerundio de Campazas, alias Zotes* (1758),

a novel which crudely satirized the bombast and ignorance of Spanish pulpit oratory. The book aroused much controversy and, though condemned by the Holy Office in 1760, contined to be read, and the absurd traditions which it criticized were soon laughed out of existence. Expelled from Spain with the rest of his order by Charles III, Isla spent the rest of his life in Italy, where he wrote a sequel to *Fray Gerundio* (1770) and a Spanish translation of Lesage's *Gil Blas* (pub. 1787).

ISLA. See ISLE.

ISLAM, the name used by Mohammedans for their religion. See MOHAMMEDANISM.

ISLAND, a body of land surrounded by water. Islands occur in rivers, lakes, and oceans. River islands are sometimes bits of resistant rock around which the stream cuts its channel. Frequently a river island is an accumulation of water-borne debris. Such an island is pear shaped and tends to migrate downstream—erosion rounds the upstream end, and deposition occurs downstream. Lake islands are usually irregularities in the lake bed that appear above water level. Oceanic islands are subclassified into those which appear on the continental shelf and those which are far from the mainland. Islands on the shelf are the result of submergence of coastal highlands, or they are the ends of peninsulas whose necks have been cut by sea action. The structure and shape of such islands is related to their parent form. Thus there are islands that are mountainous, table-like, or plains. Sand bars (tombolos) formed by current action tie some continental islands together or to the mainland. Although this form violates the definition, it is still considered an island. Continental islands may appear in groups or chains or as a single island. Oceanic islands away from continents are irregularities in the basin floor. Frequently they are volcanic mountains, or coral rings built around worn-down mountains or plateaus (see ATOLL). Sometimes the island is a combination of the two forms. Oceanic islands too, can occur singly or in chains.

The plant and animal life on islands is a reflection of their proximity to the mainland. Isolated islands possess peculiar life forms; the proportion of endemic species and genera is large, and the forms are in a number of cases distinctly archaic.

As far as man is concerned, islands are useful as military outposts, entrepôts, refueling stations, and recreational spots. If the islands are large enough they support much the same activities as mainlands. The 10 largest islands of the world in order are:

The Thousand Islands dot the St. Lawrence River

Greenland, New Guinea, Borneo, Madagascar, Baffin, Sumatra, Honshu, Great Britain, Victoria, and Ellesmere.   E. K. A.

ISLAND NO. 10, the tenth island in the Mississippi River below Cairo, Ill., near the boundary line between Kentucky and Tennessee. In the Civil War it was heavily fortified by the Confederates and defended by forces under General Mackall. The Federal forces advanced on it in March, 1862, with an army under General Pope and seven gunboats under Commodore Foote. The gunboats bombarded the works for weeks without effect, but the construction of a canal, behind the Confederate position, the island lying at the end of a long peninsula, finally cut them off. Two gunboats, commanded by Captain Walke and Lieutenant Commander Thompson, gallantly ran by the batteries on the nights of April 3 and 7 and co-operated in an assault by troops which had been transported through the canal. Forced to evacuate by Pope's landing (April 7), the Confederates were penned in the almost impassable morasses, and about 7,000, nearly the entire force, were taken, together with a great quantity of supplies.

ISLAND UNIVERSE. See GALAXY.

ISLANDS, BAY OF, in the Gulf of St. Lawrence, on the W coast of Newfoundland. The Humber River flows into it. Some of the islands in the bay rise to heights of 500 feet.

ISLAY, southernmost island of the Inner Hebrides, Scotland, in Argyllshire; 61 miles W of Kintyre and one mile SW of Jura, from which it is separated by Islay Sound; area, 375 sq. mi.; pop. about 5,000. On the western coast is a peninsula known as The Rhinns of Islay, which is formed by Loch Indal on the north and Loch Gruninart on the southwest. The island's highest elevation is about 1,600 feet. The industries of the island include dairy farming, stock raising, distilling, iron and lead mining, and slate and marble quarrying. The island has 60 square miles of peat bog. Oats and barley are raised. Bowmore, Port Ellen, Port Askaig, Bridgend, Port Charlotte, Portnahaven, and Kilchoman are the chief towns. On the Oa, a small peninsula to the south, is a memorial tower honoring American soldiers and sailors lost on the transport *Tuscania*, which was torpedoed during World War I. Islay was the seat of the Macdonalds and the Campbells, "Lords of the Isles."

ISLE, Spanish **Isla,** French **Île.** When used as a part of the name of a place, see entry under the principal word: PINES, ISLE OF; MAN, ISLE OF.

ISLE ROYALE NATIONAL PARK, a forested island in NW Lake Superior, a part of Michigan, 50 miles NW of Keweenaw Point. The largest island in Lake Superior, Isle Royale comprises 133,838 acres; it is 45 miles long and nine miles across at its widest point. Inaccessibility and the severe winter climate have kept the island one of the few remaining wilderness areas of continental United States. The first white visitor to Isle Royale was probably an Indian trader, Etienne Anton Brulé, in the 17th century. The island became an American possession through the efforts of Benjamin Franklin, who had heard of rich copper deposits there and insisted that the island be ceded to the United States through the Treaty of Paris (1783). The Ojibway Indians controlled the island until 1842 when they ceded it to the Federal government. Mining of copper was carried on (1846–83) and some pre-Columbian copper pits also have been found. The park, established in 1940, has dense woods through which herds of moose roam. There are also interesting rock formations, a pageant of wild flowers, beautiful inland lakes, fine harbors, and good fishing grounds which attract many visitors to the camps in the area. Passenger service to Copper Harbor was started in the late 1930's.

ISLES OF THE BLEST, or **FORTUNATE ISLES,** were, according to ancient Greek conception, situated at the western extremity of the known world,

and were the abode of those happy mortals who the gods decreed should be exempt from death. Homer appears to identify them with the Elysian Fields. Later ages identified them with the Canaries or Madeira. The Avalon of the King Arthur cycle is also a homologue of this classic myth. Compare, too, the Babylonian "isle of the blessed," with its four encircling rivers, and the herb of life growing in the midst, and note its similarity to the biblical story of the garden of Eden. The ancient Egyptians put their Amenet (Amenthes), or world of the dead, in the west. See ATLANTIS; ELYSIUM.

ISLINGTON, metropolitan borough of London, England, two miles N of St. Paul's; is bounded on the E by Stoke-Newington and Hackney, on the S by Shoreditch and Finsbury, and on the W by St. Pancras. It was the residence of Sir Walter Raleigh, Charles Lamb, and Oliver Goldsmith. Institutions include two colleges, several large hospitals, and Holloway and Pentonville prisons. The Caledonian cattle market is located here; it has a large Agricultural Hall where fairs are held. Metal goods, woolen and cotton textiles, and printing type are manufactured in Islington. Pop. (1950 est.) 240,370.

ISLIP, town, New York, in Suffolk County, on Long Island, the S shore of Great South Bay, and the Pennsylvania Railroad; 45 miles E of New York City. It was founded in 1683 by William Nicoll and named for Islip, England, home of some of the early settlers. Islip consists of an aggregation of villages; the incorporated ones are Brightwaters, Ocean Front, and Saltaire. Bay Shore is the chief shopping center. The villages of Islip, Sayville, and Bayport are the principal mainland summer resorts. The products of the area include fish, oysters, clams, dairy goods, radio parts, beeswax, knitted goods, and small boats. Pop. (1950) 5,254.

ISMAIL PASHA, 1830–95, khedive of Egypt, succeeded his uncle, Said Pasha, as viceroy in 1863, and in 1866 assumed the hereditary title of "khedive," and from 1873 possessed virtually sovereign powers. He initiated internal reforms, and spent large sums on roads, railways, telegraphs, and harbor works. In 1874–75 he annexed Darfur and other districts in the Sudan and endeavored, without much success, to suppress the Sudanese slave trade. In 1875, under pressure of financial difficulties, he sold 177,000 shares in the SUEZ CANAL to the British government for £4,000,000, but Ismail's reckless expenditure led eventually to a dual British and French control. His arbitrary dismissal of Nubar Pasha's ministry in 1879 led next to the interference of the European governments. Ismail was deposed by the sultan (June, 1879), Tewfik, his eldest son, being proclaimed khedive.

ISMAIL. See IZMAIL; IZMAIL REGION.

ISMAILIA, town, Lower Egypt, on the Suez Canal, 93 miles by rail NE of Cairo, and about 50 miles either way from the Red Sea and the Mediterranean, on the NW shore of the salt lagoon called Lake Timsah. Ismailia was the scene of the first scientific attack on the malaria-carrying mosquito (*anopheles*). The town was laid out in 1863 in connection with the construction of the Suez. Pop. (1947) 66,338.

ISMENE, in ancient Greek legend a daughter of Oedipus and Jocasta, and sister of Antigone.

ISMID. See IZMIT.

ISNA. See ESNA.

ISOBAR. See WEATHER FORECASTING.

ISOBAR, in chemistry. Isobars are the species of atoms which have the same atomic weight but different atomic numbers. For example, one of the isotopes of calcium (atomic number 20) and one of the isotopes of argon (atomic number 18) both have the atomic weight 40; therefore they are considered as isobars. Other examples of isobars include isotopes of zinc and germanium having the atomic weight 70, and of tin and antimony having the atomic weight 121.

ISOBUTYLENE, a gaseous HYDROCARBON of the olefin series. It is obtained as one of the products of cracking petroleum (see PETROLEUM, *Increasing Yield of Gasoline*). Isobutylene, $(CH_3)_2C = CH_2$, is important in the manufacture of synthetic RUBBER and high octane gasoline; see ISO-OCTANE.

ISOCHRONISM, the property possessed by any vibrating or oscillating system—e.g., a tuning fork or pendulum—which oscillates in the same time whatever the range of oscillations. For the two cases mentioned the isochronism holds only for a certain small range of oscillation. Theoretically the cycloidal pendulum (see CYCLOID) has perfect isochronism through large arcs. In virtue of their practical isochronism, tuning forks, stretched strings, and vibrating columns of air in organ pipes and trumpets give notes whose pitch, which depends on the period, is independent of the intensity. The dynamical condition for isochronism is that the force which resists the displacement is proportional to the displacement. See ELASTICITY; SOUND.

ISOCLINAL FOLDS, in geology, folds of rock strata in which the crumpling has been so pronounced

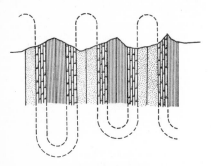

Isoclinal folds

that the sides of the folds are practically parallel to each other. The folds may be upright, horizontal, or oblique.

ISOCLINIC LINE, in terrestrial magnetism, a line on a map joining points on the earth's surface at which magnetic inclinations of a dipping needle from a plumb line are equal. Such inclinations may be ascertained by means of a magnetic needle which is supported at its center by a pivot. See ISOGONIC LINE; TERRESTRIAL MAGNETISM.

ISO-COMPOUND, an organic compound having a branched chain structure rather than a straight chain. For example isobutane has the structure

$$CH_3—CH—CH_3$$
$$|$$
$$CH_3$$

while butane (normal butane) has the structure $CH_3CH_2CH_2CH_3$. See ISOMERISM.

ISOCRATES, 436–338 B.C., one of the 10 Attic orators, was a native of Athens, and was taught by Prodicus, Gorgias, and Socrates. He early began to teach the art of rhetoric, first at Chios and afterward at Athens. From 392 onward he was occupied with his school. He did not appear as a public speaker, but composed speeches on topics of the day, which he published as pamphlets. In these, his one idea was to unite Greece in some common enterprise, preferably war against Persia. Twenty-one of his speeches and nine letters are extant. His style is smooth and ornate. He observes metrical effects, avoids hiatus between successive words, and attains to perfect lucidity and grace of expression, though he lacks the force of Demosthenes.

ISODIMORPHOUS SUBSTANCE. See ISO-MORPHISM.

ISOGONIC LINE, a line connecting points of equal magnetic variation. True North and Magnetic North are not in the same direction; the difference be-

tween the true meridian and the direction the compass points is called variation, or declination. This difference has been measured for most regions of the

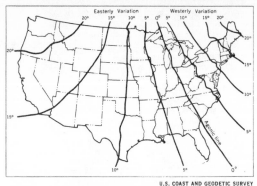

U.S. COAST AND GEODETIC SURVEY
Chart of isogonic lines in the U.S. in 1945

earth's surface, and it is indicated conveniently by means of isogonic lines. Thus at all points in a given area where the variation is 10° East, the line connecting these points indicates that, all other factors disregarded, the compass needle will point 10° East of North. The isogonic line connecting points where the difference between True and Magnetic North is 0° is called the agonic line. In the United States it runs generally from northern Lake Superior through northeast Indiana and along the southwest border of South Carolina. As the earth's magnetic field changes, the isogonic lines move, so charts with isogonic lines are always dated. The change in declination in the eastern United States was about five degrees for the period 1880–1940. At London the magnetic needle moved west 35 degrees, 1580–1818, and since then has moved back east about 14°. Anyone using the magnetic compass, especially where the variation is large, should, for accurate results, take into account the amount of variation in his general locality; this he can see on a chart showing the isogonic lines. Easterly variation is always subtracted, westerly added; e.g., if the true heading to a point is 90° and the variation is 17° E, the magnetic heading (the heading as shown on the magnetic compass) will be 73°. See COMPASS.   H. L. H.

ISOLATION. See SEGREGATION.

ISOLATIONISM, advocacy of political or economic isolation; a traditional American policy of avoiding "entangling alliances." The term itself is relatively new, having come into use in derogation of opponents of President WILSON's internationalism after World War I. Political isolation was a desideratum from the earliest days of the republic, however, having been advocated by WASHINGTON, Jefferson, and others of the founding fathers and finding early expression in coolness toward the alliance with France and in the policy of neutrality with regard to the war in Europe in the 1790's. The policy was based on a belief that the United States had nothing to gain and much to lose by being drawn into the alignments and recurrent conflicts of the Old World; that continental America was protected geographically by the broad oceans; and that peace was essential to the development of the nation, whose ample domain contained vast wealth that merely awaited exploitation.

During the 19th century the policy was nurtured by the country's rapid development; but it was thrown into question by the acquisitions in the Pacific following the Spanish-American War and by commitment to the OPEN DOOR policy in China. Interrupted by the nation's participation in the first World War, isolationism regained popularity during the ensuing period of disillusionment and revulsion against war. Wilson failed to win America to the League of

Nations, and the Senate blocked membership in the World Court. In the 1930's, as war in Europe was again imminent, the popular desire to prevent American involvement was expressed in neutrality legislation and other ways. But after World War II when it appeared that geographical isolation had been largely destroyed by the advent of new weapons and war-making techniques, the United States inevitably assumed a larger role in international affairs and strongly supported the United Nations.

IRVING FRYER

BIBLIOG.—J. F. Rippy and A. Debo, *Historical Background of the American Policy of Isolation* (1924); R. L. Buell, *Isolated America* (1940); W. Johnson, *Battle Against Isolation* (1944).

ISOLEUCINE. See AMINO ACIDS.

ISOMER. See ISOMERISM.

ISOMERISM is a phenomenon associated with organic chemistry in which two or more individual carbon compounds may exist, even though they contain the same numbers of atoms of the same elements. Such compounds are said to be *isomeric* or to be *isomers*.

Isomerism may be of two main kinds: (1) that in which the atoms are arranged in quite different positions in relation to the whole molecule; and (2) that in which the atoms occupy the same relative positions in the molecule, but have particular positions in three-dimensional space. The latter type of isomerism is usually called *stereoisomerism*.

In the first type, the isomers may have totally different properties. For example, the formula C_2H_6O may stand for ethyl alcohol, CH_3CH_2OH, or for dimethyl ether, CH_3OCH_3, depending upon how the atoms are distributed in the molecule. These compounds behave quite differently. The atoms of some compounds may be arranged in straight chains or in branched chains. Such isomers have properties that differ from each other less markedly. Thus pentane, C_5H_{12}, one of the components of gasoline, may exist in three isomeric forms:

$$CH_3—CH_2—CH_2—CH_2—CH_3,$$
$$CH_3—CH—CH_2—CH_3, \text{ and}$$
$$|$$
$$CH_3$$

$$CH_3$$
$$|$$
$$CH_3—C—CH_3$$
$$|$$
$$CH_3$$

The kinds of isomers existing in gasoline are important, since the rapidity of combustion (accounting for "knocking") varies with each isomer. In modern PETROLEUM refining, methods are used to control the kinds of isomers which go into gasoline.

The larger the number of carbon atoms in an organic compound, the greater the number of isomers. The great number of organic compounds known depends to a large degree on the existence of isomers (see ORGANIC CHEMISTRY).

In stereoisomerism, isomers exist when the atoms or groups of atoms attached to a particular carbon atom in a compound may be arranged in space in more than one way. Compounds containing *asymmetric* carbon atoms—i.e., carbon atoms to which are attached four different atoms or groups of atoms—may exist in stereoisomeric forms. Thus, lactic acid,

$$CH_3CH(OH)COOH,$$

contains a carbon atom attached to four different groups: CH_3, H, OH, COOH. These groups may be arranged in two ways in space:

$$\begin{matrix} \text{COOH} & & \text{COOH} \\ | & & | \\ \text{H—C—OH} & \text{and} & \text{HO—C—H} \\ | & & | \\ \text{CH}_3 & & \text{CH}_3 \end{matrix}$$

Hence two isomers exist, mirror images of each other. Spatial formulas are necessary to adequately recognize them. The isomers of lactic acid and of other compounds containing asymmetric carbon atoms may be distinguished by using polarized light, one isomer (dextro-rotary) rotating the plane of polarized light

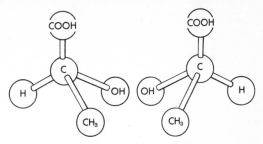

The Two Isometric Forms of lactic acid are mirror images of each other

to the right, the other (levorotary) to the left. (See POLARIZATION OF LIGHT.) Many natural occurring compounds, such as sugars, proteins, and drugs, owe their physiological action to only one of a number of stereoisomers.

Another type of stereoisomerism is exhibited by some organic compounds which contain double bonds. Maleic and fumaric acids, for example, have the same groupings, but different spatial arrangements, hence are stereoisomers. Maleic acid has the structure

$$\begin{matrix} \text{H—C—COOH} \\ || \\ \text{H—C—COOH} \end{matrix}$$

with two similar groups on the same side of the molecule ("cis"). Fumaric acid has the structure H—C—COOH with similar groups on op-

$$\begin{matrix} \text{H—C—COOH} \\ || \\ \text{HOOC—C—H} \end{matrix}$$

posite sides of the molecule ("trans"). J. M. D.

ISOMETRIC DRAWING. See MECHANICAL DRAWING.

ISOMORPHISM. In 1819 E. Mitscherlich, on examining the arsenates and phosphates of sodium, observed that substances having similar chemical constitution and having the same number of atoms per molecule also have similar crystalline forms (see CRYSTALLOGRAPHY). Other pairs of substances, such as potassium sulfate (K_2SO_4)-potassium chromate (K_2CrO_4) and potassium perchlorate $(KClO_4)$-potassium permanganate $(KMnO_4)$, resemble each other in chemical structure and also have similar crystalline forms. Such pairs (or groups) of substances are said to be *isomorphous*.

Isomorphous substances are usually capable of forming "mixed crystals." Thus crystals formed from a solution containing a mixture of magnesium sulfate and zinc sulfate are of uniform composition throughout and have practically the same form as the crystals of either salt.

Chrome alum and potassium alum are isomorphous substances. When a crystal of the former is placed in a saturated solution of the latter, the crystal readily grows by forming a shell of potassium alum and retains its characteristic shape.

A crystal, dropped into a supersaturated solution of its isomorph, will cause CRYSTALLIZATION.

Isomorphism is useful as a means of mineralogical classification. It has been used as an aid in determining the atomic weight of an element from its equivalent weight. Not all substances having similar chemical structures are isomorphous. Among the few exceptions are sodium nitrate $(NaNO_3)$ and calcium carbonate $(CaCO_3)$ which are not generally regarded as belonging to the same crystalline system. Likewise not all substances having the same crystalline structure are isomorphous, for example argentite (Ag_2S) and galena (PbS).

A special case of isomorphism known as *isodimorphism*, is illustrated by mercury and cadmium. These metals, although they possess different crystalline forms, can be dissolved in each other to produce two series of solid solutions. Solutions containing a higher percentage of cadmium than mercury form crystals which are isomorphous with cadmium; solutions containing a higher percentage of mercury form crystals which are isomorphous with solid mercury. Thus mercury and cadmium are considered as isodimorphous substances.   J. M. D.

ISONZO RIVER, ancient *Sontius*, NW Yugoslavia and NE Italy, rises in the Val Trenta NW of Monte Tricorna in the Julian Alps; flows S 85 miles through the Plezza Basin, past Caporetta, Tolmino, Canale, and via canals through the plain of Udine; and empties into the Gulf of Trieste at Sdobba. It was an Austrian river until 1918, when it became Italian. During World War I it was the scene of 12 major Italo-Austrian battles. After World War II most of the area through which the river flows became a part of Yugoslavia.

ISO-OCTANE, a colorless liquid HYDROCARBON belonging to the methane series. Chemically, it has the formula $(CH_3)_3CCH_2CH(CH_3)_2$, and is one of the isomers of octane, C_8H_{18}. (See ISOMERISM). Iso-octane is a highly desirable component of gasoline, since its presence improves the anti-knock qualities of the gasoline. It has an *octane-number* 100, making it superior to almost all hydrocarbons. ISOBUTYLENE and isobutane, both obtained from petroleum, may be combined in the presence of a catalyst to form iso-octane. (See PETROLEUM, *Distillation Products*.) During World War II large quantities of iso-octane were synthesized and blended with commercial gasolines to make aviation gasoline.

ISOPODA, an order of the class CRUSTACEA (lobsters, crayfish, and barnacles). Most members of the order are marine, a few are parasitic upon other crustaceans or upon fish, several are inhabitants of fresh water, and some are terrestrial. There are about 3,000 known species. None of the animals undergoes metamorphosis and, except for size, the young are like the parents.

One of the most common members of the group is the sow bug, *Oniscus asellus*. Large specimens may be two-thirds of an inch long and one-third wide. The body is oval and flattened, and the surface is rough. It is dark gray with white spots on the back. These crustaceans may be found under stones, logs, and other objects that help them to retain moisture, for the sow bugs respire by means of gills and die in a dry environment.

ISOPRENE. See RUBBER.

ISOPROPYL ALCOHOL. See PROPYL ALCOHOL.

ISOSTASY. See GEODESY, *Isostasy*.

ISOTHERM. See WEATHER FORECASTING.

ISOTOPE. Isotopes are atoms of the same element having identical chemical properties but differing in mass or atomic weight. The existence of isotopes was discovered in 1912 by J. J. THOMSON through the use of the MASS SPECTROGRAPH, an instrument which he had devised in 1911. This instrument provided Thomson with the means of determining the relative masses of atoms and molecules by measuring the amount of deflection they produce on positive rays in a magnetic and an electric field. By means of the mass spectrograph Thomson discovered that the element neon, which has an atomic weight of 20.2, is composed of a mixture of atoms of atomic weight 20 and 22. Later, neon atoms of atomic weight 21 were discovered. Ordinary neon consists of a mixture of atoms, 90 per cent of atomic weight 20, 9.73 per cent of atomic weight 22, and 0.27 per cent of atomic weight 21.

The improvement of the mass spectrograph by FRANCIS W. ASTON in 1919, and later by others, led to the discovery of a large number of isotopes, including many that are quite rare.

The existence of atoms of different weight belonging to the same element is explained by a difference in the number of neutrons in the nucleus of each kind

of atom. Oxygen atoms of atomic weight 16, 17, and 18 are known to exist. Since oxygen has an atomic number of eight, the external structure of each kind of oxygen atom is identical, with two electrons in the first shell and six electrons in the outer shell. Therefore, each kind of oxygen atom has the same chemical behavior. It has eight protons in its nucleus but the number of neutrons is eight in the atoms having an atomic weight of 16, nine in those of atomic weight 17, and ten in those of atomic weight 18.

The existence of isotopes explains why the atomic weight of most of the elements is not a whole number. Thus chlorine which has an atomic weight of 35.457 is a mixture of atoms, 75.4 per cent of atomic weight 35 and 24.6 per cent of atomic weight 37.

Separation of Isotopes. The separation of the isotopes of an element is a difficult operation since their chemical properties are practically identical. Hydrogen, the lightest of the elements, may be separated into its isotopes of atomic weight one and two by fractional electrolysis of water. Molecules of water containing the heavier atoms decompose less readily. The last small residue of water when electrolyzed separately yields "heavy" hydrogen atoms, called DEUTERIUM. The ratio of heavy to light hydrogen atoms in ordinary hydrogen is about 1 to 6000. A third isotope, TRITIUM, having atomic weight 3, has been produced synthetically. Special methods of separating the isotopes of uranium were developed to obtain U-235 for the ATOMIC BOMB. The "electromagnetic method" takes advantage of a difference in deflection when ions of the isotopes are passed through an electromagnetic field. The "gaseous diffusion method" involves the diffusion of gases of different density through a porous barrier, the gases being a mixture of uranium hexafluorides containing both the lighter and heavier isotopes.

Radioactive Isotopes. Decay of radioactive elements results in various series of radioactive isotopes; see RADIOACTIVITY. Other radioactive isotopes, such as tritium and carbon-14, are formed by the action of cosmic rays on the atmosphere. In addition, scientists have produced several hundred radioisotopes artificially. Altogether, over 1000 stable and radioactive isotopes have been identified. Carbon-14 is used for "tracers" or "tagged atoms" in plants and

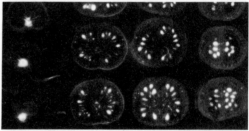

Radioactive Isotopes of zinc in slices of green tomato show localization of zinc in specific tissues

animals to study the development of normal and abnormal tissues, and to observe body functions. It is also applied in the dating of fossils; see CHRONOLOGY. Radioactive phosphorus-32, iodine-125, and others, are also used in "tracer" experiments to learn how plants produce food and how certain drugs combat disease. For a listing of isotopes see the table with the article on ELEMENT.

ISPAHAN. See ISFAHAN.

ISRAEL, the name given to JACOB in connection with a prominent episode in his life (Gen. 32:24–30), and became the collective name of the nation that sprang from him through his 12 sons. After the revolution under Rehoboam it was adopted as the distinctive designation of the northern kingdom, but subsequent to the Babylonian exile it regained its national significance.

ISRAEL

UNITED PALESTINE APPEAL

Combination of rich coastal plains, arid hills, and barren desert

ISRAEL, Medinat Israel or **State of Israel,** the Jewish state proclaimed at Tel Aviv on May 14, 1948, in accordance with the United Nations partition plan, approved November 29, 1947. Israel lies on the western edge of Asia bordering the Mediterranean Sea. On the north it is bounded by Lebanon and Syria, on the east by Jordan, on the south by Sinai, Egypt, and the Gulf of Aqaba. According to the 1947 U.N. plan the state was to include 5,579 sq. mi. and was to consist of three parts of Palestine: the northern part, west of the Jordan river and around the shores of the Sea of Galilee; the western part, from Haifa and the plain of Esdraelon in the north to the Rehovoth area in the south; the southern part, consisting of the desert of Nageb or Negev which has an outlet to the Red Sea. Israel's area, as tentatively determined by the armistices with the Arab states in 1949, includes the territory agreed upon by the U.N. plan, and in addition Western Galilee and a corridor to Jerusalem. The *de facto* area of Israel is 7,100 sq. mi. and its estimated population is 1,250,000 (1950). The final frontiers of the state have not yet been agreed upon. The national flag of the new state is white with two horizontal blue stripes; the blue Star of David is in the center. For the topography, climate, plants, and animals of Israel see PALESTINE.

People. Between 1920 and 1946 the total number of Jewish immigrants was about 376,000, or an average of over 8,000 per year. After the creation of the new state of Israel the number of immigrants rose to a rate of several thousand every week. The government reiterated its determination to permit immigration of all Jews who wish to come to Israel. The large immigration imposed a severe burden on Israel and created its most serious economic problem. The state was not prepared to provide housing and employment opportunities for such a large population increment. There was not enough capital at hand to provide employment opportunities as fast as the immigrants arrived. Most of them came from Europe, but many came from central Asia (Bukharans), from southeastern Arabia (Yemenites), from Iraq, and from North African countries.

The natural rate of increase of the Arabs as a result of excess of births over deaths is very high, but this was offset by the thousands of Arabs who fled Israel in the spring of 1948 at the start of the Israel-Arab war. According to the November, 1948, census the Arabs in Israel numbered about 65,000. By 1950 this figure had increased approximately to 165,000 through the legal return of some who fled, through illegal crossing of the borders, and through the cession to Israel of various areas inhabited by Arab peasants. The Arabs who fled and had not returned were estimated at some 650,000; they now live in Syria, Lebanon, and Jordan.

In addition to the Jews and Arabs, there are some 50,000 Christians in Israel. The official language of the land is Hebrew, but Arabic and English are often used in everyday life. See HEBREW LANGUAGE AND LITERATURE. The largest cities are TEL AVIV, 300,000 (1950), HAIFA, 155,000 (1950), and JERUSALEM (Jewish) 120,000 (1950). The first two are located on the Maritime Plain, which borders the Mediterranean Sea.

ECONOMIC LIFE

Agriculture. Israel is primarily an agricultural nation and its most important crops are citrus fruits, cereals, grapes, olives, vegetables, and tobacco. The most important agricultural section of the country is the Maritime Plain which is about five miles wide in the north and gradually broadens to a width of about twenty miles in the south. On the Galilean hills, cereals, olives, vines, apricots, and figs are produced, and sheep and goat herds graze on the poorer soil. The Esdraelon Valley is a rich producer of grains and other agricultural crops. The greatest detriment to agriculture is the shortage of water. To increase the land under cultivation the government provided for a water supply for Nageb, an irrigation project of 25,000 acres in the Beisan Valley, the drainage of the Huleh swamps in Galilee, the damming of the Na'aman region and Ga'aton Springs, and adapting the Kourdaneh waters for irrigation.

Although Israel is primarily agricultural, it requires considerable food imports. To reduce dependence on imported food the government has encouraged the expansion of agriculture through loans and subsidization, in addition to irrigation projects. As a result of these efforts the area cultivated in 1949 amounted to more than double that of 1948.

The important citrus industry was badly damaged by the Israel-Arab hostilities in 1948–49. The war also damaged the orchards with the result that the crop of apples and plums was poor. Government assistance was extended to the citrus industry. By the end of 1949 the yield of citrus, grain, vegetables, livestock, dairying, poultry, eggs, and fisheries had increased.

Agricultural production is mainly based on cooperative or group farming. There are three general types of co-operative farming: the *Kibbutz* is a communal farm settlement where everything is owned and operated collectively; the *Moshav* is operated by individual family units, in which large-scale farming, buying, and marketing are done co-operatively; the *Moshav-Shifti* is the combination of the above two types. Co-operative farming enabled people to settle on land with less capital investment per person than would be needed in individual farming; it made it possible for people to improve their standards of living with much less average monetary incomes than would otherwise be possible.

Industry. The most important industries are in metals, textiles, building materials, leather, wood, chemicals, paper, and printing. In recent years industry has become the largest contributory to the national income. The most significant expansion of industries occurred in respect to food-processing, textile, metalworking, and chemical enterprises. By the end of 1949 there were 76,000 industrial workers, an increase of 14,000 over the previous year. The Israel-Arab war has adversely affected industrial enterprises: the main plant of Palestine Potash, Ltd., was destroyed completely, and the oil refineries at Haifa had to be closed down. The government encouraged industry by economic policies protecting it against competitive imports. A number of new plants came into existence in 1950.

Mining. The principal mineral products of Israel are limestone, sandstone, gypsum, sulfur, and potash. Minerals are mainly found near the DEAD SEA.

Commerce. Israel's foreign trade is characterized by a wide gap between imports and exports, the former being larger than the latter. In 1949, manufactured goods comprised 58 per cent of the total imports; food, 26 per cent; and raw materials, 16

Emek Valley, formerly a malaria infested region, is now the granary of Israel

The New City of Jerusalem came into existence in 1857 when Jews first built outside the Old City walls and has been greatly modernized since 1920

Desert Orange Groves have been made possible by extensive irrigation projects in Israel

president of the state.

On February 16, 1949, the assembly passed the Transition Law, which laid the foundation for the permanent organs of the state. The legislative authority of the government is a single-chamber assembly elected for a four-year term. The executive authority rests with the president and with the cabinet. The president appoints the prime minister who in turn selects the members of the cabinet. The cabinet, headed by the prime minister, administers the government and is responsible to the assembly under the parliamentary system. The judiciary consists of two kinds of courts, civil and religious, and each has its respective jurisdiction. The local government consists of municipal corporations, local councils, and village councils.

History. Immediately after the proclamation of the new state of Israel on May 14, 1948, large scale military operations were started by the Arab nations. The armed forces of Lebanon, Saudi Arabia, Jordan, Iraq; and Egypt attacked Israel from the east, south, and north. The Jewish troops were more effective than the divided and weak forces of the Arab League, and the course of the war was marked by almost continual successes for the Israel forces. From the beginning of the war, the United Nations tried to bring about peace between the contending forces. In May, 1948, the Security Council appointed Count Bernadotte of Sweden as mediator for Palestine. By virtue of the Security Council Resolution of May 29, 1948, a four-week truce went into effect on June 11. Despite many violations, the truce lasted until July 8, when hostilities were resumed. A second truce went into effect on July 17. The Israeli government on July 26 decreed that the New City of Jerusalem was a Jewish-occupied area; previously Israel had been forced to surrender the Old City to the forces of King Abdullah of Jordan.

Count Bernadotte's efforts to negotiate a peace came to an end in September, when he was assassinated by a Zionist terrorist. Negotiations were continued by his successor RALPH BUNCHE. The truce of July 17 broke down in October, when the Israeli forces achieved some of their greatest successes of the war, capturing Beersheba from the Egyptians, driving the Arab forces out of Galilee, and occupying part of Jordan. On November 16, the Security Council called for the establishment of an armistice. By the beginning of 1949, the Israeli government controlled the area over which it claimed jurisdiction, except Nageb where fighting was still in progress. The Jewish forces not only had succeeded in repulsing the Arab troops but in many cases pushed them back to the frontiers. Between February and July, 1949, general armistices were signed by Israel and the various Arab states.

Relations between Israel and the Arab states continued to be strained even after the establishment of the armistice. The United Nations Conciliation Commission made many attempts to bring about a peace settlement between Israel and the Arab states instead of a mere armistice. Such a peace settlement

was not arrived at because of disagreements regarding the future of Jerusalem, territorial adjustments, and Arab refugees. The Old City of Jerusalem, taken by Arab forces in 1948, was included in the part of Palestine annexed by Jordan in 1950. The refugee problem was especially acute because of the great importance attached to it by the Arab states. They demanded that Israel should repatriate the 650,000 Palestinian Arab refugees. The Israel government maintained that it could not repatriate more than 100,000.

On May 11, 1949, Israel was admitted to United Nations membership, having been already recognized by many nations. By the middle of 1949 the state of Israel was properly functioning. The year of 1949 was a period of transition and adjustment from war conditions to peace. Considerable reduction of Israel's armed forces took place. In 1950 the government continued to be concerned with the economic status of the country, and absorbing Jewish immigrants into the national life. In the 1951 elections, Prime Minister Ben-Gurion's Mapai party won the greatest number of seats but failed to gain an absolute majority in the Knesset. See JEWS, HISTORY OF; JUDAISM; PALESTINE; ZIONISM.　　　　G. B. DE H.

BIBLIOG.—Marshall N. Dana, *Their World and Ours* (1949); L. Larry Leonard, *The United Nations and Palestine* (1949); S. Rolbant, *Mapai* (1949); Chaim Weizmann, *Trial and Error* (1949); Edward A. Norman, *Israel After Two Years* (1950); M. Pearlman, *The Army of Israel* (1950).

ISSUS, an ancient city in SE Cilicia, at the head of the Gulf of Alexandretta, and at the northern end of the pass through Mount Amanus known as the Syrian Gates. It is famous for Alexander's defeat of Darius Codomanus, gained in a neighboring valley in November, 333 B.C.

ISSYK KUL, a brackish lake, U.S.S.R., situated in NE Kirgiz Soviet Socialist Republic, between the Zailiski Ala Tau on the N and the Terskei Ala Tau on the S. Its length is about 125 miles, its greatest breadth, 35 miles; its basin is over 2,000 square miles in area. It is estimated that the banks of the lake were once 200 feet higher than at present. Its name is Kirgiz for "warm lake." Its entire area is never completely frozen even in the coldest weather.

ISSYK-KUL REGION, U.S.S.R., an administrative area of the Kirgiz Soviet Socialist Republic; bounded on the N by Frunze Region and the Kazakh Soviet Socialist Republic, on the W by Tien-Shan Region, and on the S and E by the Chinese province of Sinkiang. The capital of the Region is Przhevalsk.

ISTAKHRA. See PERSEPOLIS.

ISTANBUL, vilayet, NW Turkey, lying in Europe and Asia, E and W of the Bosporus, bounded on the N by the Black Sea, E by Izmit, S by the Sea of Marmara, and W by Tekirdag; area 2,118 sq. mi. (1,293 sq. mi. in Europe); pop. (1945) 1,074,091. The surface of the vilayet is mountainous, the foothills of the Istranca Mountains extending southeast from the Bulgarian frontier. Several small streams drain into the Black and Marmara seas, and several lakes are located in the northeast section of the vilayet. Lands along the streams are richly fertile, producing tobacco, maize, sugar beets, wheat, and barley. There are orchards bearing tropical and semitropical fruits, fig, olive, and almond groves, and vineyards of yellow and white Sultana grapes, which are dried to make white raisins. Garden vegetables are produced for Istanbul markets. Sheep and goats are grazed in the hills. The industries are centered in the city of Istanbul, and include glassworks, firearms factories, flour mills, tanneries, match and cigarette factories, cotton, woolen, and silk textile mills, and the manufacture of leather goods, gold and silver embroideries, and carpets and rugs. Most of these products, especially tobacco and rugs, are exported. Ports on the Black and Marmara seas, in addition to Istanbul and Üsküdar, are Anadolu, Silivri, Sile, Kilyos, and Buyuk.　　　　K. E. H.

"House in the Desert," Israel's first film, shows the blessing of a newly founded Israeli home

ISTANBUL, or **CONSTANTINOPLE**, ancient **Byzantium**, a great historic city, for 1,000 years capital of the Byzantine Empire, then of the Eastern Roman Empire, and (until 1923) of the Ottoman Empire; situated in NW Turkey, Istanbul Vilayet, at the S extremity of the Bosporus, which connects the Black Sea with the Sea of Marmara. More than half of the population of the city is Mohammedan. Pop. (1945) 845,316.

., The city consists of three main sections, Stamboul, Üsküdar (Scutari), and Galata and Pera. On the European side Stamboul is separated by the Golden Horn from the twin cities of Galata and Pera. The Golden Horn, a narrow four-mile-deep inlet of the

PHILIP GENDREAU
Istanbul, with Sea of Marmara in background

white marble. The Mosque of Suleiman the Magnificent is the largest and the Mosque of Eyoub is the most sacred to the Turkish people.

Educational Institutions. The University of Istanbul, the Woman's College, and Robert College provide higher education. There are primary schools and mosque colleges for men which teach theology and law. Other educational institutions are classical, civil service, commercial, medical, engineering, and military colleges.

Economic Life. Istanbul has few industrial establishments, but the transshipment of materials through the port is considerable; its market supplies to a great extent all the countries bordering the Black Sea and, to some extent, those of Asia Minor. Industries include tanneries, flour mills, brick and tile and marble-cutting works, match and tobacco factories, manufacturers of fine morocco leather goods, saddles, pipes, perfumes, gold and silver embroideries, and carpet-weaving plants. Exports are silk, silk goods, carpets, hides, wool, goatskins, goat's hair, madder, valonia, and tobacco products. In 1943, the government bought out the two French companies which held the concessions for the port facilities of Istanbul and next year assumed

PIX
Golden Horn, narrow inlet of the Bosporus

Bosporus, extending inland in a northeasterly direction, is the city's principal harbor. Across the Bosporus, on the Asiatic side, stands Üsküdar (Scutari).

Stamboul, the most ancient section, triangular in form, is built upon the site of the ancient Byzantium and is often referred to as the "heart" of Constantinople because of its Oriental character and picturesque appearance. The Golden Horn extends along the north of this section; the Sea of Marmara is on the south; the Bosporus is at the town's eastern apex. Across the Golden Horn lie Galata and Pera, connected with Stamboul by two iron pontoon bridges. For centuries Galata and Pera have been Istanbul's chief business and financial center. Üsküdar (Scutari), ancient Chrysopolis, is surrounded by thick groves of cypress trees.

Walls, Buildings and Churches. In ancient times Istanbul was completely surrounded by walls, built as fortifications against land and sea attack. Portions of many of these are still standing. The SERAGLIO at the east end of Stamboul was the residence of Turkish sultans from Mohammed II (1454–1840). Subsequently the Dolman Baghtche (Ba'hcheh) and Yildiz Kiosk became the official palace.

There are 270 mosques and churches in Istanbul; 14 of them are royal mosques especially built, and many of them were formerly Christian cathedrals. More than 1,000 minarets and spires rise at various high points of the city and suburbs. The most famous mosque of Istanbul is ST. SOPHIA, built entirely of

ACME
Walnut salesman at the entrance to a bazaar

the entire control of the port. Üsküdar (Scutari) is the terminus of the Turkish State Railroad extending from Ankara, the capital city, to Istanbul.

History. A band of Greeks from Megara in 657 B.C. settled on the promontory now occupied by the building and gardens of the Seraglio, and called the settlement BYZANTIUM. This settlement grew and prospered. For a short time it was under the rule of the Persians, but most of the time it was one of the states controlled by Athens. It was unsuccessfully besieged by Philip of Macedon in 340 B.C. Constantine the Great, A.D. 328, determined to make it the capital of his empire and it became known as Constantinople or New Rome. On the division of the empire, in 395, it became the residence of the emperors of the East. Its strong fortifications protected the city repeatedly against the attacks of foreign foes. The Persians were repulsed in 616, and again in 626, and the Arabs in 668–75 and again in 717–18. Terrible havoc was wrought by the Crusaders in 1203–4, when numerous ancient monuments were either destroyed or taken away. The Latin empire which they founded here lasted about 60 years. After the restoration of the Greek empire, in 1265, Constantinople remained undisturbed, save for the contentions of the Venetians and Genoese, until 1396–1401, when it was fruitlessly besieged by the Turkish sultan. It was again besieged in 1422 by Murad II, and was eventually taken in 1453, after a heroic defense for 40 days by the numerically inferior Greeks and Italians.

In the years following its capture by the Turks, Constantinople was historically of importance not so much as an individual city as the symbol of Turkish power. During the Russo-Turkish War, in 1878, the Russians advanced close to the city, and imposed the peace of San Stefano. During the BALKAN WARS of 1912–13 the Balkan Allies nearly reached the walls of the city, and in World War I, the British and French attempted to capture it. The city was occupied by a Franco-British force during 1920–23; meanwhile, the capital of Turkey was transferred to Ankara. The capitulations which allowed immunity of jurisdiction to the nationals of certain foreign powers were abolished by the Treaty of Lausanne (1923), and by a revision of that treaty in 1936 the remilitarization of the straits of the DARDANELLES and the BOSPORUS was permitted. See BYZANTINE ARCHITECTURE; BYZANTINE ART; BYZANTINE EMPIRE.

G. B. DE H.

BIBLIOG.–H. G. Dwight, *Constantinople* (1926); V. Murdock, *Constantinople, the Fantastically Delicate and Dirty* (1926); G. Young, *Constantinople* (1926); G. W. Edwards, *Constantinople, Istamboul* (1930); D. L. Neave, *Twenty-six years on the Bosphorus* (1935); R. de Calri, *Conquest of Constantinople* (1936).

ISTHMIAN GAMES, one of the great athletic festivals of ancient Greece, were held, in honor of Poseidon, near the isthmus of Corinth. Their historical importance, if not actual existence, began about 580 B.C. The same contests were held as at Olympia (see OLYMPIC GAMES). The festival took place in the first and third years of each Olympiad. The prize of a victor was at first a wreath of parsley (Pindar, *passim*), and it was probably not till after Julius Caesar's day that a wreath of pine leaves was substituted for it.

ISTRATI, PANAIT, 1884–1935, Rumanian novelist who wrote in French, was born in Braïla. After a roving, adventurous life as strike leader, revolutionary and itinerant laborer, he finally settled in southern France, where he wrote exotic novels of Balkan life. He acquired an international reputation but died a pauper due to machinations of his publishers. Among his best-known works were *Kyra, My Sister* (1925), *Thistles of the Baragan* (1928) and *Balkan Tavern* (1931).

ISTRIA, a part of NW Yugoslavia and NE Italy (except for the Free Territory of Trieste), extending S from the Carnic Alps, along the W side of the Julian Alps, and comprising the Istrian Peninsula at the head of the Adriatic Sea. The region is mountainous; its highest peak is Monte Maggiore (alt.

4,580 ft.). Istria's coasts are rocky, with deeply indented inlets at the estuaries of the rivers, and there are many grottoes and underground rivers. The chief rivers are the Indrio, Idria, Isonzo, Reeca, Quieto, and Arsa. Lake Arsa is the largest inland body of water. Agriculture and cattle raising are the chief occupations; crops include wheat, maize, rye, oats, melons, figs, and fruits. There are large orchards, olive groves, and vineyards, and olive oil and wines are exported. Industries of the area include shipbuilding yards, salt refineries, and fishing. Minerals found are alum, bauxite, coal, salt, and marble. The chief towns of the region are Gorizia, Trieste, Fiume, and Pola. Ancient Istria was peopled by Illyrian tribes who were conquered successively by the Romans, Goths, and the Slavs. At the close of World War I, Istria was one of the disputed territories. It was transferred from Austria to Italy by the Treaty of Rapallo in 1920. As a result of the peace Treaty between Italy and the United Nations, the greater portion of Istria was given to Yugoslavia. See FIUME; ITALY; YUGOSLAVIA.

ITA, city, and port, SW Paraguay, in Villeta Department; on the Paraguay River, in an agricultural region. Cotton and tobacco are the city's chief exports. Pop. (1944 est.) 24,000.

ITABUNA, city, E Brazil, in the state of Bahia near the Atlantic Coast, SW of Salvador, in an agricultural section of the mountain foothills. Pop. (1940) 15,868.

ITAGAKI, TAISUKE, COUNT, 1837–1920, Japanese statesman, was born on Shikoku Island. He took an active part in the civil war against the Shogunate (1868), and after the restoration became an ardent advocate of representative government, establishing a school in his native province for teaching the people the principles of government. He organized the first political party in Japan and held several great offices of state. In 1898 he with Count Okuma formed the first cabinet of the Constitutional party. In 1900 he retired to private life.

ITAJAHY, town, Brazil, in the state of Santa Catarina, on the Itajahy River, in the wooded hills of the Serra do Itajahy, about 60 miles N of Florianopolis. Itajahy is the marketing and shipping center for an agricultural region. Pop. (1940) 13,367.

ITAJUBÁ, town, SE Brazil, in the state of Minas Gerais, NE of São Paulo in an agricultural and mining region. Pop. (1940) 14,940.

ITALIAN ARCHITECTURE. Arising from Roman ruins, Italian architecture first became prominent as a national trend in the eighth century with the emergence of the Lombard style. Predominant in northern Italy, the Lombard style's major characteristic is the use of groined vaulting. The earliest example is Sant' Ambrogio in Milan, in which a heavy vaulting is supported by thin piers running up the sides. The general type was that of a basilica with side galleries like San Michele at Pavia and the cathedrals of Parma and Modena.

Because of the prevalence of buildings constructed by the Romans, the development of the Romanesque style was slower in Italy than in other European countries. The first or Tuscan Romanesque style is closely related to the antique. The interior is flat ceiled and the roof is supported by antique columns. The exterior is in perfect harmony with the interior, and is adorned by tiers of columns and variegated marbles. The chief example, the model for central Italy, is the Cathedral of Pisa (1063–1118), with its Baptistery and celebrated leaning tower. The Florentine Romanesque bore even greater resemblance to the classic, and carried the use of marble incrustation to the highest perfection.

In southern Italy and Sicily a peculiar variety of Romanesque originated, with a strange mixture of Byzantine, Saracen, and Norman elements. The chief characteristics are the splendor of its mosaic decoration, the delicacy of its carvings and the occasional

EWING GALLOWAY-DE COU

Ornate flying buttresses of Milan Cathedral

who, after long studies at Rome, produced in his cupola of the Cathedral of Florence (1420–64) the first monument of the new style. In his churches (San Spirito, San Lorenzo), as well as in his palaces, of which the finest example is the Pitti, he adopted rather than imitated the features of Roman buildings; as did also his principal pupil, Michelozzo (Palazzo Riccardi). Classic forms were more closely imitated by Alberti, the great theorist of the early Renaissance. Their successors carried the style throughout Italy. In Lombardy it was highly decorative as in the celebrated Certosa of Pavia. In Venice, where the Renaissance was introduced latest of all, it developed into the most richly decorative of the Italian styles, as may be seen in such characteristic examples as the church of the Miracoli and the court of the Ducal Palace.

The High Renaissance had much more of the classic spirit. The decoration, less rich, was subordinated to constructive principles, resulting in a grandiose and severe style abounding in plain surfaces and colossal details. The study of Vitruvius and of the Roman ruins was accepted as a part of the training of every architect. The pioneer of the style was Bra-

use of the pointed arch. The finest examples are in Sicily, among which the Cathedral of Monreale is preeminent.

Gothic Architecture was never highly developed as a style in Italy; the Italians themselves devised the term in derision of the supposed barbaric character of Gothic. Italian Gothic was decorative rather than constructive in its character. The pervading tendency was horizontal rather than vertical; the nave only high enough to admit sufficient light; while the façade was not a constructive part of the church but free to take any form, and the towers were built apart from the church.

The mendicant orders played an important part in the introduction of Gothic into Italy. Among the principal examples are the Cathedral of Milan, begun in 1386, a compromise between Italian and Northern methods; the cathedrals of Siena and Orvieto, begun in 1245 and 1290 respectively, the most beautiful and consistent examples of the Tuscan Gothic; and the Cathedral of Florence, begun in 1232 after the plans of Arnolfo di Cambio and continued throughout the 14th century.

The Italian Architectural Renaissance began in Florence and its early works were by Florentine architects. The founder of the style was Brunelleschi,

Scene in court of the Ducal Palace in Venice

PIX

EWING GALLOWAY-B. HOLMES

Modern apartment houses on Via Flaminia, Rome

mante of Urbino, whose chief activity was at Rome, which now succeeded Florence as the center of artistic endeavor. His principal successor was Michelangelo, who in his cupola of St. Peter's created a model for the churches of the following period. The tendency was increasingly classical, and about 1450 a period of formal classicism began with stricter imitation of Roman models. The greatest representatives were Vignola, the author of the celebrated treatise on architecture, and Palladio (Basilica of Vincenza and San Giorgio Maggiore at Venice). The Baroque or declining Renaissance was a reaction against classical severity: it emphasized the picturesque rather than the monumental, and was characterized by exaggerated forms and constructions and a general disregard for architectural propriety. Its greatest representatives were Maderna, Bernini, and Borromini.

Throughout the whole history of Italian architecture the classic style has exerted a tremendous influence. Even in the 20th century Italian architects have continued the classic tradition. They have been leaders in the modern school which attempts to combine functional planning with classic proportion and detail. One of the most outstanding examples of this school is the post office at Naples, designed by Vaccaro and Franzi.   M. R.

BIBLIOG.–G. Ferrari, *Italian Rural Architecture* (1925); C. T. G. Formilli, *Stones of Italy* (1928); W. G. Thomas and J. T. Fallon, *Northern Italian Details* (1928); C. B. McGrew, *Italian Doorways* (1929); S. G. Wiener, *Venetian Houses and Details* (1929); C. Shearer, *Renaissance of Architecture in Southern Italy* (1935).

ITALIAN ART

For centuries the glories of Italian art dominated the European art world

ITALIAN ART. Subsequent to the Roman Empire, the art of Italy is best divided into six great periods: Early Christian and Byzantine, Romanesque, Gothic, Renaissance, Baroque and Rococo, and the 19th century and modern times. During the Roman Empire a crude Christian art had been developing in the Catacombs. After the conversion of Constantine (313), this art emerged above ground and became something new and vigorous. The clearest manifestation of it was in the architecture of the Christian-Roman basilica. The early Christians also created buildings of the central type, round, polygonal, or in the shape of the Greek Cross, designed for monuments or tombs. With the architecture went a new system of decoration consisting of extensive mosaics, glittering and gold-backed, portraying the lives of the saints. The greatest center for MOSAICS was Byzantium, but Italy produced many, notably in Ravenna, Rome, and later in Venice and in the south. The mosaics of San Marco in Venice were especially fine and the continued pre-eminence of Venice in glassware probably stems from the mosaic work of the 11th century. At the same time the minor arts, especially sculptured decoration of sarcophagi and carved ivories, received new development.

Romanesque and Gothic. In the Dark Ages (500–1000) Italy was overshadowed by Byzantium but in the 11th century a new art appeared in Italian Romanesque. Toward the end of this period and the Early Gothic, the cultural center of Italy was in the south, and a new sculpture appeared based upon Classic models. Romanesque architecture may be regarded as a truly Italian product. Gothic architecture in Italy, distinctly an importation from France, quickly became so Italianized as to be regarded as native. With the Gothic architecture, there came a brilliant development in the other arts, especially sculpture and painting. In the art of painting the most important phase of its tremendous progress took the form of fresco or painting on wet plaster allowing the pigment to dry in. This was popular in the Middle Ages and into the Renaissance. Paintings were also made in tempera, using egg as a medium, and applied to wooden panels. The earliest local school was probably that of Siena, but the Sienese continued the medieval tradition and their work may be regarded as the culmination of the art of Byzantium. The Florentines' greatest master was Giotto de Bondone (c. 1276–1336), a pupil of the Cimabue who is mentioned in Dante. Rome produced a vigorous local school with Cavallini in the end of the 12th century, but it was snuffed out by the chaotic conditions which existed in Rome until the time of Pope Martin V in the 15th century. Giotto had many able followers in Florence in the 14th century and he and they paved the way for the Renaissance in painting much as Niccolo and Giovanni Pisano did in the art of sculpture.

Renaissance. In the early 15th century there arose a new cultural movement in Italy, probably the most important in the arts from the Fall of Rome to the present day. Known as the Renaissance, it was marked by extreme individualism, enormous vitality, a reversion to classical models in art and to a naturalism which these models suggested. It appeared first in architecture. In sculpture, classical imitation was less obvious than in architecture, but classical naturalism appealed to the sculptors and modern sculpture began. The most important sculptor of the early Renaissance was DONATELLO (1386–1466), famous for his many monuments. A contemporary, GHIBERTI (1378–1455), did the bronze doors of the Baptistry of Florence; meanwhile, the Robbia family were popularizing the glazed terra cotta statuary that became so prevalent in Florence. The transitional figure from early to high Renaissance was Andrea Verrocchio (1435–88), and it was the great MICHELANGELO (1475–1564) who dominated the period of the high Renaissance. His contemporaries and successors were not his equal, though some like Cellini (1598–1680), executed famous works.

In painting the Renaissance was introduced by Masaccio (1401–28) who revolutionized the art almost as strikingly as Giotto had done a century earlier. Meanwhile, Botticelli's work (1444–1510) brought out the more literary and lyrical aspects of painting. All aspects of this Renaissance art were embodied in the style of the prosaic Ghirlandajo (1449–94), the illustrator of the Florentine Renaissance. The dominant figure in north Italy was Mantegna (1431–1506) and in Venice Giovanni Bellini (1431–1516), master of Giorgione (1478–1510), produced the famous Venetian style, perhaps the most influential ultimately in the history of painting.

In Florence LEONARDO DA VINCI (1452–1519) led the way in producing the High Renaissance and will always be famous for his "Last Supper." The Umbrian tradition flowered in the work of RAPHAEL (1483–1520). In Venice the outstanding figure was Titian (1477–1576), probably more studied by later artists than any painter who ever lived.

Baroque. By the end of the 16th century the Baroque period had begun. It was marked by restlessness, showiness, melodrama and a desire to surprise, but it showed extraordinary technical skill and a unity in planning surpassing that of the Renaissance. It shows clearly in the work of Maderna (1556–1629) and BERNINI (1598–1680). Sculpture in the Baroque period was marked by the same restlessness and theatricality, but probably no more clever and technical sculptor ever existed than Bernini.

In the Renaissance, Italy led the world in all the arts. In the Baroque and Rococo periods she at least held her own. In the 19th century, however, she fell far behind the rest of Europe and leadership went to France. Italy continued to produce charming and technically able painters and sculptors who could carve stone with amazing skill, but she did not lead, although she participated in some of the progressive movements in painting such as the broken color impressionism of Segantini (1858–99).

PAINTING

Painting in Italy did not figure nearly as prominently in the early Middle Ages as it did in the latter part of that period and during the Renaissance. Religious pictures were produced either in Byzantium or by local artists trained in the Byzantine manner. A certain amount of work was done in fresco, but probably fresco was regarded rather as a cheap substitute for the more highly prized mosaic. Nevertheless, interesting frescoes were produced such as those of the crypt of Anagni in the 11th century. Italian work in the period, however, stemmed from Constantinople and was comparatively unoriginal. Originality began to appear by the 12th century as well as an attempt at naturalism. To what high degree of naturalism the local artists reached in the 13th century is proved by the famous treatise on falconry written by the Emperor Frederick in the mid-13th century and profusely illustrated for him. Ornithologists have no difficulty in identifying the many varieties of birds in the margins. The best of this work was done in the south, but Tuscany began to emerge in the 13th century as the leader in the art of painting. Large crucifixes were painted, some of them violently emotional and reflecting the almost hysterical feeling inspired by St. Francis of Assisi.

Stress on Mysticism. Probably as early as 1223 Guido da Siena established a local school of painting in the town of his name. By the end of the century there were three prominent schools of painting in

"The Way to Calvary," by Giovanni de Paolo

"The David of the Casa Martelli," by Donatello

"The Madonna of Humility," by Fra Angelico

"Tarquin and the Cumaean Sibyl," by Mantegna

"Bust of a Warrior," by Pollaiuolo

METROPOLITAN MUSEUM OF ART
"The Agony in the Garden," by Raphael

NATIONAL GALLERY OF ART
"Little Boy Poised on a Globe," by Verrocchio

"Fête Champêtre," by Giorgione da Castelfranco

"Venus and the Lute Player," by Titian

METROPOLITAN MUSEUM OF ART

Detail of tomb of Giuliano, by Michelangelo

Italy, in Siena, Florence, and Rome, and a fourth was added in the 14th century in Northern Italy, the Roman school. The school was stifled, however, by the Babylonish captivity and the removal of the papacy to Avignon in 1307 and the consequent chaos in Rome. At about the same time the Sienese emerged as one of the most important. Not interested in naturalism, it laid its emphasis on mysticism and a development of line comparable to the masterpieces of Oriental painting. Indeed, it is quite possible that the influence of the Far East played a part in Sienese painting. The art may be regarded as the culmination of the line of Byzantium and its most exquisite flowering rather than looking forward to something new.

Naturalistic Trend. Originality and, above all, naturalism and solid form were developed in Florence by the first great master, GIOTTO. Sienese art was sophisticated and finished. Giotto's work was progressive and forward-looking and, in a literal sense, archaic. If any artist deserves the title of "Father of modern painting," it is he. He was famous as a painter in fresco, but he did many works in tempera. By the latter part of the 14th century, however, Giotto's influence was weakened and, for a time, the Florentine school was under the domination of Siena.

By the 15th century there was a somewhat new line-up of the Italian schools of painting. The chief schools were those of Florence, Umbria, North Italy, and Venice. The leader was Florence, which reverted to the ideals of Giotto with greater technical performance and naturalism in the work of the great MASACCIO (1401–1428) who, in his brief career of 27 years, brought about a second revolution of Italian painting. Thereafter, brilliant painters appeared in Florence in surprising numbers. They can be divided roughly into the artists who solved the scientific problems of modern painting while not neglecting the aesthetic, and those who were abreast of the times but more interested in the expression of sentiment, of spirituality and of poetry and philosophy. The work of the earlier scientists was carried on in the latter part of the century by Verrocchio, one of the subtlest of Florentine painters. Among the painters of spirituality and sentiment should be mentioned the charming and pious Dominican monk, FRA ANGELICO (1387–1455), whose frescoes are as filled with spiritual expression as painting can devise. Of the later generation of these artists, the most prominent was BOTTICELLI. He was influenced by the philosophy and poetry of his period and his masterpieces are reflections of the Neo-Platonic philosophy of Florence in this period and the idyllic poetry of writers like Poliziano. It is fair to call him the most original of the Florentines in the 15th century. Meanwhile, the other Italian schools forged ahead stimulated by Florentine contact. The true Renaissance arrived with the painting of Piero della Francesca (1420?–92) who did for the Umbrian school what all the scientific painters of Florence had done at home.

Introduction of Painting in Oil. A local center of great importance developed in Perugia where PERUGINO (1445–1524) produced one of the most tender and pious Madonna types and became a master of tri-dimensional or space composition. In northern Italy the master was MANTEGNA, eminent in form, in color, in full knowledge of the scientific aspects of painting and a strong classicist in feeling. Venice had lagged in the early 15th century but emerged as a great school in the second half of the period. This was due largely to the work of GIOVANNI BELLINI, who mastered the medium of oil painting which had begun to be practiced in Italy. Oil painting had been developed in Flanders by the Van Eycks and their successors. It came into Italy by several roads. Once observed, the beauty and advantages of it were recognized and it became the favored medium at the time of the High Renaissance except, of course, when the paintings were made in true fresco.

Da Vinci, Michelangelo, and Raphael. Giorgione, one of the most exquisite poets who ever handled a brush, bridged the gap between the 15th century and the High Renaissance. The new period, usually known as the High Renaissance, was ushered in in the 16th century. As to be expected, Florence was the leader, and the first master of the era was the incredible genius, Leonardo da Vinci. He had mastered completely all the technical problems of painting and was free to express his philosophy of art in the subtlest of composition, the most delicate nuances of expression and the most living line of any Italian artist. Chronologically, he belongs chiefly to the 15th century, artistically he was wholly of the High Renaissance. His most brilliant younger contemporary was Michelangelo, painter, sculptor, architect and poet, whose frescoes for the ceiling of the Sistine Chapel in Rome are probably the most dynamic paintings that have come down to this age. Meanwhile, another genius had appeared in Umbria where Raphael fortified his art with four years of study in Florence and then was called to Rome to paint such masterpieces as the frescoes of the Stanze of the Vatican. He was perhaps greatest as a composer, but, in religious expression, he fixed for the western world permanently its conception of the appearance of the Madonna, God the Father, and the most important saints.

The pre-eminence of Florence was wrested from her in the second half of the 16th century by Venice. Here, three of the archangels of painting appeared in rapid succession. The first was TITIAN, the greatest colorist that the Italian Renaissance produced. He painted in oil, using very large canvases and was a superb composer. He reflected the richness and opulence of his city. His younger contemporary was the dynamic TINTORETTO (1518–94) who was the most dramatic of the Venetians. His somewhat younger contemporary, PAUL VERONESE (1528–88), best reflected the pageantry of Venice, using his religious subjects as a vehicle for expressing the richness and opulence of Venice. Unlike Titian, he had little or no spiritual content, but in technique and in his sense of decoration, he was one of the greatest masters. All three great Venetians did superb murals but tended to do them in oil on canvas, abandoning the old medium of fresco.

Decline. After the High Renaissance, Italian art went into a general decline. The great figures were succeeded by mannerists, who in turn were succeeded by abler painters who were eclectics. These painters had a great vogue in their time. Their theory was to select the finest qualities of the great artists of the Renaissance and combine them in a single picture. Philosophically, this sounded logical but, in practice, it led to a mechanical feeling and a certain lack of sincerity. These painters were very highly regarded in the 19th century, then sank to a very low level in the public estimation in the 20th, and now they are beginning to come back in vogue, though will probably never be regarded as the peers of the great artists of the Renaissance. As a revolt against eclecticism, a naturalistic movement started, headed by CARAVAGGIO (1569–1609). These artists sought brutal realism but tended to confuse the ugly, the dirty and the unpleasant with the real. Using a violent chiaroscuro, they painted melodramatic episodes which made them powerful, but oversensational.

In the Baroque period in the 17th century, Italy produced many able painters whose names, however, are not nearly as familiar today as are those of the earlier artists. They were brilliant draftsmen, but tended to melodrama, violent foreshortening, an interesting and highly forced color scheme and a marked theatricality. They were particularly expert at tricky murals, intermingling uneasy architecture with ingenious but forced perspective. In the 18th century, Italy produced some exceedingly interesting rococo painting. It must be noted, however, that after the High Renaissance, the centers of gravity in painting, so to speak, had shifted from Italy to such countries as Spain with Velazquez, Flanders with Rubens and Van Dyck, and Holland with Rembrandt and Hals.

Similarly, in the 19th and early 20th centuries, Italy produced interesting painting but lost her leadership in the art. The most significant developments in 19th century painting occurred in Paris, and Italy, with the other nations, tended to conform to, or more or less to imitate, the great art of France. However, by the middle of the 20th century there was a definite resurgence of national artistic vitality. See Sculpture below.   G. H. Edgell

SCULPTURE

The first sculpture was introduced into the country by the Etruscans in the sixth century B.C. Bronze and clay were the materials of their artistry, and their sculpture in the round was worked in clay rather than stone. The best examples executed by them were the reclining images found on their sarcophagi. When Rome was in its early days of power, the art was fostered by using the Etruscan workers to apply their artistic skill. To beautify their elaborate palaces, the Roman generals brought the bronzes and marbles back from Greece. When this supply had been exhausted, they were satisfied with copies made of the Greek works, and in order to acquire more they imported Greek artists. From the work accomplished, a certain realistic quality began to appear in a product that was a combination of Etruscan, Greek, and individualistic styles.

Religious Influences and Architectural Sculpture. In the early Christian era little sculpture was produced because statues in the round were considered too closely allied with "graven images." An outlet for the art was found, however, when reliefs were executed for sarcophagi which were completely covered with classical Greek figures representing biblical scenes and expressing Christian ideas. In this style of sculpture the images were crowded closely together and there was little regard for design. Sculpture, in general, was limited by convention in the Romanesque period and confined itself to architectural ornamentation in the way of statues in niches, friezes, and other decorative embellishment. Since about the year 500 there had been practically no monumental sculpture produced, but it began to be revived on a large scale about 1100. The Gothic era brought a gradual growth of naturalism in the appearance of individual figures and there was a renewed activity in the sculpture that formed an integral part of church architecture. A classic revival gathered momentum in southern Italy during the 13th century and a sculptor appeared whose work reflected a freshness in the observation of nature. His name was Nicola Pisano (c. 1225–1278) and his quiet executions somewhat represent the Romanesque; but his son, Giovanni (c. 1240–1320), following the naturalism of Gothic, worked in contrast to the father, putting lively movement into his figures and stirring them with excited restlessness.

Renaissance, Baroque, and Classicism. Gothic motifs continued to be reflected in much of the sculpture of the 14th century, but a spirit of adventure began to make its appearance in 15th century works, and particularly in the work of Donatello (1386–1466) who broke away from classicism to substitute naturalness filled with dramatic movement. His famous creations have prompted the consideration of him as the founder of modern sculpture. However, even the strong influence of Donatello did not stifle the Gothic style, which reached its zenith in Lorenzo Ghiberti (1378–1455). The realism of Donatello was passed on, through such sculptors as Luca della Robbia (1400–1482), Desiderio da Settignano (1428–64), Antonio Pollaiuolo (1429–98), and Andrea Verrocchio (1435–88), to the great Michelangelo Buonarroti (1475–1564). This gifted man, all of whose work was designed to fit a definite part of architectural setting, brought the Renaissance sculpture to its climax and laid a foundation for the Baroque style that was to assume rapid rise in the next century as the decline of Renaissance art set in. Baroque sculpture found sure footing in Rome because its ostentatious display in restless design suited the revival spirit of the church counterattacking the Reformation. In the churches every kind of material was used to extravagance and every possible space was filled with rich workings in marbles, bronzes, and reliefs. The sculptor who dominated this era was Giovanni Lorenzo Bernini (1598–1680), who, like the other baroque sculptors, worked for effects in richness of colors and texture, combining white marble with the colored and with gilding. After the period reached the peak of its flaming spectacular show, it burned out, and decadence in sculpture, as in the other art forms, began. There was a brief moment, in the 18th century, when the ruins of Pompeii and Herculaneum were uncovered, in which a sudden and strong revival of classicism was enacted. Canova (1757–1822) led this Neo-Classic movement and, helped by many other sculptors, fought to instill a return of art to antiquity. Sculpture resumed a lifeless and artificial quality, a mere imitation of the art of the past. From the 18th century to World War II Italian sculpture seemed scarcely to struggle in the attainment of any of its former supremacy, but by the middle of the 20th century a new school of sculpture arose that acquired international influence. Leader of the new trend was Marino Marini, whose earthy, swollen figures showed traces of Chinese Ming and Etruscan style combined with a renascent humanism. Both he and Alberto Giacommetti rejected the usual emphasis on materials for a new insistence on form and human universality. R. T.

Bibliog.—C. Crichton, *Nicola Pisano and Revival of Sculpture in Italy* (1938); G. Bazin, *Italian Painting in the 14th and 15th Centuries* (1938); F. J. Mather, *History of Italian Painting* (1938); L. Schmeckebier, *Handbook of Italian Renaissance Painting* (1938); A. Blunt, *Artistic Theory in Italy 1450–1600* (1940); P. Gregory, *When Painting Was in Glory* (1941).

Italian greyhound

ITALIAN GREYHOUND, a miniature English Greyhound. Two weight classes are recognized, one including dogs of eight pounds and under, the other those over eight pounds. Colors are fawn, red, mouse, blue, cream, or white. The Italian greyhound has always been a pet rather than a sporting dog.

ITALIAN LANGUAGE. Italian is a member of the Italic subfamily of the Indo-European Languages. It was one of the latest of the Romance languages to develop from Latin, and it has always, in its purest form, adhered more closely to Latin than the other Romance languages. The earliest traces of Italian speech are found in a document dated 960. For a variety of reasons, both literary, political, and economic, Tuscan (and especially Florentine) has been the classical literary tongue of Italy almost from the beginning of the national literature. Numerous Italian dialects, however, such as Sardinian, Sicilian and Neapolitan, have shown a striking tenacity and have produced a distinguished literature of their own. The Italian alphabet has only 22 letters, k, w, x, and y being used only in a few words borrowed from foreign languages. Also lacking are diphthongs ph and th. Spoken Italian has a notable musical quality, due to the abundance of vowel sounds and to the pronounced tonic accent, usually falling on the penultimate syllable.

ITALIAN LITERATURE. Such disparate observers as Mazzini and the discredited futurist Marinetti complained that Italian literature has been conventionally regarded as a graveyard of antique giants, that even their countrymen have tended to forget that their literary tradition remained great after the High Renaissance. This conventional misconception may have been the effect of the Italian writers' tending less to form schools or cenacles and tending to demonstrate a disunity comparable to that of Italy herself, the "geographical expression" of Metternich. Nevertheless, just as Italian post-Renaissance art in its comparative weakness gloried in occasional influential figures like Bernini, Tiepolo, or Modigliani, later Italian literature presents several individualistic authors well known outside Italy. The two threads of unity which may be discerned in Italian literature are: an espousal of the cause of national unity and freedom, a cause supported even during fascism by patriotic writers outside Italy, and a serious erudition to be expected of writers who felt themselves lineal descendants of the great Roman masters.

Early Writers. Although the first genius of Italian literature was DANTE ALIGHIERI, many writers were composing in Latin, Provençal, or one of the peninsular dialects as early as the 11th century. Literature before Dante consisted largely of imitations of the lyrics of the troubadours, chivalric poems and novelle from French or British sources, local annals and chronicles, allegories, mysteries, moral and rhetorical treatises, Goliardi student songs and solemn hymns (see GOLIARDIC LITERATURE). Dialectal literature flourished. As an example of the literature inspired by popular religious sentiment and individual mysticism, the pauper saint, FRANCIS OF ASSISI (1182–1226) left his famed *Cantico delle creature*, a compound psalm thanking the Lord for the miracle of creation. These simple and beautiful praises are often viewed as the first important work of Italian literature. At the brilliant Suabian court of Frederic II of Sicily (d. 1250) poets from all over the peninsula founded a "school" which reproduced in Italian Provençal themes and forms of love poetry.

The two leading poets immediately preceding Dante were GUIDO GUINICELLI (1240–76) and GUIDO CAVALCANTI (1259?–1300), inventor of the "sweet new style" of Italian lyric, according to which woman was exalted as a vision of truth and divinity and poetry became an expression of gentle philosophy.

Dante Alighieri (1265–1321) has been described by an Italian critic as one of "those geniuses whom nature creates, as if from a passing caprice, to test the limit of her power, shattering the mold immediately afterward." It was a genius fashioned and intensified by adversity: political enmities, love unfulfilled, bitter exile. The earliest of Dante's works is the *Vita nuova* (New Life), composed about 1294–95, a prose narration of his meeting with and love for Beatrice Portinari, wife of Simone de' Bardi, but containing 25 sonnets and six other poems, most of which were dedicated to her. Also in the vernacular is Dante's *Convivio* (1307–9), a "banquet" of wisdom, com-

"Saint Francis," a painting by El Greco

posed of canzoni and tracts on metaphysics, politics, linguistics, and moral values. The unfinished *De vulgari eloquentia* (c. 1305) posits that the ideal vernacular for Italy must not be any single dialect, not even Tuscan, but must be a lofty national composite speech, by nature illustrious, cardinal, legal, and courtly. The Latin *De monarchia* (1312–13) expresses Dante's impelling desire for empire and in it he states his position that emperor and pope are reciprocally independent, each deriving his authority from God.

Dante himself called his epic work a "sacred poem" or "comedy," the adjective "divine" being added by a later generation. (See DIVINE COMEDY.) The elaborate allegory, begun after Dante's banishment from Florence and finished just before his death at Ravenna, is an encyclopedia of all the popular and scholastic wisdom of the Middle Ages. The learned allusions to contemporary persons and events, the brilliant complexities of versification, and the facts of theology contained in the work led Papini to write that to understand Dante one must be Florentine, Catholic, and a poet. Dante's visit through Hell, up the hill of Purgatory, and finally through the spheres of Heaven, at first under the guidance of Virgil and finally of Beatrice, is related in varying tones of awe, bitterness, pathos, humor, and reverence. The genius of Dante consists not merely in his ability to create a masterful consistent allegory of universal interest and fourfold meaning, but in creating the very language and versification (tercet rime) out of his own inventive faculties. As an allegory, the work is the autobiography of a middle-aged man lost in sin who reviews the entire hierarchy of moral values and the lessons of history and undergoes a gradual purification through wisdom (Virgil) and divine love (Beatrice) until the catharsis culminates in a blinding revelation of God.

Boccaccio and Petrarch. No such passionate pilgrims were the other two giants of the Trecento, FRANCESCO PETRARCH (1304–74) and GIOVANNI BOCCACCIO (1313–75), one the founder of a school of poetry and the other of the mode of novelle which flourished down into the 17th century. Son of a Florentine exile, Petrarch studied jurisprudence, took minor orders, and spent the major part of his mature life in the service of the Colonna and Visconti families. In 1327, at Avignon, he met the famous Laura de Noves, wife of Hugues de Sade, who was to serve as the inspiration of his greatest verse. The great paradox of Petrarch's outpouring of verse is that it is addressed to a woman he knew so briefly, an outpouring which continued long after Laura's death in 1348. Other poets found in Petrarch's sonnets and canzoni a model expression of the sweetness and bitterness of a love keenly felt. The *Canzoniere* set a pattern for love poetry copied for over two centuries in Italy, France, Spain, and England, when Petrarchism and Neo-Platonism were concurrent motifs of verse. Petrarch's *Triumphs* are an allegorical sequence in tercet rime and record a dream of the great figures of the past passing in review. Petrarch, like the other proto-humanists, supposed that his immortality would be due not to his vernacular writings, but rather to his many Latin works, such as the *Africa* (1538–42), an epic poem in hexameters on Scipio Africanus, or the *De viris illustribus*, a series of biographies from Romulus to Caesar in the manner of Livy.

Although no apostate among the imitators of classic forms and themes, the Florentine Giovanni Boccaccio also won his greatest fame with a vernacular work, the DECAMERON, which capitalized on the popularity of the novella form. Among his many Latin writings, the most notable were his *De casibus virorum illustrium*, stressing the vanity of human affairs, and the *De genealogiis deorum gentilium*, a thesaurus of learned mythology. His chief works in Italian were *Il Filocolo*, a version of the romance of the two unhappy lovers Fiorio and Biancofiore; the *Fiammetta*, a reminiscence of his first amorous adventure in Naples, called by one Italian critic a primitive psychological novel; *Il Filostrato*, a poem in octaves telling of the lovesickness of the Trojan youth Troilus. Boccaccio had the happy inspiration of collecting in one volume, his Decameron (1348–53), 100 folk tales of his time deriving from both European and oriental lore. The spinners of these tales are three youths and seven young women who have fled the pest-ridden city of Florence, leaving the churches to those willing to risk contagion, and have taken refuge in a villa up in fragrant Fiesole.

Illustration from the "Decameron," by Boccaccio

Their plan is to pass time by telling tales for ten days (hence the title), and these tales treat of all types of Trecento Italy, nobles, savants, priests, adventurers, faithless spouses. While they are light and licentious, one must remember, as Carducci cautioned, that they were stories for "tranquil idleness." If, as Cyrano de Bergerac wrote, imitation is the greatest tribute, then Boccaccio has been complimented in this manner by the greatest of authors: Chaucer, Hans Sachs, Lope, Molière, La Fontaine, Lessing, and even Shakespeare.

The Renaissance. While the Quattrocento did not boast the literary giants of the Trecento or Cinquecento, it was nevertheless a crucial formative period for Italian literature, a transition from medievalism to Renaissance humanism. It was a period during which manuscripts were discovered, readings established, and classics translated. Academies were founded after the influx of learned Greek refugees from the fall of Constantinople in 1453. It was a period during which the authority of the ancients rivaled that of the patristic churchmen. Humane letters superseded divine letters.

In Florence the "Platonic Academy" was headed by the scholars and translators Cristoforo Landino, PICO DELLA MIRANDOLA, and MARSILIO FICINO. The great Lorenzo Il Magnifico (1449–92) was so versatile as to compose carnival songs and spiritual hymns. With his burlesque version of a romance of chivalry, called *Il Morgante*, LUIGI PULCI (1432–84) furthered the vogue of the Charlemagne cycle and the theme of lovable but grotesque giants (Morgante, Margutte) so popularized by Rabelais. MATTEO MARIA BOIARDO (c. 1434–94) continued the Carolingian matter in his romance *Orlando innamorato* (see ORLANDO), which he infused with tried and true Celtic devices of enchanted castles, charmed rings, etc. The culmination of these verse romances came with LODOVICO ARIOSTO (1474–1532), who wrote his *Orlando Furioso* (40 of the 46 cantos appeared in 1516; the rest in 1532) ostensibly to "continue the invention of Count Boiardo." Yet his romance of knight-errantry, while containing moments of high pictorial poetry and exalting noble sentiments, nevertheless switches frequently to irony and travesty.

To TORQUATO TASSO (1544–95) writing without didactic purpose was a heresy. Composed during the Counter Reformation, when a conservative element of the clergy was trying to purify art and letters, Tasso's epic poem, *La Gerusalemme Liberata* (1575), sang of the First Crusade, and was an heroic rejoinder to the frivolous romances with which it has been vainly compared. Tasso recast in his labored octave rimes some battles and events described by medieval chroniclers of the Crusades, some poetic ornament from the classic epicists, and some of the love interest, the magic, and the varied inventions of the generation of romance writers immediately preceding him.

The 16th century gloried in other great names: Pietro Bembo's three books of dialogues, *Gli Asolani* (1498–1502) are testimony to the learned conversations on love, influenced by Petrarchism and Neo-Platonism, which one might hear in a contemporary salon. MICHELANGELO BUONARROTI (1475–1564), who jokingly cited his poems as evidences of his second childhood, wrote many compelling if labored verses (*Rime*), imbued, like his plastic works, with Neo-Platonism and a deep religiosity. BALDASSARE CASTIGLIONE also reproduced the conversation of a learned group, at Urbino, in his *Cortegiano* (Courtier). In this work (1508–24) various noblemen define the qualities and talents which must be possessed by a perfect Renaissance gentleman and gentlewoman. Benvenuto Cellini's frank and extravagant autobiography (1558–66) affords an honest portrayal of the conflicts, politics, superstitions, and gallant life of the time as seen by a sensitive if boisterous artist.

The most important prose writer of the period is no doubt NICCOLO MACHIAVELLI (1469–1527), for 14 years secretary of the Florentine Republic, from which post he watched power politics of Borgias and Medicis operating in a disunited Italy. Hence the cynicism regarding statecraft apparent in *Il Principe* (1513), akin to the cynicism about marriage and morals in his comedy *La mandragola* (Mandrake). In the *Prince* he accepts the premise that only a vigorous and shrewd monarch can win, unite, and maintain a great state such as Italy. The tractate is full of "realistic" maxims which have endeared it to tyrants like Mussolini (who called it the "statesman's supreme guide"). *Florentine Histories* show how historical laws have operated upon the politics of Florence during the Middle Ages and up to the death of Lorenzo Il Magnifico.

From the Secento to the Present. The 17th century did not engender giants after the manner of the 16th. The scientific prose of GALILEO GALILEI; GIAMBATTISTA MARINI's tardy pastoral poem on *Adonis*; Giambattista Vico's learned if obscure *Principles of a New Science*, in which he founded a new philosophy of history and thus of the human spirit—these are the varied masterpieces of the 17th century. At the end of the century and extending into the 18th, Italy had its band of Arcadians, as did France and Germany, but only one of these became renowned, PIETRO METASTASIO (1698–1782), whose musical dramas such as the *Clemenza di Tito* were consummate in the new medium. CARLO GOLDONI (1707–93), Venice's gift to the theater, composed comedies characterized by amusing situations and *brio*, and raised the level from that of the old farces of improvisation. GIUSEPPE PARINI (1729–99) left us both idealistic and satirical verse, but his biting satire on the futile everyday life of a nobleman, *Il giorno* (The Day) was symptomatic of the antiaristocratic spirit of the century. In the field of the tragic theater, Italy was a century behind France and two centuries behind Germany in giving birth to her tragic poet: like Parini, VITTORIO ALFIERI (1749–1803), witness of the French Revolution and the Terror, was against tyranny, but tyranny of the left as well as the right. Most of his moving historical dramas (*Filippo, Saul*) treat of the conflict between liberty and despotism, and were most appreciated by the patriots of the Risorgimento.

As the struggle for the liberation of Italy intensified during and after the Napoleonic period, the patriotic element in her literature became dominant. Both VINCENZO MONTI (1754–1828) and UGO FOSCOLO (1778–1827) illustrated an anomaly possible only in Italy: ardent republicans and patriots, they were yet staunch Bonapartists in their lives and their poetry. There are patriotic notes even in Foscolo's *Last Letters of Jacopo Ortis* (1802), the recital of an unhappy love affair, complete with Romantic trappings of Weltschmerz and suicide, and in his *Sepolcri*, a poetic tribute to the inspirational qualities of tombs.

In a country where classicism and erudition had taken such solid root, ROMANTICISM came to mean not merely a reaction to the authority of past literary conventions, but also to the political authority of the present. The movement centered in Milan and the leader was ALESSANDRO MANZONI (1785–1873), author of two historical Romantic dramas, the *Count of Carmagnola* and the *Adelchi*, a series of fervently Catholic *Sacred Hymns*, and Italy's greatest historical novel, *The Betrothed*, a complex, somewhat undisciplined love story of Milan in the early 17th century.

Italy has had poets who, like Marlowex or Chenier, were cut down early and yet produced enough in a short lifetime to win lasting fame. Such was GIACOMO LEOPARDI (1798–1837), the brilliant, melancholy cripple who became Italy's great pessimist. He spent his last, broken years in Naples and composed there his *Ginestra* (Broom Plant), the masterpiece in which the tender plant engulfed by the lava of Vesuvius serves as a text on the theme that nature is not a mother but a cruel stepmother. Like Leopardi, GIOSUÈ CARDUCCI (1835–1907) was well grounded in classics and became the readvocate of pagan classicism against moribund Romanticism. Professor at Bologna, poet, and essayist on a wide variety of topics, senator, Nobel prize winner (1906), Carducci achieved a perfected and varied style which enriched Italian poetry immensely.

Several competent novelists, frequently exploiting the regional vein, bridge the 19th and 20th centuries: GIOVANNI VERGA (1840–1922), author of realistic Sicilian stories (*Cavalleria rusticana*); ANTONIO FOGAZZARO (1842–1911), interested in religious and psychological problems; Matilde Serao (1856–1927), writer of sentimental tales popular among women; Italo Svevo, whose psychological novels have linked his name with that of Joyce; Giuseppe Borgese (1882–   ), whose brilliant novels (*Rube*), poems, and short stories were a prelude to his anti-Fascist broadsides (*Goliath*) written in English from America; GIOVANNI PAPINI (1881–   ), a versatile story teller and journalist. An interesting personality who lived into the Fascist period was GABRIELE D'ANNUNZIO (1863–1938), lyric poet, dramatist, novelist (*Il Fuoco*), egotistic dandy, and professional patriot; D'Annunzio was a superb stylist in whichever medium he elected. LUIGI PIRANDELLO (1867–1936) also worked in several media, but is best known as a dramatist (*Six Characters in Search of an Author*, etc.) who aimed to demonstrate that sensory reality can become as real and effective as physical reality itself.

Under the yoke of fascism, to use Salvemini's phrase, intellectual life in Italy was debased and sterile. BENEDETTO CROCE prided himself that he did not mention the word fascism for 18 years; even such irrepressible writers as Guido da Verona eulogized Mussolini, as did an entire generation of younger literary aspirants. Among the anti-Fascist writers whose works were published in Lugano and smuggled into Italy were GUGLIELMO FERRERO (*Liberazione*), Leo Ferrero, whose tragedy *Angelica* dramatizes how readily an entire populace embraces a glamorous despot, and especially the Socialist Ignazio Silone, whose bitter and despairing novels against fascism (*Bread and Wine, Fontamara*) have been acclaimed as among the greatest polemic literature. After the collapse of fascism, Alberto Moravia was among the first to increase his stature as a novelist and a new writer, Dr. Carlo Levi, won international honors with his episodic "diary," *Christ Stopped at Eboli*, written when he was banished by the Fascists to a primitive Italian province.

By mid-century the new renaissance in Italian literature that had begun just after World War II was in full swing. The most noticeable trend was toward a detailed neorealism, influenced strongly by such American novelists as Faulkner and Hemingway, and echoed in the Italian film. Leader of this movement was Elio Vittorini, whose *In Sicily* won an international audience. Vasco Pratolini's *A Hero of Our Times* and Alberto Moravia's *Woman of Rome* also typified the quality and world-wide popularity of the new Italian novel.   ROBERT J. CLEMENTS.

BIBLIOG.—Francesco de Sanctis, *A History of Italian Literature* (2 vols., 1931); S. Kennard, *A Literary History of the Italian People* (1941).

ITALIAN SOMALILAND. See SOMALILAND.

ITALICS, letters of Italian origin, as the name implies. They are said to have been in imitation of the handwriting of Petrarch, and were first used in ALDUS MANUTIUS' *Virgil* (1500). Between 1501 and 1558 six different sizes were produced.

More cursive than ordinary Roman type, and containing a large number of tied letters, italic type gradually came to be used for special purposes, such as introductions, prefaces, notes, quotations, and indexes, throughout a text of Roman type. The letters are now quite separate from each other. The type is used to distinguish words, phrases, or sentences which contrast in some way with their context, words from a foreign language, emphatic words which need the help of type to show their emphasis, and names of books and periodicals (thus, *The Old Curiosity Shop*).

ITALY

For more than 2,000 years this country has played a vital role in Western civilization's art, music, literature, and war

ITALY, a peninsular republic of S Europe, extending into the central Mediterranean Sea and including politically the large islands of Sardinia and Sicily and the smaller islands of Elba, Ischia, and Capri; area 119,764 sq. mi.; pop. (U.N. 1950 est.) 46,-131,000. The country is bounded in the north by the Alps, which separate it from France, Switzerland, and Austria and by an arbitrary boundary drawn in the Istrian Karst which separates Italy from Trieste and Yugoslavia. Its western shore faces the Ligurian and Tyrrhenian seas, and its eastern the Adriatic Sea. Italy is 708 miles long, with a width that varies from 270 miles in the north to 150 miles at the widest point of the peninsula. San Marino (area 38 sq. mi.; pop. 15,000) and the Vatican City (pop. 1,000) are self-governed areas within Italy.

PHYSICAL FEATURES

Topography. An S-curve formed by the Alps and the Apennine Mountains divides Italy into six physiographic divisions. In the north and northwest is the (1) Alpine Slope, which cuts Italy off from the rest of Europe and fringes the (2) Po Basin. The Maritime Alps curve southward and southeastward around the Ligurian coast and blend into the (3) Apennine Chain. The Apennines complete the S-curve down the peninsula and form the "toe" of Italy, ending in Sicily. Lying to the west of the chain is the (4) Tuscan Plain, between the Arno and Tiber rivers, and (5) the Plain of Rome, sometimes known as the Campagna. To the east of the chain there is (6) a narrow alluvial plain.

The Alpine Slope is composed of mountains of high relief, with glaciated ridges and valleys. The maritime section is a rugged and treeless limestone belt. The so-called Pennine Alps are a crystalline mass that rises directly from the Po River Basin. To the east the Bergamasche Alps blend into the limestone Dolomite Mountains and then into the Istrian Karst; a plateau roughened by many sinkholes. In many places the pre-World War II boundary (see *History*) ran along the crest at elevations of more than 9,000 feet. The many U-shaped valleys are too rugged for human occupation, but where there is a valley terrace or small pasture the dairy industry has developed. The valleys do not afford easy access to neighboring countries; passes near the tops of Mont Cenis, Simplon, and St. Gotthard have been tunneled for railroads. The Adige River has cut a broad valley through the limestone which ends in Brenner Pass, the most accessible route to the rest of Europe. The line of contact between the Alps and the Po Basin is

marked by a piedmont area in the west and by a series of lakes that fill ice-gouged valleys, their waters held in check by terminal moraines. Among these noted longitudinal lakes (W to E) are: Maggiore, drained by the Ticino River; Lugario; Como, drained by the Adda River; Islo, drained by the Oglio River; and Garda drained by the Minco River. Below the line of lakes lies the Po Basin.

The Po Basin, covers an estimated 26,798 square miles. It is an area of flat to rolling alluvial plains of Quaternary age. The plain is drained by the Po River, which rises in the Cottian Alps and flows first northeast, and then east to the Adriatic, entering the sea through many distributaries. There is a coastal canal that stretches along the marshy coast of of the Gulf of Venice. Streams are navigable inland from the coast for 20 to 30 miles. The Po, which receives short streams from the south slope of the basin and the longer, lake-draining streams from the north, furnishes water power for basin industries and water for irrigation farming. It is also a transportation route, being navigable north of Turin, and is connected by a deep canal with Turin and Milan. The physiography of the Po Basin is most intimately related to its streams; even now the Po, Adige, Piave, and Tagliamento are depositing alluvium and building the basin out into the Adriatic. The Po and its tributaries, in their swift descent from the mountains, carry large amounts of sediment, and the constantly shifting delta extends 100 to 300 feet farther into the sea each year.

The Apennines branch off to the southeast from the Ligurian Alps. They are divided into ranges, each different in character, that overlap in echelon fashion. In the north an old eroded peneplain of Cretaceous and Tertiary sandstones and clays gives rise to well rounded summits and gentle slopes; the crests are from 5,000 to 6,000 feet high. In the central or Abruzzi section, east of Rome, the Gran Sasso d' Italia rises 9,500 feet; this chain consists mainly of limestone eroded into bold features. The drainage divide between the Adriatic and the Tyrrhenian seas runs along the east side of the Apennines; streams of the Adriatic are short and swift, and they have deposited an alluvial plain. Streams to the Tyrrhenian Sea are few in number and follow tortuous courses. In the south the Apennines are composed of a limestone block and outcroppings of older crystalline rocks. These formations end in Mount Etna, on the island of Sicily. Below the Apennines on the west coast is a line of low, volcanic mountains formed at the joint between the Apennine system and a submerged crystalline block whose western edge forms Corsica and Sardinia.

The Tuscan Plain, or Tuscan Maremma, is an uneven and hilly region with small plains and

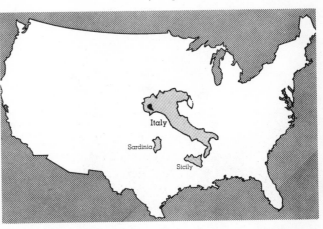

Area of Italy compared with that of the United States

swamps, lying between the Arno and Tiber rivers. Offshore is the island of Elba, composed of igneous rocks. The Arno River rises in the Etruscan Apennines and forms a great southern loop before flowing westward across the Tuscan plain past Florence and Pisa. The river has been canalized and there is traffic between Pisa and Leghorn. The irregular course of the main stream and several lesser streams is the direct result of recent volcanic activity in the area. The sub-Apennines which lie between the plain and the valley of the Tiber are volcanic in character and contain crater lakes such as Lago di Bolsena.

The Plain of Rome, or the Campagna, is composed of Quarternary igneous rocks and alluvium deposited by the Tiber. The Tiber rises in the Roman (central) Apennines and takes a right-angle course through a structural depression. It drains Lago Trasimeno, which also lies in the depression surrounded by lava. The Tiber is navigable; the waterway is between 6 and 10 feet deep as far as Rome and 3½ feet deep as far as Perugia. South of the Tiber the eruptive mountain chain again appears, here called the Alban Hills. The chain continues down the "instep" and "toe" of Italy and includes Mount Vesuvius, Stromboli, and the Lipari Islands, and Mount Etna; this is one of the principal earthquake regions of the world.

The narrow alluvial plain of the east coast has many short, parallel streams flowing to the Adriatic from the Apennines. They have deposited a flat plain from Rimini south to the "spur," the former island of Gargano, which has been joined by alluvium to the mainland. Only one stream, the Marecchia, is navigable; boats may move 10 miles upstream from Rimini. South of Gargano is the low limestone Murgia Plateau, which forms part of the "heel" of Italy. Vultura, a volcanic mountain, also lies on the eastern slope.

Climate. Because of its extent and variety of topography there are several climatic provinces in Italy. South of Naples there is a true subtropical Mediterranean climate. The winters are mild; the coldest month averages between 47° and 50° F., and there is a moderate rainfall of about 30 inches. Summers are hot and dry; both seasons are sunny. Southern Italy is almost free from storms and winds, an occasional warm, muggy wind, the sirroco, blows from the Sahara. The island of Sicily also has this type of climate. North of Naples to the Riviera there is a modified Mediterranean climate. The temperatures are slightly cooler, January averages 43° to 46° and July averages 72° to 76°. Freezing temperatures are recorded at least once a year, and the rainfall is more abundant, averaging between 32 and 52 inches. Cyclonic storms occur, and Genoa experiences a cold wind in winter similar to the mistral. Inland and upland, typical mountain climates prevail. The

higher Apennines are snow covered in winter and have occasional summer frosts. The island of Sardinia is largely mountainous, so that it too has a variety of climate, cold in the mountains and hot and humid on the coastal lowlands. The Alps are high enough to force the air to move upward, causing increased precipitation. There are some glaciated peaks, and the snowline is high. The east-west trend of the Alps guards Italy from the cold weather of central Europe. The Po Basin and the land north of the Gulf of Venice have a modified continental type of climate. The summer is long and hot; July averages 76° F. Winter temperatures fall to the freezing point, and snow is common. Unlike the rest of Italy there is a double maximum in the precipitation regime; the heaviest rainfall occurs in spring and fall, and the basin receives about 40 inches.

Plants and Animals. The characteristic vegetation of Italy is drought-resistant trees and shrubs. In the south the live oak, arbutus and oleander thrive. The mountain slopes are grass covered, but they turn brown during the hot dry summer; high valleys are green when the lowlands are seared. On the mountains there are oak, chestnut, fir, and pine. Olives, lemons, oranges, citron, cotton, and sugar cane are cultivated in the south. North of Naples the broad-leafed evergreen and drought resistant trees mingle with oak, beech, chestnut, and other plants of central European character. Again the mountains have a more luxurious and varied vegetation. Olives, grapes, and mulberries are grown, and along the Riviera bananas and date palms thrive. In the Po Basin most of the land is turned to agriculture and supports crops of wheat and corn. The Alpine slopes contain Italy's forest reserve.

Because Italy has been populated for so long there is no abundant wild life. The mountains are the home of wolf, bear, fox, vulture, buzzard, and eagle; in the streams are mountain trout. Small birds are caught for food; true game birds present are the partridge, snipe, and woodcock. The warmth of the Mediterranean Sea limits the quantity and variety of fish. Among the domesticated animals, goats and sheep are dominant in the south and cattle, in the Po Basin.

PEOPLE

Population. From prehistoric times Italy has been well populated, probably because of its nearness at all points to the sea, its fertile plains and valleys, and its equable climate. The density of population in 1948 was 381 to the square mile. This was concentrated in the larger industrial cities, in the ports, and in the grain-growing districts.

PRINCIPAL CITIES	POPULATION	
	1936 Census	1949 Est.
ROME, the capital.............	1,155,722	1,626,635
MILAN.....................	1,115,848	1,282,660
NAPLES....................	865,913	1,004,500
GENOA....................	634,646	666,200
TURIN....................	629,115	720,251
PALERMO...................	411,879	479,040
FLORENCE..................	322,535	378,796
VENICE...................	264,027	312,593
BOLOGNA..................	269,687	331,226

The Italians claim as prehistoric ancestors the earliest members of the Mediterranean peoples, who migrated to the peninsula from Africa. Other ancient tribes preceding the Romans were the Ligurians, Umbrians, Villanovans, Picenes, and Etruscans. The Etruscan civilization, the most advanced, flourished about 500 B.C. The Etruscans built walled cities, roads and bridges, were cultured and luxury-loving and skilled in the arts of working iron, gold, silver, and bronze; fine textile weaving; jewelry making; pottery firing (the beautiful black Bucchero); furniture building; and the manufacture of implements and vehicles. They were agricultural and planted vine-

BURTON HOLMES-EWING GALLOWAY

Road through an olive grove in Tuscany

B. HOLMES-EWING GALLOWAY

Farm girl

EWING GALLOWAY

Italian family harvests the hay crop on farm in Tuscany

ACME

Roman Street Vender

ACME

The Piazza Vittorio, Rome, is a crowded outdoor market

B. HOLMES-EWING GALLOWAY

Peasant woman

BURTON HOLMES-EWING GALLOWAY

Peasant family lives in thatched hut on the Campagna

DE COU-EWING GALLOWAY

Old man of Capri

EWING GALLOWAY

Fishermen of Capri spread their nets on beach to dry

yards and olive trees and raised and stored grain crops. The conquering Romans assimilated these arts and skills and promoted trade. They colonized in far countries and extended their commerce. Eventually founding an empire, they made their capital, Rome, the capital of the world. Many of the cities of southern Italy and Sicily were colonized by the Greeks, but the citizens were either absorbed among the Romans or driven out.

Religion. The religion of the state of Italy is Roman Catholic, although other creeds agreeable to public order or moral behavior are permitted. About 97.12 per cent of the people are Roman Catholics. According to the 1931 religious census there were 41,014,096 Roman Catholics, 83,618 Protestants, 47,895 Jews, and an estimated 25,000 of other creeds. Appointments of archbishops and bishops are made by the Holy See, after confirmation by the government. Catholic religious teaching is given in elementary and intermediate schools. Marriages are acknowledged if performed by priests or clergymen of sects recognized by the government; civil marriages are recognized when the proper legal formalities are followed.

Education. Primary education is free and compulsory for children aged 6 to 14. It is given in three divisions, preparatory or primary (3 yrs.), lower (3 yrs.), and higher (2 yrs.). The first grades, called the "maternal," are maintained by the municipalities. Secondary training is provided by gymnasium schools, classical lyceum schools, by the lyceum of sciences, or by the institute for teachers. Secondary technical training is given by the technical institutes, or other higher schools and institutes, with instruction in agriculture, and commercial, industrial, and nautical subjects. Higher education is offered by the 27 provincial universities and institutes. Italy has 10 universities dating from the 13th and 14th centuries. Great progress has been made in the eradication of illiteracy. In the 50 years from 1871 to 1921

Divisions and Provinces of Italy

	POP. (1948)	POP. (1949 EST.)		POP. (1948 EST.)	POP. (1949 EST.)
Abruzzi e Molise.........		1,663,000	Marches..............		1,337,000
Aquila................	378,475		Ancona..............	400,196	
Campobasso...........	418,127		Ascoli Piceno.........	331,983	
Chieti................	407,649		Macerata............	308,618	
Pescara...............	241,296		Pesara..............	336,680	
Teramo...............	274,894				
			Piedmont.............		3,425,000
Apulia (Puglia)..........		3,112,000	Alessandria...........	488,169	
Bari.................	1,178,699		Aosta...............	233,964	
Brindisi..............	303,665		Cuneo...............	610,917	
Foggia...............	624,070		Novara..............	416,657	
Lecce................	601,106		Torino (Turin)........	1,413,494	
Taranto..............	410,958		Vercelli..............	372,929	
Calabria...............		1,997,000			
Catanzaro............	712,812		Sardinia..............		1,220,000
Cosenza.............	687,956		Cagliari..............	637,046	
Reggio di Calabria.....	659,379		Nuoro..............	251,339	
			Sassari..............	345,829	
Campania..............		4,234,000			
Avellino.............	502,668		Sicily.................		4,383,000
Benevento...........	337,841		Agrigento............	469,612	
Napoli (Caserta).......	2,634,216		Caltanissetta..........	294,170	
Salerno..............	822,326		Enna...............	343,353	
			Catania..............	787,964	
Emilia.................		3,468,000	Messina.............	682,064	
Bologna.............	757,227		Palermo.............	998,943	
Ferrara..............	416,643		Ragusa..............	248,027	
Forli................	487,401		Syracuse.............	323,066	
Modena..............	498,277		Trapani..............	421,006	
Parma...............	401,827				
Piacenza.............	307,901		Tuscany..............		3,086,000
Ravenna.............	285,559		Arezzo..............	334,742	
Reggio nell' Emilia.....	396,093		Firenze (Florence)......	910,125	
			Grosseto.............	210,141	
Lazio (Latium)..........		3,242,000	Livorno (Leghorn).....	271,566	
Frosinone............	487,401		Lucca...............	375,617	
Rieti................	184,812		Apuania (Massa e Carrara)..............	206,178	
Rome................	2,077,204		Pisa................	351,049	
Viterbo..............	251,784		Pistoia..............	221,687	
Littoria..............	272,501		Siena...............	227,387	
Liguria................		1,518,000			
Genoa...............	893,183		Umbria...............		788,000
Imperia..............	163,178		Perugia..............	578,693	
Savona..............	236,394		Terni...............	216,968	
Spezia, La............	237,332				
Lombardy..............		6,231,000	Veneto...............		3,846,000
Bergamo.............	683,022		Belluno.............	238,357	
Brescia..............	842,807		Padova (Padua).......	723,059	
Como................	537,761		Rovigo..............	356,806	
Cremona.............	381,063		Treviso..............	610,654	
Mantua..............	424,070		Venezia (Venice)......	727,334	
Milano (Milan)........	2,440,478		Verona..............	647,465	
Pavia................	505,463		Vicenza.............	621,378	
Sondrio..............	156,345				
Varese...............	450,188				
Lucania (Basilicata)......		610,000	Trentino-Alto Adige.....		693,000
Matera...............	174,483		Griuli-Venezia Giulia....		925,000
Potenza..............	436,285		Vald' Aosta...........		93,000

the rate was lowered from 69 per cent to 27 per cent. Secondary and university schools are supported by the state. Women may now enter any course of study of the fine arts, literature, and journalism. Women may take degrees in the institutes enabling them to teach in normal and technical schools. They may also take university degrees in all courses of study including medicine, chemistry, and law, but may not practice law.

ECONOMIC LIFE

Italy's industrial economy is greatly handicapped by a shortage of coal and the distance from some of the great markets for raw materials. Supplementing these factors is a surplus labor supply which gives the country the highest unemployment figure in Europe. In August, 1949, there were more than 2,-340,000 persons fully unemployed; many others were working only part time. Before World War II the surplus labor problem was solved largely by emigration to the African colonies and elsewhere. The closing of these outlets during the war built up a labor supply far beyond the point where it could be accommodated by the Italian economy. The country's natural resources were insufficient to keep this rapidly expanding pool of workers fully employed.

Agriculture is the chief industry of the Italian people, with textile weaving a close second in importance. Of equal importance in third place are the country's heavy metal products and machinery works and motor vehicle plants. The great majority of Italy's population is engaged in agriculture, and about half of the people live in rural areas. Other industries include mining and quarrying; chemical trades; clothing and food industries; rice polishing; grist mills; straw hat plaiting; wineries and distilleries; bleaching and dyeing works; porcelain, chinaware, and glass factories; brick and tile kilns; cement works; and salt and sugar refineries. Factories in northern Italy were not badly damaged during World War II, although transportation difficulties and high production costs were factors in the slowness of the resumption of industry.

Deep sea fishing is engaged in, principally off the coast of Sicily, the Istrian Peninsula and Dalmatia. The greatest percentage of fish taken are tunny, anchovies, and sardines. Sponges and coral are obtained off Sicily.

Agriculture. Of the total land area of 76,625,218 acres only about 8 per cent is unproductive, although much of the soil is poor or more suited to the growing of fruits and vegetables rather than grain and fodder crops. About 43 per cent of the land is given over to grain crops. About 22 per cent is in pasturage, and 23 per cent is in forests and woodland. The chief crops are wheat, barley, rye, oats, maize, rice, beans, potatoes, sugar beets, olives, and a great variety of garden vegetables.

BURTON HOLMES-EWING GALLOWAY

Great monastery of the Franciscans at Assisi

Cultivation is carried on at several levels of altitude: citrus and tropical fruits are grown in the southern coastal areas and in sheltered valleys; the vineyard sections thrive higher among the lower mountain slopes; the chestnut groves are higher in the mountains; the grains and vegetables are grown around the rivers and in the northern plains.

Irrigation was first introduced into Italy by the Etruscans in 1000 B.C. In the 17th century the Cavour Canals provided irrigation by tapping the Po below Turin. Farther east large canals which gather overflow from the Adige and the Po provide irrigation and navigation. The area below Venice has a network of canals, and one of the most highly developed canal systems of the world is found in Lombardy and Piedmont.

Holdings of land in Italy run from small freeholds to large estates. Crop-sharing tenancy is characteristic; about 80 per cent of it is to be found among the farmers tilling small acreages. There are many reclamation projects to give families from overpopulated districts a chance to produce their own food. Aided by the Rockefeller Foundation, lakes and swamps have been drained providing many thousands of acres of tillable land. Littoria Province was created from almost the whole of the Pontine Marshes, a huge reclamation scheme carried out by the adjoining provinces of Rome and Frosinone.

Maize is the principal crop of the north, though the production of rice in the Po Valley is of considerable importance. The chief crops of the south and of the islands are olives, grapes, and wheat; together with fruits, including figs and lemons; almonds and chestnuts; tobacco; hemp; and flax. Nearly all of the citrus fruits exported from Italy come from Sicily. Italy ranks third in the world in the production of mulberry trees, providing food for the silkworms.

Farmer plowing with long-horned, white oxen

BURTON HOLMES-EWING GALLOWAY

Boys carry sulfur rocks from mine at Comitini

EWING GALLOWAY

Many of the areas along the coast are given over to growing flowers for marketing in the larger cities. Modern tools and machinery are used in most of the larger farming districts.

Large acreages are devoted to hay and grass which provide food for the large herds of cattle and flocks of sheep and goats. Northern Italy is famous for its dairy districts, especially in Lombardy, Venetia, and the valley of Aosta. The famous Parmesan cheese is manufactured from Lombardy to Emilia, Gorgonzola in Lombardy, and Gruyère in Piedmont.

Mineral Resources and Mining. Italy is a relatively poor country in mineral resources. The lack of coal has in recent years been offset somewhat by the development of hydroelectric power from the rivers of the Alps and the Apennines. The power stations of northern Italy suffered relatively little damage during World War II. The chief mineral found is sulfur, obtained mainly in Sicily, which furnishes about one-tenth of the world's supply. The principal other mineral products are iron and cupreous pyrites, zinc, lead, asphaltic and bituminous substances, gypsum, lignite, copper, silver, potash salts, aluminum talc, magnesite, a great variety of sands for pottery and glass, borax, boric acid, lime, marl, and kaolin, white and other colors in fine marble, and porphyry. The quicksilver mines of Idria, formerly Austrian and then Italian, fell within the boundaries of Yugoslavia after World War II. The mining industry of Italy is most developed in Caltanissetta, Sicily; in Florence, Arezzo, and Grosseto provinces of Tuscany; in Cagliari, Sassari and Iglesias on Sardinia; and in Lombardy and Piedmont. Boracic acid is obtained in Tuscany and statuary marble at Carrara and Massa.

Manufacture and Commerce. The cotton industry is carried on chiefly in northern Italy, Tuscany, and Campania. The breeding of silkworms occupies a great number of people in northern Italy, the manufacture of silken textiles and goods being of first importance in Como, Milan, Bergamo, Venice, and along the west coast. The manufacture of rayon is also of considerable importance. Other leading manufactures are of woolen cloth and other woolen goods, paper, olive oil, wines, confections, candies, tobacco products, hemp, rope, cord, jute cloth, linen, linen yarns and tissues, leather goods, felt hats, gloves, shoes, embroidered shawls, jewelry, processed meats, spirits, pottery, porcelains, glassware, and furniture. In the manufacture of small metal articles, pottery, enamels, faïence, and glassware requiring great artistic skill, Italy holds high rank. The chemical industry includes the manufacture of citrate of lime, citric acid, tartatic acid, oils, tars, caustic alkalies (for dyes), and tanning extracts from chestnuts and the bark of other trees. The 8,982 quarries of Italy produce the finest marble, basalt, and building stone. Apulia, Calabria, Tuscany, and Sicily are the chief olive oil producing centers.

The commercial expansion of Italy, facilitated by an extensive seaboard and good harbors and railway communication, has kept even pace with manufacturing development. In 1900 the value of imports was $340,047,133; of exports, $267,250. By 1913 foreign trade had doubled with imports valued at $702,089,724 and exports at $483,255,239. In that year imports from the United States were worth $54,107,364 and exports to the United States $76,285,278. In 1929, imports totaled $1,133,180,000 ($153,967,819 from the United States); and exports were $796,790,000 ($117,066,598 to the United States). Italy's commerce was expanded by ERP aid after World War II. In 1949, imports totaled $1,498,000,000 ($517,000,-000 from the United States); and exports were $1,-107,000,000 ($45,000,000, to the United States).

In normal times Italy's chief imports are raw cotton, raw rubber, raw wool, timber, gasoline, mineral oils, machinery and parts, paper pulp, electrical equipment, copper, brass, bronze, iron and steel (raw, scrap, and heavy manufactured articles). Exports include cotton and silk goods, cotton yarns, silk and artificial silk, olive oil, tomato paste, wines and vermouth, cheese, citrus and other fruits, both fresh and dried. Before World War I the greatest volume of trade was with Germany, Great Britain, and the United States. Between wars exports went chiefly to Germany. After World War II at least one-third of the imports came from the United States. Exports went principally to the United States, Great Britain, and Switzerland.

Transportation and Communication. The natural configuration of Italy, with the Apennine Range through the center of the country, led to the development of two great railway systems; one on the south-west along the shore of the Mediterranean and the other on the northeast following the Adriatic. The first Italian railway was built in 1839 to connect Naples with Portici, a distance of five miles. By 1869 the government was operating more than 2,400 miles of lines. This soon led to financial difficulties, and in 1885 an agreement was made with some private owners to operate the railways until 1905, when the state again took control. Of 13,450 miles of railroad in 1949 the state owned 10,190 miles. Of the total railroad mileage 3,505 miles were electrified. In 1949 there were about 106,600 miles of improved highways. Since Etruscan and early Roman times roads of the peninsula have been famous for their sturdy construction. Rome was the center of the arterial highway system, fine roads radiating in every direction. Some of the most famous were the Via Appia, Via Flaminia, Via Aemilia, Via Postuma, and Via Julia Augusta.

In 1933 Venice opened a $4,000,000 bridge for motor traffic connecting that city with the mainland, two and one-half miles across the lagoon. In 1934 two heavy motor truck roads were completed, one from Genoa to Milan (98 mi.) and the other from Genoa to Turin (102 mi.). These highways were only slightly damaged during World War II.

Inland navigation is of limited importance, the Victory Canal, connecting Lombardy and Veneto provinces was built after World War I and is about the most important canal. The aviation services are well-developed. Air lines maintain regular schedules between Rome, Vienna, Barcelona, Istanbul, Bengazi, and other foreign ports. Italy's chief ports are Genoa, Naples, Palermo, Leghorn, Venice, Messina, and Catania. Before World War II the improved port of Genoa vied with Marseilles in importance in the Mediterranean.

GOVERNMENT

Until the middle of 1946 Italy was a constitutional monarchy, although under the Fascist regime it was actually a dictatorship; in an election held on June 2, 1946, the Italian people voted to oust the monarchy and set up a republic. The old Italian constitution was the *Statuto* of 1848. The major constitutional principles were, however, unwritten and were to be found in custom and practice. The *Statuto* entrusted power to the crown and to the two houses of the parliament; the king was empowered to nominate and dismiss his ministers at his pleasure.

Executive power belonged exclusively to the king, while the legislative power was shared by him with the parliament. The king had many powers and was responsible to no one; the ministers were responsible to him. However, treaties with foreign powers required the consent of the parliament. The two houses of parliament, the senate and the chamber of deputies, were nominally on equal footing although the latter became more important. The senate was filled by appointment for life by the king from certain categories of high officials, ecclesiastics, and men of intellectual rank or large incomes (all to be over 40 years of age). Besides its legislative powers, the senate

The Castel Sant' Angelo, also known as Hadrian's tomb, was once a most imposing sepulcher. In 537 it became a fortress and the original walls which were of Parian marble, the Corinthian columns, and the fine Grecian art were stripped away and hurled unavailingly at an invading barbarian army

The Appian Way, the queen of roads, was built in 312 B.C. by the blind Appius Claudius. Its construction of lava blocks was so solid that many parts of the road are still in constant use. Tombs line the sides of the road as the Romans were eager to be buried along this most fashionable highway

Arch of Constantine, originally designed as a triumphal arch, now keeps alive the name of the ruler in whose reign the Roman Empire embraced Christianity

St. Peter's Cathedral, famous landmark of Rome erected in the 16th century, is the supreme example of Italian Renaissance ecclesiastical architecture

The Claudian Aqueduct is one of the most famous of Roman arched structures. It was erected A.D. 38 to carry water from the Sabine Hills to Rome

St. Paul's Outside-the-Walls at Rome replaces the original cathedral built A.D. 380. Its interior is impressive with mosaics, rare paintings, and fine marbles

Rome is unique among historical cities as the original center of the Roman Republic and Roman Empire. Its antiquarian interest is second to none

View of Grand Canal and Rialto Bridge in Venice

was the highest court of the land.

In 1919 universal manhood suffrage was established for election of deputies. Numerous political parties appeared, clustering for the most part around politicians with few principles and policies. Moreover, elections were almost always manipulated by government agents so that there was no real free choice. In the chamber of deputies the numerous political parties promoted governmental instability since no one or even two ever had a majority. Governmental responsibility therefore tended to fall into the hands of the leader most adept in group manipulation. Soon after World War I the parliament became almost powerless as a result of the irreconcilable conflict among the revolutionary Socialist party, the Catholic party, and the Fascist party. The result was the seizure of power by the most determined and ruthless of the political groups —the Fascists.

Under fascism the institutions of democratic government were gradually subverted and then abolished. The other political parties were made illegal so that the Fascist party stood alone; civil liberties were abrogated. All power centered in Mussolini who was the head of the Fascist party and the "chief of the government." The Fascist Grand Council was made an integral part of the government. An electoral law of 1928 provided that this council should select 400 candidates for the chamber of deputies from a list submitted by Fascist syndicates and trade unions; the electorate then was given a choice of accepting or rejecting the slate *in toto*. In 1938 the chamber was abolished and in its place a Chamber of Fasces and Corporations, the members of which were appointed, was established.

On July 28, 1943, the interim government of Marshal Pietro Badoglio announced the dissolution of the Fascist party and the unconstitutionality of the law of 1928. Many of the activities of the Italian government were subject to the approval of the Allied Commission in Italy until the peace treaty came into effect on Sept. 15, 1947. On Sept. 25, 1945, a consultative assembly was organized and Count Carlo Sforza became its president. Elections were held in June, 1946, for a constituent assembly and on the question of monarchy. On June 10, Italy became a republic since the majority of voters at the referendum had voted for a republic. Voting was compulsory for both men and women over 21.

The new constitution was passed by the constituent assembly on Dec. 22, 1947, and came into force on Jan. 1, 1948. Under its terms the parliament consists of two houses: the chamber of deputies and the senate. The former is elected for 5 years by universal and direct suffrage; the latter is elected for 6 years on a regional basis. The president of the republic can nominate 5 senators for life from eminent men. The president himself is elected in a joint session of the chamber and the senate, a two-thirds majority being required for the election. The

term of the president lasts for seven years and the president of the senate acts as his deputy. The president is empowered to dissolve the parliament, except during the first six months of his term of office. The defeat of a bill of the government does not lead to its resignation. The cabinet can be forced to resign only on a motion of censure voted by the parliament.

The constitutional court consists of 15 judges who are appointed by the president, the parliament, and the highest law and administrative courts. It is the highest court of the land and can decide on the constitutionality of laws and decrees. It is also empowered to define the powers of the state and regions, judge disputes between them, and between regions, and try the president and the ministers. The court of cassation is in Rome. The country is divided into 22 appeal courts (with one detached section) and is subdivided into 153 tribunal districts. These districts are divided into 977 *mandamenti*, each with its own magistry. There are also 101 assize courts. For civil matters there are *conciliatori* with jurisdiction in petty matters.

The nation is divided into 19 regions, each being subdivided into provinces and communes. Each region has a council, an executive, and a president of the executive. The central government supervises and co-ordinates the regional administration with the state administration. Each of the provinces are headed by a *prefetto* (prefect), who is responsible to the minister of interior in the government at Rome. The prefect represents the executive power, provides for the execution of laws, controls the police, and supervises the operation of the local government. Each province has an elective council which meets once a year. In the local government the commune, based on the French model, is the principal unit. Each commune has an elective mayor and an elective council.

The principal political party is the Christian Democrat which maintains a center position, favors moderate social reforms and is anti-Communist. The Communist party advocates extreme industrial nationalization and land redistribution; it is in constant and violent opposition to the government. The party is completely pro-Soviet in foreign affairs. The Italian Socialist party is aligned with the Communist party though members of it have withdrawn and formed parties opposing the Communists. The party follows the Communist line in domestic and foreign policy. The Socialist Party of Italian Workers represents the right-wing Socialists and is independent of the Communists. It favors political democracy and has co-operated with the Christian Democrats.

G. B. DE H.

HISTORY

The name Italy was originally applied to the southern extremity of the peninsula. During the age of the republic it was extended to the central provinces, the territory north of the Apennines being known as Cisalpine Gaul. It was in the imperial period that the name first came to include the whole peninsula.

Decline of the Roman Empire. It is difficult to fix an exact date for the end of Roman and the beginning of Italian history. Barbarian invaders first penetrated into the country early in the fifth century, but it was long before they founded a settled government, and titular "Emperors of the West" still resided in Italy. In 476, however, Odovakar (Odoacer), a Herculian chieftain, deposed the last of these emperors, and was proclaimed king of Italy by his followers, though he acknowledged the superior authority of the Eastern emperors. But under Odovakar, and under his conqueror and successor, THEODORIC, king of the Ostrogoths (493), the Roman character of the administration was little changed. Though himself an Arian, Theodoric was tolerant of Roman Catholicism; but the orthodox population, after his death (526), gladly welcomed the restoration of the authority of the Eastern emperor, Justinian.

The Lombards. Two famous Greek generals, Belisarius and Narses, reconquered Italy, the latter defeating and killing the Goth chief Totila (552). The country was now governed by a Greek official, called an "exarch," who resided at Ravenna; and Justinian's own code of law was introduced. But only a few years later appeared a fresh swarm of invaders, the Lombards. They never succeeded in conquering the whole country; the exarchate of Ravenna and the Pentapolis, on the east coast, remained subject to the empire, as did also the south, though there were Lombard dukes of Benevento and Salerno. Venice, though practically independent, and Rome, dominated by its bishops, also acknowledged the authority of the Greek emperors. Yet the Lombard dominion was much more firmly founded than those of its barbarian predecessors, and its effects upon the character and history of the country were far-reaching and permanent. The Lombards adopted the language, customs, and civilization of their subjects, and were converted from Arianism to Roman Catholicism. To a great extent Roman law and institutions survived, though modified by Lombard customary law. Government was at first decentralized, in the hands of a number of almost independent dukes; but King Liudprand (12–744) succeeded in imposing the royal authority on them.

Establishment of the Western Empire. The absence from Italy of any stable authority left room for an immense development in the power of the bishops of Rome, especially in their own city and the surrounding country. Though they still considered themselves subjects of the Eastern empire, they tried to assert their supremacy over the Eastern Church, and finally quarreled openly with the emperor, Leo the Isaurian, on the question of image worship. Liudprand espoused the pope's cause, attacked the Greek dominions, and seemed to be on the point of completing the conquest of Italy. But the popes took fright, and turned for help to the Franks, who had established a strong power in Gaul. Pope Stephen II called Pepin, king of the Franks, into Italy (754). Pepin defeated the Lombards and bestowed the exarchate and pentapolis on the papacy, which thus founded its territorial power on the ruin of the Greek. CHARLEMAGNE, son of Pepin, called into Italy by Pope Adrian (773), confirmed the grant, conquered the Lombards, and was himself proclaimed king. Finally he was crowned emperor at Rome by Pope Leo III (800); and thus the authority of the Eastern emperors was wholly shaken off and a new empire set up to embrace all Western Europe.

Period of Anarchy. This left Rome merely the nominal capital of a large empire, of which Italy was an outlying province. Her alien monarchs had little effective power, even when they were themselves in the country. Though feudalism was not so powerful as in other countries, the emperors had to contend with the Lombard dukes of Benevento and Spoleto; the Greeks, who still held the south; and the Saracens, who in the ninth century conquered Sicily and tried to conquer Italy. After the Carlovingian monarchy broke up and rival claimants struggled for both Italy and the imperial title, there was complete anarchy in Italy until the establishment of the Saxon dynasty of emperors. Then OTTO I (emperor, 962) and Otto III enforced a temporary submission upon all the country except the extreme south, and tried to reform the papacy, which had fallen under the control of the Roman aristocratic families, and was sunk in the lowest depths of vice and degradation. But directly their personal influence was removed, Italy relapsed into anarchy. The margraves of Tuscany and of the Piedmontese "march" were almost independent; while in the south appeared a new disturbing element in the Norman adventurers, who in the 11th century, led by ROBERT GUISCARD and his

Citadel of La Rocca and aqueduct at Spoleto

brother Roger, conquered southern Italy from the Greeks and Sicily from the Saracens.

Conflict of Pope and Emperor. In the latter half of the 11th century the church itself initiated that reformation which the emperors could not effect. The Hildebrandine reform (see GREGORY VII) had momentous effects on Italian affairs. In the war of INVESTITURES both parties strove to gain allies in Italy. The emperor was supported by most of the feudal nobles who resented the independence of the reforming popes. The papacy found on its side the powerful Countess MATILDA OF TUSCANY and the Normans of southern Italy. But when on the accession (1152) of FREDERICK I of Hohenstaufen (Barbarossa) to the empire, the papal-imperial quarrel broke out afresh; the strongest ally of the papacy was a new Italian force, that of the communes, which during the last century had gradually been coming into prominence. The most advanced cities were those of the coast, Venice, Genoa, and Pisa, which had wide commercial relations, especially in the East. By the end of the 11th century the chief towns of Lombardy were sufficiently advanced to form a league of their own and assist the papacy against the empire. They felt the control of imperial officials a check on their progress toward autonomy, and the feudal nobles, their natural enemies, formed the bulk of the imperial party.

Frederick's Imperial Expansion. When Frederick re-asserted imperial rights in Italy he came into conflict with both the popes and the towns. From 1159–77 the struggle raged fiercely with varying fortunes. Finally Frederick was defeated at the Battle of Legnano in 1176; and by the treaty of Constance (1183) the towns extorted practical recognition of their autonomy, the emperor retaining, however, control of the supreme courts of appeal within the cities.

Besides their claims to central Italy, there was a new subject of contention between the popes and Frederick's son, Henry VI, on account of the marriage of the latter with Constance, heiress of the Norman dynasty of Sicily, and his claim to its inheritance. Henry VI was powerful enough to disregard the papacy; but the struggle was on with renewed vigor between the popes and his son, FREDERICK II (1220). It was the great combat of civic independence and industrial progress pitted against the forces of feudalism. Frederick II died, defeated and disheartened in 1250.

Guelfs and Ghibellines. Mutual jealousies and struggles for territorial expansion and commercial predominance characterized northern Italy. Between town and town, and within each town, the fiercest party strife broke out; the parties labeled themselves "Guelfs" and "Ghibellines." Half the citizens were disfranchised, or else in exile, allied with a neighboring town or noble, only waiting for the first chance to return and oust their rivals. By the end of the 13th century, the towns, exhausted by their own internal contests, were rapidly relinquishing their independence to local tyrants. Such were the Estes of Ferrara, the Visconti of Milan, the Della Scalas, the Carraras of Mantua. The most successful were the Della Scalas and the Visconti who extended their conquests into central Italy. Both were Ghibelline, and were opposed by a Guelf league of which Florence was the moving spirit.

Florence gained a hegemony in Tuscany, which in the 14th century she gradually converted into a dominion over subject towns. After her conquest of Pisa in 1406, Florence ruled over all Tuscany except Siena and Lucca. The 14th century emperors, on their brief visits to Italy, attacked her as the bulwark of Guelfism. Venice continued to prosper, and consolidated her government into a narrow, powerful oligarchy.

The popes took advantage of the weakness of the empire, and consolidated the papal states; Emperor Rudolf of Hapsburg, in return for papal help in his election, acknowledged their sovereignty over Romagna, Umbria and the March. But when the popes fell under the influence of France, and moved their residence to Avignon (1309), their states fell into anarchy.

Renaissance. By the 15th century, however, we find Italy settling into a more tranquil condition, the minute factions into which she was split tending to consolidate into five larger states. Their subjects enjoyed a great measure of prosperity, and their wars were waged almost entirely by mercenary soldiers. There was immense commercial activity, and the 15th century saw the rise of that great intellectual and artistic movement which is called the RENAISSANCE. The towns were governed by humane "tyrants," especially in Florence, where the wealthy and clever Cosimo de' Medici, who manipulated half the finance of Europe, acquired an influence in the government, which his grandson, Lorenzo, turned into an almost absolute control. See MEDICI, LORENZO DE'.

Conflicts among City-States. The 15th century consists mainly in the development and mutual relations of the five greater states. The first important change was the rapid formation of a mainland state by Venice. The first half of the century was filled with wars between her and Filippo Maria Visconti who was succeeded by Francesco Sforza as duke of Milan.

The popes still asserted overlordship of southern Italy, and on this account frequently interfered in its affairs. Italy in this age was the prototype of Europe in a later epoch. A careful balance of power was established between the states, and maintained by an elaborate system of alliance and skillful diplomacy. Throughout the latter 15th and early 16th centuries there were frequent conflicts between the states of Italy, but changing allegiances and alliances kept any one state from attaining dominance.

North Italy made an attempt to unite against the French who after many battles were ousted. Naples became a dependency of Spain in 1540. Five

Pope Leo X

years later Venice lost her mainland possessions. The next 50 years were mainly occupied with a struggle of France, and her enemies for the Milanese duchy. Swiss mercenaries, German soldiers, French and Spanish men-at-war trampled Italy under foot, and treated her as a conquered country. The popes took sides with a view to advancing their ambitious plans for the church and for their own families. Leo X, a Medici, obtained Spanish help to restore his family to Florence, overthrowing the republic which had been established there. Florence subsequently revolted but was recaptured and was restored to the control of the Medici family.

Period of Foreign Rule. After the fall of Florence there is little real Italian history to record. Italy seemed dead, exhausted by her early development and the vehement splendor of her short life. Her brilliant people were sunk in apathy under the rule of foreign princes, who, with complete disregard for their welfare, treated her states as counters in the diplomatic game.

In Savoy and Piedmont there was a semblance of national life, because the rulers were native, and governed with commendable uprightness. Territorial expansion was their constant ambition; and though often nearly crushed by France, and losing to her the western part of their dominions, they expanded eastward into Lombardy, and took advantage of the war of the Spanish Succession to obtain Sardinia with the title of king (1719).

Venice and Genoa, losing the last of their Eastern possessions to the Turks, preserved the independence of insignificance. Milan fell to the empire on the extinction of the Sforzas, and, with the rest of the Hapsburg dominions in Italy, went to Philip II of Spain in 1541. The European powers continued to treat it as their battlefield, with constant campaigns in which the natives had no interest, but in which they suffered heavily. Till the end of the 17th century Spain ruled the peninsula: Milan, Naples, and Sicily belonged to her; the smaller princes of central Italy were under her influence; the papacy depended upon her as the leading Roman Catholic power.

War of the Spanish Succession. The war of the Spanish Succession (1700-13) led to a change in the rulers of Italy, and to a slight change in her condition.

Young Italian Noblemen and Doctors, as portrayed in a painting by Fiorenzo di Lorenzo

Italy

Austria succeeded to the Spanish dominions; and though in 1738 she had to give up the Two Sicilies to a junior branch of the Spanish Bourbons, she remained the dominant power, controlling the smaller states.

Nothing could have been worse than the administration of government by the Spanish viceroys, and southern Italy was in a constant ferment of ineffectual discontent. The Bourbon kings were an improvement, and the rule of Austria was comparatively just and humane, and was directed toward improving the material condition of the people; so also was that of the house of Lorraine, which succeeded the Medici in Tuscany in 1737. But the condition of the papal states was deplorable. The government was exclusively clerical, the Inquisition was all-powerful, and, as in southern Italy, the well-being of the people was utterly neglected, and they were sunk in laziness, ignorance, and poverty.

Napoleonic Invasions. It was the Napoleonic invasions which first stirred the lethargic mass into consciousness of life, breaking for a time the Austrian yoke, and forcing the ideas of the French revolution upon the people. In 1796 the conqueror first swept into Italy, driving the Austrians before him; Nice and Savoy he had seized for France; Lombardy and part of central Italy he constituted into the Cisalpine Republic, and the Genoese district into the Ligurian Republic, after the French model. Venice he forced to surrender its liberty, and then tossed it carelessly to Austria as a bribe for acknowledging the independence of his republics. After his departure Tuscany and Piedmont were annexed to France, the king of the latter retiring to Sardinia; republics, called the Roman and Parthenopean (in southern Italy), were founded—Ferdinand of Bourbon taking refuge in Sicily, where the British fleet protected him. When the Austrians again invaded Italy, the unstable republics fell rapidly before them; but in 1800 Napoleon returned, bringing his whole army over the St. Bernard pass. Defeating the Austrians at Marengo, he re-established the Cisalpine (now called the Italian) Republic, of which he himself became president. Venice was taken from Austria; Naples was made a kingdom, first for Joseph Bonaparte, then for Joachim Murat (1808); the temporal power of the popes was abolished.

It was for the Italians a time of great material prosperity, and of civil liberty previously unknown; though there was little political liberty, since, after Napoleon became emperor, he was crowned king of Italy, and the constitution of the Italian republic fell into abeyance. Even Ferdinand of Sicily, under pressure from England, granted a modified constitution.

Austrian Dominance. The kingdom of Italy fell with its king. The old governments were restored and former rulers came back determined to crush all popular manifestations; Austria more powerful than before proscribed all persons suspected of liberalism. The secret Italian society Carbonari fostered rebellions, which broke out in 1820–21 in Naples and Piedmont, and in the Papal States and the duchies of Parma and Modena. They were suppressed by the Austrians. The election of Pius IX (1846) who began to grant moderate reforms, led to an outburst of popular enthusiasm. Leopold II of Tuscany and Charles Albert of Piedmont promulgated constitutions.

Revolution of 1848. Mazzini, founded the Young Italian Society, with a view to improving the lot of the population. When the news of the French and Austrians revolutions of 1848 arrived, Milan and Venice rose in revolt. Charles Albert of Piedmont attacked the Austrians but was defeated in July, 1848. Pius IX and Leopold II fled from their dominions. The old policy of repression was resumed in the Austrian dominions of Italy. See VICTOR EMMANUEL II.

Only Sardinia kept her constitution, and under the government of Victor Emmanuel and CAVOUR,

THE BETTMANN ARCHIVE

The Meeting of Garibaldi and Victor Emmanuel at Teano, as portrayed in painting by C. Ademollo

regained her prosperity, and prepared for a fresh effort to liberate Italy. With the assistance of Napoleon III, Austria was attacked and several victories were gained. But Napoleon, though he wished to liberate Italy from Austria, had never intended to unite her under Savoy. Consequently peace was made and Venice was left in Austrian hands. But in the meantime Tuscany, Modena, and Parma had expelled their rulers and now asked to be united to Sardinia.

Unification of Italy. Garibaldi led an expedition into Sicily and soon conquered the mainland state. Victor Emmanuel marched across the Papal States and joined Garibaldi. Naples and Sicily declared by plebiscite their desire to be united to Sardinia; and in 1861 Victor Emmanuel assumed the throne of Italy. To obtain Venice, Italy joined Prussia in her war against Austria in 1866; and though the Italians were beaten on land at Custozza, and on the sea at Lissa, the triumph of Prussia was so complete that, by the Peace of Prague, Venice was surrendered to Italy. (See AUSTRIA; GERMANY.) Rome was less easy to secure because of the opposition of Roman Catholic opinion throughout Europe and the protection of the pope by French soldiers. It was not till the fall of the French empire, in 1871, that the Italian government could act freely. Pius IX refused to give up the temporal power and withdrew to the Vatican, where he and his successors remained until the creation of the Vatican State in 1929. See PAPACY; VATICAN CITY.

Italian Expansion. During the reign of HUMBERT I (1878–1900) the TRIPLE ALLIANCE was formed, and twice renewed, and considerable effort was made to develop a colonial dominion on the Red Sea coast, but the Italians were defeated by the Ethiopians at Aduwa (1896). When Humbert was assassinated by an anarchist on July 29, 1900, his only son succeeded to the throne as VICTOR EMMANUEL III.

The relations between the state and church were more friendly from 1905. The German demonstration at Agadir, Morocco, in July, 1911, caused Italy to turn toward Tripoli where she had certain concessions which were being abused by the Turks. She issued an ultimatum and war was declared on September 29, 1911. Italy occupied the Dodecanese Islands, and Rhodes. The powers induced the Ottoman Empire to cede Tripoli and peace was agreed upon at Ouchy, Switzerland, October 15, 1912, and signed at Berlin October 18. By this treaty Turkey acknowledged the sovereignty of Italy over Tripolitania, henceforth known as *Libia Italiana* while Italy was to surrender the Dodecanese when Turkey had completely withdrawn from LIBYA.

World War I. Despite her membership in the Triple Alliance, Italy declared her neutrality on August 3, 1914, after the outbreak of WORLD WAR I. Negotiations were opened with the Entente Powers, and on April 26, 1915, Italy signed the Treaty of London, which promised satisfaction of her territorial aspirations. On May 24 she declared war on Austria, and on August 27 on Germany. The Boselli government was much criticized but maintained itself in power until the disaster at CAPORETTO, when it fell, and a new ministry was formed by Vittorio Orlando, Oct. 30, 1917. See ORLANDO, VITTORIO EMANUELE. The fortunes of war now began to swing from the Central Powers toward the Entente, and Austria came to the verge of collapse. In September, Italy refused to consider Austria's peace offer and began on October 24, the Battle of Vittori Veneto, which was rapidly becoming a triumphal march when on Nov. 4, 1918, an armistice was signed with Austria-Hungary.

Peace Settlement. Italy at once formulated her aspirations and claims which included Trentino, southern Tyrol, Trieste, Istria, Fiume, Dalmation Islands, and the Dodecanese Islands. The east coast claims conflicted with the claims of YUGOSLAVIA and the claims to the Dodecanese Islands with the claims of GREECE. The dispute with Yugoslavia became bitter. President Wilson stood firmly against the transfer of Fiume to Italy. The Italian delegation went to Rome and, after receiving the support of the Chamber for its attitude at the Peace Conference, returned and signed the Treaty of Versailles. On its second return to Rome the Orlando government was overthrown by reason of its failure at Paris, and on June 21 Francesco Nitti became premier, with Tottoni as Foreign Minister.

Meanwhile, Fiume had again become the center of the international stage. On September 13, D'ANNUNZIO and his followers occupied Fiume until after the signing of the Treaty of Rapallo (Nov. 11), between Italy and Yugoslavia, when in December, 1920, he surrendered the city to an Italian general. See FIUME.

Nitti tried to come to an agreement with England and France in regard to the Adriatic problem. But on May 21, 1920 he resigned and Giolitti was made premier, with Count Sforza as foreign minister. The latter undertook to settle the Fiume question by making obvious concessions to Yugoslavia, which the country was in no mood to entertain.

Rise of Fascism. The unpopularity of Sforza's foreign policy became manifest and the cabinet resigned and was succeeded by a former socialist, Ivanoe Bonomi. Toward the close of 1921, BENITO MUSSOLINI became the head of the organization of the Fascisti. (See FASCISM.) Under his direction the Fascisti began their work in attempting to take over the government. In February, 1922, Bonomi resigned, and was succeeded by Facta. Owing to the inability of the government to establish order, the struggle of the Fascists and radicals for supremacy continued. The king chose to accept the resignation of the Facta government, and summoned Mussolini, who on October 22, formed a new government.

Benito Mussolini, who rose to power in Italy in 1922, appears with leading figures of Fascist party
INTERNATIONAL NEWS

A new electoral law was created which gave the Fascist government a majority of seats. In June, 1924, persons connected with the Fascist movement kidnaped and probably murdered the Socialist leader Matteotti. Three months of crisis followed in which there was a demand for the return of the old order. Nevertheless Mussolini inaugurated a broad program of fascism which was destined to transform Italian society.

Foreign Relations. 1925 was marked by a trade treaty with Germany and, in compliance with the terms of the Treaty of London, transfer of the province of Jabaland from Kenya Colony to Italian Somaliland and acquisition of the Egyptian oasis of Jarabub. This year also saw an increase in the prestige of fascism and Mussolini, both at home and abroad. Several laws were passed to extend Fascist control of Italy. Italy made a treaty of neutrality with Spain and concluded pacts of friendship and arbitration with central European states and with Germany. The conclusion of a mutually protective treaty with Albania at Tirana, November 27, 1925, produced a political upheaval in Yugoslavia on the charge that it concealed a potential protectorate over Albania.

Development of Fascism. The first half of 1927 was particularly memorable as showing the economic and cultural results of the Fascist regime. Further changes were made to consolidate the regime; such as a new constitution, changing the title of Mussolini to "Head of the Government," press censorship, and new electoral laws. Mussolini succeeded in settling the old feud between church and state which had smoldered since 1870. At the Lateran Palace in Rome, on Feb. 11, 1929, representatives of the government and the Vatican met and signed the historic document which in a limited measure, restored the temporal power of the popes. See LATERAN TREATY.

Imperial Ambitions. In 1932 the Fascist leaders indicated that they were interested in treaty revision, and in colonization in Africa which was considered pre-eminently the sphere wherein Italy claimed a right to territorial redistribution in order to employ her surplus population. In spite of Italy's participation in the disarmament conferences, Mussolini stated that "only war carries human energies to the highest level."

In 1933 far-reaching economic changes were introduced to regulate industry. In the next year working hours were reduced to 40 hours, with a pro rata reduction in wages, overtime was abolished, and extra remuneration was given to parents of large families.

Diplomatic Developments. Hitler's emergence as chancellor in January, 1933, was hailed enthusiastically by the Italian press. It seemed likely that a bloc of Italy, Germany, Hungary, and perhaps Austria could be formed. France, Poland, and the Little Entente were not pleased with these developments.

When Hitler made an attempt to incorporate Austria in Germany, Italy's sympathies began to veer from Germany toward France. Mussolini disliked the idea of a greater Germany on his northern frontier and made common cause with France in support of Austrian independence. When Hitler's promise to Mussolini to stop Nazi propaganda in Austria was broken, the duce attempted to isolate Germany in European diplomatic relations, most notably with the establishment of the Danubian economic confederation.

Ethiopian Aggression. An affray of the Eritrean-Ethiopian border on December 1935 was the pretext for resolute measures against the African kingdom (see ETHIOPIA), and early in February, 1935, Mussolini mobilized a quarter of a million troops. Ethiopia's request in March that the dispute be submitted to the League of Nations was rejected by Mussolini. During the summer months of 1935 committees of the league sought in vain to find a solution of the problem acceptable alike to both disputants. On October 2, in defiance of world opinion that the resources of negotiations had not yet been exhausted, Italian forces advanced into Ethiopia. Soon Italian and Ethiopian forces were engaged both in the north and south of the country. The Council of the League resolved on October 7 that the Italian government had violated the Covenant and committed an aggression. The Assembly agreed (Austria and Hungary dissenting) to impose financial and economic sanctions against Italy.

Marshall Emilio de Bono, Italian commander in chief in East Africa, was replaced in November by Marshall Pietro Badoglio, and as a consequence war operations which had languished after the brilliant start, assumed greater activity. By March, 1936 no serious obstacles lay between the Italian Northern forces and Addis Ababa, and the Italians believed victory within sight.

Meanwhile, in December, 1935, Foreign Minister Sir Samuel Hoare of Great Britain, and Premier Laval of France, had proposed a plan for terminating hostilities on a basis which, in effect, would have given a large area of the country to Italy, but widespread popular opposition necessitated its withdrawal. It was realized that the LEAGUE OF NATIONS was meeting its hardest test, and efforts were continued to coerce Italy into bowing to its will. But England and France failed to deter Mussolini whose animosity was roused by the league's action. With the entry of Italian forces into Addis Ababa in May the campaign was virtually concluded, and on June 1, 1936, a royal decree established the Italian East African Empire, comprising Ethiopia, Eritrea, and Italian Somaliland.

Rome-Berlin Axis. Count GALEAZZO CIANO was appointed foreign minister on June 9, 1936, and the following October he visited Berlin, where the "Rome-Berlin Axis" was consummated. In October, too, a huge rearmament program was announced by Premier Mussolini, and he went in person to Berlin in September 1937. The Italian leader announced the resignation of the country from the League of Nations.

When Austria was seized by German troops, Mussolini declined to interfere, declaring his attitude to be "determined by the friendship between the two countries consecrated by the axis." In line with this policy, too, was his action in sending large Italian forces to aid the Insurgents in Spain and the increasing ties with Germany were still further emphasized when Hitler visited Rome in May, 1938.

Mussolini played a leading part in the Munich settlement. In line with the German practice, Italy initiated in September 1938 a program of restrictive measures against Jews. An Anglo-Italian pact was signed on April 16, 1938, which recognized the *status quo* in the Mediterranean and purported to resolve mutual rivalries in Africa and the Near East, and in furtherance of his policy of appeasement of dictators, Prime Minister Neville Chamberlain, accompanied by Lord Halifax, his foreign minister, visited Rome in January, 1939. Negotiations with Mussolini produced no apparent results, due in large measure, perhaps, to the fact that at that time Italy had considerable colonial aspirations at the expense of France, the trusted ally of Great Britain.

Albanian Aggression. On April 7, 1939, Italian forces landed on the coast of Albania and quickly overcame the slight resistance that was offered. Mussolini rejected peace proposals offered by King Zog, and within a few hours the king fled into exile. On April 12 King Victor Emmanuel accepted the crown of Albania which nation became a part of Italy. The seizure was not recognized by the United States.

World War II. The ties between Italy and Germany became even closer when, on May 22, 1939, the foreign ministers of the two countries signed in Berlin a ten-year offensive-defensive military pact. Despite this undertaking, however, when hostilities began between Germany and Poland on Sept. 1,

1930, the Italian Council of Ministers declared that the stand of their country was one of nonintervention. All those with pro-Nazi leanings were dropped from the Italian cabinet, and following completion of a Turkish mutual assistance alliance with Great Britain and France, Mussolini sought to form a neutral block in the Balkans. For several months Italy played a waiting game, making threats against Germany's enemies, giving much material assistance to her ally, preserving a status of nonbelligerency.

On June 10, 1940, with France on the verge of collapse before the Nazi onslaught, Italy declared war on Great Britain and France. On June 24 an armistice with France satisfied some of Italy's territorial aspirations. Italy's entrance into the war started a series of disastrous campaigns which, by the fall of 1941, had reduced Italy almost to the status of a German vassal state. See WORLD WAR II; AFRICAN CAMPAIGN; SICILIAN CAMPAIGN; ANZIO; CASSINO.

In the fall of 1940 Italy undertook two offensives in Africa but neither of them succeeded. Her invasion of Greece on October 28 turned out to be disastrous, and only when the Nazis came to the rescue of the Italians was complete victory attained. During the winter of 1940–41 Italy fell under almost complete Nazi domination. German troops and officials entered the country and took over a great part of the government and administration. The internal economy of the country deteriorated; it was severely damaged by the war effort and by the drain of foodstuffs to Germany.

Early in 1942 the Axis counter-offensive in Africa started, and by June 21, German and Italian forces captured Tobruk. But by the spring of 1943, Italy had lost Lybia, and was faced with the defense of Sicily. Shortly after the fall of Palermo, capital of Sicily, Mussolini was replaced by Marshall Badoglio, on July 25. On September 8, Badoglio accepted unconditional surrender terms, an action denounced by the Germans, who rushed troops to Italy. After a series of campaigns the Allies captured Rome on June 4, 1944. The king conferred his authority on his son and a popular government assumed control under the supervision of the Allied Military Government. By the end of April, 1945, Allied troops had completely defeated the German forces in Northern Italy. An agreement was signed on April 29, for the unconditional surrender of the German armies in Italy to the Allies. On April 28 Mussolini, with his mistress Clare Petacci, was shot by Italian Partisans near Lake Como.

General Clark leads troops into Rome, 1944

Postwar Conditions. After the war the nation was faced with three major problems: economic reconstruction, issues relating to the constitution, and the peace treaty. The government tried to deal with the disrupted economic life. In June, 1945, the Bonomi cabinet resigned and a coalition government under Parri came into existence. After a prolonged crisis Alcide de Gasperi formed a new government. On June 2, 1946, the Italian people in a referendum decided in favor of a republic. In the newly-created chamber of deputies, the Christian Democratic party, led by Gasperi, obtained a majority.

The council of foreign ministers of the great powers met in London in the fall of 1945 but failed to come to an agreement regarding the Italian peace treaty and the disposition of Italian colonies. The terms resulting from the June, 1946, Big Four conference provided for the internationalization of Trieste, deprived Italy of her colonies, fixed the amount of reparations, transferred to Yugoslavia the Italian cities on the western coast of Istria, and determined Italy's frontiers in favor of France. The final peace conference of 21 nations did not alter substantially the terms of the treaty, which was signed by Italy on Sept. 15, 1947. American troops left Italy on Dec. 14, 1947.

On January 1, 1948, the republican constitution became effective, providing two houses of parliament of equal power, a president elected for seven years by the parliament in joint session, universal suffrage, and continuation of the LATERAN TREATY of 1929. Then with elections scheduled for Apr. 18 and 19, 1948, the Communists made a determined bid for power through the ballot, having already failed at the end of 1947 to gain their objectives by strikes. The conservatives, the center parties, and the moderate leftist parties charged that the Communists were tools of the Soviet Union. In the election the Communists were badly defeated. The Christian Democrats, led by Premier Gasperi, won 53.3 per cent of the seats in the Chamber of Deputies, and 43 per cent of those in the Senate. The Communists and leftwing socialists won 31.8 per cent of the seats in the Chamber and 31.7 per cent in the Senate. On May 11, 1948, Parliament elected Luigi Einaudi president of the republic.

In April, 1949, the government outlined a specific program for land reform. Some improvements took place with regard to industrial unemployment in the middle of that year. The chief factor in Italy's economic rehabilitation was the supply of ERP aid from the United States. In April, 1949, Italy signed the North Atlantic treaty and in August joined in the deliberations of the Council of Europe. On November 21, the General Assembly of the U.N. recommended that Libya should become independent by 1951, and Italian Somaliland should gain independence in 10 years and meanwhile should be placed under international trusteeship, with Italy as the administering authority.

On Jan. 27, 1950, the United States agreed to send military aid to Italy. Italy became a member of the unified European army and approved of German participation in it. On December 4, the United Nations again considered the membership application of Italy but, as it had before, the Soviet Union vetoed Italy's entrance into the U.N. In the same month Italy signed an agreement with Yugoslavia regarding reparations and other war claims. In January, 1951, scattered Communist riots and disturbances marked General Eisenhower's visit to Rome on a tour of European defenses. In the 1951 elections, the Christian Democrats polled 36 per cent of the vote and the Communists 38.5 per cent. De Gasperi formed a new cabinet in August.   G. B. DE H.

BIBLIOG.–R. de Cesare, *Last Days of Papal Rome, 1850–70* (1909); B. King, *History of Italian Unity* (2 vols. 1912); T. Tittoni, *Modern Italy* (1922); L. Collison-Morley, *Italy after the Renaissance* (1928); D. Randall-McIver, *Italy Before the Romans* (1928); B. Croce, *History of Italy, 1871–1915* (1929); L. Villayi, *Italy* (1929); J. P. Trevelyan, *Short History of the Italian People, from the Barbarian Invasions to the Present Day* (1929); J. I. Walsh, *What Civilization Owes to Italy* (1930); T. Hodgkin, *Italy and Her Invaders* (4 vols. 1899, ed. 1931); J. A. R. Marriott, *Making of Modern Italy* (1931); G. K. Brown, *Italy and the Reformation to 1550* (1933); D. Pettoello, *Outline of Italian Civilization* (1933); G. Salvemini, *Under the Axe of Fascism* (1936); G. Borgese, *Goliath, The March of Fascism* (1937); K. D. E. Vernon, *Story of Italy* (1939); L. Salvatorelli, *Concise History of Italy* (1940); G. Salvemini and G. LaPiana, *What to do with Italy* (1943); A. J. B. White, *Evolution of Modern Italy* (1944); C. Sforza, *Contemporary Italy* (1944); J. C. Burckhardt, *Civilization of the Renaissance* (1945); A. W. Salomone, *Italian Democracy in the Making* (1945); L. Sturzo, *Italy and the Coming World* (1945); G. Prezzolini, *Legacy of Italy* (1948); W. Hilton-Young, *The Italian Left* (1949); B. Foa, *Monetary Reconstruction in Italy* (1949); L. Oschli, *Genius of Italy* (1949); B. B. Carter, *Italy Speaks* (1947); *Italy and Italians* (1949); R. Albrecht-Carrié, *Italy from Napoleon to Mussolini* (1950); E. Fodor, *Italy in 1951* (1951).

ITAPETININGA, city, SE Brazil in São Paulo State, NW of São Paulo in an agricultural region. Pop. (1940) 13,977.

ITASCA, LAKE. See MISSISSIPPI RIVER.

ITATA INCIDENT, an affair in 1891 growing out of the attempt made by the U.S. government to seize the *Itata*, a ship which was carrying arms from the United States for Chilean insurrectionists. The so-called Congressional party, then in revolt against President Balamaceda, sent the *Itata* to San Diego, Cal., for military supplies. The ship was detained on suspicion, but was released and permitted to reach its destination; then on a demand of the American government the ship was returned with its cargo to San Diego. The Federal court held, however, that the ship should be released since the American neutrality laws had not gone into effect, no recognition of Chilean belligerency having been made by the president. The release of the ship did not appease the victorious Congressional party, and the result was strained relations with the United States; then followed the *Baltimore* affair in which 116 sailors from the U.S.S. *Baltimore* on shore leave were attacked by a mob in Valparaiso, resulting in the death of two Americans. Chile was finally forced to pay an indemnity of $75,000 because of this incident. See CHILE, *History.*

ITCH, or **SCABIES,** is a highly contagious skin disease, caused by a minute parasite which deposits eggs beneath the skin. The delicate integument between the fingers is the most usual habitat of the parasite, which may, however, invade other parts. It is communicated from one patient to another, and is most common among neglected and unwashed children. The disease is extremely rare among the better classes, and rarely seen among the poor in the United States. The irritation caused by the burrowing of the parasite leads to scratching, which spreads the disease and induces eczema. Scabies is usually easily cured by cleanliness and the application of sulfur ointment, which should be rubbed well into the affected skin for several nights in succession. In more obstinate cases treatment with naphthol or other antiseptics may be necessary. *Sarcoptes scabiei* is often wrongly called the itch "insect"; it is really a mite, and belongs to the zoological class Arachnida.

ITCH MITE. See MITE.

ITHACA, or **Itháke.** See IONIAN ISLANDS.

ITHACA, city, W New York, county seat of Tompkins County, at the S end of Cayuga Lake; served by the New York State Barge Canal and the Lehigh Valley and the Delaware, Lackawanna, and Western railroads; 28 miles NE of Elmira. Ithaca, one of the principal gateways to the Finger Lakes region, is noted for education and scenery. Three picturesque gorges with numerous waterfalls cut through the hills of the city. It was founded in 1789 by Simeon De Witt, surveyor general of New York, following a military survey of the central portion of the state. The city was named for the island of Ithaca, off Greece, famous as the home of Ulysses. Ithaca is the seat of CORNELL UNIVERSITY and Ithaca College. For a time the city was an early center of the motion picture industry; the "Perils of Pauline" was produced in Ithaca. Stewart Park, at the head of Cayuga Lake, is the principal park of the city. Its most distinctive features are the Renwick Bird Sanctuary and the Fuertes Wildfowl Sanctuary. Buttermilk Falls State Park, the Robert H. Treman State Park, and the Taughannock Falls State Park with its 215-foot falls, the highest east of the Rockies, are all within eight miles of the city. Ithaca's major manufactures include adding machines, cigars, electric meters, firearms, handbags, technical mirrors, pottery, precision instruments, cement, aerial survey maps, power drive chains, and photoengraving. Pop. (1950) 29,257.

A. M. K.

ITHACA COLLEGE. See COLLEGES.

ITHOME, mountain in Messenia, in ancient Greece, on which stood the chief fortress of the Messenians in their war with Sparta during the seventh and sixth centuries B.C. It is 25 miles from Kalámai, and is 2,630 feet in height.

ITO, HIROBUMI, PRINCE, 1841–1909, Japanese statesman, was born in the feudal province of Choshu, son of Juzo Ito, a samurai in the service of the daimyo of Choshu. He was the senior of the genro (elder statesmen), who included Yamagata, Matsukata, Saionji, and Inoue, and it was largely due to his political genius, progressiveness, and energy that Japan rose to be a great world power. He wrote the Constitution, promulgated in 1889, on which Japan's modern political system was based and which remained in effect until 1947. In 1900 he founded the Seiyukai, longest-lived and one of the most powerful of Japan's political parties, establishing the principle that the cabinet should be based on the party having the parliamentary majority. He was prime minister four times between 1886 and 1901. He saw Japan victorious in decisive wars with China and Russia, and conclude the eventful alliance with Britain. He rose through the grades of Japan's new peerage until finally Emperor Meiji made him a prince (nonimperial). After the war with Russia he became resident-general in Korea, where he instituted many reforms. He retired from that post in July, 1909, to become president of the emperor's Privy Council, but in October of the same year he was assassinated at Harbin, Manchuria, by a Korean. During his career, and notably as a member of the Iwakura mission, Japan's first embassy to the West, he visited America and Europe several times to study western civilization for the purpose of modernizing and elevating his country.

P. W.

ITÚ, or **Ytu,** town, Brazil, São Paulo State, on the Tiete River, 70 miles NW of São Paulo. The city has iron foundries and cotton textile factories. Pop. (1940) 13,977.

ITURBI, JOSE, 1895–   , American pianist and conductor, was born in Valencia, Spain, and studied at the Valencia Conservatorio de Musica, and the Conservatoire de Musique, Paris. In 1919 he accepted a teaching position at the Geneva Conservatory, but soon abandoned this for piano concert work. Acclaimed in most of the capitals of Europe, his American debut (1929) was also enthusiastically received; after that he performed, both as pianist and conductor, with most of the major American or-

M.G.M.

Jose Iturbi

chestras, appeared in movies, and made a number of recordings.

ITURBIDE, AGUSTÍN COSME DAMIÁN DE, 1783–1824, Mexican patriot leader and emperor, was born in Valladolid. He served in the royalist army against Hidalgo (1810) and Morelos (1814), and in 1820 took the royalist command against Guerrero. Iturbide tried to conciliate royalists and patriots in 1821 with his Plan of Iguala, by which the Roman Catholic religion was maintained and an independent limited monarchy set up with equal rights for Mexicans and Spaniards. The patriots accepted, but the royalists repudiated the plan and outlawed Iturbide, who now led the patriots in the occupation of southern Mexico. In August, 1821, a new viceroy, O'Donajú, recognized Mexican independence in the Treaty of Córdoba, and Iturbide entered Mexico City the next month. He was elected president Sept. 28, 1821. In 1822 he became emperor of Mexico, approved by his army and popular opinion, and confirmed by a reluctant congress. After quarreling with the congress he dissolved it in October, 1822. Revolutions recurred, under the republican Santa Anna, and in 1823 Iturbide recalled the congress and abdicated, agreeing to permanent exile. Returning to Mexico in disguise the next year, he was captured, sentenced to death as an outlaw, and shot.

ITZEHOE, town, Germany, a port in the Prussian province of Schleswig-Holstein, located on the Stor River, 44 miles by rail NW of Hamburg. Founded in 809 it was, until 1864, the meeting place of the estates of Holstein. It is a large manufacturing center, having sugar refineries, fish net factories, shipbuilding yards, and iron works. Wallpaper and portland cement are also manufactured. In the early 1930's a so-called *Hunengrab* (the tomb of a giant) containing urns, etc., was discovered in a hill overlooking the town, and the cave, subsequently enlarged, was used as a hiding place for airplanes secretly manufactured. Pop. (1946) 34,079.

IUKA, BATTLE OF, an indecisive engagement fought near the town of Iuka, Miss., on Sept. 19, 1862, between the Federals under Rosecrans and the Confederates under Price. This battle was an incident which occurred after the Confederate Bragg eluded his opponent Buell and marched toward Louisville, Ky. In dense woods near Iuka, Price attacked Rosecrans' force to prevent the latter from joining Buell. The Union Army was driven back but darkness halted operations; during the night Price retired to Baldwyn. The town of Iuka is located near the Tennessee River about 115 miles southeast of Memphis, Tenn. Pop. (1940) 1,664.

IVAN III, or **IVAN THE GREAT,** 1440–1505, grand duke of Muscovy, the first great national ruler of Russia. Succeeding his father in 1462, he inaugurated a policy of foreign conquest. He subjugated Novgorod (1470–88), acquiring the immense expanse of northern Russia from the Ural Mountains to Lapland, and later gained possession of Vyatka, Tver, Yarslavl, Rostov, and other key territories. In 1480 he released Russia from an ancient bondage by refusing to pay the annual tribute to the Tartar Khan. Ivan next invaded Lithuania (1492, 1501) and in 1503 annexed by treaty the border territories, White Russia and Little Russia (Ukraine). After his marriage to Sophia (Zoë), niece of the last Byzantine emperor, in 1474, Ivan introduced an autocratic type of government, reduced the Boyar power and set up a Byzantine-like court ceremonial. He compiled the first Russian law code, and imported foreign architects to Moscow to rebuild the Kremlin. See RUSSIA, *History.*

IVAN IV, called **The Terrible,** 1530–84, first Russian ruler to use the title of Czar (1547), was enthroned in 1544. His sinister name came from the tortures and executions he inflicted on his opponents, especially nobles. In an angry fit he killed his own son Ivan (1582). Lower classes fared no better; serfdom grew when peasants were deprived of their annual right to change their masters. Ivan's troops conquered the Volga Tartars (1552–56) and annexed Siberia (1582–83), but his long war against Livonia on the Baltic (1558–83) involved him in a war against Poland and Sweden as well, ending in his defeat. See RUSSIA, History.   ALBERT PARRY

IVANOVO, formerly **Ivanovo-Voznesensk,** city, U.S.S.R., in the Russian Soviet Federated Socialist Republic, capital of Ivanovo Region, about 175 miles NE of Moscow. It is called the "Soviet Manchester" for its extensive textile industry which began with 17th century village weaving. The first cloth factory here was opened in 1745. The Moscow fire of 1812 brought to Ivanovo refugee textile masters and capitalists who stayed here helping the city to greater growth. In the 19th century cotton was imported from Bukhara and America as Ivanovo's raw material, but in time less cotton was brought from the United States and more from Russian central Asia, while Ivanovo textiles won markets in the Near and Far East. The Soviets expanded the city's textile industry and added chemical factories and plants which manufacture machines for the region's peat-extracting industry. Ivanovo is the seat of technical schools and a medical college. Pop. (1951 est.) 300,000.

IVANOVO REGION, U.S.S.R., an administrative area of the Russian Soviet Federated Socialist Republic; bounded on the N by Kostroma Region, on the W by Yaroslavl Region, on the S by Vladimir Region, and on the E by Gorki Region; pop. (1950 est.) 1,500,000. The Region is the center of the cotton-spinning and weaving industry manufacturing about 75 per cent of all the linen produced in the U.S.S.R. Numerous textile mills are found in the capital city of Ivanovo, in Shuya, Rodniki, Teikovo, and other towns. The Region is drained by the upper reaches of the Volga River.

IVANOVO-VOZNESENSK. See IVANOVO.

IVES, BURL, 1909– , American ballad singer and actor, was born in Jasper County, Ill. In 1927 he entered Eastern Illinois State Teachers College, but after 1929 much of his time was spent as a wandering troubadour; in 1931 he forsook college entirely in order to rove the country and enlarge his ballad repertory. Spasmodically he interrupted his wanderings in order to sing on the radio, in cafes and in night clubs, and to appear on the professional stage. He gained recognition for his role in the play, *Sing Out, Sweet Land,* and his phonograph records won a large following. He published his autobiography, *Wayfaring Stranger,* in 1948.

IVES, CHARLES EDWARD, 1874– , American composer, was born in Danbury, Conn. Although the son of a musician, he was in the insurance business after his graduation from Yale University. Composing, however, was his avocation and his music became well known for its modern harmony and distinctive rhythms. His major orchestral works, such as the symphony, *Holidays,* and *Three Places in New England,* were written between 1906 and 1916 when songs began to comprise the majority of his works. In 1947 his Symphony No. 3 was awarded the Pulitzer prize. Ives' unique form and polytonality make both his instrumental and vocal works extremely difficult to play.

IVES, FREDERICK EUGENE, 1856–1937, American inventor, was born in Litchfield, Conn. While connected with the photographic laboratory of Cornell University (1874–78), he became interested in the process of half-tone photoengraving. He directed the first commercial production of half-tone plates for the Crosscup and West Engraving Company of Philadelphia in 1881, and by 1886 had perfected the now universally used pin-hole screen for reproducing the half tones of a photograph. Ives' work in color photography culminated in the trichromatic printing process, the polychrome process for obtaining a three-color effect by using only two negative elements, and a process for taking motion pictures in natural colors.

IVES, HERBERT EUGENE, 1882– , American physicist and inventor, was born in Philadelphia, Pa., son of FREDERICK E. IVES. He directed the development of the apparatus used in the transmission of photographs over telephone lines (1923) and had an important part in the first demonstration of television by wire and radio between Washington and New York (1927). He was associated with the Bell Telephone Laboratories from 1919 to 1947.

IVES, JAMES MERRITT. See CURRIER AND IVES.

IVIGTUT, mining town, S Greenland, on Ivigtut Fjord. Cryolite, important in processing aluminum, is mined here.

IVIZA. See ÍBIZA.

IVORY, a word designating the substance obtained from elephant tusks. It is loosely applied to the tusks or horns of other animals and even bone and vegetable substances. The true ivory tusk, after the removal of the outer layers, is used for both commercial and art objects. Industrially it is best known for its use in billiard balls, piano keys, cutlery handles, and buttons. Of the two kinds—hard and soft—the hard, which lacks grain, is more highly prized. Artists and turners, however, often try to avoid using the hard ivory, which cracks easily and is more difficult to carve. The main sources of the world's ivory supply are Africa and Russia. As

MET. MUSEUM OF ART

Ivory handle of a crozier

early as 1827 London, where colorful auctions are still held, was the largest market in the world. The desire of European nations to hold and expand African territories is due in large part to the profitable ivory market. Over the years hunters have destroyed elephant herds to the extent that a shortage has resulted and prices are extremely high.

The art of ivory carving is traced to prehistoric days. Carvings of horn and bone have been found in caves throughout Europe. Animal figures are most generally represented, but there are several examples of human figures done with remarkable workmanship. To the Egyptians is given the credit for first having used ivory in practical as well as artistic objects. Amulets, combs, and even pieces of furniture have been found in tombs. The Babylonians, Etruscans, Greeks, and Romans used ivory and fully appreciated its worth. Though most of the actual pieces have been lost through the ages, information, gained from early writings and the few remaining works, shows that the art of ivory carving was well developed. Inlays, jewelry, pins, and dice were made from this material. Perhaps the most fabulous use of ivory was in the huge statues used in temples. There are records describing the Greek sculptor PHIDIAS' use of ivory for his statues of Zeus and Athena. It is difficult to identify ivories done in the early Christian Era because it was not until the 14th century that pieces were signed. There are many examples of beautiful work done from the 4th century on. A great many of the religious crosses, panels, and altar figures still exist and are of the finest workmanship. During the Renaissance ivory work reached its height. Though it is still used today for art objects, the beauty of the early Christian pieces has never been surpassed. In the Orient, ivory work took on an almost religious significance. In 1263 a special bureau of 150 carvers was established. Exquisite figurines, boxes, and even chopsticks were among the finest work produced by Oriental artists. In some cases whole tusks were used, being carved with hundreds of figures portraying complete legends or histories. Beautiful sword scabbards and execution swords were carved from the whole tusk. Today it is from the East that the best ivory work is obtained. North American ivory carvings were done primarily by the Eskimos using walrus tusks. Ivory was material for artistic work but was found important for practical uses also; ivory harpoons and sewing needles, both, are still in use.   MARIE A. PUHLMANN

IVORY COAST, a colony in the federation of French West Africa; a part of the great western bulge of Africa, bordered on the S by the Gulf of Guinea, on the W by Liberia and French Guinea, on the N by French Sudan, and on the E by British Gold Coast; area 184,174 sq. mi.; pop. (1945) 4,056,000. The capital is ABIDJAN, situated near the coastal ports of Grand Bassam and Port Bouet.

The convex coast line extends from 7° 30′ to 3° 7′ W long., or about 380 miles, and has neither bay nor promontory in its entire length. Most of the coast is fronted by a submarine sand bar that is a handicap to the entry of shipping. The coastal plains extend inland some 40 miles, after which the land rises in steep slopes to a general plateau of about 1,000-foot level, broken by hills, some of which rise above 2,000 feet, and are cut by a number of valleys with a general southeastward trend. The district of Kong in the northeast is mountainous. In the western area, near the Liberian frontier, mountains reach 6,000 feet. The chief rivers are the Cavally, separating Liberia and the Ivory Coast, the Sassandra (240 mi.), the Bandama (225 mi.), and the Comoé (360 mi.), all of which drain into the Gulf of Guinea. All are interrupted by rapids in their descent from the inland plateau, and are not navigable except close to their mouths. The rivers in the extreme north drain into the Niger. The climate is generally hot and unhealthful; there is a heavy rainfall. Great primeval forests extend from the coastal plains to about 8° N lat.

The Ivory Coast's native population is made up of Negroes, with the tribes of the coast districts closely allied to the Krus and Ashantis. Most of the Negroes are fetish worshipers, but some of the northern Mandés are Moslems. The coastal tribes are peaceful. The population includes some 10,000 Europeans. The chief ports are Port Bouet, near Abidjan, Grand Bassam, Assinie, Grand Lahou, Sassandra, and Tabou. Other important centers are Ouagadougou, Bobo Dioulasso, and Bouaké. There is a central school group at Bingerville, and a number of government schools in the various districts.

The Economy of the Ivory Coast is chiefly agricultural, the indigenous crops including peanuts, corn, rice, millet, bananas, pineapples, and other fruits. Cocoa, cotton, coconuts, and coffee have been introduced. The inland mahogany forests yield fine cabinet woods. There is some native industry in cotton weaving, pottery making, and the smelting of iron. Gold is found near Grand Bassam, on the Comoé and the Bia rivers, in Indenie, and in Lobé. Manganese deposits have been located. The chief exports are palm kernels, cocoa, coffee, cabinet wood, bananas, and cotton; the chief imports are cotton fabrics, wines,

Ivory Coast natives and their hut at Port Bouet
ACME

ACME
Scene in Ivory Coast town of Grand Bassam

metal work, and automobiles. A railway running from Abidjan to Bobo Dioulasso, has been extended to Ouagadougou. There are 11,130 miles of motor roads, and the colony has telephone, telegraph, and radio communication with other French West African points. Two canals connecting the lagoons at Assinie and Grand Bassam, and Grand Bassam and Grand Lahou have been dug. There is air service from Abidjan.

Government and History. The region is ruled by a governor, assisted by a privy council and a general council consisting of 27 Africans and 18 Europeans. The seat of administration is Abidjan. Ivory Coast is represented in the French National Assembly by 2 deputies, in the Council of the Republic by 3 councilors, and in the Assembly of the French Union by 4 councilors.

Although the Ivory Coast is said to have been visited in the 14th century by Dieppe merchants, it was made known by the Portuguese navigators of the 15th century and was early frequented by traders in ivory and slaves. The French maintained settlements and trading stations at Grand Bassam from 1700 to 1707, and at Assinie from 1700 to 1704, and French traders established themselves along the coast early in the 19th century. In 1830 Commandant (later Admiral) Bouët-Willaumez began a series of surveying expeditions, and in 1842 native chiefs ceded to him territory at Assinie and Grand Bassam, which the French occupied in 1843. This area was placed under the administration of Senegal. In 1887 Captain Louis Binger began traveling the region between the coast and the Niger and by 1889 had signed protectorate treaties with the chiefs of Bondoukou and the Kong countries. During 1892 Binger explored the Ivory Coast farther, and in 1893 the country was given separate administration with Binger as governor. The Liberian boundaries were decided by agreements made in 1892 and later; the eastern frontier with the Gold Coast was defined by agreements in 1893 and 1898, and the northern frontier was decided in 1899. The colony became an autonomous unit of French West Africa in 1902. Native revolts broke out in the Upper Volta region in 1916. Following France's defeat in 1940, the colony remained loyal to the Vichy government, but two years later it joined the side of the Allies in the war. In early 1933 a part of Upper Volta became a part of the Ivory Coast, but in January, 1948, the districts of Bobo-Dioulasso, Gaoua, Koudougou, Ouagadougou, Kaya, and Tenkodogo were transferred from the colony to the reconstituted Upper Volta.   G. B. DE H.

IVORY NUT, source of vegetable ivory. Within the heavy drupelike fruit of the tagua palm, *Phytelephas macrocarpa*, are six to nine bony seeds, the ivory nuts of commerce. The tagua or ivory nut palm grows abundantly on river banks in tropical America, principally in Colombia and Ecuador, and is characterized by short, thick stems that bear erect-curving, feather-like leaves, often 20 feet long. Ivory nuts are collected in great quantities and shipped throughout the world, especially to the United States and Europe, where they are used as a substitute for true ivory in the man-

CHICAGO NATURAL HISTORY MUSEUM

Ivory nuts and fruit of the tagua palm

ufacture of chessmen, knobs, buttons, etc. The endosperm of bony content of the nut is hemicellulose.

IVORYBILL. See WOODPECKER.

IVREA, ancient **Eporedia,** town and episcopal see, NW Italy, Piedmont Division, Turin Province, on the Dora Baltea River; 38 miles NE of Turin. Interesting structures of the town are a Roman bridge crossing the river; a cathedral with two bell towers (973); St. Stephen's Church (1029); and a 14th-century castle. Important in Roman times for commanding the Great and Little St. Bernard passes, the town was the capital of the margraviate of Ivrea, established by Charlemagne. Pop. about 9,000.

IVRY-LA-BATAILLE, village, France, in the department of Eure, on the Eure River; 42 miles W of Paris. It was the scene of the signal defeat of the Catholic Leaguers under the duke of Mayenne by Henry IV of Navarre (1590).

IVRY-SUR-SEINE, town, France, in the department of Seine, on the left bank of the Seine SE of the fortifications of Paris. It manufactures earthenware, organs, and chocolates. Pop. (1946) 42,445.

IVY, the popular name of several creeping or climbing vines. Japanese or Boston ivy, *Parthenocissus tricuspidata* of the family *Vitaceae*, is widely used as a vine for wall plantings. It has glossy three-lobed or three-foliate leaves and bluish-black berries. English ivy, *Hedera helix* of the family *Araliaceae*, has three-to five-lobed triangular-ovate leaves and small, black berries. It is widely grown on walls as a ground cover in regions of mild winters, and as a potted house plant. Ground ivy, *Nepeta hederacea*, is a creeping, perennial herb of the family *Labiatae*. Its leaves are rounded and opposite, the flowers light blue and bilateral, and it is occasionally planted as an ornamental. Kenilworth ivy, *Cymbalaria muralis*, of the family *Scrophulariaceae*, is a creeping, delicate perennial herb with small blue, yellow-throated, bilateral flowers. Poison ivy, *Rhus toxicodendron*, is a native North American member of the family *Anacardiaceae*. It grows extensively in the United States in woods and open areas

and is characterized by conspicuous, three-foliate leaves and skin-irritating qualities.   H. J. FULLER

IVY POISONING, an inflammation of the skin produced by poisonous plants, especially poison oak, ivy, sumach, or dogwood. The skin becomes red and inflamed, vesicles appear in great numbers, and itching or burning is severe. The poison often is transmitted to other parts of the body by auto-inoculation. The remedies usually employed are zinc compounds, boric acid, hyposulfite of sodium, and fluid extract of grindelia robusta. Alkaline baths are usually recommended when the inflammation covers large areas of the skin. The attack begins within a few hours or days after exposure and lasts from one to four weeks. Susceptibility to poison ivy varies widely among individuals. Some are able to handle the plants with impunity while others are affected by mere proximity to poison ivy without actual contact.

IWO JIMA, or **Sulphur Island,** central of the three Volcano Islands (Kazan Retto), situated just below the 25th parallel, some 750 miles SSE of Tokyo, and 100 miles SW of Chichi, former Japanese naval base in the Bonins. The Volcano Islands were discovered by Bernardo de Torres in 1543, and were annexed by Japan in 1891. Iwo is about 15 miles long, with Suribachi (Mixing Bowl) volcano at its western end. The east shore is steep and terraced, but from these heights the island slopes gently to the west.

As late as 1921 there was no settlement, but the Japanese used it in later years as an air base to screen the approach to their naval base on Chichi and the home islands, since Iwo Jima was the only island in the Volcanos and Bonins with a surface flat enough for use as an airstrip. During World War II, as the American island-hopping campaign neared, Iwo was bombed or shelled almost daily from late in 1944 until the American landing on Feb. 19, 1945. The fight proved one of the most bitter of the Pacific campaign; the island was not completely conquered until March 16, 1945. Following its capture, Iwo was used as a base for fighter planes, which protected the flights of superfortresses over the Japanese home islands.   C. S.

IXION, in ancient Greek legend, was a king of the Lapithae, in Thessaly. He treacherously murdered his father-in-law; and, as no mortal would purify him, Zeus took him to heaven and purified him there. For attempting to make love to Hera he was bound in hell to an ever-rolling wheel.

IXTILILXÔCHITL, DON FERNANDO DE ALVA, c. 1570–?1648, Mexican historian. He was a native Mexican and a descendant of the ancient Chichimecs (so called), or the clan or tribe of Tezcuco, from which the principal war chiefs, or "kings," were chosen. He was an official interpreter to the Spanish in Mexico, and wrote historical works of great value concerning the native Mexicans and the relations between them and the Spanish after the conquest. According to Bandelier, however, he probably unduly exalts his own tribe. His history of the Chichimecs was translated and published by Ternaux-Compans as *Histoire des Chichimèques, et des anciens rois de Tuzcuco* (2 vols. 1840), and Alfredo Chavero published his *Obras históricas* (2 vols. 1891–92).

IYEYASU. See IEYASU.

Beach operations at Iwo Jima in World War II

U.S. ARMY SIGNAL CORPS

HUGH SPENCER

Leaf mosaic of English ivy growing on a wall

IZAAK WALTON LEAGUE, a nonprofit society of public-spirited men and women throughout the United States interested in the conservation of woods, waters, and wildlife. The League was organized in Chicago in 1922 by 54 outdoorsmen under leadership of Will H. Dilg. It was named in honor of the renowned IZAAK WALTON because of his philosophy of outdoor life as expressed in his writings, notably *The Compleat Angler*. In 1951, the League had 600 chapters located in 37 states, the District of Columbia, and Alaska. Headquarters are at Chicago, Ill.

IZABAL, LAKE, E Guatemala, in the department of Izabal; length about 30 miles. The lake, sometimes called Golfo Dulce (Freshwater Lake), reaches the Caribbean through its connection with Golfete Dulce (Little Freshwater Lake) and the Río Dulce, a broad river which flows into the Gulf of Honduras. On the south shore of Lake Izabal is the town of Izabal, an important lake port in Spanish colonial days.

IZALCO, volcano, W El Salvador, NW of Acajutla; altitude 7,773 feet. Continuous smoke and flames issue from the volcano, which is often called the lighthouse of the Pacific. Violent eruptions at several periods have scattered ashes over a wide area. On the slope of Izalco is the Spanish stone of conquest which the conquered Indians are said to have signed with their blood. The town of Izalco lies at the foot of the volcano.

IZARD, the name of a local race of the chamois, *Rupicapra tragus*, which is confined to the Pyrenees. It is somewhat smaller than the Alpine kind, and is of a more foxy-red color, but the distinctions are not sufficiently marked to entitle it to rank as a separate species.

IZHEVSK, city, U.S.S.R., in the Russian Soviet Federated Socialist Republic, situated on the Izh River, capital of the Udmurt Autonomous Soviet Socialist republic. The city was established in 1760. Its famed factory of hunting rifles, founded in 1807, was expanded and modernized by the Soviets along with its other industries. Many Udmurts (Finno-Ugric tribesmen formerly called Votyaks) now work in the rifle factory, the new steel mills, and the motorcycle and machine-tool factories. Izhevsk has technical schools and teachers' college. Pop. (1951 est.) 200,000.

IZMAIL, or **Ismail,** city, U.S.S.R., in the Ukrainian Soviet Socialist Republic, capital of Izmail Region, situated on the Kiliya arm of the Danube River, about 40 miles from the Black Sea. Izmail is famous for its fishing and its fruits, particularly apricots. Captured from the Turks by General Suvorov in 1790, the town was ceded to Russia in 1812, lost by her in 1856, regained in 1878, seized by Rumania in 1918, again ceded to Russia in 1940, taken by Nazi-Rumanian forces in 1941, and recaptured by the Soviets in 1944. Pop. (1950 est.) 30,000.

IZMAIL REGION, or **Ismail,** U.S.S.R., an administrative area of the Ukrainian Soviet Socialist Republic; bounded on the N by the Moldavian Soviet Socialist Republic and Odessa Region, on the E by the Black Sea, and on the S and W by Rumania. The Region is situated on the lower Danube including the Kiliysky branch of the river's delta. Fishing and trading in grain are the principal occupations of the population. The capital is Izmail.

IZMIR. See SMYRNA.

IZMIT, or **Kocaeli,** maritime vilayet, NW Turkey, bounded on the N by the Black Sea, E by Bolu, S by Bilecik and Bursa, W by the Sea of Marmara and Istanbul; area 3,130 sq. mi.; pop. (1945) 200,088. The Gulf of Izmit, at the eastern end of the Sea of Marmara, indents and cuts the vilayet almost in half and almost reaches its only river, the Sakarya. The southern half of the vilayet is mountainous, with forests of oak, fir, and beech. The northern half is agricultural, chiefly producing tobacco, small fruits, and melons. Tobacco, raw silk, silk goods, and textiles are exported.

IZMIT, ancient **Nicomedia,** city, Turkey, the capital of Izmit Vilayet, at the head of the Gulf of Izmit, 50 miles SE of Istanbul. It is an important trade center, connected by railway with Ankara (Angora), Konya, and Izmir (Smyrna). The ancient city, Nicomedia, of Bithynia, was founded by Nicomedes I in 264 B.C. upon the site of a still earlier city, Astacus. Under the Romans, it became a colony and the chief port of the Near East. It was the ancient capital of the kings of Bithynia and several later emperors, notably Diocletian. Constantine the Great made it his summer residence. Hannibal died there. Pop. about 30,000.

IZTACCIHUATL, or **Ixtaccihuatl,** an elongated volcanic peak (alt. 16,883 ft.) in central Mexico, between the states of Pueblo and Mexico, the second highest mountain in the country. With its twin peak POPOCATEPETL (17,887 ft.), 10 miles north, it forms a short spur of the Sierra Nevada. Iztaccihuatl is known as the "Sleeping Woman" because of its three rounded summits of varying heights which suggest a shrouded human figure. The most widely known of several Indian legends concerning it is that Iztaccihuatl represents a dead or sleeping princess, covered with perpetual snow and guarded by her lover Popocatepetl. A climb to either mountain usually starts from the village of Amecameca.

IZU SHICHITO, seven volcanic islands, Japan, extending southward from about 30 miles S of Tokyo Bay, E central Honshu, into the Pacific Ocean. The largest, OSHIMA, has an active volcano, Mihara, rising to 2,477 feet.

IZVOLSKY, ALEXANDER, 1856–1919, Russian statesman. He entered the Czar's foreign service as a young man; was Russia's chargé d'affaires and later minister at the Vatican; also served in Belgrade and Munich; and became successively minister to Japan and Denmark. From Copenhagen he was recalled to be minister of foreign affairs (1906–10). The defeat of Russia by the Japanese in 1904–5 shifted the Czar's main interest from the Far East to Europe and the Near and Middle East.

In 1907 Izvolsky signed an agreement with Great Britain, thus strengthening the Anglo-French Entente against Germany. By this agreement, Russia and England divided Persia between them into two spheres of influence, and Russia recognized England's dominance in Afghanistan but failed to gain anything for herself in regard to Turkey, particularly in the Dardanelles. In October, 1908, Austria-Hungary formally annexed Bosnia and Herzegovina, her foreign minister, Count Aehrenthal, having cleverly outmaneuvered Izvolsky, who had secretly suggested this annexation but on his own terms—the giving of the use of the Turkish Straits to the Russian navy. This was not achieved because such use was not dependent on Austria-Hungary's permission but on Great Britain's withheld assent. Thus the Central Powers won a bloodless victory in the Balkans, much to Russia's anger and Izvolsky's loss of prestige.

Appointed the Czar's envoy to Paris in 1910, Izvolsky, burning with a desire for revenge, did his utmost to bolster the Franco-British-Russian alliance against Germany and Austria-Hungary. Both friends and foes recognized Izvolsky's ingenuity, ambition, and flexibility. After the Romanov dynasty fell in 1917, Izvolsky remained in France until his death.

ALBERT PARRY

Iztaccihuatl, a volcanic peak in central Mexico

EWING GALLOWAY

J **J j** **J j** **J j** **J j** **J j** **J j** **J j** **J j** **J j**

J is simply a modification of *I*. It was employed for a time as the initial form of that letter. Since the 17th century the consonantal value of *i* has been assigned to *j*, and its vocalic value to the older form. The value of German *j* is the early consonantal value of *i;* it occurs also in the English word "*hallelujah*." In Spanish *j* has a sound somewhat resembling that of the German *ch*. The present English value is a compound of *d* and *zh;* it was borrowed from the French in the 14th century. The French value has now become *zh*, as in "jour." See I; G.

JABBOK RIVER, modern **Wadi Zerqa,** rises in N Trans-Jordan, and flows in a winding course SW and W into the Jordan, 30 miles N of the Dead Sea. It is mentioned in Josh. 12:2 as the boundary between the kingdoms of Sihon, king of the Amorites, and of Og, king of Bashan. On its banks Jacob wrestled with his mysterious visitant (Gen. 32:33 ff.). Its length is 110 miles.

JABLONEC, German **Gablonz,** manufacturing town, NE Czechoslovakia, Bohemia, on the Neisse River; eight miles SE of Reichenberg, Germany. It is noted for industries producing Bohemian glassware and porcelains, glass beads, glass buttons, and other clothing ornaments, and pearls and various kinds of costume jewelry. Cotton and woolen textiles and cardboard, also, are manufactured. The town was invaded in March, 1939, by the Germans but was liberated by Soviet troops in 1945. Pop. (1947 est.) 23,112.

JABNEEL, ancient **Jabneh, Jamnia,** or **Jemnaan,** a city of Judaea, or Judah, in the Land of Canaan (Palestine), near Mount Baalah, mentioned in Josh. 15:11; 13 miles S of Jaffa (Joppa). In II Chron. 26:8 it is called Jabneh, one of the cities captured by Uzziah from the Philistines. It is also mentioned in I Maccabees 4:15, 5:58, 10:69, 15:40; II Maccabees 12:8, 9:40; and in Josephus. It was sacked by Judas Maccabeus, Jewish military leader, who took it from the Syrians in 165 B.C. Later, having been rebuilt, it was recaptured by Simon of the Syrians, in 161 B.C. It was seized by Vespasian, A.D. 66, during the War of the Jews. After the destruction of Jerusalem, Jabneel, called Jamnia at this time, became famous as the seat of the Sanhedrin (ecclesiastical supreme court), and for its school of the rabbis, until the massacre of the Jews at Bether (near Jerusalem) by Hadrian in A.D. 135. The modern town of Yibna (Yebna), south of the Nahr (river) Rubin, stands near the ruins of these towns, on an elevation 170 feet above the sea.

Jabneel of Naphtali, referred to in Josh. 19:33, was in a district west of the Sea of Galilee, near the Upper Jordan. K. E. H.

JABOATÃO, town, NE Brazil, in the state of Pernambuco; on a railway near Recife, of which it is a suburb. Pop. (1940) 13,997.

JABORANDI is a woody South American shrub, *Pilocarpus jaborandi*, that was introduced into Europe in 1847. It contains alkaloids and a volatile oil. The leaves of jaborandi have marked medicinal properties. They are now seldom used since it has been discovered that their action depends upon their PILOCARPINE content (0.5 per cent in the leaf). Like pilocarpine, jaborandi leaves or their extracts exert a powerful stimulating effect on the parasympathetic nervous system.

JABOTICABAL, town, SE Brazil, in the state of São Paulo, in an agricultural region. Pop. (1940) 11,938.

JACA, ancient **Icca,** town, Spain, in the province of Huesca, on the Aragon River, 48 miles N of Huesca by rail. It is situated in the Pyrenees, near the French border, and has railway connection with France. A bishop's seat since 1063, it has a Gothic cathedral (1040), old walls, and a citadel. There is trade in grain, cattle, and herbs, and manufactures of cement, pottery, and chocolate. The inhabitants annually celebrate the Spanish victory over the Moors here in 795, on the first Friday of May. Pop. (1940) 7,663.

JACAMARS are brilliantly colored South American birds of the family *Galbulidae*, and are allied to the barbets and honey guides. The bill is long and straight, the feet weak, the flight quick and jerky. The ordinary colors are golden green above and brown or red below, but the beautiful *Urogalba paradisea* is dark blue. Their food consists of insects caught on the wing; and their nests are in holes bored into earthen banks; but little is known in detail of their habits.

JACANA, a common name given to about seven species of aquatic birds that belong to the family *Jacanidae*. Although they resemble the rails they are more closely related to the plovers. The birds are especially remarkable for their long toes and excessively long claws. This peculiar foot structure makes possible such a distribution of body weight that the birds are able to walk on lily pads and floating vegetation in lakes, swamps, or river margins. Jacanas are found in tropical regions of Africa, Madagascar, India, China, and the New World.

Mexican jacana

The Mexican species ranges from Texas into Central America.

Jacanas of all species have a horny spur at the angle of each wing and a naked leaflike structure at the front of the head with wattles at the base of the bill. The nests are fragile structures of water weeds, and the eggs are deep, olive brown with many fine dark lines over the entire surface. W. A. HILTON

BIBLIOG.–A. H. Evans, *Birds in Cambridge Nat. History* (1909); T. G. Pearson, *Birds of America* (1936); R. Hegner, *Parade of the Animal Kingdom* (1937).

JACARANDA, a genus of trees and shrubs native to the American tropics and belonging to the family *Bignoniaceae*. The plants have large compound leaves bearing numerous small, delicate leaflets. The flowers are bell-shaped, slightly bilateral, blue or violet in color, and are borne in large, showy panicles. Jacarandas are widely cultivated in Florida and California. H. J. FULLER

JACAREÍ, town, SE Brazil, in the state of São Paulo, in an agricultural region. Pop. (1940) 11,965.

JÁCHYMOV, German **Joachimsthal,** spa, Czechoslovakia, famous for its radioactive waters, NW Bohemia, 12 miles N of Karlovy Vary (Carlsbad). It is situated in the Erzgebirge at an altitude of 12,300 feet. Jáchymov is famous for its deposits of PITCH-BLENDE, the largest in non-Russian Europe, and the recovery and milling of uranium is a well-developed industry. An institute for radium research to further the work of Pierre and Marie Curie is located in Jáchymov. It was here that the tons of pitchblende needed for their radium discovery were obtained. Near by are silver mines, which have been worked for more than 300 years. The German *thaler* (silver dollar) is a corruption of *Joachimsthaler*, a silver coin originally minted here in the 16th century. In the area there are also deposits of lead, iron, and tin. Other industries include paper mills, paint works, and the manufacture of gloves, dolls, lace, and cigarettes. Pop. (1940 est.) 8,000.

JACINTH. See HYACINTH.

JACK FRUIT, the name commonly given to the fruit of the tree, *Artocarpus integer*, of the family *Moraceae*. This tree, a native of Malaya and adjacent countries, bears large, leathery leaves, and produces large, ovoid fruits weighing as much as 60 pounds. The fruits, which resemble those of the American hedge apple or Osage orange, are highly nutritious, and the trees are widely planted in the tropics. The wood of the tree resembles mahogany and is often used for furniture. The jack fruit is closely related to *A. incisa*, or breadfruit.   H. J. FULLER

JACK-IN-THE-PULPIT, or **INDIAN TURNIP,** the common name of *Arisaema triphyllum*, a plant belonging to the family *Araceae* and occurring in rich, deep woods, particularly in northeastern United States. It is one of the most conspicuous plants in the early spring flora. The plant is a perennial herb arising from an underground corm. It commonly bears two leaves, each composed of three ovate, pointed leaflets three to five inches long, and a single inflorescence or flower cluster. This structure, commonly but erroneously called a flower, is responsible for the common name of the plant. The inflorescence is a fleshy spike, called a *spadix*, which is about three inches long and bears on its basal portion tiny, naked flowers which lack both sepals and petals. Above this floriferous base, the spadix is prolonged into an erect, smooth, sterile portion, the "jack." The plants are dioecious, that is, some individuals bear only staminate, or pollen-producing flowers, while others bear only pistillate, or seed-producing flowers. From the base of the inflorescence, immediately below the floriferous zone, a conspicuous bract, or *spathe*, grows upward in the form of a narrow tube. It broadens out into an arch that overhangs the apex of the "jack." The spathe is the "pulpit" of the inflorescence. The tissues of this plant, like those of most other *Araceae*, contain numerous, sharp-pointed crystals in their cells. If the tissues are chewed, these crystals are freed from their cells and become embedded in the tongue and membranes of the mouth, thus causing a painful, burning sensation that may persist for several hours.

Jack-in-the-Pulpit. Model, below, and mature plant, right

MISSOURI C. C.

BUFFALO MUS. OF SCI

Boiling destroys the crystals and makes the corms fairly palatable. Indians formerly used them as food.
          H. J. FULLER

JACK-O-LANTERN. See WILL-O'-THE-WISP.

JACK RABBIT. See HARE.

JACKAL. The common jackal of eastern Europe, southern Asia, and India, *Canis aureus*, is an animal between two and two and a half feet long, with a bushy tail one-third of the length of the head and body. The jackal varies greatly in color in the different parts of its extensive range, but is generally light reddish brown, with a black tip to the tail. It interbreeds freely with the pariah dogs of India and Egypt, and differs from the wolves chiefly in the smaller size, shorter tail, and relative reduction of the carnassial or flesh teeth as compared with the molars. The diet is varied, the flesh of animals which the jackals have themselves killed being mingled with carrion, fruits, seeds, and sugar cane, of which they are very fond. They live in burrows and dens among rocks, and are chiefly nocturnal, going about in small companies and uttering a most unpleasant howl. In South Africa the

NEW YORK ZOOLOGICAL SOCIETY

Indian jackal

common jackal is replaced by two other related species, the striped jackal (*C. adjustus*) and the black-backed jackal (*C. mesomelas*).

JACKASS. See ASS.

JACKDAW, a member of the CROW family, found throughout most of Europe, western Asia, and northern Africa. It is a noisy gregarious bird, about 14 inches long, with glossy black plumage. It is shrewd, intelligent, and easily tamed, often making an amusing pet. Its nests are made in hollow trees, rabbit burrows, church towers, and holes or crevices in cliffs, and are constructed of sticks, straw, wool, and feathers. The eggs number from four to six. The food consists of worms, insects, parasites of sheep, and at times also eggs and young birds.

JACKSON, ALEXANDER YOUNG, 1882–   , Canadian painter, was born in Montreal where he began his art studies which were later continued at the Art Institute, Chicago (1906), and at the Julian Academy, Paris (1907–8). During World War I he was official artist for the Canadian War Memorials, and (1919–33) he was an original member of the Group of Seven, the Canadian nationalist painters whose efforts were devoted to interpretation of regional environment. Jackson was the central figure in *Canadian Landscape* (1941), a documentary film released by the Canadian National Film Board and the National Gallery of Canada. Representative of his landscapes is "Early Spring, Quebec," Art Gallery of Toronto.

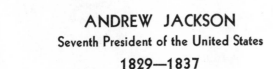

ANDREW JACKSON
Seventh President of the United States
1829—1837

JACKSON, ANDREW, 1767–1845, seventh president of the United States, was born on Mar. 15, 1767, in the Waxhaw Settlement, close to the state line between North and South Carolina. The house in which he was born disappeared long ago, and the exact location of the state line at the time of his birth is uncertain, consequently, it cannot be stated with certainty in which state he was born. Although but a boy during the Revolutionary War, he saw some service in that war and was taken prisoner in 1781. Mistreatment during the time of his captivity gave him a dislike for the British which continued throughout his lifetime.

Jackson studied law in Salisbury, N.C., and was admitted to the practice of law in that state in 1787. The next year he moved to Nashville, in what was then the western district of North Carolina, having been appointed prosecuting attorney for that district. Here his private law practice flourished, and he was soon a prosperous and prominent member of the new community. In 1791 he was married to Rachel (Donelson) Robards, the divorced wife of Lewis Robards, she being the daughter of John Donelson, one of the founders of Nashville. On account of a legal misunderstanding regarding the procurement of the divorce, the marriage ceremony was performed a second time two years later; and Jackson was thereafter acutely sensitive to any reference to the irregularity of his marriage.

When Tennessee was admitted to the Union in 1796, Jackson was a member of the convention which framed the constitution of the new state; a constitution which Thomas Jefferson described as the most nearly perfect of any that had been written at that time. Tradition credits Jackson with suggesting Tennessee as the name of the new state, but there is no written record of this. He was elected to represent Tennessee as its lone member of the House of Representatives, and served one year.In 1797 he was elected to the U.S. Senate, but resigned in 1798. From 1798 to 1804 he served as a judge of the Superior Court of Tennessee, then the highest court in the state.

In 1806 Jackson fought a duel with Charles Dickinson, in which encounter Dickinson was killed and Jackson severely wounded. Jackson's friends charged that the duel was forced on him by political enemies who thought thus to eliminate him, as Dickinson was an experienced duelist and expert shot. Jackson never fully recovered from the wound suffered in the duel; and the fact of his having killed an opponent in an affair of honor was afterward used against him by his political enemies.

Military Career. The WAR OF 1812 brought Jackson the opportunity to distinguish himself as a military hero in a way that made him not only a national figure but an international celebrity. In 1813 he led the Tennessee militia in a victorious expedition against the hostile Creek Indians in Alabama. In this campaign he displayed such military skill that in 1814 he was awarded a commission as major general in the Regular Army of the United States, commanding the Southern division. It was in this capacity that on Jan. 8, 1815, he won the crushing victory over the British under General Parkenham at the Battle of New Orleans. It was this battle which really sealed the independence of the United States. Although fought after the treaty of peace between the belligerents had been signed at Ghent, the news of the signing had not yet reached this country and the treaty had not yet been ratified by either nation. See NEW ORLEANS, BATTLE OF.

An opportunity for further military glory came when the Seminole Indians in Florida staged an uprising late in 1817. Under orders from the secretary of war, General Jackson early in 1818 marched to Florida (then a Spanish province) with a strong detachment of Tennessee and Kentucky volunteers. Here he seized the Spanish fort at St. Marks and dispersed the insurrectionary Indians; and, after seizing Pensacola, left a garrison there and returned to Tennessee. The Florida territory was soon thereafter acquired from Spain by the United States, and in 1821 Jackson was back in Pensacola as territorial governor. He found the duties of the office, however, uncongenial and unpleasant, and after a few months' service he resigned and returned home again.

Political Career. In 1823 the legislature of Tennessee elected Jackson to the U.S. Senate, and at the same time formally nominated him a candidate for the presidency. In the presidential election of 1824 there were four candidates: Andrew Jackson, John Quincy Adams, William H. Crawford, and Henry Clay. None of these candidates received a majority of the electoral votes, the vote in the Electoral College being Jackson 99, Adams 84, Crawford 41, Clay 37. The election was thus thrown into the House of Representatives for decision, the law requiring the selection to be made from the three leading candidates. Clay threw his support to Adams, who was elected President. Jackson and his supporters charged there was a "corrupt bargain" between Adams and Clay, and their cries were intensified when Adams made Clay his secretary of state.

Jackson soon resigned his seat in the Senate, but was again nominated for the presidency by the Tennessee legislature. In the 1828 election Jackson was opposed by Adams, candidate for a second term. The campaign was an exceptionally spirited one, marked by intensely acrimonious vilification and personal abuse of Jackson by the politicians and press supporting Adams. Jackson was elected, receiving 178 electoral votes to 83 for Adams. The enjoyment of his

It happened when
Andrew Jackson
was president . . .

"Downfall of Mother Bank," detail of cartoon during Jackson's campaign against Bank of the U.S.

INTERNATIONAL HARVESTER CO.

Cyrus McCormick staged first public demonstration of reaping machine at Steele's Tavern, Va., in 1831

Battle of the Alamo in 1836 resulted in death for all members of small but valiant band of Texans

"DeWitt Clinton" hauled New York State's first train in a trial run on the Mohawk and Hudson, 1831

NEW YORK CENTRAL SYSTEM

FANEUIL HALL, BOSTON

Daniel Webster's reply to Hayne in the Senate in great nullification debate of 1830

political triumph was dulled, however, by the sudden death of Mrs. Jackson in December; and a few days after her burial he set out alone for Washington for his inauguration.

The President. Andrew Jackson's first year as president was featured by the introduction of the "SPOILS SYSTEM" in the selection of governmental appointees; and in 1831 there took place the serio-comis imbroglio involving "Peggy" Eaton, wife of Secretary of War Eaton, resulting in the dissolution of Jackson's cabinet and the strengthening of Jackson's favor for Martin Van Buren which later made Van Buren president. See EATON, MARGARET; KITCHEN CABINET.

On the whole, Jackson's first term as president was popular with the people, and in 1832 he was elected to a second term by an overwhelming majority—219 electoral votes to 49 for Henry Clay. It was in 1832 that Jackson issued his famous "Nullification Proclamation," directed at the people of South Carolina in general and John C. Calhoun in particular, a state paper described as "clear in statement, forcible in argument, vigorous in style and glowing with the fire of a genuine and enlightened patriotism." The next year he took the memorable step of withdrawing the government's deposits from the Bank of the United States, an act which convulsed the financial world and brought upon him the censure of the Senate. But by 1835 he had paid off the national debt, for the first and only time in the history of the United States, and when he retired from the presidency at the conclusion of his second term in 1837 he left a surplus in the Federal treasury. However, his bank policies, and the issuance of his "SPECIE CIRCULAR" in 1836 are thought to have been important causes of the Panic of 1837. See NULLIFICATION; DEMOCRATIC PARTY.

Life at the Hermitage. Retired to his plantation home, the HERMITAGE, near Nashville, Jackson continued to take a lively interest in politics and was an active backstage factor in national affairs. Not even his influence could re-elect Van Buren in 1840, but it was his support which was partially responsible for the nomination and election of James K. Polk, a fellow Tennessean, to the presidency in 1844. Meanwhile, through his old friend, Sam Houston, he had been actively promoting the annexation of Texas. His last years were marked by increasingly bad health, a complication of physical ailments, intensified by advancing years. On June 8, 1845, he died, and was buried by the side of his wife in the garden of the Hermitage. This home, which President Jackson began in 1819 and completed in 1835, is now a public museum. Monuments have been erected in both North Carolina and South Carolina to mark what each state claims to be the site of his birthplace. See TENNESSEE for illustration.   STANLEY HORN

BIBLIOG.–*Dictionary of American Biography;* J. S. Bassett, *The Life of Andrew Jackson* (1911); C. G. Bowers, *The Party Battles of the Jackson Period* (1922); M. James, *Life of Andrew Jackson* (1938); A. M. Schlesinger, *Age of Jackson* (1945).

JACKSON, CHARLES THOMAS, 1805–80, American scientist, was born in Plymouth, Mass. He was graduated from the Harvard Medical School and practiced in Boston, but afterward became interested in chemistry, geology, and mineralogy. He claimed that the credit for the telegraph belonged to him, rather than to Morse, and also that he had discovered ether as an anesthetic. The latter claim was subsequently investigated by a committee from the French Academy of Sciences, who decided that both Morton and Jackson should be recognized. He wrote a *Manual of Etherization, with a History of its Discovery* (1863). See MORSE, SAMUEL F. B.; MORTON, WILLIAM T. G.

JACKSON, CHEVALIER, 1865– , American laryngologist, was born in Pittsburgh, Pa. and studied at Jefferson Medical College. During his 50-year practice, first in Pittsburgh and then in Philadelphia, he became a pioneer in peroral endoscopy and surgery.

He saved the lives of more than 1,000 children by extracting nails, coins, and other objects which they had swallowed. He also removed diseased tissue from the throats and larynxes of patients. To perform these operations he invented scores of instruments, the most noted being the esophagoscope and the bronchoscope. He set up a bronchoscopic clinic in Jefferson Hospital, Philadelphia, to train surgeons in these techniques and described his methods in *Peroral Endoscopy and Laryngeal Surgery* (1914), *Bronchoscopy, Esophagoscopy and Gastroscopy* (1934), and *The Foreign Body in Air and Food Passages* (1934).

JACKSON, FREDERICK GEORGE, 1860–1938, British Arctic explorer, was educated at Denstone College and Edinburgh University. He traveled in the Australian deserts, and made a famous journey across the Great Tundra and Lapland in midwinter. In 1894–97 he was commander of the Jackson-Harmsworth Polar Expedition to Franz Josef Land, where he made valuable scientific discoveries and observations. He served in the Boer War (1899–1902) and World War I (1914–18). In 1919 he commanded a number of Russian prisoners of war camps in Germany. In 1925–26 he crossed Africa from Beira to Banana Point; trekked with carriers across the Urundi and Ruanda countries, visiting the volcanic Virunda Mountains, and ascended Mount Sabinjo; from Lake Kivu he crossed the Congo forest to the Lualaba River where he hunted with the Pygmies, and descended the whole length of the Congo River to the sea; also visited the sources of the three great rivers of Africa—the Zambezi, the Nile, and the Congo. He wrote *A Thousand Days in the Arctic* (1899); *The Lure of the Unknown Lands* (1935).

JACKSON, HELEN HUNT, 1831–85, American poet and novelist, was born in Amherst, Mass. She received a sketchy education at preparatory schools in Ipswich and in New York City, then married Edward Hunt (1852), who according to a rather frail tradition was at one time loved by the poet Emily Dickinson, a lifelong friend of Helen's. After her husband's death in 1863, she began writing verse, criticism, and fiction for the New York *Nation* and *Independent.* She is also supposed to be the author of the Saxe Holm stories, which appeared in *Scribner's Monthly.* In 1875 she married a Colorado banker. While living in the West she became interested in Indian life and dedicated herself to improving the treatment of the Indians by the government. At her own expense she published and distributed *A Century of Dishonor* (1881), a sensational history of the government's relations with the Indians. She continued her campaign in *Ramona* (1884), in which she arraigned both the Spaniards and Americans for their inhuman treatment of the Indians. Primarily a thesis novel, this story of life in Old California became her best known work. The best known of her other novels is *Mercy Philbrick's Choice* (1876), supposedly based on the life of Emily Dickinson. Other works include *Verses* (1870), *The Story of Boon* (1874), *Sonnets and Lyrics* (1886), and *Between Whiles* (1887).   J. J. M.

JACKSON, HOWELL EDMUNDS, 1832–95, American jurist, was born in Paris, Tenn., and studied at West Tennessee College, the University of Virginia, and Lebanon Law School. After practicing law at Jackson and Memphis, he entered the Tennessee legislature (1880–81), and in 1881 became U.S. senator from that state. He resigned in 1886 to serve as judge of the circuit court of western Tennessee, becoming the first presiding judge of the new circuit court of appeals at Cincinnati in 1891. He was a Harrison appointee to the U.S. Supreme Court (1893–95).

JACKSON, ROBERT HOUGHWOUT, 1892– , American jurist was born in Spring Creek, Pa., and studied at Albany Law School and Chautauqua Institute. Following admittance to the bar in 1913, he practiced in Jamestown, N.Y. He served as general counsel for the Bureau of Internal Revenue (1934–36), assistant attorney general of the United

States (1936–38), solicitor general (1938–39), and attorney general (1940–41). Roosevelt appointed him associate justice of the Supreme Court in 1941. After World War II, Jackson was named chief U.S. war-crimes prosecutor at Nuremberg and wrote *The Nuremberg Case* (1947).

JACKSON, SHELDON, 1834–1909, American missionary to the Indians, was born in Minaville, N.Y. He was graduated (1855) from Union College, entered the Presbyterian ministry, and was engaged in missionary work among the Indians of the West and Southwest until 1877, when he turned his attention to the Alaskan field. In 1885 he became U.S. general agent of education in Alaska, and introduced there the public school system and the government reindeer industry. He was the author of *Alaska and the Missions on the North Pacific Coast* (1880), and of many government reports.

JACKSON, THOMAS JONATHAN, generally known as "Stonewall" Jackson, in allusion to his stubborn defense of a position in the first Battle of

CHICAGO HIST. SOC.
Stonewall Jackson

Bull Run, 1824–63, Confederate officer during the Civil War. He was born on Jan. 21, 1824, in Clarksburg, Va. (now West Virginia), was graduated with little distinction from West Point in 1846, and as a lieutenant served in the southern campaign of the Mexican War (1846–47), winning the brevet of captain at Contreras and Churubusco, and of major at Chapultepec. In March, 1851, he resigned from the army, and until the outbreak of the Civil War was professor of natural and experimental philosophy and artillery tactics at the Lexington (Va.) Military Institute, making a visit to Europe meanwhile. He deprecated secession, but was a strong believer in states' rights, and when Virginia withdrew from the Union maintained his allegiance to the state. In April, 1861, he became colonel in the Virginia army, and shortly afterward (July) was commissioned a brigadier general in the Confederate service. He showed his genius for command and his dogged intrepidity in the first Battle of Bull Run (July 21, 1861), arriving with Johnston's troops from Harper's Ferry in time to help materially toward changing the fortunes of the day. For his gallant conduct he was promoted to major general and served in the Shenandoah Valley, being worsted by General Shields at Kernstown, but defeating Milroy at McDowell, and Banks at Winchester (May, 1862). By his strategy in confusing the Federal troops that would otherwise have reinforced McClellan, he greatly aided the Confederate forces in the peninsula and then, with about 25,000 men, quickly joined Lee in the vicinity of Richmond, and took part as a corps commander in the battles of Gaines's Mill (June 27, 1862) and Malvern Hill (July 1, 1862). See BULL RUN, BATTLES OF.

Under Lee's orders, Jackson again entered the Shenandoah Valley, defeated an inferior Federal force under Banks at Cedar Mountain (Aug. 9), and after making a rapid march, debouched from Thoroughfare Gap on Pope's flank, and, together with General Longstreet, won the second Battle of Bull Run (Aug. 29–30). Lee, starting on his invasion of Maryland, detached Jackson to capture Harper's Ferry, which he did (Sept. 15), and by a forced march rejoined Lee in time to participate in the Battle of Antietam (Sept. 16–17). He commanded the Confederate right at Fredericksburg (Dec. 13), was promoted to the rank of lieutenant general, and at Chancellorsville, after making a famous flanking march directed against Hooker's right, was severely wounded in the left arm (May 2, 1863) by his own men while making a reconnaissance. After the amputation of his arm, pneumonia developed, and he died May 10, 1863.

Jackson was probably the greatest corps commander on either side during the Civil War. He had a deeply religious nature and has often been compared with the Cromwellian leaders in England. See LEE, ROBERT E. for illustration.

BIBLIOG.–M. A. Jackson, *Memoirs of Stonewall Jackson* (1895); M. L. Williamson, *Life of Thomas J. Jackson* (1918); P. A. Bruce, *The Virginia Plutarch* (1929); J. Adams, *Stonewall* (1931); A. Tate, *Stonewall Jackson, the Good Soldier* (1928, ed. 1932); J. W. Wayland, *Stonewall Jackson's Way* (1940); H. K. Douglas, *I Rode With Stonewall* (1940); H. A. Monsell, *Young Stonewall, Tom Jackson* (1942); D. S. Freeman, *Lee's Lieutenants* (1943); G. F. R. Henderson, *Stonewall Jackson and the American Civil War* (1898, ed. 1943); J. Bissett, ed., *Mysteries of Chancellorsville* (1945); R. B. Cook, *Family and Early Life of Stonewall Jackson* (ed. 1948).

JACKSON, WILLIAM HENRY, 1843–1942, American painter, photographer, and explorer, was born in Keeseville, N.Y. A self-taught artist, he began his career at 15 by working as a retoucher in a photographer's studio. After service in the Civil War, Jackson photographed the newly built Union Pacific Railroad and later became a photographer for the U.S. Geological Survey. As head of the W. H. Jackson Photograph and Printing Company (from 1879), he produced thousands of stereopticon views, used as a popular form of entertainment of the time. In 1935 his last series of murals was executed for the Department of the Interior building in Washington. In 1936 Jackson's 40,000 negatives were bought by Henry Ford for the Edison Institute. See OVERLAND TRAIL for illustration.

JACKSON, town, SE Louisiana, parish seat of East Feliciana Parish, on Thompson's Creek, about 27 miles N of Baton Rouge. The town was founded as Buncombe by John Horton who named it for his home county in North Carolina. After the Battle of New Orleans in 1815, when Andrew Jackson encamped on the creek, the town was renamed in the general's honor. Until 1908 Jackson was the seat of Centenary College. Today it is the site of a state hospital for the mentally defective. Pop. (1950) 6,772.

JACKSON, city, S Michigan, county seat of Jackson County, on the Grand River, the Grand Trunk and the Illinois Central railroads and U.S. highways 12 and 127; about 70 miles W of Detroit. It was settled in 1829 by Horace Blackman and named for Andrew Jackson. Here, "under the oaks," on July 6, 1854, at a state convention, the REPUBLICAN PARTY was born and named. The 456-acre Sparks Foundation Park in Jackson is noted for its Illuminated Cascades, a series of brilliantly colored artificial waterfalls. Jackson has railroad shops and manufactures of automotive parts, furniture, surgical garments, machine tools, tires and tubes, airplane wheels, and grinding wheels. Pop. (1950) 51,088.

JACKSON, city, SW central Mississippi, state capital and county seat of Hinds County, on the W bank of Pearl River, the Illinois Central and the Gulf, Mobile, and Ohio railroads; U.S. highways 49, 51, and 80; and the Chicago and Southern and the Delta air lines; 45 miles E of Vicksburg. Jackson, the largest city in Mississippi, spreads along high bluffs with the Pearl River forming its eastern boundary. The city had its beginnings as Le Fleur's Bluff, a trading post. In 1822 it was laid out as the seat of the state government and named for General Jackson. The old capitol was the scene of the secession convention in 1861 when Mississippi voted to sever its connection with the Union. During the Civil War Jackson was occupied by Union troops and was partially destroyed by General Sherman in 1864. Belhaven, Campbell, and Millsaps colleges are located in the city. Battlefield Park has ruins of old Confederate fortifications. Jackson has railroad shops and oil-drilling supply houses, and manufactures brick, lumber, store fixtures, cottonseed-oil products, textiles, clothing, and glass bottles. Pop. (1950) 98,271.

Jackson

JACKSON, city, S Ohio, county seat of Jackson County, on the Baltimore and Ohio, the Chesapeake and Ohio, and the Detroit, Toledo, and Ironton railroads and U.S. Highway 35; about 70 miles SE of Columbus. Jackson was founded about 1817 by Welsh settlers. It is located in a coal-mining and fruit-growing region. Pop. (1950) 6,504.

JACKSON, city, W Tennessee, county seat of Madison County, on the Forked Deer River, the Illinois Central, the Gulf, Mobile, and Ohio, and the Nashville, Chattanooga, and St. Louis railroads, and U.S. highways 45 and 70; about 85 miles NE of Memphis. Jackson is an important railroad and shipping center situated in the valley of the Forked Deer River. It was settled by North Carolinians in 1820. During the Civil War, the city was an important supply depot for the Union forces under Grant. Jackson is the seat of Union University and of Lambuth and Lane colleges. In the Catholic cemetery here is buried John Luther Jones, railroad engineer, the "CASEY JONES" of ballad fame. Jackson has railroad shops and manufactures lumber; veneer; cotton bagging; store, church, and office fixtures; cottonseed oil; and candy. Pop. (1950) 30,207.

JACKSON, FORT, a fort on the Mississippi River, 57 miles southeast of New Orleans. In the early part of the Civil War it was strongly fortified by the Confederates but was bombarded during Farragut's expedition against New Orleans and finally surrendered to Commander Porter, April 28, 1862.

JACKSON HOLE NATIONAL MONUMENT, NW Wyoming, an isolated valley of 173,064 green, fertile acres overshadowed by the high mountains of the Teton Range, through which the headwaters of the Snake River flow southward into Jackson Lake.

Jackson Hole winter feed ground for elk herd

John Colter, probably the first white visitor, came in 1807, and although a few straggling settlers came after 1883, the valley was so isolated that it became a favored haunt for fur trappers and traders as well as a convenient hiding place for cattle rustlers and other evaders of the law. A haven for wild game, it has large numbers of deer, moose, bear, and mountain sheep, and is the range of one of the largest elk herds in the United States. Geese, ducks, grouse, and sage hens live in the meadows. Interesting glacial phenomena are found in the valley. Jackson Hole was made a national monument in 1943; in 1950 most of it was incorporated into Grand Teton National Park.

JACKSONVILLE, city and port of entry, NE Florida, county seat of Duval County, on the W bank of the St. Johns River, about 28 miles from the Atlantic Coast; 359 miles N of Miami and 200 miles NE of Tampa. There is a deep channel which accommodates ocean-going vessels. The city is served by the Atlantic Coast Line, the Florida East Coast, the Seaboard Air Line, and the Southern railroads; U.S. highways 1, 17, and 90; the Delta, the Eastern, and the National air lines, and by numerous coastwise, intercoastal, and overseas steamers. Jacksonville, the largest city in Florida and the third largest

Sky line of Jacksonville over the St. Johns River

metropolis in the southeastern states, is one of the most important industrial, commercial, sales, and distributing centers of the Southeast. The port of Jacksonville, the largest in the South Atlantic area of the United States, has a developed water frontage of more than nine miles and is open to navigation during the entire year. Located not far from the Atlantic Coast, Jacksonville is situated in a low, flat region varying from 10 to 25 feet above sea level. It is surrounded by fertile farm and citrus country and by great pine forests. The forests and the city's excellent bathing beaches have made Jacksonville a popular resort to which many tourists are attracted annually between September and May. The area of the city is 39.37 square miles.

Jacksonville is the principal industrial city of Florida and of the area southeast of Atlanta, Ga. It is the second largest naval-stores market in the world, and the largest lumber port on the South Atlantic coast. The major products of the city include lumber and millwork, naval stores, pulp and paper, hosiery, cigars, chemicals, crushed oystershells, bottles, palmetto fibers, and stone, clay, and concrete products.

In 1816, Lewis Zachariah Hogans built a log cabin on his Spanish grant, overlooking the St. Johns River, and the field he tilled is now the heart of Jacksonville. About a year after Florida was bought by the United States, the city was platted and named for Gen. Andrew Jackson, first territorial governor of Florida. Jacksonville's greatest catastrophe came in 1901 when fire gutted the city and left 9,000 people homeless. Upon the devastated area a new city was built, and within a decade more than $25,000,000 had been spent to replace the burned ruins. Ten miles to the south is an important U.S. naval air station. Pop. (1950) 204,517. A. M. K.

JACKSONVILLE, city, S central Illinois, county seat of Morgan County, on the Alton, the Burlington, and the Wabash railroads and U.S. highways 36 and 67; about 35 miles W of Springfield. Jacksonville, one of the oldest and most beautiful cities in Illinois, was founded in 1825. Before the Civil War the city was an important station in the underground railroad. It was in Jacksonville that Stephen A. Douglas and William Jennings Bryan first began to practice law. The city is the seat of the Illinois, the MacMurray, and the Routt colleges and state institutions for the blind, deaf, and mentally defective. Enamel and galvanized ware, meat and poultry products, refrigerators, Ferris wheels, bridges, men's garments, and bookbinding are the principal industries of Jacksonville. Pop. (1950) 20,387.

JACKSONVILLE, city, E central Texas, in Cherokee County, on the Missouri Pacific, the Southern Pacific, and the St. Louis Southwestern railroads and U.S. highways 69, 79, and 175; about 120 miles SE of Dallas. Jacksonville is a trading and shipping center for an agricultural region which specializes in the growing of tomatoes. The city was founded in 1872. Its principal industries include the manufacture of canned goods, crates and boxes, clothing, and cotton products. Pop. (1950) 8,607.

JACMEL, seaport, on the S coast of Haiti, on a bay of the same name, about 55 miles SW of Port-au-Prince, near the beautiful Blue Lakes region. Jacmel has been a commercial center since 1689. Its chief trade is in coffee, cotton and cottonseed, beeswax, honey, turtle shells, bananas, and dried orange peel. Pop. about 12,000.

JACOB, also called **Israel,** was the founder of the Israelite nation that sprang from him through his twelve sons. One of the biblical patriarchs, he was the grandson of Abraham and the son of ISAAC. The best-known incident of his life relates his selfishness and duplicity in fraudulently securing the birthright of his twin brother, ESAU. Having preceded his brother in birth, Esau possessed first inheritance. Jacob, taking advantage of Esau's hunger, offered him a freshly cooked meal of boiled pottage in exchange for the birthright. Pursuing further his schemes, Jacob, with the help of his mother Rebekah, managed to dupe his blind father into giving him the patriarchal blessing intended for Esau. In order to escape the anger of Esau, Jacob fled to his mother's native country. There he was tricked into marrying Leah, and by her and her handmaids he became the father of ten sons. Later he acquired Rachel for his wife, who bore him JOSEPH and Benjamin. After a peaceful settlement with Esau, Jacob and his household returned to his original home. The Bible records several instances of God's messengers appearing to Jacob, the most famous of these being the herald with whom he wrestled and from whom he received the commission to change his name to Israel. He is reported to have lived to the age of 147, dying in Egypt where he had gone to join his son, Joseph. (Genesis 25 to 49.)   R. M. LEONARD

JACOBABAD, town, Pakistan, Sind, capital of Upper Sind Frontier District, 48 miles by rail NW of Sukkur, near the Baluchistan frontier; a railway junction and terminus of a highway. In 1847 it was founded by and named for General John Jacob, commandant of the Sind Horse, on the site of Khanghar, a village. Jacob died here in 1858. The town is the headquarters for caravans from central Asia, and has a thriving grain trade. Jacobabad has the most consistently high temperature of India, ranging in June from 120° to 127° F. An annual horse show is held here. Pop. (1950 est.) 15,000.

JACOBI, FRIEDRICH HEINRICH, 1743–1819, a younger contemporary of Kant, and himself a philosopher, was born at Düsseldorf. Here he held intercourse with a wide circle of literary friends, among whom were Lessing, Herder, and Goethe. In the later period of his life he was for some years president of the Academy of Sciences at Munich, where he died. He did much to direct attention to the true importance and significance of Spinoza, and also distinguished himself by acute criticism of Kant. He represents an important tendency in the thought of the period—viz., that which recognized faith rather than demonstrative science as ultimate, and insisted on the limits of the knowledge attainable by the latter. A philosophy which takes scientific demonstration for its ideal must end, according to Jacobi, either in the materialism of Spinoza or in the subjective idealism of Fichte. Scientific knowledge, he agrees with Kant, is limited to the sphere of the finite, of phenomena. It is by faith, not by logical proof, that we pass beyond the circle of phenomena to an outer reality, whether it be the reality of the external world or the higher divine reality which is revealed to us by an inner or spiritual intuition. But Jacobi did not give to this position any systematic development, and his "faith" itself remains a rather ambiguous conception.

JACOBI, KARL GUSTAV JAKOB, 1804–51, German mathematician, was born in Potsdam, studied at the University of Berlin, and was professor of mathematics at the University of Königsberg (1827–42). With NIELS HENRIK ABEL he stated the theory of elliptic functions and made the first application of these functions to the theory of numbers. He was also one of the originators of the algebraic theory of determinants and established a landmark in the history of mathematics with his theory of Abelian functions.

JACOBINS, a party that appeared in France during the Revolution. At first fairly moderate in tone, and including all deputies opposed to the government, after 1791 it became more extreme and decidedly revolutionary. During the years 1792–94 it was one of the most important influences in France, influencing opinion by means of daughter clubs in every considerable town and village throughout France. Camille Desmoulins, Marat, Danton, Pétion, and all the revolutionary leaders, were at one time members, but the dominant influence was that of ROBESPIERRE. On his fall the club was closed (1794). See FRANCE, *History*.

JACOBITES, the name applied after the revolution of 1688 to the adherents of the Stuarts, more particularly to those who rose in 1715 and 1745, or openly sympathized with them then or later. For some years the activity of the supporters of James II was confined to futile plots, such as the Assassination Plot of 1696, for which some prominent Jacobites suffered. In 1715 occurred the simultaneous rebellions in Scotland and in the north of England. The indecisive Battle of Sheriffmuir proved the end of the Scottish affair, and the English rebels surrendered at Preston. James, the "Old Pretender," who had succeeded to his father's pretensions, arrived when all was over, and was soon shipped back to France. Derwentwater and Kenmure among the nobles, and a host of minor folks, were executed, and many of the surrendered prisoners were sent to the plantations in America. It is the rebellion of 1745, with the charming personality of the "Young Pretender," "Bonnie Prince Charlie," that has touched the heart of romance. The enterprise was really hopeless from the first, but many circumstances seemed to favor it. At first fortune smiled on Charles and his Highlanders, and Prestonpans seemed the earnest of still greater victories. But the Jacobites turning back after penetrating into England as far as Derby showed the Stuart incapacity for seizing an opportunity, and, despite many gallant and romantic episodes, the remainder of Prince Charlie's life was not a menace to the government. The vengeance taken by the English government was limited by the prudence of Forbes of Culloden, and the power of the Highland chiefs was broken by the abolition of heritable jurisdictions, and by the era of prosperity which set in as soon as the Highland menace was removed. See STUART, CHARLES EDWARD; STUART, JAMES EDWARD.

JACOBS, WILLIAM WYMARK, 1863–1943, English author, was born in London. He was best known for his humorous short stories about sailors and longshoremen, the first of which were published in the *Idler* and *Today*, magazines edited by Jerome K. Jerome. The most popular collections of his stories were *Many Cargoes* (1896), *Sea Urchins* (1898), *Light Freights* (1901), and *Night Watches* (1914). His classic ghost story, "The Monkey's Paw," was dramatized by Louis N. Parker, who collaborated with him in several other one-act plays, notably *The Beauty and the Barge* (1904).

JACOB'S LADDER, an erect herbaceous plant belonging to the phlox family, *Polemoniaceae*. Jacob's ladder, *Polemonium caeruleum*, grows about 18 inches tall, his pinnate leaves, and in summer bears terminal pale-blue flowers with wheel-shaped corollas. It is easily grown in ordinary garden soil, and may readily be propagated by root division. There is a white-flowered variety, and also a variety with variegated foliage. Most of the species of *Polemonium* are natives of North America.

JACOBSEN, JENS PETER, 1847–85, Danish novelist, born in Thisted in Jutland; won fame especially after the publication of *Fru Marie Grubbe* (1876), a masterly delineation of 17th-century life in Denmark. His last romance, *Niels Lyhne* (1880; Eng. trans. as *Siren Voices*, 1896), was disagreeably pessimistic in tone, but a very brilliant piece of work. Jacobsen indeed, despite a tendency to preciosity, undoubtedly was a consummate stylist. He also wrote poems, *Digte og Udkast* (1886), and translated Darwin's *Origin of Species* (1893).

JACOPONE DA TODI, c. 1240–1306, Italian religious poet; entered the Franciscan order, and wrote religious poems infused with a most passionate asceticism. He is important chiefly as an author of *laude*, which, in their dialogue form, play a leading part in the development of the Italian drama. In some of his pieces Jacopone inveighed against Boniface VIII, and he took sides against the pope in his struggle with the Colonnas. When Penestrina, the stronghold of the latter, fell (1298), he was thrown into a dungeon, where he languished for five years, till the death of Boniface (1303). Several beautiful Latin hymns (among them the *Stabat Mater*) have been attributed to Jacopone. The first edition of Jacopone's works appeared at Florence in 1490, and a useful selection was edited by Sorio (1858).

JACQUARD, JOSEPH MARIE, 1752–1834, French inventor, was born in Lyons where at the age of eight he began to assist his father, a weaver in a silk mill. Later he became a bookbinder and a hat manufacturer, but remembering his boyhood experience in having to crouch down under a loom to tie the broken threads he determined to improve this device. In 1799 Napoleon I learned of his efforts and installed him in the Conservatoire of Arts and Industries. There he developed the Jacquard loom for weaving all kinds of figured materials, an improvement on the loom invented by Jacques de Vaucanson. See TEXTILES.

JACQUERIE, a revolt of French peasants in May and June, 1358. The name arose from the contemptuous term, "Jacques Bonhomme," by which the nobles designated the peasants. The insurrection had its source in the increased burdens laid upon the peasantry by the seigneurs after the battle of Poitiers, and came to a head in the neighborhood of Paris, from where it spread outward. The nobles, headed by Charles of Navarre, utterly defeated the peasant army near Meaux.

JADE, or **Jahde,** bay, NW Germany, in the North Sea, a few miles W of the estuary of the Weser; area 75 sq. mi. The bay is ice-free the year round and available to ships of heavy draft. On its west coast is the naval port of WILHELMSHAVEN.

JADE, a hard stone with a waxy, lustrous surface, often translucent, and capable of a high polish. The term "jade" comes from the Spanish, *piedra de ijada* or "stone of the side," a name arising from legends of jade's medical properties in curing pains. Emerald-green, or "imperial," jade is considered the most valuable. Gray, opaque jade with a fatty feeling to it is called "mutton fat," and is often carried as "finger-pieces" by Orientals because of its pleasant tactile quality. When accompanied by correct color and translucency, the sound of jade is a sign of genuineness, and because of its resonance, it is often used for musical instruments. See JADEITE; NEPHRITE.

Prized as a gem stone in the Far East, jade took the place of gold in China, where the "Jade Mountains" of West China provided a natural resource for the stone. The primitive Chinese made implements, such as celts, of jade, but the stone early became associated with pre-Buddhist religious customs and a complex symbolism was attached to its various colors. In the worship of heaven and earth the six precious tablets were of jade; heaven was symbolized by a dark green round tablet; earth by an octagonal yellow tablet; east, west, north, and south by green, white, black, and red jade respectively. Jade also became emblematic of the five cardinal virtues: wisdom, modesty, justice, charity, and courage.

Chinese jade sculpture ranges from well-shaped amulets of ring, disk, or tablet form to small figure pieces. In the Shang and Chou periods the style of jade carving was abstract and almost geometric, but later this formalism was superseded by an increasing naturalism. Chinese sculpture in jade reached its height during the Ming Dynasty (1368–1644). See CHINESE ART.

PARKE-BERNET GALLERIES

Carved white jadeite

BIBLIOG.–S. C. Nott, *Chinese Jade Throughout the Ages* (1937); A. Salmony, *Carved Jade of Ancient China* (1938); B. Laufer, *Jade* (ed. 1946); J. L. Kraft, *Adventure in Jade* (1947); H. P. Whitlock and M. L. Ehrman, *Story of Jade* (1949); S. H. Hansford, *Chinese Jade Carving* (1950).

JADEITE, a mineral of the pyroxene group which occurs in compact masses of thin-felted fibers, very tough, hard, and taking a fine polish. It was formerly confounded with NEPHRITE, a mineral of the amphibole group, the two species being included under the generic name, *jade*. Jadeite has the composition $NaAlSi_2O_6$ and is distinguished from the infusible nephrite by its ease of fusion. White, pale-green, apple-green, and emerald-green varieties of jadeite are known. The mineral is found in China, Burma, and Tibet. In China and in other Oriental countries it is worked into objects of great beauty. See JADE.

JADWIN, EDGAR, 1865–1931, American army engineer, was born in Honesdale, Pa., studied at West Point, and joined the Engineer Corps. He was one of General Goethals' assistants in the construction of the Panama Canal (1907–11), and as resident engineer of the Atlantic division built the ship's channel through Gatun Lake, the Gatun Dam, and the Atlantic breakwater. During World War I he supervised construction projects in France. Later, he was chairman of the American section of the board for the development of the St. Lawrence River project (1924–29). In 1927 as chief engineer, he secured congressional adoption of the Army Engineer Plan for Mississippi flood control. A lieutenant general, he retired from the Army in 1929 to become a consulting engineer.

JAEGER, a common name given to certain members of the order Longipennes (long-winged swimmers). The birds are characterized by their predaceous and aggressive behavior. Jaegers have a wide sistribution in the Northern Hemisphere and are most frequently found near large bodies of water. The adults are from 20 inches to 2 feet in length. The bill is dark, thickened, and hawklike; the body, sturdy and muscular. The wings are rounded and of moderate length (most of the other members of the

Jaén

order have long, pointed wings), and the tail is short and wide. There are four heavily-clawed toes on each foot; however, the hind toe is raised and is smaller than the others.

JAÉN, province, S Spain, bounded on the N by Ciudad Real, on the E by Albacete and Murcia, on the S by Granada, and on the W by Córdoba; area 5,209 sq. mi.; pop. (1949 est.) 808,020. It lies on the southern slopes of the Sierra Morena, and includes the fertile valley of the upper Guadalquivir and the highlands north of Granada. Olives, grapes, and cereals are the chief crops, and sheep are raised in the mountains. Lead mining is an active industry, especially in Linares, and La Carolina. The capital is Jaén.

JAÉN, city, Spain, capital of the province of JAÉN, on the Guadalbullon River (affluent of the Guadalquivir), about 23 miles SW of Linares. The town, built at the foot of Mount Jabalcuz, has preserved much of its medieval aspect, with ruined Moorish walls, a Gothic castle with a Moorish portal, and a Moorish castle. It also has several fine Renaissance buildings, a cathedral (1532), and is the seat of a bishop. There is trade in oil, cement, and wine. Pop. (1949 est.) 62,794.

JAFFA, or **Joppa,** seaport, Israel, on the Mediterranean near Tel Aviv, with which it was combined in 1949 as Jaffa-Tel Aviv; 54 miles NW of Jerusalem. The town is called Japho in Joshua 19:46, and it traded with Tyre and Tarshish according to II Chron. 2:16; Jonah 1:3; Ezra 3:7; and Acts 9:42. Jaffa is said to be the place where Peter restored Tabitha to life. The town was attacked by Sennacherib in 702 B.C. The Crusaders captured it in 1126 and lost it to Saladin in 1187. Richard the Lion-hearted took it again in 1191 but lost it five years later. Jaffa was sacked by the Arabs in 1722 and by Napoleon in 1799. During World War I it was occupied by British troops. There is an open roadstead for large vessels. The chief exports are oranges, olive oil, corn, sesame, wool, cotton, leather, and barley. Modern industries include the manufacture of soap, flour, and cement. Pop. (1950 est.) of Jaffa-Tel Aviv, 300,000.

JAFFNA, town, in extreme N Ceylon. It was ruled by Tamil rajahs from about 200 B.C. until A.D. 1617, when the Portuguese took possession. Missionaries of Francis Xavier made converts here as early as 1544; Portuguese missionaries built a Jesuit college and a Franciscan and a Dominican monastery. The Dutch drove out the Portuguese in 1658. With the aid of irrigation the Tamils cultivate Palmyra palms for fiber, and tobacco and curry stuffs. Pop. (1946) 62,922.

JAGERSFONTEIN, mining village, Union of South Africa, Orange Free State, 13 miles SE of Fauresmith, and 70 miles WSW of Bloemfontein. The village owes its existence to the opening in 1870 of the Klipfontein diamond mine, most valuable in the Orange Free State, which has produced the "Excelsior" stone of 917 carats. Pop. (1946) 1,903, including 645 whites.

JAGGERNAUT. See PURI.

JAGUAR, the largest of the New World members of the cat family, *Felidae*. It ranges from Texas through Mexico, Central America, and South America in sparsely settled regions. The jaguar, *Felis onca*, inhabits mainly dense forests but it also occurs in the great open plains. In many parts of Latin America the animal is known as *el tigre* but it is actually more like a leopard than a tiger.

The fur is yellow, spotted with black rosettes that are more complex than those of the leopard and cheetah. It is heavier than the leopard, the head is larger, the neck smaller, and the tail shorter. A mature specimen may be as long as six feet.

Its diet depends upon the environment; it is said to kill tapirs but its chief prey consists of small mammals and birds, and it feeds also on the capybara (the largest living rodent), fish, alligators, monkeys, and turtle eggs. If wild life is scarce it will kill cattle and

South American jaguar

horses. Unless injured or molested it is a much less dangerous beast than the smaller leopard of Africa and India. The jaguar is not as easily tamed as the cheetah or leopard, but fine specimens may be seen in zoos.

In Yucatán and other parts of South and Central America it is hunted with dogs, and often takes refuge in trees as its small domestic cousins do under similar circumstances. Within the species there appear very dark individuals but, however dark, the spotted pattern can be seen in a strong light.   W. A. HILTON

BIBLIOG.–R. Lydekker, *The New Natural History* (1901); W. J. Hamilton, *American Mammals* (1939).

JAGUARÃO, town, SE Brazil, in the state of Rio Grande do Sul; on the Uruguayan boundary; on the Pan American Highway in a mountainous region. Pop. (1940) 10,747.

JAGUARUNDI, a wildcat found in Central and South America, and in the United States only in extreme southern Texas. The jaguarundi, *Felis cacomitli*, is about 42 inches long, the tail comprising almost half of its entire length. The body is long and slender, the head comparatively small, and the legs short. Two color phases are seen in this cat, brownish gray and brownish red. In the latter phase the cat is called "eyra." Jaguarundis feed upon small mammals and birds. They are agile climbers and are difficult to tame in captivity.

JAHN, FRIEDRICH LUDWIG, 1778–1852, German patriot and father of German gymnastics, was born in Lanz. He established the first *Turnplatz,* or outdoor gymnasium, in Berlin in 1811. The physical training which he advocated was aimed to restore the patriotic spirit of the Prussian youth. He commanded a battalion in the corps of Lutzow during the War of Liberation (1813–15). After the war he was appointed state gymnastic teacher. His liberal tendencies and free-speaking manner caused the closing of the *Turnplatz* and Jahn's arrest as a demagogue (1819). He was released in 1825 and in 1848 was elected to the German National Parliament.

JAIL. See PRISONS AND PENOLOGY.

JAIL FEVER. See TYPHUS.

JAINISM, a religion of India. Like Buddhism, it grew out of revolt against Hinduism. Vardhamana, its originator, spent 12 years in strict asceticism before he proclaimed himself a prophet. He is called *Mahavīra,* which means "the great herd," and *Jina,* meaning "the conqueror"; the latter furnishes the title for the religion. The Jain doctrine holds that all spirits are eternal. The various changes through which they pass in transmigrations do not destroy their individualities. Eight reincarnations are considered by Jainism to be sufficient before the spirit attains NIRVANA and freedom from material bonds. Jainist monks take five vows: to kill no living being, to tell no lies, to steal nothing, to indulge in no sexual pleasures, and to renounce all attachments. Two different orders of Jainist monks have been in existence since the fourth century B.C.: the Digambaras, "air-clothed," who admit no women and originally went nude, but have been modified to wear as little clothing as possible; and the Svetambaras, "white-clothed," who admit women and wear complete attire. Jainism teaches that, in order to obtain salvation, all must be guided by *three jewels:* knowledge, faith, and right conduct. Since its inception in the sixth century B.C., one of Jainism's rigid practices has been kindness to animals. This belief that it is evil to kill anything has led Jains to an absurd tolerance of vermin.

JAIPUR, former feudatory state, India, now a part of Greater Rajasthan, in NE Rajputana; area 15,610 sq. mi.; pop. (1941) 3,040,876. Jaipur's center is made up of sandy and barren plains, some 1,600 feet above sea level, to the east of which are ranges of hills with a north-south direction. To the north and west a projection of the Aravalli Mountains ends in a broken chain of hills covered with a jungle growth of trees of little value. Beyond the hills lies the Rajputana Desert. The southeast area of the state is the most fertile. Agriculture is assisted by irrigation projects. Cattle are raised; and corn, wheat, barley, cotton, tobacco, and sugar cane are planted. Manufactures include pottery, brass, cottons, statuary, lacquer work, and salt from Lake Sambhar. Marble, copper, and cobalt are mined, and some precious stones are found.

The ruling dynasty claimed descent from Kush, son of Rama, king of Oudh and hero of the epic poem, the *Ramayana.* The rule was assisted by an appointive council of ministers. After the Indian Independence Act, 1947, Jaipur was treated as a viable state, but later merged with several other states to form the Greater Rajasthan Union.

Jaipur was known to the ancients as Matsya Desh, and was the kingdom of the King Virata mentioned in the *Mahabharata.* Its dynasty (the Jaipur ruler is head of the Kachwaha clan of Rajputs) was known in eastern Rajputana as early as the ninth century, and it is believed that the first maharajah was Dulha Rai, who established his capital at Amber in 1037. In 1818 Jaipur signed a treaty with the British, gaining protection in exchange for the payment of an annual tribute. During the 1857 mutiny Jaipur's ruler remained loyal to the British, and subsequently was rewarded with added territory.   C. S.

JAIPUR, city, India, the largest in Rajputana, capital of the former state of Jaipur; a railway and highway junction, situated 84 miles NE of Ajmer. It was founded in 1728 by Maharajah Jai Singh II, and is surrounded by crenelated walls, overlooking which

Beautiful Jain marble temple in Calcutta

CANADIAN PACIFIC RAILWAY

AMERICAN MUSEUM OF NATURAL HISTORY
Street scene in the Indian city of Jaipur

are rugged hills crowned with forts. Its main streets are wide and handsome. And many of its buildings being plastered with pink stucco, the town is known as the "Pink City of Rajputana." Notable are the ruler's palace in the center of the city, the open-air observatory, the college, the school of art, the public library, and the public gardens and zoo. Jaipur is a prosperous commercial center, and has industries in jewel cutting and setting, enamel and metalwork, and the treatment of marble and inlay. Pop. (1941) 175,810.

JAISALMAR, former feudatory state, India, now part of Greater Rajasthan Union; area 15,980 sq. mi.; pop. (1941) 93,246. The state comprises a part of the great Indian desert, and has a dry and healthful climate. The principal occupation is the grazing of cattle, camels, sheep, and goats, and the population is in a measure nomadic. Jaisalmar is said to have been founded by Deoraj, a prince of the Bhatti family. Jaisal, in 1156, founded the capital town named for him. In 1818 Jaisalmar entered an alliance of "perpetual friendship" with Great Britain, and in 1844, following the British capture of Sind, forts and areas formerly belonging to Jaisalmar were restored to her.

JAJCE, town, W central Yugoslavia, in the Peoples Republic of Bosnia-Hercegovina, situated at the confluence of the Vrbas and Pliva rivers, 90 miles by rail NW of Sarajevo. Features of interest include several fine mosques; catacombs built into the cliffs; a Franciscan monastery which contains the body of Tomasevic, the last of the Bosnian kings, buried in a glass casket; and a 14th-century citadel. The town has one of the largest carbide works in Europe, powered by energy derived from the falls on the Pliva River. Jajce was once the residence of the Bosnian kings. In 1463 it fell to Matthias Corvinus, king of Hungary, and from 1528 it was under Turkish rule. Austria occupied it from 1908 to 1918, when it was incorporated into Yugoslavia. Pop. (1948) 5,177.

JAKARTA. See BATAVIA.

JAKOBSHAVN, town and district, N Greenland, on a narrow bay off Disko Bay, in 69° 15′ N lat. Pop. (1946 est.) 685, including about 20 Europeans.

JALALABAD, town, Afghanistan, capital of Eastern Province, situated on a plain 1,950 feet above sea level, on the S side of the Kabul River; 96 miles E of Kabul, 76 miles W of Peshawar, and near the KHYBER PASS. It was built by Akbar in 1560. Jalalabad is a fortified town commanding the Peshawar road to Kabul, the entrances to the Kunar and Laghman valleys, and the routes to Chitral and northern India. During the first Afghan War it was the scene of a magnificent defense from November, 1841, to April, 1842, by a British force under Sir Robert Sale. Pop. about 6,100.

JALANDHAR. See JULLUNDUR.

JALAPA, town, Mexico, capital of the state of Veracruz, on the National Railway and a highway connecting Mexico City and the port of Veracruz which is about 60 miles SW. Located on the mountain slopes in the midst of luxuriant vegetation, this old Spanish city retains its stone houses, walled gardens, and Old World charm. For 200 years after the conquest, it was an Indian town until, in 1720, it was designated as a trading center for imports brought from Europe by the Spanish merchant fleet. For 60 years, it was the chief Spanish trading center of Mexico and gradually took on a European flavor. Its cool, healthful, summer climate attracts many vacationers from Veracruz. Points of interest in Jalapa are the state capitol, the old church, a convent, and a teachers' college. Jalapa is a noted coffee, orange, sugar, and tobacco market. Pop. (1950) 59,307.

JALISCO, state of W central Mexico, bordering the Pacific Ocean; area 31,152 sq. mi.; pop. (1950) 1,744,700. The state is traversed from northwest to southeast by the Sierra Madre, which, in the south culminate in volcanic peaks: Colima (alt. 12,792 ft.) and Nevado de Colima (alt. 14,220 ft.). The low coastal zone has a humid, tropical climate while the higher inland plateaus are temperate and healthful. The Río Lerma and its chief tributary the Río Verde drain much of the state. Among the numerous lakes are Chapala, about 80 miles long and from 10 to 35 miles wide, one of the most beautiful lakes in Mexico. The agricultural products of Jalisco include corn and wheat grown in the central plateau, rice and sugar cane in the south, and fruits and vegetables. Lumber, rubber, and palm oil are the chief forest products. The principal minerals are silver, gold, copper, and various precious stones. Guadalajara is the capital.

JALUIT. See MARSHALL ISLANDS.

JAM. Jams and fruit jellies consist respectively of the whole substance of fruits, or of their fluid portions only, preserved in a solution of sugar. The quantity of sugar used for one part by weight of clean fruit varies from one part in the case of harsh highly acid fruits like red currants to a half part in the case of cherries or blackberries. The process of boiling serves to dissolve the sugar in the juices that flow from the fruit, to sterilize the whole mixture, and to cause the juice to develop the all-necessary setting properties, which are due to the presence of the little-known "pectin bodies" always present in ripe fruits. The time needed for boiling varies from ten minutes to one or even two hours, according to the kind of fruit. On the other hand, if the boiling be continued too long, the setting powers of the jam may be destroyed, owing to the conversion of the pectin into pentoses. In all cases where steam heating is not available, the process is carried out over a slow fire, so as to keep up the temperature without unduly driving off steam, which invariably carries away with it the aromatic and flavoring principles of the fruit. Commercial jams are boiled for a shorter period than those prepared at home. They contain, therefore, a smaller proportion of inverted sugar and on this account homemade jam is superior from a dietetic point of view. The actual proportion of cane sugar in most homemade jams averages 20 per cent: in commercial jams, from 10 to 50 per cent.

In the preparation of jellies, the fruit is heated— and bruised if necessary— to cause the juice to flow out, and the solid portions are then removed from the mass by straining. The juice alone is subsequently boiled with sugar until ready to "jell." *Marmalade* is a kind of jam made from oranges, lemons, grapefruit, and similar thick-skinned fruits. Much aromatic flavoring matter is contained in the peel of these fruits; so that in making the preserve, in order to avoid loss of flavor by volatilization with the steam, at least part of the peel is kept separate from the pulp, and toward the end of the boiling process is added in the form of shreds.

Location map of Jamaica

JAMAICA, island in the Caribbean Sea, a British crown colony, the largest of the British West Indies islands, located about 80 miles S of the E extremity of Cuba; area 4,404 sq. mi.; pop. (U.N. 1949 est.) 1,373,000. The Turks, the Cayman and the Caicos islands, and the Pedro and the Morant cays are dependencies of Jamaica. A backbone of high land with numerous subsidiary spurs runs through Jamaica from east to west culminating in the east in Blue Mountain Peak (alt. 7,388 ft.), the highest point in the British West Indies. About two-thirds of the island is a high plateau of white limestone broken by many forested hills. From the air, Jamaica is like a rich green gem set in a blue tropic sea. The island's name, an Indian word meaning "well-watered," probably was chosen because of more than 100 swift, unnavigable rivers generally flowing north and south. The largest are the Black and the Cabaritta in the southwest, the Green in the northwest, the Salt in the south, and the Río Grande in the northeast.

Jamaica's climate is moderate for a tropical island; however, it is cool and equable in the highlands while the hot, moist coast has a mean annual temperature of 79° F. There is sunshine throughout the year except for brief periods of rain in May and October. Jamaica's luxuriant vegetation ranges from forested mountains to lush jungles and palm-fringed shores. The rich and varied plant life includes acacia, cacti, orchids, ferns, and grasses. Native trees are the coconut palm, mahogany, cedar, and ceiba.

The 1943 population of Jamaica included 598,267 males and 638,796 females. White people numbered 14,793; colored 216,250; black 965,944; East Indian 21,396; and Chinese 6,894. The chief cities are the capital, Kingston (109,056), Spanish Town (12,007), and Montego Bay (11,547).

Economic Life. Agriculture is the principal industry. Most of the important crops are grown on sugar estates or coffee and banana plantations. Livestock, too, is concentrated on estates and raised in large pens or pastures. The chief agricultural products are sugar, coffee, coconuts, bananas, logwood, pimentos, ginger, and tobacco. Before 1940, large areas were used for the growing of bananas, but because of diseased plants, the banana industry gradually has declined and banana areas now are devoted to sugar cane and citrus fruits. Included among the exports, sent largely to the United States, the United Kingdom, and Canada are: annatto, a dyestuff; cocoa, coffee, coconuts, honey, oils, goatskins, ginger, rum, sugar, bananas, tobacco, and tropical fruits and vegetables, especially mangoes, limes, eggplants, and some potatoes. Cigars are the chief manufactured product for export. The principal imports are shoes, cotton goods, medicines and drugs, food, hardware, paint, grain, and cattle feed.

Jamaica has about 2,500 miles of main roads with considerable additional mileage of cart roads and trails. A scenic highway encircles the island, and

Jamaica

Jamaica grapefruit picker
ALCOA LINE

A tourist trip down the Rio Grande on bamboo rafts
ALCOA LINE

K.L.M. ROYAL DUTCH AIRLINES
Native cart on road from Kingston to Jamaica

K.L.M. ROYAL DUTCH AIRLINES
A solitary silk cotton tree near Kingston

Montego Bay, a popular attraction for tourists
K.L.M. ROYAL DUTCH AIRLINES

Bathing beach at Dunns River Bay near Ocho Rios
K.L.M. ROYAL DUTCH AIRLINES

twisting roadways have been carved across several mountain ranges. There are 218 miles of government-owned railroads and several railroads owned by sugar companies; extensive bus service reaches many outlying communities. Steamer service connects several ports with foreign nations, and there is a considerable coastwise trade. The principal harbors are Port Morant, Kingston, Old Harbor, Montego Bay, St. Ann's Bay, Port Maria, and Port Antonio. During World War II, the United States used the area around Kingston as an important air base for the defense of the Caribbean. Kingston is a stop on the Pan American, the Royal Dutch, and the British West Indian airways plying between the United States, South America, and the adjacent islands. The government of Jamaica maintains a broadcasting station and the island is connected by cable and wireless with the other islands of the West Indies and with the United States.

The tourist trade in Jamaica is of increasing importance, because of the delightful climate which permits outdoor sports throughout the year. Modern resorts have a tropical setting. The principal seaside resorts are Kingston, Montego Bay, and Port Antonio; there are mountain resorts at Mandeville and Montague, and mineral springs at Milk River and Bath.   F. C. W.

Government and History. The administration is headed by a governor appointed by the British government in London. Under the constitution, which was formally proclaimed on Nov. 20, 1944, there is a bicameral legislature consisting of a House of Representatives of 32, elected by universal suffrage, and a Legislative Council of 15, nominated by the governor. In addition, the governor is assisted by an Executive Council of 10, of whom five are elected by the House and five nominated by the governor. Justice is administered by a high court of justice, circuit courts, and parish magistrates.

Jamaica was discovered by Columbus in 1494 on his second voyage to the New World. Villa de la Vega was founded in 1523. Very early in the Spanish regime, the native Indians were exterminated and were replaced by Negro slaves. Spanish immigration to the island was negligible, hence when the British launched an attack on it in 1655 the invaders soon won possession of the colony; British sovereignty was recognized by the Treaty of Madrid in 1670. Under the new settlers the sugar industry developed rapidly, leading to extensive importations of slaves. When the slave trade was finally abolished in 1807, there were 319,351 Negroes held in bondage. A great slave uprising occurred in 1831 during the agitation in Great Britain for the abolition of slavery; a few lives were lost and much property was destroyed. In 1833 the slaves were emancipated and compensation was provided for the owners. The result was a long period of stagnation, due partly to labor scarcity. In 1866 crown colony status was established and the affairs of the island were reorganized. In 1884 the people were granted a degree of representation in the government. Since the island is in the Caribbean storm area it has suffered many times from terrible hurricanes.

During World War I about 12,000 Jamaicans served in the British armed forces, and about 1,000 lost their lives. Also in World War II large numbers saw service on the fighting fronts. In 1940, as a part of the destroyer-base deal, Great Britain granted to the United States a leasehold for a naval and air base on Jamaica. A violent hurricane which swept across the island in August, 1951, took more than 150 lives and caused property damage estimated at more than $56,000,000. The towns of Norant and Port Royal were virtually destroyed.   F. M.

BIBLIOG.—Institute of Jamaica, *Jamaica Today* (1940); S. H. O. Oliver, *Jamaica, The Blessed Island* (1941).

JAMAICA. See QUEENS; NEW YORK, city.

JAMAICA PLAIN, formerly a village, Massachusetts, now a part of Boston.

JAMES, SAINT, called **The Greater,** d.c. A.D. 44, one of the Twelve Apostles and son of Zebedee, was the brother of John. James and John were fishermen on the Lake of Galilee, and were the partners of Simon Peter and Andrew. In company with Peter, the brothers formed what may be called the inner circle of the disciples of Christ. Probably because of their impetuosity they were surnamed Boanerges, or "Sons of Thunder." James was the first martyr among the Apostles, being put to death by Herod Agrippa (Acts 12:1–2).

JAMES, SAINT, called **The Less,** one of the Twelve Apostles, was the son of Alphaeus. He is the traditional author of the General Epistle of James. It is probable that the title of "The Less" was assigned to him either by reason of his being younger than James, the son of Zebedee, or smaller in stature.

The General Epistle of James, is the first of the so-called catholic epistles of the NEW TESTAMENT. The writer calls himself "James, a servant of God and of the Lord Jesus Christ" (1:1), and the work is addressed to the Christian Jews of the dispersion, its design being to encourage them in the midst of trials, and to warn them against various doctrinal and practical errors. The epistle shows no systematic structure, and its general style contrasts strikingly with Paul's. It contains nothing of doctrine in the proper sense, and the name of Christ is mentioned but twice. In one passage (2:14-26) it seems to conflict with Paul's doctrine of justification through faith alone (Rom. 3:28) in asserting that good works are necessary to salvation. It was this quality which led Martin Luther to speak of the letter as an "epistle of straw." But a less capricious criticism than Luther's maintains that the faith which James condemns is mere external belief, and far removed from the burning passion which alone ranks as faith with Paul. The epistle should probably be placed in a relatively late period of the Apostolic Age and as written to the Jewish Christians outside of Palestine.   R. T.

JAMES I, 1566–1625, king of England and Ireland and as James VI, king of Scotland; son of MARY QUEEN OF SCOTS and Lord DARNLEY, and grandson of JAMES V, was born in Edinburgh Castle. Until 1581 he was under the guidance of regents, of whom Moray and

James I

Morton were the most important, and his rule in Scotland was much disturbed by political and religious discontents. In 1582 during the Raid of Ruthven, James was captured by some discontented nobles, who forced him to banish Lennox and imprison Arran, his two favorites, and although the confederate lords in the following year were compelled to fly to England, they returned in 1585 and insisted upon the banishment of Arran, who had been reinstated. In 1585 he made a treaty with Queen Elizabeth which caused a complete breach with his mother, but after the latter's execution (1587), and his marriage with Anne of Denmark, he came into closer relationship with the Protestants. However, he was in constant trouble with both Roman Catholics and Presbyterians.

King of England. On the death of Queen ELIZABETH in 1603, James became king of England and Ireland. His view that he held the kingship by divine right; his impression that Puritanism was the same as Presbyterianism; his wish to tolerate the Roman Catholics; and his determination to exercise absolute power over Parliament, led to conflicts with the House of Commons which continued throughout his reign. Until 1612 he was guided in foreign politics by Robert Cecil, who, however, was unable to bring about peace between James and his first Parliament, which sat from 1604 to 1611. Over the rights of the Commons, over the question of the union of England and Scotland, and over religious matters, disputes arose; and though a Parliament met in 1614, it sat for only a few months. It was not until 1621 that James called his third Parliament. His desire for toleration of Roman Catholics was checked by the GUNPOWDER PLOT, his hopes of a close union between England and Scotland, by the narrow views of the English Parliament. From 1612 to 1618 he made strenuous efforts to bring about a marriage between the Infanta of Spain and his son Prince Charles, hoping thereby to secure the peace of Europe. He had already, by his Ulster settlement, begun in 1607, attempted to give peace to Ireland. But the native Irish disliked the settlement, and were not conciliated; and in 1618, the year in which Raleigh was executed, the Thirty Years' War broke out, and all hopes of the Spanish match were destroyed. Hoping by diplomacy to secure the restoration of Frederick to the palatinate, James sent Prince Charles and the duke of Buckingham to Spain. The mission having failed, James made a treaty with Denmark, and arranged a marriage alliance with France. War with Spain was popular in England, and the Parliament of 1624 was favorable to the king's policy. James was known as a good scholar though somewhat pedantic. His reign saw the beginning of the conflict between king and parliament, later to result in the English Civil War; and the establishment of English colonies in North America. See HARVEY AND MODERN PHYSIOLOGY (Back End Papers, Vol. 11).

JAMES II, 1633–1701, king of Great Britain and Ireland, was born in London, the second son of CHARLES I, and Henrietta Maria; and, when a mere infant, was created duke of York. During the civil war he remained in England till shortly before his father's execution, when he fled to Holland. Between 1649 and 1660 he saw service under Turenne and in the armies of Spain. At the Restoration in 1660 he was made lord high admiral of England, and won the battles of Solebay (1665) and Southwold Bay (1672) against the Dutch. In 1672 he openly professed Roman Catholicism and owing to the Test Act passed in 1673, he was obliged to resign his post of lord high admiral. The excitement over the Popish Plot necessitated his leaving England and in 1679 the Exclusion Bill, to prevent his accession, was brought forward. The same year James returned and was sent to suppress the Covenanters in Scotland, which he did with much cruelty. At the close of 1680 the Exclusion Bill was thrown out by the Lords; and after a stormy period a reaction in favor of royalty set in, which continued till the death of CHARLES II in 1685, when he succeeded to the throne.

James II

Having overcome the rising of Monmouth, James endeavored to secure the repeal of the Test Act by means of Parliament. On the failure of his attempt, he fell back on the dispensing power, set up a new Court of Ecclesiastical Commission, and issued his first Declaration of Indulgence. In April, 1688, he issued his second Declaration of Indulgence. Seven bishops petitioned against the king's illegal command, and were tried. Their acquittal was followed by an invitation to William of Orange to come over to England, and his acceptance was followed by James' flight to France. One of his daughters, Mary, married the Prince of Orange. Another succeeded to the English throne as Queen Anne. His son by his second wife, James Francis Edward, was known as the Old Pretender. Louis XIV received James kindly, and he endeavored to use Ireland as a steppingstone to the conquest of England. His defeat at the Battle of the Boyne (1690), however, destroyed his chance of success, and he returned to France where he remained until his death.

JAMES I, 1394–1437, king of Scotland, son of Robert III, was born in Dunfermline. Sent to France by his father in 1406 to escape the plots of the duke of Albany, he was captured by English sailors en route and delivered to HENRY IV. Meanwhile (1406) on his father's death, he had been proclaimed king of Scotland. As an English prisoner, till 1423, he was treated magnanimously, especially by HENRY V; he was released in 1423 and crowned at Scone in 1424. After crushing the House of Albany, he reduced the power of the feudal nobles and raised the parliamentary power of clergy and commoners; he had the Scottish statute law collected; and he introduced a system of weights and measures and one of coinage comparable to those of England. He was assassinated at Perth by Sir Robert Graham, in a conspiracy headed by the earl of Atholl. James was also a notable poet and wrote *The Kingis Quair* for his wife Jane Beaufort, daughter of the earl of Somerset.

JAMES II, 1430–60, king of Scotland, was only in his seventh year when he succeeded his father, JAMES I. A truce of nine years was made with England, dating from July 1, 1438. During the next few years Sir Alexander Livingstone and Sir William Crichton at first contended for the possession of the young king, but later acted together against all rivals. In 1439 a coalition was formed between Douglas and Livingstone against Crichton, who was overthrown in 1445, though he shortly afterward regained the king's favor. Douglas further distinguished himself by attacking and defeating the Percies. After executing Livingstone (1450), James in February, 1452, on discovering his confederacy with Crawford and Ross, murdered Douglas with his own hand. James, the ninth earl of Douglas, continuing the struggle, was defeated at Arkinholm in 1455. In 1460 the king led a force to besiege Roxburgh Castle, but on August 3 was killed by the explosion of a cannon. Important legislative enactments mark his reign, and the administration of justice was made more efficient by the establishment in 1458, of a court or committee of nine representatives of the clergy, nobility, and burghers to deal with judicial matters. Glasgow University was founded by him in 1451.

JAMES III, 1453–88, king of Scotland, was the son of JAMES II on whose death in 1460 he succeeded. Until 1466 the government was carried on by guardians. Of these the earl of Angus died in 1462, and Bishop Kennedy of St. Andrews in 1465, and up to 1483 James was occupied in making himself the real master of his kingdom. From 1465 the family of the Boyds held the reigns of power until 1469, when the king shook them off. In 1479 troubles arose in connection with James's two brothers, the duke of Albany and the earl of Mar. Both were imprisoned; but, while Mar died in confinement, Albany escaped to France. Owing to the intrigues of Louis XI, hostilities between England and Scotland recommenced in 1480 and Edward IV was assisted by Albany; but the king's death in 1483 freed James from the danger of further English invasions. His weak government provoked a rising of the nobles, which led to his defeat at Sauchieburn, near Bannockburn, and he was murdered while fleeing from the defeat. James III patronized the fine arts, and under him a vigorous national literature was developed.

JAMES IV, 1473–1513, king of Scotland, the son of JAMES III, succeeded to the throne in 1488. Possessed of many accomplishments, James had an enterprising nature and an inquiring mind, but was restless, extravagant, and headstrong. At first the insurgent lords conducted the government and acted with energy and decision. As soon as he began to govern, James placed implicit confidence in Sir Andrew Wood of Largo, who showed great skill in the development of the navy. The years 1493 and 1494 were occupied in securing the submission of John, lord of the Isles. But no sooner had James's triumph been assured than difficulties arose with England. In 1495 James received PERKIN WARBECK, and though he invaded England, a truce was concluded between the two countries on Sept. 30, 1496. In 1503 Henry VII's daughter Margaret married the Scottish king. In 1511 the relations between James and Henry VIII became strained. The capture of two Scottish ships by Sir Edmund Howard was a further cause of irritation. In 1513, when Henry was embarked upon his campaign in France, James invaded England, but was defeated and killed at the Battle of FLODDEN (Sept. 9, 1513).

JAMES V, 1512–42, king of Scotland, the son of JAMES IV, was born in Linlithgow, and it was not till 1528 that he began to govern. For many years after Flodden, the rival English and French parties struggled for supremacy in Scotland. In 1528 James escaped from the custody of the earl of Angus, overthrew the influence of the Douglases, and made peace with England for five years. He adopted vigorous measures with regard to the border chieftains, and established some sort of order in the Highlands and islands. But from 1532 the king's real troubles began. The antagonism between him and Henry VIII, the hostility of the nobles, the opposition of the reformers, were in evidence during the later years of the reign. It only required the outbreak of war between England and France in 1542 to bring about hostilities between England and Scotland. The rout of a Scottish force at Selway Moss in 1542 so overwhelmed James with shame and grief that he died in December of the same year, leaving a daughter only several days old, afterward MARY QUEEN OF SCOTS.

Henry James,

JAMES, HENRY, 1843–1916, Anglo-American novelist, born in New York City, was resident in Europe, principally England, after 1883, except for short visits to the United States. He was naturalized as a British subject in 1915. Born into a family that had wealth, leisure, and the habit of European travel, he was early exposed to that European culture which plays so significant a role in his fiction. He aspired to write in such a way that "it would be impossible to an outsider to say whether I am at a given moment an American writing about England, or an Englishman writing about America." Far from being ashamed of such an ambiguity, he told his brother that he would be exceedingly proud of it, "for it would be highly civilized." He saw as desirable a union between European culture and American idealism—between a culture that had beauty but lacked innocence, and an idealism that had innocence but lacked experience.

His first full-length novel, *Roderick Hudson* (1875), traced the disintegration of a young American sculptor in Rome. *The American* (1877) established his reputation, and *Daisy Miller* (1878) was a popular success. *French Poets and Novelists* (1878), *Life of Hawthorne* (1879), and *Partial Portraits* (1888) gave him standing as a critic. *The Portrait of a Lady* (1881), the best novel of his middle period, develops with mature power the theme he made peculiarly his own: the "international situation"—the American in Europe. In a long succession of novels and stories he portrayed the principal types involved in this drama, from the little schoolmistress of *Four Meetings* (1877), who fed her imagination on pictures of castles and cathedrals and became the predestined victim of the most obvious European scoundrels, to the middle-aged retired business man from Massachusetts of *The Ambassadors* (1903), whose experience in Paris awakens him to values in life that he is too old to make his own. James's

Americans are sometimes naïve, sometimes merely unspoiled—in either case, exposed to misunderstandings, if not actually victimized by the charming Europeans they encounter. In the issue of American versus European manners and morals, Americans usually come off the better in the earlier stories. Later it seems less a question of good and evil than of the different codes of those who live to the full and those who are held back by scruples and unconfessed fears. In James's Americans, the Puritan conscience survives in an infinitely refined form.

Only four novels—*The Europeans* (1878), *Washington Square* (1881), *The Bostonians* (1886), and *The Ivory Tower* (left unfinished at his death)—deal exclusively with American life. Of his short stories, about 80 in number, many are masterpieces. He wrote about writers and artists and their problems with superb insight, and was a master of the subtly terrifying and symbolic ghost story. The most notable of these ghost stories, *The Turn of the Screw* (1898), with its theme of evil taking possession of the souls of two children, has been given a Freudian interpretation, but chills the blood even without benefit of Freud.

In the 1890's James tried his hand at writing plays but failed of stage success. The experiment intensified his striving for dramatic structure in the fiction to which he returned. On the merits of the great novels of his final period—*The Wings of the Dove* (1902), *The Ambassadors*, and *The Golden Bowl* (1904)—critical opinion is divided. They have been held by some to be fantastic elaborations of trivial themes; H. G. Wells compared their efforts, in relation to their meaning, to a hippopotamus picking up a pea. Critics like Van Wyck Brooks, who argue that a writer cannot without loss of power cut himself off from his native soil, are driven to prove their thesis by belittling the later novels. Other critics see in them the supreme justification of James's method, and ascribe the remoteness and elaboration to approaching old age.

The question of the significance of his subject matter is crucial. He preferred to write about people with leisure to develop the delicate intricacies of personal relationships, and with the capacity to be "finely aware" of their predicaments and "richly responsible." When he tried in *The Princess Casamassima* (1886) to write of the aspirations of the working class in London, he chose as hero a most exceptional little bookbinder, who comes to care more about the beauty of the things a social revolution might destroy than about the justice to the oppressed which it might establish. We care comparatively little (James wrote in the preface) for what happens to the coarse, the stupid, the blind. The agents in any drama are interesting only in proportion as they feel their situations. James's subject is not what happened, but what someone with a fine intelligence felt about what happened. Hence the frequent indirection of his approach and his choice of a point of view—that of a fine central intelligence—features of his technique brilliantly analyzed by Percy Lubbock in his *Craft of Fiction*.

Whether his leisure-class life is beautiful or not is another point in dispute. The tendency of recent criticism is to deny its beauty, or call it "a bright jungle concealing a dim beast," and to claim that James himself knew it was not beautiful. The fascination of money in his world is that it is at once a symbol of release from the more sordid compulsions, and a symbol of damnation. In his last novel, *The Ivory Tower*, begun in 1914, there are two old dying millionaires overshadowing the story; to the daughter of one and the nephew of the other was to come the realization of "the black merciless things that are behind the great possessions."

James revisited the United States for a prolonged tour in 1904–5. Stunned by the speed and gregariousness and noise, he felt as much "a belated survivor from a lost age as Trinity Church with its diminished needle of a spire in the roaring canyons of Broadway and Wall Street." Overwhelmed by the material and political power of his country, he undertook a searching criticism in *The American Scene* (1907). When World War I broke out in 1914, James wrote to a friend that the plunge of civilization into the abyss of blood and darkness "so gives away the whole long age during which we have supposed the world to be . . . . gradually bettering, that to have to take it all now for what the treacherous years were all the while really making for and *meaning* is too tragic for any words."

Critics with a strong sense of social meanings in literature have in recent years been giving James credit for a large measure of realistic social insight. The erstwhile "snob" has been hailed as a prophet. Probably because the critics have realized, as James did, what the treacherous years were all the time really meaning, they have discerned in James what had been obscured before. It may be true, as James Huneker wrote in 1917, that the fiction of Henry James is for the future.   DOROTHY BREWSTER

BIBLIOG.–Rebecca West, *Henry James* (1916); Van Wyck Brooks, *The Pilgrimage of Henry James* (1925); P. Edgar, *Henry James: Man and Author* (1927); C. Hartley Grattan, *The Three Jameses* (1932); F. O. Matthiessen, *Henry James— The Major Phase* (1944); *The James Family* (1947).

JAMES, HENRY, 1879–1947, American writer, son of the philosopher, WILLIAM JAMES, was born in Boston and was educated at Harvard University. His principal works include an edition of his father's letters (2 vols. 1930) and two scholarly biographies. *Richard Olney* (1923) and *Charles W. Eliot* (1930; Pulitzer prize).

JAMES, JESSE WOODSON, 1847–82, American desperado, was born in Clay County, Mo., the son of a Baptist clergyman. In 1851 his father died in California, where he had gone to seek gold, and Jesse's mother, after an intervening marriage and divorce, married Dr. Reuben Samuels, a physician who maintained a small farm. At the outbreak of the Civil War, Jesse's mother and stepfather, militantly pro-Southern, were harassed by bands of Union "regulators."

Frank, 1843–1915, his brother, and Jesse left home, as a result, to join the Confederate "bushwhackers" commanded by WILLIAM CLARKE QUANTRILL. They were associated with COLE YOUNGER and other renowned outlaws, and it is supposed that they participated in the "Central Massacre" with "Bloody Bill" Anderson, in which 286 raw Federal recruits were ambushed and slaughtered.

Many apocryphal stories have survived concerning the James boys' careers as bandits, and not infrequently they were credited with robbing banks or holding up trains at the same time in widely separated locations. In the period from 1866 to 1882, while the Jesse James gang was flourishing, its score was chalked up as 11 bank robberies—seven of trains, and three of stagecoaches. Jesse's role as an avenger of wrongs done him and his family was bolstered when Pinkerton detectives bombed his home, killing a younger brother and wounding his mother. The outlaws' luck began to run out in 1876, when their raid on a Northfield, Minn., bank was vigorously resisted, several of the bandits being killed or captured. Jesse and Frank escaped, and, after an interlude of almost three years, reappeared with new followers. Demands for their apprehension became so insistent that the brothers went into hiding in 1882, Jesse going to St. Joseph, Mo., where he masqueraded as Mr. Howard. He was treacherously shot in the back and killed by Charles and Robert Ford, members of his gang, for the $10,-000 reward set upon his head. Jesse became a Robin Hood in folk song and story, represented as robbing the rich to befriend the poor. Many dime novels have been written about his exploits. See BORDER WAR.

BIBLIOG.–R. Love, *The Rise and Fall of Jesse James* (1926).

JAMES, MARQUIS, 1891–   , American biographer, was born in Springfield, Mo., and educated at Oklahoma Christian University. His career in journalism—as reporter and rewrite man for Midwest and New York papers— was interrupted by World War I, in which he served as an infantry captain in France. After the war, he was on the staff of the *New Yorker* (1925) and the *American Legion Monthly* (1923–32). His fast-paced, historically sound biographies, *The Raven: A Biography of Sam Houston* (1929) and *Andrew Jackson* (1937), were both Pulitzer prize winners. Among his other works are: *Mr. Garner of Texas* (1939); *Alfred I. DuPont* (1941); *Biography of a Business* (1942), a history of the Insurance Company of North America; *The Cherokee Strip* (1945); *Metropolitan Life* (1947), another insurance history.

JAMES, THOMAS LEMUEL, 1831–1916, American banker and legislator, born in Utica, N.Y. He became a printer's apprentice (1846–51), was the publisher of the *Madison County Journal* (1851–56) and the *Democratic-Republican* (1856–61) at Hamilton, N.Y., and was inspector of customs (1861–64), weigher of teas in the warehouse department (1864–70), and a deputy collector of customs (1870–73) in New York City. From 1873 to 1881 he was postmaster of New York City. The various important reforms effected by him in the administration of his office attracted general attention, and led to his appointment as postmaster general in the cabinet of President Garfield. He resigned after Garfield's assassination, but during his brief term of office (Mar. 1881–Jan. 1882) reorganized his department and investigated and exposed the "Star-route" frauds. From 1882 until his death he was chairman of the board of directors of the Lincoln National Bank in New York City.

JAMES, WILLIAM, 1842–1910, American philosopher and psychologist. James is probably the best-known American philosopher. He was not adept in the technical manipulation of abstruse concepts; but he grappled during all his life with the basic speculative issues confronting intelligent men of his day, and his doctrines constitute vigorous and original replies to the questions posed by the intellectual developments of the 19th century. He was one of the small group of such thinkers as Justice Oliver Wendell Holmes, Mark Twain, Walt Whitman, and Herman Melville, who brought American culture to maturity. Whether because of his vigor and ability or because he lived in a critical time, there can be no doubt that in both philosophy and psychology the work of James marks the transition from genteel, amateur dabbling to first-class competence.

William James

His grandfather, a dynamic Irishman who came to the United States in the latter part of the 18th century, had accumulated a considerable fortune which enabled William James's father, the elder Henry James, to spend his life in writing and theological speculation and which permitted William James and his brother, HENRY JAMES, the novelist, to educate themselves leisurely and liberally. During his childhood William James studied at school and with tutors in New York, where he was born, and in England, France, Switzerland, and Germany. After a year devoted to painting, he entered the Lawrence Scientific School at Harvard in 1861, and in the following years studied chemistry, anatomy, physiology, and medicine, receiving the M.D. degree from Harvard in 1869. After a period of bad health, he became instructor in anatomy and physiology at Harvard in 1873. He continued teaching there for some 30 years, beginning the teaching of psychology in 1875 and the teaching of philosophy in 1879. He resigned from Harvard in 1907; but his active teaching had been interrupted by poor health several years earlier.

Though he never received formal training in philosophy, and he shifted to the teaching of philosophy from teaching physiology, anatomy, and psychology, James was by temperament a philosopher. Throughout his education he was interested in basic, general problems and followed them persistently through the various specific subjects he studied.

James's Intellectual Life may be divided into four periods. Until about 1878 he was studying, criticizing, and searching for answers to his problems. About 1878 he arrived, as evidenced by articles published at that time, at the general position he maintained and developed during the remainder of his life. From 1878 to 1890 he worked on his great *Principles of Psychology* (1890), applying his basic point of view to many specific problems but leaving ultimate philosophical issues to one side. During the next 10 years he worked on both psychological and philosophical problems but devoted his major effort to the preparation of the *Varieties of Religious Experience* (1902). In the years after 1900 he attempted to systematize his philosophy and to state its important conclusions. During this period he published *Pragmatism* (1907), *A Pluralistic Universe* (1909), and *The Meaning of Truth* (1909).

The *Principles of Psychology* is still a valuable discussion of philosophical problems in psychology, though the parts of it which constitute scientific psychology have been superseded. In its day it was a great stimulus to psychological work in America and furnished suggestions and guidance for later studies. James was acquainted with accomplishments in psychology in England, France, and Germany; but unlike some of the importers of European scholarship, who merely repeated what they had learned, James worked over critically the products of several countries and added his own contributions. Almost all the later schools and special branches of American psychology have some roots of their development in the *Principles*.

As a Philosopher James is famous as one of the founders of PRAGMATISM, though such is his versatility that he may also be rated as the father of American Realism. The motive or need underlying his philosophical speculations can be best described in his own terms as the need to reconcile the beliefs of tough-minded people with the beliefs of tender-minded people. The tough-minded stick close to hard facts, are not interested in abstractions, and are suspicious of ideals and sentiments. Science is their characteristic product. The tender-minded are likely to form their beliefs to suit their needs and sentiments, and to assume that the real world conforms to their ideals. Religion is the prominent expression of the tender-minded way of thinking. James's lifelong effort may be characterized as an attempt to reconcile science with religion. This was indeed one of the major problems of his age; and his thinking expressed the urgent need for creating a new and significant synthesis of 19th-century science with the essentials of traditional religious and moral idealism.

James was tough-minded and a scientist; and he would not tolerate a refusal to accept the results of science or an attempt to philosophize with a bland disregard of scientific facts about the world and man. The theological speculations of his father and the poetic metaphysics of Emerson seemed to him and many of his contemporaries to be the lovable but incredible fantasies of childhood. He was convinced, however, that many scientists and their followers jumped beyond the facts of science to dogmatic materialistic and mechanistic philosophies which would lead, in life, to pessimism and despair. Such philosophies, though they are in harmony with the tough-minded temperament of the scientist, are not facts and are not proved by facts. Moreover, they constitute a picture of the world and man which cannot be used as a guide to action and life because they rule out the ideals and the beliefs on which action is based. James insisted, as against the tender-minded, that we must not reject facts or assume that facts must conform to our wishes and ideals. As against the tough-minded he insisted that, in action and in life, we use and must use beliefs and summary characterizations of the world and man which can be neither proved nor disproved by the facts, and that in evaluating such beliefs we are justified in considering their significance in action and in life.

On Freedom of Choice. The dogma that man is a mechanism having no freedom of choice and that the universe is a closed system of matter and energy in which all events are rigidly determined by past causes is not a statement of scientific fact but a world view or hypothesis congenial to many scientists because it seems to complete their tough-minded way of dealing with things and events in terms of causes and factual conditions. Such a world view cannot, however, be acted upon, because it denies that human beings can act and asserts that nothing in the universe can really be changed since everything is the inevitable consequence of past causes. If man is to act he must assume that he has the freedom to make decisions and that what he does will make some difference in the world. If we admit, as we must, that men, even scientists, act, make plans which they strive to accomplish, formulate ideals which they attempt to realize, and believe that there is a difference between success and failure, then we are entitled to believe that man is the kind of being who can do such things and that the world in which he lives is such that they are possible. The tough-minded person who objects that we cannot prove such beliefs and must consequently reject them is too tough-minded. The tender-minded person who jumps to the conclusion that the world is such that we cannot fail in our endeavors, and that the nature of things guarantees success for our plans and final triumph for all our ideals, is too tender-minded.

James faced life with enthusiasm and a sense of adventure; and he could not tolerate a philosophy which removed chance, novelty, and uncertainty from our lives, leaving everything settled by a cosmic plan, for good or ill. The reconciliation of the two points of view comes in the assertion that the universe neither rules out ideals and the possibility of their realization through effort nor guarantees that our efforts will be successful.

The Central Doctrines of James's Philosophy are closely related to the aim he pursued of reconciling science and religion. He accepted the view to which other people also were led by the theory of evolution, then revolutionizing the biological sciences, that human intelligence should not be conceived as a mirror serving to hold a passive image of the world but should be regarded rather as an organ of adjustment whose function is to guide action. His originality consisted in the way in which he developed the consequences of this view. If the function of intelligence is to guide action, then we should look to the effects of beliefs on action both to determine the meaning of beliefs and to test their truth.

James insisted that many traditional disputes could be closed and many baffling concepts clarified if the pragmatic test were used to find out the precise problem in dispute and to settle the meanings of the concepts or words. As James stated this test, the real issue in dispute between two conflicting beliefs can be found if we ask what difference in action it would make if we accepted one belief rather than the other. This difference in action is the sole point at issue; and if the two beliefs would lead to the same consequences in action then the beliefs really do not differ in meaning and the dispute has been idle controversy about words. Similarly, we can settle the meaning of any concept or word by asking how it would be applied.

The Pragmatic Test for determining which of our beliefs are true is to act on the beliefs and then see which belief guides action successfully. If a man lost in the woods has a map, then the test of the correctness of the map is whether the man using it finds his way out of the woods. According to James, all our beliefs, even the doctrines of philosophy and the dogmas of religion, are ultimately tested in this way.

When we ask, however, how we decide that a belief is responsible for the success of action or how we determine whether or not an action is successful, the pragmatic test loses its simplicity. A man with an incorrect map would probably emerge from the woods sooner or later if he walked straight, and the mere fact that he had a map in which he believed might so encourage him that he would continue to walk. Shall we say that a belief is true if the people holding it act successfully? Shall we say that a belief which encourages and cheers people is true even though it does not guide action in any specific way? James did not evade such questions but he refused to pin himself down closely in regard to them. He was convinced that what we know directly and with certainty is experience, what we perceive; that all concepts and abstract theories are hypotheses serving to guide us around in experience; and that the test of all such hypotheses consists in trying them out in practice.

James was willing to leave to his friend, CHARLES S. PEIRCE—who made important contributions both to the formation of James's views and to the creation of Pragmatism—and to his follower, JOHN DEWEY, the task of working out detailed, technically accurate statements of the pragmatic doctrine. He was convinced that he and his associates had developed a method and a way of thinking which was in essentials correct, which could combine sound reasoning with moral idealism, and which would furnish an intelligible basis for life and action in the modern age.

CHARNER PERRY

BIBLIOG.—C. H. Grattan, *Three Jameses* (1932); J. Burke, *Bundle of Life* (1934); R. B. Perry, *In the Spirit of William James* (1938); J. Nathanson, *Forerunners of Freedom* (1941); *In Commemoration of William James, 1842–1942* (1942); M. C. Otto and others, *William James, the Man and the Thinker* (1942); A. A. Roback, *Willlam James, his Marginalia, Personality, and Contribution* (1942); F. O. Matthiessen, *The James Family* (1947); L. R. Morris, *William James* (1950).

JAMES BAY. See HUDSON BAY.

JAMES, EPISTLE OF. See JAMES, SAINT.

JAMES ISLAND. See GALÁPAGOS.

JAMES ISLAND. See SEA ISLANDS.

JAMES MILLIKIN UNIVERSITY. See COLLEGES.

JAMES ORMOND WILSON TEACHERS COLLEGE. See COLLEGES.

JAMES RIVER, rises in E central North Dakota and flows S through South Dakota to empty into the Missouri 10 miles below Yankton after a course of about 600 miles. Wheat is the chief crop grown in its fertile valley. The river was formerly called the Dakota.

JAMES RIVER, in Virginia, is formed by Jackson's and Cowpasture rivers, which rise in the Allegheny Mountains and unite in the northernmost part of Botetourt County. It flows in an east-southeast direction and at Richmond falls 100 feet in six miles, then increases in volume, and for the latter part of its course becomes an imposing estuary of over 50 miles in length and of varying width, flowing through Hampton Roads into Chesapeake Bay. Its chief tributaries are the Appomattox and the Chickahominy, both made notable by operations during the Civil War. JAMESTOWN colony was founded on its banks in 1607. The river is navigable to Richmond, and is used extensively to furnish power for industry. Its total length is 450 miles.

BIBLIOG.—B. R. Niles, *The James* (1939).

JAMESON, JOHN FRANKLIN, 1859–1937, American historian, was born near Boston and studied at Amherst College and Johns Hopkins University, where he taught (1882–86). He was professor of history at Brown University (1888–1901), head of the History Department of the University of Chicago (1901–5), director of historical research for Carnegie Institution of Washington (1905–28), and became chief of the division of manuscripts of the Library of Congress in 1928. A leader in historical scholarship, he edited the *American Historical Review* (1895–1901,

1905–28) and wrote *History of Historical Writing in America* (1891) and *The American Revolution Considered as a Social Movement* (1926). Jameson edited the *Correspondence of John C. Calhoun* (1900), *Original Narratives of Early American History* (1906), and was chairman of the committee of management for the *Dictionary of American Biography*.

JAMESON, Sir LEANDER STARR, 1853–1917, British administrator in South Africa, was born in Edinburgh, Scotland, and studied medicine in London. While practicing in Kimberley, Cape Colony (1878–91), he became the friend of CECIL RHODES, then prime minister of Cape Colony, and helped him set up the chartered British South Africa Company in 1889. Rhodes appointed Jameson administrator of Rhodesia in 1891, which position he held until the unfortunate Jameson Raid. On Dec. 29, 1895, Jameson, anticipating a rebellion of the Uitlanders in Transvaal, led 600 men across the border to their aid, apparently without orders; but the rebellion was called off and Jameson forced to surrender to the Boers near Dornkop (Jan. 2, 1896). Delivered to British authorities by Boer President KRUGER, Jameson was sentenced to 15 months' imprisonment in England for violating the Foreign Enlistment Act, but was released after serving part of his term because of ill health. He returned to South Africa, where he was regarded as a premature hero, and in 1900 entered the Cape Legislative Assembly. He became Progressive leader in 1903, and was prime minister of Cape Colony from 1904 to 1908. He remained in the assembly till 1912, and then returned to England, where he had been created a baronet in 1911. Jameson supported Rhodes's ideal of a South African Union, and was instrumental in bringing it about in 1910. See SOUTH AFRICAN WAR.

JAMESON RAID. See JAMESON, SIR L. S.

JAMESONITE or BRITTLE FEATHER ORE, a sulfantimonide of lead found in ore veins in sections of England, Czechoslovakia, Bolivia, and in the United States in Sevier County, Arkansas, and in Silver City, South Dakota. It is one of the minor ores of lead.

JAMESTOWN, British coaling station, capital of the island of St. Helena, on the NW coast. It has a fortified harbor. In the neighborhood is the first burial place of Napoleon, from which his body was removed to France in 1840. Pop. about 1,500.

JAMESTOWN, city, SW New York, in Chautauqua County, at the foot of Lake Chautauqua, on the Erie and the Jamestown, Westfield, and Northwestern railroads, 70 miles SW of Buffalo. Jamestown is situated at an altitude of 1,410 feet above sea level in a region of dairying and grape culture and summer resorts. It was founded in 1806 by James Prendergast for whom the city is named. Near by on the lake is the location of the world-famous Chautauqua Institution with its summer school. Jamestown is one of the leading furniture-making centers in the United States. Other products include tools, kitchenware, washing machines, and textiles. Jamestown is inhabited primarily by people of Swedish birth and descent who saw an opportunity to continue their woodworking trades here in the city's furniture factories. Pop. (1950) 43,354. See CHAUTAUQUA MOVEMENT.

JAMESTOWN, city, SE North Dakota, county seat of Stutsman County, on the James River, the Midland Continental and the Northern Pacific railroads and U.S. highways 10, 52, and 281, about 90 miles W of Fargo. Jamestown is the commercial center of a farming area which ships livestock, wheat, barley, flax, oats, and butter. The Jamestown College is located here. Jamestown was settled about 1872 and named for one of its early settlers. Pop. (1950) 10,697.

JAMESTOWN, district, Virginia, James City County, at the mouth of the JAMES RIVER, 45 miles west of Norfolk. Here was established in May, 1607, the first successful English settlement in America. On Dec. 20, 1606, three small ships, the *Sarah Constant*, 100 tons, the *Goodspeed*, 40 tons, and the *Discovery*, 20

Old church tower at Jamestown, Virginia

tons, set out from England with some 120 men for the New World. The men were employees of the VIRGINIA COMPANY OF LONDON who had agreed to work in America as laborers and servants in exchange for food, clothing, shelter, and protection, plus a vague promise of land and a share of company profits in the future. On May 14, 1607, they landed on a small island in the James River, 32 miles from its mouth; this site was chosen because it was easy to defend, but since it was marshy it was one of the most unhealthful locations which could have been found. Rude huts were thrown up, a fort was built, and wheat was planted; an early Indian attack was repulsed, but within a few months friendly relations were established with the neighboring tribes so that the colonists were able to secure corn and meat from them. Unfortunately malaria and dysentery broke out resulting in the death of over 60 persons; added to disease was dissension, especially among the members of the seven-man council. In December, 1607, when 120 new colonists arrived only about 40 of the original group were living. Then came the destruction of the village by fire just at the beginning of the first winter.

The fate of the colony was in doubt for three years, although several new groups of colonists arrived, including the first two women in October, 1608. Malaria and other diseases continued to take their toll so that by June, 1610, only about 60 remained of the 700 who had left England. Also, enterprise was discouraged by the requirement that all supplies and produce be held in common. During these trying days Captain JOHN SMITH, who had been a member of the governing council from the beginning, assumed a position of leadership, and by his resourcefulness helped the colony through its first two years. An injury in an accident forced Smith to return to England in 1609. Famine then came to the colony in the winter of 1609–10; in June, 1610, the dispirited remnant started back to England, but when they were met by the new governor, Lord Delaware, with supplies and new colonists they returned to Jamestown. The crisis had passed but the colony increased only slowly during the following years; in 1616 the population

was only 351 and in 1624 only 1,200. One-half to two-thirds of the early groups died within a few months after arrival in the New World. Fortunately the introduction of tobacco cultivation gave the colony an economic foundation; this crop was first cultivated in 1612 by JOHN ROLFE, who is remembered also for his marriage to the Indian maiden POCAHONTAS. Other factors which promoted progress in the new settlement were the reform in the government, by which the inefficient council was replaced by a single governor, and the provision for the private ownership of land, which stimulated private initiative. In 1619 occurred the establishment of the first legislative assembly in America and the introduction of Negro SLAVERY. The terrible Indian massacre of 1622 nearly annihilated the English colonists, but Jamestown was saved through the warning of a friendly native.

In 1624 the English crown took over the colony, revoking the charter of the London Company, which had invested about $5,000,000 (in terms of present-day values) without securing any profits. In 1676 the town of Jamestown was burned during BACON'S REBELLION against Governor Berkeley; it was rebuilt but the population dwindled because of the poor location. The seat of government for Virginia was finally moved to Williamsburg in 1698, and soon thereafter the village was abandoned. Today Jamestown Island is preserved as a historical shrine; a sea wall has been built to protect the site from the erosion of the river. See VIRGINIA, *History;* UNITED STATES HISTORY. FRANK L. ESTERQUEST

BIBLIOG.–John Fiske, *Old Virginia and Her Neighbors* (1897); H. L. Osgood, *The American Colonies in the Seventeenth Century,* 3 vols. (1904–07); P. A. Bruce, *Economic History of Virginia* (1896), *Social History of Virginia* (1907), and *Institutional History of Virginia* (1910); T. J. Wertenbaker, *The Old South* (1942); W. L. Watson, *History of Jamestown* (1949).

JAMESTOWN COLLEGE. See COLLEGES.
JAMESTOWN TERCENTENNIAL EXPOSITION. See EXPOSITION.
JAMI, NUR ÉDDIN ABDURRAHMAN, 1414–92, Persian mystical poet, was born in Jam (Khurasan). At least 40 works are attributed to him. Seven of his best writings are included in a collection *Haft Aurang* ("The Seven Stars of the Great Bear"), among which are *Yusuf and Salikha* (Eng. trans. by Griffith, 1889), *Mejnun and Leila* (Ger. trans. 1890), and *Salaman and Absal* (Eng. trans. by FitzGerald, 1887). He wrote also a history of the Sufis, *Baharistan* (a didactic prose story book for his son), and other prose works. His collected works appeared in 1890.
JAMMU, town, India, capital of the state of Jammu and Kashmir, in Jammu Province on the Tavi River, a tributary of the Chenab, 80 miles due N of Amritsar to which it is linked by rail. Jammu is the maharajah's winter quarters. The town and palace stand on the right bank, and on the left bank there is a fort. Pop. (1941) 50,379. ADRIAN TROY
JAMNAGAR. See NAVANAGAR.
JAMNIA. See JABNEEL.
JAMSHEDPUR, steel city, India, Bihar Province, in Singhbhum District, 135 miles by rail W of Calcutta, and 205 miles SSE of Patna. In 1907 a steel company acquired a site in what was then a village. Steel production began in 1911, and today Jamshedpur produces about one-half of India's pig iron. The city has blast furnaces, steelworks, and rolling mills. Pop. (1941) 148,711.
JÄMTLAND, county, W central Sweden, extending along the Norwegian frontier, bounded on the N by the county of Västerbotten on the E by Västernorrland and Gävleborg, and on the S by Kopparberg; area 19,967 sq. miles; pop. (1949) 144,257. It lies on the eastern edge of the mountainous Scandinavian backbone, and forest covers the greater part. Some farming and livestock raising is carried on, particularly in the region around Ostersund, in the latitude of the Trondheim gap, where lower altitudes and a better soil make agriculture possible.

There are lumber and pulp mills. Jämtland is a popular tourist region, with a national park containing the peak of Sonfjallet (4,190 ft.). There are a number of lakes, chief of which are Kalisjö, Jormsjö, and Storsjö, on whose shore is located the capital, Ostersund.

JAN MAYEN ISLAND, a volcanic island in the Arctic Ocean, 150 miles E of Greenland, 300 miles N of Iceland; area about 144 sq. mi. The greatest height is Mount Beeren (8,350 ft.). Jan Mayen was discovered by Henry Hudson in 1607 and has been rediscovered many times since. It was named for a Dutch navigator, who reputedly used it as a whaling and sealing base (1611–36?). In 1921 the Norwegian Meteorological Institute set up a weather-forecasting station on the island, which led to the incorporation of the island within Norwegian possessions in 1929. During World War II the island was fortified to protect Allied meteorological observers and radar technicians stationed here in 1941. The radar proved valuable in the warning of Allied shipping against the dangers of German planes and submarines operating out of Norwegian ports. During the war the island was bombed frequently by German planes. The island is uninhabited except for the meteorological observers.

JANÁČEK, LEOŠ, 1854–1928, Czech composer, was born in Hukvaldy, East Moravia. At 10 he became a chorister in the community of the Austin Friars in Brünn, where he studied piano and organ under Krizkovsky. He did not enter the Leipzig Conservatory until he was 25, and made only one public appearance in Vienna at which he played his piano composition, Variations on an Original Theme (1879). In 1881 he returned to Brünn to become conductor of its Philharmonic Society and in the same year he founded his Organ School there. The Organ School was incorporated into the state in 1920 and Janáček became professor at the Conservatory of Prague. The composer's major interests were in the fields of harmony and folk music. He studied folk music seriously in relation to its affiliation with song and with folk speech, and his opera, known by its German name, *Jenufa* (1896–1903), is a true folk music drama. ANNE AND MARX OBERNDORFER.

JANDULA DAM. See DAM.

JANESVILLE, city, S Wisconsin, county seat of Rock County, on both sides of the Rock River, on the North Western and the Milwaukee railroads, and U.S. highways 14 and 51; about 13 miles N of Beloit. Janesville was founded by Henry Janes in 1835. It has been the home of Ella Wheeler Wilcox, Carrie Jacobs Bond, and Frances E. Willard. The principal products are automobiles, fountain pens, textiles, canned goods, porch shades, machinery, absorbent cotton, boxes, furniture, and prefabricated houses. Pop. (1950) 24,899.

JANICULUM, a hill on the Tiber, opposite the city of Rome, of which it commands a splendid view. It was not included within the fortifications until the time of Aurelian (c. A.D. 275).

JANINA. See EPIRUS; IOÁNNINA.

JANIS, ELSIE, 1889– , American actress, was born in Columbus, Ohio, and educated in private schools. She first appeared on the stage in *The Charity Ball* (1897). After touring in vaudeville, she starred in *The Belle of New York* (1904); but her first popular success was in *When We Were Forty-one* (1905), where imitations of popular artists proved her to be a remarkable mimic. Many plays followed, among them *A Star for a Night* and *Elsie Janis and Her Gang*. During World War I she traveled extensively to entertain the American Expeditionary Forces. She wrote *Love Letters of an Actress* (1913) and *If I Know What I Mean* (1925).

JANITZIO, a picturesque island in Lake Pátzcuaro about 235 miles W of Mexico City; area about four sq. mi.; pop. about 450. The Indians earn their living by fishing and marketing their catch weekly at the near-by mainland town of Pátzcuaro. A visit to Janitzio is a favorite excursion for tourists, who are drawn by the beauty of the scenery and the quaint and simple life of the natives.

JANIUAY, city, Philippine Islands, on Panay, in Iloilo Province, 19 miles NNW of Iloilo, the provincial capital, in a hilly area. Silk and cotton are manufactured. Pop. (1948) 44,348.

JANIZARIES, a Turkish military force organized about 1328 by the Osmanli Sultan Orkhan, who for the purpose selected from the Christian families which he had conquered, a thousand of the finest boys. These boys were trained in the Mohammedan faith and carefully educated for a soldier's life. About 1680 the force ceased to be recruited exclusively from Christian families and was voluntarily joined by young Turks and others. They received high honors and privileges and eventually became so powerful and influential that they were a source of terror and danger to the sultans. They were suppressed in 1826.

JANJIRA, small feudatory state, India, under the Kolhapur and Deccan States Agency, situated about a bay among the heights of a spur of the Western Ghats, some 40 miles S of the city of Bombay; area 326 sq. mi.; pop. (1941) 103,557. The principal industry is the cutting of firewood which is shipped to Bombay. The state came under British influence in 1870. The capital is Murad. The ruler is also chief of Jafarabad State.

JANSENISM, a religious movement in France which takes its name from Cornelis Jansen (1585-1638), who was born at Acquoi, near Leerdam, in Holland, and became professor of theology at Louvain (1617) and bishop of Ypres (1635). Certain statements in his *Augustinus* (1640) a posthumous work dealing with the writings of St. Augustine, were regarded as heretical and gave rise to bitter controversy. The distinguishing features of Jansenism were: (1) the doctrine of grace as against the Jesuit doctrine of works; (2) insistence upon a more rigid and puritanic morality; (3) emphasis upon the authority of the Bible and the early councils as against the later developments of the church; (4) attention to education. The community of PORT ROYAL DES CHAMPS, near Versailles, with its nuns and solitaries, was the center of the movement.

In 1652 a papal formulary was procured condemning five theses in the *Augustinus*, and all Catholics were required to accept this formulary. This was republished in 1661, and the nuns of Port Royal were forced to submit to much persecution because of their refusal to sign it. In 1705 a papal bull (*Vineam Domini*) repeated the demand for acceptance of the formulary, and as a result Port Royal was closed, the buildings were destroyed, and the burial ground was plowed up. The controversy broke out anew in 1713, on the discovery of Jansenist opinions in a book by Quesnel, called *Moral Reflections on the New Testament;* and a bull (the *Unigenitus*) condemned one hundred and one statements in this book. The struggle was continued in the reign of Louis XV, but without its former earnestness, having become chiefly a movement in opposition to the Jesuits and the French monarchy. Driven from France the Jansenists took refuge in Holland, where a "Jansenist" church still exists.

JANSSEN, PIERRE JULES CÉSAR, 1824–1907, French astronomer, was born in Paris. He traveled to Peru in 1857, and to the Azores in 1867, for the purpose of correcting magnetic observations; observed the total solar eclipse of Aug. 18, 1868, at Guntur in India, and initiated next morning the spectroscopic method of viewing prominences in daylight. He observed the transit of Venus on Dec. 8, 1874, at Nagasaki, Japan. In 1875, on his return from a third eclipse expedition to Siam, he was appointed director of the new astrophysical observatory at Meudon, and there devoted consummate skill to the art of solar photography. In the course of a comparative investigation of telluric oxygen absorption and the solar spectrum, he made ascents of Mont Blanc in 1888, 1890, and 1893, and erected an observatory on the summit.

JANSSENS VAN NUYSSEN, ABRAHAM, 1575?–1632, Dutch painter, was born in Antwerp, and in 1601 entered the Guild of St. Luke as a "master." A precursor of Rubens, until the rise of the latter, he was the greatest historical painter of the time. He was especially known for the quality of his light and shadow. "Burial of Christ," "Entombment," "Descent from the Cross," and "Night and Day" are representative of his best work.

JANUARY. See MONTH.

JANUARY THAW, traditionally a mild stretch of weather, lasting from one or two days to a week, late in January, particularly along the Middle Atlantic States and New England. One investigator reports "a marked crest in the graphs of the average daily mean temperatures, January 21–23," from Atlanta to Boston over a 50-year period. The storm track across the lower Great Lakes and upper New England is intensified during the winter months. In its midwinter journey a low-pressure area of large extent may draw in the mild southern air to turn the snows of upper New York and New England into deep slush. Severe weather variations are common along the track in midwinter. See WEATHER; WINTER.   V. L. S.

JANUS, one of the most ancient Latin divinities, or *numina*. He was the spirit of the doorway, invoked at entrance and exit, and for this reason each head of a household was his flamen, so to speak, and there were no priests of his worship except the Rex sacrorum. Since the door was the *initium* of the house, Janus came to be revered as the divinity presiding over all *beginnings*. The first hour of the day, the first day of the month, and the first month of the year (January) were sacred to Janus. He was the first god invoked in prayer. The Romans on the Palatine and the Sabines on the Quirinal built a temple to Janus on the road between them; this was left open in time of war against outsiders, so as to allow help to pass readily from one to another, but it was shut in time of peace in order to prevent an over-neighborliness that might breed quarrels. As the god of beginnings, Janus presided over all *januae*, or gates, in Rome; above all, it was he under whose protection was the archway out of which the army marched to war and by which it returned. The tutelary god of the gate that opened both ways was, by a natural transference of thought, himself represented by an image having a double head that looked in both directions.

JANVIER, THOMAS ALLIBONE, 1849–1913, American author, was born in Philadelphia, where he received a common-school education. He worked for the *Philadelphia Press* (1870–81); passed several years in the Southwest (1881–87); and, after a prolonged residence in New York, left America for Europe, spending the rest of his life in England and southern France. His characteristic works include romantic stories and sketches based on his travels in France and Mexico (*The Aztec Treasure House*, 1890; *From the South of France*, 1912) and satirical tales of Philadelphia Brahmins and New York Bohemians (*The Passing of Thomas*, 1901; *At the Casa Napoléon*, 1914).

JAORA, former feudatory state, India, now part of the Madhyabharat Union, comprises two separated tracts in the NW angle of Malwa; area 601 square miles; pop. (1941) 116,953. Its fertile soil produces wheat, cotton, corn, poppies, and millet. The ruler is styled nawab, and the first was Abdul Ghafoor Khan, an Afghan Moslem, who came into possession of the state about 1808. In 1818 Jaora's independence was guaranteed by the British treaty of Mandsaur. The nawab is assisted by a nominated council of five, with himself as president. The capital is Jaora (pop. about 21,000), on an Indian state railway. The people are Hindu.

EWING GALLOWAY

In a few decades Japan shed her ancestral insularity to assume a startling position in world power and world warfare

JAPAN, before World War II a great Asian empire, now an island kingdom, between the 30th and 46th parallels, consisting of the four main islands (and many small islands in adjacent waters) of Hokkaido (Yezo), Honshu or Hondo ("main island"), Shikoku ("four provinces"), and Kyushu ("nine provinces"); area 147,707 sq. mi.; pop. (1950 census) 83,199,637. Before Japan's defeat in World War II the Japanese empire included that part (Karafuto) of SAKHALIN ISLAND below the 50th parallel, the mainland peninsula of KOREA (Chosen), FORMOSA (Taiwan), the KURIL ISLANDS (Chishima), the PESCADORE ISLANDS, the RYUKYU ISLANDS, the BONIN ISLANDS, the former German Pacific islands north of the Equator mandated to Japan following World War I (Carolines, Marshalls, and Marianas—except Guam), and the mainland leased areas of KANTOSHU and the South Manchurian Railway zone; the area of this "outer empire" was 115,280 square miles.

PHYSICAL FEATURES

Topography. Japan is a very mountainous country, the only considerable plain being that of Musashi, north of Tokyo. Honshu is traversed from end to end by many broken ranges with numerous branches. In the northeast the highest summits are mostly volcanic cones superimposed on older mountains, such as Ganjusan (7,400 ft.) and Chokaisan (7,100 ft.). Iidesan, farther to the south, and not volcanic, has an altitude of 6,100 feet. Near it is Bandai (5,968 ft.), a volcano, whose explosion, in 1888, caused the loss of 460 lives. The Nikho district has several dormant volcanoes, of which Shirane (8,458 ft.) and Nantai (8,100 ft.) are the principal ones. Asamayama (*yama* means "mountain"), an active volcano (8,340 ft.), occupies the center of the axial range of Honshu. West of it extend the highlands of Nagano, and beyond is a majestic range of nonvolcanic granitic mountains, called the Japan Alps, 8,000 to 10,000 feet in height, with lofty, detached, quiescent volcanoes on the western margin. South of Asamayama is the famous Fujiyama (Fujisan—12,388 ft.), Japan's highest mountain and a beautiful and perfect volcanic cone, dormant since 1708. Shikoku has nonvolcanic ranges from 3,000 to 6,500 feet in height. Kyushu has several volcanoes, among which are Kirishima (5,574 ft.), the highest; Aso, very active, remarkable for its wide crater; and Sakurajima, which erupted violently in 1914. Hokkaido also has active volcanoes, including Tarumai.

Earthquakes are frequent throughout Japan. There are slight tremors daily, most of which are perceptible only by instruments; yearly six or seven severe shocks; and at longer intervals a terrible catastrophe, causing widespread destruction. One occurred at Tokyo (then Yedo) in 1855, another at Nagoya in 1891, and in 1896, 27,122 persons perished in a northeastern Honshu upheaval. The first on record, in A.D. 684, submerged 1,200,000 acres of land. On Sept. 1, 1923, the greater part of Tokyo was destroyed, and Yokohama was virtually wiped out; other cities and towns were devastated; 44,279 persons died. Yet another earthquake, 50 miles north of Kyoto, on Mar. 7, 1927, killed 3,017 persons, injured 3,440, and destroyed or damaged some 10,000 houses. On Dec. 20, 1946, an earthquake, described as one of the world's most severe, occurred 45 miles off the south coast of Shikoku, and was followed by tidal waves. The southern part of Honshu was most severely affected. On June 28, 1948, a series of earthquakes in the Fukui area of Honshu killed more than 3,000 persons. These seismic movements may be traced to the fact that the shores along the Pacific Ocean are slowly rising, while those bordering the Sea of Japan are sinking.

In addition to earthquakes and tidal waves, Japan is subject to typhoons, winds of cyclonic force which frequently inflict great damage. The series of typhoons recorded in September, 1912, was the worst known in the islands for 50 years; the total damage was enormous. On July 28, 1930, a typhoon struck Kyushu, the southern main island, killing 62 persons and injuring 268 more, and inflicting heavy property damage.

Rivers, Lakes, Seas. None of the many rivers are of great size, and most of them are too swift to permit navigation. The potential water-power resources of the rivers of Japan proper are estimated at 4,500,000 horsepower, most of that already harnessed being converted into electric power. The principal rivers are the Tonegawa (*gawa* means "river"), 180 miles long, in the plain north of Tokyo; Ishikarigawa, 275 miles long, in Hokkaido, which runs into Otaru Bay; the Shinano, which, after a course of 215 miles, empties into the Sea of Japan at Niigata; and the Teshio, 190 miles long, which flows into the Sea of Japan, near the northernmost point of Hokkaido.

E. PAINE

Kegon Waterfall, the outlet of Chuzenji Lake

Among the lakes, formed chiefly through the blocking of natural outlets by volcanic materials, are Lake Biwa, near Kyoto (30 mi. in length); Lake Suwa, in Nagano; Chuzenji Lake, near Nikko; Lake Inawashiro, in Fukushima; Lake Ashi-no-ko, in the Hakone Mountains; and Lake Towada, in Aomori. On Hokkaido are Lake Shikotsu, in the south; Lake Kutcharo, in the northeast; and Lake Abashiri, to the north. With the Honshu lakes are associated many of the hot mineral springs which abound in Japan, and have a high medicinal value. There are a number of fine waterfalls, notably Kegon, near Nikko, as well as many elsewhere.

The coast line of Japan is characterized by extreme irregularity, especially on the eastern shore, where the aggregate mileage is 10,309. Off this side the sea bottom descends abruptly to the Tuscarora depression, at a depth of 4,655 fathoms, which is thought to mark the origin of many Japanese earthquakes. The noted INLAND SEA (Setonaikai), with its beautiful islands and irregularity of outline, extends from the Pacific Ocean to Korea Strait (separating southern Honshu and Kyushu from the Korean peninsula); and has four narrow entrances, in one of which (Naruto Channel) is a famed whirlpool. There are numerous deep bays and excellent harbors. The Kuroshio (Black or Japan) Current, corresponding to the Gulf Stream of the Atlantic, rises between Luzon and Formosa and passes along the eastern coast of Japan and over the North Pacific, finally losing itself on the shores of North America. Its constant shift of position greatly affects climatic conditions.

Climate. Because the southward flowing Oyashio (Okhotsk) Current bathes the shores of Hokkaido and northern Honshu, the northern part of Japan is much colder than places of like latitudes in Europe and America. In Tokyo, the average temperature over a period of 30 years ranged from 37.4° F. for January, to 77.7° for August, with the July-August temperatures sometimes mounting to 80° or 90°; the average for the whole year is 56.8°. The average annual rain-

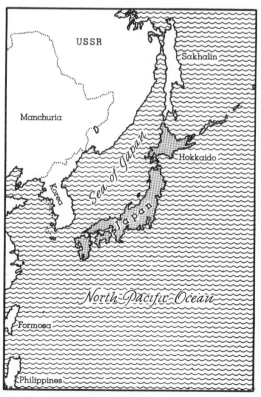

Location map of Japan

fall is 64 inches. Most of the rain falls in June and September, and there is much fine weather in spring, late autumn, and early winter. In Tokyo snow seldom lies long, but in Hokkaido the snowfall is heavy. Fogs are prevalent in summer in the northern and western parts of the empire. The country is visited annually by typhoons, mostly in September. The prevailing winds are northerly in winter and southerly in summer. The climate is healthful on the whole.

Plants. With its wide range of climate and its lofty mountains, Japan has a great variety of vegetation. There are some 3,200 species of flowering plants and 300 species of ferns. The shrubs are mostly evergreen, comprising many with beautiful flowers. Tea plantations are prominent. There are also hornbeams, maples with beautiful autumn foliage, planes, and camphor trees; and many dwarfed trees are carefully cultivated. Nonbearing plum and cherry trees are prized for their blossoms. American and European gardens have obtained many beautiful shrubs and flowers such as the *Lilium auratum*, Kerria, Pyrus, azalea, bamboos, chrysanthemums, *Rosa rugosa*, Aucuba, and Aralia from Japan.

Animals. Japan has one species of short-tailed monkey and 10 species of bats. Of carnivora the largest (except the marine carnivora) is the bear, of which there are two kinds—a small black bear peculiar to Japan, and a large brown bear (the grizzly of North America) which is common in Hokkaido. Badgers, foxes, monkeys, otters, sea otters with valuable fur, moles, rabbits and hares, squirrels, wild boar, and deer are found. Domestic animals include the horse, ox, pig, dog, sheep, and goat. Dogs of nearly all varieties are domesticated. The Tosa, or native Japanese dog, is large-sized and short-furred, with a short, curly tail—a relative of the Mongol dog. The domestic cat is remarkable in having a mere stump of a tail. Rats are numerous.

There are numerous water birds, pheasants (two species), pigeons, cranes, herons, quail, and ptarmigan. Various owls as well as the crow, kite, falcon, and eagles are found also. Songbirds are not especially numerous—the bullfinch and two varieties of *uguisu* ("Japan nightingale") being best known. Swallows, swifts, sparrows, goatsuckers, and woodpeckers are abundant, and there is a fine species of Japanese jay. Of all Japanese birds the *Icteria princeps*, a flycatcher, is the most beautiful. One variety of lark, twelve buntings, eleven thrushes, three robins, a wren, a tit, and various other small birds are native to Japan. There are many varieties of the barnyard fowl, raised for eating and eggs.

Reptiles are represented by 34 species, only one, the mamushi, being venomous. Tiny lizards, including the poisonous night variety, and frogs and toads are plentiful. Fishes of numerous kinds furnish an important foodstuff of the Japanese. Carp and goldfish are popular for their decorative appearance. Among Invertebrata there are some 400 species of butterflies, many species of beetles and spiders, and cicadas and other noisy insects without number.

Forests. As the result of its unusually humid climate, Japan possesses a large area of forest land. The types of forest growth correspond to those found in the Atlantic states, including some 60 species of conifers and pines, and oak, beech, maple, birch, and other deciduous trees; laurel, chestnut, walnut, and bamboo. The long-continued use of wood for building, fuel for heating and the manufacture of ceramics, and later for wood pulp for rayon and newsprint, and the wholesale destruction of wooden houses by fire, however, have lessened the supply of accessible timber to such an extent as seriously to affect climate and rainfall. The fertility of the soil in the river valleys having been impaired through the resulting floods, a national forestry law was passed in 1907, placing the cutting of lumber and the planting of new trees under government regulation. For the succeeding 15 or 20 years bounties were granted for the planting of camphor, oak, and other trees.

Forests are classified as crown, state, communal, temple and shrine, and private; there is a total of approximately 91,500 square miles of forest.   P. W.

PEOPLE

Population. The habitable areas of the home islands, with the exception of Hokkaido, are crowded. Hokkaido, in spite of government encouragement of settlers, has, because of the Japanese dislike for the cooler climates, large habitable areas that are only sparsely populated. Japan's resources are equal to feeding its expected maximum population (estimated to occur in 1970), but cannot provide a maximum standard of living for them. Territorial expansion and industrialization as the answer for population pressure ceased working for the Japanese at their defeat in World War II.

Japan had more than 250 years of internal peace under the shogunate of the Tokugawa family (1603–1867), when the Japanese were strictly secluded from the outside world. In spite of this long period of peace, the population of the islands remained static. The reasons for this nonincrease can be summed up in the economic status which permitted only a subsistence agriculture and simple handicrafts, governmental restriction of movements, pestilence, famine, national disasters, abortions, infanticide, and the government's ready use of the death penalty. According to the incomplete census of 1721, Japan's population numbered 26,065,000. Following Commodore Perry's successful efforts to open trade with Japan, the hindrances to population increase were in part eliminated, and the population rapidly increased. An incomplete census taken in 1852 revealed a population of 27,200,000, but it probably more nearly totaled 34,-000,000. In 1920, the year of the first adequate census, Japan's population numbered 55,963,053. The factors in this growth were the increase in the birth rate and the fall in the death rate. It is believed that the birthrate increase which existed until 1920 provided a momentum that will continue throughout the productive lifetime of the new generations and will insure an increase in Japan's population until 1970. The 1940 census showed a population of 73,114,308, an increase of 5.6 per cent over the census of 1935, but this rise was almost 2 per cent less than that of the five-year period 1930–35. Postwar census figures were: October, 1945, 71,996,477; April, 1946, 73,114,136; October, 1947, 78,090,955; August, 1948, 80,216,896. The sharp increase in 1947 was attributed to the heavy civilian and military repatriations, and the ensuing high birth rate.

Between 1920 and 1940 the population increasingly tended to migrate to the cities, particularly the larger cities. The urban population in 1940 was 37 per cent of the total, but decreased to 29 per cent in 1946.   P. W.

PRINCIPAL CITIES	POPULATION	
	1940 Census	1947 Census
Tokyo, the capital..............	6,778,804	5,385,071 *
Osaka......................	3,252,340	1,559,310
Kyoto......................	1,089,726	999,396
Nagoya.....................	1,328,084	853,085
Yokohama...................	968,091	814,268
Kobe.......................	967,234	607,202

*—1950 census

The Japanese are a composite people predominantly of southern Mongoloid type akin to the Malayans, but with a strong intermixture of northern Mongoloids much like the Koreans. There is evidence also of an underlying aboriginal element brought about by mixture with the Ainu—a generalized Caucasoid type. Long contact with China and Korea led to a great deal of borrowing of cultural elements and considerable intermarriage, particularly

EWING GALLOWAY

Japanese farm woman

EWING GALLOWAY--B. HOLMES

Cultivated rice fields in the Matsui district of Honshu

EWING GALLOWAY

A resident of Kobe

EWING GALLOWAY

Interior of a stockbroker's office in the city of Kobe

EWING GALLOWAY

Young girl of Yokohama

E. GALLOWAY--D. DICKASON

Hardware piled high on a peddler's pushcart in Yokohama

OFFICIAL U.S. NAVY PHOTO

Young Japanese repatriate

ROBERT D. HALL

Rice ration queue in the village of Chiba near Tokyo

Japan

in the upper or ruling class. As a result the population can be roughly divided into two types—one with the sharp features characteristic of Caucasoids, and a second with the broader face, flatter features, and more yellowish-brown skin color of the southern Mongoloids. See PEOPLES OF THE WORLD; RACE.

FAY-COOPER COLE

Religions. The three great religions of Japan are Buddhism, Confucianism, and Shintoism, though the three faiths are not exclusive of one another, and it is quite possible for a Japanese to belong to all three at the same time.

Shinto is the indigenous religion of Japan, and began as a primitive type of nature worship. All natural objects and phenomena were identified with spirits so that the religion represented the extreme to which polytheism might go. The gods were innumerable, and the chief among them all was the sun goddess. During the seventh and eighth centuries, Shintoism became more systematized and gradually the primitive nature worship came to be perverted into a deification of the ruling house of Japan by means of making the sun goddess the ancestor of the emperors. Ancestors, and particularly dead emperors, came to be worshiped, and even the living emperor was regarded as a deity. State Shintoism became a propaganda tool of the government, and was used as an aid in securing absolute obedience to the authority of the emperor, and in building up an extreme nationalistic psychology among the people, based on the Shintoistic doctrine of a divine race ruled by a divine emperor who could do no wrong. Prior to and during the course of World War II, state Shintoism was fostered by the government of Japan, attaining great influence over the people and inspiring them to extreme efforts and sacrifices in support of the war. The defeat of Japan and the subsequent denial by the emperor of his divinity had the effect of weakening state Shintoism's hold upon the people.

Buddhism was introduced into Japan sometime during the sixth century A.D., probably by way of Korea. It was a branch of the northern form of the religion, and in Japan it was split up into a number of more or less distinct sects. Buddhism developed a more elaborate ritual and a more highly organized priesthood than did Shintoism. However, it lacked the patronage bestowed by the government upon Shintoism, particularly during time of war, and although claiming many adherents it was useless as a political force in fostering the spirit of nationalism.

Confucianism, although not strictly a religion but rather a way of living, has also had a long history in Japan and a great influence upon the life of the Japanese. China, with its older civilization, has always

PAUL'S PHOTOS

A Shinto priest in his clerical robes

exercised a great influence upon Japanese culture, and the ideas and ideals of Confucius, imported from China, likewise have had a profound effect upon the thought and life of the Japanese. Loyalty to rulers and filial piety are the principal duties enjoined upon adherents to the tenets of the great Chinese teacher.

Although Christianity was introduced in 1549 by Francis Xavier, the Christians were severely persecuted with the result that Christianity died out except in the region near Nagasaki where several thousand Roman Catholic Christians were found when Japan was opened up to Western trade and influence in 1859 (the date when the trade treaty with the United States went into effect). Missions were established by the Greek church, the Roman Catholics, and a number of the Protestant denominations, including the Protestant Episcopal, Methodist, and Congregational churches. Although the Japanese government tolerated these activities, more and more restrictions were placed upon the missionaries, particularly the mission schools and colleges, as antiforeign sentiment developed prior to the outbreak of World War II. During the war the missionary institutions and property were confiscated and utilized by the government. The outstanding Japanese Christian leader has been TOYOHIKO KAGAWA.   W. G. D.

Education. The education of children is compulsory in Japan; all boys and girls on reaching the age of six are obliged by law to attend school for nine years. Literacy is estimated at more than 99 per cent of the entire population, based on the fact that an average of about 99.5 per cent of the children of school age are in constant attendance at school. The schools are in two general divisions: governmental (central, prefectural, municipal) and private. The former are under the supervision, more or less direct, of the Ministry of Education, while the latter have to conform to the standards established by the ministry. There are four main categories of schools; primary; middle or high school; higher, or college and university; and specialized schools. Schools of all these categories are in both of the two divisions previously mentioned, though the number of governmental is greater than of the private institutions.

There are about 50,000 schools altogether, with some 18,000,000 students; in addition, there are about 2,000 kindergartens. Numerous army and navy schools, as well as military instructors in the civilian schools, were abolished as a result of Japan's defeat in World War II. Also, militaristic and ultranationalistic teachings were expunged from the textbooks. There is a marked shortage of teachers.

PAUL'S PHOTOS

A Buddhist priest in his imposing costume

EWING GALLOWAY

Physical training in a Japanese grade school

The primary schools number about 21,000, with approximately 12,000,000 pupils; this number is constantly increasing because of the high postwar birthrate. Primary schools throughout the country suffered extensive damage from American bombing during the war, but by 1947 considerable rehabilitation was in progress. The great majority of these schools are operated by the cities, towns, and villages; before the war, Tokyo, for example, had 590 elementary day schools and 77 evening schools, as well as 285 kindergartens, all belonging to the municipality; also there were numerous private schools in the same category. In addition to the usual studies, vocational training for the boys and domestic science for the girls are stressed. Six years' attendance is compulsory in this category, and primary schools are in general coeducational.

In the secondary category, in which three years' attendance is now compulsory, there are about 12,000 middle schools, with about 7,500,000 students. Courses vary from three to six years, and standards and curricula correspond generally to those of American high schools. In addition, there are normal schools and thousands of specialized schools for both sexes, devoted to technical, industrial, domestic, and other training.

In 1950, Japan had 52 schools ranked as universities; of these, seven were national universities, 31 were national, prefectural, or municipal universities of one or two faculties, and 14 were private universities. The national universities were located at Tokyo, Sapporo, Kyoto, Fukuoka, Nagoya, Osaka, and Sendai. Among the private schools are some under Christian auspices, and several whose students prepare to become Buddhist priests. Prior to World War II, only 10 universities were coeducational; in 1946, 36 universities became coeducational. University courses vary from three to five years; thus a complete education takes from 16 to 18 years. University professors number about 4,000, and the students about 350,000. The leading university, Tokyo, has seven comprehensive faculties and many attached institutes. Prior to World War II there were about a thousand foreign teachers in Japanese schools.

An American education mission visited Japan in 1946; its recommendations included replacing the ideographs by the Roman alphabet, decentralization of authority, and lengthening the compulsory period. The latter two were effected in 1947. Education, revered from the earliest times, was established as a system in the Imperial Court in the fifth century. The modern system was founded in 1872.

Economic Life

Fisheries. Before World War II Japan had the world's greatest fishing industry, some 650,000 of her employables being fishermen; and employment in seasonal fishing and workers in aquiculture and fish-processing industries brought the total engaged in fishing to more than 1,500,000 persons. About 475,000 Japanese fishermen now are part owners of small fishing boats of five tons or less. These are principally engaged in coastwise fishing. But almost 10,000 deep-sea fishing vessels ranged the Sea of Okhotsk, the Bering Sea, the Pacific Ocean to the Californian and Australian coasts, the Antarctic, the China and Yellow seas, and the Indian Ocean. Prior to World War II the Japanese obtained great quantities of oil and other products from their whaling industry, which was carried on in the Antarctic with a fleet of large, modern mother (or factory) ships of 16,000 to 18,000 tons, each with its flock of whaling boats. From 1946 the Japanese again engaged in this industry.

In Japan fish largely take the place of beef; and besides the fish eaten fresh—some of the choicer kinds being eaten raw—large amounts, both edible and inedible, are prepared by manufacture for future domestic consumption and export. The fish products other than food are isinglass (manufactured from the bladders of sturgeon, cod, carp, and other fish), fish and whale oil, glue, and fertilizer.

Coastal fishing catches are sardine, sea bream, yellowtail, cuttlefish, mackerel, prawn, shrimp, tuna, trout, and herring. Among the deep-sea catches are crab, salmon, whale, tuna, bonito, sardine, flatfish, and sea bream. Aquiculture's chief product is varieties of edible seaweed, much of it cultivated in shallow bays and inland waters. Pearl culture is carried on near Toba, Mie Prefecture.

Prior to World War II the far-ranging fishing fleets of Japan were causes of international friction, and, following their defeat, Japanese fishermen were largely restricted to coastal waters. In 1946 they were permitted to fish in the area of the Bonin Islands, some 750 miles south of Tokyo, and other high seas south of Japan. The great Japanese fishing fleet was considerably reduced in size by air and naval action during World War II.

Mining. Japan is only moderately wealthy in mineral resources. Her coal reserves are estimated at only 6,000,000 metric tons; enough, at the present rate of consumption, to last for 200 years. Two-thirds of the domestic coal is produced near the great Yawata industrial region of northern Kyushu, while Hokkaido produces about one-fifth in a single large field (Ishikari) in the west central part of the island.

EWING GALLOWAY

Miike mine, the largest coal mine in Japan

Japan

In October, 1946, two coal seams were discovered in Okayama and Shimane prefectures, in western Honshu. Japan's petroleum supplies are not large, the principal producing areas being in northwestern Honshu. However, Japan, prior to and during World War II, was producing synthetic gasoline in large amounts from coal and, in Manchuria, from shale. The iron ore reserves are estimated at 60–80,000,000 metric tons, mostly magnetite and hematite, with the chief producing areas at Kamaishi and Muroran. In sulfur and limestone, Japan is self-sufficient; she is semisufficient in manganese, chromium, and copper, and has small amounts of phosphate rock. China clay, pottery materials, abrasives, mica, silver, and semiprecious stones are found; and there are abundant supplies of such building materials as sand, gravel, clay, stone, and limestone, but little gypsum or asphalt.

Agriculture and Stock Raising. Nearly half of the people are agriculturists, although only about 16 per cent of the land is arable. Because of the frequent severe storms and the denudation of forest lands, the rivers of Japan are subject to flood and deposit large quantities of gravel and sand in their lower courses. This increases the natural barrenness of the soil caused by the superposition of ash, lava, and other volcanic products over the original sedimentary and metamorphic rocks of the islands. More than one crop a year raised on some of the land brings the arable percentage of the land to about 19 per cent. Some farm families subsist on little more than an acre of land and the average-sized farm is less than three acres. As a result there is little land available for the raising of forage crops, and the intensive farming is done with hand labor, assisted in many cases by the primitive tools of a century or more ago. A good part of the soil is of tertiary and alluvial deposits, not rich, but forming a deep, friable, easily worked mold. The natural qualities of the soil are supplemented with fertilizers, largely derived from fish, also the so-called night soil (human excrement), and chemical fertilizers. The rotation of crops is not well suited to rice cultivation, and over half the rice land lies fallow through the winter. The system of two crops growing on one space at the same time is used in some places.

Of the approximate 5,500,000 families on the land before World War II, about 1,700,000 owned their property, another 2,300,000 families owned a part of the land they tilled, and the other 1,500,000 families were tenants. Rentals were high, most tenants paying more than 50 per cent of their crops for the privilege of tilling the soil. In the 20 years that preceded the Japanese attack upon Pearl Harbor, the farmers made their discontent increasingly felt through their associations. However, following the Manchurian invasion and the subsequent war with China, the government dissolved many of these groups, and many of the gains made by the farmers were lost. After World War II, the United States occupation authorities demanded land reforms from the parliament (Diet); a land reform bill was passed in December, 1945, and revised in October, 1946. By August, 1950, the Japanese government had bought and resold some 5,300,000 acres of farmland to former tenant farmers.

Rice is the chief crop, and the staple article of food, its growth being facilitated by the mild climate and the tendency of the streams to build up their lower courses. It is sown in seedbeds and the plants are set out in early summer. It must be kept growing in a few inches of water for several months. As rice land must therefore be flat and conveniently situated for irrigation, the valleys of even small streams have been terraced on the slopes. The rice fields amount to about 7,822,000 acres, with a yield of about 342,061,000 bushels. Sericulture is decreasing because of the competition of rayon and nylon, and during World War II the government subsidized the conversion to food crops of some of the areas planted to

EWING GALLOWAY

Japanese Farmer and his wife pedal a crude water wheel to pump water to their rice paddy near Osaka

mulberry trees; however, Japan is still the world's largest producer of silk. Barley, wheat, millet, buckwheat, corn, and many varieties of beans and peas are also produced everywhere. The staple vegetables are the large white radish (*daikon*) and potatoes, but many others are grown. Persimmons, oranges, apples, strawberries, loquats, plums, pears, grapes, watermelons, bitter oranges, figs, and peaches are the best fruits.

The culture of tea, introduced from China in 770, is universal in the middle and southern districts; the total acreage devoted to tea being in the neighborhood of 99,000 acres. Tobacco is under a government monopoly in all stages. The tobacco grown is of a somewhat inferior kind, remarkable for its mildness and dryness. The sweet potato and soybean form a large part of the food of the population of southern Japan, and the culture of the ordinary potato is extensive in the north. The Japanese government devotes much attention to agriculture and large sums are spent annually on agricultural laboratories, schools of agriculture, exhibitions of produce, agricultural associations, experiments, and the like.

Despite low-rate, long-term agricultural loans, and because of the high taxes and meager returns, Japan's farming inhabitants have been slowly moving to the better-paying urban industries. Most farmer families increase their income by engaging in allied industries, such as fishing, sericulture, forestry, and small home manufactures.

There is little area available in agricultural districts for the raising of stock. Also the Japanese eat comparatively little meat. But there has been a slow increase in the amount of stock raised, principally in northern Honshu and Hokkaido. Japan's dairy cattle number less than 125,000; some beef is produced; and there are some chickens raised. Horses have been more widely bred—for farm transport and as a military adjunct. Some of the upland mulberry areas have been converted to sheep grazing.

Manufactures. Manufactures in Japan are sharply divided into the old historic industries and those introduced since the imperial restoration of 1868. The former industries, some originating in China, were improved by the Japanese through long and laborious effort, and attain high artistic value. Many brocades and other rich and beautiful stuffs were made for the ceremonial robes of daimyo and priests, and for other uses. The art of sword making, developed to a high pitch in feudal times, has declined. Lacquer has been made in Japan for more than 1,200 years; it is often ornamented with beautiful designs, in which mother-of-pearl, gold in the form of dust or leaf, and ivory are utilized. The best-known kinds of art pottery come from Satsuma, Kaga, Kyoto, and other ancient centers. Painting and carving have attained a remarkable degree of excellence. Other art products are enamels (cloisonné) on earthenware and copper; articles in bronze, iron, and other metals; and embroidery. (See JAPANESE ART.) The paper of Japan is made from the inner bark of the paper mulberry and other trees, and is extensively used for interior partitions, windowpanes, handkerchiefs, napkins, umbrellas, and, when treated with wax, for waterproof clothing. A variety known as Japanese vellum is highly valued by art publishers. These historic industries are worked at largely in the home and by women. Modern industries range in size from the small two-man shop to immense factories employing thousands, many providing dormitories, club rooms, movies, radio, and other social facilities for workers.

Modern industries, based on American and European models, were established by the government as early as 1875, for the purpose of decreasing the huge preponderance of foreign imports that followed the restoration. They included spinning and weaving, shipbuilding, gas manufacture, and the making of cement, glass, safety matches, and brick. In 1880 many of the state industries were thrown open to private purchase, the government reserving only the salt, tobacco, and camphor monopolies, military supply works, printing offices, a steel foundry, and a mint. Although the quality of Japanese industry was for some time below the standard of American and European work, a surprising increase in excellence of products occurred during the early 1930's, so that Japanese products were on a near par with those of older industrial nations.

Much of the new industry was first sponsored by the government, and the development of industry gradually changed the hitherto feudal life of Japan's people. Supplementing the government in its introduction of new industries were a few financially powerful families in a class called *zaibatsu*. Both they and the government furthered industrial knowledge by sending talented young men to the universities and great industrial works of the United States and Europe.

The first of these new manufactures were household wares, clothing, building materials, and agricultural implements of Japan's own medieval style for the home market; raw and woven silk, cotton and woolen textiles; and pottery, toys, buttons, and matches for both domestic and foreign markets. A small iron industry, and the mining of coal, copper, and sulfur were early established.

After 1910, when Japan assumed full control over its own customs tariff, the government applied protective tariffs which aided in the growth of manufactures. A great impulse to the development of Japan's manufactures was given during the days of World War I as the result of the withdrawal of European and, later, United States goods from the Far Eastern market. Japanese goods were still inferior, and when in the 1920's European and American goods reentered this market they did so at the cost of Japanese industry. A period of retrenchment followed, relieved by the building demands following the great earthquake of 1923 and the increased demand for raw silk and cotton textiles; in meeting these demands Japanese manufacturing efficiency was increased and costs were lowered. After 1929 there was a spectacular development of industry. Japan rose from 15th of the nations producing steel in 1913 to sixth in 1936, surpassed only by the United States, Germany, Russia, the United Kingdom, and France.

For the most part the industries grew up around the large cities, usually seaports. Among Osaka's widely diversified industries the chief was cotton spinning; others were blast furnaces and steel mills. Osaka is the port for the old capital, Kyoto, which is famous for its silk weaving and artistic trades. Tokyo, present capital, also grew with vast industries, important among which was airplane manufacture. Inland, near the sources of Japan's hydroelectric power, pottery and textiles were produced, and these were distributed through the port of Nagoya. An aluminum industry also was developed.

Japan's heavy industries have concentrated near the principal mines. Moji, Yawata, and neighboring cities in northern Kyushu are the centers of the steel industries. In the northern island of Hokkaido, Muroran also has produced steel, obtaining its ore from the Kutchan mine and from Korea and China. Hakodate and Otaru, Hokkaido's other manufacturing cities, produce canned fish, lumber, cement, and hemp.

During the 1930's, Japan's industry was rapidly converted to a war basis to supply her armies in the invasion of Manchuria in 1931, and of China in 1937. Heavy industries were built beyond her peacetime consumption, and following her defeat in World War II, the occupation forces drastically reduced production in these industries. Japan is not a country with large natural resources, and at the height of her production much of the supply of coal and iron ore was imported, as was most of the petroleum.

Without large resources in coal and petroleum, Japan utilizes in great measure her swift-flowing rivers, and has put to use a far greater percentage of the potential water power resource than has the United States. Most of Japan's water power is converted to hydroelectric power, which is used by the railways and most of the country's industries.

In 1948 Japan had some 100,000 industrial plants in operation. Industrial production, however, was estimated to be only about 15 per cent of the average production during 1930–34. The greatest recovery in 1948 took place in the manufacture of metals, machinery, and chemicals. The textile industry continued its slow postwar comeback.

Commerce. The situation of Japan is most favorable to foreign commerce, its island character, limited area of tillable land, and proximity to countries rich in natural resources suggesting a comparison with Great Britain. The growth of Japan's commerce, owing to her peculiar history, is mainly confined to the past 70 years. Until the conquest of Korea about the fourth century A.D., Japan had little intercourse with the outside world. Thereafter Korean weavers, embroiderers, architects, and other skilled workers introduced Chinese civilization; and by 750 Osaka, Hakata, and other ports were in trade with Korean and Chinese merchants. The exports were probably seaweed, military arms, lacquerware, and gold and silver; the imports, silk textiles, embroidered goods, and coin. During the Middle Ages, Japanese commerce developed through the stages of piracy, guilds, and interprovincial rivalry, until in 1541 Portuguese traders were driven by storm upon the Japanese coast. During the succeeding century the Portuguese, Spanish, English, and Dutch kept up a flourishing trade, bringing in brocades, silks, sugar, sheep, goats, potatoes, and tobacco in exchange for gold and silver. The closing of the ports in 1638 to Europeans limited the foreign commerce of Japan to two Dutch and 10 Chinese ships annually; and this condition existed until Commodore Perry in 1854 negotiated a treaty with the United States.

Between 1859 and the beginning of World War II Japan's foreign trade mounted steadily. In 1868 the imports and the exports were valued at only $13,115,-000. Japan's rapid development of manufacture provided goods for export in great quantity, but the scarcity of raw materials necessitated heavy imports also. As a result, between 1929 and 1939 Japan had an excess of exports over imports in only two years—1938 and 1939; and only in 1939 was the excess of important proportions.

In the decade ending in 1940 the changing needs of Japan's growing heavy industries were sharply reflected in her imports. During World War II Japan's imports were food from Indochina, petroleum from conquered Indonesia, and heavy war goods from Manchuria. Her exports during this period were concentrated on supplies to her armed forces.

In the postwar period, Japan's trade, particularly its imports, was closely tied to the United States. The trend after 1947, however, was for a wider dispersion of Japan's trade. The principal postwar exports of Japan were textiles, machinery, ceramics, drugs, and chemicals. Imports were limited to essential commodities, chiefly foodstuffs, medicines, and industrial raw materials. In 1948 foodstuffs and industrial raw materials made up approximately 93 per cent of the value of all imports. Imports in 1948 were valued at $682,613,000, and exports at $258,621,000; in 1949, imports at $510,943,000, and exports at $865,518,000. Much of the country's postwar trade was financed by funds appropriated by the United States.

Communications. The large number of ports in Japan, the rough configuration of the country, and the short distances from inland areas to the seacoast districts have encouraged water transportation. But the four main islands have some 594,490 miles of highway, much of which is paved. And the total railway mileage is 15,250 miles, of which 10,890 miles are government-owned and 4,360 miles privately owned. Some 3,000 miles are electrically operated. Because of the mountainous character of the country there are innumerable railway tunnels. The railways are a popular form of conveyance in Japan, and they yearly carry more than 1,600,000,000 passengers. The first railway in Japan was the Tokyo-Yokohama line (18 mi.), built in 1872. Bicycles, many with package trailers or sidecars, are a much used form of individual transportation. Motor trucks, busses, taxis, and motorcycle sidecar and rearcar delivery vans are widely used.

The Japanese postal system was instituted in 1871, and the government assumed full control of the mails in 1879. Japan is a member of the Universal Postal Union, and of the International Telegraph Union. The first telegraph line, connecting Yokohama and Tokyo, was constructed in 1869. There are some 84,000 miles of telegraph trunks, and the telephone system has more than 975,000 subscribers. Japan has had direct radio communication with all important countries except the U.S.S.R. and Australia, and domestic radio receiver sets are in universal use. Japan's first commercial radio station, operated by the Tokyo newspaper *Mainichi*, began daily broadcasts on Sept. 1, 1951. Before World War II, Japanese air lines provided extensive foreign service. After their defeat, the Japanese were permitted only limited domestic air travel.   C. S.; P. W.

ADMINISTRATION

Government. The constitution of February 11, 1889, drafted by Prince Ito, was modeled upon that of Prussia. Although the constitution incorporated certain provisions for the protection of the subjects, it was nothing more than a democratic façade for an autocratic regime operating through the emperor. The emperor was held to be of divine origin, and therefore his person was regarded as sacred. In addition to being the sovereign head of the state he was the chief priest of state Shintoism. He exercised the whole of the executive powers with the advice of the ministers who were appointed by himself and were responsible to him. The emperor had the power to declare war, make peace, conclude treaties, and was in supreme command of the army and navy. He also exercised the legislative power, with the Diet's consent, gave sanction to laws, convoked the Diet, and might dissolve the House of Representatives. In reality however, the emperor was merely the instrument of forces working behind

and through him. He was a convenient symbol of supreme authority and of national unity.

The Diet consisted of the House of Peers and the House of Representatives. The former consisted of imperial princes, subject princes, other members of the nobility, persons nominated by the emperor for meritorious service to the state or for erudition, and representatives of the highest taxpayers. The House of Representatives was elected by the people (general manhood suffrage was introduced in 1925). The cabinet consisted of the prime minister and other ministers appointed by the emperor. The fact that the ministries of war and navy were filled by high military officers gave the army and the navy great power over the cabinet.

A new constitution was promulgated on November 3, 1946, and became the supreme law of the land on May 3, 1947. The new constitution drastically changed the status of the emperor, who became a constitutional monarch. He is the symbol of national unity, deriving his position from the sovereign will of the people. The emperor himself, at the end of 1945, divested himself of the attributes of divinity. His functions are purely ceremonial and his office remains hereditary. Peers and peerages were specifically abolished.

The sole law-making authority became the Diet consisting of a House of Representatives and a House of Councilors, with the ultimate power residing in the former. The 466 members of the House of Representatives are elected for not more than four years by universal suffrage, including women, of persons over 20. The lower house controls the budget and approves treaties with foreign powers. A bill passed by the House of Representatives and rejected by the House of Councilors will become law if passed again by the lower house by a two-thirds majority. The House of Councilors has 250 members, 100 of which are elected at large and 150 from prefectural districts. Its members are elected for six-year terms, half of them being elected every three years.

The executive power rests with the Cabinet, headed by the prime minister, which is chosen by the Diet from its own members. The Cabinet is responsible to the Diet; on a vote of no-confidence by the Diet, the Cabinet must resign or dissolve the lower house. Judicial power is vested in a supreme court which has the power to declare any law unconstitutional. Members of the supreme court are appointed by the Cabinet and enjoy conditional life tenure. Below the supreme court are courts of cassation, courts of appeal, district courts, and lower courts. The courts are bound to defend the civil rights of the people as granted by the bill of rights of the constitution, and those provisions of the constitution which grant powers to the regional or local governments. Japan is divided into prefectures, municipalities, towns, and villages, and each of them has a representative assembly. The governors of the prefectures and the municipal mayors are elected.

In the January 23, 1949, election the Democratic Liberals won a decisive victory. They formed a coalition government with the Democrats and members of the Green Breeze party. The Democratic Liberal party is conservative and advocates return to free enterprise. The Democratic party advocates strict economic controls but does not favor nationalization. The Green Breeze party is composed of conservative elements but has no specific platform. The Social Democrat party advocates socialism but rigidly opposes political collaboration with the Communist party which advocates the doctrines of the Soviet Union.

Until the peace treaty provided for the withdrawal of the Allied Powers, the latter exercised full, but self-limited, government to insure that Japan would become a democracy. The Supreme Commander for the Allied Powers was the sole executive authority for

U.S. ARMY SIGNAL CORPS

Japanese Woman, wearing native costume and carrying baby in traditional manner, casts vote at polls

the Allied Powers in Japan. He was advised by the Allied Council for Japan, which had no executive authority, and the Far Eastern Commission, whose recommendations were forwarded to the Supreme Commander. U.S. state and defense department officials served on the Commission.   G. B. DE H.

Armed Forces. In 1862 the government of the shogun began the introduction of the European military system. In 1873 military conscription was adopted and was gradually extended during the next two decades. The Japanese took the German military system as their model. The fighting efficiency of the modernized army was proved in the Sino-Japanese War of 1894–95 and the great Russo-Japanese War of 1904–05. Under the Japanese military system which prevailed up to World War II, all males between 17 and 40 were liable for service. The normal peacetime strength of the army was about 15,000 officers and 242,000 men, including the air forces. The Manchurian invasion (1931) and the Chinese "incident" (1937) demanded larger forces and at the beginning of World War II it was estimated that the Japanese army numbered between 2,500,000 and 3,000,000 men.

The character of the Japanese soldier was unique among modern armies, and the civilized world was shocked when it was revealed that Allied forces had taken but a handful of Japanese prisoners because the Japanese soldier's fanatical patriotism demanded that he fight no matter how hopeless the odds. Only the Imperial rescript, admitting Japanese defeat and broadcast by the emperor, induced the army to surrender.

The Japanese navy took the British navy for its model, just as the army was patterned after the German army. The navy gave a good account of itself in both the Sino-Japanese and the Russo-Japanese wars. The strength of the Japanese navy was extended before and during World War I. But at the Washington Naval Conference of 1921–22 Japan agreed to the 5–5–3 ratio in capital ships, by which her strength was limited to three-fifths that of either the United States or Great Britain. The Japanese brought an end to naval limitation by walking out of the London Naval Conference of 1935–36. At the time of her attack on Pearl Harbor (Dec. 7, 1941) the Japanese had at least 10 Washington treaty battleships (with two more under construction—completed during the war), 9 aircraft carriers, 45 cruisers, 126 destroyers, and 70 submarines. At the end of the war there remained only 1 battleship, 2 heavy aircraft carriers, 2 light carriers, 2 heavy cruisers, a few submarines, destroyers, and auxiliary vessels.

Both the army and navy were rapidly demobilized under Allied orders after the war; under the new constitution promulgated by the emperor on Nov. 3,

1946, Japan renounced war as a policy of state and abolished its armed forces. The Allied Supreme Command later authorized a coast guard of 125 vessels and a national rural police force; in 1950 the latter was increased to 75,000 men.   C. S.

HISTORY

Prehistoric and Legendary Period. The origin of the Japanese people is a mystery that has fascinated but baffled many ethnologists and historians of many lands, including the Japanese themselves. The earliest known inhabitants of the Japanese islands were of two neolithic cultures, as indicated by human remains and pottery and other relics found in mounds, caves, pits, shell heaps and other neolithic sites. The first culture, called Jomon, was one of the highest neolithic kinds yet found in the world. It is surmised that it went through a very long period of development in Japan by a Caucasoid people who in the remote past migrated across the northern part of the Eurasian continent and spread over the islands. The early Japanese called them Emishi; their descendants are the AINU, now living in scattered groups in Hokkaido. The people of the second culture, called Yayoi, also of an advanced type, are thought to have been of Mongol stock from the Asian mainland, and to have coalesced with the Jomon people. Other aborigines, whom the Japanese found in Kyushu, called Kumaso, are conjectured to have been carried there by the Black (Japan) Current from Borneo. They disappeared, though they may have been identical with the Hayato, a race of captive slaves mentioned in Japanese annals from prehistoric times down to A.D. 694. How much, if anything beyond intermarriage to a small extent, these various peoples had to do with the formation of the Japanese, or Yamato, is problematical.

One thing seems to be certain about the Yamato people, namely that they are not composed of any one greatly predominant original stock. At some undetermined period, possibly between 25 and 30 centuries ago, several waves of migrants arrived in the islands, from perhaps three sources: northeast Asia, via Korea, of Mongol or Tungusic stock; somewhere in China; and the islands or mainland of southeast Asia, carried by the Black Current, with some of these people being carried by the northwest branch of the current to participate in populating Korea. In the course of time there was much migration back and forth between Korea and southwest Japan. These peoples—which, if any, was the more numerous is unknown—settled in Kyushu, Izumo in western Honshu, and Shikoku, and coalesced into the Yamato. Through succeeding centuries they drove the Emishi into eastern and northern Honshu and finally into Hokkaido. The story is allegorically and incompletely told in two histories, the *Kojiki* and *Nihongi*, compiled A.D. 712 and 720 respectively. Prominent in these records is a queen or princess, chief of the strongest of the migrant peoples, named Amaterasu Omikami, literally, Heavenly Shining Great Female Person (the so-called "sun goddess"). One of her descendants, Prince Iware, became the first emperor of the Yamato, with the name JIMMU.

Earliest Historic Age (660 B.C.–A.D. 592). Jimmu was proclaimed emperor at Kashiwabara in the Yamato region, south of the present Osaka, in west central Honshu. The date of this, 660 B.C., is that given in the *Nihongi*, but its accuracy is doubted; some historians think there is a possible discrepancy of several centuries. The dynasty founded by Jimmu has continued, in the same family though not always from father to son, to the present day, and is one of the chief sources of pride, as well as of national cohesion and strength, of the Japanese people; it is the oldest lineage known to the world.

There is some surmise that Yamato was the name given, in the earliest time, to the whole of Honshu, or all the islands; but later it was restricted to the region where Jimmu was named emperor. At some unknown time the people began to call their country NIPPON (Nihon), or Dai Nippon, apparently about 2,000 years ago. Neither Jimmu nor his early successors ruled over the whole of what is now Japan; consolidation of the empire was gradual, through a period of centuries.

This age, down to the end of the sixth century A.D., saw the growth of the family system, another great source of strength of the nation to the present time. It began with eight main families, or uji, from which came the military chieftains and administrators. Around these families grew countless others, many of Korean and some of Chinese ancestry.

Also evolved in this period was Shinto, at first the primitive religion of the Japanese, which became the national cult whose main concept is reverence for the imperial family and reverence for and communion with the spirits, or souls, of those who have gone before. The first recorded mention of the word Shinto, in the Nihongi, is that "Emperor Yomei (A.D. 586-7) believed in the Buddhist law and reverenced Shinto." The definite beginning of Shinto probably was when Emperor Suinin, A.D. 11, founded the Imperial Shrines of Ise, dedicated to Amaterasu Omikami; the mirror, one of the three imperial treasures, was then enshrined as her symbol by the emperor, and has been preserved there ever since. Imperial enthronement, marriage and burial rites have been completely Shinto, down to the present day. BUDDHISM, also to have a profound effect on all Japan's future, was introduced from Korea, A.D. 552 (or 538); at first it was received with skepticism, but it became firmly established during the next century, and since then has been the religion of the Japanese. See SHINTOISM.

Previously, A.D. 405 (or 379), a Korean scholar, Atogi (or Achiki) arrived, and he began teaching the Chinese classics at the imperial court. This was the beginning, as far as is known, of Japanese education, though the Japanese court had been using the ideographs at least as early as the second century B.C.

Another event of this era was the Great invasion of Korea by the celebrated Empress JINGO, widowed consort of Emperor Chuai, and herself of Korean royal descent, in or about the fourth century A.D. Thereafter Japan exercised ascendancy over a large part of the peninsula for several centuries. It can be said that circumstantial evidence plays a considerable role in Japanese history down to the end of the fourth century A.D.

Nara Epoch (593-781). Though Japan's first great capital was not founded at Nara until 710, the events of this epoch centered in the district around Nara. The outstanding personalities were Prince Regent Shotoku and Kamatari, and the outstanding events were the establishment of Buddhism, the rise of the Fujiwara family, of which Kamatari was the head, and the partial adoption of the Kung Fu-tse (Confucius) doctrine, whose main concept governs family relations.

Shotoku (572-621) was one of the great men of Japanese history; his integrity, learning and statesmanship were of the highest; tradition says he was born at a stable door, hence his youthful name, Umayado. Shotoku was chiefly instrumental in establishing Buddhism, and caused the building of the first great temple, Shitennoji, at present Osaka, and the Horyuji (A.D. 607), near Nara, which remains as the world's oldest wooden building. Countless other temples arose in the empire, which then comprised the southwestern half of the islands. With Buddhism came a tremendous influx of culture from China, with which the Japanese combined their own culture and built their own civilization. It is an irony of history that Buddhism, which looks askance at woman, was established during the reign of a female sovereign, Empress Suiko (A.D. 593-628), and further enhanced during the reign of Empress Kogyoku (642-645).

Among his many activities, Shotoku issued (604) Japan's first constitution, ethical injunctions in 17 articles. Several of its provisions were for the welfare of the common people. The great statesman Kamatari brought about the sweeping Daika (great change) reforms (645), in reality a comprehensive national and provincial administration. The Fujiwara were powerful thereafter for centuries; they continued influential to the present day; and Prince Konoye, three times premier in the years before World War II, was head of one of the Fujiwara five family divisions. It became the custom for imperial consorts to be taken from the Fujiwara family. Japan's first code of laws was compiled in 667; it was greatly elaborated in the Daiho (701) and Yoro (718) civil and penal codes; later revisions were made in the 9th and 10th centuries.

Cultural and commercial intercourse was carried on with China and Korea, but Japan lost her influence in the latter following a naval battle (662) near the peninsula, in which her forces were soundly beaten by the Chinese. During the Nara era proper, music, painting, literature, and other forms of art, as well as agriculture, sericulture and architecture flourished. Highways were constructed, and gold, silver, and copper coins came into general use. There was a great uprising by the Emishi in eastern Honshu in 774, not suppressed until 794 when the imperial forces pushed the aborigines into the northern part of the island. A noted scholar, Kibi no Makibi (693-775), invented, to supplement the ideographs, the kana syllabary, still in constant use. Also in this era occurred the only known case of a subject who tried (in vain) to usurp the throne, that of a priest, Doken, lover of the reigning Empress Shotoku (765-770) and famed in Japanese annals for his extraordinary sex appeal. Previously the imperial lady had had a torrid liaison with a Fujiwara statesman.

Heian or Earlier Kyoto Age (782-1185). Emperor Kwammu, whose reign began in 782, did not occupy Kyoto, his newly constructed capital, until 795. The name of this long era came from the main palace, Heian-jo (Peace and Tranquility Castle, or Palace) and an alternate name of the capital, Heian-kyo. With the wealth of palaces, splendid temples and shrines, luxurious dwellings and gardens that were built, as well as a numerous population, it became one of the world's great cities, and one of the most beautiful, which it still is. Luxury prevailed in this setting, and art and literature reached a high level. One of the world's great books, Genji Monogatari, was written (about 1020) by a court lady, Murasaki Shikibu. The original Imperial University, adjoining the main palace, taught law, mathematics, and Chinese classics; Sugawara Michizane (845-903) was one of the outstanding scholars in Japanese history. Trade and agriculture, and the welfare of the people, prospered during the earlier part of the era, but later declined. Intercourse with China, especially regarding Buddhism and philosophy, as well as trade, went on intermittently. Buddhism acquired great power; one of Japan's most renowned priests, Kobo Daishi (Kukai), founded the famed monastery on Mount Koya, and another noted temple, Enryakuji, was built on Mount Hiei, near Kyoto, among many others. It became a rather frequent practice for emperors to abdicate and enter retirement palaces or the priesthood, sometimes, however, retaining the actual power. The slave class, composed of war captives and degraded persons and their descendants, passed out of existence in the 10th century, absorbed into the common people.

The Fujiwara remained pre-eminent until the 11th century, when they began to be eclipsed by another great family, the Minamoto, descended from Emperor Saga (810-823); its famous descendants were the Ashikaga and Tokugawa shogun dynasties. The Minamoto waged a bitter war with the Taira family, in which the latter, under Kiyomori (1118-81), was temporarily victorious. This epoch, known as Gen-

Daibutsu, huge figure of Buddha at Kamakura

Pei, was the source of some of Japan's great stage dramas; it also caused the rise of the SAMURAI, or bushi (whence bushido, the code of loyalty of the samurai). The Taira were crushed (1185) by the revived Minamoto under Yoritomo, first of the shoguns.

Kamakura Era (1186-1334). Yoritomo, while maintaining deep respect toward the emperor, founded (1180–84) a military-civil administration, known as Bakufu, at Kamakura, which accordingly became the political capital and a great city (now a noted seaside resort), though Kyoto remained the imperial capital. Emperor Go-Toba appointed Yoritomo as shogun in 1192, marking the emperors' loss of administrative power until the Meiji Restoration (1867).

Education made great advances, as the terakoya (Buddhist temple schools) began to flourish, and the Ashikaga College was founded. The austere life of the Kamakura samurai, as well as a new influx of Chinese culture, gave a fresh impetus to art and literature. Fine arts, artisanry, and popular industry progressed. The Kamakura Daibutsu (Great Image of Buddha), one of the world's great works of religious art, is ascribed to Yoritomo.

The third shogun, Sanetomo, was assassinated (1219), ending Minamoto rule. Thereafter the country was governed, mostly well, by the Hojo line of regents in the name of a succession of child shoguns, until 1333. Regent Tokimune's administration was noted for the repulse of Kublai Khan's attempts to subjugate Japan (1274 and 1281). The Zen introspective doctrine of Buddhism rose to fame in this era. A new code of laws, named Joei, enacted in 1232, remained in force until the Meiji Restoration. See SHOGUN.

Muromachi, or Later Kyoto Age (1335-1573). The downfall of the Hojo and the foundation of the Ashikaga dynasty of shoguns had their cause in a complicated conflict (1318–1392) between two rival branches of the imperial family for the throne; they eventually coalesced in Emperor Go-Komatsu. Takauji, head of the Ashikaga, played an opportunistic role in the struggle, and was nominated shogun in 1338. He established his Bakufu in the Muromachi district of Kyoto, giving the name to the era, though in reality it was the Ashikaga age. Takauji appointed a junior Ashikaga line to govern northeastern Japan from Kamakura, and they held the office until 1439, when it was taken over by the Uesugi family as the result of an Ashikaga family feud.

Takauji and his successors down to the sixth shogun, Yoshinori (assassinated, 1441), gave a comparatively capable administration. The remaining nine shoguns were incompetent, and the country fell into constant disorder. In this period the DAIMYO (feudal barons) came into prominence—the emergence of families who, through preceding centuries had amassed wealth and land. For both prestige and security they built castles on their fiefs all over the country. Samurai, discontented farmers and others flocked to the standards of these daimyo, especially the ablest and strongest, for livelihood, protection, or adventure. Towns and then cities grew up around the castles, and many of the daimyo, such as Uesugi, Takeda, Oda, Hojo (of Odawara), Date, Hatakeyama, Shiba, Shimazu, Ouchi, and others, became so powerful that they were almost independent in their own domains, and made their voices heard in Kyoto in affairs of state. Moreover, many of the great Buddhist temples and monasteries became centers of armed strength, due partly to the abbots' ambitions and partly to the need for protection; especially the Mount Hiei temple and the Ishiyama monastery at Osaka. Looting and armed conflict were rife throughout the country, and natural calamities occurred from time to time; central authority was almost nonexistent. The Civil War of Onin, breaking out in 1467 and involving Kyoto and many of the provinces, lasted for 30 years. The questions of provincial land tenure and taxes, that have plagued Japan throughout her history down to the present time, were intensified during this era. The daimyo fought with one another and with the great abbots.

In the midst of all this, the shoguns indulged in the greatest luxury and extravagance, especially the eighth shogun, Yoshimasa (1435–90). All his time and great sums were spent on costly palaces, temples, pavilions, landscape gardens, and lavish entertainments. When he could extort no further taxes from the people, he obtained funds totaling more than $2,000,000 (a large sum in those days) from the Ming emperor of China. Corruption and intrigue prevailed, and the emperors and people were impoverished. A redeeming feature was that Yoshimasa and other shoguns patronized the fine and esthetic arts, such as all kinds of works of art, cha-no-yu (tea cult), incense burning, and ikebana (flower cult). Japan began to produce the finest swords and lacquerware the world has known. Great artists, such as Sesshu and Motonobu, flourished.

Some elements, such as powerful daimyo and temples, and wealthy merchants, as well as the shoguns, prospered from lucrative trade with China, despite the general lawlessness and depression. Japanese pirates, existing from the remote past, became very active in the 16th century, harrying the east Asian seaboard and especially the China coast.

The stormy era of the Ashikaga shoguns closed in 1573 when the 15th and last, Yoshiaki (1537–1597), fled from Kyoto, ending one of the worst periods in Japan's history.

War and Final Reunification, and the Coming of the European (1573-1602). This quarter of a century was dominated by three men: Oda Nobunaga (1534–82), of Taira ancestry and daimyo of Owari; Toyotomi Hideyoshi (1536–98), named Nakamura Hiyoshi in his childhood and later Hashiba, the son of a small farmer; and Tokugawa Ieyasu (1542–1616), of Minamoto ancestry, originally a small daimyo called Matsudaira Motoyasu, whose crest was the famous aoi-no-mon (three hollyhock leaves). These three soldier-statesmen shaped Japan's history for three centuries.

Nobunaga's great fidelity to the imperial house was well known, and Emperor Okimachi called on him to restore order in Kyoto. He did so (1568), and appointed Hideyoshi as governor of the capital. The latter, having entered Nobunaga's service as a sandal bearer, had rapidly risen to be his counselor, and throughout the rest of Nobunaga's career was his chief lieutenant and adviser. From 1573, when Yoshiaki fled, Nobunaga was de facto shogun, though he did not receive the actual title. With friendly daimyo, including Ieyasu, as allies, Nobunaga had subjugated hostile barons and restored order in about half the empire when (1582) he was assassinated by a sulky general. Nobunaga had subdued also the numerous militant Buddhist strongholds, including the great monastery on Mount Hiei, comprising some 3,000 buildings, which he burned to the ground, most of the monks and their families being killed in the battle. This ended forever any pretensions by the Buddhists to political power.

Meantime the Portuguese had arrived in Japan, the first (c. 1542) landing after a storm on Tanegashima, an island off Kyushu, and carrying muskets. These firearms aroused the intense interest of the Japanese, who promptly copied them. More came, mostly for trade, and in 1549 the great Spanish Jesuit, St. FRANCIS XAVIER, arrived. Thereafter Portuguese and Spanish missionaries made great efforts to convert the Japanese, attaining considerable success, though also the arrogance of some of them aroused resentment. Nobunaga showed great tolerance to the foreign propagandists, and in the year of his death there were about 150,000 Japanese Christian converts. He died before the political implications of the missionaries' activities became apparent.

Hideyoshi succeeded to Nobunaga's power and completed the latter's work of national reunification by bringing under his unquestioned rule all the great daimyo—who, however, were left largely to their own devices within their own domains. Little attention was paid to Hokkaido, as a land of aborigines, until the 19th century. Small, ugly, and of humble origin, Hideyoshi rose to become one of the greatest men the Orient has ever known, thanks to his sagacity, military genius, able statesmanship, and patronage of art and industry. He undertook many measures for the welfare of the empire, and encouraged trade, including foreign commerce not only with Korea and China but also the Philippines, Siam, Cambodia, and Annam. Among the interesting new things brought in were tobacco (c. 1590), by the Portuguese, and various fruits and vegetables. Japan entered a period of prosperity that lasted for centuries. The emperor conferred on Hideyoshi the title of kwampaku (imperial regent), but not that of shogun—apparently because Hideyoshi did not desire it. Later he became known as the taiko (Great Prince). He built the Juraku and Momoyama palaces, the Daibutsu (Great Image of Buddha) of Kyoto, and the castle of Osaka. The palaces, including that of the castle, were embellished with the screen and wall paintings of Kano Eitoku and other great artists of the time, solid gold metalwork, and spacious landscape gardens. The splendor of the Momoyama palace, near Kyoto, was unrivaled, and this period of Japanese art is known as the Momoyama epoch. The Osaka castle, the greatest of its kind, was destroyed with the downfall of the Toyotomi family (1615), but the enormous size of the stones in its outer walls still excite wonder. The cost of all this was vast, added to by sumptuous cherry blossom viewing and tea cult parties, and other entertainments and pageantry, as well as the distribution of huge sums of gold and silver money. Unlike the Ashikaga shoguns Yoshimitsu and Yoshimasa, who impoverished the people, however, the taiko paid for it largely out of great wealth he acquired from foreign commerce and newly exploited gold and silver mines. Culture spread throughout the country, and fine porcelains, rivaling in beauty those of China, were produced. Books began to be printed with movable metal type late in the 16th century. Such printing was evolved in Korea early in the 15th century, and the Japanese knew of it but preferred their wood block printing, with which they produced books in the 10th century, if not earlier.

In 1577 Hideyoshi told Nobunaga that he intended eventually to subjugate China, subduing Korea as a preliminary. Fifteen years later he began to carry out this plan, and he was confident of success in two years, as a letter exists in which he stated the emperor of Japan would enter Peking in 1594 and he would present to the emperor the 10 provinces around the Chinese capital. The taiko's army of 200,000 men easily occupied the whole peninsula in 1592, but he made the strange mistake of not ensuring his command of the sea. A Korean fleet of armored vessels (the first used in warfare) of Chinese design sank and scattered the Japanese shipping. This made the situation of the Japanese army untenable, and after defeating a Chinese army of about 100,000 men sent to aid the Koreans, the Japanese managed to return home, leaving a small force in south Korea. Hideyoshi's army invaded Korea again (1597–98), this time crushing the Korean fleet and defeating another Chinese army; but the death of the taiko in 1598 brought the project to an abrupt end. The miseries suffered by the Koreans from these invasions caused them to hate the Japanese for generations.

Toward the Roman Catholic missionaries and their Japanese converts, Hideyoshi was, at first, tolerant; but later, suspicious of Spanish schemes of conquest, he subjected them to severe restrictions.

Age of the Tokugawa (1603-1867). This was an era of unbroken peace, and, generally, of prosperity, except for occasional famines and financial crises. It also was a period of complete national isolation, lasting more than two centuries, that is unique in world history.

Like Nobunaga, Hideyoshi left no worthy heir, so Ieyasu grasped the power, overcoming, with the aid of friendly daimyo, powerful barons who supported the Toyotomi family in the decisive battles of Sekigahara (1600) and Osaka castle (1614–15). He was nominated shogun in 1603, and founded the Tokugawa shogunate (Bakufu), in Yedo (now Tokyo) as the capital. Here he and the second shogun, Hidetada, built a castle of great strength, which became the nucleus of an immense city.

At first Ieyasu was tolerant toward the Jesuits and other missionaries, but later turned against them. He welcomed Dutch traders, who arrived in 1600 and 1611; and English East India Company merchants who appeared in 1613. Will Adams, an English pilot, who arrived in 1600, became the adviser and trusted friend of the great shogun, who gave him the rank of feudal baron, an estate in Miura Peninsula, and a lovely Japanese wife—one of the most romantic episodes in Japan's early intercourse with the West.

The English and the Dutch confined themselves strictly to trade; the Spanish confined themselves to feverish Christian propaganda and conducted their activities in such a way as to convince the Bakufu that Spain would seize any opportunity to try to conquer Japan; and the Portuguese took part in both propaganda and trade. In the result, the English voluntarily departed, due to trade losses; the Spaniards and Portuguese were expelled in 1624 and 1638, respectively; and the Dutch were allowed to trade only at the small island of Deshima, from 1640 to the end of the Tokugawa era. Ieyasu died in 1616, and his successors, Hidetada and Iemitsu, interdicted Christianity, not because of intolerance of the religion but because of their deep suspicion of the motives of the Spanish and Portuguese. Many of the missionaries and hundreds of Japanese Christians were executed for disobeying these edicts. This culminated in the Shimabara revolt (1637–38), in which, it is said, some 37,000 Japanese Christians perished. Christianity disappeared from the Japanese scene for the remainder of the Tokugawa era, except clandestine vestiges. Besides expelling the foreigners, the shogun forbade all Japanese to leave the country, or if they did, to return, under penalty of death. Only a few daring spirits evaded this edict. Some trade continued with China, and a trickle of Western trade and learning came in through the Dutch at Deshima.

The earlier shoguns devised effective measures for keeping the daimyo in subjection, and enacted numerous new laws. Among these was a constitution, an expansion of the Tokugawa family laws, which served until the MEIJI Restoration. Rules were made for the guidance of the emperors, in impoverished seclusion at Kyoto, which in effect limited them to issuing the commission for each new shogun, and to ceremonial functions. However, notable literary works by the Tokugawa daimyo Mitsukuni and several scholars of the 18th century, exposing the shoguns' usurpation of the emperors' prerogatives, paved the way for the Meiji Restoration.

Hideyoshi's grouping of the people into four great classes, samurai, farmer, artisan, and merchant, became firmly established in the Tokugawa era. The haughty samurai, including the daimyo, pretended to look down on the merchants, but often had to go to them for money. Gradually matrimonial alliances took place between them, and some samurai even turned trader. To the four classes mentioned there was added another, the *eta*, a pariah stratum that had formed of descendants of slaves, criminals, and others, who were handlers of animal carcasses, and hides, and corpses, and other so-called unclean occupations; later, in the Meiji period, these people were given legal equality with all other classes, but for many years chafed under the nickname shin-heimin (new common people). The merchants became wealthy and actually the most powerful class; from them came the great merchant families of the Tokyo era. There was much luxurious living, especially in the Genroku era (1688–1703).

Under the patronage of the merchant and artisan classes, the kabuki drama achieved an eminence, continuing into the Meiji era, that rivaled the theater of any other country. Chikamatsu was the great playwright. The famous ukiyoe art flourished. Highly cultured courtesans, forerunners of the GEISHA of today, also flourished. A decline in the status of women, that began in the Ashikaga age under the influence of Buddhism and Confucianism and the domineering attitude of the samurai, was accentuated in the Tokugawa era; the actual influence of women generally, however, was not much diminished.

Toward the middle of the 19th century the Tokugawa shogunate approached its downfall. Besides the old age weakness of the system itself and general unrest, the chief causative factors were the powerful demand, centering around some daimyo and Kyoto court nobles, for the restoration of administrative power to the emperor, and the American action, under the threat of Commodore PERRY's naval force, that compelled Japan to open the empire to foreign intercourse (1854). Finally the 14th and last of the Tokugawa shoguns, Keiki (Yoshinobu), abdicated on Oct. 14, 1867, and the 122nd sovereign, Emperor Meiji (Mutsuhito) (1867–1912), recovered the imperial prerogatives after a lapse of 675 years.

The Tokyo Era (from 1868) has been the most eventful in Japan's history. In the tremendous reaction due to the abolition of feudalism, innumerable reforms were carried out. The old class distinctions, including that of the samurai with his "topknot" and

two swords, were abolished, and the daimyo and kuge (Kyoto court nobles) alike were gathered into a new peerage of five ranks. Emperor Meiji took the epochal and symbolic step of moving to Yedo, which was renamed Tokyo (eastern capital), where he occupied the splendid, ancient palace of the shoguns, making it the imperial capital; the castle was removed, but the great outer walls, with their old pines, towers, and moats, were left intact. The emperor issued several memorable edicts and promulgated a new constitution in 1889, written by HIROBUMI ITO, later Prince Ito; he and several other leading Meiji reformers became known as the genro (elder statesmen), who advised the emperors on important state affairs, and the last of whom, Prince Saionji, died in 1940. An entirely new government on Western lines was established, administrative, legislative, and judicial, with the emperor as sovereign head of state; the Teikoku Gikai (Imperial Parliament), with the House of Representatives elected by popular vote, was convened in 1890. A privy council and other governmental bodies were set up. A modern army and navy

Landing of Commodore Perry at Yokohama on Mar. 8, 1854

were organized. Complete new codes of law were established, as well as modern education, public hygiene, and other systems. Treaties were signed with the United States, Britain, and other Western powers —later revised, to delete some extraterritorial provisions. Measures were enacted to encourage industry, trade, and finance. The result was that during the period embracing the two world wars Japan became one of the great powers; her commerce spread all over the world and her navy and mercantile marine were third only to those of America and Britain. In politics, a variety of parties was formed at first, but in 1900 Prince Ito founded the conservative Seiyukai, which continued for four decades; during the same period the other chief, and liberal, party had various names, the last being Minseito; there were proletarian and several other smaller parties. Universal male suffrage was enacted in 1924. Democratic government came into power for about two decades, especially under Premiers Hara (1918–21) and Hamaguchi (1929–31); both Hara and Hamaguchi were assassinated. At other times the cabinets tended to be bureaucratic. The last democratic cabinet (1931–32) ended with the assassination of Premier Inukai, May 15, 1932, by a band of young army and navy men. During the preceding years numerous ultranationalistic groups had been formed, and there were other assassinations. The extremists continued to foment national unrest, enhanced by many years' irritation over intermittent political party corruption and governmental incompetence to carry out agrarian reform; various cabinets, several headed by

Japan

generals or admirals, followed one another during the ensuing decade, midway in which occurred, on Feb. 26, 1936, a mass assassination of cabinet and other high officials by army and civilian conspirators, 19 of whom were executed. See EXTRATERRITORIALITY.

Japan engaged in a series of foreign wars during the Tokyo era. These began with the first war with China (1894–95)—Japan's first foreign war since the Empress Jingo and Hideyoshi invasions of Korea centuries before. The results were that the Chinese claim to suzerainty over Korea was quashed and Japan annexed Formosa (Taiwan), which during the next half century she transformed into a treasure island of prosperity, and the Boko (Pescadores) Islands. Previously (1889), the Ryukyu Islands, over which China claimed suzerainty but which had been part of the domain of the daimyo of Satsuma since the 17th century, had been organized into the metropolitan prefecture of Okinawa and part of Kagoshima Prefecture. Japan also obtained Liaotung Peninsula, Manchuria, but was coerced into withdrawing by France, Germany, and Russia, after which Russia turned around and herself occupied the southern end (Kwantung) under a lease from the Peking government; Russia established there a naval and military base at Ryojun (Port Arthur) and a seaport at Talien Wan (Russian Dalny; Japanese Dairen), to which she constructed a great extension of the Chinese Eastern Railway (Manchuria). Next, Japan took part in an allied expedition to relieve the Peking legation quarters besieged by the "Boxers" (1900), in which Japanese troops were preponderant though the expedition was commanded by a German general, Graf von Waldersee. Japan and Britain entered into an alliance (1902–1911) to protect their mutual interests. Russian penetration into Korea, menacing Japan, precipitated the spectacular RUSSO-JAPANESE WAR (1904–5); the result was that Japan ousted Russia from Korea and south Manchuria and obtained the south half of the Russian railroad (renamed South Manchuria Railway), the Kwantung lease, and valuable fisheries rights on Russia's Pacific seaboard, as well as regaining the south half of Sakhalin (Karafuto). In 1875 Japan had waived her claim to Sakhalin in return for Russia's abandoning to Japan her claim to the Kuril Islands. Prince Ito, who had been sent to Korea as resident general, was assassinated (1909) by a Korean, at Harbin; this was followed, in 1910, by Japan's annexing the peninsula. Under the Anglo-Japanese alliance, greatly strengthened in 1911, Japan entered (1914) the war against Germany and Austria, chasing the German fleet from the Pacific and convoying Anzac troopships to Europe; she also took Tsingtao from Germany, later returning it to China. Under a League of Nations mandate Japan obtained Germany's Pacific islands north of the Equator. She also participated in an allied expedition to Siberia to restore order out of the chaos

Ruins of Tokyo after the earthquake of 1923

caused by the Bolshevik revolution, and sent further troops to protect Japanese residents, hundreds of whom had been massacred by the Communists (1918–20). See SINO-JAPANESE WAR.

The Washington Conference (1921–22) resulted in the four-power Pacific treaty, the nine-power "open door" treaty on China, and produced the Washington naval treaty, under which Japan was constrained to accept a naval position inferior to that of the United States and Great Britain. One of the greatest earthquakes in world history in 1923 devastated Tokyo and Yokohama, which, however, were soon rebuilt on modern lines. Emperor Taisho died in 1926 and the present emperor Hirohito ascended the throne.

Manchuria. Numerous clashes between the Japanese and Chang Hsueh-liang, de facto ruler of Manchuria, led to Japan's occupying that country in 1931 and setting up the satellite empire of Manchukuo (1932–45); severe fighting occurred between Japanese and local Chinese forces at Shanghai. Prefaced by Japan's so-called "21 demands" on China (1915)—later pared down to three—this Manchurian exploit caused the United States to take great umbrage, and the resulting tension with Japan grew steadily until the explosion 10 years later. There were two classes of Japanese expansionists: the so-called "south seas" and "continental." The latter (of whom General Doihara was a typical example), taking Manchuria as a starting point, began to meddle in north China. This led to clashes with the Chinese, including the massacre of Japanese at Tungchou, east of Peiping.

In 1933 Japan withdrew from the League of Nations, angered by that body's censure of her actions in Manchuria based on the report of the commission headed by Lord Lytton. An Anglo-Japanese trade conference of the same year failed because Japan rejected the British proposal to divide the world's cotton-goods markets. Next year, Japan gave the required notice of termination of the Washington naval treaty, which, with the London naval treaty, expired at the end of 1936. A naval conference held in London, December, 1936–January, 1937, was abortive mainly because the United States and Great Britain rejected Japan's demand for naval parity. Japan, now free to do as she pleased, proceeded to strengthen her army and navy. In 1936, Japan joined Germany in the anti-Comintern pact, which displeased the Soviet Union.

War with China. From 1933 to 1937 the Japanese steadily infiltrated into Hopei and Chahar and demanded the establishment of an autonomous North China—a demand rejected by Chiang Kai-shek. A frontier clash near the Lukoukiao (Marco Polo) bridge, southwest of Peiping, in 1937, rapidly expanded into the second Sino-Japanese war. The Japanese speedily

Defeat of Russian fleet at Battle of Tsushima

occupied Peiping and most of north China, Shanghai, and many important inland cities, as well as railroads and other lines of communication. The Chiang Kai-shek regime retreated to the Szechuan interior city of Chungking, on the Yangtze, and held out there. A stalemate resulted subsequently. Throughout this war, never declared as such by either Japan or China, there was much intermittent fighting.

Japan and the Western Powers. The Japanese sinking of the American Yangtze gunboat, *Panay*, in 1937, the Japanese blockade of the British concession in Tientsin (1939), as well as Japan's altercation with Great Britain and the United States over war supplies being sent to China over the Burma Road, worsened Japanese relations with the United States and Great Britain. The United States on July 26, 1939, gave six months' notice of termination of the basic treaty with Japan, and Britain acted similarly. On September 27, 1940, Japan entered into a military alliance with Germany and Italy (the so-called Berlin-Rome-Tokyo axis). The purpose of this act, as avowed by Yosuke Matsuoka, Japanese foreign minister, was to keep the United States out of the European war, already in progress; but obviously it was also to strengthen Japan's own position. Then, on April 13, 1941, Japan entered into a five-year neutrality treaty with the Soviet Union. This treaty ended a state of semiwar between Japanese-led Manchurian forces and Soviet-backed Mongolian forces, and also included an agreement to divide China. Matsuoka also signed an agreement with Vichy France, whereby Japan was given the right to occupy the strategically important French Indochina, which she proceeded to do in the fall of 1940. See AXIS POWERS.

In the meantime the United States had been imposing various restrictive measures against Japan, such as embargoing the export of airplane fuel, steel, and other war materials. On July 25, 1941, all Japanese assets in the United States were impounded ("frozen"); Britain and the Netherlands took similar action at the same time. Japan immediately responded with a like measure against the three countries. Prince Konoye initiated lengthy conversations in Washington in the endeavor to reach an amicable settlement, or at least a *modus vivendi*, with the United States, while at the same time preserving intact Japan's position in Asia. The United States maintained that Japan's actions in China violated the Nine Power treaty and demanded that Japan withdraw from China, as well as Indochina. Finally, the third Konoye cabinet (July–October, 1941), deciding it could do nothing to make a satisfactory arrangement with the United States with regard to China, resigned on October 16. Gen. HIDEKI TOJO, who had become war minister in the Konoye cabinet on July 18, 1941, became premier. The emperor expressed the desire that Tojo continue the conversations with the United States. A special envoy, Saburo Kurusu, was sent to Washington in November to collaborate with the Ambassador Admiral Kichisaburo Nomura in the conversations with the American government. Yet in the same month the plan to attack Hawaii, the Philippines, and Dutch and British possessions was approved and the fleet for attacking Pearl Harbor moved to the Southern Kuriles. Kurusu and Nomura had their first conference with Roosevelt and Hull on November 17. Nine days later Hull handed Nomura the American terms, which included respect for the territorial integrity of China and the withdrawal of foreign troops from China and Indochina. Tojo described these proposals as an "ultimatum." On December 7, 1941, Japan attacked Pearl Harbor. Forty-five minutes after the attack a note from the Japanese government was handed to Hull by Nomura and Kurusu, in which Hull's proposals of November 26 were rejected.

Japan at War with America and Britain. The surprise attack on Pearl Harbor plunged Japan into war with the United States, the British Empire, the Netherlands, and their allies. In rapid succession Japan occupied Guam, Hong-Kong, the Philippines, two Aleutian islands, Siam, the Malay Peninsula, Singapore, Burma, the Netherlands East Indies, and various Pacific archipelagos. These successes gave Japan control over a vast territory and a tremendous number of people, and access to such important raw materials as petroleum, rubber, tin, and copper. Japan put into full swing the ambitious project that she called the "new order" and "co-prosperity sphere" in East Asia, establishing hegemony over that vast area. However, she was halted in her advance to Australia and New Zealand in the crucial Battle of the CORAL SEA, May, 1942, and to the east in the important Battle of Midway, June, 1942. (See MIDWAY, BATTLE OF.) The tide set in against Japan with the American occupation of Guadalcanal, in the Solomons, toward the end of 1942. Thereafter, under the commands of Gen. Douglas MacArthur and Adm. Chester W. Nimitz, Japan was turned back and ousted one by one from her newly-won lands. On Nov. 26, 1943, Roosevelt, Churchill, and Chiang Kai-shek issued the Cairo declaration that unrelenting pressure would continue against Japan, that all territories unlawfully acquired by Japan would be returned to their rightful owners, and that Korea would become independent. Roosevelt and Churchill signed the Yalta agreement with Stalin in February, 1945, which included a secret provision for the Soviet Union's entry into the war against Japan. The defeat of Japan came with the Battle of OKINAWA, intensive American bombing of Tokyo and other cities, and the blasting of HIROSHIMA and NAGASAKI with atomic bombs, the first used in warfare, dropped by American planes in August, 1945. Just at this time the Soviet Union entered the war. Japan surrendered on Sept. 2, 1945, with the signature of a formal document on board the American battleship *Missouri* in Tokyo Bay, under the terms of the POTSDAM DECLARATION. See WORLD WAR II.

Postwar Japan. The emperor ordered the Japanese people to co-operate with the occupation authorities headed by General MacArthur, and the occupation proceeded smoothly. The basic policy pursued by the occupation authorities aimed to insure that Japan could never again be a menace to peace and security; to establish a democratic government; to demilitarize the nation and to eliminate the influence of militarism; to encourage the development of civil liberties; to permit an economy that would satisfy the peacetime needs of the people. The United States and the British Commonwealth sent occupation troops to Japan and the demobilization of the Japanese forces proceeded rapidly. Early in 1946 the war crime trials opened and by 1948 former Premier General Tojo and other wartime leaders, accused as war criminals, were tried before an Allied court in Tokyo. The emperor, however, was absolved of war responsibility.

After surrender political parties came into existence and the press became free. General elections were held on April 10, 1946, but no single party won an overwhelming victory. The Liberals, Progressives, and Socialists became the major parties and the Liberal leader formed a coalition government. Attempts were made to deal with the economic dislocations caused by the war and to decentralize Japanese industries. Although food prospects improved, the difficulty of restoring the country's economic life continued as the major problem facing the government. On May 3, 1947, the new constitution became effective and the nation's political life changed drastically as a result of it.

Settlement of the terms of the peace treaty for Japan remained in abeyance in 1948 because of

Kanda Ward section of Tokyo after B-29 raids

disagreements between the United States and the Soviet Union. Some progress was recorded in the economic recovery of Japan in 1948, but the government failed to curb inflation, and it was difficult to find a greater foreign market for Japanese goods. The program of purchasing land for redistribution to landless tenants moved ahead. Less drastic action was taken in the attempt to break up excessive concentrations of industrial power. In October, 1948, the Diet elected the leader of the conservative Democratic Liberal party as premier.

Occupation policy in 1948 shifted away from the punitive and reform measures of previous years, and emphasized economic reconstruction. The Democratic Liberal party again won victories in the elections of 1949 and 1950. After the 1950 election, General MacArthur ordered the Japanese government to ban members of the Communist party from public affairs; in December he declared that Japan might have to rearm against the threat of international lawlessness. The dismissal of General MacArthur in April, 1951, almost led to the resignation of the Japanese Cabinet. General Matthew Ridgway replaced MacArthur.

Early in 1951, the United States initiated discussions concerning a peace treaty with Japan. On Sept. 8, 1951, 49 of the 52 nations represented at the Japanese peace conference in San Francisco signed the treaty ending the war with Japan; the U.S.S.R., Poland, and Czechoslovakia abstained from signing. The treaty was to become effective when ratified by Japan, the United States, and a majority of the nations which signed. Provision was made that if a majority of the nations had not ratified the treaty within nine months, individual countries could bring it into force for themselves. The treaty also provided that Japan might make separate peace treaties with countries that did not sign at San Francisco.

Under the terms of the treaty, Japan again became a fully sovereign nation; the treaty recognized Japan's right to rearm, and placed no restrictions on Japan's industrial development or arms production. Japan accepted the principles and obligations of the U.N. Charter, and could apply for U.N. membership. Allied occupation troops would leave Japan within 90 days after the treaty took effect; however, Japan might make treaties for foreign armed forces to be stationed in its territory for defense. Japan was reduced to its four home islands, and renounced all claims to its former island possessions.

The treaty recognized that Japan should pay reparations, but suggested that Japan, because of its economy, pay indirect reparations through service and labor. Japan could make separate trade agreements with Allied powers. Five hours after the peace treaty was signed, the United States and Japan signed a treaty for the maintenance of U.S. defense forces in Japan.   G. B. DE H.

Japanese Archaeology

BIBLIOGRAPHY

HISTORY: F. Brinkley, *A History of the Japanese People* (1915); J. and R. K. Reischauer, *Early Japanese History* (1937); S. Hishida, *Japan Among the Great Powers* (1940); Y. S. Kuno, *Japan's Emergence as a Modern State* (1946); K. S. Latourette, *Short History of Japan* (1947); F. J. Horner, *Case History of Japan* (1948); N. F. Busch, *Fallen Sun* (1948); C. Yawaga, *Japan Since Perry* (1949); G. B. Sansom, *The Western World and Japan* (1950); H. Feis, *The Road to Pearl Harbor* (1950).

EMPIRE: T. A. Brisson, *Japan in China* (1938); A. M. Young, *Imperial Japan, 1926–1938* (1938); W. H. Chamberlain, *Japan over Asia* (1939); F. Whyte, *Rise and Fall of Japan* (1945); N. J. Nanporia, *Japanese Paradox* (1947); D. H. James, *Rise and Fall of the Japanese Empire* (1951).

POLITICS AND ECONOMICS: J. M. Maki, *Japanese Militarism, Its Cause and Cure* (1945); J. F. Embree, *The Japanese Nation* (1945); G. C. Allen, *Short Economic History of Modern Japan, 1867–1937* (1946); E. Ackerman and others, *Japan's Prospects* (1946); E. M. Martin, *The Allied Occupation of Japan* (1948); A Roth, *Dilemma in Japan* (1948); W. M. Ball, *Japan—Enemy or Ally* (1949); T. A. Bisson, *Prospects of Democracy in Japan* (1949); J. B. Cohen, *Japan's Economy in War and Reconstruction* (1949); N. Ike, *Beginnings of Political Democracy in Japan* (1950); E. O. Reischauer, *United States and Japan* (1950).

CULTURE AND RELIGION: B. H. Chamberlain, *Things Japanese* (1925); J. W. T. Mason, *The Meaning of Shinto* (1937); D. C. Holtom, *National Faith of Japan* (1938); G. B. Sansom, *Japan, A Short Cultural History* (1943); G. T. Trewartha, *Japan, a Physical, Cultural, and Regional Geography* (1945); E. F. Briggs, *New Dawn in Japan* (1948); H. Wakefield, *New Paths for Japan* (1948); H. Means, *Mirror for Americans: Japan* (1948).

JAPAN CURRENT. See OCEAN.

JAPAN SEA, Nihon-kai, a body of water some 1,100 miles NE to SW and 500 miles E to W, having an average depth of 4,500 feet, lies between Japan and the Asiatic mainland, with Korea and Russia sharing the W coast. There are three main entrances: Korea (Tsushima) Strait, in the southwest between Korea and Kyushu; Tsugaru Strait, on the east between Honshu and Hokkaido; and Soya (La Perouse) Strait, on the northeast between Sakhalin Island and Hokkaido. There is another entrance at the far north, the narrow Tatarski Channel, between Sakhalin and the Siberian mainland. In World War II the sea provided Japan with a protected route between the home islands and Korea and Manchuria. The sea has valuable salmon, crab, and other fisheries. The major ports on the sea are Vladivostok (Russia), Chongjin or Seishin, and Fusan (Korea), and Niigata, Tsuruga, and Otaru (Japan).

JAPANESE ARCHAEOLOGY. The archaeological remains of the Japanese people date from a few centuries before the Christian epoch. The most remarkable are the sepulchers of the mikados, known as *misasagi*. They take the form of huge double mounds enclosing a megalithic vault of unhewn stone without mortar. Some of the largest are as much as 80 or 90 feet in height. They are usually terraced, and ringed with rows of curious earthenware tubes about a foot in diameter, associated by tradition with the clay figures of men and horses set up in former times around these mausoleums as substitutes for living victims. Neither the tombs of the mikados nor those of the nobles have any inscriptions. They have, however, yielded a large number of objects of antiquarian interest, such as wheel-made pottery of somewhat rude workmanship, earthen and stone sarcophagi, iron swords and spearheads, armor skilfully adorned with gold and silver, horsegear of good workmanship, and jewelry. This style of sepulture fell into disuse about the eighth century, under the influence of Buddhist ideas.

The antiquarian remains of the Ainu people are found in shell mounds, resembling the kitchen middens of Denmark. They consist of shells, fragments of broken bones, implements of stone and horn, and handmade pottery—all indicating a much lower grade of civilization than that of the Japanese. Stone celts, arrowheads, etc., similar to those of other parts of the world, have been found everywhere in Japan.

Recently, archaeological sites apparently belonging to early Japanese immigrants from the mainland have been found in the vicinity of Tokyo.

JAPANESE ARCHITECTURE. Prior to the time of man-made buildings, the Japanese, like primitive people elsewhere, made their dwellings in natural caves. The entire country, there is reason to believe, was laid over with dense forestry; so it was but natural that, when inventive minds began to plan the formation of things by hand, wood should have been used to fashion a place in which to live. The first structures were but huts, simply constructed, shaped after the style of tents, with two poles set upright into the ground, a third placed across the tops of these, and two rafters, sloping to the ground, attached to each end. Several beams tied to the rafters formed a support for thatching, thus constituting walls and roof. These huts were first built as housing for spirits of the dead and were made into shrines. Later, when the structures were used as homes, they were raised from the earth on stiltlike foundations. Nature's gift of huge supplies of timber proved the best protection possible in a land visited by numerous earthquakes, since no other natural material could have withstood so well the shocks of earth's rumblings. With the advance of time a distinction was made between homes and shrines—the roof decorated with projections in the form of horns was forbidden to the ordinary dwelling and reserved only for the shrine. These shrines are rebuilt even today as a reminder to the people of the beauty and sanctity of the ancient times. Korean influence began to show in the architecture after the invasion of Korea, and coloring was introduced; but buildings remained extremely simple, including imperial palaces, largely because the court was moved at the death of each ruler.

Period of Chinese Influence, 552-889. When Buddhism was brought to Japan in 552, the influence of Chinese architecture came with it. Its appearance was most marked in the Buddhist temples; while the Shinto shrines and the private homes continued the native style. Gradually there was a blend, resulting from the absorption of the Chinese influence into the Japanese culture. Much of the Chinese design was not suited to the steep slopes and rapidly changing countryside of Japan. Sensitive to the blending of landscape with architecture, the Japanese rejected the dignity and severity of Chinese formalities for their own native sense of the picturesque. From Korea came temple builders, tile artisans, and painters. The building of temples introduced pillars with entasis, tile floors and tiled roofs, and brackets that supported wide, sloping eaves; and the several-storied pagoda made its appearance. With the rise of esoteric Buddhism a drastic change in religious architecture followed, and temples were erected on the very tops of mountains. An effort to bring together the two religious beliefs of Shintoism and Buddhism resulted in an elaborateness of temple buildings; curvature in the roofs was introduced, and the sloping roofs were widely extended—far over the ends of the structures.

Nationalization Period I, 890-1185. Although the homes of the common people continued in simplicity and retained the thatched roofs in this period, the wealthy aristocracy built elaborate temples, both private and public, and constructed magnificent mansions for themselves. This latter class developed a style called *shinden-zukuri*, which consisted of a group of rectangular buildings all joined together by long corridors. The buildings were so placed that they formed three sides of a square, in the center of which was made a lake containing an island to be reached by several ornamental bridges. This period ushered in a dignified and graceful architecture that reflected a true and distinctive Japanese taste. It was all an outgrowth of a strong reaction against imported culture which resulted in an assertion of native tendencies.

The light and lenient quality of the easygoing Jodo sect that sprang up was represented in the almost extreme decorations of the interiors of temples, meant to signify the joys of the Buddhist paradise. Fences formerly used to enclose the shrines disappeared and were replaced by corridors. The two horizontal beams supported by two poles, symbol of former shrines, were supplanted by gates with eight and four posts.

Chinese Influence Period II, 1186-1572. The power of the country fell from the hands of the aristocracy and passed to the warrior class, called *samurai.* While the *shinden-zukuri* style of the previous period continued to be favored by the aristocracy, the samurai developed a simplification called *buke.* In the place of several buildings connected by corridors, the *buke* style built several rooms under one roof, thatched or shingled, and a single house would be surrounded by a ditch and a fence. In temple buildings two styles were in greatest evidence: the *wa-yo,* the Japanese style of the previous period; and the *kara-yo,* a Chinese style brought in by the introduction of the Zen sect of Buddhism. The *wa-yo* permitted much freedom in planning and in the distribution of the various buildings belonging to the temples; the *kara-yo* demanded an arrangement of the buildings that would preserve symmetry throughout. Later there was a merging of the two, resulting in a mixed style. Before the period ended, the samurai were all but forgotten, and a life of luxury prevailed during which the wealthy and powerful vied with each other in the building of mansions. The samurai style gave way to one called *shoin-zukuri* which brought several innovations into the homes—shelves added to walls, entrance rooms, tiny verandas, and sliding paper screens and wooden panels decorated with colorful landscapes.

Nationalization Period II, 1573-1867. When Hideyoshi rose to power the art style called *Momoyama* evolved in its grandeur. This became an age for the common people; and the tea ceremony, which formerly had belonged only to the upper classes, became a pastime for everyone. The result was a widespread development of the ceremonial teahouses called *chaseki.* Space for the tea ceremony was built simply, containing shelves, tiny cabinets, and a raised platform to support flowers; characteristically a real tree trunk, natural and untrimmed, served to bring the outdoors inside. There came into construction a new type of shrine, consisting of two buildings, one for the sanctuary, the other for worshiping, and the two connected by a sunken room which was stone-paved. The period saw co-operation grow between architecture, sculpture, and painting, until all three functioned together for the production of greater harmony. There was a development of the addition of a

Religious Architecture of Japan is represented by Kondo or Golden Hall of Horyuji Temple at Nara

study room to dwelling houses, ceilings were decorated with paintings, and a common practice developed of covering the floors with wadded mats. A notable change in domestic architecture took place when the recurrence of fires brought about increased use of tile roofs and mud walls. Another outstanding development of the period was the building of mausoleums.

Western Influence, 1868-1926. The country's people leaned so far in the direction of Western culture, when those ideas began to penetrate the land, that the native architecture was threatened. Architects from other countries brought the knowledge of building with stone, bricks, and iron; and factories, stores, and entertainment structures appeared throughout Japan. The wealthy built homes after the Western style, and the middle classes sought to arrange at least a part of their homes in this fashion. But when the earthquake and subsequent fire destroyed many of these buildings in 1923, the development of special types of structure was a natural result.

Contemporary. Nationalism again asserted itself when Japan seceded from the League of Nations. A natural result was the revival of native styles in architecture with a return to traditional types. What the outcome of World War II will reflect in the country's architecture is a matter for conjecture and only the passing of time will tell.

Homes. Because of its distinctive nature, the traditionally styled Japanese house should receive special mention. It should be made clear that, to the Japanese, the terrain on which the home is to be built, largely determines the type of architecture, for architecture and landscape must blend into one harmonious whole. The picturesque sense of the people demands that there be a strong relationship between a building and the trees surrounding it; its relationship to inclines and to lakes and waterfalls determines the basic features of house plans. Generally the homes are built on foundation stones. Although the buildings are not attached to the ground, they are weighed down against the danger of winds, by heavily tiled roofs. Walls are made of mud mixed with short rice straw to bind them together and given a smooth coating of plaster, sand, or certain kinds of clay. Ceilings are made of wood in which the same type of grain is used throughout; for variety, ceilings of different rooms sometimes vary in grain. Few walls are built within the structure, but sliding screens, paneled, papered, or painted, are made to move easily between grooves on ceiling and floor. When occasion demands, a house can be made into one huge room or many smaller ones.

A very important part of the home is the recessed alcove, a small room whose floor is about four inches higher than the floor of the house. The back wall of the alcove supports picture scrolls, and on its floor are placed a vase of flowers and an incense burner. Shelves line the walls of the alcove for the purpose of holding various ornaments. The entire alcove is considered sacred and regarded with reverence.

Because it is customary to remove the shoes before entering a home, the front entrance (extended as a shelter under which vehicles may be drawn) is also an important feature. A Japanese home and its garden have always been woven into an inseparable unit. The two are connected by a small walk, usually lined with a fence. In order to give the effect of living close to nature—a factor always regarded in the country's architecture—the side of the house nearest the garden is often closed with sliding screens, and these may be removed to furnish the satisfaction of sharing the garden and the home at once.

JOAN C. CAMERA

BIBLIOG.–C. Dresser, *Japan; its Architecture, Art and Art Manufacturers* (1882); R. A. Cram, *Impressions of Japanese Architecture and the Allied Arts* (1930); J. Horada, *The Lesson of Japanese Architecture* (1936); B. Taut, *Fundamentals of Japanese Architecture* (1936); A. L. Sadler, *A Short History of Japanese Architecture* (1941).

JAPANESE ART

Of incredible delicacy and beauty are the Japanese paintings, carvings, ceramics, known only recently to the Western world

JAPANESE ART. The Western world has only begun to appreciate the arts of the Far East. There are two reasons for this late appreciation: great mental differences and the lack of complete, accurate translations of the important Oriental books. The artists who produced the masterpieces of the Orient were saturated with Buddhist, Taoist, or Shintoist philosophies—teachings involved, obscure, and devoid of logical premises to the Western mind. But even before Buddhism was officially introduced into Japan, handicraft produced objects of artistic nature.

Pre-Buddhistic Age. The first-known form of art in the country was practiced in what is now called the New Stone Age. Its products are two types of pottery. The earlier consisted in vessels of a dark-gray material, which were characterized by handles usually formed into heads of animals and by a simple ornamentation of artistically curved lines. The other type is distinguished by its red color, lack of design, and the beauty of its form. In the following Bronze Age, instruments such as bells, arrowheads, spears, and daggers were produced. Of these the bells are of chief interest since they depict the life of the age in their designs representing hunting scenes, agricultural activity, and architectural styles. Articles found in the burial mounds of Japan show that its people next passed through an Iron Age when swords, helmets, and other armor were made and carved with rich decoration. Trappings for horses are among the most beautiful articles surviving from the period. Bit cheek pieces, stirrups, bosses, and saddles were made of hammered iron covered with a copper sheet coated in gold. Other items yielded by the burial mounds are clay figures, crudely formed from red terra cotta, of men and women, as well as of horses, birds, and houses, which were used in the funeral ritual and were set upon the mounds. Precious stones of excellent workmanship have also been found, and necklaces of variously colored glass, beads, and rings.

METROPOLITAN MUS. OF ART
Bronze temple bell

Periods of Art. Before the introduction of Buddhism into Japan, which occurred in 552, there was no organized religion in the land except Shinto, the cult of ancestor worship. Buddhism came by way of China, through Korea, and into Japan. From that time to the present the progress of art may be assigned to several definite periods: Suiko Period (552–645); Nara (646–793); Heian (794–893); Fujiwara (894–1185); Kamakura (1186–1333); Muromachi (1334–1573); Momoyama (1574–1614); Yedo (1615–1866); Meiji-Taisho (1867–1926); and the Contemporary era.

Religious Influence. With the advent of Buddhism, appreciation of the arts in Japan grew rapidly. At first only the monks of the Buddhist monasteries had either the time or the inspiration to execute artistic objects. Through them others were taught, and art received a powerful impetus. Much of the most impressive work done in the Suiko period was industrial. Gilt-bronze banners, adorned with decorative metal fittings, fashioned with Buddhist and animal figures, are striking examples. Embroidered tapestries were the work of court ladies, who employed brilliantly colored threads in representations of flowers, birds, goblins, and Buddhas. The Nara period brought yet a greater advance in the decorative arts when the artists were appointed under patronage of the imperial court. Textile artists were sent out into many provinces to teach the art of weaving. The variety of fabrics produced included rough silk, silk, twill, brocade, gauze, and many others. Dyeing processes enlarged the field of colors, and the motifs adopted in textile weaving were landscape, floral, animal, and plant. Carved and inlay work of the period, using sandalwood, mother-of-pearl, and tortoise shell, are exemplified in the decorative designs of the musical instruments. Of the Heian period, an era of esoteric Buddhism, but few examples remain to indicate the practice of minor arts. These are carved Buddhist symbols, used in worship or peculiar to the decoration on the costumes of the monks.

Effects of Chinese Art. The next 292 years is called the Fujiwara period, after the family of that name which assumed an important role in the rule of the country. This period saw the rise of a true national spirit and an expression of this spirit in the arts. Industrial arts made extraordinary progress, and the advance in lacquerwork was most remarkable. Numerous utensils—trays, mirror stands, tables, toilet boxes, clotheshorses—were given backgrounds of plain black LACQUER, sprinkled with flecks of gold, and ornamented with designs of mother-of-pearl, gilt metals, or gold lacquer. The Sung Dynasty of China had a close relationship with Japan in the Kamakura period. This, together with the introduction of a new form of Buddhism, Zen, brought the delicate splendor of Chinese art to the country and caught the fancy of its people. Lacquerware, with its elaborate designs of nature's outdoor life, continued to be a favorite work with artists. In the art of metalwork, sword making reached a new peak and reflected the skill of the craftsmen, as did the new highly decorative body armor. POTTERY attained a more important place in this period. Incense boxes were numerous, made of white porcelainware introduced by priests coming from China.

The beginnings of the Muromachi period were filled with imperial disorganization and civil war; but progress in the arts was far from lacking. The important artists of the era were Shinsai and Michinaga, both receiving the patronage of the shogun, Yoshimasa. Raised gold lacquerwork was developed at the same time that the *togidashi* style was born. The latter style consisted of a gold lacquer design furnished by an artist-painter, applied to a lacquered background, coated with a layer of transparent lacquer, and burnished evenly into the surface. This style was effected in both flat and raised forms. The practical need of arms during the period furnished further development of metalwork, and the designs became more and more intricate and artistic.

Spread of Art to the Masses. Hideyoshi became the political leader in the Momoyama period and his prolific imagination afforded the development of art on a large scale. The minor arts found new application not only in architectural ornamentation, but also in the development of the tea ceremony. Lacquerware assumed importance both in decorating the interiors of buildings and in the making of tea utensils. Ceramics found special favor with the tea cult when Chojiro produced his soft-textured tea bowls of red glaze. New color schemes were applied in metalwork and added vivid display to the trappings of architecture. The Yedo period was the first in which the arts made any spectacular progress with the masses of the country. It was an era of peace, a time when the plebeian class had freedom to devote to cultural things. The art of ceramics developed every kind of pottery: earthenware (glazed and unglazed), stoneware, and porcelainware. Some of the finest examples of color in Japanese porcelain were produced during this period. One of the country's great ceramists, Ninsei, founded a famous pottery kiln; Kaki-e-mon gave his name to a type of enameled porcelainware; Iro-nabeshima ware, Satsuma ware, and Ko-Kutani ware were developed. The height of elaborate gold lacquerwork was attained in this Yedo period by such artists as Kajikawa Kyujiro, Igarashi Doho, Ogata Korin, and Yamada Jokasai, who invented delicately artistic methods for their craft. Gold leaf, embroidery, brocade, and silk fabrics were woven into colorful tapestries and costumes, with special designs often painted in.

Contact with the West. The year 1868 was one of many changes. The city of Yedo became Tokyo, marking the beginning of the Meiji-Taisho period. Western influences began seriously to affect the country's arts, but soon there was a return to normalcy, and harmonization between the new and the old was accomplished. Contemporary minor arts in Japan are making new progress. Metalworkers produce utensils, vases, and other vessels in bronze. Every form of textile fabric is dyed and woven after European methods, but worked in the intricate and delicate designs peculiar to Japanese artistry. Ceramics continue to be noted for their beauty of color and form.

PAINTING

No knowledge is had regarding the type of painting that had developed prior to the introduction of Buddhism in Japan, but it is most probable that it consisted only in decorative form. In the Suiko period, artists were invited from Korea to bring the art of painting into the country, and the crown prince of Japan moved about the Kinai provinces establishing art as a profession existing for the purpose of painting Buddhist images in the temples. The Korean painters worked after the manner of the Chinese School of the Six Dynasties. Two styles of painting were in use in the Nara period: the line composition of the original Chinese, and the Indian chiaroscuro. The court took painting under its wing by creating a special art department within its confines. Documents of the era furnish the knowledge that pictures were painted on folding screens and that numerous paintings were made depicting Buddha and his disciples, as well as frescoes containing scores of Buddhist figures. Mention is made of 17 different kinds of colors in use. During the Heian period, painting, previously practiced exclusively by the Buddhist priests, spread into the ranks of the aristocracy. This led to the first painting of nonreligious pictures, and also to the rise of Japan's first important artist, Kose Kanaoka. Kanaoka, at the imperial command, painted at the palace; and his images of horses and of famous scholars were in great demand.

Introduction of Picture Scrolls. A different departure from Buddhist painting marked the Fujiwara period when Eshin Sozu, a Buddhist priest, depicted religious beliefs in storytelling form with colorful landscape backgrounds. A striking feminine beauty characterized the paintings of the age; representations of Amida, with purely feminine pose and expression, were favorite pictures. In secular painting, for the first time romantic stories were painted on picture scrolls. The Fujiwara era saw art progress to the extent that several artists became influential enough to found their own schools. The paintings of the Kamakura age, following the trend of the previous period, were primarily Buddhistic. The most noteworthy development was made in the picture scrolls, which assumed a purely Japanese character; and such a multitude of scrolls appeared that this is known as the picture scroll age. These scrolls were vivid in their renditions of legendary, historical, and religious topics. For the first time, because of the military spirit of the period, the Japanese warrior appears in paintings. Near the end of this era, Eiga, who had received his training under various Chinese artists, painted in a style that laid the path for a revival of Chinese forms.

Ink Paintings. The following Muromachi period was marked by such great art progress that it closely corresponds to the European Renaissance, and the greatest of this progress was made in the art of painting The Chinese artists who were imported at this time were responsible for the adoption of ink instead of color in paintings. The black and white ink paintings were brought to such perfection in the period of Muromachi that their expression has not since been equaled. Josetsu was one of the great artists of this age, and his pupil, Shubun, even outshone him. Almost every leading Japanese artist in the Muromachi period studied under Shubun. But the most important figure of the time was Sesshu (1420–1506) who is still considered one of the greatest landscape masters ever to use a brush in Japan. His training, acquired by studying the style of both Josetsu and Shubun, soon gave in to his own originality. He studied closely the Chinese styles of the Sung and Yuan dynasties also, and succeeded in completely Japanizing them. His sensitive portrayal of nature, in deep and light tones, made his ink paintings creations of beauty which gained the admiration of the Japanese, as well as the Chinese people. The period produced also a famous family trio of landscape painters: No-ami, Gei-ami, and So-ami—father, son, and grandson respectively. The Kano school, which was a blending of Chinese styles with their adaptions by Japanese masters, was founded in this era by Masanobu and his son Motonobu, and became the most important school in the two following periods.

A newness of aesthetics was achieved in the painting executed during the Momoyama period. Feelings of importance and desires to display bigness stirred the minds of the powerful military leaders. These found expression in the building of huge mansions to magnify all this greatness and resulted in a remarkable development of architectural painting which took its form in scenes painted on the sliding screens used for partitions between rooms, and on walls. For this work rich colors on gold-leaf background were used, and ink paintings in black and white served as contrast. The most important artists of Momoyama painting were Eitoku (1543–1590) and Sanraku (1559–1635). Both worked in the style of bigness that was the spirit of the age, painting walls and screens with mammoth pictures of trees, flowers, plants, and general outdoor life. The old schools, still adhering to religious painting, were in the state of decadence; but the new ones were alive with beginnings, full of promise.

First Japanese Prints. The Kano school was greatest in importance during the period called Yedo. Its painters were inspired with the religion of Confucius; and, because it was an age in which Chinese classics commanded deep admiration, the painters worked with the classics as their inspirational source. Chinese subjects appeared in great number—Chinese sacred animals, Chinese landscapes, Chinese kings. Kano Tannyu (1602–1674) became the third of the three greatest masters of Kano, sharing the honors with Motonobu and Eitoku. Before the Yedo era, painting belonged to the court and the aristocracy; but now it became a privilege of enjoyment for the common people also. The genre painting (which consisted of two types: that painted by hand and that printed with blocks) became their favorite art. Famous beauties, scenes of love, and actors of the theater were the popular subjects. It was Motonobu, working from 1688 to 1703, who produced the first black and white prints,

which he embellished by hand with a dull-red finish. He produced the first picture books, which had a tremendous reception from the masses. From that time there was a continuous development of Japanese prints, from the early tinted products to the beautifully colored Japanese prints so widely known today. In the production of a color print it is necessary to have close co-operation, from beginning to end, between the three artists required: painter, engraver, and printer. It is because of this complicated process that the prints have become highly prized possessions. To this period belong Hokusai (1760–1849) and Hiroshige (1797–1858) who are considered unequaled in the art of color block printing. The Nangwa school of the Yedo period also deserves mention, for through its influence the literary style of painting developed among Confucianism scholars. One of the important figures of the school was Taiga (1723–76) whose work reflects a poetic imagination. Other schools found favor with the masses also—for example, the Maruyama and the Shijo.

The Meiji-Taisho period ushered in Western influences and saw art instructors from Western countries teaching in Japan. Japanese painters learned the art of oil painting and began to adopt ideas from the West in their work. The government established the first art school and appointed the well-known Kano Hogai (1828–88) and Hashimoto Gaho (1835–1908) as instructors. Exhibitions of artists' work were held for the first time, and further aesthetic appreciation of the people was given greater encouragement. The period gave rise to such artists as Taikan, Kogyo, Seiho, and many like them. It is still too soon to give a definite picture of contemporary painting. There is much complication in styles resulting from imitations and study of the art of the West, and Cubism, Impressionism, Realism, and other schools.

SCULPTURE

The Japanese sculpture which preceded the year 552 apparently was not an art in itself, but served merely as decorative work to other mediums, such as architecture, and was executed in a type of relief. In the Suiko period, however, sculpture became an independent art and figures were made chiefly of bronze and wood. The technique used in making bronze casts consisted in shaping the desired image out of earth, covering it with wax, and placing a layer of earthen material over it. The wax was then melted out through a heating process, and molten bronze was poured into the cavity. As in the other arts, subjects were Buddhist. Wood sculptures were fashioned from single blocks and decorated in color. Both types reflected an expressionless style similar to the flatness of Egyptian art. The Nara period introduced a development of fullness in its sculpture, replete with well-rounded curves. Large Buddhist figures made their appearance, cast in bronze, and smaller ones were done in repoussé work. In the latter part of the period the use of bronze and wood declined, while clay became the most popular material with sculptors, followed closely by dry lacquerwork.

Symbolism and Demand for Religious Figures. A complete understanding of symbolism, during the Heian period of esoteric Buddhism, gave rise to exalted statues, many-armed and many-headed. Wood supplanted other materials in use, and sculpture for the first time worked to obtain effects of the natural wood without using artificial color. Also for the first time, images cut from rock appeared, and Buddhist figures were often carved on open cliffs. Although sculpture did not prosper as well as painting in the Fujiwara period, it did advance. Wood was used exclusively and joinery (in which different parts of the final piece are made separately) was introduced. Craftsmen making their complete livelihood from this art came into being, and the profession of sculpturing was born in Japan. The reconstruction work of Buddhist monasteries fur-

"Waves at Matsushima," screen painting by Korin, portrays one of most famous views of Japan

JAPANESE ART

The art of Japan utilizes suggestion rather than factual statement, but shows a passion for perfect detail

Inlaid sword guard, 17th century

Buddhist wood statue

"Courtesan," 18th century

"Evening Rain at Massaki," print by Hiroshige

Imari ware produced in 18th century

nished rapid progress for the sculpture of the Kamakura era, since religious figures were in great demand. The martial spirit of the age gave rise to images showing heroic action. Because gods were considered by people of this time to be more human, the practice began of making figures on which the clothes could be changed. This resulted in the nude sculptures of Buddhist and Shinto images, for which costumes were made as for living men. The Kamakura age left the names of two great sculptors, Unkei and Kwaikei, who developed their art in wood.

Buddhism declined in the next period, giving way to Zen Buddhism which stressed the importance of individuality. Portrait sculpture, therefore, was the most popular form in the Muromachi period, and most of the pieces represented the figures of founders of Zen temples. Confucianism gained many followers during this era and resulted in numerous sculptures of Confucius. Portraiture developed in wood, slightly decorated in color. Degeneration of sculpture as a separate art set in during the period known as Momoyama, and was developed almost completely as architectural decoration. This decline continued through the Yedo era, when little was done except the making of masks, and extended well into the Meiji-Taisho period, the beginning of which saw sculpture at the lowest ebb since its origin. Then, with the revival of nationalism in the late 19th century, sculpture also was revived and was included in the studies of the Tokyo Art School. As in painting and the minor arts, sculpture followed Western methods. By the contemporary age it had begun to regain its place in the field of art and was sharing in the numerous art exhibitions held throughout Japan.

JOAN C. CAMERA

BIBLIOG.–M. Anesaki, *Art, Life, and Nature in Japan* (1933); L. Binyon, *Painting in the Far East* (1934); K. Toda, *Japanese Scroll Painting* (1935); H. Minamoto, *Illustrated History of Japanese Art* (1935); N. Tsuda, *Handbook of Japanese Art* (1935); B. Samagama, *History of Buddhist Art in Japan* (1940); N. Tsuda, *Ideals of Japanese Painting* (1940).

JAPANESE BEETLE, a hemipterous insect reported as occurring in the United States (New Jersey) for the first time in 1916. The adult Japanese beetle, *Popillia japonica*, is about half an inch long and has a metallic green head and thorax and brown wing covers. The abdomen has two white spots at its tip and a row of white spots on each side. The curved, white larvae or grubs have well-developed legs. Both larvae and adults feed on practically all kinds of plants, the larvae especially attacking the roots of grass. Control consists for the most part in killing the grubs by spraying with chemicals. Recently a species of *Tiphia* wasp and the *Centeter* fly have been imported to combat this pest. These insects lay their eggs on the adult beetle. The maggots that emerge enter the body of the beetle, eventually killing it.

U.S.D.A.

Japanese beetle

JAPANESE DEER, a small deer of Central Asia that has been introduced into British parks. This deer, *Sika nippon*, stands about three feet high, has a brown coat in winter and in summer a reddish coat with spots. It differs from deer of the genus *Cervus* in its smaller size, longer tail, spotted summer coat, and simpler antlers.

JAPANESE EXCLUSION. See IMMIGRATION.

JAPANESE LANGUAGE AND LITERATURE. The Japanese language belongs structurally, like Korean and Manchurian, to the Altaic family, and like other Altaic languages delights in long, involved sentences, the introductory details being heaped up to an extraordinary length, so that when the final verb is reached many of these are apt to be already forgotten. The verbs, which are burdened with untranslatable honorific endings, come at the close of the clause. Grammatical gender is unrecognized; case is indicated by separable particles; there are no articles; prepositions follow the words they govern. The language, though difficult to master, is easily pronounced and musical.

The introduction of Chinese civilization in the sixth century was followed by a wholesale absorption of Chinese words and characters, but the language remained grammatically unchanged, as obscure and involved in its idioms and constructions as before. Chinese ideographs are said to have been reduced to a phonetic syllabary by the Buddhist priest Kobodaishi in 810. In process of time this system, the *Hiragana*, was rendered more complex by the addition of variants; and this led, apparently, to the introduction of another and simpler alphabet, entirely without variants, known as the katakana character. The revolution of 1868 caused the language to become more Chinese in vocabulary than ever, from the necessity of coining a host of new scientific terms, although many European words were also transferred *simpliciter*. A movement, powerfully supported, has been on foot for many years to introduce the Roman alphabet, a reform which would save much tedious labor, since Japanese youths have to spend years in learning Chinese ideographs.

Other languages spoken in the Japanese Empire are Luchuan, a very closely related sister tongue; Aino or Ainu, the language of the aborigines of Yesso, of ill-ascertained affinities; and the Chinese and Malay dialects of Formosa. Ordinary Japanese writing is a mixture of the Chinese ideographic character for the roots of words, and a phonetic syllabic character called *kana* for the terminations and particles—as we write "8th," which is a combination of an Arabic ideograph with Roman phonetic characters. There are 47 syllables, represented by several hundred kana.

Literature. The earliest extant book, a mythological and historical work called the *Kojiki*, belongs to A.D. 712. It is written in a strange compound of Japanese and Chinese. The *Nihongi*, composed in Chinese, followed in 720. It is also a history. Both contain a number of more ancient poems of an unimaginative primitive kind, which are the oldest extant specimens of any Ural-Altaic language. Another archaic monument is the *Norito*—liturgies of the Shinto religion, belonging probably to the seventh and eighth centuries.

The old poetry of Japan is contained chiefly in the collections called the *Manyoshiu* (collection of 10,000 leaves) and *Kokinshiu* (ancient and modern collection), made in the ninth and the tenth century respectively. Japanese poetry has no rhyme, accent, or quantity. It is distinguished from prose by the regular alternation of phrases of five and seven syllables, and by the exclusion of words of Chinese origin. There are no epics, no didactic, philosophical, or satirical poems, and indeed no long poems of any kind. The favorite meter is a stanza of 31 syllables, which constitutes the entire poem. Praise of love or wine, longing for absent dear ones, elegies, sententious ejaculations, emotion at the various aspects of nature —these are the favorite subjects of the Japanese poet.

Classic Prose. The great age of prose was the Heian period (794–1185). It has left us a considerable mass of fiction, essays, and a few quasi-historical works, containing a strong element of romance. Curiously, the two greatest writers of this time were women—officials of the mikado's court. One, Murasaki no Shikibu, is famous for a portentously long novel of Kyoto court life, named the *Genji Monogatari*, and the

Detail of scroll, a part of the "Heike Monogatari," depicts burning of the Sanjo Palace

other, Sei Shonagon, for a series of charming essays and sketches called *Makura no Soshi*. From the end of the Heian to the beginning of the Yedo period Japanese literature did not flourish. It has left us the *Heike Monogatari* and the *Taiheiki*, two histories in which are recorded, with much rhetorical flourish and embroidery of romantic details, the wars that then devastated Japan. The principal literary interest of these periods attaches to some essays, tales, and sketches by a Buddhist priest named Kenkoboshi (14th century).

The drama dates from about the same time. As in other countries, it was at first associated with religion. The *No* are short lyrical pieces of six or seven pages, which could be acted in an hour. Two or three hundred of these remain, most of them belonging to the 15th century. Their subject is usually some monkish legend, but they are not without poetic merit.

The Yedo Revival. The political movement which culminated in the establishment of the Tokugawa shogunate was accompanied by an intellectual revival. Chinese political and moral philosophy were earnestly studied, and a literature which derived its inspiration from this source was the result. It was the day of the *Kangakusha* (Chinese scholars), as they were called. The number of their works is appalling. They comprise commentaries on the Chinese classics, moral treatises, works on government, history, and philosophy, and they have done much to mold the national character and determine the moral standards of the modern Japanese. There was a revival during the Yedo period of the Shinto religion. It had a literature of its own in a pure Japanese style, illustrated by the great names of Motoöri and Hirata. The popular literature of Japan during the Yedo period is extremely voluminous.

A popular drama (*Joruri*), suited to a less refined public than the audiences of the *No*, was created toward the end of the 17th century by Chikamatsu. In the 17th and 18th centuries Saikaku, Jisho, and Kiseki produced numerous stories and sketches, more notable for their literary merit than for their moral tendency. The end of the 18th and the beginning of the 19th century is illustrated by the names of Kioden, Bakin, and Tanehiko, writers of romantic stories replete with wonderful incidents. The *Hiakkenden*, one of Bakin's works, is contained in 106 volumes. Novels of sentiment were largely written in the first half of the 19th century, when there also flourished Samba and Ikku, two humorists of no small merit. The *Hizakurige* of the latter is a most amusing book. It relates the picaresque adventures of two worthies named Yaji and Hida on their travels along the great highways of Japan.

Fiction received a fresh impulse from the stirring of national thought caused by contact with European ideas in the second half of the 19th century.

Notable protagonists of contemporary trends in fiction are the neo-Realist Kikuchi Kan (1,888–   ), called the dean of Japanese writers; Hayashi Fusao (1906–   ), author of *The Threads of Destiny of the City* and other proletarian novels; and Yokomitsu Richii 1898–   ), leader of a school of extreme Impressionists.   **S. W. X.**

BIBLIOG.–Z. Kincaid, *Kabuki, the Popular Stage of Japan* (1925); F. A. Lombard, *An Outline History of Japanese Drama* (1929); G. B. Sansom, *Japan: A Short Cultural History* (1943).

JAPANESE SPANIEL, or **JAPANESE CHIN,** the oldest breed of toy dogs, thought to have originated in China. The Japanese spaniel is a lively little dog,

Japanese spaniel

alert and sensitive. Its long, straight, silky coat may be either black and white or red and white. The large, round head has a short, turned-up nose, small V-shaped ears, and large, dark eyes. The compactly built body is square; the twisted tail is covered with long hair. An outstanding characteristic of this dog is its Oriental appearance.

JAPANNING is the process of producing, by the aid of heat, a hard coating of colored varnish upon metal, wood, leather, or papier-mâché. Articles so coated resemble the lacquerwares of Japan and China (see LACQUER). A good brown japan is prepared by separately heating equal quantities of amber and asphaltum, and adding to each one-half the quantity by weight of boiled linseed oil. Both compounds are then mixed together. For black japan asphaltum is mixed with gum, linseed oil, and turpentine, or the metal may be given a preliminary coating of black paint, then treated with brown paint. Only one coating of brown japan is given to cheap goods, but for better wares two or more coatings are applied. After each coating the articles are heated for ten or twelve hours in an oven at from 135° to 165° F., or higher.

The japanned surface is then rubbed with fine ground pumice, next with rottenstone, and the final polish is given to it by the palm of the hand. If gold or bronze bands or floral decoration are to be added, these are first painted on in japanner's gold size; then the gold leaf is applied or bronze powder dusted on, after which the objects are again placed in the oven. After they are removed the gilt or bronzed portions receive a protecting coat of white spirit varnish.

JAPHETH, or **JAPHET,** according to Gen. 10:1–5, the second son of NOAH, and the ancestor of a number of tribes who came to occupy "the isles of the Gentiles." Among his sons was Javan (i.e., Ionia, Greece). The term Japhetic or Japetic was at one time used loosely for peoples of the European stock (nearly as Aryan and Indo-European now), as opposed to Semitic and Hamitic (Asiatic and African).

JAPURÁ RIVER, also **Yapurá,** or **Caquetá,** South America, one of the most important of the northern tributaries of the Amazon, rises in the Colombian Andes, and follows a SE course through Colombia and W Brazil. Its upper course lies through a deep rocky gorge over a series of rapids culminating below the Arataicoara reefs in a magnificent cascade 100 feet high. In its lower course the river becomes sluggish and develops numerous lateral channels which connect with the Amazon. The Japurá is 1,700 miles long and is navigable for about half its length.

JAQUE, airfield, SE Panama, near the Pacific Ocean and the Colombian border. The site, comprising 310 acres, was leased in 1947 by the United States for the defense of the Panama Canal.

JACQUES-DALCROZE, ÉMILE, 1865–1950, Swiss composer and educator, was born in Vienna. Educated at the conservatories of Geneva, Paris, and Vienna, he was a pupil of Bruckner and Delibes. His books, *Méthode Jaques-Dalcroze* (1907–14) and *Rhythm, Music, and Education* (1922), explain his educational system of rhythmic gymnastics. Called eurhythmics, the method teaches musical rhythm in correlation with exercise and has influenced both ballet and physical training. He founded the Institut Jaques-Dalcroze at Geneva on the eurhythmic theory and has been its director since 1915. Many branches of the school have been established in Europe and America. His compositions include the opera, *Sancho Panza* (1897) and the choral work, *Festival Vaudois* (1903).

JARABE TAPATIO, the national dance of Mexico, combines characteristics of both Spanish and Mexican dances. Performed by a couple, it is a pantomime of courtship. The man feigns pursuit of the girl and finally tosses on the floor his sombrero around which the girl dances, performing intricate steps on the brim. The music is in either double or triple time, and is usually played by harp, violin, and guitars. At the end of the dance the musicians play the "diana," a fast Mexican melody symbolizing a happy climax and the approval of the audience.   RUTH FISCELLA

JARARACA, a venomous South American pit viper that is related to the FER-DE-LANCE.

JARDINE, WILLIAM MARION, 1879–   , American educator and public official, was born in Oneida County, Idaho, and studied at the Agricultural College of Utah, where he taught (1904–6). From 1907 to 1910 he was assistant U.S. cerealist in charge of dry-land investigations and in 1910 became agronomist at the Kansas State Agricultural College and Experiment Station. He was acting director and dean of the Kansas Experiment Station and dean of the State Agricultural College (1913–18), and president (1918–25). Jardine served as secretary of agriculture (1925–29) in President Coolidge's cabinet. In 1934 he became president of the Municipal University, Wichita, Kan.

JARGON, or **JARGOON,** is a colorless, yellowish, smoky, or gray ZIRCON, obtained from Ceylon. Its only value is as a source of zirconium oxide which is employed as a refractory. Jargon is found in worn pieces in river sands, and when polished has a fine diamond-like luster.

JARNAC, town, France, in the department of Charente, on the river Charente; seven miles by rail SE of Cognac. It is a wine and brandy center. Here (Mar. 13, 1596) the Duke of Anjou defeated the Huguenots under the Prince of Condé and Coligny. Pop. about 3,500.

JARO, city, Philippine Islands, Leyte Province, 15 miles W of Tacloban. It was captured by U.S. forces on Oct. 31, 1944. Pop. (1948) 19,650.

JARO, former city, Philippine Islands, on Panay, now consolidated with Iloilo. It is an old Spanish settlement and episcopal see.

JARRAH, an Australian tree of great economic value on account of the hardness and durability of its wood. See EUCALYPTUS.

JARROW, port and municipal borough, NE England, Durham County, on the Tyne Estuary; six miles SE of Newcastle, five miles E of Gateshead, and three miles SW of South Shields. The parish church of St. Paul has incorporated parts of the Benedictine monastery, which was founded in 685 by Ceolfrid and was the scene of the labors of the Venerable Bede. The town has shipbuilding, ironworks, marine engine construction works, a chemical plant, blast furnaces, and steel rolling mills. Paper is manufactured and coal exported. Pop. (1950 est.) 28,570.

JARVES, JAMES JACKSON, 1820–88, American art collector, was born in Boston, the son of a pioneer glass manufacturer. After traveling in South America, he settled in Hawaii, founding in 1840 *The Polynesian,* first newspaper in the islands. He held several posts representing the Hawaiian government in Europe; and, while a U.S. vice-consul in Florence, he made a valuable collection of paintings and other art objects. In 1881 he presented his collection of Venetian glass to the Metropolitan Museum of Art, New York City. Yale University came into possession of a large share of his Italian masterpieces. His books include *History of the Hawaiian or Sandwich Islands* (1843) and *Art Studies, the Old Masters of Italy* (1861).

JARVIS, JOHN WESLEY, 1780–1840, American artist, born in South Shields, England; was taken to Philadelphia when five years old. He studied under Stuart, Martin, Malbone, and other artists of the day, and became well known as a portrait painter. His pictures, which are pleasant in coloring, include portraits of Governor De Witt Clinton and Bishop Benjamin Moore. Examples of his work are to be seen in the City Hall, New York, in the Metropolitan Museum of Art, and in the collection of the New York Historical Society.

JARVIS ISLAND. See HOWLAND, BAKER, AND JARVIS ISLANDS.

JASHAR, BOOK OF, or **Jasher,** an ancient Hebrew collection of songs, no longer extant. It is mentioned twice in the Old Testament, both times in connection with the quotation of a lyrical passage; also in the Septuagint of I Kings 8:12, 13. In Josh. 10:12, 13, the verses about the sun standing still upon Gibeon are cited from the book; while in II Sam. 1:18 it is named as the source of David's elegy on Saul and Jonathan.

JASHPUR, former feudatory state, India, now part of Central Provinces and Bihar, at SW border of Bihar; area 1,955 sq. mi.; pop. (1941) 223,612. The state is almost equally divided between high- and lowlands, and in the east is a plateau about 2,200 feet above sea level, from which rises its highest point (3,527 ft.). Gold has been washed from the sands of the Ib River for many years. The forests grow many sal trees, and the exported products of the jungle include lac, timber, silk cocoons, and beeswax. Elephants, bison, and other big game are found. The people are chiefly aboriginals.

JASMIN, JACQUES, real name **Jacques Boé,** 1798–1864, Gascon barber-poet, a native of Agen. He was apprenticed to a hairdresser, and in his *Soubenis*

(1830) has given a humorous account of the poverty and privations of his early life. His first volume, entitled *Papillotos* (Curl Papers), appeared in 1835. He was made a chevalier of the Legion of Honor in 1846, and in 1852 his works were crowned by the French Academy and a prize was awarded him. His most attractive poems are short epic narratives, now serious, now gay, dealing with lowly peasant life, in his own Gascon dialect. They charm by their spontaneity and simplicity, and belong to the remarkable achievements of dialect literature. Jasmin published altogether four volumes of verse, and greatly enhanced his reputation by reciting his own poems in public. Among his best pieces are *The Charivari* (1825), a mock-heroic poem; *The Blind Girl of Castel-Cuillé* (1835), translated by Longfellow; *Franconetto* (1840); *The Son's Week* (1849).

JASMINE, or **JESSAMINE**, a genus of plants of the olive family, including many cultivated varieties, most of them shrubs with long twining branches and bearing fragrant flowers. The flowers are salver-shaped, the corolla being white or yellow in color; the stamens, two in number, are included in the tube of the corolla; and the leaves are usually pinnate. The common jasmine, *J. officinalis*, has been naturalized in southern Europe, and the essential oil is usually distilled from this variety and from *J. grandiflorum*, a native of the East Indies. The commercial oil of jasmine, however, is merely oil of ben or the like, flavored with jasmine. Other well-known naturalized species are *J. sambac* and *J. humile*. The Cape jasmine, *Gardenia jasminoides*, a Chinese shrub, brought to America about the middle of the 18th century, is a double-flowered variety that grows out of doors along the southern seaboard, and is cultivated elsewhere in greenhouses. The Carolina jasmine, *G. sempervirens*, or yellow jasmine, is a native climbing plant of heavy fragrance found throughout the South Atlantic states.

JASON, in ancient Greek legend, the leader of the Argonautic expedition, was the son of Aeson and Polymede. His father's half brother, Pelias, tried to kill him, but he was rescued and was brought up by the centaur Chiron. Having grown to manhood, Jason demanded his father's kingdom from Pelias, who promised its restitution on condition that Jason secure the golden fleece from Colchis. This he accomplished with the help of the other heroes who had been his fellow pupils with Chiron, and with the aid of Medea, the daughter of the king of Colchis, whom he made his wife. When, upon his return to Iolcos, Jason found that Pelias had killed his father, Medea in revenge persuaded Pelias' daughters to cut their father in pieces and boil him in a cauldron in the hope of restoring his youth. For this crime Jason and Medea were driven from Iolcos, and went to Corinth where, after some years, Jason abandoned Medea for Creusa, the king's daughter. Medea avenged herself by sending Creusa a poisoned robe, which burned her to death, and by killing her own and Jason's children. Accounts of Jason's death vary. Some writers attribute it to grief caused by Medea's vengeance. See ARGONAUTS.

JASPER, WILLIAM, c. 1750–79, American Revolutionary soldier, was born in South Carolina. As a sergeant in the 2nd South Carolina regiment, he distinguished himself at Fort Moultrie by recovering the flag under fire of the British (1776). For his daring Governor Rutledge presented him with a sword and offered him a lieutenant's commission. Jasper declined it because of his poor education but continued to distinguish himself as a scout. He was killed at Savannah.

JASPER, city, NW central Alabama, county seat of Walker County; on the Frisco, the Illinois Central, the Southern, and the Alabama Central railroads, and U.S. Highway 78, about 35 miles NW of Birmingham. Jasper is a railroad center located in a region of coal mines, sandstone quarries, and natural gas wells. The city, settled in 1815, is located on the site of a former Indian trading center. Jasper's chief manufactures are lumber, cotton textiles, hosiery, and leather goods. Pop. (1950) 8,589.

JASPER, city, SW Indiana, county seat of Dubois County, on the Southern Railroad, about 50 miles NE of Evansville. This industrial city is located in a farming region producing chiefly corn, wheat, and strawberries; coal mines are near by. Jasper was founded in 1818 but in 1838 received a large group of German immigrants who have molded the life of the city. St. Joseph's Church, begun in 1868 and built over a period of years by members of the congregation, is of particular interest: the roof of the church is supported by four large trees. Jasper has canning plants and factories making furniture, plywood, veneer, and other wood products. Pop. (1950) 5,215.

JASPER, an abundant mineral, generally regarded as one of the varieties of QUARTZ, composed chiefly of silica mixed with clay or other substances, and essentially similar to flint, chert, and chalcedony. There are many kinds of jasper, some of them of one color, as red, yellow, green, white, etc., and some variously striped, spotted, or clouded with different colors. Jasper occurs in veins and embedded masses in many rocks, and is common in the shape of pebbles. It takes a high polish. The variety known as *porcelain jasper* is found in places where coal seams have taken fire, and is thus simply a baked clay. Sometimes it has a banded pattern (striped jasper or ribbon jasper); at other times a wavy or concentric one, with spots and flakes of various colors. *Egyptian jasper* is a yellow-brown variety found on the banks of the Nile. Radiolarian cherts, which are gray, yellow, or red, and banded, are also known as jaspers.

JASPER NATIONAL PARK, Canada, in the province of Alberta, lies along the E slope of the Canadian Rockies NW of Banff National Park. It is the largest national park in Canada and contains an area of 4,200 square miles. Noted for its rugged beauty, the park contains majestic peaks, beautiful alpine valleys, sparkling lakes, glittering ice sheets, and forested mountains. The first settlement in the area was Jasper House, a trading post, established in 1813 by the North West Company and operated at one time by Jasper Hawes for whom the region is named. The park, established in 1907, is traversed by motor highways and is served by the Canadian National Railway. Administrative headquarters are located in the town of Jasper.

JASPERWARE, a form of porcelain. See WEDGWOOD.

JASSY. See IASI.

JÁSZBERÉNY, town, E central Hungary, on the left bank of the Zagyva River, 40 miles E of Budapest.

NATIONAL PARKS BUREAU, CANADA
Maligne Lake in Jasper National Park, Alberta

It has manufactures of cloth and wine and a large trade in corn, cattle, and horses. Pop. about 35,000.

JATAKA, the title of a book on the Buddhist religion containing 550 legends dealing with the early life of Buddha. This collection of stories was known in 350 B.C. and though the legends were originally written in the Pali language, they were soon adopted into the Persian and European cultures and formed the bases for many folk and fairy tales. Bas-reliefs dating from the third century B.C. illustrating many of these tales have been found. The first English translation of the Jataka was completed in 1913 by E. B. Cowell and his assistants.

JATS. See GYPSY.

JAÚ, city, SE Brazil in the state of São Paulo, in an agricultural region. Pop. (1940) 18,665.

JAUNDICE is a condition in which the coloring or pigment matter normally eliminated through the bile backs up into the blood and other tissues. Bile pigments produce a typical yellowish color of the skin and mucous membranes, particularly visible in the whites of the eyes. Jaundice is a symptom that can be caused by a wide variety of mechanical conditions, infections, and diseases.

One important cause of jaundice is obstruction to the normal flow of bile from the gallbladder into the intestines. This can come from such things as gallstones, a clump of parasites, inflammation of the lining of the bile duct, or pressure on the duct from something outside it, such as a tumor. In the obstructive type of jaundice the color of the skin can vary all the way from a lemon yellow to a deep olive green or bronze color. Discoloration is usually associated with a distressing itching of the skin. Because the bile is no longer emptying into the intestinal tract the stools become pale or slate gray in color. The heart rate is slow and there is frequently a tendency to easy bleeding because the normal clotting of the blood is delayed. The amount of yellow color in the skin does not necessarily reflect the amount of bile pigments in the blood, which can be discovered accurately only by chemical tests of the blood serum. When the particular cause of the obstruction has been discovered and if the condition has lasted for a long time without signs of improvement, surgery is usually necessary. Sometimes the obstructing gallstone or other foreign body can be removed and drainage restored. In some cases the entire gallbladder has to be taken out or other surgical procedures employed. When the jaundice has not lasted too long and successful surgery is possible, the jaundice disappears entirely without serious lasting effects.

Jaundice can be produced also by certain toxic or infectious states. Some poisons, such as trinitrotoluene (TNT), act on the liver so that the bile pigments are not passed through and accumulate in the blood. In other cases excessive bile coloring matter is produced by increased destruction of red blood cells, the original source of this material. If not eliminated rapidly enough the bile pigments accumulate and produce jaundice. Infectious hepatitis, which was quite common during World War II, especially among military personnel in many parts of the world, is a common cause of jaundice. This is probably due to an infectious disease involving the liver and is accompanied by jaundice as well as other symptoms.

A hereditary disease which seems to run in families can cause jaundice. Jaundice in newborn infants usually comes from an excessive destruction of the red cells due to incompatability between the blood of the infant and of the mother. (See BLOOD GROUPS, Rh Factor.) Another disease in which jaundice is present is acute yellow atrophy of the liver. The cause of this condition is not known but it comes from a severe disorder in the liver which prevents the elimination of bile pigments.   EDWIN P. JORDAN, M.D.

JAUNPUR, city, India, United Provinces, capital of Jaunpur District, on the left bank of the Gumti River, 37 miles NW of Benares. Jaunpur was the capital of an ancient Moslem kingdom and has many splendid architectural sights, including a mosque built in 1376 and a bridge over the Gumti built between 1569 and 1573. Jaunpur, less prosperous than formerly, produces perfumes and papier-mâché articles. Pop. (1941) 44,833.

JAURÈS, JEAN, 1859–1914, French political leader, was born in Castres, department of Tarn. He was educated at the Ecole Normale Supérieure, became professor of philosophy at the University of Toulouse (1883) and in 1885 was elected to the Chamber of Deputies. In 1892 he championed the cause of the workmen in the Carmaux strike, and in the following year became the leader of the Socialist group in the Chamber. He was an earnest defender of Dreyfus, a bitter opponent of militarism, and an advocate of arbitration. His attacks on militarism aroused such resentment that he was assassinated by a half-demented fanatic at the outbreak of World War I. He contributed largely to *Histoire socialiste, 1789–1900* (12 vols., 1901–8), and to various periodicals.

JAVA ❖ Chief Island of Indonesia

Java was at one time the center of a vast Indian empire which covered most of southeastern Asia

JAVA, perhaps from Sanskrit **yava** "millet" or from the Polynesian place-names **hava** and **sava,** an island off SE Asia, a part of the Netherlands-Indonesian Union, the Republic of Indonesia; now divided into three provinces—West Java, Central Java, and East Java; one of the islands of the Greater Sunda Group, lying between Sumatra on the W and the small island of Bali on the E, separated from them respectively by the straits of Sunda and Bali; area 50,745 sq. mi.; pop. (1949 est.) 50,000,000. Java is bounded to the north by the Java Sea and to the south by the Indian Ocean; extending 600 miles from 105° 12′ E and 5° 52′ S to 114° 35′ E and 8° 47′ S, with a width varying from 45 to 120 miles. It includes administratively a number of insular dependencies: Madura (Madoera), Bawean (Bavian), the Karimon Java (Karimoendjowo) Islands, the group of 80 islands ("Thousand Islands") northwest of Batavia Bay, Nusa (Noesa), Kambangan, and others. Fourth in size, Java is first in importance and population in Indonesia. The capital, BATAVIA (Jakarta), is the seat of the central government for the Republic of Indonesia.

Topography and Climate. Java's mountain system is part of the volcanic fringe of the Malay Archipelago. It consists of a continuous chain beginning at a point some 50 miles inland from Sunda Strait, ending at the very edge of Bali Strait, and lying somewhat south of center. In West Java it is a massif or mountainous mass of connected ranges enclosing upland basins and becoming narrower in Middle Java. In East Java the chain separates into individual peaks. The system has three groups distinct from the central chain: two on Sunda Strait and one on the north coast, northeast of Semarang. On the south the main range is flanked by a limestone ridge which slopes down to the Indian Ocean. Of the 112 volcanic centers, 12 are in various states of activity. The principal peaks are Semeru (Semeroe), also known as Mahameru (Mahameroe) (12,057 ft), Slamet or Slamat (11,259 ft.), Merapi, near Jogjakarta (11,460 ft.), and Merapi, in East Java (11,453 ft.). The majority of the plains are along the northern shore. The upland valley of Kedu (Kedoe) lies in Middle Java and is the most densely populated tract in the entire island.

The watershed is mostly to the north; of Java's eight important watercourses five empty into the Java Sea and three into the Indian Ocean. The long-

Buffalo cart is a familiar sight on Java roads

est river is the Solo, 336 miles. The others, with the exception of the Brantas in East Java, are short, and while in the main they are navigable for small craft their greatest use is for irrigation.

The temperature averages 80° at sea level with a decrease of 1° for each 300 feet altitude. The humidity is high. There are two seasons, wet and dry. The west monsoon brings the rains which are practically continuous from October to April.

Plants and Animals. Animals found on the island include the tiger (rare), civet, ichneumon, wildcat, and common cat; the one-horned rhinoceros; the banteng or wild ox; several species of deer; two species of wild pig, the galeopithecus, a flying lemuroid; the porcupine; the scaly anteater; hares; badgers; rats; mice; and shrews. Bats in great numbers have created guano deposits. The dugong, a large aquatic mammal, frequents the coastal waters. The bird population numbers around 400 species, including parrots, swifts, thrushes, trogons, orioles, doves, pigeons, the green peacock, and two species of fowl. Crocodiles infest the rivers. Lizards are numerous. The great python, the cobra, and one kind of adder are found. Fishes are abundant and play an essential part in the native diet. Java has crabs, lobsters, and crayfish. Insects include beetles, scorpions, centipedes, hornets, ants, termites, moths, mosquitoes, and about 500 species of butterflies. The chief draft animal of southeast Asia, the carabao, is present in large numbers. Early in Java's history the Indians brought over zebus and a small breed of horses. Later imports have been cattle from Europe, swine from China, and horses from Arabia.

Java has over 5,000 species of plants, most of them represented in the world-famed Botanical Gardens of BUITENZORG. The flora is South Asian but in the east and southeast, or near the demarcation line formed by Bali Strait, Australian affinities are perceptible. As the island's climatic zones include one of high peaks where conditions are Alpine and frosts occur, many trees and plants of the temperate and subtropical belts grow here: the oak, chestnut, maple, an elm (the *anggrang*); the yew, fig, laurel, rhododendron, azalea; the whortleberry, raspberry, and blackberry; the myrtle, elder, and barberry; the honeysuckle, lily of the valley, lobelia, sow thistle, foxglove, and wood sorrel; the guelder-rose and the so-called Javanese edelweiss; the ironwood, acacia, and magnolia; the jasmine. The Tengger country has fields of rye and truck gardens of European produce. Mosses and lichens are present. Among the timber trees the rasamala and the teak are most important with forests of the latter covering extensive areas in central and eastern Java. The teak is used locally as common

lumber and not as a precious wood. Southeast Asian plants and trees of the island are the alang-alang, pepper vine, bamboo, rattan, Casuarina, palm, and sugar palm.

Population. Ethnically the Javanese are predominantly Malayan with a greater amount of the pro-Malayan element in the Tengger mountain area. They are divided into three main groups: the Sundanese who occupy the southern half of West Java; the Javanese who, except for a Madurese enclave on the northeast coast, occupy the rest of the island; and the Madurese who occupy Madura and the enclave. Besides these there are two statistically negligible groups: the Badui in Sundanese territory, and the Tenggerese in Javanese territory. On the area roughly equal to that of New York state Java supports more than 50,000,000 people. It has 7 per cent of the territory and 67 per cent of the population of the Republic of Indonesia. As plantation agriculture is conducted mainly at both extremities of the island, leaving the rest to intensive tillage dominated by paddy rice, population density per square mile varies greatly, the lowest being in West Java (630) and the highest in Jogjakarta government (1,300). Attempts to relieve the overcrowding through voluntary emigration to the more sparsely settled Indies have met with indifferent success.

The important cities of Java are: Batavia (with its suburb, Meester Cornelis), 533,015; SURABAYA (Soerabaja), 341,675; SEMARANG 217,796; JOGJAKARTA (Djokjakarta), 135,469; BANDUNG (Bandoeng), 166,-815; SURAKARTA (Soerakarta), 165,484; and CHERIBON (Tjirebon), 54,079. Java has 80 per cent of the Chinese of the Republic of Indonesia. There are also Arabs, mostly from Hadhramaut, and a number of Indians.

Javanese, Java's vernacular, is a descendant of Kavi, a Malayo-Polynesian language with a large Sanskritic vocabulary. The modern language is richer in Malay and even Arabic words but retains from the older tongue its two forms: vulgar and polite. It is written in the Arabic characters and, to a slight extent, in a modified form of the Indian alphabet. Of late a Romanization of it has been introduced. Standard Malay is understood in Java as it is in most of the Indies.

Education and Religion. In Java as in the rest of the Netherlands Indies, government policy has not

Court dancer in traditional Javanese dance pose

favored a large degree of education. The system organized in 1872 placed emphasis on the primary grades beyond which most of the few who attend do not go. Schools are divided not by race but by language, vernacular, Dutch, or Chinese, the individual being free to attend any of these types. Natives leaving the primary school may attend native trade, agricultural, or normal secondary schools; or, by attending what is known as a "link school," pass over to the secondary school system. Higher education is provided at the Government University at Batavia, which has faculties in law, civil service, arts, and agriculture, and a technical college at Bandung. Besides the public schools there are private and missionary schools subsidized by the government. There are also schools for the training of railway and public service experts.

With the exception of two small groups, the Badui and the Tenggerese, who combine a primitive animism with Hinduism, the Javanese are Mohammedan. They do retain, however, particularly in eastern Java where the Moslem influence has been weaker, many pagan superstitions and customs.

Minerals. Java is the least favored of the Indies in mineral wealth. Coal is found in many places though in strata too thin to warrant exploitation. There are deposits of lignite in Bantam. Tin is exploited and exported, and the oil deposits on Madura are worked on a small scale. Other minerals include marble, clay, limestone, salt, saltpeter, sulfur, asphalt, naphtha, and manganese.

Agriculture. Java has the four requirements to ideal farmland: favorable climate, freedom from seasonal change, abundant rainfall, and a fertilizing volcanic ash. The Javanese are essentially an agricultural people. Rice, their staple food, can be raised the year round in the lowlands as well as in terraced fields on mountain sides, and in such amounts that enough is left above the island needs to export to the other Indies or even to China. Other important crops are corn, cassava, and soybeans. These and crops like sweet potatoes and peanuts, are "native" cultures. "Non-native" or plantation cultures include sugar, rubber, cinchona, coffee, tea, cacao, tobacco, and kapok.

Industry in Java is in a transitional stage. Although manufacturing is still largely of the "cottage" type such as weaving (mostly on hand looms), hat plaiting, batik cloth, and copper work, the island has for a long time held a position of world importance in the refining of sugar and the production of quinine. In recent years other industrial developments have been attempted, the tendency receiving an additional impetus from the 1929 crisis and the ensuing sugar slump. New developments include paper mills, textile mills, soap factories, and breweries, a tire and rubber plant in Buitenzorg, an automobile assembly plant in Tanjong Priok, and a shoe factory near Batavia. For many years sugar was Java's main item of export. Since the 1929 slump, however, it has lost some of its importance, the 1,576,159 tons exported in 1939 representing 6 per cent of the world's market compared with 11 per cent in 1929. Other exports are coffee, cinchona, indigo, nutmeg, mace, cloves, cinnamon, pepper, tea, rice, copra, cacao, tapioca, tin, rubber, cochineal, hides, tobacco, arrack, and cubebs. Exports in 1938 amounted to $385,734,420 and were to the United States, England, the Netherlands, India, and Japan. Java is dependent on the outside world for textiles, paper, oil, automobiles, and fertilizer. Imports in 1938 totaled $268,587,900 and were mostly from England.

Communications. The railroad network traverses Java lengthwise with two main lines, one in the north and one in the south, with linkage through the transversal valleys. A spur of the north branch extends into Madura, the two-mile gap between island and mainland being bridged by a ferry at Surabaya. In 1940 Java had 16,850 miles of highway and 3,378 of

NETHERLANDS INFORMATION BUREAU
Headquarters of the Peoples' Council in Java

rail. The telephone system has more than 100,000 miles of wires, and the wireless station at Bandung is one of the world's largest. Java is linked to the other Indies by steamships; the chief harbors are Batavia Semarang, Surabaya, and Cheribon. International airports are located at Batavia and Surabaya, with Batavia the main terminus for both international and domestic air routes. International air lines provide service to Australia, the Philippines, and China, and to Africa and Europe by way of India and Pakistan. Domestic air lines have a network of some 13,000 miles in Indonesia.   ADRIAN TROY

Government. For administrative purposes Java is divided into three provinces: West Java, Central Java, and East Java (including Madura). Java is a part of the Republic of Indonesia which came into existence on Aug. 15, 1950. The island is governed under the provisional constitution of the Republic of Indonesia which was to be in effect until a constituent assembly framed a constitution for the Republic. Under the present constitution a strong central government administers the 10 provinces of Indonesia. See INDONESIA, REPUBLIC OF, *Government*.

History. Before the appearance of the Portuguese the history of the island consists of two periods; the era of Hindu influence and the succeeding Mohammedan domination. Java's earliest civilization derives from India; Hindus visited the island as traders and priests as early as the first century A.D. A number of coastal states in the 5th and in the 7th centuries were established by the Hindus. By the 14th century Java, under the kingdom of Majapahit, established hegemony extending from the Malay Peninsula to the Moluccas. Under the Majapahit kingdoms (1293–1520) a considerable civilization was built up by the Hindus. Both Hinduism and Buddhism shaped the cultural tradition of the country. The Hindu-Javanese era has left a permanent impression on the island. The next conquerors were Moslems from India under whom the island was split up into many kingdoms and provinces. Mohammedanism had been introduced in Java and gradually the great majority of Javanese became Moslems.

The first of the occidental powers to arrive in Java were the Portuguese (c. 1511). The Dutch traders arrived in 1596. The Dutch East India Company, founded in 1602, developed and protected the island against Spanish, Portuguese and British competitors, until the dissolution of the Company in 1799. In 1610 the first Dutch governor general was appointed and by 1745 Dutch authority, largely through the East India Company, was recognized over the whole of the northeast coast. During the Napoleonic wars France laid claim to Java and for a very brief period governed the island. The presence of the French brought in the British, who defeated the French at Welteverden in 1811 led by General Stamford Raffles. Raffles, under the control of the governor general of India, ruled the island until 1816. In that year Java was restored to the Dutch who soon had to face a rebellion started by Dipa Negara. From 1830 to 1839 the government exploited native labor to produce not only for island needs but for European markets as well. In 1854, however, progressive administration was introduced. Between 1903 and 1918 the natives obtained the right to participate in the administration of the island. In the meantime the demand for home rule grew among the moderates, while the extremists demanded independence. Revolutionary movements in 1927 and in 1933 placed the Dutch government of the island in a temporarily precarious position.

After the outbreak of the Second World War, the Dutch government intensified its efforts to protect the island. However, the fall of Singapore and a naval defeat in the Java Sea made the defense of the island impossible. The first Japanese landings occurred on Feb. 29, 1942, and by March 10 virtually all resistance had ceased. The capitulation of the Japanese in the latter part of 1945 was followed by the restoration of Dutch authority. But a revolutionary nationalist movement seized power in Java; the Indonesian Republic, proclaimed on August 17, 1945, claimed jurisdiction over the island. In March, 1947, the Dutch recognized the *de facto* authority of the Republic over Java. However, late in July warfare again broke out between the Dutch and the natives, and Dutch forces gained control over most of the coastal areas of Java and much of Madura. After the intervention of the United Nations, the Dutch agreed late in 1949 to the creation of the new state of Indonesia of which Java became a part. On January 30, 1950, the state government of West Java dissolved as a result of the decision of the legislature and the Indonesian government was asked to take charge of the region and to protect it against guerrilla forces and extremists. Next day East Java and Madura likewise surrendered state powers to the central government. On March 11, 1950, Java became a single state of the Indonesia Republic through the merger of West, Central, and East Java (including Madura). See INDONESIA, REPUBLIC OF.   G. B. DE H.

BIBLIOG.–A Cabaton, *Java and the Dutch East Indies* (1911); D. M. Campbell, *Java, Past and Present* (1915); H. S. Banner, *Romantic Java* (1927); E. S. Klerck, *History of the Netherlands East Indies* (1938); J. S. Furnivall, *Netherlands India* (1939); R. Kennedy, *The Ageless Indies* (1942); H. W. Ponder, *Javanese Panorama* (1942); F.-C. Cole, *Peoples of Malaysia* (1945); B. A. Ubani and others, *Indonesian Struggle for Independence* (1946); J. W. Fabricius, *Java Revisited* (1947); D. Wehl, *The Birth of Indonesia* (1948); J. F. Collins, *The United Nations and Indonesia* (1950).

JAVA SEA, also known as the **Sunda Sea,** the body of water which lies between Java and Borneo, and reaches from Sumatra on the W to Celebes on the E. During World War II, on Feb. 27–28, 1942, an engagement between Allied and Japanese ships was won by the Japanese, resulting in the loss to the Allies of 16 ships, including five cruisers.

JAVA SEA, BATTLE OF THE, naval engagement of World War II, fought on Feb. 27-28, 1942, between Allied and Japanese forces. Rear Adm. Karel Doorman of the Dutch navy commanded the Allied force, which included five cruisers and nine destroyers: the Dutch light cruisers *De Ruyter* and *Java;* the Australian light cruiser *Perth;* the British heavy cruiser *Exeter;* the American heavy cruiser *Houston,* which had her afterturret out of commission because of damage received on 4 Feb. when an explosion was caused by a bomb hit inflicted by Japanese naval planes off Madoera Strait; the Dutch destroyers *Witte de With* and *Kortenaer;* the British destroyers *Jupiter, Electra,* and *Encounter;* and four American destroyers of the 1,200-ton type dating from 1918, the *Edwards, Alden, Ford,* and *Paul Jones.*

There were three phases of the battle. First, on the afternoon of February 27, Doorman fought for two hours with the covering force of the Japanese Java invasion convoy, apparently 5 heavy cruisers and 6 destroyers. *Kortenaer* and *Electra* were sunk; *Exeter* badly damaged. *Jupiter* was torpedoed, probably by a submarine, and sank just after this fight. Second, at about 11:15 P.M., *De Ruyter* and *Java* were sunk, and two Japanese destroyers were put out of action. Third, on February 28, all Allied naval vessels were ordered out of the Java Sea. The American destroyers *Edwards, Alden, Ford,* and *Paul Jones* had a skirmish at night in the Bali Strait but escaped uninjured. *Houston* and *Perth* reached Sunda Strait where they encountered a large enemy force during darkness. *Perth* was sunk almost immediately, but *Houston* fought for more than an hour, sank two transports, used almost all her ammunition, and had her captain killed, before she sank. Of her crew of 882, only 368 reached land, and 76 of these died in prison camps. *Exeter* and *Encounter* had been joined by an American destroyer, the *Pope,* and these three vessels were sunk. The battle delayed the invasion of Java for 24 hours, at a cost of five cruisers and five destroyers.   J. B. HEFFERNAN

JAVARY RIVER or **Jabary,** South America, flows NW to form a part of the boundary between Brazil and Peru and unites with the Marañon at Tabatinga, Brazil. The Javary is navigable for about 300 miles.

JAWHAR, former feudatory state, India, under the Gujarat States Agency; merged in 1948 with Bombay Province; area 308 sq. mi.; pop. (1941) 65,126. Its chief exercised full criminal and civil jurisdiction, and the state paid tribute neither to the British nor to another state. The capital was Jawhar (pop. 13,370). Jawhar's chief products are rice and millet, timber, and charcoal. Primary education was free within the state.

JAXARTES. See SYR DARYA.

JAY, JOHN, 1745–1829, eminent American statesman and diplomat, of Huguenot descent, was born in New York City on Dec. 12, 1745. He graduated from Kings College (now Columbia University) in 1764, and was admitted to the bar in 1768, being for a time the partner of ROBERT R. LIVINGSTON. Through force of character and exceptional ability he soon won a high place in the community both as a citizen and as a lawyer, and by his marriage (1774) with the daughter of William Livingston became allied with one of the most influential families in the colony. In the period immediately preceding the outbreak of the American Revolution he ardently embraced the Whig or Patriot cause, but allied himself with the conservative rather than with the radical elements of the opposition to the arbitrary measures of the British ministry. During the Revolution he was a member of the Continental Congress (1774–77 and 1778–79), was its president during the second period, drafted the "Address to the People of Great Britain," which was issued by Congress (1774) and which Jefferson, when ignorant of its authorship, declared to be "a production certainly of the finest pen in America," the "Address to the Canadians" (1775), and other important state papers; and was one of the most influential leaders of the Whigs in New York, being a member of important executive committees and of several provincial conventions, the chairman of the special committee which drafted the first state constitution of New York (1777), and the first chief justice of the state (1777–79).

CHICAGO HIST. SOC.
John Jay

Diplomat of the New Nation. Jay was one of the ablest and most conspicuous of the American diplomats during the Revolutionary period. From 1779 to 1782 he was the representative of the United States in Spain, but the Spanish government, though sharing as the ally of France in the war against Great Britain, persistently refused to acknowledge the independence of the United States and never recognized Jay as a member of the diplomatic corps; and Jay, whose position had been a difficult and trying one, left Madrid without having accomplished either of his principal objects—the securing of financial assistance and the negotiating of a treaty of alliance and friendship. It is mainly owing to him, however, that the United States did not make damaging concessions to Spain with regard to the navigation of the Mississippi River. See JAY-GARDOQUI NEGOTIATIONS.

In 1782–83 Jay was one of the American peace negotiators at Paris, and as such, quickly perceiving the true policy of the French government in the negotiations, was largely responsible for the decision of the American negotiators to deal directly and independently with the English and thus to disregard the instructions of Congress, which directed them to maintain confidential relations with the French ministers and "to undertake nothing in the negotiations for peace or truce without their knowledge or concurrence; and ultimately to govern yourself by their advice and opinion." To Jay, more than to any one of his associates, undoubtedly belongs the chief credit for the success of the negotiations. See PARIS, TREATY OF.

After his return to the United States Jay was secretary for foreign affairs of the Confederation (1785–9), and exerted a powerful influence, as the author, with Hamilton and Madison, of the famous *Federalist* papers and as a member of the N. Y. Constitutional Convention, to secure the ratification by New York of the Federal Constitution of 1787. After the organization of the new national government (1789), Jay was the first chief justice of the U.S. Supreme Court (1789–95); "his general learning and ability," says Daniel Webster, "and especially the prudence, the mildness, and the firmness of his character eminently fitted Mr. Jay to be at the head of such a court." See SUPREME COURT OF THE UNITED STATES; FEDERALIST PAPERS.

In 1794 as envoy extraordinary of the United States, though still retaining his position as chief justice, Jay negotiated with the British government what has come to be known as JAY'S TREATY. The treaty, when its contents became known, was vigorously denounced by the Democratic-Republicans, Jay himself being virulently attacked, but it was finally ratified by the U. S. Senate. During the early years of the national government Jay was one of the foremost leaders of the Federalist party and from 1795 to 1801, as a Federalist, he was governor of New York; he then retired to his estate at Bedford, N. Y., where he died May 17, 1829.

Among the published works of John Jay are: the *Federalist* or *The New Constitution*, papers by Alexander Hamilton, James Madison, and John Jay (1888–1945), *Correspondence and Public Papers of John Jay* edited by H. P. Johnston (1890–93), *Diary, During the Peace Negotiations of 1782* (1934), and *Some Conversations of Dr. Franklin and Mr. Jay*, a manuscript written by John Jay in Paris during 1783–84 (1936).

BIBLIOG.–W. Jay, his son, *Life of John Jay* (1883); W. Whitelock, *Life and Times of John Jay* (1887); G. Pellew, *John Jay* (1890, ed. 1909); E. Wildman, *The Founders of America in the Days of the Revolution* (1924); S. F. Bemis, ed., *The American Secretaries of State and Their Diplomacy* (1927); F. Monaghan, *John Jay, Defender of Liberty* (1935); J. J. Ide, *Portraits of John Jay (1745–1829)* (1938).

JAY, a familiar bird belonging to the CROW family, *Corvidae*. These birds usually have short wings, a long tail, an erectile crest, and plumage in which blue is the prevailing tint. Jays occur in most temperate and warm countries and are active, noisy birds, taking their name from their harsh call note. They feed upon insects, nuts, berries, and the eggs and young of other birds. The typical and most familiar jay of the United States is the blue jay, *Cyanocitta cristata*, which is resi-

CHICAGO NAT. HIST. MUS.
Northern bluejay

dent throughout the year in practically all parts of the country. Canada has a subarctic species, gray, and with a rounded topknot, the Canada jay, *Perisoreus canadensis*, which is noted for its impertinent familiarities about camps and lumbermen's cabins in the forest. The jays of Europe, represented by the common but shy and wary *Garrulus glandarius*, are more varied with less blue in their feathers; many related species inhabit the Orient. In captivity jays display many amusing and imitative traits.

JAY, FORT. See GOVERNOR'S ISLAND.

JAY-GARDOQUI NEGOTIATIONS, the attempt made by JOHN JAY (1784–6) to settle the question of Mississippi navigation and other matters in dispute with Spain. The negotiations between Jay and the Spanish representative, Diego de Gardoqui, resulted in a draft treaty by which the United States would give up for 30 years the right to the navigation of the lower Mississippi (over which Spain claimed exclusive control, since she held both banks), in return for favorable commercial privileges in Spanish home ports; the disputed boundary was to be compromised on terms favorable to the United States. The Westerners, whose livelihood depended on access to New Orleans, were highly incensed because their interests had been sacrificed to the commercial Eastern states; consequently the Southern states blocked ratification of the treaty. Finally in 1795 Spain yielded on the matter of free navigation of the Mississippi.

JAY'S TREATY, a treaty between the United States and Great Britain, negotiated in November, 1794, by JOHN JAY, representing the United States, and Lord Grenville, representing Great Britain. Soon after the close of the American Revolution, relations between the United States and Great Britain became strained, owing largely to the failure of Great Britain, in contravention of the treaty of 1783, to surrender the Western posts held by her or to render compensation for slaves carried away by the British troops at the close of hostilities, Great Britain justifying her course on the ground that several states of the United States had prevented the payment by Americans to British creditors of debts contracted before the Revolution. During the revolutionary turmoil in Europe, moreover, while the United States was weak, both France and Great Britain took advantage of her weakness and imposed burdensome restrictions on her commerce; Great Britain, for instance, ordering in 1793 the seizure of neutral vessels carrying provisions to French ports, and frequently impressing into her service American sailors from American ships. During this period the question of foreign relations was carried into politics, the Federalists being inclined to favor Great Britain as against France; the Republicans, France as against Great Britain. In 1794 war with Great Britain seemed imminent, and it was largely to avert war, for which the United States was unprepared, that Washington sent Jay, then chief justice of the United States, to negotiate a treaty. This treaty did not fully meet all the points in dispute. Nothing, for instance, was said about impressment, and no compensation was granted for the transported American slaves, but Great Britain agreed to evacuate the Western posts on June 12, 1796, and arrangement was made for the settlement by commission of pecuniary claims of Americans against Englishmen, and of Englishmen against Americans. Disputed boundary questions were also to be referred to joint commissioners. The commercial clauses of the treaty on the whole gave Great Britain the advantage, and it was these clauses which were received with greatest hostility by Americans, one of them, and the most unjust, being wholly rejected. When the provisions of the treaty became known in the United States, opposition on the part of the Republicans burst forth with unexampled fury. Jay's motives were traduced and he was charged with having been corrupted by British gold; even President Washington was virulently attacked, and the Republican press teemed with bitter and sensational articles assailing the treaty and its sponsors. Finally, however, on June 24, 1795, the Senate ratified the treaty, with reservations as regards the most objectionable of the commercial clauses, and in the following year (May, 1796) after the House of Representatives had vainly asserted a right to share in the treaty-making power, an act was passed making appropriations for carrying the treaty into effect. Although the United States was forced to make burdensome concessions, it is probable that, in view of her weakness at the time, the treaty was as good a one as could then have been negotiated; but it left various questions unsettled and merely postponed hostilities, which were probably inevitable. The Republican campaign against it did much to weaken the confidence of the country in the Federalists. The text of the treaty may be found in MacDonald's *Select Documents of United States History 1776-1861* (1898); see also the various biographies of Jay, Trescot's *Diplomatic History of the Administrations of Washington and Adams* (1857), and for able defenses of the treaty see Alexander Hamilton's *Works* (the series of letters signed "Camillus"), and the *Works* of Fisher Ames, who made the most famous speech during the debates in the House of Representatives.　　　　　　　　　S. W. X.

JAZYGES, a Sarmatian tribe occupying a district near the Black Sea. See SARMATIA.

JAZZ ❖ An American Art Form

In New Orleans of the early 1900's a new music was born—part African, part European, with a new spirit of improvisation

JAZZ. Early in the 17th century when the first 20 Africans set foot on Virginia soil, there was sown a rhythmical seed destined to enter into the very warp and woof of American music. The white man's hymns: baptismal, funereal, and call to worship—slow in tempo, while appealing poetically to the Negro in a new-found Christianity—were so lacking in rhythm that the primitives sang from four to nine notes of the pentatonic scale to every one note of their written score—a spirit of improvisation that became the folk-roots of jazz.

American, lent to instrumental music a quality in keeping with the singing of forebears—the essence of jazz.

Origin. Jazz first flourished in American cities; but its inception can be traced to the shout songs in the cotton fields of Dixie, the stomps and pats of Louisiana canebrakes, the banjo songs of the Kentucky tobacco cabins that inspired STEPHEN C. FOSTER's minstrel songs; and traced even farther back to the *bamboula*, the *calinda*, the *counjaille*, and African tribal songs in which the king of instruments is the drum. In the late 1890's and early in the 20th century, Scott Joplin wrote masterpieces of ragtime, *Euphonic Sounds* and *Maple Leaf Rag*—too full of syncopation for the average musician of that era. Later, other composers simplified ragtime, representing the pulse beat of a virile America, but lacking in tone color. In the 1890's Tennessee's governor had a brother named Joe Turner who under the peonage system carried Negroes to the penitentiary and labor camps. Out of this unhappy environment a folk song with three-line stanzas was born called *Joe Turner*. This melody, along the Ohio and Mississippi rivers and as far west as Texas, was sung by various names. Many spirituals sung by the unsophisticated carried the minor 3rd and flatted 7th, exaggerated by quarter tones, but were deleted from the scores of scholarly composers.

It was in 1909 that this tone color (now known as blue notes) was written into a campaign ditty called *Mister Crump*, and published in 1912 as *The Memphis Blues* with the three-line stanzas of *Joe Turner* as a pattern which, when written into music, made a twelve-bar strain. In these folk blues there is a wait or gap between the singer's lines which has to be filled in by some instrument when accompanying. In *The Memphis Blues* orchestration this gap was bridged by what became the original "jazz break" in American music, first played by HANDY's band with tenor saxophone. In 1913 Ed V. Cupero's band and orchestra featured this blues with the George Evans "Honey Boy" Minstrels who sang: "When the big bassoon seconds the trombone's croon, it moans just like a sinner on Revival Day." This first blues was recorded by James R. Europe's band that carried the jazz and blues to Europe during World War I.

Development. Blues became a musical form—jazz the method of interpretation. Interpretation grew from raucous clarinets, as in the *Livery Stable Blues*, first played on Victor records in 1917 by the Dixieland Jazz Band, into Whiteman's Symphonic Jazz in 1922 with John Alden Carpenter's *Krazy Kat*, flowering into full manhood with GERSHWIN's *Rhapsody in Blue*. The primitive blues were played in the major keys with the tonic, subdominant and dominant, for chord structure. Very seldom was the minor mood used, thereby avoiding sadness. In the major moods there were quick transitions in and out of the minor which gave what is called the "blue note." This musical form was the expression of illiterate Negroes, those known as the "men farthest down," who laughed at trouble and sang in joyous tones to disguise their heavy hearts which meant to say, "I'm going to live anyhow 'til I die." Consequently the blues, first cousins to the spirituals, were born of suffering. The Negro had known what it meant to be sold away from his family and later to be denied the blessings of a nominal freedom. The white man listened to his music as a thing apart, beautiful, but still the Negro's music. Then came World War I that tore Yankees away from loved ones and sent them to foreign shores, and this Negro music, with its power to dispel melancholia, became American.

Arranged by W. C. HANDY

W. C. HANDY

Improvisation expanded these hymns into spirituals. Improvisation also expanded the cries of field-hands, stevedores and roustabouts, quarrymen, and steel drivers like John Henry, into work songs. It is but natural that while using instruments to replace voices that this improvisation, so characteristically Afro-

The Jazz Age had ushered in prohibition, bootlegging, highjacking, gang wars, and fads that make men uncomfortable and willing to listen to distorted music in order to keep from thinking. Bert Williams, the great comedian, said "When you see a friend falling on an icy pavement your first impulse is to see if he is hurt, but the next is to say that 'you sho did look funny falling.' " That is the underlying purpose of jazz. Syncopation, a Negro characteristic, was not enough to satisfy without offbeat rhythms and bass notes on unaccented beats.

With World War II terminated, jam-sessions that knew no color line sprang into vogue, where each race imitated the other and learned from each how to bring from instruments notes which the masters never dreamed possible.

The vaudeville stage, dance halls, and phonograph records were educational factors in the early propagation of this distinctive music. Chicago was the mecca for New Orleans jazz bands. Now 25 years of radio and thousands of motion picture theaters equipped for sound pictures enable the smallest child to point out that which is blues and jazz without having to read its definition.   WILLIAM C. HANDY

HOT JAZZ

The term "hot jazz" describes qualitative jazz music, just as the term "classical" implies a superior musical quality to the term "semiclassical" or "light classical." Considered in this sense, hot jazz has become an identifying label for various styles and interpretations of jazz which both critical opinion and the concensus of hot jazz fans regard as contemporary music worthy of serious musical attention. It is this special meaning which has resulted in the world-wide usage of the phrase "hot jazz" to describe a kind of music originated in the United States that is both aesthetically and technically superior to "popular music" or "dance music." The finest hot jazz musicians have achieved technical and musical standards of performance equal to that sought by performers in so-called serious music. The best hot jazz, then, combines *quality* of music and performance: this difference of *degree in quality* sets off hot jazz.

Definition. Jazz music differs from classical in the following characteristics: (1) Rhythm. A rigid 4/4 beat (occasionally 2/4 or 8/8) combined with polyrhythms or cross rhythms, more commonly known as syncopation, and the use of free rubato. (2) Harmony. The blues triad (dominant, subdominant, tonic), which has been intermixed with harmonies stemming from European traditions, including polyphony and polytonality. (3) Figurations. Refers chiefly to suspensions, afterbeats, passing tones, and melodic intervals. Since the use of figurations results in a mixture of concords and discords, this accounts for the disregard of the so-called pure tone and the subsequent utilization of what has come to be known as the jazz intonation, a very particular qualitative difference which cannot be judged musically inferior merely because it is different from European tradition. Swing contains all the elements of hot jazz, plus unresolved rhythm, that is, the melodic tone commences or ends on the offbeat. This added element is now an integral part of much hot jazz.

These are the simplest possible technical definitions; they do not account for factors involved in the forming of aesthetic judgments. To classify music as hot jazz, the music must contain large portions of these technical characteristics, which must be used consistently throughout the duration of any given composition or performance.

Hot jazz improvisation—not to be confused with the accepted "classical definition—consists in the performer's alteration in the melodic line and/or extension of the harmonic structure, both of which are based upon the original chords (or harmony) of the tune which is being played. In the case of the blues, which are built on three chords (blues triad), improvisation results from similar melodic and/or harmonic extension over the implicitly given set harmonic structure of the blues. Many jazzmen can improvise in this manner. Playing experience, memory, knowledge of harmony, and an intuitive taste for the right phrasing, shading, and feeling: these are the ingredients of hot jazz improvisation.

There are two types of hot jazz improvisation: contrapuntal or polyphonic improvising, which usually involves three, or at the most four, melodic instruments backed by a rhythm section; and solo improvising against a rhythm section, or as in the case of big bands, against the harmonizing of the brass and/or reed sections as well as the rhythm section. The so-called New Orleans and Dixieland styles are examples of contrapuntal improvising; the full-size swing band with featured soloists is an example of solo improvising. Solo improvising also is found, of course, in small bands, since the polyphony of three or four melodic voices is seldom sustained for the duration of a tune's performance.

History. The roots of hot jazz were planted and began growing in the 19th century. The port city of New Orleans was the nerve center of this growth. From the religious hymns, spirituals, work songs, and plantation songs, quadrilles, marches, coon songs, and blues of southern United States came the inspiration for this new American music—hot jazz.

The early history of hot jazz falls naturally into two periods. The first major period is unquestionably identified with New Orleans (1895–1917). The segregated Storyville vice district of that city (1903–17) contributed the economic base which nurtured early hot jazz performers. With the closing of Storyville during World War I, many of the best performers of the new music made their way up the Mississippi to Chicago. The second major period (1918–30) centered in that city. The feverish postwar activity in Chicago was intensified by the economic support it gained from the gangster-prohibition era and the support which the Negro population of Chicago gave to its own musicians. Beginning in the mid-twenties, New York City gradually became another center of hot jazz activity; thereafter, hot jazz was widely dispersed, centering now here, now there, but never concentrated as it had been in New Orleans and Chicago. Hot jazz became the new music of all America.

The Small Band. On the whole, the small band (up to eight pieces) has more consistently maintained the musical quality of hot jazz than has the big band. However, the latter has contributed much toward the establishment of an economic base for the jazzmen themselves, for it was not until recent years that small band combinations could find audiences large enough to support them on a broad national scale. Earlier many small bands had existed, but their support was local.

The important small bands, with dates indicating their peak period of performance, are the following:

In the New Orleans period, Buddy Bolden (1890–1905); Jack Laine (1890–1917); the Eagle Band (1911–17); the Olympia Band (1911–17); the Tuxedo Orchestra (1915–18). In addition there were more or less unorganized groups under the leadership of whatever musician happened to obtain a job and the Original Creole Band (1912–17), which performed on vaudeville circuits from California as far east as Cleveland and New York during those years.

In the Chicago period, King Oliver (1918–25); Sidney Bechet (1917–18); Johnny Dodds (1924–30); Original Dixieland Band (1914–20); Louisiana Five (1914–20); Jimmie Noone (1927–30); New Orleans Rhythm Kings (1921–23); Wolverines (1923–24); Armstrong Hot Five and Hot Seven (1925–28). The Chicago Rhythm Kings and McKenzie and Condon's Chicagoans (1927–28) made a few recordings but were not actual organized groups.

By far the greatest number of small bands since

King Oliver's Creole Jazz Band, 1922, with Louis Armstrong, front foreground, on slide trumpet

that time have been recording groups only; that is, the units were not organized for public performance but for the recording studio only. The importance and influence of such groups has been great. Among these are Muggsy Spanier who (1939–40) had a unit which performed publicly as well as recorded; numerous units under Red Nichols and Miff Mole (1925–50); James P. Johnson (1944–45); Lu Watters (1943–51); and the extraordinary work of pianist Max Miller (1937–51) who, with various groups, has left his impress both as leader and composer. These, and numerous other small groups, have demonstrated the vitality of hot jazz, both in public performances and through recordings.

Big Bands. Big bands often gave experience to the individual musicians who comprised the small units. An individual jazzman may also gain his public reputation during the time he plays with a well-known big band. In addition, big bands popularized some aspects of hot jazz and won many converts to small bands, since it is easier for music-minded Americans to appreciate the big-band style, which is more in the conventional European tradition.

The big band began to take shape in Chicago. Elgar's Creole Band (1916–28) gave what were probably the first jazz concerts at Chicago's Orchestra Hall (1917–18). Other important big bands of the Chicago period include Charlie Cooke (1922–30); Erskine Tate (1922–34); Freddie Keppard (1926–30); Sammy Stewart (1924–29); Carroll Dickerson (1925–28); Jimmie Wade (1926–28); Hugh Swift (1925–28); Louis Armstrong's Sunset Stompers (1927); Earl Hines (1929–34); Ben Pollack (1927–29). But elsewhere other important big bands included the following: Fletcher Henderson (1927–36); DUKE ELLINGTON (1927–40); Charlie Johnson (1926–27); Luis Russell (1928–32); McKinney's Cotton Pickers (1927–34); Andy Kirk (1928–40); Don Redman (1932–40). All dates refer to peak periods.

Big bands became tremendously popular during the 1930's. Swing, the new name for big band hot jazz,

was started on its way to this popularity by clarinetist BENNY GOODMAN, whose band first gained a national hearing on a series of radio broadcasts during the 1933–34 season. Among the other leaders who have left their impress on big band jazz since then are Artie Shaw, Bob Crosby, The Blue Rhythm Band, Stan Kenton (who has unsuccessfully tried to adapt European symphonic harmonies to jazz), Woody Herman (who led the most brilliant performing band of the forties), and Bunny Berigan, one of the handful of greats and perhaps the greatest trumpeter.

Instrumentalists. A critical account of some of the important performers in hot jazz will effectively point up specific suggestions for further acquaintance with this music through recordings. Because the best hot jazz is infrequently heard in public places or on the radio, recordings serve as an excellent basis for a better understanding.

The hot jazz artist with the most sustained and consistent achievement of high quality playing is Sidney

Sidney Bechet, greatest of jazz artists by virtue of his consistently high level of performance

Bechet. He began playing professionally at the age of 14; in 1919, at the age of 22, he was acclaimed as an extraordinary artist by the Swiss conductor and critic of classical music, Ernest Ansermet, when Bechet was featured in London concerts by Will Marion Cook's orchestra. Bechet's first recordings date back to 1922, when he played in a studio recording group named Clarence Williams' Blue Five. Since then, Bechet has left a brilliant account of his performances both as a clarinetist and soprano saxophonist. Although widely acclaimed among jazz fans, his name is not generally known. Yet no other hot jazz instrumentalist can match his musical achievements; no other has played so well for such a long span of time. Bechet's best recordings include "Lonesome Blues," "Buddy Bolden's Story" (a heart-felt traditional blues of which Bechet is one of the very few living exponents, and which puts to shame the phony attempts of George Gershwin), "Panama," "Blues in Thirds," "Chant in the Night," "Ole Miss," "Indian Summer," "Nobody Knows the Way I Feel," "Really the Blues," "Blues in the Air."

Hot Jazz Exponents. From left to right, Woody Herman, Chubby Jackson, Bill Harris, Dave Tough

Goodman's Quartet, 1938. Left to right, Teddy Wilson, Lionel Hampton, Gene Krupa, Benny Goodman

Trumpeter Louis Armstrong wielded a tremendous influence on many other instrumentalists, and was himself the best trumpeter in the 1925–30 period when competition was keen. Unlike Bechet, Armstrong failed to maintain the high level of his performances, although he still plays a very fine horn. The best Armstrong recordings all were made in the 1920's: "Keyhole Blues," "Once in a While," "Savoy Blues," "Drop That Sack," "West End Blues," "Two Deuces," "Knee Drops," "Weather Bird," "Basin Street."

Other trumpeters whose names should be remembered include Bunny Berigan, Muggsy Spanier, Cootie Williams, Roy Eldridge, Red Nichols, Sidney de Paris, Bix Beiderbecke, Tommy Ladnier, Red Allen, John Nesbit, Bobby Hackett, Max Kaminsky. The consistency of performance of these men, as all players in jazz, cannot always be vouched for. Some, in fact most, hot jazz musicians play much better at one period in their lives than in another. Any reference to musicians in this article should take that into consideration.

Top trombonists include Bill Harris (in his dramatic "Everywhere"), Jimmy Harrison, Miff Mole, Jack Teagarden. Among the best clarinetists are Pee Wee Russell, Irving Fazola, Barney Bigard, Johnny Dodds, and of course Goodman and Shaw. Since the tenor, alto, and baritone saxophone, in addition to the now rarely used soprano sax, are used as solo instruments in hot jazz, there are numerous excellent performers. Among them are Coleman Hawkins, Harry Carney, Ben Webster, Johnny Hodges, Sidney Bechet, and Ernie Caceres.

Recordings. Many of these men, together with other fine performers on the piano, string bass, drums, guitar (the usual rhythm section) may be heard in what might be called all-star groups on recordings. Anyone wishing to gain a better understanding of, and acquaintance with, hot jazz will do well to secure the following recordings of high musical merit: "Basin Street Blues," "Peg o' My Heart," "Beale Street Blues," "St. Louis Blues," "Memphis Blues," by various studio combinations on the Commodore label; by trumpeter Bunny Berigan and his band, "In the Dark," "Davenport Blues," "In a Mist," "I Can't Get Started," "Candlelight," "Caravan," "Flashes," and "Blues," this last by a studio all-star group on the Victor label; clarinetist Pee Wee Russell, solos in all the Commodores mentioned above, in addition to "The Last Time I Saw Chicago," "Bugle Call Rag," and "Muskrat Ramble"; by the late Thomas (Fats) Waller, some wonderful pipe organ and piano work, "Go Down Moses," "Loveless Love," "St. Louis Blues," and "Carolina Shout"; by the late Leon (Chu) Berry, "Body and Soul," "Sunny Side of the Street," "Blues in C# Minor," "Ain'tcha Comin' Home," and "Ghost of a Chance." The great Ellington band of the thirties and very early forties produced "Ko Ko," "Warm Valley," "Bundle of Blues," "Crescendo and Diminuendo in Blue," "Merry Go Round."

Typical of the enthusiastic playing of the Bob Crosby orchestra of the thirties is "Dogtown Blues," "South Rampart Street Parade," "Gin Mill Blues," "Milk Cow Blues," "Song of the Wanderer." Both large and small units under the leadership of Benny Goodman waxed hot jazz of the calibre of "Soft Winds," "Six Appeal," "Sugar Foot Stomp," "Rose Room," "Jumpin' at the Woodside," and "Clarinet a la King." Some of the finest polyphonic improvising on records (but not available to the public) is found on radio transcriptions—unfortunately. Unfortunate also is that limited space allows only a suggestion of the wealth of hot jazz.   PAUL EDUARD MILLER

BIBLIOG.–W. Handy, *Father of the Blues* (1941); W. Hobson, *American Jazz Music* (1941); F. Ramsey and C. Smith, *Jazzmen* (1941); H. Panassie, *Real Jazz* (1942); R. Goffin, *Jazz: From the Congo to the Metropolitan* (1944); D. Dexter, *Jazz Cavalcade* (1946); P. E. Miller, *Yearbook of Swing* (1938), *Yearbook of Popular Music* (1943), *Esquire's Jazz Books* (1944–45–46); R. Blesh, *Shining Trumpets* (1946); W. Sargeant, *Jazz: Hot and Hybrid* (1946); M. Mezzrow, and B. Wolfe, *Really the Blues* (1946); E. Condon, *We Called It Music* (1947); P. E. Miller and R. Venables, *Esquire's Jazz Book* (London, 1947); R. De Toledano, ed., *Frontiers of Jazz* (1947); A. Lomax, *Mister Jelly Roll* (1950).

JEALOUSY arises when another person or condition endangers affection or esteem which one desires for oneself. The jealous person may react not only to the one who is usurping his possession, but also toward the one whose affection or esteem he seeks. The emotional state arising from jealousy may dominate its victim's thoughts or it may be merely fitful.

Jealousy may grow out of a specific situation or it may be a response to vague conditions. The responses to jealousy may be of the vengeful type or merely a tendency to grieve and to feel self-pity. Sometimes jealousy in children results in a return to more infantile habits such as bed wetting, fears that had been outgrown, or new symptoms such as lying and tattling.

Jealous children have been found to be more selfish, pugnacious, and fearful, and to have a greater attachment for one parent than nonjealous children. They also exhibit more behavior problems such as nightmares, destructiveness, and attention-getting activity. Jealousy occurs in children on all levels of intelligence. It is most frequent when the age difference between two children in a family is less than eighteen months or more than forty-two months.

            FRED McKINNEY

JEANNE D'ARC. See JOAN OF ARC.

JEANNETTE, city, SW Pennsylvania, in Westmoreland County; on the Pennsylvania Railroad and U.S. Highway 117, about 20 miles SE of Pittsburgh. The city grew about a glass factory built in 1889 on a farm site and named for the wife of one of the factory promoters. Jeannette is an industrial city whose industries have been aided by coal and gas found near by. Glass, rubber products, iron castings, generators, and cement are the chief manufactures. Pop. (1950) 16,172.

JEANS, Sir JAMES HOPWOOD, 1877–1946, English physicist and astronomer, was born in Southport, London and studied at Trinity College, Cambridge. He was professor of applied mathematics at Princeton University (1905–9), Stokes lecturer in applied mathematics at Cambridge (1910–12), and research associate of the Mount Wilson Observatory (1923–44). His work in dynamics, radiation, and atomic physics led to such works as: *Dynamical Theory of Gases* (1904); *Theoretical Mechanics* (1906); *Mathematical Theory of Electricity and Magnetism* (1908); *Radiation and Quantum-Theory* (1914); *Problems of Cosmogony and Stellar Dynamics* (1919) for which he received the Adams prize of Cambridge University; *Astronomy and Cosmogony* (1928). Among his popular books for the layman were: *The Universe Around Us* (1929); *The Mysterious Universe* (1929); *The Stars in Their Courses* (1931); *The New Background of Science* (1933); *Physics and Philosophy* (1942); *The Growth of Physical Science* (1947). Among his honors were the Royal medal of the Royal Society (1919), the gold medal of the Royal Astronomical Society (1922), the Franklin medal of the Franklin Institute (1931). He was knighted in 1928. Jeans was president of the Royal Astronomical Society (1925–27) and of the British Association for the Advancement of Science (1934). His contributions to applied mathematics, theoretical physics, stellar dynamics, and theoretical cosmogony were important, and in a number of books he gave the public an idea of the astronomical consequences of the new atomic theories. He was an interesting and prolific writer.   EVERETT I. YOWELL

JEBAIL, also **Jebeil,** or **Djebeil,** coastal town of Lebanon, 18 miles NW of Beyrouth (Beirut), near Mount Lebanon. Because it is the site of ancient Byblos it has been the scene of continuing French and Lebanese excavations since the early 1920's. It has been proved that the site was occupied, except for certain gaps, from at least 4000 B.C. into medieval times. Byblos played a leading role among the Phoenician towns which traded with Egypt. Egyptian inscriptions have been found in the excavations, the earliest dating from the time of King Khasekhemui (c. 2775 B.C.). Rib Addi, king of Byblos at the time of the "first great internationalism," is often mentioned in the Tell-el-Amarna letters. The remains of the later-first-millenium Phoenician town seem largely to have been destroyed by subsequent early Christian and medieval building activities.

JEBBA, town, W Africa, Nigeria, on the bank of the Niger River, 70 miles N of its junction with the Benue. The town is an important trading and textile center, and is connected by rail with Lagos, the capital. Pop. about 15,000.

JEBEL ED DRUZE, province, S Syria, occupying a high, isolated tract of land rising at the S extremity of the great basalt plateau of Hauran, and bordered on the S by Trans-Jordan; Pop. (1943) 80,128. The region is hilly, with peaks attaining to 6,000 feet above sea level. It is fertile, and sufficient rainfall permits the cultivation of grains such as wheat and barley. The inhabitants are engaged principally in agriculture and stock raising. The capital and chief town is Es Suweida. Under French-mandated Syria, Jebel ed Druze was largely autonomous, before 1936 excluded altogether from Syria and afterward retaining autonomous administrative and judicial powers. It was the center from which spread the Syrian revolt of 1925–27. In 1945 the region was fully incorporated into the republic of Syria. See DRUSES; SYRIA.

JEBEL SHAMMAR, a province of Nejd, Saudi Arabia; pop. about 200,000. It is crossed by two granite ridges, the Jebel Shammar (6,000 ft.) and Jebel Selma. Much of the land surrounding the capital city, Hail, is desert, but the valleys are fertile. Jebel Shammar was formerly an emirate of the kingdom of Hejaz and Nejd. It became a part of Saudi Arabia in 1921.

JEDBURGH, royal and small burgh, SE Scotland, county town of Roxburghshire, on the Jed River; 50 miles SE of Edinburgh. The remains of an abbey built of Old Red sandstone by David I in 1118 are said to be Scotland's most perfect example of Saxon and early Gothic architecture. There are also ruins of a castle built in the 12th century by David I. The town was frequently sacked and burned during the Border Wars. The expression "Jeddart Justice," meaning to hang a man first and try him afterward, is a reflection of the rough life of the border towns during James VI's reign. Jedburgh is the birthplace of Sir David Brewster, and Mary Somerville; it was at various periods of its history the residence of Mary, Queen of Scots, Prince Charles Edward Stuart, Wordsworth, and Burns. The house occupied by Mary in 1566 is now a museum of relics pertaining to her life. The town was one of the first in Scotland to establish the manufacture of woolen textiles, which is still its principal industry. In the vicinity are orchards. Pop. about 4,000.

JEDDA. See JIDDA.

JEFFERS, ROBINSON, 1887–   , American poet, was born in Pittsburgh, Pa., and was educated at Occidental College (Calif.). A resident of California for many years, he has used the country surrounding his home at Carmel as the background for many of his poems, giving the sea, the redwood forests, and the mountains a powerful symbolic role in such lyrics as "Boats in a Fog" and "Granite and Cypress" and in his tragic, allegorical narratives, "Tamar," "Roan Stallion," "Cawdor," and "Give Your Heart to the Hawks." His works include *Roan Stallion, Tamar, and Other Poems* (1925), *The Women at Point Sur* (1927), *Cawdor, and Other Poems* (1928), *Descent to the Dead* (1931), *Thurso's Landing* (1932), *Give*

Your Heart to the Hawks, and Other Poems (1933), *Medea* (1946), and *The Double Axe* (1948).

JEFFERSON, JOSEPH, 1829–1905, American actor, was born in Philadelphia, descendant of a long line of theatrical people. At the age of three he made his first stage appearance as the child of Cord in Kotzebue's *Pizarro*. A year later he enacted a miniature Jim Crow to Thomas D. Rice's adult version.

CHICAGO HIST. SOC.

Joseph Jefferson as he appeared in "The Rivals"

As he grew older, he followed his father on tours throughout the country until the latter's death in 1842. Jefferson then became a member of a group of itinerant players barnstorming in remote regions of the South and Southwest, and eventually made his way to Mexico with the victorious U.S. Army.

On his return to the United States, Jefferson acted in Philadelphia and New York without attaining notable prominence. One of his parts was that of Marroll in Philip Massinger's *A New Way to Pay Old Debts*, starring Junius Brutus Booth as Sir Giles Overreach. In 1856 he acted in London, where his great grandfather had performed in the time of Garrick. The following year he joined Laura Keene's stock company at her theater in New York, achieving his first pronounced success as Dr. Pangloss in *The Heir-at-Law*. This character was to be one of the four or five with which his name became associated and to which he practically restricted himself in later years. In 1858 he triumphed as Asa Trenchard to Sothern's Lord Dundreary in *Our American Cousin*, and in the next year first assumed the part of Caleb Plummer in *The Cricket on the Hearth*.

On his way back home from a trip to Australia and New Zealand, Jefferson stopped in London, and at the Adelphi Theater there in 1865 he played the title role of *Rip Van Winkle* in an adaptation of Washington Irving's story written by Dion Boucicault from an earlier play in which Jefferson had appeared in Washington. The improved vehicle had a long run, and was so successful on its presentation in New York (1866) that Jefferson confined himself to the part of Rip for nearly 15 years. In 1880 he produced Sheridan's *The Rivals* in Philadelphia with himself as Bob Acres. Thereafter he was to be seen chiefly in one of these two roles. His concentration on the character of Rip arrested Jefferson's growth as all-round comedian, but his interpretation of the shiftless town loafer who awoke after 20 years of slumber became more polished with the years until it assumed its place as one of the legendary performances of theatrical history. In 1889 Jefferson bought an estate at Buzzard's Bay, Mass., where his neighbors and intimates were Grover Cleveland and Richard Watson Gilder. He also won some distinction as a painter. His *Autobiography* (1890) is a valuable mirror of his life and times.

BIBLIOG.–William Winter, *The Jeffersons* (1881); E. P. Jefferson, *Intimate Recollections of Joseph Jefferson* (1909).

U.S. NAVAL ACADEMY

Louisiana Purchase Treaty, signed at Paris in 1803, added vast territories to the United States

Frigate "Philadelphia" was boarded and burned in Tripoli harbor, 1804, by a force led by Decatur

ANHEUSER-BUSCH, INC.

JOS. BOGGS BEALE

Lewis and Clark Expedition, 1803-6, crossed the continent, making a study of area west of the Mississippi and blazing the trail for settlers

Burr-Hamilton Duel in 1804 resulted in death of Hamilton

© CAMPBELL PRINTS, INC.

Robert Fulton's "Clermont" made its maiden voyage on the Hudson River in 1807

☆ ☆ ☆ ☆ ☆ ☆ ☆ ☆ ☆   ☆ ☆

THOMAS JEFFERSON
Third President of the United States
1801—1809

BOWDOIN COLLEGE

JEFFERSON, THOMAS, 1743–1826, third president of the United States, is credited with being the father of architecture in America, a musician, a philosopher, and an inventor. He was definitely a product of the great appreciation of man and his nature, the theory of progress, and the world-wide approach of that theory which burst upon the earth in the last part of the 18th century. He must, also, be remembered as a great Virginia gentleman.

No man has been responsible for so many of the fundamental things that have gone into American governmental theory and practice; for example, the decimal system, the basic money system, and the theory for the admission of new states into the Union. Jefferson had absolute faith in the freedom of speech and the press, believing that each would contribute to the education of the citizenry, and that democracy would, therefore, be successful, since it would be based upon a trained citizenry. In a sense he is the father of the public school system in the United States, and is the man who worked out the land measurement principles on which public land has been divided and private individuals have been made owners of these lands.

Thomas Jefferson was born at "Shadwell" in Goochland (now Albemarle) County, Va., then the outskirts of the western frontier, on Apr. 13, 1743, to Jane Randolph and Peter Jefferson. Tradition holds that the first Jefferson in the colony came from Wales, but the genealogy of Jefferson is traced back to a Thomas Jefferson, who lived in Henrico County in 1677. Peter Jefferson was deputy surveyor in Albemarle and assisted in continuing the boundary line between Virginia and North Carolina and made the first correct map of Virginia. Thomas Jefferson had great regard for his father's map; he inherited his father's mathematical mind and his love for exploring the unknown. Coming from the aristocracy of the lowland countries, the background of his mother, Jane Randolph, is contrasted with the rugged frontier life of his father. Eight of the ten children born to Peter Jefferson survived his death in 1757, Thomas, the elder of his two sons, was left 2,750 acres of land and a family reputation of high repute in the community.

The education of Thomas Jefferson was started at "Tuckahoe," on the James, near Richmond, where his father had moved in keeping a promise to William Randolph to be guardian of Randolph's son. When Jefferson was nine the family returned to Albemarle County and this became his permanent home. Here he continued the study of Latin and Greek. Jefferson mastered the classical tongues and gained much from the literature of Greece and Rome. He entered the College of William and Mary in 1760 and graduated two years later. His scientific interest was aroused by Dr. William Small, teacher of mathematics and philosophy, who introduced him to Gov. Francis Fauquier and to George Wythe, the most noted teacher of law in Virginia at that time. Under Wythe, Jefferson prepared himself for the practice of law. He was admitted to the bar in 1767, and though he disliked the practice of law was successful until he abandoned his profession for the cause of the Revolution.

Religious and Ethical Beliefs. With Jefferson natural freedom, moral freedom, and political freedom all went hand in hand and irresistibly followed upon one another. Jefferson hesitated to discuss his religion freely and publicly. He repeatedly told his friends, "Say nothing of my religion. It is known to my God and myself alone. Its evidence before the world is to be sought in my life; if that has been honest and dutiful to society, the religion which has regulated it cannot be a bad one." Jefferson formulated a stern code of personal conduct and self-discipline. He abstained from the use of tobacco, never played cards or gambled, and did not allow himself to become embroiled in personal quarrels. It was important to him that the mind of man be freed from the bonds of superstition and religious ignorance as it was that man be left to worship as he pleased or to worship not at all.

It has been inferred that Jefferson's morals and political philosophy were influenced by his sojourn in France. But true historical facts disprove this. Despite his evident skepticism in regard to the theological aspect of religion, Jefferson was deeply interested in morality. Abandoning all hope of finding the answers to the many questions of dogma on which the churches of his day differed, he limited his reading on religion to moral aspects, wherein he was convinced that all religions were essentially alike. Thus, his religion came to take on the form of an ethical code, based, however, on a belief that the essential morality had back of it an eternally unchanging basis. Jefferson thus discovered a sort of universal morality in man. Man's morality is part of his nature. Here we have an approach to the Christian concept of a light "which lighteth every man that cometh into the world" (John 1:9). His final deductions seem to be the result of reasoning from what he considered sound experience and his final acceptance was the notion of a universal morality based on eternally unchanging principles. We must, therefore, consider Jefferson as a moralist. The paraphrase of Jefferson's moral principles as found on the monument to his honor in Washington reads: "I know but one code of morality for men whether acting singly or collectively."

Life at Monticello. On Jan. 1, 1772, Jefferson married Martha (Wayles) Skelton, the daughter of Martha Eppes and John Wayles of Charles City County. She was the widow of Bathurst Skelton. Six children were born to them, only two of whom,

Thomas Jefferson designed Monticello (above), his home in Virginia. In 1776, he drafted the Declaration of Independence (right), on which he conferred with Franklin. Jefferson arrived in Washington (above right) for his inauguration as president in 1801. After retirement in 1809, he designed and supervised much of the building of the University of Virginia. Below are the serpentine wall and original University plan

PHOTOS FROM VA. CONSERVATION COMM.:
BETTMANN ARCHIVE; VA. STATE CHAMBER

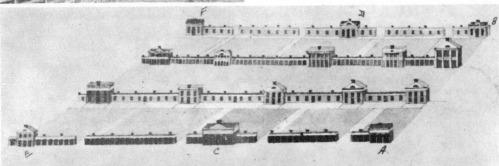

Martha and Mary, lived to maturity. Martha Skelton was reputed to have been very beautiful and their union was exceedingly happy. They began married life at MONTICELLO, consisting then of the southeastern pavilion. It took a generation to complete the building operations of this home.

Jefferson was elected justice of the peace and church vestryman in 1768. In May, 1769, he was elected to the House of Burgesses and continued to be elected until the House ceased to function in 1775, though he did not attend in 1772. He was appointed county lieutenant of Albemarle in 1770 and the College of William and Mary appointed him surveyor of the county in 1773. He was intimate with Patrick Henry and seems to have been sympathetic with him, as the representative of the upper counties of Virginia in his views against the aristocracy.

Jefferson and the Revolution. Jefferson was not an effective speaker. His greatest contribution in legislative work came through committee work and the fruits of his prolific pen. He is credited with having drafted the address adopted by the committee appointed to write the address to Dunmore rejecting Lord North's conciliatory offer. His paper to the Virginia Convention, which he was prevented from attending in 1774 because of illness, "A Summary View of the Rights of British America," is considered by many his greatest contribution to the American Revolution next to the Declaration of Independence.

In 1775 he was chosen to a seat in the Continental Congress; appointed chairman of the committee to draft the DECLARATION OF INDEPENDENCE, and chosen by the committee to write the Declaration. In 1776 he was elected to the Virginia legislature, giving up his seat in the Continental Congress and declining a proffered election to serve with Benjamin Franklin and Silas Deane as commissioners to France, because he felt he could best serve the "cause" in furthering the "reformation" of Virginia. While serving in the legislature he began the revision of the laws of Virginia, proposed the Statute for Religious Freedom, Bill of Universal Diffusion of Knowledge, and the bill to abolish primogeniture and entail.

He was elected governor of Virginia in 1779 to succeed Patrick Henry. During his second term (1780–81) Virginia was overrun by the British and much of their success was blamed on Jefferson, but most of the criticism, no doubt, was unfounded. He declined renomination for a third term, but was unanimously elected to the legislature. During this period he wrote *The Notes on the State of Virginia*. This book went through many editions and was later printed in France. Through it Jefferson became known as a universal scholar and because of it he is today famed as a pioneer American scientist.

Jefferson was elected delegate to Congress in June, 1783, and during this term he served on almost every important committee and drafted in the neighborhood of 31 state papers, one of the most important of which was his report on the coinage system, advocating the adoption of the dollar, and its division into tenths and hundreths (dimes and cents). His report of Mar. 22, 1784, contained practically all of the features of the Northwest Proviso or the Ordinance of 1787, and, had it been adopted as Jefferson first wrote it, slavery would have been forbidden in all of the Western Territory after 1800 and the secession of any section of that territory would have been illegal. He drew up a report on the definitive treaty of peace which was adopted, and his report of Dec. 20, 1783, was agreed to as the basis for procedure in negotiating treaties of commerce. In 1784 Congress appointed Jefferson, with Adams and Franklin, to negotiate treaties of commerce with foreign countries.

He was appointed minister to France to succeed Franklin in 1785 and remained in France until October, 1789. Though successful there, his stay was always overshadowed by Franklin's popularity and reputation.

Jefferson and Hamilton. Soon after his return to his home, Monticello, from France Washington offered Jefferson the appointment of secretary of state, being temporarily administered by John Jay. He was reluctant to enter politics again, but for patriotic reasons he accepted and became the first secretary of state under the Constitution on Mar. 22, 1790. While Jefferson approved the new Constitution, he urged that a bill of rights be included in it, which was later added. He did not like the ever-continuing Senate with but one third of the Senate being elected every two years, and was opposed to the president being eligible for re-election. All three of these reactions reflected Jefferson's basic fear that a monarchy might be established in America.

Hamilton at this time was serving as secretary of the treasury. Jefferson differed completely with Hamilton on his theories of foreign policies and his financial measures and he led the group opposing Hamilton. This marked the beginning of political parties in the new government. The Jefferson group stigmatized the Hamiltonians as monarchists, and claimed for themselves the title of Republicans. As time went on, the Hamiltonian party became the Federalist party and the Jeffersonian party became known as the Democratic Republicans.

The most crucial question confronting Jefferson as secretary of state grew out of the policy of neutrality adopted by this country toward France, the country America owed so much and with whom we were in alliance. At the time of the French Revolution, Jefferson was determined that the United States should take no action which would oppose the principle of the French Revolution, yet he shared the conviction of Washington and Hamilton that American politics should be for America and French politics should be for France. This policy was accepted by Washington in his Farewell Address. Jefferson resigned the secretaryship on Dec. 31, 1793.

Vice-President and President. In 1796 John Adams was elected president and was the Federalists' candidate. Jefferson, the Republican candidate, was elected vice-president. Out of his experiences as presiding officer of the Senate came his *Manual of Parliamentary Practice*, later published in many editions and translated into several languages; it is still the basis of parliamentary procedure in the Senate. Because Adams and Jefferson were political enemies, though good friends, Jefferson played little part in the administration. Jefferson approved Monroe's mission to France which aroused so much hostile comment from the Federalists, in their efforts to align the United States with Great Britain. The French issue, however, lost the limelight when the Federalists succeeded in passing the Alien and Sedition Acts. In answer to these came the KENTUCKY RESOLUTIONS of 1798, which Jefferson is credited as being the author, and the Virginia Resolutions, drawn up by Madison.

In 1800 the Federalist party lost prestige and the Republican candidates, Jefferson and Aaron Burr, received an equal number of votes. It then devolved upon the House of Representatives to make one president. Jefferson was chosen president and was re-elected in 1804, at which time John Adams voted for him as a Republican elector from Massachusetts. The two great achievements of his administration were the LOUISIANA PURCHASE in 1803 and the LEWIS AND CLARK EXPEDITION in 1804. See AMERICAN PRESIDENT; UNITED STATES HISTORY; DEMOCRATIC PARTY; EMBARGO; IMPRESSMENT; TRIPOLI WAR.

Educator and World Citizen. Jefferson retired to Monticello in 1809 and from then on his chief public interest was education. He wrote to Du Pont de Nemours in 1816, "Enlighten the people generally and tyranny and oppressions of both mind and body will vanish like evil spirits at the dawn of day." In 1814 he became associated as a trustee with the unorganized Albemarle Academy, which later became Central College, the nucleus from which the University of

Virginia developed. In the building of the University of Virginia many of the specifications were drawn by Jefferson himself and a great many of the structures on the campus were built under his direct supervision. See AMERICAN ARCHITECTURE; COLLEGES, *Virginia, University of.*

Jefferson was a world citizen, but at the same time he was an American. He reflected at all times the great fundamentals of American nationalism. Jefferson is best understood when one reads his writings, constantly keeping in mind world events as they occurred when he wrote. When one realizes that he was a living witness of both the American and French revolutions, watched from day to day the growth of his own United States and the evolution of Europe during and after the Napoleonic Wars, one appreciates that he can probably be considered the greatest constructive statesman of his time, a statesman who never lost faith in concept of progress, and who, late in life, was able to write to his friend, John Adams, "You and I will yet look down from heaven with joy at the fulfillment of our great dreams." A historical coincidence from which many American orators have taken inspiration is the fact that Jefferson and Adams died on the same day, the 50th anniversary of the promulgation of American independence, July 4, 1826. *The Papers of Thomas Jefferson* have been published by the Princeton University Press (1950-   , ed. J. P. Boyd).

Monticello, President Jefferson's home, is preserved by the Thomas Jefferson Memorial Association. In Washington, D.C., the JEFFERSON MEMORIAL, a circular colonnaded structure, was dedicated on the 200th anniversary of his birth.   ELBERT D. THOMAS

JEFFERSON AS A SCIENTIST

Thomas Jefferson was a philosopher and a humanitarian, a scholar and a great leader. He had a thorough understanding and appreciation of the principles of science and of the practical value of precise knowledge. To a man of lesser stature, his own achievements in the field of science would have been significant. To him they were, for the most part, incidental.

Perhaps the most serious scientific study by Thomas Jefferson of which there is a record is that connected with the introduction of the decimal system into American coinage and weights and measures. His recommendation of the establishment of the dollar as the central monetary unit with a ten dollar gold coin and a one-tenth dollar silver and one-hundredth dollar copper coin was eventually adopted by Congress. His arguments against continuing the use of the pounds and pence system of the British were convincing. It is unfortunate that his equally valid argument favoring a decimal system of weights and measures was not likewise adopted.

Jefferson approached the problem of weights and measures in 1790, at a time when this question was a live international, as well as an important American, issue. The Colonial system, borrowed from the English, varied from place to place and was unsatisfactory. The French had not yet adopted the meter though this was already under discussion. Jefferson wanted to find a unit of length which could be duplicated anywhere on the earth. His fundamental unit of weight is the ounce, which is the weight of water required to occupy a cubic inch. Thus he had his fundamental unit of time, length, and mass. The second is the appropriate fraction of the mean solar day. The inch is 1/50 of the length of a rod, which suspended at one end, will beat a second; the foot is 10 such inches, which works out to be almost identical with the English foot. The ounce, being the weight of a cubic inch of water, is almost identical with the English ounce.

Jefferson developed this system in detail with recommendations of multiples and submultiples of the various units, comparing their values precisely with those that were in existence in various British systems. He thus had a series of weights and measures similar in principle to those later adopted by the French in their metric system, which, if it had been introduced at that time, would have eased the tasks of generations of industry and would have relieved the headache of many a schoolboy.

Especially interesting was the true grasp of the methods of science which Jefferson showed in this discussion of weights and measures. It was a matter of major importance with him that his fundamental units should be such that they could be precisely duplicated without reference to artificial standards. There was no such basis for the British system of weights and measures. The French advocated a unit of length based on the length of a quadrant of the earth's surface. Jefferson pointed out that the size of the earth is much more difficult to measure precisely than is the length of a second pendulum. He was careful to explain that each of his units could be determined by a direct physical operation, such as measuring the length of a pendulum or building a cube with a one-inch edge and weighing the water that it would contain. These were important points, and as history has shown, his fundamental basis for the unit of length was a sounder one than that which was later chosen by the French, and which is now used in the American weights and measures. It has become necessary for Americans practically to make use of a replica of the French meter as the basis of their system of measurement.

Other Scientific Contributions of Thomas Jefferson were his development of methods of determining longitude, his invention of a plow, and his study of natural history with particular relation to the remains of prehistoric mammals. More important was his interest in stimulating the use of scientific observations as practical assets.

Of especial interest is Jefferson's concern with the encouragement of inventions, through the development of a patent system. He saw the high importance of reward to inventors. He wanted to guarantee these rewards and, at the same time, to set up a legal system that would give an equitable adjustment of claims of different inventors. Of equal interest was his concern with obtaining a detailed census. In 1800, as president of the American Philosophical Society, Thomas Jefferson sent a memorandum to the House of Representatives in which he called attention to the great value that might come to the nation by learning more details with regard to its population. He wanted not only an enumeration of the number of citizens, he wanted also to know their ages, where they had come from, and what their occupation was. Thus, he pointed out on behalf of the society, we might learn what the relative conditions of health are in various parts of the country, and where within the nation we should look to find persons capable of doing appropriate tasks.

Most particularly, however, Jefferson was primarily an advocate of freedom. To him, anything that would advance freedom was something to be encouraged. He saw such advance in education. He saw it in the growth of industry. He saw it in the development of science. To Jefferson, the great task of the American nation was to show the world a way of developing a life of greater value than had been possible under the old restrictions of Europe. These ideas are epitomized in the inscription which Jefferson wrote and caused to be placed over his grave: "Here was buried Thomas Jefferson, author of the Declaration of American Independence, of the Statute of Virginia for religious freedom, and father of the University of Virginia." "Because of these as testimonials that I have lived," Jefferson said, "I wish most to be remembered." See THE DECLARATION. OF INDEPENDENCE (Back End Papers, Vol. 13); RICHMOND; VIRGINIA.

ARTHUR H. COMPTON.

BIBLIOG.—*Jeffersonian Cyclopedia* (1900); G. Chinard, *Thomas Jefferson, the Apostle of Americanism* (1929); E. D. Thomas, *Thomas Jefferson, World Citizen* (1942); M. G. Kimball, *Jefferson: The Road to Glory, 1743–1776* (1943); H. W. Van Loon, *Thomas Jefferson* (1943); C. G. Bowers, *Thomas Jefferson* (3 vols. 1945); M. Kimball, *Jefferson: War and Peace, 1776–1784* (1947); D. Malone, *Jefferson and His Time* (1948–   ); M. Beloff, *Thomas Jefferson and American Democracy* (1949); A. Koch, *Jefferson and Madison* (1950).

JEFFERSON BARRACKS, a U.S. military post located about 10 miles south of St. Louis on the Mississippi River, established by the War Department in 1826 and named in honor of Thomas Jefferson. During the Civil War it was a general military hospital, and later it was used as a garrison for troops. It has an arsenal and powder magazine and a national cemetery. During World War II it was first used as a reception center for the Air Corps and later it became an important induction center for selectees.

JEFFERSON CITY, city, central Missouri, state capital and county seat of Cole County, on the S bank of the Missouri River, on the Missouri Pacific and the Missouri-Kansas-Texas railroads and U.S. highways, 50, 54, and 63; about 110 miles W of St. Louis. Jefferson City is the trading and distributing center for a large agricultural area. The city's location makes it the northern gateway to the beautiful Ozarks region. Jefferson City was laid out as the City of Jefferson to serve as the state capital in 1822. It was named for Thomas Jefferson and incorporated as a city in 1825. The new capitol built in 1918 is beautifully located on a bluff 150 feet above the river. The Lincoln University for Negroes is located here. Shoes, clothing, grain and dairy products, brick, furniture, and machine tools are the chief manufactures. Pop. (1950) 25,099.

JEFFERSON, FORT. See FORT JEFFERSON NATIONAL MONUMENT.

JEFFERSON MEMORIAL, in Washington, D.C., is located on the south side of the Tidal Basin, 3,000 feet south of the Washington Monument and on the center line of the White House. In 1934 Congress created the Thomas Jefferson Memorial Commission and in 1936 authorized expenditure of $3,000,000 for this structure. In 1938 ground was broken and on April 13, 1943, the 200th anniversary of Jefferson's birth, the building was dedicated by President Roosevelt. Architects were John Russell Pope (1874–1937) and his surviving associates Otto R. Eggers and Daniel Paul Higgins. The landscape architect was Frederick Law Olmstead.

The building is a domed Pantheon-type structure, a form admired by Jefferson, and similar to the central building designed by Jefferson for the University of Virginia. The circular peristyle surrounding the monument presents a new version of the type which Jefferson called the "perfect model" of a circular building. There are two circular terraces around the monument. Three broad flights of steps with intervening terraces and platforms lead from the edge of the Tidal Basin to the great portico. Twelve Ionic

columns, eight of which are across the front of the portico, support the pediment, on which there is sculptured in high relief, by Adolph Weinman, a group of some of the signers of the Declaration of Independence. From the portico which is 93 feet in length and 23 feet in depth, other monuments and several houses of government can be seen: the Washington Monument and White House to the north, Lincoln Memorial to northwest, and the Capitol dome, to northeast. The colonnade around the Jefferson Memorial has 54 columns, each 43 feet high and weighing about 45 tons. The circular memorial room is 82 feet in diameter and has floors of pink and gray Tennessee marble. A heroic statue by Rudolph Evans dominates the room.

JEFFERSON RIVER, one of the three head branches of the Missouri River, rises in SW Montana, and after a circuitous course joins the Madison and Gallatin at Three Forks to form the Missouri. Its length is 150 miles and its drainage area 9,400 square miles.

JEFFERSON TERRITORY, a spontaneous political organization of the region which later became the state of Colorado, existing from 1859 until 1861. The region was part of Kansas Territory, but the settlers who came in the Pike's Peak gold rush felt that they were too far from the seat of government. A meeting in Denver, 1858, elected a delegate to Congress and requested the establishment of a new territory; no action was taken because of the controversy over slavery. The inhabitants of the region therefore organized a provisional government and formed the Territory of Jefferson. Two sessions of a territorial legislature were held prior to 1861, when Congress created the Territory of Colorado. See COLORADO, *History*.

JEFFERSONVILLE, city, S Indiana, county seat of Clark County, on the Ohio River opposite Louisville, Ky., on the Baltimore and Ohio, the New York Central, and the Pennsylvania railroads, and U.S. Highway 42. It was founded in 1802 and laid out according to plans drawn by Thomas Jefferson. An Army quartermasters' supply depot is located here. Soap products, steel, and boat building are the chief manufactures. Pop.(1950) 14,685.

JEFFREY, FRANCIS, LORD JEFFREY, 1773–1850, Scottish literary critic, was born in Edinburgh. A lawyer by profession, he was appointed lord advocate (1830) and had a share in the passing of the Reform Bill (1832). He is chiefly known, however, for his connection with the *Edinburgh Review*, which he founded with Sydney Smith and Lord Brougham in 1802. Under his editorship (1803–29) the magazine became notorious for its attacks on the "Lake poets," which provoked Byron's satire, *English Bards and Scotch Reviewers*, and led Tom Moore to challenge Jeffrey to a duel.

BIBLIOG.–R. Noyes, *Wordsworth and Jeffrey in Controversy* (1941).

JEFFREYS OF WEM, GEORGE JEFFREYS, LORD, 1648–89, lord high chancellor of England, born in Acton, near Wrexham, Denbighshire. He was called to the bar (1668), appointed common serjeant of the City of London (1671), recorder of the city (1678), and chief justice of Chester (1680). He prosecuted Lord William Russell for his share in the Rye House Plot, and presided at the trial of Algernon Sidney. In July, 1685, after Monmouth's Rebellion, he conducted the "Bloody Assize," when 320 executions for high treason were ordered by him. On becoming lord chancellor (1685) he endeavored to rule the House of Lords; and, as James II's right hand, he secured the committal of the seven bishops to the Tower (1688). Like the king himself, Jeffreys had to flee (1688); but being discovered in disguise at Wapping, he was arrested, and was placed in the Tower, where he died.

JEFFRIES, JAMES, 1875–   , American heavyweight boxer, was born in Carroll, Ohio. He won the

The Jefferson Memorial in Washington, D.C.

world's heavyweight championship from Bob Fitzsimmons in 1899, retired in 1905 and lost to Jack Johnson in an attempted comeback (1910).

JEFFRIES, JOHN, 1744–1819, American physician and scientist, was born in Boston, Mass., graduated from Harvard, and later studied medicine in England and Scotland. A Loyalist, he went to England after service as a British army surgeon during the Revolutionary War. He supplied financial backing for FRANÇOIS BLANCHARD, French balloonist, with whom he made two ascents for scientific purposes. On Jan. 7, 1785, they made the first balloon trip across the English Channel, from Dover to the forest of Guînes, France. Jeffries returned to Boston about 1790 and established a medical practice there.

JEHLAM. See JHELUM RIVER.

JEHOIAKIM, or **ELIAKIM,** king of Judah, 608–597 B.C., was the son of Josiah, and the successor of his brother Jehoahaz. He began his reign as the vassal of Necho, king of Egypt; but about 605 Nebuchadnezzar of Babylon, who had defeated Necho at Carchemish, laid siege to Jerusalem, and shortly reduced it, carrying away many captives, among whom was Daniel. Jehoiakim was reinstated; but his revolt three years later was the signal for a renewed attack by the Babylonian vassals, during which he was slain, and Jerusalem eventually taken and plundered. See II Kings 23:34 to 24:5; II Chron. 36:4–8.

JEHOL, province, NE China, just N of the Great Wall, bounded on the N and NW by Chahar and Inner Mongolia, on the E by Liaopei, on the SE by Liaoning, and on the S by Hopeh; area 72,008 sq. mi.; pop. (1947 est.) 2,185,000. It was once a part of Chihli, metropolitan province of the old Chinese Empire. The chief rivers of Jehol are the Lwan and Laoha. The products of the province include fruits, melons, grains, millet, tobacco, cotton, and indigo. The capital and chief town is Chengteh (Jehol), on the Lwan, 130 miles northeast of Peiping. In March, 1933, Japanese troops invaded the province, thereafter making it a part of the puppet state of Manchukuo. It was captured by Soviet troops and returned to the Chinese government in April, 1945. See MANCHURIA.

JEHOSHAPHAT, VALLEY OF, (Joel 3:2), identified with the gorge NE of Jerusalem, between the Mount of the Temple and the Mount of Olives, the dry bed of the brook Kedron forming its lower part. The garden of Gethsemane and the village of Siloam are in the valley. Some hold that Joel referred to the valley of Berachah, in which Jehoshaphat gained a memorable victory (II Chron. 20:26).

JEHOVAH, the most sacred of the names given in the Old Testament to the Supreme Being, regarded also as the God especially of the Jewish people. So holy was the name esteemed that the Jews were afraid to allow it to escape their lips, and therefore took means to mispronounce it by altering its vowel points to those of Adonai, or, when the two occur together, of Elohim, less sacred names for God. This practice arose from their having misinterpreted such passages as in the book of Deuteronomy: "If thou wilt not observe to do all the words of this law that are written in this book, that thou mayest fear this glorious and fearful name, THE LORD THY GOD" (Deut. 28:58). What the real vowel points, and consequently the proper pronunciation, should be is now doubtful. Many critics contend for Hebrew, *Yahveh,* some for *Yahvah,* and some for *Yahavoh.* It is generally derived from *havah,* an old form of *haiah,* meaning "He is." The import of the name is explained in the book of Exodus: "And God said unto Moses, I AM THAT I AM. . . ." (Exod. 3:14), thereby predicating self-existence or existence in a sense in which it can be applied to no created being.

JEHOVAH'S WITNESSES, a religious group whose central organization is the Watch Tower Bible and Tract Society, incorporated by "Pastor" Charles Taze Russell (1884), who was succeeded by "Judge"

Joseph F. Rutherford (1916), and he by Nathan H. Knorr (1942). The organization for foreign work is the International Bible Students Association. The Witnesses have clashed with the police and with local, state, and national government on many occasions, on account of their energetic methods of propaganda and their resistance to military service and to the usual symbols of civic loyalty. They teach that, while man is not radically bad, all human institutions and social processes, including governments and churches, are dominated by Satan, and that the state of the world is destined to become worse and worse until the coming of the Kingdom with power soon. The control of the movement is highly centralized. The only literature produced is that from headquarters; selling it and getting subscriptions to the *Watch Tower* (published since 1879) and *Consolation (Golden Ages* from 1916, present name since 1937) is the chief activity of the 7,627 full-time workers (4,204 in the United States) and the 106,000 part-time workers. No membership roll is kept and there are no other statistics. Witnesses are not pacifist because of conscientious objection to the use of force, but are opposed to any war supported by government because all governments are evil.   W. E. GARRISON

JEHU. See BIBLE, *Principal Persons.*

JEJUNUM. See INTESTINE; DIGESTION.

JELLACHICH, JOSEPH, BARON, 1801–59, Austrian general, was born in Peterwardein. Having won the entire confidence of the Croatians, he was in 1848 appointed Ban of Croatia; by this appointment Austria secured the support of the Slavonian Croatians against the Magyars of Hungary. Jellachich took an active part in the suppression of the Hungarian rising of 1848–49.

JELLICOE, 1st EARL, JOHN RUSHWORTH, 1859–1935, British admiral. He entered the navy in 1872, rose through the ranks, and was second sea lord of the admiralty 1912–14. Shortly after the outbreak of World War I, Jellicoe was placed in command of the Grand Fleet. He was in supreme command in the Battle of Jutland, May 31–June 1, 1916 (see JUTLAND, BATTLE OF). He served as first lord of the admiralty from November, 1916, to December, 1917. In 1919 he was made admiral of the fleet and in 1920 was appointed governor general of New Zealand. Following his retirement from public life in 1924, he was created viscount Brocas of Southampton and first earl Jellicoe. He wrote: *The Grand Fleet 1914–16, Its Creation, Development and Work* (1920); and *The Crisis of the Naval War* (1920).

JELLY is a state of matter in which a liquid is solidified by the addition of a comparatively small amount of some colloid substance such as gelatin or silicic acid. Jellies do not flow, possess the incompressibility of liquids, and though elastic to torsional or tensile stresses, exhibit the property to but a small extent.

The best-known jellies are those composed of gelatin and water, with more or less flavoring matter, that are used as articles of food or confectionery (see JAM); the vegetable jellies, such as that of agar-agar, used as culture media in bacteriology; and the purely inorganic jellies, such as those formed when solutions of silicic acid are allowed to stand.

JELLYFISH, a name properly applied to members of the coelenterate class, Scyphozoa. However, it is sometimes given to the medusae of the Hydrozoa, the siphonophores (such as the Portuguese man-of-war), and the ctenophores. Of the true jellyfish a familiar example is *Aurelia flavidula,* often thrown up in thousands on the Atlantic beaches in August. These flattened, dying examples differ in several respects from the living creatures found in the open sea. In this natural habitat the body consists of a strongly curved "umbrella" of jelly, whose margin is fringed with tentacles. Through the translucent jelly there radiate blue canals, 16 in number, 8 being branched and 8 unbranched. Conspicuous also are the four yellowish

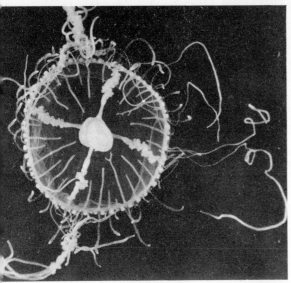

RALPH BUCHSBAUM

Jellyfish from the shallow waters of Bermuda

or pink horseshoe-shaped reproductive organs. On the undersurface is the mouth, surrounded by four frilled lips that bear stinging threads. The umbrella contains muscular fibers, and the jellyfish swims by alternately expanding and contracting these. Although *Aurelia* in Northern seas seldom exceeds eight inches in diameter, other species are sometimes enormous. An outstanding example is *Cyanea arctica*, which occasionally may be six and a half feet wide, with tentacles reaching over 100 feet in length. In the larger forms the stinging cells are extremely powerful. The special interest of *Aurelia* lies in its larval development. See LARVA.

BIBLIOG.—R. Buchsbaum, *Animals Without Backbones* (1938); L. A. Borradaile and F. A. Potts, *The Invertebrata* (1946).

JEMAPPES, town, SW Belgium, Hainaut Province, on the Haine River, and the canal from Mons to Conde; three miles W of Mons. It has a glass factory, chemical works, breweries, and, in the vicinity, extensive coal mines. It is famed for being the scene of the victory of the French over the Austrians on Nov. 6, 1792, when Dumouriez, with 46,000 men, defeated the duke of Saxe-Teschen. In May, 1940, the town was abandoned to the Germans during the retreat of the British troops from Flanders. It was liberated by the British on September 5, 1944. Pop. (1949 est.) 12,812.

JEMISON, MARY, called **the White Woman of the Genesee,** 1743–1833, Shawnee Indian captive, taken when she was 15 years old. She lived her life among the Indians and married twice, having two children by her first husband and six by her second. A tract of land along the Genesee River, granted to her in 1797, was confirmed by the New York legislature in 1817. Dr. James Everett Seaver recorded her story as *A Narrative of the Life of Mrs. Mary Jemison* (1824).

JENA, university town, Germany, in the eastern part of the state of Thuringia, in the valley of the Saale River, surrounded by a desolate plateau, on the left bank of the Saale, 12 miles E of Weimar. On the right bank of the river lies East Jena, connected with Jena proper by the Kamsdorfer bridge. Jena has many interesting buildings, among them the late Gothic town church, St. Michael (15th century), the Catholic church (11th century), the town hall (14th century), and the university library. The town is best known for its university founded in 1558 (see JENA UNIVERSITY). Here in the old ducal palace, Goethe wrote his idyll

Optical works in Jena before World War II

ACME

of village life, *Hermann und Dorothea*, and on a riverside path, the famous poem "Der Erlkönig." Here also Schiller wrote the historical play *Wallenstein*. The ancient moat that once circled the old town is now a fine parkway. The former residence (1672–90) of the dukes of Saxe-Jena contains the scientific collections of the university. Jena's most handsome street is the Fürstengraben, which is lined with chestnut trees and runs past the university and the botanical gardens. Among Jena's cultural institutions, aside from the university, are an observatory, a municipal library, the botanical gardens, several museums, a planetarium, and a fine theater. The great Carl Zeiss optical factories are located in Jena, along with an important optical school near by. During World War II the factories were targets for Allied bombs. The factories, normally employing some 12,000 workers, produced binoculars, bomb sights, cameras, range finders, and gun sights. Jena also produces machinery, chemicals, cement, glass, vaseline, sausages, soap, and books.

Jena, first mentioned as early as 1145, received its municipal rights in 1284. In 1485 it came under the control of the Ernestine branch of the Wettin family, and in 1672 it became the center of the duchy of Saxe-Jena. In 1690 it fell to Saxe-Eisenach and Saxe-Weimar, but by 1741 it was controlled by the latter alone. Jena is famous as the scene of the Battle of Jena, a term often applied as a collective name to two separate engagements fought on the same day, Oct. 14, 1806—one at Auerstädt, 14 miles to the north, between 30,000 French under Davoût and 48,000 Prussians under the duke of Brunswick; the other, on the heights round Jena, between 70,000 Prussians under the prince of Hohenlohe and 90,000 French under Napoleon. In both the Prussians were totally defeated. Pop. (1946) 70,578.

JENA UNIVERSITY. The Friedrich Schiller-Universitaet at Jena, Germany, was founded in 1558. Over 2,000 students were enrolled at the start of World War II under five faculties: theology, law and economics, medicine, philosophy, and mathematics and natural science. Among the famous men who have taught at Jena are Fichte, Hegel, Schelling, Schlegel, Haeckel, Eucken, and Schiller, for whom the university was later named.

JENGHIZ KHAN. See GENGHIS KHAN.

JENKINS, ALBERT GALLATIN, 1830–64, American Confederate soldier, was born in Cabell County, Va., studied at Jefferson College and Harvard Law School, and served in Congress (1857–61). Becoming a captain in the Confederate army, he led bold raids in the mountains of Virginia and in 1862 served in the Confederate Congress. Commissioned a brigadier general, he commanded a raid, riding 500 miles through Virginia and into Ohio. He fought at Chambersburg, Gettysburg, and in western Virginia. He was killed near Dublin, Va., in action against Crook.

JENKINS, CHARLES JONES, 1805–83, American legislator, was born in Beaufort District, S.C.,

and moved to Georgia in 1816. He was educated at Union College, Schenectady, N.Y.; practiced law at Augusta, Ga.; was a member of the state legislature (1836–42 and 1843–51); a justice of the Georgia Supreme Court during the Civil War (1860–65), and governor of Georgia (1865–68). In the last-named office he unsuccessfully attempted, by means of a lawsuit before the U.S. Supreme Court, to prevent Secretary of War Stanton from carrying out the Reconstruction Acts in Georgia. In 1868 he was removed from office by General Meade. In 1872 he received two of Georgia's electoral votes for the presidency, and in 1877 was president of the state constitutional convention.

JENKINS, THORNTON ALEXANDER, 1811–93, American naval officer, was born in Orange County, Va. He became a midshipman in the U.S. Navy in 1828; served on the coast survey (1834–42); investigated the lighthouse systems of Europe (1845), and drafted the act of 1852 organizing the lighthouse system of the United States. He served through the Civil War, during which he was flag captain to Farragut in the *Hartford*, and commanded a division at Mobile Bay. He was promoted commodore (1866) and rear admiral (1870), and was in command of the Asiatic station when he retired (1873).

JENKINS, town, SE Kentucky, in Letcher County, on the Chesapeake and Ohio Railroad and U.S. highways 23 and 119; about 28 miles SW of Shelby. Jenkins, situated in the Cumberland Mountains, was laid out in 1911 by a coal company. The mining of coal is the town's chief industry. Pop.(1950) 6,921.

JENKINS' EAR, THE WAR OF, was fought between England and Spain in 1739–1741. Thinking that Captain Jenkins of the ship *Rebecca*, had been engaged in smuggling in Spanish waters near the entrance to the gulf of Florida, the Spaniards in 1731 captured and mistreated him. On finding no positive proof against him, they cut off his ear and told him to give it to the king of England. Jenkins' story (which may have been mere fiction) at first produced no results, but when in 1738 he related it to Parliament it served as an incident to bring about a war which had long been brewing.

The war was begun over a question of trade. The Spanish colonies in the New World still produced a great deal of gold and silver and, in addition, were the source of a lucrative trade in commodities for which there was a great demand in Europe. Since the trade was so profitable, Spain wished to monopolize it. England, on the other hand, wished to share in it. In the Treaty of Utrecht of 1713 England had been given permission to send one ship yearly for trade in Spanish America. Before long the Spaniards accused the British of taking unfair advantage of the privilege by reloading the one ship over and over again from other ships. In an effort to stop this practice the Spanish authorities resorted to the right of search and too often the crews of English vessels were subjected to torture. Walpole, the British prime minister, had done his best to prevent war over this question, but the story of what had happened to Jenkins roused the war spirit to a point where he could no longer resist it and the war broke out in 1739.

A British fleet commanded by Admiral Vernon captured Porto Bello in the Isthmus of Panama; Anson raided the western coast of South America; a combined British and Colonial fleet tried unsuccessfully to attack Cuba. Spanish attacks on Gibraltar, and Portuguese attacks on Montevideo were equally unsuccessful. Neither side prosecuted the war with vigor and neither gained any decisive victories, and the issues of the war were soon merged in the War of the Austrian Succession.   ARVEL B. ERICKSON

JENKINTOWN, borough, SE Pennsylvania, in Montgomery County, on the Reading Railroad, five miles N of Philadelphia. Jenkintown, a residential suburb, is the seat of the Beaver College for women. Pop.(1950) 5,130.

JENNER, EDWARD, 1749–1823, English physician and surgeon, was born in Berkeley, Gloucestershire, and studied under John Hunter in London and at the University of St. Andrews. While practicing in Berkeley he found that cowherds and milkmaids who had suffered from cowpox (a disease of cows' udders closely resembling smallpox) were immune to smallpox during the periodic epidemics of that disease. He continued his observations and experiments over a period of 16 years. At length in 1796 he made his crowning experiment on an eight-year-old boy, thereby demonstrating the prophylactic power of inoculation with cowpox vaccine, and in 1798 published *An Inquiry into the Causes and Effects of the Variolae Vaccinae.* Although the evidence accumulated by Jenner seemed conclusive, yet the practice which he advocated met with violent opposition not only from the ignorant populace but from the learned members of the Royal Society. It was not until 1800, when vaccination was given an excellent trial during a smallpox epidemic in Vienna, that 70 London physicians signed a declaration of their confidence in it. Parliament showed its gratitude by voting Jenner a grant of $50,000 (1802) and a second grant of $100,000 (1807) for his contribution toward founding the science of preventive medicine.   M. E. C.

BIBLIOG.–H. E. Sigerist, *The Great Doctors* (1933); F. R. Moulton and J. J. Schifferes, eds., *The Autobiography of Science* (1945).

JENNER, Sir WILLIAM, 1815–98, English physician, was born at Chatham, and early began the investigations which enabled him practically to prove the difference between typhoid and typhus fevers. He held various professorships connected with medical theory and practice at University College, London, from 1849 to 1872. He was president of the College of Physicians (1881–88). He published *Diphtheria: Its Symptoms and Treatment* (1861); *Lectures and Essays on Fevers and Diphtheria, 1849-79* (1893).

JENNEY, WILLIAM LE BARON, 1832–1907, American architect and engineer, was born in Fairhaven, Mass. In 1856 he was graduated from the École Centrale des Arts et Manufactures in Paris. After the Civil War, in which he enlisted and became chief engineer of the XV Army Corps, he established himself as an architect and enginner in Chicago. In 1883 Jenney was commissioned to build the Chicago branch of the Home Insurance Company of New York, and this gained for him a great reputation. The 10-floor building was the first real introduction to the skyscraper, and used a skeleton metal construction as the basis for design, each story being carried independently on a framework of metal. After its erection, Jenney's services were constantly being sought, and he designed several other buildings in Chicago. His *Principles and Practice of Architecture* was published in 1869.   JOAN C. CAMERA

JENNINGS, HUGH AMBROSE, known as **Hughie,** 1870–1928, American baseball player and manager, member of Baseball Hall of Fame, was born in Pittston, Pa. A star shortstop for Baltimore (1893–99), he later became manager of the Philadelphia Phillies (1901–2) and the Detroit Tigers (1907–20); he won American League championships for Detroit in 1907, 1908, and 1909. His lifetime batting average was .314.

JENNINGS, SARAH, DUCHESS OF MARLBOROUGH, 1660–1744, entered the service of the royal household, and became the intimate friend of the Princess Anne. On the accession of Anne to the throne she exercised over the young queen a profound influence. In 1678 she was married to John Churchill, later duke of Marlborough, and she greatly promoted her husband's career. She retired from the queen's service in 1711, and survived her husband for nearly a quarter of a century. See MARLBOROUGH, DUKE OF.

JENNINGS, city, SW Louisiana, parish seat of Jefferson Davis Parish, on the Southern Pacific Railroad and U.S. Highway 90, about 38 miles W of

Lafayette. Jennings, located in a rice and oil country, was settled in 1882. Oil was found here in 1901, the first discovery in the state. The manufacture of oil well supplies is the chief industry. Pop. (1950) 9,663.

JENSEN, JOHANNES VILHELM, 1873–1950, Danish writer, was born in Farso, Himmerland, and was educated at the University of Copenhagen, where he studied medicine. His early work includes tales about his home province, *Himmerland Stories* (1898); novels and novelettes reflecting his travels in America (*Madame d'Ora*, 1904) and the Orient (*Exotic Stories*, 1907–9); and an imaginative portrait of Christian II, *The Fall of the King* (1899–1902). With *Det tabte Land* (1909) he began a long series of historical novels illustrating the evolution of the cave dweller into the discoverer and master builder. This brilliant fictional panorama was completed in 1920; it was published in English as *The Long Journey* (1922–24). Much of Jensen's later writing was in the form of "myths," an art form of his own devising, which he made the vehicle for his views on life and art. More serious works, as *The Transformation of Animals* (1927) and *Stages in the Development of Mind* (1928), witness his life-long interest in Darwinian evolution. He received the Nobel award for literature in 1944.

JENSON, NICHOLAS, d. 1480, French printer, was born in Sommevoire. Apprenticed to the trade of making dies for coinage, he later became master of the French royal mint and by order of Charles VII of France he was secretly sent to Mainz to learn the new art of cutting punches and letters for printing. In 1470 he set up his own printing shop in Venice. He became so noted for the design of his roman type, the beauty of his books, and the accuracy of their texts, that he was named a count by Pope Pius IV shortly before his death. See PUBLISHING AND BOOKSELLING for illustration.

JEOPARDY means peril or danger. It refers to the situation in which a person is put when regularly charged with a crime before a tribunal competent to try him as used in Article V of the United States Constitution providing "no person . . . . shall be subject for the same offence to be twice put in jeopardy of life or limb." A person is in legal jeopardy when he is put upon trial, before a court of competent jurisdiction, upon an indictment or information which is sufficient in form and substance to sustain a conviction; and a jury has been charged with his deliverance. There are a number of circumstances under which the discharge of the jury amounts to an acquittal. There are other situations in which there is no acquittal if the jury is discharged without the consent of the defendant as in the case of the illness of a juror, or the judge, the absence of a juror, extended disagreement among jurors, the discharge of the jury during the trial, or when the court lacks jurisdiction. In these cases, a new trial does not impose a double jeopardy.

JEPHTHAH. See BIBLE, *Principal Persons.*

JEQUIÉ, town, E Brazil, in the state of Bahia; on a railroad and a highway, SW of Salvador. Pop. (1940) 13,403.

JERABLUS. See CARCHEMISH.

JERÂSH. See GERASA.

JERBA. See DJERBA.

JEREMIAH, c. 650–c. 585 B.C., Hebrew prophet of the Old Testament, was the son of Hilkiah. He was of priestly descent and lived in Anathoth, about three miles from Jerusalem. He was called to the prophetic office in the 13th year of King Josiah. Recognizing the king's reform to be largely external, Jeremiah made it a special task to proclaim the necessity of internal acceptance of the divine law to a people disloyal in heart. Under the rule of Jehoiakim, Jeremiah lived in imminent danger of death because of his fearless preaching, and he was treated with unspeakable cruelty when Zedekiah reigned. He was kindly dealt with, however, by the Babylonians when Jerusalem fell, and was permitted to retire to Mizpah. But he was afterward taken to Egypt, where, according to tradition, he was stoned to death in the city of Tahpanhes.

The Book of the Prophet Jeremiah consists largely of threatenings of judgment upon a people who had broken God's covenant, together with promises of a new and better covenant. It gives an account of Jeremiah's sufferings and his warnings to foreign nations. The arrangement of the book is by no means chronological. The first draft, written at Jeremiah's dictation by Barush, was destroyed by King Jehoiakim (Jer. 36:23). A second draft, containing considerable additions to the first, is probably to be identified with the larger part of the present book. The Septuagint version of the book seems to presuppose a very different text from the Hebrew. It is somewhat shorter and the arrangement of the material is quite different. It was probably made from a Hebrew text belonging to a time previous to the final redaction.

The Lamentations of Jeremiah is a short poetical book consisting of five elegies expressive of the sufferings of the people of Jerusalem during and after the Chaldean siege (587 B.C.). In the English Bible, as in the Septuagint, it follows Jeremiah, in accordance with the tradition that it was written by that prophet; in the Hebrew canon it forms one of the five Megilloth (Rolls). Some modern criticism has reversed the judgment of tradition, placing its date about half a century after the destruction of Jerusalem and considering it a compilation of many of Jeremiah's utterances.

R. T.

JEREMIAH'S GROTTO. See GOLGOTHA.

JEREZ DE LA FRONTERA, city, S Spain, in the province of Cádiz; 30 miles by rail NE of Cádiz. Features of interest are the Alcazar, the church of San Miguel (1482); and several other ancient churches. The town gave its name to sherry wine, and still produces it in large quantities. It is one of the most important commercial cities in southern Spain. Originally a Roman colony, Jerez was taken by the Moors in 711, and played a prominent part in the struggle between the Christians and the Moors. Pop. (1949 est.) 104,958.

JEREZ DE LOS CABALLEROS, town, Spain, in the province of Badajoz; 100 miles NW of Sevilla. It was the birthplace of Balboa, the explorer, and was a stronghold of the Knights Templars. It has trade in grain, cork, and flour. Pop. (1940) 12,486.

JERICHO, ancient city in the part of Palestine now controlled by Jordan; five miles N of the Dead Sea and 15 miles NE of Jerusalem. During its long history Jericho ("City of Palms") was destroyed by invaders' armies and rebuilt on or near the same site as many as 17 times. Although Jericho is today only a large oasis, it was once a beautiful metropolis with avenues of tall palms, fragrant gardens, sumptuous villas, vineyards, and fig and olive groves. In

TWA AIRLINES

Ruins of the walls of Jericho in Palestine

pre-Israelite times it was dedicated to the worship of Astarte, moon goddess. The Canaanites made Jericho one of their chief cities. About 1479 B.C. the Egyptians captured it. In the 13th century B.C. it was attacked by JOSHUA (successor to Moses) and miraculously destroyed by him; he forbade rebuilding it, under penalty of anathema. The territory was given to the tribe of Benjamin, and five centuries later was captured and the town was rebuilt by Hiel of Bethal (I Kings 16:34). It was at Jericho in 586 B.C. that the Babylonians defeated ZEDEKIAH (II Kings 25) and brought to an end the kingdom of Judah; they carried away the population into Babylonia. After Babylonia was conquered by the Persians, the surviving Jewish prisoners were returned to Judah, among them 345 who came originally from Jericho. Again the town was rebuilt. After Alexander's conquest of Persia (333–323 B.C.), Jericho became a cultural center with a fine university. When Herod the Great (d. 4 B.C.) came into power he rebuilt Jericho in Greco-Roman style, and made it his winter residence. The Jericho which Jesus visited on His way to Jerusalem, had theaters, a hippodrome, a university, and resplendent palaces, temples, and synagogues. It was here, according to the New Testament, that Jesus gave sight to blind Bartimaeus and near here upon the mountain top that He resisted the tempting of Satan. It was upon the road to Jericho that He set the scene for His parable "The Good Samaritan." The Jericho which the Crusaders attacked in the 11th century and controlled for a time, was built upon the present site of Er Riha, farther west. Jericho was in the hands of the Moslems from A.D. 636. In the 20th century archaeologists (particularly Ernst Sellin, in 1910, John Garstang in the 1930's) have made extensive excavation in the mound of ancient Jericho, now known as Tell-es-Sultan. Seventeen settlements have been uncovered proving its extreme antiquity and existence through various periods of history from the Neolithic and Chalcolithic Ages onward. An unbaked pottery head with polished shell eyes, found in one of the lowest stratas, dates from about 5000 B.C. and is considered one of the oldest art objects known to man and one of the earliest representations of the human form yet found in Palestine. Semitic sculptures, pottery, and other relics found are thought to be about 3,600 years old. There is also a considerable variety of later archaeological material, much of it now in the Jerusalem museum. Three miles north of Jericho the remains of an eighth century Umaiyad castle, Khirber Mefjer, and the mosaic floors of a 10th century Byzantine synagogue have been found. Pop. about 1,000.

K. E. H.

JEROBOAM I. See BIBLE, *Principal Persons.*

JEROME, SAINT, in full **Sophronius Eusebius Hieronymus,** c. 346–420, one of the greatest of the Latin fathers, was born of a Christian family at Stridon, a frontier town between Dalmatia and Pannonia. In early youth he went to Rome, where he received a liberal training under Donatus the grammarian, Victorinus the rhetorician, and Bishop Liberius; here also he was baptized. An earnest seeker after truth, he traveled to Treves, then to Aquileia, in furtherance of his studies; then to the East, where an impressive dream drew him from the classics and turned him more zealously to the Bible and the gospel. Ascetically inclined, he lived for a while in the desert near Antioch, and there, as a means of self-discipline he learned Hebrew from a converted Jew. Thereafter he became a presbyter at Antioch, resided for a while in Constantinople, and in 382 returned to Rome and became secretary to Bishop Damasus. Here he undertook the revision of the old Latin version of the New Testament; but his labors tended to awaken resentment among both clergy and laity. Jerome left Rome in 385, and in the following year settled at Bethlehem, where he founded a monastery, chiefly through the beneficence of a Roman lady named Paula, who likewise founded a convent for women. Here Jerome labored for 34 years, completing his translation of the Bible, and here he died. He is usually reckoned the pre-eminent scholar of the Western Church. There are editions of his works (polemical, exegetical, and versions) by Erasmus (1516), the Benedictines (1693 f.), Vallarsi (1734 f.). F. A. Wright translated *Select Letters* (1933). His feast is celebrated on September 30.

BIBLIOG.–P. Monceaux, *St. Jerome: The Early Years* (1933); Sister Jamesetta Kelly, *Life and Times as Revealed in The Writings of St. Jerome Exclusive of his Letters* (1944).

JEROME, JEROME KLAPKA, 1859–1927, English author and playwright, was born in Staffordshire. He began working at the age of 14, educated himself by reading in the British Museum and after experience as a railway clerk, stock company actor, reporter, and schoolteacher, entered journalism, contributing a column to *Home Chimes* (1886), and editing a monthly magazine, *The Idler* (with Robert Barr, 1892–97), and a weekly paper, *Today* (1893–97). Meanwhile, his whimsical stories and sketches, *Idle Thoughts of an Idle Fellow* (1886) and *Three Men in a Boat* (1889), established his reputation as one of the foremost British humorists. Besides a dozen volumes of fiction Jerome produced 19 plays, the most notable being the allegorical *Passing of the Third Floor Back* (1910), a dramatization of his short story with the same title.

BIBLIOG.–A. Moss, *Jerome K. Jerome* (1929).

JÉRÔME BONAPARTE. See BONAPARTE, JÉRÔME.

JEROME OF PRAGUE, d. 1416, a Bohemian pre-Protestant reformer and martyr. He was of knightly family. Having become widely known as a scholar with a conspicuous gift of eloquence, he incurred the hostility of the ecclesiastical authorities by spreading the teachings of Wycliffe and by championing the cause of JOHN HUSS. Huss and Jerome put new vigor into an old strain of religious reform in Bohemia, and both were ardent Bohemian patriots. Jerome went to the Council of Constance (1415) to support Huss, who had gone there under the emperor's safe-conduct but was burned at the stake nevertheless. Ten months later, Jerome also was tried for heresy, condemned and burned.   W. E. GARRISON

JERRY O'CONNELL DAM. See DAM.

JERRYMANDER. See GERRYMANDER.

JERSEY, largest of the Channel Islands, belonging to Great Britain; lies about 15 miles W of the coast of Normandy, 18 miles SE of Guernsey, and 95 miles S of Weymouth, England; area, 50 sq. mi.; pop. (1948) 57,133. It is rectangular in shape; its rock-bound coasts are high on the north, but stretch out south for a long distance as low, jagged reefs. The people of Jersey are mostly of Norman extraction, and speak a mixture of Norman French and Early English. They engage in fishing, granite quarrying, and agriculture. Quantities of tomatoes, potatoes, orchard fruits, and flower bulbs are grown for English and French markets. A valuable and widely celebrated breed of small milch cow (see CATTLE) is raised.

Although Jersey has been attached to the Crown of England since the Norman Conquest it has its own separate existence and is administered according to

Castle Mont Orgueil on the Isle of Jersey

ACME

Jersey

its own laws and customs. The island has a legislative body known as the States Assembly; the head of the administration, however, is the lieutenant governor, who is appointed by the Crown. St. Helier on St. Aubin's Bay is the chief port and the island's capital; at St. Brelades on the southwest coast is an 11th-century church; and at Gorey on the east coast is Castle Mont Orgueil, once a Roman stronghold. In 1940, just before the invasion by Nazi military forces, most of the inhabitants, the military garrison, and the best of the Jersey herds and their registration records were evacuated to England. It was cleared of Germans by English troops in May, 1945, at the end of World War II. See CHANNEL ISLANDS. K. E. H.

JERSEY, a plain-knitted, elastic fabric with a faint rib on one side. It is made from wool or rayon and sometimes cotton. Weights vary according to use, which includes women's dresses, sportswear, lingerie and blouses. Because of the looped construction of this fabric, it is subject to "runs" when breakage occurs. Jersette is a woven nonrun fabric imitative of jersey. Jersey may be knit in tubular form, flat or in tricot knit, which is a type of run-resistant warp knitting. Glove fabrics are usually done in this weave.

JERSEY CITY, city, E New Jersey, county seat of Hudson County, is situated on a peninsula between the Hudson River and New York Bay on the E and the Hackensack River and Newark Bay on the W; opposite Manhattan with which it is connected by vehicular tunnels, the passenger tubes of the Hudson and Manhattan railroad, and by ferries. Jersey City is served by the Baltimore and Ohio, the Central of New Jersey, the Delaware, Lackawanna, and Western, the Erie, the Hudson and Manhattan, the Lehigh Valley, the New Jersey and New York, the New York Central, the New York, Susquehanna, and Western, and the Pennsylvania railroads, U.S. highways 1 and 25, and by numerous steamship lines. Pop. (1950) 299,017.

Jersey City covers an area of 20.2 square miles with a water front of 11 miles. The main business and industrial section occupies the eastern portion of the peninsula adjacent to the Hudson River, while the residential section is laid out on the higher ground to the west. There are 26 parks in the city, the most important of which is Lincoln Park with 287 acres. Jersey City is the seat of a state teachers college, St. Peters College, the Hudson College of Commerce and Finance, and the John Marshall College of Law.

Buildings. One of the outstanding buildings in the city is the Colgate-Palmolive-Peet plant, which covers seven blocks with 44 buildings. The Medical Center of Jersey City is the largest hospital in the state. Four main buildings of light yellow brick and terra cotta form the most imposing segment of the city's sky line. In the main branch of the public library of Jersey City is one of the world's most complete exhibits of precious and semiprecious stones. The Department of Labor maintains a Safety Museum in Jersey City.

Industry. Jersey City, the second largest city of New Jersey, is an important commercial and industrial center. Its shipping activities are comparable in volume to those of New York City. The manufactures of Jersey City are extremely varied and numerous. More than 5,000 different articles are made including cans, metals for welding, castor oil, boilers and tanks, macaroni and egg noodles, cheese, lamps and electrical fixtures, pharmaceuticals, patent medicines, iron products, soap, steel barrels, matzoths, chemicals, electric elevators, cosmetics, paint and varnish, slippers and sandals, cork, cigars, and cigarettes.

History. The site of Jersey City, formerly known as Paulus Hook, was settled as early as 1630. In 1779, during the Revolutionary War, it was the scene of a brilliant exploit by Major Henry Lee, "Light Horse Harry Lee," who with 200 men descended on the British stationed here, to capture the entire garrison.

Colgate-Palmolive-Peet plant in Jersey City

The city was laid out in 1804, incorporated as the "City of Jersey in the County of Bergen" in 1820, and as Jersey City in 1838. Annexations of territory and the filling in of tidal lands have increased the size of Jersey City until it is now more than 100 times bigger than the original settlement of Paulus Hook. Jersey City adopted the commission form of government in 1913. A. M. K.

JERSEY SHORE, borough, N central Pennsylvania, in Lycoming County, on the Susquehanna River, the New York Central and the Pennsylvania railroads and U.S. Highway 220; about 12 miles SW of Williamsport. Jersey Shore was settled in 1800. The borough has railroad shops and manufactures of steel and wire. Pop. (1950) 5,595.

JERSEYVILLE, city, SW Illinois, county seat of Jersey County, on the Alton Railroad and U.S. Highway 67; about 21 miles NW of Alton. Jerseyville is the shipping center for the apples grown in the surrounding area. The city was settled in 1823. Shoes, flour, seed cleaners, and concrete products are the principal manufactures of the city. Pop. (1950) 5,792.

JERUSALEM, ancient city and capital of Palestine, located about 15 miles W of the northern extremity of the Dead Sea, 33 miles from the Mediterranean, and at a maximum altitude of 2,528 feet. It is connected by rail with Jaffa and all-weather motor roads link it with Damascus, Jaffa, Jericho, Hebron, and other cities of Palestine. The population of the city is very heterogeneous and is composed of many different religious groups, including Jews, Mohammedans, Roman Catholics, Orthodox Christians, Copts and Protestants. The population (1946 est.) was 160,000, more than half being Jewish.

The industries of Jerusalem are confined mostly to the production of pottery and of articles made of mother of pearl and carved olive wood which are sold to the numerous tourists and pilgrims who visit the city. There is also considerable buying and selling of merchandise which is produced outside Jerusalem.

Climate and Topography. The climate of Jerusalem is temperate. The elevation and sea breezes serve to modify the summer heat and the nights are generally cool. The mean annual temperature of the city is 62.8° F., the lowest mean monthly temperature (47.2° F.) being in February and the highest (76.3° F.) being in August. The mean annual rainfall is approximately 26 inches, the rainy season lasting from November to April. Snow falls during January and February about two years out of three, but it seldom remains long on the ground.

The city rests on a spur of the principal range of the Judean hills. This plateau is divided on the south into two ridges, the one to the east being known as Moriah and the one to the west as Zion. On the western side of the city is the valley of Hinnom, or Wadi Er Rababi, and to the east is the Kidron Valley, or Jehoshaphat, beyond which lies the Mount of Olives which rises considerably above the level of the city. Both valleys unite not far from the southern extremity of the city near the Pool of Siloam and drain the district into the Dead Sea. Within the city, the Tyropoeon Valley runs southeast, joining the other two valleys of the city. In early times all three valleys were much deeper than they are now, having accumulated large quantities of rubbish through the centuries.

The inner city is surrounded by an irregular quadrangular stone wall about 38 feet high which was originally built by Suleiman the Magnificent in 1542 and has since been restored. This wall, which is approximately two and one-half miles in circuit, is pierced by eight gates, the Jaffa Gate on the western side of the city being the one most used. Before 1858

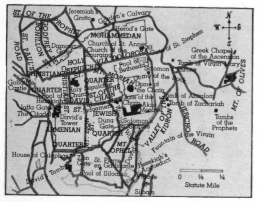

Detail of Via Dolorosa, above; the location of features of interest in and about Jerusalem, below

the city was almost wholly contained within these walls but, since that time, Jerusalem has grown beyond the walls, the suburbs occupying a larger area than the old city. There is a great contrast between the suburbs outside the walls with their comparatively recent buildings and wide well-paved streets, and the city inside the walls with its old houses and dirty streets, which are so narrow and poorly paved that automobiles cannot be driven in the old city.

Interesting Features. Many Christian, Jewish, and Moslem visitors come to the city annually because of its close associations with the religions of all three groups. Of paramount interest to most Christians is the Church of the Holy Sepulchre which is, in reality, not one church but a group of connected and superimposed churches, or chapels, under the control of different religious groups, including the Armenians, Catholics, Copts, and Greeks, The Church of the Holy Sepulchre contains what is, according to tradition, the tomb in which the body of Jesus was laid, and also the traditional site of Calvary and other shrines which tradition connects with events in the trial, crucifixion, and resurrection of Jesus. The site of the Church of the Holy Sepulchre was determined by Helena (c. 248–328), the mother of Constantine, who visited Palestine and determined a number of the places connected with the life of Jesus. The earliest church on the site was consecrated in 336 but was destroyed by the Persians in 614. The present structure dates from 1810 but contains parts of a Romanesque church erected by Crusaders in the early 12th century. Some scholars have questioned the authenticity of the church as marking the site of Calvary. Outside the wall of the city and not far from the Damascus Gate, there is a tomb close to a rock

cliff which is known as Gordon's Calvary. Many Protestants believe that this place more nearly corresponds with the biblical description of Calvary and the tomb of Jesus than does the location of the Church of the Holy Sepulchre.

Of great historial and political interest is the Haram-esh-Sherif, exceptionally holy to both Jews and Moslems. It is the site of Solomon's Temple and of the later Temple erected by Herod; on the site now stands the beautiful Moslem shrine known as the Dome of the Rock, an octagonal building dating from 691, and second in importance to Moslems only to the Great Mosque at Mecca. Within the Dome of the Rock is a rock which, according to one legend, Mohammed ascended to visit the seven heavens of Islam. According to Jewish tradition, Abraham prepared to sacrifice Isaac upon this rock. Also in the area is a portion of the foundation wall of the Temple known as the "Wailing Wall" of the Jews.

Jerusalem is now altogether different from the city which Jesus saw, since all of the houses and even the fortifications which he knew were destroyed centuries ago. Because of accumulated débris, the remains of the city of Jesus' time lie several feet below the level of the present city. However, at one place in the city it is possible for the visitor to descend below street level and see part of a very old street which Biblical archaeologists agree dates back to the time of Jesus. Very possibly, Jesus may have walked along this street while He was in Jerusalem, and it may be that He followed it on His way to Calvary. Other features of interest in and about Jerusalem are the *Via Dolorosa*, which is supposed to mark the route along which Jesus passed to Calvary; the Pool of Bethesda; the Tomb of David; the Tomb of the Virgin Mary; the Grotto of Jeremiah; and the Garden of Gethsemane on the Mount of Olives. There are also other shrines and churches of interest both within and outside the walls of the city.

History. In the modern city many of the holy places stand on the very ground wherein must lie the remains of early Jerusalem. Since there is aversion to distrubing the holy places, full scale archaeological excavation has not been done in the important areas. A small group of pottery dating to before 3000 B.C. was secured from the hill of Ophel. The first Egyptian mention of Jerusalem dates to about 1900 B.C. Seven of the Tel-el-Amarna tablets of Egypt refer to an imminent attack upon the city and the request of its inhabitants for the help of the Egyptians in repelling the invaders. The location of the Canaanite town (and the town in later periods) was limited to a certain area by reason of the water supply. Two springs were the main source of water; the one, Gihon, was in the Kidron Valley, and the other, En-rogel, was at the juncture of the Kidron and Hinnom valleys. The hill between these valleys and above the springs, Ophel, or the "Eastern Hill," was the site of the early Jerusalem. By the time of Jesus, the use of aqueducts and cisterns had allowed the city to spread to the north and west. The city was the chief stronghold of the Jebusites when the Israelites invaded Palestine and was finally taken by DAVID (c. 1000 B.C.). Following its capture, David made the city the political and religious center of his kingdom. His son, SOLOMON, built the Temple, the Royal Palace and other magnificent buildings, and fortified the city.

Jerusalem declined in political importance after the revolt of Jeroboam and the northern tribes, though its religious prestige endured. Joash, king of Israel, took the city during the reign of Amaziah (c. 790 B.C.) and destroyed much of the northern wall which was repaired later by Uzziah. Sennacherib laid siege to the city but was repelled. Jerusalem was sacked and its Temple, Palace, and walls destroyed in 586 B.C. by NEBUCHADNEZZAR, but, in 536, a group of exiles returned under Zerubbabel and a new Temple was completed in 515 B.C. Nehemiah

Arched Gate in Jerusalem leads to site of Solomon's Temple and present Moslem Dome of the Rock Mosque

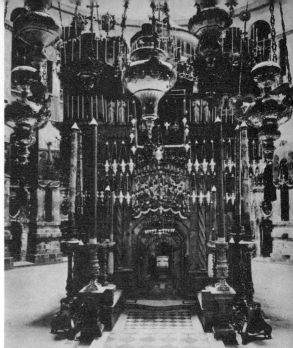

Holy Sepulchre, according to tradition, was the tomb in which Jesus was laid after the Crucifixion

Walls of Jerusalem during an Easter pilgrimage

Garden of Gethsemane and Church of All Nations

David Street, market street of the Walled City

Zion Square in the modern section of Jerusalem

rebuilt the wall about 445 B.C. Alexander the Great entered Jerusalem without damage to the city in 332 B.C. The Temple was desecrated and the walls destroyed by Antiochus Epiphanes in 168 B.C., but the Jews, under Judas Maccabaeus, took the city and restored the Temple in 165 B.C.

Pompey captured the city in 63 B.C. and, in 37 B.C., Herod became king. He reconstructed the Temple and the fortifications and made Jerusalem a strong and imposing city. After a long siege, Jerusalem fell to Titus A.D. 70, and great damage was done. However, it was not until after the unsuccessful revolt of the Jews under Bar Kochba (A.D. 132) that the city was completely destroyed. A new city, Aelia Capitolina, with pagan temples was built on the ruins of the old. Christian churches were erected under the reign of Constantine and later Christian emperors. In 637, the Romans lost control of the city to Omar, and Jerusalem came under the domination of Islam. Mosques were erected, including the Dome of the Rock. Great destruction to Jerusalem resulted from the entry into the city in 1099 of the Crusaders, under GODFREY OF BOUILLON. Jerusalem was conquered by Saladin in 1187, and, except for two short periods during the 13th century, remained under the control of the Moslems until its capture by British forces under ALLENBY near the end of World War I. The city became the capital of the British mandated territory of Palestine.

Under British rule, the water supply of the city was greatly improved and Jewish immigration increased greatly up to the outbreak of World War II. A Hebrew University was founded on Mount Scopus near Jerusalem in 1925; it is regarded as one of the outstanding institutions of higher learning in the Near East.

Jerusalem has been the center of much of the strife between the Arabs and the Jews. Disputes between the two groups over the rights to the Wailing Wall caused serious riots in 1929. Despite a ruling by the British that the Arabs were the rightful owners of the Wall, other riots continued during succeeding years. All attempts to reconcile the two factions failed to achieve lasting results.

In recent years Jerusalem has been shaken by conflicts between the British and the Jews and open warfare between the Jews and Arabs. On July 22, 1946, the King David Hotel in Jerusalem was dynamited by a Jewish terroristic organization, killing many persons, including several British officials. On Nov. 27, 1947, the Assembly of the United Nations proposed the establishment of Jerusalem as a holy place and the creation of an international regime for the city. A new wave of violence then broke out between Arabs and Jews in Jerusalem. On May 15, 1948, the British terminated their mandate, leaving Jerusalem with neither *de facto* nor provisional authority. The United Nations had agreed on the necessity of saving the sacred shrines of the city, but had not been able to organize an international police force. With the withdrawal of the British troops the ARAB LEAGUE states launched an immediate invasion of the new state of ISRAEL with Jerusalem as their first objective. Bitter fighting then broke out in Jerusalem until the conclusion of the truce. In January, 1950, the Israeli government announced that it would continue to oppose the U.N. efforts to internationalize Jerusalem, and claimed that modern Jerusalem should be an Israeli city. Later that month the Israeli parliament proclaimed Jerusalem the capital of the state.

W. G. D.; F. M.; G. B. DE H.

BIBLIOG.–G. A. Smith, *Jerusalem: the Topography, Economics and History from the Earliest Times to A.D. 70* (1908); G. G. Atkins, *Jerusalem Past and Present* (1918); W. L. Phelps, *City of the Great King* (1926); J. Baikie, *Ancient Jerusalem* (1930); P. Loti, *Jerusalem* (1930); L. G. Farmer, *We Saw the Holy City* (1944); H. Kendall, *Jerusalem City Plan, Preservation and Development* (1948); B. H. Vester, *Our Jerusalem* (1950).

JERUSALEM CHERRY, a small shrub, which may reach four feet in height, but which is usually smaller when used as a pot plant in greenhouse and window garden. It has shining green, entire leaves, and scarlet or yellow globular fruit.

JERUSALEM CORN. See SORGHUM.

JERVIS, JOHN, EARL OF ST. VINCENT, 1735–1823, British admiral, was born in Staffordshire. He took part in the expedition to Quebec (1759) and at Ushant (1778), and was in command at the reduction of Martinique and Guadeloupe (1794). He won a great naval victory over the Spaniards off Cape St. Vincent in 1797, for which he was created earl of St. Vincent. He served as first lord of the admiralty (1801–3) reforming corrupt methods in the dockyards. He commanded the Channel fleet (1806–7) and became admiral of the fleet (1821).

JERVIS, JOHN BLOOMFIELD, 1795–1885, American civil engineer, was born in Huntington, N.Y. He began work as an axeman on the survey of the Erie Canal (1817) and within two years became sectional resident engineer. A pioneer in modern engineering, he designed one of the first railroads in the country (1825–30), in Pennsylvania. He was the first to use reservoirs to supply water to higher levels on the Chenango Canal (1833–36), and supervised construction of the Croton Aqueduct for New York City's water supply (1836–43), and the Cochituate Aqueduct for Boston (1846–48). Later he supervised the construction of several Middle Western railroads. Port Jervis, N.Y., was named for him.

JERVIS BAY, Australia, New South Wales, in Vincent County, 90 miles SW of Sydney; one of the safest and most commodious harbors in the world. It is about 10 miles long and its width varies from 2 miles at its entrance to 10 miles. The port for the national capital territory of Canberra is to be located on Jervis Bay.

JESSAMINE, or **CAROLINA YELLOW,** a climbing shrub of the family *Loganiaceae* that thrives in southern United States, growing in low altitudes from Virginia and Arkansas south to Florida and Texas. In eastern Guatemala the jessamine ascends to nearly 7,000 feet. Its evergreen leaves are usually opposite, sometimes whorled, and the showy bright yellow clusters of funnel-shaped, five-lobed flowers are very fragrant. Yellow jessamine, *Gelsemium sempervirens*, is one of the best known plants of the South, where it is found covering river banks or forming thickets on the borders of pine woods. Another species, *G. Rankinii*, is found on the Coastal Plain from North Carolina south to Florida and Louisiana. True JASMINE, or jessamine, *Jasminum officinalis*, of Europe, is a member of the Olive family, *Oleaceae*.

JESSE, an Old Testament personage, was the father of King DAVID, and the grandson of Boaz and Ruth.

JESSELTON, seaport on the NW coast of British North Borneo. It is the principal west coast town. From here a railway runs 127 miles to Melalap in the interior. It was occupied by the Japanese during World War II.

JESSUP, PHILIP CARYL, 1897–   , American author and diplomat, was born in New York City and studied at Hamilton College, Yale, and Columbia Universities. He joined the Columbia faculty (1925), and was professor of international law (1935–46). He served as legal adviser for many international groups, and was the U.S. representative on the U.N. Security Council (1948). He was named U.S. Ambassador-at-large (1949). He wrote many international law texts and other works, including: *Law of Territorial Waters and Maritime Jurisdiction* (1927); *International Security* (1935); *Elihu Root* (2 vols. 1938); *Modern Law of Nations* (1948).

JEST BOOK. Many current stories and jests can be traced back through the monkish *raconteurs* of the Middle Ages to the East. The fact is, that the humorous situations which appeal to men's minds are few and simple, and recur in all countries and among all races; and this is particularly true of practical joking. Collections of jests and humorous stories may be acknowledged compilations, extracted from literature, history, tradition, and experience; but they are frequently fathered upon some notorious local or national jester. Among such jest books are Tarlton's *Jests: a Hundred Mery Talys* (first extant ed. 1611), to which reference is made in *Much Ado about Nothing;* and Joe Miller's *Jest-Book, or the Wits Vade Mecum* (1739). These, however, are only a few of the vast number of jest books, a type of literature to be found in nearly all countries, and which prepared the way for the realism of the modern novel. See HUMOR IN LITERATURE AND ART.

JESTER is properly a teller of *gestes* or heroic deeds. But in the decay of minstrelsy a *geste* came to mean a witty story of sally, and a *gestour* such a domestic fool or buffoon as great personages used to keep for their private entertainment. This custom can be traced in the Roman Empire, was widespread in the Middle Ages, and lasted through the Renaissance. Among famous fools are Thévenin de St. Leger, the fool of Charles V of France; Triboulet, the fool of Louis XII, celebrated by Rabelais; Will Somers, the fool of Henry VIII; and Archie Armstrong, the fool of James I. As a court institution the fool does not seem to have outlived the commonwealth. The earliest fools were probably real "naturals," or half-witted folk; in later cases the folly was mainly assumed, and served as a cloak for plain-speaking and ribaldry. So it is with the fools who figure in *As You Like It, Twelfth Night, King Lear,* and other plays of Shakespeare and his contemporaries. The description of Touchstone in *As You Like It* fixes the type. The traditional getup of the court fool, the parti-colored garments, the hood with cockscomb and asses' ears, the bauble or *marotte,* was probably borrowed in the 14th century from that of the so-called Feast of Fools. This was a New Year revel practiced by the inferior clergy of cathedral establishments, in burlesque of divine service. The hoods probably represented beast masks of sacrificial origin, worn by heathen revelers at the same period of the year. They therefore form a link between the court fool and the grotesque buffoon, with skin cap and hanging cow's tail, who, under the name of "fool" or "squire," makes his appearance in morris dances, mummers' plays, and other diversions of the folk.

JESUITS or **SOCIETY OF JESUS,** a religious order of the Roman Catholic Church.

The History of the Order up to 1556 is very closely linked with the life of its founder, St. IGNATIUS OF LOYOLA (1491–1556). While studying in Paris, Ignatius associated himself with a group of six companions: four Spaniards, Diego Lainez, Francis Xavier, Nicholas Bobadilla and Alfonso Salmerón; a Portuguese named Simón Rodriguez; and a Savoyard named Pierre Le Fèvre. This group formed the nucleus of what was later to develop into the Jesuits, or Society of Jesus, and each contributed to the early expansion of the Order. On Aug. 15, 1534, Ignatius and his companions took vows of poverty and chastity in a chapel on Montmartre, Paris, resolving that they would go to the Holy Land for the purpose of converting the Moslems. The war against the Turks prevented them from carrying out this plan but they did keep together as a group, working on various religious projects in or near Venice, the port from which they had intended to sail for Palestine.

It was not until 1538 that the plan to form a permanent religious organization developed. A formula for the proposed new order was brought to Rome and presented to Pope Paul III (1468–1549) in 1539 by Ignatius and his associates. Although the plan met with considerable papal opposition at first, it was finally approved, and, on Sept. 27, 1540, the pope issued a bull officially recognizing the organization

"Miracle of St. Ignatius de Loyola," by Rubens

of the Jesuits. The formula which Ignatius had drawn up and submitted to the pope as the rule of the order became known as the *Constitutions.* Although it was frequently revised by Ignatius himself during his lifetime, the *Constitutions* have remained essentially unchanged ever since his death, continuing to be the rule by which the order has always been governed. Ignatius was elected, against his will, general of the new order in 1541 and continued to hold that position, despite his desire to resign, until his death.

In his position as leader, Ignatius directed the affairs of the Jesuits from Rome, which became the headquarters of the new organization. Although the order has always been pledged to do whatever the pope might command, Ignatius was the principal director of its early activities and much of the work of the Society was concerned with the two major interests of its founder, i.e., foreign missions and the education of youth. During the lifetime of Ignatius, the order expanded rapidly, until, by the time of his death in 1556, there were about 1,000 Jesuits working not only in Spain but also in Germany, Italy, Portugal and in mission stations in Brazil, India and Japan.

The History of the Jesuits after the Death of Ignatius, although marked by still further expansion, was also characterized by the growth of antagonism to the organization. By 1616, the Jesuits numbered 13,112 members and, by 1710, the membership had risen to 19,978. With the increase in numbers there came also an increase in the power and influence of the order throughout Europe. As avowed supporters of papal supremacy, the Jesuits came into conflict with those who were influenced by the rising spirit of nationalism. During the first half of the 17th century, trouble developed between the pope and the Republic of Venice, and the Jesuits, who supported the papacy, were banned from the Venetian States.

The close relationship of the order to the pope made its position in France very insecure at times, though the influence of the Jesuits was powerful enough in that country to be a strong force in combating the spread of Protestantism by the Huguenots. The Jesuits in France were much opposed to the movement known as Gallicanism, which advocated the independence of the Church from the pope and the subordination of papal authority to that of the general ecclesiastical councils. Also, the Jesuits and the Jansenists in France bitterly denounced each other, the latter maintaining that the casuistry of the Jesuits constituted an abuse of the confessional. Aroused by the influence which the Jesuits exerted over education, both the University of Paris and the Sorbonne denounced the Society in France. The French philosophic party opposed the

Jesuit Saints, with Ignatius Loyola at top left, in detail of fresco at Loyola Univ., Chicago

order on the grounds that it represented a powerful factor in the preservation of Catholic education and thought in the country. The enmity of the mistress of Louis XV (1710–74), Mme. de Pompadour (1721–64), was aroused when the Jesuits refused her the sacraments. All of these forces working together finally resulted in the suppression of the order in France by Louis XV in 1764. See JANSENISM.

The Jesuits had already been expelled from Portugal and her colonies by Pombal (1699–1782), the minister of King Joseph. Before long, as a result of action taken by Bourbon courts, the order was also suppressed in Modena, Naples, Parma and Spain, as well as the Spanish colonies. Acting from motives of political expedience and in an effort to insure the unity of the Church, Pope Clement XIV (1769–74) finally issued a brief (July 21, 1773) which suppressed the order entirely. Although the papal brief was strictly observed in all Catholic countries, two non-Catholic governments refused to publish it, thereby permitting the Jesuits to function as educators in those countries, though without authority from Rome. Catherine II (1729–96) of Russia and Frederick the Great (1712–86) of Prussia refused to comply with the pope's edict, because they could not afford to dispense with the educational activities of the Jesuits.

The suppression of the Society did not last long, a limited reorganization of the order being obtained by the Duke of Parma in 1792. Pope Pius VII (1800–23) allowed the Jesuits to reorganize in part of Russia and Lithuania in 1801, and in 1804 the Society was permitted to return to Naples. The complete restoration of the order took place on Aug. 7, 1814, when the pope issued a bull which granted full recognition of the order in all countries. There have been no more efforts at suppression from Rome and the

Society has spread over the world, becoming the largest religious order of the Roman Catholic Church.

The Organization of the Order is based upon the *Constitutions* of Ignatius and the power of the general ("Father General") of the Society is limited by that document. The ordinary judicial and executive powers reside in the general who is elected for life by the general congregation of the order. The general congregation, which possesses legislative power, is composed of the general or his representative, the five assistants of the general who compose his advisory council, the heads of the provinces (provincials) and two representative deputies from each of the provinces. The general congregation is empowered to depose the general under certain conditions but this has never been done. Although the general consults with his advisory council on all important matters, he is not required to follow its decisions. The general has no authority to change any of the rules of the *Constitutions*, only the general congregation having the power to do so.

The Jesuits are divided into four classes. The *novice*, who first undergoes a short period of trial as a postulate, engages exclusively in spiritual exercises such as prayer, reading, and meditation. After two years of this training, the novice takes the vows of chastity, obedience, and poverty, which entitle him to become a *scholastic*. In this class, he studies, teaches, and undergoes additional spiritual training before becoming either a *coadjutor* or a *professed father*. The coadjutors are ordained priests who do not have the health or the ability necessary to meet the high standards required to become a professed father. The general and all high officials of the order are selected from the class of professed fathers, who are required not only to reaffirm the three vows of the novice but also to take a special vow of obedience to the pope.

The geographical divisions of the order are the *provinces* and the *assistantships*, the latter being large groupings of the provinces based on linguistic similarities. The provinces are under the control of the *provincials* who are appointed by the general of the order. The assistantships are headed by the *assistants* who also compose the advisory council of the general. The assistants are elected by the general congregation.

The Spiritual and Intellectual Training of the Jesuits is largely governed by the rules of the order. The spiritual discipline is based upon the *Spiritual Exercises*, a manual of devotions written by Ignatius in a cave near Manressa soon after his conversion and subsequently revised by him a number of times. A novitiate of the Society devotes much of his time to spiritual development and 30 days of the first year of his training are spent in complete silence, putting into practice the *Spiritual Exercises* of Ignatius. At least eight successive days out of every year thereafter must be devoted to a similar retreat, conducted in accordance with the *Spiritual Exercises*.

The intellectual training of the Jesuits is very thorough, necessitating years of study with emphasis being placed on the study of philosophy, theology, the humanities, and science. After five years of study, a Jesuit is often allowed to teach in some college of the order, at the same time devoting himself to further study. Following a period of teaching, he prepares himself for advancement to holy orders by the study of theology and allied subjects.

The Work and Influence of the Jesuits has been chiefly in two fields of endeavor, i.e., education and missions. The Jesuits founded schools and colleges in many of the principal cities of Europe and for many years they were the dominant force in education on that continent. This fact resulted in antagonism on the part of some established schools, and also those who were opposed to the teaching of the doctrine of papal supremacy. Despite opposition, however, the influence which the Jesuits exerted through education was very great. Not only was the scholarship of the Jesuit teachers very high, but also the Society perfected a system of instruction which proved to be very effective and efficient. Jesuit teachers put into practice their techniques of education in over 600 institutions of learning during the 17th and 18th centuries. During this period, no other organization had a greater part in the education of European Catholics than did the Jesuits. The dogmatic theology of the Society owed much to Thomism and the Scholasticism of the 14th and 15th centuries, and such Jesuit theologians as FRANCISCO SUAREZ (1548–1617) and Leonard Lessius (1554–1623) exerted considerable influence upon the philosophical and theological thought of their time.

The Jesuits have always excelled in missionary work as well as in learning. One of the greatest of all missionaries was the Jesuit FRANCIS XAVIER (1506–52) who founded missions in the following places, Goa in India, Malacca on the Malay Peninsula, and a number of places in Japan. The missions established in Japan (1549) grew rapidly, numbering 200,000 converts by 1579, but persecutions followed the early successes of the missions and they were nearly destroyed in the first part of the 17th century. Even though all the Jesuit priests were killed, Christianity survived despite great opposition in Japan, native Christians being found in that country when it was opened up to western trade in the 19th century.

In China, the Jesuits under the leadership of Fathers Matteo Ricci (1552–1610) and Adam Schall secured many converts but persecutions developed which greatly retarded, but never destroyed, the missionary work of the Society. In India, Robert de' Nobili made many converts after years of patient effort during which he lived as a Brahmin. In the New World, the Jesuits established missions in the possessions of France, Spain and Portugal, the work of Father José de Anchieta (1530?–97) in Brazil being especially noteworthy. During the 17th century, the Jesuits worked with the Indians of New France, establishing missions and aiding greatly in the exploration of unknown territory. Outstanding among these early Jesuit missionaries to North America were Fathers Charles Albanel (1613–96), Claude Jean Allouez (1622–89), Jean de Brébeuf (1593–1649) and Jacques Marquette (1637–75).

The order is still distinguished by its foreign missionary work and its educational activities in many countries. In the United States, the Jesuits maintain many educational institutions, outstanding among them being Fordham and Georgetown universities. Jesuit scholars have made noteworthy contributions to many fields of learning, particularly the sciences.

There are 55 provinces of the Order, eight of which are in the United States; over 30,000 members, with 7,000 in the United States; and nearly 5,000 members serving in 44 missions widely distributed throughout the world.   W. G. D.

BIBLIOG.–G. Smith, ed., *Jesuit Thinkers of the Renaissance* (1939); J. J. Daly, *Jesuit in Focus* (1940); J. Brodrick, *Origin of the Jesuits* (1941); F. J. Corley and R. J. Willmes, *Wings of Eagles* (1941); M. P. Harney, *Jesuits in History* (1941); J. Brodrick, *Progress of the Jesuits* (1947); E. Kenton, *With Hearts Courageous* (1948).

JESUITS' BARK. See CINCHONA.

JESUP, MORRIS KETCHUM, 1830–1908, American philanthropist, born in Westport, Conn., was engaged in the banking business in New York in 1852–84, became president of the American Museum of Natural History in 1881, and of the Chamber of Commerce in 1899, both in New York; and retained both offices till his death. He was also president in 1881–1903 of the New York City Mission and Tract Society, for which he built the DeWitt Memorial Church. He gave to the Union Theological Seminary, Syrian Protestant College at Beirut, and was a liberal patron of charitable, scientific, and educational institutions. To the Museum of Natural History he gave $1,000,000 in life and bequeathed $1,000,000.

JESUS CHRIST

The ethical ideals of Western civilization are based on the life and teachings of Jesus

JESUS CHRIST, the founder and foundation of the Christian religion. The name "Jesus" is the Greek form of the Hebrew "Joshua." "Christ" is not a name but a title, from a Greek word meaning "the anointed one"; it is the equivalent of "Messiah," which is from the Hebrew word meaning "one sent." Even when the two are used together they are not properly a compound name, like Pontius Pilate, as is shown by the fact that they can be, and often are, used in either order—either Jesus Christ or Christ Jesus. A more accurate English form would be "Jesus the Christ."

Summary of His Life. The external facts of his life, so far as known, can be briefly stated. He was born in the town of Bethlehem in Judea, about six miles south of Jerusalem, lived to the age of 30 in

NATIONAL GALLERY OF ART

"Bust of the Christ Child," by A. della Robbia

humble circumstances in the village of Nazareth in Galilee, about 60 miles north of Jerusalem, where he was known as the son of a carpenter and probably worked as a carpenter himself. He became convinced that he was called to a heavenly mission and journeyed south to the "wilderness of Judea" where his cousin, JOHN THE BAPTIST, was preaching "Repent, for the kingdom of heaven is at hand," and was baptized by John. He then returned to Galilee and spent three years going about Palestine with a small band of companions, preaching "the kingdom of God" and gaining reputation as a miracle-worker. During this itinerant ministry he won much popular acclaim but gained no substantial body of adherents. He seems not to have wished to consolidate a party about him other than the twelve who were to become his APOSTLES and a group of 70 about whom nothing is reported except that he once sent them out to spread his teaching. He incurred the active hostility of the priests, scribes, and higher Jewish officials because he subordinated ritual and ceremonial law to purity of life, justice, and consideration for the poor, and the suspicion of the Roman authorities because the status

Although of royal lineage, Joseph was a humble carpenter. As a child, Jesus helped him in his workshop

When he became 30, Jesus went into towns around and about Galilee to teach, turned water into wine

News of his miracles spread near and far. Wherever he went the sick were brought to him, made well by the touch of his hands

To prove his resurrection Christ appeared as man in the upper room of the Apostles, the first church of Christianity

THE LIFE OF JESUS CHRIST

Galilee in Judea lay far off the main routes of travel, away from the pagan world of the ancient Roman Empire. Sheltered among rocky hills for over a thousand years, the Galileans were able to develop noble ideas about God, truth, and justice, later transformed into the peerless rules of conduct taught by Jesus Christ. In such formative surroundings Jesus moved as a child. His boyhood was a happy one spent in the congenial home made for him by his beloved mother, Mary, and in helping the humble and good Joseph with carpentry work. But in the minds of his parents hovered the prophecy of Simeon foreshadowing the great role their son was to play in the world of men—the wonderful and sorrowful events leading to the crucifixion and resurrection. Unusual phenomena accompanied Christ's death. The earth quaked; rocks split open on Calvary

Many flocked to hear the wonderful words of the Galilean. The Sermon on the Mount was delivered to his 12 disciples

Rulers who feared this miracle worker and his promised kingdom had him crucified. Hanging from the cross, he uttered the most sorrowful words heard on earth, "My God, My God, why hast Thou forsaken me?"

of messianic king, which came to be ascribed to him, seemed to threaten a popular revolt. A combination of these suspicions and hostilities led to his arrest, trial, and execution by the usual Roman method of crucifixion.

His most intimate associates, though ready at the time of his death to concede that the whole enterprise had failed, became convinced within two or three days that he was still living and that he had been raised to life from the tomb in which he had been placed. They reported seeing him and talking with him several times in the next six weeks, and some of them said that at least they saw him ascend from the earth toward heaven and disappear in a cloud. They were so sure of his RESURRECTION that it became a central feature of the message they began to proclaim; and they were so sure that what he had taught and what they were now prepared to teach about him was the key to salvation for all who would believe it that they were willing to risk their own lives in spreading this gospel. Most of them not only risked their lives but actually lost them at the hands of mobs whose convictions or prejudices were affronted by the new teaching, or governmental authorities who regarded it as socially dangerous.

Hub of Christian Calendar. Modern chronology takes the birth of Christ as the base line from which to reckon the dates of all other events as so many years before or after Christ. But since, at the time when this system was being put into operation, his birth was believed to have occurred a little later than what now seems to have been the actual time, the curious result is that the birth of Christ must now be dated about 4 B.C.

Writings Concerning Christ. The source material for present knowledge of the historical facts about the life of Jesus is limited to writings which were produced within the Christian movement at least one generation after his death. By far the most important sources are the four GOSPELS which are the first four books of the New Testament. To these must be added some passages in the Acts of the Apostles and in the Epistles of the Apostle Paul. No contemporary neutral or unfriendly writer mentions Jesus, and no official document contains any allusion to him. (Letters purporting to have been written by Pontius Pilate and others are transparent forgeries of later date.) This is not surprising in view of the circumstances of his life and the conditions of the period. Jesus was not a public figure of any recognized importance in his own time. His life was spent in rural places and villages, except for two (possibly four) brief visits to Jerusalem, one when he was 12 years old, the other beginning five days before his death. No other character of that time and region and in similarly humble station is mentioned in any contemporary writing that is extant. But this lack of disinterested testimony creates no valid presumption that he was not an actual historical person.

Real Historical Person. The existing documentary evidence, though friendly and not strictly contemporary, is varied and excellent. The separate Gospels show enough consistency with one another to produce a harmonious impression and to confirm one another's witness that such a man really lived; they contain enough verbal identities to prove that they made free use of source materials older than the Gospels themselves, so that their testimony is closer to the events than their dates of composition; and they present enough dissimilarities and contradictions to refute any suggestion that the writers were in collusion to foist a fictitious character upon the world as a historical person. The prompt rise of the church and the rapid spread of Christianity are evidence of some tremendous impetus. If there were no surviving records of such a historical person as Jesus, it would be necessary to posit one as the only reasonable hypothesis upon which Christianity could be explained. It is sometimes said that the Apostle PAUL

created the Christian religion. This is partly true, in the sense that he was the chief agent in freeing it from Jewish limitations, making it into a world religion, giving it a body of doctrine, and making the church a concrete and expanding institution. But he did all this on the foundation of a historical Jesus, whom, to be sure, he had never seen except in a vision, but in

ART INST. OF CHICAGO
"Pietà," by Alfeo Faggi

testimony to whose reality he was willing to die—and did. Moreover, the personality of Jesus as portrayed in the Gospels is not one that could have been invented, either individually or in collaboration, by the men who wrote those books. For these and other reasons, the historical reality of the man Jesus is no longer seriously questioned by responsible scholars.

Sequence of Events by Critical Methods. But with the application of critical methods to the study of the Gospels, many of the details concerning the life of Jesus become less certain as matters of historical fact. A systematic and consecutive "biography," in the ordinary sense of that term, is impossible. The most obvious method of trying to produce one from the available materials is to make a mosaic of passages from the four Gospels, arranging the episodes and discourses in what seems the most probable chronological sequence in view of the differences of order in the different documents. This was first tried by Tatian, near the end of the second century, about the time it was being decided, by the preponderance of opinion, that the four Gospels as now known should be accepted as *the* Gospels to the exclusion of their many competitors which were to be regarded as apocryphal (though some of these continued to be held in favor by the churches in some regions until much later). A more popular method has been that of making a "harmony" of the Gospels, setting the material of the four in parallel columns with duplicate accounts of the same incident or sayings opposite to each other, and arranging the items in the order which involves the least dislocation of their order in any one Gospel. Many such harmonies have been made and new ones are constantly being published. They are useful tools for study, but they are not biographies. They are convenient devices for visualizing the agreements and differences among the Gospels. (See GOSPELS, HARMONY OF THE.) The four Gospels were written for different purposes. They describe the life and work of Jesus from different points of view and embody differences of emphasis and interpretation which are blurred by any attempt to blend them into one composite picture.

Oral Tradition and the "Q." It is evident that before any memoranda of the life of Jesus had been reduced to writing there had come to be a body of oral tradition—stories of what he had done, and some crystallized and memorized formulations of notable things he had said. Since Jesus and his disciples spoke Aramaic, and since this was the language also of the earliest converts in Palestine, such an oral tradition would doubtless be in Aramaic. Critical study of the Gospels has brought most scholars to the conclusion that the next step toward putting this material into form for preservation and transmission was the making of a written collection of the sayings of Jesus, generally referred to as "Q" (for *Quelle*, source). This is a hypothetical document, or series of documents; it does not now exist. That it once existed is presumed chiefly because of the similarities between Matthew and Luke who, since apparently neither of them copied from the other, must both have copied from some common source. This hypothetical document was probably made up of sayings, or "logia," of Jesus. (Some very ancient fragments of this kind have been found on papyrus in Egypt, containing materials that never got into the present Gospels as well as variant forms of some that did.) The earliest oral tradition was undoubtedly in Aramaic, but the written Gospels as we have them are in Greek. There is a theory, held by only a very few scholars, that our present Greek Gospels are translations from Aramaic originals. These "Aramaic originals" are hypothetical, like "Q"; they do not now exist. The vast majority of scholars hold that they never existed and that they are an unnecessary and misleading hypothesis. But somewhere between the earliest Aramaic oral tradition and the Greek written Gospels, two things happened: what had been in Aramaic was translated into Greek; and what had been oral was reduced to writing. The translation probably came first. "Q" was probably a collection of the sayings of Jesus that had been put into Greek.

The Writing of Mark. Now begins the process of writing the Gospels that we have. Mark was the first. It was written about A.D. 70, something like 40 years after the death of Jesus. It is a straightforward, fast-moving narrative of incidents in the life of Jesus, not including many of his sayings. As regards events and episodes, it was the source-book from which Matthew and Luke drew. Because these three give very similar views of the objective events in the life of Jesus, they are called the Synoptics. Mark was a Palestinian Jew who took a Roman name. Legend identifies him with a minor figure (Mark 14:51) in the scene of the arrest of Jesus on the night before his crucifixion, but there is no historical evidence for this identification; and even if there were, it would not qualify him as an eyewitness. But a few years later he was in the company of the Apostle Peter at Jerusalem, and it has been commonly assumed that he got his data from Peter. At any rate, he framed a clear factual story that sounds as though it rested upon an eyewitness account of the events. It evidently represents the commonly accepted body of tradition in regard to the events in the life of Jesus as these were remembered and told by the Apostles and other brethren in Jerusalem 10 or 20 years after the crucifixion. Mark wrote his Gospel for Gentile Christians, to give them the essential facts about the Jesus who was the object of their faith. He gives very little theology. He records that a voice from heaven, at the time of the baptism, said, "This is my beloved Son." He quotes Peter's "Thou are the Christ." But he does not develop the ideas of Sonship or Messiahship. He says that Jesus spoke many parables, but he does not tell many of them—practically none except those of the sower and the mustard seed. He reports many miracles of healing. But he has no infancy narrative, says nothing about the descent of Jesus from Abraham and David (a matter that would mean little to the Gentiles), and lays great emphasis upon Jesus' challenge of old Jewish customs and his exaltation of moral purity and humane attitudes above conformity with the ceremonial law. Only Mark puts this challenge into the crisp and unforgettable declaration that "the Sabbath was made for man, and not man for the Sabbath."

The Synoptics. The authors of the first and third Gospels, called Matthew and Luke, had Mark before them when they wrote their accounts, a little later. They also had the collection of sayings of Jesus, "Q,"

and each of them had some material not possessed, or at least not used, by the other. Luke has much more of such unique material than Matthew. In the main sequence of events, they both follow Mark. Neither of them uses every episode in Mark, but between them they do, almost completely. There is only one solitary incident or unit of teaching in Mark that is not found in one or both of the other two. (That one is the healing of a blind man, Mark 8:22–26.) While the order of the events (based on Mark) is nearly identical in the three Synoptics, the sequence of the sayings and teachings (based on "Q") varies some, and there is a difference of emphasis.

Matthew's Gospel. The Gospel of Matthew (probably not written by the Apostle Matthew) was written for Jewish Christians in Palestine after the fall of Jerusalem in A.D. 70. Its central point is that Jesus is the promised Messiah of Israel, and that the old hope of a messianic king and a restored Hebrew monarchy governed from a liberated and glorified Jerusalem has been fulfilled by being absorbed into something on a vastly larger scale and on a higher spiritual level by the inauguration of a new kingdom on new principles—the Kingdom of God. The old order is doomed. The earthly Jerusalem, its selfish rich and its seekers of place and power had already suffered the woes which the writer records as having been predicted for them. But though a new order has arisen under a greater Messiah than Israel had expected, this new and better regime has its roots in the old. Matthew traces the lineage of Jesus from Abraham, and makes much of the belief that certain events occurred "in order that the prophecy might be fulfilled." Only Matthew quotes Jesus as saying, "Think not that I came to destroy the law or the prophets; I came not to destroy but to fulfill."

Gospel of Luke. Luke, himself a Gentile, wrote

"The Entombment," by Fra Angelico

CINCINNATI ART MUSEUM

"Crucifixion with View of Toledo," by El Greco

specifically for his Greek friend Theophilus but in general for the instruction of Gentile Christians. He gives the clearest picture of the humanity of Jesus and stresses the universality of his message and work. He traces the genealogy of Jesus from Adam—through Abraham, to be sure, though from his Gentile point of view Abraham was only incidental to the fact that Jesus was, through a long line of ancestors, ". . . . the son of Adam, the son of God." He is not concerned about noting, as Matthew does, that there were 14 generations from Abraham to David, 14 from David to the carrying away into Babylon, and 14 from that event to Jesus. (In fact, these figures do not check by Luke's table, which has 42 generations between David and Jesus.) Luke gives the fullest and most picturesque narrative of the infancy. Strangely enough, only Luke tells the lovely stories of the annunciation, the visitation, the birth of John the Baptist, the angels and shepherds at Bethlehem, and the visit to Jerusalem at 12 years old. Just as strangely, only Matthew tells of the visit of the wise men (the "Three Kings" of legend) to Bethlehem. This suggests the richness and diversity of the traditions and also the fact that they had not been combined.

Luke indicates in his opening verses how near he and the other writers of Gospels stood to the events, even though once removed from them: "Inasmuch as many have undertaken to compile a narrative of the things which have been accomplished among us, just as they were delivered to us by those who from the beginning were eyewitnesses and ministers of the word, it seemed good to me also, having followed all things closely for some time past, to write an orderly account for you, most excellent Theophilus, that you may know the truth concerning the things of which

you have been informed" (Revised Standard Version of 1946). Yet he is willing to omit the visit of the Magi from the East, and he does not mention a "flight to Egypt" to escape the wrath of Herod but has the family go directly from Bethlehem to Jerusalem for the circumcision and purification, after which they immediately "returned into Galilee, to their own city, Nazareth." Matthew, on the other hand, tells of a flight to Egypt "to fulfill what the Lord had spoken by the prophet, Out of Egypt have I called my son," and gives the impression that the family had never been in Nazareth until after the return from Egypt, and that they went into Galilee only because they were afraid to return to Judea for fear Herod's son would carry on the vendetta.

Writing Ascribed to John. The Fourth Gospel bears the name of John, but most scholars agree that it certainly was not written by the Apostle of that name, though perhaps by some other John who lived in Ephesus near the end of the first century. It is even further than the other Gospels from giving a biography of Jesus. It does not even try to do this. The author says: "These things are written that you may believe that Jesus Christ is the Son of God, and that believing you may have life in his name." Its purpose therefore is not biographical or historical but evangelistic; and since the evangel, as the author understood it, rested upon the eternal Christ and his identification with God, more than upon the earthly life of the human Jesus, it is also theological and metaphysical. No infancy narratives are given, but the author makes his beginning before the dawn of time and affirms that before creation there existed the *logos*, or divine Word, which "became flesh and dwelt among us." Aside from the crucifixion and resurrection narratives and the events immediately before and after them, the Fourth Gospel omits the greater part of what the three Synoptics include and is made up chiefly of materials not found in them.

Of the 46 units into which the Fourth Gospel may be divided, 31 are unique, only 15 are paralleled in the Synoptics, and only 6 of these 15 deal with events or sayings before the Last Supper on the night before the crucifixion. It may be argued that the author had the Synoptics before him when he wrote and deliberately omitted what had already been satisfactorily recorded. Obviously, any arrangement of the Fourth Gospel's materials in a chronological scheme derived from the Synoptics is largely conjectural. The difficulty is increased by the fact that the Fourth Gospel speaks of two journeys to Jerusalem which are not mentioned by the others, and much of the teaching that it reports is said to have been delivered in the course of these journeys. It is these additional journeys to Jerusalem—one to attend a passover, the other to attend "a feast of the Jews"—that require the supposition that the ministry of Jesus extended over three years. Eighteen months would be sufficient for everything recorded by the Synoptics.

It may be added that the early church soon followed the author of the Fourth Gospel in showing little interest in the earthly life of Jesus except for his birth and death. By the time the Apostles' Creed began to take form, in the second century, the Christian mind was prepared to pass immediately from "born of the Virgin Mary" to "suffered under Pontius Pilate," when it recited the historical foundations of its faith.

Harmonizing the Four Gospels. It may be useful to give a skeleton outline of the life of Jesus as it appears in a "harmony" of the four Gospels, even though, as has been stated, the Gospels were not designed for use in making such a composite picture and the relation of the resulting synopsis to the actual course of events must therefore remain to some extent conjectural. The following outline is based largely upon *A Harmony of the Gospels*, by Stevens and Burton. The material falls into nine main divisions:

1. Thirty years of private life—birth at Bethlehem in Judea, early infancy in Egypt, childhood and

young manhood at Nazareth, broken only by a visit to Jerusalem in boyhood.

2. Opening events of ministry—journey to Judea for baptism by John the Baptist, calling of the earliest disciples, return to Galilee, the first miracle (water into wine) at Cana.

3. Early ministry in Judea—a tour of preaching and baptizing converts in Judea, Jesus acclaimed by John the Baptist as the Christ and the Son of God, return to Galilee by way of Samaria, conversation with the Samaritan woman to whom Jesus says plainly that he is the Messiah.

4. First phase of ministry in Galilee—report of John the Baptist's imprisonment, the calling of four disciples, a preaching tour with miracles of healing.

5. Second phase of ministry in Galilee—widening fame, choice of the Twelve, Sermon on the Mount, two preaching tours, miracles and teaching by the Sea of Galilee, the sending out of the Twelve to preach the Kingdom and heal the sick.

6. Third phase of ministry in Galilee—retirement to northern Galilee, journey through coastal region of Tyre and Sidon, return through Decapolis, Messiahship asserted and death foretold, the Transfiguration, continued miracles and teachings, a visit to Jerusalem for the Feast of Tabernacles and return to Galilee.

7. Ministry in Perea—a slow and circuitous journey from Galilee, through the region east of Jordan, to the vicinity of Jerusalem, with many miracles and parables by the way and the raising of Lazarus at the end.

8. Passion week—Sunday, triumphal entry into Jerusalem; Monday, cleansing the Temple; Tuesday, parables of warning, questions and controversies with Jewish rulers, destruction of Jerusalem foretold; Wednesday, a day of retirement, perhaps at Bethany; Thursday, the Last Supper; Friday, trial, crucifixion, and burial; Saturday, the day in the tomb.

9. Final 40 days—resurrection; appearance to the Marys, to two disciples walking to Emmaus, to the disciples in Jerusalem, to Thomas with the others, to seven by the Sea of Galilee, to the eleven on a mountain in Galilee; ascension, from a place near Jerusalem.

The Revolutionary Religion. Jesus was, as has been said, both the founder and the foundation of the Christian religion, but the foundation goes deeper. Like every other religion, CHRISTIANITY rests upon some universal need and capacity of man. Specifically, Christianity is related historically to the Hebrew religion, in which it was cradled and from which it emerged with some difficulty. Jesus himself was a Jew by birth and religion. He never repudiated the Hebrew religion, and he met his death while at Jerusalem in attendance at one of its great historic feasts. Either early or late in his ministry (it is a controversial question), he came to consider himself the promised or expected Messiah of Hebrew thought, Jehovah's special representative whose function it was to usher in a new age. Jewish expectation, after the political downfall of the nation, was focused upon a restoration of the glory and prestige of Israel, involving freedom from the conqueror's yoke and the rehabilitation of the Davidic monarchy at Jerusalem; but at its best this expectation rose above mere political independence and included a moral and spiritual revival, the reign of righteousness and peace, and the extension of the beneficent regime to the fulfillment of the promise to Israel that "in thee shall all the nations of the earth be blest." From the beginning of his consciousness of mission, Jesus definitely set aside all political and military methods. As soon as any attention was directed toward him as a possible "redeemer of Israel," he made it clear that he would not be another Judas Maccabeus. The Romans could never feel quite sure of this, and their suspicion of his revolutionary purposes became a factor in his death. This refusal to head either a Jewish

underground or an open revolt also cost him some of the popular following that was ready to respond to a patriotic Jewish leader. But he also broke with certain aspects of the Jewish regime as it was. His seeming indifference to some requirements of the ceremonial law provoked the PHARISEES, who were strict legalists and experts in ethical and ceremonial casuistry; and his low valuation of the Temple-centered ritual and his condemnation of priestly greed and lust for power enraged the SADDUCEES who, as Temple functionaries, had come to terms with the Roman overlords and made comfortable and profitable places for themselves within the status quo.

Christ and Judaism. Jesus's own religion was, at bottom, Judaism. He knew and respected the Law, was familiar with the words of the prophets, recognized that Israel had been the chosen people of Jehovah. But his dominant thought came to be of the fatherhood of God and the brotherhood of man—ideas not absent from Judaism, but overshadowed by ritual requirements and national exclusiveness. A common hypothesis now is that though Jesus did not *radically* renounce Judaism, there were built up in his own mind, and in the minds of his followers after his death, conceptions of his unique and exalted nature, of the nature and extent of the Kingdom of God, and of the means and processes of individual salvation by acceptance of the benefits of his death, all of which involved a radical separation from Judaism. On the basis of the purely historical evidence, it is impossible to say how much of this transition occurred in the mind of Jesus himself as he became aware of his own relation to God, the imminence of his death, and the total meaning of his mission, and how much

NATIONAL GALLERY OF ART

"Christ Appearing to the Virgin," a painting by the Flemish master, Rogier van der Weyden

of it was a post-crucifixion development in the minds of his followers. That problem has theological implications which are beyond the limits of this article. See BIBLE; MARY; THE SERMON ON THE MOUNT (Back End Papers, Vol. 4).   W. E. GARRISON

BIBLIOG.–G. Papini, *Life of Christ* (1921); E. Bosworth, *Life and Teaching of Christ* (1939); W. Elliot, *Life of Christ* (1939); A. C. Garrett, *Man From Heaven* (1939); A. F. Gilmore, *Who Was This Nazarene?* (1940); W. Lowrie, *Short Story of Jesus* (1943); M. Komroff, *One Story* (1943); M. Goguel, *Life of Jesus* (1944); B. Forbush, *Toward Understanding Jesus* (1946); R. F. Grewen, *Know Your King* (1946); J. Shepard, *Christ of the Gospels* (1946); H. E. Fosdick, *The Man from Nazareth* (1949); E. J. Goodspeed, *Life of Jesus* (1950); F. Mauriac, *Life of Jesus* (ed. 1950).

JESUS CHRIST IN ART. The figure of Christ has been one of the central motifs of Western art. The first drawings of Christ are attributed to his disciples, and picture him with the long light brown beard and fine features that have become traditional. In the early Christian church, representations of the Christ were banned; it was not until the 4th century that his figure is found in frescoes and painted on sarcophagi. He is most often pictured as the Good Shepherd, though three scenes from his life, "Christ Raising Lazarus from the Dead," "Healing of the Paralyzed Man," and "The Miracle of the Loaves," were favorite episodes with the first Christian artists. In the Byzantine period, from A.D. 600 until A.D. 1000, Christ was usually pictured in the role of "Lord of the Universe." Though the first paintings of Christ during the period of Primitive Christianity were crude, the look of compassion and suffering was portrayed by the artists; but in the Byzantine era, the figure of Christ became stylized and without individual expression. In the 11th and 12th centuries, Christ again became a more lifelike figure, with soft eyes and delicate features. In the sculpture of this time the Passion of Our Lord is represented; a bust of Christ by an unknown French artist of the 12th century, now in the Louvre at Paris, is one of the finest pieces of Christian sculpture. With the early Renaissance, representations of the Christ increased both in number and in beauty of execution. Giotto's Christ is both strong and delicate; pity and pain have left their mark on the face. Leonardo da Vinci's drawing, "Study for the Christ," now at a museum in Venice, is a magnificent example of Renaissance art, as is Raphael's drawing, "Head of Christ." The first Flemish painters gave Christ Teutonic features; the Christs of Hans Memling and of Holbein are less delicate than the Italian versions of the Savior. The Spanish painter, Juan de Juanes, pictured Christ with liquid Spanish eyes. The pictures of Christ that are most familiar to Americans are those of the German J. M. A. Hoffman, who painted in the 19th century, which are found in most Protestant religious literature. Today the figure of Christ is not often found in the work of modern masters, though a fine painting, "Head of Christ," by Pablo Picasso, shows that the inspiration of Jesus Christ is not dead among the new artistic generation. See ECCLESIASTICAL ART; MADONNA IN ART.   HELEN STEWART

JESUS SIRACH. See ECCLESIASTICUS.

JET is a kind of lignite or brown coal, which is rendered black by fossilization and by impregnation with bituminous matters. It burns with a smoky flame, breaks with a conchoidal fracture, is easily cut, and takes a fine polish. Some specimens, when examined under the microscope in thin sections, show the cellular structure of fossil wood. Formerly much jet was extracted from the dark bituminous shales of the Upper Lias near Whitby in Yorkshire. It is also obtained in the department of Aude, in France, in the amber-bearing clays and sands of northern Germany, and in several other places. Only the harder kinds are of any value. Jet ornaments were valued in early times and have been popular in more recent periods. Imitations of jet are made from vulcanite or celluloid, or from black wax covered with glass.

JET PROPULSION

Development of the jet engine made possible speeds that man had only dreamed of in olden times

JET PROPULSION. The principle of jet propulsion is most readily explained by reference to the open-tube toy balloon. When inflated and released, the balloon is propelled by reaction to the high velocity jet stream from its tube. The escaping air pushing one way is the "action," while the resulting thrust against the inside surface of the balloon opposite the tube is the "equal and opposite reaction." If the tube of the balloon were tied, to prevent the escape of air from within, no "action" would result, consequently no "reaction." Likewise, sphere A, containing compressed air, will not move of its own accord, but sphere B, having an opening which permits the escape of compressed air at high velocity,

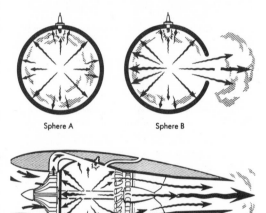

Sphere A   Sphere B

Jet Propulsion Motor

GENERAL ELECTRIC CO.

The principle of jet propulsion

will move as a result of reaction to the flow of air through the opening.

It might be said that jet propulsion is the application of Newton's Third Law of Motion to the propulsion of vehicles or other devices by means of high-velocity fluid flow through an orifice or jet nozzle. Like the toy balloon, which propels itself by reaction to the jet stream from its tube, so all jet engines are propelled by high-speed release of fluid from the engine through an orifice or nozzle.

Types of Jet Engine. There are several forms of the jet, or reaction engine. Strictly speaking, the rocket is a reaction engine, since its principle of operation is based upon the Third Law of Motion. It differs from the other forms of reaction engine, however, in that it contains within itself the oxygen required for the combustion of its fuel. Because it does not depend upon oxygen from the surrounding air for its propulsive energy, a rocket can travel in a vacuum. Other types of jet engine make use of the oxygen in the air which enters the engine from the surrounding atmosphere, consequently they must travel in air. The V-2 rocket bomb, which the Germans used so effectively during the latter part of World War II, is a practical example of the application of rocket power for propulsion.

The Simplest Form of jet engine is called the ramjet, or athodyd (from Aero-Thermo-Dynamic-Duct). It has no moving parts, but consists simply of a specially-shaped tube or pipe, open at both ends. It is equipped with a fuel injector and a spark plug. The athodyd is not capable of moving by itself from

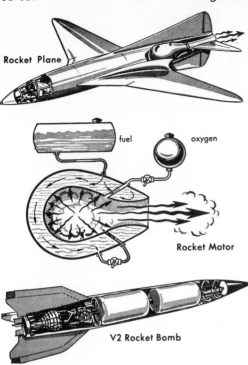

fuel   oxygen

Rocket Plane

Rocket Motor

V2 Rocket Bomb

GENERAL ELECTRIC CO.

Representative types of jet engines

a standstill, but must be launched or driven by some means until it reaches a considerable velocity, when air which enters the front opening compresses itself by ram action. Then fuel can be injected and burned to increase the volume of gases and make possible a jet velocity higher than the velocity at which air enters the pipe.

The pulse-jet, or aeroresonator is constructed fundamentally the same as the athodyd, except that its front opening is equipped with a shutter-like cover. When launched or driven by some external means to a velocity which will cause the pressure of ram air to open the shutter-valves, fuel is injected and the fuel and air mixture exploded, causing the shutter-valves to close due to the resulting higher internal pressure. (It is possible that the pulse-jet engine could be designed to start itself from standstill.) Expansion of gases from the combustion chamber takes place through a nozzle, thereby producing the high-velocity jet which drives the engine forward. With this release of gases, the internal pressure drops below the ram-air pressure, causing the shutter-valves to reopen, and the cycle is repeated. World War II's V-1 flying bomb was the first-known practical application of the pulse-jet engine.

The Gas-Turbine Jet-Propulsion Engine does not depend upon ram-air pressure for its operation. Instead, pressure is developed by means of its compressor. This high-speed rotor compresses the atmospheric air that enters the engine, and directs it into the combustion chambers, where it is mixed with injected fuel and ignited. The combustion of fuel with the compressed air results in expansion, or increased volume. All or part of the combustion gases are directed through a turbine, which converts some of the energy of the hot gases into power to drive the compressor. The gases exhaust from the turbine through a jet nozzle, where high-velocity discharge produces the thrust which propels the engine and its vehicle.

Performance of Jet Engines. There are several operating characteristics to be considered for any type of internal combustion engine, such as fuel con-

sumption, air flow, efficiency, etc. Here a brief summary of elementary relationships is presented.

The jet engine generates useful thrust (and, therefore, reaction) by producing a jet nozzle exit velocity considerably greater than the velocity of the vehicle it propels. This is illustrated by the fundamental equations:

$$F = \frac{W_a}{g} \ (V_1 - V_2)$$

for engines using atmospheric air, and

$$F = \frac{W_a}{g} \ (V_1)$$

for engines which carry their own air or oxygen, where

F   = thrust, in pounds,
W_a = flow of fluid from nozzle, in pounds per second,
V_1 = velocity of fluid from nozzle, in feet per second,
V_2 = velocity of vehicle, in feet per second,
g   = 32.2, the acceleration of gravity, in feet per second per second.

(The first equation is true only if we assume that the flow of gas from the nozzle is equal to the flow of air entering the engine. Actually, the flow from the nozzle is greater than that which enters the engine, because a certain amount of fuel has been added during the combustion process. However, the equation is sufficiently accurate for illustration purposes.)

BOEING AIRPLANE CO.

B-47, a 60-ton, 6-jet, 600-mile-per-hour bomber, takes off from a very short runway with the aid of eighteen JATO (jet-assisted take-off) rocket units

Engine Efficiency. When the *useful power output* of any jet or reaction engine is to be considered, the velocity of the engine and its vehicle must be known, since the useful power output from the engine, P_1, is equal to the thrust in pounds multiplied by the velocity of the vehicle in feet per second

$$P_1 = F \times V_2, \text{ in foot-pounds per second}$$

One horsepower is equal to 550 foot-pounds per second, so the power output would be one horsepower when $F \times V_2 = 550$. Consequently, the thrust F equals one pound when $V_2 = 550$ feet per second, and since 550 fps is equivalent to 375 miles per hour, then one pound thrust represents one propulsive horsepower at 375 mph. Below 375 mph, a pound of thrust generates less than a horsepower, and at speeds above 375, more than a horsepower. An engine which produces 4000 lbs. thrust at 375 mph is developing 4000 propulsive horsepower, but if its thrust is 4000 lbs. at 750 mph, it is developing 8000 horsepower.

The power input to the engine, P_2, is equal to the mechanical equivalent of the heat value of the fuel consumed by the engine.

$$P_2 = W_f \times h \times J, \text{ in foot-pounds per second,}$$

where W_f = flow of fuel, in pounds per second,

  h = heat value of fuel in Btu per pound,

  J = 778, the mechanical equivalent of heat, in foot-pounds per Btu.

Since the over-all efficiency of a jet engine and its vehicle is simply the ratio of the useful power output from the engine to the power input to the engine, it is a measure of the ability of the engine-vehicle combination to convert the heat available in the fuel into useful work.

$$\text{Over-all Efficiency (engine and vehicle)} = \frac{\text{output}}{\text{input}}$$

$$= \frac{F \times V_2}{W_f \times h \times J}$$

Obviously, the over-all efficiency of any jet-propulsion engine-vehicle combination increases as the velocity of the vehicle approaches the velocity of the jet. At sea level, the present-day simple-cycle turbo-jet airplane will have an over-all efficiency ranging from 5 per cent at 200 miles per hour to 13 per cent at 600 miles per hour. The effect of altitude upon the over-all efficiency is beneficial. The same turbo-jet airplane that has a sea-level efficiency of 13 per cent at 600 miles per hour will yield about 15 per cent at 50,000 feet altitude at the same speed.

One might be inclined to look with disfavor upon a propulsive system which converts such a small percentage of fuel energy into useful power, but a comparison of over-all jet-propulsion efficiency with the over-all efficiencies of other propulsive systems, and a consideration of the relative over-all costs per ton-mile, serves to prove the practicability of jet propulsion. The over-all efficiency of the engine itself is the efficiency with which the engine converts the power input from the fuel into a form of power which is useful for propulsion.

$$\text{Over-all Engine Efficiency} = \frac{W_a (V_1 - V_2)}{2g \times W_f \times h \times J}$$

The propulsive efficiency is a measure of the ability of the engine-vehicle combination to convert the engine's propulsive power into motion of the vehicle.

$$\text{Propulsive Efficiency} = \frac{2 V_2}{V_1 + V_2}$$

The over-all engine-vehicle efficiency, which is defined earlier, is simply the product of engine efficiency and propulsive efficiency.

Over-all Efficiency (engine and vehicle)

$$= \frac{W_a (V_1^2 - V_2^2)}{2 g \times W_f \times h \times J} \times \frac{2 V_2}{V_1 + V_2}$$

$$= \frac{W_a (V_1 - V_2) \times V_2}{g \times W_f \times h \times J}$$

$$= \frac{F \times V_2}{W_f \times h \times J}$$

Other forms of reaction engine, such as the rocket, ram-jet or pulse-jet, do not convert fuel energy into useful propulsive power as efficiently as the gas turbine except at extreme speeds and altitudes.

Turbo-Jets in America. In the United States gas-turbine jet engine development was stimulated by World War II's demand for faster warplanes. In 1941, drawings of a British engine, designed by Group Captain, now Commodore Frank Whittle of the Royal Air Force, were turned over to the General Electric Company to be used as the basis for the design of a new engine. Less than six months later the first gas-turbine jet engine to be built in the United States successfully passed its tests, and in October, 1942, the P-59 Bell Airacomet, this country's first jet-propelled airplane, was ready for flight.

Within a decade some half-dozen American companies were regular turbojet producers, largely for high-speed military aircraft, for which at this time turbojets appeared most suitable. In 1949, the Douglas 558-2 Skyrocket, an experimental Navy plane with rocket booster engine, exceeded the speed of sound at sea level—763 mph. These efforts were stimulated by foreign advances, such as Soviet jet fighters capable of over 600 mph. The first fight between jets was reported in Korea in 1950, the planes being a U.S. F-80 Shooting Star and a Soviet-built MIG-15.

In commercial aviation, air lines at first doubted

GENERAL ELECTRIC CO.

J-47 axial-flow turbojet engine, rated at 6,000 lbs. thrust (with water injection), powers B-47 and F-86

Republic F-84 Thunderjets have proven valuable as ground-support weapons in the Korea fighting

that turbojets were economical for scheduled long range transport. The first all-jet airliner was the British de Havilland Comet, flown in 1949, and capable of 500 mph. The same year A. V. Roe Canada, Ltd., introduced its commercial jetliner Avro-102. The U.S. was quicker in accepting the jet-assisted take-off (Jato), and the jet-propeller combination.

Historical Background of Jet Propulsion. Sir Isaac Newton (1642–1727) formulated the fundamental laws which express the relationships between force and motion. These Laws of Motion are three in number. The third one, which serves as the basis for the theory of jet propulsion, is simply this: To every action there is an equal and opposite reaction.

Examples of Newton's Third Law of Motion appear frequently in our everyday lives. The recoil of a rifle is the reaction to the force, or action, which drives the bullet from the barrel. The force which propels a canoe through the water is the reaction to the push of the paddle against the water. The force which tends to drive a fire hose nozzle backward is the reaction to the force which drives the jet of water forward.

Although Newton's Laws of Motion were written after 1660, the principles of jet propulsion were recognized centuries earlier. About 100 B.C., Hero, the Alexandrian philosopher, designed and demonstrated the first-known jet, or reaction, engine. It consisted of a hollow ball to which were attached a pair of diametrically opposite bent tubes. With the ball supported so that it was free to turn, and steam supplied to the inside of the ball through the hollow legs which supported it, the reaction of the jets of steam from the tubes would spin the ball on its axis. Hero's engine was called the

GENERAL ELECTRIC CO.
Hero's Aeolipile

Aeolipile. Some types of rotating lawn-sprinkler operate in a similar manner.

In 1680 Newton, in his desire to apply his Third Law of Motion, drew plans for a jet-propelled carriage. The engine was to consist of a firebox under a large sphere which had a nozzle projecting from the rear. The sphere contained water for the generation of steam, which when directed backward through the nozzle, would propel the carriage forward. The principle of Newton's proposed engine is that on which aircraft jet engines are based.

The history of rockets may logically be considered an important part of the history of jet propulsion. The use of rockets dates back to several centuries B.C., when the Chinese apparently introduced this device. Rocket projectiles were used in battle in the early 19th century. During World War I their use was very limited, but rocket development progressed so fast that most military powers engaged in World War II used rockets for many purposes. See AERONAUTICS; GAS TURBINE; ROCKET. W. F. BOYLE

BIBLIOG.—A. L. Murphy, *Rockets, Dynamometers, Jet Motors* (1944); E. Hawks, *Jet Propelled Aircraft* (1945); H. S. Zim, *Rockets and Jets* (1945); G. G. Smith, *Gas Turbines and Jet Propulsion for Aircraft* (1946); J. Grierson, *Jet Flight* (1946); J. G. Keenan, *Elementary Theory of Gas Turbines and Jet Propulsion* (1946); G. P. Sutton, *Rocket Propulsion* (1949).

JETTY, an artificial obstruction, similar to a pier or breakwater, built at the mouth or from the banks of a river, across a harbor, or out from the shore line. A jetty is constructed of rubble, timber, reinforced concrete, steel and iron braced together, or a combination of these materials.

When constructed at the mouth of a river, jetties are so placed as to control the direction of the current and thereby direct its eroding action. Jetties are also extended from both banks of a river, at intervals, to contract wide, shallow channels into deeper central channels. The construction of jetties across harbors accomplishes the same results. The concave sides of a river may be protected from erosion by building a jetty from that side, deflecting the current into midstream and preventing it from cutting into the bank.

Jetties have been used for many years on seacoasts, and along the shores of the Great Lakes in North America, for the purpose of assisting the natural process of beach creation. For this type of jetty the common procedure is to construct a solid wall at right angles to the shore and extending into the water for 200 or 300 feet.

A permeable jetty, also used for "beach building," is one that is not tightly closed to the passage of littoral (shore) currents. Constructed of piles, brush and timber, or concrete blocks with lugs (so as to leave a space between each block) the permeable jetty permits the current to deposit silt, sand, etc., on the shore along both of its sides. See MISSISSIPPI RIVER.

JEVONS, WILLIAM STANLEY, 1835–82, English political economist and logician, was born in Liverpool and studied at University College, London. Returning to England after serving as assayer in the Sydney mint (1854–59), he became professor of logic, economics, and philosophy at Owens College, Manchester (1866–76), and professor of political economy at his alma mater (1876–80). He was widely known for his *Theory of Political Economy* (1871), his work on *The Coal Question* (1865), and *The State in Relation to Labour* (1882). Other works included: *Pure Logic* (1864); *The Substitution of Similars* (1869); *The Principles of Science* (1874). Jevons developed the theory of economic utility.

JEWEL CAVE NATIONAL MONUMENT, SE South Dakota, in Custer County, a cave of limestone formations consisting of a series of chambers connected by narrow passages with a network of side galleries. Its name is derived from the fine crystal encrustations which ornament the cave. Discovered by Albert and Frank Michaud, prospectors, it became a national monument in 1908. The Park is 1,274 acres.

JEWELL, MARSHALL, 1825–83, American politician, born in Winchester, N.H. He became a resident of Connecticut, was governor of that state as a Republican (1869–70 and 1871–72), was U. S. minister to Russia (1873–74), was postmaster general of the United States (1874–76) during part of President Grant's second term, and was chairman of the Republican National Campaign Committee during the Garfield campaign of 1880.

JEWELRY, a term referring to individual adornments made of precious materials or set with gems. Jewelry is said to be an art as ancient as vanity, and vanity is an underlying reason for the wearing of jewelry, but it is not the only one. Religion, love, and conspicuous display of authority or wealth all play a part in the design and use of jewelry.

Aside from the wearing of ornaments to enhance sexual attraction, jewelry has been important in the art of courtship. In Roman times carved portrait rings of loved ones were in style and during the Renaissance lockets containing portraits in oil or enamel were exchanged between suitors and the young women of distant lands they hoped to marry. Many jeweled cases were also created to hold portrait miniatures.

Religion also has had a strong influence on jewelry. The Egyptians chose the lotus, asp, cat, and scarab as motifs to carve on their cabochon (unfaceted) stones, because of the deep significance they had in their religion. Christian symbolism was especially profuse in the jewelry of the Middle Ages, and medieval devotional rings were widely worn. Made of gold, bronze, or ivory, they had a series of knoblike projections for counting "Aves" in prayer. Reliquary pendants and tablets enameled with religious scenes were hung on chains around the neck. In the Renaissance, however, ornaments with religious significance disappeared except for specific emblems worn by church officials.

Conspicuous display of authority and wealth is another intrinsic reason behind the wearing of jewelry. Rings have always been favored symbols of political, social, and domestic status. The key ring, for instance, was worn only by the mistress of the house and was used to seal containers of household stores against pillaging by servants. During the Renaissance massive links were formed into chains and collars and worn by gentlemen to signify their wealth and distinction. In Egypt it was the fashion to wear many rings and often even the thumb was decorated with a band. The Romans further enlarged the number of such ornaments by wearing them on the second joint of the finger as well as on the third. In the 16th century rings were worn on the joints of all fingers and if the wearer was so wealthy as to possess still more rings, they were worn on a chain or necklace.

Relation to Costume. The use of different types of jewelry has often been in correlation with fashions in costume. Bracelets, so popular in the pre-Christian era, almost disappeared in the Middle Ages because of the mode for long, flowing sleeves. Wrist ornaments were not worn again until short sleeves appeared in the 18th century. Due to the medieval custom of binding the head with close-fitting headdresses, earrings also went out of style in the Middle Ages. From primitive times, when buttons were as yet not invented, through the 17th century, the brooch was a favorite and useful ornament. Since then, except for a brief popularity during the Victorian era when shawls returned to fashion, brooches have been little worn. However, their popularity is still strong in the Highlands of Scotland where they are used to fasten the tartan.

During the latter part of the Middle Ages jewelry became more and more a part of dress. Belts, chaplets, hair nets, and necklaces of jewels were sewn on garments. In the Renaissance jewelry and costume were linked even closer. It was the fashion to adorn clothes with such myriads of tiny jewels (most often seed pearls) that surface decoration and jewelry were indistinguishable.

There have also been fashions in jewelry itself, irrespective of costume changes. The diamond, so popular in the 20th century, ranked far below the more colorful ruby and emerald in cost and favor during the Renaissance. Irregularly shaped pearls were the mode in the Baroque period. The Greeks wore only one earring instead of the pair of identical ear ornaments that are in style today. See BRACELET; BROOCH; GEMS AND ARTIFICIAL STONES; GOLDSMITHING; RING; SILVERSMITHING; BUTTON; BEAD.   M. R.

BIBLIOG.—M. von Boehn, *Modes and Manners* (1929); H. Wilson, *Silverwork and Jewelry* (1931); F. W. Burgess, *Antique Jewelry and Trinkets* (1937); W. T. Baxter, *Jewelry, Gem Cutting and Metalcraft* (1938); F. Rogers and A. Beard, *5000 Years of Gems and Jewelry* (1940); G. Pack, *Jewelry and Enameling* (1941); L. Haas, *Art Metal Work and Jewelry* (1946); M. Baerwald and T. Mahoney, *Gems and Jewelry Today* (1949); A. F. Rose and A. Cirino, *Jewelry Making and Design* (ed. 1949).

JEWETT, CHARLES COFFIN, 1816–68, American bibliographer, was born in Lebanon, Me., and studied at Brown University and Andover Theological Seminary. As librarian of Brown (1841–48) and of the Smithsonian Institution (1848–58), and superintendent of the Boston Public Library (1858–68), he devised methods of arranging and cataloguing books that were generally adopted by librarians. He published *Notices of Public Libraries in the United States of America* (1851) and *On the Construction of Catalogues of Libraries and Their Publication by Means of Separate Stereotyped Titles* (1852).

JEWETT, FRANK BALDWIN, 1879–1949, American electrical engineer, was born in Pasadena, Calif., and studied at Throop Polytechnic Institute (now California Institute of Technology) and the University of Chicago. In 1912 he joined the Western Electric Company, being promoted to chief engineer (1916) and vice-president (1922). In 1925 he became president of the Bell Telephone Laboratories, Inc., and was chairman of the board (1940–44). He saw telephone transmission efficiency improved by phantoming loaded circuits, installing vacuum-tube repeaters or amplifiers, using permalloy for loading coil cores, and adopting the dial system (see TELEPHONY). He received the Distinguished Service Medal, the Medal for Merit, the Edison, Faraday, Franklin, and Fritz medals, and the Washington award.

JEWETT, SARAH ORNE, 1849–1909, American writer, was born in South Berwick, Me., and was educated largely by her father, a wise physician, as they drove together about the countryside. Her first book, *Deephaven* (1877), was a collection of stories about Maine people, told with a realism as intimate as Mrs. Stowe's and with far greater sensitiveness to human values. Miss Jewett is at her best in the loosely connected sketches of *The Country of the Pointed*

CHICAGO NAT. HIST. MUS.
Roman silver necklace

Egyptian gold pectoral of a kneeling Isis

MET. MUSEUM OF ART
Roman serpent ring

CHICAGO NATURAL HISTORY MUSEUM
Greek gold earrings

MET. MUSEUM OF ART
Greek silver bracelet

JEWELRY

Although the origins of jewelry are lost in history, ornaments such as the nose ring, were devised many years before clothing, according to one theory. To-day's jewelry is designed principally for women, but in primitive cultures gemmed ornaments were a male prerogative, worn to show authority or wealth

CHICAGO NAT. HIST. MUS.
Indian nose ring, above

Indian pearl earring, left
CHICAGO NAT. HIST. MUS.

METROPOLITAN MUSEUM OF ART
Victorian cameo of about 1860

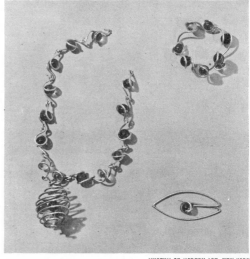

MUSEUM OF MODERN ART, NEW YORK
Modern jewelry, designed by Alexander Hammid

Firs (1896), an unassuming masterpiece, rather than in her former novels. Though she wrote about the life of a slowly stagnating province, she was not herself provincial, but brought to her exquisite art lessons learned from Flaubert and Tolstoy as well as from Thackeray and Jane Austen. She is often classed among local color writers, but she excelled all others in her ability to suffuse everyday characters and scenes with universal imaginative significance.

GEORGE F. WHICHER

BIBLIOG.–F. O. Matthiessen, *Sarah Orne Jewett* (1929).

JEWFISH, the name of several huge SEA BASS regarded as game by anglers. Perhaps the best known under this name is the great California species, *Stereolepis gigas,* which frequently exceeds 200 pounds in weight. It is a bottom feeder, and haunts the edges of the kelp growths along the coast of southern California, where it is angled for in 40–50 feet of water. When it finds the hook fast it rushes away with terrific suddenness and speed, and fights long and hard before submitting; yet it is taken by expert anglers with light rod, reel and line. The spotted jewfish, *Promicrops itaiara,* is a similar fish common on both coasts of Central America, and better known under the name "guasu" or "warsaw"; it has several large relations much liked in tropical markets. One of them, the black jewfish or black grouper, *Garrupa nigrita,* rivals the others in weight, none ever having been taken of less than 100 lbs., while several are recorded exceeding 500 lbs. It abounds in the Gulf of Mexico and about the West Indies, and occasionally strays to the Mediterranean.

JEWISH AUTONOMOUS REGION or **Birobidzhan,** U.S.S.R., an administrative area of the Russian Soviet Federated Socialist Republic, located within Khabarovsk Territory, along the Manchurian frontier and centered upon the Amur River and two of its tributaries, the Bira and the Bidzhan; area 13,800 sq. mi.; pop. (1950 est.) 150,000. Popularly known as Birobidzhan, the name of its capital city and the two rivers on which it is situated, the Jewish Autonomous Region was set up by the Soviets in 1928. It was held open for settlement for those Soviet Jews (some settlers from abroad were admitted, too) who wanted an opportunity to develop full nationhood in a state of their own. Originally an autonomous district, the settlement in 1934 became an autonomous region directly represented in the Council of Nationalities of the Supreme Soviet of the U.S.S.R. The population of the Region increased 10-fold in the years between 1928 and 1939. During World War II many refugees from European Russia swelled the ranks of the permanent inhabitants.

About one and a half times larger than Palestine, the Jewish Autonomous Region is rich in fertile agricultural land, pasture grasses, fur-bearing animals, forests, and mineral deposits. Among its natural resources are the Malikhingen iron ore deposits, richest in the Far East, which are estimated at several hundred million tons. Gold, graphite, coal, magnesites, marble, asbestos, and various building materials are also mined and quarried in the Region. Agriculture is important in the Region; by 1939 some 125,000 acres had been cleared for cultivation. The chief products include soya beans, wheat, rice, potatoes, and cabbages. The Region is noted for its honey-producing flowers and beehives. Cattle raising and fishing are other important activities.

The capital of the Jewish Autonomous Region and its cultural and industrial center is the city of Birobidzhan. Originally a small railroad station on the Trans-Siberian railway, Birobidzhan is a beautiful and spacious modern city with schools, libraries, model parks, theaters, cinemas, and industrial areas. Its factories make many varieties of wood products such as furniture, skis, and plywood; clothing, textiles, and leather goods. Before World War II, Birobidzhan's furniture factories supplied the needs of the entire Khabarovsk Territory. During World War II the town specialized in mass production of skis. Its railway-carriage and wagon-building works supply a large proportion of the rolling stock used in the Far East.

JEWISH LANGUAGE AND LITERATURE. See HEBREW LANGUAGE AND LITERATURE; YIDDISH.

JEWISH ORGANIZATIONS in the United States comprise a wide variety of agencies in the fields of religion, education, cultural activities, welfare, and civil protection. Among those organized on a strictly religious basis are the *Union of American Hebrew Congregations,* composed of reformed or liberal temples, the *United Synagogues* of America, representing the conservative synagogues, and the *Union of Orthodox Congregations.* These groups aid in the organization of local congregations, carry on educational activities, and sponsor brotherhoods, women's leagues, and young people's organizations.

Civil Protection Agencies. Several organizations operate primarily for the protection of the rights of the Jewish people, both in the United States and abroad. The *American Jewish Committee* was organized in 1906 for the purpose of safeguarding Jewish civil and religious rights, combating discrimination, and allaying prejudice. Its publications include the *Commentary* and the *Committee Reporter.* It also prepares, annually, the *American Jewish Year Book.* In 1950 the committee had a total membership of 18,500 in chapters located throughout the United States.

The *American Jewish Congress,* originally organized on a temporary basis in 1917 to send a commission to the Versailles Peace Conference, was permanently established in 1922 with the same general purposes as the *American Jewish Committee.* Composed of individual members and affiliated national organizations, it carries on activities to protect the rights of Jews, especially the right to pursue as a group the historic aims of the Jewish people, and to lend aid to Israel.

The *Antidefamation League* of B'nai B'rith, national fraternal organization, directs its efforts toward eliminating defamation of Jews and promoting goodwill among American groups, with especial emphasis on the removal of anti-Semitic material from the radio, press, movies, and theater. The *Jewish Labor Committee,* established in 1934 and composed in 1950 of 10 national trade unions, 23 central regional bodies, and 1,100 local unions, serves as the representative of organized Jewish labor and carries on "a program of improved interfaith and interracial relations within the American trade union movement, as well as a program of aid in the reconstruction of labor institutions and rehabilitation of victims

SOVFOTO

Birobidzhan Kindergarten Class enjoys outing in capital of the Soviet Jewish Autonomous Region

of fascism abroad."

The *American Council for Judaism* was organized in 1942 to advance the doctrine that Jews are a religious community, to apply that doctrine to practical problems of relief and reconstruction, and to oppose the segregating and secularizing of Jewish life through nationalistic philosophies.

Zionist Organizations. The *Zionist Organization of America* was founded in 1897 to enlist public support in the reconstitution of Palestine as a Jewish commonwealth. With a membership of 300,000 in 1951 (in some 800 chapters), the organization carries on a program of public education in regard to the purposes of the Zionist movement and sponsors cultural projects.

HADASSAH, the women's Zionist organization of America carries on a dual program of fostering Zionist ideals and supporting health and youth welfare services. In 1949, together with the HEBREW UNIversity, Hadassah opened the first medical school in Israel. Membership of Hadassah in 1951 was about 300,000 members.

Social Service Agencies. In the field of social service more than 4,000 Jewish communal organizations, loosely woven into federations and receiving support from central funds, carry on an extensive program of aid to the sick, aged, and needy. Since the first federation was established in 1895 for the purpose of raising funds, more than 70 of these agencies have been organized, operating much as community chests in supporting, co-ordinating, and controlling the social service work of their local communities. The *Council of Jewish Federations and Welfare Funds*, organized in 1932, serves as a clearing house and co-ordinating body for the federations. A co-operative association of over 200 local federations, it carries on research programs and provides aid to local agencies in fund raising and the establishment of social legislation. See ZIONISM.

The *National Jewish Welfare Board* is the national organization for the *Young Men's* and *Young Women's Hebrew Associations* and the *Jewish Community Centers*. Organized in 1917 to serve Jewish servicemen during World War I, the board had by 1946 reached a membership of 427,000 individuals, 38 affiliated national organizations, 10 regional organizations, and 288 constituent societies. The *National Conference of Jewish Social Welfare* provides a forum for the discussion of problems of Jewish welfare and the formulation of programs for Jewish social agencies.

The *National Council of Jewish Women*, established in 1893 and with a membership of 65,000 in 1946, carries on activities in the fields of overseas service, service to the foreign born, social welfare, international relations, contemporary Jewish affairs, and social legislation.

Overseas Aid. The *American Jewish Joint Distribution Committee*, established in 1914, provides aid to relieve distressed Jews in nearly 50 countries throughout the world. The committee carries on a program of war relief, economic aid and rehabilitation, and aid to refugees and emigrants both directly and through its associated organizations. The *United Jewish Appeal for Refugees, Overseas Needs and Palestine* provides funds for the *Joint Distribution Committee*, the *United Palestine Appeal* and the *United Service for New Americans*. Established on an annual basis by the participating agencies, the organization has served continuously since 1939 as a fund-raising agency.

Social Organizations. Among the Jewish social organizations are the lodges and fraternal societies organized usually for the purpose of mutual aid. At least 15 such societies exist in the United States, with a membership of somewhat over 500,000. Among the most widely known of these are *B'nai B'rith*, established in 1843 and with a membership in 1950 of 205,000 men in 950 lodges and 115,000 women in 735 chapters; the *Independent Order of Brith*

Abraham, with 25,000 members; *Brith Sholem;* and the *Free Sons of Israel*, with 11,000 members in 1950. In addition there are a number of Jewish fraternities and sororities located on college campuses throughout the United States.   C. F.

HISTORY OF THE JEWS

Jewish history tells of wanderings, of insecurity and persecution, and of the dream of an eventual homeland

JEWS, HISTORY OF THE. All primitive peoples begin their history with an account of the foundation of the world and the origins of man. The Hebrews developed several theories and blended them into a biblical narrative which deeply influenced Western religious life. In the beginning there was a divinely created pair, Adam and Eve, and they were the original ancestors of everybody. There was a single pure stock to begin from, a single language, a definite home, Eden. But as men multiplied, life became debased and cruel and the pleasant simplicity of Eden vanished. Then came the raging flood, as a punishment for the past and a lesson for the future. All mankind was destroyed, except Noah and his three sons, from which have come the known races of the earth. The descendants of Shem, the Semites, settled in western Asia; they included not only the Hebrews, but the Aramaeans, the Assyrians, and other mighty peoples. The descendants of Ham centered themselves in Africa and were fathers to the Egyptians, the Turanians, the Cushites, and their kinsmen. And the European peoples, far off to the unknown west, sprang from the loins of the kindly Japhet. So the generations passed and multiplied until, from the city of Ur, in Mesopotamia, came a descendant of Shem whose name was Abraham. To him was vouchsafed the discovery of the one true God, Yahweh, and with him the Hebrew chroniclers definitely begin the history of their people. The Old Testament is a significant account, and of historical usefulness, principally to give us an insight into the mind of the generations of the 10th century B.C. that conceived it. Some of it was borrowed from Babylonion traditions; but the moral genius of the biblical writers expurgated it, refinished it, and charged it with ethical meaning.

The one germ of authentic history that is important is that there were migrations all through the early centuries. The Hebrews were part of an engulfing flood of nomadic tribes which spilled over into Palestine. By the year 1000 B.C., large numbers of them were already established and were taking on the rudiments of a fairly united people.

The Egyptian Episode. Before the final settlement in Palestine, however, there was apparently an important stay in Egypt. Every old tradition points to such a sojourn as part of the earliest Hebrew experiences. It may be that the first arrivals in Palestine, unable to get a permanent foothold there and impelled by famine or restlessness, kept moving southward until they found their way into the hospitable delta of the Nile. Or perhaps, while most of the early Hebrews took root in Palestine, assimilating rapidly with the natives, a part of them, unable or unwilling to remain, and attracted by the luxury of Egypt, wandered southward and established themselves in Goshen in the eastern Nile delta. Such an interpretation would mean that there were Hebrews in Palestine at the same time that there were Hebrews in Egypt, and that both groups united their blood and their traditions many centuries later. This view has the authority of most modern historians.

Apparently there was a long period of oppression in the 13th century B.C. until the 19th dynasty began to founder. The last kings were not very able statesmen. Internal dissensions began to gnaw at the heart of the state. Libyan invaders came in upon the country from the west, and hordes of Cretans swept in from the sea; pirates from Cyprus and Asia Minor followed in the wake of these troubles, and all together probably gave a basis for the plague stories, which the Hebrew writers dwelt upon with relish.

The central hero of the Exodus and what follows is Moses: tradition portrays him in the dual role of leader and priest-prophet, the maker of the nation and the organizer of the Hebrew religion. In fact, the two roles were inseparably connected and arose out of each other. Moses created the Hebrew people when he united them by the bonds of religion. His immense influence easily marks him as the outstanding character in Hebrew history, one of the moral giants of all time.

Conquest of Palestine. From the desert, then, perhaps by way of Egypt, the Hebrews came to Palestine. The settlement of the country, according to the Book of Judges, was not accomplished in one violent effort. It was a slow filtering-in process, wave by wave, tribe by tribe. Hordes of land-hungry nomads fought for a foothold, fell back, returned, conquered, settled down, intermarried, assimilated, and were not certain, even after the passing of several generations, that they would succeed in rooting themselves in the soil.

From the Tel el Amarna letters it can be understood how formidable this resistance was, what serious obstacles to the path of the invaders were presented by the many cities that dotted the country, with their walls, their fortifications, and their watch towers, defended by natives, superior in culture, greater in numbers, and possessing far better weapons. The war chariots of the Canaanites were deadly effective and struck terror into the hearts of the Hebrews. Only the wretched political weakness of the natives undermined their natural advantages and brought them low. One recalls the conquest of the Celts in ancient Britain by the Saxons, dribbling in little by little, but overcoming the opposition of a whole country made feeble by internal dissension and fratricidal hostility.

Conquest was one matter; security after conquest was quite another. For generations the newcomers had no peace. They held only scattered portions of the country, and even in the days of David it was necessary to conquer Jerusalem before it could be made the country's capital. The Hebrews were often hemmed in on all sides by other alien tribes. Where there were peaceful relations, there was rapid assimilation and very often a loss of identity. Simeon could not retain its corporate existence and very early was merged in the tribes of the south. Asher took to the sea and was lost among the Phoenicians. Even Judah received a large infusion of Canaanite blood.

More often, however, relations between the newcomers and the older inhabitants were not peaceful. Warfare was constant, and no mercy was shown by either side. Captured communities were given over to massacre; men, women, and children were all exterminated "with the edge of the sword." A man's life was unsafe outside his own village. "In the days of Jael the highways were in disuse, and the travelers walked in bypaths." In the Book of Judges, which describes the long and desperate wars of the local Hebrew chieftains against the enemy tribes of Palestine, there is an idealized but fundamentally sound record of the early Hebrew struggle to maintain life and independence in the newly won communities.

The most powerful danger to the security of the Hebrews came from the Philistines, probably a non-Semitic people, hailing from Crete and the Greek islands. It was the trip-hammer blows of the Philistines which at last aroused the Hebrew tribes to the need for union.

The First National State. A powerful young farmer, Saul, gathered about him some of the stricken clans of his own tribe of Benjamin and turned with desperate fury on the foe. He crushed them so effectively that a thrill of courage ran through his people. They turned to Saul as to a savior, confident that through him their woes were to be ended. One tradition has it that after his spectacular victories over the Ammonites he was at once crowned king at Gilgal.

Saul was succeeded by David, the greatest statesman in Hebrew history. He came to a country rent with strife, bewildered by the blows of enemies. Constant warfare imperiled every man's life and threatened every man's home. David cleared the frontiers and then pushed them back until they touched the mountains in the north, and the desert in the south. He created Jerusalem and made it not only a capital but also a shrine.

David was followed by Solomon who reigned for 40 years, momentous years that changed the life of the nation. Palestine had become an important country, Jerusalem a great capital, with palaces, and buildings, and a Temple worthy of its new dignity. But there was much sorrow beneath the grandeur. Probably about this period a class of wealthy men began to develop, accumulating capital at the expense of the whole community. The poorer folks were compelled to mortgage their belongings to pay their taxes and save enough to subsist. It did not appease them to know, as the prophets afterward exclaimed, that the aristocrats ate of the finest and drank of the best; that they reclined on soft cushions in imported couches, inlaid with ivory. The class divisions, appearing so early in the history of the monarchy, were to have sorry fruits in the later day.

Solomon's successor had neither tact nor patience. As a result, the ten northern tribes seceded and set up a kingdom of their own, the kingdom of Israel leaving only the two southern tribes to go on as the kingdom of Judah. The historic rupture, never healed, destroyed a united kingdom which had endured rather precariously for some 70 years. It proved the turning point in the political history of the Hebrews. Powerful states were growing up in the east and in the west. The days of militant empire were recommencing, bespeaking woe to the smaller peoples of the ancient world. Even firmly united, made vigorous by an active sense of religious and national loyalty, the Hebrews could not long have withstood the onslaughts of their ambitious neighbors. Divided into two toy kingdoms, constantly fighting against each other and torn by rabid dynastic struggles, the Hebrews destroyed any possible hope for survival. Judah, indeed, was not so great an offender. Despite internal feuds, the monarchy remained in the line of the house of David for several centuries, until its extinction. But Israel wallowed in revolution and assassination. Nine dynasties were established in little more than 200 years; 19 kings followed each other, usually compelled to hack a bloody way to the throne. The political history of the Hebrews in these two centuries, disgraced by selfish and undisciplined turbulence, is little different from the history of any petty Oriental people. Ultimately the northern kingdom was destroyed in 732 B.C. The southern kingdom lingered longer until 586 B.C. The political story of the two kingdoms is important only because the events were the somber background against which the Hebrew prophets ministered.

Dispersion and Return. Yet the Jews survived the destruction of their national life. The miracle of such survival is more extraordinary when it is realized into what tiny fragments Judah was shattered. A remnant of the population lived on in Palestine, another was carried off to Babylon, a third fled to Egypt. All three together probably did not number more than 125,000. Yet a few centuries later, just before the Christian Era, the Greek geographer, Strabo, wrote of the Jews: "They have penetrated already into every state, so that it is difficult to find a single place in the world in which their tribe has not been received and become dominant!"

The greatest number lived in Palestine, poor, ignorant peasants who gained a precarious livelihood from the soil and who needed to be forever on guard against the raids of marauding neighbors. The Ammonites, the Moabites, and the Philistines coveted their meager harvests and neglected no opportunity to harass them. The Edomites, driven northward by the Nabatheans and other tribes which pressed on their own borders, were a particular scourge. Ezekiel curses them for their cruelty (Ezekiel 25:12–15), and the historians to whom the memory of Edomite encroachments was fresh, wrote their bitter hatred into their accounts. The glory of Judah was gone. Its survivors ceased to hope for better days as they wrestled with the soil. They intermarried and forsook the God who had evidently forsaken them.

In Egypt the situation was much more promising. Here Jews had been filtering in for centuries, and even before the destruction of Jerusalem there were flourishing Jewish communities in many parts of Pharaoh's dominions. All through the sixth century B.C. Jews fleeing from the successive assaults of Babylon settled on the east borders of Egypt. Some returned to Palestine; others drifted into other lands and were lost; still others took over completely Egyptian ways of life and were absorbed in the native population. But the majority who came settled permanently, remained faithful to their traditions, and helped to build up the wealth and strength of the Elephantine region. Several centuries later the Egyptian communities had become the leading commercial and cultural centers in the Jewish world.

The smallest number, but the most dynamic and creative, settled in Babylon. They lived together in little colonies, where they enjoyed an almost autonomous life. They kept almost desperately every custom which bound them to their past, and they worshiped Yahweh with more fervor now that they were set down in an alien environment. Their religious concepts became clearer, more mature. They began to understand the deeper significance of the prophetic messages. Yahweh was not dependent on temples and sacrifices. He was a god of the heart, as near in Babylonia as in Palestine, present wherever men sought him.

A day came when opportunity was offered by the rise of a Persian king who conquered Babylon, for some of the Babylonian exiles to return to Palestine. A goodly group decided to return and they joined with those who had remained in Palestine in the task of rebuilding the neglected country. They were especially anxious to re-establish the Temple as the center of religious life. In 516 B.C. the Temple was completed and dedicated with great joy. Humble, plain, undecorated it was, but it is difficult to overestimate its importance in Jewish history. It stood for 500 years, a century longer than its predecessor. It was the center of a restored worship, and every pious Jew contributed to its maintenance. All the sentimental yearning of the Jews scattered through the world was now focused in the Temple, which thus effectively bound together the whole Jewish people.

For more than a century after the rebuilding of the temple the Jews lived quietly by the principles of the Mosaic law. Persian dominance was not oppressive and each people within the empire pursued its ends without let or hindrance. Imperial tolerance enabled priests and scribes to regulate the minutest acts by religious rites and to make the Temple the center of existence. Gradually the Jewish state became a theocracy, with priests and law supreme.

Greco-Roman Period. The whole development seemed providential, for at the close of the long period of discipline the integrity of Jewish life was suddenly menaced by the most serious danger which it had ever faced. With the conquest of Europe and Asia by Alexander the Great and Hellenism a new, alluring way of life was placed before the ancient world. Every people, great and small, sooner or later succumbed, except the stubborn little folk of Palestine, who were also sorely tempted to follow the popular gods of the forum and the market place. For four centuries, until the destruction of the state, the nationalists waged a life-and-death struggle, first against the Greeks themselves and then against the Romans, who assimilated Greek culture. In the end, though Jewish thought was unmistakably influenced by the long contact with Hellenism and by the struggle against it, Judaism survived distinct and more militant than ever.

During the complicated politics of the Greek and Roman period the Jewish people suffered not only from the insensate feuds of the Hasmonaean princes, but also from the civil strife of their masters, during which Palestine changed hands many times.

Then, A.D. 70, the Romans, after four desperate years of siege, completely conquered Palestine and uprooted a large part of the Jewish population. The conquest was not accepted by the fanatical survivors and every few years there were new, pathetic, hopeless revolts. The final conquest came after Hadrian took over the Roman Empire A.D. 117.

End of the Jewish State. It is not improbable that a half million lives were sacrificed in the hopeless cause. Those who escaped death were rushed to the slave markets of the East or to the gladiatorial arenas in the chief cities of the West. On the site of the sanctuary a temple was built in honor of Jupiter Capitolinus. On the south gate of the city was placed the head of a boar, the emblem of the tenth legion. The very name of Judah was discarded and the province which had given the Roman legions so much trouble was renamed Syria Palestina. Jews were forbidden on pain of death ever again to set foot in Jerusalem. Only on the ninth of Ab—the traditional anniversary of the destruction of the Temple—could Jews pay for the right to weep on the site of the old sanctuary. For centuries thereafter they "bought their tears," weeping over the lost glories of the past, yet never abandoning the hope that some day a restoration would come and the Holy Land would once again rise from the ruins.

Life in the East Under Islam. In the next centuries the center of Jewish life again shifted to the East, especially to the Tigris Euphrates valley. In the seventh century a new power emerged from the Arabian desert, the army of Islam, which was destined to destroy both the Persian and the Byzantine empires, and to rule the eastern world for more than 1,000 years. The main influence in the lives of the Jews was now created by Islam. At first there were grave difficulties for all subject peoples. But after the first impetuous sweep the conquerors did not compel their subjects to adopt MOHAMMEDANISM. They were content to accept homage and a heavy tribute. Theoretically, the restrictions which were established reduced the vanquished Christians and Jews to slavery. By the Code of Omar they were not permitted to bear arms or to raise their dwellings above those of the Mohammedans. They could not worship in a loud voice, nor build new houses of prayer, nor rebuild their old ones. They could hold no judicial or administrative office, nor employ Moslem slaves. They were compelled to wear marks by which they might be easily distinguished from faithful sons of Islam. But most of these restrictions were dead letters. A schism had occurred in the Moslem world, and the califs of Baghdad, in contact with Western civilization, refused to be bound by the strict letter of the code. They overlooked many of its intolerant commands, and so long as subjects kept their peace and paid their poll tax and their ground rent, they were content. They interfered little in their affairs and allowed them to live an almost autonomous life. From the eighth century onward, therefore, the Jews of the East enjoyed a period of unprecedented peace and freedom, rivaled only in France during the tolerant and distinguished reign of Louis the Pious. It was during this halcyonic respite that the Talmudic literature was developed.

But in the 10th century, the tide turned again. The

Eastern world was engulfed in serious political troubles brought on by the inroads of the Turks. The great academies of the Jews began to founder, and one by one they closed. When the calif imprisoned the unfortunate Hai, tortured him to discover his treasuries, and then executed him in 1040, there was a real end of Jewish corporate existence in the East.

Golden Age in Spain. Meantime a new center of learning had grown up. At the other end of the world, in sunny Spain, the light which went out in Babylon was rekindled. The Babylonian scholars migrated to the West, carrying with them the precious scrolls which had been so long housed in the academies of the East. In the new country, under the tolerant rule of the Spanish Moslems, the Jewish spirit created new works of genius, and the few centuries of Jewish life in Moslem Spain are among the happiest and most fruitful in all Jewish history.

The Moslem conquest of Spain, endured for nearly seven centuries, marked a new epoch in the history of western Europe. Already with the first OMAYYAD, the romantic Abd Ar Rahman who fled from the East when his family was ruined and established himself in Cordoba in 755, a tradition of culture was begun. Under the enlightened rule of Abd Ar Rahman and his successors, Spain helped dissipate some of the darkness that enveloped the rest of Europe. Beautiful palaces and mosques, busy streets and markets, flourishing fields and orchards were the outward marks of a glorious era. The sovereigns were patrons of learning, and authors and singers laid at their feet the fruits of a rich genius. Abd Ar Rahman III, who assumed the title of calif to symbolize the passing of the Moslem headship to his brilliant Cordoba, prized a good poem above a brave deed in battle.

Jews entered fully into the life of the country and soon rose to wealth and power. Many of them became leading landowners and financiers, others prominent physicians and statesmen. They made a definite contribution to medieval civilization by serving as the intermediaries between the Arabs and the Christians; their translations and adaptations of Arabic and Greek writings bridged the Dark Ages. The admirable work of the Arabs in mathematics and astronomy, and their enlightened interpretation of the old Greek philosophers, came to Europe partly through the Jews.

The union of Hebrew and Moslem culture produced a renaissance in literature and philosophy, in science and religion. Even architecture flourished and some of the most beautiful churches in Spain speak to the modern pilgrim of their glory in a day when they served as synagogues and received the prayers of a proud and wealthy Jewish community.

Decline and Fall of Jewish Life in Spain. But by the 14th century the sun no longer shone for the Jews of Spain. The Moslems were driven back by resurgent Christian states and their leaders were not the most admirable representatives of the Christian virtues of brotherhood and tolerance. The Jews passed from comparative security to humiliation and despair. The fury of 1391 opened a period when whole communities were put to the sword. Thousands of Jews rushed to the baptismal fonts, hoping through conversion to escape. Such converts were known as Marranos, externally pretending to be Christians, but remaining Jews in secret. The Inquisition soon began to root these out and the punishment was usually death by public burning. Finally, in 1492, the entire Jewish settlement in Spain was unceremoniously expelled and one of the great periods in Jewish history came to an end.

Eclipse in Christian Europe. Meantime, Christian Europe, outside of Spain, seethed with hatred. For a time after the 11th century the story of Jewish life in France, England, and the several hundred states of the Holy Roman Empire, included a long succession of indignities and brutalities, culminating in wholesale massacres and expulsions. To be sure, the Jews were not alone in their misery. These were centuries in which civilization moved slowly and painfully. Living in an alien faith, the Jews were usually considered as outside the pale of civilization, completely at the mercy of their rulers' whim. With the exception of a brief Talmudic renaissance in the Rhine districts, in the 11th century, when Gershom and Rashi flourished, one seeks in vain for a respite.

Havens of Refuge. Fortunately, there were new areas which opened for Jews to settle. Eastern Europe once again became the leading center of Jewish life as the doors of Turkey and Poland were providentially opened. Some of the Italian states and a few of the states of the Holy Roman Empire were also temporary havens of refuge. Holland, and later England, gradually relaxed restrictions. But despite these few havens in a stormy world, Jewish existence remained too precarious to be comfortable, and the years of travail cast their shadows over the years of quiet. It was not astonishing that, with no hope for participation in the life of the country, Jews swaddled themselves in their own traditions and placed their reliance in a personal Messiah who would some day come to restore them to the ancient homeland in Palestine.

Recent Developments. The rise of capitalism and the revolutionary sentiments at the end of the 18th century improved the conditions of the Jews in Europe. The first attempt to secure legal recognition in England was under the reign of Charles II. In 1743 they were distinctly recognized as British subjects. During the reign of Queen Victoria, Jews were placed practically on the same footing as other British subjects, and a British Jew, DISRAELI, became prime minister. The French Revolution was a turning point in the history of Jews not only in France but all over Europe. For the first time in 1,000 years they became citizens of the states in which they lived. Even more important, it completely changed their economic status and opened new worlds of opportunity to them.

Chaim Weizmann, first president of Israel

The Jews were able to obtain needed economic strength in the new liberal states controlled by the middle class. They played a significant role in the development of finance, particularly through the banking house of ROTHSCHILD. In Austria and Germany the emancipation of the Jews was proclaimed after the revolution of 1848.

But at the end of the 19th century there was a new violent anti-Semitism. It was felt in Germany, Austria, and above all in Russia. It reached even liberal France, where the DREYFUS AFFAIR was a disillusionment for those who believed that it could not happen there.

In 1917 equal rights were granted to the Jews in Russia, and after World War I similar rights were gained in Rumania. But soon after the conclusion of World War I, anti-Semitism grew in some European nations, particularly in Germany. Adolf Hitler adopted anti-Semitism as one of the most important points of his political ideology. (See NATIONAL SOCIALISM.) During Hitler's rule of Germany and most of Europe, millions of Jews were killed. At the end of the war, virtually every historic Jewish community in Europe had been destroyed. Nevertheless in the British Commonwealth of Nations, the United States, and the democracies of western Europe, Jews continued to live side by side with other peoples and to participate in government and social life. However, the Jews were oppressed in the U.S.S.R. and its satellites and many of them attempted to emigrate from the latter. A significant event in Jewish history occurred in 1947 with the creation of the Jewish state of ISRAEL in Palestine. See ANTI-SEMITISM; ISRAEL; JUDAISM; PALESTINE; ZIONISM.   A. L. SACHAR

BIBLIOG.—*Jewish Encyclopaedia* (1906); Joseph Jacobs, *Jewish Contributions to Civilization* (1919); R. Kittle, *The Religion of the People of Israel* (1925); H. Graetz, *A History of the Jews* (1926); E. R. Bevan and C. Singer, *The Legacy of Israel* (1927); M. L. Margolis and A. Marx, *A History of the Jewish People* (1927); I. Abrahams, *Jewish Life in the Middle Ages* (1932); M. Steinberg, *Making of the Modern Jew* (1934); S. Baron, *A Social and Religious History of the Jews* (1937); A. L. Sachar, *Sufferance Is the Badge* (1939); M. Berger, *Beneath the Surface* (1946); J. W. Parkes, *Emergence of the Jewish Problem, 1878–1939* (1947); A. L. Sachar, *History of the Jews* (ed. 1948); A. E. Bailey and C. F. Kent, *History of the Hebrew Commonwealth* (ed. 1949); D. F. Zeiligs, *History of Jewish Life in Modern Times* (ed. 1949); I. Goldberg, *Israel* (1949); Y. J. Meek, *Hebrew Origins* (ed. 1950); H. Daniel-Rops, *Israel and the Ancient World* (1950).

JEW'S HARP, a musical instrument, perhaps so named because Jews introduced it into England. The "Jew's harp," or "Jew's trump," as it is sometimes called, consists of a small piece of iron of horseshoe shape, with a slender tongue of steel, which is made to vibrate. The instrument is held between the parted teeth, and the projecting end of the tongue of steel is twanged with the forefinger.

JEYPORE. See JAIPUR.

JEZEBEL. See BIBLE, Principal Persons in the Bible.

JEZREEL, modern **Zir'in,** a city of Canaan, situated on a W spur of Mount Gilboa. Ahab made it a royal residence (I Kings 21:1), and it was the scene of the murder of Naboth (I Kings 21:1–16) and of the tragic end of Ahab's dynasty (II Kings 9:10). The city gave its name to the valley of Jezreel, and also to the plain of Esdraelon. The former is associated with Gideon's triumph over the Midianites (Judges 6:33–7; 25) and the defeat and death of Saul in battle against the Philistines (I Sam. 29). The plain of Esdraelon (or Megiddo) was the scene of Deborah's triumph over the Canaanites (Judges 4. 5) and the defeat of Josiah by Pharaoh Necho (II Kings 23:29 f.).

JHALAWAR, former feudatory state, India, now part of Greater Rajasthan, made up of two separated tracts in SE Rajputana; area 824 sq. mi.; pop. (1941) 122,299. Jhalawar became a separate principality in 1838 when it was split off from Kotah. In 1896 its ruler was deposed because of misrule, and the government came into the hands of the British resident. A

year later the greater part of the state was returned to Kotah, and in 1899 the two separated tracts became a new state. The chief town, Patan (pop. 6,059), founded in 1796, is the center of trade. The principal exports are oilseeds and cotton. The ruler belongs to the Jhala clan of Rajputs.

JHANSI, city, India, United Provinces, capital of Jhansi District, about 60 miles SE of Gwalior. A railway center, Jhansi is also the trading center for a large agricultural area. It has manufactures of brass, silk, and rugs. Founded by a Mahratta prince, Jhansi was made his capital, and for its protection a fort was built on an eminence commanding the city. In 1806 the British promised protection, and in 1817 the prince ceded his rights to Bundelkhand to them. In 1853 the rajah died childless, and the British annexed the city and area. Pop. (1941) 103,254.

JHELUM RIVER, or **Jehlam,** also **Bitasta,** the ancient **Hydaspes,** India, in Punjab Province, the most westerly of the five streams which give that province its name. It rises in the mountains of Kashmir, flows south and northwest for about 100 miles, passing Anantnag and Srinagar, then takes a southwest course, and enters the plain of the Punjab about 250 miles from its source; after a further course of 200 miles it joins the Chenab below Jhang Maghiana. Its total length is about 490 miles.

JIBOUTI. See DJIBOUTI.

JICARILLAS, a division of the Apache Indian tribe now confined to the Jicarilla Reservation in New Mexico. They formerly dwelt in tents somewhat like those used by the Indians of the Plains. They make excellent basketry.

JIDDA, or **Jedda,** seaport of SW Saudi Arabia, in Hejaz, on the Red Sea. It is the port for pilgrims (about 80,000 annually) bound for the holy city of Mecca, 50 miles east. Originally, Jidda was probably settled by Persian merchants; and during the 15th century it was a center of trade between India and Egypt. It has a seawater converting plant, which purifies drinking water. Exports are coral, cotton goods, cutlery, hardware, mirrors, leather goods, dates, coffee, and hides. Jidda is open to foreigners; therefore its population includes Arabs, East Indians, Persians, and others. Pop. about 30,000.

JIG, a species of dance tune of a merry buoyant character. It is usually written in $6/8$ or $12/8$ time; but Bach, Händel, and other early composers, who frequently introduced the *giga* into their suites, wrote it in various times, such as $9/8$, $12/16$, $3/4$, etc. It was originally a form of country dance, but on introduction into the United States it became famous as part of the MINSTREL SHOW through Daddy Rice.

JIG, in machine tooling, is a frame or body into which work is fastened to guide the cutting tool. The use of jigs tends to increase production by eliminating the need for measuring each piece of similar work and

Rotating jigs used in aircraft construction

BOEING AIRCRAFT CO.

to lower manufacturing costs by permitting employment of semi- or unskilled workers.

Depending upon the shape of the part being machined, the jig may be a simple plate fastened on top of the work, or, when it is a drilling jig and holes are to be drilled from different angles, a box-jig is used. This type is constructed either as a casting or built up of steel plates welded or screwed together into a box form. The work is enclosed in this jig and holes are provided for the escape of chips. The holes or channels for guiding and supporting cutting tools have bushings of hardened-tool steel or case-hardened machine steel.

Jig boring machines are used for accurately finishing holes and surfaces in definite relation to one another, the finished piece being used as a plate jig.

The jig should always be rugged enough to stand rough handling by an awkward operator. See MACHINE TOOLS.

JIGGER. See CHIGOE.

JIGUANÍ, town, E central Cuba, in Oriente Province; on a railway and a highway, NE of Santiago de Cuba in an important sugar-producing region. Pop. (1943) 13,995.

JIHLAVA, or **Iglau,** town, S central Czechoslovakia, Moravia, on the Jihlava River; 110 miles SE of Prague (Praha). Its industries are sawmills, breweries, shoe and tobacco factories, and manufactures of linen and woolen cloth, plush, glass, and pottery. There are silver mines in the vicinity. The town has a large trade in timber and cereal grains. Jihlava is first mentioned in the 12th century. Here in July, 1436, the Hussite wars were ended by the Compact of Jihlava, agreed upon by both Hussites and Catholics. Jihlava became thoroughly Protestant between the years 1560 and 1623. It was occupied by the Swedes for a short time (1645–47) during the Thirty Years' War. Here the Austrians defeated the Bavarians in December, 1805. Upon the collapse of the Austro-Hungarian Empire in 1918, the town came under Czechoslovakian administration. Pop. (1947 est.) 23,413.

JIHUN RIVER. See AMU DARYA.

JILOLO ISLAND. See HALMAHERA ISLAND.

"JIM CROW" LAWS, a term applied to legislation to prevent contacts between Negroes and whites implying social equality. After the emancipation of the slaves all the southern states passed such legislation in order to hold the Negro "in his place." These laws require the separation of the races in public conveyances, and in such public places as schools, prisons, hospitals, restaurants, hotels. Intermarriage is prohibited, usually "a person of color" being defined as one possessing one-eight part of Negro blood. Most northern states have "equal rights" laws or constitutional provisions establishing the principle of equal treatment for all without regard to race or color; in practice, however, many of the objectives of the "Jim Crow" laws are secured through social pressure. The decision of the U.S. Supreme Court in 1883 invalidating the Federal Civil Rights Act of 1873 made possible the passage and enforcement of these laws. In recent years the Supreme Court has become increasingly critical of "Jim Crow" legislation. In 1917 it declared unconstitutional city ordinances requiring the residential segregation of races. In 1944 the court held the exclusive white primary unconstitutional; in 1946 it held that the segregation of Negroes on interstate buses is an unconstitutional burden on interstate commerce. See NEGRO.   F. M.

JIMÉNES. See XIMÉNEZ DE CISNEROS.

JIMÉNEZ DE QUESADA, GONZALO, 1497-1579, Spanish conquistador of New Granada (now Colombia). Sent to Santa Marta to be chief justice of the colony, he led an expedition into the interior (1536), following the valley of the Magdalena, crossed the mountains, and finally reached a cultivated plain, where in 1538 he founded Santa Fé de Bogotá, as a Spanish fort. He was assisted in his conquest of the Chibcha Indians by their internal conflicts. Jiménez returned to Spain and in 1549 was made a marshal and returned to Bogotá. In 1567 he started a three-year search for El Dorado.

JIMMU, or **JIMMU TENNO,** fl. 7th century B.C., the first emperor of Japan, who founded the imperial dynasty and Empire of Japan (*Dai Nihon Teikoku*) by ascending the throne at Kashiwabara, near where the capitals of Nara and Kyoto were established in later centuries, in Yamato province, west central Honshu, on Feb. 11, 660 B.C. This Japanese official date is based on ancient records, and some historians doubt its strict accuracy. Japanese chronology starts with that year, so that 1947 is the Japanese 2607. The date February 11 was chosen by Emperor Meiji to promulgate, in 1889, the modern constitution of Japan, which remained the basic law until superseded by the new constitution Emperor Hirohito promulgated in 1946, for which he chose the date November 3, Meiji Tenno Day. See JAPAN, History.

Jimson weed, or thorn apple

JIMSON WEED, also called **Thorn Apple,** a poisonous weed growing in fields and wastelands throughout southern United States. The weed is a coarse annual with a stout stem, spreading branches, and strong-scented foliage. Its funnel-shaped flowers, borne in the axils of the branches, develop into hard, prickly fruits. Jimson weed is cultivated for the alkaloid *stramonium*, which is extracted from the inflorescence and dried leaves and is used medically as a substitute for *belladonna*. All parts of the plant, when eaten, are narcotic and poisonous to both animals and man. With some individuals, contact with the leaves and flowers may cause a severe dermatitis. Jimson weed, *Datura stramonium*, belongs to the genus *Datura*, which contains a number of poisonous species. One particularly harmful species is *D. arborea*, a subtropical shrub used by Amazon tribes as a narcotic herb.

JIND, former feudatory state, India, now part of the Pepsu Union; in SE Punjab; area 1,299 sq. mi.; pop. (1941) 361,812. Jind is one of the three Phulkian states, of which the other two are PATIALA and NABHA; it became a separate state in 1763 when Rajah Gajpat Singh established a principality that was recognized by the Mogul in 1768. The state came under British influence in 1809, and its rulers since have been conspicuously loyal to the British, in the 1857 Mutiny being the first in the field with loyal troops. Following the Mutiny, Jind was rewarded by the addition of the Dadri territory of some 600 square miles. The capital since 1827 has been Sangrur, which has connections with British railways.

JINGO, or **JINGO KOGO,** d. A.D. 269, most celebrated female sovereign in Japanese history, who ruled the southwestern half of what is the present empire, from A.D. 201 to 269, according to ancient records; some historians place the period about a century later. The outstanding event of her reign was her invasion of Silla, southeastern kingdom of Korea, which she led in person and which caused her absence from Japan for several years. This expedition had far-reaching effects in the intercourse it brought about between Japan and Korea. From about this time Japan maintained suzerainty for centuries over Mimana, a small state in south Korea. Japanese historians do not list Jingo among the reigning sovereigns. She was descended from a Korean prince, and in her lifetime was named Okinaga Tarashi. The old annals say that in addition to being able, courageous, and ambitious, the empress was extremely beautiful. So far as is known she is the only Japanese sovereign to have gone outside the empire while ruling it. Jingo was the third consort of Emperor Chuai and mother of Emperor Ojin, who in a later period was deified as Hachiman, god of war, and whose ancient shrine stands in Kamakura. See JAPAN, *History*.

JINN, a class of supernatural beings in Arabic mythology, created out of fire 2,000 years before Adam. They are supposed to haunt all the places of the earth and to be able to assume any form they desire. There are good and bad jinn, the latter being subject to Idlis. Although the jinn are above all the usual laws of nature, man can control them by means of talismans; and thus Solomon held them all in subjection. The old French translators of the *Arabian Nights* used *génie* (familiar spirit) to represent the Arabic word.

JINNAH, MOHAMMED ALI, 1876–1948, Moslem leader and first governor general of the Dominion of PAKISTAN, was born in Karachi, India. Educated in Karachi and Great Britain, he became an advocate of the Bombay high court in 1906 and served on the Imperial Legislative Council (1910–19). In 1913 he joined the Moslem League three years later became its permanent president. At that time the leading Moslem advocate of concord with the Hindus, Jinnah was instrumental in getting the Congress party and the Moslem League to hold several joint sessions during World War I.

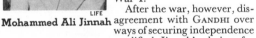
LIFE
Mohammed Ali Jinnah After the war, however, disagreement with GANDHI over ways of securing independence modified Jinnah's desires for Hindu-Moslem harmony. In 1930 he demanded separate electorates for Hindu and Moslem communities and equality for Moslems in the sharing of offices in the central and provisional government. After the spectacular victories of the Congress party in the 1936–37 elections, the Moslem League became increasingly fearful of Hindu predominance in the government. In 1940 demands for an independent state of Pakistan were launched by Jinnah, to be created seven years later. Jinnah's dream became reality shortly before he died. See INDIA for picture.

JINSEN. See CHEMULPO.

JIPIJAPA, city, W central Ecuador, in the province of Manabí; on the Seco River and a highway; NW of Guayaquil and near its port of Cayo. Jipijapa is Ecuador's largest coffee center; the city also exports tagua nuts and "Panama" hats. Pop. (1944 est.) 22,097.

JITOMIR. See ZHITOMIR.

JIUJITSU or **JUJITSU,** the Japanese art of self-defense, is of great antiquity, but was practiced only by the SAMURAI, the governing and military caste of Japan; it was an essential part of their elaborate training, and the exclusive knowledge of it was considered necessary to their predominance. In the late Japanese renaissance much wider functions were given to it; originally for self-defense purely, it came to be valued as a means to general physical efficiency, and, finally, in the development of character, the training was thrown open to the whole people.

The history of jiujitsu is complex. It is not unlike the *pancratium* of the ancient Olympic games, but no relationship has been traced. Probably it was imported to Japan from China, but it has been very greatly modified in the course of years by the Japanese. Moreover, many formal and ritualistic elements have been incorporated into it. At the end of the 19th century it began to attract attention outside of Japan. Schools were established in the United States and England and on the Continent. Its popularity is growing in America today, and it is given official attention in certain of the universities and police forces.

Jiujitsu means literally "the gentle art." It opposes knowledge and skill to brute strength, and seeks to make man independent of weapons and mere physical force, its principle being to use a man's weight and strength against himself. An opponent's blow that cannot be resisted can be turned to his own downfall.

It will be easily seen that the qualities to be cultivated are quickness and suppleness and a delicate perception of balance. Stiffness is unpardonable, and it is a great mistake to offer a dull resistance to the stress of assault instead of yielding to it and cultivating an elastic and aggressive recovery.

The first thing that must be learned is the art of falling without shock or injury. A man usually falls on a joint—i.e., either on the base of the spine, the elbow joint, or the wrist. Thus injury is caused. In the jiujitsu method of falling, the violence of the shock is taken by pads of muscle on the arm, leg, or foot.

The next thing that must be known is anatomy. The jiujitsu expert knows those points of the body which, upon pressure, produce temporary paralysis: the exposed nerve at the elbow sometimes called the "funny-bone," the armpit, the complex of nerves above the stomach (the solar plexus), the wrist and ankle bones, the nerves of the upper arm, the tendon running downward from the ear, and the Adam's apple. Moreover, the expert must know the points where pressure may most easily disturb balance, particularly the back of the knee joint and the base of the spine.

Judo is a popularized form of jiujitsu designed not for sport but for self-defense, especially against a larger man. As in jiujitsu the main principle of judo is to use the strength of an adversary to his own disadvantage; however, American judo (sometimes termed "hand-to-hand combat" in the U.S. Army) also employs such elements of rough-and-tumble fighting as kicking, choking, and gouging, and in some cases includes the use of a club.   L. S. B.

JIVAROS, or **Jeveros,** a South American people of the Upper Marañon. They were reduced by the Spaniards after the conquest of Peru, but revolted in 1599. They have fixed homes, cultivate several economic plants, and possess the secret of mummifying human heads, which in the process are reduced to about the size of a large orange, without losing the features and expression of the living subject.

JOAB. See BIBLE, *Principal Persons*.

JOACHIM, d. 1202, founder and abbot of the monastery of Giovanni del Fiore (or Floris) in Calabria, was celebrated as interpreter of the Apocalypse, mystic, and prophet. His principal works, the *Concordia Utriusque Testamenti* and a commentary on the Revelation, arranged the divine governance of the world in three stages corresponding to the persons of the Trinity—the Old Testament, the New Testament, and an impending final dispensation of the Holy Spirit. He found many followers, especially among the Franciscans; one of whom, Gherardo di

Pull right arm as right foot advances kick ankle

REAR CHOKE HOLD defense

FRONT CHOKE HOLD defense

THE DEVIL'S HANDSHAKE

Action against the throat

Throw right foot over, twist, and throw

Pull right arm, yank right knee up, and lift

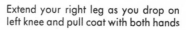

Action against the elbow

Extend your right leg as you drop on left knee and pull coat with both hands

Toe hold against attack from rear

Borgo San Donnino, in 1254 re-edited Joachim's commentaries as the *Evangelium Aeternum*.

JOACHIM, JOSEPH, 1831–1907, Hungarian violinist, was born in Kittsee, near Pressburg. He studied under Boehm of Vienna; and with David at Leipzig, and became the foremost violinist of his time as well as a great teacher. He was leader of the grand-duke's orchestra at Weimar (1849), director of concerts at the court of Hanover (1854–66), and in 1868 was appointed director of the high school for music at Berlin. He became an incomparable exponent of classical works for the violin. As a teacher and founder of a system of violin technique he was equally famous. His compositions include overtures, concertos, pieces for violin and piano, etc., but his greatest work is his Hungarian concerto (op. 11) for violin and orchestra. Brahms' violin concerto was dedicated to Joachim.

JOACHIMSTHAL. See JÁCHYMOV.

JOAN, called **The Fair Maid of Kent,** 1328–85, was the daughter of Edmund of Woodstock, son of EDWARD I. She appears to have formed a liaison with the Earl of Salisbury, and then to have married Sir Thomas Holland. She became countess of Kent (1352), and on Holland's death, married the Black Prince (1361), and became the mother of RICHARD II.

JOAN OF ARC, SAINT, or **Jeanne d'Arc,** the **Maid of Orléans,** 1412–31, French national heroine and patroness of France, was born in Domrémy. Deeply religious, at the age of 13 she maintained that she received visions and heard the voices of several saints who prompted her to free her country of the English domination under which it lay. By the time she was 16, the voices and visions increased to such an extent that she felt bound to bend every effort in the deliverance of France. Overcoming the violent opposition and ignoring the ridicule of her family, friends, churchmen, and courtiers, she managed to see the dauphin of France for a personal interview. She was forced to withstand investigations and examinations from ecclesiastical courts, but at her ardent and continuous pleas Charles gave her a small army. With these followers, when she was 17, she broke the siege of Orléans. By this accomplishment she brought France to a reawakening and evoked live hope from a dying spirit. The revived spirit roundly defeated the English at Loire and the dauphin was crowned CHARLES VII at Reims. In the defense of Compiègne Joan was captured by the English, taken to Rouen, and confined in chains. Brought before the tribunal of the Inquisition, she was questioned by the infamous Bishop of Beauvais, Cauchon, who was but a tool of the English. The judges were astounded at every turn by the readiness of her answers, but they were determined to quiet this young girl. She was finally condemned to die by burning at the stake on the counts of heresy, supporting witchcraft, having her hair cut off, and wearing the clothing of men. She met her death by burning on May 30, 1431. Twenty-four years later, at the request of the king of France, Pope Callistus III appointed a special commission of investigation which rehabilitated her. She was beatified in 1909, and in 1920 Pope Benedict XV canonized her a saint of the church. Her feast is on May 30. W. Trask compiled and translated an autobiography, *Self Portrait* (1936). See HUNDRED YEARS' WAR. For illustration, see FRANCE, History. R. M. LEONARD

BIBLIOG.–A. B. Paine, *Girl in White Armor* (1927); M. Monahan, *My Jeanne d'Arc* (1928); J. Eaton, *Joanne d'Arc* (1931); C. F. Oddie, *Story of Saint Joan* (1931); W. P. Barrett, trans., *Trial of Jeanne d'Arc* (1932); M. Williams, *Joan of Arc* (1932); E. Everett-Green, *Heroine of France* (1933); M. D. Holmes, *Joan of Arc* (1934); J. d' Orliac, *Joan of Arc and Her Companions* (1934); D. M. H. Bronky, *Joan of Arc, 1412–1431* (1935); M. Waldman, *Joan of Arc* (1935); S. Fumet, *Joan the Saint* (1937); Chroniques de Saint-Denis, *Joan, the Maid of Orleans* (1938); V. M. Sackville-West, *Joan of Arc* (1938); J. I. Lane, *St. Joan of Arc* (1939); O. Rutter, *Land of Saint Joan* (1941); A. Buchan, *Joan of Arc and the Recovery of France* (1945); E. C. Wagenknecht, ed., *Joan of Arc* (1948).

ART INSTITUTE OF CHICAGO
"Joan of Arc at the Court of Chinon"

JOANNA I, 1326?–1382, queen of Naples from 1343 to 1382, was crowned on the death of Robert of Anjou. When her husband Andrew died mysteriously in 1345, his brother, Louis I of Hungary, drove Joanna and her second husband out of Naples. They returned in 1352. Married two more times, Joanna caused further trouble by repudiating her heir, Charles of Durazzo, naming Louis of Anjou as her successor. Pope Urban VI supported Charles when he invaded Naples and had Joanna executed.

JOANNA II, 1371–1435, queen of Naples from 1414 to 1435. Dominated by unscrupulous favorites, she made intrigue and murder commonplaces in her reign. She first named Alfonso V of Aragon as her heir, but later quarreled with him and settled the dispute with her Anjou heirs.

JOANNES DAMASCENUS, known also as **Chrysorrhoas,** d. c. 754, theologian, hymn writer, and one of the later Greek fathers, was a native of Damascus, and flourished during the first half of the eighth century A.D. His later years were passed in the most stringent self-discipline in the monastery of Santa Saba, near Jerusalem. His memory is best preserved by his hymns, several of which have been rendered into English, notably " 'Tis the day of Resurrection" and "Come ye Faithful, Raise the Strain."

JOÃO PESSÔA, or **Paraíba,** city, NE Brazil, capital of Paraíba State, about 10 miles from the seacoast and 50 miles N of Recife. Founded in 1585 by João Tavares, the city has been known by several names under the Dutch and Portuguese regimes. In 1930 it was again renamed for João Pessôa, an associate of the revolutionary leader, Getulio Vargas. The city has beautiful parks, fine colonial buildings, and a state normal school. Cotton and sugar are shipped from the port of Cabedello near by. Pop. (1948) 109,761.

JOASH, or **JEHOASH.** See BIBLE, *Principal Persons.*

JOB, book of the Bible, forms a dramatic episode of the tribulations of its central figure, Job, in the Bible. The design of the story concerns a problem found in the earliest histories of man: why the difficulty of human suffering exists, and, more particularly, why the righteous and innocent must bear a share of it. Job, formerly a wealthy man, suffers first the loss of his possessions and then the loss of his family; afterward he is afflicted with serious bodily ills. All of this is considered by the writer to be a test of Job's integrity and faith in the help of God. The moral of the story is brought to light by a visit from three of his friends who point out to Job the traditional view that suffering is a penalty for sin and that his sorrows are the unmistakable evidence of something ungodly in his life. Job, however, insists that he is righteous, but asserts that if it is God's attempt to try his patience he will continue to prove himself. Persisting in his belief of God's power, Job passes through the trials and ultimately regains double his former possessions. Critics assign various dates for the writing, ranging between the ninth and the fourth centuries B.C. The general tone of the work agrees with the period after the Hebrew captivity, when the question in men's minds concerned a point of justice. Why, they asked, should those born in exile, and consequently not responsible for the evils of which the exile was believed a penalty, continue to suffer? Jewish tradition has claimed that Moses himself was the writer. From the Book of Job has come the phrase "the patience of Job."   R. M. LEONARD

JOB ANALYSIS, sometimes erroneously called JOB EVALUATION, is the process of critically evaluating the operations, duties, and relationships of occupations or jobs. It may serve one or both of two general functions, a *personal function,* and a production or *engineering* function.

The term "job" is not synonymous with the term "occupation." A job is a specific task at which the worker temporarily may be engaged within an occupation or position. An occupation or position is a continuing assignment sufficiently unlike all other assignments that the transfer of an experienced worker to that assignment from another assignment would involve special training rather than simply casual instruction; or sufficiently unlike other assignments that the conditions surrounding the performance of its duties involve different degrees of skill, effort, responsibilities, and working conditions.

Personnel Function. For the personnel function, job analysis may be used: (1) to provide occupational descriptions or written records of duties, responsibilities, working conditions, and requirements of the occupation as an aid in selecting, placing, transferring, and promoting employees; (2) to provide information necessary in standardizing the jobs and in setting up general employee training programs so that each employee may know the extent of his duties and the proper relation of his job to others in the organization; (3) to aid in developing or revising organizational structures; and (4) in training executives in the job requirements and organizational relationships of their subordinates.

The personnel function usually may be served by adequate *Occupational Descriptions.* Each description usually should include: date; occupational title and code number; department; number of workers; general description of regular duties; occasional duties; percentage of time on such duties; names of parts, materials, tools, and equipment used; how the work is checked or inspected; nature and extent of supervision received and given; responsibilities; potential accident and health hazards; special talents or experience required; promotional possibilities; and working conditions including disagreeable features, general surroundings, hours worked, vacations and other privileges, wage rates, and methods of payment.

In addition to this factual data, the personnel department will need *Occupational Specifications,* which are written records of the requirements sought in the *workers* assigned to the occupations. They may include: age range; physical qualities required; sex; possibly race and nationality; educational background; kind and extent of previous experience; any special in-service training; personality requirements; a list of aptitude and performance tests, with critical scores, which the applicant

A Time and Motion Study of machine operation is conducted as a part of job analysis, below

		SUBJECT CHARTED	BRUSH HOLDER ASSY.	PROCESS CHART *John A. Patton* MANAGEMENT ENGINEERS, INC.		SUMMARY			
OPERATION		ASSEMBLY COMPLETE			METHOD	PRES.	PROP.	SAVING
CHARTED BY		METHODS IMPROVEMENT TRAINEE			NO. OF OPERATIONS	32	17	15
CHART NO	1	SHEET NO.	1		NO. OF MOVES	5	0	5
DATE	9-1-47			CAN I ELIMINATE?	NO. OF STORAGES	0	0	0
PLANT		COMPANY		CAN I COMBINE?	NO. OF INSPECTIONS	0	0	0
DEPT.				CAN I CHANGE SEQUENCE?	MAN HOUR PER 20 POS.	0.6	0.35	0.25
				CAN I SIMPLIFY?	DISTANCE TRAVELED	15	0	15'

P.L.	DIST. IN FEET	TIME IN MIN.	OPER. MOVE STORAGE INSPECT.	DESCRIPTION OF PRESENT METHOD	P.L.	DIST. FEET	TIME MIN.	OPER. MOVE STORAGE INSPECT.	DESCRIPTION OF PROPOSED METHOD
1	3'		○●△□	LIFT PAN OF BRUSH HOLDERS TO BCH	1			●○△□	PICK UP BRUSH HOLDER AND PIN
2	3'		○●△□	LIFT BOX OF BRUSH LEVERS TO BCH	2			●○△□	POSITION BRUSH HOLDER AND PIN IN FIXTURE
3	3'		○●△□	LIFT BOX OF SPRINGS TO BENCH	3			●○△□	PICK UP SPRINGS AND BRUSH LEVER
4	3'		○●△□	LIFT BOX OF PINS TO BENCH	4			●○△□	POSITION SPRING & LEVER OVER PIN
5	3'		○●△□	LIFT BOX OF WASHERS, SCREWS, COTTER PINS & CTS. SCREWS TO BCH	5			●○△□	PICK UP WASHER AND COTTER PIN
6			●○△□	PICK UP BRUSH HOLDER AND BRUSH LEVER PIN	6			●○△□	POSITION WASHER & INSERT COTTER PIN
7			●○△□	INSERT PIN TO BRUSH HOLDER	7			●○△□	PICK UP SCREWDRIVER
8			●○△□	TAP INTO BRUSH HOLDER TO START	8			●○△□	SPREAD COTTER PIN
9			●○△□	LAY ON BLOCK	9			●○△□	REPEAT #1 THRU 8 ABOUT 20 TIMES
10			●○△□	PICK UP HAMMER & CENTER PUNCH	10			●○△□	TURN ASSY. 90°
11			●○△□	PUNCH END OF PIN	11			●○△□	PICK UP R.H. MACH. SCREW & WASHER
12			●○△□	PEEN OVER HEAD OF PIN	12			●○△□	SCREW INTO BRUSH HOLDER
13			●○△□	LAY DOWN PUNCH AND HAMMER	13			●○△□	REPEAT #10 THRU 12 ABOUT 20 TIMES
14			●○△□	REPEAT 6 THRU 13 ABOUT 20 TIMES	14			●○△□	PICK UP 1/4 CAP SCREW & WASHER
15			●○△□	TURN OVER (1) ASSY.	15			●○△□	SCREW INTO BRUSH HOLDER
16			●○△□	PICK UP SPRING	16			●○△□	DROP THRU CHUTE TO PAN
17			●○△□	DROP SPRING ONTO PIN	17			●○△□	REPEAT #14 THRU #16 ABOUT 20 TIMES
18			●○△□	PICK UP BRUSH LEVER				○○△□	
19			●○△□	SLIDE BRUSH LEVER OVER PIN AND THRU SPRING				○○△□	
20			●○△□	PICK UP WASHER					
21			●○△□	PLACE WASHER OVER PIN					
22			●○△□	PICK UP COTTER PIN					
23			●○△□	SLIDE COTTER PIN INTO HOLE IN PIN					
24			●○△□	PICK UP SCREWDRIVER					
25			●○△□	SPREAD COTTER PIN					
26			●○△□	REPEAT 15 THRU 25 ABOUT 20 TIMES					
27			●○△□	PICK UP #10-24 R.H. MACH. SCREW AND WASHER					
28			●○△□	SLIDE WASHER ONTO SCREW					
29			●○△□	PICK UP SCREWDRIVER					
30			●○△□	SCREW INTO BRUSH HOLDER					
31			●○△□	REPEAT 27 THRU 30 ABOUT 20 TIMES					
32			●○△□	PICK UP C' SCREW AND WASHER					
33			●○△□	HOLD BRUSH HOLDER AND SCREW IN C' SCREW					
34			●○△□	PICK UP WRENCH					
35			●○△□	TIGHTEN C' SCREW					
36			●○△□	LAY DOWN WRENCH AND THROW ASSY. IN PAN					
37			●○△□	REPEAT 32 THRU 36 ABOUT 20 TIMES					
37			TOTAL						

JOHN A. PATTON, MANAGEMENT ENGINEERS, INC.

Engineering Job Analysis. On process chart, 20 operation elements were eliminated; time for 20 pieces was nearly halved by a careful analysis of work

should pass; and possible sources of supply. These specifications may be shown as portions of the occupational descriptions or on separate specification sheets.

Engineering Function. In the production or engineering function, job analysis is used largely in industrial engineering for improving methods and reducing costs. The engineering job analysis, therefore, consists of descriptions of the detailed elements on specific jobs or tasks. The elements usually are grouped into relatively few classifications which include: (1) *Operations* or changes in the condition of the material or part; (2) *Transportations* or changes in location of the material or operator; (3) *Storages* of the material, and idle periods of the operator which are enforced by the nature of the operation; (4) *Inspections* to control the quantity and quality of the product; and (5) miscellaneous avoidable and unavoidable *Delays* or interruptions which disturb the normal progress of the process or operation. Such an analysis usually will include a sketch of the item or product and special charts showing the elements of the process or operation in sufficient detail that it could be reproduced accurately at some later time.

Operator and hand movement diagrams often are produced photographically by making time-exposure still-pictures of short operation cycles. These are called *Chronocyclegraphs*.

Moving pictures (and occasionally other devices) are convenient for making *Micromotion Analyses* of very rapid operations. Such films are analyzed frame by frame, and the data are transferred to *Simo-Charts* (simultaneous motion charts) which show the time relationships of very minute movements of various body members. See INDUSTRIAL PSYCHOLOGY; INDUSTRIAL ORGANIZATION and MANAGEMENT.

JOB EVALUATION or occupational rating, sometimes erroneously called job analysis, is the process of establishing consistent and justifiable relationships between the *values* of occupations or positions requiring different degrees of skill, effort, responsibility, and working conditions. It is concerned with the minimum requirements of the occupation itself, and not with the degree to which an individual meets those requirements. Without job evaluation, wage rates on similar occupations occasionally are found to vary as much as 200 or 300 per cent; but with good job evaluation, such variations seldom should be more than 20 or 25 per cent within a labor grade or class, and these can be justified only by merit differentials.

A complete job evaluation program should serve the following purposes: (1) discover the relative minimum requirements of the respective occupations within a plant or industry; (2) determine consistent relative base values for all present incentive or non-incentive occupations in a company or industry, between jobs in one department, between departments, and between hourly rated and salary rated occupations; (3) determine the proper relative value for any new or revised occupation; (4) convert permanent relative index (or point) values into corresponding current actual money values; (5) provide a foundation for a sound over-all labor policy involving hiring rates, labor grades, and rate ranges; (6) provide a basis for systematic *merit rating* of the workers; (7) aid management in correcting any inequalities in present wages; (8) provide a basis for intelligent discussions in wage rate disputes, and thereby reduce such disputes to a minimum; and (9) obtain other benefits associated with job or occupational analysis which is a prerequisite for any job evaluation program.

Relative values can be established by a simple *Ranking* method in which the occupational names are arranged in the order of increasing importance according to the opinion(s) of the person(s) doing the evaluation; then allowable index or monetary values, from the lowest to the highest, are distributed rather uniformly over this list. Occupational *Classification* is a variation of the Ranking method, in which the occupations are sorted into several predetermined classifications with corresponding ranges of values.

Point Rating plans are used in most installations. Guided by predetermined definitions and value scales, the committee assigns numerical (point) values to the job for each of at least five job attributes or factors: (1) physical demand or effort; (2) skill; (3) mental requirements; (4) responsibility; and (5) working conditions. In one published plan, these point scales are in terms of cents per hour or dollars per week; but in most plans, obvious relationships between points and money purposely are avoided to reduce the influence of existing wage rates on the opinions of the evaluating committee. Any additional job factors, as used in many plans, merely are subdivisions of the above five.

To insure an over-all consistency, these point values usually are reviewed simply by ranking the occupations under each factor at a time. The final results should be tabulated on a *Summary Sheet* which becomes a master list of evaluated occupations as well as a guide in evaluating new or revised occupations.

The *Wage Survey* of actual base rates then is made on all evaluated jobs within the plant and, if possible, on similar key jobs in other companies. These base rates are plotted on a scatter diagram against corresponding point values and a smooth curve (usually a straight line) is drawn to show the central trend. Similar surveys should be made every six or twelve months to keep the wage structure in line with current economic trends.

The occupational *Rate Ranges* then should be established for each job or labor class. In one method, additional curves are drawn plus and minus 10 per cent (or 15%) from the central curve. In another method, the point scale is divided into ranges or labor grades, and corresponding monetary ranges determined from the survey curve. Each occupation then is assigned to the labor grade within which its point value falls, and at certain time intervals, each worker's base rate may be adjusted within the available range according to the supervisor's merit rating of the worker's performance.

The *Job Specification Sheets* then should be prepared for the employment department and the departmental managers. These are discussed in detail under the section on JOB ANALYSIS.

Although a systematic (point rating) evaluation plan may be used to guide the judgment of the persons making the evaluations, the final values still reflect personal opinions. Job evaluation therefore should be done, not by one person, but rather by a committee of experienced persons who can examine each job objectively. Especially in the larger companies, job evaluation has proved indispensable in establishing sound wage structures. See WAGE.

JOB TRAINING. See MANUAL TRAINING AND INDUSTRIAL EDUCATION; VOCATIONAL EDUCATION.

JOB'S TEARS, a corn plant of India. It is a grass, sometimes rising to the height of eight feet, with the stout habit of maize, to which also it is botanically allied. The name is derived from the tear-like form of the hard, shining, bluish-white seeds, which are sometimes made into bracelets and necklaces, and are also an article of food.

JOCASTA, the mother and wife of Oedipus.

JODELLE, ÉTIENNE, 1532–73, French poet and dramatist, was a member of the PLÉIADE, the literary circle directed by RONSARD. As director of pageants and spectacles at the court of Henry II, he composed a quantity of circumstantial verse, but is best known as the author of *Cléopâtre* (1552), the first French tragedy in a classic vein.

JODHPUR, or **Marwar,** former feudatory state, India, now part of Greater Rajasthan Union, bordering Sind on the W; Jaisalmer and Bikaner on the N; Jaipur, Ajmer Merwara, and Udaipur on the E and

SE; and the small states of Sirohi, Palanpur, and Sabar Kantha on the S; area, 36,120 sq. mi.; pop. (1941) 2,555,904, 86 per cent of whom are Hindus.

Jodhpur is largely a sandy, arid plain, dotted with conical hills, the highest of which reach 3,000 feet. There is little rainfall, and the only important river is the Luni, which overflows its banks in flood, enriching an area in which wheat and barley are produced. The state is served by a railway entering Sind, and connects with another in Ajmer. Besides wheat and barley, important crops are millets and pulses. Marble quarries along the northern and southeastern borders furnish fine stone, and Salt Lake, at Sambhar, and two smaller salt lakes within Jodhpur's borders furnish large quantities of salt. Manufactures include leather boxes, brass utensils, turbans, scarves, and embroidered silk.

Government and History. Jodhpur has a state council of six members, with the maharaja as president; there is a consultative committee representing the Sardars, who make up the majority of the people; and there is a representative advisory assembly of 64 members, of whom 14 are state officials, 41 elected, and 9 nominated. The Jodhpur rulers are the head of the Rathor Rajputs, and claim descent from Rama, the diefied king of Oudh; their ancestry is readily traceable to the fifth century.

Jodhpur was established (1212) after the downfall (1194) of the Rathor dynasty of Kanauj when Sivaji, a grandson of the last king, entered Marwar on a pilgrimage to Dwarka. But the state was not fully established until Rao Chanda, 10th in line of descent from Sivaji, finally conquered Marwar. In 1561 the state was invaded by Akbar, and in 1679 Aurangzeb sacked the larger towns, Aurangzeb demanded that the Rathors embrace Mohammedanism. Resentment against this edict cemented relations among the ruling houses of Udaipur, Jodhpur, and Jaipur to an effort to throw off the Mohammedan yoke. The three states reached an agreement that princes of Jodhpur and Jaipur should marry the princesses of Udaipur, and that the offspring of the Udaipur princesses should succeed to the states in preference to other children. This agreement provided fuel for so much weakening dispute that the Rajput states came under the domination of the Mahrattas. Jodhpur came under British protection in 1818, and during the Mutiny of 1857 rebelled.   C. S.

JODHPUR, city, India, capital of the former feudatory state of Jodhpur. Founded in 1459 by Rao Jodha, the city is situated about 100 miles W of Ajmer. The town is circled by a strong wall, which has a number of fine gates. A fortress, situated on an elevated rock, contains the maharaja's palace. Jodhpur has a number of palaces belonging to the state's nobles, and several fine temples. Jaswant College, situated here, is affiliated with Allahabad University. Jodhpur is a rail junction and a trading center. Pop. (1941) 126,842.

Jodhpur women carry water containers on heads

JODL, ALFRED GUSTAV, 1892?–1946, German chief of staff, served with the Bavarian army during World War I and later with the German ministry of war and intelligence service. He became Hitler's chief military adviser (1942) and his chief of staff. In this capacity he approved all Nazi war orders including that of mass civilian execution. Jodl led the German delegation which signed Germany's surrender at Reims, France (1945). The International Military Tribunal judged him in a military sense the actual planner of the war and condemned and hanged him. See GERMANY, History, for illustration.

JOE-PYE WEED. See EUPATORIUM.

JOEL, whose book is the second of the Minor Prophets, was the son of Pethuel (Bethuel). Nothing is known of his personality, but it is commonly accepted that he belonged to Judah; his thoughts center around Jerusalem. The date is much canvassed; the traditional view was that Joel lived in the days of Joash, and accordingly must have been one of the first "literary" prophets; but recent scholarship, arguing from the absence from the book of any reference to Assyria, to Israel (the northern kingdom), or to a king, combined with the mention of priests and fasts, tends to assign a post-Exilic date. The style is pure and clear, but lacks the creative originality of Hosea or Amos.

JOFFRE, JOSEPH JACQUES CÉSAIRE, 1852–1931, French military leader and marshal, during and after World War I called "the victor of the Marne," and "the savior of France." He was born in Rivesaltes, educated at the College of Perpignan, and entered the École Polytechnique. During the Franco-Prussian War (1870–71), he joined the army as a second lieutenant and participated in the defense of Paris. After the war he completed his studies at the Polytechnique and was promoted to lieutenant (1872) and captain (1876). His long career as an army engineer in the French colonies included participation in the defense of Pontarlier (1874), the occupation of Formosa (1885), a distinguished role in the occupation of Timbuktu, and service in the Madagascar campaign (1897). After a professorship at the War School, he was promoted general of brigade (1900) and general of division (1905). In 1911 he became commander in chief of the French forces and was chief of the General Staff when World War I began in 1914. He was placed in command of both French and British forces on the western front. Historians and strategists differ in their appraisal of Joffre's military genius and his handling of vast responsibilities. Although he must share honors with General Galliéni (the military governor of Paris who directed the troops rushed to the front in commandeered taxicabs in Sept., 1914), his generalship checked Von Kluck's armies and pushed them back to the Aisne. (See MARNE, BATTLES OF THE.) Joffre was popular with the troops from whom he exacted every sacrifice, but his efforts to wear down the enemy with annihilating blows were unsuccessful. Although he kept his title of commander in chief, he was replaced in the field by General Nivelle in 1917, and was appointed advisor to the general staff of the war office. In the spring of 1917 as a member of a French commission he toured the United States where he was hailed as a hero and a symbol of victory. He wrote *My March to Timbuctoo* (1915) and *Personal Memoirs of Joffre, Field Marshal of the French Army* (2 vols. 1932). See WORLD WAR I, 1914.   W. P. S.

BIBLIOG.—C. Dawbarn, *Joffre and His Army* (1916); G. Hanotaux and J. G. A. Fabry, *Joffre* (1921); R. Recouly, *Joffre* (1931).

JOGJAKARTA, or **Jokyarta,** also **Djokjarta,** or **Jokjarta** (the name is usually shortened to *Jokya*), city in Central Java, lying 20 miles inland at the foot of Mount Merapi, 260 miles SE of Batavia on the Batavia-Surabaya railroad. It is linked by rail to Semarang via Magelang. Jogjakarta was the residence of the Dutch governor and of the two native nominal rulers. The old Dutch town and fort are separate from Jogjakarta proper. The points of interest within the city are the sultan's palace in the "kraton," a citadel a mile square in the center of the city, and the native market; outside the city lie the ruins of the Tamansarie or water gardens, which a Portuguese designed around 1750 for Sultan Mangku Bumi, and the Hindu ruins of Borobudur (Boroboedoer). Jogjakarta is the center of a small batik industry. Japan occupied the town and government in March, 1942. Following the Japanese evacuation the town became the temporary capital of the Indonesian Republic and the headquarters of President Soekarno. Pop. (1930) 136,649. ADRIAN TROY

JOGUES, ISAAC, 1607–46, was born in Orléans, France. A Jesuit and ordained priest, he was sent to North America (1636) as missionary to the Hurons. In 1642 he, with some Hurons, fell into a Mohawk ambush and was taken prisoner and tortured. Efforts made to ransom him were fruitless, but in 1643, through the help of Dutch settlers, he escaped. After a stay in Europe he returned to Canada, where he was of assistance in concluding peace between the French and Mohawks (1646). Hearing that peace was likely to be broken, he set out for the Mohawk country, and was again made prisoner, near the present Auriesville, N.Y. He wrote a *Journal* of his captivity and also a *Description of New Netherlands in 1642.* He was canonized in 1930.

JOHANNESBURG, largest city of the Union of South Africa, Transvaal Province, mining center of the Transvaal gold fields; 30 miles SW of Pretoria. It is situated at an altitude of 5,735 feet, and is connected by rail with Pretoria, Delagoa Bay, Port Elizabeth, and Capetown. The city is modern and progressive, with broad streets, and contains many handsome government and other buildings. The University of Witwatersrand (founded 1921) with a faculty of 324 and a student body of 2,650, is located here; and there are an art gallery, a library, and an observatory. The fortress erected by the Boer government is now dismantled. Near the suburb of Krugersdorp stands the National Boer Monument, erected to commemorate the declaration of independence of 1880. In 1886 the site of Johannesburg was bare, open veldt; but in that year the Transvaal government proclaimed certain farms on the famous Reef of Witwatersrand as public gold fields, and the ground was selected as the site of the new town. A dynamite explosion wrecked part of the town in 1896. During the SOUTH AFRICAN WAR, on May 29, 1900, it was occupied by the British under Lord Roberts. Pop. (1946) 322,268 Europeans, and about the same number of natives, chiefly workers in the mines.

JOHANNISBERG, village, Germany, in the Prussian province of Hesse-Nassau, at the southern slope of the Taunus, on the right bank of the Rhine River, three miles NE of Rüdesheim. The vineyards from which the famous Johannisberger wine is de-

rived surround the Johannisberg Castle (1757–59), situated on a hill overlooking the Rhine. It was presented in 1807 to Marshal Kellermann by Napoleon I, and in 1814 by the Austrian emperor, Francis I, to Prince von Metternich. Pop. about 1,400. See RHINE OR RHENISH WINES.

JOHN, SAINT, one of the Twelve Apostles of Christ, was born probably in Bethsaida of Galilee. He and his brother James, also an apostle, were the sons of Zebedee and Salome. It was while pursuing his occupation as a fisherman on the bank of the Lake of Galilee that he was attracted to follow Christ. Probably because of their impetuosity, of which instances are recorded in New Testament writings, the brothers were given the name of "Sons of Thunder" by their leader. John apparently overcame his excessive impatience. To him was assigned the title "the disciple whom Jesus loved." Also to him was given the place of distinction at the Last Supper; and it was John to whom Christ committed the care of his own mother at the time of the crucifixion. The Epistles and the Gospel which bear his name have been attributed to him by many, and general tradition has identified him as the author of the Apocalypse. After the death of Christ, John seems to have remained in Jerusalem where he still lived when Paul visited that city for the second time after his conversion (Gal. 2:9). The subsequent history of John is involved in obscurity. Tradition has always assigned him the death of a martyr. See JAMES, THE GREATER, SAINT.

The Epistles of Saint John, three letters among the New Testament writings, traditionally have been attributed to the Apostle John. The identity of thought and method of expression in the first of these writings, when compared with the Fourth Gospel, is thought by most critics to be sufficient in establishing the author of both works as the same writer. This letter was written to the Christians of Asia Minor to strengthen their belief against the preaching of heretics. The Second Epistle is addressed "to the Elect Lady and to her children," a phrase of obscure meaning thought to refer to an individual or to the whole church. A letter of exhortation, it stresses charity for the neighbor. Sent to a certain Gaius, the Third Epistle is a request for hospitality on behalf of those teaching the word of Christ. The last two epistles are the shortest writings in the New Testament. Not as well authenticated as the First, similarities of expression in the Second and Third Epistles lead to ascribing all three writings to the same author.

The Gospel According to Saint John. See BIBLE; GOSPEL; GOSPELS, HARMONY OF THE; JESUS CHRIST; NEW TESTAMENT. R. T.

JOHN I, SAINT, d. 526, pope, was born in Tuscany, Italy. His accession to the throne in 523 had been preceded by a reunion between the Eastern and Western churches. Theodoric, king of the Ostrogoths and of Italy, provoked by that peace, became infuriated when news reached him that the Byzantine emperor, Justin, was persecuting the followers of ARIANISM in his domain. An Arian himself, Theodoric demanded that John intercede for the Arians in the East. The first of the popes ever to travel to Constantinople, John received a tremendous welcome there, where he sought clemency for the Arians. Theodoric's infuriation grew when he learned of the obeisance paid to the pope, and when John returned to Rome he was imprisoned by the emperor. The pope died during this incarceration.

JOHN. See POPE.

JOHN VIII, d. 882, pope, was born in Rome, Italy. The first pope to meet death by the violence of assassination, his entire pontificate, which began in 872, was surrounded with bloodshed. Believing that Louis the German would be capable of quelling the disorders in Italy, the pope sided with him over the claims of Charles the Bald for the title of emperor.

Johannesburg, the "Golden City"

John held the coronation of Louis in Rome on the Christmas of 875. Louis failed to send his armies to support the pope, and the Italian disorders only multiplied under the violence of Charles' soldiers. The return of the Saracens added to the turmoil, and the pope's efforts to obtain peace were ignored. A courageous and fearless man, John himself became a military and naval leader, eventually repelling the Saracens. Lambert, the duke of Spoleto, invaded Rome, took the pope prisoner, and sought papal backing for Carloman of Bavaria. John escaped to France and crowned Louis the Stammerer as king of that country in order to gain his assistance. When help was not accorded him, John had no other choice but to accept Carloman as emperor. Uprisings in Rome, promoted by a faction of aristocrats, caused the pope to oust their leader, FORMOSUS, who was later to become pope himself. Violence followed John to his grave, when his enemies poisoned him and, before death came to him in that fashion, broke his skull with a sledge.   R. M. LEONARD

JOHN XII, c. 937–964, pope, was born in Rome. His father, Alberic II of Italy, secured the promises of influential friends, before his own death, that his son would be elected the next pope. Under these circumstances John XII came to the papal throne in 955, at the approximate age of 17. The youth's profligacy ushered in a pontificate of wild orgies and shameful simonies. In order to protect himself from the invasion of the king of Italy, Berengarius, John asked for help from OTTO I, king of Germany, and one of Alberic's former enemies. The pope crowned him emperor, but when Otto's power grew too great, the treacherous John secretly negotiated with Adalbert, the son of Berengarius. The discovery of this led to Otto's march on Rome and John was forced to flee. A council of German and Italian bishops was convened to examine the evidences of the pope's numerous crimes, and this resulted in John being summoned to defend himself. The pope retaliated with a message threatening to excommunicate the council members if they elected another pope. Uncanonically, they chose another ruler, but the people of Rome, zealous for traditions, demanded the return of the rightful pope. John was restored and relentlessly punished his antagonists. Debauchery once again returned to the papacy and continued until the end of John's reign.   R. M. LEONARD

JOHN XV, or **XVI,** d. 996, pope, was born in Rome. Because some of the papal catalogues listed a John (John XV) as the successor to the antipope Boniface VII, the numeration of popes who have assumed the name of John has been thrown into confusion. Such a pope John never existed, however, and rightfully the papal ruler from 985 to 996 is John XV, although by reason of this error in listings he is sometimes referred to as John XVI. Under his reign the first solemn canonization of a saint was held, which had previously been performed by bishops or synods, in 993. The person thus solemnly declared was Bishop Ulrich of Augsburg.

JOHN XXII, 1249–1334, pope, was born in Cahors, France. One of the most tireless popes of the Avignon papacy, during his 18 years of rule, which began in 1316, he issued some 60,000 papal documents. Believing sincerely that the papal throne should be kept at Avignon, John created 23 French cardinals in order to insure it. In spite of the fact that the citizens of Rome fought for the return of the tiara to their city, they were quick to react when the excommunicated and notorious Sciarra Colonna "elected" an Italian as pope. With great violence they forced "Nicholas V" to flee the city. Louis of Bavaria, seeking the Imperial title, enlisted the services of this Colonna, and together they called a "General Council" for the purpose of deposing the pope. They were aided in their plans by a group of heretical Franciscans who sought a return of Christendom to the austerities of early Christians. Relation-

ship between church and state provoked numerous controversies during John's reign and accusations of heresy were directed from every quarter against various persons. The pope himself was not to escape such accusations when, in a sermon, he stated that the Beatific Vision was attained at the time of death and lasted until the Last Judgment. Although he declared this to be merely a private opinion and not a dogmatic definition, cries of heresy brought such reverberations that the pope had to make a public profession of belief that all the saints in heaven see God "face to face." A small crusade was organized under John and accomplished a few minor victories over the Turks.   R. M. LEONARD

JOHN, 1167?–1216, king of England, born probably in Oxford, was the youngest son of HENRY II, and ascended the throne in 1199. In 1189 he joined Philip of France in a coalition against his father. During RICHARD I's absence in the Holy Land he

 attempted to secure the crown; and when Richard was in captivity, he allied himself with Richard's enemy, Philip of France. In 1203 John put to death Arthur, the son of his brother Geoffrey; and the death of John's able mother, Eleanor of Aquitaine, in 1204 was the signal for the conquest of Normandy, Anjou, Maine, and Touraine by the French king. In 1205 a struggle began between the papacy and the English king over the election

King John

to the archbishopric of Canterbury. The pope, INNOCENT III, put aside John's candidate, and consecrated STEPHEN LANGTON (1208). On the refusal of John to receive Langton, Innocent laid England under an interdict, and in 1212 excommunicated the English king. John then yielded, and agreed to hold his kingdom as a fief of the papacy. But the English barons and clergy now determined to resist John's tyranny, and the defeat of his forces at Bouvines, on July 27, 1214, by Philip, and his own failure to hold Poitou, encouraged the English barons. On June 15, 1215, John was compelled to sign the MAGNA CHARTA, but he had no intention of keeping his promises, and civil war soon broke out. The barons were aided by the French prince Louis, to whom they offered the English crown. In the struggle Hubert de Burgh successfully defended Dover for John, who, however, died suddenly at Newark. See ENGLAND, History; MEANING OF THE MAGNA CHARTA (Back End Papers, Vol. 6); PHILIP II.

JOHN II, called **the Good,** 1319–64, king of France in 1350. Being hard pressed by the king of Navarre and the English, and accused of maladministration of the finances, he surrendered the management of them to the States-General. Defeated at Poitiers (1356), he was taken prisoner to England, but returned after the treaty of Bretigny (1360). But the Duke of Anjou, whom he left as hostage, having fled, John thought it his duty to go back to England, where he finished his days. See FEUDAL SOCIETY for illustration.

JOHN III, SOBIESKI, 1624–96, king of Poland, was born in Olesko in Galicia. By his brilliant victories over the Swedes, Tartars, Turks (at Chotin in 1673), and Cossacks he gained for himself the throne of Poland (1674). Europe owes to him the relief of Vienna (1683), when it was besieged for the last time by the Turks. He was a man of culture, fond of books and of scientific research. See POLAND, History.

JOHN I, called **the Great,** 1357–1433, king of Portugal, was born in Lisbon, the natural son of Pedro I. Grandmaster of the Knights of Aviz from 1364, he drove the regent from the throne in 1384, and after successfully defending Lisbon against

John of Castile, who claimed the succession, was unanimously elected king of Portugal at Coimbra in 1385. His title to the throne was reinforced by a great victory at Aljubarrota over the Castilians, in the same year. During John's reign, permanent alliance was made with England (1386), when he married Philippa of Lancaster, daughter of John of Gaunt; Castile was pacified (1411), and Ceuta taken from the Moors (1415). John was succeeded by his son Edward; another of his sons was Prince HENRY THE NAVIGATOR.

JOHN II, called **the Perfect,** 1455–95, king of Portugal, was born in Lisbon, the son of Alfonso V. Succeeding to the throne in 1481, he immediately began to centralize royal power by decreasing the power and property of the feudal nobility. He crushed a revolt headed by the Duke of Braganza in 1483, executing the ringleaders. During his reign the Treaty of Tordesillas was signed with Castile, settling the disputes of both kingdoms to New World colonies (1494); Portuguese navigation flourished; DIOGO CAM and BARTHOLOMEW DIAZ made their discoveries.

JOHN III, 1502–57, king of Portugal, was born in Lisbon, the son of Emmanuel I, whom he succeeded in 1521. During his reign Portugal's title to Brazil was confirmed (1524); the Inquisition was begun in Portugal (1536), and the Jesuit order was introduced.

JOHN IV, called **the Fortunate,** 1603–56, king of Portugal, born in Villaviciosa, became duke of Braganza in 1630. He became the first Braganza ruler of Portugal in 1640, when a coup d'état made Portugal independent of Spain. Alliances with England and France made possible the victory over Spain at Montijo (1644), which strengthened Portugal's freedom. Also during John's reign the Portuguese of Brazil became independent of Holland (1654).

JOHN V, 1689–1750, king of Portugal, was born in Lisbon, and succeeded his father, Pedro II, in 1706. He maintained the English alliance in the War of the Spanish Succession, but was decisively defeated by the Spanish at Almanza in 1707, and made peace with them in 1715. John held an elaborate court at the Mafra palace, which he built. He was a zealous church supporter, and was called "Most Faithful King" in a papal bull issued in 1748.

JOHN VI, 1769–1826, king of Portugal, was born in Lisbon, the son of Pedro III and Maria I. He began to rule in 1792, when his mother became insane, and was officially regent from 1799. He supported Britain during the Napoleonic Wars until 1801, when he submitted to Napoleon by the Treaty of Badajoz. In 1807 the French invaded Portugal, and John moved his government to Rio de Janeiro. He became king in 1816, on his mother's death, and returned to Portugal in 1821. He accepted a liberal Portuguese constitution in 1822 but altered it in favor of absolutism the next year.

JOHN, AUGUSTUS EDWIN, 1879–   , English painter and etcher, was born in Tenby, Wales. He studied art at the Slade School, London, and later worked in Paris, where he was greatly influenced by the postimpressionists. At the age of 20 he began to exhibit at the New English Art Club; in 1908 he held his first one-man show, at the Chenil Gallery, Chelsea, evincing an extremely individualistic personality, and tendencies toward brilliant coloring and distortion for the sake of emphasis. After 1901 a major portion of his work was done in the medium of etching, one of the more important of these being the portrait of W. B. Yeats. In his oils he won especial renown for such gypsy scenes as "The Mumpers" and for such portraits as "The Smiling Woman," Thomas Hardy, G. B. Shaw, Lloyd George, and the portrait series of 1919 Peace Conference members. In 1928 he was elected a Royal Academician; he resigned in 1938, but was re-elected in 1940.

JOHN B. STETSON UNIVERSITY. See COLLEGES.

JOHN BROWN UNIVERSITY. See COLLEGES.

JOHN BROWN'S BODY, the title of a song popular in the Northern states during the Civil War, sung as a verse to "The Battle Hymn of the Republic" by Julia Ward Howe. It was based on the story of JOHN BROWN, American abolitionist.

JOHN CARROLL UNIVERSITY. See COLLEGES.

JOHN CRERAR LIBRARY. See CRERAR LIBRARY.

JOHN DAY RIVER, NE Oregon, rises in several branches in the Blue Mountains and flows W and N for about 250 miles to join the Columbia River at the Canadian border. The river was named in honor of John Day of Virginia who was a scout with the Astor overland expedition in 1811.

JOHN DORY. See DORY.

JOHN HENRY, American Negro folk hero, symbolizes the sacred relation between man and his work and represents the last stand of mankind against the machine. Though his feats have become legendary and many of them are undoubtedly apocryphal, John Henry was an actual historical figure, unlike PAUL BUNYAN, JOE MAGARAC, and PECOS BILL.

John Henry was a steel-drivin' man—the greatest one among epic hammer men. He helped dig the Big Bend Tunnel on the Chesapeake & Ohio Railroad, in West Virginia. It has been said of John Henry that "he used to keep six men runnin' just to carry his drills back and forth from the man that sharpened 'em."

He drove steel so magnificently that one day he was pitted against a steam drill. He used a twenty pound hammer, according to legend, and drilled two holes, even seven feet, making 14 feet in all. The steam drill made one hole nine feet deep. John Henry dropped dead when he had won the contest. This happened in 1870. That is the true legend of John Henry. Those who give accounts of his working in the cotton fields and on Mississippi River packets distort the story.   JULIAN LEE RAYFORD

BIBLIOG.–G. B. Johnson, *John Henry: Tracking Down a Negro Legend* (1929); Roark Bradford, *John Henry* (1931); L. W. Chappel, *John Henry: A Folk Lore Study* (1933).

JOHN MAURICE OF NASSAU, 1604–79, Dutch field marshal and governor, was born in Dillenburg. After service in the Thirty Year's War, he went to Brazil for the Dutch West India Company as governor general of their holdings. A successful administrator (1637–44), he forced the Portuguese back, built forts, gained the confidence of the natives and the support of the colonists. Returning to the Netherlands, he was active in the campaigns of 1645–46, and became governor of Cleves, Mark, and Ravensburg (1647). He was made a prince of the German empire (1652), commander in chief of the land forces of the Netherlands (1665), field marshal (1671), and served in the Dutch war against Louis XIV (1674).

JOHN OF AUSTRIA, DON, 1546–78, Spanish general, natural son of the Emperor Charles V, was born in Ratisbon, and passed as the son of a Spanish nobleman named Quijada. Appointed when only 22 by Philip II, commander of the forces against the rebel Moors of Granada, he triumphantly subdued them. As generalissimo of the combined fleets of Spain and Italy he gained a great naval victory over the Turkish fleet in the Gulf of LEPANTO (1571). After the refusal by Philip to allow him to accept the proffered sovereignty of Albania and Macedonia, he commanded an expedition against the Moors in Africa, and took Tunis and Bizerta. In 1576 he became governor of the Netherlands, which were then in a state of rebellion. After taking Namur, Louvain, Nivelle, and other towns belonging to the insurgents, he died, it is said, from the effects of poison.

JOHN OF BOHEMIA, 1296–1346, the blind king, was son of the Emperor Henry VII, and became king of Bohemia through his marriage with the heiress to the throne. There was a fierce contest between the houses of Austria and Bavaria for the Bohemian empire, and John achieved the victory for Bavaria in 1322 at Mühldorf. He became an ally of the French king in the war against England, and was slain at Crécy. See BOHEMIA.

JOHN OF BRIENNE, 1148–1237, king of Jerusalem and emperor of the Latin empire of Constantinople. As king of Jerusalem (1210–25), he took part in the Fifth Crusade, led by Andrew, king of Hungary, and besieged Damietta which capitulated in 1219. In 1225 he married his daughter Yolanda to the German emperor Frederick II. Frederick then claimed John's throne, but John, refusing to give up his throne, led the papal forces in the quarrel between Pope Gregory IX and Frederick and was defeated. In 1229 the barons of Constantinople elected him emperor during the minority of Baldwin II. In this capacity he defeated the united forces of the Greeks and Bulgarians. See CRUSADES.

JOHN OF DAMASCUS, SAINT, 676–770, last of the Greek church fathers, was born in Damascus, Syria. Though his father was a Christian, he held a high official position among the Saracens; John himself became chief councilor when his father died. Privately tutored by a monk named Cosmas, John was later ordained priest by the patriarch of Jerusalem, John V. His writings on theology were not original, but he is considered the first theological encyclopedist, and his work strongly defended the doctrine regarding image worship. John organized the complete doctrine of the Greek fathers and the councils of the church in his chief work, *The Fountain of Knowledge.* His feast is celebrated on March 27.

R. M. LEONARD

JOHN OF GAUNT, DUKE OF LANCASTER, 1340–99, fourth son of EDWARD III, was born in Ghent. He married Blanche (d. 1369) the heiress of the duchy of Lancaster, in 1359, and was himself created duke of Lancaster in 1362. After the close of the Black Prince's expedition to help Pedro the Cruel of Castile, John married Constance, daughter of Pedro, and in 1372 assumed the title of king of Castile, but in 1387 resigned all claims in favor of his daughter, Catherine. His defense of Wycliffe, the religious reformer, made him famous. He exercised great influence in England but failed to win the confidence of the House of Commons. After 1389 his influence was used to promote peace between RICHARD II and the nobles. In 1394 his wife Constance died, and in 1396 he married Catherine Swynford, by whom he had already three sons and one daughter, known as the Beauforts. These children were legitimatized by Richard II, and in the following century figured prominently in English affairs. His eldest son, Henry Bolingbroke, became king as HENRY IV. See ROSES, WARS OF THE.

JOHN OF LANCASTER, DUKE OF BEDFORD, 1389–1435, third son of HENRY IV, king of England. He was created duke of Bedford (1414) by his brother, HENRY V, after whose death (1422) he became regent of England. In the struggle for the French crown after the death of Charles VI, he commanded the English army in France and in 1422 proclaimed HENRY VI, a child of nine months, king of France. He defeated the French at Verneuil (1424) but the rise of JOAN OF ARC (1429), and the desertions of the dukes of Brittany and Burgundy ended his success.

JOHN OF LEIDEN, properly **Johann Bueckelszoon,** or **Bockhold,** 1510–36, a notorious fanatic, was born in Leiden. Having joined the Anabaptists, he established himself in the city of Münster, where he set up a peculiar commonwealth in preparation for the new Zion which he prophesied as about to come. After committing gross excesses and cruelties for two years, he was captured by the bishop of the city, and with his followers put to death. See ANABAPTISTS.

JOHN OF NEPOMUK, SAINT, c. 1340–93, Bohemian Christian martyr, was born in Nepomuk. He is the subject of the famous legend concerning his martyrdom. When John was elected the vicar general of Bohemia, he was also the Bohemian queen's confessor. When he refused King Wenceslaus' demand to relate what the queen had told him in confession, the king became so enraged that he had John tortured and drowned in the Moldau River. John was canonized in 1729, became the patron saint of Bohemia and of confessors, and his feast day is kept on May 16.

JOHN OF SALISBURY, c. 1115–80, English scholar, taught for a time in Paris, apparently returning to England about 1147. He acted as secretary successively to Archbishop Theobald and THOMAS A BECKET, accompanied the latter on his virtual exile in France, and witnessed his assassination (1170). In 1176 he became bishop of Chartres. In his *Polycraticus* he sets forth his views on contemporary life, and in his *Metalogicus* deals with contemporary education and thought.

JOHN OF THE CROSS, SAINT. See CRUZ, SAN JUAN DE LA.

JOHN THE BAPTIST, the forerunner of JESUS CHRIST, was the son of Zacharias, a priest, and Elisabeth, a near relative of Mary, the mother of Jesus. The date of his birth is uncertain, but it probably took place in Hebron, about six months before the birth of Christ. Little is told of the Baptist's early life, save that from the time of his birth he was a Nazarite (Luke 3:2, 7:33) and lived in the desert; but his "shewing unto Israel" (Luke 1:80) was the beginning of a short ministry of amazing energy and power, the whole land being shaken by his demand of repentance, his proclamation of the kingdom of God, and his rite of baptism. He baptized Jesus, but asserted, both on that occasion and later, his own inferiority and the preparatory character of his work. Jesus' testimony to his greatness, John's arraignment of Herod, and his consequent imprisonment and execution (Matt. 14), are known to all.

JOHNS HOPKINS UNIVERSITY. Incorporated in 1867, Johns Hopkins University was founded as the result of a bequest by JOHNS HOPKINS, a Baltimore merchant, who left the bulk of his estate for the establishment of a university and a hospital. Instruction in liberal arts began in 1876 both on the undergraduate and higher level. The university has two campus groups: Homewood, occupied in 1916, and that centering about the Johns Hopkins Hospital. Both locations are in the city of BALTIMORE, Maryland. The Medical School, established in 1893, and the School of Hygiene and Public Health (1918) are located near the hospital. The Johns Hopkins Hospital School of Nursing has been in existence since 1889, although it is not a formal part of the university.

The Homewood group includes the College of Arts and Sciences, the Graduate School of Engineering and the School of Business (1922). These three divisions are open only to men. The rest of the university is coeducational. The School of Higher Studies of the Faculty of Philosophy administers work leading to the advanced degrees. The College for Teachers dates from 1924. In 1951 plans were announced for ending the graduate-undergraduate student distinction in order to grant speedier degrees.

JOHNSON, ALLEN, 1870–1931, American teacher, historian, and biographer, was born in Lowell, Mass., and graduated from Amherst College. After further study in the United States and Europe, he was professor of history at Iowa (now Grinnell) College (1898–1905), Bowdoin College (1905–10), and Yale University (1910–26). He edited *The Chronicles of America* (50 vols. 1918–21) at Yale, and became editor (1926) of the *Dictionary of American Biography*, six volumes of which were published before his death. He was the author of *Stephen A. Douglas: A Study in American Politics* (1908); *Readings in American Constitutional History* (1912); *Jefferson and His Colleagues* (1921); *The Historian and Historical Evidence* (1926); with W. A. Robinson, *Readings in Recent American Constitutional History, 1876–1926* (1927).

☆ ☆ ☆ ☆ ☆ ☆ ☆ ☆ ☆   ☆ ☆

ANDREW JOHNSON
17th President of the United States
1865—1869

MESERVE COLLECTION

JOHNSON, ANDREW, 1808–75, 17th president of the United States, was born in Raleigh, N.C., on Dec. 29, 1808. His father died when Andrew was four years old, and at the age of ten the boy was apprenticed to a tailor. He had received no schooling but managed in his spare hours to learn to read. About 1825 he became a journeyman tailor, and in 1826 married Eliza McCardle, who taught him to write and figure.

Johnson's political career began in 1828 with his election, by a workingmen's party, as alderman of Greenville, Tenn.; he was then mayor (1830–3), and a member of the Tennessee House of Representatives (1835–9) and Senate (1841). From 1843 to 1853 he was a Democratic representative in Congress, and from 1853 to 1857 governor of Tennessee. In 1857 he became a member of the U.S. Senate.

Though a States' Rights Democrat in politics, Johnson joined Brownlow and others in ardent support of the Union on the approach of the Civil War. From 1862 to 1864 he was the military governor of Tennessee, a position of extreme difficulty, the duties of which he discharged with such efficiency and courage that he attracted the attention of the whole North. In 1864, though still essentially a Democrat, he was nominated for the vice-presidency, on the ticket with Lincoln, by the Republicans, who wished thus to recognize the Unionist element in the South.

Johnson's succession to the presidency (1865), upon the assassination of President Lincoln, was regarded with considerable misgiving. Within two weeks of his inauguration the Civil War was virtually brought to a close by the surrender of the Confederate General Johnston (April 26, 1865). Upon the president, in conjunction with Congress, devolved the reconstruction of the Southern states. At first Johnson's attitude toward the South and the late leaders of the Confederacy was intensely bitter—"traitors must be punished and impoverished," he said. Within less than two years, however, this attitude was completely changed, becoming one of tolerance, leniency, and conciliation. Johnson's policy was now substantially what Lincoln's had been, but he was without Lincoln's shrewdness and consummate tact. Moreover, he was a Southern Democrat among Northern Republicans, and inevitably came into conflict with Congress, which contended that reconstruction belonged properly to the legislative branch of government. Bill after bill passed by Congress was vetoed by the president, often in messages of great power and of remarkable cogency of reasoning, but his veto was usually overridden. The president further weakened his position both in Congress and in the country at large by a speech-making tour (1866), in which he cast discretion to the winds, bitterly attacking his political opponents, frequently by name. Eventually he was impeached, chiefly for having disregarded the TENURE OF OFFICE ACT, passed primarily to compel his retention of Secretary of War Stanton in the cabinet. After a sensational trial before the Senate, he was acquitted (May 26, 1868), the vote of 36 to 19 for conviction failing by one, of the requisite two-thirds.

After the expiration of his term of office, Johnson was defeated as a candidate in turn for U.S. senator and for representative in Congress, but was elected to the Senate in 1875. He died on July 31, 1875.

Though opinionated, stubborn, and lacking in personal magnetism, Johnson was a man of the strictest integrity, and of considerable ability, and sincerely and earnestly wished to serve the best interests of his country. The position taken by him in his contest with Congress has been defended by leading scholars and authorities on the Constitution.

For the events of Johnson's administration and for his portrait, see UNITED STATES HISTORY. See also ANDREW JOHNSON NATIONAL MONUMENT; IMPEACHMENT; RECONSTRUCTION.   H. L. H.

BIBLIOG.–G. E. B. Clemenceau, American Reconstruction, 1865–1870, and the Impeachment of President Johnson (1928); R. W. Winston, Andrew Johnson, Plebeian and Patriot (1928); H. K. Beale, Critical Year (1930); G. F. Milton, Age of Hate (1930); L. P. Stryker, Andrew Johnson (1936).

JOHNSON, BYRON BANCROFT, known as Ban, 1864–1931, American baseball executive, member of Baseball Hall of Fame, was born in Norwalk, Conn. He founded the American league in 1900, led it for 27 years, and inaugurated the World's Series between the National and American league champions.

JOHNSON, CAVE, 1793–1866, American political leader, was born near Springfield, Tenn., studied at Cumberland College, and practiced law in Tennessee. A Democrat, he was representative in Congress (1829–37, 1839–45). As postmaster general (1845–49) under Polk, he introduced the use of postage stamps and worked for the systematizing of the mails. He served as a circuit judge in Tennessee (1853) and kept his interest in politics, being influential in causing his state to support Buchanan in 1856.

JOHNSON, CHARLES SPURGEON, 1893– , American Negro educator, was born in Bristol, Va., and received his doctor's degree at the University of Chicago. He joined the faculty of Fisk University in 1928, and assumed its presidency in 1946. He was a member of the executive committee of UNESCO. His writings include: The Negro in American Civilization (1930), The Negro College Graduate (1936), To Stem the Tide (1943), and Into the Main Stream (1946).

JOHNSON, EASTMAN, 1824–1906, American artist, was born in Lovell, Me. He studied in Düsseldorf's Royal Academy, and in Holland, France, and Italy. Both his portraits of famous persons and his genre paintings brought him success.

It happened when
Andrew Johnson
was president . . .

UNION PACIFIC RAILROAD

Construction Crews rushed work on the Union and Central Pacific railroads to link the coasts by rail

U.S. Mail Service utilized stagecoaches to speed delivery of mail to points not reached by railroad

LESLIE'S ILLUSTRATED NEWSPAPER

Armies of the United States took part in the Grand Review at Washington in 1865. A Brady photo

METROPOLITAN MUSEUM OF ART

Transatlantic Telegraph achieved continuous transmission in 1866. The first message from England over newly laid cable had been received in 1858

HARPER'S WEEKLY

Ku Klux Klan became active during the reconstruction era

Alaska, which became a treasure land and sports-man's paradise, was acquired from Russia by treaty

U.S. FOREST SERVICE

U.S. Senate, as a court of impeachment for trial of Johnson in 1868, acquitted him by one-vote margin

F. J. MEINE--HARPER'S WEEKLY

JOHNSON, GUY, c. 1740–88, American colonial leader and Loyalist, son-in-law of Sir WILLIAM JOHNSON, was born in Ireland and came to America at an early age. He succeeded Sir William as superintendent of Indian affairs (1774–82). After the Revolution broke out, Johnson went to Montreal, organized the Indians, and helped to defend St. John's. In 1776 he attempted to promote co-operation between the British and the Indians on the New York frontier and in 1779 fought with the British and Indians at the battle near Newtown, N.Y. He then aroused the Indians to raid colonial settlements in the vicinity of Niagara (1779–81). At the close of the Revolution he went to England.

JOHNSON, HERSCHEL VESPASIAN, 1812–80, American lawyer and legislator, was born in Burke County, Ga. He was graduated from the University of Georgia in 1834, and became one of the most prominent lawyers of the state. He was a member of the U.S. Senate (1848–49); governor of Georgia (1853–57), and a candidate for the vice-presidency on the ticket with Stephen A. Douglas in 1860. He subsequently served in the Confederate Senate.

JOHNSON, HIRAM WARREN, 1866–1945, American political leader, was born in Sacramento, Calif. He studied at the University of California and in his father's law office, was admitted to the bar in 1888, and came into public notice as prosecuting attorney in the San Francisco graft investigations (1906–8). He served as governor of California (1911–17) and U.S. senator from California (1917–45). Johnson was a founder of the PROGRESSIVE PARTY in 1912, but returned to the Republican fold. He supported Franklin D. Roosevelt in 1932, later becoming a severe critic of the New Deal. During both World Wars Johnson was an isolationist, and opposed both the League of Nations and the United Nations.

JOHNSON, HUGH SAMUEL, 1882–1942, U.S. Army officer and lawyer, was born in Fort Scott, Kansas. After graduation from West Point, he served at posts in the United States and Philippines; during this period, he wrote two popular books for boys. He took part in the Mexican Border Expedition (1916) and in World War I originated the plans for the selective draft, formulated its rules and policies, and supervised their execution. He also served as representative of the Army General Staff on the War Industries Board. He resigned from the service in 1919 to enter private business. As NRA administrator (1933–34), Johnson became a figure of national importance.

JOHNSON, JAMES WELDON, 1871–1938, American Negro author, was born in Jacksonville, Fla., and educated at Atlanta and Columbia universities. From 1906 to 1912 he served as American consul in Puerto Cabello, Venezuela, and Corinto, Nicaragua. In 1916 he became secretary of the National Association for the Advancement of Colored People, which post he retained until 1930, when he became professor of creative literature at Fisk University. His most notable books include two volumes of poems, *Fifty Years, and Other Poems* (1917) and *God's Trombones* (1927); *Black Manhattan* (1930), a sociological study; and two autobiographical works, *The Autobiography of an Ex-Colored Man* (1912), and *Along this Way* (1933).

John Rosamond Johnson, 1873– , his brother, was a versatile musician and composer. The Johnsons collaborated on the Negro anthem, *Lift Every Voice and Sing* (1900). They also worked together on such popular songs as *Under the Bamboo Tree* and compiled collections of Negro spirituals.

JOHNSON, Sir JOHN, 1742–1830, American Tory leader, son of Sir WILLIAM JOHNSON. He inherited his father's title and estates in the Mohawk Valley, N.Y.; became identified with the powerful Tory element in that region; and in 1776, with several hundred followers, went to Canada, where he organized the "Royal Greens," of which he was made colonel. He laid siege to Fort Stanwix (1777), and defeated General HERKIMER, but was defeated in turn. In 1779 he was beaten at Newtown (now Elmira) by General Sullivan.

JOHNSON, JOHN ARTHUR, known as **Jack,** 1878–1946, American Negro heavyweight boxer, was born in Galveston, Tex. The first Negro to hold the world's heavyweight boxing championship, he won the title by defeating Tommy Burns in 1908 and knocking out Jim Jeffries in 1910 when the latter emerged from retirement. Johnson lost the title to Jess Willard in 26 rounds at Havana, Cuba, in 1915.

JOHNSON, JOSEPHINE WINSLOW, 1910– , American novelist, was born in Kirkwood, Mo. She was educated at Washington University, in St. Louis, where she majored in English literature. Her first book, *Now in November* (1934), a story of farm life in the Middle West, was awarded the 1935 Pulitzer prize for the novel. She was the author of a volume of short stories, *Winter Orchard* (1935); *Year's End* (1937), poems; and the novels, *Jordanstown* (1937) and *Wildwood* (1946).

JOHNSON, LOUIS ARTHUR, 1891– , American lawyer, was born in Roanoke, Va. He began a law practice in Clarksburg, W. Va., in 1912 and was elected to the state legislature. He served in World War I and was national commander of the American Legion in 1932. In 1937 he was made assistant secretary of war, resigning in 1940. Named secretary of defense in 1949, he resigned after heavy public criticism in 1950 and returned to private law practice.

JOHNSON, MARTIN, 1884–1937, American explorer and author, was born in Rockford, Ill. He spent 27 years in the South Seas, Australia, Africa, and the East Indies, photographing savage tribes and wild animals in their native surroundings. His greatest achievement was a motion picture of African wild life (1924–29) which he made for the American Museum of Natural History. He published *Cannibal-Land* (1917), *Safari* (1928), *Congorilla* (1931), and other books about his travels.

Osa Johnson, 1894– , his wife, accompanied him in his expeditions and collaborated with him on his books. Under her own name she published *Jungle Babies* (1930), *Jungle Pets* (1932), and *Tarnish* (1945). She wrote the autobiographical *I Married Adventure* (1940), *Four Years in Paradise* (1941), and *Bride in the Solomons* (1944).

JOHNSON, REVERDY, 1796–1876, American lawyer and statesman, was born in Annapolis, Md., and studied at St. John's College. Admitted to the bar in 1815, he practiced in Baltimore after 1817, and became an outstanding constitutional lawyer. He served in the state senate (1821–28) and the United States Senate (1845–49), and was President Taylor's attorney general (1849–50). Pro-South in sympathy, Johnson was counsel for the defense in the Dred Scott case (1857), but opposed secession. He was a delegate to the fruitless peace conference of 1861, and helped to keep Maryland from seceding. Lincoln sent him to investigate New Orleans' complaints against General Butler in 1863. Again a senator after the Civil War (1863–68), he supported Andrew Johnson's reconstruction policy and was influential in securing Johnson's acquittal when he was impeached. He was minister to Great Britain (1868–69), and negotiated the rejected Johnson-Clarendon Treaty for settlement of the Alabama and other claims. He resumed his practice in 1869.

JOHNSON, RICHARD MENTOR, 1781–1850, ninth vice-president of the United States, was born in Kentucky. He was a representative in Congress (1807–19), and took part in the War of 1812 as a colonel of Kentucky volunteers. He distinguished himself in the Battle of the Thames (Oct. 5, 1813), in which he is said to have personally slain the Indian chief Tecumseh. From 1819 to 1829 he was a member of the U.S. Senate; from 1829 to 1837 a representative in Congress; and from 1837 to 1841 vice-president of the United States. He failed as candidate for the vice-presidency in 1840, and the Democratic presidential nomination in 1844.

JOHNSON, SAMUEL, 1709–84, English writer and lexicographer, was born in Lichfield, Staffordshire. He studied at Pembroke College, Oxford. After teaching (1732–3) at Market Bosworth, in Leicestershire, he published (1735) a translation of Lobo's *Voyage to Abyssinia.* In the same year he married, and set up a school at Lichfield. In 1737 he went to London in company with David Garrick, and in the following year obtained regular employment on the *Gentleman's Magazine.* He edited its parliamentary reports from 1738 to 1741, and contributed them from July, 1741, to March, 1744.

In May, 1738, Dr. Johnson published his first poem, *London,* in imitation of the third satire of Juvenal. Its success won him the friendly interest of Pope. In 1742 he was employed on the catalogue of the Harleian Library. Two years later appeared his *Life*

Samuel Johnson

of Savage, afterward included in the *Lives of the Poets;* it brought him at once into note. His reputation grew so steadily that in 1747 several London booksellers contracted with him for a *Dictionary of the English Language.* This did not appear till April, 1755. Its definitions are often prejudiced, and its derivations are worthless; but it everywhere affords evidence of Johnson's vigorous and acute intellect, and is of great historical importance as a record of the language in the 18th century.

Johnson, however, had not devoted the eight years entirely to the *Dictionary.* In 1749 he published the *Vanity of Human Wishes,* an imitation of the 10th satire of Juvenal, and his best poem. In February of the same year Garrick staged *Irene,* a tragedy in blank verse, written mostly at Lichfield by 1737; but it was not a success. In March, 1750, Johnson started the *Rambler,* a periodical on the model of the *Spectator,* and it appeared regularly every Tuesday and Saturday till March, 1752. In 1753–54 he contributed to the *Adventurer,* and in 1756 he began to edit the *Literary Magazine.* In 1758 he started another periodical, the *Idler,* which appeared weekly from April, 1758, to April, 1760. In 1759 he wrote *Rasselas, Prince of Abyssinia,* in the evenings of a week.

In 1762 he was granted a pension of £300 by Lord Bute; and from this time dates his literary dictatorship, which was confirmed by the founding of the Literary Club in 1764. His edition of Shakespeare appeared in eight volumes in 1765. The text is sometimes faulty; but Johnson recognized the value of the first folio (1623), and he has no superior in sagacious comment. On the whole, his was the best edition of Shakespeare which had yet appeared. In 1769 he was appointed professor in ancient literature to the Royal Academy. Then for some years his sole work was four Tory pamphlets, published together in 1776, under the title *Political Tracts.*

In 1773 Johnson was induced by Boswell, whom he had known since 1763, to set out on the memorable tour to the Hebrides. Both travelers have left records of their experiences—Johnson's *Journey to the Western Islands of Scotland* appearing in 1775. In 1774 he toured with the Thrales (whom he had met in 1765) in North Wales, and in 1775 he visited Paris with them.

But Johnson was yet to write his greatest work, the *Lives of the Poets.* The first four volumes appeared in 1779, and the remaining six in 1781. Altogether there are 52 lives, and of these only one—that of Young—is by another hand. With all its faults, the *Lives of the Poets* remains one of the greatest

monuments of English criticism. The accounts of Dryden and Pope are masterpieces; but there is matter for question in his criticisms of those poets who, like Milton and Gray, did not conform to the classical manner of the 18th century. He was buried in Westminster Abbey.

Great as Johnson is as a writer, there is much truth in Macaulay's remark, that "Boswell's book had done for him more than the best of his own books could do." His prose style has been the subject of much unjust ridicule. It is massive rather than heavy; and the rapidity with which he wrote would alone prove that it was not labored. See BOSWELL, JAMES; DICTIONARY. For illustration see ENGLISH LITERATURE.

BIBLIOG.–R. Lynd, *Dr. Johnson and Company* (1928); E. S. Roscoe, *Aspects of Dr. Johnson* (1928); C. Hollis, *Dr. Johnson* (1929); H. Saltpeter, *Dr. Johnson and Mr. Boswell* (1929); S. C. Roberts, *Eighteenth Century Gentleman* (1930 ed. 1933), *Doctor Johnson* (1935); H. Pearson and H. K. Lunn, *Skye High* (1938); W. B. C. Watkins, *Perilous Balance* (1939); H. K. Lunn, ed., *Johnson Without Boswell* (1941); J. C. Bailey, *Dr. Johnson and his Circle* (1944); B. H. Bronson, *Johnson and Boswell* (1944); J. W. Krutch, *Samuel Johnson* (1944); S. C. Roberts, *Samuel Johnson* (1944); T. De Quincey, *Dr. Johnson and Lord Chesterfield* (1945); B. H. Bronson, *Johnson Agonistes, and other Essays* (1946); W. T. Cairns, *Religion of Dr. Johnson* (1946); Boswell, *Life of Samuel Johnson* (1791, ed. 1946), *London Journal, 1762–1763* (1950).

JOHNSON, THOMAS, 1732–1819, American jurist, born in Calvert County, Md. He practiced law in Annapolis, and was a prominent leader in Maryland during the Revolutionary War. He was a member of the Continental Congress (1774–77), and nominated Washington to be commander in chief of the Continental army. He was the first state governor of Maryland (1777–79), and an associate justice of the U.S. Supreme Court (1791–93).

JOHNSON, TOM LOFTIN, 1854–1911, American political leader, was born in Georgetown, Ky. He became a clerk in a street railway office in Louisville (1869–75), and invented several street railway appliances. Afterward he bought a street railway in Indianapolis, and then became interested in similar railways in Cleveland, Detroit, and Brooklyn (N.Y.). He was a member of Congress from 1891 to 1895, and mayor of Cleveland, Ohio, from 1901 to 1909. His principal work as mayor was the securing of a franchise tax, by which the city of Cleveland obtained a legal valuation of railway properties, and his victory in obtaining a three-cent fare. He was well known as an advocate of the single-tax theory, and as an adherent of Henry George. See CLEVELAND, Ohio.

JOHNSON, WALTER PERRY, known as **the Big Train,** 1887–1946, American baseball player, member of Baseball Hall of Fame, was born in Humboldt, Kan. A right-hander, he was conceded to be the fastest pitcher in the history of baseball. With Washington, a club which was generally in the second division, throughout his major league career, he won 413 games, pitched two no-hit games and 114 shutouts. He was manager of Washington (1929–32) and Cleveland (1933–35).

JOHNSON, Sir WILLIAM, 1715–74, American colonial soldier and statesman, was born in Smithtown, county Meath, Ireland. He came to America in 1738 to undertake the management of a large tract of land in the Mohawk Valley, which his uncle, Admiral Sir Peter Warren, had acquired partly from his wife (a daughter of Stephen De Lancey of New York) and partly by purchase. He settled at "Warrensburg," 24 miles west of what is now Schenectady, and opened trade with the Indians, whom he treated kindly and justly, with the result that he won their confidence and was adopted and made a sachem by the Mohawks. Governor Clinton appointed him colonel of the Six Nations (1744), and as commissioner of New York for Indian affairs he was a strong opponent of the French. He had been put in charge of all the New York forces on the frontier when the peace of Aix-la-Chapelle ended King George's War.

In 1753 and again in 1754 his influence with the Indians averted a rupture between them and the colonists, and in 1755 General Braddock put him in charge of all the affairs of the Six Nations. With the rank of major general, he led the colonial troops against Crown Point in 1755, and defeated DIESKAU at Lake George, for which victory Parliament created him a baronet and awarded him £5,000.

From 1756 until his death Johnson was "colonel, agent and sole superintendent of the affairs of the Six Nations and other Northern Indians" under the king's commission. On the death of General Prideaux at the siege of Fort Niagara (1759) Johnson took command and forced the surrender of the garrison, and in Amherst's Canadian expedition (1760) he commanded the Indians. For these and many other services he received from King George 100,000 acres of land north of the Mohawk, a tract afterward known as "Kingsland" or the "Royal Grant." He planned and practically built at his own expense the village of Johnstown. In 1768 he negotiated the important treaty of Fort Stanwix with the Indians. He married (1739) Catharine Wisenburgh, a German settler's daughter, and she bore him two daughters and a son. After she died he had several mistresses, one of them "Molly" Brant, a sister of JOSEPH BRANT, the Mohawk sachem, and by her he had eight children, whom he calls his "natural children" in his will.

A. C. Flick prepared Johnson's *Papers* (1933) for publication by the Division of Archives and History and also directed A. W. Lauber in the preparation of *Papers* (12 vols. 1939). See AMHERST, JEFFREY.

S. W. X.

BIBLIOG.–A. Pound and R. Day, *Johnson of the Mohawks* (1930); F. W. Seymour, *Lords of the Valley* (1930).

JOHNSON, WILLIAM, 1771–1834, American jurist, was born in Charlestown, S.C., studied at Princeton, and read law under Charles Cotesworth Pinckney. After serving in South Carolina's legislature (1794–98) and Court of Common Pleas (1798–1804), he was appointed to the U.S. Supreme Court by Jefferson, serving from 1804 to 1834. A personal friend of Jefferson's, he was often pro-Federalist in his court decisions. Johnson wrote *Sketches of the Life and Correspondence of Nathanael Greene* (1822) and a eulogy of Thomas Jefferson (1826).

JOHNSON, WILLIAM SAMUEL, 1727–1819, American jurist, legislator, and educator, was born in Stratford, Conn., the son of Samuel Johnson (1696–1772), an Episcopalian minister and the first president of King's (later Columbia) College. William Samuel was educated at Yale College and Harvard. He became a prominent Connecticut lawyer and served in the colonial assembly (1761–65), gaining a reputation for conservative and mildly pro-British political views. He was sent to the Stamp Act Congress in 1765 and was colonial agent to London (1767–71), becoming a Superior Court justice (1772–74) on his return to the colonies. In 1774 he declined election to the Continental Congress, and the next year retired from the upper house of the assembly, after serving on a fruitless peace embassy to General Gage. He was arrested in 1779 on suspicion of correspondence with the British, but was cleared of the charge and released. After the Revolution, Johnson was a popular member of the Congress of the Confederation (1785–87), and introduced at the Federal Constitutional Convention (1787) the Connecticut compromise on representation in the legislature. He was a U.S. senator (1789–91); and was first president of the newly renamed Columbia College (1787–1800), resigning because of illness. See CONSTITUTION OF THE UNITED STATES.

JOHNSON C. SMITH UNIVERSITY. See COLLEGES.

JOHNSON CITY, village, S central New York, in Broome County, on the Delaware, Lackawanna, and Western and the Erie railroads and U.S. Highway 11; three miles W of Binghamton. With Binghamton and Endicott, Johnson City forms the group known as the "Triple Cities." The village was laid out in 1891 and named for George F. Johnson, an industrialist, who incorporated his ideas on labor and social welfare in the setting up of the village's factories and plants. Shoes, shoe lasts, felt, spools and spindles, and blacking are the major industries. Pop. (1950) 19,249.

JOHNSON CITY, city, NE Tennessee, in Washington County, on the Clinchfield, the Southern, and the East Tennessee and Western North Carolina railroads, U.S. highways 11, 19, and 23, and the American Airlines; 86 miles NE of Knoxville. Johnson City, beautifully situated amid mountain scenery, is the second largest hardwood flooring center in the United States and one of the outstanding burley tobacco centers in the Appalachian region. It was settled about 1777 but no center was founded until the arrival, in 1854, of Henry Johnson, who became the city's first mayor. Johnson City is the seat of the East Tennessee State Teachers College. Hardwood flooring, furniture, textiles, rayon yarn, hosiery, foundry products, and fabricated steel are the principal manufactures. Pop. (1950) 27,864.

JOHNSON GRASS, a common pernicious weed belonging to the family *Gramineae*. The plant is a large, coarse perennial grass with a loose, spreading panicle. It is of Mediterranean origin but has become naturalized in many parts of the world, including the United States. In some districts it is regarded as a hay and pasture grass, but in other areas it has become a troublesome weed. It is classified as *Holcus halepensis* and is closely related botanically to the sorghums.

H. J. FULLER

JOHNSON NATIONAL MONUMENT. See ANDREW JOHNSON NATIONAL MONUMENT.

JOHNSONBURG, borough, NW Pennsylvania, in Elk County, on the Clarion River; the Baltimore and Ohio, the Erie, and the Pennsylvania railroads; U.S. Highway 6; and the American Airlines; about 60 miles E of Oil City. The borough was founded in 1810 by David Johnson. Paper pulp manufacture is the principal industry. Pop. (1950) 4,567.

JOHNSTON, ALBERT SIDNEY, 1803–62, American soldier, prominent as a Confederate general in the CIVIL WAR, was born in Washington, Ky. He was graduated from West Point in 1826, was chief of staff to Gen. Henry Atkinson in the Black Hawk War (1832), and resigned from the service in 1834. In 1836 he moved to the Republic of Texas and soon rose from the ranks to the command of the Texan army (1837). He was severely wounded in a duel with Gen. Felix Houston, whom he had displaced, and resigned within a few months. He was secretary of war of Texas (1838–40), and after the annexation of Texas served for a time as colonel of a Texan regiment in the northern campaign of the Mexican War. In 1855–57, as colonel in the regular service, he commanded the Department of Texas, and in 1857 led an expedition against the rebellious Mormons in Utah, winning a brevet of brigadier general for his skill and conduct. He was placed in command of the Department of the Pacific (1860), but when Texas seceded he adhered to his state, resigned from the army in May, 1861, immediately after the outbreak of the Civil War, and assumed command of the Department of Kentucky and Tennessee. He commanded the Confederate army in the Battle of SHILOH (April 6–7, 1862), until mortally wounded early in the afternoon of the first day. Though his brief experience in actual warfare on a large scale was not sufficient thoroughly to test his capacity, he has been ranked by competent military critics as in natural endowments the ablest of the Confederate generals, with the probable exception of Lee.

JOHNSTON, ALEXANDER KEITH, 1804–71, Scottish cartographer, was born in Kirkhill, Edinburgh, and studied at the University of Edinburgh. With his brother in the firm of W. and A. K. Johnston (1826), he published the *National Atlas* (1843), one of the most accurate atlases to that time. Appointed royal geographer of Scotland, he brought out his *Physical Atlas of Natural Phenomena* (1848), a fine early physical atlas in English. His other important works are the *Dictionary of Geography* (1850; 1877) and *The Royal Atlas of Modern Geography* (1861; 1905).

JOHNSTON, ERIC ALLEN, 1896–   , American industrialist and publicist, was born in Washington, D.C., but moved, when he was six years old, with his family to Spokane, Wash., where his father soon died. Working his way through the University of Washington, he achieved success through his leadership in several industrial concerns. In 1931 he was elected president of the Spokane Chamber of Commerce, and in 1942 was chosen president of the U. S. Chamber of Commerce. He held several government posts during the war and succeeded Will Hays as president of the Motion Picture Producers and Distributors of America in 1945. In 1951 he obtained a leave of absence to become head of the Economic Stabilization Agency. He wrote *We're All in It* (1948), a discussion of international politics.

JOHNSTON, JOSEPH EGGLESTON, 1807–91, American soldier, a prominent Confederate general in the CIVIL WAR, was born in Prince Edward County, Va., and was graduated from West Point in 1829. He was an aide (1836–37) to Gen. Winfield Scott during the Seminole War, earning the brevet of captain; was engaged in surveying the boundary between the United States and Canada (1843–44); and served with distinction in the southern campaign of the Mexican War, holding the rank of lieutenant colonel of voltigeurs (April 1847–August 1848), and winning the brevet of major and colonel at Cerro Gordo, where he was seriously

CHICAGO HIST. SOC.
Joseph Johnston

wounded, and the brevet of lieutenant colonel at Chapultepec. In 1858 he was acting inspector general of the forces sent against the rebellious Mormons in Utah, and in 1860 became quartermaster general of the U.S. Army with the rank of brigadier general.

Johnston resigned from the army in April, 1861, became a major general in the Virginia army, and shortly thereafter was commissioned a brigadier general by President Davis, being the only U.S. officer of such high rank to enter the Confederate service. He was the ranking officer in the first Battle of BULL RUN (July 21, 1861), arriving so opportunely as to change the fortune of the day. He opposed General McClellan in the Peninsular campaign, but was forced by a wound received at Seven Pines (May, 1862) to give way to General Lee. Johnston commanded the Confederate army opposed to General SHERMAN in the Atlanta campaign, but his cautious policy met with much popular criticism, and he was superseded by the more venturesome Hood in July, 1864. Early in 1865 he was placed in command of the Confederate forces in the Carolinas, and once more was opposed to Sherman, to whom he finally surrendered on April 26, 1865 (a little more than two weeks after the surrender of Lee). After the war he was a Democratic representative in Congress (1879–81), and was a U.S. commissioner of railroads during Cleveland's first administration (1885–89). Johnston was rated by Sherman as equal in generalship to Lee, but much of his great reputation after the war was due to the fact that he never lost a battle. On the other hand, he was overly cautious, and bickered constantly with other commanders and President Davis.

JOHNSTON, MARY, 1870–1936, American author, was born in Buchanan, Va., and was privately educated. Her first novel, *Prisoners of Hope*, appeared in 1898, followed by *To Have and to Hold*, which was published as a serial in the *Atlantic Monthly*, where it attracted much attention. These and *Audrey* (1902) were romances of colonial life in Virginia. Among her other novels are *Sir Mortimer* (1904); *Lewis Rand* (1908); *The Long Roll* (1911); *Hager* (1913); *The Witches* (1914); *Michael Forth* (1919); *Sweet Rocket* (1920); *Silver Cross* (1921); *1492* (1922).

JOHNSTON, town, N Rhode Island, in Providence County, five miles SW of Providence. The first settlement was made here in 1650. In 1759 Johnston was separated from Providence and incorporated as a separate town. It was named for Augustus Johnston, attorney general of the Rhode Island Colony. The manufacture of worsted yarns is the dominant industry. Pop.(1950) 12,725.

JOHNSTON CITY, city, S Illinois, in Williamson County, on the Chicago and Eastern Illinois and the Missouri Pacific railroads, six miles S of West Frankfort. Johnston City was incorporated in 1896. Coal mining and grain farming are the chief industries. Pop. (1950) 4,479.

JOHNSTON ISLAND, or **Cornwallis,** consisting of two small sand bars in a coral reef, 800 miles WSW of Pearl Harbor and 700 miles E of the 180th meridian. It was discovered in 1807 by a British vessel, the *Cornwallis,* and was named after her captain, Charles James Johnston. It was long the site of many disputes between American companies wishing to exploit its deposits of guano. A claim for the island by Great Britain in 1898 was never pursued. In 1934 Johnston became a base for the United States Navy and in World War II a strategic stop-over for planes flying between Hawaii and the South Pacific. On Apr. 1, 1946, naval installations suffered damage when the fringe of a tidal wave which swept the eastern Pacific inundated Johnston Island.

JOHNSTOWN, city, E New York, county seat of Fulton County, on Cayadutta Creek and the Fonda, Johnstown, and Gloversville Railroad, 40 miles NW of Albany. Johnstown is situated amid the beautiful scenery of the Mohawk Valley in the Adirondack foothills, four miles from the Mohawk River and 10 miles from the Adirondack State Park. It was founded by Sir WILLIAM JOHNSON in 1760. In Johnstown on Oct. 25, 1781, was fought the last real battle of Revolutionary War. Johnson's Hall, the home of Sir William which he built in 1762, is maintained as a state historic site, the only baronetical mansion in the United States. Johnstown is one of the leading centers of the glove-making industry which had its beginnings in this vicinity in the early 1800's. Other important products include gelatin, leather novelties, knit goods, and paper products. Pop. (1950) 10,923.

JOHNSTOWN, city, SW Pennsylvania, in Cambria County, on the Conemaugh River at the mouth of Stony Creek, the Baltimore and Ohio and the Pennsylvania railroads, and U.S. Highway 219; about 75 miles SE of Pittsburgh. Johnstown is one of the leading coal-mining and steel-producing centers of the state. The city is beautifully located in a level valley surrounded by the Alleghenies. The first settlement here was made in 1791 by Joseph Johns for whom the city was named. On May 31, 1889, heavy rains caused a poorly engineered reservoir dam, 12 miles above the city, to give way. The resulting flood submerged Johnstown and caused between 2,000 and 3,000 deaths. Grandview Cemetery, which overlooks the city, has the graves of 777 unidentified victims of the flood. In 1936, another flood resulted in the loss of eight lives and property damage estimated at $40,000,000. Subsequent work by U.S. Army engineers has eliminated possibilities of future disasters. Iron, steel, mining equipment, electrical supplies, machine tools, clothing, radiators, and clay products are the chief manufactures. Pop.(1950) 63,232. See FLOOD AND FLOOD CONTROL.

JOHORE, or **Johor,** a sultanate occupying the S extremity of the Malay Peninsula from 2° 40′ S to Cape Romania (Ramunya), a member of the Malay-

BRITISH COMBINE

Native houses in a clearing in Johore

operations of joiner's work, the most important is the making of joints. See CARPENTRY; CABINETMAKING; INLAYING.

JOINT, in geology, a fissure in the earth's crust, usually vertical, at least in rocks that have not been much disturbed. Joints are usually open, though their width may be very small. They develop more readily in rocks that are hard and coherent; in sands, clays, and gravels they are absent or rare. In bedded sediments the joints are perpendicular to the bedding planes, and frequently run in two directions, one set being nearly at right angles to the other. Joints may be produced by compression, by tension, or by torsion. In the last-named case it is the tension produced by the torsion that causes the joints. Tension joints frequently form along the crests of anticlinal folds and run parallel to the axes of the folds. If an anticlinal fold also "plunges," that is, if its axis departs from the horizontal, a second set of joints roughly at right angles to the first is likely to form. Tension may also be caused by the shrinking produced in mud by drying, or in shales by consolidation, thus causing tension joints to appear. Similar results often follow the cooling of hot lava, especially basalt, which commonly acquires a columnar structure made up of hexagonal prisms. Joints of this type are perpendicular to the cooling surface. The GIANT'S CAUSEWAY, on the shore of Ireland, is a well-known example of this prismatic structure.

Compression joints are generally the results of the shearing effect of opposing pressures. Such joints generally form in a plane at an angle of 45° with the direction in which the pressure is exerted, and are common on the limbs of folds and in the neighborhood of intrusions.

Joints may be enlarged by weathering, and may be filled with debris or by the deposition of mineral matter from solution. In the latter case they are

an Federation (1948); area about 7,500 sq. mi.; pop. (1947) 738,251, including about 310,000 Malays and 325,000 Chinese. Johore includes Muar Province and all the small islands lying close to the coast below 2° 40′ S. With the exception of Mount Ophir (Gunong Ledang, alt. 4,187 ft.), the sultanate is low-lying, marshy on the littoral, and heavily forested with clearings for settlements and plantations. The rainfall is 97.28 inches yearly, and the temperature averages 98 to 65° F. Communications are: by road, 929 miles of paved highways in 1940; by rail, 120 miles of the Penang-Singapore railroad in Johore; and by river, mostly for the rubber traffic. The country produces rubber, pineapples, minerals, timber, gambier, coffee, and pepper. Since 1914 a British adviser to the sultan has been appointed. Japan occupied Johore in January, 1942. The capital is Johore Bharu (New Johore). ADRIAN TROY

JOHORE BHARU, or **New Johore,** capital of the sultanate of Johore, located on the S shore, facing Woodlands on Singapore Island on the other side of the Strait of Johore. The palace built by Sultan Abubaker is beautiful and modern. There are public offices, commercial buildings, and several sawmills. Johore Bharu is a free port and a station on the Penang-Singapore railroad. Pop. (1941) 97,634.
ADRIAN TROY

JOINDER, in law, a joining of parties as plaintiffs or defendants in a suit or a joining of causes of actions or defense; also the acceptance of an issue tendered in a cause of action. Subject to some exceptions, parties jointly concerned in the same offense may be indicted jointly or separately. When an offense is one which may be committed by more than one person at the same time, the several persons engaged in its commission may be jointly charged, even though subject to different punishments for the offense. The right to join offenses in the same indictment generally is determined by the statutes and decisions. A joinder of causes of action is the uniting of two or more demands or rights of action in one action. No question can arise as to the joinder or misjoinder of causes of action unless it is first determined that more than one cause is stated; if so, the question as to the propriety of the joinder then arises. In determining whether more than one cause of action is stated, the main test is whether more than one primary right or subject of controversy is presented. PAUL PIKE PULLEN

JOINERY is the art of making and fitting the interior woodwork of a building, as opposed to carpentry, which concerns itself with the framework essential for the stability of the structure. Joiner's work, which in its finer branches is often spoken of as cabinetmaking, includes doors, windows, wooden stairs and their accessory parts. The various pieces are now cut and shaped chiefly by machinery. The actual work of the joiner is thus often confined to fixing together the component parts, which must be done with great care and exactness. Among the subsidiary

U.S. DEPT. INTERIOR

View of end ridge illustrating jointing

called *veins,* and are frequently valuable sources of metallic ores. Joints sometimes become filled with intruded igneous material, forming DIKES. C. C. G.

JOINT, or **ARTICULATION,** the approximation of two or more bones bound together and enveloped by other structures. Joints, which are usually formed of fibrous connective tissue and cartilage, are of three types. (1) *Synarthroses* are immovable joints characterized by a continuous union between bones whose edges are uneven and adapted to firm fixation. The bones in this type of joint may be united by a layer of cartilage (as in the temporary epiphyseal unions) or of thin fibrous tissue (as in the sutures of the skull). (2) *Amphiarthroses* are slightly movable joints in which the articular surfaces are joined by flattened disks of cartilage (as between the bodies of vertebrae) or by interosseous ligaments (as between the lower ends of the tibia and fibula of the leg). (3) *Diarthroses* are movable joints characterized by the presence of a joint cavity between bones whose articular surfaces are smooth and adapted for movement.

Several types of diarthroses are recognized. In a *ball and socket joint* (enarthrosis) the rounded head of one bone rests in a concave surface of another, as in the joints of the shoulder and hip. In a *hinge joint* (ginglymus) the bones fit together like a hinge, as in the jaws, ankle, and elbow. In a *pivot joint* (trochoidal) the articular surface of one bone is the edge of a disk that fits in a concave surface of another, as between the radius and ulna of the forearm. In a *saddle joint* the articular surfaces resemble saddles at right angles to each other, as in the joint of the thumb between the carpus and the metacarpus.

See Skeleton and the Dynamics of Bone; Muscle and the Muscular System; Arthritis; Bursitis; Rheumatic Fever; Gout; Dislocation.

JOINT-STOCK COMPANY is an association of individuals for the purpose of profit, possessing shares of a common capital, of which each member possesses one or more shares which are transferable by the owner. It differs from the usual partnership in that in the latter the death or withdrawal of a partner dissolves the firm; and from the usual corporation in that in the case of the corporation the stockholders are liable for the debts of the corporation only to the extent actually contributed for their share in the capital stock, while the members of a joint-stock company are liable without limit for all the debts contracted by the company. The joint-stock company cannot sue or be sued except in the names of all the members and cannot hold real estate. Real estate is usually vested in trustees appointed by the members, and active control of the company is generally exercised by a board of directors, as in corporations. In England the term joint-stock company is much more common than in the United States, but it is not an accurate term by American standards since their structure is comparable to the corporation rather than following the specifications outlined above.

As early as the 16th century trading companies pooled their funds to form joint-stock companies. The East India, Levant, Muscovy and other companies were united in this way.

The Virginia Company, chartered in 1607 to settle a colony in America was an outstanding example of this type of organization. It was financed mostly by members of the landed gentry and had funds larger than any other English trading venture. The joint-stock feature here was not merely the pooling of capital, but the labor of the colonists was also pooled on a share and share alike basis.

The joint-stock organization was used extensively in the United States during the early 19th century in order to accumulate sufficient capital to finance such relatively large-scale operations as the building of turnpikes and canals and operating business in the newly opened western territory. However, later in the century when industry, railroads, and public utilities needed even larger amounts of capital, it became necessary to attract the thousands of small investors who did not want to risk their money unless they were freed from the responsibility of assuming unlimited company debts. This fact led to the rise of the corporation form for industry, where the investors are limited in their responsibility only to the extent of the money invested, and has practically made the joint-stock type of company nonexistent in the United States. See Corporation; Industrial Organization and Management; East India Company; Virginia Company of London.   N. D.

Bibliog.–Birdseye, (New York Statutes) article "Joint Stock Associations" (1901); H. S. Miller and C. D. Campbell, *Financial Democracy* (1933); H. W. Jordan, *How to Form a Company* (1934); F. Gore-Brown, *Handbook on the Formation, Management and Winding Up of Joint Stock Companies* (1936); H. F. Williamson, ed., *The Growth of the American Economy* (1944); F. B. Palmer, *Private Companies* (annual).

JOINT-STOCK LAND BANKS were banks chartered under the authority of the Federal Farm Loan Act of 1916. The banking system of the United States as it developed during the 19th century did not provide sufficient facilities for meeting the financial needs of agriculture. Consequently during the early years of the 20th century the agricultural interests of the country were insistent in their demands for increased provisions for mortgage loans and as a result the act set up a separate system of Federal banks designed to finance farm mortgages. The law also allowed for a simpler method of mortgage financing by permitting private individuals to organize joint-stock land banks that could deal directly with the individual farmer. These banks were allowed to make loans within the state in which they were chartered and in one contiguous state. Somewhat less than 90 banks were so chartered, but not all of these opened for active business; they were most successful in the better agricultural districts of the Middle West, particularly during the land boom of World War I. In the late 1920's poor agricultural conditions and unconservative management caused many of them to get into financial difficulties, and in 1933 they were ordered to liquidate under the Emergency Farm Mortgage Act.

JOINT TENANCY. The ownership of lands or goods by two or more persons in such a way that each one is deemed to own the whole as well as an undivided share. This is the only interpretation that can be put on the mysterious phrase of Norman-French law by which joint tenancy is characterized—that the ownership is *per my et per tout*. Its one unfailing characteristic is the right of survivorship (*jus accrescendi*), the death of one of the joint tenants leaving the entire property to the survivor or survivors. Joint tenancy is characterized by the four unities: all the tenants must acquire their estate under the same instrument, at the same time, with the same interest (i.e., one estate cannot be for life and the other freehold), and with the same possession (i.e., all the tenants are seized of the whole land). A joint tenancy can be severed by partition, and converted into a tenancy in common by the alienation by a joint tenant of his share to a third person. See Tenancy; Survivorship.

JOINVILLE, FRANÇOIS FERDINAND PHILIPPE LOUIS MARIE D'ORLÉANS, PRINCE DE, 1818–1900, son of Louis Philippe of France. Trained for the navy, he distinguished himself (1838) at the bombardment of San Juan de Ulloa, and in 1845 bombarded Tangier. At the revolution of 1848 he took refuge in England. He served in the American Civil War, on the Union side, and in the Franco-Prussian War, under an assumed name, but was expelled by Gambetta. Later he was elected to the Assembly, in which he sat till 1876.

JOINVILLE, JEAN, SIRE DE, 1224?–1317, French historian, was a seigneur of Champagne, who accompanied King Louis IX in his crusade of 1248–54. His *Histoire de St. Louis* was begun when Joinville was almost 80; there is a critical edition by N. de Wailly (1874). Besides this he wrote a *Credo*, or confession of faith, in 1250.

JOINVILLE, city, Brazil, in Santa Catarina State; on the Cachoeira River, about 25 miles W of its port of São Francisco, and N of Florianópolis. Located in an important agricultural region, Joinville is a market for the surrounding area and also manufactures furniture and beverages. Pop. (1940) 16,883.

JÓKAI, MAURUS, 1825–1904, Hungarian novelist, was born in Komorn. He took part in the revolution of 1848, and as a member of parliament (1867–

96) supported Kalman Tisza, the radical leader. Besides editing several magazines, he published some 200 novels. The bulk of his fiction was written during the post-revolutionary period with the objective of enlivening the national language and literature, then at their lowest ebb. Among the most popular of his works in English translation were *The New Landlord* (1868), *Black Diamonds* (1870), and *Eyes like the Sea* (1890).

JOKJOKARTA. See JOGJAKARTA.

JOLIBA. See NIGER RIVER.

JOLIET, city, NE Illinois, county seat of Will County, on the Des Plaines River and the Illinois Waterway, served by the Alton, the Santa Fe, the Milwaukee, the Rock Island, the Elgin, Joliet, and Eastern, and the New York Central railroads and U.S. highways 6, 30, 45, 52, and 66; about 40 miles S of Chicago. Joliet is an important industrial city of the Midwest situated in an area of coal mines and limestone quarries. The first permanent settlement was made here in 1831. The new community was named for LOUIS JOLLIET, the famous French-Canadian explorer, who, together with Marquette, visited the site of Joliet in 1673. Joliet is the seat of the College of St. Francis and of two state penitentiaries. The city's schools were pioneers in music education. Pilcher Park in the city is noted for its arboretum with its many varieties of native and imported trees. More than 200 kinds of birds are sheltered in a nearby bird haven. Joliet's industries are many and varied. They include the making of wallpaper, roofing, steel, wire, chemicals, horseshoes, oil products, calendars, gas ranges, brick, tanks, beer, bakery machinery, dairy products, and work clothing. Pop. (1950) 51,601. A. M. K.

JOLIETTE, city, Canada, in the province of Quebec, county seat of Joliette County; on the Canadian National and the Canadian Pacific railways, in the Laurentian Mountains, about 36 miles N of Montreal. Barthelemi Joliette, a descendant of the explorer, JOLLIET, founded the city in 1841. It was incorporated in 1863 and for a time was known as Industry Village because of its industrial interests. Lime, steel, brick, tile, clothing, beverages, and food products are manufactured. Pop. (1949 est.) 15,000.

JOLIOT-CURIE, JEAN FRÉDÉRIC, 1900– , French physicist, was born in Paris, studied at the Paris Institute for Physics and Chemistry, and became an assistant to Marie Curie at the Paris Institute of Radium (1925). After becoming chief of research for the National Foundation of Science (1930), he embarked with his wife, IRÈNE JOLIOT-CURIE, on a scientific collaboration which paved the way for the final splitting of the atom. The experiments conducted by the Joliot-Curies led to the discovery of the neutron by Sir James Chadwick and of the positron by CARL D. ANDERSON. In 1934 they made their greatest contribution when they succeeded in producing radioactivity in nonradioactive elements. They were awarded the 1935 Nobel prize in chemistry and the Barnard gold medal of Columbia University (1940).

Soon after his appointment as professor of physics at the Collège de France in 1937, Joliot produced evidence that on the splitting of a uranium atom several neutrons are released and that these neutrons are capable of initiating a chain of reactions. During World War II he co-ordinated the work of the atomic research laboratories of the Collège de France, the University of Paris, and the National Center of Scientific Research. On the fall of France he became a leader in the university resistance movement known as the Front National and directed the laboratory manufacture of explosives for the Maquis (or guerrilla fighters). In 1944 he was appointed director of the National Center of Scientific Research and in 1946 was named French high commissioner for atomic energy, holding this post until 1950 when he was removed for his pro-Communist views. He had

FRENCH PRESS & INFORMATION SERV.

Frédéric and Irène Joliot in their laboratory

joined the Communist party in 1946. In 1951 he was awarded the Stalin Peace prize by the Union of Soviet Socialist Republics. M. E. C.

JOLIOT-CURIE, IRÈNE, 1897– , French physicochemist, was born in Paris, the elder daughter of PIERRE and MARIE CURIE. After studying at the University of Paris, she served during World War I as a hospital radiographer and then became an assistant to her mother at the Paris Institute of Radium. In 1926 she married JEAN FRÉDÉRIC JOLIOT-CURIE, with whom she established a scientific partnership that was as remarkable as that of her parents. She and her husband became world famous in 1934 when they succeeded in producing radioactive elements artificially. They won the 1935 Nobel prize in chemistry and the Barnard gold medal (1940). After 1935 Mme. Joliot-Curie was director of research for the National Foundation of Science and served in 1936 as undersecretary for scientific research. Her Communist sympathies led to her removal in 1951 from the French Atomic Energy Commission.

JOLLIET, LOUIS, 1645–c. 1700, famous French-Canadian explorer, was born in Quebec. He was educated by the Jesuits and was destined for the priesthood, receiving the tonsure and the minor orders in 1662, but yielded to the lure of the wilderness, and became one of the most adventurous of the early Canadian fur traders and explorers. He unsuccessfully attempted to discover the copper mines of Lake Superior (1669), and in 1673, with the Jesuit JACQUES MARQUETTE, he was sent by Talon, intendant of Canada, to explore the MISSISSIPPI RIVER.

Louis Jolliet

Proceeding by way of Green Bay and the Wisconsin River, on June 17, 1673, the explorers reached the Mississippi, near the place where the city of Prairie du Chien now stands; they then passed down the river to within about 700 miles of its mouth, and being convinced that it emptied into the Gulf of Mexico, returned. On their return they ascended the Illinois River, crossed the Chicago portage to Lake Michigan, and were again in Green Bay in September. In 1674 when Jolliet was almost to Montreal his canoe upset and all of his maps and records were lost. Jolliet later visited Hudson Bay (1679), received a grant of the island of Anticosti (1680), where he engaged in fisheries, explored the coast of Labrador (1694), and was in turn royal pilot for the St. Lawrence and hydrographer at Quebec. The priority of Jolliet and Marquette's discovery of the Mississippi has been denied, and it seems probable that Radisson preceded them, but they were certainly the first to pass down the river for any considerable distance.

JOLO, port of entry, Philippine Islands, capital of Sulu Province (SULU ARCHIPELAGO), on the NW coast of the island of Jolo. The town is some 540 miles by steamer from Manila, and was the old capital of the sultans of Sulu, who exerted a spiritual (and earlier a temporal) influence on Borneo. The native settlement of Jolo antedated the Mohammedan entrance during the 14th century; it was here that Sulu military efforts against the Spaniards were mounted. Although Jolo has lost more than 7,000 of its population since 1918, it is still an active trade center, and from here cattle, horses, and carabao raised on the island are exported to Singapore and other places; Jolo is also the center of the pearl industry. The town has brick walls and redoubts, built by the Spaniards, who cleared away much of the old town in 1878. Paved roads lead to other island towns. Jolo was held by the Japanese during World War II until Apr. 11, 1945, when United States troops seized the town and a near-by airfield. Pop. (1939) 12,573, mostly Moros and Visayans.

JOLSON, AL, real name **Asa Yoelson,** 1888–1950, American actor, was born in St. Petersburg, Russia. The son of a rabbi, he and his parents settled in the United States in 1893. At an early age Jolson became an entertainer in cafes and in the circus, and in 1899 he made his first legitimate theater appearance in *Children of the Ghetto.* He spent many years in vaudeville and as an end man in LEW DOCKSTADER'S Minstrels before he made his first success in 1909, singing "Mammy" in blackface. Two years later he began a long series of popular stage productions in the Winter Garden Theater which included *La Belle Paree* (1911), *Robinson Crusoe, Jr.* (1916), and *Sinbad* (1918–20). In 1921

NBC

Al Jolson

he starred in *Bombo* at a theater named in his honor. His film debut was made in *The Jazz Singer* (1927), the first talking picture, and in the next year he introduced his second famous song, "Sonny-Boy," in a motion picture, *The Singing Fool.* Many other films followed, and he developed a radio career simultaneously. He played in *Hallelujah, I'm a Bum, Go Into Your Dance,* and *Rose of Washington Square.* He returned to the stage in *Hold on to Your Hats* (1940), and dubbed in the voice for an autobiographical film, *The Jolson Story* (1947). He entertained troops in World Wars I and II and in Korea in 1950.

JOMINI, HENRI, BARON, 1779–1869, general and author of works on military tactics, was a native of Payerne (canton Vaud), Switzerland. He rose in the French military service to be chief of staff to Marshal Ney, but after the Peninsular campaign (1808), and the retreat from Moscow, he joined the Russian service. To him was largely due the Turkish capitulation at Varna (1828). He published *Principes de la stratégie* (1818), *Précis de l'art de la guerre* (1830), and histories of the revolution and Napoleonic wars.

JOMMELLI, NICCOLÒ, 1714–74, Italian opera composer of the Neapolitan school, was born in Aversa. At 16 he entered the Conservatorio de' Poveri di Gesù Cristo, but he soon changed to the Conservatorio della Pietà de' Turchini in order to study composition with Leo and Feo and singing with Prato and Mancini. In 1737 he presented his first opera, *L'errore amoroso,* under the assumed name of Valentino, because he feared public disapproval. The success of the work caused him to drop his pseudonym and present his second opera, *Odoardo* (1738), under his own name. The year after his opera, *Didone* (1748), was produced in Vienna, Jommelli was appointed second choirmaster at St. Peter's, Rome. Four years later he went to Stuttgart as the Kapellmeister to the Duke of Württemberg and his operas after this date, such as *Fetonte* (1769), show a German influence. His new style proved unpopular upon his return to Naples and his last operas, *Armida* (1770), *El Demofoönte,* and *Ifigenia in Aulide* (1773), were failures. Just before Jommelli died he composed his Miserere, a psalm for two sopranos and orchestra which is still performed in the Italian Roman Catholic Church.

JONAH, THE BOOK OF (so-called), in the Old Testament, the fifth book of the Minor Prophets. Its authorship is uncertain. It does not, in all probability, belong to the period of the prophet of that name, being apparently of a much later date. It recounts how the prophet was commanded by God to preach in Nineveh; how he fled instead to Tarshish; how on the voyage he was cast overboard, swallowed by a great fish, and liberated again after three days (ch. 1 and 2); how eventually he preached to the Ninevites, was instrumental in bringing them to repentance (3), and was displeased at the result (4). The tenor and style of the narrative seem to indicate that it was not written as a historical record, and its place among the "Twelve Prophets" can be adequately explained only if we emphasize the prophetic bearing of the story. See BIBLE; OLD TESTAMENT.

JONATHAN, eldest son of King Saul. His prowess and ingenuity were shown in his successful attack on the Philistines at Michmash (I Sam. 14), but it is the warmth and disinterestedness of his friendship with DAVID which keep his memory fresh. Along with Saul he perished in battle with the Philistines at Gilboa. His young son Mephibosheth was tenderly cared for by David (II Sam. 9).

JONATHAN, BROTHER, See BROTHER JONATHAN.

JONES, ANSON, 1798–1858, the last president of the Republic of Texas, was born in Great Barrington, Mass. He moved to Texas in 1833, took an active part in the War for Texan Independence, was the minister of Texas to the United States (1838) and was successively president of the Texan senate, secretary of state of Texas, and president of the republic (1844–46), vigorously opposing annexation to the United States. He committed suicide at Houston, Tex., in 1858. His *Memoranda and Official Correspondence Relating to the Republic of Texas, its History and Annexation, including a Brief Autobiography of the Author* (1859), is of great value to students of Texan history.

JONES, CASEY, hero of a popular ballad about a train wreck, generally identified as John Luther Jones. Born Mar. 14, 1864, in Missouri or Kentucky, he was in early life a resident of Cayce, Ky., from which town his nickname was derived. At 16 he went to work for the Mobile and Ohio, and in 1888 joined the Illinois Central as fireman, becoming engineer two years later. During his 10 years as engineer he became something of a legend, being noted for his technique in "quilling" the whistle. He drove a Consolidation freight locomotive, No. 638, and a picture of him in its cab survives. Transferred Jan. 1, 1900, to a passenger run of the Chicago-to-New Orleans Cannonball Express, he operated this train between Memphis, Tenn., and Canton, Miss. His locomotive was a McQueen 10-wheeler (4—6—0), No. 382, referred to in the song as a "six-eight wheeler." On Apr. 30, 1900, near Vaughan, Miss., he was killed in a wreck when his engine crashed into the rear of a freight train. Shortly after the wreck Wallace Saunders, a Negro roundhouse worker, composed the song, which was formalized in several versions. The most popular version was published in 1903, with words by T. Lawrence Siebert and music by Eddie Newton. Casey was buried at Jackson, Tenn. A bronze tablet in his honor was dedicated at Cayce, Ky., in 1938.   DON RUSSELL

BIBLIOG.–F. J. Lee, *Casey Jones, Epic of the American Railroad* (1939); F. H. Hubbard, *Railroad Avenue* (1945).

JONES, EDWARD BURNE. See BURNE-JONES.

JONES, Sir HAROLD SPENCER, 1890– , British astronomer royal, was born in Kensington and educated at Jesus College, Cambridge. He became chief assistant in the Royal Observatory at Greenwich (1913–23), was astronomer at the Cape of Good Hope (1923–33); and in 1933 became astronomer royal. In 1943 Jones was knighted and received medals from the Royal Society and the Royal Astronomical society. He served as president of the Institute of Navigation (1947–49). His writings include: *General Astronomy* (1922); *Worlds Without End* (1935); and *Life on Other Worlds* (1940).

JONES, HENRY, 1831–99, author of *Cavendish's Laws and Principles of Whist,* was born in London, and practiced medicine there from 1852 until 1869. A member of the "Cavendish Club" in Cavendish Square, he published in 1862 *Principles of Whist Stated and Explained by Cavendish.* In 1863 it was reissued and became the standard authority.

JONES, HENRY ARTHUR, 1851–1929, English dramatist, was born in Grandborough, Buckinghamshire. He was forced to leave school at the age of 12, and during the next 15 years supported himself by working as a draper's assistant, shopkeeper, and traveling salesman. He began writing for the stage when he was 16, sold his first script in 1879, and in 1882 achieved sensational success with *The Silver King,* a long melodrama. He attained his greatest popularity in the 1890's with such comedies as *The Dancing Girl* (1891) and *The Liars* (1897). Later successes were *Mrs. Dane's Defense* (1900), a "drawing room melodrama"; *The Hypocrites* (1907); and *Mary Goes First* (1913). His 83 plays display an unusual mastery of dramatic technique, but his opposition to progressive ideas prevented him from playing a more significant part in the development of the modern theater. His dramatic criticism was collected in *The Renascence of the English Drama* (1895) and *The Foundations of a National Drama* (1913).

JONES, HOWARD MUMFORD, 1892– , American author and educator, was born in Saginaw, Mich. He was educated at the universities of Wisconsin and Chicago. After teaching at several universities, he became professor of English at Harvard University in 1936, being dean of the graduate School of Arts and Sciences (1934–44). In 1945 he was appointed educational consultant to the Provost Marshal General's office. He was named president of the American Academy of Arts and Sciences in 1950. He wrote poems, *Gargoyles* (1918); plays; a biography of Tom Moore, *The Harp That Once* (1937); essays, *Ideas in America* (1944); criticisms, *Modern Minds* (with R. Ludwig and M. Perry, 1949); and edited many textbooks.   GEORG MANN

JONES, INIGO, 1573–1662, English architect, who obtained his early training in Italy by the constant study and imitation of the designs and monuments of ANDREA PALLADIO. It was the desire of Jones to become a scenic designer, as well as architect, and toward this end he received the patronage of James I; but he found himself continually competing with his enemy, BEN JONSON, for the favor of the king. In court pageants and masques, it was often necessary for Jones to work with Jonson. Each exerting every effort in his own art, one vied with the other to acquire the royal smile. It was Jones who effected the style change of English architecture—to the Palladian type from the style of the Transitional Renaissance. Though he received numerous architectural commissions, the rise of the Commonwealth prevented him from completing the most important ones among them. The only large scale accomplishment was that of the Banquet Hall in Whitehall. A simple church in London, St. Paul's Covent Garden, was also completed by Jones. His great plan for the Greenwich Hospital was only begun by him, and later finished by Sir CHRISTOPHER WREN; but the designs of Jones for the Queen's House, a part of the hospital scheme, were carried out after his death. The architecture of the manor house in the following Georgian Period had its style formed by Jones, who had designed several houses after the fashion of Palladio's palaces.
        JOAN C. CAMERA

JONES, JESSE HOLMAN, 1874– , American public official, was born in Robertson County, Tenn. He proved his administrative talent in his uncle's lumber business, and later became a prominent builder and banker. In World War I, he was director general of the American Red Cross's department of military relief, and assisted in setting up the League of Red Cross Societies of the World in 1919. In 1924 he bought the *Houston Chronicle* and became active in the Democratic National Committee. He was appointed the first director of the RECONSTRUCTION FINANCE CORPORATION when it was organized in 1932, and served as chairman of the board from 1933 to 1939. Roosevelt appointed Jones as Federal Loan Administrator (1939–42) and named him to his cabinet as secretary of commerce (1940–45).

JONES, JOHN PAUL, originally **John Paul,** 1747–92, American naval officer, was born in the parish of Kirkbean, Kirkcudbrightshire, Scotland.

In 1759–66 he was an apprentice to a merchant at Whitehaven engaged in the American and West Indian trade, being almost immediately sent to sea and showing a remarkable aptitude for seafaring life. He became part owner of a vessel, and engaged (1766–67) in the African slave trade, then regarded as thoroughly legitimate. In 1773 at Tobago in the British West Indies Jones accidentally, he asserted, killed the leader of a mutiny on his ship.

John Paul Jones

Rather than wait trial he left and went to Fredericksburg, Va., adding Jones to his name at this time.

Espousing the cause of the colonies on the outbreak of the American Revolution, he was consulted by the Continental Congress concerning the organization of a navy, and in December, 1775, was commissioned as a lieutenant in the newly organized naval service. He assumed temporary command of the *Alfred* and on it displayed the first flag—the "Pine Tree and Rattlesnake Flag"—ever displayed on an American man-of-war. He then commanded the *Providence* (1776), being promoted to captain, and the *Ranger* (1777–78), which cruised around the British Isles, did great damage to British shipping, even dashing into British ports, and defeated and captured the British sloop-of-war *Drake* (Apr. 23, 1778). See NAVY OF THE UNITED STATES.

Le Bonhomme Richard's Victory. After being idle for some time in France, Jones received (Feb., 1779) from King Louis XVI, then the ally of the United States, the command of a ship of 40 guns, *Le Duras,* an old East Indiaman which, in Franklin's honor, was renamed *Le Bonhomme Richard.* Three other ships, the *Alliance,* the *Pallas,* and the *Vengeance,* were placed, with qualifications, under his orders, and he, still retaining his American commission, conducted a memorable cruise of 50 days (Aug. 14–Oct. 3, 1779), during which he again made a circuit of the British Isles, and in a famous naval battle between *Le Bonhomme Richard* and the British warship *Serapis* with 44 guns, on Sept. 23, 1779, defeated and captured his antagonist, but lost his own vessel, which sank after the engagement. "I've just begun to fight," his reply to the enemy captain's "Have you struck?" has become one of the navy's classic quotations. In 1783 Jones went to Paris as agent to collect prize money. In 1788 he became a rear admiral in the Russian navy, and commanded a squadron in the Black Sea. Discharged in 1789 he returned to Paris, where he died.

The record of his burial place was lost, but after a long search conducted by Ambassador Horace Porter, his body was discovered in the Protestant Cemetery in Paris (1905), was conveyed to the United States by a squadron sent to France for the purpose, and was buried in the chapel of the U.S. Naval Academy at Annapolis, Md. Some scholars are not convinced that the body was that of John Paul Jones. See HALL OF FAME.   R. W. M.

BIBLIOG–A. F. De Koven, *Life and Letters of John Paul Jones* (2 vols. 1913); W. R. Jones, *John Paul Jones and his Ancestry* (1927); S. Spewack, *Mon Paul* (1928); P. Russell, *John Paul Jones, Man of Action* (1930); J. O. Kaler, *Life of John Paul Jones* (1932); G. M. V. C. Long, *Life of Rear-Admiral John Paul Jones* (1940); V. Thomson, *John Paul Jones, Father of the American Navy* (1942); L. Lorenz, *John Paul Jones, Fighter for Freedom and Glory* (1943); V. Brown, *John Paul Jones* (1949).

JONES, ROBERT EDMOND, 1887–   , American stage designer, was born in Milton, N.H. At Harvard University, where he was graduated in 1910, he became interested in the little theater movement, and afterward associated himself with the Washington Square Players and the Provincetown Players. In the latter group he began a long relationship with EUGENE O'NEILL, for whom he designed many stage settings, including those of *The Hairy Ape* (1921), *Mourning Becomes Electra* (1931), *Ah, Wilderness!* (1933), and *The Iceman Cometh* (1946). *The Dramatic Imagination* (1941) expresses Jones's credo of theatrical art.

JONES, ROBERT TYRE, 1902–   , American golfer, was born in Atlanta, Ga. He was educated at the Georgia School of Technology, Harvard University, and the law school of Emory University. Jones was Southern amateur golf champion 1917, 1920, 1922, national (U.S.) amateur champion 1924, 1925, 1927, 1928, 1930, British amateur champion 1930, national (U.S.) open champion 1923, 1926, 1929, 1930. In the eight national open tournaments of 1923–30 inclusive Jones finished below second place only once. This feat, called amazing by all experts of the game, was eclipsed only by Jones's winning of four major titles in the single year of 1930, a feat which brought him enduring recognition as the all-time greatest golfer. Retiring from national championship play after his "grand slam" of 1930, Jones practiced law. He wrote with O. B. Keeler *Down the Fairway* (1927) and with H. E. Lowe, *Group Instruction in Golf* (1939), *How to Play Golf* (1940).

JONES, Sir WILLIAM, 1746–94, English Oriental scholar, born in London. Called to the bar in 1774, he became commissioner of bankrupts (1776). Appointed to a judgeship in Bengal (1783), he held the post until his death. He made a careful study of Hindu law, the results of which were published in 1800 by Colebrooke as *Digest of Hindu Laws*. His translation of the *Institutes of Manu* appeared in 1794. Among his other publications are *A Persian Grammar* (1772), and translation of the ancient Arabic poems called *Moallákat* (1783). But it was as the English pioneer in the study of Sanskrit that his influence was greatest. His collected works were published in 1799 by Lord Teignmouth. In 1784 he founded the Bengal Asiatic Society.

JONESBORO, city, NE Arkansas, county seat of Craighead County, on the Frisco and the St. Louis Southwestern railroads and U.S. Highway 63; about 120 miles NE of Little Rock. Jonesboro, in a cotton and rice-growing region, was settled about 1870. It is the seat of the Arkansas State College. Jonesboro has rice mills and cotton gins and compresses and manufactures of lumber, flour, handles, crates, and brick. Pop. (1950) 16,310.

JONESBORO, the oldest town in Tennessee, formally established on Nov. 4, 1779, the seat of Washington County, the first in the United States named for George Washington. Originally this county included all of the present state and was a part of North Carolina. In 1784 delegates met at Jonesboro to organize a provisional government; they drafted an extralegal constitution for their state, which they called Franklin. John Sevier was elected governor. This government functioned until 1790, when Congress organized the "Territory of the United States South of the River Ohio," commonly known as the Southwest Territory. Andrew Jackson practiced law in Jonesboro from 1788 to 1790. The seat of the government was removed to Knoxville. The early buildings were constructed with great care and some of them are still standing. Pop. (1950) 1,126.

JONGKIND, JOHAN BARTHOLD, 1819–91, Dutch artist, considered the greatest Dutch painter of the 19th century. He went to Paris when he was 27 and studied with Jean Baptiste Isabey. Gaining recognition rapidly in France, due to the publicizing efforts of Edmond and Jules Goncourt who held the Dutch painter in great esteem, Jongkind allied himself with the Fontainebleau school. The appealing warmth of his landscape work became inseparable from the history of that medium in France. He was called the instigator of IMPRESSIONISM and to him must be attributed the highest expression of the delicate Dutch feeling for light. Keeping his tones divided, he obtained intense and transparent colors. Of his entire work, his accomplishments in scenes of moonlight are considered his greatest achievements. He was the master of Monet, Pissarro, and Sisley. Jongkind died in France. His best landscapes include "Moonlight in Paris," "Dutch Canal by Moonlight," "Course of the Seine," "Harbor of Harfleur," and "Souvenir of Havre."   JOAN C. CAMERA

JÖNKÖPING, county, S Sweden, bounded by the counties of Skaraborg and Östergötland on the N, Kalmar on the E, Kronoberg on the S, and Halland and Alvsborg on the W; area 4,449 sq. mi.; pop. (1948 est.) 266,796. The county includes a part of southern Lake Vättern, and several other smaller lakes, among which are Bolmen in the southwest and Sommen on the northeast border. Forestry is the principal industry. The industrial city of Jönköping is the capital.

JÖNKÖPING, town and lake port, S Sweden, capital of Jönköping County; at the S extremity of Lake Vättern, 230 miles SW of Stockholm. The city was originally built in the 13th century over marshes on the lake shore. It was burned in 1612 to prevent its falling into the hands of the Danes. In 1809 the peace between Sweden and Denmark was concluded at Jönköping. The town is today one of Sweden's chief industrial centers, with a fine harbor and a large shipping trade. It has the world's largest match factory, and important woolen goods mills, founded in the 17th century. Other industries include the manufacture of carpets, paper, shoes, tobacco, iron goods, small arms, and machinery. These and wood pulp are exported. The town has a noteworthy folk museum. Pop. (1949) 42,423.

JONQUIÈRE, town, Canada, in the province of Quebec, Chicoutimi County, on the Sable River and the Canadian National Railway, 213 miles N of Quebec. It is an important railroad center and

L. W. BROWNELL
Jonquils

has a large wood pulp industry. The city was named for the Marquis de la Jonquière and was incorporated in 1912. Pop. (1949) 16,000.

JONQUIL, a bulbous plant native to Europe and Asia and cultivated extensively in the United States. Jonquils have fragrant yellowish flowers growing singly or in clusters at the tops of tall scapes. The blossoms are unusual in shape, each being composed of a slender tube, six overlapping segments, and a short, cup-shaped corona of the same color as the segments. The leaves are glossy and narrow, and two to four leaves grow on each stem. Jonquils, *Narcissus jonquilla*, are grown in gardens or in greenhouses. Outdoors they are planted in moist, loamy soil or are grown in dishes of water. See NARCISSUS.

JONSON, BEN, 1573?–1637, English poet and dramatist, claimed descent from the Johnstons of Annandale. He was born probably in Westminster. He served in the English contingent in Flanders under Maurice of Nassau, and, if he spoke truth, slew a Spaniard in single fight. About 1592 he returned to London, and in 1597 he was a player, and was writing plays for Henslowe. During 1598 he killed a fellow actor, Gabriel Spencer, in a duel, stood his trial for murder, pleaded benefit of clergy, was branded in the thumb, and while in prison, became a Roman Catholic. In the autumn his *Every Man*

GAL. OF PORTRAITS

Ben Jonson

in his Humour was acted at the Globe, possibly through the good offices of SHAKESPEARE, and was followed in 1599 by *Every Man out of his Humour*. The Children of the Queen's Chapel produced his *Cynthia's Revels* (1600) and *Poetaster* (1601). The latter play was an episode in the "war of the theaters," not to be taken too seriously, in which Jonson on one side, and Shakespeare, Marston, and Dekker on the other, led the hosts. *Sejanus* appeared at the Globe in 1603. With the accession of James I began the long series of Jonson's court MASQUES, for which he provided the poetry and the learning, and Inigo Jones the architecture. In 1605 he joined Chapman and Marston in prison on account of the criticism of the Scots in their joint play of *Eastward Ho*.

Leader of the Mermaid Wits. Jonson was center, with John Donne, of a brilliant circle of wits. He was on friendly terms with Shakespeare and with BACON. He lorded it in the taverns, first at the Mermaid, somewhat later at the Dog, the Sun, and the Triple Tun, where the young poets courted him. At some uncertain date he received the appointment of poet laureate, and among his patrons were the Sidney family, the Earl of Pembroke, and Lucy, countess of Bedford, for whom and others he wrote much miscellaneous verse. The regular stage was now in the background of his interests, but *Volpone, Epicoene, The Alchemist, Catiline, Bartholomew Fayre, The Case is Altered,* and *The Devill is an Asse* were all produced between 1605 and 1615. In 1613 Jonson went to France as tutor to Sir Walter Raleigh's son. In 1618 he undertook his famous walk to Scotland, and visited William Drummond of Hawthornden. The summer of 1619 was spent with another poet, Richard Corbet, at Oxford. During the reign of Charles I his vogue diminished. The court masques began to go to other men. He quarreled with INIGO JONES. His later plays —*The Staple of News* (1625), *The New Inn* (1629), *The Magnetic Lady* (1632), *The Tale of a Tub* (1633)—show a falling away of power; and *The New Inn* was markedly unsuccessful. He withdrew from court about 1630, and in his later years was helped by the Earl of Newcastle. At his death, one of his best pieces, *The Sad Shepherd*, remained a fragment. He died at Westminster, and was buried in Westminster Abbey. It is debated whether Jonson's epitaph ("O Rare Ben Jonson") is a literary evaluation or merely a devotional formula, though there is no question that for a time, at least, he was acknowledged as the literary dictator of England. Besides the familiar lyric "Drink to Me Only with Thine Eyes," his works which show the most vitality in modern times are the comedies *Every Man in his Humour, The Alchemist, Bartholomew Fair,* and *Volpone,* one of the great masterpieces of misanthropic humor. These illustrate both Jonson's personality and his characteristic literary traits—his bluntness, sincerity, and courage, and the hard-won learning and craftsmanship with which he eked out a somewhat confined imagination.　　M. R.

BIBLIOG.–L. C. Knights, *Drama and Society in the Age of Jonson* (1937); G. E. Bentley, *Shakespeare and Jonson* (1945); G. B. Johnston, *Ben Jonson, Poet* (1945); A. H. Gilbert, *Symbolic Persons in the Masques of Ben Jonson* (1948).

JOPLIN, city, SW Missouri, in Jasper and Newton counties, on the Santa Fe, the Frisco, the Kansas City Southern, the Missouri and Arkansas, the Missouri-Kansas-Texas, and the Missouri Pacific railroads, U.S. highways 66 and 71, and the American and the Mid-Continent air lines; 140 miles S of Kansas City. Joplin is one of the leading zinc and lead mining and smelting centers in the United States. The first permanent settlement was made here in 1838 by the Rev. Harris G. Joplin. Lead mining was begun in 1848 and the mining of zinc, in 1860. In Schifferdecker Park is the Mineral Museum which contains several thousand specimens of Missouri minerals. While zinc and lead are the chief products of Joplin, explosives, lumber, meat packing products, and crackers are also important. Pop. (1950) 38,711.

JOPPA. See JAFFA.

JORDAENS, JACOB, 1593–1678, Flemish artist, was born in Antwerp where his father was a draper of poor means. At the age of 14 this boy, who was to become the greatest Flemish painter of his day, second only to Rubens, was apprenticed to Adam van Noort, quickly becoming that artist's favorite pupil. When he became 21, Jordaens married his master's daughter. He developed a great admiration for the Italian artists, but his responsibilities grew with the advent of three children and prevented his traveling to Italy to study under these masters. He studied their work and imitated it the more meticulously at home. Attaining a marvelous ability for genre work, Jordaens filled his paintings with robust, life-loving Flemish people. These paintings reflected the feasts and merry-makings he earlier enjoyed in the Van Noort household. This medium obviously gave him delight; for it gave him free reign to fancy, as is evidenced in a series of five pictures in which he interpreted the Flemish proverb "as the elders sing, the young children pipe." Of this same type, he several times painted pictures called "The King Drinks." Because portrait painting did not appeal to him, he did but a few, although his "Admiral de Ruyter" is one of his most celebrated works. The fame of Jordaens spread rapidly and he was pressed with numerous commissions. These often called for religious paintings and some of his finest accomplishments are "The Four Evangelists," "Crucifixion," "Adoration of the Shepherds," "St. Martin Healing a Man," and "Moses Striking the Rock." Jordaens was commissioned by Charles I of England to paint 22 pictures for Henrietta Maria's rooms at Greenwich; and the king of Spain ordered him to finish 12 paintings ("Metamorphoses" of Ovid) which Rubens had left uncompleted at his death.

The full achievement of Jordaens is in his color, which is sparkling and sensual. Although he was greatly influenced by Rubens, a common saying sprang up that "if Rubens painted with blood, Jordaens painted with fire." One of his strongest characteristics is his contrast of light and shade. After 1665 the power of his brush began to fade, and in his last years he became feeble-minded. The work of these years, although no match for his former accomplishments, are reflective of the genius that was Jordaens.　　JOAN C. CAMERA

JORDAN, DAVID STARR, 1851–1931, American naturalist and educator, was born in Gainesville,

N.Y., and studied at Cornell University, Indiana Medical College, and Butler University. After serving for six years as professor of zoology at Indiana University, he became president of that institution in 1885. He achieved special recognition in educational circles during the 25 years that he headed Stanford University (1891–1916). As a result of his work in ichthyology he was appointed assistant to the U.S. Fish Commission (1877–91, 1894–1909). In 1897 he was the U.S. commissioner in charge of investigating the fur seal industry in the Bering Sea controversy with Great Britain, Russia, and Japan. He also investigated the salmon fisheries of Alaska and during 1908–10 was international commissioner of fisheries. Prior to World War I he was well known as a pacifist, serving as chief director of the World Peace Foundation (1910–14) and as president of the World's Peace Congress (1915). Among his numerous books were: *A Manual of Vertebrate Animals of the Northern United States* (1876–1929); *Care and Culture of Men* (1896); *Footnotes to Evolution* (1898); *Imperial Democracy* (1899); *A Guide to the Study of Fishes* (1905); *Ways to Lasting Peace* (1915); *The Genera of Fishes* (4 pts. 1918–20); his autobiography, *The Days of a Man* (2 vols. 1922); *The Trend of the American University* (1929). In collaboration with Barton W. Evermann he wrote several books in ichthyology, the most important of which was *The Fishes of North and Middle America* (4 vols. 1896). M. E. C.

STANFORD UNIV.
David Starr Jordan

JORDAN, DOROTHEA, stage name of **Dorothea Bland,** 1762–1816, Irish actress, was born near Waterford. After playing in Dublin and Leeds, she appeared (1785) at Drury Lane as Peggy in *The Country Girl,* and took the town by storm. Her reputation was made by her charming impersonations of those characters which were of the happy, romping, tomboy order. She played for 30 years in Drury Lane Theatre, London, almost without a break. In 1811 she appeared at Covent Garden, and here (as Lady Teazle) she made her last appearance on the London stage (1814). From 1790 to 1810 she was the mistress of the Duke of Clarence (afterward William IV). She died at St. Cloud, France.

JORDAN RIVER, Arabic **Nahr Esh Sher'ia,** the largest river of SW Asia Minor; in the north it forms the boundary between Syria and Israel, and farther south, between Jordan and Israel; it is one of the world's most famous rivers because of its association with Hebrew and Christian history and because of its remarkable descent within its course of 200 miles from 260 feet above sea level to 1,292 feet below sea level. The Jordan is formed by the confluence of four streams flowing from Mount Hermon (alt. 9,232 ft.) in the Anti-Lebanon range in Syria. Its easternmost source is the Nahr Banias, six miles long, which issues from a cave near the ancient city of Caesarea Philippi (Baniyas, or Paneas). Two miles west is the spring of Ain Leddan, which bubbles up into the Nahr el Leddan, shortest of the four-pronged source of the Jordan, at Dan (Laish or Tell-el-Quady), which is on the northern boundary of ancient Israel and today marks the line between Palestine and Syria. The westernmost source of the Jordan is the Nahr Bareight, a mountain waterfall, which flows from the side of a rocky hill into a gorge and through the plateau of Merj 'Ayun, referred to as Ijon in I Kings 15:20. The longest of the mountain sources is the Hasbany, which comes 24 miles from its source near Rachaya, Syria.

After the four have united in the Jordan, the river flows through the Ard-el-Hule, a marshy stretch where rice is grown and the temperature is hot and humid. After a run of seven miles, the river widens just before entering Lake Hule (Huleh), called the "waters of Meron" in Joshua 11:5–7. Lake Hule is more than 200 feet above sea level; papyrus grows in it; and sugar cane, rice, and cereal grains thrive on its shores. The lake is 10 to 16 feet deep, four miles long, and three miles wide. A mile or two south of the lake the Jordan depression dips sharply below sea level. Cascading in falls and rapids through a narrow black basalt gorge, the river falls to 682 feet below sea level in 10½ miles between the two lakes and joins the Sea of Galilee (ancient *Tiberias,* or *Gennesaret*). This harp-shaped body of water is 13 miles long and 8 miles wide and at its lower end is 150 feet deep, at the point where the Jordan River flows out. From the Sea of Galilee south to the Dead Sea the Jordan travels a stretch of 65 miles through a fertile valley. Through this area the river has two levels. Its upper part is known as the Ghor, a rift; 150 feet lower, its lower plain is called the Zor, a depression which is about one mile wide. During the Bible days, lions, wolves, and jackals had their lairs in this region, according to Jeremiah 49:19. It is tropical and lush and covered with an almost impenetrable thicket. The average rate of descent of the river here is nine feet per mile, the valley gradually deepening to a depression of 1,292 feet below sea level, where it empties into the DEAD SEA. Through this section of the valley, which is 3 to 14 miles wide, the river twists and turns in large serpentine loops, is from 90 to 100 feet broad, from 3 to 10 feet deep, and very muddy at the lower end near the Dead Sea.

From the Sea of Galilee to the Dead Sea the Jordan receives many small streams called *wadis,* and four rivers of fair size. On the east side, just after the Jordan leaves the Sea of Galilee, the Yarmuk enters at Naharaim, where are located a large hydroelectric plant and reservoir, which generate current for a large part of Jordan. Other east side tributaries of the Jordan are the Arab, Taiyibeh, Ziglab, Jurm, Yabis (Cherith), Kufrenji, Rahib (Rajib), Jabbok (Zerka), Kufrein, Nimrin, and Rameh. From the west side the Jordan is swollen by the Jalud River, entering from the Plains of Bethshean, and by the Bira, Malih, Faria, and Qelt. For a distance of 13 miles south from the Sea of Galilee the Jordan Valley is four miles wide; after the Jalud enters it, the river widens to seven miles. Along both sides of the Jordan are the ruins of more than 50 ancient towns and villages, which flourished about 5,000 years ago. The oasis of JERICHO is now the largest settlement. On the east side of the river just before it empties into Galilee is Bethsaida (Julias), where Jesus fed the multitude (Luke 9:10–17). Beside the sea are the ruins of the town of CAPERNAUM (near Tell Hum), where Jesus entered the synagogue and taught (Mark 1:21). It is believed that Jesus was baptised in the Jordan at a point somewhere in the vicinity of Jericho.

By the time the Jordan arrives at the plains of Moab, its valley has reached its maximum width of 14 miles. This area also has many ancient sites, some of them dating from 3500 B.C. Just south of the plains of Moab the Jordan enters and is finally lost in the Dead Sea. In January and February the river, swollen

View of the Jordan River in Palestine

T.W.A. AIRLINES

with a load of melted snows from the Anti-Lebanon Mountains, overflows and floods wide stretches along its shores. See PALESTINE; GALILEE, SEA OF. K. E. H.

BIBLIOG.–N. Glueck, *The River Jordan* (1945).

JÖRGENSEN, JENS JOHANNES, 1866–   , Danish poet and novelist, was born in Svendborg, Fyn, and was educated at the University of Copenhagen. His early work, as *Vers* (1887), was naturalistic, reflecting the influence of the Brandesian determinism then prevalent. In the 1890's, however, with Sophus Claussen, Viggo Stuckenberg, and other young Danish poets, he was converted to the doctrines of the French Symbolists and founded the literary review *The Tower* (1893–95) to promote the fight against naturalism. In 1895 Jörgensen was received into the Catholic church and his later works, both verse (*Poems*, 1898; *Flowers and Fruits*, 1907; *The Brig Marie of Svendborg*, 1926) and prose (*Parables*, 1898; *Saint Francis of Assisi*, 1912; *Don Bosco*, 1929) were characterized by romantic melancholy and mysticism. His *Autobiography* (2 vols. 1928–29) is particularly valuable for its comments on modern Danish literature.

JORULLO, volcano, W Mexico, in the state of Michoacan, SW of Morelia. It was created in 1759 in an eruption in the middle of a cultivated plain and was active for more than 40 years. Until the eruption of PARÍCUTIN, Jorullo was the youngest volcano. Great damage was caused in an extensive area which had been used for the growing of sugar cane and indigo plants. The volcano reached a height of 1,300 feet above the plain.

JOSAPHAT. See BARLAAM.

JOSEPH, in the Old Testament, was the son of JACOB and Rachel. Sold to a band of merchants by his jealous brothers, he was made a slave in Egypt. While imprisoned under false accusation, Joseph interpreted the Pharoah's dream and was made his chief minister. His foresight enabled him to preserve the country through seven years of famine, during which he brought his father and brothers into Egypt. He married Asenath, the daughter of a priest, and their two sons MANASSEH and EPHRAIM are the ancestors of two of Israel's 12 tribes. His history is given in Gen. 37–50.

JOSEPH, in the New Testament, was the husband of MARY, the mother of Christ. His genealogy is traced in Matt. 1:1–15, to David, Judah, and Abraham. His residence was at Nazareth in Galilee, where he followed the occupation of a carpenter, for which Christ was also trained (Mark 4:3). When Joseph became the husband of Mary, he was somewhat advanced in age and is generally supposed to have died before Christ began his public ministry. See JESUS CHRIST.

JOSEPH I, 1678–1711, emperor of Germany, of the house of Hapsburg, and son of Leopold I, born in Vienna; was proclaimed king of Hungary (1687), and king of the Romans (1690), succeeding his father as German emperor (1705). He carried on a successful war, with the assistance of England, Holland, and Savoy, against Louis XIV, the allied armies being under the command of the Duke of Marlborough and Prince Eugène. See SUCCESSION WARS; AUSTRIA, History, *War of the Spanish Succession.*

JOSEPH II, 1741–90, emperor of Germany, son of Francis of Lorraine and MARIA THERESA, born in Vienna, was elected king of the Romans (1764), succeeding his father as German emperor (1765). Along with the sovereigns of Russia and Prussia, he signed the treaty by which Poland was divided among them (1772). On the death of his mother (1780) he came into possession of the Austrian throne. He helped in the suppression of the Jesuits; established religious toleration in his dominions (1781); was visited by Pius VI, who dreaded his reforms in convents; warred with Turkey in conjunction with Catherine of Russia. His zeal in correcting the abuses of the Roman Catholic Church caused an insurrection

in Belgium, and the same thing happened in Hungary over his attempt to establish German as a universal language in his dominions. Among his other reforms were the abolition of serfdom, curtailment of feudal privileges, the readjustment of taxation, and the framing of a new law code. See POLAND, Government and History.

JOSEPH, real name **Hinmaton-Yalatkit,** c. 1830–1904, chief of the Nez Percé tribe of North American Indians, was born in the vicinity of Wallowa Valley, Ore. Succeeding his father in 1873 as chief of the Nez Percés who ignored the treaty of 1863, by which the U.S. Government confined them to the Lapwai reservation in Idaho, Joseph became prominent after an Indian revolt in 1877. Finding his forces insufficient, he began an epic 1,000-mile retreat toward Canada, eluding notable Indian fighters, and surrendered to Gen. Nelson Miles after a five-day siege in the Bear Paw Mountains. Joseph was eventually sent to the Colville reservation in Washington, along with about 150 of his tribe. His fighting ability and integrity were highly respected by his white adversaries. See IDAHO; MONTANA for pictures.

JOSEPH, KING OF NAPLES. See BONAPARTE, JOSEPH.

JOSEPH OF ARIMATHEA, a wealthy Jew who according to all four Gospels begged the body of Jesus from Pilate and buried it in his own grounds. Joseph is described as a "councilor" which is thought by many to indicate that he was a member of the Sanhedrin. A medieval legend attributes the founding of the first British Christian church to Joseph, and Arthurian poetry credits him with bringing the HOLY GRAIL to England. Neither of these stories is sanctioned by the church. See GLASTONBURY.

JOSEPH STALIN CANAL. See BALTIC-WHITE SEA CANAL.

JOSÉPHINE, born **Marie Josèphe Rose Tascher de la Pagerie,** 1763–1814, empress of the French, the wife of NAPOLEON I, was born in Trois Islets,

Joséphine

Martinique, and went to France at the age of 15. In 1779 she married ALEXANDRE DE BEAUHARNAIS, by whom she had two children Eugène and HORTENSE (see BEAUHARNAIS, EUGÈNE DE). Despite her efforts to save her husband, he was guillotined in 1794. Joséphine, arrested also, was released through the intervention of Tallien after the 9th Thermidor. Introduced to young Napoleon by Barras, she married him in 1796, and in 1804, at his coronation, she was crowned empress of the French. When the marriage continued to prove childless, Napoleon divorced her (1809), but continued her friend, and took charge of the future of her two children. Joséphine retired to Malmaison, the neoclassical château which the emperor had bought for her, and lived on a lavish allowance from him till her death of quinsy. The correspondence of Napoleon and Joséphine was published in 1827.

JOSEPHUS, FLAVIUS, A.D. 37–c. 100, Jewish historian, was a man of high birth, and was sent on a mission to Rome in A.D. 63. When the Roman governor left Jerusalem, he accepted the management of affairs in Galilee, and defended Jotapata for 47 days against Vespasian. Titus interceded for him, and his life was spared; but he was not released from custody until Vespasian was declared emperor in A.D. 70. Thereafter he attached himself to the imperial family, taking the name Flavius out of respect to them, and living in Rome to the end of his life. His chief works (both written in Greek) are *The History of the Jewish War*, which gives a brief sketch of Jewish affairs from 170 B.C. to his own day, and a full account of the conquest of Jerusalem; and *The Jewish Antiquities*, narrating the history of the Jews from the creation to A.D. 66—the latter part treats more fully what is outlined in the other work. Josephus possesses a clear and pure style, and his descriptions are vivid.

JOSHIN, or **Sonjin**, port in NE Korea, about 135 miles SW from the Russian-Manchurian border.

JOSHUA ("Jesus," Acts 7:45), the son of Nun, according to the book called by his name (see next article), succeeded Moses as the leader of the Israelites, and completed the invasion of Canaan. After crossing the Jordan from the east he reduced Jericho and (after a reverse) Ai, defeated a large number of native kings, and occupied their territory, afterward subdividing the land among the tribes of Israel. This is not in accord with Judges 1–2, which represents the conquest as carried through by different aggregations. Joshua is said to have died at Mt. Ephraim at the age of 110.

JOSHUA, THE BOOK OF, describing the Israelite conquest of Canaan, is now regarded as the necessary supplement to the Pentateuch, and in critical works the six books are conjoined under the name of HEXATEUCH. See BIBLE; OLD TESTAMENT.

JOSHUA TREE NATIONAL MONUMENT, S California, an area of 655,961 acres of desert country in San Bernardino and Riverside counties, ranging in altitude from 1,000 feet in the east to more than one mile in the San Bernardino Mountains. The park, established in 1936, is notable for unique desert vegetation and wild life. It was named for the rare and spectacular Joshua Tree which, tradition says was so designated by the Mormons because the feathery flowers that tip its angular branches seemed to point to the Promised Land.

JOSIAH. See BIBLE, *Principal Persons*.

JOSTEDALSBRÄE, Europe's largest icefield (alt. 6,700 ft.), which includes 350 square miles of mountainous region along the SW coast of Norway, between the Nord and Sogne fjords, west of the JOTUNFJELD (Jotunheimen) Mountains. A score of famous glaciers descends from this field into the valley in Sogn og Fjordane County, the most noted being the Boium, or "Blue Glacier," and the Suphelle, in the Sogne Fjord, the Kjendal, or "frozen cascade," and Brigsdal in the Nord Fjord.

JOTUNFJELD, or **Jotunheimen**, highest mountain region of S central Norway, lying in the NW section of Opland and the E part of Sogn og Fjordane counties; area 850 sq. mi. In Norse mythology it was called the "Home of the Giants," because it contains the highest peaks of Scandinavia. These are Galdhöpig (8,097 ft.), Glittertind (8,077 ft.), Memurutind (7,966 ft.), Knutshaltind (7,812 ft.), and several other peaks to the south between lakes Gjende and Bygdin. In summer the region provides grazing for goats, sheep, and cattle.

JOUBERT, JOSEPH, 1754–1824, French moralist and critic, a native of Montignac (Périgord), became a member of the brilliant literary circles of Paris just before the Revolution. After his death Chateaubriand edited a selection of his *Pensées*, and a fuller edition was published in 1842 by Paul de Raynal. This was followed by the improved editions of Arnaud Joubert (1850) and Louis de Raynal (1862).

JOUBERT, PETRUS JACOBUS, 1834–1900, Boer commandant, was born in Cango in Cape Colony; migrated when young to Natal, later to the Transvaal. He was for a time attorney general of the republic (1874). He worked with Kruger against the annexation of the Transvaal by Sir T. Shepstone in 1877. When the flag of independence was raised in December 1880, he was appointed one of the triumvirate to whom the government of the country was entrusted. As commandant general of the Boer forces he defeated the British at Majuba Hill on Feb. 28, 1881. Joubert twice unsuccessfully sought the presidency in opposition to Kruger—in 1893 and in 1898.

On the outbreak of the Boer war (1899–1902) Joubert was again commandant general and invested Ladysmith; but ill-health compelled him to return to Pretoria, where he died.

JOUETT, MATTHEW HARRIS, 1788–1827, American artist, the son of a Revolutionary patriot, was born in Mercer County, Ky. He studied law, but found that his interest lay in the direction of art work. After service in the War of 1812, he devoted himself to the study of portrait and miniature painting, taking a brief course under Gilbert Stuart. He lived in Lexington, Ky., where and in other parts of the South he painted many portraits of which the best known is that of Lafayette.

JOULE, JAMES PRESCOTT, 1818–89, English physicist, was born in Salford, studied under John Dalton, and became secretary of the Manchester Literary and Philosophical Society. His first research was on magnetism, particularly the magnetizability of iron by electric currents, and this led to his discovery (1840) that the quantity of heat produced by the passage of a current through a conductor is directly proportional either to the square of the current in amperes or to the resistance of the conductor in ohms. In 1843 he formulated the first law of thermodynamics which stated that thermal energy and mechanical energy are equivalent and can be converted into each other. After conducting a number of experiments, which gave definite proof of the conservation of all forms of energy, whether mechanical, heat, or electrical, he set forth his findings in papers entitled "On Matter, Living Force, and Heat" (1847) and "On the Mechanical Equivalent of Heat" (1849). His name was given to the Joule unit. See ELECTRICITY: ELECTROKINETICS; THERMODYNAMICS.

BIBLIOG.–F. R. Moulton and J. J. Schifferes, eds., *The Autobiography of Science* (1945).

JOULE is the practical electric unit of work; it equals 10^7 cgs electromagnetic units of work or ergs, and represents the work done or heat generated by a watt per second, or an ampere flowing through an ohm in a second, or a coulomb passing through the P.D. of one volt. Taking Joule's equivalent (see THERMODYNAMICS) as 41.6×10^6 in the cgs system, then the joule being 10^7 ergs is the amount of heat required to raise .24 gram water 1° C. See ELECTRICITY: ELECTROKINETICS.

JOURNALISM is the term commonly used to denote the business and profession of managing and writing for newspapers and magazines; but it is now frequently broadened to include the entire field of communications, comprising newspapers, periodicals, radio, and even those phases of motion pictures and book publishing related to current news.

The basic jobs on a daily newspaper are: (1) publisher, who is the owner or one who acts for the owner or owners to determine basic policies and hire the key men; (2) business manager, in general charge of business operations; (3) circulation manager; (4) advertising manager; (5) mechanical superintendent; (6) managing editor, in general charge of editorial operations; (7) city editor, in charge of local news, with staff of reporters; (8) copydesk editor, in charge of editing all copy; (9) departmental editors, including sports, feature, picture, Sunday, state, and society editors; (10) editorial-page editor. Nearly every paper has its own variations of this pattern, and all the above have assistants or staffs. A "news editor" is often an assistant managing editor.

A typical magazine staff consists of: (1) owner, in many cases a company publishing several periodicals; (2) publisher, who may be chief owner and has primary responsibility for the magazine; (3) editor, who has general supervision of contents; (4) departmental editors; (5) art editor; (6) business manager; (7) circulation manager; (8) advertising manager. The smallest magazines consolidate these positions; larger ones multiply them. Magazine content comes from the staff-written material, contributions prepared on assignment, and "freelance" matter. Many magazines use unsolicited, or "freelance" matter, employing "readers" to choose acceptable contributions from what is submitted.

Journalism has become increasingly professional in the United States in the past 75 years by means of a higher educational level for its practitioners, the formation of journalistic societies, and the publication of professional journals. A large proportion of journalists are now college-educated. Specialized education in journalism began with individual courses in Midwestern universities in the 1870's and 1880's. The first school of journalism was established at the University of Missouri in 1908; in 1950 there were 38 such schools recognized by the Association of Accredited Schools and Departments of Journalism. Many city press clubs and state press associations were organized in the 1880's. The Gridiron Club, of Washington, D.C., was formed in 1885, the National Editorial Association also in 1885, the American Newspaper Publishers' Association in 1887, the American Society of Newspaper Editors in 1922. There are several strong regional associations of editors and publishers. Important journals are *Journalist* (1884-1907), *Fourth Estate* (1894-1927), *Editor and Publisher* (1901-current), *Journalism Quarterly* (1923-current). See MAGAZINE; NEWSPAPER.   FRANK LUTHER MOTT

JOURNALISM, EDUCATION IN. The first instruction in journalism in an American institution of higher education took place at Washington College (now Washington and Lee University), Lexington, Virginia, in 1869. By 1941 over 60 per cent of the four-year colleges and universities in the United States offered some instruction in journalism courses. The first distinct school of journalism was established in 1908 at the University of Missouri. In the following twelve years schools and departments of journalism came into being in such number that by 1920, 131 colleges and universities were offering journalism courses, and of these 28 were providing professional type instruction. In 1912 the American Association of Teachers of Journalism was established. The Association of Accredited Schools and Departments of Journalism (formerly the American Association of Schools and Departments of Journalism) consisted in 1950 of 38 schools of journalism in the U.S.

Professional level courses are usually given in the preparation and editing of material for publication, the history of journalism, the relation of the press to the community, typography, press photography, public opinion, interpretive and specialized reporting, and specialized writing for feature and women's pages. Many schools of journalism offer additional courses dealing with the methods of advertising, writing for radio, and the preparation of material for magazines and books. Some of the larger schools of journalism have a complete editorial and publication organization on the premises.   ROBERT MARSH

JOUTEL, HENRI, c. 1650–c. 1723, French explorer in America, was born in Rouen. He was a friend and fellow townsman of the explorer LA SALLE, whom he accompanied on the expedition of 1685–87, which resulted in the establishment of a temporary colony in Texas and finally in La Salle's assassination. During this period Joutel was La Salle's most trusted lieutenant; he commanded the fort on Matagorda Bay during La Salle's absences in search of the Mississippi River, and accompanied his leader on his last trip (1686–87). After La Salle's assassination, Joutel's life was also threatened; but he finally (in July, 1687), after what Parkman calls "one of the most adventurous journeys on record," reached Montreal by way of the Arkansas, the Mississippi, and the Illinois. He immediately returned to France and was seen at Rouen 35 years later by Charlevoix. His *Journal historique du dernier voyage que feu La Salle fit dans le Golfe de Mexique* (1713), an abstract of his narrative which was published in full by Margry in his *Découvertes et établissements des français* (1879), and republished in

English by the Caxton Club of Chicago, is the best contemporary narrative of La Salle's last voyage.

JOUVENET, JEAN, 1644–1717, French artist, was born in Rouen. As he came from a family of painters, his early instruction was given by his father; but when he was 17 he was sent to study in Paris under Charles Le Brun. Although he found no personal appeal in the rigid work of Le Brun, Jouvenet worked with him for almost 20 years on decorations at Versailles, learning Le Brun's complicated constructions. He became a member of the Académie when he showed his "Esther before Ahasuerus" in 1675, and six years later was appointed professor there. Until the death of his master in 1690, Jouvenet contented himself with following Le Brun's technique; after that time, his originality began to assert itself in the attainment of dramatic feeling accompanied by sensuous color and powerful effects with light and shade, but his handling retained a type of coarseness devoid of soft qualities. Four years before he died Jouvenet was seized by a paralysis that affected his entire right side. Painting with his left hand, he completed the paintings he had already begun of the "Visitation" and the "Magnificat" in the church of Notre Dame. His numerous works include "Resurrection of Lazarus," "Jesus and the Pharisees," "Descent from the Cross," "View of the High Altar of Notre Dame," and "The Money Changers Driven from the Temple."   JOAN C. CAMERA

JOVE. See JUPITER.

JOVELLANOS, city, E central Cuba in Matanzas Province; on a railroad and highway, S of the port of Cárdenas, in an important sugar-producing region. Pop. (1943) 13,324.

JOWETT, BENJAMIN, 1817–93, English scholar and theologian, was born in Camberwell and was educated at Oxford. In 1855 he became regius professor of Greek at Oxford and in 1870 was appointed master of Balliol College. Best known as an essayist and translator, he also attained renown as a teacher. His essays include the commentary, *Epistles of Saint Paul* (1855), and *On Interpretations of Scripture* (1860), for which he was tried for heresy before Chancellor's Court and later acquitted. His *Dialogues of Plato* (4 vols. 1871) is considered the classic English translation, though the work is more distinguished for its literary quality than its accuracy. He also published English versions of Thucydides (1881) and of Aristotle's *Politics* (1885).

JOYCE, JAMES, 1882–1941, Irish author, was born in Dublin. After education in Jesuit schools and at University College, Dublin, he spent most of

James Joyce

his life in Paris, Rome, Trieste, and Switzerland, where he died. A small volume of lyrics, *Chamber Music* (1907), was followed in 1914 by *Dubliners*, short stories comprising a "series of chapters in the moral history of his community," with the episodes arranged in progression from childhood to maturity. Joyce's technique, rejecting the short-story contrivances of surprise and coincidence, resembles that of Chekhov. *A Portrait of the Artist as a Young Man* (1916), an autobiographical novel, traces in the hero, Stephen Dedalus, Joyce's own emotional and intellectual growth to the point where he exiled himself from his country, to discover in "silence, exile and cunning" the mode of life or of art whereby his spirit could express itself in "unfettered freedom." Part of a first draft of this novel, edited and published in 1944 from the manuscript in Harvard College Library under the title *Stephen Hero*, offers a revealing artistic comparison with the final version. The themes are the same:

Stephen's family, his friends, the life of Dublin, Catholicism, art; the revision has greater economy and dramatic intensity, and the center of action has been shifted as far as possible inside the consciousness of the hero. A play, *Exiles*, was published in 1918.

In 1922 there appeared in Paris the work on which Joyce had been engaged since 1914, *Ulysses*. A 730-page novel about the events of one day (Thursday, June 16, 1904) in the lives of Stephen Dedalus, Leopold Bloom, his wife Molly, and certain other Dubliners, it combines psychological exploration, especially at the subconscious levels, with experiments in style that in sheer virtuosity are unequaled. Its technical and linguistic innovations deeply influenced contemporary writers; critics explained the book, with its Homeric symbolism, to a reading public intrigued by the censorship ban maintained for several years in England and the United States. In *Dubliners*, writes the critic David Daiches, Joyce is the artist observing his environment; in *A Portrait of the Artist*, he is the artist rejecting his environment; in *Ulysses*, he is the artist recreating from a distance the world he has rejected.

Joyce then spent 17 years on *Finnegans Wake* (1939), sounding still lower reaches of human dream consciousness and experimenting in language to a point where only a few philologists can follow him. Yet anyone with a sensitive ear can derive great pleasure from listening to 'the reading aloud of *Finnegans Wake*. It should be noted in considering the strange stylistic progress from *Dubliners* to *Finnegans Wake* that Joyce had very defective eyesight, and perhaps in consequence, his imagination was auditory rather than visual.   DOROTHY BREWSTER

BIBLIOG.–S. Gilbert, *James Joyce's Ulysses: A Study* (1930); H. Gorman, *James Joyce* (1939); S. Givens, ed., *James Joyce: Two Decades of Criticism* (1948); W. Y. Tindall, *James Joyce: His Way of Interpreting the Modern World* (1950).

JUAN DE FUCA, STRAIT, a passage separating the state of Washington from Canada's Vancouver Island and connecting the Pacific Ocean with the Gulf of Georgia. It was named by Capt. Charles Barkley in 1787 in honor of a Greek sailor who was said to have sailed through the strait at an earlier date. The waterway is about 100 miles long and 15 to 20 miles wide, and contains several islands which comprise San Juan County, Washington.

JUAN, DON. See JOHN OF AUSTRIA.

JUAN FERNÁNDEZ ISLANDS, a small group of volcanic islands belonging to Chile, in the South Pacific between 33° and 34° S lat. at 80° W long., about 400 miles W of Santiago; pop. about 500. The largest island of the group is MAS A TIERRA, where a Scotch seaman, ALEXANDER SELKIRK, was marooned for a number of years. It was from his experiences that DANIEL DEFOE wrote ROBINSON CRUSOE. While the islands have about 100 plants that are found nowhere else, the plants and animals are chiefly like those of Chile. The islands were discovered in 1563 by the Spanish navigator Juan de Fernández, who obtained a grant of them from the Spanish crown. Fernández stocked the islands with pigs and goats and settled

on Mas a Tierra for a time. Pirates and privateers were frequenters of the islands, and pirate gold is reputed to be buried there. Many of the early Pacific explorers, among whom were Schouten, Dampier, and Carteret, visited the islands. The islands became a Chilean possession when that country gained her independence early in the 19th century. Until the 20th century the islands were visited only by Peruvian and Chilean fishermen, although Chile has at times used the islands as a penal colony for political prisoners. Following the sinking of the German cruiser *Dresden* by the British navy in World War I, the islands were used to intern the German survivors. In 1935 Mas a Tierra was established as a national park, and in 1946 Chile built an air base on the same island.   C. S.

JUANA INÉS DE LA CRUZ, SOR, 1651–95, Mexican poetess, nun, was born in San Miguel de Nepantla. In 1669 she entered the convent of San Jerónimo where she wrote numerous poems and plays on religious themes. In spite of the pronounced gongoristic tone of her work, she is considered the greatest lyric poet of her time in Spanish and the most outstanding figure in Mexican colonial literature.

JUÁREZ, BENITO PABLO, 1806–72, president of Mexico, born of Indian parentage, at Guelatao, in the state of Oajaca, of which he was governor

PAUL'S PHOTOS
Benito Juárez

(1847–52). Forced in 1853 to leave Mexico during Santa Anna's ascendancy, he returned in 1855 to join Álvarez, became minister of justice (1855), and secretary of the interior and chief justice (1857), and finally was elected president in 1858. He had to struggle, however, against Miramon, who was recognized as the chief executive by the conservative group. At last, Dec., 1860, Miramon was utterly defeated in battle. In the civil war the treasury was exhausted and Juárez's suspension of payment of Mexico's foreign obligations caused the intervention of France, England, and Spain. A Spanish expedition invaded Mexico in 1861. England and Spain soon withdrew, however, but France engaged in a regular war, the object of which was finally the seating of the Archduke MAXIMILIAN of Austria upon the throne of Mexico, converted into an empire. After the entry of the French into the city of Mexico (1863) Juárez retreated to the northern provinces and continued the struggle. At the beginning of 1867 the French forces were withdrawn from Mexico. Maximilian was besieged by the followers of Juárez in Querétaro, and in June he was taken prisoner and shot. Juárez retained the presidency until his death. See MEXICO, History.

BIBLIOG.–J. A. Magner, *Men of Mexico* (1942); R. E. Stratton, *Juárez of Mexico* (1942); Ralph Roeder, *Juárez and his Mexico* (1947); N. B. Baker, *Juárez, Hero of Mexico* (1949).

JUÁREZ, CIUDAD. See CIUDAD JUÁREZ.

JUAZEIRO, town, E Brazil, in the state of Bahia, in an agricultural region. Pop. (1940) 10,079.

JUAZEIRO, city, NE Brazil, in the state of Ceará. Pop. (1940) 23,761.

JUBA, d. 46 B.C., king of Numidia from about 61 to 46 B.C. In the civil war between Caesar and Pompey he took the latter's side, and after the Battle of Thapsus was won by Caesar, committed suicide.

JUBA, d. c. A.D. 19, son of JUBA, was taken as a child to Rome by Caesar, and gained the favor of Augustus, who restored him to the throne of Numidia in 30 B.C. When Numidia became a Roman province in 25 B.C., Augustus gave Juba the kingdom of Mauritania in exchange for it.

JUBA RIVER, E. Africa, rising at about 7° N lat. in the highlands of Ethiopia, flows E and SE, then

ACME
"Robinson Crusoe" cave on Juan Fernandez island

Jubaland

S into Italian Somaliland, and empties at 0° 14′ S lat. into the Indian Ocean. At its mouth there is a dangerous bar covered by only a fathom of water at high tide; however, the river is navigable for shallow draft vessels 140 miles above the bar. The Yanana, the Web, and the Daua flow into the Juba. Its total length is about 1,000 miles.

JUBALAND, an area of E Africa, formerly a province of Kenya Colony (British), the larger part of which was ceded to Italy in 1925. Italy made it a part of Italian Somaliland. The valley of the Juba River is fertile; the rest of the area is semiarid. It is inhabited by Somalis, who raise cattle and camels.

JUBBULPORE, or **Jabalpur,** city, India, N Central Provinces, capital of Jubbulpore District, 165 miles NNE of Nagpur. The city has an important military cantonment and manufactures military supplies, cotton goods, carpets, glass, and pottery. Jubbulpore is an important trade center. In the early 19th century it was notorious as a haunt of the Thugs. Jubbulpore is modern, with wide, regular streets. Pop. (1941) 178,339.

JÚCAR RIVER, Spain, rises in the Sierra Albarracin, and flows S and E through remarkable defiles, and enters the Mediterranean 25 miles SSE of Valencia. Its length is 270 miles.

JUCHITÁN, town, S Mexico, in the state of Oaxaca; on the Perros River and the isthmus of Tehuantepec. An ancient town which flourished at the time of the Spanish Conquest, the city still retains its old customs and primitive industries, such as the salt manufacture by evaporation. The area produces cereals, sugar, coffee, and cacao. Pop. (1941) 14,550.

JUDAEA, one of the districts into which Palestine was divided in the time of Christ. The captives who returned from Babylon were mainly of the tribe of Judah, and settled largely in the territory of the ancient kingdom of Judah. The name Judaea sometimes connotes Galilee and Samaria as well—i.e. all Palestine west of the Jordan.

JUDAH, the fourth son of Jacob, and the eponymous ancestor of the tribe of the same name. When the Hebrews settled in Canaan as described in the Book of Joshua, the tribe of Judah pressed southward and established itself in a broad strip of territory to the west of the Dead Sea. It comprised the following four districts: the Hill Country, forming the southern portion of the great central ridge of Palestine; the Shephelah, to the west; the wilderness of Judah, or Jeshimon, to the east; and the Negeb, or South Country. The tribe seems to have absorbed large portions of the aboriginal clans. The first king of Israel, Saul, was a Benjamite; but from the accession of David, his successor, the ascendency of Judah becomes marked. The revolt of the ten tribes certainly put her supremacy in dispute; but Judah, with only one other tribe, Benjamin, on her side, was able to resist the eastern invaders for more than a century longer than did her northern rival. See Israel.

JUDAH HA-LEVI, c. 1085–?1140, Jewish philosopher, poet, and physician, born in Toledo in Spain; was the greatest medieval poet who wrote in Hebrew. His poetry, largely adopted in the liturgy of the synagogue, reflects the sufferings as well as the aspirations of his people. He died in the Holy Land while on a pilgrimage there.

JUDAISM

The Jewish religion is one of dignity and strong loyalty to a moral order sanctioned by Yahweh, the God revealed by Moses

JUDAISM: ITS HISTORY AND ITS CONCEPTS. Judaism, the religious faith of the Jewish people, one of the oldest religions of mankind. The history of the faith goes back nearly 4,000 years. Unlike many other religious experiences, it is not

"Moses on Mt. Sinai," an engraving by Gustave Doré, from "The Holy Scriptures" by Martin Luther

built around a personality as are Christianity, Mohammedanism, Buddhism, and Zoroastrianism. Great personalities have contributed to the development of the faith, but none, not even the titanic Moses, was permitted by tradition to overshadow or supersede concepts and practices.

Early Developments. Judaism grew, like so many other historic religions, out of early primitive desert experiences. The world was filled with spirits, many life-bringing, many malignant. Jinn, demons, lurked in dark places, brought plagues and pestilence, carried sickness and death. Every clan had its soothsayer or magician, calculated to win the favor of the good spirits or to destroy the influence of the unfavorable. All through the biblical narrative we have references to similar ways of life, and it is not improbable that many of them were survivals from such primitive forms. The early Hebrew must also have been polydemonic, fearful of every phenomenon, grateful for every blessing. The spirits were harsh and jealous, demanding cruelty to enemies, exulting in the complete destruction of those who sought to harm the tribes that they had chosen to protect. Perhaps there was an element of ancestor worship connected with the veneration of the spirits. Oracles from the dead occur frequently in the Bible, and the teraphim, which often resembled human form, may have been meant for ancestral images. This reconstruction may be justly challenged, for the way is tangled and the facts that throw light upon early practices are few and dim. Yet it cannot be easily denied that the earliest Hebrew religious conceptions were neither greatly in advance of nor greatly behind the conception of kindred desert tribes.

Moses and the God Idea. The development from these primitive notions to the idea of Yahweh and its ethical content may have taken place on Palestine soil, under Egyptian or Babylonian influence. But every tradition points to a remarkable religious revelation wrought by the genius of the desert chieftain, Moses, who imbued his people with a sense of their unity and sanctified the bond by a common devotion to the God, Yahweh. Innumerable legends have grown up about Moses, but discounting any idealization of character and career, most critics place him among the great religious leaders of all time.

To Moses, Yahweh was indissolubly bound up with the lives of men and the moral order of the universe. He was the sanction for all the laws which governed society. They were not made simply for the convenience of men. They were Yahweh's will and part of an inscrutable divine scheme. To break the moral law, then, was more than a crime against society; it was a sin against Yahweh. There followed from this a unique relation between Yahweh and his people. Yahweh indeed sought to help Israel. He was the Lord of hosts, fighting for his people; but never at the expense of the moral order. This was absolute and unchangeable. The moral nature of other gods was perhaps not inferior to Yahweh's; but other gods were not so bound up with the moral law. They could stretch it, change it, forget it, when their own favorites were involved. Yahweh could not unbend even for his chosen people. It is this magnificent austerity, this undeviating loyalty to a principle of law, suggested in the monumental masterpiece of Michelangelo, which raises Moses to the heights in religious history. His Yahweh was often narrow and jealous; his laws were often steeped in the primitive spirit of the desert. But he had linked his people to Yahweh and the moral law in a sublime, indissoluble trinity. The union remained the basis of the faith of the prophets, of the great teachers of mankind, when they had exalted both the concept of Yahweh and the moral code which he demanded. See JEHOVAH.

Yahweh and Baal. After many moving experiences, described in detail in the early books of the Bible, the Hebrews conquered portions of Palestine and, over a period of decades in the 13th century B.C., they took over all the land. The Books of Joshua and Judges are filled with the stories of the long, drawn-out battles for a foothold and for ultimate conquest. Once the Hebrew tribes were settled there were important effects on their social and religious outlook.

The first contact of Yahwism and the native Baalism was doubtless a dramatic clash; each people clung desperately to its gods, appealing for assistance in the hour of direst need and ruthlessly uprooting all institutions which seemed alien. But after the Hebrews had settled down to a stable life, antagonisms diminished and a process of assimilation began. By degrees, loyalty to Yahweh wavered as BAAL beckoned alluringly. Gods, shrines, festivals, habits, all found their way into Hebrew life. The assimilation has been often compared to the astonishing process by which a great body of pagan practices was built into the structure of early Christianity. Doctrines and dogmas were taken from pagan philosophies; rites and ceremonies were borrowed from pagan temples. The Church Fathers gave them new meanings and associated them with events in the history of Christianity. This religious synthesis is not uncommon wherever two civilizations come into close contact. The contact brought with it great dangers. Shrines and festivals might be assimilated without serious hurt. But there also crept into the religion of the Hebrews a pernicious polytheism which threatened to debilitate Hebrew life. For long the Hebrews lived on a plane no higher than any contemporary people. This was the background for the PROPHETS who came, aflame with anger, at the degradation of the old desert faith, demanding root and branch reformation. They were a turning point not only in Hebrew history but in the religious history of mankind.

The Prophetic Heritage. The prophets are as surely the contribution to civilization of ancient Israel as Hellenic art is the Greek contribution, and imperial law and government the Roman. Extraordinarily complex spirits they were: supreme individualists, yet preaching restraint and conformity to law; innately religious, yet despising the forms that religion often took. They smote the idea of a national god and a narrow patriotism. They labored to substitute plain, moral requirements for elaborate ceremonial and formal creed. They were the stern guardians of individual and national conduct, the living Hebrew conscience, the poets of statesmanship. And they were completely fearless in pursuing their self-appointed mission, bearing abuse with sublime patience, defying kings and priests and populace alike, eternal rebels.

They must not be identified with the generations of quacks who preceded them and called themselves prophets. Genuine prophecy was not concerned with prediction or with working charms. It was related to the reformation of the moral order. A prophet like Amos was revolted by the self-satisfaction of the leaders of his people. He challenged the complacency of those who identified goodness with ritualistic piety. Yahweh's justice could not be satisfied with empty forms. Those who brought in sacrifices did not wash away their guilt—they heightened it, for they compounded evil with hypocrisy. A prophet like Hosea tempered the emphasis upon justice with an appeal to love and mercy. He preached the doctrine of a God who cared, with all the solicitude of a loving father, for the welfare of his children. Doom was not irrevocable. It need not come if the sinner would only see the light. A prophet like Isaiah went even further. He emphasized the highest standard of conduct in a people as in an individual. When he spoke of Israel as a chosen people he did not mean that it was therefore a favorite people. Israel was chosen only in the sense that it was obliged to live above the average. And the simple democratic Micah put it all in unforgettable language: "What doth the Lord require of thee, but to do justly, to love mercy, and to walk humbly with thy God?"

The great religious geniuses of the eighth, seventh and sixth centuries B.C., AMOS, HOSEA, ISAIAH, Micah, JEREMIAH and the others, changed the religion of the Hebrews. They crystallized the progressive thought which had been developing for three centuries and gave it an expression which influenced the subsequent history of three religions. They became a model for all rebels who placed national and individual life on a moral basis, holding conscience higher than law. It is sometimes suggested that the prophets repudiated all ritual and ceremonial. Superficially it would seem so. Amos hated the festivals; the psalms and songs were din in his ears. Isaiah called the entrance of sacrifice into Yahweh's courts a desecration. Yet the prophets did not repudiate the *forms* of religion. They repudiated their abuse. When they lived, the dogmas had often become charms, magical formulas, intended to induce the deity to favorable action. There was little spirit in organized religion; it sometimes sank to heathen levels. It was the degeneration which the prophets smote without fear and without stint. They had no quarrel with a cultus practiced sincerely and with understanding hearts.

Babylonian Exile and Impact. The prophets did their work during the turbulent centuries of Hebrew national existence in Palestine. But in the eighth century the northern kingdom of ISRAEL was destroyed; two centuries later the southern kingdom of JUDAH was laid low by the Babylonians. Great numbers of the Jewish inhabitants were uprooted and resettled in Babylon. Many of the Jews were swallowed up and disappeared. A fervid minority held fast. They kept, almost desperately, every custom which bound them to their past, and they worshiped Yahweh with more fervor now that they were set down in an alien environment. Their religious concepts became clearer, more mature. They began to understand the deeper significance of the prophetic messages. Yahweh was not dependent on temples and sacrifices. He was a god of the heart, as near in Babylon as in Palestine, present wherever men sought him out.

It was during this period, too, that the institution of the SYNAGOGUE developed, destined to survive until the present time. Bereft of temples and of religious centers, each little community created its own meeting place. The exiles would congregate, usually on the Sabbath, to hear their elders read to them the prayers which had been handed down by tradition. Alms would be distributed, and perhaps there would be instruction in the ritual that was practical in a strange land. When the exile was over, the synagogue was brought back to Palestine. And when national life was again snuffed out, the synagogue went with the wandering Jews into every corner of the globe. All through the ages there was never a place where Jews could not meet to keep alive the faith of their ancestors.

The Pharisaic Developments. Meantime, there was a return to Palestine on the part of many of the tenacious exiles and national life was temporarily restored. The TEMPLE was rebuilt. The scribes, forerunners of the PHARISEES, became the interpreters of the law, the leaders in the synagogues. Zealous in their belief that the law of God must be strictly observed and that Israel must remain a separate people, they fought every attempt at religious laxness and easy assimilation with non-Jewish inhabitants and neighbors. It was due to them that, after the fifth century, Israel threw itself into complete dependence on the TORAH, the Mosaic law, as the guide for life.

The law, which had been orally preserved for generations, was now carefully brought together and consecrated as the foundation of Jewish civil and religious life. "Turn it and turn it again," the scribes admonished their people, "for everything is in it." And the Jews responded with unparalleled devotion. All existence was centered in the law. The Jews became the people of the book. The early Hebrews had created the BIBLE out of their lives; their descendants created their lives out of the Bible.

But the Torah in itself contained only general principles. These required application and elaboration. New laws were therefore deduced from the old ones, new meanings were ferreted out of every sentence. So a school of interpreters developed, the Pharisees, whose work continued for centuries and became the foundation of the TALMUD. The process was not devised by petty spirits to chain men to the letter of the law. On the contrary, it was hoped to make the ancient law practical in the life of later generations. In the field of civil law the new principles were decidedly useful. Those which were afterward embodied in the MISHNA were sound and humane and were a distinct improvement on many of the Biblical injunctions. In the field of religious practice, too, many of the new interpretations helped to enrich the spiritual life. The Sabbath became a useful day of rest, with many of its onerous prohibitions modified.

It was inevitable, however, that the endless spinning of meanings from the old texts should sometimes go to extremes and become burdensome. Hence there were protests. The Book of Jonah was such a protest, written to combat a tendency to narrow chauvinism. The Book of Ruth was a beautiful idyll which pointed out that even King David descended from a daughter of Moab and there was no virtue in a narrow exclusivism.

The two tendencies, one calling for adherence to a revealed way of life, the other opposing the imposition of dogmatic authority, produced a fundamental antimony, never to be reconciled. They continue to struggle for expression in Judaism and in all organized religions. It is easy to stigmatize the first as a harsh legalism which breeds intolerance and exclusiveness and impoverishes spiritual life by robbing it of spontaneity and freedom. Yet each type of faith is immortal and draws adherents from men of opposite temperaments. The Pharisees built their ideals upon what they accepted as a divine revelation. They insisted that men could live best only by following the precepts of this divine law as interpreted by its great teachers. Though there were occasional shortcomings, the work of the Pharisees was not stultifying, as is so often insisted by some writers. It gave solidity to the religious idealism of a number of the noblest teachers of all time. To pious souls it gave a practical outlet for high earnestness and moral zeal. In creating a clear set of principles by which to live, it helped to

link Jews scattered in all parts of the known world. Above all, it preserved Jewish solidarity in the crisis soon to follow, when nations and religions were all beset by the seductive power of Greco-Roman paganism.

Judaism and Hellenism. After several centuries of discipline, Jewish life was suddenly menaced by the power of Hellenism. For when Europe and Asia were conquered, in the fourth century B.C., by Alexander and his successors, the culture of the Greeks, not so much in its highest form, but in its degenerate form, threatened to engulf the world. Every people, great and small, sooner or later succumbed, except the stubborn little folk of Palestine. For four centuries, until the destruction of the Jewish state by the Romans, the Jews waged a life and death struggle. In the end, though Jewish thought was unmistakably influenced by the long contact with Hellenism and by the struggle against it, Judaism survived distinct and more militant than ever.

The best in the Greek spirit did not meet the best in the Hebrew spirit. It might have been possible to round out national life beautifully with the burning zeal for social righteousness of an Amos or an Isaiah, and the serene wisdom of a Socrates or a Plato, the moral fervor of a Jeremiah, and the artistic genius of a Praxiteles. But the splendid achievements of the philosophers and the artists, their search for truth and beauty, their mellowed humanistic approach, did not come to the East in the wagons of the Greek conquerors. There came instead a degraded imitation of Hellenism, externals with the glowing heart burnt out, a crude paganism, a callousness for the common weal, a cheap sophistry, a cynicism easily undermining old conceptions and older loyalties, but substituting nothing constructive to take their place. Too often the gymnasium and the amphitheater meant mere lewdness and licentiousness; the search for intellectual clarity meant dishonest banter and trickiness, the pursuit of the beautiful meant moral irresponsibility. Perhaps there would have been no revolt against all of this but for the stupidity of one of the Syrian conquerors, Antiochus Epiphanes, who usurped the throne in 175 B.C. He was not ready to let Greek culture have its way quietly. He began a systematic persecution of those who would not be Hellenized. He issued an edict prohibiting, on pain of death, further observance of Jewish practices and then added insult to injury by compelling loyalty to the pagan abominations which he substituted. This brought the Maccabean revolt, described with prophetic fervor in the Book of the Maccabees and in the prophetic utterances of the Book of Daniel. Syria was so beset by other enemies at the same time that the Jews, though greatly outnumbered, were able in 142 B.C., to win their independence and the right to their own worship.

Judaism had a new lease on life. Deeply influenced by Greek thinking, it kept to its essential monotheism, and to its ethical discipline. It had a fine vitality and, in the centuries preceding the triumph of Christianity, it even had a brief proselytizing period, one of the few in the history of the Jews. For the old paganism, especially in the Near East, was decaying, and sensitive minds were repelled by it. The uncompromising monotheism and the rational practices of the Hebrews, expounded with charm by the Hellenized Jewish writers, made a deep impression. There were great numbers of converts, if not officially to Judaism, at least to Jewish practices and ideals. The converts, referred to in the Acts as "God fearing Greeks" were welcomed by the scattered Jewish communities and freely admitted to the services of the synagogue. It was among these converts, whose spirits were leavened by Jewish concepts, that the early Christians made their first converts.

The Long Talmudic Experience. And now for hundreds of years Judaism revolved about the Talmudic law. It has grown up over the centuries and the Jews, without a land, without a common language, without cohesion that was physical, utilized it, in Heine's brilliant phrase, as "a portable Fatherland." The Talmud was not displaced until modern times. It became the citadel of Jewish life all through the bitter Middle Ages, and, in Eastern Europe down to our own day. Almost as soon as the Jewish youngster was able to lisp his alphabet he was set to pore over the pages of the bulky tomes; most often his mind was steeped in Talmudic discussions long before he had clearly grasped the Bible itself. And the study of the Talmud continued until the very day of death. Pages of the Talmud, like pages of the prayer books which had been torn and tattered in use, were reverently placed aside and buried with the dead.

The Talmud faithfully reflected the beliefs and notions of its people. In close proximity were the superstitions of the contemporary world and the most advanced ethical ideals. The Talmud attempted to mold lives in the spirit of charity and self sacrifice.

Persecution of Jews in the Middle Ages, from a painting by 19th-century Dutch artist, Karel Ooms

"He who gives charity in secrecy," the rabbis said, "is greater than Moses himself." They taught an exalted concept of God and the true meaning of tolerance. Though lovers of learning, they cherished kindness more than wisdom, a clean spirit above knowledge. Their ideals were often limited by the world in which they lived, but more often they soared high above its passions and hatreds. When they taught, the Roman empire was fast decaying and the barbarian hordes, not yet tinctured by Christianity, dissipated their energies in continuous war.

Revolts Against the Talmud. Occasionally there were revolts against the Talmud and its interpretation of Judaism. The most formidable came in the eighth century A.D., and was led by Anan ben David who insisted that the Bible alone was the supreme authority in Jewish life and that the Talmudic traditions had no validity and were not binding. Because of their strict adherence to the written word of the Torah, unchanged by any interpretation, the new sect became known as the *Bnai Mikra*, the Children of the Text, or the KARAITES. The new doctrines released the Karaites from many traditions. The dietary laws, for example, were made less stringent. Yet there was much new severity when the Talmudic modifications of the biblical word were denied authority. Fast days were multiplied; the only meat that could be eaten was deer meat; the only fowl, pigeon. Physicians were barred, for did not the Scriptures say clearly: "I am the Lord that healeth thee." The Karaite sect spread, and for a time it threatened to become supreme in Jewish life. But in the 10th century, with the rise of Saadiah, one of the ablest religious philosophers in Jewish history, and the powerful champion of Tal-

mudic Judaism, Karaism began to lose its vitality. It depended for its strength upon the very principles that weakened it. Its individualism, the idea that called it into being, prevented its organization. Hence there was a split into quarreling sects, each holding different views. After the 11th century their Karaite numbers steadily declined and the group ceased to play an influential part in Jewish life. It gained a temporary importance during the Reformation when Catholics hurled the epithet *Karaei* at Protestants, in contempt for their adherence to the biblical text, a term which the Protestants gladly accepted. But Karaism served a very useful purpose. Talmudic Judaism required periodic protests against its supremacy to prevent it from ossifying. It was helpful to remind the rabbis that, while interpretation of the Bible was highly commendable, when the process was carried too far it could easily become self-defeating.

Medieval Sorrows. The late Middle Ages were a period of ever increasing difficulty for the Jewish communities of Europe. Life became a long succession of indignities and brutalities, culminating in wholesale massacres and expulsions. As a result, Jews lost their resiliency of mind, and their power of judgment. Many Jews harkened to charlatans who promised them a way out, rascals and fanatics who claimed to be Messiahs, sent by God to usher in a new world. Other Jews swooned into an other-worldly kind of mysticism. The mystical tradition itself, climaxed in the Kabbala, was healthy and wholesome. But it often degenerated into superstition and the mumbo-jumbo of word juggling and miracle mongering. Persecution became successful beyond the fondest hopes of the Jew-baiters. They could look with satisfaction upon the medieval Jew, bent, broken, ignorant, grasping at straws. They could laugh at his pathetic claim, still fervently intoned, that he was the guardian of the prophetic spirit.

Modern Developments. At long last, in the 18th century, when the great emancipation movements began, there was release of the Jewish spirit too. A great revitalization came to Eastern Europe through the rise of Chassidism, a warm emotional faith which brought new life to thousands of neglected souls in Eastern Europe. The founder was Israel of Moldavia, reverently known as the Baal Shem Tov, the Master of the Good Name, who substituted a warm mysticism for the arid scholasticism which had engulfed so much of Jewish religious practice. Chassidism made prayer more meaningful and enriched the liturgy of the synagogue. Its emphasis upon cheerfulness and optimism dispelled the clouds which so often obscured the sun and the promise of a better tomorrow. In the literary revival of the 19th century it was natural that scenes from Chassidic life should furnish the inspiration for many a novelist and poet.

Meantime, in the heart of Lithuania came another great renaissance movement, stemming from the magnificent work of Elijah, the Vilna Gaon. Elijah had little sympathy for mysticism but he was as antagonistic to the casuistry of the scholastics. He aimed to bring life and faith back to the simple textual meaning of the Bible and the Talmud. He cut through obscurantism and word juggling and under his sure guidance arose a new respect for the law and custom of the Talmud and for rational study and practice.

Above all, through the work of MOSES MENDELSSOHN, Jews of Germany and of western Europe moved out of their spiritual ghettos and began to participate in the intellectual life of Europe. In 1783 Mendelssohn translated the Pentateuch into beautiful German prose and added a clear concise commentary. Its influence was enormous. The Jews, whose long confinement within physical and mental ghettos had corrupted their speech, learned German from the translation. They used the instrument to probe into every field, and their minds, long cut off from the channels of Western thought, were now flooded with new ideas and new points of view. Gradually the whole motif of Jewish education was changed. The Bible became important, not only for religious principles, but also for language and for its literary and aesthetic qualities. Mendelssohn thus opened a new world to his people. They became interested in Germany and in German thought. They began to long for citizenship, for participation in the life of the nation. They became Germans and Europeans. When emancipation came to the other countries of western Europe, similar developments occurred.

Reform, Orthodox and Conservative Judaism. Through the 19th century, as Judaism squarely met the currents of change, of the new science, of Darwinism, of the great social forces which were released by the political and economic revolutions, it was natural for different points of view to develop. Modern *Reform* Judaism stems from this period of transition. Its leaders sought to modify the ancient teachings in the light of the changes in each generation. They welcomed the new science, for far from harming true religion, it strengthened it. There was no fundamental conflict. Religious faith was still a necessity, for science solved none of the mysteries of life and death, the secrets of creation, the wonders of divine inspiration. As for the Bible, one could discard its limited scientific concepts and still look upon the old writ as a magnificent ethical and spiritual repository.

But *Orthodox* Jews stood by all the old traditions. They took the position that the Bible was the revealed word of God and that man was happiest if he faithfully followed its teachings. The marvels of science might improve man's physical lot, and these marvels, God's gifts, were to be gratefully accepted. But they gave no warrant for changing beliefs or practices that had come from the past. Man's mind was too limited to question the word of the divine law.

Conservative Jews followed a middle course. They used MAIMONIDES' method of rationalization. After all, they suggested, the new science was not incompatible with a view of the Bible as a verbally inspired document. The miracles and stories which did not square with science were allegories. The view that religion had developed gradually was met with the thesis that remarkably gifted religious personalities were the most important factor in the developing process. There was nothing in evolution, for example, to deny that Moses, by divine intuition, could create a religious system which was far in advance of all that subsequent ages painfully realized.

The Essence of Judaism. In contemporary Jewish life there are these mental and temperamental differences among various groups, and a great many more. But despite differences, the basic essentials remain, and they are linked with the oldest elements in Judaism. These include the belief in one God, a God of uncompromising integrity, the belief that God is best honored and respected through emphasis upon justice and mercy and love and charity, and that Israel is one of His messengers to create a better world. If the Jews are a chosen group, they are chosen only in the sense of *noblesse oblige*, of heavy responsibility. Sorrow and distress have been constant companions in the long trek through the centuries, but these experiences have been a chastening influence, serving to purify the dross, to fit the people better for the mission of helping, with other great faiths, to bring about the fatherhood of God and the brotherhood of man.   A. L. SACHAR

BIBLIOG.–M. Steinberg, *Basic Judaism* (1947); B. D. Cohen, *Judaism in Theory and Practice* (1948); A Marmorstein, *Studies in Jewish Theology* (1950); P. S. Bernstein, *What the Jews Believe* (1951).

JUDAS ISCARIOT, one of the disciples of JESUS, and His betrayer, is believed to have belonged to the village of Kerioth, now El-Karjetein in South Judah. When he became a disciple, he was chosen to carry and administer the funds (John 13:29). He displayed a grasping disposition and ultimately betrayed Jesus to the Jewish authorities for 30 pieces of silver.

Overcome with remorse at the dreadful outcome of his crime, he committed suicide, of which rash act two discrepant accounts are given (Matt. 27:3 f.; Acts 1:18).

JUDAS MACCABAEUS, the deliverer of the Jews from the Syrian yoke in the reign of Antiochus Epiphanes, was the third son of Mattathias, the priest who began the revolt. Judas met and routed in succession the Syrian generals Apollonius and Seron (I Macc. 3), and captured Beth-horon; defeated Ptolemy, Nicanor, and Georgias near Mizpeh, and Lysias at Beth-sur (164 B.C.). He then devoted himself to the purification of the temple at Jerusalem. He subsequently made successful attacks upon the neighboring tribes, Edom, Ammon, etc.; but after the death of Antiochus (164) his good fortune began to desert him. He suffered a repulse at Beth-Zacharias; and although he again defeated Nicanor at Adasa (161), his army, now shrunk in numbers, was crushed by a large force under Bacchides at Elasa, and himself slain (I Macc. 9). Judas had every gift of a great general—bodily strength, ready judgment, power of organizing, courage, zeal, and, above all, faith—and is to be regarded as one of the most heroic figures in the history of Israel. His career forms the subject of one of Handel's greatest oratorios, *Judas Maccabaeus*. See MACCABEES.

JUDAS TREE, a name sometimes applied to the elder tree, and to various trees belonging to the leguminous genus *Cercis*, each in turn reported to be the tree on which Judas hanged himself. The European *C. siliquastrum* is the species most frequently meant, and the name has been transferred to the American representative of the genus *Cercis*, *C. canadensis*, most common in the Middle West, where it reaches a height of about 50 feet, and a trunk diameter of one foot. It has pink-purple, papilionaceous flowers.

JUDD, CHARLES HUBBARD, 1873–1946, American psychologist and educator, was born in Bareilly, British India, was brought to the United States six years later, and studied at Wesleyan, Leipzig, and Yale universities. After teaching psychology at New York University (1898–1901), the University of Cincinnati (1901–2), and Yale University (1902–9), he served as professor and chairman of the Department of Education at the University of Chicago (1909–38) and chairman of the Psychology Department (1920–25). Judd's works include: *Genetic Psychology for Teachers* (1903); *The Psychology of Secondary Education* (1927); *Education and Social Progress* (1934); *Teaching the Evolution of Civilization* (1946).

JUDD, ORANGE, 1822–92, American editor and publisher, was born near Niagara Falls, N.Y., and graduated (1847) from Wesleyan University. After some years of work as a teacher he took a course at Yale (1850–53) in analytical and agricultural chemistry, and began to contribute to agricultural papers. Editor of the *American Agriculturist* (1853–83), of which he became proprietor in 1856, Judd was actively engaged in field work with the U.S. Sanitary Commission during the Civil War. He moved to Chicago, 1883, and there established the *Orange Judd Farmer* and the company by which it is published. He founded the Hall of Natural Science at Wesleyan (1871), which bears his name, and was active as a trustee of the university (1871–81).

JUDE, THE EPISTLE OF. See BIBLE; NEW TESTAMENT.

JUDGE, in our legal system, the presiding officer of a court of justice. As the administration of justice involves the determination both of questions of law and of fact, the same person or group of persons may perform both functions, or the two may be separated, questions of law being decided by one man or set of men and questions of fact, in whole or in part, by another. The former practice was followed in the Greek and Roman systems of jurisprudence and still obtains, with some modifications, in the modern systems of the Continent and of Spanish America which are derived from the

Roman law. Such persons, however numerous they may be, are known as judges. The separation of the two functions of determining law and fact in the English and American jurisprudence has resulted in vesting the latter in a separate branch of the court known as the JURY, the title "judge" being confined to the member or members of the court to whom is committed the decision of questions of law. Many questions of fact, however, are even in our system decided by the judges. The great power and divinity of the judicial office are recognized in the care exercised in every civilized country to secure fit men to perform its duties. Judges in Great Britain and the United States almost invariably are selected from the legal profession and are protected by the bar in the exercise of their high office. In many other countries the judiciary constitutes a separate profession, its members being specially trained for the performance of judicial duties. Formerly in Europe, as is still the case in some oriental states, the king or chief administered justice in person. As the "fountain of justice" he still appoints the officers who are to administer the law in his stead. In England the actual power of appointing minor judicial officers, such as county court judges, is vested in the lord chancellor, who is himself appointed by the Crown on the recommendation of the government for the time being. The judges of the High Court of Justice are appointed by royal patent. In this country the practice of filling the judicial office varies. The judges of the United States Supreme Court and of the circuit and district courts are appointed by the president subject to confirmation by the Senate. In some of the states all judges of record are appointed by the governor, whereas in many, if not most of them, all judges of whatever degree are elected by the people. In the Federal system and in some of the states judges hold office for life, but in most states for a fixed term of years. In the United States judges are removable by IMPEACHMENT and, in some if not all of the states, by vote of the legislature. See COURT; TRIAL, *Functions of Judge and Jury.*

JUDGE ADVOCATE, specialist in law on the staff of the Judge Advocate General's Corps of either the U.S. Army or Air Corps who renders legal advice and assists in administering the courts of the command to which he is attached. His counterpart in the Navy is the legal officer. In order to hold appointment from the judge advocate general, the judge advocate must be a graduate of an accredited law school or have the equivalent legal training. Aside from his administrative and advisory duties, a judge advocate may be required to act as trial counsel (prosecutor), defense counsel, or "law officer" in a court-martial. In all general courts-martial, all of these offices must be filled by judge advocates; in a special court-martial, counsels need not be judge advocates except that if the trial counsel is a judge advocate, then the defense counsel must be, also. As law officer in a court-martial, the judge advocate acts as general adviser on procedure to the court's presiding officer, and as a witness to the authenticity of the record of the trial. A routine duty of the staff judge advocate is to review the proceedings and findings of all courts-martial held in his command area and make report to his commandant as to their validity.

The Judge Advocate General is the head of the corps or office in the U.S. Army, Navy, or Air Corps whose major function is to supervise the administering of military justice. He is the custodian of all records of trials or inquiries by military courts or commissions, and of all papers relating to military reservations, parks, etc. Like the judge advocate, the judge advocate general serves as legal advisor to his commander, who is the chief of staff of his department, and at his request may even draft or propose legislation relating to the military establishment. See COURTS, MILITARY; MILITARY LAW.   L. S. B.

JUDGES, THE BOOK OF, purports to narrate the history of Israel from the death of Joshua till the time of Samuel. After an introduction (ch. 1–3:4), giving an account of the subjugation of Canaan differing from that in the Book of Joshua (see JOSHUA), it gives the histories of the several "judges" in their long-protracted struggle with internal or external foes—viz., Othniel, Ehud, Shamgar, DEBORAH (with Barak), GIDEON (with Abimelech's usurpation), Tola, Jair, Jephthah, Ibzan, Elon, Abdon, and SAMSON (3:5–16). Chapters 17–20 form a sort of appendix treating of two sinister episodes of the period. The book shows a relatively simple structure; the history of the earlier judges is largely cast according to the following recurrent cycle of events:—Israel sins, is given over to the enemy, and sore oppressed for a period; is then delivered by the particular judge, and has rest for (mostly) 40 years. Parts of the book, notably the song of Deborah (ch. 5), are undoubtedly very ancient; and the compiler, writing after the captivity of the ten tribes (cf. 18:30), seems to have availed himself of written sources throughout, though how far such sources can be identified with the various strata of the Pentateuch (see HEXATEUCH) is a moot point. See BIBLE; OLD TESTAMENT.

JUDGMENT, in law, a decision, decree, or sentence of a court; also, the obligation, as a debt, created by decree of court. There are many types of judgments, a money judgment being the most common. Certain types of judgments are denominated *decrees*, such as the *decree of divorce* and the *mortgage foreclosure decree.*

When *A* brings to a successful conclusion a lawsuit filed against *B* on some personal liability (such as that arising on *B*'s promissory note or because of personal injuries inflicted by *B*) the court enters an order directing that *B* pay *A* the amount found due *A*. This order is a *judgment. A* is the *judgment creditor* and *B* is the *judgment debtor*. In many states such a judgment is a lien on *B*'s land. That is, *B*'s land may be sold by the sheriff or other local officer to raise funds for the payment of the judgment, and *B* cannot defeat this right by selling his land, once the judgment has been rendered against him. In addition to being a lien on any real estate presently owned by the judgment debtor, a judgment also becomes a lien on any real estate afterward acquired by him unless or until the judgment is satisfied. Thus, if *A* obtains a judgment against *B* in 1942 and in 1943 *B* acquires title to a tract of land, the lien of *A*'s judgment immediately attaches to this land.

As a rule, a judgment is a lien only on the actual interest of the debtor in the land. For example, *A* bought and paid for certain land, but directed the seller to convey the title to *B*. Thereafter, *C* obtained a judgment against *B*. The court held that *B* was a mere title holder, had no beneficial interest in the land, and a judgment against him would not become a lien on the land.

A judgment exists from the time of its rendition or pronouncement by the court, and in a few states the judgment lien attaches to the judgment debtor's land as of that date. In most states, however, it is required that all judgments be entered in books which are alphabetically arranged according to the name of the judgment debtor and which are maintained by the court clerk, and a judgment does not become a lien until it is entered in these books. In some states the judgment does not become a lien until it is filed in the register's or recorder's office. A judgment is a lien on all land of the judgment debtor located in the county where the judgment was rendered. If the judgment debtor owns land in some other county of the same state, the judgment can be made a lien on the land by filing an official copy of the judgment in the proper office of such county. A money judgment can be enforced by public sale of the judgment debtor's land or personal property by garnishment of his wages or other sums due him, and in a few cases (such as nonpayment of a judgment for a malicious injury or nonpayment of alimony) by imprisonment until the judgment is paid.

The first step in the enforcement of a judgment by sale of property is the issuance of an *execution* and its delivery to the sheriff. The next step is known as a *levy*. This consists of those acts by which a sheriff sets apart and appropriates for the purpose of satisfying the command of the execution, a particular piece of the judgment debtor's property. In the case of personal property, the sheriff or other officer actually seizes the property levied on. Next, the sheriff publishes notice of the coming sale and posts copies thereof in certain public places. At the date fixed for sale, the sheriff auctions off the real estate to the highest bidder, who is actually the judgment creditor, since he can bid up the amount of his judgment without producing any cash other than the sheriff's costs. In many states there is a redemption period in sheriff's sales of land, one year being the most frequently encountered. Ultimately, if no redemption, a sheriff's deed issues to the purchaser. The duration of a judgment lien varies from state to state, with a ten year period the most common. When a judgment is paid, the judgment creditor files a formal discharge. This is known as a *satisfaction*. See DICTUM; EXECUTION; LIEN.   ROBERT KRATOVIL

JUDGMENT DAY, in Christian theology, is the time of the final determination of the destinies of men, to take place at the world's end. In the Old Testament the "day of Yahweh" was awaited as the time of Israel's salvation, but to one of the minor prophets (Amos 5:18–27) it becomes a day of judgment which will sift even the chosen nation and bring to destruction all that is unworthy. When the belief in a personal resurrection had been fully developed in New Testament times, Christ is represented as speaking of a tremendous crisis which is to take place at the end of the world, when he personally will return and bring all peoples before him to separate the good from the evil in a final arbitrament. It is manifest in several passages of the New Testament that the destinies of men are fixed by their actions during life, and that death closes their account by an immediate and particular judgment. Therefore, Judgment Day, or the Last Judgment, becomes a public verification of those destinies. It is the Christian belief that Christ is to be the principal of the final judgment and that men's ultimate fate will be determined by their relation to him.

JUDICATURE ACTS are the successive enactments of Parliament from 1873 to the present day by which the English judicial system has been reformed and changed. The practice and procedure of the High Court of Justice is now regulated by the Judicature Act of 1925 which repealed and consolidated all the former Judicature Acts and rules formulated under them.

Before the 1873 revision, justice had for many hundreds of years been administered by a great number of independent tribunals of diverse origin, some of which exercised a concurrent jurisdiction and some a jurisdiction which differed in spirit and in procedure from that exercised by others. The most important of these earlier courts were the courts of King's Bench, of Common Pleas, and of Exchequer, the High Court of Chancery, the Admiralty Court, the Court of Probate and for Divorce and Matrimonial Causes, the last two of which were derived from the older ecclesiastical tribunals. All of these were merged by the acts in question in one great court, known as the "Supreme Court of Judicature," to sit in two permanent divisions—the High Court of Justice and the Court of Appeal. The supreme judicial functions of the House of Lords and the Privy Council were not interfered with. The further important changes effected by the Judicature Acts were (1) the consolidation of law and equity jurisdiction and (2) the simplification of procedure. In all of these particulars the Acts did little more than put into effect in England reforms which had already been made in the United States.

JUDICIAL POWER. See SUPREME COURT OF THE UNITED STATES, *Organization and Business.*

JUDICIAL REVIEW is the power of the courts to pass upon the legislature acts of Congress or of states' legislatures with reference to their constitutionality, and the power of the court to enforce its decisions arising from its failure or refusal to enforce such acts or legislative enactments as it deems unconstitutional. This is a unique development in the United States and was by no means arrived at as a simple pragmatic principle of government. In the English government no such right of judicial review is effective, for Parliament is sovereign and can by legislation supersede any judicial determination. However in some countries, notably Australia and Canada, Mexico, Brazil, Argentina, Venezuela, and Austria, where constitutional governments exist, some measure of judicial review maintains.

Under the Constitution of the United States judicial review was not a specifically delegated power although its existence is inherent in the plan of delegation of powers, but it is the inevitable outcome of the courts having power to decide cases, that they should also have power to interpret and enforce the laws.

No precedent for judicial review existed in the colonial governments in this country, and state governments were framed on the theory of state sovereignty which for practical purposes meant state legislative sovereignty. However the principle of judicial review was voiced as early as 1610 in a famous dictum of Lord Coke in Dr. Banhams' Case, 8 Rep. 107, 118 to the effect that there was a common law superior to the acts of Parliament which would control in case of inconsistency. Before the crystallization of the principle of judicial review, it was not extraordinary for state legislatures to annul or modify judgments of courts, reopen private controversies and settle them by "special acts." Disregard of treaty obligations of the nation in the interest of preserving vested rights caused curbs to become necessary. One curb was the gubernatorial veto; and the other, judicial review.

The first case of state judicial review was in the case of *Holmes* v. *Walton,* decided in New Jersey (1780) where the question at issue was whether a jury of six as provided by statute was constituted so as to give a "trial by jury," and the court refused to enforce the statute. Later, in 1787, the North Carolina Supreme Court in *Bayard* v. *Singleton* (1 Martin 42) and the Rhode Island Supreme Court in 1786 in *Trevett* v. *Weedon* found state laws unconstitutional.

The Federal Judiciary Act of 1789 recognized the power of review of the constitutionality of acts of Congress and in 1795 there was a test case to review the constitutionality of the "carriage tax" passed in 1794. Judicial review then became a test of constitutionality of any law.

In the famous case of *Marbury* v. *Madison,* the United States Supreme Court assumed original jurisdiction of a case involving a constitutional question. Many important decisions have been made on the constitutionality of laws since that time. They have tended to limit the scope of judicial review, and to concern substantive matters of law rather than forms of procedure. The most widely used and significant basis for testing constitutionality was on the question of "due process of law" as judicially transcribed and interpreted.

It has been said that the argument in favor of judicial review is that it stabilizes business conditions nationally by obviating local legislative interference. The argument against it is that it delays and frustrates needed reform legislation. See APPEAL; CONSTITUTIONAL LAW; CONSTITUTION; LAW; SUPREME COURT OF THE UNITED STATES.

BIBLIOG.—H. R. Hale, *Judicial Review versus Doctrinaire Democracy,* 10 Amer. Bar Journal 882; C. G. Haines *The*

American Doctrine of Judicial Supremacy (1914); J. R. Commons, *The Legal Foundations of Capitalism* (1924); C. Warren, *Congress, the Constitution and the Supreme Court* (1925); L. B. Boudin, *Government by Judiciary*, 2 vols. (1932).

JUDICIARY. See COURT; JUDGE; SUPREME COURT OF THE UNITED STATES.

JUDITH, THE BOOK OF, one of the Old Testament Apocrypha. It records how Holofernes, at the head of 132,000 troops, had been commissioned by Nebuchadnezzar to take vengeance on the countries, including Judaea, which had not aided the king in the war against the Medes; and how, while he was besieging Bethulia, Judith, a Jewish widow, gained access to him by her beauty, and, having drugged him with wine, cut off his head. The Jews then fell upon the leaderless Assyrians, slaughtering them.

JUDO. See JIUJITSU.

JUDSON, ADONIRAM, 1788–1850, American missionary, was born in Malden, Mass. His decision to become a missionary was the occasion of the organization of the American Board of Commissioners for Foreign Missions (Congregational), which sent him out with his wife, Ann Hasseltine, in 1812. On his voyage to Calcutta, however, he became a Baptist, and after 1814 was supported by the newly organized American Baptist Missionary Union. He labored at Rangoon, Ava, Moulmein, and other parts of Burma, issuing a translation of the Bible into Burmese (1835), and a *Burmese and English Dictionary*, published (1852) after his death. His son, Edward Judson (1844–1914), was associated for over 30 years with the Judson Memorial Church, New York City.

JUDSON, EDWARD ZANE CARROL. See BUNTLINE, NED.

JUDSON, HARRY PRATT, 1849–1927, American educator, was born in Jamestown, N.Y., and graduated from Williams College (1870). In 1892 he became connected with the University of Chicago, which he served as professor of political science (1892–94), head dean of the colleges (1892–94), head of the Department of Political Science (1894–1923), dean of the faculties of arts, literature, and science (1894–1907), president (1907–1923). His publications include *Europe in the Nineteenth Century* (1894, 1901); *Growth of the American Nation* (1895–1906); *Essential Elements of a Written Constitution* (1903); *Our Federal Republic* (1925).

JUDSON COLLEGE. See COLLEGES.

JUGGERNAUT. See PURI.

JUGGLING, a form of entertainment consisting chiefly of feats of skill in tossing balls, plates, tops, knives, etc. It is often confused with CONJURING, though the two arts are quite distinct, an exhibition of juggling involving no concealment of method, and no deception, while conjuring makes use of both. The ancient jugglers, joculators, or jongleurs, seem to have given only a kind of rough and general acrobatic and gymnastic display, and to have shown in their feats none of the neatness and finish of the juggling performances of today. The Chinese and Japanese are especially successful in the art.

JUGOSLAVIA. See YUGOSLAVIA.

JUGURTHA, d. 104 B.C., king of NUMIDIA, was the grandson of MASINISSA. He was brought up by his uncle Micipsa, along with the latter's sons, Hiempsal and Adherbal, and shared with them the kingdom on their father's death. He soon murdered his cousin Hiempsal and drove Adherbal from Numidia. The Roman government intervened. Jugurtha, however, prevailed upon them to assign to him the rich western portion of the kingdom, while Adherbal received the eastern desert lands. Jugurtha then made war upon Adherbal, captured him at Citra in 112 B.C., and put him to death. The Romans declared war, and after several years he was defeated by Caecilius Metellus. He was betrayed by his father-in-law Bocchus to MARIUS, Metellus' successor, adorned Marius' triumph at Rome (104 B.C.), and was then flung into a dungeon to die of hunger.

JUIZ DE FÓRA, town, Brazil, in the state of Minas Geraes, 80 miles N of Rio de Janeiro. Located in the mountain foothills, it is an important industrial city. Pop. (1940) 72,254.

JUJITSU. See JIUJITSU.

JUJU, a name given by West African Negroes to any fetish, whether an idol, or a magic rag, or anything else used as a charm. The word also denotes witchcraft and whatever is regarded as supernatural. The "Long Juju" of the Nigerian Aros was a sacred shrine (and equally the oracle of the shrine), held in such high regard that pilgrimages were made to it from great distances. It was the scene of human sacrifices and other savage rites.

JUJUY, province, NW Argentina, bordering Bolivia on the N and W, the Argentine province of Salta on the E and S, and Los Andes Province on the S; area 16,859 sq. mi.; pop. (1947 census) 166,783. The department is traversed by ranges of the Andes (Cordillera Real) rising to 18,000 feet; the lowest point is about 1,300 feet. The chief industries are farming and cattle raising. The principal crops are wheat, corn, and sugar, which is refined at mills located within the province. An oil field extending into Salta Province produces a high grade of oil. The capital of the province is Jujuy.

JUJUY, city, Argentina, capital of Jujuy Province, on the Jujuy River; 942 miles NW of Buenos Aires. The town is located in a valley at more than 4,000 feet altitude. Founded in 1593 on the site of a former Indian village, its name probably was derived from that of an Indian chief. Jujuy has many interesting relics of colonial times. Pop. (1947) 30,764.

JUJUY RIVER, or Río Grande de Jujuy, Argentina, rises near the boundary of Bolivia, and flows into the Bermejo after a course S and E of about 300 miles.

JUKES, THE, a fictitious name given to a family which formed the subject of an exhaustive study in heredity and criminology, as its members manifested a striking disposition to crime, depravity, disease, and pauperism. This scientific inquiry was undertaken under the direction of the Prison Association of New York, and revealed the fact that this single family in 75 years had cost the community some $1,308,000. It originated from the marriage of two brothers of Dutch descent with two sisters who are known as "The Jukes Sisters." Of 1,200 descendants, some 709 were investigated, and it was found that of this number 140 were criminals and offenders, having spent an aggregate of 140 years in prisons and jails; 280 had been supported at the public expense, while a large proportion not only were of debased morals, but suffered from nervous and other diseases. The investigation was made by R. L. Dugdale, and in addition to its publication in the 30th Annual Report of the Prison Association, was subsequently printed by itself, 1891.

BIBLIOG.—A. Scheinfeld, *You and Heredity* (1945).

JULFA. See ISFAHAN.

JULIA, 1st century B.C., Roman matron, the sister of Julius Caesar, was the grandmother of Augustus.

JULIA, d. 54 B.C., Roman matron, was the daughter of Julius Caesar; she married Pompey in 59 B.C., and died in childbirth five years later.

JULIA, 39 B.C.–A.D. 14, Roman matron, the daughter of Augustus by Scribonia, was married first to Marcellus, in 25 B.C.; he died in 23 B.C. Her second husband was M. Agrippa, by whom she had three sons—Gaius and Lucius Caesar, and Agrippa Postumus—and two daughters, Julia and Agrippina. After Agrippa's death in 12 B.C., she married Tiberius, who was later emperor. Julia's immorality was famous, and in 2 B.C. she was banished by Augustus to Pandataria, an island off the coast of Campania, where she died.

JULIA, d. A.D. 28, Roman matron, daughter of Julia and M. Agrippa, married L. Aemilius Paulus. Like her mother she was openly immoral, and in

A.D. 9 was banished by Augustus to the island of Tremerus, off the Apulian coast.

JULIAN, full name **Flavius Claudius Julianus,** A.D. 331–363, surnamed the Apostate, was the son of Julius Constantius, and nephew of Constantine the Great. He and his elder brother Gallus alone of the imperial family were spared by Constantius II when on his accession he massacred all the descendants of Constantius Chlorus by Theodora. In 355 Julian was allowed to live in freedom at Athens, and in the same year was invested with the dignity of Caesar, and given the government of the provinces beyond the Alps; he was also married to Helena, Constantine the Great's youngest child. In 357 he gained a great victory over the Alemanni, and invaded their territory in that year, and also in 358 and 359. He fortified the island of Lutetia (Paris), where he usually lived, and built baths there (ruins near the Musée Cluny). In 360 his soldiers proclaimed him emperor; but on Nov. 3, 361, Constantius died, and Julian was left undisputed emperor. He had long ceased to be a Christian, and at once proclaimed a general toleration of all religions, choosing, however, his own officers from the pagans, forbidding Christians to teach rhetoric and grammar in the schools, and, to annoy them, allowing the Jews to rebuild their temple at Jerusalem. After spending some time in Antioch, he set off to invade Persia in March, 363. He took up a position before the walls of Ctesiphon, the Persian capital, and was killed in a forced retreat.

JULIAN, PERCY LAVON, 1899–   , American Negro chemist, was born in Montgomery, Ala., and studied at De Pauw, Harvard, and Vienna universities. He taught chemistry at Fisk University, West Virginia State College for Negroes, and Howard University before becoming director of research for the Glidden Company (1936) and manager of the company's chemicals development (1945). He developed from soybeans a protein substance which is widely used in the manufacture of cold-water paints, in the sizing of textiles and paper, and in the extinguishing of gasoline and oil fires. He isolated from soybean oil sterols used in the preparation of two sex hormones. These are the female hormone, progesterone, which is effective in preventing spontaneous abortion, and the male hormone, testosterone, which contributes to the vitality of older men. Julian developed the hormone, Compound S, from soybeans in 1949, as an aid in relieving arthritis.

JULIAN ALPS, a SE extension of the Eastern Alps of Europe, stretching through W Slovenia, in NW Yugoslavia, to the Kapela Plateau in Croatia. The highest peak of the range is the Triglav (alt. 9,394 ft.). From its northern slope flows the only glacier in this part of Yugoslavia.

JULIAN CALENDAR. See CALENDAR.

JULIANA, full name **Juliana Louise Emma Marie Wilhelmina,** 1909– , queen of the Netherlands, daughter of Queen WILHELMINA. She was educated under her mother's supervision and at the University of Leyden (1927–29). She married Prince Bernhard of Lippe-Biesterfeld (1937) and they have four children. During World War II she and her children resided in Canada. In 1948 she ascended the throne, following the abdication of her mother, the most important act of her early reign was the freeing of all the Netherlands East Indies (except Dutch New Guinea), which became the United States (now Republic) of Indonesia in 1949.

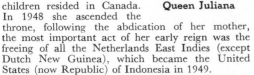

NETHERLANDS INFO. BUR.
Queen Juliana

JULIANEHAAB, town, Greenland, headquarters of a district of the same name, at the tip of a prom-

ontory jutting from the S coast. During World War II the United States established a military airfield here. The Julianehaab District (with eight outposts) has a population of about 3,600. See GREENLAND.

JULIER PASS, in the Alps of SE Switzerland, in the canton of Grisons; altitude 7,504 feet. A motor road running from Chur (Coire) to the Upper Engadine connects the Rhine and Inn valleys.

JULIUS I, d. 352, pope, was born in Rome. His reign, which began in 337, was remarkable for his adamant stand against heresies, and particularly the heresy of ARIANISM which had gained a powerful hold on Constantinople. In this age, when theologians were loudly presenting many different interpretations of Christian doctrine, Julius received the important assistance of the brilliant scholar, ATHANASIUS in the struggles with heretics and schismatics. When Emperor Constantius favored the Arians and tried to force Rome to follow their teachings, Julius defied the imperial will until his death. It is probable that the catalogue of saints' feast days originated during his pontificate.

JULIUS II, 1443–1513, pope, was born in Albissola, Italy. A prodigious worker, Julius was one of the most energetic popes in all history. Although he gained his office in 1503 through bribes and bargainings, he later issued a bull which condemned any future papal elections acquired by simoniacal means and declared such elections to be invalid. The Papal States and other properties which were the rightful possessions of the church had been widely dissipated during the reign of Pope Alexander VI, and these Julius determined to restore. His interest revolved chiefly around the temporal power of the church, and this was fortified with his unusual diplomacy which enabled him on occasion to enlist the services of one country against another, and then later reverse the process. Louis XII of France and the Emperor Maximilian were disturbed over the growing power of the pope and formulated plans for bringing it to an end. But the diplomatic skill of Julius induced the emperor to withdraw his support from France, and even persuaded Maximilian to permit the Swiss armies through the imperial dominions to fight the French. An intrepid warrior, the pope accompanied his own troops, working and living with his soldiers. The minutest details affecting the Papal States were personally examined by him, and gradually he regained all the properties which formerly had belonged to the church, constantly improved them, and eventually made them solvent. The restoration of the temporal power was achieved and Julius turned to the spiritual needs of the church. He convoked the Fifth Lateran Council in 1512 for the purpose of correcting the shameful discipline, although the indulgence of his own earlier personal life was reflected in the existence of three daughters. While he was occupied with his numerous administrative duties, the progress of art did not escape his attention. He assigned BRAMANTE the task of rebuilding St. Peter's basilica, encouraged the genius of RAPHAEL, and was responsible for calling MICHELANGELO to Rome. See MICHELANGELO (Back End Papers, Vol. 8).   R. M. LEONARD

JULIUS III, 1487–1555, pope, was born in Rome. He had served as the first president of the Council of Trent in 1545, but when the Council was forced to adjourn, during his pontificate, by the invasion of the Tyrol by French Protestant allies, with complete lack of courage he merely submitted to the force of circumstances. Julius sent Cardinal Pole, who had been his rival for the papal election, to Queen Mary of England to officiate as archbishop of Canterbury, and Pole was the last of the Catholic faith to hold that title. The five years of Julius' pontificate were marked by his indolence and the absence of interest in carrying out the duties of his office. See POLE, REGINALD, CARDINAL; TRENT, COUNCIL OF.

JULLUNDUR, or **Jalandhar,** city, India, E Punjab Province, capital of Jullundur District, 47 miles by rail ESE of Amritsar, 260 miles by rail NW of Delhi. The city is a railway junction and the site of an army cantonment. Jullundur has cotton, sugar, and silk manufactures. In 1766 it fell into the hands of the Sikhs and in 1811 was annexed by Ranjit Singh, who made it the capital of the Lahore Doab possessions. Following the end of the first Sikh War, it was annexed (1846) by the British. Pop. (1941) 135,283.

JULY. See MONTH.

JUMET, town, Belgium, in the province of Hainaut; three miles NNW of Charleroi. It has extensive coal mines, iron furnaces, and glass-making industries. Pop. (1949) 28,764.

JUMNA RIVER, or **Jamna,** India, the chief affluent of the Upper Ganges, has its source on the S slopes of The Western Himalaya, at a height of 12,000 feet. Flowing south it forms the boundary between Punjab and the United Provinces; then running southeast through the United Provinces, joins the Ganges three miles below Allahabad. It supplies the waters for the irrigation works of the East and the West Jumna canals. The chief cities on its banks are Delhi, Agra, Firozabad, Muttra, and Allahabad. It has a length of 860 miles, and drains an area of 118,000 square miles.

JUMPING. See TRACK AND FIELD SPORTS.

JUMPING BEAN, or **Mexican Jumping Bean,** the seed of a spurge, *Sebastiana pavonia,* infested with the living caterpillar of a moth, *Carpocapsa saltitans.* This curious seed, which botanically is not a true bean, has for centuries intrigued man by its erratic behavior. In the United States, where they are especially in demand, jumping beans are sold in large numbers, one company alone reporting an annual sale of more than two million beans. Not only do children and adults enjoy watching the beans jump, but they often use them for table games in which the beans represent racing animals.

Only recently have carefully conducted experiments given some explanation for the caterpillar's behavior, how it gets into the bean, and why it moves about within its dwelling. When the adult female moth deposits an egg on an immature fruit, which consists of three triangular seeds, a caterpillar eventually develops from the egg, burrows into a seed, and consumes the contents until only a thin outer shell remains. This eating stage continues as the seeds ripen, so that when they reach maturity and fall to the ground the outer shell is hard and the enclosed caterpillar is full-fed. Although the caterpillar is now prepared to become a pupa, it does not do so immediately because the need for movement still remains. Once the caterpillar pupates it can no longer move.

JUNAGADH, feudatory state, Pakistan, extending inland from the S coast of the Kathiawar Peninsula; area, 3,337 sq. mi.; pop. (1941) 670,719. The principal port is Veraval, which has rail connection with the capital, Junagadh. The chief products are cotton, Sesamum, wheat, rice, sugar cane, cereals, timber, stone, castor beans, fish, tobacco, peanuts, coconuts, and bamboo. There are manufactures of ghi, molasses, candy, copper and brass ware, dyed cloth, gold and silver embroidery, pottery, hardware, leather, and bamboo furniture. The chief town, Junagadh, is situated on the slopes of the Girnar and Datar hills, and has an old citadel that contains interesting Buddhist caves. The famous Asoka inscription, carved on a block of granite at the base of Girnar hill, is sacred to the Jains, the Shivaites, the Vishnavites, and other Hindus. The Girnar forest (494 sq. mi.), which supplies timber and other natural products, is unique as the sole remaining stronghold of the Indian lion.

Junagadh until 1472, when it was captured by the Moguls, was a Rajput state. During Akbar's reign it became a dependency of Delhi. The ancestors of the present ruler expelled the Mogul governor and established their own rule in 1735. Junagadh entered treaty relations with the British in 1807, and the state pays a tribute which is less than it collects in tribute from neighboring states. Although the state has a majority Hindu population its ruler is a Moslem, and, upon the partition of India into the two states of Pakistan and India on Aug. 15, 1947, Junagadh acceded to Pakistan.   C. S.

JUNCO, a genus of birds belonging to the Sparrow family, *Fringillidae,* and comprising 21 forms in 10 species. The name junco is also commonly applied to all birds belonging to the genus. The birds range from the arctic tree line in North America south to western Panama. Juncos are adaptable and tolerant and can survive and breed under a variety of conditions. Although they migrate from regions of extreme winter climate they are among the hardiest of the ground foraging sparrows.

Three basic types are found in the genus: the streaked-backed, dark-tailed junco; the plain-backed, partly white-tailed junco with yellow eyes; and the plain-backed, partly white-tailed junco with dark eyes.

The best known and most widely distributed form is the slate-colored junco, *Junco hyemalis,* which occurs over the entire North American continent. Although less common in the western regions, it breeds from the mountains of Pennsylvania, New England, and Michigan, northward to Labrador, Hudson Bay, and the Yukon Valley. It winters throughout eastern United States as far south as the Gulf Coast.

Slate-colored junco

This species is easily recognized in the field by its slate-colored back and head, and white belly; the short, conical, light pink bill and the white outer tail feathers, seen only when the birds dart away, also aid in identification. In winter these birds are frequently seen in small flocks hopping about on the ground in search of food. When disturbed they fly quickly as a flock to a near-by tree or bush.

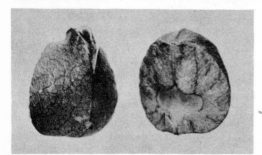

U.S.D.A.

Jumping Bean Moth Larva, dorsal view, above. Bean containing larva of jumping bean moth, below

As the breeding season approaches, the flocks migrate northward and disband into breeding pairs. The nest, made of grass, moss, and rootlets, and lined with finer grasses and long hairs, is usually placed on or near the ground. The eggs, four to five in number, are white or bluish white, finely and evenly speckled or spotted with reddish brown, sometimes blotched at the larger end.

Juncos are a useful genus, consuming great quantities of weed seeds and many injurious species of insects.   A. WOLFSON

BIBLIOG.–F. M. Chapman, *Handbook of Birds of Eastern North America* (1932); A. H. Miller, *Speciation in the Avian Genus Junco*, Univ. of Calif. Publ. Zool. (1941).

JUNCTION CITY, city, NE Kansas, county seat of Geary County, on the Kansas River at its junction with the Smoky Hill and the Republican rivers; on the Union Pacific and the Missouri-Kansas-Texas railroads, and U.S. highways 40 and 77; about 70 miles W of Topeka. Junction City, the trade center of a stock-raising and farming country, was settled in 1857. Fort Riley, a U.S. Army post, is located three miles northeast of the city. Junction City has railroad shops and makes cheese and flour. Pop.(1950) 13,462.

JUNDIAHY, town, SE Brazil, in the state of São Luis; on a railway and a highway, about 36 miles N of São Paulo, in a district producing grapes, grain, and coffee. Jundiahy, an important railway center, also has textile mills, match factories, and potteries. Pop. (1940) 29,891.

JUNE. See MONTH.

JUNE BEETLE, a green and brown beetle of southern United States. The June beetle, *Cotinus nitida*, feeds upon all sorts of soft fruits, and sometimes is so numerous as to cause notable damage to figs, peaches, and the like. Its natural home is on the ground, where it devours decaying vegetable mold. When too numerous in orchards, the beetles can be killed by placing trap-piles of spoiled fruit sprinkled with Paris green in several locations. In the northern states the name June beetle or June bug is often applied to the May beetle, *Phyllophaga*.

JUNEAU, capital city, SE Alaska, on the mainland shore of Gastineau Channel, backed by the steep-timbered slopes of Mount Juneau. Several air lines serve Juneau, and its excellent harbor handles a large volume of shipping. This largest city of Alaska has mining, fishing, fur farming, and lumbering interests, but government service is the most important economically. There are many salmon canneries in the district and a sawmill which produces most of the lumber sold in Alaska. The Alaska-Juneau mine has produced gold since the late 19th century and continues to employ about 1,000 men. Juneau began as a mining camp and was named at a miners' meeting in 1882 in honor of Joe Juneau, a wealthy pioneer prospector. During the boom period of near-by gold mines in 1916, Juneau had a population of about 8,000. The city became the capital of Alaska in 1900, although the executive offices were not moved from Sitka until 1906. The six-story Federal building was erected in 1931. Pop.(1950) 5,956.

JUNG, CARL GUSTAV, 1875–   , Swiss psychiatrist, was born in Basel; attended the universities of Basel, Zürich, and Paris; studied under Freud until 1911. In 1933 he became professor of psychiatry at the University of Technology in Zürich. Jung rejected Freud's theory of the sexual origin of psychoneuroses, emphasizing the creative impulse in man, and is best known for his classification of personality on the basis of introversion and extroversion. He is also known for his studies in word association and his theory of a "racial unconscious." Jung founded the school of analytical psychology to distinguish his point of view from that of psychoanalysis associated with the name of Freud. He wrote: *The Theory of Psychoanalysis* (1915); *Analytical Psychology* (1916); *Psychological Types* (1923); *Dream Symbols of the Individuation Process* (1937); *The Integration of the*

A. KLOPFENSTEIN
Majestic, snow-covered peak of the Jungfrau

Personality (1939); *Psychology and Alchemy* (1949). See CONSTITUTIONAL TYPES; ANALYTIC PSYCHOLOGY; INTROVERSION-EXTROVERSION.

JUNGARIA. See DZUNGARIA.

JUNGFRAU, Alpine peak, the third in height (13,669 ft.) among the Bernese Oberland. It owes its name (found as early as 1577) to the legend that no one could defile the snows of the "virgin" peak; however, it was ascended in 1811 by J. R. and H. Meyer. The usual starting point is the Concordia Inn (9,436 ft.) above the Great Aletsch glacier to the east of the peak. It can also be climbed from Grindelwald, Lauterbrunnen, and the Little Scheidegg. A railway runs from the Little Scheidegg up to the Eiger glacier.

JUNGLE, or **Jangal** (Hindustani "waste"), land covered with dense, luxuriant vegetation, such as long grass or undergrowth, or the intertropical forest.

JUNGLE CAT. See CHAUS.

JUNGLE FOWL, a name commonly given to the members of four distinct species of birds native to India and the Malayan region. The birds are closely related to domesticated poultry. It is believed that the various breeds of poultry have been derived from one species, the red jungle fowl, *Gallus ferringeus*, occurring in the Malay States and central India.

The head and neck of the male red jungle fowl are almost naked of feathers; as in domesticated fowl, the head bears a comb and wattles; the stout legs have spurs that are similar to those of fighting cocks. The upper parts are orange or purplish red with metallic iridescent reflections; the wings and tail are black, and the under parts are black with a greenish tinge. The bird bears a close resemblance to "black-breasted game" poultry, or fighting cocks. The roosters are pugnacious and, unlike the domestic breeds, are not polygamous. The hens have no wattles, the comb is short and stubby, the plumage is plain brown or black, and they are not as pugnacious as the cocks.

Jungle fowls feed upon seeds, soft vegetable materials, insects, slugs, spiders, and other small invertebrates. They do not construct nests but scratch out a basin-like depression in soft earth. From five to nine eggs are laid. These are usually white or gray and are smaller than those of the domesticated fowls. During the mating season the roosters perch near the nests and crow for long

Juneau harbor with gold mine on mountainside
ALASKA STEAMSHIP CO.

periods; the hens become aggressive in defense of their nests and young.

Three other species of jungle fowl are: (1) the Ceylon jungle fowl, *Gallus lafayettei*, having a golden-orange mantle on the back, a bright red-orange rump and breast, and paler red sides; (2) the gray jungle fowl, *Gallus sonnerati*, black or gray in color, and occurring in western, southern, and central India; (3) the green jungle fowl, *Gallus varius*, of Java, having a golden-green mantle marked with purplish blue. These last three species cannot be successfully mated with the common domestic poultry of the United States.   L. A. HAUSMAN

JUNIATA COLLEGE. See COLLEGES.

JUNIATA RIVER, Pennsylvania, has its source in the Allegheny Mountains and flows generally E by a circuitous route through beautiful scenery for about 150 miles to empty into the Susquehanna River about 15 miles NW of Harrisburg.

JUNIN, department, Peru, bounded by the departments of Huanuco on the N. Loreto and Cuzco on the E, Huancavelica on the S, and Lima on the W; area 22,820 sq. mi.; pop. (1947) 423,636. The department is crossed by a range of the Andes, contains Lake Junín, and is drained by the Mantaro River. Copper, silver, gold, salt, and coal are found in the department. Potatoes, cereals, coffee, sugar, cacao, and fruits are the principal crops. In 1944 the department of Pasco was created out of a portion of the department of Junín. The capital of Junín is Huancayo; pop. (1947 est.) 33,137.

JUNIN, LAKE, Peru, in the department of Junín, nestles in the Andes Mountains at an altitude of 13,000 feet. Its length is 37 miles and its breadth 7 miles. The Mantaro River issues from the lake.

JUNIOR COLLEGE, an institution of collegiate rank usually offering a two year course. It requires four years of high school education or its equivalent for admission, and provides for those wishing to complete their formal education at the end of two years as well as for those who intend to continue their college education elsewhere. The junior college does not grant a college degree.

Functions. The junior college meets a real need in American education. The number of pupils completing high school and wishing further education increased greatly in the 20th century. Yet many students did not need or desire the type of work required in existing colleges and universities. Furthermore, many preferred the first two years of college in a smaller institution or one nearer their homes, for financial, social, or personal reasons. However, administrators in higher education felt that colleges and universities ought not to make great changes in their curriculums, for fear of lowering standards. As a result, the junior college has grown to meet the needs of American youth for education beyond the secondary level. Its special curricular contribution has been the introduction of courses for freshmen and sophomores in areas not usually touched in the offerings of traditional colleges and universities.

The junior college popularizes higher education by extending it to secondary school graduates and mature persons who could not otherwise obtain it. The junior college also offers adequate preparation to students who wish to go on to other institutions for senior college work. It provides general education and semiprofessional courses for those finishing their formal education in the junior college. Finally, it guides the student scientifically in discovering his own skills and interests, and in preparing to make the best use of them in college and in later life. See EDUCATION IN THE UNITED STATES.

Types. Junior college is a summary term referring to a wide variety of institutions. Most of these are co-educational, but a large number in the eastern and southern states are for women, and several are military schools for men. A few junior colleges are half a century old, but the majority of them are young institutions. Most junior colleges have small enrollments, less than 200, but a few have enrollments in the thousands.

Nearly all junior colleges are two-year institutions, but a few offer three or four years of work. In some places the junior college has been an extension of the four year public high school and so closely integrated with it as to make of the two a six-year institution. In a few instances the last two years of high school work and the first two years of college work are combined in a four-year junior college.

Development. Junior colleges have come into existence in four ways. Most commonly, high schools have added two years to their offerings. Many small colleges, especially denominational ones, have reduced their courses to two years, thus making more concentrated use of their facilities. Independent junior colleges have been newly created in authorized districts, especially in California. Finally, colleges and universities, by setting apart the work of the first two years, or doing away with parts of it, have stimulated the formation of junior colleges.

A great increase in enrollments in institutions of higher learning followed World War II and junior college enrollments in 1951 had climbed to 562,786 students in 634 institutions with 13,920 full-time and 8,000 part-time faculty members. California, Illinois, and Texas had the largest enrollments, and California the largest number of institutions. See EDUCATIONAL ACCREDITING AGENCIES.

R. H. CARPENTER

BIBLIOG.–W. C. Eells, *American Junior Colleges* (1940); M. Tuttle, *Career Schools and Junior Colleges* (1945); J. A. Sexson, *The New American College; The Four-Year Junior College, Grades 11–14 Inclusive, Organized and Administered as a Single Institution* (1946); American Council on Education, *American Junior Colleges* (ed. 1948); J. A. Starrak and R. M. Hughes, *New Junior College* (1948); *Junior College Journal* (monthly).

JUNIOR HIGH SCHOOL, an intermediate school, typical in large American cities. It includes grades 7–8–9 or 7–8 in an institution designed for pupils in early adolescence. Its organization is based on the assumption that pupils will master fundamental tools and skills in the six elementary grades but will need something different from the usual high school program intended for later adolescence. Scientific studies of the biological, psychological, and social characteristics of early adolescence have indicated that pupils need special provisions in education at this stage in their development. The junior high school is an American invention to meet this need. See EDUCATION IN THE UNITED STATES.

History. Increasing school enrollments after 1890 magnified the problem of providing proper education for pupils in the intermediate grades. As the school population practically doubled in each decade up to 1940, it appeared that many pupils would not gain the greatest benefits from plunging into the traditional academic program of the secondary school designed primarily for college preparation. The increase in enrollments did not prevent educators from seeing that large numbers of pupils left school at the end of the seventh, eighth, or ninth grade. This mortality indicated that the program in the intermediate grades was ill-adapted to the needs of many youths and further that the elementary and secondary programs were not properly co-ordinated. Studies in the adaptation of instruction to INDIVIDUAL DIFFERENCES confirmed this conclusion. A new program, a new curriculum, and a new organization were needed.

The first junior high schools were established in Berkeley, California, and Columbus, Ohio in 1909–10. A year later Los Angeles, California, and Easton, Massachusetts, organized this kind of school, and St. Louis, Missouri, Rochester, New York, and Philadelphia, Pennsylvania, soon followed. By 1917 there were 557 junior high schools in cities of 25,000 or more population. By 1948, the number of junior high schools in the United States had passed 2,500.

Juniper

Programs. Administrators of junior high school programs have borrowed from both the elementary and the high school, and they have added something new. Instruction and drill in fundamental skills have been continued in varying degrees, and newer practices in ELEMENTARY EDUCATION have been adapted to the intermediate grades. From the HIGH SCHOOL has been taken the scheme of departmental organization of the curriculum found in most junior high schools. By merging these borrowings the junior high school may be said to have made progress in integrating the elementary and secondary programs.

Innovations in the intermediate program as found in junior high schools consist in new content and new methods. Curricular offerings have been enriched by studying the local community and by fresh materials in general science, general mathematics, general language, personal and vocational guidance, shop, and household arts. Extracurricular activities, tied closely to the curriculum, include taking a part in community activities and developing personal interests through hobbies. New methods include the project method, the activity method, emphasis on supervised study and good study habits, and constant attention to individual differences among pupils. Pervading all of these innovations is the aim of satisfying the distinctive needs of early ADOLESCENCE through increasing opportunities for pupil planning and activity appropriate to that stage of human development. See EDUCATIONAL METHODS.

R. H. CARPENTER

JUNIPER, the common name of plants belonging to the genus *Juniperus* of the family *Pinaceae*. Junipers are trees or shrubs with short, awl-shaped or scalelike leaves that are often prickly-pointed and evergreen, They bear small, fleshy, berry-like cones with one to three seeds. The cones are aromatic, usually bluish-green in color, and are the source of a flavoring used in GIN. *J. virginiana*, the eastern red cedar, grows chiefly on dry hills in eastern United States and is the source of

U.S. FOREST SERV.

Sierra juniper

cedarwood, highly prized in the manufacture of cedar chests, wardrobes, closet linings, and fence posts. Other juniper species are widely distributed in the United States, especially in the West, where they often occur in forests in dry, mountain regions. Several species occur in Asia. There are many cultivated junipers, some of them having a beautiful spreading habit (e.g., Pfitzer's juniper). These are widely used in ornamental plantings. Many junipers grow rapidly, and successfully withstand drought.

H. J. FULLER

JUNIPERO SERRA, MIGUEL. See SERRA.

JUNIUS, the pseudonym under which a series of political letters attacking the Tory administration generally and the Duke of Grafton particularly, were published in the London *Public Advertiser* (1769–72). Ably written, the letters are remarkable for their shrewd comment and scathing insult. The author remaining pseudonymous, a vigorous and long-lived controversy developed on his probable identity. The favored candidate was Sir Philip Francis; others were Richard Glover, the Duke of Portland, the Earl of Chesterfield, Gibbon, Viscount Sackville, Earl Temple, and Lord Shelburne. In 1949, however, a note found in the papers of Lord Shelburne established Laughlin Macleane, a regimental surgeon

NORTHWEST ORIENT AIRLINES

Junks on the Whangpoo River at Shanghai

with the British Army and later private secretary to Shelburne, as the author of the Junius letters.

JUNK, a wooden sailing vessel peculiar to the Chinese, used for river and ocean navigation. It is usually equipped with three pole masts, though one to five masts may be used. The junk is noted for its high stern and bow and its distinctive lugsails of cane or bamboo matting. Some junks are very large, their tonnage reaching 1,000 tons.

The junk of today remains practically the same as that of the 11th century, though watertight compartments are built in the holds of some seagoing types. The rudder of a large junk projects deep into the water and may weigh as many as eight tons. It can be raised by means of a windlass when the craft is in shallow water. A transverse beam, fitted to the stem head and projecting over each bow, is equipped with an anchor windlass. Single fluke anchors, often with shanks 10 to 12 feet in length, are of hardwood weighted with large stones.

The only instrument of navigation used on these vessels is the old-fashioned Chinese compass, and this is only consulted when the ship is out of sight of land.

In 1847–48 a Chinese junk, the *Keying*, sailed from Canton, China, to the Thames River, England. In heavy seas 15 men were required to work the helm. The mainsail, weighing nine tons, took two hours to hoist. Another junk, named the *Wang-Ho*, successfully sailed from China to Australia in 1908 when the vessel was 100 years old.

JUNKERS comes from the middle high German *juncherre* which means young gentlemen. Originally the Junkers were the landed gentry of Prussia, who in the 19th century had ultra-conservative views. The Junkers were concerned with the increased industrialization in Germany in the latter part of the 19th century and opposed workmen benefits. They assisted the creation of the German Socialist Act of 1878, which made illegal, church meetings, unions, pamphlets, and books which were against the existing form of state and society. Since this law, with the help of the National Liberal party and that of the Prussian Conservatives, remained in force with minor alterations, the Junkers became the most outspoken anti-socialists. During the Bismarck regime the Junkers became the military aristocracy of Germany; they supplied the high officers of the army. The power of the Junkers centered in the General Staff which they dominated during World War I. After the war their power temporarily diminished due to socialistic tendencies in the Weimar Republic. Under the Weimar Republic the Junkers often fostered and assisted counterrevolutionary movements. They made an alliance with Hitler and under his regime they assumed an important role in the army. Although some Junkers opposed Hitler, they dominated the German army during World War II. In 1945, at the Crimea Conference, the Allies announced that the destruction of the Junker General Staff was one of the war aims. With the surrender of the German army the Junker domination of military life ceased, and the class lost its former political, economic, and social power. See GERMANY, *History;* NATIONAL SOCIALISM; PRUSSIA, *History*.

JUNO, the chief goddess of ancient Rome, was identified with the Greek Hera. As a Roman goddess Juno is the counterpart of Jupiter; thus she was regarded as the queen of heaven. She was also the especial protectress of the female sex, and was worshiped under a great variety of epithets—Virginalis, goddess of maidens; Matronalis, of matrons; Natalis, of the birthday (women offered sacrifices to Juno on their birthdays); Pronuba and Juga or Jugalis, as watching over marriage; Lucina, as presiding over childbirth; and in general as Opigena or Sospita, giving help and safety. She also was the guardian of the finances of the state; and as Juno Moneta had a temple which contained the mint at Rome. See HERA; JUPITER.

JUNO, the third ASTEROID to be found, was discovered by Harding in 1804. At OPPOSITION, when it is on the opposite side of the earth from the sun, it is somewhat brighter than ninth MAGNITUDE, on the average, and its albedo, or fraction of the incident sunlight reflected in all directions by it, is 0.12. Juno's diameter of 120 miles, as measured by Barnard, places it fourth in size among the asteroids. Its orbit, traversed in a period of 1,592 days, has an eccentricity of 0.26 and is inclined 13° to the plane of the ECLIPTIC. The mean distance of Juno from the sun is about 248,000,000 miles, about 2.67 times the earth's mean distance.

JUNOT, ANDOCHE, DUKE D'ABRANTES, 1771–1813, French general, born in Bussy-le-Grand, Côte d'Or; served under Napoleon in Italy, subsequently accompanying him to Egypt (1798). In 1804 he became ambassador to Portugal, but left Lisbon to join Napoleon in Germany. Placed in command of an army for the invasion of Portugal (1807), his brilliant maneuvers, culminating in a successful dash upon Lisbon, won for him the governorship of Portugal, and the title of Duke d'Abrantes; but after a time he was forced by Wellington to leave the country. Junot was appointed governor of Illyria, but took part in the invasion of Russia. He ended his life in a fit of insanity.

JUPITER, the chief god of ancient Rome. He was the son of SATURN and Rhea, and brother and husband of JUNO. The first syllable of his name corresponds with the Greek ZEUS and the Sanskrit Dyaus ("light"), and Jupiter thus means "the light-father"; hence he was worshiped as the god of rain, storms, thunder, and lightning, under the titles of Pluvius, Tonans, Fulgurator, and Fulminator. As the greatest of the gods he was known as Optimus Maximus—"best and greatest." He was held to be the especial guardian of Rome, and as such bore the titles Imperator, Victor, Invictus, Stator, Triumphator, and was solemnly invoked by the consuls on entering office; while the triumph of a successful general was really a special thanksgiving to him. As Jupiter Capitolinus he presided over the great games at Rome; and as Latiaris, over the Latin festival. He ordered the course of events, and revealed the future by omens and portents, and so was worshiped as Prodigialis; and as the supreme upholder of justice, punished oath-breakers, who were cast down from the Tarpeian rock. His worship was under the especial care of the Flamen Dialis, the highest in rank of all the *flamines*.

JUPITER, largest and most massive planet of the solar system, is fifth in order from the sun, except for the asteroids, and nearest to the earth of the four giant planets. Being brighter, usually, than the planet Mars, or than the brightest star, Sirius, it has been known to mankind for thousands of years. At its brightest it has an apparent MAGNITUDE of −2.5, but is outshone by Venus. Jupiter is not partly self-luminous, as was once thought; its light is sunlight, about 44 per cent of that falling upon it being reflected (albedo = 0.44).

Through a large telescope the planet shows distinctive markings of dark and light bands roughly parallel to the equator. Red and brown shades pre-

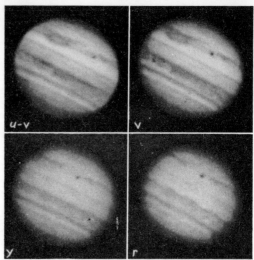

Jupiter photographed in ultraviolet, yellow, and red light. The great red spot is conspicuous in the first two, barely visible in the last one, and its change in position on the visible disk shows the rotation of the planet. Darkening of the limb, due to absorption of light by Jupiter's atmosphere, becomes more noticeable at increasing wave lengths (violet to red), which penetrate to greater depths

dominate, with green and some blue or black showing also. From observations of details in these belts, Jupiter is found to be rotating rapidly on its axis. Although the rotation is most rapid at the equator, it varies irregularly with latitude and also from one year to another, the period ranging from 9 hours 50 minutes to nearly 9 hours 56 minutes. The belts, changeable in appearance and in width, are cloudlike phenomena carried along by currents that extend deep into the planet's atmosphere. A long-lived feature is Jupiter's great red spot, some 30,000 miles long and 7,000 miles wide when first noticed in 1878, and conspicuous for several years afterward. The spot was shown on drawings made in 1859, and its position can still be identified although the color has faded and the form has become more rounded. South of the red spot is another relatively persistent long and dark marking known as the south tropical disturbance, visible since 1901. These markings have different rotation periods whose variability indicates that they are probably floating in the planet's atmosphere.

Orbit. Jupiter revolves about the sun at a mean distance of 483,900,000 miles with an average speed of 8.1 miles per second. It completes the circuit of its orbit in a *sidereal period* of 11.86 years, which is the interval between two consecutive alignments of the sun and Jupiter with the same star. The *synodic period* is 399 days; this is the interval between consecutive OPPOSITIONS, when the planet is on the opposite side of the earth from the sun. The orbit is somewhat more elongated (eccentricity = 0.48) than the earth's, and at APHELION the distance from the sun is about 47,000,000 miles greater than at *perihelion.* Jupiter's equator is tilted only about 3 degrees from the plane of its orbit, and the orbit only a little more than a degree from the plane of the ecliptic.

Physical Data. The mean diameter of Jupiter is 86,850 miles, the polar diameter being perceptibly less than the equatorial (oblateness = 0.065); but this is a small polar flattening for such a rapid rotation, and indicates that the variation in density from the center outward is relatively greater than it is for the earth. Since Jupiter's diameter is nearly 11 times as great as the earth's, its surface area is nearly

121 (=11²) times and its volume nearly 1,331 (=11³) times as great. Its mass is more than 318 times the earth's. From these relations it can be calculated (see PLANET) that the density of Jupiter is less than one-fourth that of the earth, and only 1.33 times that of water; and that the acceleration at its surface due to gravity (briefly, *surface gravity*) is 2.6 times the earth's, being greater, of course, at the poles and less at the equator.

Atmosphere. Jupiter's SPECTRUM is the characteristic solar spectrum with additional absorption bands (see BAND SPECTRUM) in the red and infrared regions that have been shown to be due to methane (CH_4) and ammonia (NH_3). At Jupiter's surface temperature of about 210° F. below zero, the methane is gaseous, but the ammonia must be crystallized except for vapor molecules in the clouds. Hydrogen must be abundant; Wildt concludes that there is a compressed layer of it nearly 8,000 miles deep, and below this a much thicker layer of ice, surrounding a rocky core whose depth is less than half the radius.

Satellites. The four largest and brightest satellites of Jupiter were discovered in January, 1610, by GALILEO with his telescope, and were called Galilean satellites, though Marius of Brandenburg claimed prior discovery. They revolve in practically circular orbits that lie very nearly in the plane of Jupiter's equator at distances from the planet that range from about one-fourth to one million miles. Their periods range from less than 2 to nearly 17 days. The fifth satellite, discovered by Barnard in 1892, is much fainter and much closer to Jupiter, making it very difficult to observe. The first determination of the velocity of LIGHT was made by ROEMER (1675) as the result of observing that the time intervals between eclipses of a Galilean satellite were greater when the earth was receding from Jupiter than when it was approaching. See BARNARD, EDWARD E.

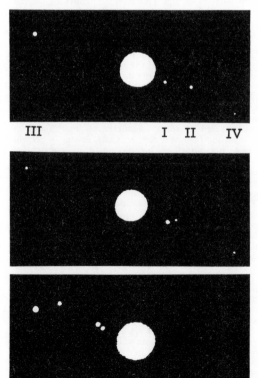

III   I   II   IV

Jupiter and Its First Four Satellites. The photograph at top was made 2 hr. 43 min. before the center one, and 8 days before the one at bottom

The remaining 6 of the 11 known satellites of Jupiter are much fainter, smaller, and far more remote from the planet than the Galilean ones; their orbits are more eccentric and much more tilted to the plane of Jupiter's equator; and three of them, VIII, IX, and XI, revolve in the retrograde direction. S. B. Nicholson discovered IX at Lick Observatory (1914), and X and XI at Mount Wilson (1938). See ORBIT; SOLAR SYSTEM; and tabular data in PLANET; SATELLITE.   A. T. M.

BIBLIOG.–H. S. Jones, *Life on Other Worlds* (1940); F. L. Whipple, *Earth, Moon and Planets* (1941); H. N. Russell, R. S. Dugan, and J. Q. Stewart, *Astronomy*, vol. I (ed., 1945).

JURA, department, E France, bounded on the N by the department of Haute-Saône, on the E by that of Doubs and by Switzerland, on the S by Ain, and on the W by Saône-et-Loire and Côte d'Or; area 1,951 sq. mi.; pop. (1946) 216,386. It is divided into three regions, a mountainous area in the south and east, the vine region in the north, and a small plain to the west. The chief rivers are the Doubs and the Ain, draining southwest toward the Rhône. Large forests furnish timber, chiefly pine; grains and potatoes are grown and vineyards are cultivated; and livestock and dairy farming are important. Gruyère cheese is a noted manufacture. Water power from the numerous streams is used to a great extent in the local industries, which include the manufacture of watches, pipes, metalwares, wood and paper products, and the polishing of precious stones. Rock salt is mined. The capital is Lons-le-Saunier.

JURA, fourth largest island of the Inner Hebrides, off the W coast of Argyllshire, SW Scotland; area 143 sq. mi.; pop. about 450. The island is 28 miles long, up to eight miles wide, and separated from Islay on the south and southwest by the Sound of Islay; from the mainland on the east by the Sound of Jura; and from Scarba, on the north, by the dangerous tidal strait of Corrievrekin. The sea loch, Tarbert, cuts from the west six miles into the center of the island. A ridge of bleak, rugged mountains extends from north to south; the highest are Beinn An Orr (2,570 ft.), Beinn Siantaidh (2,477 ft.), and Beinn Chaolais (2,412 ft.), which form the "Paps of Jura." Much of the island consists of deer forest. Fishing and granite quarrying are the chief industries. Granite and a sand used for glassmaking are exported. On the east and more fertile side of the island oats, barley, and potatoes are raised. Sheep and cattle are grazed in the highlands. Ardlussa and Feolin Ferry are the chief villages.

JURA MOUNTAINS, a range on the French-Swiss border, curves for about 190 miles in a northeasterly direction through the French departments of Ain, Jura, and Doubs, and the Swiss cantons of Vaud, Neuchâtel, and Bern. The mountains are an Alpine offshoot, composed principally of Jurassic limestone, and are made up of parallel ridges cut by transverse gorges called *cluses*. The mountains range in height from 5,000 to 2,000 feet, with the greatest heights in the southern Jura in the peaks of Crêt de la Neige (5,655 ft.), Colombier de Gex (5,548 ft.), Mont Tendre (5,519 ft.), and La Dôle (5,505 ft.).

JURASSIC SYSTEM, the division of geological strata following the TRIASSIC and immediately preceding the CRETACEOUS. (See GEOLOGIC TIME.) The system derives its name from the JURA MOUNTAINS in Switzerland, which are largely built up of rocks of this group. In America the Jurassic strata are developed on a comparatively small scale. Their presence has not been definitely established in the eastern part, but they occur in the western interior and on the Pacific Coast. Parts of the western interior, including large sections of Montana, Wyoming, Colorado, and Utah, were under water during the latter part of the period, and extensive deposits of sedimentary material containing marine fossils were laid down in these areas. California, Oregon, and Nevada were under the sea in early Jurassic times. In the deposits formed in these areas are found slates containing gold-bearing veins. In Alaska, extensive sedimentary deposits as well as some deposits of igneous material are of Jurassic age. Jurassic limestones are found in parts of Texas and extend into central Mexico.

In England, where the Jurassic is well represented, the following subdivisions are recognized, from the base upward: (1) Lias; (2) Lower Oölite; (3) Middle Oölite; (4) Upper Oölite. In Germany the Jurassic is divided into three series—the Lias, the Dogger, and the Malm (known also as the Black Jura, the Brown Jura, and the White Jura). Rocks of this system cover a wide spread in Silesia, Franconia, and northwest Germany. In France the subdivisions are very similar to those adopted in England, and a tract of these rocks surrounds the Paris basin.

The close of the Jurassic period in North America was marked by a great upheaval in the west, resulting in the formation of the Sierra Nevada and Cascade mountain ranges. In Europe there was widespread emergence of continental areas, while in Asia there was considerable folding and mountain-building in parts of Mongolia.

Life. Since the Jurassic was a period of widespread submergence of continental areas marine life was very prominent. Ammonites abounded in the warm sea waters, developing many new genera and species in rapid succession, and easily maintaining their numerical superiority over other invertebrates. Belemnites, relatives of the modern cuttlefish, also swarmed in the seas. Corals of modern types built up great banks of limestone in France and England. Echinoids, starfishes, crustaceans, crinoids, and brachiopods were also numerous. Among fishes, types related to the modern gar pike and dogfish were vastly in the majority, but a few of the *teleosts*, or modern bony fish, had at least put in an appearance. Some of the types of rays, skates, and sharks also had a rather modern aspect. Ichthyosaurs (fishlike lizards) with limbs developed into paddles and long snouts equipped with teeth for seizing their prey were found in every sea. Some of these ichthyosaurs were over 30 feet long. Long-necked turtles and some crocodilians made their first appearance late in the period.

On land, cycads, conifers, and ferns were the most numerous plant types, the cycads constituting at least 40 per cent of all living species, so that the Jurassic is often referred to as the Age of Cycads. Among the trees of this period the GINGKO has the distinction of being still represented in the modern world, although by a single species in China and Japan. Beetles and ants were plentiful, and the first butterflies appeared, an indication of the probable existence of flowering plants. Among the land reptiles, the carnivorous dinosaurs of the previous (Triassic) period still thrived, but were outnumbered by the herbivorous types, some of which attained tremendous proportions. *Gigantosaurus* from East Africa is estimated to have weighed about 50 tons. *Ornithopod* (birdfooted) dinosaurs, walking on two feet and with their front teeth replaced by a horny bill, became abundant. Descended from these ornithopods, but walking on four feet, were the strange armored dinosaurs, the *stegosaurs*, some of them larger than elephants but with brains less than three ounces in weight. See CYCADACEAE.

The restriction of land areas in the Jurassic may have forced many land reptiles to the sea in search of prey. Others, however, took to the air. Developed probably from small, active, hollow-boned reptilian ancestors, the *pterosaurs*, or winged reptiles, sailed out over the seas in large numbers. Their jaws were toothed, and their wings membranous, like those of a bat. True birds, probably descended from some common ancestor with the pterosaurs, were the most distinctive contribution of the Jurassic to animal evolution. Preserved in the fine-grained lithographic limestone of Bavaria are two beautiful fossil specimens of the oldest known birds, ARCHAEOPTERYX and

Archaeornis. They had long jointed tails, claws on both fore and hind limbs, teeth set in sockets, in reptilian fashion, but they had true wings, were clad in feathers, and walked only on their hind legs, and are therefore considered true birds. A few very small mammals were also present. See DINOSAUR; GEOLOGY.

Economic Importance. From the standpoint of economic geology, the Jurassic period is important in two ways. Fine-grained limestone, known as *freestone*, useful for carving ornamental stonework, was laid down near Portland and Bath in England, and the famous lithographic limestone of Solenhofen, Bavaria, is the only known limestone fine enough to be used in lithography. In parts of California gold-quartz veins in the Mariposa slates of the Jurassic system constitute the so-called "mother lode" from which, by weathering, the famous placer deposits of gold were derived.   C. C. G.

JURISDICTION. In its broad terms as applied to a sovereign state or nation, jurisdiction signifies the authority to make, declare, and execute laws, and the right to apply these laws to the acts of persons. A more restricted definition is the legal power of a court to hear and determine causes, that is, the authority to hear and decide a legal controversy.

Different types of courts have different powers. Certain courts in each state are given broad powers to decide suits of all kinds. These are known as courts of *general jurisdiction*. Such courts are often denominated *circuit* or *district courts*, although there is little uniformity in the nomenclature applicable to courts. Courts of *limited* or *special jurisdiction* have power to decide cases falling in particular categories only, as *probate courts* (also called *orphans' courts* or *surrogate courts*) which exercise power only over estates of deceased persons, minors and insane persons. Thus a decree of divorce handed down by a probate court would be wholly void, since it lacks power to decide controversies of this character. A court of *original jurisdiction* is the court that actually hears the case. A court of *appellate jurisdiction* is one that hears a case on appeal from a lower court.

In the United States, the jurisdiction of the Federal Courts is limited to the authority expressly conferred by the Constitution and the laws passed by Congress, as, for example, authority to hear controversies between citizens of different states. Courts and their jurisdiction vary widely from state to state. The simplest systems are found in those states which do not have large cities. Typical, perhaps, of the court systems and of court jurisdiction is that found in Wisconsin. There the *Supreme Court*, except in certain cases, has appellate jurisdiction only, coextensive with the state. Next are the *Circuit Courts*, which have original jurisdiction in all cases, civil and criminal, except probate matters. *County Court* jurisdiction extends to matters of probate and guardianship. There are also *Municipal* and *Superior Courts*, with varying jurisdiction, civil and criminal. The lowest courts are those of the Justice of the Peace whose jurisdiction is considerably limited, both by the nature of the causes which it can hear and by the amounts involved in these causes. See COURT; VENUE.   ROBERT KRATOVIL

JURISPRUDENCE, the science of law. The term is commonly employed by scientific legal writers to denote general or comparative jurisprudence, in which legal ideas common to all systems of law are analyzed, compared, and classified. It may, however, with equal propriety be applied to a particular legal system, as that of the Roman law or the common law of England and the United States, where reference is had not to the body of legal rules and principles comprised in the system but to the legal ideas which it expresses and their relation to one another. Thus a systematic exposition of the leading principles of a system, with a study of their origins, the processes by which they are developed, the social conditions by which they are shaped and their arrangement or classification in accordance with general legal principles constitutes the jurisprudence of that system.

A study of jurisprudence, whether general or local, comprehends, therefore, an inquiry into the nature and functions of law in organized society, an analysis of legal rights and obligations, a consideration of the various agencies by which the law is administered and developed, including the organization and functions of courts of justice, and, finally, an orderly arrangement of the leading principles of the law with reference to the rights and obligations which it defines, protects, and enforces. See Law; LEGAL EDUCATION.

JURUÁ RIVER, South America, rises in E Peru and flows NE through Brazil to join the Amazon in W Brazil. The river, navigable for about 500 miles, is an important link in transportation in the interior.

JURY, a selected body of men or women charged by law with the duty of settling questions of fact. The jury is an important feature of the legal systems of England and the United States, allowing the people at large to participate to a considerable degree in the administration of justice.

Kinds of Juries. Modern juries are of three types. The *grand jury*, composed of from 12 to 23 persons, has the investigative function of determining whether a crime has been committed and whether there is sufficient evidence to hold the accused persons for trial. The *petit or trial jury*, composed of 12 persons, assists the court in determining questions of fact by establishing guilt or innocence in criminal cases or deciding, in civil cases, whether damages should be paid. The *coroner's jury*, usually a body of six persons, investigates the causes of deaths by violence and fixes the responsibility therefor.

Historical Development. The modern jury system probably evolved from a system first established in Normandy by the Carlovingian kings and later developed to a high degree in England following the Norman Conquest. In earlier days issues of fact were determined by means of (1) trial by battle, whereby the contestants engaged in physical combat, with truth depending upon victory; (2) trial by ordeal, whereby the accused was submitted to various tests in which God would be relied upon to protect the innocent; and (3) trial by compurgation. In this trial the 12 compurgators, or jurors, did not determine the issues on the basis of evidence submitted, but merely swore that from their knowledge of the defendant they believed him not to be guilty of the offense charged. From this type of trial developed both the modern jury trial and the character witness system. Originally all juries had to be drawn from the vicinity in which the crime was committed or the transaction had taken place, as they would be most likely to know the parties and circumstances of the case. Today the ideal jury is one which knows nothing of the facts of the case or the parties involved until the trial begins, although modern doctrine still holds that certain cases, such as those involving real estate, should be determined by the neighbors of the parties to the suit.

Selection of the Jury. The rules of law governing the selection of jurors vary under different jurisdictions. Generally all persons between the ages of 21 and 70 are liable to jury duty unless they belong to one of the numerous exempt classes or are disqualified for insanity, conviction of crime, or a similar reason. The panel from which trial jurors are finally drawn is usually selected by lot from the eligible persons.

When 12 jurors have been called to serve on a particular case, counsel on both sides have the right to question them to discover any bias or prejudice, undue friendship for either party, previous conviction of the guilt or innocence of the accused, or other factors which would disqualify them as impartial jurors. Either side may challenge any individual juror for cause, as not qualified or not impartial, and in addition may challenge a given number—fixed by statute —of jurors without stating any cause, this being a protection against accepting jurors who are deemed

unfair although there is no specific reason for disqualification. In addition, either party may challenge the entire jury panel before the trial begins on the basis of the partiality or fraud of the officer by whom they were summoned. In complicated or difficult cases, usually of a commercial character, there may be called a "special" or "struck" jury, composed of persons of a higher degree of experience or intelligence than those composing the ordinary panel.

Once chosen, the function of the jury is to hear the entire trial, conduct its deliberations in secret, and reach a unanimous verdict. Jurors are sworn to answer truthfully all questions put to them by court or counsel regarding their qualifications to serve as jurors, and after being accepted are sworn to render a true verdict according to the evidence presented to them. The absence of a single juror suspends the hearing and the death or withdrawal of a juror at any stage of the proceedings terminates the trial. Jurors receive a stipend, fixed by law, for each day of service and are entitled to be discharged immediately following the presentation of the verdict.

Trial Procedures. Procedure during the jury trial includes the presentation of the evidence and of the arguments for the defense and the prosecution. During the trial the judge must rule on questions of law determining what may be admitted as evidence. When the judge has decided the admissibility of the evidence it is presented to the jury for decision as to its validity and credibility. Following the presentation of evidence, counsel on both sides may argue to the jury to place the evidence in proper focus and aid the jury in properly evaluating it. At the conclusion of the arguments the judge gives instructions to the jury as to the law governing the case. Often counsel on both sides submit instructions to the judge at the end of the trial, setting forth different theories of law under which the jury may decide the issues.

After receiving instructions from the judge, the jury retires to reach its verdict. Verdicts may be general, special, and general with answers to special interrogatories. A general verdict directly finds or negates all the facts in issue in a general form, such as "guilty" or "not guilty" in a criminal case or a finding for the plaintiff or the defendant in a civil case, without stating any reasons. A special verdict is comparatively rare and is a finding of the facts by the jury, leaving the court to enter judgment on those facts. A general verdict with answers to special interrogatories is quite common in modern trials and is recognized as a means of "searching the minds of the jurors." Thus, while the jury may bring in a general verdict they may be required to find specially on any matter of fact submitted to them in writing as an interrogatory. If the answer to the interrogatory is consistent with the general verdict, the general verdict is thereby greatly strengthened; but if the answer is inconsistent, the general verdict is overruled and judgment is entered accordingly.

A verdict is valid only when it is entered in the records of the court. The device of polling the jury may be used to guard against a verdict having been obtained in the jury room by illegal means, such as drawing lots, or by the use of threats. When the jury returns to the box, therefore, they may each in turn be asked whether the verdict *was* and *is* his verdict, thus giving each juror a chance to speak freely before judgment is rendered. Polling is rarely employed except in cases of capital crime. If properly reached, the verdict of a jury is final, unless set aside by the court as being manifestly against the weight of evidence. It may, however, always be set aside for grave irregularities involving prejudice to the party against whom the verdict is rendered or for bribery or other corrupt practices. A verdict must always be delivered viva voce in open court, except in certain kinds of civil cases in which a "sealed verdict" may be handed in.

In some instances a jury may be unable to reach a unanimous decision. Such a jury is referred to as a "hung" jury. Judges will permit a "hung" jury to remain in deliberation until there is no reasonable prospect of agreement, in which case the jury will be discharged from further consideration of the case.

The function of the jury in the administration of justice is a restricted one. In some courts and in many classes of cases juries are not employed, either because the questions involved are questions of law and not of fact, or because the court, not being a common-law tribunal, has developed a procedure in which the jury plays no part. This is the case with the equity tribunals and generally with the probate or surrogate courts. Even in the common-law courts proper, all questions of law and many questions of fact are decided by the court without a jury. See COURT; TRIAL; EVIDENCE; VERDICT.   J. BUCKLEY

BIBLIOG.–D. C. Blashfield, *Instructions to Juries* (3 vols. 1916); C. N. Callender, *Selection of Jurors* (1924); J. E. Johnson, Comp., *Jury System* (1928); R. von Moschzisker, *Trial by Jury* (1922, ed. 1930); A. G. Hays, *Trial by Prejudice* (1933); S. F. Brewster, *Twelve Men in a Box* (1934); A. Abbott, *Brief for the Trial of Civil Issues Before a Jury* (1885, ed. 1935); F. S. Wellman, *Gentlemen of the Jury* (1924, ed. 1937); G. de C. Pamiter, *Reasonable Doubt* (1938); C. H. Winfield, *Grand Jury* (1944).

JUS GENTIUM, a Latin term meaning the "law of nations," used by the Romans to designate that portion of ROMAN LAW which governed the relations between nations or Romans and non-Romans. The *jus gentium* became distinguishable from the *jus civile*, the civil law, over a period of time when the Romans were coming into wide contact with the legal systems of conquered and neighboring peoples. It was that part of the Roman private law which was essentially in agreement with the private law of other nations, especially the Greek law which was widely followed in commercial practice. The Romans considered that this area of agreement constituted a common groundwork of legal institutions which could appeal to the reason of all persons engaging in legal relationships, regardless of their national origin.

After the distinction between the *jus gentium* and *jus civile* had been made, the process began to reverse itself with the consequence that the *jus gentium* became used generally in place of the civil law and became recognized as part of the body of Roman law proper. In modern times, writers have sometimes confused *jus gentium* with INTERNATIONAL LAW, not realizing its more extended and integrated meaning to the Romans. See CIVIL LAW; INTERNATIONAL LAW.

     ALFRED DE GRAZIA

BIBLIOG.–C. Phillipson, *International Law and Custom of Ancient Greece and Rome* (1911); J. L. Brierly, *The Law of Nations* (1942).

JUSSERAND, JEAN JULES, 1855–1932, French historian and diplomat, was born in Lyons. He entered the diplomatic service in 1878; was chancellor of the French embassy in London (1887–90); minister to Denmark (1899–1902); and succeeded Jules Cambon as ambassador to the United States in 1903. He was an authority on the Elizabethan age and on the life and literature of medieval England. His works include: *English Wayfaring Life in the Middle Ages* (1889); *Piers Plowman* (1894); *A Literary History of the English People* (1895); *The English Novel in the Time of Shakespeare* (1896); and *With Americans of Past and Present Days* (1916), for which he was awarded the first Pulitzer prize for history.

JUSTICE. The word "justice" is derived from the Latin "justitia," which is from the Latin "jus," which means a right, or that to which one has a just claim. Justice, then, consists in rendering to each that which is his due; the administration of justice is the determination and enforcement of the rights of persons according to law or equity. Law stresses the strict rendition of what is due, while equity emphasizes the idea of fairness.

Personified, justice is commonly represented as the Roman goddess *Justitia* holding a sword (law) or scales (equity), or both, and often blindfolded (impartiality). The emblem of justice in ancient Egypt was the "feather" worn erect in her headdress by *Matt* (meaning straight), the Egyptian goddess of justice.

Justice, as a cardinal virtue, is a moral habit which inclines the will to render another what rightfully belongs to him. It is distinguished from the virtue of charity which prompts us to lend assistance to the needy from our own possessions.

The basic mental concept of the meaning of "right" and "justice" has been one of the greatest determining factors in the rise and fall of various forms of government and legal systems throughout history.

In ancient Egyptian civilization (c. 3500 B.C.) the source of all rights, laws and justice was the king, who derived his authority from the sun-god *Osiris*. The rights of the individual, therefore, were dependent upon royal decree.

Similar to the Egyptian concept of right and justice was that of Mesopotamia (c. 3000 B.C.) where the king, receiving all law from divine guidance, was the source of all rights and justice.

In Chinese civilization (c. 2500 B.C.) is found the maxim of "government of men, not laws." The idea of right and justice was perfected by Confucius (c. 500 B.C.), who held that perfect conduct consisted in "the skillful carrying out of the wishes of our forefathers." The concept of an absolute right is not to be found in Chinese justice, which is based upon arbitration and compromise.

In the Hebraic law, founded upon the Ten Commandments received by the great Hebrew leader, Moses, from Jehova (God) on Mount Sinai (c. 1250 B.C.), is to be found the idea of absolute rights resident in man himself. In seven of the Commandments is found a prohibition against the violation of these inherent rights.

Plato (c. 350 B.C.), one of the great Greek philosophers, conceived ideal justice as obtained in social harmony by the practice of beneficence. The idea of any absolute right that must be respected is lacking. Some modern writers, e.g., Herbert Spencer, Henry Sidgwick, and others, following this basic concept, have held justice to be determined by social inheritance and the natural expectations of conduct.

Aristotle, the student of Plato, recognizing man as having certain innate rights, held that justice was a certain quality by which the just claim of another was satisfied.

Modern Christian philosophy, drawing chiefly from the writings of Aristotle, the concepts of Hebraic law, and the teachings of Jesus Christ, recognizes man as a creature who is to work out his own destiny by the use of the faculties and liberty given to him by the Creator. Man, then, by necessity of nature, must have certain rights, or claims in justice, which are moral and lawful faculties of doing, possessing or obtaining something necessary or helpful for the accomplishment of that destiny. These rights may be natural, civil, religious, or acquired.

Natural rights are the gift of nature itself, antecedent to and independent of the state, that the state must not violate but rather preserve and guarantee to its citizens. Civil and religious rights are those granted to the individual by civil or religious society. Acquired rights are those which a person has gained by his own industry, by custom, or agreement, such as the right of ownership of specific goods. Justice requires that each individual be left free to exercise and enjoy all his rights as long as such exercise does not violate superior or equal rights of others or the common good.

According to this Christian philosophic concept, developed especially by so-called Scholastics under the leadership of the great medieval thinker, Thomas Aquinas (d. A.D. 1274), the state, or civil society, is instituted to preserve these rights to its subjects, to adjudge rights as between individuals, and to advance the common good by promoting the peace and prosperity of its citizens.

This Christian idea of right and justice is the general basis of the legal and governmental institutions of what is known as Western Civilization.

An outstanding example of the application of these basic Christian concepts is to be found in the establishment of the government of the United States of America. The acknowledgment of the existence of natural rights in man and the duty of government to protect them is found in the Declaration of Independence: "We hold these truths to be self-evident, that all men . . . . are endowed by their Creator with certain inalienable rights . . . . That to secure these rights, governments are instituted among men . . . . That whenever any form of government becomes destructive of these ends, it is the right of the people to alter or abolish it." The absolute guarantee of the preservation of these rights to the citizens by the Federal government is found in the Bill of Rights in the Constitution, and by the state governments in the Fourteenth Amendment to the Constitution.

The various forms of modern totalitarian governments, following the philosophic concept of those who hold that the state is the sole and only source of rights, e.g., Kant, Hobbes, Spinoza, and others, consider the state supreme and deny the value or importance of the individual and his rights except in so far as he may prove of aid or assistance to the state. See LAW; NATURAL LAW; JURISPRUDENCE; HUMANITARIANISM; EQUITY.   A. A. VAIL

BIBLIOG.–R. Stammler, *The Theory of Justice* (1925); R. Pound, *Law and Morals* (2nd ed. 1926); L. Stapleton, *Justice and World Society* (1944); F. Neilson, *In Quest of Justice* (1944); H. E. Brunner, *Justice and the Social Order* (1945); F. A. Cockin et al, *People Matter* (1945); R. Pound, *Criminal Justice in America* (1945); W. A. Robson, *Justice and Administrative Law* (2nd ed. 1947).

JUSTICE OF THE PEACE is a local magistrate, with powers partly judicial, partly administrative, who is primarily concerned with the maintenance of good order in the district over which his authority extends.

England. The forerunners of the justices of the peace in England were the conservators of the peace, and it was in 1363 that the modern term first appears on the statute book. Throughout the succeeding centuries duties of a multifarious nature were imposed on the justices of the peace, who were appointed almost exclusively from the landowning classes. The old county and other courts, which had been the organs of local government, were now extinct, and their functions in this respect devolved upon the county justices. When Parliament passed an act dealing with local administration, in nearly every case they were charged with carrying out its provisions.

In their judicial capacity the justices of the peace exercised functions scarcely less important. One magistrate had the power of investigating all criminal matters that arose within the county, and of committing suspected persons to prison. A large number of statutes authorized one or two of them sitting in petty sessions to try small offenses summarily—that is, without a jury—while at these quarter sessions two or more were competent to try any crime, however heinous, with a jury. It is only within comparatively recent times that the justices have been compelled to reserve serious offenses for trial by a superior judge at the assizes. As regards civil matters they have a statutory jurisdiction in many small cases.

In the United States the justice of the peace formerly exercised sweeping local executive and administrative powers, although his actual authority varied from state to state. Often he drew up the tax levy, collected the tax, appointed road commissioners and supervised highways, made disbursements, granted licenses to taverns, and appointed and controlled administrators, executors, and guardians. Another common function was that of performing marriages. In the administration of justice the official exercised wide powers of investigating crimes, and he could commit persons suspected of criminal acts.

In colonial times he was an appointed official but later he was elected. At present the powers of the justice of the peace are much less extensive, but in most rural districts he still has jurisdiction over misdemeanors and minor cases, involving from $100 to $300. Payment is by fee, a system which sometimes leads to abuses. The justice of the peace is today under attack because he is usually untrained in law. In many urban areas this official has been superseded by the salaried police magistrate. See POLICE COURT.

JUSTICE, U.S. DEPARTMENT OF, a major branch of the executive establishment of the Federal government, created in 1870 to conduct the legal business of the government. It is headed by the attorney general who has been a member of the president's cabinet since 1789. The attorney general is the public prosecutor and standing counsel of the United States and the legal advisor to the president and the heads of the other departments of government. He appears before the Supreme Court in cases of special importance and exercises general supervision over all U.S. attorneys and marshals. Directly under his office fall the FEDERAL BUREAU OF INVESTIGATION (FBI), the offices of the pardon attorney, the solicitor general, who has general charge of government business in the Supreme Court, and the assistant solicitor general, and the office of the assistant to the attorney general who supervises directly the administration of the departmental bureaus and divisions and maintains liaison with other branches of the government.

Under the assistant to the attorney general stand the seven divisions: antitrust, tax, claims, lands, criminal, customs, and administrative. He administers the Bureau of Prisons with 27 penal and correctional institutions, the Immigration and Naturalization Service, transferred from the Department of Labor in 1940 with 16 districts throughout the country, and the Office of Alien Property which handles all seized enemy property and which was vested in the Department in 1946.

The Board of Immigration Appeals and the Board of Parole are quasi-judicial agencies administered by the department. Certain matters such as counterfeiting, postal violations, customs violations, and internal revenue cases have been placed by statute in other departments. Matters pertaining to ESPIONAGE, SABOTAGE, and internal security fall within the Department and are assigned to the FBI, which maintains 50 district offices throughout the nation. The Antitrust Division maintains eight districts, and each year receives and investigates hundreds of complaints against monopolies or restraints of trade. It also defends or enforces the orders and processes of various federal administrative tribunals such as the INTERSTATE COMMERCE COMMISSION, the FEDERAL TRADE COMMISSION, and the FEDERAL COMMUNICATIONS COMMISSION. The Tax Division prosecutes income, estate, and other tax cases referred to it by the Treasury Department. Department examiners periodically investigate the offices of Federal district attorneys, marshals, clerks, and commissioners and the records of the Federal courts.   ALFRED DE GRAZIA

BIBLIOG.–H. Cummings and C. McFarland, *Federal Justice* (1937).

JUSTIFIABLE HOMICIDE. See HOMICIDE.

JUSTIFICATION, in law, may have either of two meanings. In *pleading*, it is the maintenance of the right of the defendant to perform the act charged by the plaintiff as a wrong. Thus, trespass may be justified by the possession of a warrant issued by a court of competent jurisdiction; or libel and slander may be justified by proving that under the circumstances the defendant had a right to make the statements in question, as in an indictment. In *practice*, justification is the proceeding by which a surety establishes his qualifications for performing his undertakings.

In theology, justification is the act of God by which

the soul is reconciled to Him. According to the terms of the Westminster Confession, justification is by faith only, and consists in "accounting and accepting . . . persons as righteous, not for anything wrought in them or done by them, but for Christ's sake alone." According to the Roman Catholic doctrine, defined by the Council of Trent, only such faith as is active in charity and good works justifies; and "justification is not remission of sins merely, but also the sanctification and renewal of the inward man, through the voluntary reception of the grace and of the gifts whereby man from unjust becomes just." See FAITH.

JUSTIN I, emperor of the East from A.D. 518 to 527, was probably of Gothic descent, and at first was a shepherd. He distinguished himself in war against the Isaurians and Persians; became commander of the imperial guards under the Emperor Anastasius; and when the latter died, Justin secured his own election as emperor. His reign is memorable chiefly for his resignation of the appointment of consuls to Theodoric, king of the Goths (522); for a war with the Persians; and for the destruction of Antioch in 525 by fire and inundations. He was succeeded by his nephew, JUSTINIAN I.

JUSTIN II, emperor of the East from A.D. 565 to 578, was a nephew of JUSTINIAN I, whom he succeeded. In his reign the Longobardi, or Lombards, deprived him, between 568 and 570, of the country now called Lombardy, and indeed of most of Italy. He also waged a disastrous war against Persia. From A.D. 574, Justin's mental condition unfitted him for rule, which was carried on by his empress, Sophia.

JUSTIN MARTYR, one of the earliest apologists of the Christian Church, was born of Greek parents in Flavia Neapolis in Samaria, c. 100 A.D. Well schooled in the prevailing philosophies of his time, and at first largely dominated by Platonism and Stoicism, he eventually became a Christian, and the ability and zeal with which he defended Christianity and assailed paganism led at length to his martyrdom in Rome (c. A.D. 148) under Antoninus Pius (or, according to Eusebius, considerably later, under Marcus Aurelius). He wrote two apologies for the Christians, the first and larger of which is addressed to the emperor, the second being in the nature of an appendix. In these he pleads for a more humane treatment of Christians, and a reconsideration of their credentials. His *Dialogue with Trypho* seeks to maintain the claims of Christianity as against Judaism.

JUSTINIAN I, in full **Flavius Anicius Justinianus,** 483–565, emperor of Constantinople and Rome, was born in Tauresium in Illyria, his family being of Gothic extraction. In 521 he was named consul, and during the remaining years of the reign of his uncle, the Emperor JUSTIN I, he continued to exercise great influence. In 527 Justin, by the advice of the senate, proclaimed him his partner in the empire. Justin survived this step but four months, and in the same year Justinian was proclaimed sole emperor, and crowned along with his wife, the famous THEODORA. His reign was marked by wars against the Persians, the Vandals in Africa, the East Goths in Italy, the West Goths in Spain, and the Bulgarians, who invaded Thrace. Due to the genius of BELISARIUS and NARSES, Justinian's armies were on the whole so successful that at the end of his reign his empire included, in addition to Thrace, Macedonia, Greece, Asia Minor, Syria, Egypt, and generally the eastern half of the old Roman empire, Africa, also, Italy, and part of Spain.

Yet his policy toward the barbarians threatening the empire, such as the Longobardi, Gepidae, Avars, and Bulgarians—viz., of playing them off against each other—was so unsound that his successors found themselves unable to retain the huge territory he had conquered. His system of frontier defense, which attempted to repel invasions by vast lines of forts and towers, subsidiary to greater fortresses, of itself showed the weakness of the empire. His administration is also

"The Emperor Justinian," as portrayed by French artist, Benjamin Constant (detail from a painting)

remarkable for its fiscal severity. He showed the same severity in his dealings with Christian sectaries, Jews, and pagans. He spent large sums in building; the Church of St. Sophia (now a mosque) at Constantinople was erected by him.

Apart from his wars, the chief event of Justinian's reign was an extraordinary riot between the so-called Blue or orthodox Christian faction and the Green at Constantinople, in January, 532, when the whole city became filled with fire and bloodshed; the Church of St. Sophia, much of the palace, and a vast number of other buildings were burned, and many thousands of people slain. These were the so-called *Nika Riots.* At length Belisarius led 3,000 veterans against the Green faction, who had fortified themselves in the Hippodrome; it was stormed, and 30,000 of the rioters were slain in one day.

Code of Justinian. It is as a legislator that Justinian has gained his most enduring renown. Immediately on his accession he set himself to collect and codify the principal imperial *constitutions* or statutes then in force. The code in which these constitutions were collected was published in 528–9, and contained a general provision by which all previous imperial enactments were repealed (see CODE). But Justinian's ambition went much further. The bulk of what might be called the *common law* was contained in the writings of the *jurists*—i.e., of text writers and commentators—and was in a state of confusion. To remedy this, Justinian resolved upon the publication of a single treatise in which the commentaries and other writings of the jurists might be digested and harmonized. This great work was completed in four years by TRIBONIAN, with the assistance of Theophilus, a celebrated professor of law at Berytus, two other professors, and eleven advocates. It was published in fifty books under the title *Digesta* or *Pandectae* in 534. Justinian resolved on the composition of a third legal work— *viz.*, a systematic and elementary treatise on the law which might serve as an introduction to the larger work. It was published by Tribonian and his colleagues on the same day as the *Digest,* under the title of *Institutiones,* and is familiar to modern lawyers under the name of "Justinian's Institutes." A new edition, in twelve books, known as the *Codex Repetitae Praelectionis,* with alterations, the most important of which were the *Quinquaginta Decisiones,* has alone come down to us, no copy of the earlier codex being extant. In later years he promulgated many corrections and reforms in works called *Novellae Constitutiones.* These

four works form the *Corpus Juris Civilis*, or "Body of Civil Law." See BYZANTINE EMPIRE; ROMAN LAW.
R. W. M.

BIBLIOG.–G. P. Baker, *Justinian* (1931); Procopius, *Secret History of Procopius* (1927; ed., 1934); J. Burnet, *Aids to Justinian* (1936).

JUSTINIAN II, surnamed **Rhinotmetus,** emperor of the East from A.D. 685 to 695, and again from 704 to 711. He succeeded his father, Constantine IV (Pogonatus). The cruelty and severity of his rule caused his deposition in 695; but in 704 he was restored by a Bulgarian force, and reigned with greater tyranny than before, which led to a military revolt in which he was killed. See BYZANTINE EMPIRE.

JUTE, a useful fiber plant naturalized from Malaya and Ceylon. Three quarters of the world's supply is raised in Pakistan. The important species are *Corchorus capsularis,* grown in uplands, and *C. olitorius,* in lowlands, both belonging to the family *Malvaceae.* Jute is a tall, shrubby annual that grows to a height of 12 feet and has small, solitary flowers. Its arrow-shaped leaves differ slightly between species.

Cultivation. Jute thrives best in hot, humid climates with rich, well-drained, sandy soils. The seed is hand-sown and cultivation is begun when the plants reach a height of six inches. As the plants bloom they are cut and immersed in water. This causes a rotting of the tissues that surround the secondary phloem, the part of the plant from which the fibers are obtained. The extracted fibers are long, lustrous, stiffened strands. They are easily spun but tend to become weakened and deteriorated when moist conditions prevail.

Uses. Jute is used for rough weaving, gunny and potato sacks, twine, carpets, and nets. Burlap makes up 70 per cent of U. S. jute imports, though the use of strong paper bags has cut down burlap production. Jute is still the most important material for wrapping cotton bales. Almost half the jute twine in the U.S. is used for rove, the packing in electric cables. The cheapest of the major fibers, jute is second to cotton in volume produced. The normal world yield is one to two million tons, mostly from Pakistan and India.

A different fiber plant is *Abutilon avicennae,* commonly called jute or China jute. It is native to China, and its lustrous gray-white strands are used extensively there for fine rugmaking.
R. L.

JÜTERBOG, town, Germany, in the Prussian province of Brandenburg, 39 miles SW of Berlin. The Church of St. Nicholas (14th century), the Rathaus (15th century), the Abbot's House, and the three medieval gates are notable features. Here in 1644 the Swedes defeated the Imperialists; and at Dennewitz, two miles to the southwest, Bülow defeated the French in 1813. Pop. (1946) 13,934.

JUTLAND, or **Jylland,** largest and only continental province of Denmark, extending from Tonder County, Slesvig (Schleswig) District, to the Skaw in Hjorring County; bounded on the S by Schleswig-Holstein; on the E by Little Belt and Fyn Island; on the W by the North Sea; area, 11,412 sq. mi.; pop. (1945) 1,826,056. It is separated from Norway by the Skagerrak and from Sweden by the Kattegat. The province is divided into 13 counties (*amter*): Aabenraa, Aalborg, Aarhus, Haderslev, Hjorring, Randers, Ribe, Ringkobing, Thirsted, Tonder, Vejle, Sonderborg, and Viborg. The eastern part of Jutland is an area of rolling hills and fields, more than 2,400 square miles of farmlands, and large stretches of woodland. In central Jutland is a series of beautiful lakes, noted for their exquisite water lilies; the chief lakes are Jul, Mos, and Satterlang. In Jutland also is the Himmelbjerg (550 ft.), second highest point of Denmark. The narrow northern area of Jutland is separated from the peninsula by Liimfjord, which runs east to enter the Kattegat at the large east coast port of Aalborg. The peninsula then narrows to a mere neck of land called the Skaw, where the tides of Skagerrak and Kattegat meet. Skagen, a popular seaside resort and fishing center, is the largest town at this point. Jutland's largest river is the Guden, 85 miles long, which drains the lakeland district around Silkebore, emptying by way of Randers Fjord into the Kattegat. Other rivers are the Ugerby and Vors in the north; the Guden, Skive, Omme, Stor, Norre, Skerne, Vejle, Holm, and Varde in the central part of the province; and the Suder, and Arn in the south. Hirshals, Hvide Sande, and Esbjerg are the only west coast harbors. Aarhus, chief trading place on the Baltic and second largest city of Denmark, is the capital of the province. Hald, one of the oldest Danish castles, is at Viborg.

Jutland is sometimes called the Cimbric Peninsula, as it is said to have been inhabited in the earliest times by the Cimbri. In the fifth century it was inhabited by the Jutes, who took part in the expedition of the Saxons to England. The Jutes were succeeded by the Danes. During World War II the province was invaded on April 9, 1940, by the Germans, who controlled it until 1945.
K. E. H.

JUTLAND, BATTLE OF, the greatest naval battle of World War I, fought off the coast of Jutland on May 31, 1916, between the British Grand Fleet under Adm. Sir JOHN JELLICOE and the German High Seas Fleet under Adm. Reinhard Scheer. The British losses were slightly larger than the German, but the British remained in control of the seas at the end of the battle, and for the rest of the war the German surface fleet lay inactive and bottled up in its bases.

Scheer, who had succeeded to the command of the German High Seas Fleet early in 1916, determined after consulting with the high command, to come to grips with the British fleet, which had made its power felt from the beginning of the war. He did not want to meet the main British force until his was more equal to it in size, but he hoped to lure some detachment into a position where, by the use of locally superior forces, it could be destroyed. Accordingly, he ordered a cruiser bombardment of Sunderland, hoping to entice Vice-Admiral DAVID BEATTY's battle cruiser fleet from Rosyth. Later, this plan was changed to a campaign against merchantmen and light ships in and outside the Skagerrak. On May 31, Vice-Admiral Franz von Hipper, commanding the Reconnaissance Forces, started for the Skagerrak, with 5 battle cruisers, 11 light cruisers, 9 destroyers, and 14 U-boats. Scheer, following with the main fleet, had as its principal component 22 battleships, protected by three and one-half destroyer flotillas.

At the same time the British Grand Fleet was emerging for one of its periodic sweeps of the North Sea. The main body, under Jellicoe, comprised 24 battleships, 3 battle cruisers, 4 armored cruisers, 25 light cruisers, 47 destroyers, and a seaplane carrier. Beatty's force, acting as vanguard, was far to the south; it was made up of 6 battle cruisers and 31 destroyers, supported at long range by the 5th Battle Squadron—4 battleships of the *Queen Elizabeth* class, under Rear Admiral Evan-Thomas.

At 2:20 P.M., May 31, when Beatty's ships were off the northwest coast of Jutland, the *Galatea* sighted Hipper's force. Beatty radioed the news to Jellicoe and headed toward the enemy. There ensued a running battle in a southerly direction, as Hipper began falling back toward the main German fleet coming up from Helgoland. Beatty's heavy ships first sighted the German battle cruisers at 3:31, and at 3:48 they opened fire, at a range of about 16,000 yards. In this first phase of the battle, with the rival fleets moving on parallel courses, the British ships were silhouetted against the light-yellow, western sky and the German gunnery proved effective. The British lost the battle cruisers *Indefatigable* and *Queen Mary,* and two destroyers, while the Germans lost two destroyers.

At 4:42 Scheer's battle fleet was sighted by the advance British vessels. Beatty immediately turned his force north in the direction of Jellicoe's approaching main British fleet. The German battle cruisers likewise turned and, supported by their battleships, continued the battle. On receipt of Beatty's wireless message, Jellicoe had immediately made for the scene of action, and had ordered his fastest vessels, the battle cruisers, up to Beatty's support.

The main portion of the battle began about 6:00 P.M., when Jellicoe's battle squadrons gradually came into action against the High Seas Fleet. The British ships were deployed across the van of the German column, and their gunnery inflicted great damage. The *Wiesbaden* and the *Pommern* were sunk, and two battle cruisers and a battleship virtually put out of action. The action between the main battle fleets lasted intermittently for about two hours, with the giant vessels visible only at periods through the mist. Both sides were endeavoring to close in with advantage, but Scheer finally broke off the fight and withdrew in the darkness and mist, utilizing a smoke-screened turning-away maneuver, which he repeated later. In the night there was a flurry of destroyer actions, but the German fleet escaped, and by daylight on June 1, no German vessels were to be seen. At 11:00 A.M. Jellicoe decided that the High Seas Fleet had succeeded in getting back home, and he returned to his own base. During the

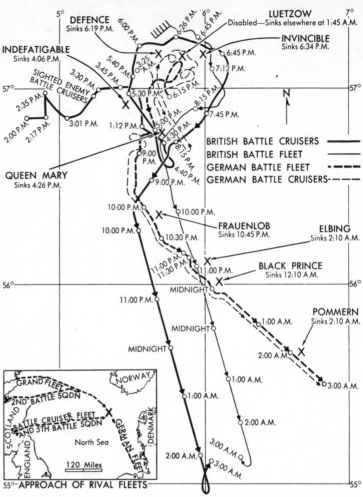

COURTESY CHICAGO TRIBUNE (REDRAWN)

The Battle of Jutland

whole fight the visibility had been very poor, and at no time was there a complete view of the battle from any one ship. Until the main action neither Jellicoe nor Scheer knew the strength of the opposing force, and even during and after it the locations of some elements were in doubt for long periods. The British lost 3 battle cruisers, including the *Invincible*; 3 cruisers; 8 destroyers; and 6,097 men killed. The Germans lost 1 battleship; 1 battle cruiser; 4 cruisers; 5 destroyers; and 2,545 men killed.   H. L. H.

BIBLIOG.–J. Buchan, *Battle of Jutland* (1916); J. R. J. Jellicoe and D. B. Beatty, *Battle of Jutland Bank, May 31–June 1, 1916* (1916); J. R. J. Jellicoe, *Grand Fleet, 1914–16* (1919); R. Scheer, *Germany's High Seas Fleet in the World War* (1920); G. Von Hase, *Kiel and Jutland* (1920); J. E. T. Harper, *Truth About Jutland* (1927); H. H. Frost, *Battle of Jutland* (1936); L. Gibson and J. E. T. Harper, *Riddle of Jutland* (ed., 1940).

JUVENAL, full name **Decimus Junius Juvenalis,** d. c. A.D. 130, Roman satirical poet. He appears to have been the son of a rich freedman of Aquinum; to have spent his life, up to middle age, mostly in the practice of declamation at Rome; and to have published his works at intervals from about A.D. 102 onward. His extant works consist of 16 satires, which were published in five books. The first includes the first five satires, and was published after A.D. 100; the second book, only the sixth (a long poem), published after A.D. 115; the third book, the seventh,

eighth, and ninth, published after A.D. 118; the fourth book, the tenth, eleventh, and twelfth, but it gives no hint of its date; the fifth book comprises the remaining four satires, and must have been published after A.D. 128. A fragment of some twenty lines was discovered in the Bodleian Library at Oxford and published in 1899.

The first nine satires are quite distinct in character from the last seven. The former are attacks, in the bitterest and most violent language, on the crime, vice, and folly of Rome; the latter are rather moral essays on various subjects. In the former, Juvenal gives a vivid picture of the state of Roman society in his day; but it is his own genuine indignation at vice, his old Roman severity of character, his love of simplicity, that impart force to his satire. He cannot, however, make his characters lifelike; his satire is not, like that of Horace, a comedy of contemporary manners. His verse is powerful, but monotonous in its rhythm. He appeals to modern readers by the similarity in many points of our present rich, affected, and luxurious civilization to that of his own day; and by the power of his epigrams, many of which are household words as quotations. Dr. Samuel Johnson imitated Satires III and X in his *London* and the *Vanity of Human Wishes*, respectively.   S. W. X.

JUVENILE COURTS. See CHILDREN'S COURTS.

JUVENILE DELINQUENCY. See DELINQUENCY, JUVENILE.

K Kk Kk Kk Kk Kk Kk Kk Kk Kk

K is the voiceless back stop; before utterance the breath is stopped by raising the back of the tongue. The sound varies according to the vowel which follows. Every *k* has a corresponding voiced stop, or *g*. In Semitic languages two *k*'s are regularly distinguished in writing. K and Q are the Latin forms of the symbols for these two *k*'s. In the Latin alphabet, and in the alphabets derived from it, the sound *k* is generally expressed by the symbol *c*, and *k* itself, for the most part, is rarely used. In the German alphabet, however, *k* is the usual sign.

In the early Semitic alphabet K faced to the left, and the perpendicular stroke was long; Hebrew ך has lost one of the side strokes, and כ is a rounding of that form. In the Greek minuscule the attempt to write K in one stroke gives a form like *u*. The Semitic name *kaph*, Greek *kappa*, means "palm" (of the hand). See ALPHABET.

K₂. See GODWIN-AUSTEN, MOUNT.

KAABA, the sanctuary at Mecca, the center formerly of pagan, now of Islamic worship. Tradition associates the Kaaba with Abraham's casting out Hagar and ISHMAEL. See MECCA.

KABAKOVSK. See SEROV.

KABARDINIAN AUTONOMOUS SOVIET SOCIALIST REPUBLIC, formerly **Kabardino-Balkar,** U.S.S.R., in the Russian Soviet Federated Socialist Republic; bounded on the N and W by Stavropol Territory, on the E by the North Osetian Autonomous Soviet Socialist Republic, and on the S by the Georgian Soviet Socialist Republic; area 4,747 sq. mi.; pop. (1950 est.) 300,000, predominantly Kabardin. The chief ethnic strain is Japhetic. Formerly an agriculturally backward land, the Kabardinian Republic has made rapid progress in farming and cattle-raising since the Russian Revolution of 1917. The greater part of the arable land of the Republic is collectivized. Irrigation of the soil has been facilitated by the harnessing of the streams descending from the mountain heights of the Caucasus. Large quantities of wheat are grown in the Nalchik plains of the Republic. The Republic is noted throughout the Soviet Union for its radioactive mineral springs with remarkable curative powers, and for its mountain ranges, ideal for mountain climbing. The highest peak in Europe, Mount ELBRUS (18,471 ft.), is located in the southern part of the Republic.

The area was formed as the Kabardino-Balkar Autonomous Soviet Socialist Republic in 1936. Late in 1944 its southwestern corner, with its Balkarian population, was ceded to the Georgian Soviet Socialist Republic. Henceforth the area became known as the Kabardinian Autonomous Soviet Socialist Republic. Its capital is Nalchik.   A. M. K.

KABBA, province, West Africa, in Nigeria, one of the Northern Provinces; area 10,577 sq. mi.; pop. about 500,000. In its northern area is the confluence of the Niger and the Benue rivers, where is located the chief town, Lokoja, established in 1860 by the first British consul. South of the river junction Kabba is divided in two almost equal parts: in the eastern section is the native state of Idah, a part of the former province of Munshi added to Kabba in 1926; west of the Niger is the native state of Igbirra. The peoples of both states are industrious, and they produce cotton, tobacco, indigo, and food crops, as well as the forest products of palm oil, kolas, shea, and rubber. Kabba, the town, 30 miles northwest of Lokoja, is a road junction and a Niger river port. Kabba Province

has many fertile river valleys, and large strips of forest; most of it lies above an elevation of 1,000 feet. In 1868 the British withdrew their consul from Lokoja, and thereafter it reverted for some time to company rule; in 1886 the company established a military center at Lokoja, which became the capital of northern Nigeria in 1900, and remained the capital until 1902.

KABINDA. See CABINDA.

KABUL, capital of Afghanistan, and chief city of Kabul Province, built 7,000 feet above sea level, on the Kabul River; 228 miles NW of Peshawar, capital of India's Northwest Frontier Province. The province of Kabul is 100 miles square, covering the plains of Koh Daiman and Beghram to the Hindu Kush Mountains on the north, extending to Jalalabad on the east, to the border of Ghazni on the south, and northwest to the Pugman Hills and including the valley of the upper Kabul River. In the fertile valleys of the Kabul wheat and barley are raised, and in the Koh Daiman every kind of fruits. The city of Kabul is situated in the center of a rich fruit-growing district. It commands passes and strategic routes from the east through the Khyber Pass into India, from the north through the Hindu Kush Range into Russia, and from the southwest through Kandahar into Iran. Kabul has manufactures of matches, buttons, leather goods, boots, and furniture. The city has an arsenal and a mint, and the most noteworthy building is the Bala Hissar, the former residence and citadel of the emir. Though Kabul has no railroad, communication with India by camel, pony, horse and donkey caravans is regular and there is a growing trade with central Asia. Exports are carpets, soap, shawls, silk and cotton goods, sugar, hardware, leather goods, tea, paper, cement, and livestock. There is also a large trade in fresh and dried fruits. A modern radio station broadcasts in Pushtu and Persian. The province and city have seen many invaders including Alexander the Great, Mahmud of Ghazni, Genghis Khan, Baber, Nadir Shad and many others. Kabul was made the capital after its capture by Baber in 1504. From 1526–1738 it was part of the Mogul Empire of Delhi. In 1839 the British supported a rival of Dost Mohammed's to the throne, and British troops occupied the city in 1842 and in 1880. From here in August, 1889, Lord Roberts set out on his memorable march to Kandahar. Pop. (1948 est.) 206,208.   K. E. H.

PAUL'S PHOTOS

Kabul Broadcasting Station is one of the many new features introduced in the Afghanistan capital

KABUL RIVER, an important stream of NE Afghanistan, rises in the Khwaja Muhammad Mountains, a branch of the Hindu Kush Range. Its total length is about 300 miles. The river basin forms the province of Kabul. From its source the Kabul flows 35 miles to the city of KABUL where it receives the first of its major tributaries, the Logar, a much larger river. Flowing on 80 miles, the Kabul passes Jalalabad where it receives another main stream, the Kunar. Smaller tributaries are the Panshir, Tagoa, Surkhab, and Swat. After flowing through the gorges of the Khyber Mountains, the Kabul joins the Indus River at Attock. From Jalalabad the river is navigable and used for commerce.

KACHH. See CUTCH.

KADAVU, or **Kandavu.** See FIJI ISLANDS.

KADESH, the name of several places in Palestine and Syria. (1) Kadesh Barnea (Gen. 14, 7), in Arabia Petraea, 55 miles south of Beersheba, was famed as the place where Moses brought forth water from a rock; there is still a clear spring. It was the headquarters of the Israelites for 40 years prior to their entry into Canaan. (2) Kadesh of Issachar (I Chron. 6; 72) is in Upper Galilee and has Jewish and Roman remains. (3) Kadesh on the Orontes has been identified with the modern Tell Nebi Mend, some 25 miles south of the city of Homs in central Syria. At Kadesh the great but indecisive battle was fought between the Egyptian king Rameses II and the Hittites (see EGYPT).   LINDA BRAIDWOOD

KADUNA, town, Nigeria, headquarters for the Northern Provinces. It is a railway junction, on the main line between Lagos on the coast and Nguru in the far northeast and the terminus of a branch line from Kagoro. It is also a highway center.

KAESONG. See KAIJO.

KAFFA, or **Gomara,** formerly an independent kingdom, E Africa, in SE Ethiopia, between 6° and 9° N lat., and 35° and 37° E long. Generally Kaffa is a plateau, scored deeply by mountain streams. It has an average elevation of 8,000 feet, with a number of peaks rising above 10,000 feet. The principal river is the Omo, which is the chief feeder of Lake Rudolf in British Kenya. Kaffa is the native home of coffee, which thrives on the mountainsides. Kaffa was conquered by Menelik in 1897, who devastated the country, killing or transporting some two thirds of the people, and imposing virtual serfdom on the rest. The present capital is Sherada, to which the government was moved from Inderacha, a thriving trading center for coffee. The natives are a copper-colored people, who speak a language varying widely from the Amharic or Galla. Some practice a debased form of Christianity; the others are pagans.

KAFFIR (Kafir) is an Arabic word meaning "an unbeliever," that is, a person who is not of the Mohammedan faith. Unfortunately this unscientific term has been widely used in anthropological literature. The word *Kaffir* designates a large number of Bantu-speaking Negroes dwelling in southeast Africa. The tribal names of these people are Pondos, Fingoes, Zulus, and Swazis. The better practice would be to use these specific names. The word *Kaffir* has entered into certain compound words, for example, Kaffraria, the land where Kaffirs dwell; "Kaffir corn" is usually Durra and Guinea corn.

KAFFIR CORN. See DURRA.

KAFFRARIA. See KAFFIR.

KAFIRISTAN, from **Kafir,** a Mohammedan word for "infidel" is the territory on the S slopes of the Hindu Kush, since 1895 a province of Afghanistan; bounded on the N by Badakshan Province, on the E by Chitral and North-West Frontier Province of Pakistan, and on the S and W by Afghanistan proper; area about 5,000 sq. mi. The area is all mountainous, with heights reaching 20,500 feet. The lower slopes support growths of wild olives and evergreen oaks, chestnut and other shade trees, and walnuts, mulberries, apricots, and apples. From 4,000 to 8,000 feet there are dense forests of pine and cedar; higher there are scrub growths of juniper, cedar, wild rhubarb, willow patches, tamarack, and birches; over 13,000 feet there are only grasses and mosses. The rivers, which teem with fish, flow for the most part into the Kabul. Animals include the wild goat and sheep, both of which are hunted by the natives during the winter; bears; and leopards. The inhabitants, pastoral tribes called Siah-Posh, are backward in civilization and practice polygamy. They were subdued by the emir of Afghanistan in 1895, after the British had disclaimed interest in the area. The emir forced them to embrace Mohammedanism.

KAFKA, FRANZ, 1883–1924, German novelist and short story writer, was born in Prague, the son of a well-to-do Jewish business man. He studied law and received his doctorate in jurisprudence in 1906. After a year of law training he took a position with an insurance company and in 1908 obtained a more desirable post with a semiofficial institution charged with the administration of the workmen's compensation laws, where he remained until forced by ill health to retire in 1918. He was a scrupulously conscientious employee, though his real interest centered on literature and writing, to which he devoted nearly all his spare time. His influences include Flaubert and Thomas Mann, Pascal and the Danish mystic Kierkegaard, his friends Franz Werfel and Max Brod; and there seems little doubt he was profoundly interested in Freud. A small book, *Observations* (1913), was assembled in 1912, but he regarded all his writings as "worthless" until *The Judgment*, a short story written in the fall of 1912, after which he wrote in rapid succession *The Metamorphosis*, one of his most powerful stories (not published until 1915), *The Stoker* (1913), which forms the first chapter of his posthumous novel *Amerika* (1927), *The Penal Colony* (1919), and the unfinished posthumous novel, *The Trial* (1925), begun in 1914. In 1917 his health, always feeble, failed altogether, and he was ordered to a sanatorium to avert tuberculosis. He tried to return to his job in Prague in 1918, but wartime shortages of food and fuel, added to the burden of earning his living, drove him finally to one sanatorium after another in a futile attempt to regain his health. In the meantime, he feverishly continued his writing. His illness, his routine job, his unhappy love affairs, his strained relations with his father, aggravated his introspective and deeply religious nature and influenced radically the aim and theme of his writings. *The Castle* (1926), his last major work and longest novel, was unfinished at his death on June 3, 1924. His friend Brod ignored his requests to burn all his manuscripts, instead publishing them posthumously in six volumes, mostly incomplete material. Kafka's writing is distinguished by the photographic clarity of his style as contrasted with the agonizing impenetrability of the underlying meaning.   ANGEL FLORES

BIBLIOG.–A. Flores, ed., *The Kafka Problem* (1946); M. Brod, *Franz Kafka* (1947).

KAGAWA, TOYOHIKO, 1888– , Japanese Christian leader, evangelist, social worker, and writer, was educated at the Kobe Theological Seminary and Princeton University. Disinherited by his wealthy family, he became a social worker in the worst slums of Kobe; aided by his wife, he spent 15 years combating moral degradation and vice conditions. Then as a "Christian Socialist" he concentrated on remedying the conditions which made for poverty; as a labor organizer he suffered several periods of imprisonment in the period after World War I, but later he became a bitter opponent of the Communists. He also helped to organize farm cooperatives. While very active in the field of public affairs he consistently refused to engage in party activity; in several emergencies, however, as after the earthquake disaster of 1923 and the Japanese capitulation of 1945, he served as adviser to the government. Until the outbreak of war in 1941 he was a strong critic of the Japanese military clique, and was arrested several times, but during hostilities he discontinued his opposition. After the war he engaged chiefly in Christian evangelistic work. He made several lecture tours to the United States. He wrote more than 50 books on religion, social and economic problems, philosophy, and other fields; he also wrote poetry and novels, some of the latter best sellers in Japan. His books include: *New Life Through God* (1932); *Love, the Law of Life* (1929, ed. 1934); *Songs from the Slums* (1935); *Behold the Man* (1941); *Meditations* (1950).   F. M.

BIBLIOG.–K. J. Saunders, *Whither Asia?* (1933); A. A. Hunter, *Three Trumpets Sound; Kagawa, Gandhi, Schweitzer* (1939); W. Axling, *Kagawa* (1932, ed. 1946).

KAGERA RIVER, or **Alexandra Nile,** headwater of the Nile, consists of two feeders, the Akanyaru and the Nyavalongo, and enters the Victoria Nyanza on the west about 1° S of the equator.

KAGOSHIMA, city, Japan, S Kyushu, capital of Kagoshima Prefecture, lies in the shelter of Kagoshima Bay. Kagoshima was the seat of the powerful daimyo (feudal barons) of Satsuma, maternal ancestors of the present empress of Japan. Their fief was the western half of the modern prefecture. Christianity made its entry into Japan when St. Francis Xavier landed at Kagoshima in 1549. The *samurai,* fierce warriors and intense patriots, grew strong in this region after the massacre, in 1638, of most of the 40,000 Christians in Japan. Kagoshima was bombarded by British ships in 1863 in retaliation for the killing of Richardson, an Englishman, by *samurai,* when he attempted to ride through the Satsuma lord's procession near Yokohama. The Satsuma rebellion in 1877 failed in a battle near Kagoshima. The city was badly damaged on Jan. 12, 1914, by the eruption of the volcano Takajima, on Sakurajima Island in the bay, opposite the city. Modern Kagoshima is the chief port in S Kyushu, manufacturing pottery and glass and trading in rice from the hinterland. Closest of the larger Japanese cities to American aircraft bases in World War II, Kagoshima suffered very heavy destruction from bombing attacks. Pop. (1947 est.) 170,416.

KAHN, ALBERT, 1869–1942, American architect, was born in Germany and came to the United States in 1891. He opened an office in Detroit (1904) and in World War I served as official architect for the Aircraft Construction Division, Signal Corps, designing numerous army airfields, naval bases, and cantonments. He pioneered in modern industrial design, combining in his factories beauty and utility. His firm had charge of the industrial building program of Russia's first five-year plan, designing and constructing over 500 buildings. It also designed over 1,000 factories and buildings for Henry Ford, and 127 major buildings for General Motors.

KAHN, JULIUS, 1861–1924, American congressman, was born in Germany and came to California at the age of five. His career was at first divided between the stage and law, but in 1898 he was elected to the House of Representatives, where he served, except for one term, till his death. A member of the House committee on military affairs from 1905, Kahn was a prominent advocate of military preparedness. He was important in drafting and promoting the passage of the National Defense Act (1915), the Selective Draft Act (1917), and the National Defense Act (1920).

KAHN, OTTO HERMANN, 1867–1934, American banker and art patron, was born in Mannheim, Germany. He learned banking in Germany, came to the United States in 1893, and became connected with the banking house of Speyer and Company, after serving five years in London for the Deutsche Bank. In 1897 he joined the banking firm of Kuhn, Loeb and Company and was its senior partner at his death. To his international fame as a great financier he added an enviable reputation as a liberal patron

of art and artists. His outstanding achievement, as director, was his reorganization of the Metropolitan Opera Company of New York. He called Gatti-Casazza and the great Toscanini from Italy, as manager and conductor, respectively.

KAHOOLAWE. See HAWAIIAN ISLANDS.

KAI ISLANDS, also **Kei,** or **Key,** Netherlands-Indonesian Union, the Republic of Indonesia, Maluku Province, a small archipelago of the Molucca Islands, in the eastern Banda Sea, 500 miles NNE of Darwin, Australia; area 572 sq. mi.; pop. about 36,000. The principal island, Great Kai, is 64 miles long; it is mountainous, with peaks reaching 3,000 feet. The neighboring islands, called Little Kai, are smaller and of low relief. The principal town and port is Tual, on Great Kai. The chief products of the islands are teakwood, copra, pepper, betel nut, and nutmeg. The Kai Islands were seized by the Japanese in 1942 and held until the end of World War II.

KAIFENG, city, central China, capital of Honan Province, situated 10 miles S of the point where the Hwang Ho (Yellow River) emerges from the Tung Kwan Gorge. The town occupies a strategic point, guarding the east end of the corridor by which China can be attacked from the west. Enclosed by massive brick and clay walls, Kaifeng is one of the most historic cities of China, having been, under its ancient name of Pienliang, the capital city of the Sung Dynasty (907–960). A noteworthy feature is a glazed blue tile pagoda, 13 stories high. Chingchow University, a government institution, is located here. Kaifeng is a crossroads for routes into Shantung Province, South Honan, and the provinces of South China and is a busy trading center for horses, mules, sheep, goats, and pigs. It is surrounded by a rich, productive agricultural area, raising millet, wheat, and cotton. There is a cotton goods manufacture. A Jewish community, called by the Chinese the "Blue Mohammedans," has existed here since A.D. 1183. The Japanese occupied the town from 1938 to 1944. It was the first provincial capital retaken by the Chinese in World War II. Pop. (1947 est.) 500,000.

KAIJO, also **Kaesong,** or **Songdo,** town, Korea, 35 miles NW of Seoul, the capital, and just four miles below the 38th parallel, demarcation line between North Korea and South Korea (see KOREA, History). Kaijo was the capital of Korea during the 10th and four following centuries. In 1951 it was the scene of truce negotiations to end the Korean War. Pop. (1949 est.) 56,000.

KAILAS, a range of mountains and its highest peak (22,028 ft.), a part of the Himalaya. The range stretches along the southwest border of Tibet, separating it from Nepal and India on Tibet's southwest and west. The Indus, Sutlej, and Brahmaputra (Tsangpo) rivers all have their sources in the range. Kailas Peak stands northwest of Lake Manasarowar; the Hindus looked upon it as sacred.

KAIPING, coal mining city, NE China, in NE Hopeh Province, about 100 miles SE of Peiping (Peking), 65 miles NE of Tientsin, and 75 miles SW of its port, Chinwangtao. The city is on the Peiping-Mukden railway, which passes through Chinwangtao, and both places are on the highway that goes northeast from Tientsin to Mukden. The walled city of Kaiping is the center of the Kailan bituminous coal field, which comprises the Kaiping, Lanchow, and Tangshan mines; Lanchow is the collective name for the Linhsi and Kuyeh mines. The Kailan mines, with a yearly output normally approximating 6,000,-000 tons, are the most productive in China proper and second in the Far East, being exceeded only by the Fushun mines in Manchuria. The Kailan reserves are estimated at more than two billion tons. The mines have been operated by the Kailan Mining Administration, an Anglo-Chinese corporation with a British manager and head office in Tientsin.

The administration developed the harbor at Chinwangtao, on Liaotung Bay, for the export of its coal, and this place, ice-free and the only good seaport in Hopeh, became one of the world's important coal shipping centers. The various mines have short railways to the Peiping-Mukden line, which carries the coal to Chinwangtao. The Kailan coal is particularly good for coking, and Japan was the biggest buyer, importing it for use in her steel industry. For this reason the mines were bombed by American planes during World War II. The mines are in territory occupied by Japan during her war with China (1937–45). They were guarded by U.S. marines after Japan's surrender. There are firebrick and cement factories at Tangshan, a colliery town adjacent to Kaiping.   P. W.

KAIPING, town, China, in S Manchuria, on Liaotung Peninsula, on the E shore of Liaotung Bay, about 20 miles S of the seaport of Yinkow and 110 miles SW of Mukden. The town is important for its marine salt production. For the tussah silk industry, see MANCHURIA.

KAIRA, town, India, Bombay Province, in the Gujarat region, capital of Kaira District, 20 miles SSE of Ahmedabad. Kaira is said to have been founded in 1400 B.C., and there is evidence of it as early as the fifth century. The town and area came under British rule in 1803. Pop. (1941) 7,311.

KAIROUAN, also **Kairwan,** or **Qairwan,** N Africa, Tunisia, 80 miles S of Tunis. It is "the Mecca of North Africa" for the Moslems and was long almost inaccessible to Christians. It is surrounded by walls, and contains a citadel and magnificent mosques, among which is that of Okbah, who founded the city about 671. His mosque is said to be one of the four gates to paradise; it was rebuilt in 1427. Kairouan is connected by rail with Tunis and the port of Sousse, 30 miles distant. Kairouan was the first capital of the Saracenic empire in Barbary; it was taken in 1881 by the French, who made many improvements, including a sterile water supply. The manufactures include morocco leather, copper vessels, potash, saltpeter, and carpets. Pop. (1946) 32,299.

KAISARIEH. See KAYSERI.

KAISER, HENRY J., 1882–   , American industrialist, was born in Canajoharie, N.Y. He spent his early career in highway construction (1914–30) and in 1931 became chairman of the executive committee of Six Companies, Inc., which built Parker and Hoover dams. He was later president of Bridge Builders, Inc., the organization which built the East Bay piers of the San Francisco Bay Bridge (1933); of the Columbia Construction Company, builders of Bonneville Dam in Oregon (1934); and of Consolidated Builders, Inc., which constructed Grand Coulee Dam (1939). Kaiser organized various companies to produce cement, ships, magnesium, and steel in World War II. In 1945 he became chairman of the board of the Kaiser-Frazer automobile corporation. In 1950 the company entered the small, low-priced car field with the "Henry J."

KAISER-FRAZER CORP.

Henry J. Kaiser

KAISER, the Teutonic equivalent for Caesar, a term used by the German and Austrian emperors.

KAISER WILHELM CANAL. See KIEL CANAL.

KAISERSLAUTERN, town, Germany, in the state of Bavaria, on the Lauter River, 42 miles by rail W of Mannheim. Notable features are the modern church of St. Mary, a Protestant church of the 14th century, and the town hall. One of the most highly industrialized towns in Bavaria, Kaiserslautern manufactures iron and metal goods, sewing machines, bicycles, textiles, shoes, furniture, and wood products. Railroad shops are also located here. Kaiserslautern, first mentioned in 882, won municipal rights in 1276.

It passed to the Palatinate of Bavaria in 1357, after having been an imperial city. From 1794 to 1814 it belonged to France, falling to Bavaria in 1816. In 1849 it was the center of revolutionary action in the Palatinate. Near here, in 1793 and 1794, the French suffered three defeats by the Prussians. During World War I it was bombed several times by the Allies. In World War II it was captured by the U.S. Third Army on Mar. 20, 1945. Pop. (1946) 70,718.

KAITHAL, or **Kythal,** town, India, E Punjab Province, Karnel District, 50 miles SW of Ambala. It was reputed to have been founded by the mythical hero Yudisthira, and traditionally connected with the monkey-god Hanuman. There are manufactures of saltpeter, lac ornaments, and toys. Kaithal fell to the Sikhs in 1767, and in 1843 it lapsed to the British. Pop. (1941) 22,325.

KAKA, or **BROWN PARROT,** a parrot-like bird of the family *Psittacidae* that inhabits New Zealand. The native Maoris call the bird the "kaka" parrot because the sound of its name resembles its harsh cry. The scientific name of the bird is *Nestor meridionalis.*

A mature bird may be between 17 and 20 inches long. The general body color is olive-brown shading to purplish red on the abdomen. The ear regions are yellow and there is a brilliant orange band across the back of the neck. Coloration is not uniform and it is not unusual to see individuals that are all yellow or red. Albino kakas are sometimes seen.

KALA-AZAR, or **Dumdum Fever,** is a disease caused by the protozoan *Leishmania donovani.* The disease is endemic to parts of India, China, the Mediterranean region, the Sudan, and South America. The parasite is transmitted to man through the bite of a sandfly of the genus *Phlebotomus.* Dogs are important animal reservoirs for the disease, which is more common in infants and children than in adults. The parasites multiply in the spleen, liver, bone marrow, and kidneys, and cause fever, anemia, emaciation, and decreased resistance to bacterial infection. Mortality is about 90 per cent in untreated cases. Specific treatment consists of intravenous injections of various antimony compounds, including antimony tartrate, neostibosan, and the diamidine compounds. Antimony therapy can save about 85 per cent of infected individuals. Different species of *Leishmania* cause the following skin diseases: Oriental sore is caused by *L. tropica;* and a South American disease, espundia, is caused by *L. brasiliensis.* Antimony is usually similarly effective in the treatment of these diseases.

KALAHANDI, former feudatory state, India, now merged with Orissa, of which it was a former state; area 3,559 sq. mi.; pop. (1941) 597,940. It has no connected authentic history, most of its people being of the aboriginal Khonds. A British railway crosses from southeast to northwest in the northern part of the state, and the capital is Bhawani Patna (pop. 7,174). The ruler is styled maharaja.

KALAHARI DESERT, a semiarid section of about 120,000 square miles in the Union of South Africa, lying between the Upper Karroo and the central plateau of South-West Africa. The Kalahari is a great basin ranging from 2,000 to 3,300 feet in elevation and bordered on all sides except the north by heights rising to 5,000 feet. It is made up of the northwest area of Cape of Good Hope Province, the south half of Bechuanaland Protectorate, and the southeast area of South-West Africa. The nomadic native population comprises Hottentots and Griquas, the latter half-caste Hottentot and Dutch.

KALÁMAI, or **Kalamata,** seaport, SW Greece, Peloponnese Division, capital of Messenia Department, located at the head of the Gulf of Korone (Bay of Messenia); 16 miles SW of Sparta. Kalámai was a Venetian town from 1685 to 1770. In 1825 it was burned by the Turks. It has a medieval castle. Silk fabrics and goods are manufactured. Oranges, figs, currants, mulberries, and olives, and other fruits are exported. The first national assembly of Greece was held here in 1921. Pop. (1950 est.) 30,000.

KALAMAZOO, city, SW Michigan, county seat of Kalamazoo County, on the Kalamazoo River, served by the New York Central, the Pennsylvania, the Grand Trunk, and the Chicago, Kalamazoo and Saginaw railroads and U.S. highways 12 and 131; midway between Chicago and Detroit. Kalamazoo, surrounded by wooded hills, is situated in a lake country noted for its growing of celery, peppermint, and grapes. The city was founded in 1829 on the site of an Indian town and trading post. The name "Kalamazoo" is from the Indian meaning "boiling pot"; it was given to the river because of the gas bubbles in the water. Kalamazoo is the seat of the Western State Teachers College and of Kalamazoo College. The manufacture of paper and paper products is the most important industry of the city. Other major manufactures include furniture, stoves and furnaces, pharmaceuticals, musical instruments, tools, taxicabs, drill presses, fishing tackle, ventilating equipment, meat products, caskets, printing equipment, and refinery products. Pop. (1950) 57,704.

KALAMAZOO COLLEGE. See COLLEGES.

KALAMAZOO RIVER rises in S Michigan, and flows NW for some 200 miles to Lake Michigan, which it enters at Saugatuck, 29 miles S of Grand Haven.

KALAMBO FALLS. See WATERFALLS.

KALANCHOE, a genus of tropical shrubs belonging to the family *Crassulaceae*, mostly natives of Asia or Africa. They have succulent leaves, and showy cymes of large purple, yellow, or scarlet flowers.

KALAT, feudatory state, Pakistan, under the Baluchistan Agency, extends W from Sind Province to Iran, and N from the Arabian Sea to the Chagai District; area 53,995 sq. mi.; pop. (1941) 253,305. Kalat holds suzerainty over KHARAN along its northwestern border, and over LAS BELA, to the southeast. It has four major districts: Makran, Sarawan, Jhalawan, and Kachhi. Kalat is a confederation of tribes, chiefly Moslems of the Sunni sect, under the Khan of Kalat. The state is mountainous, with heights reaching 10,852 feet in the north, and generally slopes southward to the coast. The chief rivers are the Mashkai, the Hingol, and the Dasht, all flowing into the Arabian Sea. Sheep raising is the principal occupation of the inhabitants.

The capital is Kalat (pop. 2,463), some 90 miles by highway south of Quetta; the chief ports on the Arabian Sea are Pasni, connected by highway with the capital, and Gwadar. The many valleys about the capital are fertile. The city of Kalat has a citadel within whose walls is the palace of the khan. The ruling family is the Ahmadzai, which came to power in 1666–67 when Mir Ahmad I defeated the Mogul governor and consolidated most of western and southern Baluchistan into a state. Kalat came under British influence by treaties made in 1854 and 1876.
                                          C. S.

KALAWAO, town, Hawaiian Islands, on Molokai Island, a leper settlement with churches, public buildings and a children's home. It was founded in 1865 by Father DAMIEN, a Belgian missionary, and is the site of a monument to his memory.

KALB, JOHANN DE, BARON. See DE KALB, JOHANN.

KALE, also called **Borecole,** a green, leafy vegetable closely related to cabbage. Kale is a hardy, nonheading plant characterized by numerous branching green leaves. It grows best in cool and temperate climates during autumn and early spring and is exceptionally resistant to extremes of cold, heat, and drought. In the United States kale is grown most intensively around Norfolk, Va., and Long Island, N.Y. It ranks low in quality among vegetable crops but because it is cheap and palatable it is used extensively as a potherb, particularly in Europe. In the

Kale, one of the most ornamental vegetables

United States it is widely used as a stock food. Kale is the popular name for the species *Brassica oleracea* var. *acephala*.

KALE-I-SULTANIEH. See CANAKKALE.

KALEIDOSCOPE, an optical instrument invented by Sir David Brewster about 1815, which became very popular as a toy. It consists essentially of a tube, within which are fixed longitudinally two mirrors at an angle—any even submultiple of 360°, in practice generally 60°—an eyepiece at one end, and an object box containing fragments of colored glass at the other. On shaking the instrument, or slowly turning it, a series of geometric patterns is presented.

KALEVALA, THE, or "Land of Heroes," the national epic of Finland, was composed by the philologist and folklorist ELIAS LÖNNROT. Lönnrot made an extensive collection of ancient popular songs which survived among the Finnish countryfolk, and from them constructed a connected narrative poem. The epic was first published in 1835. Succeeding editions by Lönnrot (1849) and A. V. Forsman (1887) included substantial additions to the original text. The *Kalevala* relates the conflicts between the brothers Wäinämöinen and Ilmarinen and their enemy Lemminkäinen. Magic, especially the magic mill Sanpo, plays a large part in the story. The meter of the *Kalevala* was adopted by LONGFELLOW in his *Hiawatha*.

KALGAN, from Mongolian **khalgha** or "gate," Chinese, **Chang-Kia-Kow,** city, China, capital of Chahar, located just inside the Great Wall of China, at an altitude of 2,800 feet, 125 miles NW of Peiping on the railroad from Peiping to Paotow (Suiyuan). Although the surrounding Hsuan-hua plain is composed of rich loess, the district's main pursuit is not agriculture but stock raising. As a result, the capital has become a collecting and distributing center for hides, wool, and similar products. Trade, however, is the chief occupation of the city. Kalgan, as its name indicates, is the gateway through which pass the goods destined to inland China and eastern Russia. Only a small part of this traffic is handled by rail and by the motor road to Ulan Bator (Urga) in the Mongolian Peoples Republic. Camels are still the usual means of transportation as they have been for centuries. Pelts, the bulk of them from the U.S.S.R., have given the city its one important industry, fur dressing. Its 20-odd factories treat the skins which are later sent to Tientsin.

Kalgan was a great emporium and a military keypoint under the Ming and Manchu dynasties. Colonization of the territory by the Chinese starting at the turn of the century has not radically modified the city, which remains largely Mongol in race and speech and Lamaite in religion. Physical change, however, occurred in the form of partial destruction during the 1924 floods. Kalgan's rise to the status of capital came when that part of Chihli Province in which it was situated was made into the provisional district of Chahar. It was maintained throughout the Japanese occupation which began late in 1937 when Inner Mongolia became Meng-Chiang, the Federated

Council of Mongol Borderland. Following Japan's surrender in August, 1945, Chinese Communists captured Kalgan. Population estimates vary from 60,000 to 150,000. The latter figure probably applies to the metropolitan area including the neighboring town of Wanchuan.					ADRIAN TROY

KALGOORLIE, town, Western Australia, in the eastern gold fields, 375 miles E of Perth. Pop. (1944 est.) 11,904.

KALI, Indian goddess of destruction, the wife of SIVA. It was in her honor that the THUGS used to strangle their victims.

KALIDASA, fl. ? 3rd century, Indian poet, belongs to the post-Vedic period of Sanskrit literature. According to tradition he lived in the first century B.C., but modern scholars place him in the third or fourth century A.D. Generally acknowledged as the greatest of the Indian poets, in both lyric and epic forms, Kalidasa is best known to the Western world for his plays, particularly the *Sakuntala*, a dramatization of the first book of the MAHABHARATA. The most notable of his other works are two heroic epics, *Raghuvansa* and *Kumarasambhava*, the plays *Vikramorvasi* and *Agnimitra*, and *Meghaduta* (The Cloud-Messenger), one of the finest descriptive poems in Indian literature.

KALIF. See MOHAMMEDANISM.

KALINGA, a term applied by the mountaineers of northern Luzon to all strange or enemy people. More specifically it refers to a collection of loosely related pagan groups residing on the eastern side of the Cordillera Central—the great mountain range which traverses most of northern Luzon from north to south. At the time of the American occupation of the Philippines they were ardent head hunters but now, due to the opening of trails, introduction of schools and missionary efforts, most of them are partially civilized.

KALINGA, one of the nine ancient kingdoms of S India, supposed to have extended from Pulicat to Chicacole along the E coast of Madras.

KALININ, MIKHAIL IVANOVICH, 1875–1946, Soviet Russian statesman, was born in the Tver (now Kalinin) Province near Moscow, the son of poor peasants. He was in school until 14, at which age he was hired as an errand boy by a nobleman who in 1889 brought him to St. Petersburg (now Leningrad). Four years later he became a factory apprentice, and in 1896 he joined an underground revolutionary group organized by Nicholas Lenin. Kalinin's first arrest by the Czar's police in 1899 began a long series of prison and exile terms, escapes, and new arrests. Between arrests Kalinin renewed his revolutionary activities as a member of Lenin's faction, later called the Communist party. After the Bolshevik revolution, in December, 1917, he was appointed the first Soviet mayor of Petrograd (now Leningrad). In March, 1919, he was made the chairman of the All-Russian Central Executive Committee of the Soviets, a post later called chairman of the Presidium of the Supreme Soviet of the U.S.S.R. and equivalent to the presidency of Soviet Russia. Becoming ill, he was relieved of his post in 1946.

KALININ, formerly Tver, city, U.S.S.R., in the Russian Soviet Federated Socialist Republic, capital of Kalinin Region, situated on both banks of the Upper Volga, and on the Moscow-Volga Canal, 300 miles SE of Leningrad. Founded in 1181, Kalinin was annexed to Muscovy in 1486. In the 18th century, the city and its surrounding area were famed for their nail-making craftsmen and for merchants who sold rural produce to St. Petersburg (Leningrad) and foreign markets. Textile mills were started here in the mid-19th century and railroad car works in 1897. The Soviets expanded both these industries and added machine-building for the textile mills and for the near-by peat fields, a chemical industry, a rubber sole and heel factory, clothing shops, woodworking shops, a plant for photoengraving equip-ment, and ship-repair yards. The city's schools include a university and a teachers' college. Kalinin is noted for its perfectly laid-out streets and long straight avenues, its cathedral (1564), palace (1763), and government buildings on Central Square of classical 18th and 19th century architecture. The square suffered the greatest destruction in the city at the hands of the Nazi invaders who wrecked the railroad-car works and several lesser factories in 1941 during World War II. Pop. (1951 est.) 250,000.

KALININ REGION, formerly Tver, U.S.S.R., an administrative area of the Russian Soviet Federated Socialist Republic; bounded on the N by Novgorod and Vologda Regions, on the W by Velikiye Luki Region, on the S by Smolensk and Moscow Regions, and on the E by Yaroslavl Region. Pop. (1950 est.) 2,250,000. In the Valdai Hills of Kalinin Region, near their highest summit, Mount Kamenik, the Volga River has its source. The green of the hill and the white of the many small lakes in the Region form a picturesque background accounting for the area's once popular name of "little Switzerland of Russia." Kalinin Region grows more flax than all of the combined countries of western Europe, and a large proportion of the entire production of the Soviet Union. Excellent soils, ample moisture, and long summer days without excessive heat make ideal conditions in the Region for the growth of long-fibered flax whose end-product is a superior linen. There are also cotton and other textile industries, machine construction, shoe and clothing plants, and woodworking factories mainly situated in the city of KALININ, the capital of the Region. The Region and its capital were renamed for MIKHAIL KALININ, former president of the U.S.S.R. During World War II the Region served as a battleground between the invading Nazis and the Soviet Army, suffering a heavy loss of lives and property.

KALININGRAD. See KÖNIGSBERG.

KALINJAR, ancient town and hill fort, India, SE United Provinces, Banda District. In 1023 it was besieged by Mahmud Ghazni, and in 1545 the Afghan Emperor Sher Shah here met his death. Kalinjar was a center of disturbance during the 1857 Mutiny against the British. The fort stands on an isolated rock that is the termination of the Vindhya Range, and overlooks the plains of Bundelkhand. Kalinjar is mentioned in the *Mahabharata*, and old inscriptions have been found in the ancient temples and caves.

KALISPELL, city, NW Montana, county seat of Flathead County, on the Flathead River, the Great Northern Railroad and U.S. highways 2 and 93; about 150 miles NW of Helena. Kalispell, located in the beautiful Flathead Valley, is 33 miles from Glacier National Park and 10 miles from the 30-mile long Flathead Lake. The city is a tourists' headquarters and a trade center for the surrounding lumber, agricultural, and mining region. It was settled in 1891 by Demers Gregg. Kalispell grew steadily with the development of lumbering and farming in Flathead County, which produces 40 per cent of Montana's lumber and has never known a crop failure. The principal products are lumber, flour, feed, beer, ice cream, and fruit. Pop. (1950) 9,737.

KALISZ, German Kalisch, town, Poland, in the province of Lodz, situated on three islands in the Prosna River, 145 miles by rail SW of Warsaw. Kalisz is an educational and industrial center, with manufactures of leather, cloth, soap, sugar, tobacco, beer, and spirits. An ancient Slav settlement, it appears as Kalisia in the geography of Ptolemy. Here in 1343 the Teutonic Knights agreed to peace terms with the Poles, and here too the Poles triumphed over the Swedes on Oct. 29, 1706. The Russians defeated the French and Saxons in the town on Feb. 13, 1813. In World War I Kalisz was heavily damaged in 1914, but later completely rebuilt. During World War II it was occupied by the Nazis. Pop. (1946 est.) 50,000.

KALKAS, or **Khalkhas,** a nomadic people, inhabiting the steppes of northeastern Mongolia. They number about 250,000.

KALKE. See DODECANESE ISLANDS.

KALMAR, coastal county, SE Sweden, on the Baltic Sea, bounded by the counties of Skaraborg on the N, Blekinge on the S, and Jönköping and Kronoberg on the W; area 4,456 sq. mi.; pop. (1949) 235,-045. The island of Öland, separated from the mainland by the Kalmar Sound, is included in the county. Forage crops, particularly oats, are grown, and sheep raising, chiefly on Öland, and dairying are important industries. There are limestone and granite quarries, sawmills and pulpmills. The capital is Kalmar.

KALMAR, seaport, SE Sweden, capital of the county of Kalmar, on Kalmar Sound, about 200 miles SW of Stockholm. It is built partly on a small island offshore, which is connected by bridge with the mainland. Notable buildings are a fine cathedral (1660–99), and Kalmarnahus Castle, a 12th-century fortress now housing a museum. There are shipbuilding yards and manufactures of tobacco, chicory, and matches, which with timber and oils make up the exports. Here in 1397, the Act of Union was drawn up among Sweden, Norway, and Denmark, conferring the three crowns on MARGARET of Denmark. Pop. (1949) 26,060.

KALMIA, a genus of hardy evergreen American shrubs belonging to the family *Ericaceae,* valuable as ornamental plants. The flowers are snowy white or pink in color, flattened bell-shaped, and arranged in terminal cymes. The most familiar species is *K. latifolia,* popularly known as mountain laurel, or calico bush, which sometimes grows to a height of 30 feet, with leaves dark green above and light green below. It ranges from New Brunswick to Louisiana, and is the most beautiful of flowering evergreen shrubs, with the possible exception of rhododendron. *Kalmia angustifolia,* known as lambkill or sheep laurel, is a smaller species with deeper rose-colored blossoms. Both species are reputed to be poisonous to livestock.

KALMUCKS, or **Kalmyks,** the westernmost of Mongols, who until World War II lived in the lowest Volga valley, around Astrakhan, along the Caspian Sea shores, and westward from there to the eastern Don area. The name "Kalmuck" means "remnant." Descendants of Genghis Khan's warriors who overran western Asia and eastern Europe in the 13th century, the remnants of this once numerous people are now scattered in the Soviet Union and can also be found as émigrés in western Europe and Turkey.

The Kalmucks migrated from northwestern China and central Asia to the Volga delta in the 17th century, bringing with them the Buddhist religion and a nomadic way of life. The Cossacks of the Don accepted them for service in their cavalry, and together with the Cossacks they fought against the Communists in the Russian civil war of 1917–20. In 1918 the Kalmucks' number was estimated at between 250,000 and 400,000. In their defeat by the Soviets and subsequent executions they lost 70 per cent of their male population. Some 5,000 managed to escape from Russia to Turkey, and thence to Bulgaria and Yugoslavia.

The rest of the Volga Kalmucks were "forgiven" by the triumphant Soviet government which, in September, 1920, organized for them an "autonomous region," renamed in October 1935 the "Kalmuck Autonomous Soviet Socialist Republic." Its population in 1939 was 220,723, of whom between 134,000 and 175,000 were Kalmucks; its capital was Elista. But arrests, deportations to Siberia, and executions of Kalmucks continued. Others perished during World War II. On the Nazis' defeat in 1943 the entire Kalmuck "republic" (which actually never had any political autonomy) was dissolved by the Soviet government on charges of collaboration with the Germans. Many Kalmucks were shot and the rest were deported to parts unknown, while the region's territory was distributed among adjacent regions.

Of the 5,000 Kalmucks who escaped westward after the civil war of 1917–20 and their descendants, in 1950 some 1,500 were in Turkey, mainly as herdsmen, 600 were in France, and 700 were in a refugee camp in Bavaria. In September, 1950, attempts were made to transfer the latter 700 to Paraguay in South America, where a farming community was to be established for them by a private corporation in co-operation with the United Nations' International Refugee Organization.   ALBERT PARRY

KALPI, town, India, United Provinces, Jalaur District, on the right bank of the Jumna, 45 miles SW of Cawnpore. The original town was on an elevated site near the river, but it was moved among near-by ravines, where a small fort was built following several Mahratta attacks. Kalpi is a trading center, chiefly in cotton, and has manufactures of paper and an excellent refined sugar. During the Mutiny of 1857–58 Kalpi was the chief rendezvous for the revolting Gwalior contingent, which was twice defeated, once after an unsuccessful attack on Cawnpore, and again in May, 1858, at Kalpi itself. The town is reputed to have been founded in the fourth century; in 1196 it fell to a viceroy of Mohammed Ghori and played a large part in the subsequent Mohammedan history. In the middle of the 18th century it fell to the Mahrattas; in 1803 the British captured it, and it remained in British hands after 1806. Pop. (1941) 11,530.

KALUGA, town, U.S.S.R., in the Russian Soviet Federated Socialist Republic, capital of Kaluga Region, situated on the left bank of the Oka River, 100 miles SW of Moscow. In 1912, retreating from Moscow, Napoleon vainly tried to break through to the Kaluga Route with its plentiful supplies. The city is noted for its greenery and several 18th-century buildings. Soviet-established industries include machine building for the U.S.S.R.'s railroads, electromechanical works, a match factory, and the manufacture of scales. Coal is mined in the area. Pop. (1951 est.) 80,000.

KALUGA REGION, an administrative area of the U.S.S.R. situated in the Russian Soviet Federated Socialist Republic; bounded on the N by Moscow and Smolensk regions, on the W by Bryansk Region, on the S by Orël Region, and on the SE by Tula Region. The capital is Kaluga.

SOVFOTO
Kalmuck farmers drinking fermented mare's milk

KALYMNOS. See DODECANESE ISLANDS.

KÁMA, or **Kámádeva,** the Hindu god of love. He is represented as riding on a sparrow, holding in his hand a bow of sugar cane and five arrows, one for each of the five senses.

KAMA RIVER, in the U.S.S.R., the most important affluent of the Volga, is 1,170 miles long and has a basin of 202,600 square miles. It rises in the swampland of east-central European Russia, flows almost due north, then northeast. Upon entering Molotov Region the Kama makes a sharp turn to the south, flowing in that direction to the city of Molotov. From Molotov to its junction with the Belaya it flows southwest. After meeting the Belaya, which brings it most of the drainage of the Bashkir Autonomous Soviet Socialist Republic, the main stream turns almost due west till it falls into the Volga 40 miles below Kazan. Large deposits of iron ore have been discovered along its banks where it parallels the Urals for some 400 miles. The Kama River, almost entirely navigable, is of immense importance as a link between the industries of the Urals and the Volga.

KAMAISHI, city, Japan, Honshu, in Iwate Prefecture, 275 miles NNE of Tokyo. Located on the east coast near the Kamaishi iron mines, the city developed into the primary steel center of northern Honshu. Its position enabled American warships to destroy the steelworks, late in World War II, by direct shelling. Pop. (1946) 26,200.

KAMAKURA, seaside resort, Japan, Honshu, Kanagawa Prefecture, on Sagami Gulf, 12 miles S of Yokohama. Kamakura's chief feature is its colossal bronze Daibutsu, or statue of Buddha, erected A.D. 1252. It is pre-eminent among the Daibutsu of Japan for its majestic serenity, and ranks among the world's masterpieces. From the 12th to 14th centuries Kamakura was the metropolis of eastern Japan, seat of the Minamoto shoguns and Hojo regents who ruled the country in the name of the imperial government at Kyoto. Among many historic edifices is the Hachiman shrine to the Japanese war god, Ojin Tenno. About 10 miles across Miura Peninsula was the great naval base at YOKOSUKA. Pop. (1946) 51,293. See JAPAN, History.

KAMARAN ISLAND, lying near the coast of Yemen, in the Red Sea, some 200 miles N of Perim; area, 22 sq. mi.; pop. about 2,200. The British took the island from Turkey in 1915. It is administered by the government of India under a civil administrator also responsible to the governor of Aden. The United States of Indonesia and India jointly maintain a quarantine station here for pilgrims journeying to MECCA.

KAMBOVE, town, Belgian Congo, Elizabethville Province, Lualaba District, Jabotville Territory, in the heart of the copper mining area of Katanga, 92 miles by rail NW of the provincial capital. It has rail connections with Benguela in Angola, and Capetown in the Union of South Africa. Kambove's chief importance is as a mining center, but it also has importance as an agricultural and commercial center. Pop. (1943) 277 whites.

KAMCHATKA PENINSULA, extending southwest from the northeastern tip of Asia. See KHABAROVSK TERRITORY; KORYAK NATIONAL DISTRICT.

KAMENETS-PODOLSKI REGION, an administrative area of the U.S.S.R. situated in the Ukrainian Soviet Socialist Republic; bounded on the N by Rovno and Zhitomir regions, on the W by Ternopol Region, on the S by Chernovtsy Region, and on the E by Vinnitsa Region. The capital is Proskurov.

KAMENSK, town, U.S.S.R., the Russian Soviet Federated Socialist Republic, in Sverdlovsk Region, about 75 miles E of the city of Sverdlovsk. Kamensk is the center of the aluminum industry of the Urals. One of its metalworks, which dates from the 17th century, is located near an iron-ore field that has deposits estimated at 80 million tons. A high grade of bauxite, necessary for aluminum production, is also mined in Kamensk. The town's population increased sharply after 1926. Pop. (1951 est.) 80,000.

KAMENSKOE. See DNEPRODZERZHINSK.

KAMENZ, town, Germany, in the state of Saxony, on the Black Elster, 20 miles NE of Dresden. Features of interest include the church of St. Mary (15th century), the church of St. Just (14th century), and the Hutberg, crowned with a monument to Lessing, who was born in Kamenz. The town has glass, machine, stove and textile manufactures, and granite quarries. Kamenz was founded early in the 13th century. In 1547, as a member of the Six-Town League, it was deprived of its municipal rights and property by Charles V for its participation in the Schmalkaldic War (1546-7). In 1635 it came under the Elector of Saxony. Pop. (1946) 14,489.

KAMERLINGH ONNES, HEIKE, 1853-1926, Dutch physicist, was born in Groningen and studied at the universities of Groningen and Heidelberg. After being an assistant at the Delft Polytechnic (1878-82) he became professor of physics at the University of Leiden and remained there until shortly before his death. In 1894 he established an especially equipped laboratory where the physical properties of matter at low temperatures might be studied. The first to liquefy HELIUM (1908), he brought it within one degree of absolute zero in attempting to solidify it. He found that at such low temperatures certain metals such as lead and cadmium lose their electrical resistance almost completely. He called this phenomenon superconductivity, and explained it as a result of the slowing down of electrons in the atoms of the metal. For these various low-temperature discoveries he received the 1913 Nobel prize in physics.

KAMERUN, a former German possession in W Africa. See CAMEROONS, BRITISH; CAMEROUN, FRENCH.

KAMES, HENRY HOME, LORD, 1696-1782, Scottish judge and metaphysical writer, was born in Kames, Berwickshire. He was raised to the bench as Lord Kames in 1752. Besides books on Scots law, he published *Essays on the Principles of Morality and Natural Religion* (1751); *An Introduction to the Art of Thinking* (1761); *Elements of Criticism* (1762); *Sketches of the History of Man* (1774).

KAMET, MOUNT, a peak of the Himalaya, in Tibet, close to the frontier of United Provinces, India, some 220 miles NW of Delhi, 25,447 feet above sea level. It is one of the highest peaks thus far climbed by man.

KAMINISTIKWIA RIVER, Canada, in S Ontario, rises in Dog Lake and flows by a winding course 60 miles SE to empty into Lake Superior through Thunder Bay at Fort William. Abundant water power is provided by its many falls and cataracts, among them the notable Kakabeka Falls, which are about 130 feet high and 150 feet wide. The name is an Indian word believed to mean, "the river with short bends and many islands."

KAMLOOPS, city, Canada, in the province of British Columbia, situated at the junction of the N and S branches of the Thompson River; on the Canadian National and the Canadian Pacific railways; 250 miles NE of Vancouver. It is an important railroad divisional point and a distributing center for a region devoted to lumbering, ranching, fruit-growing, and mining. Pop. (1950 est.) 8,500.

KAMPALA, town, E Africa, British Uganda Protectorate, Buganda Province, a few miles N of Lake Victoria; the western terminus of the Kenya and Uganda railway. It is the chief commercial center for Uganda, and is the site for Higher College, founded in 1925 and reconstituted in 1939, for the education of students of British East Africa.

KAMPEN, town, N central Netherlands, Overijssel Province, four miles above the mouth of the Ijssel River; eight miles NW of Zwolle. It is a picturesque canal city, once belonging to the Hanseatic

League. Its chief buildings of interest are two 14th century churches, and a 16th century *stadhuis*, with rich wood carving. Kampen manufactures cotton goods, damask, plush, blankets, rope, earthenware, tiles, bricks, and scythes. It has trade in dairy products. During World War II it was occupied by Germany until freed by Canadian and American troops on April 19, 1945. Pop. (1950 est.) 24,012.

KAMPERDUIN, or **Camperdown,** town, Netherlands, in the province of North Holland, on the North Sea, 25 miles NW of Amsterdam. Here Admiral Duncan defeated the Dutch fleet, on Oct. 11, 1797. See CAMPERDOWN, THE BATTLE OF.

KANAGA ISLAND. See ALEUTIAN ISLANDS.

KANARESE, a DRAVIDIAN people of South India, some ten millions in number, inhabiting the plateau of Mysore, part of South Bombay, and the Kanara country. They have an alphabet and a written literature with works dating back to the twelfth century. See DRAVIDIAN.

KANAUJ, ancient city, India, United Provinces, Farrukhabad District, on the Kali Nadi River near its junction with the Ganges, 49 miles NW of Cawnpore, Kanauj was once India's greatest capital; it is said to have been in existence as early as 900 B.C. It was a scene of intensive Brahman activity, and even today its name is given to an important division of the Brahmans of northern India. Its greatest splendor was reached under Harsha in the sixth century A.D. In 1019 it fell to Mahmud of Ghazni, and in 1194 it was taken by Mohammed Ghori. Its ruins take up a four-mile half circle and have not yet been scientifically excavated. Pop. (1941) 21,994.

KANAWHA RIVER, West Virginia, the principal river in the state and a tributary of the Ohio River. Formed by the junction of the New and Gauley rivers in the central part of West Virginia, it flows northwest and empties into the Ohio River at Point Pleasant, W.Va. About 90 per cent of its 97-mile length has been canalized by three modern locks and dams affording a minimum draft of nine feet for commercial traffic. The Kanawha Valley is rich in mineral deposits, chiefly bituminous coal and salt, and numerous chemical plants have been built on islands and along the river shores. The chief industrial center of the valley is Charleston, capital of the state, located about 58 miles from the river mouth. Locally the river is sometimes called the Great Kanawha to distinguish it from the Little Kanawha, a smaller river flowing parallel about 50 miles north.

KANAZAWA, city, Japan, N central Honshu, capital of Ishikawa Prefecture, 100 miles N of Nagoya, on the Hokuriku trunk railway and main W coast highway. Kanazawa is the largest and most affluent of Japanese cities on the Japan Sea. It has modern buildings and fine gardens, such as the 300-year-old Kenroku Park, and many temples and shrines. About 30 miles south stands Kakusan (8,865 ft.), a mountain climbed by thousands of pilgrims annually. Kanazawa's prosperity is founded on the production of silk, porcelain, rice, fans, lacquerware, and inlaid bronze. In the Tokugawa age Kanazawa was the seat of the Maeda family, among the most powerful and wealthiest of the daimyo (feudal barons) and their descendant, Marquis Maeda, was among the richest men in modern Japan. The army had a division headquarters in Kanazawa. Pop. (1947) 231,450.

KANCHENJUNGA, or **Kinchinjunga,** believed to be the world's third highest peak (28,146 ft.), in the eastern Himalaya, on the boundary between Sikkim and Nepal. The view of the peak from Darjeeling, the Indian hill-station some 50 miles southsoutheast, is one of the grandest in the world.

KANCHOW. See KANHSIEN.

KANDAHAR, second city of Afghanistan, capital of Kandahar Province, equidistant from Herat to the NW and Kabul to the NE, close to the Arghandab River. The surrounding country is an elevated plain (3,500 ft. above sea level) fertile and highly cultivated to the southwest and somewhat barren and broken by hills to the northeast. The city is like a medieval fortress, almost square and with an outer wall and a moat. Four main roads, entering each through its own gate and meeting at the central covered *chauk* (city square), divide the city into four quarters. Wells and canals from the Arghandab supply water. There are many mosques. Western goods, mostly British and Russian, are sold in some 1,600 shops. Kandahar lies in a fruit belt and ships produce to India. The rail head is New Chaman on the Baluchistan border 80 miles to the southeast, and there is a 370-mile highway to Herat and a 310-mile one to Kabul. Silk carpets of local manufacture are exported as well as cummin seed, wool, madder, and horses. The original Kandahar, the ruins of which are four miles east of the present location, is believed to have been founded by Alexander. It was at various times in Afghan, Mogul, and Persian hands. The new city was built by Ahmad Shah around 1747. The British occupied it from 1839 to 1842 and again from 1879 to 1881. Pop. (including suburbs) 77,186.   ADRIAN TROY

KANDY, city, Ceylon, built around an artificial lake, at an elevation 1,600 feet above sea level, 75 miles by rail ENE of Colombo, the capital. Among the interesting features are the botanic gardens, lying outside Kandy at Peradenia, and a number of Buddhist and Brahman temples and shrines. Tea, cocoa, pepper, cinchona, vanilla, areca nuts, coconuts, and coffee are cultivated on plantations in the surrounding country. Kandy was the capital of Ceylon kings, the last of whom constructed (1806) its lake. The town was occupied by the Portuguese in the 16th and by the Dutch in the 18th century, but the native kings were able to maintain their independence. The British gained control in 1814–15. Pop. (1946) 50,381.

KANE, ELISHA KENT, 1820–57, American Arctic explorer, was born in Philadelphia, Pa., and studied at the University of Virginia and the medical school of the University of Pennsylvania. In 1843, appointed assistant surgeon in the U.S. Navy, he went to China as physician to the Chinese embassy under Caleb Cushing. He traveled as a surgeon in China, Europe, Africa, and Mexico, and in 1850–51 was senior medical officer to the Grinnell Expedition, which searched the Arctic unsuccessfully for Sir JOHN FRANKLIN, lost since 1845. In 1853–55 Kane was commander of a second Grinnell Expedition in search of Franklin, financed privately but under Navy auspices. He sailed his ship, the *Advance*, through Baffin Bay and Smith Sound to discover Kane Basin. Winter headquarters were established in Rensslaer Bay. No trace of Franklin was found, but an exploring party reached Cape Constitution, a record 80° 10′ N lat., and discovered Kennedy Channel, an iceless channel which made probable an open polar sea. Kane deserted the frozen *Advance* in May, 1855, and led his men overland and by boat to Upernivik, a distance of some 1,300 miles made in 83 days with only one man lost. His accounts of the two expeditions, published in 1853 and 1856, were popular for years. See ARCTIC REGIONS, *Exploration*.

KANE, borough, NW Pennsylvania, in McKean County, on the Baltimore and Ohio and the Pennsylvania railroads and U.S. highways 6 and 219; about 95 miles SE of Erie. The eastern gateway to the Allegheny National Forest, Kane is a popular resort, particularly for skiing. It was settled in 1859 by Thomas L. Kane, later a general in the Union Army during the Civil War. There are gas and oil wells in the vicinity of Kane; and the most important products are oil-well machinery, brush handles, venetian blinds, luggage, clothing, glass, brass screws, and toys. Pop. (1950) 5,706.

KANEM, a native state, French Equatorial Africa, in Chad Colony, lying to the NE of Lake Chad. It came under French control in 1903. The kingdom is now a district of Chad Colony, with its capital at Mao.

KANGAROO, a pouched MARSUPIAL, generally of large size, restricted in distribution to Australia, Tasmania, New Guinea, and adjacent islands. The animals are strikingly modified for leaping; the fore limbs are small, the hind limbs very large and strong. A long, thick, tapering tail supports the animal when it sits. The ears are large and can be moved independently of each other. The coat is soft and thick. The teeth are horselike and adapted for grinding plant tissues. The females possess a large belly pouch in which the young are carried for a certain length of time after birth. At birth, the young are very undeveloped, scarcely exceeding an inch in length. The fore limbs are disproportionately developed and bear prominent claws. Immediately after birth, the single young climbs through the maze of fur to the pouch, crawls in, and grasps a nipple. The nipple swells within the baby's mouth and thus the young kangaroo remains attached for several months. At about four months, the youngster leaves the pouch to graze, but returns immediately if danger threatens.

Kangaroos belong to the family *Macropodidae* (large feet) that includes the large, familiar kangaroos commonly seen in circuses, the wallabies, or smaller kangaroos, with exceptionally large feet, and the rat kangaroos that are smaller than the others. Probably the best known is the great gray kangaroo, *Macropus giganteus*, a large, woolly-coated species of the scrublands and forests. Others are the wallaroo, *Macropus*

Young Kangaroo in mother's pouch at Melbourne is the first golden-colored kangaroo born in captivity

robustus, of the mountain ranges, and the handsome red kangaroo, *Macropus rufus*, of the open plains and tablelands.

Some species move about singly, or in pairs, others in groups of six to fifty. The larger species of kangaroos rest during the day, moving about to feed in late afternoon. They often stand on all four feet to graze but move about on the hind legs by a series of short leaps. When startled or hunted, they move by taking longer leaps. A single jump of 26 feet has been recorded, and a hunted kangaroo was observed to clear a nine-foot fence. Few however, will attempt any enclosure over five feet high.

The tree kangaroo of Queensland and New Guinea is a forest animal, well modified for an arboreal existence. The sharp claws and roughened foot pads enable the animal to climb trees with ease. The dense fur is protection against heavy rains during the wet season.

The natives used to eat kangaroos, but depletion of the animals has been primarily due to increasing demands of the fur trade. The hides and soft fur of wallabies are widely used in this industry. The ad-

vent of the automobile spelled doom for many kangaroos that might have escaped the former mounted hunters. In some parts of Australia the animals are given partial protection. However, kangaroos and wallabies do a certain amount of damage to crops and compete with sheep for herbage, so control is necessary when they become too numerous.

More than a half-million skins were marketed annually in Australia a quarter of a century ago. The larger number was converted into leather. The animals do well in captivity and a number of species are exhibited in the zoological gardens of America.

W. J. HAMILTON, JR.

KANGAROO COURT, a form of unauthorized inmate self-government, now largely abolished, but still existing in some jails and penitentiaries. In institutions where it operates, the prisoners elect a judge who presides over a "court." The setting up of rules and their enforcement are usually matters of individual whim carried out with the purpose of gaining special privilege and prestige, often through blackmail and terrorism. New inmates, in particular, unfamiliar with these arbitrary codes, are frequently subjected to abusive and demoralizing treatment. The system has been denounced as vicious and corrupt but continues to exist in unprogressive institutions.

The origin of the term "kangaroo" is obscure. Some claim it was brought from Australia—home of the kangaroo—where the practice flourished. The term has also been applied to irregular courts in frontier districts, and in the early days of the automobile to the magistrate courts which operated in conjunction with speed traps.

KANGAROO ISLAND, Australia, a part of South Australia, at the Gulf of St. Vincent, separated from Yorke's Peninsula by Investigator Strait; eight miles from the mainland; area 1,680 sq. mi. Its greatest length is 80 miles; greatest breadth, 24 miles.

KANGAROO RAT, a strikingly marked, jumping rodent, *Dipodomys*, of Mexico and western United States. The well developed hind limbs, and long tail (which acts as a balancer), are characteristic of the several species. The usual color is yellow, with a white stripe running from each side of the face, along the sides of the body, and the length of the tail. These desert rodents have external, fur-lined cheek pouches, in which they garner seeds to store in their moundlike dwellings. Kangaroo rats do not hibernate, although they are inactive during severe winter weather. W. J. HAMILTON, JR.

Long-tailed kangaroo rat

KANGHOA ISLAND. See KYODO ISLAND.

KANGRA, or **Nagar,** town, India, E Punjab Province, Kangra District, on an elevation 2,400 feet above sea level, 92 miles NE of Amritsar, an important trading center. Mahmud of Ghazni took the town in 1009, carrying off vast temple treasures; and the town was again plundered in 1360 by Feroz Shah. The district headquarters were removed from here to Dharmsala in 1855. The famous temple of

Devi Bajreshi, one of the oldest in India, and the town itself were destroyed with a large loss of life by the earthquake of 1905. The temple has since been restored.

KANGTING, or **Tatsienlu,** city in W central China; capital of Sikang Province. It is situated in some of the most mountainous country in China, at about 8,000 feet above sea level. The city is surrounded by the Chiung-lai Shan and other ranges, and is at the east portal of the 15,400-foot Dokow-la Pass; near it tower 24,900-foot Minya Konka and other peaks. A branch of the Yalung River, a tributary of the Yangtze, flows past Kangting. The city is an important entrepôt for this region of China; great trade highways, thousands of miles long, pass through it, east, south, west and northwest. Pop. about 25,000.

KANGWA ISLAND. See KYODO ISLAND.

KANHSIEN, or **Kanchow,** town, SE China, S Kiangsi Province, on the Kan River, an important tributary of the Yangtze. Kanhsien is at the head of navigation for large boat traffic on the river. It has several interesting temples, and manufactures and exports ink and varnish. Pop. (1936 est.) 100,000.

KANKAKEE, city, NE Illinois, county seat of Kankakee County, on the Kankakee River, the Illinois Central and the New York Central railroads and U.S. highways 45 and 52; about 55 miles SW of Chicago. Kankakee is the trading center for an extensive agricultural area. It was settled in 1832 by French-Canadians and "Yankee Pioneers." Old stone buildings and miles of stone fences, built by the original settlers, give Kankakee an air of old world charm. The Kankakee State Hospital is located here. Paper specialties, paint, varnish, building materials, hosiery, venetian blinds. stoves, furniture, and neon signs are some of the products of the city. Pop. (1950) 25,856.

KANKAKEE RIVER, tributary of the Illinois, formed by the union of the Kankakee and Desplaines rivers in Grundy County, Illinois. It is about 230 miles in length.

KANKAN, town, French West Africa, Guinea Colony, at the head of navigation on the Milo River. An important trade and transportation center, Kankan is the terminus of the railway from Conakry, the hub of a highway system, and has plane service to important African points. Its native population is largely Moslem. Pop. about 12,000.

KANNAPOLIS, unincorporated town, mid-North Carolina, Cabarrus County, on the Southern Railroad and U.S. Highway 29A; 21 miles NNE of Charlotte. Owned by Cannon Mills, it is the largest unincorporated town in the state. Pop. (1950) 28,448.

KANO, emirate, British West Africa, N Nigeria, making up the major part of KANO PROVINCE; area about 13,000 sq. mi.; pop. about 2,000,000. The history of the country dates back to the 10th century; it has been Moslem in religion since the 14th century. In the early 19th century, the Hausa Negroes who made up the population were overrun by the Fulahs, a Hamitic people with a strong infusion of Sudanese Negro blood; in the latter part of the century Kano established its independence and chose its own emir. In 1904 the British invaded the country and unseated the emir. Kana, at first a British protectorate, was amalgamated with southern Nigeria in 1914. The emirate is administered by the emir and a council, with the advice of the British resident.

KANO, city, British West Africa, N Nigeria, Northern Provinces, capital of KANO PROVINCE and Emirate, situated on the African plateau at an altitude of 1,570 feet, 705 miles by rail NE of Lagos, Nigerian capital and chief port. The city is inclosed within a sun-dried mud wall 40 feet thick at the base, 40 to 50 feet high, and some 12 miles in circumference. Its buildings are also of sun-dried mud. A city planning scheme has made progress in the widening of streets and adequate drainage. In the Northern Provinces Kano is supreme in commerce and in-

CHICAGO NATURAL HISTORY MUSEUM
Male weaver near Kano

dustry, most of the trade being in the hands of the Moslems. The city has been a manufacturing center for more than 1,000 years, carrying on a trade in textiles and leather. Its best known products are morocco leather—of which it supplies a large part of the European market—and the weaving and embroidery of cotton cloth. Silver, brass, and pottery are also manufactured. The livestock market deals in camels, oxen, horses, goats, sheep, and asses. Kano is unique among Negro cities in that all Europeans, including the resident, other officials, missionaries. and merchants are not permitted to live within the gates. Pop. (1946) 97,946.

KANO PROVINCE, British West Africa, N Nigeria, one of the Northern Provinces, made up of the large emirate of KANO and four smaller emirates; area 17,644 sq. mi.; pop. about 3,000,000. With some 160 people to the square mile Kano has the densest population of Nigeria. Kano Province is a part of the great central plateau, and it ranges from 1,500 to 2,000 feet above sea level. The country is rolling park savanna, has only scattered trees, and is semi-arid in the northwest. Rainfall averages 30 to 40 inches a year; the dry season extends from October to April. Agriculture and stock raising are the chief occupations, with the principal plantings millet (locally *gero*), corn, cotton, and peanuts. Sheep and goat hides and skins are extensively traded, and the chief exports are peanuts, cotton, leather, and hides and skins.

The people of Kano are Hausas and Fulahs, with the Hausas in the majority; but the Fulahs are the ruling class. The Hausas are true Negroes, the Fulahs Hamitics with a strong Sudanese Negro strain; the two people are merging. The capital is KANO. Christianity has made little progress and, since the 14th century, Mohammedanism has been the dominant religion.

By the early 19th century the invading Fulahs had completed the subjugation of the Hausa states, of which Kano was one, and the rule came under the sultan of Sokoto. However, late in the 19th century the Kano broke away and chose its own emir. The Sokoto sultan remained the supreme spiritual head, however, being known as "Lord of the Moslems" and "Commander of the Faithful." Lord Lugard sent expeditions into the country early in the 20th century to subdue uprisings and the slave trade, and Kano was for a time held as a protectorate under British suzerainty. Lord Lugard in 1914 secured the amalgamation of the northern and southern protectorates. The British rule through the local emirs, who retain a large measure of power.　　　　　　　　　　　　C. S.

KANOYA, town, Japan, S Kyushu, Kagoshima Prefecture, on Kagoshima Bay. During World War II an important Japanese air base here was heavily bombed by B-29's, and was one of the first places occupied by American forces follⁱ ving the Japanese surrender

KANSAS

The Sunflower State

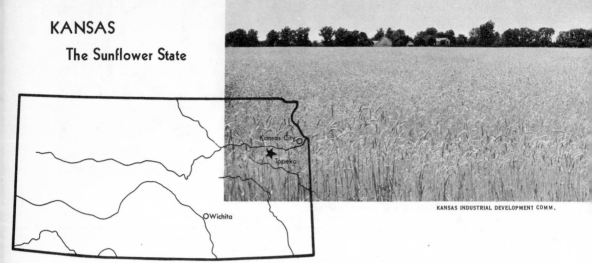

KANSAS INDUSTRIAL DEVELOPMENT COMM.

The history of Kansas, grower of much of the nation's wheat, is studded with turbulent political controversies

KANSAS, the "sunflower state," central state of the United States, containing in Smith County near Lebanon the geographical center of the nation; bounded on the N by Nebraska; on the E by Missouri; on the S by Oklahoma; and on the W by Colorado; area 82,276 sq. mi., including 163 sq. mi. of inland water surface; pop. (1950) 1,905,299. The state measures 207 miles from north to south and 409 miles at its widest point from east to west; it ranks 13th in area and 29th in population among the states. The name of the state is taken from the Kansas River, which was named for an Indian tribe. Some attribute the name to an Indian word, *Kanza*, meaning "smoky wind," probably referring to the prairie fires that once swept over the plains. The state motto is "Ad Astra per Aspera," meaning "To the Stars through Difficulties." The native sunflower is the state flower. Topeka is the capital.

Topography. Kansas belongs to the group of prairie states, yet has two distinct divisions in that the east is like the corn belt states, and the western part of the state resembles eastern Colorado. Almost the entire surface is an undulating plain, which tends to slope down gradually from the western border to the east and the south. The highest land is in the extreme west where an altitude of 4,135 feet is reached in Wallace County near the Colorado line. In the eastern part, the elevation is about 1,000 feet, except in the river bottoms. The lowest point is 700 feet, in Montgomery County two miles south of Coffeyville. High bluffs dominate many of the rivers; those along the Missouri rise to more than 200 feet.

Kansas is drained chiefly by the ARKANSAS, NEOSHO and Verdigris rivers in the south, and by the KANSAS (Kaw), REPUBLICAN, SMOKY HILL, Saline, and Solomon rivers on the northwestern boundary.

Climate. Kansas has two types of climate. The eastern half of the state is semihumid; the western half is semiarid. The state as a whole experiences long hot summers, cold winters, and sudden temperature changes, especially during the winter and early spring. The average annual temperature for 58 years was 55.0° F. Extremes of 121° and −40° have been recorded. The average annual precipitation in the eastern portion is 35.27 inches; central Kansas receives 26.45 inches; western Kansas, 19.01 inches. The snow period is from December through March; the annual average, 17.3 inches. The records refute the idea that the winters were more severe during the last generation—1945 had more snow than any previous year. Part of Kansas was in the DUST BOWL. Droughts are known in all months, but those that occur during July and August are most destructive. The prevailing wind is from the south; winter storm winds are from the north. Tornadoes are common, and frequently occur in "families"; between May and June of 1945 eight funnels caused damage in excess of $292,000. Hail and flood are other climatic disturbances. An average of 184 days are cloud free, and the growing season is long: 200 days in the southeast, 160 days in the northwest.

Plants and Animals. The native grasses, notably the bluestem, are among the most valuable assets of Kansas because they curb erosion and form the basis for the state's extensive cattle industry. The grasses are high and lush on the eastern prairies and short and coarse in the dryer sections of the west. Myriads of wild flowers thread the grass; from the pastels of spring, the flowers flame to orange, red, and purple as the grasses grow tall with the advance of summer. The two geographical divisions of Kansas are even recognized by the native sunflower which grows tall in the eastern part of the state and less tall in the western section. When the first settlers came to the state, they found few trees, as the soil and climate of the west did not encourage their growth, and the woods of the east and south had been destroyed in prairie fires set by the Indians, who sometimes held back hostile tribes by means of fire. After the Civil War, tree planting was stimulated by the Federal government which awarded 160 acres of land free to every settler who would grow 10 acres of timber on his land. Later, seedling trees were distributed extensively throughout the state.

In the 1860's, eastern Kansas was the home of bear, deer, timber wolves, and many small fur-bearing animals. On the higher prairies of the west roamed buffalo, elk, antelope, wolves, and wild horses. After the state was settled, most of the game was exterminated or fled farther west, so that only small animals and game birds remain.

PEOPLE

Population. According to the Federal census of 1950, the population of Kansas was 1,905,299, an increase of 104,271, or 5.8 per cent, over 1940 (compared with a decrease of 4.3 per cent during 1930–1940). Despite this increase, Kansas, which ranked 29th among the states in population in 1940, dropped to 31st place in 1950.

PRINCIPAL CITIES	POPULATION	
	1940 Census	1950 Census
WICHITA	114,966	168,279
KANSAS CITY	121,458	129,553
TOPEKA (Capital)	67,883	78,791
HUTCHINSON	30,013	33,575
SALINA	21,079	26,176
LAWRENCE	14,390	23,351
LEAVENWORTH	19,220	20,579
PITTSBURG	17,571	19,341
MANHATTAN	11,659	19,056
COFFEYVILLE	17,355	17,113

Education. The first schools in Kansas were religious missions among the Indians. In the 1880's Kansas became the first state to establish a statewide system of county high schools in counties of more than 5,000 population. The superintendent of public instruction heads the public school system. Attendance is compulsory for children between the ages of 7 and 16. In 1925 all higher educational institutions came under the control of a board of regents. The state supports teachers colleges at Emporia, Pittsburg, and Hays; the University of Kansas at Lawrence; and the Kansas State College of Agriculture and Applied Science at Manhattan. In addition to these there are a number of municipal junior colleges. Other important institutions of higher learning include Baker University, at Baldwin; Bethel College, near Newton; Wichita Municipal University, and Friends University, at Wichita; Washburn College, at Topeka; College of Emporia, at Emporia; Kansas Wesleyan University, and Marymount College, at Salina; Ottawa University, at Ottawa; Southwestern College, at Winfield; Bethany College, at Lindsborg; McPherson College, at McPherson; Sterling College, at Sterling; and St. Benedict's College, at Atchison. Haskell Institute, at Lawrence, is the largest Indian school in the nation. In 1945 the legislature passed an act creating a division of school reorganization within the state department of education, and county committees within each county for the purpose of reorganizing the school districts of Kansas. The aim was to do away with the one-teacher school as much as possible and to make a more equitable distribution of the tax burden for the education of the children of the state.

Public Welfare. Kansas created a Department of Social Welfare in 1939 and most of the charitable institutions of the state are directed by this department. In 1944 a Receiving Home for Children was instituted to receive delinquents from juvenile courts for scientific study and recommendation of suitable care and training. The state maintains hospitals for the insane at Topeka, Osawatomie, and Larned; the State Hospital for Epileptics, at Parsons; School for Feeble-Minded Youths, at Winfield; State Sanatorium for Tuberculosis, at Norton; State Orphans' Home, at Atchison; Kansas State Penitentiary, at Lansing; Reformatory for Young Criminals, at Hutchinson; Women's Industrial Farm, at Lansing; Boys' Industrial School, at Topeka; Girls' Industrial Farm, at Beloit; the State Soldiers' Home, at Fort Dodge; Mother Bickerdyke home at Ellsworth; a school for the blind, at Kansas City; and a school for the deaf, at Olathe.

ECONOMIC LIFE

Agriculture. Kansas is one of the foremost agricultural states. The soil is well adapted to agriculture, consisting mainly of a rich loam and having a high percentage of mineral constituents. In western Kansas, however, there is insufficient rainfall. In Kansas 91.7 per cent of all the land is divided into farms, the average containing 300 acres. Though a number of crops are grown throughout the state, it is divided agriculturally into three belts of about equal extent. In the east, the soil and climate are suited to a great variety of crops, but corn is the chief product; the middle third is the wheat belt; while the western third is best suited to grazing, although the wheat area has gradually extended westward. In recent years, Kansas has produced about one-fourth of the wheat raised in the nation, has ranked high in the acreage of corn and first in the acreage of alfalfa, and held second place in the raising of grain sorghums and sweet clover seed. Oats, barley, and rye also are important crops. Soybeans are well adapted to the climate and soil of eastern Kansas. Although soybeans are a comparatively new crop in the state, in 1950 Kansas ranked ninth in production among the states.

A great change in the state's agriculture took place in 1874 when a colony of Mennonites coming from southern Russia to the plains of central Kansas brought with them a variety of hard wheat called Turkey Red. The introduction of this variety, hardier and more drought-resistant than types previously grown in Kansas, quickly resulted in an enormous expansion of the wheat industry. Corn continued as the leading crop, however, until 1914, when wheat assumed the lead in acreage and value. Kansas is now the leading wheat-growing state.

PRINCIPAL CROPS OF KANSAS

CROP	UNIT (Thousands)	1939–1948 Average	1949	1950
Barley	Bushels	12,468	3,757	3,556
Corn	Bushels	64,779	73,196	93,188
Hay	Tons	2,604	3,299	3,273
Oats	Bushels	35,197	18,942	21,120
Potatoes	Bushels	1,920	1,114	1,060
Sorghum	Bushels	20,651	26,404	42,096
Soybeans	Bushels	1,715	3,436	6,462
Wheat	Bushels	188,577	164,208	178,060

Kansas is one of the leading cattle-producing states of the nation, and in 1951 ranked fifth in the number of animals produced on its famous bluestem pastures. Hogs and sheep also are extensively raised.

Tractors and combines have revolutionized farming methods of the state and since 1920, the number of horses and mules has been steadily decreasing. The dairy industry brings in large returns and on many farms, poultry and eggs produce 20 to 30 per cent of the farm income.

Kansas agriculture suffered from the drought cycle of 1931–37. A series of abnormally dry seasons converted a large area in the western part of the state into a near desert. Wind erosion of the soil, furthermore, resulted from destruction of the natural coverage of buffalo grass, caused by wheat planting. The Federal government and the state department of agriculture adopted preventive measures to check this erosion, and by 1938 the Kansas dust bowl had all but disappeared. Farmers of the state, moreover, have been aided by various agencies of the Federal government, and have learned from their own experience how to adjust production to climatic conditions, and that diversified crops are advantageous.

Mining. The state's mineral industry is next to agriculture in importance, and Kansas ranks among

KANSAS INDUSTRIAL DEVELOPMENT COMM.
Aerial view of the University of Kansas

Big and Little Arkansas join at Wichita. The downtown district of the city is in the background

the first ten states in the value of their total annual mineral output. In 1948, when its mineral production was valued at $363,362,000, Kansas ranked ninth. The chief mineral products are petroleum, cement, natural gas, and zinc. In petroleum production, Kansas ranks fifth among the states. The largest fields developed are in Butler, Cowley, McPherson, Marion, and Rice counties, although in recent years new fields have been opened in several counties to the west, especially in Russell County. The state also has a large supply of natural gas in many regions, and helium is produced at Dexter. The production of Portland cement is valued highly.

MINERAL PRODUCTION OF KANSAS

MINERAL	UNIT (Thousands)	1946	1947	1948
Cement........	Barrels	6,894	7,208	7,930
Clay..........	Short Tons	464	535	587
Coal..........	Short Tons	2,493	2,744	2,615
Natural Gas....	M Cu. Ft.	165,725	209,321	245,189
Natural Gasoline	Gallons	63,666	71,547	73,343
Liquefied Petroleum Gases...	Gallons	18,925	27,648	28,617
Petroleum......	Barrels	97,218	105,132	110,833
Salt...........	Short Tons	815	904	831
Sand and Gravel.	Short Tons	4,443	4,351	5,083
Stone.........	Short Tons	3,653	4,792	5,315

Manufactures. The manufactures of Kansas have been largely the outgrowth of its extensive agricultural products; they have been further stimulated by the development of rich zinc and coal mines and by the discovery of oil and gas. Kansas was organized as a territory in 1854, and at the first census thereafter (1859), the total value of all manufactured products was $4,357,000; according to the Census of Manufactures, the total value added by manufacture in 1947 was $461,061,000. This growth was largely due to the development of slaughtering, meat packing, flour mills and gristmills, and later, to the growth of the state's aircraft industry. Kansas ranks first among the states in flour milling and its extensive elevator storage system has the largest capacity in the nation. The principal milling centers are Salina, Topeka, Wichita, Kansas City, Atchison, and Hutchinson. The state in 1947 ranked seventh in meat packing, with plants located in Kansas City, Topeka, Wichita, Salina, Hutchinson, and Arkansas City. Petroleum refining is another important industry which employs many skilled men. Other leading manufactures and products are butter, cheese, and condensed milk, railroad shop construction and repairs, foundry and machine shop products, printing and publishing, bread and bakery products, wholesale poultry dressing and packing, and cement and rubber. Dehydra-

Kansas

tion plants have been established for the processing of eggs, milk, fruits, and vegetables.

The aircraft industry received a tremendous impetus during World War II, and Kansas was among the top four states in the output of military aircraft. Although Wichita was the center of this industry with four large airplane factories, a peacetime aircraft industry had been established earlier in several Kansas cities.

Various communities are notable for special products such as the manufacture of trailers at Augusta, garden tractors at Galesburg, snow plows at Wamego, strawboard at Hutchinson, pipe organs at Lawrence, locomotive parts at Atchison, paving material at Moline, stoves at Leavenworth and Wichita, furniture at Leavenworth and Garnett, soap at Kansas City, and oil field machinery at Wichita and Independence.

Transportation. The state is so situated geographically that it is traversed by several important railways, connecting the industrial centers of the Mississippi Valley with points in the West and Southwest. The principal lines are the Santa Fe; the Union Pacific; the Missouri Pacific; the Rock Island; the Missouri-Kansas-Texas; the Burlington; and the St. Louis and San Francisco. The total railroad mileage of Kansas is about 9,000 miles.

The four major air lines operating regular schedules across the state are the Continental Air Lines; the Braniff Airways; the TWA, and the Mid-Continent Airlines. The state is well covered by bus lines, both continental and those operating in conjunction with railroads. Kansas ranks second among the states in rural road mileage, having a system of 128,197 miles, one-fourth of which is hard-surfaced.

The Missouri River, on the northeast boundary, is the only navigable river; however, the operation of barges has increased, following a survey authorized by Congress in 1930, which determined the possibilities of barge navigation on the Missouri and Kansas rivers.

Tourist Attractions. The visitor to Kansas is impressed by the vast stretches of level fields rippling with wheat and the rolling pastures where beef cattle graze. Among the interesting features of Kansas are the fossils of extinct animals found in the unique chalk and rock formations of Gove County, prehistoric mounds, and areas where Indian graves and relics have been unearthed. South of Kansas City is a remnant of the Indian period, the restored Shawnee Mission, which served the Indians from 1839 to 1862 and was twice the territorial capital of Kansas. At intervals of five years, the Medicine Lodge Peace Treaty (1867), which established the southern border of Kansas and declared the area south of that border to be Indian Territory, is reenacted at Medicine Lodge. Pioneer Kansas was a crossroad for the historic trails which were traveled by the settlers of the West. Over the Santa Fe and Oregon trails, fleets of covered wagons once rumbled through the early Kansas settlements. Mormons from Nauvoo, Ill., traveled to Utah by way of the Mormon Trail which crossed the Kansas plains. Mail for the West went by Pony Express from St. Joseph, Mo., across Kansas to Sacramento, Calif., and the Holladay Overland Stage Line carried passengers over a winding Kansas route. Equally colorful was the famous Chisholm Cattle Trail over which thousands of head of half-wild Texas cattle were driven north to the railway terminus first at Abilene and later at Ellsworth and Newton. Remnants of the trail are marked through Kansas, and many Kansas cities recall their beginnings as "cow towns."

The role of Kansas in the slavery struggle is recalled by Osawatomie Memorial Park where John Brown battled a pro-slavery band in 1856. The state has placed memorials on the sites of several episodes in border warfare (see BORDER WAR). Historic markers throughout the state recall the visits of

Flour Mills at Salina, the third ranking milling center of Kansas, can produce 10,000 barrels daily

Kansas Oil Field is one of many developed since the state's first three wells were drilled in 1860

Fancy High-Heeled Boots worn by Hollywood film cowboys are produced at this boot factory in Olathe

Pipe Organs are produced in Lawrence. This tuner is testing a newly-completed instrument in the plant

Carloads of Kansas Wheat in Kansas City yards. City has world's largest grain storage facilities

Rich Grazing Lands of western Kansas provide the basis for the state's great cattle raising industry

Exact Geographical Center of the United States is designated by this marker near Lebanon, Kan.

Coronado, John C. Frémont, and the Donner Party.

An interesting scene in modern Kansas is the great area of oil wells in the northwest of the state. The U.S. Army postgraduate staff school and museum is located at Fort Leavenworth, and there are other pioneer forts and marked historic sites throughout the state. Kansas has an excellent system of state and county parks which contain recreation areas for swimming, boating, picnicking, and camping. A favorite sport in western Kansas is a jackrabbit drive to round up marauders that destroy much green wheat.   F. C. W.

GOVERNMENT

Kansas is still governed under the original constitution which went into effect when the state was admitted to the Union in 1861, but since that time 36 amendments have been adopted. Amendments may be proposed in either house of the legislature and, if approved by a two-thirds vote of each branch, must later be ratified by a majority vote of the electorate.

Modest Home in Abilene where General Eisenhower spent his boyhood is preserved as a memorial

The suffrage is granted to all citizens of 21 and over without restriction; the resident requirement is six months in the state. The legislature consists of a senate with 40 members elected for four years and a house of representatives with 125 elected for two years. Regular sessions are held biennially, beginning early in January of each odd-numbered year; the compensation of members is $3 a day for the time spent in regular and special sessions. In 1933 the Kansas Legislative Council was created; this body, known as the "Little Legislature," is composed of 15 representatives and 10 senators. It operates as a permanent joint committee, meeting four times a year to give advance consideration to problems expected to come up during the next legislative meeting. Kansas was the first state to establish such a council.

The executive department is composed of the governor, lieutenant governor, secretary of state, auditor, treasurer, attorney general, and superintendent of public instruction—all elected for two years. In addition to the normal veto power, the governor may also veto any item of an appropriation bill, but his action may be overridden by a two-thirds vote of the elected membership of each house.

The judicial power is vested in a supreme court of seven members elected for six years; in district courts, each with one judge, elected for four years, sitting in turn in each county of the district; and in probate courts and justices of the peace.

For local government the state is divided into 105 counties, each of which is further divided into townships. County government is headed by a board of three commissioners, each elected by district for four years. Other county officials, elected for two years, are a clerk, treasurer, probate judge, a register of deeds, sheriff, coroner, attorney, clerk of the district court, and surveyor. The township officers, also elected for two years, are a trustee, clerk, treasurer, two or more justices of the peace, two constables, and one road supervisor for each road district. Cities are divided into three classes: first class, all over 15,000; second class, 2,000–15,000; third class, under 2,000. State laws provide for different governmental forms for each class. The city-council plan is the normal type of municipal government, but state law permits any city to adopt either the commission or the city-manager plan. Many cities have adopted the city-manager form.

Kansas is represented in the National Congress at Washington by two senators and six representatives.

HISTORY

The Spanish and French. The state takes its name from the Kansas Indians, a tribe of Siouan stock. In 1541 the Spanish explorer CORONADO, in his search for Quivira, a land supposedly rich in gold and silver, penetrated into central Kansas. Other Spanish explorers entered the territory in 1594 and 1601. Near the very end of the 17th century French fur traders began to ascend the Missouri, and it is believed that they entered what is now Kansas. In 1719 Charles Claude du Tisné visited the Osage villages near the mouth of the Osage River. The Spaniards in New Mexico thereupon bestirred themselves to drive out the intruders but they were defeated in 1720 when they attempted to assert their sovereignty over the Indians. French influence continued until Louisiana was ceded to Spain in 1762.

American Exploration and Settlement. In 1800 Louisiana was retroceded to France, only to be sold to the United States in 1803. The following year Congress divided the vast new territory into two parts, present-day Kansas being included in the Territory of Louisiana. In 1812, however, when the Territory of Missouri was created with a western boundary approximating that of the present state of Missouri, the remainder of the region was left without law or official identification for about a quarter of a century.

Main street of Dodge City, Kan., in 1878

Railroad brings Texas cattle to Abilene (left)

John Brown, the fiery Kansas abolitionist

Cowboys on pay-day visit to a frontier town

Scene at a western Kansas station of the Union Pacific Railroad in 1870

State capitol of Kansas at Topeka

Soon after the Louisiana Purchase LEWIS AND CLARK explored the territory, reaching the mouth of the Kansas River on June 26, 1804. In 1806 Capt. ZEBULON PIKE passed through present-day Kansas to the Rocky Mountains, and along the way he gave warning to Spanish agents that they were trespassing on American territory. The next important visit was made by Major STEPHEN H. LONG in 1819 while on a scientific expedition for the government. The reports made by these early explorers were very unfavorable toward the region. Hence under the supposition that the Kansas country was part of "the Great American Desert," Congress in 1830 set aside the region as Indian country; during the following decade many tribes were removed to it from east of the Mississippi.

Fort Leavenworth was established in 1827 for frontier defense; other early forts were Scott (1842) and Riley (1853). With the removal of the Indian tribes to the Kansas country many missionaries came into the region. By 1830 there were a number of trading posts in eastern Kansas, and many others came in the years following. During the 1840's many emigrants passed through the region; two-thirds of the course of the SANTA FE TRAIL ran through the present state, while the OREGON TRAIL cut across the northeastern corner. By 1854 Kansas had approximately 1,500 white persons within its borders, nearly half of whom were in military service.

The Fight Over Slavery. In 1854 came the passage of the historic KANSAS-NEBRASKA BILL, by which the territories of Kansas and Nebraska were created, with the provision (under the repeal of the MISSOURI COMPROMISE) that the new settlers might themselves determine the question of slavery. Then followed a bitter and protracted struggle in Kansas Territory between the friends and foes of slavery. One of the chief fights was over the LECOMPTON CONSTITUTION, which upheld slavery. Finally in 1859 there was drafted at Wyandotte a fourth constitution, which prohibited slavery. This document was approved by an overwhelming vote, but southern opposition kept Kansas out of the Union until secession took the slave leaders out of Congress. On Jan. 29, 1861, Kansas was admitted to statehood. See BORDER WAR; BROWN, JOHN.

During the Civil War the new state sent into the Union army more soldiers (20,097) in proportion to its population than any other state. Yet the border war continued; bands of marauders from Missouri, containing Jesse and Frank James, and Coleman Younger, made raids into Kansas, culminating in Quantrill's Raid on Lawrence (Aug. 21, 1863) in which about 150 persons were shot down.

Kansas After the Civil War. After the end of the Civil War peace came to "Bloody Kansas" so that the state attracted a large number of settlers and made rapid progress. National attention was now directed toward central and western Kansas as settlers, encouraged by the HOMESTEAD LAW of 1862, poured into this semiarid region; western posts such as forts Hays, Dodge, and Wallace were constructed to protect the pioneers. A series of INDIAN WARS extending over a decade were fought before the redmen were forced to retire to reservations. A colorful frontier town was Abilene, first terminus of the CATTLE DRIVES from Texas over the CHISHOLM TRAIL, and center for a time of the activities of "Wild Bill" HICKOK. In 1874 came the grasshopper plague which nearly devastated the western settlements.

Political Controversies. For a generation the politics of the new state were nearly as lusty as the border activities. For a time the state was governed for the most part by carpetbag politicians from the East. Then came a period of political radicalism featuring a succession of movements: Grangerism in the 1870's, the Farmers' Alliance in the 1880's, Populism in the 1890's, and Progressivism in the years after 1900. The targets of these movements were the railroads, the banks, and monopolies in general. Colorful leaders of this period were "Sockless Jerry" Simpson and Mrs. Mary Elizabeth Lease; the latter, a flaming orator, stumped the state denouncing the "money power" and urging the Kansas farmers "to raise less corn and more hell." In 1893 disputed elections led to the organization of separate legislatures by the Populists and the Republicans, and the state militia was called out to preserve peace. Another political movement led to state-wide prohibition, a policy maintained until 1949. A well-known figure of the anti-saloon movement in the 1890's was CARRY NATION.

Twentieth Century. In World War I 80,261 men from the state saw service in the armed forces of the nation; Kansas soldiers participated in the Saint Mihiel and Argonne offensives. In 1919 Governor Henry J. Allen during a coal strike used volunteer miners and the state militia to keep the mines open; in 1920 he called a special session of the legislature to set up the Court of Industrial Relations, which was vested with the power to control strikes and to fix minimum wages for workers in vital industries. Bitterly opposed by organized labor, this court was crippled by a decision of the U.S. Supreme Court and was abolished by the state legislature in 1925. In 1924 the activities of the KU KLUX KLAN brought out the third party candidacy of WILLIAM ALLEN WHITE for the governorship; he was unsuccessful. In 1936 Gov. Alfred M. Landon, who had sponsored a cash policy for state administration in 1933, was the unsuccessful Republican candidate for the presidency of the United States.

During the 1930's Kansas suffered a succession of drought years and the southwestern part of the state was part of the "DUST BOWL." The next decade, however, brought favorable climatic conditions and bumper crops. During World War II about 199,000 Kansas men and women served in the armed forces. In 1948 the state voted to end its 68-year era of prohibition. In 1951 central and eastern Kansas suffered heavily in floods which caused nearly one billion dollars damage, took 69 lives, and forced 500,000 persons from their homes.   F. M.

BIBLIOG.–S. T. D. Robinson, *Kansas; Its Interior and Exterior Life* (1856); F. W. Blackmar, *Kansas: A Cyclopedia of State History* (3 vol., 1912); W. E. Connelley, *History of Kansas* (1928); L. H. Blanchard, *Conquest of Southwest Kansas* (1931); A. Roenigk, ed., *Pioneer History of Kansas* (1933); S. A. and R. M. Baldwin, eds., *Illustriana Kansas* (1934); C. D. Clark and R. L. Roberts, *People of Kansas* (1936); E. N. Dick, *Sod-house Frontier, 1854–1890* (1937); M. E. Whittemore, *Sketchbook of Kansas Landmarks* (1937); Federal Writers Project, *Kansas: A Guide to the Sunflower State* (1939); W.S. Campbell, *Short Grass Country* (1941); F. B. Streeter, *The Kaw* (1941); I. Bliss and W. M. Richards, *Four Centuries in Kansas* (1944); W. G. Clugston, *Facts You Should Know About Kansas* (1945); S. Vestal, *Short Grass Country* (1945); A. B. Stevenson, *Sunflower Sheaf* (1946); W. A. White, *Forty Years on Main Street* (1937); *Autobiography* (1946); A. B. Martin and L. K. Chesney, *Kansas Government* (1947); W. B. Bracke, *Wheat Country* (1950); *Kansas Facts* (Annual).

KANSAS CITY, city, NE Kansas, county seat of Wyandotte County, situated at the confluence of the Kansas River with the Missouri River, on the Santa Fe, the Great Western, the Rock Island, the Kansas City Kaw Valley, the Kansas City Southern, the Kansas and Missouri Terminal, the Missouri Pacific, and the Union Pacific railroads and U.S. highways 24, 40, 50, 69, 73, and 169; adjoining Kansas City, Mo., and 62 miles E of Topeka. Improvement of the Missouri River channel between St. Louis and Kansas City has linked the city with the great inland waterways system which serves many ports, including those of the Gulf of Mexico and the Great Lakes. Kansas City, the largest city (1940), and the manufacturing center, is located at the eastern boundary of Kansas in the heart of the central plains region, which is rich in agricultural produce and natural resources.

Kansas City has an area of 20.4 square miles. It is built partly on elevated and partly on low ground. The Kansas River and the hills divide the city into five distinct sections. There are more than 330 acres of public parks within the city limits and the 1,400-acre Wyandotte County Park and Lake are just outside the city. Kansas City is the seat of the St. Augustine Seminary, the Baptist Theological Seminary, and a municipal junior college. Since 1905 the School of Medicine of the University of Kansas has been located in Kansas City.

Ranking after Chicago and Omaha, Kansas City has the third largest meat packing industry in the United States. Fourteen companies, including four of the nation's greatest meat packers, have plants in Kansas City. In the yards and packing houses, which cover many acres, several million head of stock are handled each year. In addition to cured and fresh meats, the principal products of the meat packing industry, at least 140 by-products used in agricultural, industrial, commercial, and scientific fields are made here. Kansas City has car construction and repair shops, oil refineries, grain storage reservoirs, and manufactures of structural steel, foundry and machine shop products, soap, fiber box and bag products, wagons, walnut lumber, flour, commercial chemicals, brick and terra cotta, seat covers, soybean products, dehydrated eggs, trailers, building materials, and many other products.

On June 26, 1804, Lewis and Clark passed through what is now Kansas City on their expedition to the Pacific Coast. The first village settlement on the site of Kansas City was made in 1843 by the Wyandotte Indians. The Wyandottes were a highly civilized people for whom Kansas City was originally named. In 1855 the Indians sold their claim to the land. The first white settlement was laid out in 1857, and Kansas City was incorporated in 1858. Eight individual towns were merged at separate times to form the present corporate limits of the city. Kansas City suffered heavy damage during the Kansas River flood in 1951. Pop. (1950) 129,552.   A. M. K.

KANSAS CITY, city, W central Missouri, in Jackson County, on the Missouri River, at the mouth of the Kansas River (locally known as the "Kaw"), adjoining Kansas City, Kans. Kansas City is a port of entry and the second city in Missouri in size and importance. It is situated in the heart of a great agricultural area and near a considerable mineral wealth, including oil, lead, zinc, bauxite, coal, and gas. Pop. (1950) 456,622.

Kansas City is served by 12 trunk line railroads, the Burlington, the Alton, the Great Western, the

Municipal Air Terminal at Kansas City, Missouri

Milwaukee, the Frisco, the Kansas City Southern, the Missouri-Kansas-Texas, the Missouri Pacific, the Rock Island, the Santa Fe, the Union Pacific, and the Wabash; U.S. highways 24, 40, 50, 69, 71, and 169; four major air lines: the Braniff, the Continental, the Mid-Continent, and the Transcontinental and Western; and numerous river barge lines. Near the geographic center of the United States, "the gateway to the southwest," Kansas City is one of the great markets and transportation centers of the country. More than 7,000,000 passengers enter and leave the city annually by the numerous railroads, which handle more than 40,000,000 tons of freight. The Union passenger station, built in 1914, is one of largest in the country. South of Union Station rises the 280-foot Liberty Memorial erected to honor the Missourians who were killed during World War I.

Features of Interest. The city is built on three levels—the highest comprises the residential section; the middle level, the retail district; and the low-lying tracts around the Kansas River are occupied chiefly by railroad yards, the stockyards, wholesale houses, and manufacturing establishments. Kansas City is noted for its many miles of continuous boulevards which lace together the various sections of the city. The diversified character of the terrain of Kansas City has made possible drives of beauty and interest, such as the Cliff Drive, which is three-and-a-half miles long. Through the center of the city, extending from north to south and connecting Cliff Drive with Swope Park, is the nine-mile Paseo Parkway. Swope Park, which comprises 1,334 acres, is the largest park in Kansas City and one of the largest in the United States. Altogether there are some 3,500 acres of public parks in Kansas City.

Kansas City is the seat of Rockhurst College; the University of Kansas City, established in 1935; and a state teachers' college. Among the cultural institutions of the city are the Atkins Museum of Fine Arts and the Nelson Gallery of Art, which contain extensive collections of paintings and sculpture. The Kansas City Art Institute, an endowed school of fine and industrial arts, is housed in a group of buildings, the first of which is a remodeled brick residence of Flemish design. Developed in 1939, the Kansas City Museum stresses the science and history of the Middle West.

Industries. Kansas City is one of the leading agricultural and industrial centers in the United States. It is the leading hay market and seed distribution center of the country, the second largest general livestock market, and the first market in stock and feeder

Modern Municipal Auditorium, Kansas City, Mo.

cattle, horses, and mules. The Kansas City stock-yards, center of the city's economic life, are situated on the state line with about 62 per cent of their area on the Kansas side. Food has long been the principal industry of Kansas City; more than 40 per cent of all products manufactured in the city's industrial area are classed in the food group. Here are found large meat-packing plants, food processing factories, and grain elevators. Kansas City ranks second in the nation in the production of flour made from the millions of bushels of wheat grown in the neighboring plains. Another prominent market is the city's whole-sale and retail market for fruits and vegetables. Recently modernized, produce is a 25-million-dollar-a-year industry. World War II brought many new industries to Kansas City ranging from gunpowder and ammunition plants to a giant airplane engine plant, an aluminum foundry, a shell case manufacturing plant, and a B-25 bomber plant. Another important marketing center firmly established in Kansas City is the garment industry.

Government and History. Kansas City adopted the council-manager form of government in 1926, but under the subversive control of the Pendergast machine the city suffered more than a decade of ruinous government. There is a city council of nine members elected for two-year terms on a nonpartisan ballot. The city manager, who is appointed by the city council, appoints, supervises, and removes the heads of the departments.

The first permanent settlement within the present limits of Kansas City was established by French fur traders about 1821. In 1838, lots were surveyed and the name "Town of Kansas" (from the Kansas River) was adopted. Kansas City was incorporated as a town in 1850 and chartered under its present name in 1875. Before 1850, Kansas City was practically the exclusive eastern terminus on the river for the Santa Fe trade and a great outfitting point for emigrants to California. Whisky, groceries, and notions were staples sent to Santa Fe. Wool, buffalo robes, dried buffalo meat, Mexican silver coin, gold and silver dust and ore came in return. In 1860 the trade employed 3,000 wagons and 7,000 men, and amounted to millions of dollars. By 1866 the first railroad reached Kansas City from St. Louis; the packing industry dates from 1867. In 1951, flood waters of the Kansas River caused heavy damage in the city; an accompanying fire destroyed seven square blocks. A. M. K.

KANSAS CITY, UNIVERSITY OF. See COLLEGES.

KANSAS INDIANS, also called **Kansa** or **Kaw,** a tribe of Siouan stock, originally found near the mouth of the river named for them. These Indians were aloof and independent without friendly relations with the neighboring tribes, except with the Osages with whom they were closely related through linguistic ties and intermarriage. They lived in earth lodges

Kansas, University of

which formed permanent villages; their economy was based on the cultivation of crops and the buffalo hunt. Government was in the hands of five hereditary chiefs. The custom of scalp taking, an outgrowth of the earlier practice of head hunting, had religious significance since it built up status for the warrior in the future life. In 1815 the Kansas Indians made a treaty of peace and good will with the U.S. government; 10 years later by another agreement they abandoned their original homeland and accepted a reservation beginning 20 leagues up the Kansas. In 1846 they were moved to the vicinity of Council Grove; in 1859 their reservation was reduced, and in 1873 they were moved again, this time to Indian Territory in present-day Oklahoma. At the time of their removal the tribe, which 40 years earlier had numbered about 1,600, now was reduced to about 200 poverty-stricken persons. Through intermarriage tribal identity has been lost. CHARLES CURTIS, vice-president of the United States, was of Kansas descent.

F. M.

KANSAS-NEBRASKA BILL, a bill for the organization of the territories of Kansas and Nebraska (with limits much larger than those of the present states), passed by Congress in 1854. It embodied the principle of "squatter" or popular sovereignty, and repealed the Missouri Compromise of 1820, its most significant clause being that it is "the true intent and meaning of this act not to legislate slavery into any Territory or State, nor to exclude it therefrom, but to leave the people thereof perfectly free to form and regulate their domestic institutions in their own way, subject only to the Constitution of the United States." The bill was passed after a bitter and prolonged debate in both the House and the Senate, and chiefly through the efforts of Senator STEPHEN A. DOUGLAS.

The Kansas-Nebraska Bill re-opened, in all its rancor, the slavery controversy, which had been temporarily checked by the MISSOURI COMPROMISE; it completed the disintegration of the old WHIG PARTY; led to the organization of the REPUBLICAN PARTY; probably did more than anything else to bring about the defeat of the Democratic party in 1860; and may fairly be said to have hastened the outbreak of hostilities between the North and the South.

KANSAS RIVER, locally known as the **Kaw,** formed by the junction of the Smoky Hill and Republican rivers, in Geary County, Kans., near Junction City. It takes a northeasterly course to Manhattan, and then flows east and joins the Missouri River at Kansas City, Kans. Its chief tributaries are the Big Blue and Grasshopper rivers. Its length is nearly 300 miles or, with the Smoky Hill, nearly 900 miles. In 1951 flood waters of the river covered 1,500,000 acres in Kansas and Missouri, and caused damage estimated at nearly one billion dollars.

KANSAS STATE COLLEGE OF AGRICULTURE AND APPLIED SCIENCE. See COLLEGES.

KANSAS STATE TEACHERS COLLEGE. See COLLEGES.

KANSAS STATE TEACHERS COLLEGE OF EMPORIA. See COLLEGES.

KANSAS, UNIVERSITY OF. Located in Lawrence and Kansas City, Kans., the University of Kansas is one of the leading educational institutions of the West. Provision for the university was made in the constitution of the Kansas Territory in 1855 and in the state constitution in 1861. Instruction was begun in 1866. Following early growth, the university was reorganized in 1891 into schools of arts, law, fine arts, and pharmacy. The Graduate School was added in 1899, Nursing, 1906, Education, 1909, and Business, 1924. The University Extension Division has been in operation since 1909. Radio broadcasts on the university station carry language instruction and general educational programs to the community. The Dyche Museum of Natural History is located at the university. Kansas is one of the higher institutions belonging to the Association of American Universities.

KANSAS WESLEYAN UNIVERSITY. See COL-LEGES.

KANSU, a province of NW China, bounded on the NW by Sinkiang, on the W and SW by Tibet, on the S by Szechwan, on the E by Shensi, and on the N by Inner Mongolia; area 151,160 sq. mi.; pop. (1947) 6,256,000. A longitudinal chain, the Nanshan, with parallel subsidiary ranges in the southeast portion, constitutes Kansu's mountain system. The western half of the province is drained by small rivers flowing into the lakes of Inner Mongolia, the east half by the Hwang Ho (Yellow River) and its tributary the Wei Ho. Because of the proximity of the northern steppes, the winters are cold. The summers are hot and at times rainy.

Of the various racial elements, Tibetan, Turki, Mongol, and Chinese, the latter is the largest, and Mandarin is the dominant speech. More than one-half of the population is Mohammedan. Among the non-Chinese Moslems, the Dungan, believed to be of western Tartaric origin, have periodically revolted against the Chinese, particularly in 1820, 1861–78, 1895–96, and 1937. Lamaism is represented among the Tibetans and the Mongols. LANCHOW (pop. about 368,600), on the Hwang Ho, is the capital. Other important towns are Kanchow, Chungwei, and Kung-chang.

Agriculture is concentrated in the sandy tract north of the Nanshan Range. Wheat, millet, corn, sorghum, and tobacco are the main crops. The opium poppy is grown everywhere except in Moslem districts. The northern grasslands are given over to cattle raising, and woolen and camel hair cloths are manufactured locally. Salt, iron, kaolin. mercury, gold, and coal are found. Petroleum deposits have been worked since 1938 and Lanchow has an oil-cracking plant. The highway to Sergiopol in the U.S.S.R. was finished in 1939. The Lung Hai railroad, which is eventually to reach the capital, was completed to Tienshui in southern Kansu in 1944. Lanchow is an air base.

Kansu as such is of recent formation (1911). The territory, however, dates back to the dawn of Chinese history. It was the corridor through which Buddhism, Nestorian Christianity, and the Tartar invasions reached China. During the Sino-Japanese War (1937–45) Kansu was an important war production area.

ADRIAN TROY

KANT, IMMANUEL, 1724–1804, German philosopher and teacher, was born in Königsberg in the province of Prussia, fourth of the 10 children of Johan Georg Cant (Immanuel early changed the spelling of his own name), a harness-maker of Scotch descent,

and Anna Regina Reuter. Members of the pietistic movement, which insisted upon the personal appropriation of religion, his parents lived a simple life described by the philosopher as a moral atmosphere, the homely discharge of duties, strict conscientiousness, and deep piety. He speaks reverently of his mother, and although she died when Immanuel was only 14, her influence is shown in the actions of his life and in his writings.

Immanuel Kant

Study and Tutoring. Through the efforts of his mother, Kant, at the age of eight, entered the Collegium Fredericianum, the equivalent of the American high school, where he underwent further religious training and received instruction in the Latin language and literature, developing a taste for the beauty and spirit of the classics which laid a basis for the broad humanistic culture so noticeable in his conversations and lectures. In 1740 Kant entered the University of Königsberg, a school of mediocre standing, and although he matriculated as a theology

student, he became more interested in mathematics and physics, studying under Martin Knutsen, a lecturer in philosophy. The importance of mathematics is evident in Kant's constant demands for exact definitions and demonstrations which have mathematical certainty; and his entire philosophy reveals the action of a mathematical mind. Knutsen, who encouraged his students in original thinking rather than mere learning, was a decided intellectual inspiration, and taking interest in the young student placed his entire library at Kant's disposal.

Attended by poverty during his last years at the university, Kant, after the death of his father in 1746, earned his living as a family tutor, the regular course in that day for one without private means. He disliked the work, and wasted his abilities, yet his position with the family of Count Kayserling was of great social value to him, developing his excellent conversational powers, and the ease, culture, and polish which made him a favorite among the cultivated families of Königsberg. Except for a brief sojourn as tutor with a country family 50 miles distant, Kant remained the whole of his long life within the confines of the city. Nine years of tutorship also enabled him to pursue his studies, and he published during that time three minor works on mathematics, physics, and astronomy.

With the publication of a thesis in 1755, he was at last able to finish his university career, and was accepted by the university as a private lecturer. In addition to his lectures for the school, he gave public lectures, attracting by his skill many people of high rank as well as regular students, the honorarium from which constituted a large part of his income. While he was twice refused a professorship at Königsberg, he declined all offers from elsewhere, and after 15 years was awarded the chair of logic and metaphysics.

Growth of Reputation. The *Critique of Pure Reason*, an attempt to survey and arbitrate the boundaries between sense and intellectual knowledge, was first published in 1781. Treating such concepts as time, space, unity, matter, motion, eternity, and God, it asks the question: "How far is knowledge *a priori*, which possesses objective validity, possible by means of these concepts?" The book met with little attention until the publication, in 1783, of *Prolegomena*, intended as an introduction to the *Critique*. A second edition of the *Critique*, published in the same year, had an extraordinary reception, a fact surprising in view of the book's earlier obscurity. By 1793 Kantian philosophy was included in the curriculum of the major universities, and Königsberg became the destination of scholars, students, and the curious from all parts of Europe. So universally was his system acclaimed as the final achievement of philosophy, that Kant himself, in later years, was convinced that there could be little further progress.

In 1792, the moral rationalism of Kant's philosophy, which holds that man sins as a result of free choice rather than an original corruption of human nature, involved him in an altercation with the German government. After an unsuccessful attempt to ban his book, *On Religion Within the Limits of Reason Alone* (1794), the government exacted from him a pledge not to write or lecture on religious subjects, a pledge which he kept until the death of Frederick William II, in 1797, released him from the obligation.

Old age brought increasing weakness to the philosopher. He persisted in his severe regimen: rising, eating, working, and exercising at precise and unvarying hours; but long hours at his desk were nullified by lack of strength, and his declining years produced nothing of major importance.

Science and Religion. Kant's writings and lectures were of such influence on the scientific, religious, and philosophical thinking of Europe, that they are ranked by historians with the events of the French

Revolution as the most important factors in determining the cultural characteristics of the 19th century.

In *Universal History of Nature and Theory of the Heavens* (1755), a scientific treatise, Kant endeavors to explain the structure of the cosmos, especially our own planetary systems, in accordance with the physical principles of Newton. This work displays a vivid and fertile imagination, searching almost into the fantastic for possible ideas concerning the development of the earth and cosmos, insisting, however, upon a complete separation of the religious and scientific aspects. He anticipated the view, later worked out systematically by the critical philosophy, that natural science and religious faith are not contradictory, but are in fact, completely indifferent to each other.

Of religion itself he wrote: "The germs which lie in man need only be more and more developed; for the grounds of evil are not found in the natural endowments of man. The source of evil is found in the fact that human nature is not subject to rules. There are in man no germs except for that which is good."

The need for a critical philosophy, according to Kant, arises from questions unanswerable through experience alone: "Human reason, in one sphere of its cognition, is called upon to consider questions, which it cannot decline, as they are presented by its own nature, but which it cannot answer, as they transcend every faculty of the mind." Again in the *Critique of Pure Reason*, Kant wrote: "For human reason, without any instigations imputable to the mere vanity of great knowledge, unceasingly progresses, urged on by its feeling of need, towards such questions as cannot be answered by any empirical application of reason, or principles derived therefrom; and so there has ever really existed in every man some system of metaphysics."

Kant's early scientific writings are little read, and his major works, *Critique of Pure Reason* (1781; 1783), *Prolegomena* (1783), *Foundations of the Metaphysics of Ethics* (1785), *Critique of Practical Reason* (1788), and *Critique of Judgement* (1790), are philosophical or metaphysical in character, but all are permeated by the basic concepts of physical science, and it is generally agreed that the influence of his philosophical system owes much to its exceptional use of the empirical as well as the speculative method. See HISTORY; PHILOSOPHY; SCIENCE AND SCIENTIFIC METHOD; THEISM.   WILLIAM R. SPARKS

BIBLIOG.–G. Whitney and D. Bowers, eds., *Heritage of Kant* (1939); J. Benda, *Living Thoughts of Kant* (1940); A. Pap, *A Priori in Physical Theory* (1946); H. J. Paton, *Categorical Imperative* (1948); H. K. Smith, *Commentary to Kant's Critique of Pure Reason* (1950).

KANTOSHU, or **Kwantung**, former leased territory, China, in S Manchuria, Liaoning Province, occupying the S tip of Liaotung Peninsula; area 1,336 sq. mi.; pop. (1941) 1,493,491. With a group of small adjacent islands, it was first leased in 1898 to Russia for a period of 25 years. Following the Russo-Japanese War, in 1905 it was transferred with the South Manchurian Railway in a lease to Japan for 99 years. Port Arthur, the naval port, has a fine, deepwater harbor. Dairen is the chief seaport.

The principal products of Kantoshu are cereal grains, tobacco, soybeans, salt fish, millet, maize, wheat, buckwheat, rice, hemp, and garden vegetables. There are salt-refining plants, iron foundries, flour mills, breweries, and tanneries. Bean oil, leather goods, cement, paper pulp, glass, soap, peanuts, and bricks are manufactured.

In 1932, when Japan established the puppet state of Manchukuo (Manchuria) revenue from the ports of Kwantung was cut off from China. The territory was liberated from Japanese control at the end of World War II and returned to Chinese control except for DAIREN and PORT ARTHUR, which were shared with the U.S.S.R. See MANCHURIA.   K. E. H.

KAOLACK, town, French West Africa, Senegal, 90 miles SE of Dakar, to which it is connected by rail. Kaolack is a highway junction and a thriving trading center.

KAOLAN. See LANCHOW.

KAOLIANG. See SORGHUM.

KAOLIN, or **CHINA CLAY**, is a hydrated aluminum silicate, finely powdered, of white or faintly yellow color, very soft, and slightly greasy to the touch. It has a hardness of 2 to 2.5, a specific gravity of 2.2 to 2.6, and a chemical composition approximating $H_4Al_2Si_2O_9$. It softens, but is still infusible at 1880° C. It absorbs moisture readily, so that it can be molded in the solid.

Kaolin is attributed to the weathering of pegmatite veins, and to the weathering or other alteration of granite, quartz-porphyry, or gneiss amphibole. It is rarely found sufficiently pure for commercial use without washing to clear it of particles. After being suspended in water, it is allowed to settle in shallow ponds or settling tanks, and is then dried on racks or in filter presses. It is used in the manufacture of PORCELAIN and pottery (along with feldspar, flint, etc.) and in the preparation of sizes for smooth-faced printing paper, employed for illustrated books with process engravings. It is also used for sizing and loading cheap cotton goods. Much alum is prepared from kaolin by the action of strong sulfuric acid. It is also used in making ultramarine pigment and as a filler in rubber articles. See PAPER AND PAPER MANUFACTURE.

Output of china clay or kaolin in the United States during 1948 reached a record peak, 1,568,000 tons. Georgia produced 72 per cent of the total output, with South Carolina, Alabama, Florida, and North Carolina ranking next. Imports from abroad that year came, in small quantities, from the United Kingdom, Canada, France, and Czechoslovakia.

KAPITZA, PETER, 1894–   , Soviet physicist of Byelorussian descent, specializing in atomic research and related problems, graduated from the Polytechnic Institute of St. Petersburg (now Leningrad). He worked with Professor Abram F. Joffa in that city's Physico-Technical Institute. In 1921 he moved to England where he entered the Cavendish Laboratory, Cambridge, as an associate of Lord ERNEST RUTHERFORD. Returning to the Soviet Union in 1934, Kapitza was given unlimited facilities to continue research in his homeland. He headed the Moscow Institute of Physical Problems, his major achievements being his work on low temperatures and its application in the liquefying of air, also the discovery and investigation of hyperfluidity of liquid helium. In the early 1940's he built new instruments for the cosmic ray observations carried on in high mountains by Abram and Artemy Alikhanov. In 1946 he was elected a member of the National Academy of Sciences.

KAPOK, or "silk-cotton," a material used for stuffing seats and pillows, obtained from the kapok tree, a tall evergreen of the East and West Indies and other tropical regions. It belongs to the bombax family.

KÁPOSVÁR, town, SW Hungary, on the Kapos River, 126 miles SW of Budapest. Features of interest include a cathedral, and castle ruins. The town is located in a horse raising district, and other agricultural industries are carried on. Pop. (1949 est.) 33,000.

KAPPEL, or **Cappel**, village, Switzerland, in the canton of Zurich, 10 miles S of the city of Zurich. It was the scene of battle during the Swiss civil war against the Roman Catholics when Zwingli, a noted Protestant leader, was killed (Oct. 11, 1531). Pop. (1941) 700.

KAPTEYN, JACOBUS CORNELIS, 1851–1922, Dutch astronomer, was born in Barneveld and studied at Utrecht. A member of the observing staff at Leiden Observatory (1875), he became professor of astronomy at Groningen (1878), and later assisted Gill in preparing a photographic catalogue of the southern stars, Kapteyn reducing Gill's plates with an instrument of his own design which gave spherical coordinates. The catalogue contained 454,875 stars, an average of 32 per square degree, and Kapteyn believed it to be complete down to photographic magnitude 9.2. He also obtained parallaxes of 248 stars from plates taken for him by Duner. In 1904 Kapteyn announced the theory that proper motions do not occur at random, but in two preferential directions, opposite and parallel to the Milky Way.

It was Kapteyn's belief that if complete data on certain areas of the sky were obtained through the joint investigations of several observatories, valuable information of the structure of our sidereal system would result. He chose 206 regions, uniformly distributed over the sky, and 46 special areas in interesting parts of the sky for such a study; the plan is now being carried on by a number of observatories.

EVERETT I. YOWELL

KAPUAS RIVER, Borneo, rises in the central part of the island and flows in a generally SW direction to the sea. It is navigable for small boats to Benut (400 mi.).

KAPURTHALA, former feudatory state, India, merged with other states in 1948 to form the Pepsu Union, comprises three detached pieces on the great Jullundur Doab; area 645 sq. mi.; pop. (1941) 378,380. The chief crops are wheat, grain, corn, cotton, and sugar cane; the principal exports are wheat, sugar, tobacco, and cotton. The most important commercial town is Phagwara, which manufactures farm implements, metal housewares, and has a sugar factory. The town is also notable for its grain markets. Saltanpur, in the southern part of the former state, is famous for hand-printed cloths. The former capital, Kapurthala, has electric lights, waterworks, and other modern conveniences.

Although the ruler of Kapurthala was a Sikh, the population is largely Moslem. The ruler granted the people of the state a legislative assembly in celebration of his diamond jubilee of rule (1916). Although the rulers of Kapurthala revolted against the British in the first Sikh war, they remained loyal thereafter; as a reward, the British remitted in perpetuity the state's yearly tribute, and granted the ruler a private estate of 700 square miles. In 1947, Kapurthala acceded to India, and in 1948 became part of the Pepsu Union.   C. S.

KARA HISSAR. See AFYON KARAHISAR.

KARA-KALPAK AUTONOMOUS SOVIET SOCIALIST REPUBLIC of the U.S.S.R. in the Uzbek Soviet Socialist Republic; bounded on the N, E, and W by the Kazakh Soviet Socialist Republic and on the S by the Turkmen Soviet Socialist Republic and Bukhara and Khorezm Regions; area 79,631 sq. mi. (more than one-half the territory of the entire Uzbek Soviet Socialist Republic); pop. (1950 est.) 435,000 including Karakalpak, 39.1 per cent, Kazakh, 27 per cent, Uzbek 26.4 per cent. The chief ethnic strain of the population is Turco-Tartar. A large area of the Kara-Kalpak Republic is covered by the KYZYL KUM ("red sands") Desert situated between the AMU DARYA (Oxus) and SYR DARYA. The greater part of the Aral Sea, into which the Amu Darya flows, is situated within the territorial confines of the republic.

Irrigation, largely from the Amu Darya, has played an important role in developing the agriculture of the Kara-Kalpak Republic. Fine crops of melons, figs, pomegranates, grapes, and vegetables are grown here. Kara-Kalpakia is the largest karakul sheep producing area in the Soviet Union, largely because of its extensive tracts of rich pasturage. Cotton is also grown. There is some irrigation. The climate of the republic is dry; rainfall averages four inches annually.

The area of the republic was absorbed into Russia in 1867, forming part of the former province of Turkistan. It was founded as an autonomous soviet socialist republic in 1932. The principal cities of the Kara-Kalpak Republic include Nukus, the capital, Turtkul with large cotton factories, Khiva, Chimbai, formerly the administrative center, and Urgench.

A. M. K.

KARA SEA, a branch of the Arctic Ocean, situated along the northern border of the Russian Soviet Federated Socialist Republic where the sea is encircled on the E by Novaya Zemlya and on the W by Severnaya Zemlya. The Kara Sea is open for navigation from six to eight weeks every year in the months of July through August. Igarka is its chief port.

KARACHAYEV AUTONOMOUS REGION, a former political division of the U.S.S.R., which was situated in the Russian Soviet Federated Socialist Republic, in the N Caucasus; area 3,821 sq. mi.; pop. (1939) 157,000. The Region was founded in 1926, with its capital at Mikoyan-Shakhar (now Klukhori). The principal ethnic strain of its people, 83.3 per cent of whom are Karachai, is Turco-Tartar. The Region was dissolved during World War II for opposition to the Soviets. Its land was transferred to STAVROPOL TERRITORY and the GEORGIAN SOVIET SOCIALIST REPUBLIC.

KARACHI, third largest seaport and chief airport of the Indian subcontinent; capital of Pakistan (since Aug. 15, 1947) and of Sind Province and headquarters for Karachi District, situated shortly inland from the Arabian Sea close to the Baluchistan border and N of the large Indus delta. The city is connected by rail with Hyderabad, from where there is rail transport to the Punjab, Rajputana, Baluchistan, and the United Provinces. The airport at Karachi serves routes from Europe, Egypt, Malaya, China, Japan, Australia, and America. The airport facilities were vastly enlarged by the demands of World War II. The climate is superior to that of the rest of Sind, the city being cooled by sea breezes. The rainfall, however, is slight, averaging only five inches annually. The merchants of Karachi have their businesses mainly along the city's famous Bandar Road. The shipping quarter is on the former island of Kiamari, which became a part of the mainland with the building of a mole in 1850. The harbor has a depth of 32 feet and some 9,000 feet of wharfage. The completion (1912) of the upper Chenab section of the Punjab triple project irrigating some 2,000,000 acres and the Sukkur Dam project (1932) have made Karachi the greatest wheat port of the subcontinent, although the largest export is raw cotton. Other exports include raw wool and animal hides. Among the imports are manufactured cotton goods, sugar, iron and steel (distributed throughout the northwestern part of the subcontinent and into Baluchistan, Afghanistan, and areas of Iran and central Asia).

Among the notable buildings are the clock tower monument to Sir William Merewether, the Sind and Mohammedan colleges, several schools and hospitals, and Frere Hall, an auditorium and public library before which stands a statue of Queen

City auditorium stands on Bandar Road, Karachi

Victoria presented (1906) by the Prince of Wales (later George V). Industrial establishments include the government arsenal and printing press, and manufactures of tin, cotton, and flour. Fishing is important.

In 1795 Karachi was seized from the Khan of Kalat by the Mirs of Sind. In 1836 it was taken by the British, and in 1842 was ceded to the British government, which made it the provincial capital. Upon the partition of the subcontinent on Aug. 15, 1947, Karachi became the capital of the Dominion of Pakistan and the residence of the governor general. The population increased greatly during World War II. Pop. (1941) 359,492.   C. S.

KARADAGH. See MONTENEGRO.

KARAFUTO. See SAKHALIN ISLAND.

KARAGANDA ("Black Land"), city, U.S.S.R., in the Kazakh Soviet Socialist Republic, capital of Karaganda Region, situated on the Akmolinsk-Balkhash rail line. The city is the center of the Karaganda coal area, the third largest Soviet coal basin, with deposits estimated at 53 billion tons. Here some of the best seams are so close to the surface that they can be worked directly by steam shovels that gouge out the coal and load it onto trains alongside. Karaganda's coal, known since 1854, was mined by an English company before the Russian Revolution. The Karaganda coal basin supplies coking coal to the Urals and the Asiatic republics, and produces fuel for the railways and nonferrous metal industries of the Kazakh Soviet Socialist Republic. The city's industries also include a steel plant, machine-building factory, brick and cement works, and a flour mill. Karaganda, like Magnitogorsk, sprang from the empty steppe during the Soviet Five-Year Plans. Pop. (1950 est.) 200,000.

KARAGANDA REGION, an administrative area of the U.S.S.R., in the Kazakh Soviet Socialist Republic; bounded on the N by Akmolinsk and Pavlodar Regions, on the NW by Kustanai Region, on the W by Aktyubinsk Region, on the SW by Kzyl-Orda Region, on the S by South Kazakhstan and Dzhambul Regions and Lake Balkhash, on the E by Semipalatinsk Region, and on the SE by Taldy-Kurgan Region. Pop. (1950 est.) 460,000.

KARAGEORGE, or **CZERNY GEORGE,** 1766–1817, Serbian leader and founder of the Karageorgevich dynasty of Serbia and Yugoslavia, was born of peasant parents. With the assistance of Russia he led Serbian forces against the Turks and wrested Belgrade from them, ruling it from 1806 to 1813. He became lord of Serbia in 1804, and hereditary supreme commander in 1808. When Russia withdrew its support, he was compelled to flee to Vienna and was succeeded by MILOSH OBRENOVICH; returning in 1817, he was murdered by Obrenovich's orders. The Karageorgevich dynasty included his son, Alexander Karageorgevich (1842–58), grandson Peter I (1903–21), great-grandson Alexander II (1921–34) and great-great-grandson Peter II (1934–45).

KARAITES, a Jewish sect who adhere to the strict letter of Scripture, and reject oral tradition and depreciate the Talmud. The schism arose at Bagdad about the middle of the eighth century A.D., under the leadership of Anan ben David. He led his adherents to Jerusalem, whence they were scattered at the time of the Crusades. They are most numerous in South Russia, especially the Crimea.

KARAKORAM, a great mountain range of India, in Kashmir, extending, in the Muztagh Ata Range, into Sinkiang (China), and separated from the western end of The Himalaya, to the south, by the Indus River Valley. It contains the second highest known peak of the world, K₂ (GODWIN AUSTEN, or Dapsang), and has a number of other peaks reaching well over 25,000 feet. On the north the upper Yarkand Darya Valley, almost parallel to the Indus, separates the range from the western Kunlun. The Karakoram Range is almost 450 miles long, and the Karakoram Pass (35° 53′ N lat., 80° 18′ E long.) is the principal commercial route from India to Sinkiang. It is traversable throughout the year, although it is some 18,500 feet above the sea. Distaghil, in the Gilgit Agency at the northwest end of the Karakoram Range, reaches 25,868 feet.

KARAKORUM, the name of two ancient Asiatic capitals, in Mongolia, both now in ruins, in a region between the Gobi Desert on the south and the U.S.S.R. on the north. The older city, also called Holin, was located on the left bank of the Orkhon River, 210 miles southwest of Urga (Ulan Bator.) It was the capital of Uighur, a Turkish kingdom of the seventh to ninth centuries. The second capital was situated on the right bank of the Orkhon River, 15 miles southeast of the first. The Mongolian capital of Genghis Khan, it was founded in 1234 and continued as the capital until the 15th century. Marco Polo visited there in 1275. Later it was destroyed by Kublai Khan. In 1890 Heikel and Radlov explored the ruins of the two cities and discovered many valuable Turkish, Mongol, Persian, Tibetan, and Chinese relics and historical inscriptions of the eighth century.

KARAKUL. See PERSIAN LAMB.

KARAMANIA, a central plateau of S Asia Minor, occupying a part of the modern Turkish vilayet of Konya. It was in existence in the 13th and 14th centuries as an independent province under Turkish protection. Its capital was Laranda, the modern Karaman.

KARAMZIN, NICOLAI MIKHAILOVICH, 1766–1826, Russian historian, was born near Simbirsk on the Volga. He spent two years in the army but left it to devote himself to literature. He made his reputation as a stylist with *Travels from Moscow* (Eng. trans., 3 vols. 1803), and in the same year he was appointed imperial historiographer and at once began his great *History of Russia* (11 vols., ed. 1850–53), which he continued until his death, bringing it down to 1613. It is the first systematic history of Russia, and Karamzin was one of the creators of modern Russian prose. His other works include the novels *Poor Lisa* (1792); *Natalya, the Boyar's Daughter* (1792); *Martha the Viceregent* (1793).

KARAULI, former feudatory state, India, now part of Greater Rajasthan; in E Rajputana, bordered by Jaipur, Bharatpur, and Dholpur, and with the Chambal River dividing it from Gwalior on the SE; area 1,242 sq. mi.; pop. (1941) 152,413. The state is largely made up of hills and broken ground. Iron ore and building stone are found; the principal crop and native food is millet. The state has many small manufactures of weaving, dyeing, woodworking, and stone cutting. The people are mostly Hindu. The state was founded in the 11th century and in 1817 came under the protection of the British. The capital was Karauli (pop. 19,177), some 75 miles southwest of Agra. The ruler was styled maharaja, and was entitled to a 17-gun salute.

KARAWALA, a small viper of southern India and Ceylon, closely related to the American copperhead and of similar appearance. The karawala, *Hypnale nepa,* is about 18 inches in length.

KARBALA, also **Kerbela,** or **Mechhed-Hosain,** city, SW Iraq, capital of Karbala Province, on the eastern edge of the Syrian Desert in the midst of date palm groves, 20 miles W of the Euphrates near the ruins of Babylon and 60 miles SW of Baghdad. The town centers around the shrine of Hosain, the son of Ali, and is an important place of pilgrimage second only to Mecca and Najaf, for Shiite Mohammedans, who also carry their dead here for burial. The mosque which contains the tomb has gold-plated domes and minarets. Karbala is a prosperous trade center. Dates, hides, raw wool, cereal grains, and religious objects are exported; sacred bricks and shrouds stamped with verses from the Koran are the chief manufactured products. Pop. (1935) 65,000.

Karelia

KARELIA. See KARELO-FINNISH SOVIET SOCIALIST REPUBLIC.

KARELO-FINNISH SOVIET SOCIALIST RE-PUBLIC, or **Karelia,** one of the constituent republics of the U.S.S.R.; bounded on the N by Murmansk Region of the Russian Soviet Federated Socialist Republic, on the E by the White Sea and Archangel Region, on the S by Leningrad Region, and on the W by Finland; area 73,515 sq. mi.; pop. (1950 est.) 600,000. Lying on a glaciated bed of granite and dotted by innumerable lakes, with vast stretches of coniferous forest, Karelia is often called "the land of lakes, forests, and granite." The largest lakes in Europe—lakes Ladoga and Onega—are found here. Numerous rivers, excellent sources for hydroelectric power, form the connecting links between the republic's 26,000 lakes and the large bodies of water contiguous to it, namely, the White Sea and the Gulf of Finland. Two-thirds of Karelia's surface is covered with dense growths of pine, fir, and birch, constituting the basis of its chief industry—timber. Winter months in Karelia are severe, although somewhat mitigated in the south by proximity to the Baltic; summer months are rainy and frequently cool. The Karelians are the creators of the great epic poem, *Kalevala* (see KALEVALA, THE), from which Longfellow borrowed the rhythm for *Hiawatha.* Their chief ethnic strain is Finno-Ugrian.

Economic Life. Lumbering is the backbone of the republic's economy. Karelian industries dependent upon timber production are sawmilling, concentrated at the river mouths on the White Sea coast; the tar, pitch, and turpentine industries; and the paper and cellulose industries, now the largest in the Soviet Union. The Soviets, since the first Five-Year Plan, have expanded the machine-building and shipbuilding industries considerably. Fishing is carried on in the lake regions and along the White Sea coast.

The republic is rich in deposits of diabase, porphyry, sandstone, mica, marble, pegmatites, titano-magnetites, nonferrous metals, and peat. The mining and extraction of these minerals is an important phase of the Karelian economy. Uranium and thorium are found.

The soil and climate of Karelia are not advantageous to large-scale development of agriculture, except in the south of the republic where substantial crops of potatoes and vegetables are grown. Some barley, oats, rye, and wheat constitute the lesser crops of the region. The livestock are chiefly dairy cattle. In the north, reindeer are bred.

History. The Karelians are mentioned as early as the ninth century, once forming a strong and independent state. In the 14th century the Karelian state

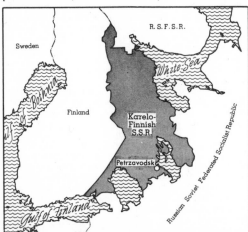

Location map of the Karelo-Finnish S.S.R.

SOVFOTO
Rafting the timber cut from forests of Karelia

was partitioned between the Swedes and the Russians; the western part fell to the former, while the eastern part fell to the Russian principality of Novgorod. Karelia was totally absorbed by the Russians in the 18th century. In 1939 the Soviet invasion of Finland was launched from Karelia, and in 1940, after the Finnish defeat, 16,000 square miles of Finnish territory were seized. With the additional territory, Karelia became a Union Republic. During World War II, Finnish and German forces invaded the republic. On June 29, 1944, the Soviet army recaptured Petrozavodsk, the capital, and soon afterward the remainder of the republic. In 1945 the Vyborg and Keksgolm areas, acquired from Finland under the Armistice terms of 1944, were taken from Karelia and incorporated into the Russian Soviet Federated Socialist Republic. The ceded area totaled 2,925 square miles with an estimated population of 150,000.   K. E. H.

KARENNI, plateau, 3,000–4,000 feet above sea level, between Lower Burma and Siam. The country is divided into several petty states under the control of the Burma government. The plateau is fertile and well cultivated. It is inhabited by the Red Karen tribe.

KARENS, a tribe of semi-aborigines on the eastern frontier of Burma and the western border of Siam, and in the Irrawaddy delta. Their prehistoric home was apparently in southwest China. The some 2,000,000 Karens received a bloc of seats in Parliament by the 1948 Constitution. In 1948 they joined the revolt against the government and in 1949 announced the creation of an independent Karen state.

KARIKAL, a small colony of French India, on the Coromandel coast, below Pondichéry, within the limits of the Tanjore District, Madras Province; area 53 sq. mi.; pop. (1948), 70,541. The chief town, Karikal (pop. 23,008), located on one of the mouths of the Cauvery River, is connected by rail to Peralam and carries on a trade with Ceylon and Malaya. The area was promised to the French by the rajah of Tanjore in 1738, but the French needed to use force to occupy it the following year. The British captured the settlement in 1760, but restored it in 1765; the British again took Karikal in 1768, retaining it until the final restoration in 1817. Karikal is one of five colonies comprising French India, the capital of which is at Pondichéry. The settlement is governed by an administrator subordinate to the governor of French India. See INDIA, FRENCH.

KARIMATA ISLANDS, or **Carimata,** an archipelago of about 60 small islands belonging to the Republic of Indonesia, lying 75 miles off the W coast of Borneo and some 400 miles SE of Singapore; area 57 sq. mi.; pop. about 500. The chief occupations of the inhabitants are fishing and iron mining. The largest island of the group is Great Karimata; its capital is Padang. The Karimata Islands were occupied by the Japanese during World War II.

KARLFELDT, ERIK AXEL, 1864–1931, Swedish poet, was born in Karlbo. He won early in his life a popularity which is accorded to few poets in modern times. His genius for humor and whimsy first appeared in *Fridolin's Ballads* (1898) and was continued with a deepening range in *Fridolin's Pleasure Garden* (1901), *Flora and Pomona* (1906), and *Flora and Bellona* (1918). Karlfeldt's baroque affectations and his complex Swinburnian rhythms are lost in translation, and he received only limited recognition abroad, though he ranks as one of the greatest Swedish poets. Much of his life was devoted to the activities of the Swedish Academy, to which he was elected in 1904 and of which he was permanent secretary after 1912. The Nobel prize for literature, which he had refused during his lifetime, was awarded him posthumously in 1931.

KARLI, a renowned Chaitya cave temple, 25 miles southeast of Bombay, India. It is cut in a rocky wall 850 feet high, and the interior, 126 feet long, 45½ feet broad, and 46 feet high, is adorned with richly carved columns and has a shrine at one end.

KARLINGS. See CARLOVINGIANS.

KARLOVCI, German **Karlowitz,** Hungarian **Karlocza,** town, E Yugoslavia, Peoples Republic of Serbia, in the Autonomous Province of Vojvodina, at the foot of the peak of Fruska Gora, on the right bank of the Danube River, 45 miles NW of Belgrade. It is the seat of a Greek Orthodox patriarch and a Serbian Orthodox metropolitan, with a cathedral and a palace. A famous red wine is produced here, and other industries include fishing, and hog raising. The Treaty of Karlowitz was signed here Jan. 26, 1699, when Turkey made peace with Poland, Austria, and Venice, and signed a short truce with Russia. The Turks renounced their control of Hungary, with the exception of the Banat, and relinquished Transylvania, among other provisions. In World War II Karlovci was occupied by the Italians in 1941. Pop. (1948) 5,520.

KARLOVY VARY, German **Karlsbad,** or **Carlsbad,** famous health resort, Czechoslovakia, in W Bohemia, on the Cheb (Eger) River, at the southern

CZECHOSLOVAK STATE RAILWAYS
"Market Spring" bath house in Karlovy Vary

foot of the Erzegebirge; 116 miles NW of Prague (Praha). The little town, 1,225 feet above sea level, is squeezed into the narrow and romantic valley of the Tepl, and is surrounded by pine-clad mountains. The waters of its famous "Sprudel" are warm and alkaline-saline; they are said to be beneficial for rheumatism, dyspepsia, and gout. Porcelain, goldsmith's work, liqueurs, needles, ornaments, and costume jewelry are manufactured. Salt and mineral water from the springs are exported. The waters were discovered by and named for Charles IV of Bohemia in the 14th century. Pop. (1947) 30,915.

KARLSBAD. See KARLOVY VARY.

KARLSBURG. See ALBA IULIA.

KARLSKRONA, or **Carlskrona,** fortified island seaport, SE Sweden, capital of Blekinge County; 47 miles SW of Kalmar and 300 miles SW of Stockholm.

It is built partly on several small islands in the Baltic off the southern coast and partly on the mainland. Entrance to its harbor is protected by forts on Aspö and Kungsholm islands. The dry docks are constructed of solid granite. Since 1860 Karlskrona has been the chief station of the Swedish fleet. There is a large airfield. The town has shipbuilding yards, an arsenal, a naval school, and hospital. There are manufactures of naval equipment, clothing, hats, metal goods, porcelain, canvas, leather goods, woolen textiles, tobacco, and matches. Granite is quarried near by. Exports include granite, dairy products, and timber. Pop. (1949) 30,639.

KARLSRUHE, town, Germany, capital in the state of Baden, in the Rhine plain, near the N end of the Black Forest, 34 miles SW of Heidelberg. It is connected by canal with the Rhine, six miles west, on which is situated its port in the industrialized Muhlburg area. The old town is built in the shape of a fan, with 32 streets radiating from the 18th century castle at its center, but the new sections such as Muhlburg, Daxlanden, Grunwinkel, and the garden suburb of Ruppurr are constructed along traditional lines. A continental air lines stop, Karlsruhe has a large airport and is a rail and road communications center. Its cultural history is embodied in its historical and natural history museums, colleges, library, art gallery, and observatory. The town is an industrial center, manufacturing railway engines and cars, machinery, tools, chemicals, surgical instruments, leather, cement, and food products. Founded in 1715, Karlsruhe became the cultural center of Baden, and the residence of the margraves of Baden. During World War II the castle, and in large part the town, were left in ruins, an air attack in 1942 causing the principal damage. The town fell to Allied forces in April, 1945. Pop. (1946) 172,343.

KARLSTAD, port city, Sweden, capital of Värmland County on the island of Thingvalla and the N shore of Lake Vänern at the mouth of the river Klar; 160 miles W of Stockholm. Two large bridges join the island with the mainland. The seat of a bishop, the town has a cathedral. Known in medieval times as Thingvalla, it was incorporated as Karlstad in 1584. It has been rebuilt since a fire in 1865 and is an important industrial center, with manufactures of heavy machinery, tobacco, matches, and textiles; there are sawmills and pulp and paper factories. Karlstad has railway connections with Oslo and Stockholm; there is shipping by way of Lake Vänern and the Göta Canal. Its mineral springs (iron) are important. Here was signed in 1905 the agreement dissolving the union of Norway and Sweden. Pop. (1949) 34,382.

KARLUK, or **Karluck,** village, Alaska, on the NW coast of Kodiak Island, on Shelikof Strait opposite the Alaska Peninsula. Behind the village is a rugged mountain mass 1,600 feet high, called Karluk Head. Most of the natives of the village engage in fishing. Pop. (1939) 189.

KARMA. See BUDDHISM.

KARMÖ ISLAND, or **Carmo,** at the mouth of Bokn Fjord, Norway, off the SW section of Rogaland County. It has herring fisheries and copper mines. The chief towns are Skudesnaes, at the southern end, and Kopervik, centrally located. Pop. (1946) 14,290.

KARNAK, a great temple in Egypt situated on the right bank of the Nile, in 25° 50' N lat., one and a half miles N of the modern village of Luxor. An avenue of ram-headed sphinxes leads up to the great gateway of Ptolemy III Euergetes (d. 222 B.C.), which opens on to the beautiful temple of the Theban deity Chensu, dedicated by Ramses III (20th dynasty). Slightly to the northeast are the ruins of the main temple. The great propylaea leading from one court to another are of magnificent proportions, the total breadth of the largest being 370 feet and its height 142½ feet, while its depth is 60 feet. The processional hall surpasses all in size. There is a central avenue of 12 columns 80 feet high, with nine lines of smaller columns on either side—134 in all and the whole is profusely decorated with carving and brilliant coloring. It was erected by Seti I and finished by Rameses II (19th dynasty). East of the hall is a court surrounded by Osiride figures in which are two huge red granite obelisks, erected by Queen Hatshepsut (18th dynasty). Other temples lying near the main building are those of Ptah and Hathor, of Amenhotep III, and of Harmhab.

Hypostyle Hall in Temple of Ammon at Karnak, Egypt

KÁROLYI, MICHAEL, COUNT, 1876–   , Hungarian Socialist statesman, of a famous family of Hungary, was educated in Budapest. He traveled extensively and in 1905 was elected to Parliament. He was president of the Hungarian Agricultural Society in 1909, but later resigned and allied himself with the Radicals. After the outbreak of World War I he seceded from the Independents and founded the Károlyi party (Socialist) in order to break with Germany and negotiate for a separate peace. In 1918 when the war was plainly lost he became premier and later was proclaimed president of the People's Republic of Hungary. Károlyi's efforts to restore order and contentment were thwarted by Bolshevist propaganda and in 1919 he handed over the reins of government to BÉLA KUN and went into exile. During the HORTHY regime, he was found guilty of treason and his estates were confiscated. He returned early in 1947 to take a post in the coalition government's foreign office; but resigned and returned to exile when Soviet influence became powerful in the government of Hungary later in 1947.

KARRER, PAUL, 1889–   , Swiss chemist, was born in Moscow, Russia, reared in Aagau Canton, Switzerland, and educated at the University of Zürich. After serving as an assistant to Paul Ehrlich at the George Speyer Haus für Chemotherapie in Frankfurt am Main he returned to Zürich as assistant professor of organic chemistry (1918). In 1919 he became professor and director of the university's Chemical Institute. He was noted for his research on the carotinoids and flavines, discovering that some of these such as carotene and lactoflavine act as precursors of Vitamins A and B₂. In 1938 he synthesized the compound alpha-tocopherol which has the fertility potency of Vitamin E. In 1937 Karrer shared the Nobel prize in chemistry with WALTER N. HAWORTH.

KARROO, tablelands, Union of South Africa, forming two successive terraces between the seashore and the high veld of the interior of Cape of Good Hope Province. The Little Karroo is the first terrace, its northern buttress being the Zwaarteberg Range, average elevation 1,000 to 2,000 feet. The Great Karroo (average width, 60 mi.; height, 2,000 to 3,000 ft.) is bounded on the north by the Sneeuwberg Range. In the summer, except for the limited irrigated areas, the Karroo is desolate and arid, its only trees being a species of acacia. When the rains come, however, the Karroo appears a vast ocean of green, spangled with innumerable brilliant flowers. The irrigated areas are among the most productive of Africa. During the season of rain large flocks of sheep are grazed in the Karroo.

KARS, highland vilayet, in E Turkey, at the SE end of the Black Sea on the border of the Georgian and the Armenian Soviet Socialist Republics; area, 6,700 sq. mi.; pop. (1945) 383,222. The vilayet is very mountainous, some of its peaks reaching 10,000 feet, and is heavily forested with fir and birch. The principal rivers are the Arpa-Chai, which receives the Kars River and then joins the Aras (Araxes) and flows into Iran, and the Jura, which rises near the Allaheukher Dagi at an altitude of 10,217 feet and flows north and northeast into Georgia. The province has a wealth of minerals including coal, copper, lead, and silver. There are many small lakes including Cildir Gölü, lying at an altitude of 9,975 feet. The climate shows extremes of heat and cold. Agriculture and trade are the chief occupations of the people, although the Kurdish population are nomadic and pastoral, raising horses, sheep, cattle, and goats on the gentle slopes of the mountains. Barley, maize, and some wheat are the chief crops. There are also vineyards. The principal towns of the vilayet are Kars, the capital, Ardahan, and Kagizman. Kars has been invaded many times by Kurds, Turks, and Russians. It became Russian after the Russo-Turk War of 1877–78 but was returned to Turkey in 1921 by a treaty with Soviet Russia.   K. E. H.

KARS, city, NE Turkey, capital of Kars vilayet, on the Arpa-Chai River, 25 miles W of the frontier between the Georgian and the Armenian Soviet Socialist Republics; 135 miles SW of Tbilisi (Tiflis), Georgia. There is an ancient citadel and an 11th-century cathedral. During the 9th and 10th centuries, Kars was the capital city of an independent Armenian principality. In 1828 it fell before the Russians under Paskevitch, but was later restored to Turkish rule. In 1855 it was brilliantly defended for six months by the Turks under the British General, Williams, but was finally forced again to surrender to the Russians. It was the scene of severe fighting in World War I, but in 1921 was returned to the Turks. Carpets, woolen goods, and felt are manufactured. Southeast of here, near the Iranian border, is Mount ARARAT, sacred mountain of Armenia and traditional landing place of Noah's Ark. Pop. (1945) 22,264.

KARSHI, formerly **Bek-Budi,** U.S.S.R., in the Uzbek Soviet Socialist Republic, capital of Kashka-Darya Region, on the Karshi River and rail lines extending to Bukhara and Shakhnisyabz, 100 miles SE of the city of Bukhara. Situated in the fertile Karshi oasis, Karshi produces poppies, fine fruits, and tobacco. It is famous as the favorite residence of Tamerlane. Pop. about 14,200.

KARST, a descriptive term for topography characterized by caverns, depressions, and underground drainage. Karst topography develops in areas of pure limestone and abundant precipitation; it is the result of ground water solution. The main forms, known as sinks in the United States and *dolinas* in Italy, are depressions formed by the collapse of a cavern roof. They may be shallow or deep and are steep sided with circular or irregular outlines. Frequently karst areas are covered with a soil mantle such as the sandy soils of Florida or the red porous soils of Cuba. The term was taken from the Karst, a denuded limestone plateau and hill region behind the Adriatic shore of Yugoslavia. Other European examples are the heel of Italy, the lowland of Apulia (Italy), the *causses* of France, and Derbyshire (England). On the plains bordering the Gulf of Mexico there are large karst areas including the famous arid peninsula of Yucatán. Central Kentucky is underlain by limestone formations, and the famous cave area is the result of underground solution (see MAMMOTH CAVE NATIONAL PARK).

KARTIKEYA, the Hindu god of war, according to some legends was the second son of SIVA and Parvati. In others he is of miraculous birth without any direct intervention of a woman. He is renowned for prowess in battle.

KARUIZAWA, one of the leading summer resort towns of Japan, E central Honshu, situated on high moorland in the mountains of E Shinano Prefecture, about 80 miles NW of Tokyo and on the main railroad and highway routes from Tokyo to the Sea of Japan coast. The town's population varies with the seasons; the townsfolk themselves number several thousand.

KARUN RIVER, W Iran, rising in the Zerdeh Kuh Mountains (13,450 ft.) of the Bakhtiari Range. In its upper course running 100 miles west of Isfahan, the river is known as the Ab-i-Kurang. It flows west and south past Shuster and Ahwaz and empties into the Shatt Al Arab at Khorramshahr, 45 miles from the Persian Gulf. The Karun is navigable as far as Shuster, although navigation at Ahwaz is impeded by rapids. There are many mountain tributaries; the most important is the Ab-i-Diz, which enters at Dizful. The river has been open to foreign commerce since the turn of the 20th century. Its total length is about 465 miles.

KASABA, also **Kassaba, Casaba,** or **Turgutlu,** city, W Turkey, Manisa Vilayet, 35 miles (60 mi. by rail) E of Izmir (Smyrna). Kasaba is in the center of a fruit-growing district producing the famous variety of pears and melons (Casaba) which, with cotton, silkworms, and raw silk, make up the chief exports of the town. There are cotton gins, a bazaar, and two handsome mosques. Pop. (1945) 22,719.

KASAI RIVER, or **Cassai,** rises in Angola (Portuguese West Africa) at about 12° S lat. and 18° W long., and flows E then N, forming the boundary between Angola and the Belgian Congo for nearly 300 miles. After a farther course in a northwest direction of more than 500 miles, during which it is swollen by a number of affluents, it is joined by the Kwango (Cuango) and enters the Congo at Kwamouth. After the junction with the Kwango, the Kasai is sometimes called the Kwa. Wissman explored the river in 1885, and it is navigable to the falls bearing his name.

KASBIN. See KAZVIN.

KASCHAU. See KOSICE.

KASHAN, city, N central Iran, on the route between Teheran, Qum, and Isfahan; 95 miles NW of Isfahan. It is a very ancient city, and was once the most important center of ceramic art in Persia, producing pottery and glazed tiles of exquisite beauty for export to European and Asiatic markets. Today the city still manufactures tiles and porcelains, as well as carpets, silks, satins, velvets, embroidered articles, cottons, brocades, brass and copper ware, and silk carpets. The last are very valuable and much in demand in Mohammedan countries. Rose water is exported and cobalt is mined at Kamsar, 19 miles south of Kashan. The town had many disastrous earthquakes. Pop. about 45,000.

KASHGAR, or **Shufu,** city, NW China, in W Sinkiang Province, the chief city of the Kashgaria District, on the Kashgar (Kizil) River; 100 miles NW of Yarkand (Soche), at the S foot of the Tien Shan. The city is located in a fertile oasis, the largest of Sinkiang, at the western extremity of the arid Tarim Basin, and is the junction of several ancient and important commercial caravan routes between Russia, India, and China, communicating with Kashgar via high passes—the Terek, the Karakorum, the Burzil, and Hunza—and the long roads across western China. An improved motor road connects Kashgar with the Sinkiang capital, Tihwa, but oxcart and camel are still the principal means of transport. Kashgar is composed of an old town, built in 1513 and encircled by a massive high clay wall, and the new town extending five miles east beyond the Kashgar River. In the old town is a governor's palace and a caravanserai, built by Yakub Beg (1864–77); the new town, built in 1838, is also walled and contains the palace of the Amban (Chinese governor). It is a picturesque place, with its arched gates, wide market place, and willow-shaded mosques.

A polyglot population, like that of the whole of western Sinkiang, is in Kashgar predominantly Uighur (Chinese Wei-wu-erh), who are a Sunni Moslem sect, merchants and farmers. Kashgar has a university and a government-built radio station. Its industries include the manufacture of carpets, cottons, woolens, felt boots, porcelains, jasper, jade, and gold and silver articles and cloth. In addition to these products, exports are tea; rhubarb; silk, wool, and cotton textiles; and sheepskins. The surrounding region produces oats, corn, wheat, barley, rice, cotton, millet, garden vegetables, and a variety of fruits— peaches, pears, grapes, plums, and melons. In the vicinity are two great copper mines, producing ore of 40 and 20 per cent purity. Coal, oil, and iron are also exploited, and there are smelting works.

The Chinese maintained a garrison at Kashgar as early as the eighth century, but Chinese rule in the far western town was often only nominal and the Chinese merely traders at the oasis. It was the capital of the Turkish kingdom of Uighur in the 10th and 11th centuries, fell to Genghis Khan in 1219, and to Tamerlane in the 14th century. It was visited by Marco Polo in 1275. Kashgar's situation made it a hub of political as well as commercial interests from Russian Turkistan (Kirgiz, Tadzhik), Afghanistan, and India. In the latter half of the 19th century overlapping British and Russian interests met for a time at Kashgar, and both countries had consuls in the city. In the 1860's the rebel Yakub Beg overthrew the Manchu Chinese rule and set up a government at Kashgar. The city had a comparatively large Russian colony which dwindled in the years following the birth of the Soviet Union, and again revived with the establishment of a consulate in 1925. In 1934 Kashgar was the refuge for several months of Ma Chung-ying, leader of the Moslem revolt of the 1930's against the Sinkiang administration. Pop. (1936 est.) 80,000.

                                   K. E. H.; D. M.

KASHGARIA, a name applied to Chinese Turkistan, the modern SINKIANG. The term now refers to an area of western Sinkiang. See KASHGAR.

KASHING, an important commercial town, SW China, in N Chekiang Province, on the Grand Canal, midway between Shanghai and Hangchow, with which it is connected by rail. Kashing is the trading center for a rich farming and silk-producing region and exports large quantities of raw silk. It was attacked by the Taipings in 1852 and partially destroyed. Japanese troops occupied the city from September, 1937, until the close of World War II in 1945. Pop. (1936) 60,000.

KASHIPUR, town, India, United Provinces, Naini Tal District, 80 miles ENE of Meerut. It is identified as the former capital of the Govisana (Aryan) kingdom, and pilgrims resort to its many Hindu temples. It has some importance as a trading center, and is a railway junction point.

KASHKA-DARYA REGION, an administrative area of the U.S.S.R. in the Uzbek Soviet Socialist Republic; bounded on the N by Samarkand Region, on the NW by Bukhara Region, on the SW by the Turkmen Soviet Socialist Republic, on the SE by Sukhan-Darya Region, and on the E by the Tadzhik Soviet Socialist Republic. Pop. (1950 est.) 405,000.

KASHMIR AND JAMMU, largest Indian native state, bounded by the North-West Frontier Province to the W, Punjab to the S, Afghanistan to the NW, Sinkiang (Chinese Turkistan) to the N, Tibet to the E; area 85,900 sq. mi.; pop. (1941) 4,021,616. Mountainous all over, except for the submontane tract of Jammu in the south, Kashmir and Jammu has the second and fifth highest peaks in the world: GODWIN-AUSTEN (K₂, 28,250 ft.) and NANGA PARBAT (26,629 ft.). India's longest river, the INDUS runs through the state. Jammu (pop. 50,379) is the terminal of the country's only railroad, a 16-mile spur from Sialkot (Punjab). Srinagar (pop. 207,787), the summer residence, is reached from Rawalpindi (Punjab) by a

Natives pole their boat on river at Srinagar

200-mile motor road. Srinagar's location on a marshy stretch of the Jhelam is in contradistinction to the state's salubrius climate. Scenery, abundance of game, historical landmarks, Hindu shrines, and the houseboats of Dal Lake, have made Kashmir a world-famed vacation land.

Ethnically present-day Kashmir and Jammu is largely Aryan with a small admission of Sinitic, the Tibetans of Ladakh and Baltistan. Kashmiri, the vernacular, belongs to the Indo-Aryan group, while the Tibeto-Burmese is represented by the dialects of Ladakh and Baltistan. Burushaski, an unclassified language, is spoken by some 20,000 people in the Gilgit district.

The fertile soil grows native foodstuffs and many temperate zone fruits and vegetables, and early in the 20th century Kashmir produced wine. Carpet-weaving has replaced shawl-weaving as the leading industry. Other native crafts are woodcarving, saddlery, making gold and silver jewelry, woolen fabrics, copperware and papier-mâché articles, and embroidering on silk.

Government and History. In the government the maharaja is assisted by an executive council. The state assembly of 40 elected and 35 nominated members meets twice each year. Indian government control is exercised through a resident stationed at Srinagar and a political agent at Gilgit. The maharaja is a Hindu ruling a predominately Moslem population; this condition has caused frequent revolts. The ruler is entitled to a salute of 21 guns.

Buddhism came about 245 B.C. and existed with the Brahmanism of the early tribes: Naga (Sanskrit "serpent"), Gandhari, and Khasa, until the Mogul invasion introduced Mohammedanism, the faith predominant to this day. Besides adherents of the three religions mentioned—Mohammedans, Hindus, and Buddhists—Kashmir has Sikhs and Indian Christians. In 1846, Gulab Singh, ruler of Jammu, who had

Girls of Kashmir tend cows beside a country road

been active in the peace negotiations between Sikhs and British, was allowed, as a reward for his efforts, to purchase the territory the British had just taken from the Sikhs in lieu of war indemnity. With the purchase went the title of maharaja and a guarantee of the country's independence. Subsequent conquests by Gulab Singh and his descendants further

enlarged Kashmir, which now includes: Jammu, Kashmir (i.e., the portion taken from the Punjab after the 1846 war), Ladakh, Baltistan, Gilgit, and the Shin states of Yaghistan. At the partition of India (Aug. 15, 1947) into the two states of Pakistan and India, Kashmir and Jammu indicated a preference for an independent state. However, before the end of 1947 the state acceded temporarily to India, promising its predominantly Moslem population a plebiscite. Thereupon a war between unofficial Pakistan and official Indian forces broke out. The dispute between India and Pakistan about Kashmir was brought before the United Nations in 1948 and prolonged negotiations for a peaceful settlement were begun with a marked bitterness of feeling on both sides. The Pakistan prime minister refused to attend the British Commonwealth Conference in January, 1951, unless it was agreed that the conference would try to settle the Kashmir dispute.

ADRIAN TROY; G. B. DE H.

BIBLIOG.—E. F. Neve, *Things Seen in Kashmir* (1931); D. Norris, *Kashmir, The Switzerland of India* (1932); R. C. Kak, *Ancient Monuments of Kashmir* (1933); C. A. Wood, *Through Forest and Jungle in Kashmir and Other Parts of North India* (1933); J. P. Hewett, *Jungle Trails in Northern India* (1938); P. Marsden, *Kashmir Calls* (1946); S. N. Sarker, *Kashmir* (ed. 1947); K. A. Abbas, *Kashmir Fights for Freedom* (1948).

KASKASKIA, historic village, Illinois, in Randolph County, located eight miles NW of Chester. In April, 1703, the Jesuit Father Gabriel Marest moved his mission from the Lake Peoria region to the right bank of the Kaskaskia River above its junction with the Mississippi, following the migration of the Kaskaskia Indians to this new location. At first Kaskaskia was primarily an Indian village but with a few French residents. About 1717 a French village appeared apart from but near to the Indian encampment. In 1723 the French numbered 196; in 1752 there were 350 whites and 246 Negroes. Kaskaskia became the capital of the Illinois country with a French commandant subject to the governor of Louisiana. A French population of several thousand persons grew up in the rich American Bottoms along the east bank of the Mississippi extending for about 50 miles below St. Louis, including the villages of Cahokia (near the present East St. Louis), Ste. Genevieve, and Prairie du Rocher. A French fort was maintained at Kaskaskia from 1733 until 1755, when the garrison was moved to Fort de Chartres. After the Treaty of Paris (1763) the British took possession of Kaskaskia and the whole Illinois country. On July 4, 1778, GEORGE ROGERS CLARK captured the village, making it the headquarters of a county of Virginia. During the period of British rule and the first decade of American occupation the population of the village decreased, many of the French inhabitants fleeing to the Spanish settlement at St. Louis. After 1790 a few Americans replaced the French. In 1809 with the creation of Illinois Territory Kaskaskia became the territorial capital; in 1818 it became the first capital of Illinois, but two years later the state offices were moved to Vandalia. The village then lost population, and later the Mississippi began to encroach on the site until it was completely obliterated. The ruins of the old fort have, however, been left, and they now constitute the Fort Kaskaskia State Park. The new community of Kaskaskia is on Kaskaskia Island, the only section of Illinois lying west of the main branch of the Mississippi.

F. M.

KASKASKIA RIVER, Illinois, flows into the Mississippi River at Chester, after a course of 300 miles. It is navigable for 150 miles.

KASSA. See KOŠICE.

KASSAI. See KASAI RIVER.

KASSALA, town, Africa, in the Anglo-Egyptian Sudan, capital of Kassala Province, situated on a plain at the foot of the Ethiopian highlands, some 1,700 feet aboke sea level, on the bank of the Gasc (Mareb) River, 15 miles W of the Eritrean frontier,

250 miles E of Khartoum. Kassala has rail connections with Sennar, on the Blue Nile, and with Port Sudan, on the Red Sea 310 miles north-northeast. It is a trading center for animal hides and skins, gold dust, and ivory. Kassala was established in 1840 by the Egyptians as a fortified place for the protection of the newly acquired territory near the Ethiopian frontier. In 1885 it was captured by the Mahdi, from whom it was taken by an Italian force in 1894. Italy returned it to Egypt in 1897. During World War II the Italians again took the town in 1940, and in the following months the town exchanged hands several times between the British and Italians before the final defeat of the Italians in East Africa. Pop. (1938) 31,210.

KASSALA PROVINCE, Africa, the most fertile division of the Anglo-Egyptian Sudan, bordered on the E by the Red Sea, on the N by Egypt, on the W by the provinces of Berber and Khartoum, on the SW by Fung Province, and on the S and SE by Ethiopia and Eritrea; pop. (1948) 675,000. The coastal area is mountainous with some heights rising more than 7,000 feet. The principal river is the Atbara, which is fed from the Ethiopian highlands through the Gasc (Mareb). The province has a light rainfall, and cultivation largely depends upon the flooding of the Gasc and other rivers. The chief crops are white durra and cotton.

KASSEL, or **Cassel**, ancient **Castellum Cattorum**, city, Germany, in the state of Hessen, on the Fulda River, 124 miles NE of Frankfurt am Main. Before World War II, it was a combination of medieval and modern, with the old section lying along the river and the new on higher ground above it. The principal square, left in ruins by the war, was flanked by the former palace of the electors (1769 and 1821), and two museums; the most imposing buildings were those of the administration and the law courts (1876-80). The picture gallery contained a splendid collection including works by Rembrandt, Van Dyck, Franz Hals, Rubens, and others. The Academy of Fine Arts (1777) was housed in the palace where Jérôme, Napoleon's brother, lived as king of Westphalia. The Karlsaue contained the Orangery palace (18th century), largely destroyed during World War II. About three miles west is the castle of Wilhelmshöhe, surrounded by woods and fine gardens, where Napoleon III was detained (1870-71) after the battle of Sedan, and where William II and his family frequently spent part of the summer.

Originally a Roman settlement, Kassel in 913 was the site of a royal palace, becoming a town in 1189. After the 13th century it became the seat of the landgraves, and after 1685 owed much of its prosperity

Medieval Lions Castle in Kassel, Germany

EWING GALLOWAY

to the influx of refugee French Huguenots. During the Seven Years' War it was occupied by the French from 1757 to 1762, and from 1806 to 1813 was the residence of King Jerome of Westphalia. In 1867 it became the capital of Hesse-Nassau. During World War II Kassel was subjected to severe Allied air raids, which destroyed most of its industrial installations. The Henschel works, largest locomotive construction plant in Germany, is located in Kassel, and contributed the "Tiger Tank" to the Nazi war effort. In May, 1943, factories situated along the river front, were inundated by the unleashed water of the Eder Valley Dam, blasted by R.A.F. flyers. In normal times Kassel's manufactures include railroad cars, machinery, airplanes, automobiles, textiles, tobacco, china, and silver and gold wares. The city fell to the U.S. Third Army on April 2, 1945. Pop. (1946) 127,568.   K. E. H.

KASSERINE PASS, North Africa, NW Tunisia, the scene of an American setback in the Tunisia campaign, during World War II. Kasserine is one of four passes leading northwest toward Tebessa, Algeria, and Thala, Tunisia. At Kasserine the main road branches, one fork leading to Thala, the other to Tebessa. A battalion of the 1st Infantry Division was in position north of the pass blocking the Thala road, and an engineer unit on the south blocked the Tebessa road. Minefields had been laid and the position seemed strongly defended. Two other near-by

U.S. ARMY SIGNAL CORPS

U.S. Infantry Unit advances over Kasserine Pass

passes also were protected. The 1st Armored Division was concentrated. some distance to the rear ready to move up in any direction.

During the night of Feb. 19-20, 1943, German units infiltrated up gulches to high ground on both sides of Kasserine Pass into American forward positions. Some reached unoccupied ground from which they could fire down on antitank defenses below.

At daybreak on the 20th, German tanks and infantry moved against the pass and the defenders retreated. When a strong force then moved through the pass the situation became serious, for this threatened to force a general Allied withdrawal to a new defensive position in Algeria.

The Germans quickly pressed their advantage on the 20th and that night was one of apprehension and some confusion for the Allies, but also one of unflagging effort. British infantry and armor came up to assist and delay the enemy's advance until 6:00 P.M. of the 21st, by which time the infantry could establish defensive positions. An armored combat command, supported by 1st Division troops, moved toward Kasserine. The German attempt to break through was frustrated by the combined efforts of all forces, although fighting continued throughout the 22nd. Early on the 23rd the roads east from the pass were full of Axis vehicles headed away from the battle area. Despite a low ceiling, scores of Allied planes hammered the withdrawing enemy forces and ground pressure was also increased.

All available Allied forces pursued on the 25th, but the advance was difficult and slow through extensive minefields expertly planted. By late afternoon British and Americans had complete possession of Kasserine again and the heights on both sides. Contact with the enemy was lost on the 26th, for the

Germans successfully disengaged. See AFRICAN CAM-
PAIGN.   JOSEPH I. GREENE

KASSON, JOHN ADAM, 1822–1910, American diplomat, was born in Charlotte, Vt., and studied at the University of Vermont. After practicing law in Missouri and Iowa and becoming active in the new Republican party, he was first assistant post-master general of the United States (1861–62) and negotiated postal treaties in Europe (1867). He was a congressman (1863–67, 1873–77, 1881–84); minister to Austria-Hungary (1877–81) and to Germany (1884–85); special envoy to the Samoan International Conference (1893); special commissioner in negotiating several reciprocal trade agreements (1897–1901); and a member of the Joint High Commission which studied American-Canadian questions (1898). He wrote a history of the Monroe Doctrine (1904).

KASTAMONU, vilayet, N central Turkey, comprising parts of the ancient lands of Paphlagonia and Pontus; bounded on the N by the Black Sea, E by Sinope, SW by Corum, S by Cankiri, and W by Zonguldak; area 20,000 sq. mi.; pop. (1945) 384,109. The vilayet is entirely mountainous, lying in the western end of the Smali Anadolu Range; its highest peak is Ilgaz Daglari (8,415 ft.). Rivers of Kastamonu include the Daday, Gök, Devrik, Kocacay, Sovanli, and Kizil. Fertile valleys along these rivers produce cereal grains, cotton, tobacco, and tropical and semi-tropical fruits. Large flocks of sheep and goats are grazed on the mountain slopes. There are mineral springs and extensive forests are utilized for making one of its chief exports: charcoal. Industries of the vilayet include the manufacture of copper wares, cotton and woolen goods, and there are tanneries and lumber mills. The capital and chief city is Kastamonu; important Black Sea ports are Ayancik, Ineboli, Abana, and Cide. Exports are cereal grains, fruits, opium, raw cotton, wool, goat hair and mohair, and charcoal.

KASTAMONU, ancient **Castamon,** capital of Kastamonu Vilayet, N central Turkey, on the Gök River, a tributary of the Kizil; 76 miles SW of Sinope and 110 miles NE of Ankara (Angora). The town was once a Byzantine city, becoming Turkish in 1393. It is said to be the first Turkish town in which Kemal Atatürk cast aside his fez and donned the Western felt hat. It is situated in the midst of forest, which furnishes wood for two of its industries: the manufacture of charcoal and the lumber mills. The town also has manufactures of cotton cloth and goods, copper wares, leather goods, and it trades in grain, fruits, opium, raw cotton, wool, goat hair, mohair, and lumber. Ineboli is its port on the Black Sea. Pop. (1945) 12,565.

KÁSTRON, also **Khios,** or **Castro,** capital and chief E coast seaport of the Aegean island of Chios (Khíos). It has a good harbor. There are Hellenic remains; by many Kástron is claimed to be the birthplace of Homer. It once had a flourishing school of sculpture. The town was occupied during World War II by German troops. Pop. (1950 est.) 23,000.

KASUR, city, Pakistan, West Punjab Province, Lahore District, situated on the bank of the old bed of the Beas River, 34 miles SE of Lahore. It is a rail junction point and has an active trade in grain and cotton. There are manufactures of leather goods and cotton. Pathans from across the Indus settled here during the Mussulman period. Pop. (1941) 53,101.

KATAHDIN, MOUNT, the highest mountain in Maine, 5,370 feet above sea level, located in Piscataquis County, 77 miles NW of Bangor. It is a gray granite monolith rising from wooded and lake-dotted surroundings, and is included in the area of the Baxter State Park.

KATANGA, district, S central Africa, Belgian Congo, Elisabethville Province; pop. about 1,000,000 including 10,000 whites. The district is hilly, containing the lower reaches of the Mitumba Range; the main headwaters of the Congo River have their sources here. The Lualaba (upper course of the Congo) is navigable as far as Bukama, railway terminus. The chief town, Elisabethville (white pop. 5,494), is the capital of both the district and the province and was founded in 1910. Other towns of importance are Kolwezi, KAMBOVE, Jadotville, Luena, and CHINKOLOBWE.

The district, geographically, is a continuation of the Rhodesian plateau, and is suitable for agriculture. Stock is raised. The area is best known for its production of minerals. The world's largest deposits of copper are here, and other minerals found include tin, cobalt, coal, iron, gold, platinum, diamonds, uranium, and radium. Impetus to the mining operations of the district was given by the building of a railway in 1913, which connected with the main lines of the Union of South Africa. The railway has been extended since to give outlets for the district's mineral products through Beira in Mozambique (Portuguese East Africa), and through Benguela in Angola (Portuguese West Africa). The principal company exploiting the minerals of the district is the Union Minière du Haut Katanga, with headquarters at Elisabethville.

Katanga was secured for the then Congo Free State by the expedition of Captain W. D. Stairs, in 1891–92, whose entrance into the area forestalled Cecil Rhodes' plan to add the Katanga area to Great Britain's south African possessions. Atomic experiments during World War II gave a great impetus to the mining of uranium at Skinkolobwe, and American and English engineers were sent to the district to speed production. The uranium ore had been refined at Oolen, Belgium, before the war. Following Belgium's early defeat, the ore was shipped to Canada for processing. To facilitate progress, air fields were established at Bukama and at Elisabethville.   C.S.

KATHA DISTRICT, in Upper Burma, traversed by the Irrawaddy River; area 8,917 sq. mi.; pop. about 255,000. The district is made up of hilly country between the Chindwin and the Irrawaddy, and (east of the Irrawaddy) a part of the Shan plateau, on which was the famous ruby mine whose operations were stopped in 1927 after the flooding of the world markets with synthetic stones. Gold, copper, and lead are found but are not worked. Jade, soapstone sapphires, spinels, and other colored stones are worked by the natives. Salt is obtained from brine wells. The chief crop in the low sections is rice, and crops grown in the hills include tea, cotton, Sesamum, and hill rice. The people are about one-half Burmese, one-third Shans, and Saks (Lui), who are found only here. More than a third of the area is made up of the former state of Wuntho which was incorporated with Katha District in 1890 when its ruler was deposed by the British.

KATHERINE. See CATHERINE.

KATHIAWAR PENINSULA, W India, bounded on the N by the Rann of Cutch, on the E by Ahmedabad District (Bombay Province), and the Gulf of Cambay, and on the S and W by the Arabian Sea; area 20,911 sq. mi. Kathiawar was formerly divided into 188 feudatory states and chiefships; in 1948 these were merged to form the United State of Saurashtra. Cotton is the chief crop, and the peninsula is threaded with railway lines. There are many notable antiquities, including the Asoka stone inscription, Buddhist caves, and Jain temples. The Portuguese possession of Diu is in the extreme southern part of the peninsula.

KATKOFF, or **KATKOV, MIKHAIL NIKIFOROVICH,** 1820–87, Russian journalist, was born in Moscow. He studied in Moscow and Berlin and in 1845–50 was professor of philosophy at Moscow University. He founded (1856) the *Russki Viestnik,* to advocate reform; but, alarmed by an insurrection in Poland, he became the apostle of the Russification of the whole empire. Through this and the *Moscow Gazette,* which he acquired in 1863, he gained great influence throughout Russia.

KATMAI NATIONAL MONUMENT, SW Alaska, on the northern extremity of Alaska Peninsula and near Shelikof Strait. The monument, established in 1918, contains Mount Katmai, a volcano, and the Valley of Ten Thousand Smokes, a volcanic region of great beauty and scientific interest. Mount Katmai, about 7,500 feet high, exploded violently in 1912, producing a vast new crater three miles in width. During the eruption darkness extended for more than 100 miles and ashes, to a depth of from 6 to 10 feet, covered a large area. The valley became a great volcanic surface, shrouded in shifting clouds of steam ejected from millions of vividly colored fumaroles. Since this eruption Katmai has been inactive for the most part. Within the crater is a mile-long lake containing a small island. The fumaroles of the valley are nearly inactive. Much wild game lives on near-by wooded mountain slopes, and there is an abundance of fish in Naknek Lake which lies partially within the 2,697,590-acre park area. The park is so undeveloped and inaccessible that only well-outfitted expeditions can visit the region.

KATMANDU, city, capital of the independent state of Nepal, situated in an isolated, fertile valley of the central Himalaya midway between Tibet and India, at 27° 36′ N lat. and 85° 24′ E long., 75 miles N of the Indian frontier, on the Baghmati River. There is telephone communication with India, and an Indian railway extends north to Amlekganj, from which there is a motor road 27 miles north to Bhimphedi. A ropeway for the carriage of goods to the Katmandu Valley has been built north of Bhimphedi. The town has many temples, and some 5,000 brick houses of two to four stories, many decorated with picturesquely carved wooden balconies and projecting windows. The people are chiefly of Mongolian stock, but are primarily Hindu in religion. The town is said to have been founded in 723. It is the residence of the British envoy. Pop. about 109,000.

KATOWICE, German **Kattowitz,** city, Poland, capital of Slask Province (formerly Upper Silesia), six miles SE of Bytom (Beuthen). The center of one of Europe's foremost coal-producing areas, Katowice also has steel, iron, zinc, and chemical plants. It is an important railroad junction. The schools of the town include an Institute of Social Economy. After World War I Katowice with its area was the scene of bloodshed between Germans and Poles disputing over Upper Silesia. The area went to Poland by plebiscite in 1921. In World War II Katowice was held by the Germans until captured by the Soviet Army early in 1945. Pop. (1946) 128,290.

KATRINE, LOCH, border lake of W central Scotland, lying between Sterlingshire and SW Perthshire, five miles E of Loch Lomond. It is 364 feet above sea level and has a maximum depth of 468 feet. The lake is eight miles long with an average breadth of a mile and is drained by the Black Avon through Loch Vennachar into the River Teith. The

View of Loch Katrine and Ben Venue

Trossachs, a valley famous for its beauty, lies between the eastern end of Loch Katrine and Loch Achray, to the south. Rising above Loch Katrine to the southwest is Ben Venue (2,393 ft.) and to the northeast, Ben Ledi (2,875 ft.). Near the head of the loch at its northeastern end is Stronachlacher, a summer resort town. Since the middle of the 19th century Loch Katrine has furnished Glasgow with most of its water supply. The raising of the surface of the lake has submerged the "Silver Strand" and reduced the size of the "Ellen's Isle" of Scott's *Lady of the Lake.*

KATSINA, or **Katsena,** town and ancient state, British West Africa, N Nigeria, Northern Provinces, a part of Zaria Province, near the S edge of the Sahara Desert; area about 10,000 sq. mi. With origins dating back as far as the second century A.D., the state of Katsina gives evidence of having been rich and important. It was peopled by the Hausa race and attained its greatest affluence between the 14th and 18th centuries. British rule was accepted peaceably by the Hausa at the beginning of the 20th century, and although the state today has no political existence and its physical boundaries are not delineated on maps, more than a million Hausa recognize the emir as their leader. From 1907 to 1946 the Emir was Alhaji Muhammedu Diko, a progressive leader who helped modernize northern Nigeria; he was succeeded by his English-educated son, Nagago, in 1946.

The city of Katsina is 100 miles northwest of Kano and its ancient wall still survives and bears witness to the former importance of the city; the population of 100,000 in the 18th century has diminished to less than 10,000. Cattle raising and cotton growing are the main occupations of the people of the region.

KATSURA, TARO, PRINCE, 1847–1913, Japanese statesman and soldier, was born in Choshi. He was educated in a Prussian military school and entered the Japanese army in 1867. He served in the War of the Restoration, and became military attaché to the Japanese legation in Berlin, 1875-78. He was vice-minister of the war office for Japan, 1886–91, and was governor general of Formosa (1896); chief commandant Tokyo Bay defense (1896–98); war minister (1898–1900); and premier of Japan (1901–6). On the downfall of the Saionji ministry in 1909, he served as premier until 1911 and again in 1912–13.

KATTEGAT, or **Cattegat,** a large sound running NW and SE between E Denmark and SW Sweden, connecting with the Baltic Sea through the Great and Little Belts via the Öresund (a narrow sea passageway between Copenhagen and Halsingborg), and with the North Sea through the Skagerrak. The sound is 150 miles long, 88 miles at its widest, and has a depth of 13 fathoms and an area of 1,000 square miles.

KATTOWITZ. See Katowice.

KATYDID, a popular name for a group of large arboreal Grasshoppers. It is derived from the song of a male, which has been syllabled as "Katy-did, Katy-didn't" and is produced by the rasping of the wing covers. The females answer by a single sharp "chirp," produced by a sudden jerk of the wings. The katydids sing with great persistency in the autumn, sometimes both by day and by night, the day note differing perceptibly from the night note.

KATYN-BAZHI. See Belukha.

KAUAI ISLAND. See Hawaiian Islands.

KAUFFMANN, ANGELICA, 1741–1807, Swiss painter, was born in Coire. She studied under her father, an undistinguished artist, with whom she did some decorative work in a parish church and in the castle of Schwarzenburg. After painting a number of portraits, she went to Florence and devoted some time to the training of her voice, but eventually moved to London. Here she became a successful portrait painter and was elected a member of the Royal Academy. In 1781 she married a Viennese painter named Zucchi, and spent her last 25 years in Rome. The popularity of her work did not long survive her.

KAUFMAN, GEORGE S., 1889–   , American playwright and journalist, was born in Pittsburgh and educated at the public schools. After working as a stenographer, surveyor, and salesman, he obtained the post of columnist on the *Washington Times* in 1912. He later worked on the *New York Tribune* and *Evening Mail* and finally on the dramatic staff of the *New York Times*. Kaufman began his dramatic career with *Someone in the House* in 1918. Though tremendously prolific (from 1920 Kaufman has averaged some two plays a year), he has written only one play (*The Butter and Egg Man* in 1925) without one or more collaborators. He has been unusually successful as a writer of both comedy and musical comedy, and has specialized in mild political satire and drawing room themes. He was awarded the Pulitzer prize in drama for 1932 for *Of Thee I Sing* (in collaboration with Morrie Ryskind and George Gershwin) and again in 1937 for *You Can't Take It with You* (with Moss Hart). He and Hart also received the Cooper McGrue prize for *Once in a Lifetime* (1930). Other important Kaufman collaborations have been *Merton of the Movies* (1922), *The Royal Family* (1927), *Dinner at Eight* (1932), *I'd Rather be Right* (1937), *The Man Who Came to Dinner* (1939), *The Late George Apley* (1944), *Guys and Dolls* (1950), *The Small Hours* (1951).

KAUFMANN PEAK. See Lenin, Mount.

KAUKAUNA, city, E Wisconsin, in Outagamie County, on the Fox River, the North Western Railway and U.S. Highway 41; about 100 miles NW of Milwaukee. Kaukauna is a thriving market center for the surrounding agricultural and dairying region. The land site was bought from the Indians for two barrels of rum in 1793. Cheese, lumber, paper, and beer are the chief manufactures. Pop. (1950) 8,337.

KAUNAS, Russian **Kovno,** city, Lithuania (Lithuanian Soviet Socialist Republic), situated at the confluence of the Neman and the Viliya (Neris) rivers and on rail lines to Königsberg and Riga, 55 miles W of Vilnyus (Wilno), the capital. Kaunas is the chief industrial center of the republic. It has railroad shops, metalworking factories, textile mills, and chemical works. It is the seat of the national university founded in 1922 (in 1940 certain faculties of the university were transferred to Vilnyus to form the University of Vilnyus) and of the National Museum. Kaunas was an important medieval trade center and a stronghold against the Teutonic Knights. The city was brought under Russian control by Catherine the Great after the third partition of Poland in 1795. In 1812 Napoleon passed through Kaunas on his way to Moscow. During World War I the city suffered great damage being captured by the invading Germans in 1915. After the capture of Vilnyus, the traditional capital, by the Poles in 1919, Kaunas became the provisional capital of the newly-independent Lithuanian Republic. A period of rapid

A modern university building in Kaunas
LITHUANIAN CONSULATE

growth set in. Modern state and public buildings were erected and industry expanded. The traditional capital city was restored in 1939 and the following year Kaunas was occupied by the Soviet Union along with the rest of Lithuania. The city was held by the Germans from 1941 to 1944 during World War II. Pop. (1950 est.) 120,000.   A. M. K.

KAUNITZ, WENZEL ANTON, PRINCE VON, 1711–94, Austrian statesman and diplomat, was born in Vienna. After serving Maria Theresa on numerous diplomatic missions, he became ambassador to France (1750). In 1753 he was appointed chancellor of state and foreign minister. From then until his retirement in 1792 Kaunitz directed Austrian policy, serving Maria Theresa, Joseph II, and Leopold II. His was the leadership which shaped the coalition against Frederick the Great.

KAURI PINE, a large coniferous tree native to New Zealand. These trees grow to heights of 120 to 180 feet and are from 5 to 12 feet in diameter. The straight-grained wood, which is capable of attaining a high polish, is exported for use in shipmasts, deck boards, furniture, and paving blocks. These pines also yield a resin, kauri gum, used as an ingredient in fine varnishes for exterior and marine work.

KAUTSKY, KARL, 1854–1938, German Marxist, was born in Prague, and in 1874 joined the Social-Democratic party in Vienna, in time becoming one of its leaders as well as an outstanding theoretician of the Second International. He knew Marx and was associated with Engels in London, where in 1883 he founded *Die Neue Zeit,* a socialist organ, which later (1890–1917) he edited from Stuttgart. In a vigorous controversy, Kautsky attacked Bernstein's "revisionist" Marxism, and reaffirmed the necessity of revolution. Yet, as time went on, he was increasingly inclined to moderation and compromise. Thus in 1904 he tried to reconcile the Bolsheviks and the Mensheviks, the two factions of the Russian Social-Democrats.

In 1917 he was one of the founders and leaders of the Independent Social-Democratic party in Germany. He was against violence and for a peaceful development of socialism, and this determined his negative attitude toward both the German and Russian Communists. The Communists, in turn, attacked him. After World War I, Germany's first moderate Socialist government gave him access to the archives of the Imperial foreign office, and the result was the collection of documents edited by Kautsky and associates, published in English as *The Guilt of Wilhelm Hohenzollern* (1920). The Nazis, as they rose to power, hated him as much as the Communists always did. In 1938 the aged Kautsky fled first Vienna and then Prague before Hitler's troops; he died destitute in Amsterdam in October. His widow Louise was arrested by the Nazis in 1944, and perished in a concentration camp one month later.   Albert Parry

KAVÁLLA, or **Cavalla,** seaport, NE Greece, Macedonia, Kaválla Department, situated on the Gulf of Kaválla on the Aegean Sea. It is an ancient Byzantine town built in an amphitheater on the slopes of Mount Symbolon. The town has a good harbor. Surrounded by fields of a tobacco growing district, Kaválla is a center for trade in tobacco, a product exported in large quantities. The town formerly belonged to Turkey but was allotted to Greece at the close of the Balkan War of 1912–13. In 1941 it was occupied by Bulgaria, which surrendered Kaválla to Greek Partisans in 1945. The ancient Roman town of Neapolis, where St. Paul landed on his way to Philippi, is near here; there are numerous Roman ruins. Pop. (1950 est.) 50,000.

KAW RIVER. See Kansas River.

KAWASAKI, city, Japan, E central Honshu, in Kanagawa Prefecture. It is built partly on reclaimed land on the west shore of Tokyo Bay at the mouth of the Rokugo (Tama) River, and separates the cities of Tokyo and Yokohama. Kawasaki is one of the largest oil refining and storage depots in Japan. It has important radio and phonograph and sugar-refining industries. Kawasaki made a remarkable growth from a small place in the early 1900's; its population doubled between 1930 and 1940. About a third of the city was destroyed by American bombing in World War II. Pop. (1947 est.) 252,923.

KAY, JOHN, fl. 1733–64, English inventor, was born in Walmersley, near Bury. He invented the extended lathe, the fly-shuttle (1733), and the card-making engine, which revolutionized the staple manufactures of England.

KAYAK, the long, narrow, decked skin canoe of the Eskimos. The *kayik* (*caique*) of the Bosporus and the Yakut *kayik* are the same word, although applied to vessels of wood, some of them seven tons burden. The occupant of the Eskimo kayak wears a sealskin or sealgut coat, which, itself waterproof, fits over the sides of the circular hole after he is seated, making the canoe secure against the entrance of water. An average kayak measures: length, 17 ft. 9½ in.; greatest breadth, 1 ft. 11 in.; greatest girth, 4 ft. 8 in.; weight, 60 lbs.

KAYES, town, French West Africa, in Sudan Colony, at the head of navigation from the sea on the Senegal River, immediately below Felu Falls; 460 miles SE of St. Louis. It was once the capital of the former French colony of Senegambia-Niger. It is connected by rail with Dakar (385 mi. east), and with Bamako (250 mi. southeast). There are air flights from Kayes giving connection with the principal African air routes. Pop. (1945) 18,730.

KAYSERI, or **Kaisarieh,** vilayet, S central Turkey, bounded on the N by Yozgat, NE and E by Sivas, S by Maraş and Seyhan (Adana), W by Nigde and Kirsehir; area 5,369 sq. mi.; pop. (1945) 371,125. The surface of the vilayet is mountainous; its highest peak is Erciyas Dagi (Mount Argaeus). The chief rivers are the Kizil, Samanti, Delice, and Seyhan, and their small mountain tributaries. In the fertile valleys drained by these rivers, cotton and madder (much of which grows wild) are the chief crops, and there are large orchards producing semitropical fruits and wine and raisin grapes. Sheep, angora goats, and some cattle are grazed on the lower mountain slopes. The leading industries of the vilayet are cotton spinning, the manufacture of cotton textiles, carpet weaving, and aircraft construction. Exports are raw wool, raw cotton, angora wool, lambskins, hides, madder, gums, gallnuts for tanning, nitre, fresh and dried fruits, raisins, and wines. The region was once a part of the kingdom of Cappadocia and became a Roman province A.D. 18. The chief town is Kayseri.

KAYSERI, or **Kaisarieh,** ancient **Caesarea Mazaca,** city, E central Turkey, chief town of Kayseri Vilayet, S of the Kizil Irmak River, at the N foot of the peak of Erciyas (Mount Argaeus); 160 miles SE of Ankara (Angora). An important trade center since Roman times, Kayseri is the center of the Turkish cotton textiles industry and an aircraft factory is located here. It is surrounded by extensive orchards and vineyards, from which dried fruits and raisins are exported. Kayseri was once the residence of the kings of Cappadocia; as Caesarea Mazaca it became a Roman province A.D. 18. It is the seat of a Greek bishop, an Armenian archbishop, a Roman Catholic bishop, and headquarters for an American mission. Carpets, hides, raw cotton, and cotton goods are also exported. Pop. (1945) 57,698.

KAZAK, a powerful grouping of tribes living in the steppe lands of central Asia between European Russia and China. Their number is estimated at about 3,000,000, most of whom are seminomadic herdsmen. In spring and summer they move over an immense territory seeking pasturage for their herds and flocks. In winter they reside in settlements along the rivers and water courses.

The people are organized in clan groups made up of families tracing relationship through the male line. Above these units are phratries consisting of related clans, and these (formerly) were sometimes joined together into tribes. The latter were important units of the troops which under Genghis Khan and his successors surged toward Europe in the 12th and 13th centuries.   FAY-COOPER COLE

BIBLIOG.–M. C. and F.-C. Cole, *The Story of Man* (1937).

KAZAKH SOVIET SOCIALIST REPUBLIC, or **Kazakhstan,** one of the constituent republics of the U.S.S.R., situated in SW Soviet Asia; bounded on the NW, N and NE by the Russian Soviet Federated Socialist Republic, on the SE by the Chinese province of Sinkiang, and the Altai and Tien Shan (mountains), on the S by the Turkmen, the Uzbek, and the Kirgiz Soviet Socialist Republics, and on the W by the Caspian Sea; area 1,066,533 sq. mi.; pop. (1950 est.) 6,600,000, including 57 per cent KAZAK, 20 per cent Russian, and 14 per cent Ukrainian. Kazakhstan has a diversified topography, attributable to its immense size (it is the second largest republic in the U.S.S.R.). There are in the north the rolling and fertile Turgai steppes, in the south and southeast the snow-capped Altai and Tien Shan, and in the center, the hilly regions. A semidesert area, Kazakhstan contains the deserts of Kara Kum in the south and the Kyzyl Kum, east of the Aral Sea, both of which are extremely sandy and swept by hot winds. The mountain areas, much of which are covered with green pasturage, are ideally suited for the raising of great herds of livestock, a major factor in the Kazakhstan economy. In the foothills are fruitful oases, counterbalanced in other parts by extensive salt marshes and sun-scorched plains. The republic has 135,000,000 acres of arable land, and 430,000,000 acres of steppe and mountain pasture. The area is drained by the SYR DARYA, the IRTYSH, the ILI, the URAL, and other rivers, making possible the development of vast irrigation projects. The climate in the northern steppe region is cold temperate with cool summers, and in the desert regions it is warm temperate with hot summers. The administrative center of the Republic is ALMA ATA, the Hollywood of the Soviet Union. Other important cities are AKTYUBINSK, KUSTANAI, AKMOLINSK, KARAGANDA, SEMIPALATINSK, DZHAMBUL, PAVLODAR, GURYEV, PETROPAVLOVSK, and Ust-Kamenogorsk, all capitals of some of the republic's administrative regions.

Natural Resources. Kazakhstan is rich in natural resources. In the mountain and table land regions are large coal and oil reserves, and gold, nickel, copper, iron, tin, bauxite, chromites, phosphorites, rare metals, mineral salt, and large deposits of construction materials. The coal fields in the Karaganda Region are

Alma Ata, capital of Kazakh S.S.R.

SOVFOTO

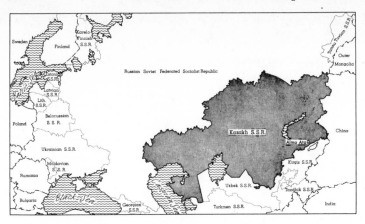

Location map of Kazakh Soviet Socialist Republic

The republic has four major railroads, the two most noted are the Chkalov (Orenburg)-Tashkent railroad and the Turkestan-Siberian railroad. New highways and railroads are being constructed under the fourth Five-Year Plan. Previous to and during World War II, Kazakhstan delivered military supplies to the Chinese government armies along the great trade routes leading into the interior of China.

History. The Kazakhs were first mentioned in the 11th century, and in the early 13th century came under the rule of Genghis Khan, the Mongol conqueror. Under the Khans the Kazakhs were organized into the Golden Horde, and subdivided into three divisions known as the Great Horde, the Middle Horde, and the Little Horde. The main divisions were further broken down into smaller units, the smallest being the aul, composed of 5 to 15 tents or "Kibitkas." The area fell piece-meal to the Russians between 1730 and 1819. Soviet power was established in Kazakhstan in 1920. In 1924 Kazakhstan became an autonomous republic of the Russian Soviet Federated Socialist Republic, and in 1936, it became a Union Republic of the Soviet Union.

S. W. X.

the third largest in the Soviet Union, outstripped in importance only by the DONETS and KUZNETSK basins. On the shores of Lake Balkash is the Kounrad copper mine, one of the largest in the Soviet Union. Near the Caspian Sea lies the great Emba oil field. A pipe line runs through the field to Orsk in the northwest and across Siberia in an easterly direction.

Economic Life. Food processing is one of the country's largest industries. There are sugar refineries, fruit and vegetable canning factories, creameries, and meat-packing plants. Other industries include chemical plants, steel mills, tanneries, tobacco plants, and consumers industries, as hosiery, footwear, and woolen and cotton fabric factories. Fishing has become an important industry, particularly along Lake Balkash, the Aral Sea, and the Caspian Coast. In 1939 the total area under cultivation in Kazakhstan was 17,-000,000 acres, an increase of 70 per cent over the 1914 level. Huge new tracts of steppe were brought under cultivation during World War II to compensate for the loss of the Ukraine and Belorussia (White Russia). In the northern steppe, Kazakhstan's largest crop area, wheat, millet, and barley are grown. In the irrigated sections of the south, the chief crops are cotton, rice, sugar beets, rubber-bearing plants (kok-sagyz, a kind of dandelion), and oil-giving legumes. The republic has numerous orchards, famed for their apples and other fruits. The breeding of livestock is one of Kazakhstan's greatest industries. With over 10 million head of cattle, the republic is one of the largest stock-raising areas in the U.S.S.R. Horses, Astrakhan sheep, goats, and, in the mountains, deer, are bred.

KAZAN, city and river port, U.S.S.R., in the Russian Soviet Federated Socialist Republic, capital of the Tatar Autonomous Soviet Socialist Republic, situated on the Volga River and at the junction of several railroads. Kazan was the capital of the Kazan Khanate conquered by Ivan the Terrible in 1552. Today it is a major industrial center with wharves extending more than three miles along the Volga. Its old soap works have been developed into a large chemical industry. Half the pelts taken by the enormous Soviet fur-trapping industry are dressed here at a single huge plant. Other industrial establishments include leather factories, wagon-building and engineering works, synthetic rubber plants, raw-film establishments, condensed milk enterprises, and one of the largest Soviet factories for the manufacture of typewriters with Latin characters used by the various national groups of Turkic origin. Asphalt is processed in the city from the local oily substances.

Kazan's historic buildings include the ancient

Kazakh farm workers cut melon crop for drying

SOVFOTO

Karaganda, center of Kazakh coal industry

SOVFOTO

Sky line of Kazan displays the spires and towers of many historic citadels and churches

Tatar Suyum Bek Tower, Czar Ivan's citadel, Tatar mosques, and 16th century Russian churches. The city is the seat of one of Russia's oldest and best universities, Kazan University, where Lenin and Leo Tolstoy studied. There are also more than 20 other colleges and research institutes using both the Russian and the Tatar languages. Pop. (1951 est.) 500,000.

KAZAN RIVER, Canada, Northwest Territories, rises in the SE corner of the Mackenzie District and flows in a circuitous route 450 miles NE through the barren Keewatin District to empty into Baker Lake.

KAZBEK, mountain peak (alt. 16,345 ft.) of the Caucasus Mountains, U.S.S.R., Russian Soviet Federated Socialist Republic, in the North Osetian Autonomous Soviet Socialist Republic. It is an extinct volcano, a double cone in shape, with steep slopes. It was scaled for the first time in 1868. The Georgian military highway runs through the Daryal Pass (7,805 ft.) at the eastern foot of the mountain. Its glacial formations give rise to the Terek and Argun rivers. The Kazbek has given rise to many primitive legends and has inspired much native poetry.

KAZEMBE. See CAZEMBE.

KAZERUN, town, SW Iran, Fars Province, 70 miles W of Shiraz; 96 miles NNE of Bushire. It is situated in the midst of a tobacco growing district near the Daryacheh Famur, a large salt lake. Other products grown near by are cotton, poppies for medicinal opium, and almonds. A fine quality of cotton stuffs is manufactured. From Kazerun there is road connection with Ahwaz, Bushire, and Shiraz, with which it has trade. Numerous ruins date from prehistoric times. Pop. about 15,000.

KAZVIN, also **Kasbin,** or **Qazvin,** city, NW Iran, built on a S slope of the Elburz Mountains; 90 miles NW of Teheran. The surrounding district grows grain. Kazvin was founded in the fourth century by Shapur II and there are ruins of a royal palace and mosque built by Haroun al Raschid in the eighth century. It was invaded in the 13th century by Mongols. Kazvin is a crossroads for caravan routes from Teheran, Pahlevi, Tabriz, and Hamadan and has a thriving trade in raw silk, rice, carpets, grain, fruits (fresh and dried), and fish (from Gilan). There are manufactures of cotton goods and ironware; the city is a carpet-weaving center. Pop. (1945 est.) 60,000.

KEA, a parrot-like bird of the family *Psittacidae.* The common name is derived from its call-note. It is native of New Zealand where it is also known as the kea parrot or mountain parrot, *Nestor productus.*

The feathers of the body are dull olive-green edged with black. The rump and undersides of the wings are a bright orange-red, and the tail is blue with a broad band of dark brown at its tip. Unlike the bills of most parrots the kea's bill is relatively long with the sharp upper mandible only slightly curved over the lower. See PARROT.   L. A. HAUSMAN

KEALAKEKUA BAY, Hawaiian Islands, on the W coast of Hawaii Island, noted as the scene of the murder on Feb. 14, 1779, of the famous explorer Captain James Cook.

KEAN, CHARLES JOHN, 1811–68, English actor, son of EDMUND KEAN, was born in Waterford, Ireland, and entered upon a stage career in opposition to his father's wishes. He became popular in melodramatic roles, and in 1830 toured the United States. In 1833 he appeared as Iago in support of his father as Othello, and also played Hamlet and other Shakespearean parts.

KEAN, EDMUND, 1787–1833, English actor, was born in London, son of a strolling actress. He made his first great success as Shylock at Drury Lane on Jan. 26, 1814. He met with equal success as Richard III, Othello, and Lear, and also played Hamlet and Macbeth with convincing power. At the close of his engagement at Drury Lane, he toured the United States, returning in 1825. Kean's tempestuous personal life, aggravated by his heavy alcoholic indulgence, had its effect upon his physical powers, and he collapsed while playing Othello in Covent Garden in 1833. He was a powerful and subtle tragedian endowed with magnificent voice and stage presence.

KEARNEY, DENIS, 1847–1907, American labor agitator, was born in Oakmont, county Cork, Ireland. Restrictions in the conduct of his business as a drayman impelled him in 1877 to begin a movement in San Francisco against Chinese labor and other grievances. Through his leadership in the Workingmen's party of California, which worked with the Granger party, some measures favorable to labor were accomplished. Kearney claimed his stress on the need for the exclusion of the Chinese had made Chinese immigration a national question.

KEARNEY, city, S Nebraska, county seat of Buffalo County, on the Platte River, the Burlington and the Union Pacific railroads and U.S. highways 30 and 83; about 185 miles SW of Omaha. Kearney is the trade center of a wheat and stock-raising region. It has alfalfa feed mills, foundries, and machine shops. Kearney was founded in 1872 and named for Gen. Stephen Watts Kearny; the name of the town was at first spelled without the second *e.* Seven miles southeast of the city Fort Kearny was built in 1846 for the protection of wagon-train travelers (see KEARNY, FORT). Pop. (1950) 12,115.

KEARNY, PHILIP, 1814–62, American army officer, was born in New York City. He studied for the law at Columbia College, but inheriting a million dollars in 1836, applied for a commission in his uncle STEPHEN W. KEARNY's 1st Dragoons, and served on the frontier (1837–39). In 1839 he was sent by the War Department to study cavalry techniques at Saumur, the French cavalry academy. He served with the French in Algiers (1840). Returning to America, he became aide de camp to General Macomb, and later to General Winfield Scott; he was brevetted major after losing an arm at Churubusco in the Mexican War. From 1859 to 1861 he served in Napoleon III's cavalry in Italy. At the beginning of the Civil War he commanded the 1st New Jersey brigade in the Army of the Potomac; he became commander of cavalry in the Army of the Potomac in May, 1862, and took an important role in cavalry strategy in the Peninsular Campaigns. Before he received a commission of major general dated July 4, 1862, he was shot while in enemy territory near Chantilly. General Winfield Scott once called Philip Kearny "a perfect soldier."

KEARNY, STEPHEN WATTS, 1794–1848, American army officer, was born in Newark, N.J. He left his studies at Columbia College to join the Army in the War of 1812 as first lieutenant in the 13th Infantry. He was captured at Queenstown Heights, but exchanged and promoted to captain in 1813. He remained in the Army; was brevetted major in 1823; became lieutenant colonel of the 1st Dragoons (1833) and colonel of Dragoons (1836). In 1842 he was appointed head of the Third Military Department; and in 1846 assumed command of the Army of the West and was promoted to brigadier general. He led the Army of the West across the country to New Mexico, occupied SANTA FE in August, 1846, and was military governor of New Mexico till September, writing a code of laws for the Territory of New Mexico. He served in California at San Pasqual (1846) and San Diego (1847); later he was brevetted major general for his bravery at San Pasqual. As military governor of California (March-June, 1847) Kearny was responsible for the arrest of FRÉMONT on charges of insubordination. He served for short periods in 1848 as military and civil governor of Vera Cruz and Mexico City, but retired to St. Louis after contracting a fatal tropical disease.

KEARNY, town, NE New Jersey, in Hudson County, at the head of Newark Bay between the Passaic and the Hackensack rivers, on the Central of New Jersey, the Delaware, Lackawanna, and Western, and the Erie railroads; opposite Newark and adjoining Harrison. Although Kearny is a residential suburb of both Newark and New York City, it is an important manufacturing center. First settled about 1765, Kearny was a part of Harrison until it was incorporated as a separate town in 1871 and named for Gen. Philip Kearny, Union officer in the Civil War. Linoleum, electrical parts, celluloid, aeronautical and marine appliances, railroad supplies, tools, and brushes are some of the major products. Pop. (1950) 39,952.

KEARNY, FORT, a military post on the Missouri River near the site of present Kearney, Nebr., established in 1846. The site was selected by Col. Stephen Kearny and Nathan Boone in 1838, but the construction was delayed eight years. But hardly had the blockhouse been completed when it was decided to abandon it for a new fort much farther west for the protection of· emigrants on the OREGON TRAIL. In June, 1848, Lt. Daniel P. Woodbury selected the new site on the Platte river near the present city of Kearney; the post was established as Fort Childs but was usually called new Fort Kearny. The fort had two corner blockhouses of heavy timber, powder and guard houses, a lookout, barracks, and officers' quarters. During the Civil War the regular troops were withdrawn and the fort was garrisoned by volunteers, including some former Confederate soldiers. When the railroad displaced the wagon train the usefulness of the fort was at an end, hence it was abandoned in 1871. The site is now the Fort Kearney (see KEARNEY) State Park with an area of 80 acres.

KEARNY, FORT PHIL, military post on the BOZEMAN TRAIL, located in northern Wyoming about 23 miles southeast of Sheridan. The fort was built in 1866 amid constant attacks from the Sioux. It was abandoned in 1868 under the terms of the treaty of Fort Laramie. The FETTERMAN MASSACRE occurred near this post.

KEARSARGE, a chain-armored, wooden corvette of the U.S. Navy, built at Portsmouth, N.H., and launched in September, 1861. She was placed under the command of Capt. John A. Winslow, who blockaded the *Florida* and the *Rappahannock* in the harbors of Brest and Calais respectively, and on June 19, 1864, off Cherbourg, France, sank the Confederate cruiser, *Alabama*. The *Kearsarge* was destroyed upon the Roncador reef in the Caribbean Sea, Feb. 2, 1894. See ALABAMA CLAIMS.

KEATS, JOHN, 1795–1821, English poet, was the son of a London hostler. While he was still a small child, his mother, a frail passionate creature whom the boy adored, was left a widow with four little children. When Keats was only 15, his mother died, and he turned to the dream world of books for escape and consolation. Here he rapidly discovered Homer's works, in translation, Virgil's *Aeneid*, Spenser, Shakespeare, the golden myths of Greece and the fairyland realms of medieval romance.

In 1810 the boy left school and for a time was apprenticed to a surgeon. Next, he studied medicine in a London hospital, passed his examinations, and set up as an apothecary. His mind and heart were set on poetry, however, and after a single nerve-wracking, albeit successful, experience in surgery, he abandoned all thoughts of a medical career. In 1817, *Poems by John Keats* appeared, to be ignored by the public and the critics as though it had never been published. His only literary champion at the time was Leigh Hunt, who himself was in temporary disfavor with the bigwigs in the world of letters.

In 1818 *Endymion*, a much more ambitious volume, appeared, to be assailed instantly by some of the cruelest criticism ever visited upon a young poet. Indeed, Shelley referred to these critics as "murderers," claiming that their savage attacks hastened Keats' death. Meanwhile, the poet's personal life was an unhappy one: his brother, Tom, died of tuberculosis; another brother, George, who had sailed for America, was having a difficult financial time; and his sister was away. London was lonely indeed. A year later (1819), Keats met Fanny Brawne, whom he loved with a hectic and consuming passion whose only safety-valve was his poetry. During this period he produced his finest work: "The Eve of Saint Agnes," "Ode to a Nightingale," "Ode on a Grecian Urn,"

STANFORD U. PRESS-EARLE V. WELLER
John Keats

"Ode to Autumn," and the immortal sonnets.

By this time, it was obvious to his friends that the passionate young poet was ill with the same dread disease that had taken his mother and brother. He was persuaded to go to Italy, and there he died in February, 1821, in the arms of Joseph Severn.

Before he left for Italy, his third and last volume, *Lamia, Isabella, The Eve of Saint Agnes and Other Poems* appeared, but he never had a chance to enjoy the favorable response which the book received, for by the time his contemporaries began to regard his poems seriously, he was already too ill to take notice.

Keats said of himself: "I was never afraid of failure; for I would sooner fail than not be among the greatest." Poetry was his very life's blood. He poured himself, hot and throbbing, into every poem he wrote. His poetry preached by carrying its own beauty, alive, like a sacred flame in the vessel of the senses, into the heart. He summed up his own credo of poetic faith: "Beauty is truth, truth beauty." His poetry was beginning to deepen with the dark and tragic implications of our common humanity when he was cut off in the full flush of his youth.

More than any other poet of his time, Keats restored that faith in the pure enchantment of poetry which had passed out of the English world with the passing of Chaucer, Spenser, Marlowe, and Shakespeare. What he wrote, in his brief 25 years, remains unsurpassed·for sheer felicity and natural magic.

JOSEPH AUSLANDER

BIBLIOG.–Sir Sidney Colvin, *John Keats: his Life and Poetry* (1917); Amy Lowell, *John Keats* (1925); J. M. Murry, *Studies in Keats* (1930); R. J. Caldwell, *John Keats' Fancy* (1945); H. E. Rollins, ed., *Keats' Circle* (1948).

KEBLE, JOHN, 1792–1866, English clergyman and poet. He was educated at Oxford, where he was tutor from 1818 to 1823. In 1831 he was called to the professorship of poetry at Oxford and for 10 years served in that capacity. Keble's first poetical work, *The Christian Year*, appeared anonymously in 1827. Its excellence was recognized by critics, and its influence was marked. His *Lyra Innocentium* (1846) is considered by many the finest fruit of his genius. Among his other contributions to literature are his edition of *Hooker's Works* (1836); *Life of Bishop Wilson*

(1836); a metrical version of the *Psalms—The Oxford Psalter* (1839).

Keble's name is associated with the OXFORD MOVEMENT. Newman dated the movement from Keble's sermon on "National Apostasy" preached at Oxford in 1833, and four of the famous *Tracts for the Times* were Keble's. The conversion of Newman to Catholicism in 1845 saddened him, but he gave himself to the maintenance of the High Anglican principles which he held so firmly. Keble College, Oxford, opened in 1869, was erected in the "poet's honor and to perpetuate his teaching."

BIBLIOG.–E. F. L. W. Irwin, *John Keble* (1932); K. Ingram, *John Keble* (1933).

KECSKEMÉT, city, S central Hungary, 65 miles SE of Budapest by rail. Essentially a farming town, its growth was due to the gathering of people for defense purposes. It is the main market for the surrounding plains, whose produce includes corn, tobacco, and fruit, especially apples and apricots. Industry such as leather working and milling is located here, and there is also trade in cattle. Pop. (1949 est.) 87,500.

KEDAH, Malayan sultanate, in the Malayan Federation, on the W coast of the Malay Peninsula, bounded to the N by the small state of Perlis, to the NE by Siam, to the E by Kelantan, to the S by Perak, to the SW by Province Wellesley, and to the W for 120 miles by the Strait of Malacca; area 3,660 sq. mi.; pop. (1941 est.) 520,719, including 337,456 Malays, 107,223 Chinese. The territory includes the group of islands (largest one, Lang Kawi) adjacent to the shore in the north. Except in the south the littoral is swampy, rising inland to a fertile plain and hilly ground in the east. There are a number of small rivers, the most important of which is Sungai Kedah, and the state is traversed by the western branch of the Singapore-Bangkok railway. In 1941 there were 174 miles of canals and 423 miles of paved roads. The chief industries are rice and rubber cultivation. There are coconuts, tapioca, betel nut, and fruit plantations. The main exports are rubber, rice, tapioca, and tin ore. Alor Star (pop. 25,000), 10 miles inland on the Kedah River, is the capital. A former tributary of Siam, Kedah came under British suzerainty in 1909. Formerly one of the unfederated states of Malaya under British suzerainty, Kedah in 1946 became a member state of the British controlled Malay Union, which in 1948 gave way to the Malayan Federation. ADRIAN TROY

KEELBOAT. Significant in the transportation history of the American West was the keelboat, a light shallow boat 40 to 80 feet long and 7 to 10 feet across with a cargo box or a passenger cabin at a central position. A heavy barge type of keelboat was used on the deeper streams and rivers. Since its primary importance was to navigate upstream where flatboats were helpless, the keelboat was equipped with both poles and oars, sometimes aided by square sails, and driven by sweating crewmen bearing down against the current at an average rate of 15 miles daily. A round trip between New Orleans and Louisville required three or four months upstream and four weeks downstream.

The keelboat era on the Ohio and Mississippi rivers was 1795–1840, with some two or three thousand men engaged in this traffic by 1815. In western history, it meant a wild, colorful phase of frontier life, for the crewmen were often former Indian fighters, border toughs, and half-savage Creoles from Canada. Most famous of all was the boastful, often vicious, and adventurous MIKE FINK, a former Indian fighter, whose crowded life became an important part of American folklore. The keelboatmen were noted for their wild adventures ranging from pitched battles against offending townsmen along the river shores to conflicts against scheming river pirates; their dancing, fiddling, tall tales, racing, drinking, gambling, and wrestling matches marked them off as a distinct group of frontiersmen. The keelboat served to tie the South and the Old Northwest commercially and to some extent culturally. With the coming of the steamboat, which solved the basic difficulties of upstream travel, the keelboat was forced into the smaller streams and finally eliminated as a major factor in river navigation. H. WISH

BIBLIOG.–Walter Blair and Franklin J. Meine, *Mike Fink, King of Mississippi Keelboatmen* (1933); Leland D. Baldwin, *The Keelboat Age on Western Waters* (1941).

KEELER, WILLIAM HENRY, known as **Wee Willie,** 1872–1923, American baseball player, member of Baseball Hall of Fame, was born in Brooklyn, N.Y. An outfielder for the New York Giants, Baltimore Orioles, Brooklyn Superbas, and New York Highlanders (1892–1910), he was regarded as the game's greatest place hitter and bunter. Known for his motto, "Hit 'em where they ain't," he was National League batting champion in 1897 and 1898. His lifetime batting average was .345.

KEELEY, LESLIE E., 1832–1900, American physician, was born in St. Lawrence County, N.Y., and studied at Rush Medical College in Chicago. After serving as assistant surgeon in the Civil War, he practiced medicine at Dwight, Ill., where, about 1890, he opened a sanitarium for curing drink and drug addicts, later known as the Leslie E. Keeley Company. Keeley, author of *The Non-Heredity of Inebriety* (1896) claimed that the Keeley Cure was achieved by using a compound containing bichloride of gold.

KEELING ISLANDS. See COCOS ISLANDS.

KEELUNG. See KIRUN.

KEELY MOTOR, a well-known mechanical fraud based on the invention of one John W. Keely (1837–1898), of Philadelphia, who claimed that his device for generating power would revolutionize the science of mechanics and enable all mechanical operations to be carried on at greatly reduced expense. Although a stock company was formed to exploit the scheme, and its capital largely subscribed for, the nature of the motor was kept secret, and it was not until after the inventor's death that the machinery was examined in detail and it was discovered that the power which was generated in demonstrations of the motor came from compressed air in a mechanism carefully concealed. The invention was before the public from about 1874 until Keely's death in 1898.

KEENE, CHARLES SAMUEL, 1823–91, English humorous artist, was born in Hornsey, Middlesex. His first drawings were made for the *Illustrated London News*, but from 1851 he was most closely associated with *Punch*, holding a foremost place among British artists in black and white. He illustrated Douglas Jerrold's *Curtain Lectures* and Charles Reade's *The Cloister and the Hearth* (in *Once a Week*). A collection of his drawings, entitled *Our People*, appeared in 1881.

KEENE, FOXHALL PARKER, 1866–1941, American polo player, was born in San Francisco, Calif., and graduated from Harvard University. The outstanding player in the early history of polo in the United States, Keene was the country's top ranking player from 1888 to 1918; rated at 10 goals 14 years

F. J. MEINE

A keelboat on the Mississippi River

and at nine goals 16 years, he was a member of several international teams.

KEENE, LAURA, real name **Mary Moss,** c. 1826–73, American actress, was born in Chelsea, London, England. She scored her first success in London, in 1851, as Pauline in *The Lady of Lyons*. She soon became a favorite in the United States, and established her own theater in New York City, where, in 1858, she produced *Our American Cousin*. It was at a performance of this play by her company, at Ford's Theater, Washington, that Lincoln was assassinated.

KEENE, city, SW New Hampshire, county seat of Cheshire County, on the Ashuelot River and the Boston and Maine Railroad, 50 miles SW of Concord. Keene is a thriving market center for the surrounding agricultural and resort region. The first permanent settlement was made here in 1750. Keene was named for Sir Benjamin Keene, a prominent British diplomat of that time. The city is the seat of the Keene State Normal School, one of the largest in New England. Pine timber and feldspar and mica quarries are found in the vicinity of Keene, and the city has manufactures of chairs, shoes, toys, drilling machinery, and fabrics. Pop. (1950) 15,638.

KEENE TEACHERS COLLEGE. See COLLEGES.

KEENE'S CEMENT. See CEMENT; GYPSUM.

KEEP. See CASTLE.

KEEWATIN. See NORTHWEST TERRITORIES.

KEF, or **Le Kef,** town, Tunisia, 95 miles by rail SW of Tunis, built on the site of the ancient *Sicca Veneria* of the Romans. Lying at the juncture of several trade routes, Kef has regained a part of its former importance. It was a famous Carthaginian city, and in addition to many Roman ruins in the neighborhood an ancient Christian basilica has been found by French archaeologists. Pop. about 9,000.

KEFAUVER, CAREY ESTES, 1903–   , American official, born in Madisonville, Tenn., studied at Tennessee and Yale universities, and began to practice law in Chattanooga in 1927. As a congressman (1939–49), he advocated streamlining government and wrote *Twentieth Century Congress* (with J. Levin, 1947). Becoming U.S. Senator from Tennessee in 1949, he headed (1950–51) the Senate committee investigating organized crime and wrote *Crime in America* (1951). See TELEVISION.

KEFIR. See MILK, *Fermented Milks.*

KEFLAVIK, seaport, Iceland, situated on the island's SW peninsula, 20 miles across the bay and some 30 miles by highway from Reykjavik, the capital. It is a resort of fishing boats from other parts of the island during the cod fishing season. The surrounding area is barren, except for some fringing grazing land, and is made up of lava rock. Harbor and dock facilities were enlarged in 1944, and during World War II an American flying field was built here, a stepping stone on the airplane ferry service to Britain. Pop. (1946 est.) 1,500.

KEI ISLANDS. See KAI ISLANDS.

KEIGHLEY, municipal borough, NE England, Yorkshire, in the West Riding, on the Aire River; 17 miles NW of Leeds. It has textile factories, iron foundries, and manufactures of sewing and washing machines and tools. It is linked by canal to Hull and Liverpool, where the manufactured goods of Keighley are shipped for marketing. Pop. (1950 est.) 56,690.

KEIJO. See SEOUL.

KEITEL, WILHELM, 1882–1946, German field marshal, was born in Helmscherode. He entered the army (1901) and was a captain on the general staff during World War I. He remained in the army, became a major general in 1934, and chief of the administration department in the War Ministry (1935–38). Named chief of the supreme command (1938) and a member of the cabinet (1939), he accompanied Hitler on many important missions. Keitel made the military arrangements for the seizure of Austria, Czechoslovakia, and Poland; he directed the campaigns against Norway, the Netherlands, Belgium, and France. After reading the armistice terms to the French at Compiègne, he became a field marshal (1940). He was reported to have retired because of his health when the 1944 bomb plot against Hitler failed; two weeks later, Hitler named him to a "court of honor" to determine the loyalty of all field marshals and generals. He signed the unconditional surrender of Germany in Berlin (1945) as chief of the supreme command. Declared guilty on four counts by the United Nations War Crime Commission in 1946, he was hanged.

KEITH, JAMES FRANCIS EDWARD, known as **Marshal Keith,** 1696–1758, Scottish nobleman, second son of William, ninth Earl Marischal, was born in Inverugie Castle, near Peterhead, Scotland. He took part in Mar's rebellion at Sheriffmuir (1715) and in the expedition which failed at Glenshiel (1719). Then escaping to the Continent, he served for nine years in the Spanish army, but in 1728 transferred his services to Russia. In 1747 he took service under Frederick the Great of Prussia, who created him field marshal, and under whom he served in the Seven Years' War, falling at Hochkirch (1758). His military career in the Prussian army is described in Carlyle's *Frederick the Great*, and in the anonymous *Memoir of Marshall Keith* (1869).

KEKULÉ, FRIEDRICH AUGUST, 1829–96, German chemist, was born in Darmstadt. In 1856 he became lecturer at Heidelberg, in 1858 professor of chemistry at Ghent, and in 1865 professor of chemistry at Bonn, where he remained till his death. Kekulé's work was almost entirely on organic chemistry, centering mainly on the constitution of carbon compounds, in particular of benzene. His theories in this respect were the foundation of the most far-reaching advances and discoveries. Kekulé was also a great teacher, and wrote an unfinished but model *Lehrbuch der organaschen Chemie* (3 vols. 1861–67).

KELANTAN, Malayan sultanate under British protection, one of the states of the Malayan Federation, on the W coast of the Malay Peninsula; bounded on the N and NE by the China Sea, on the E by Trengganu. on the S by Penhang, on the W by Perak, on the NW by Kedah and Siam; area 5,720 sq. mi.; pop. (1940 est.) 390,332, including 338,922 Malays and 30,913 Chinese. The northern half is a cultivated plain; the southern one is hilly (Bukit Temiang, 4,082 ft.). The climate is mild. There is a navigable river, the Kelantan, 120 miles long, and a network of creeks. The eastern branch of the railroad from Singapore crosses the country. The main industry is rice cultivation, and there is some silk weaving and a good deal of fishing and cattle-breeding. Rubber, coconuts, betel nuts, bamboo, pepper, and sugar cane are produced. There is little mining but gold, tin, iron, and galena are found. The chief exports are rubber, iron ore, copra, cattle, and areca nuts. Kota Bharu (pop. 14,843), terminal of both Siamese and Malay railroads, is the capital. Kelantan came under British suzerainty July 15, 1909. Before that it had been a dominion of Siam. During World War I the sultan revolted against British rule. Previously an unfederated state, the British in 1946 made it one of the newly created states of the Malayan Union, which in 1948 gave way to the Malayan Federation. ADRIAN TROY

KELAT. See KALAT.

KELLER, GOTTFRIED, 1819–90, Swiss novelist, was born in Glattfelden, near Zürich. He studied art, but the success of a volume of poems (1846) gave him a definite bent toward literature. His major work, *The Green Henry*, was a vast, autobiographical novel, whose hero, a civil servant, dedicated himself to the promotion of a new, Christian humanism and of a democratic spirit that would be at once militant and amicable. First published in 1854, the book was rewritten in 1879 to include new chapters in the hero's life. It is unquestionably the greatest Swiss novel and has been acclaimed as one of the masterpieces of modern European literature. Among his other works are *Seldwyla Folks* (2 vols. 1856–74), a collection of humorous and imaginative sketches, and *Zürich Novelettes* (1877), which deals with specific problems of the philosophy embodied in *The Green Henry*. Keller was Staatsschreiber, or cantonal secretary, at Zürich from 1861 to 1876. His collected works were issued in 10 volumes (1889–1904).

BIBLIOG.–E. Ackerknecht, *Gottfried Keller* (1939).

KELLER, HELEN ADAMS, 1880– , American writer, was born in Tuscumbia, Ala. She became totally deaf and blind at 19 months, after an attack of brain congestion.

ERICH KASTAN

Helen Keller

In 1887, through the intervention of Alexander Graham Bell, she became the pupil of Anne Sullivan (later Mrs. John Macy), who was sent from the Perkins Institute. She rapidly learned a manual deaf-and-dumb language and the Braille alphabet; in 1890 she learned to speak articulately from Sarah Fuller of the Horace Mann School in Boston. Miss Keller attended Radcliffe College (1900–1904), with Miss Sullivan, her constant companion, to take notes for her, and graduated with honors. She served for a time on the Massachusetts Commission for the Blind; started a $2,000,000 Helen Keller Endowment Fund for the American Foundation for the Blind; lectured in America, Europe, and Japan, and in World War II helped blinded veterans. In 1951 she made a tour of Africa to help handicapped Negroes. Her writings include: *The Story of My Life* (1902); *Optimism, an Essay* (1903); *The World I Live In* (1908); *Out of the Dark* (1913); *Midstream—My Later Life* (1930); *Peace at Eventide* (1932); *Helen Keller in Scotland* (1933); *Helen Keller's Journal* (1938); *Let Us Have Faith* (1940). See MACY, ANNE SULLIVAN. C. A.

KELLERMANN, FRANÇOIS CHRISTOPHE, DUKE DE VALMY, 1735–1820, French general, was born in Strasbourg. He entered the French army in 1752, served through the Seven Years' War and the Polish campaign of 1771, and in 1785 became maréchal-de-camp. He was an ardent supporter of the Revolution, was general of the army in Alsace, and in 1792, by his stubborn defense of Valmy, demoralized the Prussian forces. He commanded the army in the Alps and in Italy, and in 1804 Napoleon made him marshal of France; in 1809 he became duke of Valmy; and in 1812 he was in command of the Rhenish reserves. He voted for Napoleon's deposition and at the Restoration embraced the Bourbon cause.

KELLEY, EDGAR STILLMAN, 1857–1944, American composer and author, was born in Sparta, Wis., and received his musical education in Chicago and in Stuttgart (1874–80). In 1896–99 he was instructor in composition in the New York College of Music; in 1901–2 acting professor of music at Yale; and in 1902–10 a teacher and conductor in Berlin, Germany. In 1910 he became associated with the Cincinnati Conservatory. He was a member of the National Institute of Arts and Letters. Among his chief musical compositions are incidental music for *Macbeth, Ben-Hur* and *Prometheus Unbound; Puritania* (opera); *Symphony, New England; Alice in Wonderland; Pilgrim's Progress*. His symphonic poem *The Pit and the Pendulum* was performed at the Cincinnati May Festival in 1925. He wrote *Chopin the Composer* and *History-of Musical Instruments*.

KELLEY, HALL JACKSON, 1790–1874, American promoter of Oregon settlement, was born in Northwood, N.H., attended Middlebury College,

and taught in the Boston public schools (1818–23). Organizing the American Society for Encouraging the Settlement of the Oregon Territory, he planned to lead a colonizing expedition there in 1832. When this failed, he went alone to California where he met the trader Ewing Young, who accompanied him to Oregon (1834). He returned to Boston (1836) and became a hermit. A fanatic, he exerted influence in favor of American settlement of Oregon.

KELLEY, OLIVER HUDSON, 1826–1913, American agricultural organizer, was born and educated in Boston and became a Minnesota frontier farmer in 1849. He joined the Bureau of Agriculture in 1864, and was sent to the West and South to make a survey of agricultural conditions. On tour he conceived the idea of a social and fraternal organization of American farmers, which he called the National Grange of the Patrons of Husbandry. In 1867 Kelley and six others secured a charter for the Grange, and Kelley became its first secretary, retiring in 1878. He wrote *Origins and Progress of the Order of the Patrons of Husbandry* (1875). See GRANGE, THE.

KELLEY, WILLIAM DARRAH, known as **Pig Iron Kelley,** 1814–90, American politician who supported the Pennsylvania pig-iron interests, was born in Philadelphia, Pa. He became a jeweler by trade, but in 1840 entered the law office of James Page, and in 1846 was appointed judge of the Philadelphia Court of Common Pleas. He left the Democratic party in 1856 for antislavery and protectionist reasons, joined the Republicans, and in 1860 was elected to Congress, where he served for 20 years. He was prominently associated with protectionist legislation.

KELLGREN, JOHAN HENRIK, 1751–95, Swedish poet and critic, was born in Floby, West Gothland, and was educated at Abo University, where he became a lecturer in 1774. In 1778, with his friend Karl Peter Lenngren, he founded the periodical *Stockholmsposten*, which became an influential medium of philosophical and literary discussion. Gustavus III made the poet his librarian in 1780 and his private secretary in 1785. Gustavus and Kellgren collaborated in the operas *Gustaf Vasa, Aeneas i Kartago, Gustaf Adolf*, and *Drottning Kristina*, the King providing the plots and Kellgren the lyrics. Kellgren's style is still regarded as classical, and his satires, especially *Mina Löjen*, are among the best in Swedish literature. His reputation as a critic has declined, but during his lifetime he was regarded as a sort of Scandinavian Voltaire.

KELLOGG, EDWARD, 1790–1858, American economist, was born in Norwalk, Conn. Forced to suspend business in the financial panic of 1837, Kellogg denounced the evils of the existing financial system and recommended a revolutionary new system. His theories were expressed in *Currency: the Evil and the Remedy* (1844), revised in 1849 as *Labor and Other Capital*, and pamphletized by his daughter in 1883 as *A New Monetary System*. Kellogg's theories influenced several political groups, most notably the Greenbackers.

KELLOGG, FRANK BILLINGS, 1856–1937, American lawyer and public official, was born in Potsdam, N.Y. His family moved to Minnesota when he was a small boy and there he was educated. He was admitted to the bar in 1877 and for three years served as city attorney of Rochester, Minn. In 1887 he moved to St. Paul, where he formed a law partnership with C. K. Davis and C. A. Severance. He was special counsel for the U.S. government in a number of important cases; was U.S. senator from Minnesota (1917–23), a delegate to the Pan-American congress in Chile (1923), and ambassador to Great Britain (1923–24). He succeeded Charles E. Hughes as secretary of state (1925–29). His term of office was memorable for the aggressive stand which he took on the protection of American life and property in Mexico, in favoring intervention in Nicaragua, and in attempting to solve the Tacna-Arica dispute between Chile and Peru. His greatest achievement was the drawing up, with Aristide Briand of France, of the KELLOGG-BRIAND PACT; this multilateral treaty for the renunciation of war was signed in Paris in 1928 by 15 leading nations. Kellogg was awarded the 1929 Nobel peace prize and served as a judge of the Permanent Court of International Justice (1930–35).

KELLOGG, city, NW Idaho, in Shoshone County; on the Union Pacific Railroad and U.S. Highway 10, about 73 miles E of Spokane, Wash., in an important lead and zinc mining area. Established in 1893 as Milo, the city was renamed the following year in honor of the discoverer of Bunker Hill Mine. Incorporated in 1907, the city is the trading and supply center of a large mining and lumbering region. Pop. (1950) 4,913.

KELLOGG-BRIAND PACT, or Pact of Paris, was signed on Aug. 27, 1928, by 15 nations, and ultimately by another 48. The treaty followed considerable diplomatic negotiation. ARISTIDE BRIAND, French foreign minister, in 1927 proposed a treaty outlawing war between France and the United States. U.S. Secretary of State FRANK B. KELLOGG responded with a suggestion for a pact of this sort that would be open to all nations. Article I of the resulting treaty provides that the contracting parties "condemn recourse to war for the solution of international controversies, and renounce it as an instrument of national policy in their relations with one another." Article II provides that settlement of disputes among the parties "shall never be sought except by pacific means." The pact contains no provision for enforcement, and, as was made clear during the negotiations, does not prevent recourse to war in self-defense. The tribunal which sentenced the Nazi war criminals at Nuremberg in 1946 held that the treaty (of which Germany was a signatory) had outlawed war and that therefore "aggressive war" was illegal.   IRVING FRYER

BIBLIOG.–D. H. Miller, *Peace Pact of Paris* (1928); J. T. Shotwell, *War as an Instrument of National Policy* (1929); J. E. Stoner, *S. O. Levinson and the Pact of Paris* (1943).

KELLOGG FOUNDATION, a philanthropic foundation established in 1930 by W. K. Kellogg for the purpose of "receiving and administering funds for the promotion of the health, education, and welfare of mankind, but principally of children and youth, without regard to sex, race, creed, or nationality, in whatever manner the Board of Trustees may decide." Prior to World War II the foundation carried out most of its activities within the state of Michigan. Since then, however, expenditures for national programs have far exceeded state activities, and substantial international programs have been established. The Kellogg Foundation functions through the following six divisions: General Education, Medical Education, Public Health, Nursing Education, Hospitals, and Dental Education. Grants are made for the development and strengthening of graduate and postgraduate courses of professional schools. The foundation spends from two to four million dollars annually, nationally and internationally. Headquarters are at Battle Creek, Mich.

KELLS, EDMUND C., 1856–1928, American dentist, the founder of dental roentgenology (x-ray technique). He was born in New Orleans, La., and studied at the New York Dental College. He started his dental practice in New Orleans, where he lived until his death. Soon after the discovery of the x-ray (1895), Kells began the practical application of the x-ray as a means of revealing anatomical and pathological conditions of the teeth and jawbones, which heretofore had been hidden from view. His studies in this field included the development of stereoscopic radiography. In his zeal to develop the beneficial uses of the x-ray, Kells did not realize the danger attached to excessive exposures. As a result, its destructive effects caused his death.

                              FLORIS VAN MINDEN, D.D.S.

KELLS, market town and urban district, E Eire, in Leinster Province, County Heath, on the Blackwater River; 10 miles NW of Navan. It contains interesting antiquities such as the remains of an ancient monastery where the Book of Kells was found, a round tower, St. Columba's house, and three or four Roman crosses. Pop. about 2,500.

KELLY, CHARLES E., nicknamed **Commando Kelly,** 1921– , American army hero of World War II, was born in Pittsburgh, Pa. A technical sergeant in the 36th (Texas) Division of the Fifth Army, "Commando" Kelly received the first Congressional Medal of Honor awarded in Italy (Mar. 11, 1944) for his bravery at Altavilla, where on one day, Sept. 23, 1943, he volunteered for repeated patrols and is credited with killing 40 Germans. For additional heroism at the Rapido River, Cassino (Jan. 21–22, 1944), he received the Silver Star.

KELLY, COLIN PURDIE, 1915–41, first American flying hero of World War II, was born in Madison, Fla. Graduating from West Point in 1937, he was commissioned a second lieutenant in the infantry. Later he was transferred to the Army Air Forces, becoming a captain in 1940. On Dec. 10, 1941, his B-17 dropped three bombs on the Japanese heavy cruiser *Ashigara* off Aparri, Luzon, P.I. Attacked by four Japanese fighter planes, he crashed on Mount Arayat, Luzon; six of his men bailed out safely. Kelly was awarded the Distinguished Service Cross posthumously. His body, buried anonymously in U.S. Military Cemetery No. 1 in Manila, was identified in 1946.

KELLY, GEORGE, 1887– , American playwright, was born in Philadelphia. The brother of Walter Kelly, famous for his vaudeville sketch "Virginia Judge," he had little formal education and early began an acting career, playing in his own one-act sketches. His most successful plays were *The Show-Off* (1942, revived in 1950), a portrait of an egoist, and *Craig's Wife* (1925, Pulitzer prize), a character study of a shrewish, selfish woman.

KELLY, HOWARD ATWOOD, 1858–1943, American surgeon, was born in Camden, N.J., and studied at the University of Pennsylvania where he became associate professor of obstetrics (1888–89). On the founding of the Johns Hopkins Hospital (1889) and of the Johns Hopkins Medical School (1893) he assumed the chair of gynecology and obstetrics and until his retirement (1919) helped revolutionize the study and practice of these specialties. At the Howard A. Kelly Hospital, which he founded in 1892, he invented new instruments for the successful performance of abdominal operations and was one of the first to use radium in the treatment of cancer. He was also gynecological surgeon to the Johns Hopkins Hospital (1899–1919) and consulting gynecologist after 1919. Among his numerous books were *Operative Gynecology* (2 vols. 1898), *Medical Gynecology* (1908), *Appendicitis and Other Diseases of the Vermiform Appendix* (1909), *Diseases of the Kidneys, Ureters and Bladder* (with C. F. Burnam, 2 vols. 1914), *A Scientific Man and the Bible* (1925), and *Electrosurgery* (with G. E. Ward, 1932). At his death Kelly was the last of the "big four" (Kelly, William S. HALSTED, William OSLER, and William H. WELCH) who had extended the fame of Johns Hopkins.

KELLY, JAMES EDWARD, 1855–1933, American sculptor, was born in New York City, and while apprenticed to a wood engraver studied in the schools of the Academy of Design. In 1875, with Edwin A. Abbey, he established at New York his famous wood-engraving studio, where Cole and other well-known engravers were associated with him. He subsequently turned his attention to sculpture and exhibited his statuette, "Sheridan's Ride," at the Academy of Design, 1879. Other works are the bas-reliefs for the Monmouth monument, statue of "General Grant at Donelson" (1886), "General Sherman," and "Colonel Roosevelt at San Juan Hill."

KELLY, MICHAEL, known as **King,** 1857–94, American baseball player, member of Baseball Hall of Fame, was born in Troy, N.Y. An all-around player, he was an outfielder, shortstop, and catcher with Cincinnati, Chicago, Boston, and New York. His sale to Boston in 1887 for $10,000 was one of the biggest deals of baseball's early history; that year he batted .394 and stole 84 bases. He inspired the popular song, "Slide, Kelly, Slide!"

KELLY, WILLIAM, 1811–88, American inventor, was born in Pittsburgh, Pa. Becoming interested in the manufacture of iron kettles, he purchased iron-ore land near Eddyville, Ky., and developed the Suwanee Iron Works and Union Forge (1846). The process of decarbonizing melted pig iron by means of a current of air originated with him in 1847 when he was attempting to find a substitute for charcoal. He later discovered that this process could be utilized in converting melted iron into malleable steel quickly, cheaply, and in vast quantities. The first steel blown commercially by the Kelly "air-boiling" process was produced by the Wyandotte Iron Works (1864). During his lifetime Kelly succeeded in securing recognition of his priority, but today the process is known as the Bessemer method because it was developed independently in England by Sir HENRY BESSEMER.

KELP, a name applied to certain large brown algae, especially of the genera *Nereocystis, Laminaria, Macrocystis, Postelsia, Pelagophycus,* and related genera. These plants grow in extensive beds, usually in the shallower portions of the ocean. They are anchored to rocks by holdfasts and often possess air bladders that give them buoyancy in the water. They are usually extensively branched and frequently have leaflike organs. Some are utilized commercially as sources of IODINE and fertilizer for soils, and many are valuable as sources of food for fish and other aquatic animals. See ALGAE.

CORNELIA CLARKE
Bladder wrack, a kelp

H. J. FULLER

KELPIE, an Australian breed of sheep dog, descended from the dingo and smooth-coated collie. It is a smooth-haired, prick-eared dog about the size of a Scotch collie, and in color is red, blue, black and tan, or solid black, the last-named variety being known as the barb. The kelpie possesses qualities superior to those of the Old-World sheep dog for the particular circumstances of the large sheep runs of Australia.

KELPIE, in Scottish tradition a terrifying aquatic creature emerging from its native element to pursue human prey. By some it is identified with the water horse which lured its victims to the body of water where it dwelt and there devoured them.

KELSO, town, Scotland, in Roxburghshire, at the junction of the Tweed and the Teviot; 42 miles SE of Edinburgh. Its chief points of interest are the ruins of the abbey, founded by David I about 1130 and destroyed by the English in 1545, and the museum, which contains objects of local interest. The abbey was one of the strongest in Scotland. Floors Castle, the magnificent seat of the dukes of Roxburgh, is not far from the town. Pop. about 3,800.

KELSO, city, SW Washington, Cowlitz County; on the Cowlitz River, the Great Northern, the Northern Pacific, and the Union Pacific railroads, and U.S.

highways 99 and 830, about 50 miles N of Portland. Founded in 1884 by Peter Crawford, the settlement was named for his former home in Scotland. Kelso is an important lumber center and a headquarters for smelt fisheries. Pop. (1950) 7,345.

KELT. See SALMON.

KELTS. See CELTS.

KELUNG. See KIRUN.

KELVIN, WILLIAM THOMSON, 1st BARON, 1824–1907, British physicist and mathematician, was born in Belfast, Ireland, and studied at the University of Glasgow and St. Peter's College, Cambridge. Appointed professor of natural philosophy at the University of Glasgow in 1846, he held this position until his retirement in 1899. His jubilee in 1896 was attended by hundreds of scientists from all parts of the world who honored him for his investigations in the fields of thermodynamics and electricity. In 1904 he made his last academic contribution as chancellor of the University of Glasgow.

Kelvin first attracted attention in the field of thermodynamics with the heat-absorption phenomenon known as the Thomson effect (1856). He next propounded the doctrine of the dissipation of energy which maintained that, although the total amount of energy might remain constant, the useful amount was continually diminishing. In his study of the compression of gases he discovered the Joule-Thomson effect which pertained to the thermal changes gases undergo when forced under pressure through a small porous aperture. As a result of these experiments he found that absolute zero is −273° C., and he accordingly proposed that scientists use for certain measurements the absolute or Kelvin temperature scale. Kelvin's work in electricity was based on his mathematical theories of magnetism and electric oscillations. He served as electrical engineer in connection with the laying of the short-lived Atlantic cable of 1858, and it was largely because of his experiments that success crowned the cable layers' efforts in 1866. Among his inventions which assured the development of submarine telegraphy were the mirror galvanometer, the siphon recorder, and the curb transmitter. He also devised an improved mariner's compass, a tide predictor, a harmonic analyzer, and a deep-sea sounding machine which made navigation less hazardous.

Kelvin was interested in such other branches of science as geology, and through application of thermodynamics he concluded that the earth had solidified from a molten mass between 20 and 40 million years ago. He also propounded an atomic theory in which the properties of atoms were explained by their having been formed from "vortex-rings." His fellow scientists elected him president of the British Association for the Advancement of Science (1871) and of the Royal Society (1890–95). Outstanding among his publications were the *Baltimore Lectures on Molecular Dynamics and the Wave Theory of Light* (1885) which he had delivered the previous year at Johns Hopkins University. With P. G. Tait he wrote *A Treatise on Natural Philosophy* (1879–83). See ELECTROMETER AND ELECTROSTATIC VOLTMETER; ELECTROMOTIVE FORCE; ENERGY.   M. E. C.

BIBLIOG.–A. Russell, *Lord Kelvin* (1938).

KELVIN TEMPERATURE SCALE. See ABSOLUTE TEMPERATURE.

KELVIN'S REPLENISHER. See ELECTROSTATIC MACHINE.

KEMAL ATATÜRK, MUSTAPHA. See ATATURK.

KEMALIYE, or **Egin,** town, E central Turkey, Malatya Vilayet, on the Euphrates (at this point the Kara Su), 140 miles SW of Trabzond (Trebizond). The town was originally settled by Armenians in the 11th century. Pop. (1940 est.) 23,000.

KEMBLE, ADELAIDE, 1814?–1879, English singer and author, daughter of CHARLES KEMBLE and sister of FRANCES KEMBLE, was born in London. She sang in grand opera in Germany and in Paris (1837–

38), and made her English debut in *Norma* at Covent Garden, London, in 1841. After a short but triumphant musical career she retired from professional life in 1842 and the following year married Edward John Sartoris. The best known of her graceful writings is *A Week in a French Country House.*

KEMBLE, CHARLES, 1775–1854, British actor, youngest brother of JOHN PHILIP KEMBLE and SARAH SIDDONS, was born in Brecon in South Wales. After playing in Newcastle, Edinburgh, and other towns, he joined his famous brother at Drury Lane (1794), playing secondary parts. His chief laurels were won in comedy. In 1840 he retired from the stage.

KEMBLE, ELIZABETH, 1761–1836, English actress, daughter of ROGER KEMBLE, and sister of Mrs. Siddons, made her first appearance on the stage as Portia, at Drury Lane, in 1783. In 1785 she married the actor, Whitlock, and in 1792 went with him to the United States, where she became very popular. She returned to London in 1807, reappeared at the Drury Lane, and soon thereafter retired.

KEMBLE, FRANCES ANNE, known as **Fanny Kemble,** 1809–93, English actress and writer, daughter of CHARLES KEMBLE, was born in London. She made her first appearance on the stage in 1829, when her Juliet at Covent Garden proved an extraordinary success. With her father she went to the United States in 1832, and two years later married Pierce Butler, of Philadelphia, thereafter making her home in that city and on the Butler plantation in Georgia until 1847, when she left her husband and returned to England. In 1849 she returned to the United States, secured a divorce from Butler, and made her home in Lenox, Mass. Except for brief appearances on the stage and as a Shakespearean reader, she lived subsequently in retirement. Sheridan Knowles' play *The Hunchback* was written for her and in it she achieved her greatest triumph. She published poems, two plays, and six autobiographical works, the best known being *Records of a Girlhood* (1878), *Records of a Later Life* (1882), and *Further Records, 1848–83* (1890).

KEMBLE, JOHN PHILIP, 1757–1823, English actor, was born in Prescott, Lancashire. In 1783 he surprised London by his powerful performance of Hamlet at Drury Lane, after which he played leading tragic roles (Macbeth, Coriolanus, Cato, Othello) for some years. He became manager of Drury Lane (1788–1802), and from 1803–8 was manager and part owner of Covent Garden Theatre, when he ranked as England's greatest living tragic actor, as his sister, Mrs. SIDDONS, was the greatest actress. The O. P. ("Old Prices") riots occurred in 1809, in consequence of his having raised the admission rates to Covent Garden; but he speedily overcame his unpopularity by the magnificent acting of his riper years. He retired from the stage in 1817.

KEMBLE, ROGER, 1721–1802, English actor, was born in England. He married, in 1753, the actress Sarah Ward, and became the head of an illustrious family of actors, most celebrated among them SARAH KEMBLE SIDDONS and JOHN PHILIP KEMBLE.

KEMEROVO, formerly **Shcheglovsk,** city, U.S.S.R., in the Russian Soviet Federated Socialist Republic, capital of Kemerovo Region, situated on the Tom River. An industrial center situated in the heart of the tremendous Kuznetsk Coal Basin, Kemerovo has coke-manufacturing plants, zinc works, and extensive chemical industries. The city was built in a land scarcely inhabited even by nomads before World War I. Pop. (1951 est.) 200,000.

KEMEROVO REGION, an administrative area of the U.S.S.R. in the Russian Soviet Federated Socialist Republic; bounded on the N by Tomsk Region, on the W by Novosibirsk Region and Altai Territory, on the S by the Oirot Autonomous Region, on the NE by Krasnoyarsk Territory, and on the E by the Tuva Autonomous Region; area 36,900 sq. mi.; pop. (1950 est.) 2,000,000. The Region's terrain is mostly hilly steppe. Kemerovo Region includes the famous KUZNETSK Basin or Kuzbas, foremost coal mining and industrial center developed by the Soviets during their several Five-Year Plans. Iron ore is also mined. Steel mills, a chemical industry and production of zinc are the most prominent industries in the development of the Region. The main line of the Trans-Siberian Railroad traverses the northern part of the Region, with branch lines connecting the new industrial centers. These include KEMEROVO, the capital of the Region, ANZHERO SUDZHENSK, LENINSK KUZNETSKI, PROKOPEVSK, and STALINSK.

KEMI RIVER, Finland, rises in the northern portion of the country and flows in a southwesterly direction to empty at the port of Kemi in the Gulf of Bothnia.

KEMMEL, MONT, a knoll on Flanders Plain in Belgium, five miles SW of Ypres. During World War I it was of strategic importance in the defense of the YPRES sector.

KEMMERER, EDWIN WALTER, 1875–1945, American economist, was born in Scranton, Pa., and studied at Wesleyan and Cornell universities. After teaching economics and history at Purdue University (1901–3), he served as financial adviser to the U.S. Philippine Commission on the establishment of the gold standard (1903) and was chief of the currency division (1904–6). He was later professor of economics and finance at Cornell (1906–12) and at Princeton University (1912–28), becoming Walker professor of international finance (1928–43). He advised several Latin American and European countries on currency and banking and wrote: *Money and Credit Instruments in their Relation to General Prices* (rev. ed. 1909); *The A.B.C. of the Federal Reserve System* (1918); *Kemmerer on Money* (1934); *The A.B.C. of Inflation* (1942).

KEMPENER, PIETER DE, 1505–80, Flemish painter, was born in Brussels. Though there is little known about the facts of his early life, research shows that he came from a wealthy family of tapestry workers and painters. After study in Italy, where he did a portrait of Charles V, he went to Seville where he lived for 25 years and did most of his best work. He became one of the leading exponents of the school of painting in Seville and was so identified with the art of Spain that he is often referred to under his Spanish pseudonym Campana Pedro. Many of his paintings for churches, such as the famous "Deposition from the Cross," have been lost. Even though most of his paintings are in Spain, he was recognized throughout Europe as a master of his art.

KEMPENFELT, RICHARD, 1718–82, British rear admiral, fought in Pocock's actions with D'Aché off Cuddalore, Negapatam, and Pondicherry in India (1758 and 1759). In December, 1781, he signalized himself by scattering a French convoy escorted by a powerful fleet, and capturing several merchant ships. In 1782 he perished on board the *Royal George,* which capsized off Spithead.

KEMPER, JAMES LAWSON, 1823–95, American soldier and political leader, was born in Madison County, Va. He served (1847–48) in the Mexican War and for many years was a member of the Virginia legislature, being for two years speaker of the lower house. In the Civil War he served in the Confederate army, rising from the rank of colonel (1861) to that of major general (1864), and being severely wounded in Pickett's famous charge in the Battle of Gettysburg. He was governor of Virginia (1874–78).

KEMPIS, THOMAS A, born Thomas Hammerken, or Hammerlein, c. 1380–1471, German ecclesiastic, mystic, and generally acknowledged author of the devotional classic, *The Imitation* (or *Following*) of *Christ.* Born at Kempen, in the Lower Rhine District, he was educated at Deventer in the Netherlands, partly by the Brothers of the Common Life. He entered the Augustinian convent at Mount Saint Agnes, near Zwolle in the Netherlands in 1399, took his vows in 1406, and became an ordained priest about 1413. In 1425, he was made subprior of the convent and, in 1448, was re-elected to the same position. Practically his entire life was spent in this same convent where he was engaged most of the time in writing or copying religious works. He died in the convent and his remains, after several removals, were finally placed in Saint Michael's Church at Zwolle.

Thomas à Kempis

The writings of Thomas à Kempis consist for the most part of treatises on monasticism and devotional essays designed to cultivate the spiritual life. Many of his works have been translated into English, and *The Imitation of Christ*, originally written in Latin, has been translated into almost every common language. This book of meditations and spiritual advice is simply written, revealing the spirit of pious sincerity of its author. It calls upon the reader to practice humility and self denial in following the example of Christ. The author maintains that only through suffering and renunciation can the lusts of the world be overcome. The mystical quality of the writing and the earnest appeal to sacrificial Christian living have made this work one of the most universally read and deeply appreciated of all devotional booklets. The work has often been published as a prayer book, and it has been incorporated in many sets of religious books and classics. Its popularity has been widespread and continuous since its publication in 1441

Although Thomas à Kempis has been generally recognized as the writer of *The Imitation of Christ*, its authorship has frequently been disputed by scholars. According to one theory, advanced by Albert Hyma in 1925, the work represents a collection of writings by early members of the Brethren of the Common Life, assembled by Thomas à Kempis and published under his name. Another theory, held by Joseph Malaise, and presented in his work *The Following of Christ* (1939), maintains that *The Imitation of Christ* was derived chiefly from the writings of Gerard Groote, the founder of the Brethren of the Common Life.   W. G. D.

KEMPTEN, town, Germany, in the state of Bavaria, on the Iller River, 80 miles by rail SW of Munich. Features of interest in the town include the St. Mang Church (15th century), the St. Lorenz Church (17th century), and the former castle (17th century) of the abbatial princes. Its manufactures include machines, textiles, wood products, paper, and beer; and there is trade in dairy products. Kempten was founded on the site of the Roman colony of Cambodunum, later becoming the seat of the principality of Kempten. The Benedictine abbey was founded in 773, and its abbot in 1360 was made a prince of the empire. Kempten became Lutheran in 1527, and in 1535 joined the Schmalkaldic League. It fell to Bavaria in 1803, along with the abbey. Pop. (1946) 36,862.

KEN, THOMAS, 1637–1711, English prelate and hymn writer, was born in Hertfordshire; was rector of Little Easton, Essex (1663–65), and of Brightstone, Isle of Wight (1667–69). Thereafter, until 1672, he was a prebend at Winchester, and rector at E. Woodhay, Hampshire. In 1679–80 he was chaplain at The Hague to Mary, princess of Orange, and in 1683 chaplain with Lord Dartmouth at Tangier. He was appointed (1685) bishop of Bath and Wells. He attended Charles II in his last hours. Under James II he was one of the "seven bishops" sent to the Tower, and in 1691 was deprived of his see as a nonjuror. Ken wrote many beautiful hymns, including "Awake, My Soul, and with the Sun," "Evening Hymn," and especially the familiar doxology, "Praise God, from whom all blessings flow."

KENAI PENINSULA, S central Alaska, between Cook Inlet and Prince William Sound, extends about 150 miles into the Gulf of Alaska. It is irregularly shaped and has a coast line of more than 1,000 miles. Mountainous, dotted with lakes, and edged by great fjords, the peninsula is one of the most famous big game areas in Alaska. The climate is comparable to that of Massachusetts. Some of Alaska's finest agricultural land is located here, and there are coal mines and gold deposits, some fur farming, and extensive fish canning interests. The chief towns are Anchorage (pop. 11,254), Seward (pop. 2,063), and Kenai (pop. 281).

KENDAL, or **Kirkby Kendal,** market town and municipal borough, NW England, Westmorland County, on the Kent River nine miles SE of Lake Windermere and 38 miles SE of Carlisle. The town has a 13th-century Gothic church, and near by are the ruins of Kendal Castle, noted as the birthplace of Queen Catherine Parr (1509), last queen of Henry VIII. Kendal is one of the oldest manufacturing towns of England, producing fine woolens, tweeds, hosiery, carpets, boots, shoes, fishhooks, paper, and gunpowder. Pop. (1946) 18,555.

KENDALL, AMOS, 1789–1869, American statesman, was born in Dunstable, Mass., and studied at Dartmouth College and in a law office in Groton. Moving to Kentucky in 1814, he spent a year tutoring in Henry Clay's household, and from 1816 to 1829 co-edited the *Argus of Western America*, a pro-Jackson paper published at Frankfort. On Jackson's election, Kendall became fourth auditor of the Treasury (1829–35), and was later postmaster general (1835–40). Perhaps the most influential of Jackson's "KITCHEN CABINET," Kendall worked actively against the national bank, and is supposed to have drafted many of Jackson's public speeches. After several editing ventures, he became SAMUEL F. B. MORSE's business agent (1845), took care of the telegraph patents and organized Morse companies, and gradually made a substantial fortune. Remaining a Jacksonian Democrat, he supported Lincoln's war policy and opposed secession. He founded Columbian Institution for the Deaf and Dumb, which became Gallaudet College in 1864. He wrote a life of Jackson (1843) and his own *Autobiography* (1872). Kendall has often been mentioned as the author of the anonymous "Diary of a Public Man," an on-the-spot account of Washington in the hectic year before the Civil War (1879; ed. 1946).

KENDALL, EDWARD CALVIN, 1886–   , American biochemist, was born in South Norwalk, Conn., and studied at Columbia University. He served as a research chemist with Parke, Davis and Company (1910–11) and with St. Luke's Hospital, New York City (1911–14). In 1914 he became professor of biochemistry at the University of Minnesota and head of the chemical section of the Mayo Clinic in Rochester, Minn. In 1919 Kendall isolated in crystalline form the hormone of the thyroid gland and named it thyroxin. He shared the Nobel prize in medicine (1950) for his discoveries of hormones of the adrenal cortex, their structure, and biological effect in arthritis treatment. See CORTISONE.

KENDALL, GEORGE WILKINS, 1809–67, American journalist, born in Amherst, N.H. After working as a printer in various newspaper offices at various places, he, in association with F. A. Lumsden, founded (1837) the *New Orleans Picayune,* one of the most influential journals in the South. He served on the staff of General Taylor during the Mexican War, and wrote for his paper articles concerning the military operations which attracted much attention; he was, indeed, probably the first of the modern type of war correspondent in America. He published *Narratives of the Santa Fé Expedition* (2 vols. 1844; enlarged ed. 2 vols. 1856), which was, for a time, extremely popular; and *The War between the United States and Mexico* (1851).

KENDALL, HENRY CLARENCE, 1841–82, Australian poet, was born in Ulladalla, New South Wales. His principal works—*At Long Bay, Leaves from an Australian Forest* (1869) and *Songs from the Mountains* (1880)—abound in vigorous, realistic description of the bush country. Kendall's complete works were edited by B. Stevens (1920).

KENDALL, WILLIAM SERGEANT, 1869–1938, American artist, was born in Spuyten Duyvil, N.Y. After attending the Art Students League in New York, he studied with Thomas Eakins and later in France. Though he worked with figure, landscape and portrait, he was best known for his drawings and portraits of children. In 1905 he became a member of the National Academy and during his lifetime had the pleasure of seeing his work acclaimed in America and abroad. "The End of Day," "Psyche," and "Crosslights" are among his best paintings.

KENDALLVILLE, city, NE Indiana, in Noble County, on the New York Central and the Pennsylvania railroads and U.S. Highway 6; about 26 miles N of Fort Wayne. Kendallville is the trade center of an agricultural community situated in a delightful lake country. It was founded in 1832 by David Bundle. Refrigerators, cheese, windmills, coolers, brass and copper rivets, pumps, brushes, brooms, steel tanks, artificial bait, and machinery for making concrete are some products of the city. Pop. (1950) 6,119.

KENEH. See QENA.

KENILWORTH, market town and urban district, central England, Warwickshire, on the Leam River, a tributary of the Avon; five miles NW of Warwick and five miles SW of Coventry. It is famous for the ruins of the castle, the setting of Scott's novel, *Kenilworth.* The castle was built in 1120 by the Norman, Geoffry de Clinton. Simon de Montfort acquired it in the 13th century, holding it against Henry III, until the king's followers defeated de Montfort at Evesham in 1266. The castle passed into the possession of John of Gaunt in the 14th century and it remained a crown estate until Queen Elizabeth bestowed it upon Robert Dudley, Earl of Leicester. Here in 1575 Leicester entertained his sovereign with splendid pageants. During the Reformation the castle was sacked by Cromwell. Close to the castle are the remains of an Augustinian abbey founded in 1122. Pop. about 8,200.

KENMORE, village, NW New York, in Erie County, on the Niagara River, six miles N of Buffalo of which it is a residential suburb. Kenmore was incorporated in 1899. Its population increased by about one-third during World War II. Pop. (1950) 20,066.

KENNEBEC RIVER, Maine, flows from Moosehead Lake in a southerly course and enters the Atlantic Ocean near Bath. Its total length is about 150 miles. The principal tributary, the ANDROSCOGGIN, joins the Kennebec near Bath. A dam at Bingham forms Wyman Lake. The site of an unsuccessful English settlement in 1607 and the first shipbuilding in North America is at the mouth of the Kennebec. In 1775 Benedict Arnold led his ill-starred expedition up the Kennebec to attack Quebec. Sailing ships, built along the banks of the Kennebec, went around the world in the 19th century, and Bath is still famed as a builder of ships for the U.S. Navy. AUGUSTA, the state capital, is on the Kennebec.

BIBLIOG.–R. P. T. Coffin, *The Kennebec* (1937).

KENNEBUNK, town, SW Maine, in York County, on the Mousam River, the Boston and Maine Railroad, and U.S. Highway 1; about 25 miles SW of Portland. Kennebunk is situated in an agricultural and shore resort region. It is one of the oldest towns in Maine having been settled in about 1643. Shipbuilding and a thriving West Indies shipping trade made Kennebunk a town of some importance until the beginning of the Revolutionary War. Fine colonial homes are still in evidence in Kennebunk. Trunks, shoes, twine, leatheroid, and farm products are the principal manufactures of the town. Pop. (1950) 4,273.

KENNEDY, CHARLES RANN, 1871–1950, Anglo-American dramatist, was born in Derby. After a long career in England as actor, producer, and playwright, he went to the United States, settling first in Millbrook, N.Y., where he was instructor of dramatics at Bennett Junior College, and later in Los Angeles. His best-known play, *The Servant in the House* (1908), was a modern morality in which the character of a whole household was reformed through the influence of an unobtrusive, Christlike servant. Kennedy's later works, many of which were in the same vein, include *The Terrible Meek* (1911), *The Necessary Evil* (1913), *The Chastening* (1922), *Old Nobody* (1927), and *Sonnets for Armageddon* (1943).

KENNEDY, JOHN PENDLETON, 1795–1870, American writer, was born in Baltimore. After graduating from Baltimore College, he practiced law in Baltimore until 1838. He was a member of Congress from 1837 to 1845 and was secretary of the navy in 1852–53, supervising Perry's expedition to Japan and Kane's expedition in search of Franklin. His works include *Swallow Barn* (1832), a group of Irvingesque sketches of country life in Virginia; two historical romances, *Horse-Shoe Robinson* (1835) and *Rob of the Bowl* (1838); political satires and treatises in behalf of the Whigs; and a life of the Virginia political leader, William Wirt (1849). It was through Kennedy, who was among the first to appreciate his genius as a storyteller, that Poe was appointed to the staff of the *Southern Literary Messenger.* He became acquainted with Thackeray during his sojourn in America and provided him with some of the historical material for his novel, *The Virginians.*

BIBLIOG.–E. M. Gwathmey, *John Pendleton Kennedy* (1931).

KENNELLY, ARTHUR EDWIN, 1861–1939, American electrical engineer, was born in Bombay, India, and studied at University College School, London. On coming to the United States he became an electrical assistant to Thomas A. Edison (1887–94) and then established with Edwin J. Houston the engineering firm of Houston and Kennelly. He was professor of electrical engineering at Harvard University (1902–30) and at Massachusetts Institute of Technology (1913–24). Becoming an authority on the transmission of electric waves, he arrived in 1902 at the same explanation that OLIVER HEAVISIDE did in suggesting the existence of an ionized atmospheric region favorable to radio-wave propagation. This region, located from 60 to 200 miles above the earth, is often called the KENNELLY-HEAVISIDE LAYER and serves as a mirror in that it enables radio waves to be reflected and thus bend as they travel around the planet's curves. Kennelly wrote: *The Application of Hyperbolic Functions to Electrical Engineering* (1911); *Artificial Electric Lines* (1917); *Electrical Vibration Instruments* (1923); *Electric Lines and Nets* (1928).

KENNELLY-HEAVISIDE LAYER, in physics, a layer of ionized (electrically charged) air in the upper atmosphere which reflects radio waves back to earth. Prof. A. E. Kennelly of Harvard and O. Heaviside, an English engineer, in 1902 independently announced such findings. Research since that time confirms there are two electrically charged regions and sometimes three (depending on conditions) which are located at heights of about 60, 130, and 185 miles, respectively. See ATMOSPHERE; IONOSPHERE.

KENNESAW MOUNTAIN NATIONAL BATTLEFIELD PARK, NW Georgia, Cobb County, near the village of Kennesaw about 25 miles NW of Atlanta. The park, comprising 60 acres, was the scene of one of the most decisive battles of the Civil War. It embraces Cheatham's Hill on which the most desperate action of the Battle of Kennesaw Mountain took place June 27, 1864, between the Union forces commanded by General Sherman and the Confederates under Gen. Joseph E. Johnston. The park, established in 1917, includes the main Union and Confederate earthworks.

KENNETH I, called **Mac Alpin,** d. c. 860, king of the Scots, was a son of Alpin, king of Dalriada. He conquered the Picts (846); became Ard-Righ, or ruler of the united monarchy; established his chief seat at Scone, and six times invaded Northumbria.

KENNETH II, d. 995, king of the Scots, was a son of Malcolm I. He succeeded to the throne in 971, warred against the Strathclyde Britons, overran Northumbria to the Tees, and established his sway over the Lothians. He was treacherously slain by Fenella, the daughter of a chief of Angus.

KENNETT, city, SE Missouri, county seat of Dunklin County, near the St. Francis River, on the Frisco Railroad, 100 miles S of Cape Girardeau. Kennett, laid out on the site of an Indian village, was incorporated in 1846 and named for the mayor of St. Louis, Dr. Luther M. Kennett. Cotton is the principal product of the area. Pop. (1950) 8,685.

KENNETT SQUARE, borough, SE Pennsylvania, in Chester County, on the Pennsylvania Railroad and U.S. Highway 1; about 33 miles SW of Philadelphia. Kennett Square is the major shipping center for the most important mushroom-growing section in the United States. It was settled in 1705 and named for a village in Wiltshire, England. The chief products include road building machinery, fiber products, bakelite, and phenolite products. Pop. (1950) 3,699.

KENNEY, GEORGE CHURCHILL, 1889–   , U.S. air force officer, was born in Yarmouth, Nova Scotia, of American parentage. A graduate of Massachusetts Institute of Technology, he served as a combat pilot in World War I. He entered the regular army in 1920, served in various assignments and became commander of the 4th Air Force in 1942. As commander of the Allied Air Forces in the Far East, he directed the air war against the Japanese in World War II. Kenney's inventions advanced the science of air warfare. He became general (1945), headed the Strategic Air Command (1946–48), and the Air University from 1948 until retirement in 1951.

KENNINGTON, a suburb of South London, England, within Lambeth Borough, in Surrey, two miles SW of St. Paul's. It had a royal palace until the reign of Henry VII.

KENNY, ELIZABETH, c. 1886–   , Australian nurse, was born in the New England section of New South Wales. After receiving her training at the Toowoomba District Hospital she became a "bush nurse" and was assigned to the district around Clifton. In 1910, when called upon to care for a victim of infantile paralysis, she chanced on the method of treatment which was to make her name famous 30 years later. This method was one of physical therapy. It consisted of wringing out woolen strips in hot water and wrapping them periodically around the aching parts so as to relieve muscular spasm during the acute stage of the disease. As the pain subsided, passive exercise of the muscles was introduced until the patient could move the limb or other afflicted part himself. Both the application of heat and the system of muscle re-education overcame spasm (involuntary muscle contraction) so that nerve impulses could be transmitted in a normal manner. When applied during the early stage of infantile paralysis it enabled many patients to be spared the crippling aftereffects of the disease.

ACME
Elizabeth Kenny

Sister Kenny's attempt to spread the message of her revolutionary discovery was interrupted by World War I, during which she served as an Army transport nurse. After the war she financed the work through royalties received from a transport stretcher which she had invented and patented. In 1933 she established her first clinic in Townsville, Queensland, but encountered opposition from conservative physicians who maintained that the correct treatment was immobilizing the affected parts, thus preventing the normal muscles from pulling the affected ones.

Sister Kenny encountered the same hostility among physicians when she went to England in 1937, and it was not until 1939 that this opposition was finally overcome not only in Australia but in other parts of the British Empire. While on a visit to the United States in 1940 she was invited by the National Foundation for Infantile Paralysis and the University of Minnesota to demonstrate her method at the Minneapolis General Hospital. After her method had been formally recognized by the American Medical Association, the work of training nurses and physiotherapists in it was carried on at the Elizabeth Kenny Institute in Minneapolis. In 1950 the U.S. Congress voted Sister Kenny the privilege of entering and leaving the country without passport or other official documents. She returned to Australia in 1951. Sister Kenny was the author of *Treatment of Infantile Paralysis in the Acute Stage* (1941) and an autobiography, *And They Shall Walk* (1943).   M. E. C.

KENORA, town, Canada, in the province of Ontario, capital of the Kenora and Patricia districts, on the N extremity of the Lake of the Woods near the E branch of the Winnipeg River, on the Canadian Pacific Railway and the Canadian Pacific Airlines, about 146 miles N of the Minnesota border. Kenora is the shopping and distributing center for a large district and has a growing tourist trade which is attracted to the near-by forests, lakes and streams. Fishing is a major industry and there are pulp and paper mills and a flour mill at near-by Keewatin. Kenora was settled as a trading post of the Hudson's Bay Company about 1860 and became an Ontario town in 1892. Originally called Rat Portage, it was united with Norman in 1892 and the new name was coined from the first two letters of Keewatin, Norman, and Rat Portage. Pop. (1949 est.) 9,012.

KENOSHA, city, SE Wisconsin, county seat of Kenosha County, on the W shore of Lake Michigan and the North Western Railway, 55 miles N of Chicago and 35 miles S of Milwaukee. Kenosha is a port of entry with a good harbor and a highly industrialized commercial center. It was founded by John Bullen, Jr., in 1835 as "Pike" village. In 1837 the village was renamed "Southport" and in 1850 it was incorporated under the present name. The principal products include fire trucks and apparatus, automobiles, machinery supplies, copper wire, mattresses, bed springs, brass rods, and dairy supplies. Pop. (1950) 54,368.

KENRICK, FRANCIS PATRICK, 1796–1863, American Roman Catholic theologian, born in Dublin, Ireland. He was educated in Rome, ordained a priest, and came to America where he taught in the newly established seminary at Bardstown, Ky. (1821). He was appointed coadjutor bishop of Philadelphia (1830) and became archbishop of Baltimore (1851). He was interested in education, poor relief, temperance, and unionism, and was an advocate of moderation during the nativist riots. Of his published works the better known are *Theologia Dogmatica* (4 vols. 1839–40) and *Theologia Moralis* (2 vols. 1841–43). He also wrote various treatises on sacraments and on the history of the Roman Catholic Church.
R. J. PURCELL

KENRICK, PETER RICHARD, 1806–96, American Roman Catholic prelate, brother of FRANCIS P. KENRICK, was born in Dublin, Ireland, studied at Maynooth College, and was ordained a priest in 1832. He came to Philadelphia the following year, where he was rector of the theological seminary and filled other important offices in the diocese until his consecration as coadjutor bishop of St. Louis, 1841. He was made bishop in 1843 and archbishop in 1847, celebrating his golden jubilee in 1891. He performed distinguished services for the sick and wounded in the Civil War.

KENSICO DAM. See DAM.

KENSINGTON, west side parliamentary borough and residential suburb of London, England, four miles SW. of St. Paul's. Kensington Gardens (275 acres), the picturesque grounds of Kensington Palace, adjoin Hyde Park. The Albert Memorial (1876) opposite the Royal Albert Hall is a conspicuous object in the gardens. Other buildings of interest are the Church of St. Mary Abbots, Christ Church, Brompton Oratory, the Imperial Institute, the British Museum of Natural History, the Victoria and Albert Museum, and the Imperial College of Science, the Royal College of Art, the house of the Royal Geographical Society, and Holland House. The palace was slightly damaged during some of the air raids of World War II. Pop. (1950 est.) 178,870. See LONDON.

KENT, CHARLES FOSTER, 1867–1925, American educator and writer on biblical history and literature, was born in Palmyra, N.Y. He graduated from Yale (1889; Ph.D., 1891), taught at the University of Chicago, and was professor of biblical literature at Brown University and Yale. Between 30 and 40 volumes on Hebrew history and personalities were written by him.

KENT, EDWARD AUGUSTUS, DUKE OF, 1767–1820, fourth son of George III and father of Queen Victoria. He served with Grey's West Indian expedition (1794); and was later created duke of Kent and Strathern, and made commander in chief in North America (1799). St. John's Island was renamed Prince Edward Island in his honor.

KENT, JAMES, 1763–1847, American jurist, was born in Fredericksburgh, N.Y., the son of Moss Kent, a lawyer, and Hannah Rogers Kent. He was graduated from Yale College in 1781, read law with Egbert Benson, and was admitted to the New York bar in 1785. At Poughkeepsie, where he practiced (1785–93) with Gilbert Livingstone, he became a Federalist. It was the FEDERALISTS who persuaded the state Constitutional Convention to vote for a Federal constitution in 1788. Kent served three terms in the state assembly (1790, 1792, 1796); he was defeated by his brother-in-law in a race for Congress in 1793. Moving his practice to New York City, he became a professor of law at Columbia College (1793–98), served as master in chancery (1796–98), and was New York City's recorder (1797–98). In 1798 he resigned all three positions when he was appointed to the state Supreme Court, of which he became chief justice in 1804. But it was as chancellor of the New York Court of Chancery (1814–23) that Kent virtually introduced equity jurisdiction into the United States, drawing on the great precedent of British equity and adapting it to the American Constitution. His decisions, as recorded by court reporter William Johnson, remain a permanent record of the beginnings of New York equity; he originated the New York practice of written decisions.

Retiring upon reaching the age limit of 60, Kent resumed his professorship at Columbia. His lectures were the basic material for his *Commentaries on American Law* (1826–30), a careful, conservative study treating international law, United States constitutional law, municipal law in various states, personal rights, personal property, and real property. An omnivorous reader with a startling memory, Kent impressed readers and fellow-lawyers by his rich command of the literatures and legal systems of other countries and epochs.   C. A.

KENT, MAID OF. See BARTON, ELIZABETH.

KENT, ROCKWELL, 1882–   , American painter, etcher, and illustrator, was born in Tarrytown, N.Y. His formal training began at the age of

WHITNEY MUSEUM OF AMERICAN ART
"The Trapper," by Rockwell Kent

15, when he enrolled in William Merritt Chase's summer art school. Later he studied with Robert Henri, Kenneth Hayes Miller, and Abbott H. Thayer, attributing his greatest inspiration to the last of these. The urge to travel drew him from Columbia University on extensive trips to North and South America, Greenland, and Europe. He interspersed his tours with exhibitions of his works. During his later years he became identified with various leftist movements and organizations. His paintings of his travels provoked but slight comment; "Winter" is perhaps the finest, and he became best known for his illustrations in magazines and books. He wrote several books, which he also illustrated: *The Seven Ages of Man* (1918); *Wilderness: A Journal of Quiet Adventure in Alaska* (1920); *Voyaging Southward from the Strait of Magellan* (1924); *N By E* (1930); *Salamina* (1935); *This is My Own* (1945). His collected etchings are published in *Rockwellkentiana* (1933). Among the other numerous books Kent has illustrated are Chaucer's *Canterbury Tales;* Melville's *Moby Dick;* Casanova's *Memoirs;* and Whitman's *Leaves of Grass.*

JOAN C. CAMERA

KENT, maritime county, SE England, bounded on the N by the Thames River, Essex, and the North Sea, E by the Strait of Dover, S by the English Channel, SW by Sussex, W by Surrey, and NW by London; area 1,525 sq. mi.; pop. (1950) 1,554,000. Included with Kent on the north coast are the Isles of Sheppey and Grain; at the northeast point, the Isle of Thanet. Just off the east coast are the GOODWIN SANDS. The North Downs, rising to 800 feet at Westerham, traverse the county from east to west; the Romney Marsh occupies the southernmost tip; and the WEALD, a plateau, runs through the central part of Kent, bordered along its south side by forest ridges

Kent countryside near Sittingbearne in spring
BRITISH COMBINE

of oak and beech. Minerals found in the north and in the Weald are coal and iron. Agriculturally Kent is one of England's most fertile shires, hence its name: "Garden of England." Its rivers are the THAMES, MEDWAY, Stour, Rother, and Darent. Kent is England's leading hop-growing shire, two-thirds of its area being devoted to the cultivation of hops. There are also extensive vineyards and orchards producing small fruits in the northern and central districts. Other crops include wheat, oats, barley, potatoes, peas, beans, beets, and turnips. Large quantities of market vegetables are grown in the region surrounding London. Bee culture is widely practiced. Kent is also pastoral; the chalk downs and alluvial lands afford excellent grazing for the Southdown and Kent breeds of sheep. Romney Marsh, a tract of 47,000 acres reclaimed from the sea, furnishes rich pasturage for dairy cattle. The oysters and shrimps of Whitstable, and other coastal spots are famous. Manufacturing industries of the county are the construction of marine engines and equipment, shipbuilding, iron founding, salt refining, cement works, breweries, and munitions factories. Bricks and tiles, pottery, paper, cotton and silk thread, and cotton, woolen, and silk textiles are manufactured. There are also fisheries, fish canneries, wineries, establishments producing cheeses, and fruit canneries.

The capital of Kent is MAIDSTONE. The cathedral city, CANTERBURY, on the Medway, is a religious center and gives its title to the primate of England. There are large government establishments at WOOLWICH, SHEERNESS, ROCHESTER (another cathedral city), and Chatham; the last two are the chief manufacturing cities. MARGATE, RAMSGATE, and DOVER are the important ports; Dover is the chief harbor for continental traffic. Other important towns are FOLKESTONE, Sheerness, and Tunbridge Wells. The northwest tip of the county is included in the administrative county of London.

Antiquities and History. Kent possesses a great wealth of monastic remains, ancient castles, medieval ruins, and Saxon and Roman antiquities. The greatest Roman highway, Watling Street, extends across the county from Dover to London. At almost every town are ruins of monasteries and abbeys. England's oldest complete Roman structure is a lighthouse which still stands near Dover.

The county of Kent covers approximately the same area as the Anglo-Saxon kingdom of that name, which lasted from the fifth to the ninth century. It suffered from Danish invasions in the 10th century and was invaded by the French in the 13th century. Among historical events associated with the county is the murder of Thomas à Becket in Canterbury Cathedral (1170), and the subsequent penance of Henry II; the rebellions of Wat Tyler (1831) and Jack Cade (1450); the burning of Sandwich by the French in 1450; and the appearance of the Dutch in the Medway in 1667. Because of their aircraft factories, airfields, munitions works, and other important war industries, most of Kent's cities sustained heavy damage during World War II from German air raids and later from flying robot bombs. Of all England's southeast counties, Kent probably took the brunt of the destruction during 1940–45, because it lay in the direct path from the French coast to London. K. E. H.

KENT, city, NE Ohio, Portage County; on the Cuyahoga River, the Erie, the Baltimore and Ohio, and the Wheeling and Lake Erie railroads, about 10 miles NE of Akron in a dairying and truck-farming region. Kent was founded in the early 1800's, incorporated as a village in 1867, and chartered as a city in 1920. It is the seat of Kent State University (1913). The city has railroad shops, a tree conservation industry, and manufactures flour, automobile bodies, iron products, electric motors, air compressors, and locks. Pop. (1950) 12,418.

KENT ISLAND, Maryland, Queen Anne County, the largest island in Chesapeake Bay, about 15 miles in length and five miles in width; pop. (1950) 2,205. The first colony within the present boundaries of Maryland, it was settled by Claiborne in 1631. At one time it had sufficient population to be represented by a burgess elected to the Virginia Assembly. The island was formerly called Winston's on the map of John Smith. Peach trees have been planted on the island, but the seafood industry is the chief source of income. Love Point, on the north, is a summer resort, and Matapeake is the terminus of the Annapolis ferry. A bridge across Kent Narrows connects the island with the mainland.

KENT STATE UNIVERSITY. See COLLEGES.

KENTEI MOUNTAINS, in N central Mongolian Peoples Republic near its boundary with the Chita Region of the Russian Soviet Federated Socialist Republic, about lat. 49° N, and between long. 106° 20′ and 110° 20′ E. They are divided into the Great Kentei, to the north, and the Little Kentei, to the south. Between the two, to the east, is the sacred mountain in which tradition places the tomb of Ghengis Khan.

KENTIGERN, SAINT, or **SAINT MUNGO,** 518?–603, the apostle of Cumbria and bishop of Strathclyde. When driven from the realm by King Morken, he took refuge with St. David in North Wales, and became head of the monastery named after his disciple and successor, St. Asaph. Recalled by King Roderick, Kentigern founded Glasgow Cathedral. His day is that of his death, January 13.

KENTON, SIMON, 1755–1836, American pioneer, was born in Fauquier (or perhaps Culpeper) County, Va. At the age of 16, believing that he had killed his opponent in a fight, he fled across the Alleghenies to the region about the headwaters of the Ohio, and there engaged in trade with the Indians. He was associated with SIMON GIRTY, George Yeager, and other pioneers, winning a reputation during the Revolution by his frontier service with Boone and Clark. He was captured and tortured by the Indians; but his life was spared through Girty's influence, and he escaped. He served in Wayne's campaign against the Indians (1793–94), and later fought with the Kentucky Volunteers in the War of 1812. His land in Kentucky, to which he had neglected to secure title, was seized by settlers; and in 1820 he moved to the vicinity of Zanesville, Ohio. He was granted a pension by Congress in 1824. See KENTUCKY, High Lights of History, for illustration.

CHICAGO HIST. SOC.
Simon Kenton

KENTON, city, NW Ohio, county seat of Hardin County, on the Scioto River, the Erie and the New York Central railroads and U.S. highways 30 and 68; about 55 miles NW of Columbus. Kenton is the commercial center of an agricultural region which specializes in onion growing. It was laid out in 1833 and named for Simon Kenton, the Indian fighter. Agricultural products, machine tools, sluice gates, electric cranes, candy, and toys are manufactured in the city. Pop. (1950) 8,475.

KENT'S CAVERN, or **Kent's Hole,** hillside cave SW England, near Torquay. It has yielded (1865–80) bones of the cave lion, cave hyena, mammoth, woolly rhinoceros, wild bull, Irish elk, reindeer, grizzly bear, wildcat, horse, and beaver, intermingled with shells, ashes, charcoal, and human implements of stone and bone—the latter including two harpoon heads made from a reindeer's antler, several bone awls, and a bone needle. Archaeologists surmise that the latter was made by people similar to the "reindeer men" of the French caves; and that human life was contemporaneous with various species of now extinct mammals.

KENTUCKY
the Bluegrass State

Famous for its race horses, its tobacco, its frontier history, is this 15th state of the Union

Covington

Louisville   ★ Frankfort

CHESAPEAKE & OHIO RAILWAY

KENTUCKY, officially the **Commonwealth of Kentucky**, the "Bluegrass State," an east central state of the United States, irregular in shape; separated on the N from Illinois, Indiana, and Ohio by the Ohio River; bounded on the E by Virginia and the Big Sandy River, which separates Kentucky from West Virginia; on the S by Tennessee and Virginia; and on the W by the Mississippi River which separates the state from Missouri; area 40,395 sq. mi., including 286 sq. mi. of water surface; pop. (1950) 2,944,806. From north to south, Kentucky varies in length from 171 miles between Cincinnati, Ohio, and the Tennessee border to about 40 miles in the west near the Tennessee River; from east to west, the state is 458 miles wide. Kentucky's motto is "United we stand, divided we fall." The state flower is the goldenrod and the state song is "My Old Kentucky Home." Frankfort is the capital city.

Topography. Kentucky lies wholly within the Mississippi basin, and more than 90 per cent of the area is in the watershed of the Ohio River. In general, its surface is a tableland, sloping from the Alleghenies northwesterly toward the Ohio. The northeastern section, termed the Bluegrass Region, has an elevation of somewhat less than 1,000 feet, and consists chiefly of gently undulating land. This region is partially surrounded by an area known as the "Knobs," where the surface is broken by cone-shaped eminences, capped with sandstone, which rise to a height of about 1,200 feet. In the eastern and southeastern parts of the state lies a plateau region, ranging from 1,000 to 1,500 feet in altitude, and dominated on the southeast border by the Cumberland and Pine mountain ranges, some of whose crests rise to 3,000 feet. In the Big Black Mountains, on the Virginia border, the altitude reaches 4,100 feet. This region has considerable mineral wealth, chiefly coal and iron, and is heavily timbered.

Western Kentucky, except the part west of the Tennessee River, is similar in structure, the elevations ranging from 400 to 600 feet. Between these two areas extends a limestone plateau, which slopes from about 1,200 feet in the east to 600 feet in the west, and which is dotted by many pits or sinkholes, through which the surface water has made its way until numerous underground passages and caverns have been formed. More than 500 of these caverns have been partially explored. See MAMMOTH CAVE NATIONAL PARK.

The OHIO RIVER, which marks the northern boundary, and the Mississippi, on the western boundary, are the principal waterways of the state. The chief tributaries of the Ohio are the BIG SANDY, KENTUCKY, LICKING, GREEN, TENNESSEE, and CUMBERLAND, all of which are navigable. In general, the rivers cut deep and have steep, rocky banks. There are several natural bridges in the state.

Climate. The climate of Kentucky is transitional; the northern part of the state is continental in character, more like Illinois and Indiana, and the southern part is semitropical, more like Tennessee and Virginia. The average annual temperature for a period of 57 years was 56.7° F. Temperatures of 100° are rare, but 80° has occurred during the winter season. The greatest extremes recorded are 114° and −30°. The average annual precipitation is 45.24 inches; fall is the driest season. Snowfall amounts to 13.2 inches. Because the winters are not severe, tobacco beds are begun in early February and plowing for grains is started in February and March. The average number of cloud-free days is 162. The growing season extends from April 15–23 to October 13–21. Prevailing winds are from the south and are of low velocity.

Plants and Animals. Kentucky is famed for its bluegrass which flourished in limestone soils in the open spaces as soon as forests were cleared. The grass receives its name from the blue anthers of the blossoms which the plant produces in May, giving it the famous steel-blue cast. The Appalachian region produces a variety of mountain shrubs—rhododendron, dogwood, red bud, mountain laurel, and azalea, and the yellow poplar flowering tree. Luxuriant climbing vines bear colorful flowers, and some yield small berries which attract the birds. Among the common vines are the grape, wisteria, trumpet vine, Virginia creeper, and the poison ivy. Goldenrod, the state flower, blue ageratum, and purple ironweed grow rank along the roadways in late summer. When the pioneers first pushed their way into the wilderness, hardwoods covered the whole of Kentucky. Now not more than one-fourth of the state is forested and much of this land has been cut over. Oak, chestnut, and yellow poplar grow densely in the eastern river valleys of the Big Sandy, Upper Licking, Cumberland, and Kentucky rivers. Among the other varieties of trees which are scattered over the state are chestnut, maple, ash, gum, hickory, beech, pine, spruce, elm, cedar, and birch. Kentucky was late in establishing a policy of conservation, and commercial exploitation was the general rule throughout the 19th century. Now large areas are being protected in the Cumberland and the Jefferson national forests.

The animal life of Kentucky once included the bison, which disappeared about 1820; the beaver, which survived until the 20th century; the panther (here called "painter"), which is now extinct; passenger pigeons; and the Carolina Louisiana parakeet, which is now almost destroyed. There are still a few wild turkeys and ravens in remote areas of the state. About 300 species of birds have been found in Kentucky, including blue herons, American egrets, Kentucky warblers, mockingbirds, bluebirds, and cardinals. The small animals are numerous; among them are red and gray foxes, minks, muskrats, raccoons, opossums, and red and gray squirrels. The muskellunge, locally called the jackfish or jack salmon, is one of the principal fishes of Kentucky. Snakes include four poisonous ones: the timber rattler, copperhead, cottonmouth, and coral. The state fish and game commission is active in the preservation of wild life, and many game refugees are maintained.

PEOPLE

Population. According to the Federal census for 1950 the population of Kentucky was 2,944,806, an increase of 99,179, or 3.5 per cent, over 1940.

PRINCIPAL CITIES	POPULATION	
	Census 1940	Census 1950
LOUISVILLE	319,077	369,129
COVINGTON	62,018	64,452
LEXINGTON	49,304	55,534
OWENSBORO	30,245	33,651
PADUCAH	33,765	32,828
ASHLAND	29,537	31,131
NEWPORT	30,631	31,044
BOWLING GREEN	14,585	18,347
HENDERSON	13,160	16,837
MIDDLESBOROUGH	11,777	14,482

Education. Attendance is compulsory in both cities and rural districts for the entire school term for children between the ages of 7 and 14. Separate schools are maintained for white and for colored children. Following recommendations by a commission which had studied educational conditions in Kentucky, the legislature adopted a new school code in 1934. This provided, notably, for an appointive state board of education of seven members, with overlapping terms; for a commission to co-ordinate activities of the institutions of higher learning; and for high training requirements for Kentucky teachers.

The University of Kentucky, at the head of the state's educational system, is located at Lexington. (See KENTUCKY, UNIVERSITY OF.) There are state teachers' colleges for training white teachers at Bowling Green, Richmond, Murray, and Morehead. The Kentucky State Industrial College for Negroes, at Frankfort, trains Negro teachers. Higher education is also afforded through private and denominational colleges and universities, among which are Transylvania University at Lexington; the University of Louisville, and a branch college, the Louisville Munic-

J. B. Speed Memorial Art Museum, Louisville
CAULFIELD AND SHOOK FROM EWING GALLOWAY

ipal College for Negroes, at Louisville; Berea College, at Berea; Georgetown College, at Georgetown; Centre College, at Danville; Asbury College, at Wilmore; Kentucky Wesleyan College at Winchester; and Union College, at Barbourville. Most of the junior colleges in the state are supported by religious denominations.

Public Welfare. The charitable and penal institutions are managed by a state board of charities and corrections, composed of eight members, who serve gratuitously. The Kentucky Institution for the Education of the Blind (1842) is at Louisville; colored blind children are cared for in a separate building. Other institutions are the Kentucky School for the Deaf, at Danville; the Eastern, Western, and Central state hospitals, at Lexington, Hopkinsville, and Lakeland, respectively; the Institution for Feeble-Minded Children, at Frankfort; and the School of Reform for boys and girls, at Greendale. There are also the Kentucky Confederate Home, at Pewee Valley; and the Kentucky Home society for colored children, at Louisville. The State Penitentiary is at Eddyville, and the Women's Prison is at Pewee Valley.

ECONOMIC LIFE

Agriculture and Stock Raising. Kentucky is essentially an agricultural state, and about three-fourths of its land area is in farms. The soil of Kentucky is almost entirely residual, being formed from disintegrating limestone, shale, and sandstone. The very fertile soil of the famous Bluegrass Region, embracing about 10,150 square miles in the northeastern part, is a heavy clay loam formed from a phosphatic blue limestone. Along the rivers are alluvial deposits of great fertility, aggregating about 800 square miles. The soils of the northwest, formed from weathered limestone, are less fertile, yet only a few thousand square miles of the total area are unsuited to agriculture. In the western section generally the soil is a soft, yellowish silt.

The most important cash crop in Kentucky is tobacco, which accounts for one-third to one-half of the annual cash income of the state's farmers. Tobacco production in the state has prospered as a result of such factors as favorable soil, a sunny, equable climate, ample railway facilities, and a growing popular market; by the end of the Civil War, and for many years after, Kentucky produced more of the crop than any other state, and more recently has been outranked only by North Carolina. Burley—formerly grown in the state only in the Bluegrass Region, the best burley area in the nation—is now cultivated in nearly all the counties. Lexington, in the heart of the Bluegrass, is one of the great tobacco markets of the world. Because of their long dependence on tobacco as the chief cash crop, Kentucky farmers have been somewhat slow in diversifying their crops. An economic collapse in the state's dark-tobacco regions because of a reduced foreign market after World War I, however, resulted in the development of dairying, legume production, poultry farming, and small fruit orcharding in those regions. Corn, which can be raised in all sections, is usually the most valuable crop grown, but little of it is marketed as such, since the major part is fed to livestock. Kentucky formerly was an important hemp producing state, but with the decline of sailing vessels after 1860, the demand was lessened. During World War II, the need for replacing the hemp of the Far East again stimulated production in Kentucky. For many years whisky has been an important product, furnishing farmers with a steady market for corn and rye and keeping grains in production when other crops might have been grown. Of inestimable value in the development of the state's agriculture has been the Kentucky Agricultural Experiment Station, established in 1885 and co-operatively maintained at Lexington by the state and Federal governments.

The raising of livestock in Kentucky has had the

Berea College Students at work on school farm, with college buildings in the background. Handicrafts are an important part of school curriculum

Mountain Chair Maker turns wood with a foot lathe

Coal Mine in Floyd County is representative of the many hillside mines in eastern section of Kentucky; men of the area are employed there irregularly

Bardstown Distillery, part of a great Kentucky industry

Sorghum Cane Grinder is operated by horse-drawn sweep in production of molasses on a Kentucky farm

Tobacco is Kentucky's most important single crop. This is the sales floor of a warehouse in Lexington

advantages of a mild climate, the excellent pastures of the Bluegrass Region, streams of pure water, and a large yield of corn and other forage crops. The state led in the raising of mules until the end of the 19th century. Great numbers of cattle, sheep, hogs, and horses are pastured in the Bluegrass. Dairying has been of increasing importance in recent years, and the raising of turkeys and other fowls is also a valuable enterprise. Kentucky is famous for its fine horses. The Bluegrass Region probably offers the best pasture for horses in the nation, and many of the greatest thoroughbreds in turf history have come from here.

PRINCIPAL CROPS OF KENTUCKY

CROP	UNIT (Thousands)	1939–1948 Average	1949	1950
Barley......	Bushels	1,719	1,638	1,480
Corn.......	Bushels	74,129	88,762	78,810
Hay........	Tons	2,258	2,635	2,633
Hemp.......	Pounds	2,699	88	—
Oats........	Bushels	2,078	3,328	2,832
Popcorn.....	Pounds	9,384	12,852	16,837
Potatoes.....	Bushels	3,615	2,730	2,418
Soybeans....	Bushels	1,102	2,202	1,890
Sweet Potatoes	Bushels	1,248	913	870
Tobacco.....	Pounds	386,325	438,245	364,450
Wheat.......	Bushels	5,260	5,268	3,900

Manufactures. Much of the industrial importance of the state is attributable to its agricultural wealth and its mineral resources, affording a supply of cheap fuel, and to its efficient means of transportation, particularly over its many rivers. The tobacco industry is one of the state's oldest and most lucrative enterprises. The leading producer of burley, which forms the bulk of the average American cigarette, the state has ranked near the top in cigarette output, and Kentucky factories also make pipe tobaccos and snuff, from dark tobacco, and chewing gum. Of first-rate importance, too, is the distilling industry, and Kentucky bourbon whisky has long been famous. The name "bourbon" is derived from that of the Kentucky county to which a number of Pennsylvania "moonshiners" moved after the suppression of the Whisky Insurrection in 1794. The state ranked second in the manufacture of distilled liquor before national prohibition, and the product regained its importance after repeal of the 18th amendment.

The grain raised in the state is utilized in flour and grist-mills, and the slaughtering and meat packing industries centering at Louisville are supplied by livestock from Kentucky farms. The numerous tanneries prosper largely because of the native supply of oak bark. The lumber and timber industry is considerable; near the forests are many planing mills. Iron and steel mills are important, and utilize iron ore deposits found within the state. Clay near at hand is used in tiles, bricks, and pottery. Near Louisville and Ashland are large oil refineries.

Other manufactures and products include foundry and machine shop output, printing and publishing, men's clothing, carriage and wagon making, bread and bakery products, boots and shoes, cooperage, confectionery, patent medicines, paints and varnish, cotton goods, furniture, woolen and felt goods, cordage, and marble- and stonework. The leading manufacturing city is Louisville, where the bulk of the tobacco industry is located, as well as the larger share of the clothing, flour, and meat manufacturers. Other important centers are Covington, Newport, Paducah, Owensboro, Ashland, Henderson, and Lexington.

Mining. Kentucky has great wealth in its mineral resources, which have not been completely developed. The leading mineral product is bituminous coal, in the output of which Kentucky forged to third place among the states of the nation in 1946–48. There are two great coal fields in the state, one a part of the Middle Appalachian fields, and the other a section of the Eastern Interior field. Formerly the western section had the largest output of coal, but recent development and low cost production possible in the eastern mines have brought their yield to four times that of the west. Next in importance are petroleum and natural gas. Kentucky ranked seventh among the states in the total value of mineral production in 1948, with an output valued at $506,249,000.

MINERAL PRODUCTION OF KENTUCKY

MINERAL	UNIT (Thousands)	1946	1947	1948
Clay..............	Short Tons	735	787	802
Coal..............	Short Tons	66,552	84,240	82,000
Iron, Pig.........	Short Tons	624	661	799
Natural Gas.......	M Cu. Ft.	70,396	96,459	70,095
Natural Gasoline...	Gallons	9,062	9,577	10,182
Liquefied Petroleum Gases...........	Gallons	44,800	50,136	56,407
Petroleum.........	Barrels	10,578	9,397	8,551
Sand and Gravel	Short Tons	2,163	2,454	2,066
Stone.............	Short Tons	4,745	4,990	6,154

Transportation. Kentucky is well favored with means of water transportation, having about 4,000 miles of navigable rivers. The Ohio River on the north and the Mississippi on the west have been of great commercial and industrial importance from the earliest pioneer days. The Cumberland and Tennessee rivers are navigable for steamboats across the state. The Kentucky and Licking are each similarly navigable for 60 miles, and the Green for 100 miles. Canals around the falls on the Ohio at Louisville and at various points on the other rivers facilitate traffic. Railway construction began late, but there was considerable activity from 1880 to 1890, after which rapid progress followed. There are about 3,500 miles of steam railway and more than 400 miles of electric tracks. The principal lines are the Illinois Central, the Louisville and Nashville, the Chesapeake and Ohio, and the Cincinnati Southern. The railroads serve only about 20 per cent of the communities, the lowest percentage among the states. Kentucky maintains about 6,000 miles of highways but there is a total highway mileage of more than 60,000 within the state. Louisville is the hub of air line transportation. The state is served by the Eastern, the American, the Chicago and Southern, and the Delta air lines.

Tourist Attractions. Kentucky has a number of unique attractions which have added to its fame. For more than a century, Mammoth Cave has been renowned as a world wonder which attracts explorers and tourists alike. Kentucky's early associations with Abraham Lincoln have been preserved in the ABRAHAM LINCOLN NATIONAL HISTORICAL PARK, embracing Sinking Spring Farm, which belonged to Lincoln's father. A memorial building on the side of Abraham Lincoln's birthplace encloses a log cabin believed to be that in which he was born. Kentucky's Bluegrass horse farms continue to foster national interest in racing thoroughbreds. Since 1875 the famous Ken-

Churchill Downs, scene of the Kentucky Derby

CAULFIELD & SHOOK, INC.

Echo River, underground stream, Mammoth Cave

Tobacco field and corn patch on a mountain farm

Cumberland Gap from pinnacle on Pine Mountain

Horse farm at Fayette in the Bluegrass Region

"My Old Kentucky Home" at Bardstown

Waterfall in Cumberland Falls State Park

tucky Derby has been held at Churchill Downs in Louisville. Thousands of racing enthusiasts are attracted annually to this spectacular event.

Kentucky has a fine system of state parks which preserve scenic and historic points of interest. Blue Lick State Park is the site of the last battle of the Revolutionary War in the West (1782). The Pioneer Museum in the park houses pioneer relics and the Hunter collection of prehistoric remains discovered at the licks. Pioneer Memorial State Park, near Harrodsburg, encloses several historic shrines. A fort and palisades have been reconstructed on the site of old Fort Harrod. The Taylor Mansion, built in 1830 by Maj. James Taylor, houses relics of George Rogers Clark, Abraham Lincoln, and the Confederacy. The cabin in which Lincoln's parents were married in 1806 has been moved to the park from Beach Fork settlement and enclosed within a brick building. A memorial to Clark and an early cemetery also lie within the park.

An ancient buried city, disclosing more than 100 burials and many artifacts, has been excavated on the high bluff above Wickliffe. Several buildings which once belonged to Shakertown colony (1800) are still standing near Bowling Green. Berea is the seat of Berea College (1853), the oldest and largest of Kentucky's mountain schools. At Berea also are the Churchill Weavers, a celebrated institution devoted to preserving the art of hand-weaving and the traditional patterns used by the Kentucky mountaineers. The visitor who wants to see all of rural Kentucky should follow the back roads and trails which lead past picturesque mountain cabins where pioneer modes of life still are followed.

The two beautiful capitols of Kentucky may be seen at Frankfort, capital of the state, lying in the pleasant Kentucky Valley. The old capitol, of Greek Revival style, is now the State Historical Museum. Completed in 1830, it was the scene of many historic events until replaced in 1909 by the modern building of Bedford stone. Here also is Liberty Hall, a fine ante-bellum home of John Brown, the first U.S. senator from Kentucky. A memorial and the grave of Daniel Boone are in Frankfort cemetery. Louisville, the largest city of Kentucky, has many beautiful buildings of the pre-Civil War period such as the Benjamin Smith Home and the Ford Mansion. It is the site of the University of Louisville, on whose campus is the Speed Memorial Museum; the Filson Club which collects Kentuckiana; and Churchill Downs. Historic houses dot the Kentucky countryside and grace many Kentucky towns. Some of the finest examples of the ante-bellum period may be seen at Lebanon.

GOVERNMENT

The present constitution was adopted in 1891 and only a small number of amendments have since been ratified. Amendment is by three-fifths vote of each house of the general assembly and by majority vote of the electorate. A constitutional convention may be called by a majority of both houses of the general assembly at two successive sessions, and if the proposal is then approved by a majority vote of the electorate (equal to at least one-fourth the qualified voters at the last election).

The general assembly is composed of a senate of 38 members elected for four years and a house of representatives of 100 elected for two years. Regular sessions are held biennially in the even-numbered years, beginning early in January and lasting for not more than 60 days. The compensation is $10 a day for all time spent in regular and special sessions. All revenue bills must originate in the lower house.

The executive department consists of the governor, lieutenant governor, secretary of state, treasurer, auditor, attorney general, superintendent of public instruction, and commissioner, all of whom are elected for four years and ineligible for immediate re-election.

In case of vacancy the lieutenant governor succeeds to the governorship, unless such vacancy occurs during the first two years of the term, in which case a special election is held. The governor has the usual veto power over legislation and in addition he may veto items in appropriation bills; his veto may be overridden by a majority vote of all elected members of each house.

The judiciary is headed by the court of appeals, consisting of seven judges elected by districts for eight-year terms; the senior judge serves as the chief justice. In addition there are circuit courts, quarterly courts, county courts, justices of the peace, police courts, and fiscal courts. The counties are grouped into judicial circuits, except that counties of 150,000 population constitute separate districts.

In 1936 the state government was modernized after an extensive study of its operation. A new department of welfare was created, the powers of the department of health were expanded, the state tax commission and the department of revenue and taxation were consolidated into a single department of revenue, power was added to the efficiency department to improve the civil service, and a department of conservation was established. Another innovation was the establishment of a legislative council, an advisory body which studies and reports on the working of the legislature, prepares and submits programs for the general assembly, and promotes interstate comity.

For local government the state is divided into 120 counties, each of which is under the administration of a county court headed by the county judge. The county court collects and expends moneys and exercises considerable discretion in the regulation of local affairs. Other county officials are the sheriff, clerk, attorney, jailer, coroner, surveyor, and assessor, all elected for four years. Since Kentucky is southern in influence it does not have township organization, but the county is divided into magisterial districts, each with a justice of the peace. The cities are divided into six classes according to population, with different forms of government provided for each. State law does, however, permit each city to choose the commission or the city manager form.

All persons, with insignificant exceptions, of 21 and over may vote. Residence requirements are one year in the state, six months in the county, and sixty days in the precinct. The capital is at Frankfort.

HISTORY

The Dark and Bloody Ground. The state takes its name from the Indian word, *Kan-tuck-hee*, to which various meanings have been assigned, the one most commonly accepted being "dark and bloody ground." While there were few Indians living within its borders at the coming of the whites it had long been fought over by the northern and southern tribes. It is possible that La Salle may have entered the territory as early as 1669, but in any event other French explorers were in the region within a few years. English interest in the country beyond the mountains was stimulated when they learned of these explorations by their rivals. Gabriel Arthur penetrated to northeastern Kentucky with a party of Indians in 1673, and it is believed that he was the first Englishman within the present-day state. During the next 70 years little attention was given to the area. In 1742 John Peter Salley with a party of Virginians entered the region, where he was captured by the French; after his release his account aroused interest in Kentucky. The French then took steps to assert their sovereignty, starting a race for control which soon led to the FRENCH AND INDIAN WAR. In 1750 the Loyal Land Company of Virginia sent out an expedition under Dr. Thomas Walker; this party passed through CUMBERLAND GAP, and erected a log house on the Cumberland River near present-day Barbourville, but abandoned it after a few days because of an Indian alarm. The next year the Ohio Company sent out

KENTUCKY
High Lights of History

DETAIL, MURAL BY GILBERT WHITE; KENTUCKY HIST. SOC.
Daniel Boone explored Kentucky in 1767

FROM PAINTING BY G. C. BINGHAM; WASHINGTON U.
Boone led settlers through Cumberland Gap, 1773

FROM A PAINTING, KENTUCKY HISTORICAL SOC.
Portrayal of Simon Kenton's capture by Indians

KENTUCKY HIST. SOC.
First State House in Frankfort, 1794

DETAIL OF MURAL, CAPITAL HOTEL, FRANKFORT
In 1862, Morgan's cavalry made a 24-day raid into Kentucky, disrupting Union activities in the state

NATIONAL PARK SERV.
Birthplace of Abraham Lincoln (from a sketch)

Ohio River wharf and waterfront at Louisville

Christopher Gist to Kentucky, but settlement had to await the termination of the struggle for political control.

Early Settlements. Even after Great Britain secured possession of the western territory in 1763 a British proclamation forbade settlement beyond the mountains. Nevertheless during the 1760's Kentucky was visited by many hunters and adventurers, including John Raines, John Finley, and DANIEL BOONE. During these years Boone spent much time in Kentucky, acquiring a familiarity with the country which made him such a valuable scout. In 1773 Judge Richard Henderson of North Carolina organized the TRANSYLVANIA COMPANY, which secured a large land grant, made a treaty with the Cherokees, and commissioned Boone to blaze a trail into Kentucky; the result was the establishment in May, 1775, of the settlement called Boonesboro. Meanwhile a Virginia group was also active. In 1774 James Harrod led a party of surveyors down the Ohio and up the Kentucky to the present site of Harrodsburg, but were forced to retire at the outbreak of DUNMORE'S WAR. By June, 1775, they were back, and they established Harrodsburg. In the rivalry that followed between the Virginia and North Carolina settlements the former gained the upper hand, partly through the leadership of GEORGE ROGERS CLARK. The Transylvania Company was declared illegal. Kentucky County was established as a part of Virginia. During the early years of the American Revolution the western settlements were little molested by the Indians, but after 1778 they were constantly harrassed by tribes acting under British instigation. Major attacks on the settlers were made in 1778 and 1782. On Aug. 19, 1782, occurred the Battle of Blue Licks in which the Kentuckians were routed by the Indians and British with a loss of about 70 killed and captured.

In 1780 settlement received a great impetus; 300 boats came down the Ohio with some 3,000 persons. In that year Kentucky County was divided into Lincoln, Fayette, and Jefferson counties. After the end of the Revolutionary War, settlement was further stimulated by the cessation of Indian troubles. Then followed nearly a decade of political controversy because of the dissatisfaction with distant Virginia authority. Some people desired to set up a new state within the Union, others talked of complete independence, and there were even rumors of a movement to join Spain, which then controlled New Orleans. For a long time Virginia refused to consent to separation, but finally did so in 1789. On June 1, 1792, Kentucky entered the Union as the 15th state.

The Young State. In 1798 and 1799 the KENTUCKY RESOLUTIONS were passed. The first constitution, which provided for the choice of state officers by electors, was superseded in 1799 by a second constitution, which provided that such officers be chosen directly by popular vote.

Kentucky

The breaking out of the WAR OF 1812 brought 18,200 Kentuckians into the field, though no battle occurred within the state. Within the next few years the passing of Louisiana into the hands of the French, the closing by the French intendant of the Mississippi, and the discovery of the plottings of AARON BURR for the establishment of a new nation west of the Alleghenies, all had a large influence on the fortunes of Kentucky.

The scarcity of money due to fraudulent banking and excessive speculation led in 1822 to the passage of relief measures by the legislature. The court of appeals declared these measures unconstitutional; the legislature then abolished the court and established a new one. "New Court" and "Old Court" were made political issues in 1826, the result being a legislature which repealed the act creating the new court. Between 1828 and 1830 the common-school system of Kentucky was established. In 1830 the legislature prohibited the importation of slaves except those owned by *bona fide* emigrants. A third constitution, adopted in 1850, extended the list of offices filled by popular election to include justices of the state courts, and provided for a permanent school fund.

Civil War. At the outbreak of the Civil War, Kentucky at first refused to take sides. Governor Magoffin protested to both the Federal and the Confederate governments against the military occupation of any part of the state, and endeavored to have Kentucky named as the mediator between North and South. His wishes were not complied with, however, and the elections held in the spring and early summer of 1861 gave evidence that not only were the people opposed to maintaining a position of neutrality, but that they largely sympathized with the Union cause. The first important engagement fought in the state was at Mill Spring on Jan. 19, 1862, between the Confederates under Zollicoffer and the Federals under Thomas. In this battle the Federals were successful, and the Confederates were driven out of eastern Kentucky. Another engagement took place at Perryville on Oct. 8, 1862, in which the Federals under Buell won a strategic victory over the Confederates under Bragg. This victory gave the Federals undisputed possession of the state, and broke up the attempt to organize a Confederate provisional government. (See CIVIL WAR.) A law of 1872 gave Negroes the right to appear as witnesses in court, and another of 1874 provided for Negro education in separate schools. The present constitution was adopted in 1891.

Twentieth Century. In 1899 the Republican candidate for governor, W. S. Taylor, was declared elected by a small majority over William Goebel, Democratic candidate. The latter contested the election in the legislature; but before the final decision he was shot (Jan. 30, 1900) and killed. Several men were arrested for the crime, and Caleb Powers, secretary of state, was three times tried and found guilty. In 1907, occurred the first raids in Kentucky of the NIGHT RIDERS, bands of armed men who for several years terrorized certain sections of the southwestern United States. The Lincoln Memorial at Hodgenville was formally presented to the nation in 1916, and in that year an extensive forest conservation plan was adopted.

During World War I, 75,043 Kentucky men served in the armed forces. During 1927 steps were taken to promote the purchase of 7,200 acres overlying Mammoth Cave, to be turned into a National Park and game preserve.

In the boom years preceding and immediately following World War I, coal developments in southeastern Kentucky grew rapidly. Thousands of miners and their families moved into Harlan and the neighboring counties, so that in less than 20 years Harlan grew from 10,000 to 70,000 inhabitants, most of them concentrated in the coal camps. When the depression fell, many industries, reducing their operations, cut down on fuel purchases and the coal piled up at the mines. Many mine operators were forced to close down and thousands were out of work or on short time. Strikes, riots, and shootings followed.

The Shields-Nickell Governmental Reorganization Act of 1936 modernized the state government. In 1936 a gold bullion depository was built at Fort Knox by the U.S. Treasury Department. Kentucky suffered heavy loss in the great floods of 1937. (See FLOOD AND FLOOD CONTROL.) In World War II, about 294,-000 Kentucky men and women served in the armed forces. In June, 1949, the University of Kentucky announced that Negroes would be admitted to classes with whites.　　　　　　　　　　　F. C. W.; F. M.

BIBLIOG.–W. E. Connelley and E. M. Coulter, *History of Kentucky* (1922); W. R. Thomas, *Life Among the Hills and Mountains of Kentucky* (1926); D. H. Davis, *Geography of the Blue Grass Region* (1927); M. W. Lafferty, *Lure of Kentucky* (1939); Writers' Project, *Kentucky: A Guide to the Bluegrass State* (1939); J. W. Coleman, *Slavery Times in Kentucky* (1940); R. Newcomb, *Old Kentucky Architecture* (1940); J. F. Thomas, *Big Sandy* (1940); T. D. Clark, *Exploring Kentucky* (1939); *Kentucky* (1942); A. F. Harlow, *Weep no More My Lady* (1942); J. Magill, *Pioneer to the Kentucky Emigrant* (1942); F. G. Davenport, *Ante-bellum Kentucky* (1943); H. W. Beers, ed . *Kentucky* (1945); T. C. Cherry and A. M. Stickles, *Story of Kentucky* (ed. 1945); H. W. Schacter, *Kentucky on the March* (1949); G. Champion and C. A. Keith, *Living in Kentucky* (1950).

KENTUCKY DERBY. See DERBY, KENTUCKY; HORSE RACING.

KENTUCKY RESOLUTIONS, passed by the legislature of Kentucky in 1798 and 1799, were directed against the ALIEN AND SEDITION ACTS. The first series, originally drafted by Thomas Jefferson, was passed by the House on Nov. 10, 1798, and by the Senate on Nov. 13, and was signed by Governor Garrard on Nov. 16. The resolutions asserted "that whensoever the general government assumes undelegated powers, its acts are unauthoritative, void, and of no force; that to this compact (the Constitution) each State acceded as a State, and is an integral party, its co-States forming, as to itself, the other party; that the government created by this compact was not made the exclusive or final judge of the extent of the powers delegated to itself, but that, as in all cases of compact among parties, having no common judge, each party has an equal right to judge for itself, as well of infractions as of the mode and measure of redress." Copies of the resolutions were sent to the other state legislatures, only seven of which replied, and these condemned the resolutions. In November, 1799, the Kentucky legislature reaffirmed these views. Similar resolutions were passed by the Virginia legislature. See VIRGINIA RESOLUTIONS; STATES' RIGHTS.

KENTUCKY RIFLE. See RIFLE, KENTUCKY.

KENTUCKY RIVER, Kentucky, is formed by the junction of three forks at Proctor in Lee County, and runs in a winding NW course of about 250 miles to Carrollton, where it joins the Ohio River. It is navigable for steamboats to Frankfort. The river, which takes its name from the state, flows through a rich agricultural and mineral region, with beautiful scenery. Along the banks of the river were located two of the first Kentucky settlements; Fort Boonesboro, laid out in 1775 by Daniel Boone; Harrodsburg, just west of the upper Kentucky, established in 1774. At one time steamboats navigated the river as far as Beattyville, and in the early days flatboats floated to market over its course. The deep cut channel and palisades rival in beauty the palisades of the Hudson.
BIBLIOG.–T. D. Clark, *The Kentucky* (1942).

KENTUCKY STATE COLLEGE. See COLLEGES.

KENTUCKY, UNIVERSITY OF. Chartered in 1865, the University of Kentucky at Lexington was originally the agricultural and mechanical arts departments of another institution, Kentucky University, which is no longer in existence. The state voted to assume complete control over the school in 1878 and re-established it on its present site as the College of Agriculture and Mechanical Arts. The present name

was adopted in 1916. Instruction in arts and sciences dates from 1865; agriculture, engineering, education, and law were added in 1908; commerce and a graduate school in 1925. There is an Experiment Station Farm on the main campus, a forest and additional agricultural station at Quicksand, Ky., and another station at Princeton, Ky. The Agriculture Extension Division works through field agents among the farmers of the state. Other activities of the university include bureaus of business research, curriculum service, engineering research and development, government research, and school service.

KENTUCKY WESLEYAN COLLEGE. See COLLEGES.

KENYA, a great volcanic mountain, now extinct, in British East Africa, Kenya Colony, lying immediately S of the Equator in 37° 20' E long. and reaching 17,040 feet above the sea, one of Africa's greatest heights. It is cleft at the summit into two points, and there are 15 glaciers, most of them within an area of one square mile. A number of early efforts to climb the peak failed, but H. J. Mackinder first attained the summit in 1899. Four ascents were made in 1929 and 1930 by Eric Shipton, and a group of Italians made a successful climb in 1933.

KENYA COLONY AND PROTECTORATE, British dependency of E central Africa, on the Indian Ocean; area 224,960 sq. mi., of which about 2,000 sq. mi. are in the protectorate; pop. (1948 census) 5,373,078. Kenya is governed as a crown colony although an important 10-mile coastal strip and the adjacent islands are under the sovereignty of the Sultan of Zanzibar, from whom they are leased.

Topography and Climate. The coastal area has no deep indentations. Geographically Kenya may be divided into four areas: the low coastal region; the arid northern section; the uplands, which include Mount KENYA (17,040 ft.); and the GREAT RIFT VALLEY, extending through Lake Rudolf south into Tanganyika, a region of generally level floor. Ridges divide the valley into basins, each of which has a lake with no outlet. Mount Kenya is an extinct volcano, and Mount Teleki, at the south end of Lake Rudolf, last erupted in the 19th century. The Equator passes through the center of Kenya, and the lowlands and the

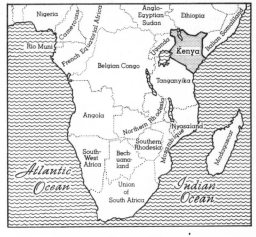

Location map of Kenya

shore of Lake Victoria have a typical tropical climate. The northern lowlands are hot and dry; in some of these districts rain does not fall for years on end. The highlands, the areas occupied by the white settlers, have a more amenable temperature, although malaria is prevalent. Here the rainfall is from 40 to 100 inches a year and the average yearly temperature is 66° F.

Plants and Animals. The coastal lowlands are swampy and have dense forests of mangroves, some

Camel safari on way to wells in northern Kenya

coconut palms, rubber vines, and patches of sandalwood, copal, and teak. The lowlands (up to 3,000 ft.) have dense thickets and thorn bushes and a few forest patches of giant euphorbia, baobab, acacia, and rubber vines. From 3,000 to 9,000 feet Kenya is largely grassland, with some acacia forests along the streams and some papyrus swamps. The eastern slopes of the mountains (6,000 to 10,000 ft.) have rain forests of camphor, hardwood, yellowwood, and giant bamboos; the dryer western slopes have much African cedar. In higher zones (11,000 to 14,500 ft.) giant senecio, lobelia, and tree heaths grow.

Kenya is noted for its big game, and the lion, leopard, cheetah, giraffe, buffalo, rhinoceros, hartebeest, eland, oryx, kudu, sable, baboon, colobus monkey, squirrel, dormouse, and elephant (the last now rather rare) are found. There are more than 40 kinds of snakes, including the deadly mamba, the tree cobra, and the puff adder. Centipedes, scorpions, and mosquitos and other insects in addition to the tsetse fly infest the coastal region. Among the birds are the ostrich, stork, bustard, secretary, tawny eagle, vultures, fancolin, guinea fowl, wild pigeon, pelican, flamingo, heron, ibis, and cormorant.

People. Kenya is a borderland between Negro and Hamitic people, with Bantus in the south; Kavirondo east of Lake Victoria; Nilotic tribes in the northwest; and Gallas and Somalis, some of whom are nomads, between the Tana River and the Somaliland border. Swahilis, a mixture of Bantu and Arab blood, and Arabs, are found along the coast. Indians, who were brought to Kenya as railway construction laborers and are now farm laborers, merchants, traders, and professional people, are limited to the lowlands by governmental edict. The Europeans have settled principally in the uplands. The population in 1948 included some 24,000 Arabs, 98,000 Asiatics (mostly Indians), and 30,000 Europeans.

The principal towns and their nonnative populations (1947) are: NAIROBI, 54,579, the capital since 1907; MOMBASA, 41,893, the chief port with Kilidini as its harbor; and KISUMU, 5,563, a Lake Victoria port and a rail terminal. Other cities are LAMU, on the island of that name; MALINDI, on the coast, the "Melind" of Milton's *Paradise Lost;* Nakuru; Eldoret, peopled mostly by Dutch-speaking South Africans; Kibuyu, a noted missionary station 15 miles north of Nairobi; and Thika, a coffee center.

Religion and Education. Among the natives in the coastal areas Mohammedanism has made considerable progress, but the inland natives are largely pagan. There are a number of British, French, Swedish, and American mission stations.

In 1948 Kenya had 58 government schools, 12 of which were for Europeans, 20 for Indians, 7 for Arabs and Somalis, and 19 for Africans. There were about 2,400 nongovernmental schools, of which 2,238 were African. There were also a few private schools.

Agriculture. Agriculture is the chief industry of Kenya. During the building of the railway that connects Uganda with the coast late in the 19th century, it was discovered that the uplands were ideal for the

Kenya Colony

growing of farm products, and subsequently the area was colonized by Europeans, some of whom came from the Union of South Africa, and by the Indians who had been brought to labor on the railway; Indians have been restricted to the lowland areas. In later years the government has encouraged the natives to raise more than for their own needs, and native products now swell the considerable agricultural exports of the colony. Labor has been the main problem of farm production, the native not taking easily to the regulated work of planned farming. The government in 1920 forbade the use of compulsory farm labor. The chief crops in the order of their importance are coffee, sisal hemp, corn, wheat, coconuts, and sugar cane. Because of the wide range of climates afforded by the mountain slopes and plateaus, production is varied. Other products are flax, cotton, peanuts, potatoes, beans, essential oils, and cashew nuts.

Commerce. The chief imports of the colony are grain, flour, tobacco, cement, tools and implements, electrical goods, machinery, cotton and woolen goods, silk, jute bags and sacks, wearing apparel, chemicals, drugs, dyes, paints, oil, paper, and motor vehicles. The principal exports are coffee, sugar, tea, tobacco, sisal hemp, fibers, hides and skins, wattle bark and extract, sodium carbonate, pyrethrum, wool, and gold. Some 68 per cent of the imports come from the United Kingdom and British possessions, and Iran and the United States furnish a large part of the remainder. Export customers are the United Kingdom and possessions (79 per cent), the United States, and other countries.

Communications. Kenya has some 1,625 miles of railway, all of which is one meter gauge. A survey for the first railway from Kisumu on Lake Victoria to Mombasa on the Indian Ocean was made in 1892, and the line was built between 1896 and 1901. A number of other lines have been built since; the chief of these extends from Nakuru to Kampala, in Uganda, a line that in importance now supersedes the first railway.

The best harbor along the eastern seaboard of Africa is Mombasa's Kilidini Harbor, which affords berth for the larger deep-sea vessels. Lamu, on the island of that name, and Malindi are also ports of some importance. Kisumu is the principal Lake Victoria port. Motor roads give entrance into Somaliland, Ethiopia, Uganda, Northern Rhodesia, and Tanganyika. Telephone and telegraph lines total more than 26,000 miles; there is cable communication between Zanzibar and Mombasa; and radio stations are at both Mombasa and Nairobi. Plane service from Mombasa, Nairobi, and Kisumu connect with the chief African air lanes.

Government. The Executive Council consists of 12 members and the governor; the Legislative

Sewing class at the gold mines in Kakamega

Council is composed of 11 elected European members, 5 elected Indian members, 1 elected Arab member, 1 Arab nominated to represent Arab interests, 4 Africans nominated to represent the interests of the African community, 7 *ex officio* official members, and 9 or fewer nominated official members. The governor presides over this body. Legislation is made by means of ordinances promulgated by the governor, with the Legislative Council restricted to giving its advice and consent.

Kenya is administratively divided into five provinces: the Coast, with the capital at Mombasa; Central, with the capital at Nyeri; Rift Valley, with the capital at Nakuru; Nyanza, with the capital at Kisumu; and Northern Province, with the capital at Isiolo. In addition there is an extra-provincial district: Masai.

The administration of the colony was reorganized in 1946. The departments of the government came under the members of the Executive Council who became responsible to the governor. A Development and Reconstruction Authority was also established. The supreme court is at Nairobi and there are district courts presided over by magistrates. The currency is based on the English pound. The budget of the colony is divided into two parts: the ordinary budget and a fund for reconstruction and development.   G. B. DE H.

History. The interior lands now making up Kenya Colony were occupied by African tribes and the long coastal area had long been owned by the Sultan of Zanzibar, where, however, only a weak control was exercised. The sultan's long association with the British Indian government encouraged him to offer to the British in 1877 a 70-year lease to these coastal lands, an offer the British refused. Stanley's explorations of that period, however, disclosed the richness of the area. A group of British business men, headed by Sir William Mackinnon, in 1888 formed the Imperial British East Africa Company under a royal charter. German interests in their Tanganyika colony were expanding during this same period and agreements made with them in 1886 and in 1890 brought the present area of Kenya under undisputed British sway.

On July 1, 1895, the country was formally transferred to the British crown, and the foreign office assumed responsibility for its administration. Construction of a railway, begun in 1896, was completed in 1903. Subsequently the white settlements grew in size. On April 1, 1905, the colony, known as the East African protectorate, was transferred from the au-

Sisal fiber is brushed preparatory to baling

thority of the British foreign office to that of the colonial office. In 1906 the region was placed under the control of a governor and commander in chief. By 1912 Kenya had become self-supporting. World War I imposed a temporary setback in the area's development. After the war the white settlers were restive while the Indians—who had been brought into the country to work on the rail construction—demanded political rights. In 1920, the region, except the dominions of the Sultan of Zanzibar, was annexed to the crown under the name of the "Colony of Kenya," thus becoming a crown colony. The territories on the coast rented from the Sultan became the Kenya protectorate. In 1923 the British government issued a white paper asserting that the native interest in the colony would remain paramount, and that when Indian and European interests were in conflict, the European interest would prevail. In 1925, the greater part of Jubaland was transferred to Italy, in accordance with the Treaty of London (1915) which had brought Italy into World War I.

Because of the activity of Germans in Tanganyika and the Italian aggression in Ethiopia, conscription was adopted in Kenya in 1936. The Kenya Legislative Council in 1945 abolished the office of chief secretary and set up in its stead an executive council. The British government in 1946 established the Colonial Development Company, with a fund of $400,000,000, to develop British colonies, particularly in Africa. In September, 1947, the British government announced that military supply bases would be established in Kenya. Plans for a Central African federation which would become a British dominion were proposed in March, 1949. It was also proposed that Kenya, Tanganyika, and Uganda form an East African federation which could unite with the proposed dominion.   C. S.; G. B. DE H.

BIBLIOG.–Norman Leys, *Kenya* (1924); W. McGregor Ross, *Kenya from Within* (1927); M. R. Dilley, *British Policy in Kenya Colony* (1938).

KENYON COLLEGE. See COLLEGES.

KEOKUK, city, SE Iowa, county seat of Lee County, on the Mississippi River at the mouth of the Des Moines River, the Burlington, the Rock Island, the Toledo, Peoria, and Western, and the Wabash railroads, and U.S. highways 61 and 218; about 43 miles SW of Burlington. Keokuk is situated at the foot of the Des Moines rapids in the Mississippi around which a canal was built by the Federal government in 1877. When the canal proved to be insufficient, the Mississippi River Power Company constructed, in 1913, a great dam and hydroelectric power plant across the Mississippi at Keokuk. In return for the privilege of operating the power plant, the power company built here for the U.S. government a drydock and lock, among the largest ever constructed. The first permanent white settlement on the site of the city was made in 1820. In 1837 the city was laid out and named for Keokuk, chief of the Sauk and Fox Indians. Keokuk was an early home of Samuel Clemens (Mark Twain). It was here that Twain worked in his brother's print shop and did

Coffee bean picker on a Kenya plantation

some of his earliest writings. Keokuk is the site of the National Cemetery in Iowa. The city is situated in the Iowa corn belt and manufactures awnings, boxes, buttons, corn products, castings, shoes, feeds, canned goods, and calcium carbide. Pop.(1950) 16,144.

KÉOS. See CYCLADES ISLANDS.

KEPHALLENÍA. See CEPHALONIA.

KEPLER, JOHANN, 1571–1630, German astronomer, was born in Württemburg. He studied at the University of Tübingen, became mathematical lecturer in the gymnasium at Gratz in 1594, and while there published his *Mysterium Cosmographicum* (1596), in which he attempted to establish a mystical geometry of the heavens. In October, 1600, he went to Prague as TYCHO BRAHE'S assistant and a year later succeeded him as imperial astronomer. He observed in 1604 the temporary star in Serpens and published in 1606 a treatise connecting the apparition with the "Fiery Triangle" of astrological import. His *Astronomia Nova* (1609) contained the laws that the planets describe ellipses with the sun as a focus and that the radius vector of each planet sweeps over equal areas in equal times.

YERKES OBSERVATORY

Johann Kepler

In 1612 Kepler became professor of mathematics at Linz. In 1618–21 he published an epitome of the Copernican astronomy, and in 1619 his *Harmonices Mundi, Libri V*, in which he announced his third law, that the squares of the planetary periods are as the cubes of their distances from the sun. At Ulm, where he had sought a refuge from war troubles, the Rudolphine Tables appeared in 1627. They represented a reform of astronomy based upon Brahe's observations and remained standard authority for a century. Kepler wrote also two works on optics, the *Paralipomena* to Vitellio (1604), and *Dioptrice* (1611), recommending in the latter the construction of telescopes with two convex lenses; *Stereometria*, which gives him a place among the founders of the infinitesimal calculus; and *De Cometis* (1619–20) treating the great comets of 1607 and 1618. A complete edition of his works was published by Frisch in eight volumes. See KEPLER'S LAWS.

BIBLIOG.–H. S. Williams, *The Great Astronomers* (1930).

KEPLER'S LAWS of planetary motion, resulting from his long study of the extensive series of accurate observations on the planets made by Tycho Brahe, apply to every planet. They are stated as follows:

1. The orbit of a planet is an ELLIPSE with the sun at one of its two foci.

2. The radius vector of the planet (a line drawn from the sun to the planet) sweeps over equal areas in equal times. (*Law of Areas.*)

3. The squares of the orbital periods P of any two planets are in the same ratio as the cubes of their mean distances a from the sun; i.e., $P_1{}^2/P_2{}^2 = a_1{}^3/a_2{}^3$, or $(P_1/P_2)^2 = (a_1/a_2)^3$. (*Harmonic Law.*)

The mean distance a is half the major axis of the orbital ellipse. If the second planet is taken to be the earth, with $P_2 = 1$ and $a_2 = 1$, the harmonic law then states for a *single planet* the relation between its period (in years) and its mean distance from the sun in terms of the earth's distance (astronomical unit); viz., $P^2 = a^3$. Making use of his laws of motion, Newton was able to show from the first two of Kepler's laws that a planet is kept in its orbit by a force directed toward the sun and that this force of attraction decreases as the distance from the sun increases, but more rapidly—i.e., the force varies inversely as the square of the radius vector; and from the third law, that the force is proportional to the masses of the planets. Newton's modification of the harmonic law is then: $m_1P_1{}^2/m_2P_2{}^2 = a_1{}^3/a_2{}^3$. This work was the basis of Newton's great generalization, the *law of universal gravitation*, the foundation of all studies of motions in the solar system and in the systems of double and multiple stars. A. T. M.

KEPPLER, JOSEPH, 1838–94, American cartoonist, was born in Vienna, Austria. After studying art in Italy, he came to the United States in 1868 and settled in St. Louis where he established a German periodical. When this enterprise failed, Keppler moved to New York and worked as a cartoonist. In 1877 he, together with Adolph Scharzmann, founded *Puck*, a weekly comic illustrated paper which inaugurated a new type of humor in America. Through Keppler's influence, *Puck's* cartoons emphasized jokes with the common man as the hero. They were in the German tradition of genial, droll humor, and they and *Puck* were the prototype for the comic supplement of today's Sunday newspapers.

KERAK, ancient **Kir-Hareseth, Kir-Haresh,** or **Kir-Heres,** formerly the capital of Moab, town in Trans-Jordan, Syria, 10 miles E of the Dead Sea. The fort, founded by the Crusaders in 1131 and captured by Saladin in 1188, still stands.

KERALA, ancient kingdom of S India, one of the divisions of the Dravida country. It corresponds with the British districts of Malabar and Kanara.

KERAMA ISLANDS, a group of small islands in the Ryukyu chain, 20 miles W of the S tip of Okinawa, and 400 miles SSW of Kyushu, Japan. The chief islands are Tokashiki (from whose cliffs 200 civilians jumped into the sea rather than be taken prisoner by the Americans in World War II), Aka, Mae, and Zamami, on all of which the chief occupations are farming and fishing. In World War II these rocky islets were used by the American Army as a springboard for the assault on strategic OKINAWA.

KERASUN. See GIRESUN.

KERATITIS, inflammation of the CORNEA.

KERBELA. See KARBALA.

KERCH or **Kertch,** city, seaport, and fortress, U.S.S.R., in the Russian Soviet Federated Socialist Republic, at the eastern extremity of Crimea Region, on the Strait of Kerch or Yenikale, (20 mi. broad and 22 mi. long), which connects the Black Sea and the Sea of Azov. The largest industrial center in the Region, Kerch has oil fields, shipyards, stone quarries, iron works, and manufactures of flour and tobacco. Fishing is also an important industry. In the sixth century B.C. Kerch was known as Pantikapaeum. It fell to the Turks in 1475, to the Russians in 1771, and in 1855 was destroyed in the Crimean War. Many *chefs d'oeuvre* of Graeco-Scythian art have been found in Kerch. These include catacombs, with curious wall paintings and sarcophagi, mostly

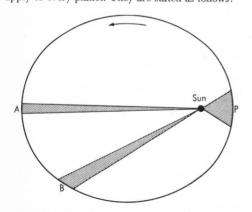

Kepler's Second Law. If the three shaded regions are equal in area, an asteroid moving in this elliptical orbit traverses arcs A, B, and P in equal time intervals, and therefore with greater speed at perihelion P than at aphelion A

assigned to the fourth century. During World War II the Germans destroyed all of Kerch's industrial establishments during their occupation (1942–44). Pop. (1951 est.) 100,000.

KERENSKY, ALEXANDER FEDOROVICH, 1881–   , Russian revolutionist and statesman. Born in a nobleman's family, a graduate of the St. Petersburg (now Leningrad) University, he began to practice law in 1904, devoting himself to the cause of the oppressed peasantry and working classes. In 1913 he was elected to the 4th Duma (Russian parliament) from the town of Volsk, Saratov Province on the Volga. During World War I he dis-
tinguished himself in the Duma by his able speeches against the pro-German elements in the Czar's govern-
ment and his exposure of corruption among high officials.

ACME
Kerensky

One of the leaders in the resistance to the Czar's de-
cree dissolving the Duma on Mar. 12, 1917, he became a member of the new provi-
sional government formed after the overthrow of the Czar. As minister of justice, one of his first acts ordered the release of all political prisoners.

He began to lose his popularity when, as minister of war and navy, he tried to lead the army in the unsuccessful Russian offensive in July, 1917. His fatal error was in not realizing that the Russian people were extremely tired of the war and longed for peace at any price.

On July 20, 1917, Kerensky succeeded Prince George Lvov as premier of Russia. He postponed the elections for the Constituent Assembly; failed to di-
vide the large estates among the peasants and to counteract the growing Bolshevik propaganda. In September he became commander in chief of all armed forces. Because he was more a brilliant orator than a man of action, he was unable to stem the rising Bolshevik revolt and was finally overthrown by NIKOLAI LENIN in November, 1917, thus opening the Soviet era in Russia's history.

Kerensky fled from the capital, first to South Russia, and later to Western Europe. Coming to the United States shortly before World War II, he settled in New York and became an influential anti-Soviet leader. His books include: *The Prelude to Bolshevism* (1919); *The Catastrophe* (1927); *The Crucifixion of Liberty* (1934).

KERGUELEN ISLAND or **LAND,** or **Desolation Island,** an archipelago in the Indian Ocean, con-
taining, besides the main island, some 300 islets, extending from 48° 39′ to 49° 44′ S lat., and from 68° 42′ to 70° 35′ E long. The group is volcanic in origin, and its face is mountainous (Mt. Ross, 6,100 ft.) and glaciated, with many cascades and deeply indented shores, providing excellent, sheltered harbors on the northeast. The annual average temperature is 39° F., but summer temperatures mount to more than 65°. Rain is almost constant. The peculiar Kerguelen cabbage (*Pringlea antiscorbutica*) is valued by sailors as a preventive of scurvy. Seals, whales, and fish are abundant in neighboring waters, and since 1907 a settlement has grown up at Port Jeanne d' Arc of those engaged in fishing and related industries. The island was discovered in 1772 by Yves Joseph de Kerguelen-Trémarec, a French navigator, and was visited by Captain Cook in 1776 and by the *Challenger* in 1874. Kerguelen was annexed by France in 1893 and made a dependency of Madagascar in 1924.

KERKI REGION, a former administrative area of the Turkmen Soviet Socialist Republic, U.S.S.R.; bounded on the N and E by the Uzbek Soviet Socialist Republic, on the W by Chardzhou Region, and on the S by Afghanistan. Kerki Region was incorpor-
ated in 1947 with Chardzhou, from which it had been separated in 1943.

KERKRADE, town and customs station, SE Netherlands, in the province of Limburg, on the German frontier, 15 miles E of Maastricht. It is the center of a rich coal-mining region. Pop. (1950 est.) 42,340.

KÉRKYRA. See CORFU.

KERMADEC ISLANDS, a group of small vol-
canic islands, lying 700 miles NE of New Zealand, to which they belong, astride the 30th S parallel in the South Pacific Ocean; area 13 sq. mi.; pop. about 25. The chief islands are Raoul (Sunday) which, in 1944, had a population of 20; Macauley; Curtis; and L'Esperance. The soil is fertile, but immigration to the group has been limited by the lack of adequate anchorages and the severe prevailing winds. The islands are used as a radio observatory station by transpacific air lines.

KERMAN, city, SE Iran, chief town of Kerman Province, 225 miles NE of Bandar Abbas on the Persian Gulf. The town has an ancient 11th-century mosque, a 12th-century stone monument, and other remains of archaeological interest. Kerman was visited by Marco Polo in 1271. It was once noted for its rose gardens, which furnished flowers for attar of roses. Today, however, the making of perfume is almost a lost art. Modern manufactures of Kerman in-
clude felt, carpets of exceptional beauty, brassware, exquisite embroideries, and goats hair shawls, that are second in texture and color only to those of Kashmir. Pop. (1942 est.) 50,000.

KERMAN PROVINCE, ancient **Caramania,** SE Iran, bounded on the E by Baluchistan, S by the Gulf of Oman, SW by Laristan, W by Fars and Yezd, and N by Khurasan; area 115,000 sq. mi.; pop. (1940 est.) 600,000. The Dasht-i-Lut, a desert waste, occupies the north and northeast; the remainder of the province is largely barren. The climate is hot and dry. In the south and southeast sections there are a number of rivers. Wheat, barley, and cotton are the chief crops; cultivation is aided by irrigation. The principal exports are cattle, cotton, gums, dates, henna, fruit, silk and woolen goods, carpets and shawls. Ruins of villages and forts indicate that the province was at one time a prosperous region.

KERMANSHAH, a province, NW Iran, bounded on the N by Kurdistan, on the N and E by Hamadan, on the S by Luristan, and on the W by Iraq; pop. about 425,000, mostly Kurds and Lurs. It is one of the richest sections of Iran, producing wheat, corn, rice, almonds, clover, castor beans, fruits, gums, and poppies for medicinal opium. There is extensive pasturage to support the great flocks of sheep, which furnish wool for export. Lambskins, silk, and carpets are also exported. Mules and camels are still used for transportation on the ancient caravan routes centering at the capital, KERMANSHAH.

KERMANSHAH, city, W Iran, capital of Ker-
manshah Province, 75 miles SW of Hamadan, and 270 miles SW of Teheran. It is an important caravan center on the road between Teheran and Baghdad (220 mi. SW) and a center for pilgrims to the sacred cities of Iran, Turkey, the Caucasus and other points in Russia, and central Asia. Kermanshah was founded in the fourth century. Horses, carpets, grains, fruits, gum, and medicinal opium are sold in the bazaars. The city has a governor's palace, an arsenal, many mosques and caravansaries, and a large oil refinery. It is known for its sweet breads. Kermanshah was occupied in 1915 by the Turks. Pop. (1942) 89,000, chiefly Kurds and Lurs.

KERMES, or **CHERMES,** an evergreen shrub of Palestine and the Mediterranean countries. It is infested with an insect (*Coccus ilicis*) from which is ob-
tained a scarlet dyestuff, now largely superseded by COCHINEAL. The name Kermes is also applied to the insect and to the dye.

KERMES MINERAL, or **Sulfuretted Antimony,** an amorphous, reddish white sulfide of antimony (Sb_2S_3), used in medicine as an ingredient of compound antimony pills.

KERMISS. See KUMISS.

KERMIT, town, W Texas, county seat of Winkler County; on the Texas-New Mexico Railway, about 160 miles W of San Angelo and eight miles from the border of New Mexico. Kermit is a trading center near oil fields and has manufactures of carbon black and oil-well supplies. Pop. (1950) 6,912.

KERN, JEROME, 1885–1945, American composer, was born in New York City and studied at the New York College of Music. After a long apprenticeship in song plugging, interspersed with trips to Europe and the writing of scores for third-class musicals, he became increasingly successful as a composer. His first Ziegfeld show, the *Follies* of 1916, was followed by *Sally* (1920), which contained the well-known song, "Look for the Silver Lining," and *Sunny* (1924), starring Marilyn Miller. His tunes for *Show Boat* (1926) have become popular classics and his songs for *The Cat and the Fiddle* (1927), *Roberta* (1933), and *Very Warm for May* (1939) are equally famous. Many of his musical comedies were reproduced in films, in addition to the new scores he prepared especially for motion pictures.

Jerome Kern

KERNER, ANDREAS JUSTINUS, 1786–1862, German lyric poet. He practiced medicine and was one of the chief poets of the "Swabian School." He published *Reiseschatten von dem Schattenspieler Luchs* (1811); *Romantische Dichtung* (1817); *Der letzte Blumenstrauss* (1852); as well as a book on animal magnetism, *Die Seherin von Prevorst* (1829). In conjunction with Uhland and Schwab he issued *Der poetische Almanach* (1812); *Der Deutsche Dichterwald* (1813).

KERNSTOCK, KAROLY, 1873–   , Hungarian artist, was born in Budapest. For a time he studied in Munich, but later went to Paris where he became the pupil of Adolphe Bouguereau. Kernstock took the doctrines of Post-Impressionism and Fauvism, in which he had become passionately interested, back to Hungary with him, and there founded the Post-Impressionist group called "The Eight." A painter with the qualities of frankness, power, and movement in his work, he made frequent choice of athletes and horses for the themes best to express those qualities, as in "Nude" and "Horsemen." Because motion and rhythm take first importance in Kernstock's work, color serves merely a functionary purpose. He accomplished some excellent stained glass work in "County House" in Debrecen.   JOAN C. CAMERA

KEROSENE is a mixture of hydrocarbons obtained by the fractional distillation of petroleum. It is an oily liquid boiling in the range 200–300° C. and has a specific gravity of approximately 0.8. At one time kerosene was used in lamps for illumination and as a fuel, but modern methods of heating and lighting have greatly diminished its importance. Higher boiling kerosenes may be used as diesel fuels, but most kerosene is "cracked" to gasoline. See PETROLEUM.

KÉROUALLE, LOUISE RENÉE DE, 1649–1734, mistress of Charles II of England and mother of the first duke of Richmond, was a native of Brittany. She was created duchess of Portsmouth and duchesse d'Aubigny. She retired to France after the death of Charles in 1685. Her influence was an important factor in preserving peace during the constant friction between Charles and Louis XIV.

KERRARA. See HEBRIDES.

KERRVILLE, city, S central Texas, county seat of Kerr County; on the Guadalupe River and the Southern Pacific Railroad, about 65 miles NW of San Antonio in a hilly region devoted to stock raising. Kerrville is one of the state's leading wool and mohair markets and is also a resort for hunters and campers. The city has creameries and hatcheries and ships goats, sheep, and cattle. Pop. (1950) 7,691.

KERRY, maritime county, SW Ireland, Munster Province, bounded on the SW, W, and N by the Atlantic and the River Shannon estuary; on the E by Limerick; on the SE and S by Cork; area 1,814 sq. mi.; pop. (1946) 133,818. The coast line is unusually irregular and broken. Almost half the county extends west into two large peninsulas, which are indented by bays and inlets. The best-known of these bays are Ballyheige, Tralee, Brandon, Dingle, St Finan's and Ballinskellig; the 30-mile deep estuary of the Kenmare River is on the southwest; the great bay formed by the estuary of the River Shannon is on the north; and along the west coast are Smerwick, Castlemaine, and Valentia harbors. The surface of Kerry is low along the north coast, but in all other sections it is mountainous, with numerous scenic glens. The principal range is MacGillicuddy's Reeks, with the culminating peak Carrantuohill (3,414 ft.) the highest peak of Ireland. Mount Brandon (3,127 ft.), the second highest, rises from the northernmost peninsula. Other lower ranges of hills are the Clanaruddery, Mangerton, Derrynasaggart, Caha, Iveragh, Mullaghanattin, Stack, Beenoskee, Baurtregaum, and the Mish mountains. There are remnants of a great forest of fir, birch, and yew trees in these highlands. Kerry's lakes all lie in the southern part of the county and include the celebrated trio of KILLARNEY—Leane and Upper and Lower Muckross—and Derriana, Cleonaghlin, Currane, Caragh, Annascaul, and Gimitane. The county is well drained by the Blackwater, Gale, Cashen, Smearlagh, Feale, Flesk, Maine, Laune, Roughty, Inny, Kenmare, and other small streams. Off the coast lie the islands of Magharee, Blaskets, Skellings, Valentia, Puffin, Scariff, and Deenish; and in the Killarney lakes are Muckross and Innisfallen. Marble, amethysts, sulfur, coal, limestone, and slate are the minerals found.

The county is more pastoral than agricultural, but oats, barley, and potatoes are produced in the more fertile valley sections. Goats, sheep, and the well-known Kerry cattle—a small, black, curly-horned breed—are raised. Industries are farming, deep-sea fishing, the quarrying of slate and limestone, and a few manufactures of coarse woolens, linen goods, and fancy carved wooden articles. TRALEE is the county town and Killarney, Ballybunion, Dingle, and Kenmare are the other important towns. There are fisheries at Valentia and Dingle; salmon fisheries at Kenmare and Killarney. Coastal resorts are Derrynane, Glenbeigh, Parknasilla, Waterville, and Tarbet. There are mineral springs at most of these towns.

Antiquities of interest include Staigue Fort, one of the most remarkable ancient fortifications of Ireland; the Ogam Stones; numerous round towers; ecclesiastical ruins, including the ruins of Derrynane Abbey; and, at Listowel, the last castle to hold out against Elizabeth in the Desmond rising. Kerry was made a shire by King John in 1210. After its conquest by the English in the 17th century, it was long dominated by the Orange party.   K. E. H.

KERRY BLUE TERRIER, an active, hardy, extremely intelligent dog that had its origin in county Kerry, Ireland. Remarkable for their trailing ability and endurance, kerries have long been used for hunting, retrieving, herding, as watchdogs, and in England as police dogs. Their gentle, lovable disposition makes them exceptionally good companions. In height the kerry measures about 18 inches at the shoulder and in weight ranges from 32 to 38 pounds. The soft, wavy coat may be various uniform shades of blue, parts of the head, ears, feet, and tail generally being lighter or darker than the rest of the body. The long, strong head has a flat skull, clean cheeks, small dark

'Kerry blue terrier

to hazel eyes, and medium-sized ears that are carried forward. Straight legs, muscular hind quarters, well-knit, sloping shoulders, a strong, straight back, deep ribs, and a moderately long tail, carried straight up, are other characteristics of the kerry.

KERSHAW, JOSEPH BREVARD, 1822–94, American soldier, was born in Camden, S.C. He was a member of the state Senate (1852–57). During the Civil War he served on the Confederate side, becoming a brigadier general in 1862, and taking a conspicuous part in the Peninsula Campaign and in the battles of Fredericksburg, Gettysburg, and Chickamauga. He was elected president of the state Senate (1865); was a judge of the state Circuit Court (1877–93); and was postmaster of Camden, S.C. (1893–94).

KERST, DONALD WILLIAM, 1911– , American physicist, was born in Galena, Ill., and studied at the University of Wisconsin. He joined the faculty of the University of Illinois in 1938 as an instructor in physics and became professor in 1943. He invented the betatron in 1940, built another in 1943, and a third, more than 100 times the size of the first, in 1950. The betatron accelerates electrons to speeds at which they attain energies of 20,000 electron volts. It was an integral factor in the development of the atomic bomb. In 1950 Kerst won the Comstock prize and the Weatherill medal for his work.

KERULEN RIVER, E Asia, a headstream of the Amur River, rises at an altitude of 8,146 feet in the Kentei Range NE of Urga (Ulan Bator), NE Mongolian People's Republic. After flowing south for 150 miles, it picks up the Tsenkhir at Bayan Munkhu, then turns northeast and skirts the northern edge of the Gobi Desert and passes the town of Kerulen (Bayan Tumen) 40 miles west of the Manchurian border. In Manchuria it traverses the Hulun Nor (lake), to a junction at Chalainoerh with the Hailar (another headstream of the Amur), becoming then the Argun. The total course of the Kerulen is about 600 miles.

KESSELRING, ALBERT, 1887– , German general, was born in Franconia and served as a pilot in World War I. Through the influence of Goering he became chief of the general staff of the Luftwaffe (1936) and proposed air tactics involving a high degree of teamwork for planes. Although he was unsuccessful at the time and resigned to take an army command at Dresden, his theories resulted in the *rollender einsatz* or rolling attack successfully applied in Poland and France. He commanded Air Fleet I at Berlin (1939) and directed operations between Danzig and Brest-Litovsk in Poland. He commanded Air Fleet II against Holland and Belgium and became field marshal general (1940) just as he was meeting his first defeat at Dunkirk, followed by the disastrous Battle of Britain. He commanded aviation in the central Russian sector (1941–42) then became

chief of the Luftwaffe in Italy (1942). As commander of the Tenth Army and supreme commander in Italy he opposed the Allied advance until the surrender (1945). He was brought to trial (1947) on charges of complicity in the Ardeatine cave massacre near Rome and other executions of Italian civilians. His death sentence was commuted to life imprisonment.

DON RUSSELL

KESTREL, a falcon distinguished by its bell-like note and plumage pattern. The kestrel, *Falco tinnunculus,* is widely distributed over Europe, Asia, and Africa and has even been taken in Massachusetts. In North America, however, the species is replaced by the sparrow hawk and similar forms. Kestrels are chiefly brown, with dark spots, and have a broad subterminal black band on the tail; the females are darker and more distinctly barred than the males. The name "windhover" is given on account of the habit of hanging in mid-air with the head against the wind. The kestrel feeds chiefly on mice, ground squirrels, and insects.

KESWICK, market town and urban district, NW England, Cumberlandshire, 209 miles NW of London. The town is located in the center of one of the most scenic areas of the British Isles, in the valley of the Greta River, on the northeast end of the lake called Derwent Water, near the peak of Skiddaw (3,054 ft.) and other high points of the Cumbrian Mountains. To the south and southeast are Borrowdale and the famed falls of Lodore. Keswick is a popular tourist center partly because of the "Keswick Convention," a religious festival held here. Near the village is a Druidical circle, measuring 100 by 108 feet, with 38 stones in the outer circle and 10 within it. Ruskin once called the view from "Friars' Crag" at the north end of Derwent Water the "finest in all England." Southey resided here in Greta Hall from 1804 until his death in 1843 and was buried in Crosthwaite parish. Shelley lived here for some time at Chestnut House. Pop. about 4,600.

KETCH, in its older sense, a stoutly-built square-rigged, two-masted craft, at one time common in the Mediterranean and used especially as a bomb vessel. The term is applied at the present day, especially in Europe, to a two-masted, fore-and-aft-rigged craft, in which the mizzen is considerably shorter than the main mast.

KETCHEL, STANLEY, known as the **Michigan Assassin,** 1886–1910, American middleweight boxer, was born in Grand Rapids, Mich., of Polish parentage. He claimed the world's middleweight championship in 1907 after defeating Jack Sullivan. He lost the title in 1908 when badly defeated by Billy Papke, but regained it by soundly whipping Papke two months later. Going out of his class, Ketchel knocked down Jack Johnson, heavyweight champion, in 1909, but lost by a knockout in the 12th round. Ketchel was shot and killed in 1910.

KETCHIKAN, town SE Alaska, on the W coast of Revillagigedo Island, separated from the main-

Ketchikan Fishing Boats are part of industry which makes port the second largest town in Alaska

land by Behm Canal. The second largest settlement in Alaska, Ketchikan is an important port and fishing center and is served by the Alaskan Coastal Airlines and the Pan American Airways. It was founded as a mining camp during the gold rush of the 1890's. Although gold mining is still important, the major industries are salmon and halibut fishing and fish canning and freezing. The town's Indian name is said to mean "spread wings of a prostrate eagle." Pop. (1950) 5,305.

KETONE, an organic compound in which two organic groups are united to a carbonyl (CO) group. The general formula for ketones may be indicated as R-CO-R', where R and R' represent any carbon-containing groups. The simplest and most important ketone is ACETONE, or dimethyl ketone, which has the formula CH_3-CO-CH_3. Other examples include methyl ethyl ketone ($CH_3COC_2H_5$), ACETOPHENONE or methyl phenyl ketone ($CH_3COC_6H_5$), and benzophenone or diphenyl ketone ($C_6H_5COC_6H_5$).

The ketones have generally pleasant odors. Some of them are used in preparing PERFUMES and artificial flavorings. Civetone, a cyclic ketone, is a constituent of many expensive perfumes. Acetone and other simple ketones are important solvents for lacquers, plastics, guncotton, etc. Ketones also offer convenient starting points for the synthesis of more complex organic compounds. See ORGANIC SYNTHESIS.

Several methods for preparing ketones are in use. Some ketones are prepared by the oxidation of alcohols. Thus acetone may be prepared from isopropyl alcohol: $CH_3CHOHCH_3 + O \rightarrow CH_3COCH_3$. The heat decomposition of some salts of organic acids produces ketones. Calcium acetate, for example, produces acetone when heated:

$$(CH_3COO)_2Ca \rightarrow CH_3COCH_3 + CaCO_3.$$

In their chemical properties, the ketones closely resemble the ALDEHYDES.   J. M. D.

KETOSE, a member of a class of CARBOHYDRATES whose members contain a ketone-alcohol group,

$$-\overset{\overset{\displaystyle H}{|}}{C}-\overset{\overset{\displaystyle O}{||}}{C}-$$
$$HO$$

Fructose is an example. These compounds exhibit the chemical characteristics of both KETONES and alcohols.

KETTERING, CHARLES FRANKLIN, 1876– , American electrical engineer and inventor, was born near Loudonville, Ohio, and studied at Ohio State University. While employed by the National Cash Register Company he invented an electrically operated cash register, the forerunner of various electric accounting and auditing machines. In 1910 he organized the Dayton Engineering Laboratories Company and spent the next seven years in inventing such devices as an improved ignition system for automobiles (1910) and an automobile self-starter (1911). He also devised from this ignition and battery starter the Delco equipment for providing cheap

GENERAL MOTORS
Charles Kettering

electric light and power for farms, rural schools, and motion picture houses. When the General Motors Corporation acquired his laboratory and manufacturing interests in 1917, Kettering became general manager of the corporation's research laboratories and was made a vice-president and director of the corporation itself. In 1947 Kettering resigned as vice-president and became research consultant to the corporation. In these capacities he directed the development of ethyl gasoline, which eliminated the knock of

automobile motors, and collaborated with E. I. du Pont de Nemours and Company in the development of Duco finish, which reduced the time of painting an automobile from 17 days to only a few hours. He furthermore devised or improved automobile lubrication, crankcase ventilation, and silent gearshifting. Such other forms of transportation as trains and boats were indebted to him for so improving the diesel motor that its weight per horsepower was reduced from 200 to 17 pounds.

Kettering invented a "buzz bomb" (1912) and during World War I a pilotless plane which could carry 200 pounds of high explosives 200 miles and drop the charge automatically. During World War II he was chairman of the National Inventors' Council which acted as a clearinghouse on all suggested inventions for fighting the war more efficiently. Besides developing the hypertherm, a machine to treat diseases by artificially induced heat, and the electric refrigerating machine known as Frigidaire, he established at Antioch College in 1930 a laboratory to find the secret of photosynthesis and thus enable man to utilize solar energy. Kettering received many honors in recognition of his inventive genius, including the Washington and John Scott medals, and the 1949 gold medal of the International Benjamin Franklin Society, awarded him for his outstanding contributions to industrial progress.   M. E. C.

KETTERING, municipal borough and market town, central England, Northamptonshire, 14 miles NE of Northampton and 75 miles NW of London. Manufactures include boots and shoes, the chief items, and plush, lace, silk, woolens, brushes, clothing, and leather goods. There are iron foundries. The first Baptist Missionary Society in England was founded here in 1792. During World War II, the town suffered damage from bombing. Pop. (1950) 37,120.

KETTLE CREEK, BATTLE OF, an engagement of the American Revolution fought Feb. 14, 1779, in Wilkes County, Georgia, between loyalists and American militia. After the British captured Savannah they overran the up-country until a detachment of about 700 men was defeated by the Americans at Kettle Creek. The British lost 70 killed, including their commander, while the Americans lost only 9 killed.

KETTLEDRUM. See DRUM.

KEUKA LAKE, or **Crooked Lake,** New York, lying in Steuben and Lake counties. This Y-shaped lake, the only one of the Finger Lakes with an irregular outline, is about 20 miles long and less than two miles wide. It lies in a pleasant valley about 700 feet above sea level and is about 200 feet deep. It is connected with Seneca Lake by a meandering stream which flows for seven miles, falling 271 feet in its course.

KEW, suburban metropolitan district, SE England, included in Richmond Borough, Surrey, on the Thames, six miles SW of Hyde Park. The Royal Botanic Garden of 11 acres was founded in 1759 by the dowager princess of Wales, and in 1840 Queen Victoria presented them for public benefit. Improvements have been made and land added until the area now occupies 288 acres. The Temperate House is among the largest plant houses in the world. Connected institutions are the herbarium museum of economic botany, the botanical library, the Jodrell Laboratory, and a valuable collection of botanical paintings. In 1897 Queen Victoria gave Kew Palace (through the 18th century a royal residence) to the nation. At Kew Observatory chronometers and other scientific instruments are tested. The churchyard of St. Anne, built in 1713, contains the grave of Thomas Gainsborough. Although the vicinity was raided by German bombers during World War II, the gardens and palace were not damaged.

KEWANEE, city, N Illinois, in Henry County, on the Burlington Railroad and U.S. Highway 34, about 130 miles SW of Chicago. Kewanee is situated in a coal-mining and corn and hog-raising region. It was settled in 1854. Valves, fittings, steel boilers, conveyors, pumps, trailers, work gloves, and farm machinery are the chief products of the city. Pop. (1950) 16,821.

KEWEENAW PENINSULA, Michigan, extends NE into Lake Superior, sheltering Keweenaw Bay to the E. The peninsula was formed by volcanic action and consists of the famous Michigan Copper Range from which more than 8,500,000,000 pounds of ore have been taken. The west shore is bold and rocky; the east shore is lower and is indented. Manitou Island lies off Keweenaw Point, the northernmost projection of the peninsula. Settlements on the peninsula—Houghton, Lake Linden, Larium, Trimountain, Baltic, Hancock, Calumet, and Copper Harbor at the tip of Keweenaw Point—are connected by state highway 26, and are served by the Copper Range and Mineral Range freight railroads. Keweenaw Waterway crosses the peninsula from Keweenaw Bay on the southeast to open water in Lake Superior on the northwest. It is a 25-mile-long sheltered passage used by lake freighters during the stormy months of October and November. See COPPER AND COPPER MINING.

KEWEENAWAN SYSTEM, the uppermost system of rocks laid down in the PROTEROZOIC ERA. These rocks are exposed in the Lake Superior region, where they rest unconformably on the upper HURONIAN rocks. They consist largely of lava flows, together with sandstones, conglomerates, and limestones. The lava is believed to have issued from huge fissures, the outpourings during the early part of the period having occurred so frequently that there was no time for the accumulation of erosion products between layers. The Keweenawan lava beds constitute one of the greatest outpourings of lava in geologic history. In northern Michigan and Wisconsin the system attains a thickness of about 50,000 feet, of which about 35,000 feet is lava. The system encloses the remarkable copper deposits of Michigan. At Keweenaw Point, Michigan, the rocks contain the world's largest known native copper deposits.

KEY, DAVID McKENDREE, 1824–1900, American politician and jurist, born in Green County, Tenn. He graduated from Hiawassee College in 1850 and practiced law in Chattanooga, Tenn. He was a lieutenant colonel in the Confederate army during the Civil War, a member of the constitutional convention of Tennessee (1870), a member of the U.S. Senate (1875–77), postmaster general in the cabinet of President Hayes (1877–80), and judge of the Eastern District of Tennessee (1880–95).

KEY, FRANCIS SCOTT, 1780–1843, American lawyer and poet, was born in Frederick County, Md. He was graduated from St. John's College, Annapolis, studied law, practiced in Frederick, Md., and in Washington, D.C., and became district attorney of the District of Columbia. While detained as a visitor on board a British vessel, during the bombardment of Fort McHenry, near Baltimore (1814), he witnessed the action celebrated in his song, "The Star-Spangled Banner," written the next morning.

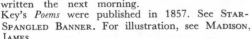
CHICAGO HIST. SOC.
Francis Scott Key

Key's *Poems* were published in 1857. See STAR-SPANGLED BANNER. For illustration, see MADISON, JAMES.

KEY. See LOCKS AND KEYS.

KEY, in engineering, a mechanical means of fastening together two or more parts in machinery, particularly to extend force from one part to another, as a key between shaft and flywheel. Types and designs are many, but great care is taken to provide a strong key without sacrificing strength in the parts keyed together. Splines are really multiple keys.

KEY, in music, signifies the scale in which a composition is written. (See SCALE.) Key is also a name given to the outward termination of the levers in keyboard instruments and, to the levers controlling valves in the certain wind instruments.

KEY DWELLERS, the name given by archaeologists to an extinct race formerly inhabiting the islets or keys (Sp. *cayos*) lying off the southwestern coast of Florida. The fact of their existence became known to science in 1895, since which time their settlements have been carefully investigated. Their islands were to a great extent artificial, being enlargements of tiny reefs or shoals by means of a remarkable series of shell-mound embankments, pyramids, and canals. The civilization of the key dwellers shows an affinity with that of Central and South America.

KEY ISLANDS. See KAI ISLANDS.

KEY WEST, city and port of entry, and international airport of entry, S Florida, county seat of Monroe County, on Key West Island, the most westerly of a group of coral islands lying between the Gulf of Mexico and the Atlantic Ocean; on U.S. Highway 1 and a National Airlines route, about 170 miles S of Miami and 90 miles N of Havana, Cuba. Key West, the southernmost city of the United States, is situated 100 miles off the mainland with which it is connected by the highway. Formerly, a line of the Florida East Coast railroad extended to Key West. When the hurricane of 1935 destroyed the line, the great "overseas highway" was put up in its place. Tremendous concrete arches sunk into the water carry the road from key to key. Key West has an excellent harbor which is protected by Fort Taylor, a Coast Guard base. Steamers connect the city with Havana and other Gulf ports. The Federal government maintains here a Navy yard, Army and Marine barracks, a lighthouse, an airport, a fort, and a biological station. The U.S. Naval Station operates a radio station and a fueling port for destroyers. From 1830 to 1870, Key West was the largest cigar manufacturing center in the U.S. When fire destroyed the cigar factories, the industry was moved to a new location. Today Key West has an extensive resort trade and small industries of fishing, canning, sponging, and commercial and sport fishing.

Key West was settled in 1822. Its name is an English version of the Spanish name for the island, *Cayo Huesta* (bone island). "Key" is a corruption of *Cayo* meaning island. Key West was an important U.S. naval base in World War II. After the war it was the center of submarine and antisubmarine development. President Truman's "Winter White House" was at Key West. Pop. (1950) 26,433.   A. M. K.

KEYES, ROGER JOHN BROUNLOW, ADMIRAL LORD, 1872–1945, British naval officer. He entered the British navy in 1885 and was in charge of the submarine service (1910–14). In World War I, he was chief of staff of the Eastern Mediterranean Squadron (1915); grand fleet captain (1916–17); rear admiral and director of plans of the Admiralty (1917). In 1918, he commanded the operations against Zeebrugge and Ostend. Named admiral of the fleet in 1930, he retired in 1935 but was recalled to service in 1940. As director of Combined Operations (1940–41), he organized and trained the British commando units. He was a member of Parliament (1934–43).

KEYNES, JOHN MAYNARD, 1883–1946, British economist, son of John Neville Keynes, English logician, and husband of Lydia Sopokova, famous Russian dancer. Prominent among 20th-century economists for both his contributions to economic theory and his influential role in the fiscal policies of several governments, Keynes was educated at Eton and King's College, Cambridge. In 1906 he launched his political career with a two-year term in the India office of the British civil service. His first spectacular government service occurred during World War I when he served in connection with loans to the Allies, as chief representative of the treasury at the Paris Peace Conference and on the Supreme Economic Council. When his views on reparations were attacked, Keynes resigned his position, but during the 30's his doctrine was particularly influential in the economic policies of Great Britain, Germany, and the United States. In 1940 the British economist was drafted back into the treasury where, during the war, he served as director of the Bank of England, economic ambassador to the United States, and chief negotiator for the British loan of $4,000,000. Made baron of Tilton in 1942, Lord Keynes was a leading advocate of world economic co-operation and one of the writers of the BRETTON WOODS agreement in 1944. His views on economic theory opposed the classical assumption of full employment and the classical stress upon the importance of "cost" in maintaining full employment. Skeptical of automatic adjustments, Keynes advocated government interference, particularly in regard to government spending in time of depression. His many books include: *The Economic Consequences of the Peace* (1919); *The End of Laissez-faire* (1926); *A Treatise on Money* (1930); *The General Theory of Employment, Interest and Money* (1936); *How to Pay for the War* (1940).   M. SHEPHERD

BRITISH INFO. SERV.
John M. Keynes

KEYPORT, borough, central New Jersey, in Monmouth County, on Raritan Bay and the Central of New Jersey Railroad, 11 miles SE of New Brunswick and 23 miles SW of New York City. Although white settlers came to Keyport as early as 1665, the first permanent settlement dates from 1821. Keyport is noted as a resort and boatbuilding center and has manufactures of cork and tile. Pop. (1950) 5,888.

KEYSER, city, NE West Virginia, county seat of Mineral County, on the N branch of the Potomac River and on the Baltimore and Ohio and the Western Maryland railroads, and U.S. Highway 220, about 28 miles SW of Cumberland, Md. Keyser lies among hills that were strategic strongholds during the Civil War. It was founded in 1802 and named for William Keyser, vice-president of the Baltimore and Ohio when the city was incorporated. Keyser is the seat of the Potomac State School of the West Virginia University, a junior college. The city has railroad shops, knitting mills, pottery plants, and a woolen mill. Pop. (1950) 6,347.

KEYSTONE STATE, popular name of PENNSYLVANIA.

KHABAROVSK, city and river port, U.S.S.R., in the Russian Soviet Federated Socialist Republic, capital of Khabarovsk Territory, situated at the confluence of the Amur and the Ussuri rivers, on the Trans-Siberian railway at its junction with the Amur railway, and on several modern highways including the new 5,100-mile Moscow-Khabarovsk road. A metropolis of the Far East and an important industrial center, Khabarovsk has automobile repair factories agricultural engineering works, machine-building, chemical, flour-milling, meat-packing, and soap, furniture, and leather factories. In addition, there are large oil and petroleum refineries which make the city the petroleum center for the entire Far East. Khabarovsk is also the seat of four institutes of higher learning including a medical and technical college. Founded in 1858, the city has made a remarkable growth since 1926. Pop. (1951 est.) 300,000.

KHABAROVSK TERRITORY, U.S.S.R., an administrative area of the Russian Soviet Federated Socialist Republic, situated at the eastern extremity of the Soviet Union; bounded on the W by the Yakut Autonomous Soviet Socialist Republic and Chita Region and on the S by Manchuria and Primorski Territory. Khabarovsk Territory consists of the Chukot National District, the lower portion of Kamchatka Peninsula, the Koryak National District, Sakhalin Island, the Jewish or Birobidzhan Autonomous Region, and the Kuril Islands. The Territory has the largest population of any administrative area in the Far East; its area is only slightly smaller than that of the Yakut Autonomous Soviet Socialist Republic. The principal rivers of the Territory are the Amur and the Issuri. The Sea of Okhotsk, the Bering Sea, the Bering Strait, and the Arctic Ocean wash the shores of Khabarovsk Territory, much of which is mountainous. Gold mining and fur trade are important in the north. Coal comes from Buryea and iron ore from the lower Amur area. Oil as well as coal are plentiful on Sakhalin. Farming has recently been developed in the south. Timbering, fishing, and hunting prosper all over the Territory. Enormous industrial strides have been made by the chief city of the Territory, KHABAROVSK, and by the cities of Komsomolsk, Birobidzhan, and Nikolaevsk. Pop. (1950 est.) 1,250,000.

KHABOUR RIVER, or **Khabur,** Asia Minor, rises in the Karaca Mountains (alt. 6,000 ft.) of SE Turkey. It flows southeast into Syria and bends southwest through Mesopotamia to join the Euphrates at Buseire (Bessireh) after a course of 200 miles.

KHAIBAR PASS. See KHYBER PASS.

KHAIFA. See HAIFA.

KHAIRAGARH, former feudatory state, India, now part of Central Provinces and Bihar; area 931 sq. mi.; pop. (1941) 173,713. It is mainly a fertile plain on which rice, cotton, and wheat are grown. The chief trading center is Donargarh (5,856), serviced by a railway; the capital and residence of the rajah is Khairagarh (5,015). Primary education in the state is free.

KHAIRPUR, feudatory state, Pakistan, an intrusion into Sind Province, bounded on the E by Jodhpur and Jessalmere and on the N, S, and W by Sind districts; area 5,989 sq. mi.; pop. (1941) 305,787. The north of the state is largely desert, with an extreme maximum summer temperature of 119° F., and a minimum winter temperature of 40° F. There is little rainfall. The principal occupation is agriculture, with the production of grain, oil seeds, and tobacco aided by five irrigation canals from the Indus and the eastern Nara, an old bed of the Indus. Manufactures include cotton, silk, and woolen fabrics, lacquer work, carpets, and pottery, and there are goldsmiths. Carbonate of soda and Fuller's earth are found. The chief exports are indigo, grain, and oil seeds.

Khairpur pays no tribute. The state came into being at the fall of the Kalhara dynasty of Sind in 1783, when Mir Fatehali Khan Tal-

Karl Marx Street, Khabarovsk, left; Khabarovsk woman and child, right

PAUL'S PHOTOS-SOVFOTO

pur established himself as ruler of Sind; subsequently his nephew, Mir Sohrah Khan Talpur, founded the Khairpur branch of the family. The British recognized the state by treaty in 1882. The ruling family are Moslems, as are some 83 per cent of the people. The principal language is Sindhi; Urdu and English are also spoken. In 1947 Khairpur became affiliated with the Dominion of Pakistan.　　　C. S.

KHAKASS AUTONOMOUS REGION, U.S.S.R., in the Russian Soviet Federated Socialist Republic; bounded on NW and W by Kemerovo Region, on the SW by Oirot Autonomous Region, on the S by the Tuva Autonomous Region, and on the E by Krasnoyarsk Territory; area 19,261 sq. mi.; pop. (1950 est.) 300,000, including 57.7 per cent Khakass. The principal ethnic strains of the Region are Turkic and Mongol. The Region is drained by the Abakan and the Chulym rivers. About 60 per cent of its entire area is forested, primarily by cedar, fir, and larch trees. Hunting, trapping, and lumbering are among the principal occupations of the Region. Fur farms, where valuable fur-bearing animals are bred, have been established. Resin is obtained from the forest trees, and the lumber industry has expanded rapidly. The Abakan River is used for floating timber to the sawmills at the town of Abakan, the capital of the Region. Vegetables, orchards, oats, barley, and wheat are the chief agricultural products of the Khakass Autonomous Region. Its Abakan steppe has long been famous for the horses and cattle which are bred here. The Khakass Autonomous Region was founded in 1930. Its people had no written language; one has since been worked out by Soviet philologists. A. M. K.

KHAKI, originally a stout twilled cotton, but now made also of wool, and in various shades, such as light brown, olive drab, or dust color. It was first used by British troops in India in 1848. The olive drab shade was adopted by the U.S. Army in the Spanish-American War, and is still used for the service uniform.

KHAMIL. See HAMI.

KHAN TENGRI, highest mountain in the central Tien Shan system, situated E of Lake Issyk Kul, and S of the Ili River, on the border between the Kirgiz Soviet Socialist Republic and Sinkiang. Its highest point reaches 23,622 feet.

KHANIA, or **Canea,** a department of Greece occupying the western end of the island of Crete, bounded on the N and W by the Sea of Candia, and S by the Mediterranean; area 921 sq. mi.; pop. (1940) 126,632. The region is mountainous, traversed by the White Range, which rises to more than 7,000 feet and is usually snow-capped. The tending of orchards and vineyards is the leading occupation. Large flocks of sheep and goats are grazed. The chief city of the department is Khania or Canea (pop. 28,213), which is the principal seaport and the capital of Crete. It is situated on the northern coast, 64 miles west of Hèrákleion (Candia). Khania was the ancient Cydonia, one of the seats of Minoan culture, and in ancient times was held by Greeks, Romans, Saracens, Byzantine lords, and Venetians, the latter taking it in 1204 and holding it for four centuries. In 1669 it was captured by the Turks, who rebuilt the city of Khania in white limestone in oriental style. After the Balkan War of 1913 Turkey surrendered her control over the entire island to Greece. Khania's fine harbor is protected by an ancient mole 1,200 feet long, which was built by the Venetians in the 13th century. The town of Khania is a Greek bishop's see, has an arsenal, and many interesting antiquities, including vaults hewn from subterranean rock, which were once used for grain storehouses. Industries include tanneries, a soap factory, and olive oil refineries. There is trade in leather goods, fruits, olive oil, and soap. During World War II the city of Khania was bombed and shelled by both German and Allied forces and much of the city was damaged.　　　K. E. H.

KHANTY-MANSI NATIONAL DISTRICT, formerly **Ostyako-Vogul;** U.S.S.R., in the Russian Soviet Federated Socialist Republic; bounded on the N by the Yamalo-Nenets National District, on the W by the Komi Autonomous Soviet Socialist Republic and a minute part of Molotov Region, on the S by the Regions of Sverdlovsk, Tyumen, and Omsk, on the NE by Krasnoyarsk Territory, and on the E by Tomsk Region; area 293,360 sq. mi.; pop. (1950 est.) 110,-000. The District, traversed by the Ob River, was founded as the Ostyako-Vogul National District in 1930. The name of the District was changed in October, 1940, in accordance with the Soviet policy of using the native names of the national groups concerned. The capital is Khanty-Mansisk, a fur-trading center. The principal ethnic strain of the District is Finno-Ugrian. Its inhabitants, known anthropologically as the Ostiaks and Voguls, engaged in fishing, hunting, and the breeding of reindeer.

KHARAN, feudatory state, Pakistan, one of the three states of Baluchistan, with Pakistan Baluchistan to the N, Iran to the W, and Kalat to the S and E; area 14,210 sq. mi.; pop. (1941) 33,763. The state is hemmed in by mountains, heights on the northern border reaching 9,852 feet, on the east 7,236 feet, and on the south more than 6,000 feet. A number of streams drain to the low center of Kharan, where they are lost in a swampy area. The people are Moslems, of the Sunni sect. Kharan became a recognized state in 1940, but remained under the suzerainty of Kalat. Upon the division of India into the independent countries of Pakistan and India on Aug. 15, 1947, Kharan acceded to Pakistan.

KHARBIN. See HARBIN.

KHÂRGA, EL, oasis and town, Egypt, in the Western Desert at 25° 26′ N lat. and 30° 33′ E long., 440 miles S of Cairo. The fertile oasis is about 100 miles long and from 15 to 50 miles wide. It is surrounded by a chain of limestone hills and is extremely fertile. Dates, cotton, wheat, barley, vines, and vegetables are grown. The able excavations of Gertrude Caton-Thompson and Elinor Gardner have given evidence that Khârga Oasis was inhabited by prehistoric men over a long period of time. Ruins of later historical settlements have been found by others. Chief among these are the ruins of the Temple of Hibis, the Temple of Nadura, and the Christian Necropolis, which contains several hundred brick tombs. Khârga is the chief town of the oasis. It has narrow roofed-in streets resembling tunnels, two mosques, and a government building. Pop. oasis 8,500; town 5,500. See ARCHAEOLOGY; EGYPT.
　　　LINDA BRAIDWOOD

KHARKOV, city, U.S.S.R., in the Ukrainian Soviet Socialist Republic, capital of Kharkov Region, situated at the junction of main-line railways from Moscow, Kiev, Rostov, Stalingrad, Crimea Region, and Kherson, 460 miles S of Moscow. The fourth city of the Soviet Union and a great commercial and industrial center, Kharkov is the "Pittsburgh" of the Ukraine. It is the gateway to the coal fields of the Donets Basin and the iron areas of the south with which the city is connected by a 124-mile railroad carrying the U.S.S.R.'s greatest freight traffic. Kharkov is the third most important engineering center of the U.S.S.R. and the site of one of the three largest tractor plants in the Soviet Union. Its other industrial establishments include plants manufacturing locomotives, turbines, mining and electrical equipment, food products, shoes, and clothing. Kharkov is also one of the Ukraine's cultural centers, the seat of a university founded in 1805, a women's medical institute, and many technical colleges.

Kharkov was founded in the early 17th century, destroyed by the Crimean Tartars, and rebuilt in the 18th century. Under the Soviets the city served as capital of the Ukraine until 1934. At that time the capital went back to the more ancient historical city of Kiev. Twice held and captured by the Nazis during World War II, Kharkov suffered great destruction. Pop. (1950 est.) 800,000.　　　A. M. K.

Factory in Kharkov, the "Pittsburgh" of Russia

KHARKOV REGION, an administrative area of the U.S.S.R. in the Ukrainian Soviet Socialist Republic; bounded on the N by the Russian Soviet Federated Socialist Republic and Sumy Region, on the W by Poltava Region, on the S by the Regions of Kirovograd and Dnepropetrovsk, and on the E by Voroshilovgrad Region. The Region is traversed for a short distance by the Dnepr River, by the upper reaches of the North Donets, and by the Sula, the Psyol, and the Vorskla rivers, tributaries of the Dnepr. The natural resources of the Region include coal, peat, phosphorites, and iron clay. Grain and sugar beets are the principal agricultural products. The capital and industrial center of the Region is the city of KHARKOV.

KHARPUT, or **Harput,** city, E Turkey, Malataya Vilayet, 60 miles NW of Diyarbekir. It is situated on a high, fertile plain (alt. 4,350 ft.) near the Murat Suyu (upper headstream of the Euphrates), and is an important station on the route from Samsun to Sivas and Diyarbekir. The city was the scene of a brutal Armenian massacre in 1895. It has a Jacobite convent with a rare collection of manuscripts, and a Protestant college, founded by missionaries from the United States, is located here. Pop. (1940 est.) 35,000.

KHARTOUM, city, capital of the Anglo-Egyptian Sudan and of Khartoum Province, on the left bank of the Blue Nile, just above its junction with the White Nile, at 15° 36′ N lat. and 32° 32′ E long., at an altitude of 1,250 feet, 1,345 miles by rail and river steamer S of Cairo and 430 miles by rail SW of the Red Sea harbor at Port Sudan. Khartoum is strategically placed to receive the trade of the central and southern provinces, and the rail and river steamers give easy access to world markets. On the north shore of the Blue Nile lies Khartoum North, at which is the chief rail station; Omdurman, the old Mahdi capital and the largest Anglo-Egyptian city (about 117,000) lies

Sudanese school in native quarter of Khartoum

on the right bank of the Nile at the junction of the Blue and White Nile. On the two-mile esplanade fronting the Blue Nile are Khartoum's handsomest buildings, built of brick and stone and including the governor general's palace and the palace of the governor of Khartoum Province. At one end of this esplanade is the extensive zoological garden. Gordon Memorial College, formerly a secondary school, has assumed the status of a university. See GORDON, CHARLES G.

In 1822 the Egyptians established a fort at the present site of Khartoum, and from this outpost grew the city, which in 1830 became the capital for Egypt's Sudanese possessions. Khartoum was long the center of an extensive legitimate trade and a slave mart. In 1884 General Gordon was ordered here to evacuate the Egyptian residents before the threat of the Mahdi (Dervish) uprising. From their headquarters at Omdurman the Mahdists besieged Khartoum, taking it and killing Gordon on Jan. 26, 1885. They then destroyed almost every building in the city. General (later Lord) Kitchener captured the city from the Mahdi successor in 1898 and planned the present city in the design of the British Union Jack. In 1899 the railway from Wadi Halfa reached Khartoum, and in 1906 the line to Port Sudan on the Red Sea was completed.   C. S.

KHASI STATES, a former group of 25 petty states, India, in SW Assam Province; area 3,700 sq. mi.; pop. about 180,000. The Khasi and Jaintia Hills, rising in the southeast to 6,433 feet, extended over most of the states. Shillong, the capital of Assam Province, lies within the former states. Although the chieftainships were largely hereditary, most chiefs had little power because of the democratic culture of the tribes. The British captured the area in 1833; the states acceded to India in 1947.

KHATANGA RIVER, U.S.S.R., issuing from various lakes and flowing N and NE through the Taimyr National District of the Russian Soviet Federated Socialist Republic into the Khatanga Gulf, Arctic Ocean, after a course of about 600 miles. The gulf, which lies on the eastern side of the Taimyr Peninsula, is about 200 miles long.

KHATMANDU. See KATMANDU.

KHAYA, a genus of tall trees belonging to the family *Meliaceae,* and closely allied to the mahogany tree. One species, *K. senegalensis,* the Senegal mahogany, is valuable for its timber.

KHAYYAM, OMAR. See OMAR KHAYYAM.

KHAZAR, the name of a people and an empire powerful from about A.D. 600 to 1000 in the area of the Caspian Sea. Prior to that time they had important relations with Persia, often acting as an ally. When the hordes of Attila and later the Turks overran their country they became, for a time, a subject people. For this reason they sometimes were called "White Huns" or "Turks from the East." In the seventh century they reassumed a place of power and influence which made them the chief bulwark against the inroads of the Mohammedan empire. Following the decline of the latter, the cities of the Khazars controlled the trade routes between East and West. Traders from all near by lands, including many Jews, were found in these markets. The Jewish people became very influential and in A.D. 740 succeeded in converting the court to Judaism. A century later the incoming Slavic speaking tribesmen broke the power of the Khazars and scattered their people over central Europe, where they were known as "Jews." It is important to note that a large portion of the central European Jews are descended from the converted Khazars.

Early accounts describe these people as having fair skin but black hair. The amount of mixture caused by the frequent invasion of their land first by Persians, later by Huns and Turks must have been considerable. However the dominant type is a rather short, round headed, dark complexioned grouping, considered by anthropologists as being a variant division of the Alpine race. See PEOPLES OF THE WORLD.

FAY-COOPER COLE

KHELAT. See KALAT.

KHERSON, city and port, U.S.S.R. in the Ukrainian Soviet Socialist Republic, capital of Kherson Region, situated on the W side of the Dnepr estuary, 15 miles from the Black Sea. Kherson has shipyards, produces agricultural machinery, and has trade in grain, lumber, wool and tobacco. The city was founded in 1778 as a fort and Black Sea naval base by Potemkin, the favorite of Catherine II. Pop. (1950 est.) 100,000.

KHERSON REGION, U.S.S.R., an administrative area of the Ukrainian Soviet Socialist Republic; bounded on the N by Dnepropetrovsk Region, on the NW by Nikolayev Region, on the SW by the Black Sea, on the S by Crimea Region and the Sea of Azov, and on the E by Zaporozhye Region; area 10,600 sq. mi.; pop. (1950 est.) 700,000.

KHIBINOGORSK. See KIROVSK.

KHINGAN, or Hingan, a mountain system of Asia, continuing the Kunluns and constituting in part the E limit of the Mongolian Plateau. It is divided into two ranges: Great Khingan and Little Khingan. The former is an Archeozoic fault-block beginning with the mountainous axis of Shansi Province in China and trending to the north-northeast. Near its southern end, its spurs project east to the Gulf of Chihli. Great Khingan forms a natural boundary between Inner Mongolia and the provinces of Jehol and South Hsingan (a part of the Manchurian provinces of Liaoning and Heilungkiang). Farther north, the range runs with North Hsingan on the west and East Hsingan on the east, ending in Heiho Province, on the right bank of the Amur. Generally speaking the Mongolian side is arid with a short slope ending at an average level of 3,000 feet, while the Manchurian side falls to a lower fertile plain. The chain reaches 8,000 feet in some of its peaks. It retains a good deal of moisture and is heavily forested. Little Khingan veers sharply to the south-southeast. Except at its junction with the parent range, it never exceeds 3,300 feet in height. Its crest is the provincial boundary line separating Heiho from its south and southeast neighbors of East Hsingan, Lungkiang, and Sankiang. At its eastern extremity Little Khingan turns north to the Siberian frontier beyond which it is continued by the Bureya Mountains.   ADRIAN TROY

KHÍOS. See CHIOS; KÁSTRON.

KHIUMA, Danish Dagö, Estonian Hiumaa, island in the Baltic Sea, near the entrance to the Gulf of Finland; a part of the Estonian Soviet Socialist Republic; area 367 sq. mi.; pop. about 17,000. Its shores are rocky and rugged, and the soil is sandy and marshy and well forested. The Dagerorts lighthouse is located off the shallow and rocky shores of the west coast. The people, three-fourths of whom are Estonians, are chiefly engaged in fishing and cattle raising. Khiuma was Danish until 1645, and Swedish until 1721, when it was acquired by Russia by the Treaty of Nystad. It remained in Russian possession until 1920 when it became a part of Estonia. In World War I German forces occupied the island in October, 1917. It was invaded and occupied by the Soviet Union, along with the rest of Estonia, in 1940. During World War II the Nazis temporarily occupied the island.

KHIVA, ancient Khorasmia, the Kharizin or Khwarezin of Moslem writers, a former soviet socialist republic in Central Asia, on the lower Amu Darya (Oxus River), now part of the KARA-KALPAK AUTONOMOUS SOVIET SOCIALIST REPUBLIC. Of the population many are nomadic Turcomans, the rest (Tajiks, Uzbeks) being concentrated in the fertile oasis of Khiva proper, which is maintained by an extensive system of irrigation from the Amu Darya.

Khiva formed part of the first and second Persian empires, of the empire of Alexander, and of the caliphate of the eighth and ninth centuries. The Mongols dealt it terrific blows in the 13th century, and in 1512 it was captured by the Uzbeks. In 1872 it came under Russian control, and in 1920 it became an autonomous soviet republic, and in 1924 was included in the Uzbek Republic. See KHOREZM REGION.

KHIVA, town, U.S.S.R., in the Uzbek Soviet Socialist Republic, in the Kara-Kalpak Autonomous Soviet Socialist Republic, situated 17 miles from the Amu Darya River. Walls encircle both the town and the citadel. The 30 mosques and more than 20 *madrasas* or Moslem colleges constitute the principal buildings of the outer city. Silks, cottons, and carpets are manufactured. Khiva was once the chief town of the former Khiva Emirate. Pop. (1950 est.) 25,000.

KHODZHENT. See LENINABAD.

KHOI, walled and fortified town, NW Iran, in Azerbaijan Province, on the Kotur River, 75 miles NW of Tabriz. The surrounding area is drained by the Kotur, Aq, and Chai rivers, all of which empty into the Araxes. It is fertile and produces wheat, barley, rice, cotton, and fruits. Khoi is beautifully laid out, with fountains, gardens, modern buildings, and wide streets. Features of interest are a palace, a large bazaar, and several mosques. Khoi is an important caravan station between Tabriz, Erzerum, and Trebizond, with all of which a large trade is carried on. Khoi has long been regarded as a strategic prize by Russia and Turkey; at various times it has been occupied by the Russians, Kurds, and Turks. Pop. about 28,000.

KHOI KHOI. See HOTTENTOT.

KHOKAND. See KOKAND.

KHOLM. See CHELM.

KHOND, a pagan people numbering about one million, found in the Madras district of India. They are tall, dark skinned, and possess rather sharp features, indicating a strong Caucasoid strain although showing some mixture with an early aboriginal element. The British invaded their territory in 1835 to stop human sacrifice, for which the Khonds were notorious.

KHORASSAN. See KHURASAN.

KHOREZM REGION, or Khwarezm, an administrative area of the U.S.S.R. in the Uzbek Soviet Socialist Republic; bounded on the N and NE by the Kara-Kalpak Autonomous Soviet Socialist Republic and on the E, S, and W by the Turkmen Soviet Socialist Republic. The Amu Darya flows through the Region. Traces of ancient civilizations, dating back several thousand years, have been found here. The principal product of the Region is cotton. Its capital is Urgench. Pop. (1950 est.) 315,000.

KHORRAMSHAHR, or Mohammerah, port, one of the hottest spots in the world, SW Iran, in Khuzistan, at the junction of the Karun River Canal and the Shatt al Arab (the united Euphrates and Tigris), 35 miles NW of the head of the Persian Gulf. It is on the oil pipe line to Ahwaz, 75 miles to the northeast. There is trade in dates, wheat, medicinal opium, wool, and horses. Before World War II Khorramshahr was a very small port. Under the need to get lend-lease supplies to Russia, the Persian Gulf Command built wharves, piers, and jetties, dredged a deep water channel, and installed heavy cranes. A truck assembly factory was built. The road to Ahwaz was completely remade, and hundreds of miles of new roads constructed to carry the load of supplies to Russia. The light-weight Trans-Iranian railway was rebuilt with heavy rails and equipment and supplied with new rolling stock. The capacity of Khorramshahr at the beginning of 1941 was fewer than 30,000 tons a month. Before the end of the war the port was handling some 250,000 tons. Pop. (1942 est.) 30,000.

KHORSABAD, town, NE Iraq, Mosul Province, on the Khosr River; 13 miles NE of Mosul. The ancient Assyrian city of Dur Sharrukin, founded in the eighth century B.C. by Sargon II was excavated here (1843–51), and many of the sculptures, inscriptions, and other antiquities unearthed were sent to the Louvre. Noteworthy among the buildings uncovered are the royal palace, built upon a series of terraces and rich with carved stairways; gates and corridors bearing the Assyrian winged bull; and a huge temple. Later finds include hundreds of cuneiform tablets in the Elamite language and a list of kings from 2200 to 730 B.C.

KHOTAN, or **Hotien,** area, W China, SW Sinkiang; about 40 miles wide and extending about 700 miles N across the desert of Takla Makan to the Tarim River; pop. (1936) 220,000. The Khotan River, formed by the Yurung Qash and the Qara Qash which rise in the Karakoram Range and unite at Khitatoi, flows north through the area to the Tarim. The district is the largest and most important of a group of oases along the southern section of the Takla Makan and is very fertile along the rivers and the northern slopes of the Kunlun Mountains. Wheat, rice, millet, oats, Indian corn, cotton, olives, apricots, peaches, and apples are grown along the rivers. The chief towns are Khotan or Hotien (pop. 5,000), Yurung Qash, Qara Qash or Moyu, and Langhru. The area is rich in jasper, gold, and jade. It is part of an ancient kingdom which included the Yarkand (Soche) River, and most of the Kunlun Range. It was held by China until the seventh century, when it was conquered by the Arabs. In the 10th century it became a part of Kashgar. Genghis Khan conquered Khotan in the 13th century and it was visited by Marco Polo in 1274. Ruined cities of the vicinity were discovered by Sven Hedin in 1895, and visited later by Stein, who brought away many interesting relics.

The town of Khotan or Hotien, the chief industrial city of Sinkiang, is situated 200 miles southeast of Yarkand (Soche) on the Yurung River. It was an early center of Buddhism. Manufactures include the making of leather goods, paper, silk, cotton and linen fabrics, felts, carpets, metal work, and articles of gold, jasper, and jade. Dried fruits, olives, jade articles, carpets, and raw silk are the principal exports.

K. E. H.

KHUFU. See CHEOPS.

KHURASAN, or **Khorassan,** largest province of NE Iran, bounded on the E by a southern tip of the Turkmen Soviet Socialist Republic and by Afghanistan, on the S by the Iranian province of Kerman, on the W by Yezd, Isfahan, and Kashan, on the NW by Teheran and Mazanderan, and on the N by Asterabad (Gurgan); area 125,000 sq. mi.; pop. about 1,000,-000. It is drained by the Atrek, Kashaf, Hari, Kara Su, and Qaleh rivers. One-third of the province is a vast salt waste; of the remainder a large portion consists of plains of shifting sands. The Kavir desert occupies the central western boundary and the Lut desert is on the south. Khurasan's fertile districts are in the north, where the highest part of the Elburz Mountains, the Ala Dagh, crosses the province. Salt, iron, lead, alum, gold, copper, and precious stones are found. The chief crops are wheat, rice, cotton, hemp, tobacco, aromatic and medicinal herbs, pistachio nuts, and fruits. Silk is also produced. Camels, horses, and donkeys are raised for market. The province was invaded in the 13th century by Genghis Khan and by Tamerlane about 1360. Important towns are MESHED, the capital, Damghan, Buynurd, Shirwan, Birjand, Yazdan, NISHAPUR, and Qain. Carpets, hides and skins, medicinal herbs, gums, timbers, cotton stuffs, and raw silk are exported. The Khorassan turquoises are in great demand; the mines near Nishapur have been in operation for several centuries.

K. E. H.; C. S.

KHUZISTAN, or **Arabistan,** province, SW Iran, between the head of the Persian Gulf and the S slopes of the Bakhtiari Mountains; bounded on the W by Iraq and the Shatt al Arab River, on the N by Luristan and the Bakhtiari Range, on the E by Isfahan, on the SW by Fars, and on the S by the Persian Gulf; area 25,700 sq. mi.; pop. (1940 est.) 400,000, of whom 100,000 are nomads. Khuzistan was part of the biblical Elam and the ancient land of Suziana. It is mountainous, but the valleys are exceedingly fertile, the southern area consisting of well-drained plains. The KARUN and Karkeh are the principal rivers. Wheat, corn, barley, rice, cotton, sesame, beans, sugar cane, dates, linseed, pulse, indigo, opium, pepper, and tobacco are raised. There is a large trade in raw wool. Shushtar is the capital and chief commercial city and has extensive oil fields. Other important towns are AHWAZ, Dizful, Ram Hormuz, and the two ports, KHORRAMSHAHR on the Shatt al Arab and BANDAR SHAH on the Persian Gulf.

KHWAREZM. See KHOREZM REGION; KHIVA.

KHYBER PASS, or **Khaibar,** a narrow defile through the Safed Koh Mountains, Pakistan, extending between North-West Frontier Province and Afghanistan. It forms part of the route between PESHAWAR and KABUL, and at Jamrud, the eastern end, is 450 feet wide; at the fort of Ali Masjid, 9½ miles farther on, it is only 40 feet wide. A railway runs

PAN AMERICAN AIRLINES
Section of Khyber Pass. A mule pack travels through the winding road in the Safed Koh Mountains

its length. The summit of the pass is at Landi Kotal, which is 1,700 feet higher than Dhaka Fort at the western end of the pass. Khyber is the only pass on the northwestern frontier of Pakistan and India practicable for the passage of artillery and is consequently of great strategic importance. It was forced by British troops during the Afghan wars of 1839–42 and 1878–80, and again in the Afridi campaign of 1897. The scenery is wild and picturesque.

KIAKHTA. See KYAKHTA.

KIANGAN, village, Philippine Islands, Luzon, 150 miles N of Manila. Gen. Tomoyuki Yamashita of the Japanese army made his headquarters here late in World War II when the remnants of his army were fleeing northward from Baguio. Kiangan was captured by American troops on July 15, 1945, after a slow and perilous advance up the mountain valley in which the village is located.

KIANGSI, a province of central China, part of the territory formerly known as Kiang-nan; area 66,830 sq. mi.; pop. (1947 est.) 13,794,000. Except in the northeast, it is mountainous. The mountain system consists of short chains trending mostly northeast by southwest, and of a larger range, the Tayuling, which forms a natural separation from Fukien to the east. Drainage is mainly by rivers, the Kan and others, which flow north into the considerable Poyang Lake. North of the latter, through a tea-growing district whose chief town is the treaty port of Kiukiang, the Yangtze runs for about 75 miles. The main crop is

rice. Other yields are sugar, tobacco, wheat, legumes, silk, cotton, and lumber. Coal, iron, and copper are found. Porcelain is manufactured at Kingtehchen (Fowliang). A good deal of the traffic is by waterways. NANCHANG, the capital (pop. 500,000), is linked by rail to Hangchow in Chekiang, and to Chuchow on the Canton-Hankow line. The second largest town, KANHSIEN, is in the southern part of the province which from 1930 to 1934 was known as "The Chinese Soviet Republic." The seat of the New Life movement originated by Chiang Kai-shek was at Nanchang.
ADRIAN TROY

KIANGSU, littoral province, China, fronting the Yellow Sea between Shantung to the N and Chekiang to the S, with Honan to the NW and Anhwei to the W for a hinterland; area 42,056 sq. mi.; pop. (1947 est.) 36,469,300. Smallest of all the Chinese provinces, Kiangsu is the most highly populated, averaging 867 inhabitants per square mile. Mandarin is the vernacular for Nanking and the northern section. Elsewhere in the delta Wu dialects are spoken. Kiangsu consists for the most part of a coastal plain irrigated by lakes, reservoirs, rivers and canals. The latter include the GRAND CANAL which intersects the province lengthwise. The important water traffic is supplemented by 400 miles of rail. A line connects the new port of Haichow in the north with inland China.

Here are located the four treaty ports, SHANGHAI, NANKING, SOOCHOW, and CHINKIANG, half the foreign population of China, and many of the native textile mills. The mineral wealth includes salt, coal, iron, marble and graphite. Long contact with the West has given Kiangsu the greatest concentration of native and foreign industry in the entire country.

History. Kiangsu was ravaged by the Chang-mao tseh or Taiping Rebellion of 1850–1864. It went through the events which culminated in the 1927 upheaval, and it was in Japanese hands for most of the 1937–45 period. Nanking, the provincial capital, also served as the national capital from 1927 to 1937 and from 1945 to 1949.
ADRIAN TROY

KIANGTU, or **Yangchow,** a walled city, E China, in the province of Kiangsu, on the Grand Canal near the Yangtze River, N of Chinkiang and 35 miles NE of Nanking. Kiangtu was the ancient capital of the Yang dynasty. Marco Polo held office here in the middle of the 13th century. The town was captured by the Japanese in 1938 and not liberated until the end of World War II. Pop. (1936) 100,000.

KIANGYIN, town, E China, in the province of Kiangsu, situated in an important position commanding a narrow part of the Yangtze River not far from its mouth and 100 miles NW of Shanghai. Kiangyin was occupied by the Japanese in May, 1942, but recaptured in August of the same year by Chinese troops. It was used as a strategic naval base on the Yangtze between Nanking and Shanghai by the United States Navy during the last few months of World War II.

KIAOCHOW. See TSINGTAO.

KIATING. See LOSHAN.

KICKAPOO INDIANS, a tribe of Algonquin linguistic stock, first visited about 1667 by the French Jesuit ALLOUEZ near the Fox-Wisconsin portage. During the 18th century with the decline of the Illinois Indians the Kickapoos moved southward into present-day Illinois and Indiana. They fought with the British against the Americans during the Revolution, took part in TECUMSEH's war, and again sided with the British in the War of 1812. In 1819 by the Treaty of Edwardsville they surrendered their lands; over their strenuous objections they were removed to a reservation in present-day Kansas. A small group of Kickapoos participated in the BLACK HAWK WAR. In 1852 a large part of the tribe moved into northern Mexico, from which after the Civil War they made raids into the United States. In 1873 they were persuaded to settle on a reservation in Indian Territory near the Sauks and Foxes, their old neighbors. Be-

cause of white depradations on their lands an uprising was threatened in 1889, but was averted when the government agreed to protect Indian rights. The tribe objected vigorously when the government opened their lands to settlement in 1895, winning for themselves the name of "kicking Kickapoos." Most of the descendants, numbering about 200, now live on their allotments on the old reservation. A small group lives in northeastern Kansas and another band in Mexico.
F. M.

KICKING HORSE RIVER, Canada, in the province of British Columbia, rises on the western slopes of the Rocky Mountains and flows SW to enter the Columbia River at Golden. The roaring mountain stream with its picturesque waterfalls affords magnificent scenery for the route of the Canadian Pacific Railway, which follows the stream. Kicking Horse Pass, on the border between Alberta and British Columbia, has an altitude of 5,339 feet and received its name from the fact that a member of an early exploration party was kicked by his horse.

KIDD, BENJAMIN, 1858–1916, English sociologist, traveled extensively in Canada, South Africa, and the United States. He won distinction by his first work, a brilliant essay on *Social Evolution* (1894). In 1908 he delivered the Herbert Spencer lecture at Oxford. His theory was that society should be interpreted in terms of biology, but he qualified the logical outcome of his argument by admitting the influence of religion in furnishing the basis of individual self-sacrifice for the public good. Other published works include *The Control of the Tropics* (1898), *Principles of Western Civilization* (1902), *Two Principal Laws of Sociology* (1909), and other sociological papers.

KIDD, WILLIAM, known as **Captain Kidd,** c. 1645–1701, British navigator and later a notorious pirate, was born probably in Greenock, Scotland, the son of a nonconformist clergyman. He went to sea in his youth, and in the war between England and France served the colonies so well that the Council of New York awarded him £150 in 1691. At the suggestion of the governor of New York and Massachusetts, he was given command of a 287-ton galley armed with 30 guns and was instructed to hunt down the pirates who were active in the Indian Ocean. He sailed from Plymouth Apr. 23, 1696, to New York City where he completed his crew. During the following year while he was cruising off the coast of Madagascar, it became rumored that the pirate hunter had become a pirate. Instructions were issued to colonial governors to arrest him on sight.

In 1699 he appeared in the West Indies, sailed up the Atlantic coast, and stopped at Oyster Bay, L.I., to take on a New York lawyer, James Emott, whom he sent to consult with the governor of Massachusetts. On July 1, 1699, Kidd reached Boston and delivered to the authorities a large quantity of goods he had captured. But he was arrested with several of his men, and sent to England, where he was tried on charges of piracy, arson, and brutality to prisoners, and more explicitly on the charge of having murdered one of his men, William Moore, whom Kidd protested was a mutineer. On this charge he was convicted after a trial which many believe was far from fair, and was hanged with nine of his men, in London, May 24, 1701. Kidd had buried some of his booty on Gardiner's Island, and this was recovered (1699).

BIBLIOG.–C. P. Mulligan, *Captain William Kidd, Gentleman or Buccaneer?* (1932); D. C. Seitz, ed., *Tryal of Capt. William Kidd* (1935).

KIDDER, ALFRED VINCENT, 1885–   , American archaeologist, was born in Marquette, Mich., and studied at Harvard University. He was distinguished for his contributions to method as well as for extensive field work. His noteworthy volume, *An Introduction to Southwestern Archaeology* (1924), was a milestone in the development of American archaeology. In 1930 he became head of the Division of Historical Research of the Carnegie Institution of

Washington. In 1947 he was awarded the Viking medal for distinguished contributions to archaeology.

FAY-COOPER COLE

KIDDERMINSTER, municipal borough and market town, W central England in Worcestershire, at the confluence of the Stour with the Severn and the Staffordshire and Worcestershire Canal; 15 miles N of Worcester. The manufacture of carpets and tapestries, introduced about 1735, is still the leading industry, with worsted spinning and dyeing, and the making of metalware following in importance. In the vicinity are iron foundries and tin-plating works. Pop. (1950 est.) 37,510.

KIDNAPING at common law is the taking by force or fraud of a person from his own country or state. During the depression of the 1930's kidnaping greatly increased and as a result many states enacted new statutes and others increased the penalties for kidnaping defining the offense in various degrees. The kidnaping of the Lindbergh baby (1932) led to the enactment of a Federal statute (the so-called Lindbergh Law) which greatly facilitated the apprehension and conviction of persons committing the offense. The common law originally applied the term to taking of children only, but it has now been extended to taking of persons of any age. At common law the offense was a misdemeanor but by statute it is a felony. The punishment varies from 10 years to life imprisonment, to the death penalty.

By statute the elements of kidnaping have generally become (1) unlawful seizure or taking without authority; (2) intent to detain; (3) actual or implied force (fear or threats of violence constitute implied force) or violence; (4) fraud; and (5) absence of consent (a minor or incompetent is incapable of consent and consent inspired by fear or fraud is not consent); (6) detention and concealment (in most states); (7) removal from the place of residence (this has been interpreted broadly to mean from any place where the victim was entitled to be, whether visiting friends, attending school, etc.; (8) transportation for any distance (even within the same town). A person entitled to custody of a child does not commit the crime of kidnaping in taking a child; but when the court has awarded custody to one parent in a divorce proceeding and the other parent takes the child, it is kidnaping. When preliminary to a divorce, custody of a young child is awarded to the mother by statute, instead of a court decree, the father does not commit the offense of kidnaping by taking the child. A parent may be kidnaping his own child, under the statutory definition of the crime, if by court order or decree, legal custody has been entrusted to another person, even though unrelated to the child. See ABDUCTION.

KIDNEYS and the Urinary System

In each kidney there are more than 1,000,-000 tubules that maintain the normal composition of the blood

KIDNEY. The kidneys are the principal organs for the removal of nonvolatile waste products of metabolism and for regulating the composition of the blood. In multicellular organisms provided with a good circulatory apparatus the quantity of inner medium is very small in proportion to the amount of protoplasm it must serve to nourish. Proper exchange of materials between protoplasm and medium determines not only the normal function of the organism but continuation of life itself. That is why partial or complete failure of either the circulation or the systems that maintain constancy of composition of the medium is serious or fatal. Removal of both kidneys results in death, though there is a factor of safety in the ability of one kidney to carry on the processes usually shared by both.

Structure. Grossly the kidneys are usually bean-shaped paired organs, in man weighing 4–6 ounces each and measuring $4\frac{1}{2} \times 2$–$2\frac{1}{2}$ inches. They are located in the upper back part of the abdominal cavity, behind the peritoneal lining, and are connected with the *urinary bladder*, which in man lies in the lower front region, by tubular *ureters*. The single channel through which the urinary bladder empties itself is called the *urethra*.

Each kidney is supplied with blood by the *renal artery*, a direct offshoot of the abdominal aorta and much larger than warranted by the size of the organ. The *renal vein* carries blood from the kidney to the inferior vena cava. In entering the kidney through the *hilus*, the depressed region toward the mid-line of the body, the branches of the renal artery, the *interlobar arteries*, spread fanwise toward the convexity of the kidney. When the interlobar arteries reach the boundary between the outer region of the kidney (the *cortex*) and the inner (the *medulla*) they divide into smaller vessels known as *arcuate arteries*. In arclike fashion these follow the cortico-medullary boundary, then further divide into *interlobular arteries*, and finally into arterioles supplying the cortex and medulla, mainly the former.

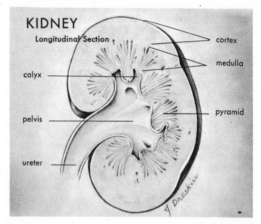

KIDNEY

Longitudinal Section

cortex

medulla

calyx

pyramid

pelvis

ureter

The cortex is composed mainly of the Malpighian bodies, or corpuscles, and convoluted tubules of the nephrons. The medulla is composed mainly of the collecting tubules. These unite and converge to form the pyramids. On the papilla of each pyramid there are numerous openings, where the tubules drain into a calyx, which in turn opens into the pelvis

The kidney is a glandular organ, which, unlike most of the other glands, is derived from the mesoderm (middle layer of the developing embryo). In higher animals the element of kidney structure and function is the uriniferous tubule or *nephron* (from the Greek *nephros*, kidney). This begins as a special blood plasma filtering device, enclosed in the *Malpighian body*, 0.1–0.2 mm. in diameter, or just within visibility by the naked eye. Examined by microscope, the Malpighian body can be seen to consist of two separate structures. The inner of the two, the *glomerulus*, is a tuft of capillaries that looks like a skein but is really made up of noncommunicating channels having a common beginning, the afferent arteriole or terminal branch of the interlobular artery. The efferent arteriole is a much smaller vessel, suggesting that less blood is carried away from the glomerulus than is brought to it. The outer part of the Malpighian body is *Bowman's capsule*, a double-layered folded-in sac of flat cells around the glomerulus. The outer (parietal) and inner (visceral) layers of Bowman's capsule are continuous with each other, meeting at the neck of the glomerulus, where the latter joins its afferent and efferent vessels (see illus.). Developmentally, Bowman's capsule is the expanded blind end of the uriniferous tubule, which from that point to its mouth resembles a conventional simple tubular gland in its cellular make-up, although it is unusually long (1–1½ in.). It has a distinct twist in the cortex (*proximal convoluted tubule*), follows a straight course into the medulla and back (*loop of Henle*), then develops a second tortuous portion in the cortex (*distal convoluted tubule*), and finally empties into one of the many collecting tubules, which carry the urine into a funnel-shaped receptacle in the hilus, the *pelvis* of the kidney. Altogether there are two to four million uriniferous tubules in the two human kidneys.

Theories of Urine Formation. The theories of kidney function reflect the conflict between the mechanistic and vitalistic conceptions of protoplasmic processes. Shortly after Bowman in 1842 described the structure of the capsule bearing his name, Ludwig

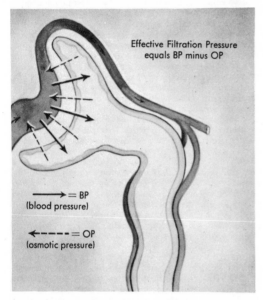

Effective Filtration Pressure
equals BP minus OP

———→ = BP
(blood pressure)

←– – – – = OP
(osmotic pressure)

Because of their effect on the filtration pressure, an increase in blood pressure or a decrease in osmotic pressure will increase the volume of fluid that filters from the blood into Bowman's capsule

propounded the theory that urine is formed by the simple process of reabsorption of water by the cells of the nephron as the glomerular filtrate courses through it. This mechanistic view is untenable, because urine is not simply a concentrated blood plasma. Certain filterable blood constituents are entirely absent from normal urine, others are found in unequal multiples of their concentration in the blood.

Heidenhain solved this problem by proposing a "secretory" theory: the glomerular cells secrete water and salts and the rest of the tubules the so-called organic substances. The "modern" theory of Cushny is a compromise in that it postulates pure mechanical filtration in the glomeruli, and secretion as well as absorption in the tubules. To explain the inequality in absorption, Cushny introduced the concept of "threshold" substances—constituents of the plasma and glomerular filtrate which are found in the urine only if their concentration exceeds a certain value. Otherwise threshold substances are completely reabsorbed into the circulation.

Glomerular Function. Although there exist different views concerning the multiple types of activity observed in the "glandular" stretch of the nephron, there is almost unanimous agreement about the contribution of the visceral layer of Bowman's capsule and the glomerular wall. The two constitute

a double membranous filter, through which blood plasma and the smaller molecules dissolved in it are squeezed out of the blood capillaries by the "hydrostatic" pressure generated by the pumping power of the heart. The filter itself is, biologically speaking, passive or inert. No work need be done by the cells of the filter, and no more oxygen is consumed when the volume of glomerular filtrate is increased. In fact, when a perfused isolated kidney is poisoned with cyanide, abolishing the respiration and therefore the activity of its cells, the "urine" collected from such a kidney is essentially blood plasma minus its proteins. Also, if the permeability of the filter is increased through disease and the urine contains protein, the latter is usually blood albumin rather than globulin (molecular weight of albumin being 68,000, that of globulin, 104,000). Furthermore, even a normal glomerulus permits purified egg albumen (molecular weight, 35,000) to pass through.

In general, as would be expected, the quantity of glomerular filtrate, and eventually the volume of urine, varies directly with the capillary blood pressure. However, the effective filtration pressure is the difference between the capillary pressure (60–90 mm. Hg) pushing outward and the osmotic pressure of the blood proteins (25–30 mm. Hg) pulling inward. This means that it should be possible to increase the quantity of glomerular filtrate by diluting the blood with salt solution, or by lowering its protein concentration while the capillary pressure remains unchanged, and such is found to be the case. Conversely, if the capillary pressure falls to a level lower than that of the osmotic pressure of the plasma proteins, urine formation should stop (as there will be no effective filtration pressure left), and it does. Finally, by blocking the ureter, one can raise the pressure in it, and when the intraureteral pressure reaches about 40 mm. Hg it stops rising, indicating that no more glomerular filtrate is being formed.

Perhaps the most convincing bit of evidence that the formation of urine starts with a plasma ultrafiltrate is the direct analysis of this fluid. This is accomplished by the proper illumination and magnification of the kidney of the living frog, in which micropipettes are inserted by delicate manipulation into the space between the parietal and visceral layers of Bowman's capsule, and the contents aspirated. Chemical microanalysis reveals that the fluid is identical with frog blood plasma, except for the absence of proteins.

The quantity of blood pumped through the kidneys is truly prodigious. It varies greatly, but for man per 24 hours the lowest estimate is about 500 liters, the highest, 5,000 liters. Since the total volume of blood in the body is about 5 liters, it means that all the blood is passed through the kidneys 100 or more times each day. In other words, the kidney circulates —per minute—2–10 times its own weight of blood. How much of the blood plasma is filtered through has been determined with fair accuracy by the inulin clearance method described below. It amounts to 0.001 cu. mm. per glomerulus per second, 120 cc. of filtrate for the two human kidneys per minute, or about 170 liters per 24 hours. The daily volume of urine voided is 1–2 liters. Therefore about 99 per cent of the water in the filtrate is returned to the circulation by absorption from the convoluted tubules. To understand the intimate relation between normal heart activity and kidney function, one must only recall that the filtering membranes of the nephron are passive and that the driving force that creates the pressure in the glomeruli comes from the beating heart.

Tubular Functions. While the glomerular portion of the nephron is a passive filter, the convoluted tubules are capable of: (1) partial or complete reabsorption into the circulation of certain plasma constituents; (2) non-reabsorption of some waste products and substances "foreign" to the blood; (3)

secretion of other substances, either already found in the glomerular filtrate and not reabsorbed, or large molecules delivered to the urine exclusively by the tubular cells; and (4) synthesis or manufacture of substances not found in the blood.

A good deal has been learned about the tubules by studying aglomerular kidneys found in certain fishes. Such kidneys evidently produce urine by a process of secretion, as there is no glomerular filtrate from which anything can be absorbed. In a negative way, experiments with aglomerular kidneys reveal the existence of substances which cannot be secreted by the tubular epithelium. One such substance now used extensively in investigations into kidney function is *inulin*, a polysaccharide with a molecular weight of 5,100. Aglomerular kidneys cannot "clear" the blood plasma of inulin, whereas kidneys provided with a glomerular system remove inulin in direct proportion to its concentration in the plasma. Comparison of excretion of inulin and other recognized "threshold" substances shows that inulin is not absorbed by the tubules. We thus have in inulin an inert, nontoxic, easily analyzable material, which is neither absorbed nor secreted by the tubules, yet passes freely through the glomerular membranes.

The method of plasma clearance (C), in which removal of inulin is often used as a standard, involves determinations of the concentration (U) of a certain substance in the urine, the concentration (P) of the same substance in the blood plasma, and the rate of urine secretion in cc. per minute (V). The formula is:

$$C = \frac{U \times V}{P}$$

In simple terms, clearance stands for the volume of blood plasma required to furnish the quantity of a particular substance secreted in the urine per minute, if all the substance were removed from the plasma. Since blood leaving the kidney always has some of the substance in question, the plasma is never completely "cleared," and the clearance volume is therefore smaller than the circulation volume. However, the plasma clearance can be equal to the volume filtered through the glomeruli if the material is neither absorbed nor secreted but merely concentrated in passing through the tubules. Inulin, being such a substance, has a plasma clearance identical with the filtration rate. Other urinary constituents, with plasma clearances lower than that of inulin, must be reabsorbed in the tubules, while substances whose plasma clearance is higher must have their concentration in the urine augmented by tubular secretion.

By this simple procedure it can be determined to what extent the cells of the uriniferous tubules participate in lowering or raising the concentration of the different plasma constituents as the glomerular filtrate is moved on toward the collecting terminals. Glucose, an important normal constituent of the blood plasma, is usually found in the urine only in traces. Its plasma clearance is therefore close to zero. But the ability of the tubule cells to reabsorb glucose is not unlimited. Its concentration in the plasma is ordinarily 80–120 mg. per 100 cc. When it rises above 160–170 mg. glucose begins to appear in the urine in larger and larger amounts. The critical concentration is what Cushny called the "threshold." Incidentally, glycosuria resulting from hyperglycemia causes such a concentration of glucose in the tubular fluid (often from 500–700 mg. per 100 cc. in the plasma and glomerular filtrate to over 5,000 mg. per 100 cc. in the urine) that the absorption of water is also decreased, probably through osmotic retention of water in the tubules. Such an "obligatory" volume leads to an invariable association of glycosuria with polyuria, or an increase in the daily volume of urine (from 1–2 liters to 5–6 liters and more). The profuse volume of urine and the resulting abnormal thirst are often the first symptoms of *diabetes mellitus*, with its concomitant hyperglycemia. See DIABETES.

Urea, an important waste product of protein metabolism, whose concentration in the blood plasma is 0.03 per cent, may be found in the urine in a concentration of 3 per cent, or 100 times greater than in the glomerular filtrate. If no urea were absorbed during the passage of the filtrate through the tubules such an excretion would require at least 100 liters of capsular fluid for one liter of urine. But, compared to inulin, the urea clearance of the plasma is only 0.6, which figure means that some urea re-enters the blood from the tubules (by absorption or diffusion). Therefore the actual volume of glomerular filtrate should be 1 2/3 greater than 100 liters, or about 170 liters, as indicated above.

By contrast to urea, the clearance of creatinine, another constant end product of protein catabolism, is slightly higher than that of inulin. Creatinine therefore is secreted by the tubule cells. Among the many other substances with a plasma clearance higher than that of inulin, diodrast stands out as an index of maximum secretion. Diodrast, an organic molecule containing two atoms of iodine, is subject to accurate chemical analysis and, like inulin, is inert and harmless. Its plasma clearance is enormous, six to seven times greater than inulin's, the plasma being almost completely cleared of diodrast when the concentration of the latter is under 10 mg. per 100 cc. Under such conditions plasma clearance becomes close to identical with the volume of blood flowing through the kidneys. Determinations of diodrast clearance have been used for that purpose and yield values of up to 700–800 cc. of blood plasma or 1,300 cc. of whole blood per minute. The total volume of blood pumped by the heart at rest is 3–5 liters per minute. Based on that figure, the kidneys get 25–40 per cent of all the blood circulating through the body.

Certain urinary constituents are not found in the blood at all. With respect to them there can be no question of reabsorption or secretion. They must be synthesized by the tubular cells. Hippuric acid, for instance, first discovered in horse urine, is excreted when benzoic acid, found in the diet of herbivorous animals, accumulates in the blood. It is a combination of benzoic acid and glycocol, a simple amino acid. Furthermore, the blood of the renal vein contains two to three times as much ammonia as does the blood of the renal artery. Ammonia is therefore manufactured by the cells of the tubules, which thus act as "sparers" of the fixed alkalies of the blood plasma. In ACIDOSIS, when the excess of organic acids, such as beta-hydroxybutyric and diacetic, have to be excreted, they are removed as ammonium salts. The rate of excretion of ammonia can be used as an index of acidosis for this reason. Because of the acid-base regulating function of the kidney there is no such thing as a "normal" reaction of urine. It is true that the urine of carnivorous animals is usually acid, while that of herbivorous animals is alkaline. However, the reaction of the urine is not due to a peculiarity of their kidneys but to the nature of their foods. Human urine is usually acid, but can easily become alkaline on a diet that is largely vegetarian.

Another way in which the tubule cells regulate the normal reaction of the blood is by selective or differential reabsorption of the different acid salts. Blood plasma (and glomerular filtrate) contains NaH_2PO_4 and Na_2HPO_4 in a ratio of 1:4, but in the urine their ratio may become 9:1. In a similar manner an excess of sodium chloride in the diet results in a decreased reabsorption of this salt from the capsular fluid.

Lastly, the kidneys maintain the normal concentration of the plasma constituents, in general, by variation in the volume of urine. Larger water intake leads to a greater water loss. In this respect the sweat glands and the kidney are complementary to each other. In hot weather, when large amounts of sweat are secreted, the urine is scanty and highly colored. In the winter relatively larger volumes of pale urine are produced by the kidneys. A temporary increase in the rate of urine formation is called *diuresis*, and drugs that bring it about are designated as Diuretics. It is interesting to note that some diuretics, usually salts, increase the volume of urine without a simultaneous rise in the oxygen consumption of the kidney. Evidently it is a matter of simple dilution of the proteins in the plasma, which, as already indicated, leads to an increase in effective glomerular filtration pressure. Water likewise dilutes the blood proteins, and its action as a diuretic resembles that of salts, which draw water from the tissues into the circulating blood. Other diuretics do elevate the oxidative rate of the kidney and therefore exert their effects on the cells of the tubules. These effects can be to increase the secretory activity or to decrease the absorbing power for either dissolved constituents or water.

There is evidence that the absorptive function of the cells is under endocrine control. A condition in man referred to as *diabetes insipidus* results in voiding enormous volumes of urine (as high as 25 liters daily). Experimentally such a state can be produced in animals by a circumscribed injury to the base of the brain at the funnel-like stalk of the hypophysis (Pituitary Gland). It probably involves an interruption of the nervous pathway from the supraoptic nuclei to the posterior lobe of the hypophysis, interfering with the production of the so-called antidiuretic substance. Pituitrin, an extract of this part of the hypophysis, has been successively used to reduce the flow of urine in diabetes insipidus. The adrenal cortex produces a hormone that furthers reabsorption of sodium chloride from the glomerular filtrate (see Adrenal Glands). Extirpation of the adrenals is fatal, but, during the severe depression that precedes death, animals lose large amounts of sodium chloride in the urine, and simultaneously retain potassium. Desoxycorticosterone, extracted from the adrenal cortex, restores the sodium absorbing power of the tubule cells, both in experimental deficiency and in spontaneously occurring Addison's disease.

The question of nervous control of the kidney remains unanswered. Nerve fibers have been traced to the kidneys, and diuresis has been developed in animals as a conditioned reflex. The dependence of urine formation on blood flow makes it possible, however, to explain diuresis of obviously nervous origin by invoking vasomotor effects in the kidney itself and elsewhere in the body.

Clinical Renal Function Tests. The plasma clearance test for urea is often used to measure normality of kidney function. Urine is collected for two hours, and at the end of the first hour blood is drawn and *P* value determined. From the urine collected *U* and *V* are determined, and the plasma clearance (see formula above) obtained is expressed as the percentage of the mean normal values. When the urine flow exceeds 2 cc. per minute the normal plasma clearance for urea is 60–95 cc. per minute; when the rate of urine formation is under 2 cc. the clearance varies from 40 to 65 cc.

Another test pertains to the ability of the kidneys to concentrate urea. After the bladder has been emptied 15 grams of urea in 100 cc. of water is taken by mouth, and three consecutive hourly samples of urine collected. Normal kidneys will deliver urine containing 4 per cent urea or better, but even if marked diuresis is induced the percentage of urea should not fall below 2.

A dye, phenol red or phenolsulfonphthalein (usually called PSP), whose plasma clearance is about three times that of inulin, has also been used for testing renal function. When 6 mg. of this dye dissolved in 1 cc. of water is injected subcutaneously it appears in the urine in 5 to 10 minutes. Normally 40–60 per cent of the dye is excreted in the first hour, an additional 20–25 per cent in the second hour. Lower values indicate approaching or existing tubular deficiency.

Hypertension of Renal Origin. Although it had been known from a long time that raised arterial blood pressure was often associated with kidney diseases, it was only recently that a direct connection between the two was established experimentally, by the Goldblatt operation. This involves a partial clamping of the renal arteries, resulting in *ischemia* (greatly reduced circulation) of the kidneys. Shortly after the operation the animal's blood pressure begins to rise to abnormal levels. Denervation of the kidney does not modify the effects of the operation. A substance has been extracted from ischemic kidneys which has pressor (arterial blood pressure raising) properties. *Renin*, as this substance is called, is obtained from the cortex of the kidney, probably from the cells of the proximal convoluted tubules. Renin, it seems, does not act on the blood vessels directly. It is an enzyme and converts a serum globulin, the *angiotonin precursor*, into effective *angiotonin* (also called hypertensin), which is capable of causing vasoconstriction and thus hypertension. The normal kidney produces another enzyme, *angiotonase*, which inactivates angiotonin. Renal ischemia may raise the blood pressure through an increased formation of renin or a decreased production of angiotonase, or both. The Goldblatt operation is ineffective after extirpation of the adrenal cortex, whose hormone appears to further the production of the angiotonin precursor. The latter, however, is probably manufactured by liver cells, as it disappears from the blood after extirpation of the liver.

Spontaneously occurring high blood pressure in man has not been linked with renal ischemia, but the feasibility of producing chronic hypertension in laboratory animals has stimulated attempts to develop means of overcoming this condition. See Blood Pressure.

Accessory Structures. The urine in its final concentration and chemical make-up accumulates in the funnel-like pelvis of the kidney, and from here is carried by the ureters to the bladder. Both the ureters and the bladder resemble the gastro-intestinal tract in the anatomical arrangement of an outer muscular coat and inner mucous membrane, as well as in their innervation and physiological properties (see Stomach). The smooth muscle in the walls of the ureters undergoes periodic contractions resulting in peristaltic waves (in man once a minute), which propel the urine toward the bladder. The stimulus probably comes from the distention of the pelvic end of the ureter by the urine pushed on by the secretory pressure in the tubules of the kidney. The ureters pass through the bladder musculature obliquely, making a backflow difficult or impossible.

The urinary bladder, like the stomach, is as big as its contents. It is capable of relaxing sufficiently to accommodate an increasing volume of urine without any increase in intravesicular pressure. Distention of the bladder produces an uncomfortable state that expresses itself in a desire to micturate (empty the bladder). This condition is usually reached in man when the volume of urine exceeds 300 cc. or when the pressure in the bladder is about 180 mm. of water. This can be seen in the operation of the so-called automatic bladder of patients who have recovered from the shock of a complete severance of the spinal cord. In such an individual the bladder reflexly empties itself after a certain amount of liquid has been introduced into it via the urethra, or when an equal quantity of urine has been delivered to it by the ureters.

In the normal individual an increase in bladder tonus may lead to a higher pressure with smaller than usual amounts of urine, and, conversely, a conscious contraction of the external sphincter of the bladder may allow an accumulation of as much as one liter of urine. As in the alimentary canal, the innervation of the bladder wall is opposite to that of the internal sphincter. The parasympathetic innervation causes contraction of the bladder and relaxation of the sphincter, the sympathetic does the reverse. The urethra simply serves as a conduit for the urine that has passed the internal and external sphincters. By means of a catheter (a thin, flexible tube) passed up the urethra into the bladder, it is possible to empty the bladder, to collect urine as it is formed, or to introduce liquids into the bladder.

A cystoscope is a metallic endoscope, carrying prisms and mirrors, through which the interior of the bladder can be illuminated and visually explored. It is usually employed for detection of abnormalities in the mucous membrane of the bladder. When one looks through a cystoscope at the opening of the ureters into the bladder one can see that urine is delivered in discrete spurts coinciding with the peristaltic waves. The employment of phenol red for renal function testing, mentioned above, permits one to see whether the dye is excreted by both kidneys, or only by one.

Voluntary control of the external vesicular sphincter, like that of the external anal sphincter, is bound up with the proper stage of development of the cerebral cortex, and is usually reached in infancy or early childhood, depending, in part, upon training in that direction. Nocturnal ENURESIS (bed-wetting) occurring during sleep in older children who are quite capable of sphincter control in the daytime is a condition that sometimes requires psychiatric treatment. However, it may be due to a weak sphincter or too great a depth of sleep, and can then be overcome by simply avoiding any intake of liquids after the middle of the afternoon.

Composition of Urine. As already suggested, to maintain the constancy of the blood the composition of urine must be highly variable. However, under normal conditions certain substances are always found in the urine. The amounts of these substances may or may not depend upon the composition of the diet. Other constituents are found in the urine only in disease.

Freshly passed urine is usually clear, has an amber color and a characteristic, not unpleasant, aromatic odor. Upon standing urine may become clouded and acquire an offensive odor due to formation of products of decomposition, mainly ammonia. The specific gravity of the urine varies from 1.012 to 1.030, a mixed 24-hour sample usually having a specific gravity of 1.020. Very high specific gravities are often associated with glucose and low ones with albumin, both abnormal constituents. The reaction of human urine is usually acid, but may sometimes be alkaline; the pH is usually about 6.0, but even in health may range from 4.7 to 8.0 (a 2,000-fold variation in hydrogen ion concentration).

The percentage concentration of the many urinary constituents is inversely related to the volume of urine, which in turn depends upon the water intake and the activity of the sweat glands. Therefore the quantity of these constituents is best expressed in terms of the range of their removal from the body in 24 hours. The chief nitrogenous end products are urea, uric acid, and creatinine. In mammals urea excretion varies with the protein metabolized, in man usually amounting to 20–35 grams per day. Uric acid excretion is related to the quantity of nucleoproteins in the diet. Its daily range is 0.5–1.0 g. Creatinine is one constituent whose excretion (1.0 to 1.6 g.) is independent of the amount of protein in the diet, thus representing a measure of what used to be called endogenous protein metabolism. About 0.5 g. of ammonia, produced chiefly by the kidney cells, is excreted daily. Amino acids, though not waste products, are also found in the urine, not being completely reabsorbed from the glomerular filtrate.

The daily excretion of inorganic constituents is related to their intake. The normal range for sodium chloride is 10–15 g.; for phosphorus, about 2 g. of P_2O_5; for sulfur, 1.5–3.0 g. of SO_3; for potassium, 2 g. of K_2O; for calcium and magnesium, about 0.2 g. of the corresponding oxide. In addition there are small amounts of iron, glucose, pigments, hormones, and enzymes. Certain drugs and toxins are also cleared from the blood by the kidneys.

Glucose appears in the urine whenever its concentration in the blood exceeds the normal threshold. Pathologically *glycosuria* is caused by the hyperglycemia of diabetes. The urine then also contains "acetone bodies" (acetone, diacetic acid, and beta-hydroxybutyric acid), as well as large amounts of ammonia. When poisoned with phloridzin the kidney tubule cells fail to reabsorb glucose from the glomerular filtrate, and glycosuria is then associated with (indeed causes) hypoglycemia.

Protein, usually serum albumin, is an abnormal constituent of the urine, though there is a condition called *physiological*, or *orthostatic, albuminuria*. It is commonly seen in some young persons after standing. As a rule albumin in the urine means an increased permeability of the glomerular capillaries, and is caused by inflammatory or degenerative lesions in the kidney.

Hemoglobinuria occurs whenever red blood cells are destroyed in the circulating blood and free hemoglobin is dissolved in the plasma. The breakdown of red blood cells may be caused by certain poisons and toxins or by micro-organisms, such as the plasmodium of MALARIA. The urine containing hemoglobin is red or dark brown, hence the term "blackwater" fever.

Creatine, as distinguished from creatinine to which it is closely related chemically, is normally present in the urine of boys up to the age of about seven years, then disappears permanently. In girls *creatinuria* not only lasts till puberty but reappears periodically in each menstrual cycle as well as during pregnancy and after delivery.

Alkaptonuria is a harmless condition representing a recessive inheritable Mendelian character. Alkapton (homogentisic acid) is formed as a result of an anomaly in protein metabolism, and when present in the blood finds its way into the urine.

Diseases of the Urinary System. An inflammatory lesion of the kidney is usually called *nephritis*, while a degenerative one is known as *nephrosis*. The term *Bright's disease* is applied by some writers to nephritis, by others to nephrosis, by still others to both. The important distinction is between involvement of the glomeruli and that of the tubules. Glomerular deficiency leads to retention of salts and water, the urine being dark and concentrated. Tubular lesions result in a decreased absorption of the glomerular filtrate, and the urine is abundant and of a low specific gravity. Nephritis may be acute or chronic. The latter is often associated with (caused by or causes) circulatory disturbances, such as edema or dropsy, hypertension, and heart disease.

Uremia is a condition of renal failure associated with the retention of nitrogenous waste products, especially urea. Uremia may be an important factor in the production of eclampsia, a serious complication of pregnancy.

Stones, or *calculi*, may form from crystals of sparingly soluble urinary constituents that are precipitated in the renal pelvis, ureters, or urinary bladder. They are usually composed of ammonium magnesium phosphate, calcium phosphate, calcium oxalate, and ammonium urate. The entrance of a stone into the ureter may cause extreme pain, usually called *renal colic*. Surgical intervention is often required to remove kidney stones.

The kidney is subject to infectious disease, either via the blood stream (hematogenous infection) or by way of the urethra, bladder, and ureter (ascending infection). *Pyelonephritis* is an example of an ascending infection of the kidney.

The mucosa of the urinary bladder is sometimes injured by sharp stones and is also subject to infection via the urethra. *Cystitis*, or inflammation of the bladder

KIDNEY FUNCTION

All of the blood in the body is passed through the kidneys 100 or more times each 24 hours. During this time the kidneys remove from the blood about 170 liters of fluid. From this they produce about 1–2 liters of urine, returning 163–169 liters of fluid to the blood

In this way the kidneys perform two functions that are essential to maintenance of life. From the blood they remove urea, uric acid, creatinine, and other non-volatile waste products of metabolism, excreting them as urine. Equally vital is their role in maintaining the normal composition of the blood by regulating its water and salt concentration and its acid-base balance

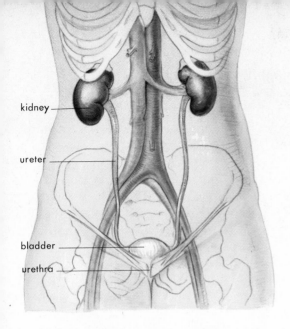

kidney

ureter

bladder

urethra

THE URINARY SYSTEM

Urine continuously secreted by the kidneys is conveyed in the ureters to the urinary bladder, where it is stored until eliminated through the urethra

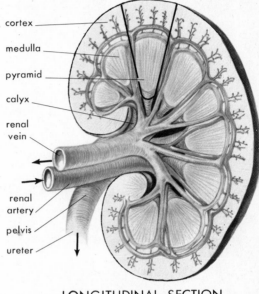

cortex

medulla

pyramid

calyx

renal vein

renal artery

pelvis

ureter

LONGITUDINAL SECTION OF KIDNEY

glomerulus

cortex

medulla

calyx

collecting tubule

to pelvis

J. Dreskin

MODEL SHOWING STRUCTURE OF ONE PYRAMID

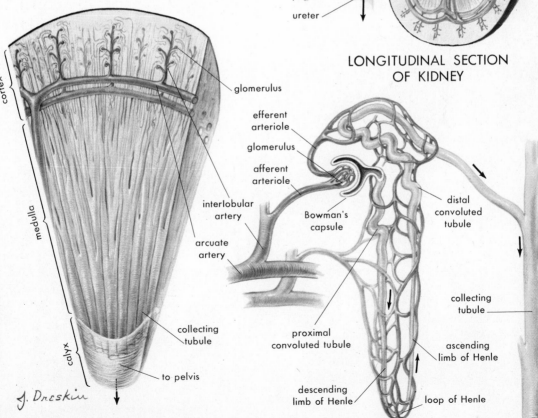

efferent arteriole

glomerulus

afferent arteriole

interlobular artery

arcuate artery

Bowman's capsule

distal convoluted tubule

collecting tubule

proximal convoluted tubule

ascending limb of Henle

descending limb of Henle

loop of Henle

to calyx

NEPHRON

PRODUCTION OF URINE

Course of Certain Substances Through a Nephron

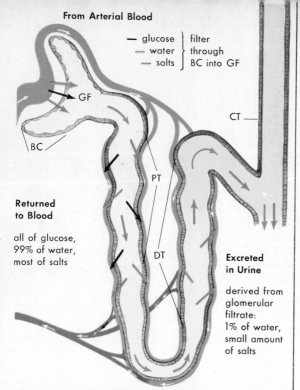

From Arterial Blood

— glucose } filter
— water } through
— salts } BC into GF

GF

BC

PT

CT

DT

Returned to Blood

all of glucose,
99% of water,
most of salts

Excreted in Urine

derived from
glomerular
filtrate:
1% of water,
small amount
of salts

HIGH THRESHOLD SUBSTANCES

glucose, water, sodium,
potassium, calcium,
magnesium, chloride } are filtered through the
glomerulus, returned to blood
by reabsorption from tubules

The various activities that are shown in the three nephrons actually are carried on simultaneously in each of the 1–2 million nephrons in each kidney

Fluid, some of which is destined to be excreted as urine, filters from the blood through the wall of Bowman's capsule, forming the glomerular filtrate

In its passage along the tubule, this fluid is made more concentrated by reabsorption of water

Its composition is further changed by reabsorption of some of the substances dissolved in it, and by addition of some wastes not found in the blood but synthesized and secreted by the cells of the tubule

Reabsorption from the tubule is influenced by hormones of the pituitary, adrenal, and thyroid glands

Key to labels in diagram at left {
BC = Bowman's capsule
PT = proximal convoluted tubule
DT = distal convoluted tubule
CT = collecting tubule
GF = glomerular filtrate }

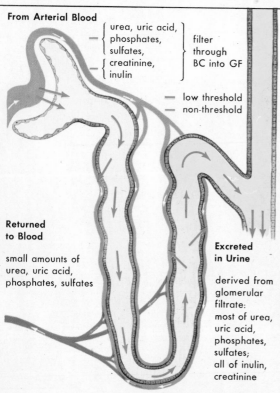

From Arterial Blood

— { urea, uric acid,
phosphates,
sulfates,
— { creatinine,
inulin } filter
through
BC into GF

— low threshold
— non-threshold

Returned to Blood

small amounts of
urea, uric acid,
phosphates, sulfates

Excreted in Urine

derived from
glomerular
filtrate:
most of urea,
uric acid,
phosphates,
sulfates;
all of inulin,
creatinine

LOW and NON-THRESHOLD SUBSTANCES

urea, uric acid,
phosphates, sulfates
creatinine, inulin } are concentrated in the urine
because they are reabsorbed
only in small amounts if at all

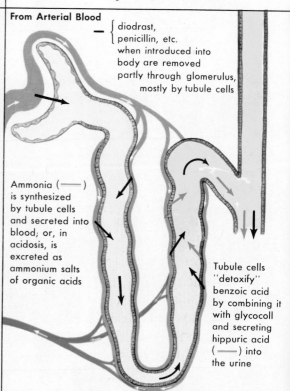

From Arterial Blood

— { diodrast,
penicillin, etc.
when introduced into
body are removed
partly through glomerulus,
mostly by tubule cells

Ammonia (——)
is synthesized
by tubule cells
and secreted into
blood; or, in
acidosis, is
excreted as
ammonium salts
of organic acids

Tubule cells
"detoxify"
benzoic acid
by combining it
with glycocoll
and secreting
hippuric acid
(——) into
the urine

SECRETED SUBSTANCES

Some of the substances that may appear in the urine are removed from the blood by tubule cells; and some are manufactured by the tubule cells

lining, produces a characteristic burning pain relieved by micturition (urination).

NATHANIEL KLEITMAN

BIBLIOG.–H. W. Smith, *The Physiology of the Kidney* (1937); *Lectures on the Kidney* (1943); C. H. Best and N. B. Taylor, *The Physiological Basis of Medical Practice* (ed. 1950); J. F. A. McManus, *Medical Diseases of the Kidney* (1950); R. L. Cecil, *A Textbook of Medicine* (ed. 1951).

KIDNEY STONES are hard, round or irregular bodies usually formed in the pelvis of the kidney, which is the cone-shaped space inside the kidney emptying into the ureter (duct which leads to the bladder). What causes kidney stones to form is not known exactly though slowed circulation of urine, chronic infection, vitamin deficiency, climate, heredity, and disturbed excretion of certain salts through the kidneys may all be at fault in certain cases. The theory dealing with crystallization of salts is favored.

Stones may occur at any age but are most common between 25 and 40. They are somewhat more common in men than in women. Frequently kidney stones grow slowly and cause few, if any, symptoms at first. Sometimes kidney stones "pass," that is, are carried down the ureter into the bladder and out of the body without pain. Frequently, however, they get caught on the way out and cause excruciating pain. At such times the stones are usually in the ureter between the kidney and bladder. It is important that they be carried out, otherwise they may produce serious complications by blocking the flow of urine and leading to infection.

The location of most stones can be discovered by the use of x-ray, especially by a technique called pyelography, in which the ureters may be visualized. With proper equipment and skill many stones can be removed or assisted to "pass." When kidney stones are discovered it is desirable to try to prevent the formation of additional stones. Since the causes of stone formation are not completely known, this may be difficult. Frequently, however, it seems that the formation of stones is delayed or prevented by regulating the acidity of the urine through the careful choice of diet. The elimination of infections elsewhere in the body and sometimes the use of vitamins may also be helpful.

EDWIN P. JORDAN, M. D.

KIDNEY VETCH, or **WOUNDWORT,** *A. Vulneraria,* is a species of the genus *Anthyllis,* family *Leguminosae.* It resembles clover in structure, but is pubescent with sparsely arranged leaves. Flowers vary from pale yellow to red and appear in heads at the end of branches. This plant which is about a foot high is cultivated in Europe and western Asia for forage. It is deep-rooted and adaptable.

KIDRON, modern **Wadi en Nar,** a stream in Palestine, flowing through the valley of Jehosaphat, then E between Jerusalem and the Mount of Olives, to the Dead Sea. The stream bed is dry except in the rainy season of winter. It is the "brook Kidron" of the Bible, and is known in its upper course as Wadi el Joz, in the central portion as the Wadi Sitti Miriam, and in its lower course as the Wadi en Nar.

KIEFT, WILLIAM, d. 1647, Dutch merchant who was director general of New Netherland from 1638 to 1647. His administration was marked by a disastrous Indian war (1643–45), growing out of Kieft's attempt to tax the Indians along the Hudson, and of the unprovoked massacre (1643), sanctioned by Kieft, of 110 peaceful river Indians who had come to the Dutch for protection against the Iroquois. This period also saw beginnings of a movement to establish a representative system in New Netherland, two representative bodies, the Twelve Men and the Eight Men being chosen by the commonalty, 1641 and 1643 respectively, to advise and co-operate with the director. Kieft was autocratic, domineering, and quarrelsome, as a result of which he was very unpopular. He died in a shipwreck while returning to the Netherlands.

KIEKIE, a New Zealand shrub, belonging to the family *Pandanaceae.* It is a high climber, bearing a large quantity of edible berries crowded on a spadix. The young spadices are made into a jelly, which has a strawberry-like flavor.

KIEL, city and seaport, Germany, capital of the province of Schleswig-Holstein, near the Baltic end of the Kiel Canal on Kiel Bay, 70 miles N of Hamburg. The old town is situated between the lake of Little Kiel in the west and the harbor to the east. North of the old town is the suburb of Düsternbrook, and east, across the harbor, are the wharves of Gaarden. The fine harbor, with an average depth of 40 feet, can accommodate the largest ships. Before World War II Kiel's greatest industrial activity was centered in the shipyards, arsenal, and naval maintenance works. Other industries include oil works, flour mills, sawmills, iron foundries, and chemical plants. Kiel was known in the 10th century as Kyl, a word apparently derived from the Anglo-Saxon *kille* meaning a haven for ships. It was a member of the Hanseatic League and long a center for trade with the Scandinavian countries. In 1773 it was made part of the kingdom of Denmark. With the rest of Schleswig-Holstein it passed to Prussia in 1866. It has been a first-ranking German naval base for many years, the most important in the Baltic area. During the greater part of World War I the German fleet was virtually imprisoned at Kiel by the British. The port was the scene of the German naval mutiny in October, 1918. In World War II Kiel suffered heavy damage from frequent air attack and was left practically in ruins. Among the numerous buildings destroyed by bombs are the St. Nikolas Church (14th century); the Church of the Holy Ghost (13th century); and most of the city's museums, including the Vaterländisches, the Thaulow, and the Kunsthalle. Pop. (1946) 213,299.

KIEL CANAL, formerly **Kaiser Wilhelm Canal,** Germany, in the province of Schleswig-Holstein, extends from near Brunsbüttelkoog on the Elbe River to Holtenau on Kiel Bay and provides the shortest and the cheapest route for shipping between the Baltic and North seas. Constructed at sea level, with locks at either entrance, the canal is 61 miles long. Passage occupies from 8 to 10 hours and the use of pilots is compulsory. In normal years about 50,000 ships use the canal each year. The Kiel waterway was begun in 1887, and opened in 1895. It was originally 72 feet wide at the bottom, 219 feet at the surface, and 29½ feet deep, but in 1914 alterations were completed making it 150 feet at the bottom, 335 feet at the surface, and 45 feet deep. The canal is owned by the government and is administered by the federal canal office. Under the terms of the Treaty of Versailles (1919) it was opened on an equal basis to the ships of all nations at peace with Germany; however, in 1936 the German government resumed full control. During World War II canal installations were damaged by frequent Allied bombing and by mines laid by aircraft. See CANAL.

Water Front Promenade at Kiel as it appeared before its destruction by bombing in World War II

EWING GALLOWAY

KIELCE, province of SW Poland; area 9,898 sq. mi.; pop. (1946) 1,173,300. The area's black earth soil covers part of the province. Potatoes are an important crop. The chief minerals of Kielce are iron, lead, and copper; zinc, cola, calamine, marble, gypsum, clay, and sulfur are also found. Its principal industries are potteries, tanneries, tile works, sawmills, flour mills, and the manufacture of metal objects. The administrative center is the city of Kielce. In World War II the province was occupied by the Nazis.

KIELCE, town, Poland, capital of Kielce Province, on the Lysa Gora, 105 miles S of Warsaw. Kielce's forested highlands contain iron, copper, marble, and lead. The city's industrial establishments include sugar factories, cement works, and textile plants. Kielce was founded in 1173 by Gedeon, bishop of Kraków. It was occupied by the Germans in World Wars I and II. Pop. (1946) 49,960.

KIERAN, JOHN FRANCIS, 1892– , American sports writer famed for his encyclopedic knowledge of popular matters, was born in New York City. After his graduation from Fordham University he was briefly a country school teacher, poultryman, and sewer-construction timekeeper before joining the sports staff of the *New York Times* in 1915. During World War I he served overseas with the 11th Engineers. After the Armistice he was employed by the *New York Herald Tribune*, the Hearst newspapers, the *New York Times* (1927–43), and the *New York Sun* (1943–44). In 1938 he made his first appearance on *Information Please* and became a regular participant on the program. He wrote *Footnotes on Nature* (1947).

KIERKEGAARD, SÖREN AABYE, 1813–55, Danish philosopher, was born in Copenhagen and lived most of his life there, becoming one of the greatest Protestant theologians. He was brought up in a strict Christian environment and when his father once cursed God it had a profound influence on Kierkegaard's life. As a young man he became engaged to Regina Olsen but broke the engagement after many months of struggle with himself. He wrote several volumes about this relationship, all of which were dedicated to Regina, in an attempt to explain himself to her. Later in life he quarreled with the newspapers

Sören Kierkegaard

and waged a war against religion as exemplified in the national Danish Church.

His Viewpoint. Kierkegaard was concerned with what he must do and not with what he could grasp with his understanding. He searched for a truth which was true for him and for which he was willing to live and to die. Kierkegaard's philosophical viewpoint was existential (see EXISTENTIALISM) according to which existence is more important than essence which is universal, cognitive, and objective. Subjectivity was for him the highest expression of truth. Central in Kierkegaard's thought is the stress on the existential as against the systematic and on the individual as against the institutional. By making the individual the supreme category, Kierkegaard opposed Hegel, according to whom man found ethical significance through identification with social, political, and religious institutions, Kierkegaard wanted to transcend rather than to transform the world of fact. He wished to reform man, each individual, and not society as a whole.

On Religion. According to Kierkegaard life outside religion is characterized by doubt, sensuality, and despair. While doubt is merely an expression of thought, despair involves the whole personality. Despair is defined by him as sickness unto death. To be healed of this sickness is the Christian bliss. Despair is sin, and sin does not lie in the intellect—in doubt

—but in the will—in defiance. The opposite of sin is not virtue but faith, which is man's relation to the divine. Kierkegaard maintains that man can have no objective knowledge of the truth of Christianity. One cannot believe because understanding approves. Furthermore, there would be nothing to faith if God's existence could be proved. Thus knowledge and faith are polar opposites.

According to Kierkegaard the paradoxical character of Christianity consists in the constant use of time and the historical in relation to the eternal. Infinite God cannot be reduced to finite human standards. The Tertullian position of Kierkegaard is expressed in his assertion that the absurd is the object of faith, and the only object that can be believed. Since the fundamental nature of Christianity is absurd it creates objective uncertainty. Such a predicament raises faith to its highest intensity. For faith is the result of the contradiction between the infinite passion of the individual's inwardness and objective uncertainty. Kierkegaard further maintained that to become a true Christian it is necessary to achieve contemporaneousness with Christ in his suffering and humiliation. According to Kierkegaard it is not easy to become a Christian, for "Narrow is the gate and straitened the way that leadeth unto life." The Church's this-worldliness was the main reason for his attack on Christendom. Christianity for Kierkegaard meant dying to this world. The central theme of his conception of Christianity is the solitary individual facing his destiny before God. The relation between historical truth and the eternal, and the relation between man and God is incommensurable.

Kierkegaard's Influence. Kierkegaard represents a reaction to Hegelianism and to Protestant and Catholic orthodoxy. His influence on recent philosophical and religious thought has been considerable. In the United States his theological views had considerable influence on Paul Tillich and Reinhold Niebuhr. His influence on literature has found eminent expression in the works of Franz Kafka. In the past 10 years practically all of Kierkegaard's works have been translated into English, mostly by Walter Lowrie and D. F. Swenson.

GEORGE B. DE HUSZAR

BIBLIOG.–W. Lowrie, *Kierkegaard* (1938); D. F. Swenson, *Something About Kierkegaard* (1941); R. Bretall, ed. *A Kierkegaard Anthology* (1946); R. Jolivet, *Introduction to Kierkegaard* (1950).

KIESELGUHR. See DIATOMACEOUS EARTH.

KIEV, Ukranian **Kyjiv,** the third largest city of the U.S.S.R., capital of Kiev Region, beautifully situated on the right bank of the Dnepr River and at the junction of the Warsaw-Kharkov railway, 205 miles N of Odessa. The oldest city in the Soviet Union, Kiev is known as the "Mother of Russia." The city, which is surrounded by large tracts of forests, consists of three sections, Podol (now Petrovskij), the commercial district, Old Kiev, and Pechersk. Kiev has innumerable buildings of historical interest, among them the 11th-century cathedral of St. Sophia, the oldest in Russia, with 19 spires; St. Michael's Monastery (1108); All Saints' Church (11th century); and the Pechersk (cave) Monastery, celebrated for its catacombs, which was built by the Greeks on a high bluff above the Dnepr. Kiev rivals Kharkov as a center of Ukrainian culture. It is the home of the Ukrainian Academy of Sciences and the Ukrainian National Library, which preserves the literature of the ancient Ukrainian language. The city has 40-odd schools and colleges, of both arts and sciences. There are also several theaters, an art gallery, many museums, an observatory, and botanical gardens.

The industrial area of Kiev is concentrated in the western and southern suburbs. Its manufactures include machinery, sugar, chemicals, cloth, tobacco, leather, pottery, metal goods, shoes, candies, food

PAUL'S PHOTOS-SOVFOTO

Business section of Kiev, Ukrainian capital

products, and beer. There are shipbuilding yards and railroad repair shops.

History. By the ninth century Kiev was already established along a great trade route running from Scandinavia to Byzantium. In 882 the city became the capital of the first organized Russian state known as Kiev-Rus. One of its rulers, Vlademin the Holy, introduced the Greek Orthodox Church here in 988, making Kiev Russia's leading spiritual center. In the 13th century the city was captured by the Tartars under Batu, grandson of Genghis Khan, who ravaged it so completely that it did not recover for a hundred years. In 1320 the city came under the rule of Lithuania, passed to Poland in 1569, and in 1688 was returned to Russian rule. Kiev, as a part of the Ukraine, fell under the control of the Polish-Lithuanian alliance during the war between Russia and Poland in the 17th century, but resumed its status as a Russian city in 1793 when Poland was partitioned. Kiev was the scene of much fighting during the Revolution of 1917 from which the Ukraine emerged as a Union Republic within the Soviet Union. In 1934 the capital of the Ukraine was removed to Kiev from Kharkov which had served as the center of government since 1923 when the Ukraine joined the Soviet Union. During World War II the Nazis occupied and ravaged Kiev from September, 1941, to November, 1943. The city's main thoroughfare, Kreshchatik, lined with numerous fine buildings, was completely laid waste, and the famous Pechersk Monastery, reduced to ruins. An estimated 200,000 persons were killed by the Nazis, and more than 100,000 taken into Germany as slave laborers. When Kiev was recaptured by the Soviet Army, only 50,000 survivors of the Nazi holocaust were found in the city. Following the recapture of the city, the Soviets outlined a three-year plan for its reconstruction. Pop. (1950 est.) 820,000.   A. M. K.

KIEV REGION, an administrative area of the U.S.S.R. in the Ukrainian Soviet Socialist Republic; bounded on the N by the Belorussian Soviet Socialist Republic, on the W by the Regions of Vinnitsa and Zhitomir, on the S by the Regions of Kirovograd and Odessa, and on the E by Chernovtsy and Poltava Regions. The Region is drained by the Dnepr and the Desna rivers. With the exception of the Pripet and the Irpen marshes, its terrain is one of extremely rich black-loam steppes. Wheat, sugar beets, apples, and tobacco are the principal products. The Region's natural resources include granite, labradorite, kaolin and other clays, peat, graphite, and lignite coal. The capital of the region is the city of Kiev. Pop. (1950 est.) 3,500,000.

KIGOMA, town, E Africa, Tanganyika Territory, on Lake Tanganyika, 15 miles N of the fifth parallel S. It is the western terminus of the Central Railway which crosses Tanganyika from DAR ES SALAAM on the Indian Ocean and it has steamer connections with Albertville, on the western shore of Lake Tanganyika, and road connections with Uganda to the north. Pop. about 15,000.

KIKUYU, district, British East Africa, central Kenya Colony. Mount Kenya rises to 17,040 feet and most of the area is above 6,000. The land was preempted for white colonization, although the Kikuyu people claimed it as their own. The rainfall is abundant and the soil is rich, producing corn, sweet potatoes, beans, millet, yams, and coffee. Because of the elevation the climate is temperate.

KILAUEA, an active volcano, HAWAIIAN ISLANDS, on the island of Hawaii, 4,090 feet above sea level on the E side of the higher Mauna Loa and independent of it as to the source of lava flow. Its depth in 1936 was more than 1,300 feet and its crater was 19 acres in area. Violent eruptions occur more often in the inner pit, Halemaumau, while the main crater emits occasional nonviolent lava flows. The eastern side of Mauna Loa is a national park and a modern concrete road brings visitors to within a safe observing distance of Kilauea. Notable eruptions occurred in 1790, 1823, 1832, 1840, 1868, and 1920 with decided signs of activity in 1889, 1892, 1894, 1902, 1907, 1919, and 1926.

KILDARE, inland county, E Ireland, Leinster Province, bounded on the E by the counties of Dublin and Wicklow, S by Carlow, W by Leix and Offaly, N by Meath; area 654 sq. mi.; pop. (1946) 68,834. About 40,000 acres of the northwest section of the county are taken up by the Bog of Allen; the rest of its surface is flat or slightly undulating. Throughout the central part of the county is the plain of Curragh, which covers about 4,800 acres. Race horses are trained here. The principal rivers are the Liffey, BOYNE, Greese, Blackwater, and Barrow. Near Mullingar are three well-known fishing lakes, Ennel, Owel, and Derrevaragh. The Royal Canal traverses the northern boundary line, connecting Dublin with the River Shannon at Cloondara. Farther south the Grand Canal, also connecting Dublin with the Shannon, passes through the Liffey Valley, crossing the Bog of Allen into Offaly. Agriculture is the leading industry and the chief crops are oats, barley, turnips, and potatoes. Cattle and sheep are grazed. Cotton and woolen fabrics and paper are manufactured, and there are grist mills, distilleries, and breweries. Extensive ruins and other antiquities—such as standing stones, raths, earthworks, a Franciscan abbey at Castlemot, and an Augustinian nunnery at Graney—are found throughout Kildare. The county town, Kildare, was founded by St. Bridget in the fifth century as a religious community. It has an ancient cathedral which has been destroyed and restored many times, a roundtower with a Roman Cross, and remains of a 13th-century castle. Other towns of Kildare County are Athey, Naas, Newbridge, and Maynooth. Punchestown is a famous racing town. Tourists, especially naturalists, are attracted to Kildare because of the great profusion of wildflowers—primroses, violets, bluebells, pansies, roses, honeysuckle, the rare wild fuchsias and orchids, and the almost extinct golden kingcups.   K. E. H.

KILGORE, city, E central Texas; on the Missouri Pacific Railroad, about 80 miles SE of Dallas and about 30 miles from the Louisiana border in an extensive oil field. Kilgore's main interests are concerned with the oil industry. The city has sawmills, oil refineries, and manufactures tanks, explosives, and oil field supplies. Pop. (1950) 9,638.

KILIMANJARO, volcanic mountain (now extinct), the highest peak (19,455 ft.) in Africa, in Tanganyika Territory near the Kenya border, 160 miles WNW of the coastal city of Mombasa. Its two peaks, Kibo (the highest) and Mawenzi, are linked by a saddle at about 14,000 feet. Kilimanjaro's heavily forested base is the site of a game reserve. Its first discovery by a white man was in 1848; its summit was first reached by Dr. Hans Meyer in 1889.

KILKENNY, inland county, SE Ireland, Leinster Province, bounded on the N by Leix, E by Carlow, SE by Wexford, S by Waterford, W by Tipperary;

Kilkenny

area 792 sq. mi.; pop. (1946) 66,683. The surface of county Kilkenny is for the most part flat, occupied as it is by the southern end of the Irish central plain. The low, isolated hills of the Booley, Margy, and Naman mountains are in the southern part. The county touches the sea only through Waterford Harbor, estuary of the Nore River. The tributaries of this river, the Kings, Suir, and Barrow, drain the county, the Suir separating it from Waterford and the Barrow separating it from Carlow. Agriculture is the chief occupation of Kilkenny; crops include wheat, oats, barley, turnips, and potatoes. Sheep, Kerry cattle, pigs, and poultry are raised, and beekeeping is widely practiced. There are a few industries, such as flour mills, distilleries, breweries, leather tanneries, and mining. Anthracite and soft coals, iron, silver, manganese, and copper are the minerals found. A fine quality of black marble and an unusual kind of black limestone in which shells have been embedded are quarried for ornamental purposes. Blue slates are quarried for flagstones. The county is rich in antiquities: cromlechs, raths, dolmen, ruins of ancient Norman castles, and 11th-, 12th-, and 13th-century ecclesiastical remains, including the Abbey of Jerpoint near Thomastown. Kilkenny boasts five almost perfect round towers. A profusion of myrtle, arbutus, and heath bloom throughout the year in the highlands. KILKENNY is the county town; Thomastown and Carrick rank second in importance. K. E. H.

KILKENNY, town and borough, SE Ireland, Leinster Province, seat of county Kilkenny, on both banks of the Nore River; 80 miles SW of Dublin. Among the town's interesting buildings are the cathedral of St. Canice, founded in 1255, when the see of Ossory was transferred hither from Aghaboe; the fortress-castle built by Strongbow in the 11th century and now modernized; the churches of St. John and St. Mary; and two monasteries dating from the 13th century. In 1642 Kilkenny was the place chosen for a Confederate Catholic Parliament. In 1650 the town was captured by Cromwell. The Tholsel (market house) has a curious cupola. Swift, Congreve, and Berkeley were educated at the grammar school, which was founded in 1684. Industries include grist mills, breweries, and distilleries and factories producing blankets, coarse woolens, and coarse linen cloth. Near by are marble quarries and the limestone caverns of Dunmore. Coal is mined. Pop. (1946) 10,291.

KILLARNEY, LAKES OF, in SW Ireland, Munster Province, county Kerry, three connected lakes occupying a length of 17 miles by a breadth of from one to three miles; 186 miles SW of Dublin. They are famous for the wild beauty of their surrounding mountains, glens, and waterfalls. Lough Leane, the largest of the three, is about six miles long, covers 5,000 acres, and is surrounded by the peaks of Mac-Gillicuddy's Reeks, Currantuohill, Torc, and Mangerton. Lake Leane is drained into Dingle Bay by the Laune River and contains, among several wooded isles, Ross Island, immortalized by Thomas Moore. Upon Ross Island is Ross Castle, ancient stronghold of the O'Donoghues. Innisfallen, another island, has the ruins of the sixth century abbey founded by St. Finian, in which was compiled the *Annals of Innisfallen.* Upper Muckross Lake, sometimes called Lough Torc, covers 680 acres and is separated from Lough Leane by Muckross Peninsula, upon which are the remains of Muckross Abbey, built in 1440. There is also a well-preserved round tower here. Near the north shore of Muckross Lake rises Torc Mountain, from which falls the famed Torc cascade; farther north, alongside Mangerton Peak (2,756 ft.), is a deep tarn called the "Devil's Punch Bowl." A winding channel three miles long, connects Muckross with Lake Leane. Lower Muckross covers 430 acres, has several small isles, and is also almost entirely enclosed by lofty mountains. Trout and salmon abound in the waters of this trio of lakes. The town of Killarney, 20 miles southeast of Tralee and 44 miles northwest of Cork,

IRISH TOURIST ASSN., INC.

Lower Lake Killarney in county Kerry

is the tourist center for the lakes. It has modern hotels and manufactures of arbutus-wood articles, which are sold for souvenirs. K. E. H.

KILLDEER, one of the common, larger PLOVERS of the family *Charadriidae.* It is well known because of its loud-whistled, half plaintive call, *kill-dee, kill-dee,* and its extensive geographic distribution. The adult birds are ten and one-half inches long. A killdeer, *Oxyechus vociferus vociferus,* can be recognized by its brown back, rufous rump, and white underparts with two black bands, one around the neck, and the other on the upper part of the breast. The male, female, and immature birds have the same coloration and show no change between winter and summer plumage. Even the downy young resemble their parents except for having only a single black band.

Killdeers breed commonly in plowed fields, pastures, lakesides and meadows, often far from water. The nest is a small depression on the ground, usually in a gravelly spot, and is sometimes lined scantily with bits of grass. The four, large tan eggs are spotted with chocolate brown, chiefly at the larger end. Incubation is usually shared by the sexes, although the male may have the larger part, if not the entire role. When disturbed on the nest the bird leaves immediately and flutters along the ground with tail spread

CRUICKSHANK-NAS

Killdeer on the nest

and wings drooping, thereby feigning injury. The performance is conspicuous and tends to draw the intruder away from the nest. When not nesting, killdeers are usually found in flocks, which scatter while feeding but unite when taking wing. They can run rapidly on the ground. When flying singly the flight is erratic.

The killdeer is a very useful species. Its food is primarily animal matter (97.72 per cent), consisting of worms and insects. The stomach of one bird contained 300 mosquito larvae; other injurious insects that are eaten in large numbers are: alfalfa weevils, grasshoppers, cotton-boll weevils, and ground beetles.

The species breeds throughout temperate North America, the Bahamas, central Mexico, and southern Lower California. It winters from southern British Columbia and northern United States as far south as northern Venezuela and Peru. Migration occurs in the spring and in the fall. A. WOLFSON

BIBLIOG.–A. C. Bent, *Life Histories of North American Shore Birds,* U.S. Nat'l Mus. Bull., 142 (1927), and 146 (1929).

KILLER WHALE. See WHALE.

KILLIECRANKIE, PASS OF, a mountain pass, Scotland, in Perthshire, in the valley of the Garry, three miles SE of Blair Athol. At the northern end of the pass was the scene of the battle fought between the Jacobites under Graham of Claverhouse and the Royalists under Hugh Mackay, on July 27, 1689.

KILLIGREW, THOMAS, 1612–83, English dramatist, was born in London, son of Sir Robert Killigrew. He became page to Charles I and was the companion of Charles II in exile. After the Restoration he served as groom of the bedchamber and queen's chamberlain, and the King permitted great license to his witty and often acidulous tongue. His best known play, *The Parson's Wedding,* is more noted for its bawdiness of situation and language than for its dramatic worth. His other plays include *Pandora, Celia and Clorinda,* and *The Princess.*

KILMARNOCK, burgh, SW Scotland, Ayrshire, on Kilmarnock Water and the Irvine River; 12 miles NW of Ayr and 33 miles SW of Glasgow. It has coal and iron mines, and its important industries are locomotive building and engine repair shops, iron foundries, and tanneries. There are also manufactures of tweeds, woolen fabrics, carpets, boots, shoes, china and earthenware, leather goods, shawls, cottons, laces, lace curtains, and other articles of lace. It is noted for its dairy products and cheese fair. Kilmarnock has a technical institute. The Burns Memorial Museum here contains original manuscripts and all editions of his works, including priceless first editions. Pop. (1950 est.) 42,700.

KILMER, JOYCE, 1886–1918, American poet, was born in New Brunswick, N.J., and studied at Rutgers College and Columbia University. Much of his poetry was written after he became a convert to Catholicism, and his poetry shows the influence of such Catholic poets as Belloc, Chesterton, and Coventry Patmore. Many critics consider his early poetry as far too sentimental, but he was killed in action while serving in the U.S. Army in France, before he was able to complete his development as a poet. Kilmer is best known for the popular poem, *Trees.* This poem was set to music and quite possibly has had a larger audience than any other modern American poem. His books include: *Summer of Love* (1911); *Trees and Other Poems* (1914); *Main Street and Other Poems* (1917). In addition, he edited anthologies of Catholic poets and wrote a volume of essays, *The Circus and Other Essays* (1921).

Aline Murray Kilmer, 1888–1941, his wife, was also a poet. Among her works are *Candles That Burn* (1919); *Vigils* (1921); *The Poor King's Daughter, and Other Poems* (1925); *A Buttonwood Summer* (1929).

KILN, a furnace or oven of brick or stone for burning, baking, hardening or drying various materials. There are two types of kilns; those in which the furnace, or heat source, is beneath or surrounding the oven (brick and pottery kilns are of this type) and which include drying kilns, such as for hops, wood, etc., and those kilns in which the materials come into contact with the fire. Lime-kilns are of this class.

Joyce Kilmer

KILO, properly a prefix used in the METRIC SYSTEM to denote 1,000—as kilogram, 1,000 grams; kilometer, 1,000 meters. It is used alone as an abbreviation for kilogram—as 10 kilos, for 10 kilograms.

KILOGRAM, the weight of 1,000 grams, approximately 2.2 pounds. See METRIC SYSTEM.

KILOWATT, a unit of measurement of electrical energy. Its significance is 1,000 watts, and it is equivalent to 1.3406 horsepower. Occasionally the term kilowatt is used to denote kilowatt hour.

KILOWATT-HOUR, a common unit of measurement of electrical power, equivalent to the work accomplished by the expenditure of power at the rate of one kilowatt for one hour. This is the unit for metering and billing electrical energy. Sometimes the term kilowatt-hour is shortened to kilowatt.

KILPATRICK, HUGH JUDSON, 1836–81, American soldier, was born near Deckertown, N.J., and was graduated from West Point in 1861. He served in the Union army throughout the Civil War, rising from the rank of first lieutenant to that of major general of volunteers, and distinguishing himself as a cavalry officer, especially at Aldie, Va., Gettysburg, Pa., Resaca, Ga., and Fayetteville, N.C. He commanded Sherman's cavalry during the March to the Sea, and through South Carolina and North Carolina; and in March, 1865, was brevetted major general in both the regular and the volunteer service for gallant and meritorious services during the campaign in the Carolinas. He was U.S. minister to Chile in 1865–70 and 1881, and died at Valparaiso.

KILPATRICK, WILLIAM HEARD, 1871– , American educator, was born in White Plains, Ga. He studied at Mercer and Columbia universities, and was acting president of Mercer (1903–5). In 1909 he joined the faculty of Teachers College, Columbia University, and was professor of the philosophy of education (1918–38). He served as president of the Board of Trustees of Bennington College (1931–38). Kilpatrick wrote: *Foundations of Method* (1925); *Remaking the Curriculum* (1936); *Selfhood and Civilization* (1941); *Intercultural Attitudes in the Making* (1947).

KILPATRICK, OLD, and **NEW.** See OLD KILPATRICK; NEW KILPATRICK.

KILRAIN, JAKE, 1859–1937, American heavyweight boxer, was born in Greenpoint, N.Y. One of the outstanding fighters in the bare-knuckle era of boxing, he fought a draw with Jem Smith, the English titleholder, for the heavyweight championship of the world in 1887. When John L. Sullivan defeated him in 75 rounds at Richburg, Miss., in 1889, Sullivan claimed the world's title because of Kilrain's draw with Smith.

KILSYTH, burgh, Scotland, in Stirlingshire; on the Kelvin, 12 miles NE of Glasgow. Remains of the Wall of Antoninus are near the town. Near here, in 1645, Montrose defeated the Covenanters in a battle which was disastrous for the latter. Pop. about 7,500.

KILUNG. See KIRUN.

KILWA, or **Kilwa Kivinje,** minor seaport, East Africa, Tanganyika Territory, 200 miles S of Zanzibar. Good highways give access through the interior to Manda on Lake Nyasa and important coastal towns. Kilwa is well laid out and has a number of well-built European homes. On Kilwa Island, lying in the south part of the bay, is the ancient city of Kilwa Kisiwani, now but little populated, said to have been founded in the 10th century by a Persian prince (ruins of his palaces and mosques remain). Vasca da Gama visited the port as early as 1502, and levied a tribute upon the sultan. The port was known to the Portuguese as Quiloa. The sultan's failure to pay the tribute resulted in the Portuguese taking the town in 1505. The Arabs later took the port, and from it carried on a trade with the interior.

KIMBALL, DAN ABEL, 1896– , American official, was born in St. Louis, Mo. A pilot in World War I, he became executive head of a jet engineering firm in 1944. A leader in the development of rockets and jet engines, he was made Navy Assistant Secretary, then Navy Under Secretary in 1949. In 1951 he was named Secretary of the Navy.

KIMBALL, SUMNER INCREASE, 1834–1923, superintendent of U.S. Life Saving Service, was born in Lebanon, Me. He was graduated from Bowdoin College in 1855; was admitted to the bar (1858); practiced law at North Berwick, Me.; and was a member of the Maine legislature (1859). After serving as acting register, acting solicitor, and acting comptroller of the Treasury (1861–71), he became chief of the U.S. Revenue Marine Service (1871), and general superintendent of the U.S. Life Saving Service, which he headed from its organization as a separate bureau in 1878 until 1916.

KIMBERLEY, gold field, Australia, in Western Australia, Kimberley Division, 300 miles SE of Derby; area about 35,000 sq. mi. The first discovery of gold in Western Australia was made in this division in 1882, and in 1886 what was known as the Kimberley gold field was proclaimed and reserved for gold mining. It is still worked to a limited extent.

KIMBERLEY, formerly **Colesberg Kopje,** and **New Rush,** chief town and diamond-mining center, Union of South Africa, Cape of Good Hope Province, located on the inland desert plateau at an elevation of 4,050 feet; 646 miles by rail NE of Capetown and 914 miles SW of Bulawayo. It was named after Lord Kimberley, British colonial secretary (1870–74). Now among the largest towns of British South Africa, it has fine public buildings, churches, hospitals, free library, botanical gardens, public waterworks—supplied from the Vaal River—and electric lighting.

In 1867 an ostrich hunter, named O'Reilly, obtained from a Dutch farmer some diamonds which had been found by children on the banks of the Vaal.

HOMER SMITH

Conveyor cars at diamond mine in Kimberley

Two years later the "Star of South Africa," valued at $100,000, was dug out of the wall of a mud hut at Du Toit's Pan, and within four years 10,000 diggers were working in the wet or alluvial diggings along the banks of the river. Finally, the matrix of the diamonds was discovered in pipes or funnels of unknown depth—probably the craters of ancient volcanoes. The surface of the diamond-bearing country is red sand; below this is a deposit of lime, and then the "blue ground," or diamond-bearing earth. The chief mines are the Kimberley, De Beers, Bultfontein, Du Toit's Pan, and Wesselton, all within a three-mile radius. The output is regulated by the De Beers Company, and has had an average annual value of between $25,-000,000 and $40,000,000. The open diggings in the alluvium along the river bank are operated by independent diggers.

On Oct. 15, 1899, Kimberley was besieged by the Boers, and was not relieved until Feb. 16, 1900. Although forced to close during World War I, the Kimberley mines (as well as others in South Africa) were kept working during World War II, because of the importance of diamonds in highly precise instruments. Pop. (1946) 52,499.   G. A.; C. S.

KIMMEL, HUSBAND EDWARD, 1882– , American naval officer, was born in Henderson, Ky., and was graduated from the U.S. Naval Academy (1904). He advanced through the grades to rear admiral (1937) and admiral (1941). In World War I he was executive officer of the battleship *New York* in the North Sea and experimented in using motion pictures in spotting shots. Praised for his bold and imaginative plans in maneuvers (1939), he was assigned to command the Battle Force (1939) and the Pacific Fleet and Combined U.S. Fleet (1941), which command he held when the Japanese bombed Pearl Harbor (Dec. 7). Kimmel was immediately relieved and after a report by a commission headed by Justice Roberts was allowed to retire (1942) and was employed as a consulting engineer. When court-martial charges were withdrawn, he demanded a court of inquiry, which acquitted him. The verdict was set aside in 1946 when the Congressional Pearl Harbor Investigating Committee placed the chief blame for the Pearl Harbor disaster on Kimmel and Major General W. C. SHORT. However, they were blamed for errors in judgment, not dereliction of duty.

KIMOLOS. See CYCLADES ISLANDS.

KIN, NEXT OF, the nearest relatives of a deceased person, no distinction being made between paternal and maternal relatives, or between whole and half blood. The relationship is reckoned by degrees—i.e., parent and child are one degree, grandparents and brothers and sisters are two degrees, uncles or aunts three degrees, and first cousins four degrees. In each case the reckoning is to the common ancestor and then down. The Statutes of Distribution have in some cases created an artificial class, who are termed next of kin, but only for purposes of interstate succession. A husband is not next of kin to his wife, or *vice versa*. In the United States, next of kin are determined by the laws of the various states. Practice in general, is the same as under the common law of England. See DESCENT AND DISTRIBUTION.

KINABALU, MOUNT, or **Kinabulu,** highest peak (13,455 ft.) on the island of Borneo, in British North Borneo, 140 miles NE of Brunei.

KINCARDINE, town and port of entry, S Canada, in the province of Ontario, Bruce County; on the E shore of Lake Huron at the mouth of the Penetangore River, and on the Canadian National Railway, about 160 miles NW of Toronto. Founded in about 1848 and incorporated as a village in 1858, the town was first named Penetangore. Gradually it was called Kincardine after the township which had been named for a governor general of Canada. The city is a farm trading center and a popular summer resort. It has wood-working plants, textile mills, and salt works. Pop. (1949 est.) 2,785.

KINCARDINE, or **The Mearns,** maritime county, NE Scotland, bounded on the E by the North Sea, S and W by Angus (Forfar), N by Aberdeenshire; area 388 sq. mi.; pop. (1950 est.) 28,800. The western half of the shire is occupied by the Grampian Hills, a high range culminating in the peak of Mount Battock (2,555 ft.), which rises at the corner of the three shires: Angus, Aberdeen, and Kincardine. The coast line of Kincardine is very rugged, with few breaks in the 250-foot cliffs; but the northwestern section belongs to the beautiful valley of the Dee River, and the southwest is a fertile area comprised of 50,000 acres and known as the "How (Hollow) of Mearns." Rivers of the county are the DEE, which forms part of the northern boundary line, the North Esk, Feugh, Dye, Carron, Cowie, and Bervie. Kincardine's most scenic section is the wild and picturesque Glen Dye; Den Fenella has a noted cascade. Agriculture and livestock grazing are the leading occupations of the people, with some salmon and haddock fishing along the coast. Oats, barley, and wheat, and potatoes and other rootcrops are grown. Kincardine is one of the principal Scotch cattle raising counties, and large flocks of Blackface and Cheviot sheep are grazed in the western highlands. Industries are flax spinning and woolen textile mills, tanneries, distilleries, and granite quarries. The county, once a part of Pictavia, was occupied by the Romans, as is evidenced by such antiquities as ancient stone circles, tumuli, cairns, and the remains of medieval castles. Stonehaven is the county town and chief port; other manufacturing towns are Inverbervie, Banchory, Laurencekirk, Gourdon and Johnshaven. There is an academy at Stonehaven.   K. E. H.

Kinchinjunga

KINCHINJUNGA. See KANCHENJUNGA.

KINDERGARTEN. Kindergartens existed in this country as early as the 1860's. They were based almost entirely upon the principles of FROEBEL, who is considered the founder of the kindergarten. The value of play was recognized, but it was a rather regimented play. The child was presented with a set of "gifts" and "occupations" in a prescribed order, designed to bring about the gradual unfolding of his nature.

Under the early influence of JOHN DEWEY and Patty Smith Hill, among others, this emphasis upon accurate work with set materials was gradually broadened. There has been a repudiation of the viewpoint that the child's nature can gradually be brought to unfold under the influence of a set of didactic materials. Rather, it is held now that the child develops as the result of experiences in the real world.

Dr. MARIA MONTESSORI was another early pioneer in the kindergarten movement. Though she contributed some valuable ideas about the importance to the child of self-help and real responsibility in the school room, her rigid use of play materials, like Froebel's, has been largely repudiated.

As early as 1873 there was a kindergarten in a public school. Between 1880–90 kindergartens were adopted with rapid progress into the public school system. In 1913 the Division of Kindergarten Education was created in the United States Bureau of Education, Department of Interior. Today by far the majority of the existing kindergartens are in the public school system.

For the past two or more decades, the kindergarten has been thought of as a part of the public school. Five-year-old children came to kindergarten in order that they might have a gradual introduction into school life. Reading was not taught, but "reading readiness" was emphasized. The actual program and methods varied somewhat according to whether the underlying philosophy stemmed more from Dewey or from Froebel. Many kindergartens tended to stress accurate handwork and finger dexterity, giving the children cut-out work, sewing, and coloring according to set patterns, and teaching them patterned games. Kindergarten teachers whose philosophies stressed *experience* for the child took him on trips into the surrounding neighborhood, gave him opportunities and materials for free dramatic play, and encouraged him to paint and draw freely in his own original way.

Today the trend is in this latter direction. In fact, there is a tendency now to consider the kindergarten not as something distinct from "school" that is to follow, but as an integral part of early childhood experience. Curriculum plans are made for kindergarten, first, and second grades somewhat as an entity, with social studies the core, and play the method of learning. "Social studies" at these age levels, of course, mean exploration and understanding of the immediate environment—home, school, and neighborhood. There is even apparent a trend to include earlier ages in the movement, those previously considered nursery school ages. As a matter of fact, there is not too great a distinction today between the philosophy and methods of the nursery school and kindergarten. Both, at different age levels, are working for the development of the total child.

BARBARA BIBER

BIBLIOG.–*Childhood Education* (monthly).

KINDLER, HANS. 1893–1949, American conductor, was born in Rotterdam, Holland. Educated at the Rotterdam Conservatory, at the age of 18 he appeared as solo cellist with the Berlin Philharmonic Orchestra. In 1914 he came to America. When the war began, he remained here and won recognition as a cello virtuoso. A desire to conduct led him (1929) to abandon his concert career in order to devote full time to the baton. In 1931 he founded and became the conductor of the National Symphony Orchestra in Washington, D.C.

NEW YORK CENTRAL

KINEMATICS

The study of motion, as related to machines and machine operation, an essential branch of engineering

KINEMATICS, the study of motion as related to machines. The objective in the design of a mechanism is the attainment of a certain desired type of motion in a certain location from a given available motion at some other location, as in the rotation of locomotive driving wheel from the reciprocating piston in the steam cylinder. Discussion and explanations are confined to a few relatively common mechanisms of everyday interest and importance. Those mechanisms which involve gears and gear trains are not discussed in this section. See GEAR AND GEARING.

Automotive Steering Gear. When an automobile is driven around a curve (Fig. 1) all wheel centers

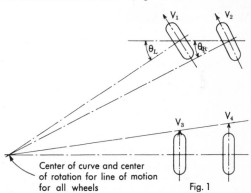

Fig. 1. For smooth tire action on a turn, the front wheels must follow arcs with a common center

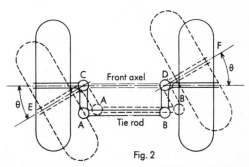

Fig. 2. A tie rod equal in length to the distance between the pivot centers would give equal angles

must be moving about the center of the curve or some of the wheels will be dragged sideways. The steering gear should turn the front wheels so that the extended wheel axes intersect at a point which falls on the extended axis of the rear axle. (The mechanism usually used is the Ackermann Steering Gear, Fig. 3.) Consider Fig. 2. If the tie rod ends A and B are directly behind the spindle bearings C and D, a parallel bar linkage is present, with AB parallel to CD regardless of the position of the linkage. If the left wheel turns so that its axle is at EC the right wheel will turn so that its axle will be at DF. Since EC and DF are parallel, their extensions will not intersect and the front wheels will "skid." The right wheel should turn less than the left. To accomplish this the tie rod ends are moved in toward the center of the axle (Fig. 3). Then when the left wheel turns through, say 22 degrees, the right may turn through only 19 degrees. Of course the position of the tie rod ends in the design is determined by the radii of the curves around which the car must travel.

The variation from the theoretically correct angles which should be turned by the two front wheels is very small, about 1 per cent with proper design. The simplicity of this gear and its satisfactory performance have established its widespread use.

Belt Arrangements. Where it is necessary to transmit power between shafts so far apart that a gear system would be impractical, or where precise timing between shafts is not necessary, the use of belts is economical. The velocity ratio between the shafts will be approximately the inverse ratio of the pulley diameters used. This ratio is not strictly exact because of the thickness of the belt and because of slip and creep of the belt. When it is desired to have two pulleys rotate in the same direction, an open belt arrangement is used (Fig. 4). Crossed belts (Fig. 5) give opposite directions of rotation. Lengths of belt required can be easily calculated. If D_1 is the diameter of the small pulley, D_2 is the diameter of the large pulley, and X is the distance between shaft centers, then for an open belt,

$$L = \frac{\pi}{2} D_2 + \frac{\pi}{2} D_1 + 2\sqrt{X^2 + \left(\frac{D_2}{2} - \frac{D_1}{2}\right)^2}$$

and for a crossed belt,

$$L = \frac{\pi}{2} D_2 + \frac{\pi}{2} D_1 + 2\sqrt{X^2 + \left(\frac{D_2}{2} + \frac{D_2}{2}\right)^2}$$

Pulleys on shafts not in the same plane may be connected by a belt, provided the arrangement is such that the belt when approaching a pulley has its center line in the plane of the central plane of the pulley (Fig. 6). If this precaution is not observed the belt will pull off. Note that in the arrangement of Fig. 6 the belt will stay on only for the direction of rotation shown. A drive can be made reversible if guide pulleys are used so that regardless of direction of rotation, the belt as it approaches a pulley will always satisfy the above requirement. Fig. 7 is an example.

When the usual flat belts are used, pulleys are often crowned to form a double cone (Fig. 8). A snug belt will lie flat on the cone with the approaching part of the belt constantly thrown to a larger diameter of the cone. Section CD approaching the pulley is, therefore, pulled toward the crown and tends to run along the dotted path.

Belts may be made of leather, rubber, some type of fabric, combinations of rubber and fabric, or even steel, depending upon the application. Belts may be flat or the cross section may have a variety of shapes such as round or trapezoidal. V-belts (usually of trapezoidal cross section) are widely used in both single and multiple belt arrangements, depending upon the power to be transmitted. Rope drives may be considered to come under the general classification of belt drives, the belt in this case having a circular cross section.

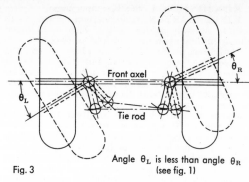

Fig. 3

Angle θ_L is less than angle θ_R (see fig. 1)

Fig. 3. A calculated, shorter tie rod swings the wheel axles to the angles that give a common center in all positions. This prevents side crawling

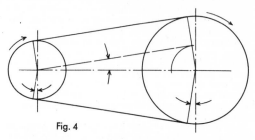

Fig. 4

Fig. 4. Pulleys for open belts must be designed for efficient belt contact. The relative diameters of the pulleys and center distance control this contact

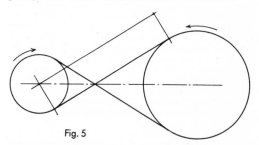

Fig. 5

Fig. 5. Crossed belts give effective contact but will be subject to belt wear at the crossing if reversal of belt is too abrupt or belt is too loose

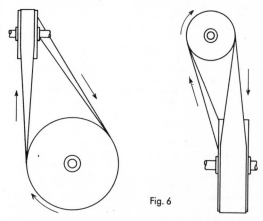

Fig. 6

Fig. 6. Shafts and pulleys at right angles may be accommodated if the belt approaches the pulley in line with the face of the pulley. Belt must ride snugly and the pulley faces should be crowned

Cams. A cam and follower arrangement offers a simple means of converting one form of motion to another. Very complex motions can be obtained which, if obtained by other means, might be much more difficult and costly. Fig. 9 illustrates a flat-faced follower moving in a straight path, and a pivoted roller follower which moves on the arc of a circle. The cams here are called disk cams since they can be considered to have been cut from disks. It should be noted (Fig. 10) that a flat-faced follower cannot follow a concave cam profile properly, and that certain limits are present on the curvature of the cam when a roller follower is used. The cylinder cam is another common form. In this type grooves for guiding the follower are cut in a cylinder (Fig. 11) and the cylinder cam rotates about its center line.

Still another type is the translation cam (Fig. 12). As the wedge is drawn to the left with a motion of translation, the follower is forced to rise. In this type, translation in one direction may be converted to translation in another direction or to oscillation if the follower is pivoted.

Follower motions of a specified amount and in a specified manner are the first considerations in a cam design. The motion of the follower is usually planned on a displacement diagram, which is merely a schedule of distance moved by the follower corresponding to each angular movement of the cam. If cam rotational speed is constant, each angular interval of the cam can be calibrated as a time interval, and the displacement diagram becomes a diagram of distance versus time. The slope of the displacement curve is then velocity, and the rate of change of slope is acceleration. Such information is useful in considering the type of curve to be used. Motions can be of wide variety. When the displacement curve is a straight line, the velocity of the follower is constant. If the displacement curve is a parabola, acceleration will be constant. Combinations of these two, with a constant acceleration at the beginning and end of motion and a constant velocity in the central portion, result in a very smooth movement. If acceleration of the follower is constant, the force of the cam on the follower to produce that acceleration is constant also.

Other curves may be used, depending on the application of the design. Involutes or simple harmonic (sine) curves are examples. The variety of choice is great. With the displacement diagram determined, the next step is the application of the diagram to a "base circle" to form the required cam profile. The method of application and the final shape of the cam depend upon the type of follower to be used—whether flat-faced, roller, straight line or pivoted.

Positive motion cams do not depend upon gravity or spring force for the return of the follower toward the cam center. In Fig. 13, definite constraint and positive motion are imparted to the follower for both outward and return motion.

Chains. Chains give positive drive between shafts and transmit power over longer distances than might be practical using gears. In some applications, chain drives may be preferred over gear drives when either might be feasible, as in the "silent chain" cam shaft drive of some automotive and diesel engines. Many chain and sprocket forms are available, a few of which are illustrated. In Fig. 14 is pictured a chain type which is used in rough service applications as in mill, mine and factory conveyors and elevators, substantially a slow speed, heavy duty chain.

Higher speed chains are made more accurately and of better materials so that less noise and wear will result. A common form is the "silent chain" (Fig. 15). The silent chains obtain relatively quiet operation because of the sliding action of engagement, the large surface contacts, and automatic adjustment of the chain position relative to the sprocket during operation.

Geneva Wheel. In some instances intermittent angular motion in one direction is required from a steadily rotating driver. The Geneva Wheel (Fig. 16) gives the driven wheel D one quarter turn for each complete revolution of B. It should be noted that the velocity of point A, the center of the driving pin, should be directed along the slot in D as A first engages the slot. Smooth action depends upon this. Then as the pin leaves the slot one quarter turn of D later (at A') it emerges with velocity again along the slot. These considerations serve to fix the pivot for B at point O at the intersection of perpendiculars to the velocity vectors at points A and A'.

Such devices are used in the film drives in motion picture projectors, in indexing equipment used with machine tools, in clocks and watches, and in can-making machinery.

Locomotive Valve Gear. The modern valve gear for locomotives is the Walschaert gear. There are also the Baker, the Young, or the Southern. The Walschaert gear is driven by two members—the

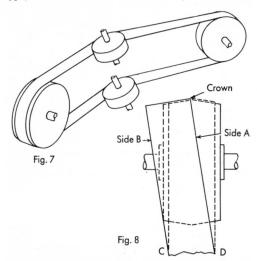

Fig. 7

Fig. 8

Figs. 7 and 8. Idler pulleys in planes of belt travel (left). Crowned pulley rim forces tensed belt toward greatest diameter of the double frustum

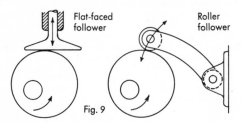

Flat-faced follower   Roller follower

Fig. 9

Fig. 9. The motion given the follower by the cam must follow a designed pattern, which is provided by the profile of the cam and the shape of follower

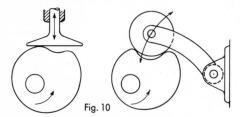

Fig. 10

Fig. 10. Followers shaped as the ones shown cannot operate successfully. The one to the left will pound. The arm to the right will be badly pulled because the cam's force is nearly in line with it

Fig. 11. A cylindrical or barrel cam being milled in a vertical milling machine. Rotation of the cam and the travel of the table are under exact control

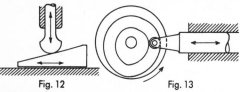

Fig. 12   Fig. 13

Figs. 12 and 13. Reciprocating wedge to the left gives "uniform motion" to its follower. Face cam to the right gives the same motion through rotation. A uniform or constant velocity is necessarily jerky

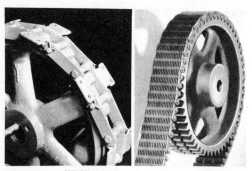

Figs. 14 and 15. Chain links (left) with tabs for attaching conveyor elements such as bearings for shafts holding trays. Silent chain (right) delivers smooth power while carrying heavy loads

Maltese Cross or Geneva movement as used in motion picture projectors for intermittent film travel

Fig. 16

Fig. 16. Intermittent motion is variously obtained. In rotating parts, the machining must be exact

crosshead and a crank pin on the drive wheel. Reversing and control of valve port characteristics are obtained by shifting the lever which controls the position of the slide block in the curved link. This link has a radius equal to the length of the radius rod. A typical gear is shown in the photograph at the head of this article.

The Walschaert type of gear has largely supplanted earlier types such as the Stephenson link gear which was driven by cams on the axle between the driving wheels. The Walschaert gear is mounted entirely outside of the driving wheels, making the parts easily accessible. It also allows greater displacements of the valve, and certain sliding parts of earlier types have been eliminated. The various parts of the Walschaert gear are pin connected.

Quick-Return Mechanisms. In some machine tool work it is desirable that the cutting stroke of the cycle be traversed at a relatively slow speed and the remainder completed rapidly. A common example is in the shaper. A common form of shaper mechanism is diagrammed in Fig. 17. Crank 2 is driven at a uniform angular rate. Link 4 oscillates between the extreme positions shown, the end traveling from R to L during the cutting stroke of the ram while the end of the crank 2 moves from M to N. The return of the ram is accompanied by the return of the end of 4 from L to R and the continued movement of the end of crank 2 from N to M. It is evident that the ratio of cutting time to return time is the ratio of angle α to angle β. There are other ingenious variations.

Radial Engine. The radial engine is probably best known from its use in aircraft. Usually it is air-cooled and is built in single or multiple banks of 3, 5, 7, or 9 cylinders. The crankshafts, of course, must be connected in such a way as to stagger the cylinders and to give approximately equal spacing to firing impulses.

Ratchets. When oscillating motion is to be converted into intermittent angular or linear motion in one direction, ratchets may be used. The downward motion of the handle of the jack (Fig. 18) raises the center slide. When the handle is raised, the lower pawl prevents the slide (and the load on top of it) from dropping downward between lifting strokes. Ratchet and pawl arrangements may be designed that will advance the driven link on both the forward and return motions of the driver, as in Fig. 19.

Several forms of so-called silent ratchets have been devised. Fig. 20 depicts a type very similar to the free wheeling device used in automobiles. Rotation of the driving shaft clockwise wedges the small rollers into the small end of the tapered slot which is cut in the driven member. The friction developed forces the driven member to rotate with the driver shaft. When the driving shaft drops in speed, it turns counterclockwise relative to the driven member and the rollers move back into the larger end of the slots. The rollers then may roll freely, no wedging action takes place, and the driven member coasts or "free wheels."

Scotch Yoke. A link may be made to reciprocate with simple harmonic motion by means of a Scotch Yoke device. In Fig. 21, arm 2 rotates at constant speed, giving point P a constant magnitude of velocity V_p. Only the horizontal component is transferred to 4 at all times, since motion is transferred only along the common normal which is always parallel to X–X. Thus rod 4 reciprocates with a variable velocity which at each instant is the projection on a horizontal diameter of the constant velocity of point P around the crank circle. Such motion is simple harmonic by definition, and can be put in equation form as a sine function. If a curved slot is used instead of a straight one many variations may be obtained.

Straight Line Mechanisms. In an application where output motion on a straight line is desired, many forms of mechanisms are available—some

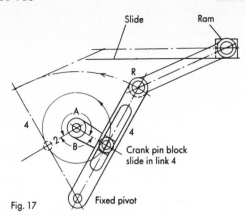

Fig. 17

Fig. 17. The ram of the shaper has a slower power stroke for cutting, through angle A; and a quick-return stroke, angle B. Shaft turns at uniform speed

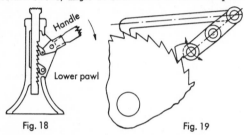

Fig. 18　　　　　　　Fig. 19

Figs. 18 and 19. Lifting jack (left) by moving pawl, gives straight-line motion. Rocker arm with pawls (right) gives continuous rotation to ratchet

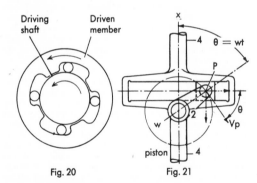

Fig. 20　　　　　　　Fig. 21

Figs. 20 and 21. Snug ring (left) will be turned by shaft and rollers until its speed is greater than that of the shaft. Scotch yoke (right) on crank pin

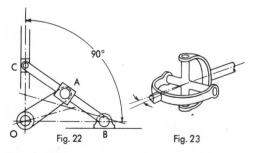

Fig. 22　B　　　　Fig. 23

Figs. 22 and 23. Straight-line motion (left) by oscillating crank and sliding blocks. Elementary Hooke's joint (right) connects out-of-line shafts and is the original of the common universal joint

exact and some only approximate. The Scott-Russell mechanism (Fig. 22) draws an exact straight line at C passing through O and perpendicular to OB as slider B moves in its path. Essential dimensions are that OA=AB=AC. Note that for a typical position, a semicircle with A as center passes through B, C, and O. Therefore, angle BOC is always a right angle, since it is an angle inscribed in a semicircle.

Approximate straight line mechanisms are very common. In general, they give very satisfactory results when used within the range for which they are designed, and they are often simpler than an equivalent exact linkage might be. The Watt linkage was very cleverly devised when Watt needed some sort of guiding linkage for the straight line piston motion in his early steam engines. No method was available for producing smooth plane surfaces such as a crosshead guide might require, so the Watt linkage was used, consisting only of turning joints.

Steam and diesel engine indicators require a device which reproduces a small straight line motion of an indicator piston to a larger scale for recording on a card. The indicator linkage is typical (Fig. 23). The end of the pointer which touches the drum moves on an approximate straight line parallel to the indicator piston movement, and the ratio of magnification for all positions is substantially constant. The errors involved are negligible from a practical standpoint.

Universal Joints. The Hooke's joint is probably the most common form of coupling connecting shafts which intersect but are not colinear. Fig. 24 shows the essential features. The cross in the middle may be replaced by a solid piece of any shape provided the spacing is maintained for points 1, 2, 3, and 4, which are the bearings for the yokes and are points on the circumference of a circle.

If θ is the angle between the intersecting shafts, it can be proved that in 90 degrees of rotation of shaft A at constant angular velocity, shaft B varies in angular velocity between a minimum of ω_a (cos θ) and a maximum of $\dfrac{\omega_a}{\cos \theta}$. Constant velocity ratio is thus not transmitted by a single joint. A second point can be added. The second will exactly compensate for the variation due to the first joint, leaving the angular velocity ratio a constant from the first drive shaft to the final driven shaft. The require-

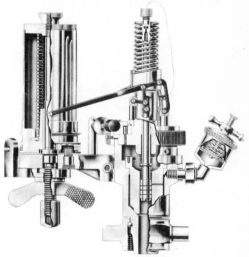

Fig. 24. Indicator for getting indicator cards for reciprocating engines gives straight-line motion to pencil located at the left hand end of arm. Pencil rises and falls with changes of pressure

ments are that the joints be used with the yokes parallel at the ends of the intermediate shaft, that the intermediate shaft make the same angle with the driver shaft as with the driven shaft, and that all shafts lie in the same plane. Many automotive and machine tool drives use this arrangement.

In order to secure a constant velocity ratio with only one coupling, other forms of universal joints have been devised. An example is the Bendix-Weiss type illustrated in Fig. 25 a and b. The Bendix-Weiss

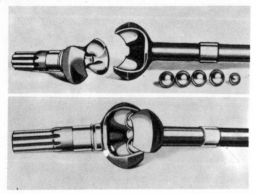

BENDIX AVIATION CORP.

Fig. 25, a and b. Universal joints, used to drive out-of-line shafts, are more compact in automotive and aviation design. (a), joint disassembled. Joint assembling at (b) shows smoothly fitting parts

joint has been extensively used in the front axles of multiple wheel drive vehicles.

Variable Speed Transmissions Without Gears. Certain transmission designs offer an infinite variation in the speed ratios between two shafts through the use of belt, friction, or chain drives. Friction cone drives utilize a system in which a belt may be moved longitudinally along the space between two conical members, transmitting motion from one to the other through friction between the belt and the cones. Assuming the top cone to be the driver, maximum angular velocity of the lower driven member is attained when the belt is shifted to the extreme left. In this position, the belt attains maximum velocity from the driver, since it contacts the driver at its maximum radius. This maximum belt velocity is

LINK-BELT CO.

Fig. 26. Variable speed transmission is shown in this ghost photograph. Sliding laminations in the chain links accommodate themselves to the teeth in the cones as the latter are moved in or out

transferred to the lower cone at its minimum radius, giving a higher angular velocity of the driven member. Similarly, minimum speed of the lower cone will be obtained with the belt shifted to the extreme right. Directions of rotation of the two members are opposite.

A variable speed drive can be made by placing wide-angle cones, on two parallel shafts, vertices inside, riding a wide V belt between the pairs of cones. By mechanically adjusting the distances between the cones on the shafts the diameters ridden by the belt are changed as required by shaft-speed changes. The adjustment, of course, must not stretch or slack off the belt. By putting "teeth" in cone faces, similar to the teeth in bevel gears, a chain drive can be used as shown in Fig. 26.   WILLARD L. ROGERS

BIBLIOG.–I. H. Prageman, *Mechanism* (1943); J. H. Billings, *Applied Kinematier* (1943).

KINESHMA, town, U.S.S.R., the Russian Soviet Federated Socialist Re¹ blic, in Ivanovo Region, situated on the Volga River, about 300 miles NE of Moscow. Kineshma has textile mills, machine-building and wood-working plants, and a dye factory. Pop. (1951 est.) 100,000.

KINETIC ENERGY. The term kinetic energy, as we use it today, means the energy a body possesses by virtue of its speed. It is defined as one-half the product of the mass of the moving body and the square of its speed. According to the Law of Conservation of Energy, this kinetic energy may be converted into other forms. As an illustration, we may consider a swinging pendulum. At the bottom of its swing its speed is a maximum and its kinetic energy is a maximum. At the extreme ends of the swing the speed is zero, but the potential energy, the energy the pendulum bob has¹ y virtue of its position, is a maximum. This potential energy is equal in magnitude to that of the kinetic energy, assuming negligible frictions from bearings and air.

The concept of kinetic energy had its origin in the consideration of collision phenomena in 1668 by the celebrated Dutch physicist, Huygens. At that time it was apparent that in collision phenomena the momenta of the colliding systems were conserved; that is, the total momentum after impact must be the same as before impact.

About 30 years later, considering perfectly elastic impact, Huygens concluded that the sum of the masses multiplied by the square of their speeds must be the same after impact as before. The name kinetic energy was supplied by Lord Kelvin in 1856. The French physicist G. G. Coriolis (1792–1893) later indicated that the concept could be more conveniently applied to one-half the produce of the mass and the square of the speeds. This may be illustrated by considering the case of a falling body. Let the mass of the body be m grams and its position above the earth surface indicated by h centimeters. The work done in elevating to this position is

$$w = m \, g \, h \text{ ergs}$$

where g is the acceleration of gravity and mg is the force in dynes. If the body is allowed to fall unimpeded to the earth, it acquires a speed equal to

$$v = \sqrt{2 \, g \, h} \text{ centimeters per second and obviously a}$$

kinetic energy equal to

$$\tfrac{1}{2} \, m \, v^2 = \tfrac{1}{2} \, m \, (2 \, g \, h) = m \, g \, h \text{ ergs.}$$

Thus the kinetic energy which it requires when it again reaches the earth is equal in ergs to the potential energy or energy of position at the elevation h.

There is also an angular kinetic energy associated with rotating bodies, such as a flywheel or the armature of an electric generator. This is expressed as

$$\text{kinetic energy of rotation} = \tfrac{1}{2} \, I \, W^2$$

where I is the moment of inertia of the rotating body and the analogue of mass, and W is the angular speed in radians per second.   B. J. SPENCE

KINETIC THEORY OF GASES. This theory states that all gases are composed of very tiny particles called MOLECULES. Gases owe their property of filling the containing vessel to the motion of the molecules produced by heat. If the velocity of motion is sufficient to overcome the cohesive forces between them, the molecules will move in straight lines until they come in contact with other molecules or with the wall of the containing vessel. They will then rebound and proceed in a straight course until the next collision occurs. The free motion is modified only by the attractive forces between molecules in contact (cohesion) and by the volume of the molecules, which reduces the free space through which they can move. Molecules actually move only very short distances without encountering other molecules, and so, evidently, can move only very limited distances in a straight line. The average distance is known as the mean free path of the molecule. The countless impulses given to the walls of the vessel by the rebounding molecules add up to make the pressure of the gas. See BROWNIAN MOVEMENT.

Ideal Gas Laws. For a mathematical discussion of the kinetics of gases it is convenient to take for consideration the behavior of an ideal or perfect gas, in which only the weights and energies of the molecules are involved. In an ideal gas the molecules are assumed, for the purposes of calculation, to have mass and velocity but no volume and are perfectly elastic. See IDEAL GAS LAW.

It may be assumed that a one centimeter cube of such an ideal gas contains n molecules each of mass m and mean velocity of u. When a molecule moves in a straight line to the wall of the cube and rebounds, the change of momentum is $2mu$. (Momentum equals mass times velocity.) Since the velocity is u, the molecule traverses u centimeters per second or moves one centimeter from wall to wall u times per second, giving a total change of momentum of $2mu^2$ per second. Since at any instant $\frac{n}{6}$ molecules are traveling toward each of the six sides of the cube, they exert a total change of momentum on one wall of $\frac{n}{6} \times 2mu$ or $\frac{1}{3}nmu^2$. This is identical with the pressure of the gas per square centimeter, and thus p (pressure) $= \frac{1}{3}nmu^2$. The total mass in the unit cube nm represents the density of the gas. The density of the gas may also be considered to be the ratio of the total mass M to its volume v. Therefore $\frac{M}{v}$ may be substituted in the last equation for nm, and the expression now becomes $p = \frac{1}{3}\frac{M}{v}u^2$ or $pv = \frac{1}{3}Mu^2$. Since the kinetic energy, which is constant at any given temperature, is $\frac{1}{2}Mu^2$, the expression $\frac{1}{3}Mu^2$ is likewise constant. Hence pv = a constant. This is

BOYLE's LAW. Also since the kinetic energy $\frac{1}{2}Mu^2$, is proportional to the absolute temperature, T, $\frac{1}{3}Mu^2$ is also proportional, and hence pv = a constant $\times$ T, which is Boyle's and Charles' laws combined. This is written pv = RT where, if the mass of the gas is one gram molecule for a perfect gas, R is equal to 1.985 calories per degree or 83×10^6 c g s units.

Applications. The various forms of the above equation permit the calculation of some interesting facts concerning the behavior of gases. For instance, from the form $p = \frac{1}{3}nmu^2$, if the density (nm) of the gas at a given pressure is known, the mean square speed for the molecules of the gas can be calculated for the temperature to which the data refer. For hydrogen at 0° C. and 760 mm. (or 1,014,000 dynes per square centimeter) pressure, the density is .00008987 g/cm³, and consequently the mean square speed of the molecule is 1,840 meters per second, about five or six times the velocity of sound in air. By theoretical and experimental investigations it has been shown that for hydrogen under standard conditions the mean free path is .000185 mm., and the number of collisions for an individual molecule is about 9,480,000,000 per second.

AVOGADRO's LAW may be derived from the above. For two gases at the same temperature and pressure the kinetic energies of the molecules will be equal since these are dependent on the temperature. If we designate the gases as 1 and 2, we can write $p_1v_1 = \frac{1}{3}n_1m_1u_1^2$ and $p_2v_2 = \frac{1}{3}n_2m_2u_2^2$. Now p_1v_1 and p_2v_2 are the same, and $m_1u_1^2$ and $m_2u_2^2$ are the same, hence n_1 and n_2 must be equal. Therefore all gases under the same conditions of temperature contain the same number of molecules, which is Avogadro's law.

The total pressure of two mixed gases may be expressed as $p_1 + p_2$, which is equal to $\frac{1}{3}n_1m_1u_1^2 + \frac{1}{3}n_2m_2u_2^2$ or $p + \frac{1}{3}mu^2(n_1 + n_2)$. Thus if the number of molecules in a space is increased at constant temperature, the pressure is increased in proportion to the total number, whether the molecules are similar or not. This is Dalton's law of PARTIAL PRESSURES.

Deviations from Ideal Conditions. To account for the discrepancies that occur between the behavior of the ideal gas and of actual gases, allowances must be made for the size of the molecules and for the cohesive forces between them. Since actual molecules have size, they occupy a portion of the space in which they are moving and thus reduce the volume by an amount (b) equal to their volume. If the intermolecular forces are not negligible, they will retard the velocity of molecular motion and thus reduce the pressure on the walls of the containing vessel. This reduction may be formulated as $\frac{a}{v^2}$ where a is a constant. The resulting gas equation will then have the form $(p + \frac{a}{v^2})(v - b) = RT$, which is known as van der Waals' equation. This equation gives opportunity to calculate with considerable accuracy the critical temperature and pressure of a gas. To get the values of a, b, and R for specific gases, it is necessary to make three observations of the pressure, temperature, and volume of each gas.   P. A. BOND

BIBLIOG.—E. H. Kennard, *Kinetic Theory of Gases* (1938); S. Chapman and T. G. Cowling, *Mathematical Theory of Non-Uniform Gases* (1939); M. C. Sneed and J. L. Maynard, *General Inorganic Chemistry* (1942).

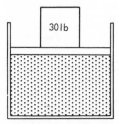
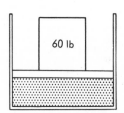

By Doubling the Pressure on a given mass of a gas, the volume is reduced one-half. Same number of molecules is now confined in half as much space

KINETOSCOPE. See MOTION PICTURES.

KING, a title expressing the rulership of a male sovereign. In early times it was usually bestowed upon the chief warrior of a tribe, and conferred despotic power over the lives and property of his subjects. While generally hereditary, it was often based upon and usurped by force of arms. Among civilized nations of the present day, the title of king is a recognized sign of independent sovereignty; though in some cases, such sovereignty is nominal. The modern king's authority is greatly restricted; and under most national constitutions an unworthy king may be deposed by the representative body, and a successor elected. See SOVEREIGNTY; MONARCHY; DIVINE RIGHTS OF KINGS.

KING, CLARENCE, 1842–1901, American geologist, was born in Newport, R.I. He was graduated from the Sheffield Scientific School of Yale (1862), and after crossing the continent (1863), for much of the distance on foot, assisted J. D. Whitney in making a geological survey of California. From 1867 to 1872 he was in charge of what was known as the Geological Survey of the Fortieth Parallel—the survey of a belt of territory, 105 miles wide, comprising an area of 86,390 square miles, between the meridians 104° and 120° W—and from 1879 to 1881 he was the first director of the newly organized United States Geological Survey. After resigning as a director he was a mining engineer until his death. He published *Mountaineering in the Sierras* (1872), *Systematic Geology* (1878), and a valuable paper, "The Age of the Earth," in the *American Journal of Science* (1893). A volume of *Memoirs* was published posthumously (1904).

KING, ERNEST JOSEPH, 1878–   , U.S. naval officer, was born in Lorain, Ohio, and graduated from the U.S. Naval Academy. He served at sea during the Spanish American War, was commissioned an ensign in 1903 and advanced through the grades to rear admiral in 1933. As commander of the submarine base at New London, Conn., he engineered the salvaging of the S-51 and S-4 in 1926. After winning his wings as a naval aviator at the age of 49, he became captain of the aircraft carrier *Lexington* in 1930, chief of the Bureau of Aeronautics (1933–36), and vice admiral commanding the Aircraft Battle Force in 1938. He was promoted to admiral in 1940 and named commander in chief of the Atlantic Fleet. In 1941, he became commander in chief of the U.S. Fleet and chief of naval operations, the first naval officer in history to hold these two assignments simultaneously. As commander in chief of the U.S. Fleet during World War II, he placed emphasis on carriers and full cooperation with army land-based aircraft. Promoted to the rank of fleet admiral when that rank was created in 1944, he retired in 1946.

U.S NAVY

Ernest J. King

KING, RUFUS, 1755–1827, American political leader, was born in Scarboro, Me. He was graduated from Harvard in 1777, studied law under Theophilus Parsons, was admitted to the Massachusetts bar in 1780, and soon attained considerable prominence. In 1784–87 he was a member of the Confederation Congress, where he strove to secure the exclusion of slavery from the Northwest Territory, introducing a bill for that purpose, which was not passed, but which in substance became part of the famous Ordinance of 1787. He was an influential member of the Constitutional Convention of 1787, and in the Massachusetts convention, of which he was a member, did much to bring about the ratification by that body of the Federal Constitution. He moved to New York (1788); was a Federalist member from that state to the U.S. Senate

(1789–96 and 1813–25), in which he was conspicuous as a defender of the Jay Treaty of 1794 and as an opponent of slavery. He was U.S. minister to Great Britain (1796–1803 and 1825–26), and was the Federalist candidate for vice-president in 1804 and 1808, and for president in 1816. A six-volume *Life and Correspondence of Rufus King* (1894–1900) was edited by his grandson, Charles R. King.

KING, THOMAS STARR, 1824–64, American clergyman, lecturer, and author, was born in New York and was well known as a lecturer from 1845 to 1860. His activity in the presidential campaign of the latter year had an important part in keeping California in the union. He is best known as an author by *White Hills, their Legends, Landscape, and Poetry* (1859).

KING, WILLIAM LYON MACKENZIE, 1874–1950, Canadian liberal statesman, was born in Berlin (now Kitchener), Ontario, and studied at the universities of Toronto and Harvard. After editing the *Labor Gazette* (1900–1908), King entered Parliament and was first minister of labor (1909–11). From 1914 to 1917 he investigated industrial relations for the Rockefeller Foundation and in 1919 became leader of the Liberal party. He was prime minister, president of the Privy Council, and secretary of state for foreign affairs (1921–30, except for a few months). King was appointed a member of the Council and vice-president of the League of Nations Assembly at Geneva

FROM "FACES OF DESTINY," BY
YOUSUF KARSH (ZIFF-DAVIS)

Mackenzie King

in 1928 and 1936. He again headed the government in 1935 and in 1940 was confirmed in his leadership of Canadian participation in World War II. A conference between King and President Roosevelt resulted in Canada and the United States forming a joint defense board in 1940. Though his plan in 1944 to send home service troops abroad created a vigorous protest in the province of Quebec, the House supported him. In 1945 he was again continued in office, was chairman of the Canadian delegation to the U.N. Conference at San Francisco, and participated in the Atomic Energy Conference at Washington. To King belongs the honor of having the longest career in public life of any Canadian. He retired in 1948. See CANADA, History.   H. W.

KING, WILLIAM RUFUS DEVANE, 1786–1853, vice-president of the United States, was born in Sampson County, N.C., studied at the University of North Carolina, and was admitted to the bar (1806). After serving as congressman (1811–16), he was secretary to the legation in Naples (1816–18). Returning, he established his home in Dallas County, Ala., and became one of the first U.S. senators from that state (1818–44), being president *pro tempore* (1836–41). After service as minister to France (1844–46), he returned to the Senate (1848–52). Elected vive-president under President Pierce (1852), he died in office.

KING COBRA. See COBRA.

KING COLLEGE. See COLLEGES.

KING CRAB, or HORSESHOE CRAB, a hardshelled arachnid found in the shallow waters of the Atlantic from Nova Scotia to Florida. Although superficially it resembles a crab, the king crab is actually closely related to the spiders and scorpions. It is a large, dark brown, shelled animal, often measuring as much as two feet in length. King crabs burrow in the sand and feed upon worms and other small animals. They comprise a single genus, *Limulus*, of which

ALLAN D. CRUICKSHANK-NAS

King crabs

there are five species. *L. polyphemus* is the common king crab of North America. See ARACHNIDA.

KING GEORGE V LAND. See ANTARCTICA.

KING GEORGE'S WAR, a war in America (1744–48) between England and her American colonies on one side and France and her American colonies on the other; in reality a part of the War of the Austrian Succession. On the part of the English, the New England colonists fought almost alone, though several of the other colonies furnished money contributions. The most important event of the war was the capture of Louisburg (1745) by New England and chiefly Massachusetts troops, under Sir William Pepperell, seconded by a British fleet. The place was, however, restored to France by the treaty of Aix-la-Chapelle (1748). The war was marked by the usual border fighting in which Indians took part, and was the next to the last of the series of wars fought by the English and the French for the possession of America. See AUSTRIA, History; LOUISBURG.

BIBLIOG.–R. G. Thwaites, *France in America, 1497–1763* (1905); H. L. Osgood, *The American Colonies in the Eighteenth Century* (1924).

KING-HSIEN, formerly **Ningpo,** "Calm Waters," river treaty port, China, in Chekiang Province. A station on the railroad from Hangchow to the west, it lies on one of the mouths of the Yangtze 12 miles south of its seaport, Chinhai. The city is five miles around and is circled by a wall pierced by six gates. The streets are wide and lined with noteworthy buildings which include among others one of the largest libraries in China. Local products are confectionery and gold, silver, and lacquer work. Its ivory carving has made it "the City of Mah-jong." Trade is largely limited to traffic from Shanghai. The Portuguese held King-hsien in 1522–1545, the British in 1841–42, and the Japanese for most of the 1937–45 hostilities. Pop. about 218,000.   ADRIAN TROY

KING ISLAND, 140 miles S of Melbourne, Australia, in Bass Strait, 50 miles from the NW point of the island of Tasmania; area 400 sq. mi. King Island has a rich deposit of tin. A British vessel touched here in 1802. The island belongs to Australia and is administratively a part of the state of Tasmania.

KING KARL'S LAND, or **King Charles Land,** a group of three islands (Swedish Foreland; King Charles Island; Abel Island) lying in the east central portion of the Spitsbergen Archipelago, separated from the main islands by the Olga Strait; total area 128 sq. mi.

KING PHILIP'S WAR, an Indian war (1675–76) in New England, the most destructive in which the English colonists were involved in the 17th century. During the early decades of English settlement in New England the Indians had been generally friendly, the most notable trouble being the PEQUOT WAR, in which the Pequot tribe was almost entirely destroyed in 1637. Massasoit, chief of the WAMPANOAG tribe, had been friendly to the whites, and had given them food and assistance. Massasoit died in 1661 and was succeeded by Wamsutta. The latter also died

King William's War

in 1662 and was succeeded by his brother Metacom (English name Philip). Philip had been known as friendly to the English, but he seems to have seen clearly that the settlement of the country must result in the destruction of his own people, and as time went on he fell under the suspicion of the English.

The actual outbreak of what is known as King Philip's War was probably accidental (1674), arising from the murder of Sausamon, a converted Indian, and the consequent English executions and Indian reprisals. Philip and his people were at once driven from their ancestral properties, and he himself fled to the Indians of the interior. The Nipmucks, a powerful tribe of central Massachusetts, now began a series of devastating attacks upon the frontier settlements, in which 12 of the English towns were entirely destroyed and more than half were made the scene of burning and massacre. Philip himself appeared at the burning of Brookfield (1675), of Lancaster (1676), and of Bridgewater (1676). The greatest disaster was on Sept. 18, 1675, when Captain Lathrop's company, the "flower of Essex," was almost entirely destroyed at Bloody Brook, near Deerfield, which had been burned a fortnight before. "New England had never seen so black a day," writes Cotton Mather in the *Magnalia*.

The superior power of the English, however, gradually overcame resistance. The Narragansetts, who were planning to join the war, were put down by a strong expedition under Colonel Winslow in the winter of 1675. The Indians were attacked in their stronghold in the frozen swamps of Kingston, R.I., and their power entirely broken. The Nipmucks also were several times beaten, and Philip fled to his old abode at Mount Hope, R.I., where he was hunted down and killed (Aug. 12, 1676) by a party under Capt. Benjamin Church. It does not appear that he really planned and aroused a great conspiracy, but when hostilities began he was a powerful influence in exciting the Indians to rise against the English.

BIBLIOG.–John Fiske, *The Beginnings of New England* (1889); George W. Ellis and John E. Morris, *King Philip's War* (1906); James Truslow Adams, *The Founding of New England* (1921 and 1926).

KING SALMON, CHINOOK, or **SPRING SALMON.** See SALMON.

KING SNAKE, or **CHAIN SNAKE,** a terrestrial snake found in the United States from New Jersey to Florida and westward to the Mississippi Valley. This nonpoisonous reptile is black with cross stripes of white or yellow, the stripes joining along each side to form a chain. Large specimens usually measure not more than six feet in length and two inches in diameter. King snakes make good pets, for they are docile toward man and thrive in captivity. They are, however, extremely antagonistic toward all other species of snakes, attacking even the most formidable of their relatives. Curiously enough, they appear to be immune from the venoms of such poisonous snakes as the rattlesnake, copperhead, and moccasin. Experiments with cobra venom, however, have proved fatal to the king snake. In addition to its diet of snakes and lizards, the king snake feeds upon small rodents and birds. Common representatives are Say's king snake, *Lampropeltis getulus sayi*, of the Mississippi Valley, and Boyle's king snake, *L.g. boylii*, of southwestern United States.

KING WILLIAM'S WAR, a war (1689–97) in America between the English and the French and their Indian allies; in reality a part of the War of the League of Augsburg. On the French side the war was vigorously conducted by Count Frontenac, governor of Canada, who in the winter of 1690 sent three expeditions against the New York, New Hampshire, and Maine frontiers; an English fleet under Sir William Phipps sailed up the St. Lawrence in order to capture Quebec, whose fortifications, however, proved too strong for the assailants (1690); and there were the usual bloody border conflicts, in which both sides were assisted by the Indians. The war was terminated by the treaty of Ryswick. Both the French and the British colonies were left almost entirely to their own resources in this war; while the course of the fighting was quite favorable to the French, no decisive results were attained. In 1702 the fighting was resumed, the new struggle being called QUEEN ANNE'S WAR.

KINGBIRD, one of the larger of the tyrant FLY-CATCHERS, *Tyrannus tyrannus,* very numerous and familiar throughout most of North America. It is grayish slate color above, white below and grayish on the breast; has a black tail tipped with white and a concealed orange-red crest. It is strong and swift in flight, catching its insect prey on the wing.

KINGFISHER, a common name given to about 200 species of birds of the family *Alcedinidae.* The family has a world-wide distribution and is thought to have originated in the Malayan area. An Australian kingfisher is called LAUGH-ING JACKASS. Many of the species in Europe and Asia are forest birds that nest in hollow trees and feed upon insects, smaller birds, and lizards. There are only two genera in the western hemisphere and members of both are true "fishers." The birds may be found near fresh water. The nests are tunnels burrowed into banks of lakes, ponds, and streams.

CHICAGO NAT. HIST. MUS.
Eastern belted kingfisher

These birds are solitary fishers and fight any other kingfishers that trespass upon their established territory. They perch in an upright position on a limb that overlooks the fishing area. Observers report that the birds can dive from a height of 40 feet or more without injuring themselves. Contrary to popular belief the kingfishers do not appreciably destroy game fish. They feed primarily upon aquatic insects, crustaceans, frogs, chubs, and minnows. The prey may be speared on the bill but usually it is taken between the mandibles. The bird may eat the catch on its perch or, in the nesting season, carry the food to the young. If a fish is caught it is battered to death and then swallowed head first. Indigestible parts, such as bones, scales, and teeth, are regurgitated.

The two most common North American species are: the eastern belted kingfisher, *Megaceryle alcyon alcyon,* ranging over most of North and South America; and the western belted kingfisher, *Megaceryle alcyon caurina,* of northwestern North America, south to California.

The eastern belted kingfisher is about 14 inches long. The bill and head are large, the feet relatively small, and the tail short. The upper parts are gray-blue and the under parts, white. The tail and wings are tipped with white feathers and there is a broad blue-gray band across the chest (the belt). In addition to the bluish belt the female has a reddish-brown stripe on the lower part of the breast. The nest burrows may be from 4 to 15 feet in length. The eggs are laid in an enlarged part of the tunnel. The western belted kingfisher differs from the eastern form only in being larger, especially the wings.   A. P.

KINGLAKE, ALEXANDER WILLIAM, 1809-91, English historian, born in Taunton. About 1835 he made an extended tour in the East, which he described in *Eothen* (1844), which became well known. He also wrote a history of the Crimean War.

KINGLET, a small greenish-gray or olive-green bird with a golden or orange-colored crown patch. Kinglets belong to the family *Sylviidae,* which is represented in North America by kinglets and the blue-gray gnatcatcher.

The golden-crowned kinglet, *Regulus satrapa satrapa,* is probably the best known of the group. The diminu-

tive bird is about four inches in length, just a little larger than the HUMMINGBIRD. In winter the kinglet may be seen on lawns, particularly among small evergreens and cedars, often coming close to the house. Old orchards are also frequented by the birds. They feed upon insects, insect eggs, and larvae. The male has a bright orange crown patch that is usually concealed by overlying head feathers. The spot is evident if the bird is seen from above or if it raises its head feathers in alarm or anger. The female has a bright lemon-yellow crown patch. Kinglets are very active birds and as they move about on branches and twigs they constantly flit their wings.

Golden-crowned kinglet

The ruby-crowned kinglet, *Corthylio calendula calendula,* another North American species, is similar to the golden-crowned except that the male has a bright red crown patch which the female lacks. The golden-crowned's song is soft and lisping. The song of the ruby-crowned bird commences with several thin, high, notes that are followed by a warbled, varied melody, uttered with astonishing vigor for such a small bird. Kinglets range southward from Canada through the Allegheny and Rocky mountains into South Carolina on the east coast and into Central America on the west.   L. A. HAUSMAN

BIBLIOG.–F. H. Knowlton, *Birds of the World* (1909); E. H. Forbush and J. B. May, *Natural History of the Birds of Eastern and Central North America* (1943); L. A. Hausman, *The Illustrated Encyclopedia of American Birds* (1944).

KINGMAN REEF, northernmost of the LINE ISLANDS, about 900 miles S of Honolulu, in the central Pacific. It was annexed by the United States in 1922. The triangular reef encloses a lagoon that has been utilized as a landing spot for transpacific planes and, during World War II, for American naval planes.

KINGS, two books of the BIBLE, were originally one book. In the Hebrew canon they are numbered among the so-called Former Prophets; in the Septuagint they appear respectively as III and IV Kings. They narrate the history of Israel from the death of DAVID till the dissolution of the southern kingdom (Judah) in 586 B.C., and thus cover a period of some 400 years. The compiler has used various historical documents, and expressly names the "Acts of Solomon," the "Annals of the Kings of Israel," and the "Annals of the Kings of Judah" as sources utilized by him. See OLD TESTAMENT.

KINGS BAY, a horseshoe-shaped inlet about 15 miles long and 3 to 8 miles wide on the NW coast of West Spitsbergen Island, at the foot of the Kingsbrae glacier. It was the point of departure of AMUNDSEN (1925) and BYRD (1926) on their flights to the North Pole, about 750 miles away.

KING'S BENCH, an English court of great antiquity and importance, which existed from the 12th century to the reform of the English judicial system in 1873-75—a period of 700 years. It originated in a gradual differentiation of the functions of the great royal court of the Norman period—the *Curia Regis*—and exercised a general jurisdiction both original and appellate. As a court of first instance it was usually presided over by a single judge, but appeals were heard by the full bench of the court under the name of King's Bench Division, a title retained in the High Court of Judicature. See JUDICATURE ACTS.

KINGS CANYON NATIONAL PARK, E central California, a mountain wilderness cut by two great canyons of the Kings River and dominated by the snow-laden peaks of the high Sierras. The thickly forested mountains are adorned with gemlike lakes and latticed with sparkling streams with here and

Windy Cliff in Kings Canyon National Park

there a green meadow. Within the park limits is the General Grant Grove of giant redwoods. The park offers excellent fishing, scenic trails, and well-equipped campgrounds. Included in the 452,984-acre area is the former General Grant National Park, established in 1890, which became a part of Kings Canyon National Park in 1940.

BIBLIOG.–J. and J. Muench, *Along Sierra Trails: Kings Canyon National Park* (1947).

KING'S COUNTY. See OFFALY.

KING'S LYNN, or **Lynn Regis,** municipal borough and seaport, E central England, Norfolk; 42 miles NW of Norwich and 100 miles N of London. King's Lynn was originally a Saxon town, built at the mouth of the Great Ouse River where it flows into The Wash and the North Sea. On the opposite side is West Lynn, a manufacturing suburb. Interesting buildings are an ancient market, a guildhall, a Perpendicular parish church, and the Decorated cruciform-shaped All Saints cathedral. Sandringham House, one of the country residential estates of the English royal family, is in the vicinity. Parts of old city walls, built in the 15th century, are still standing. Industries of King's Lynn are railway coach, automobile, and farm implements factories, iron and brass foundries; oil cake, grist, and flour mills; shipbuilding yards; a chemical plant; breweries; fisheries; and manufactures of rope, sailcloth, and jam. It has a fine harbor, covering about 100 acres, and modern docks and warehouses. Pop. (1946) 24,875.

KING'S MOUNTAIN, town, S central North Carolina, in Cleveland County; on the Southern Railroad and U.S. highways 29 and 74, at the base of King's Mountain for which it was named, about 28 miles W of Charlotte near the South Carolina border. The city is a textile center and also has a sawmill and cottonseed oil mill. Pop. (1950) 7,206.

KING'S MOUNTAIN, BATTLE OF, an engagement of the American Revolution fought Oct. 7, 1780, in what is now York County, S.C., about a mile and a half south of the North Carolina boundary between the American militia under Col. ISAAC SHELBY, Col. William Campbell, and Col. JOHN SEVIER, and a band of American Loyalists led by Major Patrick Ferguson. Lord Cornwallis, after the British victories at Camden and Fishing Creek, sent Ferguson with a detachment of about 1,000 men into western North Carolina. The mountain men of the western Carolinas

Kingsley

and Virginia (including settlers in the present states of Tennessee and Kentucky) hastily organized a militia army of about 2,000 men to meet the danger. Overtaken by the pursuing Americans, Ferguson took up a defensive position atop King's Mountain, where he was surrounded and attacked. The assault up the hill by the mountain men was aided by the cover of trees and shrubs, while the Loyalist bayonet attacks were thereby impeded. Many of the Loyalists were killed, including their commander. Capt. Abraham DePeyster surrendered after succeeding to the command. The British loss was 389 killed and wounded and 716 prisoners; the Americans lost but 28 killed and 90 wounded. This battle ended, for the time being, Cornwallis' subjugation of North Carolina. The battleground has been preserved as King's Mountain National Military Park (1931; area 4,012 acres). See REVOLUTION, AMERICAN.   F. M.

KINGS RIVER, central California, rises on the western slope of the Sierra Nevada and empties into the great Central Valley. The river takes a semi-circular course across the valley, flowing through the heart of the Fresno raisin district. Its canyon has a depth of 8,000 feet at one point, making it the deepest stream-cut gorge in North America. Where the river leaves the mountains it has deposited a vast alluvial fan that prevents drainage to the south from joining the San Joaquin River. During floods excess water drains into ephemeral Tulare Lake, where it is impounded for future irrigation. The Kings River Reclamation Project, authorized in 1940 as part of the comprehensive plan for the Central Valley, supplements the Friant-Kern Canal, and provides for irrigation, flood control, and 125,000 kilowatts of electricity. See RECLAMATION.

KINGSBURY, FORREST ALVA, 1883–   , American psychologist, was born in Oelwein, Iowa, and studied at Central College, Yale University, and the University of Chicago. He taught philosophy and education at Grand Island College (1911–15) and at Ottawa University (1915–18). In 1920 he began teaching at the University of Chicago, becoming dean of the College of Literature and Science (1924–27) and acting chairman of the Department of Psychology in 1939. He is known for his contributions in the field of psychological tests, job analysis, personnel rating scales, business psychology, and history of psychology. He wrote *Group Intelligence Scale for Primary Grades* (1924).

KINGSFORD, village, S Upper Michigan, in Dickinson County, on the Menominee River about two miles S of Iron Mountain of which it is an industrial suburb. The village, incorporated in 1923, developed about an automobile plant and its allied industries which include a sawmill, drying kilns, a chemical plant, and woodworking factories. The river furnishes hydroelectric power for industries. Dairy, fruit, and truck farms are in the surrounding region. Pop. (1950) 5,038.

KINGSLEY, CHARLES, 1819–75, English novelist and reforming clergyman, was born in Holne Vicarage, in Devonshire. Kingsley was a man of great enthusiasm, very earnest, highly excitable, and incapable of doubting the righteousness of his own views. He and F. D. Maurice were among the few members of their church who faced squarely the implications of the Chartist agitation in the 1840's and tried to devise a Christian answer to the problem in what they called Christian Socialism. Kingsley's intense energy carried him into a multitude of activities, from the co-operative movement and sanitary reform to the professorship of modern history at Cam-

Charles Kingsley

bridge. He was also an ardent upholder of what he conceived to be the Protestant view of life and a special enemy of celibacy. He described wedlock as "spiritual" and "paradisiac." He could be equally extravagant in his condemnation of "Papists" and even went so far as to accuse Newman of fostering a disregard for truth. The end of this calumny was Newman's *Apologia pro Vita Sua.*

Kingsley wrote a number of well-known poems, such as "The Sands of Dee," and several fine children's stories, of which the most famous is *The Water Babies* (1863). He also wrote historical romances, such as *Hypatia* (1853) and *Westward Ho!* (1855) and unremittingly Victorian novels of purpose, such as *Alton Locke* (1850) and *Two Years Ago* (1857). Kingsley was by no means an original thinker, nor was he always a wise or even fair controversialist, but he had great energy, which he used to further much-needed reforms, and he had a certain gift for historical romance.   ARTHUR MIZENER

KINGSLEY, HENRY, 1830–76, younger brother of CHARLES KINGSLEY. Colonial life is depicted in his fresh and vigorous *Geoffrey Hamlyn* (1859). His best novel is *Ravenshoe* (1862). His other novels include *Austin Elliot* (1863), *The Hillyars and the Burtons* (1865), *Silcote of Silcotes* (1867), and *Grange Garden* (1876).

KINGSLEY, MARY HENRIETTA, 1862–1900, English traveler and author, niece of Charles and Henry Kingsley, was born in London. She wrote the racy *Travels in West Africa* (1897), *West African Studies* (1899), and *The Story of West Africa* (in the Empire Series, 1900). She died at Simon's Town, South Africa, and was buried at sea.

KINGSLEY, SIDNEY, 1906– , American playwright, was born in New York City. After graduating from Cornell University, where he was active in student dramatics, he joined a stock company in the Bronx, played bit parts on Broadway, and worked for Columbia Pictures as a reader and scenarist. His works include *Men in White* (1933, Pulitzer prize), a play about hospital life; *Dead End* (1936), a melodramatic presentation of social contrast on the East Side of New York; and *The World We Make* (1939), dealing with the rehabilitation of a psychoneurotic girl; and *Darkness at Noon* (1951), an adaption of the Arthur Koestler novel, which won the Drama Critics Award for 1950–51.

KINGSMILL ISLANDS. See GILBERT ISLANDS.

KINGSPORT, city, NE Tennessee, in Sullivan County, on the Holston River, the Clinchfield Railroad, U.S. highways 11 and 23, and the American Air Lines; about 100 miles NE of Knoxville. Kingsport is an industrial center located in the heart of the Appalachian Mountains in a region rich in natural resources. The city was planned and laid out in 1916. Cotton textiles, camera film, cellulose acetate yarn, foundry and machine products, shale, cement, pulp and paper, and books are the major manufactures. Pop. (1950) 19,571.

KINGSTON, city, Canada, in the province of Ontario, county seat of Frontenac County, at the NE extremity of Lake Ontario and the S terminus of the Rideau Canal, and the mouth of the Cataraqui River, on the Canadian Pacific and Canadian National railways, about 160 miles NE of Toronto. Once strongly fortified, Kingston was the site of Fort Frontenac, built in 1673, demolished during KING WILLIAM'S WAR, and rebuilt by Frontenac in 1695. During the remainder of the French occupation, the fort guarded the St. Lawrence route from Indian attacks. In 1758 the British under General Bradstreet captured and destroyed the fort. In 1784 the present city of Kingston was built on the site. From 1841 to 1844 it was the capital of Canada. Old landmarks of Kingston are the government building and Fort Henry, which was built during the War of 1812. The city is an important educational center and the seat of Queen's University (1841) and Royal Military College (1875). Kingston has dye and chemical works, a large dry dock, and extensive interests in shipbuilding. Flour, nylon yarn, cotton textiles, woolens, leather, aluminum, and steam engines are the chief manufactures. Pop. (1949 est.) 32,742.

KINGSTON, capital and chief port of Jamaica and the largest city of the British West Indies, is situated on a landlocked harbor on the S side of the island. As the chief commercial and social center of Jamaica, Kingston has a thriving foreign trade and draws many cosmopolitan visitors who are attracted by its delightful climate and lush tropical beauty. Kingston's harbor admits the largest ocean vessels and handles much of the trade of the island. The city is served by three air lines: the Pan American, the Royal Dutch, and the British West Indian Airways. A curving road leads eight miles southwest to the naval station at Port Royal, the headquarters for the British naval forces. During World War II, the United States used this area as one of the most important outposts of defense in the Caribbean.

Old Port Royal was once the most flourishing English city in the New World and was the headquarters for buccaneers and pirates until it was ruined by an earthquake in 1692. When Port Royal was swept by fire in 1703, Kingston became the business center and was made capital of the island in 1872. In 1907 Kingston suffered a devastating earthquake which killed 1,500 Negroes and destroyed much of the business section of the city. Since that time the city has been largely rebuilt along modern lines. Features of special interest are the Institute of Jamaica with its notable library and museum, the quaint public market, several ancient churches, and the lovely Hope Botanic Gardens, noted for the fine

K.L.M. ROYAL DUTCH AIRLINES
Hope Botanic Gardens in Kingston, Jamaica

collection of orchids and other flowering plants gathered from all over the world. Pop. (1943) 109,056.   F. C. W.

KINGSTON, city, SE New York, county seat of Ulster County, on the W bank of the Hudson River at the mouth of Rondout Creek, on the New York Central and the New York, Ontario, and Western railroads and U.S. highways 9 and 209; about 15 miles NW of Poughkeepsie and 90 miles N of New York City. Kingston is picturesquely situated amid mountains. Several miles west of the city are the first ranges of the Catskill Mountains where is located the Ashokan Reservoir, source of water supply for New York City. In 1609 Henry Hudson established a trading post here and in 1614, the Dutch put up a small fort. The first settlement was made by the Dutch in 1652, but it was abandoned because of the Indians. In 1664 Kingston became the possession of the British, who named it for Kingston Lisle, family seat of Gov. Francis Lovelace, first governor of the territory. Kingston was burned by the British in 1777 during the Revolutionary War. The Senate House, built in 1676, one of the oldest public buildings in the

United States, was the scene of the first meeting of the state senate. It is now a museum which houses interesting collections of Colonial, Revolutionary, and Civil War relics. Kingston is both a summer resort and industrial community. Bricks, road-building machinery, shirts, knit goods, hotel equipment, and iron castings are some of the products of the city. Pop. (1950) 28,817.   A. M. K.

KINGSTON, borough, NE Pennsylvania, in Luzerne County, on the N branch of the Susquehanna River, opposite Wilkes-Barre, on the Delaware, Lackawanna, and Western and the Lehigh Valley railroads and U.S. Highway 1. Kingston was founded in 1769 by 40 settlers from Connecticut. It was known at first as the "Forty Township." The Indian Massacre of 1778 occurred near Kingston in the Wyoming Valley. Anthracite coal mining is the principal industry of the borough. There are railroad shops, silk and knitting mills, and clothing plants. Pop. (1950) 21,096.

KINGSTON-ON-THAMES, municipal and parliamentary borough, SE England, Surrey County, a residential suburb of London, 12 miles SW of Charing Cross. It includes Norbiton and part of Kingston Hill and is connected by bridge with Hampton Wick. The old Royal Chapel of St. Mary, in which several Saxon kings were crowned, was destroyed in 1730, but the coronation stone is preserved opposite the court house. The queen's promenade and Canbury Gardens extend along the river. Industries include oil cake and flour mills, iron foundries, aircraft factories, and the manufacture of machines, farm machinery, and paper. Pop. (1950 est.) 42,140.

KINGSTON-UPON-HULL. See HULL.

KINGSTOWN, or **Dun Laoghaire,** residential suburb and seaport, E central Eire, county Dublin, located at the SE end of Dublin Bay, five miles SE of Dublin. It has a splendid harbor with about 259 acres of docks and is a yachting rendezvous and favorite boating resort. It has fisheries and a large cattle market. Prior to being renamed "Kingstown" after a visit from George IV in 1821, it was called Dunleary (Dun Laoghaire). It is a mail steamer station connected with Holyhead, Wales.

KINGSTOWN, seaport, West Indies, capital of St. Vincent, one of the Windward Islands, beautifully situated at the head of a picturesque bay on the SW coast. The city has steamer and ferry service and is on the British West Indian Airways. Features of interest are the government offices, the library, the cathedral of St. George, and the Botanic Gardens. Arrowroot, rum, sugar, and spices are the chief exports. Pop. (1946) 4.811.

KINGSVILLE, city, S Texas, Kleberg County; on the Missouri Pacific Railroad and U.S. Highway 77, about 40 miles SW of Corpus Christi and 20 miles from the Gulf of Mexico. Kingsville is the headquarters for the famous King Ranch, one of the largest cattle ranches in the world which, at its peak, embraced 1,270,000 acres. The first unit of this vast property was acquired in 1854 by Richard King, a onetime Rio Grande steamboat captain. Workers on the ranch include many descendants of the original families which Captain King brought from Mexico. Thousands of calves are branded at two great round-ups which take place in February and August. The ranch area has vast grass fields, date and palm groves, and truck gardens. Kingsville is a market center for farm products, and has railroad shops, cotton gins and cottonseed oil mills. It is the seat of Texas College of Arts and Industries, founded in 1925. Pop. (1950) 16,898.

KINGTEHCHEN. See FOWLIANG.

KINKAID, THOMAS CASSIN, 1888–   , U.S. naval officer, was born in Hanover, N.H., and graduated from the United States Naval Academy. In World War I, he was assigned to duty with the British Admiralty (1917–18). Named a rear admiral in 1942, he commanded the North Pacific naval forces and directed the campaign which drove the Japanese out of the Aleutians and Alaska in 1943, the same year he was named vice-admiral. As commander of the Naval Forces of the Southwest Pacific (1943–45), he directed the Battle of Surigao Strait (October 1944) which completely defeated the Japanese navy's southern division. Made an admiral (1945), he commanded the Eastern Sea Frontier, Gulf Sea Frontier, and 16th Fleet from 1946 until his retirement in 1950.

KINKAJOU, a Central and South American mammal, *Potos flavis,* of the family *Procyonidae.* The

CHICAGO NAT. HIST. MUS.
Kinkajou

kinkajou, although related to the raccoons, is, however, more like a domestic cat in size and form. The face and ears are short, the eyes very bright, and the head well-rounded. Its tail is prehensile, and the feet have short, sharp claws; both are used for grasping when the animal climbs. The body is covered with woolly, yellowish-brown hair. The kinkajou is an excellent climber and is most active during the night. It feeds upon fruits, birds, and small mammals, and sometimes becomes a pest near cultivated orange and banana groves, on which it thrives. The animal may be tamed readily when captured young, and often becomes a good pet. In certain localities it is known as Jupura, El Cuchumbi, or Tubamono.   W. A. HILTON

KINO, EUSEBIO FRANCISCO, c. 1645–1711, Jesuit missionary explorer, was born in Segno, Italy, and entered the Jesuit order in 1665. He went to Mexico City in 1681, and in the same year published his observations on the 1680 comet. He went with the Atondo expedition to Lower California in 1682, to head the Jesuit mission, but drought forced the abandonment of the settlement in 1685. In 1687 he traveled to Pimería Alta (now northern Sonora and southern Arizona), where he made his home for the rest of his life. In more than 50 expeditions from the Mission Dolores in Sonora, he and his comrades crossed the Devil's Highway and explored the country between the Magdalena and Gila rivers; and explored (1701–2) the Colorado from the Gila's mouth to the Gulf of California, proving that Lower California was a peninsula. Kino's map of Pimería Alta (1705) was authoritative for many years.

KINROSS, inland shire or county, W central Scotland, bounded on the E and S by Fife, W by Clackmannan, N by Perth; area 82 sq. mi.; pop. (1950 est.) 7,600. Kinross is the second smallest in area and the smallest in population of the Scottish shires. The shire has a fertile central plain containing Loch Leven, which is surrounded by the Ochills and the East Lomonds. The Leven, the chief river, flows from LOCH LEVEN into Fifeshire. Kinross is about 70 per cent cultivated, and cattle are raised in the low ranges of hills. Minerals found are coal, basalt, and fire clay; limestone is quarried. Woolen goods, tartan shawls, damask, and linen goods are manufactured. The chief town and county seat is Kinross, situated at the west end of Loch Leven.

KINSEY, ALFRED CHARLES, 1894–   , American biologist, was born in Hoboken, N.J., and educated at Bowdoin and Harvard universities. In 1920 he joined the staff at Indiana University, becoming a professor in 1929. He led biological explorations to Mexico and Central America in 1931–32 and 1935–36. From 1938 he headed a Rockefeller Foundation project to study human sex behavior and published the first part of his findings as *Sexual Behavior in the Human Male* (1947).   M.R.

KINSHA KIANG. See YANGTZE KIANG.

KINSHIP is a term which refers to people related by blood, or in some societies by marriage. To Europeans this generally means that descent is reckoned through both the father's and mother's line and hence includes all relations so far as they can be traced. The mother's and the father's brothers are all called "uncles"; their sisters are "aunts," and their offspring are "cousins." These biological relationships are recognized and usually carry with them socially determined prohibitions or duties which become weaker with the lessening of the actual degree of blood relationship.

Such a situation does not hold for all societies. Among some peoples, as in Melanesia, fathers' and mothers' brothers may be sharply differentiated and hence be addressed by different terms. The same applies to their sisters and their offspring so that in place of our "uncle," "aunt," and "cousin" eight names may be in use. Still more important is the fact that individuals in some classifications have reciprocal rights and privileges, and also are subject to certain restrictions. Actual brother and sister may be completely separated from each other; marriage with cousins on the mother's side may be prohibited while persons in the father's line may be preferred mates.

In some areas individuals claiming descent from a common ancestor may form a CLAN and hence be considered related. This relationship may, however, be restricted to one line. Among the Menangkabau of Sumatra, children belong to the mother's clan and family, never to the father's. The biological relationship is understood, but children inherit through the mother and belong to her unit. Since marriage is prohibited within the clan the children cannot seek a mate with anyone in the mother's line, yet marriage with a member of the father's clan is proper. Such a system affects residence. Here the husbands are visitors in the homes of their wives, but the children belong to and live in the maternal family home. From this it appears that in this society the mother's kin group becomes an enlarged matrilineal family.

Among some peoples a woman when married becomes a part of the husband's group. The reverse is true among the Ifugao of northern Luzon, where allegiance to one's "blood group" is so strong that in case of disputes the wife will side with her people even if this results in the breakup of her immediate family.

In many lands kinship groups are held responsible for the acts of their members. This may result in feuds, such as those of the Irish or Kentucky clans.

Usually a person is born into such a social unit, but adoption or the exchange of blood may cement a relationship as strong as that of actual descent.

All this implies that the European idea of family is not universal, and that many peoples attach social obligations to those in varying degrees of kinship.

FAY-COOPER COLE

BIBLIOG.–W. H. R. Rivers, *Social Organization* (1926); E. M. Loeb, *Sumatra* (1935); F.-C. Cole, *Peoples of Malaysia* (1945).

KINSTON, city, SE North Carolina, county seat of Lenoir County, on the N bank of the Neuse River, on the Atlantic Coast Line and the Atlantic and East Carolina railroads and U.S. highways 70 and 258; about 75 miles SE of Raleigh. Kinston is one of the leading leaf tobacco markets of the United States. It was settled in 1762 and named in honor of George III of England. After the Revolutionary War, the name was altered to Kinston. Near by was fought the Battle of Wise Forks in 1865, one of the last Confederate victories of the Civil War. Kinston has tobacco auctions, warehouses, and tobacco stemmeries, and cotton and lumber mills. Pop.

KINTYRE, or **Cantire,** area, SW Scotland, the peninsular district of Argyllshire, bounded on the N by Loch Fyne, E by the Kilbrannan Sound, S by the North Channel, W by Gigha Sound and the West Loch of Tarbet; area 462 sq. mi. It is connected with the mainland of Argyllshire by the Isthmus of Tarbet. The chief industries are fishing, farming, and stone-quarrying. The Mull of Kintyre, a promontory at the southern end of the peninsula, is only 13 miles from the Irish coast across the North Channel. Campbeltown, on the east coast, is the leading town and port.

KINZIE, JOHN, 1763–1828, American pioneer, was born in Quebec, Canada, of Scottish parents, and was taken to New York at an early age. He ran away when 10 years old, was employed as a jeweler in Quebec for some years, and then became an Indian trader. The trading post on Lake Michigan that he established in 1804 was located on the present site of CHICAGO. He founded other posts in the West, but returned to Chicago, where he died.

KIOTO. See KYOTO.

KIOWA INDIANS, a small, warlike tribe of North America forming a distinct branch of the Uto-Aztecan family, formerly called the scourge of the Plains. Their homeland was in the region where the great desert country and the buffalo plains meet. About 1700 they were found in western Montana, where they formed part of a group called the Snakes. Later in the 18th century they lived in the Black Hills region, but soon moved southward to the headwaters of the Platte River; during the period of white settlement they wandered about between northern Kansas and Mexico. At first they engaged in bloody warfare with their neighbors, the Comanche, but soon the two tribes entered into a confederation. During the 1840's they came into conflict with the settlers moving into Texas; a decade later they joined with the Comanches, Apaches, and Cheyennes in trying to prevent the entry of the eastern tribes into Indian Territory. Again during the Civil War these tribes carried on a border warfare. By the treaty of Medicine Lodge, Kansas, in 1867 they agreed to go to a reservation in Indian Territory; this treaty was not enforced until General Custer led an expedition against them. In 1874 they left their reservation and took a leading part in a major Indian outbreak; they were finally defeated and their leaders were deported to Florida. The Kiowas are dark in complexion and are heavily built. They speak an independent stock language noted for its harsh, guttural sounds. They had the ghost dance religion and had a peyote cult. More than any other hunting tribe they had a sense of historical sequence; they kept a calendar on which they recorded by a crude system of pictographs the most important events of each year. They have clung tenaciously to their old culture and have resisted the decay so common among most tribes. Their reservation was thrown open to white settlement in 1901. The Kiowas have since accepted American citizenship. They live around Fort Sill, Okla., and now number about 1,300.   F. M.

KIPLING, RUDYARD, 1865–1936, English novelist and poet, born in Bombay, India, Dec. 30, 1865. He was educated in England at the United Service College, Westward Ho, experiences of his school days there being subsequently utilized by him in his tale of schoolboy life, *Stalky and Co.* (1899), in which tale he figures as "Beetle." In 1882 he went to Lahore as subeditor of the *Civil and Military Gazette,* where he remained until 1899. During these years he wrote, for the most part as contributions to the *Allahabad Pioneer,* the stories and verse afterward published in volume form as *Departmental Ditties* (1886), *Plain Tales from the Hills* (1888), *Soldiers Three, The Story of the Gadsbys, In Black and White, Under the Deodars, Wee Willie Winkie, The Phantom*

Rudyard Kipling

'*Rickshaw* (1888–89). Before returning to England at the close of 1889, he made a tour of China, Japan, and America, and it was not long after his return that he published his first long novel, *The Light that Failed* (1891). The next six years were spent partly in England and partly in travel in America, South Africa, Australia, and New Zealand. In the course of them he married (1892) Caroline Starr Balestier, with whose brother, Wolcott Balestier, he collaborated in a novel called *The Naulahka* (1893). His other publications during this period were *Life's Handicap* (1891), *Barrack-room Ballads* (1892), *Many Inventions* (1893), *The Jungle Book* (1894), *The Second Jungle Book* (1895). Shortly after his return to England in 1896, he published a volume of poems, *The Seven Seas.* In 1897 he was specially elected to membership of the Athenaeum Club and in 1907 he received the Nobel prize for literature.

Among the best known of his other works are *Captains Courageous* (1897); *The Day's Work* (1898); *From Sea to Sea* (1899), a reprint of newspaper articles; *Kim* (1901), considered his greatest novel; the children's books *Just-So Stories* (1902) and *Puck of Pook's Hill* (1906); *Actions and Reactions* (1909); *Rewards and Fairies* (1910); *Diversity of Creatures* (1917); *Limits and Renewals* (1932); and *Something of Myself* (1936).

BIBLIOG.–H. Brown, *Rudyard Kipling* (1946).

KIRBY, WILLIAM, 1817–1906, Canadian poet, was born in Kingston-upon-Hull, England, and went to Canada in 1832, where he was occupied in the customs service at Niagara, Ontario, for a long period. He was editor and proprietor of the *Niagara Mail* from 1841 to 1861. His published works include *U. E., a Tale of Upper Canada,* verse (1859), *Chien d'Or* (1879), one of the best of Canadian romances, several dramas and many miscellaneous poems.

KIRBY-SMITH, EDMUND, 1824–93, Confederate soldier, was born in St. Augustine, Fla., and was graduated from West Point (1845). He served in the Mexican War and resigned his commission as major to join the Confederacy. He was brigadier general at Bull Run and major general in command of the Army of East Tennessee, operating around Cumberland Gap, when ordered to assist Bragg's advance into Kentucky (1862). He won a victory at Richmond and seized Lexington and Frankfort. After the Battle of Perryville his Army of Kentucky was moved south and became a corps in Bragg's army in the Battle of Murfreesboro. Promoted lieutenant general and general, Kirby-Smith commanded the Trans-Mississippi Department (1863), where he defeated Banks's Red River expedition (1864). Kirby-Smith surrendered to Gen. E. R. S. Canby at Baton Rouge May 26, 1865. He was an able commander, successful in many independent harassing campaigns. He served as chancellor of the University of Nashville (1870–75) and professor of mathematics at the University of the South (1875–93). See RED RIVER CAMPAIGN; CIVIL WAR.   DON RUSSELL

KIRCHHOFF, GUSTAV ROBERT, 1824–87, German physicist, was born in Königsberg and studied at the University of Königsberg. While teaching physics at the University of Breslau (1850–54) he became acquainted with ROBERT BUNSEN and followed him to the University of Heidelberg as professor of physics. From 1874 to 1887 he held a similar position at the University of Berlin and was associated with Hermann von Helmholtz in much of his research. In 1859 Kirchhoff made a discovery which explained the Fraunhofer lines of the solar spectrum and with Bunsen invented the spectroscope. This instrument enabled them to announce to the Berlin Academy of Sciences the existence of the elements cesium (1860) and rubidium (1861). Kirchhoff described the principles of spectroscopy in *Untersuchungen über das Sonnenspektrum und die Spektren chemischer Elemente* (1861–63). The Kirchhoff laws of electricity, optics, and radiation were named for him. See ELECTRIC CIRCUIT; SPECTRUM AND SPECTROSCOPY.

KIRCHHOFF'S LAWS. See ELECTRIC CIRCUIT; SPECTRUM AND SPECTROSCOPY.

KIRGIZ SOVIET SOCIALIST REPUBLIC, or **Kirgizia,** one of the constituent republics of the U.S.S.R.; situated in the E Soviet central Asia, bounded on the N and NE by the Kazakh Soviet Socialist Republic, on the E by the Chinese province of Sinkiang, on the S by the Tadzik Soviet Socialist Republic, and on the W by the Uzbek Soviet Socialist Republic; area 78,624 sq. mi.; pop. (1950 est.) 1,-500,000. Kirgizia lies largely in the area of the PAMIR and TIEN SHAN mountains, with snow-capped peaks and mighty glaciers. The northern mountain slopes are covered with rich growths of coniferous forests, while the southwestern slopes are covered with growths of walnut. The area is also one of extensive plateaus, torrential rivers, deep valleys, and lakes, the largest of which is ISSYK KUL. The inhabitants of Kirgizia are mainly concentrated in the partially-enclosed Chu and Talas river valleys in the north, along the shores of Lake Issyk Kul in the east, in the southwestern part of the fertile Fergana Valley, and in the valleys of the south. The mountain slopes and plateaus are covered with fine pasturage, totaling some 27,000,000 acres, making possible the raising of vast numbers of livestock.

Economic Life. Kirgizia is rich in mineral resources, with large deposits of coal, oil, sulfur, molybdenum, antimony, limestone, mercury, lead, and gold. The Tien Shan mountains of the republic are estimated to contain more rare metals than all the rest of the Soviet Union combined. The fourth Five-Year Plan (1946–50) stipulates an annual coal production of 1,600,000 tons; reserves are estimated at 10 billion tons. The Dzhergalan coal fields in northern Kirgizia have large deposits of high-caloric coal, and the Uzgen Basin in the southern part of the republic has large deposits of fine coking coal. Kirgizia is the chief source of coal for the Central Asian republics. The growing mining industry produces gold, oil, sulfur, and rare and nonferrous metals.

Formerly a nomadic people, the Kirgiz cast aside their old ways after the Revolution and settled down to the promotion of large-scale industry and agriculture. In 1937 an estimated 2,500,000 acres of land were under cultivation. With the aid of the Federal government large irrigation projects have been completed, adding some 750,000 acres to the cultivated area. About 4,000 irrigation canals have been constructed. Chief crops include sugar beets, tobacco, poppies, cotton, rice, grapes, mulberry leaves, apples, and apricots. Thousands of acres of sugar beets, never

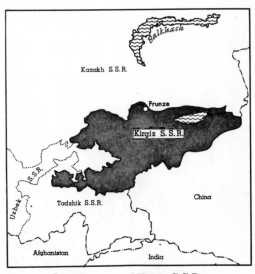

Location map of Kirgiz S.S.R.

SOVFOTO

Kirgiz Collective Farmers prepare to take their stock to neighboring pastures for summer months

before grown in Kirgizia, were planted in the irrigated valley of the Chu River. In the northern areas wheat and barley are grown, and in the southwest, maize. The newly discovered rubber-bearing dandelion, kok-sagyz, is grown here in huge quantities.

The breeding of livestock plays an important role in the Kirgiz economy. The republic possesses over 3,000,000 head of livestock, chiefly horses, cattle, sheep, goats, hogs, and camels.

History. The Kirgiz have inhabited this mountain region since the 13th century. The area was annexed by the Russians in 1864, and made part of the Turkistan Province. In 1920 an autonomous republic was formed, and in 1926 it became the Kirgiz Autonomous Soviet Socialist Republic, which in December, 1936, achieved the status of a full Union Republic. The Kirgiz are a Turco-Tartar people, who resemble the Kazakhs in general appearance. They are only two decades removed from a nomadic mode of existence. Kirgizia was one of the most backward areas of the former czarist empire. Driven from their fertile valleys to the mountain slopes, the Kirgiz wandered about with their flocks and herds and domestic belongings. They engaged little in agriculture, and what ground they did cultivate they tilled with the most primitive implements. There was no industry except for a few small handicraft establishments and coal mines of the most backward kind.

The inhabitants of the republic are 66.6 per cent Kirgiz, 11.7 per cent Russian, and 11 per cent Uzbek. Before the Russian Revolution of 1917 the Kirgiz were rapidly declining in population, decreasing by 10 per cent between 1903 and 1913. During the 12 years preceding the 1939 census the Kirgiz population increased by 45 per cent.　　　A. M. K.; K. E. H.

Theater in Frunze, capital of Kirgiz S.S.R.

SOVFOTO

KIRIN, or **Girin,** province, China, in central Manchuria, bounded on the N by Sunkiang, E by Khabarovsk Territory, S by Korea and Antung, W by Liaopei, and NW by Nunkiang; area 112,743 sq. mi.; pop. (1947) 5,122,000. The province is mountainous, with dense forests of pine, fir, and spruce. The northern range of the Changpei Mountains runs along the southern border between Kirin and Korea. Many minerals are found in the province, the most important being coal and iron. The chief rivers are the Sungari, with the tributaries Hurka and Ussuri in whose basins lie the principal agricultural and grasslands sections of Kirin. The chief crops are millet, maize, wheat, barley, pulse, and potatoes. In the west is another pastoral region of plains and hills, where great herds of cattle and flocks of sheep are grazed. Through the fertile central part of the province are a number of large connected lakes. Changchun, the capital and chief commercial city, is situated at the western end of the province; Huichun, Yenki, Tumen, and Wangching are in the east. The province is subdivided into 20 counties.

KIRIN, also **Chilin,** or **Yungki,** city, China, Manchuria, former capital of Kirin Province. An important rail center, it lies on the Sungari River at the apex of the Sungari Reservoir. Once the fortress of a tribal ruler, Kirin is now a clean, modern, landscaped city. The surrounding mountains are heavily wooded and rich in minerals, of which silver is mined. Lumber, from the vicinity and from the Chientao area, is the main product followed by tobacco and hemp. Boats for the river traffic are built locally. Other industries are paper, textiles, hosiery, matches, and cement. Pop. (1940) 173,624.　　　ADRIAN TROY

KIRJATH JEARIM (Josh. 9:17), town on the N border of Judah, Palestine; 10 miles NW of Jerusalem. Here the Ark remained for some years (Sam. 7:1–2).

KIRK, ALAN GOODRICH, 1888– , American naval officer, was born in Philadelphia, Pa., and was graduated from the U.S. Naval Academy (1909). He was promoted through the grades to admiral (1946). He was naval attaché at London (1939–41) and commanded the amphibious force, Atlantic Fleet (1943) during the invasion of Sicily. As commander of naval task forces he directed the naval phase of the landings in Normandy (1944) and exercised overall command of the naval contingents used in crossing the Rhine (1945). He retired (1946) and served as ambassador to Belgium and Luxembourg (1946–49). He was a special United Nations representative (1947) and became ambassador to Soviet Russia in 1949.

DON RUSSELL

KIRKCALDY, or **KIRKALDY, Sir WILLIAM, OF GRANGE,** c. 1520–73, Scottish soldier, was involved in the murder of Cardinal Beaton in 1546. He served as secret agent for Edward VI, and was later in the service of the king of France. Returning to Scotland in 1557, he joined the Protestant leaders, opposing Mary's marriage to Darnley, taking part in Rizzio's assassination, and helping to defeat Mary's forces at Langside. He transferred his sympathies to Mary while she was imprisoned in England, and held Edinburgh Castle for her till 1573, when he surrendered and was executed.

KIRKCALDY, large burgh and seaport, E central Scotland, on the SE coast of Fifeshire, 26 miles N (across the Firth of Forth) of Edinburgh. High Street, four miles long, gives Kirkcaldy the often-used name of "lang toun." As an industrial center Kirkcaldy's manufactures include cotton goods (sheeting and toweling), linen, sailcloth, net, rope, pottery, machinery, and iron and steel goods. It is foremost in the production of linoleum and oilcloth. There are coal and iron mines near by, iron foundries, bleaching and dye works, and breweries. Kirkcaldy has a good harbor, and fisheries. Adam Smith was born here, and Thomas Carlyle and Edward Irving were schoolmasters here for many years. The town has two noted castles: Ravenscraig, on the shore west of town, said to be the "Ravenshaugh" of Scott's *Rosabelle*, and Balwearie. The seaport of Dysart, which was merged with Kirkcaldy in 1930, has a salt refinery. Pop. (1950 est.) 49,300.

KIRKCUDBRIGHT, small burgh and county town, SW Scotland, in Kirkcudbrightshire, at the mouth of the Dee River; six miles N of Solway Firth and 30 miles SW of Dumfries. It has a good harbor. The estuary is divided at its head by St. Mary's Isle, a peninsula, upon which is the manor house of the earls of Selkirk, where Burns first gave the famed "Selkirk grace." Bomby Castle, founded in 1582 by Sir Thomas McClellan, is north of town. Dundrennan Abbey, built in 1140, is considered Scotland's finest example of 12th-century ecclesiastical architecture. Here Mary, Queen of Scots, spent her last night in Scotland before going to the Tower of London. Pop. about 2,000.

KIRKCUDBRIGHTSHIRE, maritime county, SW Scotland, including the lighthouse islands of Hestan and Little Ross, bounded on the N by Ayr, E by Dumfries, S and SW by Solway Firth and the Irish Sea, and W by Wigtown; area 989 sq. mi.; pop. (1950 est.) 30,700. It is often called the Stewartry of Kirkcudbright and East Galloway because of its once being a part (with Ayr and Wigtown) of the ancient kingdom of Galloway. Its 50-mile coast line along the Solway Firth (which separates it from Cumberlandshire, England, on the southeast) is irregular and rocky and contains numerous caves which served in ancient times as the storehouses of smugglers. The Kells range of mountains runs along the northwest; the culminating point is Merrick (2,754 ft.), the highest peak of Scotland. The rivers of the shire are the Dee, Cree, Nith, Fleet, Ken, Doon, and Urr; the best known scenic sections are the glens Trool, Ken, and Doon. Lochs Grennoch, Dee, Trool, and Urr are the largest lakes. About 35 per cent of the county is under cultivation, the grassy highlands being more suited to grazing cattle and sheep. Pigs and horses are also raised, and bees are kept. The principal crops are oats, barley, wheat, and potatoes. There is a large trade in dairy products and honey. The industries of the shire include grist mills, granite quarries, and manufactures of woolen goods and paper. There are salmon fisheries. Throughout the shire are the remains of many ancient castles. The county seat and chief port is KIRKCUDBRIGHT, situated at the head of the Dee estuary. Other important towns are New Galloway, Castle Douglas, Dalbeattie, Gatehouse of Fleet, and Creetown.   K. E. H.

KIRKDALE CAVE, limestone cavern, England, Yorkshire, in the North Riding, one mile WSW of Kirkby-Moorside. It owes its fame to the discovery in 1821 of fossil remains of mammals now extinct in Great Britain.

KIRKE, Sir DAVID, 1596–1656, English adventurer, born in Dieppe, France. In 1627 he sailed for New France with his brothers Lewis and Thomas, in command of a small fleet. Letters of marque enabled them to capture 20 Quebec-bound French vessels near Newfoundland, and to reduce French stations in Nova Scotia. In 1629 Kirke forced Champlain to surrender Quebec. Though French possessions taken after April 24, 1629, were restored, Kirke was knighted for his efforts. In 1637 Charles I gave him a grant of all Newfoundland to exploit the fisheries. Kirke's lands there, confiscated by the Commonwealth, were largely restored to him later.

KIRKE, PERCY, 1646?–91, English soldier, colonel of "Kirke's Lambs," served under Monmouth, and was appointed to command at Tangier (1680). The regimental symbol, "the Paschal Lamb," provided the above nickname for his men, who, after Sedgemoor and Monmouth's defeat (1685) became a synonym for ferocity because of the treatment of the rebels. Kirke helped William III against James, and raised the siege of Derry.

KIRKENES, town and port, NE Norway, in Finnmark County, situated above the Arctic Circle, at the point where several inlets cut the S shores of Varangerfjord; four miles from the Russian border and 60 miles NW of Murmansk. In peacetime it is an export center for a large tonnage of iron ore, mined at Bjoernevatn, close by. During the Nazi occupation of Norway from 1940 through World War II, Kirkenes was used by the Germans as a submarine base, airfield, shipping center, military camp and dump, and harbor from which to harass Russian-bound supplies from the United States and England. It was one of the first towns of Norway recaptured from the Germans on Oct. 25, 1944, by the Soviet army in their drive down the Scandinavian Peninsula. In their retreat the Germans destroyed many things in their path. The town suffered 900 bombing attacks, first by the Germans, then by the Russians. Pop. about 1,000.

KIRKLAND, CAROLINE MATILDA, nee **Stansbury,** 1801–64, American author, was born in New York City and was married to Prof. William Kirkland of Hamilton College. With him she moved to central Michigan about 1839, and experienced in that wild country the frontier life which is so humorously described in her volumes, *A New Home: Who'll Follow?* (1839), *Forest Life* (1842), and *Western Clearings* (1846). Her later life was passed in New York City.

KIRKLAND, JOSEPH, 1830–94, American author, was born in Geneva, N.Y. He was the son of Caroline Kirkland, and his boyhood was passed with his parents in the backwoods of central Michigan. From 1842 to 1856 he lived in New York City, returning to the west in the latter year. He served through the Civil War in the 12th Illinois Volunteers, and was promoted to major. After the war he practiced law in Chicago. *Zury: The Meanest Man in Spring County* (1885) and *The McVeys* (1888) are studies of early prairie life in Illinois. Kirkland also published *The Captain of Company K* (1891), and a history of Chicago.

KIRKLAND, SAMUEL, 1741–1808, American missionary and educator, was born in Norwich, Conn., and graduated (1765) at Princeton, immediately taking up work among the Six Nations. He was ordained a Congregational minister, and worked among the Indians in the neighborhood of Oneida, N.Y., for the greater part of his life. He was able during the Revolution to secure the neutrality of the Oneida Indians, and after the war labored for the civilization of the Indians generally. Hamilton Oneida College, now Hamilton College, in Clinton, was founded by him in 1793.

KIRKLARELI, or **Kirk-Killise,** town, NW Turkey, Kirklareli Vilayet, on a tributary to the Ergene River; 35 miles E of Edirne (Adrianople). It is situated on the western slope of the Istranca Mountains and commands the southern outlet of the Fakhi Pass into Bulgaria. The shortest route from Shumen in northeastern Bulgaria, to Istanbul (Constantinople) lies through Kirklareli. It is known as the "town of 40 churches" because of its many mosques. Wines, brandies, cereal grains, tobacco, butter, and cheese are exported. About two-thirds of the population is Bulgarian. Pop. (1945) 14,275.

KIRKSVILLE, city, NE Missouri, county seat of Adair County, on the Burlington and the Wabash railroads and U.S. Highway 63; about 60 miles N of Moberly. Kirksville is situated in a rich farm and coal-mining region. It was laid out in 1841 as the county seat. According to local accounts, Mr. and Mrs. Jesse Kirk, tavern keepers here, gave the commissioners a turkey dinner on condition that the town be named for them. Kirksville is the seat of the Northeast Missouri State Teachers College and of the Kirksville College of Osteopathy and Surgery, original center of osteopathic healing. Shoes, pickles and foodstuffs, dairy goods, and drug sundries are the chief products. Pop. (1950) 11,110.

KIRKWOOD, DANIEL, 1814–95, American astronomer, was born in Maryland. He became professor of mathematics at Delaware College (1851), and in 1854 president of that institution. In 1856 he was appointed professor of mathematics at the University of Indiana. In 1891 he accepted the appointment of lecturer on astronomy at the Leland Stanford University, California. He published (1867–88) *Comets and Meteors* and *The Asteroids*. He anticipated, in 1861, the relationship between comets and meteors established in 1866; criticized effectively Laplace's nebular hypothesis; and explained the lacunae in the distribution of asteroidal orbits, and in Saturn's ring system, by the commensurability of the periods of the missing bodies with those respectively of Jupiter's and Saturn's satellites.

KIRKWOOD, SAMUEL JORDAN, 1813–94, American public official, was born in Harford County, Md., moved to Richland County, Ohio, and was admitted to the bar (1843). After moving to Johnson County, Iowa (1855), he served a term in the state Senate and was governor (1860–64). Kirkwood's vigorous support of President Lincoln during the Civil War made him one of the prominent war governors. He filled an unexpired term in the U.S. Senate (1866–67), again became governor of Iowa (1876–77), but resigned to enter the Senate where he served until he was appointed secretary of the interior in President Garfield's cabinet (1881–82).

KIRKWOOD, city, E Missouri, in St. Louis County, on the Missouri Pacific and the Frisco railroads, 14 miles W of St. Louis of which it is a residential and business suburb. In 1853, after work on the Missouri Pacific had begun, a group of St. Louis businessmen bought 240 acres here and laid out a town. Kirkwood was incorporated in 1865. The principal products include lime, cement, and lumber. Pop. (1950) 18,640.

KIROV, formerly **Vyatka,** city, U.S.S.R., in the Russian Soviet Federated Socialist Republic, capital of Kirov Region, on the Vyatka River, about 500 miles E of Moscow. Situated in an oil-rich area known as the "second Baku," Kirov is a railroad and river junction, with railroad shops, machine-building and woodworking industries, flaxworks, fur and tobacco industries, and tanneries. It is the seat of several colleges and technical schools, an institute of country study, a research institute, and a museum. Kirov was founded in the 12th century by merchants from Novgorod, and called Khlynov. In 1489 it was absorbed by Moscow, and in 1780 received the name of Vyatka. After the Russian Revolution, it received its present name in honor of Sergei Kirov, assassinated Soviet leader. Pop. (1950 est.) 200,000.

KIROV REGION, formerly **Vyatka,** an administrative area of the U.S.S.R. in the Russian Soviet Federated Socialist Republic; bounded on the N by Arkhangelsk Region and the Komi Autonomous Soviet Socialist Republic, on the NE by the Komi-Permyak National District, on the SE by the Udmurt Autonomous Soviet Socialist Republic, on the S by the Tatar and the Mari Autonomous Soviet Socialist Republics, on the SW by Gorki Region, and on the W by the Regions of Kostroma and Vologda; area 40,734 sq. mi.; pop. (1950 est.) 2,250,000. Kirov is drained by the Kama and the Vyatka rivers. Rich deposits of iron ore are found in the northeastern area of the Region, and phosphorites abound in the upper reaches of the Kama River. Kirov Region is also noted for its dense woods, which provide the raw materials for the many sawmills and woodworking industries. The Region is one of the primary areas in the Soviet Union where flax is grown. The capital is the city of KIROV.

KIROVABAD, formerly **Gandzha** or **Giandzha,** and **Elizabetpol,** city, U.S.S.R., in the Azerbaijan Soviet Socialist Republic. The second largest city of the Republic, Kirovabad produces seed oil, cotton, broadcloth, clothing, silk, carpets, and sandals. There are many orchards, vineyards, and truck gardens in the vicinity. The area is rich with copper, iron, alumina, pyrites, and barites. An ancient city founded in the 12th century. Kirovabad was won by the Russians in 1804. Pop. (1950 est.) 110,000.

KIROVOGRAD, formerly **Elizabetgrad,** city, U.S.S.R., the Ukrainian Soviet Socialist Republic, capital of Kirovograd Region, 150 miles NW of Kherson. The principal manufactures of the city are farm machinery, flour, bricks, clothing, buttons, and pitched-paper roofing. Lignite is mined near by. Kirovograd is the seat of several technical schools. The city was founded in 1754 as a fort against the Crimean Tartars. Pop. (1950 est.) 100,000.

KIROVOGRAD REGION, an administrative area of the U.S.S.R. in the Ukrainian Soviet Socialist Republic; bounded on the N by the Regions of Kiev and Poltava, on the W by Odessa Region, on the S by Nikolayev Region, and on the E by Dnepropetrovsk Region. It is noted for the grain of its fertile steppes, and for its lignite coal. The capital city is KIROVOGRAD. Pop. (1950 est.) 1,100,000.

KIROVSK, formerly **Khibinogorsk,** town, in the U.S.S.R., the Russian Soviet Federated Socialist Republic, in Murmansk Region, on Kola Peninsula, beyond the Arctic Circle. The world's largest deposits of apatite, estimated at two billion tons, are mined in the Khibin Mountains near by, supplying the U.S.S.R. with rich superphosphates. Uranium, nepheline, and other minerals are also found here. In addition to mining, Kirovsk is engaged in the manufacture of fertilizers. Pop. (1951 est.) 45,000.

KIRRIEMUIR, burgh and market town, NE Scotland, Angus (Forfar) County, five miles NW of Forfar. Linen weaving is the principal industry. It is the birthplace of J. M. BARRIE, who immortalized the town as "Thrums." Pop. about 3,800.

KIRSCH, or **Kirschwasser,** a colorless fruit brandy made from a wild black cherry known as the morello cherry. Its alcoholic proof varies from 86 to 90 degrees. It is served as an after-dinner drink at room temperature.

Kirsch is made principally in France, Germany, and Switzerland. One of the most famous of the German "cherry waters" is the Black Forest kirsch or schwartzwalder. See BRANDY.

KIRUN, also **Kürun, Keelung, Kelung,** or **Kilung,** seaport, NE Formosa, Taihoku Province, 20 miles by rail ENE of the city of Taihoku. Located near the rich coal, sulfur, and gold mines in northern Formosa, it is the chief port of that island and consequently was heavily bombed during World War II. Pop. (1940) 100,151.

KIRUNA, town, N Sweden, in the county of Norrbotten, situated about 100 miles N of the Arctic Circle. Kiruna is the center of one of the world's richest iron districts. The ore comes from the near-by twin mountains of Kirunavaara and Loussavaara whose iron content is so high that magnetic compasses run wild within several miles of the mountains. The town was founded with the opening of the iron mines in about 1900. Three years later the Lapland Railway, one of the most northerly railways in the world, was opened to link the ore of Kiruna with the ice-free Norwegian port of Narvik on the Atlantic for export. Some of the ore is shipped from the Swedish port of Lulea on the Baltic, the southern terminus of the railway. Pop. about 18,000.

KIRYU, city, Japan, central Honshu, Gumma Prefecture, 80 miles by rail NW of Tokyo. A silk weaving center of the Kwanto Plain since the feudal age, it has well-equipped mills which turn out silk and satin textiles. Grapes are grown in quantity. Pop. (1946) 86,836.

KISFALUDY, KÁROLY, 1788–1830, Hungarian author, was born in Tete. In 1804 he joined the Austrian army as a cadet and was disinherited by his father when he resigned his commission in 1811. Compelled to earn his own living, he first tried painting, then turned to writing. He wrote verse, stories, and dramas, eventually achieving success with his play, *The Tartars of Hungary* (1819). He is regarded as the founder of the Hungarian national theater. As editor of *Belletristic Review*, he exercised a great influence on literary trends.

Sandor Kisfaludy, 1772–1844, his brother, was a poet. He is best known for the lyrics in *Himfy's Love* (1807) and for *Legends of the Olden Time in Hungary* (1807). The Kisfaludy Society, a literary academy named in honor of the brothers, was founded in 1837 to promote national literature.

KISHANGARH, former feudatory state, India, now part of Greater Rajasthan; in two tracts in central Rajputana, the S tract separating the two parts of Ajmer Merwara; area 837 sq. mi.; pop. (1941) 104,-427. The northern tract is mainly sandy, infertile soil; the southern, flat and fertile, is irrigated from tanks and wells and produces cotton. There are cotton-pressing and ginning mills. Kishangarh, the capital, is connected to Ajmer city by rail. Maharaja Kishan Singh, a second son of Udai Singh of Jodhpur, founded Kishangarh in 1611. The state has had treaty relations with the British since 1818. Kishangarh rulers belong to the Rathor clan of Rajputs.

KISHINEV, Rumanian **Chisinau,** city, U.S.S.R., capital of the Moldavian Soviet Socialist Republic, situated on the Byk River, an affluent of the Dnestr, 95 miles NW of Odessa. The high or new city stands on a hill 740 feet above sea level; the low town or old Kishinev is on the right bank of the Byk. The city is surrounded by many picturesque orchards, vineyards, truck gardens, and tobacco plantations in an area noted for its winding vales and steep hills. The principal industries of Kishinev include the manufacture of brandy, leather, soap, and woolens. The city was founded in the 15th century and acquired by the Russians in 1812. Alexander Pushkin, the great Russian poet, lived here from 1820 to 1823. Upon the fall of the Russian Empire, Kishinev was united to Rumania along with the rest of Bessarabia. Jews formed an exceptionally large proportion of the city's population, but the pogroms of 1904 and 1905, many emigrations, and the Nazi-Rumanian rule in 1941–44, drastically reduced the community. Under threat of invasion, Rumania ceded the city to the U.S.S.R. in 1940, retaking it during World War II. On recapturing Kishinev on Aug. 24, 1944, the Soviet army found a great part of the city destroyed. Pop. (1950 est.) 110,000.

KISHM ISLAND, largest island in the Persian Gulf, belonging to Iran, lying on Ormuz Strait and separated from the Iranian mainland by narrow Clarence Strait; area about 500 sq. mi.; pop. about 15,000, mostly Arabs. The island is made up largely of flat-topped hills, generally under 500 feet but with one rising to 1,300 feet. The southern hills are made up of rock salt, which is quarried. Kishm is barren and arid except for cultivated spots near the villages, and the climate is extremely hot between May and October. The capital and chief town is Kishm (pop. about 3,000), on the northeast coast. Basidu, a British naval base for a brief time early in the 19th century, is on the northwest coast.

KISHON, the river of central Palestine which drains the plain of Esdraelon, and falls into the Bay of Acre. Here Sisera was defeated (Judg. 4:7, 13), and ELIJAH destroyed the prophets of Baal (I Kings 18:40).

KISKA ISLAND, near the western extremity of the ALEUTIAN ISLANDS, 750 miles E of the Kamchatka Peninsula, and 140 miles N of the 50th parallel, N Pacific Ocean. It is volcanic in origin and its topography is rugged, high, and glaciated; the main peak is Kiska volcano, at the northern end of the island. The extremely adverse weather (including persistent fog, rain, snow, and hail), the summer menace of the mosquito, and the deep and sheltered harbor make it valuable only as a military outpost.

It was such an outpost of the United States, feebly manned, when the Japanese invaded and seized the island in 1942. It was recaptured, in August, 1943, after heavy bombing of its installations by American troops who suffered more casualties from the weather than from the enemy. Kiska was used as an air base during the remainder of World War II.

KISKUNFÉLEGYHÁZA, or **Félegyháza,** town, central Hungary, Pest County, situated between the Tisza and Danube rivers; 66 miles SE of Budapest. It is an old town, dating from 1743, when it was colonized after fierce Turkish raids. It is surrounded by a richly fertile section, which produces tobacco, rice, and rye, and has vast orchards and vineyards. The town has a large cattle market, wineries, distilleries, and factories producing tobacco products and canned fruits. Pop. (1949 est.) 39,000.

KISLOVODSK, town, U.S.S.R., the Russian Soviet Federated Socialist Republic, in Stavropol Territory, situated on the northern slopes of the Caucasus. Kislovodsk is a noted health and pleasure resort famous for its mineral water "Narzan." It is beautifully surrounded by mountains, some of which are 9,000 feet high. Pop. (1951 est.) 50,000.

KISMAYU, or **Chisimaio,** seaport and district, East Africa, Somaliland, in JUBALAND, on the E Indian Ocean. The port lies 10 miles south of the mouth of the Juba River, and has the finest harbor north of Mombasa. Kismayu was first occupied by the Portuguese in the 16th century. In 1905 the British leased a five-acre strip in the harbor to Italy for a landing stage, and in 1925 the port and most of Jubaland were transferred to Italy in fulfillment of one of the conditions of the Treaty of London (1915) for Italy's entrance on the side of the Allies in World War I. During World War II British forces occupied the town in February, 1941.

KISMET, a word used by Mohammedans for "fate" or "destiny." One of the leading precepts of Mohammed was that the decree of God, as preordaining the whole of a man's life, both here and hereafter, must be submitted to by the faithful with absolute resignation. Such a doctrine, apparently paralyzing to human endeavor, has had among the Mohammedans precisely the opposite effect, having been the chief inspiration of that almost unexampled courage which won for their religion its early triumphs, and made it one of the great spiritual powers of the world.

KISPEST, (Little Pest), a SE suburb of Budapest, Hungary, on the Puszta Szent Lörincz. It has factory and residential districts. Pop. (1949 est.) 65,000.

KISSING, the custom of pressing the lips to those of another person. Lombroso considered it as originating in a maternal caress but later becoming an expression of affection. From the Roman custom of greeting friends by kissing arose the kiss of peace as a symbol of Christian brotherhood. The custom is rarely witnessed outside the areas dominated by Caucasoid peoples.   FAY-COOPER COLE

KISSING BUG. See ASSASSIN BUG.

KISSINGEN, BAD, town and watering place, Germany, in the state of Bavaria, beautifully situated on the Franconian Saale, surrounded by wooded hills; about 60 miles E of Franfurt am Main. It is noted for its saline baths (51.3° F.), and its elaborate health facilities. Pop. (1946) 8,575.

KISTNA RIVER, India, rising in the Western Ghats at an altitude of 4,500 feet, flows SE and, breaking through the Eastern Ghats, empties by two main outlets into the Bay of Bengal after a course of 800 miles. The Kistna is unnavigable for the greater part of its course but is of great use for irrigation. It is connected by a canal with the Godavari River. Its drainage area is about 98,000 square miles.

KISUMU, town, British East Africa, Kenya Colony, capital of Nyanza Province, situated at the head of Kavirondo Bay, NE of Lake Victoria. The railway connects it with Nairobi and Mombasa.

"KITCHEN CABINET," an informal group to whom President ANDREW JACKSON turned for advice. Jackson relied on this group because he had little confidence in his official cabinet, most of whom he had appointed for political reasons. The term "Kitchen Cabinet" was first used by Jackson's opponents in derision because the members of this unofficial group usually entered the White House by a back door in order to avoid publicity. The most important men in this group were AMOS KENDALL, a New England editor and writer who composed many of the president's state papers and provided pro-Jackson propaganda, DUFF GREEN, editor of the *United States Telegraph*, FRANCIS PRESTON BLAIR, Sr., editor of the *Globe*, William B. Lewis, a friend and neighbor who managed Jackson's political campaigns, A. J. DONELSON, Jackson's nephew and private secretary, Isaac Hill, MARTIN VAN BUREN, and JOHN H. EATON. After the reorganization of Jackson's cabinet in 1831 the Kitchen Cabinet declined in importance. The term has since been applied to similar unofficial groups which have had influence with other presidents.   FRANK L. ESTERQUEST

KITCHEN GARDEN. See GARDENS AND GARDENING.

KITCHEN MIDDEN, KITCHEN MOUND, SHELL MOUND, are terms used by archaeologists to denote the domestic refuse heaps of certain primitive races. They were first studied by the Danish professors Forchhammer, Steenstrup, and Worsaae, who published the result of their investigations in 1860.

These heaps, containing rude implements of bone and wood, fragments of pottery and broken animal bones—presumably the débris from daily meals—may belong to any period of man's history, and need not denote a prolonged residence in their neighborhood of the race who reared them. The rudeness of the great majority of the implements found in the heaps, and the kind of life otherwise implied, indicate a low state of civilization. Thus, the Danish mounds might be mementos of the savage Fenni described by Tacitus; while J. Milne is inclined to ascribe the shell heaps of Japan to the aboriginal Ainu.

The formation of such kitchen middens is still going on among primitive peoples—notably among the Eskimos. According to Petroff's description of what he saw among the Aleuts, quoted by Professors Keane and Windle: "A family of three or four adults, and perhaps an equal number of children, will leave behind them a shell monument of their voracity a foot or eighteen inches in height after a single meal. The heaps of refuse created under such circumstances during a single season were truly astonishing in size."

Kitchen middens are numerous in America, from Alaska to Tierra del Fuego, both on the Pacific and the Atlantic Coast, and even inland on the shores of large streams. Special excavations have been made in the larger mounds of Georgia, Florida, Long Island, British Columbia, and Alaska. In Europe such mounds are found along the coasts of the British Isles, in Denmark, France, Portugal, and Sardinia. See ARCHAEOLOGY.

KITCHENER, city and customs port, Canada, in the province of Ontario, county seat of Waterloo County, on the Canadian National Railway; 60 miles W of Toronto. It is connected by electric lines with Waterloo, Galt, Preston, and Hespeler. Power, transmitted from Niagara Falls, is employed in the manufacture of furniture, tires, rubber and leather footwear, shirts, foundry and packing products, vacuum cleaners, and buttons. A Pennsylvanian was the first settler (1806), and the town was called Sand Hills and later Mount Pleasant. A number of settlers came direct from Germany in 1830 and the name was changed to Berlin. During World War I, the city was renamed in honor of Field Marshal Lord Kitchener. St. Jerome's College is located here. Pop. (1949 est.) 42,212.

KITCHENER OF KHARTOUM, HORATIO HERBERT KITCHENER, EARL, 1850–1916, British soldier and administrator, was born in Crotter House, Ballylongford, county Kerry, Ireland, second son of Lieut. Col. Henry Horatio Kitchener of Leicestershire and Anne Frances Chevalier of Aspall Hall, Suffolk. After receiving his early education in France, he enrolled in the Royal Military Academy at Woolwich in 1868. While visiting in France two years later, he served for a short time in the Second Army of the Loire, and was in the retreat of the French forces following the disastrous battle at Le Mars. After completing his course at the academy, Kitchener received a commission in the Royal Engineers in 1871. He was engaged on the Palestine survey from 1874 to 1878, and from 1878 to 1882 was on the Cyprus survey.

NATL. PORTRAIT GALLERY
Kitchener

In Egypt. In 1882 Kitchener was appointed to a cavalry command in the Egyptian army. He took part in the Nile expedition (1884–5) for the relief of Gen. CHARLES G. GORDON at Khartoum, gaining the brevet rank of lieutenant colonel; was governor general of the Red Sea Littoral and commandant of Suakin (1886–8); and was severely wounded in an attack on Handub (1888). He received the rank of colonel in the British army in 1888, and became adjutant general of the Egyptian forces. In command of a brigade of Sudanese he participated in the actions at Gamaizieh (1888) and Toski (1889). He was in temporary command of the Egyptian police in 1890–91, and in 1892 succeeded Lord Grenfell as sirdar (commander in chief) of the Egyptian army.

Kitchener at once began the restoration of the Sudan to Anglo-Egyptian rule. He completed the reorganization of the khedive's forces, and organized the Dongola Expeditionary Force (1896), clearing the entire province of Dongola of the Mahdist troops by the end of September. In recognition of this service he was advanced to the rank of major general. The next two years were devoted to completing the work so auspiciously begun. The Sudan Military Railway was constructed under his direction; on April 8, 1898, he defeated the Mahdist forces on the River Atbara; on Sept. 2 he won the great victory at OMDURMAN; and two days later entered Khartoum. For these signal accomplishments he was raised to the peerage as Baron Kitchener of Khartoum, and received a formal resolution of thanks and a grant of $150,000 from the British Parliament. During a flying visit to England he raised $500,000 for the foundation of a college at Khartoum in memory of General Gordon.

South African War. Upon the outbreak of the South African War (1899), Kitchener was made chief of staff to Lord Roberts, whom he later succeeded as first in command of the South African forces. He demoralized the organized guerrilla warfare of the Boers by a system of blockhouses and extensive drives; and eventually brought the war to a successful conclusion (see SOUTH AFRICAN WAR). On the termination of hostilities he was made a viscount, was voted a grant of $250,000, and was again thanked by Parliament for his services to the empire. Upon his return to England he was appointed commander in chief in India (1902), where he remained for seven years, completely reorganizing the service. He was promoted to the rank of field marshal in 1909, and was named to succeed the duke of Connaught as commander of the Mediterranean forces. He made a brief visit to America in 1910, and in 1911 returned to Egypt as British consul general and agent. In 1914 he was made an earl.

World War. At the opening of the first World

Kite

War, in 1914, Earl Kitchener was appointed secretary of state for war, a position which he retained in Asquith's coalition cabinet of 1915. He immediately set about the enormous task of raising a British army for the war, and in less than 18 months organized and equipped 5,000,000 troops. He was sent successively to France, to Gallipoli, and the Near East, rendering important services. He was drowned while on his way to Russia, on June 5, 1916, when the cruiser *Hampshire* was sunk, presumably by a mine, off the Orkney Islands.   R. W. M.

BIBLIOG.–G. C. A. Arthur, *Life of Lord Kitchener* (3 vols. 1920); R. B. B. Esher, *Tragedy of Lord Kitchener* (1921); C. R. Ballard, *Kitchener* (1930, ed. 1936); A. O. Cooke, *Story of Lord Kitchener* (1919, ed. 1936); A. Hodges, *Lord Kitchener* (1936); H. G. De Watteville, *Lord Kitchener* (1939).

KITE, a lightly framed aerial sail, controlled from the ground by means of a cord, and lofted against the wind by a runner while paying out cord as his kite rises in the air. The kite, which takes its name from the great soaring bird, is of ancient Eastern origin, probably as nearly prehistoric as the first man-made fiber cord, sennit, with which the aborigine of the Pacific, the Malayan, the Chinese, Japanese, and Korean first flew their kites to ward off evil spirits. In form, kites range from the simplest, tailless variety to the most ornate, tail-swinging sort flown to guard the family from devils of the air. In the Far East kite flying is both a sport for the young and old and, on occasion, borders on ceremony. Days are set aside for kite flying by whole villages.

Every boy with space to run has taught himself the art of kite making, fastening the light strips of wood with tacks and cord to get the lines desired, and pasting the thin paper over and around the outlining cord. He then attaches his two, three, or four guy

THE BETTMANN ARCHIVE

Chinese kites were made to resemble huge birds

lines to the sticks and meets them at the proper distance to the reeled twine. Until experience has taught him how to attain a balanced flight, he usually tails his kite with a string of rags. Even then his kite may show the malicious spirit of the inanimate by diving, looping, crashing, or entangling itself in roof tops or wires. Building and flying kites is a lesson in craft and patience which every American boy must learn for himself.

Kites have had some practical value in warfare. They have been used to carry aloft signal devices and aerial cameras, and man-carrying kites were used in the Russo-Japanese War. Since the coming of aerial warfare, they have been of value as antiaircraft targets, being towed and controlled in flight maneuvers from the deck of a ship while the gun crews practiced on them. In meteorology, Benjamin Franklin's kite and string drew electricity from the clouds. This was an original and notable experiment, one of many in his study of the weather. Later the kite became an instrument carrier for the meteorologist. From the earliest studies of flight, kites have been used to study air conditions, helping to develop the glider which in turn made flying possible. There are many types of kite design. See FRANKLIN, BENJAMIN.

KITE, a term which, though strictly applicable only to the rare European red kite, *Milvus milvus,* is generally applied to a group of birds of prey distinguished from the buzzards by the long forked tail, elongated wings, short metatarsus and toes, and claws of only moderate length. The European kites are very miscellaneous feeders, but depend largely on offal, and in the Eastern tropics they are valuable as scavengers. The nest is usually placed in a tree, and consists of a mass of sticks lined with rags and paper; the eggs are three to four in number.

In America, four allied species called kites occur in the warmer parts of the United States, but their habits are more like those of ordinary hawks. The beautiful swallow-tailed kite, *Elanoides forficatus,* found as far north as Minnesota and South Dakota, is chiefly black, with purple and green reflections, and is remarkable for its wonderful agility on the wing. The Mississippi kite, found as far north as South Carolina and Illinois, is slate blue with a black tail. The white-tailed kite extends westward to California. The everglades kite is a Florida species.

KITTANNING, borough, W Pennsylvania, county seat of Armstrong County, on the E bank of the Allegheny River, the Pittsburgh and Shawnee, and the Pennsylvania railroads, and U.S. Highway 422; about 40 miles NE of Pittsburgh. Kittanning is situated in a rich farming and dairying district in which there are deposits of coal, natural gas, fire clay, and limestone. It was settled in 1798 on the site of a large Delaware Indian village. Face and fire brick, cement blocks, tile, and leather and foundry products are the principal manufactures. Pop. (1950) 7,731.

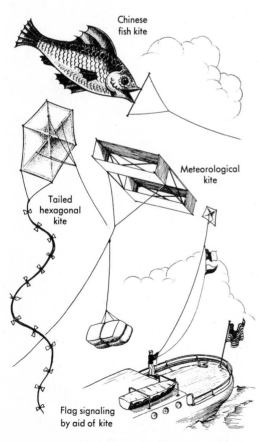

Chinese
fish kite

Meteorological
kite

Tailed
hexagonal
kite

Flag signaling
by aid of kite

Various types of kites

Delaware Water Gap in the Kittatinny Mountains

KITTATINNY MOUNTAINS, in New York, New Jersey and Pennsylvania, part of the Appalachian system and an extension of the Blue Ridge Mountains, is a ridge from 1,200 to 1,800 feet in height, noted for beautiful scenery, including the famous Delaware Water Gap. The region has numerous summer resorts. See DELAWARE RIVER.

KITTATINNY PENEPLAIN, or **CRETACEOUS PENEPLAIN.** At least three times in early geologic history the Appalachian region was the seat of great dynamic changes. Each time the strata were subjected to folding, and rugged mountain ranges were developed. But beginning with the Mesozoic era, an extremely long period of continental stability was inaugurated, during which time the processes of EROSION succeeded in planing off the folds and reducing the area to near base level. The streams of this region, having completed their work of erosion, now flowed sluggishly to the sea. Later, as a result of general continental uplift, this peneplain was elevated several hundred feet, and the rejuvenated streams began to carve valleys anew. The truncated folds beneath the alluvium were uncovered, the softer strata were readily attacked, and gradually, by differential erosion, great and deep valleys were sunk into the old plain. The position and former extent of this plain are now marked only by the crests of the greater ridges of harder rocks that still reach up nearly to the level of the original plain. This second cycle of erosion was interrupted by another period of continental uplift, and a third erosion cycle which is still in progress began.

Some of the more powerful rivers, such as the Delaware, Susquehanna, and Potomac, which have their origin west of the Appalachians, cross the mountain ranges through water gaps almost as if the mountains were not there. The explanation for this phenomenon is that the rivers had established their valleys before the mountain ranges had formed. Another factor which probably assisted these great streams to hold to their courses in spite of the mountain-building was that during uplift the area was tilted in the north toward the southeast and in the south toward the southwest. The smaller streams of the region, in the main, adjusted their courses to conform to the new topography.

Because of the numerous remnants of this old plain still existing as crests in the Kittatinny Range, this region, a relic of a former erosion cycle, is known as the Kittatinny peneplain.   C. C. G.

BIBLIOG.–Bailey Willis, *Physiography of the Northern Appalachians,* Natl. Geog. Soc. Monographs, vol. 1; Ver-Steeg, *Wind Gaps and Water Gaps of the Northern Appalachians* (1930).

KITTERY, town, SW Maine, in York County, at the mouth of the Salmon Falls River where it flows into the Piscataqua River, near U.S. Highway 1, connected by interstate bridge with Portsmouth, N.H., about 50 miles S of Portland. The interests of Kittery center about the Portsmouth Navy Yard, an important naval base, which is spread over several islands in the Piscataqua River. Kittery, founded in 1622, was the first colonial town to be chartered by the Massachusetts Bay Colony. Since

pioneer days, Kittery has been interested in shipbuilding. The *Ranger,* first ship to fly the U.S. flag and commanded by JOHN PAUL JONES, was built here in 1777. Among the interesting colonial buildings in the town is Pepperell House, built in 1682. Fort McClary, built in 1682 and 1812, is one of the outstanding landmarks. Before the Revolutionary War it was called Pepperell's Fort and Fort William, after Sir William Pepperell who was born in Kittery. The town is a summer resort and a headquarters for fisheries. Pop. (1950) 8,380.

KITTREDGE, GEORGE LYMAN, 1860–1941, American scholar and critic, was born in Boston, Mass., and graduated from Harvard University. After teaching Latin for several years at Phillips Exeter Academy, he returned to Harvard in 1888 as an instructor of English literature; became assistant professor in 1890, and was professor from 1894 until his retirement in 1936. Kittredge, an authority on Middle English and Elizabethan literature, was the author of such scholarly works as *The Language of Chaucer's Troilus* (1894); *Chaucer and His Poetry* (1915); *Shakespeare* (1916); *Witchcraft in Old and New England* (1929). He ed-

BACHRACH
George Kittredge

ited *The Complete Works of Shakespeare* (1936), a standard text.

KITTY HAWK, a windswept peninsula in North Carolina, Currituck County, E of Albemarle Sound. Here WILBUR and ORVILLE WRIGHT made their first experiments with gliders, 1900–3, and made the first successful heavier-than-air flight, Dec. 17, 1903. Near by are two high sand dunes known as Kill Devil Hills, on one of which is the Wright Memorial Monument, crowned by a three-way beacon. It was erected by the Federal government in 1932 and is surrounded by a 350-acre park.

KIUH-FU, walled prefectural town, China, in Shantung Province, about 10 miles NE of Yenchow. From one of the five city gates, located in the southwest and in former days opened only for imperial visits, a tree-lined avenue leads to a complex of temples erected to CONFUCIUS, who was born here in 551 B.C. Kiuh-fu is also the residence of his lineal descendants, whose graves, grouped around the burial mound of their ancestor, are in a grove a short distance north of the town proper. Pop. about 25,000.
ADRIAN TROY

KIUKIANG, port, China, in the N part of Kiangsi Province, on the Yangtze River. On the near-by Kiukung Shan range are grown the teas which at one time were the district's chief item of export. Since the latter's decline, porcelain from Kiutochen is at the head of the list followed by paper and grass cloth. There are two modern factories. Water traffic is by Poyang Lake, at the northern end of which the town is located, and by the Yangtze. Kiukiang is linked by rail to Nanchang, the provincial capital, and to Hangchow in Chekiang. The small foreign colony includes missionaries heading a few churches and schools. The mountain resort of Kuling (or Lushan) is situated 15 miles to the south. Kiukiang was in Japanese hands from 1938, during World War II. Pop. about 80,000.   ADRIAN TROY

KIUNGSHAN, or **Kiungchow,** city, SE China, in Kwangtung Province, capital of the Island of Hainan, near the N coast at the mouth of the Limu River; three miles from the port of Hoihow. Kiungshan was seized by Japanese forces on Feb. 15, 1939, and occupied by them throughout World War II until October, 1945. The town manufactures an excellent grade of paper. Exports are sugar, sesame, grass cloth, pigs, and poultry. Pop about 70,000.

KIWANIS INTERNATIONAL, a fraternity of business and professional men which originated in Detroit, Mich., in 1915. The title was adopted from an Indian word meaning "to make one's self known" or "to impress one's self." It is based upon the principle of service, uniting for constructive service groups of men who eat together once a week. It develops friendships and encourages leadership; seeks to build better communities through intelligent and unselfish loyalty. The first club was chartered Jan. 21, 1915, in Detroit. Membership now numbers over 201,000 in over 3,200 clubs. Headquarters of Kiwanis International is 520 North Michigan Avenue, Chicago.

KIWI, a common name given to members of the genus *Apteryx* that are inhabitants of New Zealand. They are primitive flightless birds about the size of a domestic chicken. The wings are small in relation to body size and there is no external evidence of a tail. The bill is long and slightly decurved with nostrils at the tip and stiff hairlike feathers at the base. The brown or gray body-feathers are also coarse and hairlike in texture. The feet and legs are strong, and the toes bear sharp claws that are good weapons against natural enemies. Kiwis are swift runners but in an open space an active man can overtake one. They roam the deep forests and mountainsides, almost to the snow line. Earthworms seem to be their favorite food. The birds are said to stamp upon the ground, causing such vibration that the earthworms are induced to come to the surface. When a worm is seized, the kiwi does not jerk it from its burrow, but pulls steadily until the whole worm is exposed. In New Zealand a single worm may provide a sizable meal, for some species are a yard or more in length. The birds also feed upon beetles and other insects, seeking them out with the long bill that seems to have a tactile as well as olfactory function. Kiwis are most

GOVT. OF NEW ZEALAND
Kiwi, a flightless bird of New Zealand

active during the night but feed in the early morning and evening. During the day they hide under roots of trees or in hollow logs.

The female lays one or two eggs in a breeding season. The eggs are the largest of those of any living bird. Some weigh almost a pound, about one-fourth the body weight of the mother.

The common name was given to the bird by the Maoris (native inhabitants of New Zealand) because it imitates the call of the male. The Maoris hunted the birds for food and used the skins for feathered garments. The hunting activities of the Maoris, in addition to predations of dogs, cats, and foxes, made the kiwis nearly extinct. Extreme measures have been adopted by the government to conserve the birds.

W. A. HILTON

BIBLIOG.—*New Zealand Birds*, New Zealand Native Bird Protective Society (1936); R. Hegner, *Parade of the Living* (1937).

KIZIL IRMAK, or **Red River,** the ancient Halys, the longest river of Turkey, rises in the Karabel Range at an altitude of almost 7,000 feet, in E Turkey about 70 miles NE of Sivas. Its total length is 593 miles. From its source the river flows west and southwest and then describes a deep curve northwest, north, and northeast through central Turkey. Then, after a sharp bend northwest, the river flows generally northeast and empties into the Black Sea between Sinop and Samsun at Bafra Burnu. The chief tributaries are the Delice, Devrek, and Geuk Irmak (Daday). In ancient times the Halys was the border separating Lydia from Persia.

KIZIL KUM. See KYZYL KUM.

KJÖLEN, mountain belt lying along the boundary between Norway and Sweden. The name Kjölen (the Keel) is given to the whole of the main highland mass of the Scandinavian Peninsula; but its usage is restricted chiefly to that portion of it which lies north of 63° N lat. There are a number of heights of more than 6,000 feet, including Jaeggesvarre (6,283 ft.) and Okstinderne (6,273 ft.) in Norway; Sulutjälma (6,158 ft.) on the frontier; and Kebnekaise (6,965 ft.) and Sarjektjakko (6,971 ft.) in Sweden.

KLADNO, town, W Czechoslovakia, Bohemia; 19 miles by rail NW of Prague (Praha). It has iron and coal mines, iron furnaces, and iron and steel works. During World War II it was one of the first cities seized by the Germans in 1939. It was released by the Russians in 1944. Pop. (1947) 40,692.

KLAGENFURT, town, Austria, capital of the province of Carinthia, situated in beautiful mountain scenery, on the Glan River, 115 miles by rail NW of Trieste. The town is connected with Worther See by the Lend Canal, two and one-half miles long, as well as by tram and railway. Among interesting features are the Landhaus, old assembly house with twin towers and a picturesque courtyard, and a museum containing Roman relics from the region. In the central Neuer Platz is the Dragon Fountain with its grotesque dragon's head. Klagenfurt received municipal rights in 1338 and in the 16th century replaced St. Veit as the capital of Carinthia. Rebuilding has modernized the town. Pop. (1948) 65,799.

KLAIPEDA. See MEMEL.

KLAMATH FALLS, city, SW Oregon, county seat of Klamath County, on the Upper Klamath Lake, the Great Northern, the Southern Pacific, and the Oregon, California, and Eastern railroads and U.S. Highway 97; about 180 miles SE of Eugene. Klamath Falls is the center of an agricultural, lumbering, and industrial region situated on the eastern slope of the Cascade Range at an altitude of 4,100 feet. It was laid out in 1878 and incorporated in 1889. CRATER LAKE NATIONAL PARK and a famous duck-hunting area are near by. The manufacture of lumber is the chief industry. Pop. (1940) 16,497.

KLAMATH INDIANS, a North American tribe of the Lutuami linguistic stock whose home is in southern Oregon on the upper headwaters of the river named for them. The Klamaths and the related Modocs of northern California were called "pit Indians" because their homes were roofed-over pits sunk about four feet into the ground; the interior was about 20 feet across with sleeping bunks and facilities for storing dried meats, seeds, acorns, and roots. Baked grasshoppers were a great delicacy. They believed in an existence after death, and they had many creation myths and other legends. This tribe was first described by Peter Skene Ogden, who visited the Oregon country in 1826. Frémont also visited the tribe in 1843 and 1846. The Klamaths lived at peace with the incoming white settlers. The Klamath Indian Reservation of over a million acres was set aside for them and other tribes in 1864; only about one-fourth of the land has been allotted, the rest being reserved for timber and grazing lands. The Klamaths have made good progress as agriculturalists; some are employed in lumber mills and logging camps. In all about 35 tribes are represented on the

Klamath Reservation. The Klamaths number about 1,200.

KLAMATH LAKE, UPPER, at the eastern base of the Cascade Mountains in Oregon and California, source of the Klamath River. The lake is about 8 miles wide and 40 miles long; it is the largest natural body of fresh water west of the Rocky Mountains. Klamath Lake has a capacity of 524,800 acre-feet of water, and is the main source of supply for the Klamath Irrigation Project. Water is diverted through Clear Lake and Gerber reservoirs to 74,046 acres of land southeast of Klamath Falls. About 25,000 people have located within the project and are engaged in growing potatoes, alfalfa, and barley. The northern shore of the lake is bordered by the Klamath Indian Reservation. Lower Klamath Lake, connected to the upper lake by a narrow neck, formerly was a breeding place for water fowl, especially the white pelican; since 1917 the land has been drained and used for agriculture. See RECLAMATION.

KLAMATH RIVER, Oregon, rises in Upper Klamath Lake in the SW part of the state and flows SW about 275 miles by a circuitous route through canyons in the Cascade and Coast ranges of NW California to empty into the Pacific Ocean. The river was named for the Klamath Indians of the region.

KLAPROTH, MARTIN HEINRICH, 1743–1817, German chemist, was born in Wernigerode, Harz. Apprenticed at the age of 16 to an apothecary, he acquired an excellent chemical background which enabled him about 1775 to establish his own laboratory in Berlin. His careful analyses led to the discovery of uranium in pitchblende and of zirconium in zircon. He also verified the discovery of titanium by an English clergyman, William Gregor (1761–1817), and studied the properties of tellurium which had been originally discovered by Baron Franz Joseph Müller von Reichenstein (1740–1825). His reputation as the foremost mineralogical chemist of his day was established by the treatise, *Beiträge zur chemischen Kenntniss der Mineralkörper* (6 vols., 1795–1815). After 1810 he held the first professorship of chemistry at the University of Berlin.

KLAUS, KARL KARLOVICH, also known as **Carl Ernst Claus,** 1796–1864, Russian chemist, was born in Dorpat (Tartu), Estonia. On completing his education at the University of Kazan he was appointed assistant professor of chemistry there (1838) and professor (1844). In 1852 he went to the University of Dorpat as professor of pharmacy and director of the university's Pharmaceutic Institute. He made important analyses of the residues from platinum ores and in 1844 discovered the element ruthenium in osmiridium.

KLAUSENBURG. See CLUJ.

KLAUSTHAL-ZELLERFELD, or **Clausthal-Zellerfeld,** town and health resort, Germany, in the Prussian province of Hanover, in the Upper Harz Mountains, 19 miles by rail S of Goslar. It is the center of one of the principal mining districts in Germany and has a mining school (founded 1775). Minerals found are copper, silver, zinc, and lead. Klausthal was founded in 1550 near the site of Zellerfeld, founded in the 12th century. The two communities were amalgamated in 1924. Pop. (1946) 11,310.

KLEBS, EDWIN, 1834–1913, German pathologist, was born in Königsberg and studied at the universities of Königsberg, Würzburg, and Berlin. He was an assistant to Virchow at the University of Berlin (1861–66). and became professor of pathological anatomy at the universities of Bern (1866), Würzburg (1872), Prague (1873), and Zürich (1882). In 1895 he went to the United States to teach pathology at the Rush Medical College in Chicago but returned to Germany a few years later. A pioneer in bacteriology, he investigated the bacilli causing typhoid, anthrax, malaria, and traumatic infections. In 1883 he described the club-shaped bacillus causing

diphtheria; this was later isolated from other bacteria by Friedrich Löffler and is today known as the Klebs-Löffler bacillus. His monographs on gunshot wounds were largely based on his experience as an army surgeon during the Franco-Prussian War. He also wrote two textbooks on pathology.

KLEE, PAUL, 1879–1940, Swiss painter, was born in Bern. A pupil of Stuck, he anticipated the Surrealists as early as 1902 with his dreamlike fantasies and Surrealist objectivity. His style also included absolute abstraction, however, and in 1911 he founded the German abstract school, the *Blaue Reiter*, with Vassily Kandinsky and Franz Marc. The majority of his rather small paintings are now classed with the French Surrealist school. See EXPRESSION-ISM; MODERN ART for illustrations.

KLEIN, CHARLES HERBERT, known as **Chuck,** 1905– , American baseball player, was born in Indianapolis, Ind. An outfielder, he played with Philadelphia (1928–33, 1936–39, 1940–44), Chicago (1934–36), and Pittsburgh (1939) of the National League. Named the league's most valuable player in 1931 and 1932, he was the leading batsman in 1933. His lifetime batting average was .320.

KLEIST, EWALD CHRISTIAN VON, 1715–59, German poet, was born in Zeblin. Joining the army of Frederick the Great, he was mortally wounded at Kunersdorf. His best known poem is a descriptive lyric, *Springtime* (1749).

KLEIST, HEINRICH VON, 1777–1811, German poet and dramatist, was born in Frankfort-on-the-Oder. He served for a time in the army, studied law and philosophy, lived for a while in Switzerland, where he wrote in 1803 *Die Familie Schroffenstein*, a tragedy. Returning to Germany, he wrote several other plays, including *Das Käthchen von Heilbronn* (1808) and *Prinz Friedrich von Homburg* (1810). Dissatisfied with his own achievements and tormented by an illicit love affair, he shot his married inamorata and himself.

KLEM, WILLIAM, known as the **Old Arbiter,** 1874– , American baseball official, was born in Rochester, N.Y. A minor league (1902–4) and National League umpire (1905–40), he was appointed supervisor of National League umpires in 1941.

KLEPTOMANIA is pathological stealing of a compulsive and irrational nature. It is more common in children than in adults, and often the articles that are stolen have little value and are neither wanted nor needed. This tendency to steal is irresistible, contrary to the person's conscious wishes, and beyond his intent or control. The act often gives temporary relief, in a substitute fashion, for tension which has arisen as a result of forbidden and therefore repressed wishes. A cure of this antisocial behavior, however, is usually brought about only after the underlying conflict has been resolved. See OBSESSION.

KLEVE, or **Cleves,** town, Germany, in the Prussian province of Rhine, near the Netherlands frontier, about two miles S of the Rhine River and 40 miles by rail NNW of Krefeld. Agricultural implements, tobacco, and boots and shoes are manufactured, and there is trade in cattle and wine. Originally a Roman settlement, the town became the seat of the counts of Cleves in the 11th century. The town and neighboring territory, comprising the duchy, passed by treaty in 1614 to the electorate of Brandenburg. A part was ceded to France in 1795 and the remainder in 1805, and the whole returned to Prussia in 1815, with the exception of a small portion belonging to the Netherlands. Anne of Cleves, daughter of Duke John, was the fourth wife of Henry VIII of England. The town suffered heavily from air attacks in World War II. Pop. (1946) 20,000.

KLINGER, FRIEDRICH MAXIMILIAN VON, 1752–1831, German writer, was born in Frankfort-on-the-Main. In 1775 he won a prize for his tragedy *Die Zwillinge*, and a year later published *Sturm und Drang*, a drama whose title came to symbolize the

A gold mining dredge in a Klondike stream

movement of the same name, organized in opposition to all conventional restraint and deriving from the doctrines of Rousseau and Lessing. Having been a soldier in Germany, Klinger went to Russia in the same capacity in 1780 and eventually rose to the rank of lieutenant general. From 1803 to 1817 he was curator of Dorpat University. His novels include *Fausts Leben* (1791), *Geschichte Giafars des Barmeciden* (1793), and *Der Weltmann und der Dichter* (1798).

KLINGER, MAX, 1857–1920, German painter and sculptor. His work is original and bizarre. Among his etchings, "Eve of the Future" (1882), the series entitled "Life" (1882) and "Death" (1889) are remarkable. As a painter his most noted work is "The Judgment of Paris." "Beethoven," "Pietà," and "Salome" are representative of his ability in the art of sculpture.

KLONDIKE, a region, NW Canada, in Yukon Territory, comprising the valley of the Klondike River and near-by valleys where the discovery of rich placer gold diggings in 1896 precipitated one of the greatest gold rushes in history. The news spread quickly to the United States and thousands soon were on their way through the perilous Chilkoot and White passes to the upper Yukon River. They descended the river in boats to Dawson which quickly became a city of 10,000 persons. Fortunes were scooped from Bonanza and Eldorado creeks, while less fortunate miners wandered down the Yukon to streams in Alaska. Gold production reached its height in 1900 when 1,350,057 ounces of fine gold, valued at $22,000,000, were taken. Since then, the production of gold gradually declined, slumping to less than $1,000,000 annual valuation. In the 1930's, the discovery of new gold reserves, the improvement in mechanical equipment, and the rise in price increased the value of production, so that it reached a valuation of $3,000,000 in 1942. Writings about the Klondike are voluminous, some of the best being early books of personal adventure.   F. C. W.

KLOPSTOCK, FRIEDRICH GOTTLIEB, 1724–1803, German poet, was born in Quedlinburg. He studied in the classical school at Schulpforta and was a theology student at Jena for a time, then moved to Leipzig, where the first three cantos of his religious epic *Messiah* were published in the review, *Bremer Beiträge,* in 1748. The remaining 17 cantos were published at intervals until the final one appeared in 1773, Klopstock having in the meantime gone to Copenhagen to complete his work under a pension granted by Frederick V of Denmark. Though Klopstock devoted much of his creative energy to his epic, he possessed a strong lyric gift and by his *Odes* (1747–71) did much to emancipate German literature from the French forms of verse.

KLOSTERNEUBURG, town, Austria, in the province of Lower Austria, on the Danube River,

five miles by rail NW of Vienna. Its most notable feature is the famous foundation of the Augustine Canons, founded in 1114 by Leopold III, with a 12th-century church, an art gallery, the famous Verdun Altar (12th century), and a library containing more than 30,000 volumes, including many rare manuscripts. The town is noted for the manufacture of fine wines. Pop. about 14,000.

KLYSTRON. See ELECTRONICS.

KLYUCHEVSKAYA, MOUNT, volcanic mountain, U.S.S.R., the Russian Soviet Federated Socialist Republic, in Khabarovsk Territory, on the Kamchatka Peninsula. It is the highest volcano on the continent and has a height of 15,666 feet. Klyuchevskaya erupted 19 times in two centuries, the last time in 1932. Its snow-capped peak rivals the Japanese FUJIYAMA in grandeur.

KNELLER, Sir GODFREY, 1646–1723, portrait painter, was born in Lübeck, Germany. He was a pupil of Rembrandt and Ferdinand Bol at Amsterdam. His real career began after he went to London (1675) and was introduced (1678) to the court of Charles II. He was pre-eminent in his profession, and painted people of distinction in England and in foreign countries. For Mary II he executed the "Beauties" at Hampton Court. His last public work was the portraits of the Kit-Cat Club; his most important, an equestrian portrait of William III at Hampton Court. He formed the first practical scheme for an institution to teach art (1711).

KNICKERBOCKER, a name applied to the descendants of the Dutch settlers of New York. The nom de plume of Diedrich Knickerbocker was used by WASHINGTON IRVING in his *Knickerbocker's History of New York* (1809).

KNIFE, a blade with a cutting edge, usually having some type of a handle. Special types of knives are made for various trade and domestic uses, and are generally cataloged as household, professional and industrial knives. Several kinds of specially treated steel are used for knife manufacture, with carbon and stainless steel the most widely employed.

Knives for household use are classed as table, paring, carving, bread, etc. For professional use, there are surgical knives (doctors'), palette knives (artists'), cleavers (butchers'), etc. Pen and pocket knives are used for miscellaneous purposes. Hunting knives are useful when camping and for performing work too heavy for a folding pocket knife.

Industrially, knives are used in many operations, by hand and as part of a machine. Planing mills, paper-cutting, trimming, wood-veneer and plywood-cutting machines employ specially forged and shaped knives to perform specialized cutting duties. The two latter machines use knives made of alloy steel, 48 to 134 inches long, having a beveled edge. Individual

Specially forged knife of a veneer "slicer"

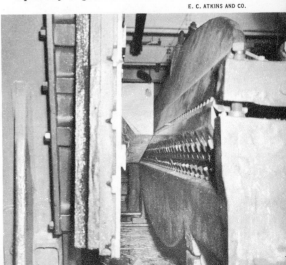

Knight

blades are detachable. Lathes and "slicers" equipped with these knives cut veneer from a rough log in continuous sheets. See CUTLERY.

KNIGHT, DANIEL RIDGWAY, 1840–1924, American painter, was born in Philadelphia. He studied at the Philadelphia Academy of Fine Arts, at the École des Beaux-Arts in Paris, and under Gleyre and Meissonier. He received the Cross of the Legion of Honor (1892). He established his studio at Poissy. His pictures, mainly of the peasant girls and the beautiful landscape of the neighborhood of Poissy, possess charm and delicacy of color and sentiment. Among the best known are: "Washerwomen" (1875); "Chatterboxes" (1885); "En Octobre" (1887); "Summer Evening" (1898); "Quietude" (1900).

KNIGHT, FRANK HYNEMAN, 1885–   , American economist, was born in McLean County, Ill., and studied at Milligan College, the University of Tennessee, and Cornell University. His doctorate thesis, later published as *Risk, Uncertainty and Profit* (1921), was judged the most remarkable Ph.D. thesis ever written in economics and a distinct contribution to theoretical economics. After teaching at various universities, he became a professor of economics at the University of Chicago in 1928. Many scholars rate him the most outstanding economic theorist of the modern era. Much of his later work was devoted to the relationships between the ethical and economic aspects of society, and interpreting social and economic trends in the western world. He translated Max Weber's *Economic History: The Ethics of Competition and Other Essays* (1935) and wrote *The Economic Order and Religions* (with T. W. Merriam, 1945) and *Freedom and Reform* (1947).

KNIGHT, MELVIN MOSES, 1887–   , American economist, was born in Bloomington, Ill., studied at Texas Christian University and Clark University. After teaching at various universities, he joined the faculty of the University of California in 1928, becoming professor of economics in 1930. A distinguished authority in the field of economic interpretation of history, he wrote *Economic History of Europe to the End of the Middle Ages* (1926), *Economic History of Europe in Modern Times* (with H. E. Barnes and F. Flugel, 1928), *Introduction to Modern Economic History* (1937).

KNIGHT, RICHARD PAYNE, 1750–1824, English archaeologist and numismatist, and classical scholar, who bequeathed his collection of coins, medals, pictures, prints, and drawings, valued at $250,000, to the British Museum. He wrote *An Account of the Remains of the Worship of Priapus* (1786), *An Analytical Enquiry into the Principles of Taste* (4th ed. 1808), and *The Progress of Civil Society* (1796).

KNIGHT, SARAH, 1666–1727, American diarist, was born in Boston, Mass., and was the daughter of Thomas Kemble, a Boston merchant. Her husband dying, she moved to Norwich, Conn., about 1715, and there conducted large real estate operations. During a journey on horseback from Boston to New York in 1704, she kept a humorous record of her misadventures. The diary was later published by Theodore Dwight as *The Journals of Madame Knight* (1825).

KNIGHT AND KNIGHTHOOD. Knighthood was a great institution of feudal society which included certain aspects of military organization, of land tenure, and of conduct and manners. A knight was a man who subscribed to the customs and duties of this institution.

Origins. The origins of knighthood are difficult to ascertain, but are to be sought in both the Gallo-Roman and Frankish-Teutonic institutions. By the 10th century it had become customary for a large class of landholders to surrender their lands to some powerful leader, or lord, in return for protection. Simultaneously the invading Franks and Teutons were introducing an element of their military organization described by Tacitus as the *comitatus;* the higher born youths of these eastern groups were trained in the use of arms and then admitted into

Knights jousting in a friendly tournament

the military organization with attending ceremony at which time they also swore enduring loyalty to their military chief. From the fusion of these two institutions knighthood gradually developed and was eventually sanctified by the spiritualizing influence of the church.

The old English term *cniht* was originally applied to the adolescent boy and to designate a retainer or servant; at the same time the Latin term *miles*, meaning soldier, and translated in old English as *thegn*, was used to designate a military retainer of the king or a lord. Eventually *cniht* (later "knight") was substituted for *thegn*. On the continent, however, the inauguration of the use of cavalry in the eighth century, created a class of warrior horsemen designated as chevaliers—from whence "chivalry." The Germans likewise had a term for a military horseman, *Ritter*.

Prerequisites of Knighthood. As indicated it was customary for a knight to hold land in fief and to be born into the noble class. Before attaining knighthood, however, the young man had to serve an apprenticeship as a page, or valet, while he learned the rules of conduct, and then as a squire or shield bearer for a knight while he learned the art of war. He also had to pass through the ceremony of knightly investiture, known as "adoubement," later as "dubbing," which usually took place at Christmas, Easter, or Pentecost, but also irregularly on the field of battle. In the earlier period the ceremony was simply a blow or three blows administered by the investing lord with his fist, or, more usually, with his sword accompanied by appropriate words. Later the rituals became more elaborate and included feasts at court, the giving of arms, spurs, and armor, and the performance of certain religious devotions.

Although the institution of knighthood was thus originally firmly rooted in fiefdom, two factors later arose which served to divorce it from feudalism. The progressive subdivision of land holdings through inheritance resulted in many of the noble class having insufficient means to support them in the full panoply of a knight while primogeniture had the effect of depriving many younger sons of the nobility of any fortune at all. Secondly there were the soldiers of the Crusades who either were propertyless to begin with or were forced to dispose of their holdings in order to obtain the supplies and equipment necessary. It was impossible to withhold the honor of knighthood from these individuals, who were literally outside of the system of feudal land tenure, if they fulfilled other prerequisites and rendered distinguished service to their sovereign or church.

The Knightly Orders. It was in all probability within the ranks of these fortuneless knights that the code of chivalry began to be developed, and it was from such servants of the Cross that the great orders of monastic knights were recruited. Within these orders, of which the Knights HOSPITALLERS, the Knights TEMPLARS, and the TEUTONIC KNIGHTS were foremost, the military aspects were fused with monastic discipline. The Hospitallers and the Templars, for example, took vows of celibacy, and all submitted to strictly defined *regula* or constitutions which did not prescribe fealty to a particular temporal lord, but demanded obedience to the church and to the crusading ideals of medieval Christianity. The earliest order was that of the Knights Hospitallers, founded about 1048 by a band of volunteers for the care of sick and infirm pilgrims; the Knights Templars was formed about 1118 for the defense of the Holy Sepulcher and for the protection of pilgrims; and the Teutonic Knights, founded about 1191, had as an objective service in the Holy Land against the Moslems.

Chivalry. The code of early feudal knighthood stressed loyalty to the military leader, performance of the obligations of feudal tenure, and personal courage, but religious devotion, human kindness, mercy, and humility were notably absent from the actions of the knights. At the beginning of the 11th century the continent was relatively safe from foreign invasion, but was threatened by internal strife and war. At this time the church through the medium of the Crusades adopted warfare as its own and introduced the concepts of humility, service, and protection of the weak to knighthood by making service to God part of their sworn duty. In addition to this combining of religion and militarism, a devotional attitude toward the Virgin Mary arose among the knights, particularly within the crusading orders, which served to give rise to a code of service to women and to exalt romantic love. In spite of the romanticizing of the "chivalrous knight" which has occurred in legend and story, this code had many defects. The knights recognized their chivalrous duty only within prescribed limits; to outsiders they remained cruel enemies or, at best, faithless friends. The romantic attitude toward women seldom was extended to include wives, who were acquired for the sake of the property they brought and not as objects of love; consequently the code eventually became a basis for a system of extra-marital relations, each knight presumably having a "lady-love"—not his own wife and often the wife of someone else—to whom he dedicated poems and madrigals and for whose favor and honor he performed feats of prowess in the tournaments. However, in spite of its defects, Christian chivalry served to bring civil order to Europe and to meliorate the savage militaristic barbarousness of early feudalism.

Decline of Knighthood. The expulsion of the crusaders from the Holy Land in 1291 ended the real era of knighthood. In the 14th century the outward symbols—the tournaments, the apprenticeship system, the religious devotions—appeared more elaborate than ever, but the Christian immorality of the romantic attitudes, the changing techniques of warfare, the rise of commercialism and towns, the commutation of personal services for a tax (*scutage*) all contributed to its obsolescence as a useful social institution. See CHIVALRY; FEUDAL SOCIETY; MIDDLE AGES; SCUTAGE; SEISIN; SERF AND SERFDOM; TOURNAMENT.   M. R.

KNIGHT SERVICE, the tenure by which in feudal days a tenant-in-chief held his property of the king—i.e., for each knight's fee he had to provide one fully-armed knight. He was also liable to the feudal aids, which were abolished in 1660. See KNIGHT AND KNIGHTHOOD; FEUDAL SOCIETY.

KNIGHTS HOSPITALLERS. See HOSPITALLERS.

KNIGHTS OF COLUMBUS. See COLUMBUS, KNIGHTS OF.

KNIGHTS OF LABOR, organized in 1869, was a union of all labor—skilled and unskilled—excluding only bankers, lawyers, gamblers, stockbrokers, and saloonkeepers. Under TERENCE POWDERLY, using the strike when necessary but preferring negotiation and arbitration, it secured higher wages, shorter hours—the eight-hour day was its goal—and better working conditions. Its success during the early 1880's attracted 700,000 members in 1885, but its radical ideas on private property, unsuccessful strikes in 1886, the failures of co-operatives sponsored by the union, and national depression caused a rapid decline in membership. By 1890 the appeal to skilled workers of the craft unions of the American Federation of Labor was fatal to the Knights.   FRANK L. ESTERQUEST

KNIGHTS OF PYTHIAS is a fraternal order founded in 1864 in Washington, D.C. Originating among clerks in government offices, it soon extended its membership to anyone having sound health and a belief in a supreme being. Ritual was based on the story of *Damon and Pythias*, and elaborate ceremonies were developed. The society expanded rapidly during the remaining years of the 19th century and several subsidiary orders, such as the Uniform Rank of the Knights of Pythias and the Pythian Sisters, were established. In recent years the size and strength of the organization has greatly decreased. Membership in 1951 totaled 300,000. Headquarters are at Minneapolis, Minnesota. See SECRET SOCIETIES.

KNIGHTS OF RHODES AND MALTA. See HOSPITALLERS.

KNIGHTS OF ST. JOHN OF JERUSALEM. See HOSPITALLERS.

KNIGHTS OF THE GOLDEN CIRCLE was a secret order existing in the United States before and during the early years of the Civil War. Composed of active sympathizers of secession, it gained its greatest strength in the North where its ultimate goal was the establishment of a Northwest Confederacy. Members carried on a program of terrorism and opposition to the Union cause which was for the most part ineffectual, and the society went out of existence during the latter part of the war. See SECRET SOCIETIES.

KNIGHTS TEMPLARS. See TEMPLARS.

KNITTING, the forming of a looped web or fabric, may be done by hand or on a frame.

Hand Knitting has for appliances two or more straight needles of bone, wood, or steel, the fabric being, by the aid of these, made up from one continuous thread. A series of loops is formed on each needle by passing the thread round a pin and drawing it through the previously made loop. Each stitch so worked is then slipped off and left hanging free. The first row being completed, a second row is worked below it in a similar manner; and so on to any length. If two needles only are used, the fabric formed will have a selvage or edge on each side; if four needles, a continuous circular web, as of a stocking, may be knitted. Variations in width to any extent may be obtained by increasing or decreasing the number of stitches in a row; and alternations in design may be effected by looping the thread in different ways or by the introduction of threads of various colors.

Framework Knitting was introduced about the year 1589 by William Lee of Nottinghamshire, the mechanical principles of whose invention remain almost unaltered to the present day. By providing, in the "hand stocking frame," a needle for each loop, so that all the loops in one row were formed simultaneously, the speed of knitting was increased from 100 stitches per minute by hand to 600 stitches per minute on the frame. The first fabric thus produced was a flat piece, circular work not being accomplished until later. The frame was of a coarse gauge—having only sixteen needles in three inches—and necessitated the thread being laid over the needles by hand. Frames are now at work with as many as 45 needles to the inch. Thread carriers were also introduced, to enable the thread to be laid mechanically at the same time as the loops were being formed.

In order to vary the stitch produced on the hand frame, a "tuck" presser was added in the year 1745. This had its edge cut instead of plain, and so could press any one needle beard, or leave one open, and thus allow the old and new loops to remain together

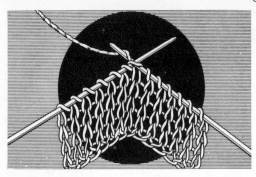

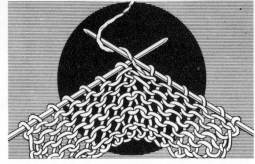

Hand Knitting. Needle containing the stitches is held in left hand. Right-hand needle is inserted into a loop; the yarn is thrown around it and brought through the loop, forming a new row of loops on the right-hand needle. Knitting one row and purling the next forms the plain or stockinette stitch, left. Purling stitch reverses knitting stitch, forming a row of loops with a crosswise appearance, right

on the needles for one or more rows. In this way were introduced fancy designs, which were further developed by the use of different colored yarns at different courses.

Ribwork was the first variation from a plain fabric, and was produced on a hand frame by the addition of a rib machine invented by Strutt about 1758. By forming certain loops (as in plain work) to the front of the web, and others (termed rib loops) to the back, a ribbed and much more elastic fabric was produced. Another method of making ribwork is to have a second set of needles working at right angles to the ordinary frame needles, and forming a series of loops depending from the sinker loops of an ordinary plain course. The method of producing those open-work designs, from which the modern lace hosiery has developed, was introduced about 1763. Certain loops are removed from one needle and added to an adjoining one, the empty needle forming a small hole in the fabric.

Warp Knitting. The first great variation in frame-work knitting was made by the adoption of "warp" threads, one to each needle, instead of the one thread to each row, as in the former (plain-knitting) methods. The warp threads are laid alternately on the needles to right and left, thus forming a series of loops without the intervention of sinkers, which are dispensed with altogether. This system was perfected by the invention of the Dawson wheel, which enabled the threads to be laid in any direction at any course.

Mechanical Frames. The first stocking frame was driven by steam power in 1828, and from that date the hand stocking frame and hand warp frame were gradually superseded by the rotary frames and looms, the machines of today. Hand frames are now only in use for exceptional work, as in the glove and fancy shawl trades, where great manipulation of the threads and variation of the loops are required.

Circular Knitting. About 1830 a French inventor introduced a machine for circular knitting by means of a series of bearded needles radiating outward from

Knitting machines for sweater fabrics

a revolving ring, the loops being formed by sinkers which also revolve. Ten years later a machine was introduced in Nottingham which performed similar work, but of smaller diameter, by means of vertical needles and bladed sinker wheels. A machine on this principle is still known as the English loop-wheel circular frame. A still greater improvement was the adoption in 1848, of a self-acting or "latch" needle, which formed a loop without the aid of the sinkers and pressers indispensable to the bearded needle. About 1870 an automatic machine, called the Griswald knitter, was introduced, which was of the latch-needle type, but differed from the older latch-needle circular frame in having the needles stationary, and in being worked by revolving cams. When put out of the reach of the cams, as is possible at will, the needles are idle; knitting movements take place only when the needles are in the working position. Either flat or circular fabrics can be made on this machine, which has been improved, by successive inventions, so as to produce also either plain or ribbed material. No circular "shaped" fabrics have as yet, however, been made automatically.

KNOCK-KNEE is a deformity in which the legs, instead of being parallel when extended with the feet pointing forwards, diverge so that when the knees touch each other the internal malleoli of the ankles are some distance apart. See RICKETS.

KNOLLS ATOMIC POWER LABORATORY, at Schenectady, N.Y., is a government-owned national laboratory established primarily for research in the development of useful power from controlled nuclear fission processes (see URANIUM). Construction was begun in 1947, the laboratory to be built and operated by the General Electric Company under contract with the U.S. Atomic Energy Commission. The company also operates the Hanford Engineer Works, at Richland, Wash., which is engaged in similar research and development in addition to its primary function of the production of PLUTONIUM. See articles on the ARGONNE and the CLINTON laboratories.

KNOSSOS. See CNOSSUS.

KNOT, the conventional nautical mile, is assumed to be 6,080 feet. A statute mile is 5,280 feet. For navigating purposes, a mile of latitude and a minute of latitude are considered to be of equal value. Consequently the nautical mile is the length of a minute of the meridian, and, strictly speaking, is different for every latitude. In the United States the sea mile is calculated at 6,082.66 feet. For charting and other purposes 10 cables make one knot, though a cable, as a measure of distance, is generally assumed to be 600 feet. A knot is so called from the fact of knots being made in the log line, which was used to ascertain the rate at which a ship was progressing through the water. See LOG.

KNOTS. The proper use of cordage in hauling, lifting, and staying is immensely important in industry both for efficiency and safety. This discussion deals with those knots and hitches known for their advantages in holding fast and loosening readily. Of prime importance to the rigger is the requirement that his knots shall be safe—his own life and that of his mates often depend on his rope skill. Safety is of first rank in requirements.

Next to safety is commercial speed, both in tying a knot and in knowing that it can be easily and quickly opened. Generally, but few knots are required if properly applied, each in its proper place.

One of the good common knots is the clove hitch which can be applied to pull in either direction, either singly or on both strands leading from it, at once. It can be picked off the floor with a single hand. This method is of course applicable only where the knot is to be slipped over an object like the end of a gin pole where the rope is to be used similarly to a guy line. Pick up the bight of the rope in your right hand, palm downward, as in Fig. 1A; you may leave it lying on the floor, or draw it across the left palm for support only, it does not matter. Now turn the right hand palm up, holding the rope loosely; this causes the parts 1 and 2 to cross, as in Fig. 1B; now push the hand forward till the backs of the fingertips rest on Part X, and as you turn the hand back, palm downward, hold part X in position, and swing the elbow out till the hand stands 90° to the right with the original position at start, with the fingertips now resting on Part 2; pick up Part 2, twist it clockwise and your clove can be picked up quickly, with a little practice, after the detailed moves are mastered. In places where an end is not available the clove must be tied in a slower manner, but the knot and its action are the same.

The ordinary *bowline* can be tied very quickly also. It is valuable because it is easily opened after moderate strain. The loop, however, will cut the stranding line under it if the strain be heavy. Grasp the end of the rope in the right hand, and using both hands, tie an ordinary "thumb knot" as shown in Fig. 2A. Next, throw a loop in the standing line by rolling the thumb knot over, and it will appear as shown in Fig. 2B. Now pass the end of line under the standing line and around to the left, and back down through the loop as in Fig. 2C and the bowline is complete. It can be tied very quickly by this method. While both hands are required, one does not even need to see the rope while tying it by this method. The knot is usually easily released by rolling part X up the standing line in the direction of the arrow.

Another good knot that opens easily is sometimes called the *weaver's knot*, Fig. 3, and is said to be used by that trade because it lies so flat when pulled taut. It holds perfectly, and even after strain opens nicely.

The *sheepshank*, Fig. 4, is a knot that is not used as often as its worth would indicate, but is highly valuable in its proper application. It can be used in pulling heavy machines into place where hauling room is restricted. The hauling rope can be shortened by two men in the matter of seconds. Fig. 5 shows a fairly fast method of making the sheepshank. Three loops are laid one over the other in the manner shown in the photographs. By reaching through the top of the last-formed loop and under the first loop to be formed, and grasping the middle loop, two sides of the middle loop may then be pulled through outside loops. This method works well only on small rope, and when both ends or at least one end of the rope is free, or when there is sufficient slack in the rope to allow the three loops to be quickly formed.

Another quickly placed hitch is the *Blackwall hitch*, used on a hook. It is safe, and can be put on with speed. Simply wind one turn of the line clockwise over the bottom of the hook, leaving the long part at the back leading off to the left, while the short end, nearest the operator, leads off to the right. Now loosen the turn well and slide it back, around the shank of the hook, as shown in the sketch. The load

line now pinches across the short part and locks it on the hook. The heavier the strain, the tighter is the pinch. It is safe if kept tight, loosens at once when the strain is released. It should be lashed in place to the hook, if used where the strain is intermittent.

The *stopper hitch* is another that is very valuable in its place. If a line is stretched partially between two supports, and it is wished to tighten it more, the stopper is used to attach another line to it and pull up the slack in the direction the line is stretched. Properly attached, the hitch does not slip, and is easily released. It is easiest to use when the second line is somewhat smaller than the line to which it is attached, so that the pulling line can wrap securely around the line to be tightened.

The *becket hitch*, not illustrated, is another very handy knot used on the becket of one of a pair of rope blocks. It is simply a clove hitch tied with the short end of the line, around itself, after passing

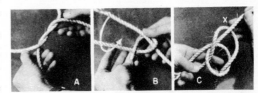

Fig. 1

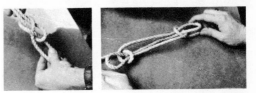

Fig. 2

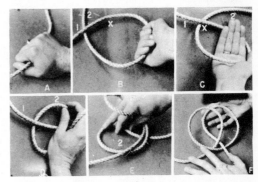

Fig. 3   **Fig. 4**

Fig. 5

POWER PLANT ENGINEERING

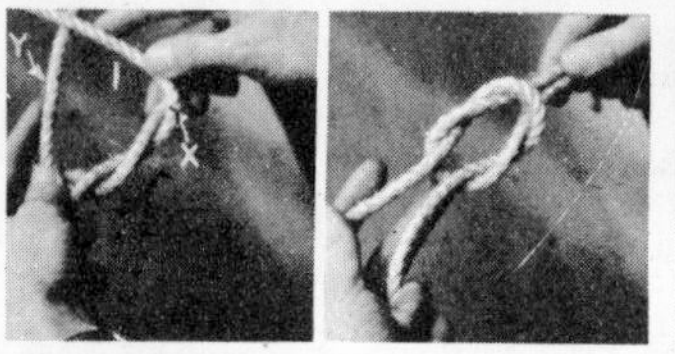

Fig. 6 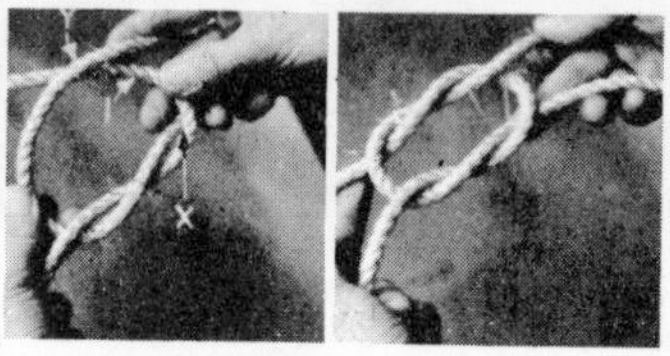   Fig. 7   Fig. 8

through the becket. Its virtue lies in the fact that it will pull up very flat, thus permitting the two blocks to come very close together when pulled "two blocks," as the rigger calls that situation. It aids the job when head room is needed.

The common two half hitches will hold the maximum power of the line it is used in, but in such a job, an axe is needed to open it. For that reason, it should be used only in light to medium strains.

The *square knot*, Fig. 6, is easily confused with the *granny knot*, Fig. 7. The latter is sure to slip and is highly dangerous. (The granny will hold on pack thread, but not with rope. On high work or on heavy pulls, it is deadly.) The square knot is safe in most places, but cannot be readily opened. The *timber hitch* is another valuable knot and widely used, as it will hold well, is easily applied, and as easily opened. See Fig 8.

Much good can be accomplished by the proper use of hitches, totally aside from the knots used in them. For instance, several turns of rope may be used around a hook and its load, with only one part having a knot in it. It is a good plan to have one part go around the load only, so that part can bind the load tight in the hitch. Always let the knot be in that unhooked part, so that the knot, aided by the friction between the rope and the load, will not pull up so tight that it is hard to open. If the knot is placed in a part that gets the direct pull, perhaps all the pull, it will be hard or commercially impossible to loosen.

Courtesy of POWER PLANT ENGINEERING

KNOW-NOTHING PARTY, more properly the **Native American,** or **American Party,** a party first organized in the United States in 1852, under the official title, "The Supreme Order of the Star-Spangled Banner"; originally a secret association, whose members, refusing to give information about the organization and disclaiming all knowledge concerning it, were popularly called "Know-nothings." Their object was to secure the government to those whom they considered genuine Americans, their fundamental doctrine being "Americans should rule America." Roman Catholics and recent immigrants they regarded with distrust and hostility, and they advocated extending the period required for naturalization to 21 years. In this they had the sympathy of large numbers of Americans—opposition to immigrants had broken out sporadically from the time the national government was organized; the course of political events having been such as to cause large numbers of the members of the older parties to waver in their allegiance, the new party rapidly gained recruits, and soon became powerful, carrying various state elections and electing a number of representatives in Congress. In 1855 the governors and a majority of the legislators of Massachusetts, New Hampshire, Connecticut, New York, Rhode Island, California, and Kentucky were Know-nothings. The slavery question split the party, however, and although in 1856 the party participated in the national campaign, its candidates for the presidency and the vice-presidency, Millard Fillmore and A. J. Donelson, received the electoral votes (8) of only one state, Maryland, though they received a popular vote of 874,534. After this election, the party rapidly disintegrated.

KNOWLEDGE. One of the amazing characteristics of man is his thirst for knowledge. He wants to know his world, himself and the why and wherefore of things that happen. Nothing in all of nature possesses this characteristic—unless it be the dim light possessed by certain animals in their recognition of their own species and the objects of hunger and fears.

More amazing is the fact that man seems to think that he can know, that knowledge is possible. The average person as well as the technically trained scientist assumes this. The interplay of man's life with things and people reveals how much is taken for granted as knowledge: he thinks he knows what people mean by their words and their actions, he thinks he knows what day it is, and that tomorrow will surely follow today. Much of knowledge is hardly distinguishable from belief. When man believes something with sufficient assurance he comes to believe his beliefs as having the stature of knowledge. Often he learns that such knowledge may not be knowledge at all but only the reflection of prejudices, hopes, likes or dislikes.

For many people knowledge is undisciplined. It is incoherent and inconsistent. It lacks the kind of highest assurance which can stand up under searching criticism. Philosophers are keenly aware how wide is the area of pseudo-knowledge, of superstitions, of plain ignorance that poses as knowledge. They make it a special study and call it by a special name: *epistemology* (from the Greek word which means knowledge). They ask how it is possible to know anything; how one can recognize truth from error; how to distinguish belief or faith from knowledge; how to set up tests to recognize it from mere opinion; and how the mind works when its ideas are said to be logical and its conclusions convincing enough to be called knowledge. It is the goal of thought on this subject to attain the kind of knowledge which can stand the tests of criticism, the kind that makes intelligible the whole of human experience.

Agnosticism and Skepticism. There are, of course, those who say that genuine knowledge is impossible. Such people are called agnostics (from the Greek word meaning no knowledge). The philosopher points out to such people that their position is self-contradictory since they assume knowledge in the denial of its possibility. In other words, an agnostic (as defined) asserts knowledge when he claims he cannot know, thus affirming what he denies! It would be much better, then, to be a skeptic; for the skeptic does not say he cannot know; he only says that he is never certain of knowing. There are two kinds of skeptics: the extreme and the mild. The extreme skeptic keeps himself locked up in uncertainty, thus shutting the door even to the very possibility of knowledge. His very attitude prevents any degree of assurance of knowing. Moreover, if he says that he is skeptical about everything, then, logically, he must be skeptical about his very skepticism. An extreme skeptic is thus in the same dilemma as the agnostic. Life demands adjustments without the absolute assurance of knowledge. For that purpose nature has provided adequate means of responses which perform immediately without waiting for the delayed action of critical reason and certain knowledge. To live, man must be heroic; he must take action even though he is not sure of the outcome; must make decisions even before the evidence is in. An extreme skeptic could not live with such skepticism. Knowledge is an adjunct to living. The mild skeptic, however, has a much better case. He would like to know but he is cautious; he wants more evidence at certain points; he would reserve judgment if it is possible; he moves slowly to his conclusions. Unless there is skepticism at least to some degree, man would be altogether naïve. A naïve person doubts nothing and thus runs riot in his thinking. Believing everything is believing nothing—a sure sign of having no knowledge.

Descartes. Skepticism (or doubt) has its limits. On the one side, too much of it makes for the impossibility of any knowledge; too little of it, on the other side, invites error and lack of understanding. All knowledge demands the belief that knowledge, to some degree, is possible. This, of course, can be denied. But to deny everything indiscriminately is a form of madness. Somewhere along the line one has to make a positive statement that seems reasonable. One such statement is the affirmation of the possibility of knowledge. One of the great modern philosophers, René Descartes, found, after much searching self-criticism, that he must assert the knowledge of his own existence on that ground that all his doubting implied a doubter, his own person. From that reasonable premise he moved on in his thinking. Knowledge is always a matter of degree: from the assurance of sheer faith to conclusions reached by approved methods of testing. The more certain knowledge becomes, the higher is the degree of probability.

Logic and Pragmatism. What is known as scientific knowledge, in the strictest sense, may be defined as that body of conclusions derived from data which have been carefully observed and capable of confirmation by others particularly if the factors can be controlled. There is a growing body of such knowledge. However, it would be foolish to deny that knowledge is possible without all such testing. A person, conceivably, may know something without being able to lay bare all the relevant factors or reasons. A mystic, for example, who claims privileged knowledge by a direct experience cannot be ruled out if he is unable to clarify by evidence outside the range of that experience. Yet, it is well to check his claims by an appeal to other areas of experience to see how matters stack up altogether. It is one of the tests of the truth of any claim to knowledge that the claim will harmonize with the whole of experience and reasonableness. Unless this be so, knowledge itself would be impossible. For to know implies orderly relationships, harmony, and fitness. The knowledge-claim of a person who is said to be insane raises doubts because it reveals a lack of fitness to the larger patterns of human experience. The study of how the mind works in such orderly relationships of ideas as these, and moves on to conclusions, is called *logic*. To such a study, Aristotle, the ancient Greek philosopher, contributed greatly in his analysis of the forms of the reasoning processes and of the rules to validity of inferences. It is known, however, that fitness is not enough. A person, it is clear, may have a harmony of ideas and not have knowledge since such a harmony may have no contact whatever with the world outside the ideas. Accordingly, philosophers add other tests, such as the practical working of ideas in terms of living situations (a test called pragmatism or workableness) and the correspondence of the ideas to data lying beyond the mind itself (known as the *correspondence* test of truth).

See AGNOSTICISM; DEDUCTION; EMPIRICISM; INDUCTION; INTUITION; LOGIC; MYSTICISM; NOMINALISM; PRAGMATISM; RATIONALISM; SCHOLASTICISM; SKEPTICISM; and the related biographies: ARISTOTLE; BERKELEY, GEORGE; HEGEL, GEORG WILHELM; HUME, DAVID; KANT, IMMANUEL; LEIBNITZ, GOTTFRIED WILHELM VON; LOCKE, JOHN; PLATO; SOCRATES; SPINOZA.

VERGILIUS FERM

BIBLIOG.—F. R. Tennant, *Philosophy of the Sciences* (1932); W. T. Stace, *Theory of Knowledge and Existence* (1932); A. J. Ayer, *Foundations of Empirical Knowledge* (1940); L. Wood, *Analysis of Knowledge* (1941); G. Berkeley, *Principles of Human Knowledge* (latest ed. 1942); R. Kroner, *Primacy of Faith* (1943); C. I. Lewis, *Analysis of Knowledge and Valuation* (1946); Bertrand A. Russell, *Human Knowledge* (1948); John Dewey and A. F. Bentley, *Knowing and the Known* (1949); E. Cassirer, *Problem of Knowledge* (1950); A. J. Ayer, *Language, Truth, and Logic* (1951).

KNOWLES, JAMES SHERIDAN, 1784–1862, British dramatist, was born in Cork, his father being first cousin of Richard Brinsley Sheridan. He became acquainted with Hazlitt and Charles Lamb, and made an appearance on the stage. For many years he taught in Belfast and in Glasgow. *Caius Gracchus*, his first great success (produced in Belfast, 1815), was followed by other plays, such as *Virginius* (1820), *The Hunchback* (1832), *The Love Chase* (1837). His dramas are of genuine merit, but as an actor he was less fortunate. In later life he became a Baptist and lectured on "No Popery" at Exeter Hall, London.

KNOX, FRANK, full name **William Franklin,** 1874–1944, American newspaper publisher and cabinet officer, was born in Boston. After graduation from Alma College, he fought with the Rough Riders in the Spanish-American War. Leaving his newspaper business, he enlisted as a private in World War I at the age of 43 and attained the rank of major. Knox was general manager of all Hearst newspapers (1928–31) and bought the *Chicago Daily News* (1931) in which he remained interested until his death. When Franklin Roosevelt was elected president, he became a fervent anti-New Dealer, and was Republican vice-presidential candidate in 1936. Always a believer in a big navy, he was named secretary of the navy by President Roosevelt (1940). Despite the losses at Pearl Harbor in 1941, he was influential in building the American fleet into the two-ocean navy that was the greatest naval force in history.

KNOX, HENRY, 1750–1806, American soldier, born in Boston, Mass., where for many years he was a bookseller. In the pre-Revolutionary controversies between the colonists and the British government, his sympathies were strongly with the colonists, and during the Revolution he was a conspicuous officer on the American side. He served as a volunteer in the Battle of Bunker Hill, became successively a colonel of artillery (Nov., 1775), a brigadier general and chief of artillery of the Continental army (Dec., 1776), and a major general (March, 1782); brought the artillery arm of the service to a high degree of efficiency, and took a prominent part in Washington's campaigns. In May, 1783, he was instrumental in founding the SOCIETY OF THE CINCINNATI; on Aug. 25, 1783, he received from Sir Guy Carleton the surrender of New York City, and from Dec., 1783, to June, 1784, he was commander in chief of the U.S. Army. He was secretary of war under the Confederation government (1785–89), and, after the organization of the national government, was the first secretary of war, in the cabinet of President Washington (1789–94), the navy being also under his jurisdiction. He passed his last years at Thomaston, Me., where he died. See WASHINGTON, GEORGE, for illustration.

KNOX, JOHN, 1505?–72, Scottish churchman, reformer and leader in the founding of PRESBYTERIANISM in Scotland. He was born in Giffordgate, Haddington, not far from Edinburgh. Little is known about his early life. His grammar school education was received at Haddington, and he entered the University of Glasgow in 1522 where he studied for an unknown period of time without receiving a degree. It is believed that he was admitted to minor orders and a record has been found which indicates that, about 1543, he was an apostolical notary. In 1544, he was serving as a tutor in Longniddry House near Haddington.

Apparently, at some time during this early period of his life, Knox must have embraced Protestantism for, when he finally did emerge from comparative obscurity, it was in the company of the Scottish reformer, George Wishart (1513?–46), whose preaching and martyrdom influenced Knox to take a positive stand in behalf of Protestantism. From 1546 on, Knox became the dominant spirit in the Reformation in Scotland. When Cardinal Beaton (1495–1546) was murdered in retaliation for the execution of Wishart, Knox joined the reformers who had taken possession of the Castle of Saint Andrews where the murder had taken place. Knox preached against "popery," arousing his Protestant followers by his powerful denunciations of Catholicism, but on July 31, 1547, the castle was captured by the French and Knox was forced to remain for some 19 months on the Loire River as a galley slave before his release was finally secured at the request of Edward VI (1537–53). Knox left France for England (1549) where he allied himself with Cranmer and other English reformers and served as one of the chaplains to Edward VI. Although he declined both a vicarage and a bishopric in the recently established Church of England, Knox preached in a number of different churches including Berwick near the Scottish border, Newcastle and London. His preaching exerted considerable influence on the development of the REFORMATION in England, and he was successful in his attempt to introduce liberal changes into the second revision of the English prayer book.

PRESBY. HIST. SOC.
John Knox

Adoption of Calvinism. When Mary Tudor (1516–58) came to the throne in 1553, Knox left England for the Continent, living successively in Dieppe, Geneva, and Frankfort-on-the-Main. He returned to Scotland in 1555 for a visit of several months after which he went back to Geneva and served as the pastor of the English church in that city for three years. It was in Geneva that he met Calvin, whom Knox came to regard as an authority on matters pertaining to the relationship between church and government. CALVINISM was later introduced into Scotland through Knox. While in Geneva, Knox wrote one of his most famous works, the *First Blast of the Trumpet Against the Monstrous Regiment of Women*. This tract was an attack against women who took part in government (specifically Mary Tudor, Mary of Guise, and Mary Stuart) and so aroused Queen Elizabeth that she later refused Knox permission to enter England on his way to Scotland.

The influence of Knox in Scotland had been largely the result of his correspondence, but in 1559 he returned to his native country and from that time on took a personal part in the reform movement. The preaching of Knox had much to do with arousing the reformers to revolt, and the result was a series of riots in which images were destroyed and monasteries wrecked. The death of the Queen Regent (Mary of Guise) brought the disturbances to an end (June, 1560) and a free Parliament was convened to establish order. Parliament discarded the old religion and established the Reformed Kirk in Scotland based on the principles of Calvinism. In all this, Knox played a most active part, both the *First Book of Discipline* and the *Confession of Faith* of the Reformed Kirk being the result of his ideas and personal influence.

Flight From Assassination. When Mary Stuart (1542–87) came to the throne in 1561, Knox extracted from her a promise to uphold Presbyterianism and the laws against the Catholics. Difficulties soon arose, however, between Knox and the Catholic queen, whom Knox accused of frivolity in living, and heresy in allowing the mass to be said privately in the palace. His denunciations of the court alienated the more moderate Protestants who were seeking to control the government in the queen's name, and Knox retired largely from direct interference in public affairs between 1563 and 1565. Following the marriage of the queen to Lord Darnley (1565), Knox again became politically active as the supporter of Murray (1531?–70), half brother of Mary, during his opposition to the Catholics and his regency following the abdication of Mary (1567). The assassination of Murray (1570) was a great blow to Knox, and was followed by misunderstanding and hostility between Knox and some of the members of the General Assembly. To escape the danger of assassination, Knox went to Saint Andrews where he continued to preach with vigor even though he was so weak that he had to be assisted into the pulpit. Toward the end of 1572 he went to Edinburgh where he died on November 24th.

Personal Qualities. Knox was a man of stern, uncompromising convictions who refused to let anything stand in the way of expressing his beliefs or carrying out his objectives. He did not hesitate to attack those in authority if, by doing so, he believed that he might advance the Protestant cause. Although the methods which he used to obtain his aims were extreme and at times even violent, Knox openly and fearlessly expressed his convictions leaving no one in doubt as to his views on any question. He not only made enemies by his harsh and violent denunciation of all who opposed his aims and beliefs, but he also was capable of inspiring those who chose to follow him with an aroused zeal and sense of purpose which made him the unquestioned leader of the Protestant forces in Scotland. The convictions held by Knox were the dominant influence in the formation of the Scottish Church, having much to do with both the determination of its Presbyterian form of organization and its theology.

As a writer and historian of his times, Knox also excelled. His works include a monumental biography and history of religion in Scotland during his time entitled *History of the Reformation of Religioun in the Realme of Scotland*. This work, begun about 1560, was first published (incomplete) in London in 1584. See SCOTLAND for illustration.   W. G. D.

KNOX, PHILANDER CHASE, 1853–1921, American lawyer and political leader, was born in Brownsville, Pa. He was graduated from Mt. Union College, Alliance, Ohio, in 1872, studied law in Pittsburgh, was admitted to the bar in 1875, and became one of the leading lawyers of Pennsylvania, devoting his attention particularly to corporation law. He was elected president of the Pennsylvania Bar Association in 1897. He carried through the legal negotiations incidental to the formation of the United States Steel Corporation (1900). In 1901 President McKinley appointed him attorney general, an office which he continued to hold under Theodore Roosevelt until his election to the U.S. Senate in 1904. As attorney general he was active in forming the Department of Commerce and Labor, in enforcing the antitrust laws, and in securing clear title for the United States to the Panama Canal property. In 1909 he was appointed secretary of state by President Taft. He was active in negotiations with the powers for the establishment of a permanent international court of justice. He was the author of a resolution declaring peace with Germany, which, though vetoed by President Wilson, formed the basis of the later peace treaty.

KNOX COLLEGE. See COLLEGES.

KNOX, FORT, a military post at Vincennes, Ind., constructed in 1788 by Maj. J. F. Hamtranck and named for Henry Knox, then secretary of war under the Confederation government. The fort was abandoned after Gen. Anthony Wayne's victory over the Indians at FALLEN TIMBERS in 1794. Previous to the construction of Fort Knox, Vincennes had been a French village for several decades. In 1777 the

THOMPSON'S, KNOXVILLE
The University of Tennessee at Knoxville

British governor Henry Hamilton had built a small stockaded fort at Vincennes, which he called Fort Sackville. This fort was captured by George Rogers Clark in February, 1779. See VINCENNES.

KNOX, FORT, a permanent United States military post located about 30 miles south of Louisville, Ky. The site was purchased by the Federal government in 1917 and used as a training camp during World War I. In 1932 it was a made a permanent military post and the name was changed from Camp Knox to Fort Knox. It was an important training center during World War II. In 1936 the U.S. Treasury Department built the Gold Bullion Depository to store the Federal gold reserve. The treasure house, 100 feet square, is of bombproof construction, and its walls and roof are faced with huge granite blocks. Atop each corner of the building are machine-gun turrets where guards keep vigil against intruders who might attempt to scale the high iron fence. Interlaced steel coils with openings too small to admit a man's hand are set in the concrete of the walls as an added protection. Constant inspection of the interior of the two-story vault, which is 60 feet long and 40 feet wide, is maintained by means of an open space under the floor and one over the ceiling; mirrors and brilliant lights make every corner visible. Supersensitive microphones in the vault are connected with the central guardroom. At the end of 1950, approximately $12,500,000,000 in gold of the $23,000,000,000 in monetary gold held by the United States was kept in this depository.
F. M.

KNOXVILLE, city, S central Iowa, county seat of Marion County, on the Burlington Railroad, 33 miles SE of Des Moines. Knoxville is situated in an agricultural and coal-mining region. It was settled in 1846 and named for Henry Knox, a Revolutionary general who became the secretary of war and had jurisdiction over the navy. Knoxville manufactures overalls and beverages. Pop.(1950) 7,625.

KNOXVILLE, city, E Tennessee, county seat of Knox County, on the N bank of the Tennessee River, the Louisville and Nashville and the Southern railroads, U.S. highways 11, 25, and 129, and the American, the Delta, and the Pennsylvania-Central air lines, 160 miles E of Nashville. Knoxville, the key city of eastern Tennessee, is located in the Tennessee Valley in the Great Smoky Mountain region. It is an important industrial metropolis and a tobacco, livestock, and produce market. In the vicinity of Knoxville, within a 100-mile radius, are found 40 different minerals including copper, coal, iron, and zinc; and marble is quarried. Knoxville is the headquarters of the TENNESSEE VALLEY AUTHORITY. The

city's location amid beautiful mountain scenery annually attracts more than one million tourists. Knoxville is less than one hour's drive from the Great Smoky Mountain National Park. The University of Tennessee and Knoxville College are located in the city. One of the finest collections of the history and genealogy of the southern states is housed in the Lawson McGhee Public Library in Knoxville. Textiles, clothing, marble products, plastics, aluminum, agricultural products, flour, cement, lumber, and machinery are some of the major manufactures of the city.

The first permanent settlement in Knoxville was made in 1786 by Gen. James White, who received a land grant from the state of North Carolina, of which Tennessee was then a part, for his services in the American Revolution. The city was incorporated in 1815 and named for Gen. Henry Knox, secretary of war in Washington's cabinet. When Tennessee was admitted into the Union in 1796, Knoxville became the first capital of the newly formed state. During the Civil War, Knoxville was taken and held by the Union forces under General Burnside. Pop. (1950) 124,769.
A. M. K.

KNOXVILLE COLLEGE. See COLLEGES.

KNUDSEN, WILLIAM SIGNIUS, 1879–1948, American industrialist, was born in Copenhagen, Denmark, and came to the United States at the age of 20.

GENERAL MOTORS
William Knudsen

He rose from superintendent with a Buffalo bicycle factory (1902) to production manager with the Ford Motor Company (1914), vice-president of the Chevrolet Motor Company (1922), and executive vice-president of the General Motors Corporation (1933). Because of his reputation as an efficiency expert he was appointed president of General Motors in 1937. He served during World War II as director general of the Office of Production Management (1941–42) and director of production for the War Department (1942–45), holding the rank of lieutenant general in the U.S. Army.

KNYPHAUSEN, WILHELM, 1716–1800, German soldier who, with Gen. De Heister, commanded the Hessian troops in the American Revolution. He took part in the attack on Fort Washington, and in the battles of the Brandywine, Germantown, and Monmouth, and was in command at New York (1779–80) during Sir Henry Clinton's absence in South Carolina. He was subsequently military governor of Cassel.

KOALA, or **NATIVE BEAR,** a clumsy and heavily built MARSUPIAL, chiefly arboreal in habit, found in eastern Australia, where it makes its home in the eucalyptus or "blue gum trees." The body is about two feet long and has thick, woolly fur, ashy gray in color above and white beneath. The ears are large and fringed, and the cheeks pouched for storing food. There is

AUSTRALIAN NEWS BUR.
Koala, or "native bear"

EWING GALLOWAY

Cotton bales are unloaded on Kobe water front

EWING GALLOWAY

Bundles of bamboo stored in a Kobe lumber yard

no tail. The koala, *Phascolarctus cinereus*, resembles the PHALANGERS, to which it is related. It is purely herbivorous.

KOBE, chief seaport and sixth largest city of Japan, S Honshu, capital of Hyogo Prefecture, on the NW shore of Osaka Bay at the E end of the Setonaikai (Inland Sea), about 20 miles W of Osaka. It includes the old city of Hyogo. Picturesquely situated along the shore and on lower slopes of the small, steep Rokkosan Range to the north, Kobe is on the Tokyo-Osaka-Kyushu trunk railroad and the main Tokyo-Osaka-Shimonoseki highway and is connected with Osaka by two fast interurban electric railroads, besides having modern bus, streetcar, and subway transportation. Kobe has a first-class harbor and is one of the world's great ports. It is an important transshipment center for cargo to and from other ports in Japan and in northern China, Formosa, Manchuria, and Korea. Kobe is one of Japan's main shipbuilding ports, and has other important diversified industries. Imports comprised great quantities of raw cotton from the United States and India, raw wool, steel and other metals, petroleum, bean cake fertilizer and coal from Manchuria, chemicals, and many other industrial materials for distribution to Osaka and elsewhere as well as Kobe's own plants. Exports included cotton, wool, rayon, and silk textiles and yarn, condensed milk and other canned goods, and a great variety of other manufactures. During World War II American planes rained thousands of tons of bombs on war industrial areas, laying over half the city in waste. Features of interest include the Sannomiya Shinto shrine, a Daibutsu (large statue of Buddha), and the historic (1336) Minatogawa battleground. The climate is temperate and equable, rather hot in August and with an occasional typhoon in the rainy month, September.

Anciently called Fukuhara, the city was the seat of the powerful feudal baron, Taira Kiyomori, who ruled Japan early in the 12th century. Modern Kobe grew into an important trading port after Japan was opened to foreign intercourse in 1854, expanding as Osaka became a great manufacturing center. Osaka eventually developed its own port, which became the third greatest in Japan, but Kobe continued to rival Yokohama as the empire's premier port. Kobe took and held the lead when Yokohama was crippled by the 1923 earthquake and much of its trade, especially the valuable raw and manufactured silk shipments from north and west central Honshu, was diverted to Kobe for some years. Kobe's foreign residents included several thousand Americans, Europeans, and Asiatics, especially Chinese and Indians. In the early days of extra-territoriality, which ended in 1899, the westerners resided in a settlement near the water front, much as a similar community lived in Yokohama. There are several Roman Catholic and Protestant churches for foreign and Japanese Christians. Pop. (1947) 607,202.   P. W.

KOBENHAVN, or **Kjöbenhavn.** See COPEN-HAGEN.

KOBERGER, ANTON, ? –1513, German printer, active in Nuremberg. Founder of the House of Koberger, he was among the first of the early printer-publishers to issue advertising listing his books and to maintain sales agencies in the principal European cities. The earliest work of his press is dated 1472 and by Koberger's death 236 separate productions are known to have been published. The most famous of these is the profusely illustrated *Nuremberg Chronicle*. See BOOK for illustration.

KOBLENZ, or **Coblenz,** city, Germany, in the Prussian province of Rhine, at the confluence of the Moselle and Rhine rivers, 55 miles SE of Cologne. A beautiful tree lined promenade stretches along the Rhine northward to the Moselle, culminating at the Kaiser Wilhelm I monument. Noteworthy buildings are the St. Castor Church, originally founded in 836, rebuilt in the 12th century; the Church of Our Lady, founded in 1182; the old Market-House (15th century); the palace (1778–86); and the castle (1280) of the electors of Trier (Treves). Koblenz is an important center for Rhine and Moselle wines, being situated in a rich vineyard region. Industries include the manufacture of machinery, pianos, boats, sugar, dyes, paper, and chemicals. On the right bank of the Rhine stands the famous and once mighty fortress of Ehrenbreitstein, situated on a rock 385 feet above the Rhine, a testimonial to the power of the medieval robber barons. The former fortress of Asterstein lies to the south of Ehrenbreitstein. A southern suburb of the city, Oberwerth, is situated on the Rhine island of the same name.

In Roman times Koblenz was a settlement called *Confluentia*. It became an important town in the Frankish kingdom, passing in 1018 to the archbishopric of Trier. During the Thirty Years' War it was taken successively by Sweden (1632) and by the imperial forces (1636). In 1794 it fell to France, and in 1815 it became the seat of the Prussian government in the Rhineland. In World War I it was bombarded

Koblenz, heavily damaged in World War II

U.S. ARMY SIGNAL CORPS

by the Allies, and following the conclusion of peace (1919) it was occupied by U.S. forces until 1923, and by the French until 1929. It was the seat of the Inter-Allied Rhineland Commission. In World War II the city fell to the 87th Infantry Division of the U.S. Third Army on Mar. 17, 1945, after a violent all-day assault. Allied air attacks caused considerable destruction; St. Castor's was severely damaged. Pop (1946) 91,103.

KOBURG. See COBURG.

KOBYLA GORA. See LANDSBERG AN DER WARTHE.

KOCAELI. See IZMIT.

KOCH, FRED CONRAD, 1876–1948, American biochemist, was born in Chicago, Ill., and studied at the universities of Illinois and Chicago. After serving as a research chemist with Armour and Company (1902–9) he joined the faculty of the University of Chicago in 1912, and became professor of biochemistry in 1923. He also served as chairman of the Department of Physiological Chemistry and Pharmacology from 1926 until his retirement in 1941. He did important research on the thyroid, sex, and pituitary hormones, methods for analyzing blood and urine, and conversion of certain sterols into Vitamin D through exposure to ultraviolet rays. His principal publication was *Practical Methods in Biochemistry* (1934).

KOCH, ROBERT, 1843–1910, German bacteriologist, was born in Klausthal, Hanover, and studied

LAMBERT PHARMACAL CO.

Robert Koch, the great bacteriologist, calls his wife to witness isolation of the tubercle bacillus

at the University of Göttingen. After serving on the staffs of the Hamburg General Hospital and the Lagenhogen Lunatic Asylum he volunteered as an army surgeon in the Franco-Prussian War; then practiced medicine at Bomst and began the study of bacteria. His first contribution to the new science of bacteriology was the isolation of *Bacillus anthracis* (1877), the cause of anthrax; six years later he proposed a method of preventive inoculation against this disease, so frequently transmitted from sheep and cattle to man. He also formulated four postulates on the etiology of bacteria-borne diseases (see BACTERIA, *Bacteria in Disease*) and demonstrated the existence of several bacteria which cause wound infection. He was appointed to the Imperial Board of Health at Berlin (1880), where he developed methods of water filtration and disinfection by steam. In 1882 he announced the isolation of tubercle bacillus (or Koch's bacillus). He was director of the German Cholera Commission (1883) which visited India and Egypt to study Asiatic cholera, and identified its cause in the comma bacillus. He was also the first to observe the bacillus now known as the Koch-Weeks bacillus, the cause of an epidemic form of conjunctivitis.

Koch was appointed professor of hygiene at the University of Berlin and director of its Hygienic Institute (1885); and director of the Berlin Institute of Infectious Diseases (1891–1904). In 1890 he produced tuberculin, which proved of great value in diagnosing tuberculosis. In the 1890's he also studied Asiatic diseases (malaria, leprosy, bubonic plague) and African diseases (black-water fever, Rhodesian red-water fever). In South Africa (1896), he devised a method of preventive inoculation against rinderpest. His last assignment took him to German East Africa, where he studied sleeping sickness (1906). Koch received the 1905 Nobel prize in physiology and medicine for his work on tuberculosis.   M. E. C.

BIBLIOG.–P. De Kruif, *Microbe Hunters* (1926); H. E. Sigerist, *The Great Doctors* (1933).

KOCHER, EMIL THEODOR, 1841–1917, Swiss surgeon, was born in Bern and studied at the universities of Bern, Berlin, Paris, and London. From 1872 to 1911 he was professor of surgery at the University of Bern and director of its surgical clinic. He developed a method of setting shoulder dislocations, devised operations for hernia and cancer of the stomach, and discovered a way to transplant the thyroid gland. In 1878 he performed the first successful operation for the removal of goiter; and thereafter, as he lived in one of the principal goiter belts of the world, repeated this difficult task more than 2,000 times. In 1912 he prepared a sterilized coagulene, injections of which would accelerate coagulation in cases of internal hemorrhage. Considered the leading European surgeon of his day, he was elected president of the First International Congress of Surgeons (1905) and was awarded the 1909 Nobel prize in physiology and medicine.

KOCHI, city, Japan, S central Shikoku, capital of Kochi Prefecture, about 110 miles SW of Kobe. The city is a trading center for rice and Kochi paper, a noted type of native Japanese paper. Its manufactures of plywood, textiles, cement, and chemicals caused it to suffer 55 per cent destruction from American bombing in World War II. Pop. (1947) 147,120.

KOCK, CHARLES PAUL DE, 1794–1871, French novelist, was born in Paris. He published about 100 novels, in which, in witty, vulgar, and realistic fashion, he described low and middle class life in Paris. Many of his novels were translated into English. His best known works include *André le savoyard* (1825); *Le barbier de Paris* (1826).

KODAK, in photography, a trade mark, which applies to a number of cameras as well as a range of products and services. Originally the word "kodak" applied to a portable, boxlike camera, developed in 1888 by GEORGE EASTMAN, in which roll film was used. The celluloid film had been invented in 1885 by Rev. Hannibal Goodwin. The roll film camera made possible modern amateur photography and was important in the growth of the motion picture industry. See PHOTOGRAPHY.

KODÁLY, ZOLTÁN, 1882– , Hungarian composer, was born in the tiny town of Kecskemét. His family wished him to be a scientist, so in 1900 he entered the University of Budapest. But he also enrolled in the Budapest Conservatory as a composition pupil of Hans Koessler, in whose class were also ERNST DOHNÁNYI and BÉLA BARTÓK. Koessler was a German, but he awoke in his students an enthusiasm for the national music of Hungary in its purity, which was in danger of being lost to the world, distorted as it was in existing collections by gypsy mannerisms and foreign influences. Like Bartók, Kodály began to travel through his country's villages, taking down by hand or by phonographic recordings, the folk music of his people. Several thousand of these were analyzed and correlated and some were published jointly by Kodály and Bartók. As a youth Kodály had greatly admired Brahms and Debussy, an admiration reflected in his early works. But when his thought became imbued with the distinctive and melodic rhythms of his native music, his style took on these contours even when he did not use specific folk tunes as a basis. He settled down to composition, giving up the idea of a career as a scientist, and accepted a professorship at the Budapest Conservatory in 1906, where he taught for many years. His reputation began to spread when a number of his compositions were performed in Budapest in 1910. His first and second String Quartets carried his name farther afield. The performances of his works at festivals of the International Society for Contemporary Music in 1923 and 1924 made him an international celebrity. The composition of his choral masterpiece, *Psalmus Hungaricus*, was the result of a commission to celebrate the 50th anniversary of the union of the cities of Buda and Pest in 1923. Only three years later his humorous opera, *Háry János*, was produced. Among Kodály's major works are the *Marossázék Dances* (1929); *Dances from Galanta* (1933); the ballet, *Kuruc Mese* (1935); *Felszállott a páva*, variations for orchestra (1939); *Concerto for Orchestra* (1940); *Missa Brevis* (1944); and *Tombeau des Martyrs* (1945). Though Kodály is not a revolutionary composer, he assimilated such modern techniques as neomodalism (from the Hungarian folk song), polyharmony, and harmonic counterpoint. His style is varied, but always colorful and vibrantly alive.   IRWIN FISCHER

KODAMA, GENTARO, VISCOUNT, 1852–1906, Japanese soldier and statesman, was born in Choshu. He supplemented his Japanese training by study in the United States (Rutgers College) and in Europe. In 1872 he entered the Japanese army, and was a captain in the Civil War (1877). He became vice-minister of war (1892), governor general of Formosa (1897), minister of war (1900), and minister of home affairs (1903). For his success in restoring order in Formosa he was appointed vice-chief of the general staff. He prepared the plans on which the war with Russia was fought, and during the war showed himself to be one of the ablest of the Japanese strategists. In 1906 he became chief of the general staff, and was created viscount.

KODIAK ARCHIPELAGO, SW Alaska, including Kodiak, Afognak, and several small volcanic isles, lying S of Cook Inlet in the Gulf of Alaska and separated from the Alaska Peninsula by Shelikof Strait; about 200 miles SW of Seward; pop. about 2,500. Kodiak, the largest island, is about 100 miles long and 50 miles wide. It contains excellent harbors and is a stop on the Pacific Northern Airlines. The island is treeless, except along the eastern coast, but luxuriant grasses make it a fine grazing land. Although Russian traders passed this way in 1762, it was not until 1784 that Shelekhov returned to make the first Russian settlement in America at Three Saint's Bay, named for his ship. In 1792, the settlement was moved to the present site of Kodiak village. It served as the

headquarters of the Russian-American Company of fur traders until 1804, when the headquarters was transferred to Sitka. In 1912 a serious eruption of Mount Katmai on the Alaska Peninsula covered Kodiak Island with volcanic ash and drove the inhabitants to the mainland for several years. On their return, they utilized the ash as the basis for excellent roads. The Russian, Aleutian, Indian, and American inhabitants of the island are largely engaged in fishing as the Karluk River is one of the best salmon streams in Alaska. The island also has salmon canneries and packing plants and some fur farming. An experiment station of the U.S. Department of Agriculture has been maintained here since 1908. The island is famous as the home of the Kodiak bears. During World War II, Kodiak was an important air base and distribution point for military supplies. Of the 13 villages in the Kodiak Archipelago, the largest are: Kodiak (1,635) Karluk (41) Old Harbor (122), and Alitak on Kodiak Island, and Afoguak (159) on Afognak Island, lying north of Kodiak.   F. C. W.

KODIAK BEAR. See BEAR.

KODOK. See FASHODA.

KOENIG JOSEPH PIERRE, 1898–   , French army officer, was born in Alsace. After service during World War I, he was with the Chasseurs Alpins and the Foreign Legion (1918–40). Escaping after the Battle of France (1940), he distinguished himself in Free French Africa as the hero of Bir Hacheim, a Libyan oasis defended from Rommel's attacks for 16 days. He became assistant chief of staff (1943) and representative of the French Committee of National Liberation (1944). As commander of the French Forces of the Interior, he directed the sabotage of German equipment and the capture of some 50,000 square miles of French soil. Lt. Gen. Koenig was appointed French representative on the Allied Control Commission for Germany (1945), and commander of French occupation forces in Germany (1946). He helped in 1948 to plan a West German government.

KOEPANG, or **Kupang,** seaport, Netherlands-Indonesian Union, the Republic of Indonesia, Sunda Kechil Province, former capital of Netherlands Timor in the Lesser Sundas; located at the W tip of the island, on Koepang Bay, at the N end of the strait which separates the mainland from Semaoe (Semau); seat of the resident. Koepang has a harbor and is the more important of the only two ports in Dutch territory (the other one is Atapupu or Atapoepoe on the northern coast near the Portuguese border). Koepang is a place of call for the ships of the Royal Packet Navigation Company which connects Koepang to the other Lesser Sunda Islands, to Celebes, and to Java. It is a difficult harbor during the northwest monsoon. Koepang has an annual rainfall of 57 inches and a yearly average of 80 days. The Japanese occupied Koepang in 1942, holding it until 1945. Pop. about 7,000.   ADRIAN TROY

KOESTLER, ARTHUR, 1905– , European author, was born in Budapest, Hungary. Educated at the University of Vienna, he served as correspondent for the German paper, *Volkische Zeitung* (1926 –30); covered the Spanish Civil War for the London *News Chronicle* (1936–38); and edited an anti-German newspaper in France from 1938 until captured by the Nazis (1940). Released through British aid, he joined the Volunteer French army and in 1941 became a private in the British army. He became a British subject in 1948. Although a Communist for several years, he left the party at the time of the Moscow

ALASKA STEAMSHIP CO.
Harbor of Kodiak, largest village in the Kodiak Archipelago

trials (1936–37) and many of his novels (*Darkness at Noon*, 1941; *Arrival and Departure*, 1941; *The Age of Longing*, 1951) underline the moral disintegration that Communism engenders. His nonfiction works, such as *The Yogi and the Commissar* (1945) and even *Insight and Outlook* (1949), also have incisive anti-Communist themes.

KOFFKA, KURT, 1886–1941, American psychologist, was born in Berlin, Germany. Educated at the University of Berlin, he became Neilson research professor of psychology (1927) and professor (1932) at Smith College. One of the founders of GESTALT PSYCHOLOGY, he theorized that behavior cannot be analyzed into separate conscious elements but must be seen in terms of wholes. He wrote *The Growth of the Mind* (1924) and *Principles of Gestalt Psychology* (1935).

KOFU, city, Japan, Honshu, capital of Yamanashi Prefecture, 80 miles W of Tokyo, on the upper reaches of the Fuji River, on a small plateau in the center of one of the most mountainous areas of Japan, and on one of the main central railways from Tokyo. Kofu is noted for its silk textiles, grapes, wine, and rock crystal jewelry and signature seals. During World War II about three-fourths of the city was destroyed. Pop. (1950) 87,195.

KÖHLER, WOLFGANG, 1887– , American psychologist, was born in Reval, Estonia, and studied at the University of Berlin. He was director of the Tenerife Anthropoid Station (1913–20), director of the Psychological Institute at Berlin (1920–35), and became professor of psychology at Swarthmore in 1935. A founder of the Gestalt school of psychology, he studied learning phenomena in apes. He introduced the term "insight" into psychology and wrote: *The Problem of Form in Perception* (1924); *Mentality of Apes* (1925); *Gestalt Psychology* (1929); *Dynamics in Psychology* (1940). See GESTALT PSYCHOLOGY.

KOHLRABI, a biennial vegetable closely related to cabbage. The kohlrabi is a stout plant with an

Kohlrabi, a relative of the cabbage

edible stem that is enlarged at the surface of the ground. This tuber-like tissue is white or purple in color and has large leaf scars on its sides. The thin leaves, growing from the top of the tubers, are characterized by irregular margins and slender petioles. Kohlrabi thrives best in rich, well-drained loams in cool climates. It is grown in spring or autumn and cut at the ground level when the tubers are about the size of baseballs. When used as a vegetable the tubers are peeled, cut into small squares and boiled like cauliflower. Although kohlrabi is widely used as a vegetable in Europe, its chief use in the United States is for stock food. Kohlrabi, *Brassica caulorapa*, belongs to the family *Cruciferae*.

KOIL. See ALIGARH.

KOK-SAGHYZ. See RUBBER.

KOKAND, or **Khokand,** town, U.S.S.R., the Uzbek Soviet Socialist Republic, situated in Fergana Region and the fertile Fergana Valley, near the Syr Darya. A beautiful town, surrounded by luxuriant gardens, Kokand has many fine structures, including the former palace of the Khans, similar in architecture to the mosques in Samarkand. Kokand is the center of a large cotton industry; silk and flour are also produced. The early history of Kokand is uncertain, but after 1218 it came under the domination of the Mongols, achieving independence only in 1700. It fell to the Russians in 1875, and in March, 1876, the khanate of Kokand was absorbed into the general government of Turkistan, as the province of Fergana. Pop. (1951 est.) 75,000.

KOKCHETAV REGION, an administrative area of the U.S.S.R. in the Kazakh Soviet Socialist Republic; bounded on the N by North Kazakhstan Region and the Russian Soviet Federated Socialist Republic, on the W by Kustanai Region, on the S by Akmolinsk Region, and on the E by Pavlodar Region. Its capital is the city of Kokchetav.

KOKO NOR. See TSING HAI.

KOKOMO, city, N central Indiana, county seat of Howard County, on the Wildcat River, the Pennsylvania and the Nickel Plate railroads, and U.S. highways 31 and 35; about 50 miles N of Indianapolis. Kokomo is an industrial city surrounded by a rich agricultural country. It was laid out about 1843 on the site of an Indian trading post and named for a Miami chief. The first practical automobile in the United States was successfully tested in Kokomo by its inventor, ELWOOD HAYNES, in 1894. Other first products developed in the city include pneumatic rubber tires, aluminum castings, aerial bombs, stainless steel, gas and smoke shells, and life-saving crafts. Kokomo manufactures steel, automobile parts, radios, stoves and ranges, pottery, special precision instruments, and cotton garments. Pop.(1950) 38,672.

KOKURA, city, Japan, at the N tip of Kyushu, Fukuoka Prefecture. Kokura is noted for its manufacture of a distinctive cotton cloth used in the making of boys' school uniforms. Its steel and chemical industries caused it to suffer considerable damage in World War II from American bombing attacks directed principally at Yawata and Moji, between which cities Kokura lies. Pop. (1947 est.) 167,996.

KOLA NUT. See COLA NUT.

KOLA PENINSULA, U.S.S.R., forming the greater part of Murmansk Region in the Russian Soviet Federated Socialist Republic, on the White and Barents seas. The peninsula's greater part is beyond the Arctic Circle, but the Gulf Stream reaches Kola Bay which thus never freezes. The Khibin Mountains in the center of the peninsula, with summits over 3,000 feet, abound in valuable apatite. Copper, nickel, granite, and marble are also extracted on Kola, and there is much fishing and timbering. The main cities are the port of MURMANSK, KIROVSK, and Kandalaksha. Besides Russians, Saamis (Lapps) live on Kola.

KOLABA, or **Colaba.** See BOMBAY.

KOLAR, city, India, in Mysore State, capital of Kolar District, 43 miles by rail E of Bangalore. Gold was discovered in the district in 1876, and Kolar has grown up among the mines. Silver is also mined. Sugar cane and cotton are raised in the district, and there are industries of sugar refining and silk and cotton weaving. Pop. (1941) 133,859.

KOLBERG, or **Colberg,** Polish **Kolobrzeg,** town and seaside resort, Poland, in the province of Pomorze Zachodnie, situated at the entrance of the Persante River into the Baltic Sea, 75 miles by rail NE of Stettin (Szczecin). Notable buildings in the town include the Gothic St. Mary's Cathedral (1280), the St. Nicklas Church, and the old town hall. A large beach-park extends along almost the entire coast line of Kolberg; to the west is the Forest Maikuhle, and to the east the Town Forest. The town's industries include iron-founding, manufactures of machines, boats, lumber, and tobacco, and fishing. Kolberg received its municipal rights in 1255, and joined the

Hanseatic League in 1284. In 1631 it fell to Sweden and in 1653 to Brandenburg. During the Seven Years War it was taken by the Russians in 1761, and in 1806–7 withstood the French siege. Formerly German, Kolberg came under Poland in August, 1945. Pop. (1946) 2,816.

KOLDING, town and seaport, Denmark, in Vejle County, on the SE coast of Jutland at the mouth of the Kolding River, 13 miles SW of Frederica. Notable are the ruins of Koldinghus, a castle founded in 1248, whose north wing contains a museum; and a 13th century stone church, the oldest in Denmark. Its harbor, located on Koldingfjord, an inlet of the Little Belt, is ice-free and does a flourishing trade in cattle, dairy products, grain, and fish. Pop. (1945) 27,660.

KOLHAPUR, former feudatory state, India, now merged with the Province of Bombay, largest state of the former Kolhapur and Deccan States Agency; area 3,219 sq. mi.; pop. (1941) 1,092,046. Kolhapur extends eastward from the heart of the Western Ghats into the Deccan plain. Along the spurs of the Ghats there are wild hills and valleys where the only production is timber. One-tenth of the state is reserved forest. The eastern part is a well cultivated plain watered by occasional rivers. The chief crops are rice, millet, tobacco, oilseeds, and cotton; there are manufactures of coarse cotton and woolen goods, sugar, oilseeds, pottery, and hardware. Bauxite is found in the mountains of the western part; iron ore is also found, but it is not worked.

As a feudatory state, Kolhapur had a legislative assembly of 51 members, of whom 4 were *ex officio* members of the executive council, 6 nominated officials, 7 nominated nonofficials, 25 elected, and 9 other nominated members. The state paid no tribute. The capital was KOLHAPUR. The ruling family were descendants of Shivaji, founder of the Mahratta empire. The British sent expeditions to curb piracy in the state in 1765 and 1792. Claiming mismanagement, the British early in the 19th century appointed an officer to manage the state. In 1947 Kolhapur became a part of India, and in 1949 merged with the province of Bombay.   C. S.

KOLHAPUR, city, India, capital of the former state of Kolhapur, 97 miles W of Bijapur. Kolhapur has the remains of several Buddhist shrines dating from the third century B.C. There are a number of fine public buildings and manufactures of pottery, lace, paper, and textiles. Pop. (1941) 93,032.

KOLHAPUR AND DECCAN STATES AGENCY, India, a former agency within the political boundaries of Bombay Province; it was made up of 6 salute, 11 nonsalute states, and 1 estate. The chief state was KOLHAPUR, whose capital (Kolhapur) was the headquarters for the Indian government agent. In 1948 all states of the agency except Kolhapur were merged into the province of Bombay.

KOLIN, town, Czechoslovakia, E Bohemia, on the Elbe River; 38 miles E of Prague (Praha). It is situated in a rich agricultural area. Sugar beets, the chief crop, make Kolin the center of the Bohemian sugar refining industry. Kolin also has flour mills, breweries, and manufactures of starch, chemicals, farm machinery, sirup, and spirits. Here, on June 18, 1757, Frederick the Great was defeated by the Austrians, under Marshal Daun. The town was annexed in 1939 by the Germans and captured in 1944 by the Soviet army. Pop. (1948) 19,820.

KOLLAR, JAN, 1793–1852, Czech poet, was born in Hungary. His writings, imbued with nationalistic fervor, were an impetus to the Panslavic literary movement. *Daughter of Slavia* (1824), a sonnet cycle, is his most important work. He also edited several collections of folk songs.

KÖLLIKER, ALBERT VON, 1817–1905, German-Swiss anatomist, was born in Zürich, studied at the universities of Berlin and Heidelberg, and was professor of anatomy at the University of Würzburg (1847–1902). As a pioneer in cytology he was the first to show that the ovum is fertilized by a spermatozoon originating in the testicular cells. He also developed a theory of the mechanism of the generative process and was a forerunner of the modern geneticists in regarding the nuclei of the ovum and spermatozoon as the carriers of inherited characters. In 1861 he published the first work on comparative embryology, *Entwicklungsgeschichte des Menschen und der höhern Tiere.* His *Handbuch der Gewebelehre des Menschen* (1852) was the first formal textbook on human histology. He helped edit the *Zeitschrift für wissenschaftliche Zoologie* for almost half a century after its founding in 1849.

KOLMAR. See COLMAR.

KÖLN. See COLOGNE.

KOLOMNA, town, U.S.S.R., the Russian Soviet Federated Socialist Republic, in Moscow Region, at the confluence of the Moscow and Oka rivers, 60 miles SE of the city of Moscow. Kolomna is the seat of a Greek orthodox bishop and has a 14th century church, as well as a beautiful cathedral and the ruins of the fortified kremlin. The town has a huge machine-building plant, founded in 1863, and enlarged by the Soviets, which produces Diesels, trolley cars, and locomotives. There are also shipyards, a phonograph plant, cement and lime works, meat packing plants, and mills. The celebrated marmalade called "pastilla" is made here. Pop. (1951 est.) 100,000.

KOLOMYYA, Polish **Kolomyja,** town, U.S.S.R., in the Ukrainian Soviet Socialist Republic, on the Prut River, 122 miles SE of Lvov. It has petroleum, ceramic, chemical, and textile industries, and a large agricultural trade. An ancient town, Kolomyya was ravaged in the 15th and 16th centuries by incursions of Moldavians and Tartars. In World War I it was bitterly contested by Russian and Austro-Hungarian forces. Prior to 1920 it was an Austrian possession in East Galicia. From 1920 to August, 1945, Kolomyya was Polish. Pop. (1950 est.) 40,000.

KOLOZSVAR. See CLUJ.

KOLYMA RIVER, U.S.S.R., the Russian Soviet Federated Socialist Republic, rises in Khabarovsk Territory, W of the Kolymski Mountains, flows north, and after an abrupt westward turn enters the Yakut Autonomous Soviet Socialist Republic to flow north until it empties into the Kolymski Gulf of the Arctic Ocean. The entire course of the Kolyma River is more than 1,000 miles. Its upper reaches have extensive gold deposits. The Omolon is one of the Kolyma's tributaries.

KOMANDORSKIE OSTROVA. See COMMANDER ISLANDS.

KOMÁRNO, German **Komorn,** Hungarian **Komárom,** town, S central Czechoslovakia, on the left bank of the Danube 65 miles NE of Budapest, Hungary. Because of its strategic location, it has become an important industrial and commercial center, with a flourishing trade in wine, wood, and grain. Komárno's history is one of conflict: it successfully resisted the Turks in 1594 and 1663, made a stubborn but unsuccessful resistance to the Austrians in the 1848–49 revolution, and, following World War I, was awarded to Czechoslovakia in 1921. In November, 1938, it was given to Hungary by an Italian-German agreement, but reverted to Czechoslovakia upon the collapse of the Nazi regime in 1945. Pop. (1947) 17,465.

KOMI AUTONOMOUS SOVIET SOCIALIST REPUBLIC, U.S.S.R., in the Russian Soviet Federated Socialist Republic; bounded on the W by Archangel Region, on the N by the Nenets National District of Archangel Region, on the E by the Urals, and on the S by the Region of Kirov and Molotov and the Komi-Permyak National District of Molotov Region; area 144,711 sq. mi.; pop. (1950 est.) 450,000, including Komi 92.3 per cent, Russians 6.1 per cent. The chief ethnic strain of the inhabitants is Finno-Ugrian. The Komi were formerly known as Ziryans.

A large part of the republic is situated above the Arctic Circle; a vast tundra region, it is rich in wild life, including arctic fox and hare, reindeer, wolf, and ermine. Almost two-thirds of the republic is covered by extensive tracts of coniferous forest, abounding in fur-bearing animals and birds. Komi winters are long and severe, with the temperature sometimes dropping as low as 50° below zero F. In the summer months of July and August the temperature rises to an average of 70° F., bringing with it luxuriant vegetation. Komi is unusually rich in mineral resources, including huge deposits of coal (Pechora Coal Basin) estimated at 100 billion tons, and in oil, iron ore, manganese, and many other important minerals. During World War II the completion of the Northern Pechora Railroad (746 miles) gave impetus to Komi coal production, making possible a continuous supply of coal to many northern cities, including Leningrad. Agriculture, largely mechanized since 1936, has made rapid progress. Grains, hemp, flax, and potatoes are grown. Timber is by far the largest export crop of the area. Livestock breeding is increasing, particularly horses and cows. The Komi Autonomous Soviet Socialist Republic was formed in 1936. Komi has a branch of the U.S.S.R. Academy of Sciences. The capital of the republic is Syktyvkar.   A. M. K.

KOMI-PERMYAK NATIONAL DISTRICT, U.S.S.R., in the Russian Soviet Federated Socialist Republic; bounded on the N by the Komi Autonomous Soviet Socialist Republic and on the W by Kirov Region, and enclosed on the E and S by Molotov Region; area 8,916 sq. mi.; pop. (1951 est.) 201,000. The majority of the natives are Finno-Ugrian. The district was created in 1925, the first of the national districts which constitute the lowest major type of autonomous unit in the Soviet Union. The capital of the Komi-Permyak National District is Kudymkar.

KOMOTAU, or **Chomutov,** town, NW Czechoslovakia, in the province of Bohemia, at the S foot of the Erzegebirge, 79 miles by rail NW of Prague (Praha). It has lignite mines, distilleries, breweries, vinegar works, railroad shops, and manufactures of woolen and linen textiles and paper. Pop. (1947) 30,806.

KOMPONGCHAM, town, French Indochina, Cambodia, on the Mekong River, 50 miles NE of Pnompenh and 120 miles NW of Saigon. It is in the center of a rubber cultivating region.

KOMSOMOLSK, city, U.S.S.R., the Russian Soviet Federated Socialist Republic, in Khabarovsk Territory, situated on the lower reaches of the Amur River and at the junction of strategic railroads and highways. A major industrial center, Komsomolsk has the largest steel mills and shipbuilding yards in the Soviet Far East. Other industrial establishments of the city include a cement mill and building-stone plant, petroleum refinery, plants manufacturing gas-generator engines and storage batteries; a cellulose, paper, and pulp mill; brick works; railway repair shops; ship repairing yards; sawmills; a sugar refinery; a fish cannery; and machine-building plants. The city was built in the 1930's on the site of a fishing village by the Komsomol—the Communist League of Youth. It was once inhabited to the extent of 70 per cent by young people. Pop. (1951 est.) 150,000.

KONAKRY. See CONAKRY.

KONEV, IVAN STEPANOVICH, 1895–   , Soviet marshal of World War II. A peasant's son, he rose in the Red army from the ranks. In 1941–44 he commanded troops fighting the Nazis in the Ukraine and southern Poland. In the spring of 1945 his forces liberated Prague and captured Berlin together with Marshal Zhukov's troops. Konev's armies were the first to make junction with U.S. troops—with the American First Army in April, 1945. Commander of Soviet occupation troops in Austria (1945), Konev became commander in chief of the Soviet army in 1946 and was also identified as supreme commander of East European satellite forces in 1951. ALBERT PARRY

KONG, inland town, French West Africa, NW Ivory Coast Colony, 260 miles NNW of Abidjan, capital of the colony. It was reached by Capt. L. E. Binger in 1888 when it was an important trading center for the natives of the surrounding region. Although less important since, Kong still handles trade in cloth and gold. Pop. about 15,000.

KONIEH. See KONYA.

KÖNIG, FRIEDRICH, 1774–1833, German printer and inventor, was born in Eisleben. During 1809–10 he developed a hand-turned printing press incorporating a reciprocal cylinder which rolled the paper upon the inked type placed on a flat platen. A year later he applied steam power to this type of press, which was then capable of printing 1,100 copies of a newspaper in an hour. The first steam-cylinder presses were installed by the *London Times* in 1814. In 1818 König established in Oberzell, near Würzburg, a printing-press factory which became known throughout Europe.

KÖNIGGRÄTZ. See HRADEC KRÁLOVÉ.

KÖNIGSBERG, Russian **Kaliningrad,** port and fortress city, U.S.S.R., in the Russian Soviet Federated Socialist Republic, on the Pregel River, four-and-one-half miles from the NE end of Frisches Haff, and 25 miles from the Baltic Sea with which it is connected by the Königsberg Canal (1894–1901) to Pillay, its outer port. The Pregel flowing westward through the city, divides itself into the Old and New Pregel. Between the two portions of the river is situated Kneiphof Island, the center of the city, which contains the 14th-century Gothic cathedral. The Old Town lies to the north of the island and contains the castle, which was once the headquarters of the grand master of the Teutonic Knights, and from 1525 to 1618 the residence of the dukes of Prussia. Löbenicht, another old section of the city, lies to the east of the Old Town. Other features of the city are the Albertus University (founded in 1544; completed in 1862), with an observatory and a botanical garden, and the palace chapel where Frederick I crowned himself king of Prussia (1701) and in which William I was crowned (1861). Immanuel Kant, greatest of German philosophers, was born in Königsberg, and taught at the university.

Local industries produce locomotives, ships, chemicals, machinery, books, amber products, pianos, flour, beer, wood, and vinegar. There are exports of grain, livestock, wood, flax, flour, chemicals, and textiles. Pop. (1950 est.) 150,000.

History. Königsberg was originally a fortress established by the Knights of the Teutonic Order in 1255. It was named in honor of King Ottokar II of Bohemia. The fortress was razed in 1258, and reestablished as a town in 1286, soon to be followed by the companion communities of Löbenicht and Kneiphof.

Harbor of Königsberg, now Russian Kaliningrad, on the Pregel River. This is a prewar view of city

EWING GALLOWAY

Königshütte

In 1724 all three communities were united. In 1340 it joined the Hanseatic League. In the 19th century Königsberg was made into a powerful fortress city. It was occupied by the Russians in 1758 and in 1806 by the French. In World War I it was threatened by the Russian invasion of East Prussia in August, 1914. In World War II the all-out assault on Königsberg by the Soviet army began on April 8, 1945; it was captured two days later, with 42,000 men surrendering to the Soviets. The city was severely damaged in the the fighting, but reconstruction was begun soon after its capture. Formerly the capital of the Prussian province of East Prussia, Königsberg was awarded to the Soviet Union in August, 1945, and renamed by the Soviets in July, 1946.　　　　A. M. K.

KÖNIGSHÜTTE. See KRÓLEWSKA HUTA.

KÖNIGSMARK, PHILIPP CHRISTOPH, COUNT, 1662–94, Swedish army officer, entered the service of the Elector of Hanover, was accused of an intrigue with Sophia Dorothea, wife of George of Hanover (afterward George I of England), and is supposed to have been assassinated on the discovery of the affair.

Countess Marie Aurora Königsmark, d. 1728, his sister, was mistress of Augustus II, elector of Saxony, and mother of Maurice of Saxony.

KÖNIGSSEE, a lake, Germany in Upper Bavaria, two and one-half miles above Berchtesgaden, at an altitude of 2,000 feet. It is shut in by rocky mountain walls 4,500 feet high, is 17 miles in circuit, and 610 feet deep.

KONITSA, town, Greece, in Epirus, in the department of Ioánnina, situated in the high basin of the Pindus Mountains formed by the Voyutsa River, about 12 miles from the Albanian border and 30 miles NW of Ioánnina. The town is isolated, with little means of modern transportation, although it has connection by motor road with Ioánnina and also with interior Albania. It was the scene of several battles between government and guerrilla troops in the general fighting taking place along the Albanian frontier during 1947 and 1948.

KONIYA. See KONYA.

KONKAN, a maritime tract along the coast of the Indian Ocean, India, Bombay Province, extending W to the Western Ghats, and taking in the Bombay districts of Thana, Kalaba, and Ratnagiri, and the feudatory states of Jawhar, Janjira, and Sawantwadi. The country is generally level and fertile, and produces rice, coconuts, and millet. Until about 1812, when they were forcibly stopped, Konkan was the abode of pirates plying against coastwise ships.

KONOYE, FUMIMARO, PRINCE, 1891–1945, Japanese statesman, was the son of Prince Atsumaro Konoye and protégé of Prince Saionji. He studied at Kyoto Imperial University and was graduated from law school in 1917. In 1919 he attended the Paris Peace Conference and, after several years in the home ministry and as a member of the House of Peers, he became president of that body in 1933. He was appointed premier (1937–39) and again in 1940 following Yonai's resignation. In 1941 he resigned and formed a new cabinet which lasted but three months. He was ordered arrested as a suspected war criminal Dec. 6, 1945, but on December 16 he committed suicide rather than surrender.

KONRAD. See CONRAD.

KONSTANTINOVKA, city, U.S.S.R., in the Ukrainian Soviet Socialist Republic. The city is situated in the Donets coal basin near rich deposits of phosphates. Chemical and metal works, a zinc plant, glass factories, and the manufacture of leather and ceramic goods are the principal industries of Konstantinovka. The University of Kharkov has a branch here. Konstantinovka and its industries were wrecked by the German invaders in World War II. Pop. (1950 est.) 100,000.

KONSTANZ, or **Constance,** city, Germany, in the state of Baden, lies at the NW extremity of Lake Con-

BRITISH COMBINE

Konya, Iconium of ancient days, contains many beautiful mosques. This is the Cifteminareler mosque

stance, where the Rhine flows from that body of water; 89 miles E of Basel (Bâle). The city contains many interesting old buildings, among which is the Münster, begun in the 11th century and altered in the 15th and 17th centuries; the Church of St. Stephen (15th century); Wessenberg Haus, containing the public library and picture gallery; the Kaufhaus (14th century), now a restaurant; the Rathhaus, containing the archives of the city; Hotel Barbarossa, in which Frederick I signed the peace with the Lombards (1183); the Rosgarten, once the guild house of the butchers; and the Dominican Monastery, in which Huss was imprisoned. John Huss and Jerome were burned for heresy here in 1415 and 1416. Constance dates from the third century. It was made subject to Austria in 1548, and in 1815 became a part of Baden. The chief industries are textile factories, iron works, chemical works, and carpet weaving. Pop. (1946) 39,323.

KONTI, ISIDORE, 1862–1938, American sculptor, was born in Vienna, Austria. He studied at the Imperial Academy of Art in Vienna, spent some years in Italy, came to America in 1890. A number of groups for the Columbian Exposition at Chicago (1893) assured his reputation as an artist of great ability. These were followed by "The Despotic Age," in the St. Louis Art Museum; the "Edward Beagle" and "Kit Carson" monuments in Washington (National Museum); "West Indies" for the Dewey arch in New York City; four groups for the Pan-American Exposition in Buffalo (1901); the two cascades for the great fountain at the St. Louis Exposition (1904); "Justinian the Great," "Alfred the Great"; a relief and a group—"South America" for the Pan-American Building in Washington and the McKinley monument in Philadelphia.

KONYA, also **Koniya,** or **Konieh,** vilayet, S central Turkey, bounded on the N by Ankara (Angora), E by Kirsehir and Nigde, SE by Içel, SW by Antalya, W by Isparta and Afyon Karahisar, NW by Eskisehir; area 500,000 sq. mi.; pop. (1945) 667,268. Part of the Taurus (Toros Daglari) mountain range, with peaks rising to heights of 4,000 to 5,000 feet, and the greater part of the Great Central Steppe (Konya Ovasi) are included in this vilayet. Though it is drained by several small streams, including the Çarşamba and the Buzakci, the lakes—Beyşehir, Akşehir, Çavuşcu, Tuz, Sugla, Tuzlu, Tersishan, and Ak—are depended upon for irrigation. The people are mostly engaged in agriculture, raising wheat and other cereal grains. The vast orchards of the vilayet produce citrus fruits, large golden plums, and apricots. Sheep, goats, and cattle are grazed in the highlands. Industries are carpet weaving and the manufacture of cotton, woolen, and silk textiles. Exports are salt, mercury, chrome ore, gold, medicinal opium, raw cotton, cereal grains, raw wool, and livestock. The capital and chief manufacturing center is KONYA. Karaman is also a woolen textiles manufacturing town.

KONYA, also **Koniya,** or **Konieh,** town, S central Turkey, capital of Konya Vilayet; 143 miles S of Turkey's capital city, Ankara. Built at an altitude of 3,320 feet, Konya is situated at the southwestern edge of the Great Central Steppe, in the midst of orchards known since the Middle Ages for their luscious fruits. It is an important rail and highway station connected with Baghdad and Barra (Iraq) and Istanbul. One of its many beautiful mosques contains the tomb reputed to be that of the founder of the whirling dervishes. Other noteworthy buildings are an ancient Byzantine church, massive government offices, called Konaks, and the remains of the palace of Sultan Ala-eddin, who reigned 1219–1236. The town is commercially important, controlling the trade of an extensive area. Grains, salt, fruits (fresh and dried), woolen goods, carpets and rugs, and colored leather goods are exported. From the capture of Nicaea by the Crusaders (1097) down to the time of Genghis Khan, Konya—called in ancient days ICONIUM—was the capital of the Seljuk (Turkish) sultans. Paul and Barnabas, on their first missionary journey, preached here, according to Acts 13:51. It is the seat of a Greek archbishop. Pop. (1945) 58,834.

KOOMASSIE. See KUMASI.

KOOMISS. See KUMISS.

KOORINGA. See BURRA.

KOOTENAY, or **KUTENAI INDIANS,** a distinct linguistic stock of North American Indians, comprising the Kitunahan family, living in the southeastern corner of British Columbia, the northern part of Idaho, and the northwestern corner of Montana. They formerly lived east of the Rocky Mountains but were driven westward by their traditional enemies, the Blackfeet, some time before the coming of the white men. In recent years, however, these two groups have been on friendly terms. There are two tribes, the Upper and Lower Kootenay; the latter were the more primitive and nomadic, relying on fish for food and canoes for transportation. They had a simple social system without clans or castes. There was no chief for the whole tribe, but each band had its own leader, originally hereditary. They lived at peace with the incoming white settlers, and have since made a good adjustment to civilization. They are noted for

Kootenay National Park extends along the Banff Windermere Highway. This is rugged Sinclair Canyon

BRITISH COLUMBIA TRAVEL BUREAU

their intelligence, morality, and hospitality. They number about 1,000, divided almost equally between the United States and Canada. In the United States a group resides on the Flatheed Reservation in Montana and another group in northern Idaho. See INDIANS, AMERICAN.

KOOTENAY LAKE, Canada, in the province of British Columbia, in Kootenay District, lying between the Purcell and Selkirk mountains. Irregular in shape, the lake is about 60 miles long and from one to four miles wide, having an area of 191 square miles. Kootenay Lake receives the waters of the KOOTENAY RIVER and empties into the COLUMBIA RIVER.

KOOTENAY NATIONAL PARK, W Canada, in SE British Columbia, extends for a width of about five miles on each side of the Banff-Windermere Highway for a distance of 60 miles, preserving the beauty and the wild life along this scenic roadway. Features of the park are Radium Hot Springs, rugged canyons, scenic waterfalls, and a lake fed by icebergs. The park was established in 1920 and contains an area of 587 square miles.

KOOTENAY RIVER, Canada, in the province of British Columbia, rises in the Rocky Mountains, and flows at first S, nearly parallel to the Columbia River; then makes a loop into Montana and Idaho, recrosses the Canadian boundary, flows through Kootenay Lake, and joins the Columbia after a course of 400 miles. Throughout its basin gold is found, and there are rich deposits of iron. Its navigation is obstructed by rapids. The United States portion of the river is spelled Kootenai.

KOPAIS. See COPAIS.

KOPPARBERG, county, Sweden, bounded by the counties of Jämtland on the N, Gävleborg on the E, Värmland, Örebro, and Västmanland on the S, and the Norwegian frontier on the E; area 11,649 sq. mi.; pop. (1949 est.) 260,472. The surface slopes from an altitude of 3,000 feet in the northwest to the lowlands of the southeast; a great part is forested in conifers. The Dal River flows through the county from the northwest to Lake Syljan and then southeast into Gävleborg, joined by the Vaster Dal south of Syljan. Agriculture is concentrated mainly in the Syljan region and along the river valleys; forage crops and cereals are grown and dairy farming carried on. FALUN, the capital, once the center of the Swedish copper industry, has iron and pyrite mines, iron foundries, and the manufacture of railway rolling stock. Other industries include iron and steel works in the Grangesberg mining district and lumber, pulp, and paper mills at Domnarvet and other places. The region of Lake Syljan is a popular summer resort.

KÖPRÜLÜ. See VELES.

KOPTOS. See KUFT.

KORAN, the sacred book of Islam, is made up of revelations which its founder, MOHAMMED, professed to have received from time to time direct from God, and which were compiled after his death by his secretary Zair-ibn-Thabit, who was commissioned to perform the task by Abu Bekr, the first caliph. About 17 years later Othman, the third caliph, had the text carefully revised, and put forth the edition which has been used ever since. See MOHAMMEDANISM.

The Koran is written in Arabic and consists of 114 suras, or chapters, which vary in length from a few lines to many verses. In the earliest compositions we discover the fragmentary impassioned utterances of an embryo prophet—appeals to his countrymen to return to the worship of God, "the Compassionate, the Merciful." In the second group the unity of the God-head is proclaimed, idolatry is denounced, and vivid pictures are drawn of judgment, of heaven, and of hell. In the third group Mohammed lays stress on the divine character of his mission. In the next group —Mecca suras—we find a militant Islam appealing to the arbitrament of the sword. Finally, in the Medina suras, we have Islam triumphant; fasts, festivals, and the pilgrimage to Mecca are instituted, and the slaughter of all "infidels" is authorized. The style is difficult and the meaning is often obscure; but there are passages of surpassing power and grandeur, of true poetry, and of lofty moral teaching.

KORAT, or **Khorat.** See NAKHON RATCHASIMA.

KORCE. See CORIZZA.

KORCULA, in Italian **Curzola,** island in Yugoslavia, situated in the Adriatic Sea off the coast of Dalmatia, between the islands of Mjlet and Havar; area about 100 sq. mi.; pop. (1948) 25,860. Its surface is mountainous, but grapes, olives, and almonds are grown. Slate and limestone are quarried, and boatbuilding and fishing are carried on. Its varied history has included domination by many different peoples, Austria being the last before the creation of Yugoslavia in 1918. The capital, Korčula (pop. 2,000), ancient Corcyra Nigra, is on the north coast of the island, with houses mostly built of marble and a fine Gothic cathedral. Here, in 1298, the Genoese took Andrea Dandolo and the traveler Marco Polo prisoner. In World War II the city was occupied by the Italians.

KORDA, Sir ALEXANDER, 1893–   , British motion picture producer and industrialist, was born in Turkeve, Hungary, and educated at the Royal University, Budapest. Losing interest in his intended journalistic profession in 1915, he entered Hungary's motion picture industry. He established himself internationally by writing and directing pictures in several European capitals and in Hollywood. In 1932 he aided in organizing, and became chairman and managing director of, London Film Productions, Limited, which released such popular films as *The Private Life of Henry VIII, Catherine the Great*, and *The Scarlet Pimpernel*. After associating himself with several Hollywood firms from 1935, he founded Alexander Korda Films there in 1940. He again allied himself with British films in 1946, by organizing the new and independent London Film Productions.

KORDOFAN, province, N central Africa, Anglo-Egyptian Sudan, lying between the provinces of Darfur and White Nile; area 130,000 sq. mi.; pop. about 1,300,000. It is generally a low, barren, rolling desert, punctuated only by isolated hills, the chief of which, the Dar Nuba in the south central part of the province, reaches a maximum elevation of 4,760 feet. Although its eastern border skirts the Nile River at an average distance of 25 miles, the irrigation in Kordofan is poor (consisting mainly of intermittent streams which flow only during the summer rain season) and drainage is inadequate, resulting in an abundance of swamps. The water table is at from 50 to 200 feet, but the shallow wells sunk by the natives yield only enough water for drinking purposes. Located between latitudes 10° and 15° N, Kordofan records temperatures no higher than 105° F. Wild fauna include the elephant, rhinoceros, lion, giraffe, buffalo, cheetah, leopard, and several species of antelope. The natives use oxen and camels for domestic purposes.

Kordofan is peopled chiefly by Arabs and Nubas; the former are nomadic and deal in cattle and camels; the latter are more settled and tend to live in villages. The Arabs live in huts made of mud, wattles and stones, while the Nubas build structures of mud and brick. A small amount of gold dust, iron, and hematite is found. The chief product of the province is gum arabic, found in both northern and southern parts of the region. Peanuts, cotton, tobacco, millet, and watermelon are the secondary agricultural products, and in the northwest part of the province date palms are found. The capital of Kordofan, El Obeid, is linked by rail with Khartoum and is a center of the road network which spans the province. Egypt took control of the province in 1821 but a revolt led by Mohammed Ahmed in 1882 gave Kordofan independence until only 1899, when it came under the newly created Anglo-Egyptian Sudan.   G. A.

U.S. ARMY SIGNAL CORPS

After World War II this ancient Asian country emerged into international affairs as a major strategic region

KOREA, or **Chosen,** an ancient country consisting of a large peninsula projecting S from the E central seaboard of Asia, and situated between Japan to the E, China to the W, and Manchuria and Asiatic Russia to the N, in one of the world's most strategic positions; it is bounded on the N by Manchuria and at the NE tip by Russia, E by the Sea of Japan (Nippon-kai), S by Korea and Cheju (Quelpart) Straits, W by the Yellow Sea (Hwang Hai) and NW by Korea Bay; area, 85,246 sq. mi.; pop. (U.S.D.S. 1946 est.) 27,900,000. The peninsula is separated from Manchuria by the YALU RIVER flowing west into Korea Bay and the Tumen River flowing east into the Sea of Japan; the Tumen, in the last 10 miles of its course, separates Korea from Siberia.

PHYSICAL FEATURES

The peninsula constituted about one third of the area of the Japanese Empire before World War II. Its length is approximately 600 miles from north to south, and its average width is 140 miles. The coast line has a circuit of some 1,700 miles. The east coast has few indentations, and sweeps down from the north in a tremendous inward curve forming a gulf sometimes called the Gulf of Korea; this is directly across the peninsula from Korea Bay. There are few good harbors on the east side. The west and south coasts are liberally indented, with multitudes of small peninsulas and islands of varying sizes, and many good harbors. Korea's largest island, rocky Cheju (known to Occidentals as QUELPART), of volcanic origin, lies about 70 miles off the south coast; some 280,000 Koreans live on its gale-swept area of 700 square miles. The peninsula's tidal rise and fall presents striking contrasts; it is 30 feet at Chemulpo (Jinsen) Bay in the west, six feet at Fusan on the south coast, and one foot at Wonsan (Genzan) in the east.

Mountains. A series of great mountain ranges and plateaus extends from the far northeast to the south coast, dominating the eastern half of the peninsula. In the north, one of these ranges connects with the lofty CHANG PAI SHAN (Long White) range across the frontier of Manchuria. At the junction stands Mount Paik-tu (White Head), an 8,993-foot peak that has been sacred to uncounted tribes since the earliest times and about which many legends have gathered. In this mountain, amid scenes of wild beauty, rise the Yalu and Tumen rivers, within a short distance of each other. The peak thus stands at the head of two great valleys, one stretching west and southwest to the Yellow Sea, and the other northeast and east to the Sea of Japan, through which runs the modern Korea-Manchuria boundary. The primeval forests of the Changpai Shan region have long been a refuge of borderland bandits. On the east coast, midway between north and south and about 50 miles southeast of Wonsan, stands the cluster of peaks called Keumkang, or Diamond Mountain, better known among world travelers as Kongo-zan, the Japanese version of the name. The scenery here is among the most magnificent in the world, and venerable Buddhist monasteries form part of the impressiveness of the region. The average height of the peaks is about 5,000 feet. Spur chains stretch across the peninsula from the main range in the east, in several places, especially in the northwest and south, where they reach the sea. The Korean peaks stand from 3,000 and 4,000 feet to over 8,000 feet above sea level, and there are many of 6,000 and 7,000 feet.

Rivers. Among the numerous rivers rising in the Korean mountains, the Tumen, about 200 miles long, is the only one of importance flowing into the Sea of Japan; the others are short coastal streams. The many flowing west and south, however, include several large rivers. The Yalu (Korean Amnok or Apnok; Japanese Oryokko), which is about 500 miles in length and reaches Korea Bay at Yongampo, is the longest in the peninsula. Also in the northwest, the Taidong (Tatong or Daido-ko), about 170 miles long, passes the ancient city of Pyongyang into Korea Bay at Chinnampo. In the center of the peninsula the historic Han, whose main stream is about 120 miles long, flows through the capital, Seoul, into the Yellow Sea

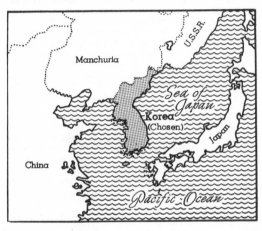

Location map of Korea

at Chemulpo. In the south the Naktong (Rakuto), some 170 miles in length, empties into Korea Strait near Fusan. Other large rivers include the Siemjin (Senshin), Keum (Kin-ko), and Chingchong (Seisenko). All these rivers are navigable for boat traffic for varying distances, and are important transportation routes. Korea has no lakes of any size.

The western half of the peninsula consists largely of vast, undulating, agricultural lands. These plains spread from the mountains, through the river valleys, westward to the Yellow Sea, and are studded with populous cities, towns, and farming communities. Generally they are fertile, especially in the south and north. The valleys are separated by irregular hill ranges.

Climate. The peninsula has a north temperate continental climate, moderated especially from the central region to the south, by its position between the two seas. A branch of the Black Current (Kuroshiwo, or Japan Current) adds mildness along the southwestern seaboard. The climate is generally healthful and invigorating, and is delightful in spring. In winter it is quite cold, especially in the north, where there is a heavy snowfall and the Yalu and Tumen are frozen for four or five months, while the Han is usually frozen for about two months. In the south the snowfall is light. It is hot and somewhat

rainy in summer; there is considerable humidity in midsummer. Rather strong northwesterly winds blow across the peninsula in winter, reversing to temperate southeasterly winds in summer.

PEOPLE

The Korean people, the story of whose origin is partially revealed by myths and legends, are a composite of aboriginal Ainu with peoples who migrated from Manchuria, Mongolia, and China, as well as some Japanese and Malayans. Twenty centuries or more ago there was much interchange between Korea and western Honshu and Kyushu in Japan; Japanese of high rank and their followers emigrated to Korea, while many Koreans, some as emigrants and some as prisoners, went to Japan, in some cases founding noble families. Present day Koreans are of good physique, medium to tall in height, with straight black hair, brown skin, and the Tungusic features common to northeast Asian peoples.

The Korean language is surmised to be of Tungusic or Ural-Altaic origin. It resembles Japanese in both syntax and pronunciation, and the Korean, Japanese, and Ryukyu languages belong to the same group. Like Japanese, the Korean spoken language bears little resemblance to the Chinese; but like both Chinese and Japanese, the Koreans use the same ideographs for their written language. This is supplemented by a phonetic alphabet, called unmun, invented by Korean scholars in the 15th century, in much the same way that the Japanese use their kana phonetic syllabary.

Living Conditions. The staple food of the Koreans is rice, with vegetables, highly seasoned meat and fish, fruit, and cakes of various kinds. Honey is much used. The Korean pickle jar is famous. Semi-delicacies include roast duck and, as with the Japanese, raw fish. Their dress is somewhat like that of the Chinese, generally a jacket or shirt, baggy trousers, or skirts, various over-garments, and slipper-like shoes—some with high tops—for both sexes. White is the prevailing color. The men are noted for their broad brimmed hats with smallish crowns, and their long tobacco pipes. Korean dwellings are generally one-storied, ranging from the luxurious tiled houses of the rich to the thatched huts, usually small, of the lower classes. Characteristic is the under-floor heating, contrived centuries before American central heating; the system, called ondol, consists of a kind of furnace from which hot air and smoke flow through passages under the floor.

Population. The Koreans are prolific; the peninsula's population in 1910 was 12,934,282; in 1940 it had jumped to 24,326,327. In 1949, before the start of open warfare in Korea, it was estimated that the total population was 29,291,000.

The capital is SEOUL (Keijo, pop. 1,141,766), a walled city founded in the 14th century, on the Han

A small Korean farm village near Seoul

Korean boys study wireless code in school

River, near the coast in the west central part of the peninsula; near Seoul is Kimkokri, a royal burial place. Seoul's port is CHEMULPO (Inchon or Jinsen, 215,784). Other important cities are Pyongyang (HEIJO, 285,965), capital of North Korea, on the Taidong River; CHINNAMPO, port for Pyongyang; Fusan (400,156), on Korea Strait, the country's chief seaport; Chongjin (SEISHIN, 200,000), port on the northeast coast; TAIKYU (269,113), important commercial and administrative center in the southeast.

Religion. Superficially Buddhism is the religion of Korea, and throughout the country there are many old temples, pagodas, and monasteries with their priesthood—as well as a profusion of other historic structures and objects, such as statues, monuments, towers, royal palaces and tombs, and objects of art. But Buddhism now is only a shadow of the magnificence and power it attained in the Korai era (10th to 14th centuries). Confucianism, also brought from China centuries ago, is still honored among the cultured classes. The religion of the Korean masses is the most ancient of all, indigenous to the country: a kind of animism, the worship of heaven and earth, mixed with superstition. Second strongest is Christianity, which gained a foothold in the mid-19th century, despite massacres of French and other missionaries and Korean adherents. In 1948 the Christian population of Korea was estimated at 666,000, with Presbyterians leading.

Education. The schools and their students, in 1937, comprised: 505 elementary, with 89,831 students; 2,509 common, with 861,389; 16 middle, with 7,778; 27 higher common, with 15,269; 30 girls' high, with 11,924; 22 girls' higher common, with 7,148; 6 normal, with 3,758; 67 business, with 18,264; 116 elementary industrial, 5,942; 15 colleges, 4,250; 1 university preparatory, 448; and the Imperial University of Korea, with 542 students. These figures include schools established by Christian missions.

South Korea in 1948 had 3,415 elementary schools, with 2,708,301 students; 240 middle schools, with 266,784 students; 202 technical schools, with 122,-547 pupils; 18 normal schools, with 14,000 pupils. There were 41 colleges and universities with 21,250 students. An adult education program was introduced in the campaign against illiteracy, which was reduced from 44 per cent in 1947 to 29 per cent in 1948. The whole South Korean educational program was disrupted by the war which began in 1950. An effort was made, however, to continue the program even though the country was swept by destruction.

ECONOMIC LIFE

Agriculture. From time immemorial, Korea has been an agricultural country and rice has been the most important food crop. More than one third of the cultivated land consists of paddy fields, devoted to rice. Other important food crops are wheat, rye, soya and other beans, millet, corn, kaoliang (a kind of

Korea

corn or sorghum), barley, potatoes, a variety of cabbage, green peppers, garlic, and many other vegetables. Large orchard crops include apples, peaches, persimmons, apricots, pears, pinenuts, chestnuts, ginkgo, and walnuts. Cotton and tobacco are other important crops; some hemp and flax are grown. One of the most interesting Korean products is the root of a small plant, ginseng, credited with remarkable tonic and stimulative properties, and popular with the Chinese, who import much of the Korean crop. Honey, of which the Koreans are fond, is extensively produced. Mulberry trees are cultivated, to provide the material for the native paper, and food for silkworms. The cultivated land is about 12,000,000 acres, or about 22 per cent of the total area of Korea, and about 73 per cent of the population are engaged in agricultural and allied pursuits. During the three decades following the annexation of Korea by Japan in 1910, the Japanese made great efforts to increase productivity. This met with much success, in rice, soya beans, cotton, apples, and sericulture.

Partition of the country into North and South Korea also divided the growing areas of the country. Most of the rice and barley lands are located in South Korea; most of the millet, wheat, soybean, and corn area in North Korea. With the help of long summers and heavy rain, two crops a year can be grown in the south; a shorter growing season and less rainfall provide only one crop a year in the north. Despite a drought which reduced rice production in some areas, South Korea achieved self-sufficiency in foodstuffs in 1949. The South Korean government in 1949 enacted a land reform bill for the distribution of farmland to self-tilling farmers. The amount of land affected was estimated at 1,470,000 acres, or nearly 30 per cent of the country's arable land. The beginning of war in 1950 completely altered the picture.

Livestock is scarce in Korea. In 1947 South Korea had 1,400 milch cattle, 640,500 work cattle, 374,000 pigs, and 36,000 work horses, mules, and donkeys.

Minerals. Korea produces nearly all important minerals, in moderate quantities, especially gold. In modern times the gold mines have been worked by foreign concessionaires, chiefly American, British, French, and Japanese, rather than Koreans; the best mine, at Unzan, was operated by an American syndicate. In the prewar decade, Korea's mineral production was valued at about $60,000,000 annually, of which over half was represented by gold. Other minerals include coal, iron, copper, silver, graphite, lead, tungsten, zinc, limestone, alunite, marble and salt. From olden times, Korean artisans have produced the finest brass, seen in utensils and the fittings on the famous cedar chests and cabinets.

Forestry. Through the centuries the Koreans denuded their mountain and other forest lands of trees, especially in the central and southern regions, with the usual results of soil erosion and floods. In the northern mountains and along the upper reaches of the Yalu and Tumen rivers, however, extensive forests remain, which are among the greatest timber resources in the world. Joint Japanese, Korean, and Chinese enterprises have done some exploitation in this region. During the annexation period, much afforestation was carried out. The forestry areas comprise over 70 per cent of the total area of the country. The trees include spruce, birch, larch, pine, oak, alder, maple, and bamboo.

Fisheries. The Korean waters abound in fish. The sardine catch is the largest and most valuable; mackerel, sciaena, Alaska pollack, herring, cutlass fish, and shrimp are also important. Others include sea bream, yellowtail, cod, shark, mullet, and lobster, eel, and some whales. There is also a large edible seaweed crop. Much of the sardine catch is turned into oil and refuse-cake fertilizer. In former times the Koreans paid little attention to fishing, but since 1910 the value of the products of this and allied industries has risen from about $5,000,000 annually

Young Korean athlete

Korean athletes in formation on the Seoul stadium field

Korean woman of Seoul

A ceremonial warrior dance on a traditional Korean holiday

A member of the "yangbans"

The 500-year-old Suwon Gate to the walled city of Seoul

Fusan factory worker

U.S. ARMY SIGNAL CORPS PHOTOS

Long waiting line outside the railroad station at Seoul

Oxcart laden with lumber on way to market

to about $80,000,000. A picturesque feature is the thousands of women divers of Cheju Island, who bring up abalone and other shellfish and edible seaweed.

Manufacturing and Commerce. Industrial manufactures during the prewar decade were valued at about $375,000,000 annually of which the so-called cottage industries, producing a great variety of goods, comprised about one-third. This contrasts with the estimated value of $15,000,000 in 1911. Leading industries are in foodstuffs, chemicals, machinery, tools and metal goods, textiles, printing and bookbinding, ceramics, flour, cement, pig iron, aluminum, fertilizer, yarn and cloth, fish oil, paper, tobacco, and opium and derivatives.

After its incorporation in the Japanese Empire in 1910, when its exports and imports totaled about $25,000,000, Korea's overseas trade was mostly with Japan until Korea achieved independence. Division of the country into North and South Korea directed, North Korean trade toward China and the Soviet Union. In 1949, South Korean exports were valued at $14,334,000, and imports at $138,809,000. The United States was the chief source of imports for South Korea (68 per cent), and Hong Kong was the chief market for exports (63 per cent). Japan occupied second rank as supplier and market. Dried shellfish was the most important export.

Transportation and Communications. The railroads, postoffice (posts, telegraphs, and telephones), highways and radio were operated by, or under the control of, the government general. The peninsula is covered by a network of modern railroads, serving all parts of the country except some mountainous regions in the east and north. In 1940 there were about 3,000 miles of government-owned railroads, and some 1,200 miles of company-operated lines, all of which were built by Japan. In 1949 the South Korean railway network consisted of about 3,600 miles of track. The peninsula has about 17,500 miles of highways, but there are few all-weather routes. The present system, in which the national highways link the chief cities and seaports, was constructed while Korea was under Japanese control. In 1949 South Korea had only 27 miles of paved highway.

Korea formerly had more than 16,300 miles of motorbus routes. In 1939 there were some 106,000 tons of steamships and 45,000 tons of sailing ships. In 1949 South Korea had six freight vessels, supplying weekly passenger service and biweekly freight service to all major ports; some old landing craft (LST) also were in use. There were commercial airports at Pyongyang (North Korea) and Seoul, with international service from the latter.

Korea had a fully-equipped modern postal, telephone, telegraph, and radio system before it was disrupted by the war. In 1949 there were 13 radio stations operating in South Korea.

Korea

ADMINISTRATION

For centuries Korea was a subject kingdom of China. From 1876 the nation established treaty relations with Japan and the Western powers. In 1905 it became a Japanese protectorate and in August, 1910, it was formally annexed by Japan. After the collapse of Japan in 1945, American and Soviet troops entered Korea and for military convenience the country was separated into two portions by the 38th parallel of latitude. Although the Allied nations promised complete independence to Korea after five years of tutelage, American-Soviet negotiations broke down in May, 1946, and the 38th parallel came to separate two distinct zones, having different governments.

In North Korea, the Soviet forces established a Communist provisional government as early as August, 1945. The subsequent Supreme National Assembly proclaimed, in September, 1948, the Korean People's Republic with a constitution that resembled those of the Soviet satellites in Eastern Europe. The government was headed by a president, a prime minister, and a cabinet. The Communist North Korean government was recognized by Soviet Russia which withdrew its armed forces by December, 1948.

Under the auspices of the United Nations, South Korea held an election in May, 1948, for a National Assembly. The Assembly adopted a constitution and elected Syngman Rhee president. The prime minister was to be assisted by a cabinet of eight members. The constitution provided for a National Assembly of 300 members, with seats reserved for Koreans living in the North if and when the region north of the 38th parallel decided to join the South in a united nation. In August, 1948, the Republic of Korea formally came into existence and the American military government ceased. The new nation was recognized by the United States and most other countries not in the Soviet sphere.

HISTORY

The first kingdom of Korea was founded over 42 centuries ago, according to legend, by a leader named Tan-gun, with his capital at Pyongyang. This dynasty is supposed to have lasted 12 centuries, but there is little to indicate what transpired during that period. Stone relics exist, including an altar on Kang-wha Island at the mouth of the Han River, attributed to Tan-gun, and what purports to be his grave near Pyongyang. This kingdom was overthrown by a Chinese leader, Ki-tze (Kii-cha), who established in 1122 B.C., according to Chinese history, a new kingdom that embraced the northwestern part of the peninsula and considerable territory north of the Yalu River, in Manchuria. Ki-tze brought with him several thousand followers, as well as the ideograph and other elements of Chinese civilization. He named the kingdom Chosen (Land of Calm, or Fine, Morning), with the capital, it is surmised, at Pyongyang, where his tomb exists, and his dynasty ruled for nine centuries. Chinese invasion then led to the region's being turned into the prosperous Chinese colony of Lakliang, also with its capital at Pyongyang; this lasted for about two centuries, but thereafter until the 19th century China claimed suzerainty over Korea, sometimes with and sometimes without the Koreans' acquiescence.

Strife Among the Kingdoms. Late in the first century B.C. a people from the Sungari Valley moved in and formed a kingdom which they called Korai (or Kokuli, Kaoli); this was the origin of the westernized name, Korea. At about the same time the kingdoms of Silla in the southeast and Paikche in the southwest were formed from Tungusic tribes who through previous centuries had populated the eastern side of the peninsula and the three Han states (from which arose the term Han, sometimes applied to Korea) that had been settled in the south. Also the small state of Imna (Mimana) had grown up on the

Korea

south coast, where Japanese colonists settled with the tribes there, and which was a Japanese protectorate through the first six centuries after Christ. During the ensuing epoch of 10 centuries there was almost incessant strife among the three kingdoms, first one and then another gaining the ascendancy. In the first half of the period Japan played a dominant role in the affairs of the peninsula, largely due to the celebrated invasion by the Japanese Empress Jingo, herself of royal Korean descent. However, Korean civilization began to flourish, and the advent of Buddhism, from China, into Korea, which in turn passed it on to Japan, was an event of enormous importance to both countries. The Koreans had considerable trade and cultural intercourse with both Japan and China.

Koli and Yi Dynasties. Early in the 10th century the whole peninsula was unified under the Koli dynasty, founded by Wang Kien (or Wang Kon), as the kingdoms of Korai, Paikche and Silla crumbled; the territory beyond the Yalu was lost to the Khitan empire. The capital was at Songdo (Kaijo) in central Korea, not far from the west coast. There was internal peace, and the Korean race was consolidated, with one language. Yi (Li) Taijo overthrew the Koli kingdom in 1392 and established his own, to which he restored the name of Chosen. This Yi dynasty ruled until 1910, when Korea was annexed by Japan; for a short period at the end it was called the Han empire, but Japan again restored the name Chosen.

The Golden Age and After. From the 10th to 15th centuries was Korea's golden age. Buddhism, in the Koli era, became all powerful. Religion, philosophy, and education flourished. Fine porcelains, literature, paintings, sculpture, metal wares, textiles, and architecture as well as the first movable metal type and the first armored warship, were produced. The country suffered terrible invasions by the Mongols, Manchus, and the Japanese under Hideyoshi. From the 16th century a decline set in. Slavery, civil corruption, and poverty prevailed, and the country was shut in until treaties were made with Japan (1876), the United States (1883), and other nations.

Korea Under Japan. In the 19th century Russia began to compete with Japan and China for control of Korea, which led to the China-Japan War (1894–95), the Russo-Japanese War (1904–5) and annexation by Japan (1910). As part of the Japanese Empire until 1945 Korea enjoyed great prosperity, but many of the people were dissatisfied, and her politicians maintained an independence movement in both China and the United States. Occasional disturbances in the peninsula, notably riots in Seoul and other cities in 1919, were harshly suppressed by the Japanese authorities.

World War II. Korea escaped damage in World War II, and the Cairo declaration of 1943 stated that Korea "in due course" should become independent; Russia later adhered to this. Russia, having entered the war against Japan on the eve of the latter's surrender, in 1945, occupied northern Korea down to the 38th parallel; American forces occupied the southern half, including Seoul, under Roosevelt-Truman-Stalin agreements. The United States, Russia, Britain, and China agreed that a trusteeship of Korea should be administered by the United States and Russia while a democratic government of Korea was being established. The American and Soviet commanders, however, could not agree on which Korean political parties should participate in such a government, and a stalemate ensued. An interim Korean assembly was set up in the American zone in December, 1946. At the instance of the United States, the United Nations in 1947 sent a commission to Korea to arrange for national elections and to establish a provisional government for the whole country. Russia refused to permit the commission to enter the Russian zone; in early 1948 the commission admitted failure. In May, 1948, a "People's Republic" was established

U.S. ARMY

In the Korean War Americans and South Koreans teamed up against Communist aggressors

in northern Korea; in August, 1948, the "Democratic Republic of Korea" was established in the American zone. Although the National Assembly in November, 1948, by a vote of 88 to 3 with 117 abstentions, requested that the American troops stay, the forces were withdrawn on June 29, 1949, leaving behind only an advisory mission.

The border between northern and southern Korea became a source of constant friction. This erupted into open warfare on June 25, 1950, when northern Communist forces, led by armored columns, invaded South Korea. The lightly armored southern troops offered only slight opposition as the northern Communist forces swept southward. A cease-fire resolution of the United Nations Security Council was ignored. On June 27, President Truman ordered U.S. air and naval forces under General DOUGLAS MACARTHUR to help South Korea repel the invaders, and also ordered the Navy to prevent invasion of Formosa. On the same day the Security Council voted military sanctions against North Korea, and asked the member states to render assistance to the Republic of Korea. On June 30, President Truman authorized MacArthur to send ground forces to Korea. The Communist advance in South Korea continued in spite of American troops and the warships of the U.S., Australia, and Britain. In July, MacArthur was named U.N. commander of forces fighting the Communist aggressor. A number of nations sent troops to the U.N. forces fighting in Korea. Nevertheless, the troops fighting in South Korea were forced back to a small beachhead. In September the U.N. forces launched a counteroffensive, with an amphibious landing at Inchon, which drove the Communist invaders back. In October, the U.N. forces crossed the 38th parallel and invaded North Korea.

Early in November, U.N. forces launched an offensive designed to destroy all enemy strength north to the Manchurian border. Chinese Communist troops, which had already infiltrated to some extent, then intervened in strength and were able to shatter the main U.N. defense line and compel its forces to retreat. In December, Communist China's spokesmen at the U.N. rejected the U.N. proposal for an immediate cease-fire in Korea. In 1951, the Communist Chinese advance continued; in January the Chinese captured Seoul and drove south. The American forces and their allies pulled out of the city without risking a showdown battle. The Chinese Communists again turned down a U.N. appeal for a cease-fire in Korea. Whereupon the United States demanded that the U.N. condemn Communist China as an aggressor and apply sanctions if necessary. In February, Communist China was formally declared an aggressor in Korea by the U.N. General Assembly in spite of the efforts of conciliatory nations led by India. In the same month the U.N. forces undertook a limited offensive against the Communist forces. They drove to Seoul and stopped a

Communist counteroffensive in central Korea. Subsequently the U.N. forces started a general counteroffensive, which compelled the Communists to retreat. In March, MacArthur declared that the Korean war would reach a stalemate if the U.N. forces continued to fight a half-way war against Communist China. He asked the United Nations governments to make vital decisions in regard to the war in Korea. MacArthur's statement implying that the U.N. might soon attack Communist China proper was sharply criticized. Early in April a letter from MacArthur indorsing use of the Chinese Nationalists to open a second front against the Chinese Communists on the mainland was made public. President Truman—whose policy was opposed to an attack against China proper, the employment of Chinese Nationalist troops, and the permanent defense of Formosa, dismissed MacArthur from all his military posts in the Far East and replaced him by Lt. Gen. MATTHEW B. RIDGWAY.

In late April and again in mid-May, the Communist forces launched offensives. In each case, the drives were soon halted and by June 1, the Communists held little territory south of the 38th parallel. The U.N. General Assembly meanwhile approved an arms embargo against Communist China. Truce negotiations, inaugurated on July 10, proceeded with difficulty because of claims by both sides of violations of the truce neutrality zone, and failure to agree on a truce buffer zone or demarcation line.   G. B. DE H.

BIBLIOG.–H. B. Hulbert, *The History of Korea* (2 vols. 1905); *The Passing of Korea* (1906); J. O. P. Bland, *China, Japan and Korea* (1921); E. Keith and E. K. Robinson, *Old Korea, the Land of Morning Calm* (1924); S. Bergman, *In Korea's Wilds and Villages* (1938); A. J. Grajdanzer, *Korea Looks Ahead* (1944); *Modern Korea* (1946); U. S. Printing Office, *Korea, 1945–1948* (1948); G. M. McCune, A. L. Grey, *Korea Today* (1950); O. G. Tewsbury, *Source Materials on Korean Politics and Ideologies* (1950); G. B. Osgood, *Koreans and Their Culture* (1951).

KORINTHOS. See CORINTH.

KORITSA. See CORIZZA.

KORIYAMA, city, Japan, N Honshu, in Fukushima Prefecture, lying in an intermontane valley 120 miles NNE of Tokyo, 12 miles ESE of the large mountain lake, Inawashiro, and near the confluence of the main rivers of the region. Koriyama has small manufacturing industries and chemical plants. It was heavily bombed by the Americans in World War II. Pop. (1946) 59,609.

KÖRNER, KARL THEODOR, 1791–1813, German poet and patriot, was born at Dresden. When Prussia roused herself against Napoleon in 1813, Körner joined Lützow's *"wilde verwegene Schar,"* or black-uniformed guerrilla troops, and died a patriot's death. He occupied almost a holy place in the hearts of his countrymen by reason of the fiery patriotic songs with which he encouraged his fellow fighters. They were collected in *Leier und Schwert* (1814).

KORNGOLD, ERICH WOLFGANG, 1897–   , American composer, was born in Bruenn, Austria, the son of the music critic, Julius Korngold. A prodigy in music, he was playing the piano at the age of five, and by the age of eleven had composed the widely performed pantomime, *Der Schneeman.* At 16, he composed his first opera, *Der Ring des Polycrates,* followed this a year later with the opera, *Violanta,* and at the age of 22 produced his most important opera, *The Dead City.* He went to Hollywood in 1936 and wrote the music for many important movies. He won Academy Awards for his work on *Anthony Adverse* (1936) and *The Adventures of Robin Hood* (1938). His music for *Kings Row* (1941) and *Escape Me Never* (1946) was also outstanding.

KORNILOV, LAVR GEORGIEVICH, 1870–1918, Russian general, was born in Siberia. At the age of 19 he entered the Artillery College at St. Petersburg and at 22 obtained his commission. From 1896 to 1902 he was engaged in a number of daring missions in Persia and Afghanistan; he commanded a brigade in the RUSSO-JAPANESE WAR; was military

attaché at Peking (1907–11); and led a division in the Galician campaign early in World War I. In 1917 he was appointed generalissimo of the Russian army; he inaugurated a series of strong military measures for the restoration of discipline, and in September (1917) demanded that Premier Kerensky deliver to him all civil and military power, whereupon he was dismissed and marched with his troops on Petrograd. The movement collapsed, however, and on September 15, he surrendered to General Alexeieff. In December he aided General Kaledin in declaring war against the Bolsheviki, and in March, 1918, he was killed by a shell burst during the siege of Krasnodar in the North Caucasus region.

KÖRÖS RIVER, E Hungary, rises in the Bihar Mountains of W Rumania, and flows W through Hungary to join the Tisza (Theiss) at Csongrád, Hungary, a total distance of 350 miles. Endrod and Szarvas are the most important towns along its banks.

KORSAKOFF PSYCHOSIS. See ALCOHOLISM; DELIRIUM TREMENS.

KORTRIJK. See COURTRAI.

KORYAK NATIONAL DISTRICT, U.S.S.R., the Russian Soviet Federated Socialist Republic, situated in Khabarovsk Territory; bounded on the SE and E by the Bering Sea, on the S by the southern portion of Kamchatka Peninsula, on the SW by the Sea of Okhotsk and a portion of Khabarovsk Territory which encloses the district, on the W by the Yakut Autonomous Soviet Socialist Republic, and on the NE and N by the Chukot National District; area 119,968 sq. mi.; pop. (1926) 12,500, principally Paleo-Asiatic. The Koryak National District is mountainous, with the Kamchatka-Koryak ranges traversing it in a northerly direction. The climate is cold temperate; summers are short and cool. The Koryaks, also known as Nymylans, are akin to the Chukchis, not only in appearance but also in mode of living. Intermarriage between the two groups is not uncommon. Fishing is the chief occupation of the Koryaks, who now ply their trade on a collective basis. Modern fishing techniques have been instituted by the Pacific Institute of Fisheries. The district was founded in 1930, with its capital at Palana.

KORZYBSKI, ALFRED HABANK, 1879–1950, American scientist, born in Warsaw, Poland. Educated at Warsaw Polytechnic Institute and in Germany and Italy, he taught in Warsaw, then enlisted in the Russian army, serving from 1916 to 1917 in the United States. Later he was attached to several Polish commissions in America, settled in the country, and became naturalized in 1940. In 1921 he published *Manhood of Humanity* and devoted the next seven years to studying psychiatric patients under Dr. William Alanson White and to the investigations fundamental to his formulations in *Science and Sanity: An Introduction to Non-Aristotelian Systems and General Semantics* (1933). Founder of general semantics and of the Institute of General Semantics (1938), Korzybski wrote the article on GENERAL SEMANTICS in the American Peoples Encyclopedia.

KOS. See COS.

KOSCIUSKO, MOUNT, loftiest peak of Australia, in New South Wales, 90 miles WNW of the coastal town of Bega; it reaches an elevation of 7,328 feet. This mountain and its neighboring Alplike peaks comprise a large resort and winter-sports area much frequented by Australians.

KOSCIUSZKO, TADEUSZ, 1746–1817, Polish general and statesman, was born in Mereczowszczyno. He went to America (1776), where he served under Washington in the Revolutionary War, and became the friend of Lafayette. He was made a colonel of engineers in October, 1776, served under Gates in 1777, was commissioned to lay out the fortifications at West Point, became adjutant to Washington, was General Greene's engineer in chief during the southern campaign, and, in 1783, was brevetted brigadier general. See REVOLUTION, AMERICAN.

Kosciuszko returned to Poland in 1786, and in 1792 led a force against the invading Russians. The Polish army fought splendidly, but the king treacherously surrendered to Russia and in rage and despair Kosciuszko resigned his commission and left the country. On the outbreak of the insurrection of 1794 he returned and was made commander in chief by the nobles in Cracow. All classes rallied to nis standard, and he defeated the Russians at Raclawice,

was made dictator of Poland, defended Warsaw for two months, but was defeated, wounded and taken prisoner at Maciejowice. He was held at St. Petersburg until the death of the Empress Catherine in 1796. After triumphal visits to England and America, he settled in France and, after a long residence there, went to Switzerland, where he died. He was buried at Kraków. There is a monument

POLISH INFO. CTR.

Kosciuszko

to him at West Point. See POLAND, Government and History.

KOSHER, a Hebrew word meaning fit or proper, applied to food meeting the strict requirements of the Jewish dietary laws, which originated from considerations of health and sanitation. According to the Law (Deut. 14; Lev. 11), only the flesh of animals which chew their cud and have cloven hoofs is fit to eat. In addition the animal must be killed in a prescribed manner (instituted to lessen its suffering) by a specially trained, learned Jew (*schochat*) acting under license of a chief rabbi. Only fish with scales and fins are permitted as food; thus oysters, clams, lobsters, etc., are unkosher or *tref*. The command in Deut. 14:21, "Thou shalt not seethe a kid in his mother's milk," is interpreted as a restriction against using milk or its products, such as butter, with flesh, and even the utensils used for one are forbidden to be used with the other. Milk products cannot be eaten at the same meal with meat. Since the observance of the Mosaic Laws has become increasingly difficult for the Jew, the number of Liberal Jews, who do not believe in strict adherence to the Law, is increasing. Kosher is also used as a general term signifying anything fit opposed to that which is unfit.

KOŠICE, Hungarian **Kassa,** German **Kaschau,** town, E Czechoslovakia, SE Slovakia, lying S of the Carpathian Mountains in the Hernad River Valley; 70 miles NW of Mukačevo and 135 miles NE of Budapest. The town was founded in 1235, and has many interesting old buildings. St. Elizabeth's cathedral, begun in 1270, is considered one of the finest examples of Hungarian Gothic architecture, and contains frescoes and the tombs of Magyar noblemen. There are numerous unusual Magyar palaces and a fine museum. There are mineral springs and baths. The industries of Košice include sawmills, distilleries, tanneries, breweries, chemical plants, stoneware and pottery works, wineries, wool spinning mills, and manufactures of tobacco, paper, machinery, furniture, yarn, leather goods, and woolen and cotton textiles. In the vicinity are salt mines. As a border town Košice has long been the subject of controversy and has been held at various periods of its history by Hungarian, Russian, Austrian, and Turkish monarchs. As one of the Hungarian strongholds it was captured by the Austrians in 1848. At the close of World War I it was awarded to the Czechoslovakian Republic by the Treaty of Trianon in 1920. In 1943, Germany, having annexed Slovakia in 1938, ceded to Hungary a large section of territory along Slovakia's southern borders, which included Košice. Following World War II. the Košice area was returned to Czechoslovakia. Pop. (1947) 58,089. It is the capital of the department of Kosice.   K. E. H.

KÖSLIN, Polish **Koszalin,** town, Poland, in the province of Pomorze Zachodnie, situated at the foot of the Gollenberg Hills, five miles from the Baltic Sea and 105 miles NE of Stettin (Szczecin). Manufactures of machines, furniture, paper, sausages, fish products, and soap are the principal industries of the town. There is also trade in livestock and grain. Köslin was founded late in the 12th century by the Saxons. At the conclusion of the Thirty Years' War (1648), the town fell to Brandenburg. Formerly German, it was awarded to Poland in August, 1945. Pop. (1946) 17,115.

KOSOVO-METOHIJAN REGION. See SERBIA.

KOSSEL, ALBRECHT, 1853–1927, German physiologist, was born in Rostock and studied at the universities of Rostock and Strasbourg. He was awarded the 1910 Nobel prize in physiology and medicine in recognition of his researches on the chemistry of the cell. He formulated the *protamine nucleus hypothesis* (1896), which states that the cores (nuclei) of all protein molecules are composed mostly of the amino acids, arginine, histidine, or lysine.

KOSSOVO, S Yugoslavia, former vilayet of European Turkey, divided at the close of the Balkan Wars (1912–13) between Serbia (9,973 sq. mi.) and Montenegro (1,961 sq. mi.). There are chrome mines, and fruit, grain, livestock, and tobacco are exported. Rice and silk are cultivated. On the plain of Kossovo ("Field of the Blackbirds") Sultan Murad I destroyed the Serbian empire by defeating and killing the Serbian king Lazar on June 20, 1389. Sultan Amurath (Murad) II gained here a great victory over John Hunyadi on Oct. 17, 1448. On Jan. 31, 1946, the autonomous Kosovo-Metohijan Region in the Peoples Republic of Serbia was established.

KOSSUTH, LOUIS, or **LAJOS,** 1802–94, Hungarian patriot, descendant of an ancient family of Magyar blood, was born in Monok, county of Zemp-

lin, Hungary. He was educated at the Calvinist College of Sárospatek and the Lutheran College of Eperies, studied law in Pest, was graduated as an advocate, and took up the practice of his profession. In 1825 he commenced his political career at the diet of Pressburg as the deputy of absent magnates, and as editor of a liberal journal. After numerous attempts to suppress his paper, Kossuth was arrested in 1837 and was in prison until 1840. Following

CHICAGO HIST. SOC.

Louis Kossuth

his release in that year, he became editor of *Pesti Hirláp*,

an ultraliberal journal which had immense popularity and influence. He was elected to the Diet of 1847 and became leader of the opposition.

He was sent with other deputies to Vienna to obtain the consent of the emperor to the appointment of a representative Hungarian ministry, and, the request having been granted, became minister of finance in the new cabinet. See HUNGARY, *History*.

Upon the revolt, a few months later, of the Croats and Serbians, secretly aided by Austrian agents, Kossuth was made head of a committee of national defense, with the powers of a dictator. Russia intervened (1849), the Hungarian forces were defeated at Temesvar, and Kossuth fled to Turkey, where he was kept a prisoner in spite of Austrian and Russian demands for his surrender. He was liberated in September, 1851, upon the intervention of England and the United States, visited England and later America, where he remained until July, 1852, being received with the greatest enthusiasm. The next 10 years he spent chiefly in England, and in 1862 settled in Turin, where he died in 1894. He steadfastly refused to recognize the compromise between Austria and Hungary effected in 1867, refusing a seat in the Diet to which he was elected. He was buried at Pest.

M. R.

BIBLIOG.-O. Zarek, *Kossuth* (1937).

KOSTELANETZ, ANDRÉ, 1901– , American conductor, was born in St. Petersburg, Russia, and was educated at the St. Petersburg Conservatory of Music. The Russian Revolution indirectly forced him (1922) to follow his parents to America. After his emigration he conducted many of the major American orchestras, but his name is primarily linked with radio, a medium through which he has attempted to effect a compromise between serious and popular music. In 1938 he married the noted singer, LILY PONS.

KOSTER, LOURENZ JANSZOON. See COSTER.

KOSTROMA, city, U.S.S.R., the Russian Soviet Federated Socialist Republic, capital of Kostroma Region, situated on the left bank of the Volga near its junction with the Kostroma River, 230 miles NE of Moscow. Notable buildings of the city include the Cathedral of the Assumption, built about 1250 and rebuilt in 1775–78; the Cathedral of the Epiphany (1773); the Church of the Resurrection (1652); and the Romanov Museum. Outside the city is the Ipatiev Monastery, founded in 1330 by the Tartar Prince Zacharias Tchet. Here in 1613, Michael Feodorovitch Romanov took refuge when persecuted by the Poles, and here he received the representatives of the Muscovite boyars and clergy who induced him to accept the Russian crown, thus beginning a dynasty which was to endure until the Revolution of 1917. The Cathedral of the Trinity within the Monastery contains many objects of interest. Kostroma is a metallurgic center, and has manufactures of textiles and textile-mill machinery, excavators, boats, footwear, and food products. There is a Textile Institute and technical colleges. Kostroma was probably founded in 1152, and was a duchy until the 14th century when it was united with the Grand Duchy of Moscow. Tartar raiders repeatedly razed the city. Pop. (1951 est.) 150,000.　　　A. M. K.

KOSTROMA REGION, U.S.S.R., an administrative area of the Russian Soviet Federated Socialist Republic; bounded on the N by Vologda Region, on the W by Yaroslavl Region, on the S by the regions of Ivanovo and Gorki, and on the E by Kirov Region. The principal rivers of the Region are the Volga and its tributary, the Kostroma. The Region is industrialized, but farming also prospers. Kostroma Region was formerly part of Ivanovo Region, and later of Yaroslavl Region. Its capital is KOSTROMA.

KOTA BHARU, town, on the E coast of the Malay Peninsula, capital of the state of Kelantan, 350 miles by rail N of Singapore. A port on the South China Sea and site of an airfield, during World War II, it was taken by Japanese landing forces Dec. 9, 1941, and used by them as a base for their southward sweep to Singapore. Pop. (1947) 22,700.

KOTAH, former feudatory state, India, merged with other states in the Greater Rajasthan Union; area 5,714 sq. mi.; pop. (1941) 777,398. The country slopes gently northward from the Malwa tableland, and is drained by the Chambal and its affluents. There are extensive game preserves, most of them grass-grown. The capital is Kotah city (pop. 45,032), some 160 miles by rail southwest of Gwalior. The capital has both the old and new palaces of the ruler, as well as fine temples, modern schools, and hospitals. Muslins are manufactured. Government of the state is by a state council of three ministers, with the Maharao as president. The ruling family belongs to the Hara sect of the Chauchan Rajputs, and is an offshoot of the ruling family of Bundi. The state was founded in 1625 during the reign of Madho Singhji, the second son of Rao Ratan of Bundi. The British in 1838 detached a part of the state to form the new state of Jhalawa; this area was returned to Kotah in 1897. It became a part of the Dominion of India in 1947.

KOTELNY. See NEW SIBERIAN ISLANDS.

KÖTHEN, or **Cöthen,** town, Germany, in the state of Anhalt, situated on the river Ziethe; 31 miles by rail SE of Magdeburg. Features of interest are the Gothic Church of St. James (15th century), the Schloss (16th century), containing Naumann's ornithological collection, the Rathaus, and a technical institute. Hahnemann founded a homoeopathic academy here in 1820. There are sugar and iron works. Köthen was the capital of the duchy of Anhalt-Köthen 1603–1847. After World War II it was in the Soviet occupation zone. Pop. (1946) 33,660.

KOTKA, town and seaport, Finland, on Kotka Island and at the mouth of the river Kymmene. The chief exports are timber and wood pulp; imports are machinery, coal, and iron. Pop. (1949 est.) 23,704.

KOTOR, or **Cattaro,** seaport, SW Yugoslavia, Dalmatia; 35 miles SE of Ragusa. The town stands at the head of the Gulf of Kotor, an inlet of the Adriatic which runs 19 miles inland, and is divided into four large and several smaller basins and affords an excellent enclosed harbor for the port. The ninth century cathedral of St. Tryphon is noteworthy. Kotor was a great commercial center when controlled by Venice (1420–1797). Prior to World War I it was an Austro-Hungarian naval base, belonging to Austria from 1814 until 1918. It was given to Italy by the Germans after the partition of Yugoslavia in 1941; it was regained by Yugoslavia in 1945. Pop. about 5,000.

KOTTBUS, or **Cottbus,** town, Germany, in the Prussian province of Brandenburg, situated on the Spree River, 70 miles by rail SE of Berlin. Interesting buildings include the Cloister Church (14th century, rebuilt 16th), the Upper Church (15th century), and the museum. Kottbus is a rail and road center, and has manufactures of machinery, cotton and woolen textiles, tobacco, and brandy. It is located in a Wendish region, and the Wendish language is spoken by a number of people in the town and neighborhood. In World War II the city was captured by the Soviet army on Apr. 23, 1945, and fell within the Soviet occupation zone. Pop. (1946) 55,500.

KOTZEBUE, AUGUST FRIEDRICH FERDINAND VON, 1761–1819, German dramatist, was born in Weimar. He was a law student at Jena and Duisberg, and was a practicing attorney for a short time in Weimar. Thereafter he held a number of government posts in the service of Russia, having married a Russian noblewoman. After his wife's death, he sojourned for a while in Paris, then returned to Germany. An implacable foe of liberalism and romanticism, Kotzebue was constantly involved in quarrels. In 1800 he sought to re-enter Russia but was arrested at the border as a spy and banished to Siberia. Czar Paul, pleased with his literary work, pardoned him and installed him as manager of the German theater in St. Petersburg. Again taking up residence in his native land, Kotzebue was forced by the Napoleonic invasion to find refuge in Russia. In 1813 he was back in Germany as a representative of the Russian government, and, as before, immediately became involved in violent controversy. His attacks on the liberal publication *Burschenschaft* led to his assassination by an enraged student. Kotzebue wrote voluminously, attaining his highest popularity for light, frivolous comedies, notably *Menschenhass und Reue* (1789) and *Die deutschen Kleinstädter* (1803), which dominated the German stage at the time.

KOTZEBUE, OTTO VON, 1787–1846, Russian explorer, was born in Reval, the son of AUGUST VON KOTZEBUE. He accompanied Krusenstern on his voyage around the world (1803–6), sailed (1815–18) with Chamisso and Eschscholtz through the Arctic Ocean and the South Seas, giving his name to the sound southeast of Bering Strait, and commanded a voyage around the world (1823–26). His *Voyage of Discovery, into the South Sea and Bering's Straits* was translated by H. E. Lloyd (1821).

HARVEY AND MODERN PHYSIOLOGY
He Discovered the Circulation of the Blood

WILLIAM HARVEY (1578-1657) in a sense did
for physiology, biology, and medicine what, about a century earlier
Nicolas Copernicus (1473-1543) had done for astronomy, physics,
and other sciences.

Before Harvey made his great discovery it was known that the
blood moves in the body, but the ideas as to how it moves were
largely erroneous. After proving this to be the case, Harvey discovered that the blood flows in the blood vessels from the heart
through the body and back to the heart, thus completing its circulation. This discovery became the basis of modern physiology and
has had a tremendous effect on the whole field of biology and
medicine. It is presented and explained in Harvey's famous treatise, *Exercitatio de motu cordis et sanguinis* (*An Anatomical Exercise on
the Motion of the Heart and Blood in Animals*), which is commonly
regarded as one of the most important key works in the whole
field of biology and medicine.

The capillary channels through which the blood passes from the
arteries to the veins were, however, not seen by Harvey, though
his deductions pointed to their existence. They were discovered
four years after his death by the great anatomist Marcello Malpighi, with the aid of the microscope.

Through books, study under the leading anatomists of Italy, and
innumerable dissections of animals belonging to 80 species, Harvey
acquired detailed knowledge of the comparative anatomy of the
heart and the vascular system. He also observed closely the action
of the heart and blood in living snakes, dogs, pigs, frogs, fishes, insects, transparent shrimps, unhatched chicks, and the like. He
rounded out his investigations and experiments along this line by
such means as tying a bandage tightly around a man's upper arm
and studying the externally visible effects of this on the veins and
arteries. In addition he did significant work in the field of reproduction and embryology.

Harvey was born in Folkestone, England. He was a student at
Cambridge before going to Padua to study medicine under Fabricius. There are differences of opinion as to his expertness as a
practicing physician and surgeon. Among his patients, however,
were Francis Bacon, King James I, and King Charles I. He was
a particularly close friend of Charles whom he accompanied on a
journey to Scotland and attended at the Battle of Edgehill.

Before Harvey died, at the age of 73, he and his discovery of
the circulation of the blood had achieved the highest professional
and general recognition in his own country and throughout Europe.
See ANATOMY; ARTERIES, VEINS, AND CAPILLARIES; BIOLOGY; CIR-
CULATION OF THE BLOOD; FABRICIUS, HIERONYMUS; HARVEY, WIL-
LIAM; MALPIGHI, MARCELLO; MEDICINE; PHYSIOLOGY.

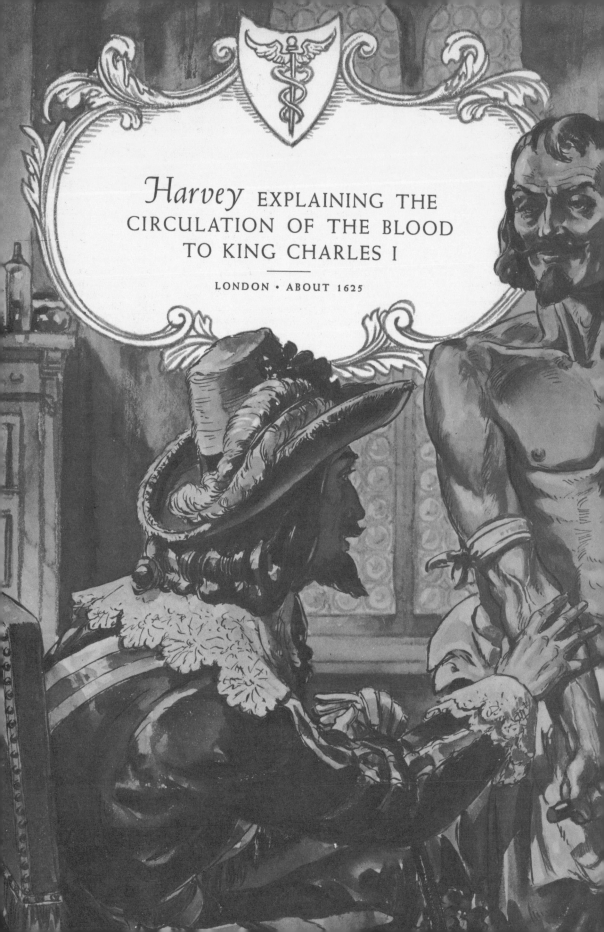

Harvey EXPLAINING THE
CIRCULATION OF THE BLOOD
TO KING CHARLES I

LONDON · ABOUT 1625